Welcome to

Life
Science

An Overview of *Holt Science & Technology: Life Science*	T2
Components Listing	T18
Correlation to the National Science Education Standards	T19

**EXPECT EXCITEMENT!
EXPECT RESULTS!**

HOLT SCIENCE & TECHNOLOGY

A Text that Grabs and Holds Your Students' Attention

Student Edition

Begins with a bang!
Each chapter begins with a brief introduction designed to pique your students' interest. Pre-Reading Questions are included so you can check students' prior understanding.

A text that motivates
Holt Science & Technology motivates your students in a variety of ways.

Visuals
- are integrated into the narrative
- clearly reveal macro-to-micro relationships
- support English-language learners and reluctant readers
- are functional, accurate, and understandable

Narrative
- contains concise, outline-style headings to help students find information easily
- presents content in a clear, logical sequence
- contains friendly language to make reading accessible and enjoyable
- incorporates analogies to help students relate concepts to the real world

HOLT SCIENCE & TECHNOLOGY

"I need a textbook that will **engage** and **excite** my students while they're learning."

Applies to real life
Some of your students may ask you why they are studying science. *Holt Science & Technology* provides answers with motivating features:

- **Start-Up Activity** stimulates your students' curiosity about upcoming chapter concepts with a hands-on activity.
- Tidbits to feed the mind are presented in small captions called **Brain Food**. There's nothing better than a fun fact to captivate a young audience!
- **Apply** poses real-world questions and asks your students to answer them by applying what they have just learned.
- **Activity** gives your students the opportunity to use their imaginations and to expand their learning.

If all the blood vessels in your body were strung together, the total length would be more than twice the circumference of the Earth.

Brings focus to the Internet
SciLinks—a National Science Teachers Association–sponsored Web service—links you and your students to interactive activities and current information directly related to chapter content. (see page T17)

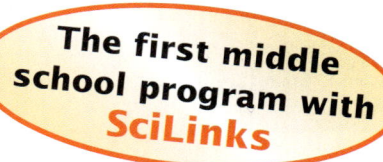

The first middle school program with **SciLinks**

Ends with enrichment
Weird Science, **Health Watch**, **Careers**, **Scientific Debate**, and other end-of-chapter features extend chapter content with real-world examples, articles, and motivating activities.

HOLT SCIENCE & TECHNOLOGY

HOLT SCIENCE & TECHNOLOGY

Focus on Reading and Understanding

Holt Science & Technology makes instruction accessible to all your students—English-language learners, special needs students, those having difficulty mastering content, students who need more practice or hands-on experience, and advanced learners.

Read for understanding

Each lesson gives you suggestions to help your students read for understanding.

- **Pre-Reading Questions** assess your students' prior knowledge and serves as a reading warm-up.

- **Reading Check-Up** allows students to see how their understanding has changed.

- highlights activities that help English-language learners grasp content.

- emphasizes key concepts in order to guide reading and ensure comprehension.

- *Directed Reading Worksheets* makes reading an active process. A variety of strategies and fun activities help your students identify the main idea, then organize and synthesize supporting information.

- *Reinforcement & Vocabulary Review Worksheets* makes reviewing and reinforcing chapter content easy. Students have opportunities to examine issues in each section from different perspectives or to benefit from a different instructional approach.

- *Holt Science Skills Workshop: Reading in the Content Area* contains activities and exercises that target the reading skills specific to the comprehension of science texts.

Prediction Guide Have students respond to the following statement before reading this section. The cells bond to e answ thei

Prediction Guide Before reading this section, ask students to answer the following question in their ScienceLog. *Amphibian* means "double life." Why would we give this class of animals such a name? After reading this section, ask students to evaluate their answers.

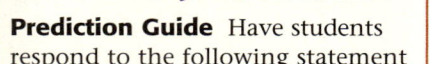

Take a minute to review your answers to the Pre-Reading Questions found at the bottom of page 320. Have your answers changed? If necessary, revise your answers based on what you have learned since you read the chapter.

1. What characteristics make an animal different from a plant?
2. How do animals know when to migrate?

> "I need a program that helps me teach **today's students.**"

Guided Reading Audio CD Program

This audio program provides students with a direct reading of each chapter using instructional visuals as guideposts. Auditory learners, students with limited reading proficiency, and Spanish-speaking students receive the explanation they need from this alternative text format.
Available in both English and Spanish.

Provide universal access

Holt Science & Technology helps all your students learn science.

- **Meeting Individual Needs** in the teacher's wrap provides engaging demonstrations and hands-on activities to help learners of all levels.
- **Reteaching** gives you alternate methods of instruction for those students who need it.
- **Homework** options use a variety of teaching strategies to complement diverse learning styles.
- *Critical Thinking & Problem Solving Worksheets* provides challenging activities connecting science concepts to the "real world." Your students learn to think through a problem and to use the scientific method and other strategies to find a solution.

> **MEETING INDIVIDUAL NEEDS**
>
> *Writing* **Advanced Learners**
> In a given temperate region, different animals have different
>
> **MEETING INDIVIDUAL NEEDS**
>
> *Writing* **Learners Having Difficulty**
> In a given temperate region, different animals have different ways of surviving cold winters. Have students list as many behaviors or adaptations for winter survival that they can think of.
> **Sheltered English**

Approach learning from different angles with these in-text features and ancillaries. You can make sure your students understand science concepts no matter what their learning styles.

GROUP ACTIVITY

HOLT ANTHOLOGY OF SCIENCE FICTION

 REAL-WORLD CONNECTION

COOPERATIVE LEARNING

HOLT SCIENCE POSTERS

 Teaching Transparency

 Science Puzzlers, Twisters & Teasers

Universal Access

HOLT SCIENCE & TECHNOLOGY

HOLT SCIENCE & TECHNOLOGY

Labs to Make Learning Active and Meaningful

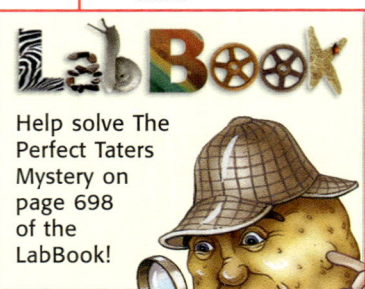

Help solve The Perfect Taters Mystery on page 698 of the LabBook!

Holt Science & Technology provides a strong yet flexible lab program that meets lab science requirements, regardless of limited lab equipment or time restrictions. Labs include clear procedures, demonstrate scientific concepts, and develop students' understanding of scientific methods. **Using Scientific Methods**

These labs have been classroom-tested, and also reviewed by an independent laboratory, for reliability, safety, and efficiency.

Terry Rakes
Elmwood Junior High School
Rogers, Arkansas

In-text LabBook
LabBook, in the back of the *Student Edition*, allows for
- more labs and activities,
- greater flexibility in lesson planning,
- a wider variety of labs,
- more detailed lab procedures and explanations,
- an uninterrupted chapter narrative, and includes
- separate *Datasheets for LabBook*.

> "I need a variety of **fun** yet **meaningful** lab activities that are **cost effective**."

Additional, in-text labs and activities

LABS AND ACTIVITIES FOR EVERY LESSON

- **QuickLabs** are easy to execute and require minimal time and materials—great for quick in-class activities, teacher demonstrations, or group presentations.
- **Start-Up Activity** stimulates your students' curiosity about scientific concepts in the upcoming chapter.
- **Activity** gives your students the opportunity to use their imaginations and expand their learning.
- **Apply** poses real-world questions and asks your students to answer them by applying what they have just learned.
- **Demonstration** and **Activity** in the Teacher's Edition give you options to demonstrate labs and procedures to the whole class or provide fun, hands-on activities.

QuickLab
Do Bacteria Taste Good?
If they're the kind found in yogurt, they taste great! Using a **cotton swab,** put a small dot of **yogurt** on a **plastic microscope slide.** Add a drop of **water,** and use the cotton swab to st... Add a... stic

Activity
...e all mammals, you have ...iaphragm. Place your hand underneath your rib cage. What happens as you breathe in and out? You are feeling the motion of your abdominal muscles, which are con...cted to ...ur dia...agm.

Lab Ratings make choosing labs easy

Lab Ratings, for all labs, make it easy for you to determine, at a glance, which labs are most appropriate for your class.

Time Required
One 45-minute class period

Lab Ratings
EASY ———————→ HARD
TEACHER PREP
STUDENT SET-UP
CONCEPT LEVEL
CLEAN UP

Science Kits, available in both consumable and nonconsumable packages, offer you all the materials you need for in-text labs and will cut your prep time significantly. Replacement materials can be ordered directly through Science Kit at www.sciencekit.com.

For a complete materials list, see page xxviii in the **Annotated Teacher's Edition**

HOLT SCIENCE & TECHNOLOGY

HOLT SCIENCE & TECHNOLOGY

Lab Manuals Extend Your Options

Whiz-Bang Demonstrations gives you a rousing way to get your students' attention at the beginning of a lesson. **65 labs in all!**

Labs You Can Eat safely incorporates food into the classroom to provide a fun inquiry-based learning tool. **25 labs in all!**

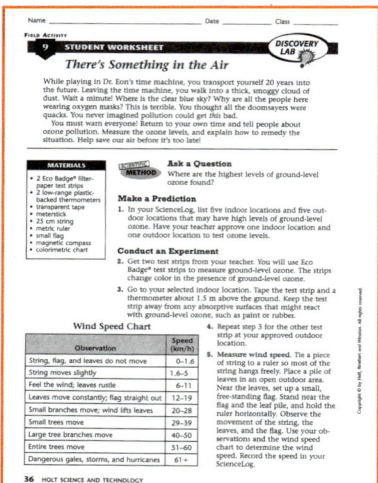

EcoLabs & Field Activities includes activities that address specific ecological questions and increase environmental awareness. **23 labs in all!**

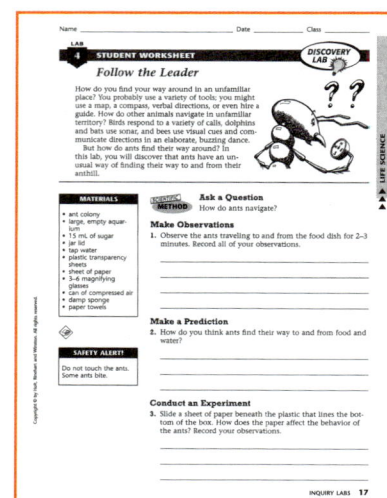

Inquiry Labs encourages your students to ask questions and investigate problems in order to find solutions. **23 labs in all!**

Long-Term Projects & Research Ideas extends and enriches chapter content with experiments, activities, inquiry-based projects, and Internet and library research. **2 for every chapter!**

T8   HOLT SCIENCE & TECHNOLOGY

Comprehensive Skill Development

Science skills ensure future success

Holt Science & Technology gives your students ample opportunities to master the skills necessary for future success in science. Science skills are developed in a variety of ways:

- The in-text **LabBook**, activities, and lab booklets provide lots of practice using scientific methods.
- The **Appendix** helps your students refresh their measuring and data-analysis skills, as well as their understanding of the **scientific method**.
- **Apply** and **Activity** allow your students to develop science skills in fun and motivating ways.

In addition, your students can find plenty of skill-building practice in *Science Skills Worksheets*. These worksheets help your students hone important science skills, such as thinking objectively, conducting research, designing investigations, keeping accurate records, and creating and analyzing graphs.

Math is covered everywhere you look!

Surface-to-Volume Ratio

The shape of a cell can affect its surface-to-volume ratio. Examine the cells below, and answer the questions that follow:

Holt Science & Technology also strengthens your students' math skills. From practice problems to reviews, math skills are continually developed:

- **MathBreak** provides practice with direct application to the science concepts being taught.
- **Math Concepts** reviews the math lessons presented in the chapter.
- **Math Refresher**, found in the Appendix, reviews basic math skills, such as averages, ratios, percentages, and more.

Math Skills for Science helps your students develop and apply basic math skills to scientific problems with two types of worksheets.

- **Math Skills Worksheets** provide a brief introduction to a relevant math skill, a step-by-step explanation of the math process, and example and practice problems.
- **Math in Science Worksheets** give your students practice using math in real-life science situations.

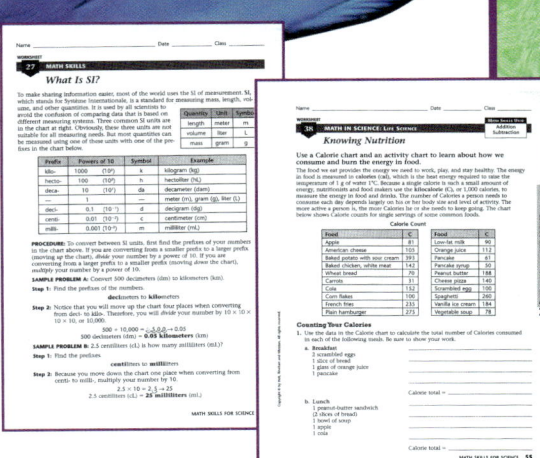

HOLT SCIENCE & TECHNOLOGY

A Versatile Teacher's Edition that is Easy-to-Use

The Chapter Organizer—your easy-to-follow road map

With such a wealth of program resources, you'll be glad to know we've included a convenient, timesaving guide suggesting how and when to use them. The **Chapter Organizer**

- integrates all labs, technology, and print resources
- is organized according to time requirements
- includes National Standards correlated by section
- Activities are leveled by ability level to help you choose which ones are appropriate.

Chapter Resources & Worksheets makes choosing teaching resources easy by showing them as reduced pages. Available resources are categorized by

- Visual Resources
- Meeting Individual Needs
- Review and Assessment
- Lab Worksheets
- Applications & Extensions

The **Chapter Background** provides additional information to help you enrich upcoming lessons.

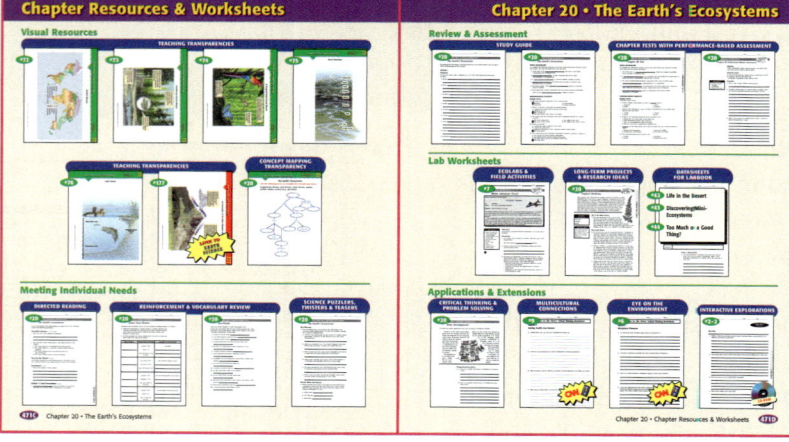

T10 HOLT SCIENCE & TECHNOLOGY

> "A teacher's edition should be **well-organized** and provide **effective** tips and techniques."

Keep the focus on the lesson
The complete lesson cycle helps you keep your students interested and involved. An array of both traditional and new teaching strategies, creative reinforcement, and thought-provoking extensions help you teach to a wide variety of learning styles, ability levels, and interests.

Fuel your presentation
Found on almost every page, fun features and intriguing stories ignite class discussion and get your students thinking.

Q: Why didn't the skeleton cross the road?

A: It didn't have the guts.

IS THAT A FACT!
Research shows that baleen-whale sounds, which scientists believe are produced by the larynx, may be the loudest sounds produced by any animal on land or in the sea. Such sounds may carry hundreds of kilometers underwater.

MISCONCEPTION ALERT
Can ancient DNA be used to produce dinosaurs as seen in the movies Jurassic Park and The Lost World? In these movies, scientists make dinosaurs by combining fragments of ancient DNA with DNA from modern-day frogs.

Science Bloopers
In 1798, when English scholars first observed the duck-billed platypus that had been sent to them by a scientist in Australia, they were convinced they were the victims of a joke. Surely, they thought, some prankster had pieced together parts of various animals. The English scholars cut and sliced the dead animal for signs of stitches holding the bill and webbed feet to its mammal-like body. It took a lot of convincing, but eventually they came to the conclusion that the animal was indeed real.

WEIRD SCIENCE
Environmental stimuli can sometimes affect flower color. Hydrangeas growing in acidic soil produce blue flowers. If the soil is made alkaline, the same plants will produce pink flowers.

Teacher's Edition

HOLT SCIENCE & TECHNOLOGY

Teaching Support that Makes Your Job Easier

Teaching Resources

Point-and-Click Planning

One-Stop Planner CD-ROM

with Exam-View® Test Generator

The **One-Stop Planner® CD-ROM with Exam-View® Test Generator** is a timesaving, all-in-one planning tool that contains everything you need on a single disc!

- **customizable** lesson plans, tests, assessment checklists, and rubrics
- a **powerful** test generator
- **printable** resources, including
  - worksheets
  - transparencies
  - Spanish transcripts
  - assessment materials
  - rubrics
  - National Standards Correlation
  - Science Fair Guide
  - Parent Letters
  - and much more!

Includes student worksheets

"I would love to **streamline planning** so I can spend more time on what I do best—teaching."

Sharpen your saw
The *Professional Reference for Teachers* provides current information about pertinent issues in science education today. In professional articles, you can learn more about the National Science Education Standards, block scheduling, classroom management, and more. A bibliography of books, lectures, magazines, and Web sites is included.

Visualize science concepts
Teaching Transparencies, many with images taken directly from the text, reinforce important science concepts and processes.

Two *Concept Mapping Transparencies* are included for each chapter—a partial map transparency to use with your students as they progress through the chapter and a completed concept map to serve as an answer key.

Bellringer Transparency Masters (found on the *One-Stop Planner CD-ROM*) help you focus your students' attention quickly at the beginning of class while you are dealing with administrative demands.

Teaching Resources

HOLT SCIENCE & TECHNOLOGY   T13

HOLT SCIENCE & TECHNOLOGY

Assessment that Accurately Measures Mastery of Content

Check progress

Self-Check encourages your students to evaluate their own learning by answering questions found intermittently within the chapter. A page reference allows them to check their own answers. After reading each lesson, your students explore, evaluate, and extend what they've learned by answering questions in the section **Review**. In the teacher's wrap, a **Quiz** provides an objective assessment of each lesson.

> **✓ Self-Check**
>
> How are the structures of arteries and veins related to their functions? *(See page 782 to check your answer.)*

Chapter Highlights lists vocabulary and provides content summaries in a concise, visual format. This helps your students organize their thoughts and synthesize information.

Study Guide contains blackline masters for Chapter Highlights and Chapter Reviews that help your students gear up for tests and quizzes.

Chapter Review question types are identical to those found on the chapter tests, making the Chapter Review an excellent resource for pretest practice.

> "I want to **make sure** my students are **learning**."

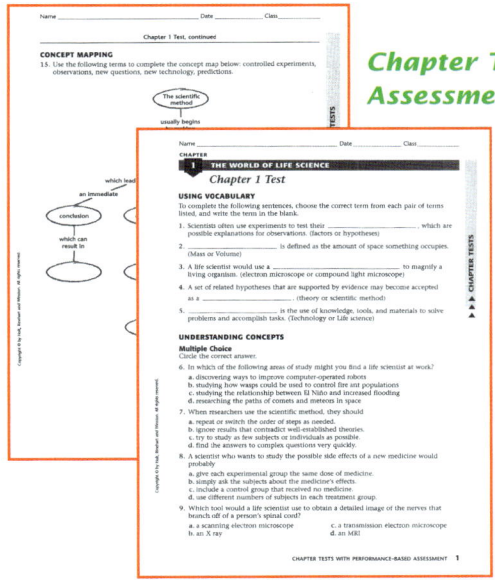

Chapter Tests with Performance-Based Assessment includes multiple-choice, concept-mapping, critical-thinking, interpreting graphics, math-in-science, and alternative assessment questions, to name a few.

Alternative Assessment in the teacher's wrap provides you with different evaluation options, such as expository writing and concept mapping, to ensure a thorough assessment.

Create your own assessments

One-Stop Planner CD-ROM

With the *One-Stop Planner CD-ROM with Test Generator*, you can create, revise, and edit quizzes, section and chapter reviews, and chapter tests, drawing from thousands of questions organized by chapter and linked to chapter objectives. Performance-based assessment is also included.

The *Test Generator: Test Item Listing* provides a printed copy of thousands of assessment items on the *One-Stop Planner CD-ROM*. This handy guide allows you to preview test items before making selections.

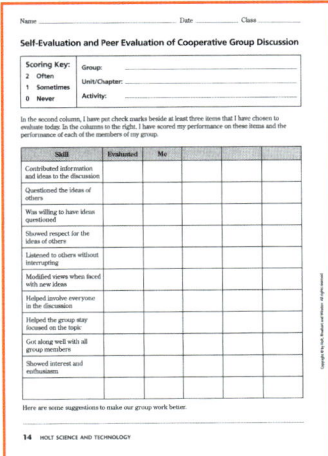

Assessment Checklists & Rubrics, available on the *One-Stop Planner CD-ROM* or as blackline masters, gives you guidelines for evaluating your students' progress, including performance and portfolio assessment tools. You can also create a customized checklist for each class, helping you gather daily scores and determine grades.

Assessment

HOLT SCIENCE & TECHNOLOGY T15

HOLT SCIENCE & TECHNOLOGY

Technology That Expands Your Options

Holt Science & Technology provides the right combination of fully integrated technology resources—including CD-ROMs, videos, and Internet products—to make your teaching more effective, efficient, and creative.

Technology Resources

Guided Reading Audio CD Program provides a direct reading for each chapter, in English and Spanish, to help struggling readers and English-language learners better understand the text.

Interactive Explorations CD-ROM Program turns a computer into a virtual laboratory where your students act as lab assistants in solving 24 real-world problems.

Science Tutor CD-ROM serves as a personal tutor for helping students practice what they've learned in their textbooks and in class by offering immediate feedback.

Student Edition, CD-ROM Version provides students with the entire textbook on CD-ROM so they have less to carry home.

Lesson Presentation CD-ROM provides you with a media-based presentation of core concepts to engage your students.

One-Stop Planner CD-ROM with Test Generator makes planning and managing lessons easier than ever with the following resources:
- printable worksheets and resources
- customizable lesson plans
- powerful ExamView® Test Generator

CNN Presents Science in the News: Video Library allows students to see the impact of science on their everyday lives with the following videos: Multicultural Connections, Science Technology & Society, Scientists in Action, and Eye on the Environment.

One-Stop Planner CD-ROM

*"I don't have time to **find** and **evaluate** the **technology** resources out there."*

Internet Resources

Online Edition is portable, expandable, and interactive, and yet it weighs nothing at all! This online learning resource gives you and your students the following:
- the Student Edition online
- interactive exercises and feedback
- presentation materials
- homework help

SciLinks is an Online service developed and maintained by NSTA that links you to the best and most up-to-date Web sites directly related to the textbook.

cnnstudentnews.com is the ultimate news and information Web site for students and teachers and includes news as it happens, classroom resources, activities, and lesson plans.

go.hrw.com enriches student learning with chapter activities and resources.

Technology

EXPECT EXCITEMENT!
EXPECT RESULTS!

HOLT SCIENCE & TECHNOLOGY   T17

The *sciLINKS* name and the *sciLINKS* logo are registered trademarks of the National Science Teachers Association. CNN and Turner Learning logos, copyright 1998, by Turner Learning, Inc. Cable News Network. Time Warner Companies. Produced in the United States of America

Life Science Components Listing

Student Edition

Annotated Teacher's Edition

Life Science Teaching Resources

- Study Guide
- Study Guide Answer Key
- Critical Thinking & Problem Solving Worksheets
- Reinforcement & Vocabulary Review Worksheets
- Science Puzzlers, Twisters & Teasers
- Chapter Tests with Performance-Based Assessment
- Directed Reading Worksheets
- Directed Reading Worksheets Answer Key
- Datasheets for LabBook
- Datasheets for LabBook Answer Key
- Test Generator: Test Item Listing

LabBank

- Labs You Can Eat
- Whiz-Bang Demonstrations
- Inquiry Labs
- EcoLabs & Field Activities
- Long-Term Projects & Research Ideas

Program Teaching Resources

- Science Skills Worksheets
- Math Skills for Science
- Professional Reference for Teachers
- Holt Anthology of Science Fiction
- Assessment Checklists & Rubrics
- Science Fair Guide
- Holt Science Posters
- Holt Science Skill Workshop: Reading in the Content Area

Technology Resources

Online Edition

Student Edition, CD-ROM Version

Science Tutor CD-ROM

Lesson Presentation CD-ROM

Teaching Transparencies with Concept Mapping Transparencies

Guided Reading Audio CD Program

Guided Reading Audio CD Program, Spanish

One-Stop Planner CD-ROM with Test Generator for Mac® and Win®

Interactive Explorations CD-ROM Program for Mac® and Win®

CNN Presents Science in the News: Video Library

- Scientists in Action
- Multicultural Connections
- Science, Technology & Society
- Eye on the Environment

HOLT SCIENCE & TECHNOLOGY Life Science

National Science Education
STANDARDS CORRELATIONS

The following lists show the chapter correlation of **Holt Science & Technology: Life Science** with the *National Science Education Standards* (grades 5–8).

The chapter correlations for the Life Science Content Standards begin on page T22.

UNIFYING CONCEPTS AND PROCESSES

Standard	Chapter Correlation		
Systems, order, and organization Code: UCP 1	Chapter 1 — 1.1 Chapter 2 — 2.1 Chapter 3 — 3.1, 3.3 Chapter 4 — 4.1, 4.2 Chapter 5 — 5.1 Chapter 6 — 6.2 Chapter 8 — 8.1, 8.2 Chapter 9 — 9.1	Chapter 10 — 10.1, 10.3 Chapter 12 — 12.1, 12.2, 12.3, 12.4 Chapter 13 — 13.2, 13.3 Chapter 14 — 14.1, 14.2, 14.3 Chapter 15 — 15.1, 15.2 Chapter 16 — 16.1, 16.2, 16.3, 16.4 Chapter 17 — 17.1, 17.2 Chapter 18 — 18.1, 18.2, 18.3	Chapter 19 — 19.1, 19.2 Chapter 22 — 22.1, 22.3 Chapter 23 — 23.1, 23.2, 23.3 Chapter 24 — 24.1, 24.2 Chapter 25 — 25.1, 25.3 Chapter 26 — 26.2 Chapter 27 — 27.2 Chapter 28 — 28.1
Evidence, models, and explanation Code: UCP 2	Chapter 2 — 2.1, 2.2, 2.3 Chapter 3 — 3.1, 3.2, 3.3 Chapter 4 — 4.1 Chapter 5 — 5.1, 5.2 Chapter 6 — 6.1, 6.2 Chapter 7 — 7.1, 7.2, 7.3 Chapter 8 — 8.1, 8.3 Chapter 10 — 10.2, 10.3	Chapter 11 — 11.1 Chapter 12 — 12.1, 12.2, 12.3, 12.4 Chapter 13 — 13.1, 13.2, 13.3 Chapter 15 — 15.2, 15.3 Chapter 16 — 16.1, 16.2, 16.3, 16.4 Chapter 17 — 17.1, 17.2 Chapter 19 — 19.1, 19.2 Chapter 20 — 20.1, 20.2, 20.3	Chapter 21 — 21.2 Chapter 22 — 22.2, 22.3 Chapter 23 — 23.1, 23.3 Chapter 24 — 24.1, 24.2, 24.3 Chapter 25 — 25.1, 25.2 Chapter 26 — 26.3 Chapter 27 — 27.1, 27.2 Chapter 28 — 28.3
Change, constancy, and measurement Code: UCP 3	Chapter 1 — 1.2, 1.3 Chapter 3 — 3.2, 3.3 Chapter 4 — 4.1, 4.2 Chapter 7 — 7.1, 7.2, 7.3 Chapter 8 — 8.1, 8.2 Chapter 10 — 10.1, 10.2 Chapter 12 — 12.2	Chapter 13 — 13.1, 13.2, 13.3 Chapter 14 — 14.2 Chapter 15 — 15.1, 15.2, 15.3 Chapter 16 — 16.1, 16.2, 16.3 Chapter 17 — 17.1, 17.2 Chapter 19 — 19.1, 19.2 Chapter 20 — 20.2, 20.3	Chapter 21 — 21.1, 21.2 Chapter 22 — 22.1, 22.2, 22.3, 22.4 Chapter 23 — 23.1 Chapter 24 — 24.2 Chapter 25 — 25.3 Chapter 26 — 26.3 Chapter 27 — 27.2, 27.3
Evolution and equilibrium Code: UCP 4	Chapter 3 — 3.2, 3.3 Chapter 4 — 4.1, 4.2 Chapter 7 — 7.1, 7.2 Chapter 8 — 8.1 Chapter 10 — 10.2 Chapter 13 — 13.1, 13.2 Chapter 15 — 15.1	Chapter 16 — 16.1, 16.3, 16.4 Chapter 17 — 17.2 Chapter 18 — 18.3 Chapter 19 — 19.1, 19.2 Chapter 20 — 20.1, 20.3 Chapter 21 — 21.2 Chapter 22 — 22.1, 22.3	Chapter 23 — 23.3 Chapter 24 — 24.2 Chapter 25 — 25.1, 25.2, 25.3 Chapter 27 — 27.2, 27.3 Chapter 28 — 28.1
Form and function Code: UCP 5	Chapter 2 — 2.3 Chapter 3 — 3.1, 3.2, 3.3 Chapter 4 — 4.2 Chapter 6 — 6.1 Chapter 7 — 7.1, 7.2 Chapter 8 — 8.3 Chapter 9 — 9.2 Chapter 10 — 10.1, 10.2, 10.3	Chapter 11 — 11.1, 11.2 Chapter 12 — 12.1, 12.2, 12.3, 12.4 Chapter 13 — 13.1, 13.2 Chapter 14 — 14.2 Chapter 15 — 15.1, 15.2, 15.3, 15.4 Chapter 16 — 16.1, 16.2, 16.3, 16.4 Chapter 17 — 17.1, 17.2 Chapter 20 — 20.1	Chapter 22 — 22.2, 22.4 Chapter 23 — 23.1, 23.2, 23.3 Chapter 24 — 24.1, 24.2 Chapter 25 — 25.1, 25.2 Chapter 26 — 26.1, 26.2, 26.3 Chapter 27 — 27.2

SCIENCE AS INQUIRY

Standard	Chapter Correlation		
Abilities necessary to do scientific inquiry Code: SAI 1	**Chapter 1** 1.1, 1.2, 1.3 **Chapter 2** 2.3 **Chapter 3** 3.2, 3.3 **Chapter 4** 4.1, 4.2, 4.3 **Chapter 5** 5.1, 5.2 **Chapter 6** 6.1, 6.2 **Chapter 7** 7.1, 7.2, 7.3 **Chapter 8** 8.1 **Chapter 9** 9.1, 9.2 **Chapter 10** 10.1, 10.2, 10.3	**Chapter 11** 11.2 **Chapter 12** 12.1, 12.2, 12.3, 12.4 **Chapter 13** 13.1, 13.2, 13.3 **Chapter 14** 14.1, 14.2, 14.3 **Chapter 15** 15.1, 15.3 **Chapter 16** 16.1, 16.2, 16.3 **Chapter 17** 17.1, 17.2 **Chapter 18** 18.1, 18.2 **Chapter 19** 19.1, 19.2 **Chapter 20** 20.1, 20.2, 20.3	**Chapter 21** 21.1, 21.2 **Chapter 22** 22.2, 22.3 **Chapter 23** 23.3 **Chapter 24** 24.1, 24.2 **Chapter 25** 25.1, 25.2 **Chapter 26** 26.1, 26.2, 26.3 **Chapter 27** 27.1, 27.2 **Chapter 28** 28.1, 28.2, 28.3
Understandings about scientific inquiry Code: SAI 2	**Chapter 1** 1.1, 1.2, 1.3 **Chapter 2** 2.2 **Chapter 3** 3.2 **Chapter 4** 4.2 **Chapter 5** 5.1 **Chapter 6** 6.1, 6.2 **Chapter 7** 7.1, 7.2 **Chapter 8** 8.1, 8.3	**Chapter 9** 9.1 **Chapter 10** 10.1, 10.3 **Chapter 11** 11.2 **Chapter 12** 12.1 **Chapter 13** 13.1, 13.2, 13.3 **Chapter 14** 14.2 **Chapter 15** 15.2 **Chapter 16** 16.2	**Chapter 18** 18.1 **Chapter 19** 19.1 **Chapter 20** 20.2 **Chapter 21** 21.1 **Chapter 22** 22.3, 22.4 **Chapter 23** 23.3 **Chapter 25** 25.1 **Chapter 27** 27.1

SCIENCE AND TECHNOLOGY

Standard	Chapter Correlation		
Abilities of technological design Code: ST 1	**Chapter 5** 5.1 **Chapter 6** 6.1 **Chapter 10** 10.2 **Chapter 16** 16.2	**Chapter 20** 20.1 **Chapter 26** 26.3	
Understandings about science and technology Code: ST 2	**Chapter 1** 1.3 **Chapter 3** 3.2, 3.3 **Chapter 4** 4.2 **Chapter 6** 6.1, 6.2	**Chapter 7** 7.2 **Chapter 12** 12.1 **Chapter 16** 16.2 **Chapter 17** 17.2	**Chapter 21** 21.2 **Chapter 26** 26.3 **Chapter 27** 27.1

SCIENCE IN PERSONAL AND SOCIAL PERSPECTIVES

Standard	Chapter Correlation		
Personal health Code: SPSP 1	**Chapter 4** 4.2 **Chapter 5** 5.1 **Chapter 10** 10.3 **Chapter 11** 11.1	**Chapter 21** 21.1, 21.2 **Chapter 22** 22.2, 22.3, 22.4 **Chapter 23** 23.1, 23.3 **Chapter 24** 24.1	**Chapter 25** 25.1, 25.2 **Chapter 26** 26.2, 26.3 **Chapter 27** 27.1 **Chapter 28** 28.1, 28.2, 28.3
Populations, resources, and environments Code: SPSP 2	**Chapter 7** 7.2 **Chapter 13** 13.3 **Chapter 18** 18.1	**Chapter 19** 19.2 **Chapter 20** 20.1, 20.2, 20.3 **Chapter 21** 21.1, 21.2	

Science in Personal and Social Perspectives (cont'd)

Standard	Chapter Correlation			
Natural hazards Code: SPSP 3	**Chapter 1** 1.1 **Chapter 8** 8.1, 8.2 **Chapter 13** 13.2, 13.3 **Chapter 15** 15.1	**Chapter 20** 20.1 **Chapter 21** 21.1 **Chapter 28** 28.3		
Risks and benefits Code: SPSP 4	**Chapter 3** 3.3 **Chapter 4** 4.2 **Chapter 6** 6.1 **Chapter 10** 10.3 **Chapter 12** 12.3	**Chapter 13** 13.1 **Chapter 15** 15.1, 15.2, 15.3 **Chapter 19** 19.1 **Chapter 21** 21.1, 21.2 **Chapter 22** 22.2	**Chapter 23** 23.1, 23.3 **Chapter 26** 26.2 **Chapter 28** 28.1, 28.2, 28.3	
Science and technology in society Code: SPSP 5	**Chapter 1** 1.2, 1.3 **Chapter 3** 3.2, 3.3 **Chapter 4** 4.2 **Chapter 5** 5.1, 5.2 **Chapter 6** 6.1, 6.2 **Chapter 7** 7.2 **Chapter 10** 10.2, 10.3	**Chapter 11** 11.2 **Chapter 12** 12.4 **Chapter 13** 13.3 **Chapter 16** 16.2 **Chapter 17** 17.1 **Chapter 19** 19.1 **Chapter 21** 21.1, 21.2	**Chapter 23** 23.1, 23.3 **Chapter 25** 25.1, 25.2, 25.3 **Chapter 26** 26.3 **Chapter 27** 27.1 **Chapter 28** 28.2, 28.3	

History and Nature of Science

Standard	Chapter Correlation		
Science as a human endeavor Code: HNS 1	**Chapter 1** 1.1, 1.2, 1.3 **Chapter 2** 2.2, 2.3 **Chapter 3** 3.2, 3.3 **Chapter 6** 6.1 **Chapter 7** 7.2	**Chapter 8** 8.1 **Chapter 9** 9.1, 9.2 **Chapter 10** 10.2 **Chapter 11** 11.2 **Chapter 12** 12.3, 12.4	**Chapter 13** 13.1, 13.2 **Chapter 16** 16.2 **Chapter 24** 24.1, 24.2 **Chapter 27** 27.1
Nature of science Code: HNS 2	**Chapter 1** 1.1 **Chapter 2** 2.2 **Chapter 3** 3.2 **Chapter 5** 5.1, 5.2 **Chapter 6** 6.1	**Chapter 7** 7.1, 7.2, 7.3 **Chapter 8** 8.3 **Chapter 9** 9.1, 9.2 **Chapter 12** 12.1 **Chapter 13** 13.2, 13.3	**Chapter 14** 14.2 **Chapter 16** 16.2 **Chapter 17** 17.2 **Chapter 21** 21.2
History of science Code: HNS 3	**Chapter 1** 1.1, 1.3 **Chapter 3** 3.2, 3.3 **Chapter 5** 5.1, 5.2 **Chapter 6** 6.1	**Chapter 7** 7.2 **Chapter 8** 8.1, 8.3 **Chapter 9** 9.1 **Chapter 10** 10.2	**Chapter 14** 14.1 **Chapter 21** 21.1 **Chapter 24** 24.1 **Chapter 27** 27.1, 27.2

Life Science

CONTENT STANDARDS

STRUCTURE AND FUNCTION IN LIVING SYSTEMS

Standard	Chapter Correlation	
Living systems at all levels of organization demonstrate the complementary nature of structure and function. Important levels of organization for structure and function include cells, organs, tissues, organ systems, whole organisms, and ecosystems. Code: LS 1a	**Chapter 2** 2.3 **Chapter 3** 3.1, 3.2, 3.3 **Chapter 6** 6.1 **Chapter 8** 8.3 **Chapter 12** 12.2, 12.2, 12.3, 12.4 **Chapter 13** 13.1, 13.2 **Chapter 14** 14.1, 14.3 **Chapter 15** 15.1, 15.2, 15.3, 15.4	**Chapter 16** 16.1, 16.2, 16.3, 16.4 **Chapter 17** 17.1, 17.2 **Chapter 18** 18.1, 18.2, 18.3 **Chapter 20** 20.1, 20.2, 20.3 **Chapter 22** 22.1 **Chapter 23** 23.1, 23.2, 23.3 **Chapter 24** 24.1, 24.2 **Chapter 25** 25.1, 25.2 **Chapter 26** 26.2, 26.3
All organisms are composed of cells—the fundamental unit of life. Most organisms are single cells; other organisms, including humans, are multicellular. Code: LS 1b	**Chapter 2** 2.2 **Chapter 3** 3.1, 3.2 **Chapter 8** 8.2 **Chapter 9** 9.2	**Chapter 10** 10.1, 10.3 **Chapter 11** 11.1, 11.2 **Chapter 26** 26.3 **Chapter 27** 27.2
Cells carry on the many functions needed to sustain life. They grow and divide, thereby producing more cells. This requires that they take in nutrients, which they use to provide energy for the work that cells do and to make the materials that a cell or an organism needs. Code: LS 1c	**Chapter 2** 2.1, 2.2, 2.3 **Chapter 3** 3.1, 3.2, 3.3 **Chapter 4** 4.1, 4.2, 4.3 **Chapter 5** 5.2 **Chapter 10** 10.1, 10.2 **Chapter 11** 11.1, 11.2	**Chapter 12** 12.2 **Chapter 13** 13.2 **Chapter 22** 22.4 **Chapter 23** 23.1, 23.3, 23.3 **Chapter 24** 24.2
Specialized cells perform specialized functions in multicellular organisms. Groups of specialized cells cooperate to form a tissue, such as a muscle. Different tissues are in turn grouped together and form larger functional units, called organs. Each type of cell, tissue, and organ has a distinct structure and set of functions that serve the organism as a whole. Code: LS 1d	**Chapter 2** 2.1 **Chapter 3** 3.1, 3.2 **Chapter 5** 5.2 **Chapter 11** 11.2 **Chapter 12** 12.3, 12.4 **Chapter 14** 14.1 **Chapter 15** 15.1, 15.3, 15.4 **Chapter 16** 16.1, 16.2	**Chapter 17** 17.1, 17.2 **Chapter 22** 22.1, 22.2, 22.3, 22.4 **Chapter 23** 23.1, 23.2, 23.3 **Chapter 24** 24.1, 24.2 **Chapter 25** 25.1, 25.2 **Chapter 26** 26.2, 26.3 **Chapter 27** 27.2, 27.3
The human organism has systems for digestion, respiration, reproduction, circulation, excretion, movement, control and coordination, and protection from disease. These systems interact with one another. Code: LS 1e	**Chapter 3** 3.1 **Chapter 22** 22.1, 22.2, 22.3, 22.4 **Chapter 23** 23.1, 23.2, 23.3	**Chapter 24** 24.1, 24.2 **Chapter 25** 25.1, 25.2, 25.3 **Chapter 27** 27.2
Disease is the breakdown in structures or functions of an organism. Some diseases are the result of intrinsic failures of the system. Others are the result of damage by infection by other organisms. Code: LS 1f	**Chapter 5** 5.1 **Chapter 6** 6.2 **Chapter 9** 9.2 **Chapter 10** 10.2, 10.3 **Chapter 11** 11.1, 11.2 **Chapter 15** 15.1, 15.3	**Chapter 22** 22.4 **Chapter 23** 23.1, 23.2, 23.3 **Chapter 24** 24.1, 24.2 **Chapter 25** 25.1, 25.3 **Chapter 26** 26.2 **Chapter 27** 27.1, 27.2, 27.3

REPRODUCTION AND HEREDITY

Standard	Chapter Correlation	
Reproduction is a characteristic of all living systems; because no living organism lives forever, reproduction is essential to the continuation of every species. Some organisms reproduce asexually. Others reproduce sexually. Code: LS 2a	**Chapter 2** 2.1 **Chapter 9** 9.2 **Chapter 10** 10.1 **Chapter 11** 11.1, 11.2 **Chapter 13** 13.1	**Chapter 14** 14.3 **Chapter 15** 15.1, 15.2 **Chapter 16** 16.2, 16.4 **Chapter 17** 17.2 **Chapter 26** 26.1

Reproduction and Heredity (cont'd)

Standard | Chapter Correlation

Standard	Chapter Correlation
In many species, including humans, females produce eggs and males produce sperm. Plants also reproduce sexually—the egg and sperm are produced in the flowers of flowering plants. An egg and sperm unite to begin development of a new individual. The individual receives genetic information from its mother (via the egg) and its father (via the sperm). Sexually produced offspring never are identical to either of their parents. Code: LS 2b	**Chapter 2** 2.1 **Chapter 5** 5.1, 5.2 **Chapter 6** 6.2 **Chapter 12** 12.1, 12.2, 12.3, 12.4 **Chapter 13** 13.1, 13.3 **Chapter 14** 14.1 **Chapter 16** 16.2, 16.4 **Chapter 26** 26.1, 26.2, 26.3
Every organism requires a set of instructions for specifying its traits. Heredity is the passage of these instructions from one generation to another. Code: LS 2c	**Chapter 2** 2.1, 2.3 **Chapter 3** 3.2 **Chapter 5** 5.1, 5.2 **Chapter 6** 6.1, 6.2 **Chapter 7** 7.2, 7.3 **Chapter 9** 9.2 **Chapter 12** 12.3 **Chapter 13** 13.3
Hereditary information is contained in the genes, located in the chromosomes of each cell. Each gene carries a single unit of information. An inherited trait of an individual can be determined by one or by many genes, and a single gene can influence more than one trait. A human cell contains many thousands of different genes. Code: LS 2d	**Chapter 4** 4.3 **Chapter 5** 5.1, 5.2 **Chapter 6** 6.1, 6.2 **Chapter 12** 12.3 **Chapter 13** 13.1 **Chapter 26** 26.1
The characteristics of an organism can be described in terms of a combination of traits. Some traits are inherited and others result from interactions with the environment. Code: LS 2e	**Chapter 5** 5.1 **Chapter 6** 6.1, 6.2 **Chapter 16** 16.4

Regulation and Behavior

Standard | Chapter Correlation

Standard	Chapter Correlation
All organisms must be able to obtain and use resources, grow, reproduce, and maintain stable internal conditions while living in a constantly changing external environment. Code: LS 3a	**Chapter 2** 2.1, 2.2 **Chapter 3** 3.3 **Chapter 7** 7.1, 7.2 **Chapter 8** 8.1, 8.2 **Chapter 10** 10.1 **Chapter 11** 11.1 **Chapter 13** 13.3 **Chapter 14** 14.2 **Chapter 15** 15.1, 15.2, 15.4 **Chapter 16** 16.1, 16.4 **Chapter 17** 17.1, 17.2 **Chapter 18** 18.3 **Chapter 20** 20.1 **Chapter 21** 21.1 **Chapter 22** 22.1, 22.4 **Chapter 24** 24.2 **Chapter 25** 25.1, 25.2, 25.3 **Chapter 27** 27.2
Regulation of an organism's internal environment involves sensing the internal environment and changing physiological activities to keep conditions within the range required to survive. Code: LS 3b	**Chapter 2** 2.1 **Chapter 3** 3.2 **Chapter 10** 10.1 **Chapter 14** 14.2 **Chapter 16** 16.1 **Chapter 17** 17.1 **Chapter 22** 22.4 **Chapter 23** 23.1 **Chapter 24** 24.1, 24.2 **Chapter 25** 25.1, 25.3 **Chapter 27** 27.2, 27.3
Behavior is one kind of response an organism can make to an internal or environmental stimulus. A behavioral response requires coordination and communication at many levels, including cells, organ systems, and whole organisms. Behavioral response is a set of actions determined in part by heredity and in part from experience. Code: LS 3c	**Chapter 2** 2.1, 2.3 **Chapter 13** 13.2, 13.3 **Chapter 14** 14.2, 14.3 **Chapter 15** 15.3 **Chapter 16** 16.1, 16.2, 16.3, 16.4 **Chapter 17** 17.1, 17.2 **Chapter 18** 18.3 **Chapter 20** 20.1 **Chapter 25** 25.1, 25.3
An organism's behavior evolves through adaptation to its environment. How a species moves, obtains food, reproduces, and responds to danger are based in the species' evolutionary history. Code: LS 3d	**Chapter 2** 2.2 **Chapter 7** 7.1, 7.2, 7.3 **Chapter 12** 12.4 **Chapter 13** 13.3 **Chapter 14** 14.2, 14.3 **Chapter 16** 16.1, 16.2, 16.3, 16.4 **Chapter 18** 18.3 **Chapter 20** 20.1, 20.2, 20.3

POPULATIONS AND ECOSYSTEMS

Standard	Chapter Correlation	
A population consists of all individuals of a species that occur together at a given place and time. All populations living together and the physical factors with which they interact compose an ecosystem. Code: LS 4a	**Chapter 3** 3.1 **Chapter 14** 14.2, 14.3 **Chapter 18** 18.1, 18.2, 18.3 **Chapter 20** 20.2, 20.3	
Populations of organisms can be categorized by the functions they serve in an ecosystem. Plants and some micro-organisms are producers—they make their own food. All animals, including humans, are consumers, which obtain their food by eating other organisms. Decomposers, primarily bacteria and fungi, are consumers that use waste materials and dead organisms for food. Food webs identify the relationship among producers, consumers, and decomposers in an ecosystem. Code: LS 4b	**Chapter 2** 2.2 **Chapter 9** 9.2 **Chapter 10** 10.1 **Chapter 11** 11.1, 11.2 **Chapter 12** 12.3 **Chapter 14** 14.1	**Chapter 15** 15.1, 15.2, 15.3, 15.4 **Chapter 18** 18.2 **Chapter 20** 20.1, 20.2, 20.3
For ecosystems, the major source of energy is sunlight. Energy entering ecosystems as sunlight is transferred by producers into chemical energy through photosynthesis. That energy passes from organism to organism in food webs. Code: LS 4c	**Chapter 2** 2.2 **Chapter 4** 4.2 **Chapter 9** 9.2 **Chapter 11** 11.1, 11.2	**Chapter 12** 12.1, 12.3, 12.4 **Chapter 13** 13.2 **Chapter 18** 18.1, 18.2 **Chapter 20** 20.1, 20.2, 20.3
The number of organisms an ecosystem can support depends on the resources available and abiotic factors, such as the quantity of light and water, range of temperatures, and soil composition. Given adequate biotic and abiotic resources and no disease or predators, populations (including humans) increase at rapid rates. Lack of resources and other factors, such as predation and climate, limit the growth of populations in specific niches in the ecosystem. Code: LS 4d	**Chapter 2** 2.2 **Chapter 12** 12.3 **Chapter 14** 14.2, 14.3	**Chapter 18** 18.1, 18.2, 18.3 **Chapter 20** 20.1, 20.2, 20.3 **Chapter 21** 21.1

DIVERSITY AND ADAPTATIONS OF ORGANISMS

Standard	Chapter Correlation	
Millions of species of animals, plants, and microorganisms are alive today. Although different species might look dissimilar, the unity among organisms becomes apparent from an analysis of internal structures, the similarity of their chemical processes, and the evidence of common ancestry. Code: LS 5a	**Chapter 2** 2.1 **Chapter 3** 3.2, 3.3 **Chapter 6** 6.1 **Chapter 7** 7.1 **Chapter 8** 8.3 **Chapter 9** 9.1 **Chapter 11** 11.1	**Chapter 12** 12.1 **Chapter 14** 14.1 **Chapter 15** 15.1, 15.2, 15.3, 15.4 **Chapter 16** 16.1, 16.2, 16.4 **Chapter 17** 17.1, 17.2 **Chapter 20** 20.1
Biological evolution accounts for the diversity of species developed through gradual processes over many generations. Species acquire many of their unique characteristics through biological adaptation, which involves the selection of naturally occurring variations in populations. Biological adaptations include changes in structures, behaviors, or physiology that enhance survival and reproductive success in a particular environment. Code: LS 5b	**Chapter 3** 3.3 **Chapter 6** 6.2 **Chapter 7** 7.1, 7.2, 7.3 **Chapter 9** 9.2 **Chapter 12** 12.3, 12.4 **Chapter 13** 13.1, 13.3 **Chapter 14** 14.2	**Chapter 16** 16.3, 16.4 **Chapter 17** 17.1 **Chapter 20** 20.1
Extinction of a species occurs when the environment changes and the adaptive characteristics of a species are insufficient to allow its survival. Fossils indicate that many organisms that lived long ago are extinct. Extinction of species is common; most of the species that have lived on Earth no longer exist. Code: LS 5c	**Chapter 7** 7.1, 7.2, 7.3 **Chapter 8** 8.1, 8.2 **Chapter 12** 12.2 **Chapter 14** 14.2 **Chapter 16** 16.2, 16.3, 16.4	**Chapter 17** 17.2 **Chapter 21** 21.2

HOLT SCIENCE & TECHNOLOGY

Life Science

Annotated Teacher's Edition

HOLT, RINEHART AND WINSTON

A Harcourt Classroom Education Company

Austin • New York • Orlando • Atlanta • San Francisco • Boston • Dallas • Toronto • London

Acknowledgments

Contributing Authors

Katy Z. Allen
Science Writer and Former Biology Teacher
Wayland, Massachusetts

Linda Ruth Berg, Ph.D.
Adjunct Professor–Natural Sciences
St. Petersburg Junior College
St. Petersburg, Florida

Jennie Dusheck
Science Writer
Santa Cruz, California

Mark F. Taylor, Ph.D.
Associate Professor of Biology
Baylor University
Waco, Texas

Lab Writers

Diana Scheidle Bartos
Science Consultant and Educator
Diana Scheidle Bartos, L.L.C.
Lakewood, Colorado

Carl Benson
General Science Teacher
Plains High School
Plains, Montana

Charlotte Blassingame
Technology Coordinator
White Station Middle School
Memphis, Tennessee

Marsha Carver
Science Teacher and Dept. Chair
McLean County High School
Calhoun, Kentucky

Kenneth E. Creese
Science Teacher
White Mountain Junior High School
Rock Springs, Wyoming

Linda Culp
Science Teacher and Dept. Chair
Thorndale High School
Thorndale, Texas

James Deaver
Science Teacher and Dept. Chair
West Point High School
West Point, Nebraska

Frank McKinney, Ph.D.
Professor of Geology
Appalachian State University
Boone, North Carolina

Alyson Mike
Science Teacher
East Valley Middle School
East Helena, Montana

C. Ford Morishita
Biology Teacher
Clackamas High School
Milwaukie, Oregon

Patricia D. Morrell, Ph.D.
Assistant Professor, School of Education
University of Portland
Portland, Oregon

Hilary C. Olson, Ph.D.
Research Associate
Institute for Geophysics
The University of Texas
Austin, Texas

James B. Pulley
Science Editor and Former Science Teacher
Liberty High School
Liberty, Missouri

Denice Lee Sandefur
Science Chairperson
Nucla High School
Nucla, Colorado

Patti Soderberg
Science Writer
The BioQUEST Curriculum Consortium
Beloit College
Beloit, Wisconsin

Phillip Vavala
Science Teacher and Dept. Chair
Salesianum School
Wilmington, Delaware

Albert C. Wartski
Biology Teacher
Chapel Hill High School
Chapel Hill, North Carolina

Lynn Marie Wartski
Science Writer and Former Science Teacher
Hillsborough, North Carolina

Ivora D. Washington
Science Teacher and Dept. Chair
Hyattsville Middle School
Washington, D.C.

Academic Reviewers

Renato J. Aguilera, Ph.D.
Associate Professor
Department of Molecular, Cell, and Developmental Biology
University of California
Los Angeles, California

David M. Armstrong, Ph.D.
Professor of Biology
Department of E.P.O. Biology
University of Colorado
Boulder, Colorado

Alissa Arp, Ph.D.
Director and Professor of Environmental Studies
Romberg Tiburon Center
San Francisco State University
Tiburon, California

Russell M. Brengelman
Professor of Physics
Morehead State University
Morehead, Kentucky

John A. Brockhaus, Ph.D.
Director of Mapping, Charting, and Geodesy Program
Department of Geography and Environmental Engineering
United States Military Academy
West Point, New York

Linda K. Butler, Ph.D.
Lecturer of Biological Sciences
The University of Texas
Austin, Texas

Copyright © 2004 by Holt, Rinehart and Winston

All rights reserved. No part of this publication may be reproduced or transmitted in any form or by any means, electronic or mechanical, including photocopy, recording, or any information storage and retrieval system, without permission in writing from the publisher.

Requests for permission to make copies of any part of the work should be mailed to the following address: Permissions Department, Holt, Rinehart and Winston, 10801 N. MoPac Expressway, Building 3, Austin, Texas 78759.

SciLinks is owned and provided by the National Science Teachers Association. All rights reserved.

Printed in the United States of America
ISBN 0-03-073173-9
1 2 3 4 5 6 7 048 06 05 04 03 02

Acknowledgments (cont.)

Barry Chernoff, Ph.D.
Associate Curator
Division of Fishes
The Field Museum of Natural History
Chicago, Illinois

Donna Greenwood Crenshaw, Ph.D.
Instuctor
Department of Biology
Duke University
Durham, North Carolina

Hugh Crenshaw, Ph.D.
Assistant Professor of Zoology
Duke University
Durham, North Carolina

Joe W. Crim, Ph.D.
Professor of Biology
University of Georgia
Athens, Georgia

Peter Demmin, Ed.D.
Former Science Teacher and Chair
Amherst Central High School
Amherst, New York

Joseph L. Graves, Jr., Ph.D.
Associate Professor of Evolutionary Biology
Arizona State University West
Phoenix, Arizona

William B. Guggino, Ph.D.
Professor of Physiology and Pediatrics
The Johns Hopkins University School of Medicine
Baltimore, Maryland

David Haig, Ph.D.
Assistant Professor of Biology
Department of Organismic and Evolutionary Biology
Harvard University
Cambridge, Massachusetts

Roy W. Hann, Jr., Ph.D.
Professor of Civil Engineering
Texas A&M University
College Station, Texas

John E. Hoover, Ph.D.
Associate Professor of Biology
Millersville University
Millersville, Pennsylvania

Joan E. N. Hudson, Ph.D.
Associate Professor of Biological Sciences
Sam Houston State University
Huntsville, Texas

Laurie Jackson-Grusby, Ph.D.
Research Scientist and Doctoral Associate
Whitehead Institute for Biomedical Research
Massachusetts Institute of Technology
Cambridge, Massachusetts

George M. Langford, Ph.D.
Professor of Biological Sciences
Dartmouth College
Hanover, New Hampshire

Melanie C. Lewis, Ph.D.
Professor of Biology, Retired
Southwest Texas State University
San Marcos, Texas

V. Patteson Lombardi, Ph.D.
Research Assistant Professor of Biology
Department of Biology
University of Oregon
Eugene, Oregon

Glen Longley, Ph.D.
Professor of Biology and Director of the Edwards Aquifer Research Center
Southwest Texas State University
San Marcos, Texas

William F. McComas, Ph.D.
Director of the Center to Advance Science Education
University of Southern California
Los Angeles, California

LaMoine L. Motz, Ph.D.
Coordinator of Science Education
Oakland County Schools
Waterford, Michigan

Nancy Parker, Ph.D.
Associate Professor of Biology
Southern Illinois University
Edwardsville, Illinois

Barron S. Rector, Ph.D.
Associate Professor and Extension Range Specialist
Texas Agricultural Extension Service
Texas A&M University
College Station, Texas

Peter Sheridan, Ph.D.
Professor of Chemistry
Colgate University
Hamilton, New York

Miles R. Silman, Ph.D.
Assistant Professor of Biology
Wake Forest University
Winston-Salem, North Carolina

Neil Simister, Ph.D.
Associate Professor of Biology
Department of Life Sciences
Brandeis University
Waltham, Massachusetts

Lee Smith, Ph.D.
Curriculum Writer
MDL Information Systems, Inc.
San Leandro, California

Robert G. Steen, Ph.D.
Manager, Rat Genome Project
Whitehead Institute—Center for Genome Research
Massachusetts Institute of Technology
Cambridge, Massachusetts

Martin VanDyke, Ph.D.
Professor of Chemistry Emeritus
Front Range Community College
Westminister, Colorado

E. Peter Volpe, Ph.D.
Professor of Medical Genetics
Mercer University School of Medicine
Macon, Georgia

Harold K. Voris, Ph.D.
Curator and Head
Division of Amphibians and Reptiles
The Field Museum of Natural History
Chicago, Illinois

Mollie Walton
Biology Instructor
El Paso Community College
El Paso, Texas

Peter Wetherwax, Ph.D.
Professor of Biology
University of Oregon
Eugene, Oregon

Mary K. Wicksten, Ph.D.
Professor of Biology
Texas A&M University
College Station, Texas

R. Stimson Wilcox, Ph.D.
Associate Professor of Biology
Department of Biological Sciences
Binghamton University
Binghamton, New York

Conrad M. Zapanta, Ph.D.
Research Engineer
Sulzer Carbomedics, Inc.
Austin, Texas

Safety Reviewer

Jack Gerlovich, Ph.D.
Associate Professor
School of Education
Drake University
Des Moines, Iowa

Teacher Reviewers

Barry L. Bishop
Science Teacher and Dept. Chair
San Rafael Junior High School
Ferron, Utah

Carol A. Bornhorst
Science Teacher and Dept. Chair
Bonita Vista Middle School
Chula Vista, California

Paul Boyle
Science Teacher
Perry Heights Middle School
Evansville, Indiana

Yvonne Brannum
Science Teacher and Dept. Chair
Hine Junior High School
Washington, D.C.

Gladys Cherniak
Science Teacher
St. Paul's Episcopal School
Mobile, Alabama

James Chin
Science Teacher
Frank A. Day Middle School
Newtonville, Massachusetts

Kenneth Creese
Science Teacher
White Mountain Junior High School
Rock Springs, Wyoming

Linda A. Culp
Science Teacher and Dept. Chair
Thorndale High School
Thorndale, Texas

Georgiann Delgadillo
Science Teacher
East Valley Continuous Curriculum School
Spokane, Washington

Alonda Droege
Biology Teacher
Evergreen High School
Seattle, Washington

Acknowledgments (cont.)

Michael J. DuPré
Curriculum Specialist
Rush Henrietta Junior-Senior High School
Henrietta, New York

Rebecca Ferguson
Science Teacher
North Ridge Middle School
North Richland Hills, Texas

Susan Gorman
Science Teacher
North Ridge Middle School
North Richland Hills, Texas

Gary Habeeb
Science Mentor
Sierra-Plumas Joint Unified School District
Downieville, California

Karma Houston-Hughes
Science Mentor
Kyrene Middle School
Tempe, Arizona

Roberta Jacobowitz
Science Teacher
C. W. Otto Middle School
Lansing, Michigan

Kerry A. Johnson
Science Teacher
Isbell Middle School
Santa Paula, California

M. R. Penny Kisiah
Science Teacher and Dept. Chair
Fairview Middle School
Tallahassee, Florida

Kathy LaRoe
Science Teacher
East Valley Middle School
East Helena, Montana

Jane M. Lemons
Science Teacher
Western Rockingham Middle School
Madison, North Carolina

Scott Mandel, Ph.D.
Director and Educational Consultant
Teachers Helping Teachers
Los Angeles, California

Thomas Manerchia
Former Biology and Life Science Teacher
Archmere Academy
Claymont, Delaware

Maurine O. Marchani
Science Teacher and Dept. Chair
Raymond Park Middle School
Indianapolis, Indiana

Jason P. Marsh
Biology Teacher
Montevideo High School and Montevideo Country School
Montevideo, Minnesota

Edith C. McAlanis
Science Teacher and Dept. Chair
Socorro Middle School
El Paso, Texas

Kevin McCurdy, Ph.D.
Science Teacher
Elmwood Junior High School
Rogers, Arkansas

Kathy McKee
Science Teacher
Hoyt Middle School
Des Moines, Iowa

Alyson Mike
Science Teacher
East Valley Middle School
East Helena, Montana

Donna Norwood
Science Teacher and Dept. Chair
Monroe Middle School
Charlotte, North Carolina

James B. Pulley
Former Science Teacher
Liberty High School
Liberty, Missouri

Terry J. Rakes
Science Teacher
Elmwood Junior High School
Rogers, Arkansas

Elizabeth Rustad
Science Teacher
Crane Middle School
Yuma, Arizona

Debra A. Sampson
Science Teacher
Booker T. Washington Middle School
Elgin, Texas

Charles Schindler
Curriculum Advisor
San Bernadino City Unified Schools
San Bernadino, California

Bert J. Sherwood
Science Teacher
Socorro Middle School
El Paso, Texas

Patricia McFarlane Soto
Science Teacher and Dept. Chair
G. W. Carver Middle School
Miami, Florida

David M. Sparks
Science Teacher
Redwater Junior High School
Redwater, Texas

Elizabeth Truax
Science Teacher
Lewiston-Porter Central School
Lewiston, New York

Ivora Washington
Science Teacher and Dept. Chair
Hyattsville Middle School
Washington, D.C.

Elsie N. Waynes
Science Teacher and Dept. Chair
R. H. Terrell Junior High School
Washington, D.C.

Nancy Wesorick
Science and Math Teacher
Sunset Middle School
Longmont, Colorado

Alexis S. Wright
Middle School Science Coordinator
Rye Country Day School
Rye, New York

John Zambo
Science Teacher
E. Ustach Middle School
Modesto, California

Gordon Zibelman
Science Teacher
Drexel Hill Middle School
Drexell Hill, Pennsylvania

Acknowledgments continue on page 853.

Contents in Brief

Unit 1 **The Study of Living Things**   2
- **Chapter 1** The World of Life Science 4
- **Chapter 2** It's Alive!! Or, Is It? 34

Unit 2 **Cells**   52
- **Chapter 3** Cells: The Basic Units of Life 54
- **Chapter 4** The Cell in Action 82

Unit 3 **Heredity, Evolution, and Classification**   102
- **Chapter 5** Heredity 104
- **Chapter 6** Genes and Gene Technology 126
- **Chapter 7** The Evolution of Living Things 148
- **Chapter 8** The History of Life on Earth 174
- **Chapter 9** Classification 200

Unit 4 **Simple Organisms, Fungi, and Plants**   220
- **Chapter 10** Bacteria and Viruses 222
- **Chapter 11** Protists and Fungi 242
- **Chapter 12** Introduction to Plants 268
- **Chapter 13** Plant Processes 298

Unit 5 **Animals**   318
- **Chapter 14** Animals and Behavior 320
- **Chapter 15** Invertebrates 342
- **Chapter 16** Fishes, Amphibians, and Reptiles ... 372
- **Chapter 17** Birds and Mammals 398

Unit 6 **Ecology**   430
- **Chapter 18** Interactions of Living Things 432
- **Chapter 19** Cycles in Nature 456
- **Chapter 20** The Earth's Ecosystems 472
- **Chapter 21** Environmental Problems and Solutions ... 496

Unit 7 **Human Body Systems**   518
- **Chapter 22** Body Organization and Structure ... 520
- **Chapter 23** Circulation and Respiration 544
- **Chapter 24** The Digestive and Urinary Systems ... 566
- **Chapter 25** Communication and Control 586
- **Chapter 26** Reproduction and Development 610

Unit 8 **Human Health**   632
- **Chapter 27** Body Defenses and Disease 634
- **Chapter 28** Staying Healthy 654

LabBook 680

Contents

Master Materials List xxviii
Science & Math Skills Worksheets xxxiv

Unit 1 ··· The Study of Living Things

Timeline 2

CHAPTER 1

Chapter Organizer 3A
Chapter Resources & Worksheets 3C
Chapter Background 3E

The World of Life Science 4
   Section 1 Asking About Life 6
   Section 2 Thinking Like a Life Scientist 10
   Section 3 Tools of Life Scientists 19

Chapter Highlights/Review 28

Feature Articles
   Career: Zoologist 32
   Science Fiction: "The Homesick Chicken" 33

LabBook
- Safety First! 682
- Does It All Add Up? 686
- Graphing Data 688
- A Window to a Hidden World 689

CHAPTER 2

Chapter Organizer 33A
Chapter Resources & Worksheets 33C
Chapter Background 33E

It's Alive!! Or, Is It? 34
   Section 1 Characteristics of Living Things 36
   Section 2 The Simple Bare Necessities of Life 40
   Section 3 The Chemistry of Life 42

Chapter Highlights/Review 46

Feature Articles
   Scientific Debate: Life on Mars? 50
   Science Fiction: "They're Made Out of Meat" 51

LabBook
- Roly-Poly Races 690
- The Best-Bread Bakery Dilemma 692

vi Contents

Unit 2 ··· Cells

Timeline 52

CHAPTER 3

Chapter Organizer 53A
Chapter Resources & Worksheets 53C
Chapter Background 53E

Cells: The Basic Units of Life 54

- **Section 1** Organization of Life 56
- **Section 2** The Discovery of Cells 61
- **Section 3** Eukaryotic Cells: The Inside Story ... 68

Chapter Highlights/Review 76

Feature Articles

- **Across the Sciences:** Battling Cancer with Pigs' Blood and Laser Light 80
- **Health Watch:** The Scrape of the Future 81

LabBook

- Elephant-Sized Amoebas? 694
- Cells Alive! 696
- Name That Part! 697

CHAPTER 4

Chapter Organizer 81A
Chapter Resources & Worksheets 81C
Chapter Background 81E

The Cell in Action 82

- **Section 1** Exchange with the Environment 84
- **Section 2** Cell Energy 88
- **Section 3** The Cell Cycle 92

Chapter Highlights/Review 96

Feature Articles

- **Across the Sciences:** Electrifying News About Microbes 100
- **Science Fiction:** "Contagion" 101

LabBook

- The Perfect Taters Mystery 698
- Stayin' Alive! 700

Contents vii

Contents

Unit 3 — Heredity, Evolution, and Classification

Timeline 102

CHAPTER 5

Chapter Organizer 103A
Chapter Resources & Worksheets 103C
Chapter Background 103E

Heredity 104

Section 1 Mendel and His Peas 106
Section 2 Meiosis 114

Chapter Highlights/Review 120

Feature Articles
Science, Technology, and Society: Mapping the Human Genome 124
Health Watch: Lab Rats with Wings 125

LabBook
- Bug Builders, Inc. 702
- Tracing Traits 704

CHAPTER 6

Chapter Organizer 125A
Chapter Resources & Worksheets 125C
Chapter Background 125E

Genes and Gene Technology 126

Section 1 What Do Genes Look Like? 128
Section 2 How DNA Works 136

Chapter Highlights/Review 142

Feature Articles
Scientific Debate: DNA on Trial 146
Science Fiction: "Moby James" 147

LabBook
- Base-Pair Basics 706

CHAPTER 7

Chapter Organizer **147A**
Chapter Resources & Worksheets **147C**
Chapter Background **147E**

The Evolution of Living Things 148

Section 1 Change Over Time 150
Section 2 How Does Evolution Happen? 158
Section 3 Natural Selection in Action 164

Chapter Highlights/Review 168

Feature Articles

Eye on the Environment: Saving at the Seed Bank ... 172
Science Fiction: "The Anatomy Lesson" 173

LabBook

- Mystery Footprints 708
- Out-of-Sight Marshmallows 710
- Survival of the Chocolates 711

CHAPTER 8

Chapter Organizer **173A**
Chapter Resources & Worksheets **173C**
Chapter Background **173E**

The History of Life on Earth 174

Section 1 Evidence of the Past 176
Section 2 Eras of the Geologic Time Scale 182
Section 3 Human Evolution 188

Chapter Highlights/Review 194

Feature Articles

Across the Sciences: Windows into the Past 198
Careers: Paleobotanist 199

LabBook

- Dating the Fossil Record 712
- The Half-life of Pennies 715

Contents **ix**

Contents

CHAPTER 9

Chapter Organizer **199A**
Chapter Resources & Worksheets **199C**
Chapter Background **199E**

Classification 200

Section 1 Classification: Sorting It All Out 202
Section 2 The Six Kingdoms 208

Chapter Highlights/Review 214

Feature Articles
Scientific Debate: It's a Bird, It's a Plane,
It's a *Dinosaur*? 218
Weird Science: Lobster-Lip Life-form 219

LabBook
- Shape Island 716
- Voyage of the USS *Adventure* 718

Unit 4 ··· Simple Organisms, Fungi, and Plants

Timeline 220

CHAPTER 10

Chapter Organizer **221A**
Chapter Resources & Worksheets **221C**
Chapter Background **221E**

Bacteria and Viruses 222

Section 1 Bacteria 224
Section 2 Bacteria's Role in the World 229
Section 3 Viruses 233

Chapter Highlights/Review 236

Feature Articles
Science, Technology, and Society: Edible Vaccines 240
Health Watch: Helpful Viruses 241

LabBook
- Aunt Flossie and the Intruder 720
- Viral Decorations 721

CHAPTER 11

Chapter Organizer 241A
Chapter Resources & Worksheets 241C
Chapter Background 241E

Protists and Fungi 242
Section 1 Protists 244
Section 2 Fungi 255

Chapter Highlights/Review 262

Feature Articles
Science, Technology, and Society: Moldy Bandages . . . 266
Across the Sciences: It's Alive! 267

LabBook
- Making a Protist Mobile 722
- There's a Fungus Among Us! 723

CHAPTER 12

Chapter Organizer 267A
Chapter Resources & Worksheets 267C
Chapter Background 267E

Introduction to Plants 268
Section 1 What Makes a Plant a Plant? 270
Section 2 Seedless Plants 274
Section 3 Plants with Seeds 278
Section 4 The Structures of Seed Plants 284

Chapter Highlights/Review 292

Feature Articles
Science, Technology, and Society: Supersquash
or Frankenfruit? 296
Careers: Ethnobotanist 297

LabBook
- Leaf Me Alone! 724
- Travelin' Seeds 726
- Build a Flower 727

Contents   xi

CHAPTER 13

Chapter Organizer 297A
Chapter Resources & Worksheets 297C
Chapter Background 297E

Plant Processes 298

Section 1 The Reproduction of Flowering Plants 300
Section 2 The Ins and Outs of Making Food 304
Section 3 Plant Responses to the Environment 307

Chapter Highlights/Review 312

Feature Articles
Weird Science: Mutant Mustard 316
Eye on the Environment: A Rainbow of Cotton 317

LabBook
- Food Factory Waste 728
- Weepy Weeds 730

Unit 5 ··· Animals

Timeline 318

CHAPTER 14

Chapter Organizer 319A
Chapter Resources & Worksheets 319C
Chapter Background 319E

Animals and Behavior 320

Section 1 What Is an Animal? 322
Section 2 Animal Behavior 326
Section 3 Living Together 332

Chapter Highlights/Review 336

Feature Articles
Eye on the Environment: Do Not Disturb! 340
Weird Science: Animal Cannibals 341

LabBook
- Wet, Wiggly Worms! 732
- Aunt Flossie and the Bumblebee 734

CHAPTER 15

Chapter Organizer 341A
Chapter Resources & Worksheets 341C
Chapter Background 341E

Invertebrates 342

Section 1 Simple Invertebrates 344
Section 2 Mollusks and Annelid Worms 352
Section 3 Arthropods 357
Section 4 Echinoderms 363

Chapter Highlights/Review 366

Feature Articles
Weird Science: Water Bears 370
Eye on the Environment: Sizable Squid 371

LabBook

- Porifera's Porosity 736
- The Cricket Caper 737

CHAPTER 16

Chapter Organizer 371A
Chapter Resources & Worksheets 371C
Chapter Background 371E

Fishes, Amphibians, and Reptiles 372

Section 1 What Are Vertebrates? 374
Section 2 Fishes 377
Section 3 Amphibians 382
Section 4 Reptiles 387

Chapter Highlights/Review 392

Feature Articles
Across the Sciences: Robot Fish 396
Weird Science: Warm Brains in Cold Water 397

LabBook

- Floating a Pipe Fish 740
- A Prince of a Frog 742

Contents **xiii**

Contents

CHAPTER 17
Chapter Organizer 397A
Chapter Resources & Worksheets 397C
Chapter Background 397E

Birds and Mammals 398
Section 1 Birds 400
Section 2 Mammals 410

Chapter Highlights/Review 424

Feature Articles
Across the Sciences: The Aerodynamics of Flight 428
Weird Science: Naked Mole-rats 429

LabBook
- What? No Dentist Bills? 744
- Wanted: Mammals on Mars 745

Unit 6 ··· Ecology
⋮ Timeline 430

CHAPTER 18
Chapter Organizer 431A
Chapter Resources & Worksheets 431C
Chapter Background 431E

Interactions of Living Things 432
Section 1 Everything Is Connected 434
Section 2 Living Things Need Energy 438
Section 3 Types of Interactions 444

Chapter Highlights/Review 450

Feature Articles
Health Watch: An Unusual Guest 454
Eye on the Environment: Alien Invasion 455

LabBook
- Adapation: It's a Way of Life 746
- Capturing the Wild Bean 748

CHAPTER 19

Chapter Organizer 455A
Chapter Resources & Worksheets 455C
Chapter Background 455E

Cycles in Nature 456

Section 1 The Cycles of Matter 458
Section 2 Ecological Succession 462

Chapter Highlights/Review 466

Feature Articles
Weird Science: Weather from Fire 470
Eye on the Environment: The Mysterious Dead Zone 471

LabBook

- Nitrogen Needs 750
- A Passel o' Pioneers 752

CHAPTER 20

Chapter Organizer 471A
Chapter Resources & Worksheets 471C
Chapter Background 471E

The Earth's Ecosystems 472

Section 1 Land Ecosystems 474
Section 2 Marine Ecosystems 481
Section 3 Freshwater Ecosystems 486

Chapter Highlights/Review 490

Feature Articles
Across the Sciences: Ocean Vents 494
Careers: Ecologist 495

LabBook

- Life in the Desert 754
- Discovering Mini-Ecosystems 755
- Too Much of a Good Thing? 756

CHAPTER 21

Chapter Organizer **495A**
Chapter Resources & Worksheets **495C**
Chapter Background **495E**

Environmental Problems and Solutions 496

Section 1 First the Bad News 498
Section 2 The Good News: Solutions 505

Chapter Highlights/Review 512

Feature Articles
Careers: Biologist 516
Scientific Debate: Where Should the Wolves Roam? . . . 517

LabBook
■ Biodiversity—What a Disturbing Thought! 758
■ Deciding About Environmental Issues 760

Unit 7 · · · Human Body Systems

Timeline 518

CHAPTER 22

Chapter Organizer **519A**
Chapter Resources & Worksheets **519C**
Chapter Background **519E**

Body Organization and Structure 520

Section 1 Body Organization 522
Section 2 The Skeletal System 526
Section 3 The Muscular System 530
Section 4 The Integumentary System 534

Chapter Highlights/Review 538

Feature Articles
Science, Technology, and Society: Engineered Skin . . . 542
Eureka!: Hairy Oil Spills 543

LabBook
■ Muscles at Work 762
■ Seeing Is Believing 763

xvi Contents

CHAPTER 23

Chapter Organizer 543A
Chapter Resources & Worksheets 543C
Chapter Background 543E

Circulation and Respiration 544

Section 1 The Cardiovascular System 546
Section 2 The Lymphatic System 554
Section 3 The Respiratory System 556

Chapter Highlights/Review 560

Feature Articles
Weird Science: Catching a Light Sneeze 564
Health Watch: Goats to the Rescue 565

- Build a Lung 766
- Carbon Dioxide Breath 767

CHAPTER 24

Chapter Organizer 565A
Chapter Resources & Worksheets 565C
Chapter Background 565E

The Digestive and Urinary Systems 566

Section 1 The Digestive System 568
Section 2 The Urinary System 576

Chapter Highlights/Review 580

Feature Articles
Across the Sciences: Quench Your Thirst! 584
Health Watch: A Voiceless Companion 585

- As the Stomach Churns 768
- Enzymes in Action 770

Contents xvii

Contents

CHAPTER **25**

Chapter Organizer 585A
Chapter Resources & Worksheets 585C
Chapter Background 585E

Communication and Control 586
Section 1 The Nervous System 588
Section 2 Responding to the Environment 595
Section 3 The Endocrine System 600

Chapter Highlights/Review 604

Feature Articles
Science, Technology, and Society: Light on Lenses ... 608
Eureka!: Pathway to a Cure 609

LabBook
- You've Gotta Lotta Nerve 772

CHAPTER **26**

Chapter Organizer 609A
Chapter Resources & Worksheets 609C
Chapter Background 609E

Reproduction and Development 610
Section 1 Animal Reproduction 612
Section 2 Human Reproduction 616
Section 3 Growth and Development 620

Chapter Highlights/Review 626

Feature Articles
Across the Sciences: Acne 630
Science, Technology, and Society: Technology in Its Infant Stages 631

LabBook
- It's a Comfy, Safe World! 774
- My, How You've Grown! 775

Unit 8 ··· Human Health
Timeline 632

CHAPTER 27

Chapter Organizer 633A
Chapter Resources & Worksheets 633C
Chapter Background 633E

Body Defenses and Disease 634
- **Section 1** Disease 636
- **Section 2** Your Body's Defenses 640
- **Section 3** Challenges to the Immune System 645

Chapter Highlights/Review 648

Feature Articles
- **Careers:** Naturopathic Physician 652
- **Health Watch:** Frogs in the Medicine Cabinet? 653

LabBook
- Antibodies to the Rescue 776
- Passing the Cold 778

CHAPTER 28

Chapter Organizer 653A
Chapter Resources & Worksheets 653C
Chapter Background 653E

Staying Healthy 654
- **Section 1** What We Put into Our Bodies 656
- **Section 2** Risks of Alcohol and Other Drugs 663
- **Section 3** Healthy Habits 669

Chapter Highlights/Review 674

Feature Articles
- **Science, Technology, and Society:** Bacteria at Your Service 678
- **Health Watch:** Meatless Munching 679

LabBook
- To Diet or Not to Diet 780
- Keep It Clean 781

Contents xix

Contents

LabBook 680

Self-Check Answers 782

Appendix 785
- Concept Mapping 786
- SI Measurement 787
- Temperature Scales 788
- Measuring Skills 789
- Scientific Method 790
- Making Charts and Graphs 793
- Math Refresher 796
- Periodic Table of the Elements 800
- Physical Science Refresher 802
- The Six Kingdoms 804
- Using the Microscope 806

Glossary 808

Spanish Glossary 820

Index 835

Answers to Concept Mapping Questions 854

The more labs, the better!

Take a minute to browse the **LabBook** located at the end of this textbook. You'll find a wide variety of exciting labs that will help you experience science firsthand. But please don't forget to be safe. Read the "Safety First!" section before starting any of the labs.

Safety First! **682**

CHAPTER 1 The World of Life Science
Does It All Add Up? 686
Graphing Data 688
A Window to a Hidden World 689

CHAPTER 2 It's Alive!! Or, Is It?
Roly-Poly Races 690
The Best-Bread Bakery Dilemma 692

CHAPTER 3 Cells: The Basic Units of Life
Elephant-Sized Amoebas? 694
Cells Alive! 696
Name That Part! 697

CHAPTER 4 The Cell in Action
The Perfect Taters Mystery 698
Stayin' Alive! 700

CHAPTER 5 Heredity
Bug Builders, Inc. 702
Tracing Traits 704

CHAPTER 6 Genes and Gene Technology
Base-Pair Basics 706

CHAPTER 7 The Evolution of Living Things
Mystery Footprints 708
Out-of-Sight Marshmallows 710
Survival of the Chocolates 711

CHAPTER 8 The History of Life on Earth
Dating the Fossil Record 712
The Half-life of Pennies 715

CHAPTER 9 Classification
Shape Island 716
Voyage of the USS *Adventure* 718

CHAPTER 10 Bacteria and Viruses
Aunt Flossie and the Intruder 720
Viral Decorations 721

CHAPTER 11 Protists and Fungi
Making a Protist Mobile 722
There's a Fungus Among Us! 723

CHAPTER 12 Introduction to Plants
Leaf Me Alone! 724
Travelin' Seeds 726
Build a Flower 727

CHAPTER 13 Plant Processes
Food Factory Waste 728
Weepy Weeds 730

CHAPTER 14 Animals and Behavior
Wet, Wiggly Worms! 732
Aunt Flossie and the Bumblebee 734

CHAPTER 15 Invertebrates
Porifera's Porosity 736
The Cricket Caper 737

CHAPTER 16 Fishes, Amphibians, and Reptiles
Floating a Pipe Fish 740
A Prince of a Frog 742

Contents

CHAPTER 17 Birds and Mammals
What? No Dentist Bills? 744
Wanted: Mammals on Mars 745

CHAPTER 18 Interactions of Living Things
Adaptation: It's a Way of Life 746
Capturing the Wild Bean .. : 748

CHAPTER 19 Cycles in Nature
Nitrogen Needs 750
A Passel o' Pioneers 752

CHAPTER 20 The Earth's Ecosystems
Life in the Desert 754
Discovering Mini-Ecosystems 755
Too Much of a Good Thing? 756

CHAPTER 21 Environmental Problems and Solutions
Biodiversity—What a Disturbing Thought! 758
Deciding About Environmental Issues 760

CHAPTER 22 Body Organization and Structure
Muscles at Work 762
Seeing Is Believing 763

CHAPTER 23 Circulation and Respiration
Build a Lung 766
Carbon Dioxide Breath 767

CHAPTER 24 The Digestive and Urinary Systems
As the Stomach Churns 768
Enzymes in Action 770

CHAPTER 25 Communication and Control
You've Gotta Lotta Nerve 772

CHAPTER 26 Reproduction and Development
It's a Comfy, Safe World! 774
My, How You've Grown! 775

CHAPTER 27 Body Defenses and Disease
Antibodies to the Rescue 776
Passing the Cold 778

CHAPTER 28 Staying Healthy
To Diet or Not to Diet 780
Keep It Clean 781

Contents

Start your engines with an activity!

Science is an activity in which investigation leads to information and understanding. The **Start-Up Activity** at the beginning of each chapter helps you gain scientific understanding of the topic through hands-on experience.

A Little Bit of Science 5
Lights On! 35
What Are Plants Made Of? . . 55
Cells in Action 83
Clothing Combos 105
Fingerprint Your Friends . . 127
Making a Fossil 149
Earth's Timeline 175
Classifying Shoes 201
Our Constant
 Companions 223
A Microscopic World 243
Observing Plant Growth . . 269
Which End Is Up? 299
Go on a Safari! 321
Classify It! 343
Oil on Water 373
Let's Fly! 399
Who Eats Whom? 433
A Classroom Aquarium . . . 457
A Mini-Ecosystem 473
Recycling Paper 497
Too Cold for Comfort . . . 521
Exercise and Your Heart . . 545
Changing Foods 567
Act Fast! 587
How Grows It? 611
Invisible Invaders 635
Conduct a Survey 655

QuickLab

See for Yourself 20
Starch Search 43
Do Bacteria Taste Good? . . 66
Bead Diffusion 84
Take Your Chances 112
Mutations 139
Could We Run
 out of Food? 161
Thumb Through This . . 189
Evolutionary Diagrams . 205
Spying on Spirilla 226
Moldy Bread 257
Observe a Mushrooom . 259
Moss Mass 275
Thirsty Seeds 302
Which Way Is Up? 308
How Long Is a Minute? . . 330
Sticky Webs 360
Body Temperature 376
Bernoulli Effect 404

Not all laboratory investigations have to be long and involved.

The **QuickLabs** found throughout the chapters in this book require only a small amount of time and limited equipment. But just because they are quick, don't skimp on the safety.

The Human Population . . 435
Combustion 460
Pond Food
 Connections 487
Trash Check 510
Pickled Bones 527
Power in Pairs. 531
Why Do People Snore? . . 559
Break It Up! 569
Knee Jerks 594
Where's the Dot? 597
Life Grows On 625
It's Only Skin Deep 641
A Healthy Diet 662

MATHBREAK

Averages 16
Finding Area 24
How Much Oxygen? 43
Surface-to-Volume Ratio . . 65
Cell Multiplication 92
Understanding Ratios . . 110
Genes and Bases 131
Building a Human
 Chain Around a
 Giant Sequoia 211
Airborne Organisms . . . 224
Sizing Up a Virus 233
Multiplying Yeasts 258
Practice with Percents . . 273
Bending by Degrees 307
Speeding Squid 352
A Lot of Bones 380

Science and math go hand in hand.

The **MathBreaks** in the margins of the chapters show you many ways that math applies directly to science and vice versa.

Ants for Dinner! 416
Energy Pyramids 441
Gallons Galore 461
Rainfall 480
Water Depletion 501
Runner's Time 533
The Beat Goes On 553
How Much Water? 578
Time to Travel 589
Chromo-Combos 613
Counting Eggs 617
Epidemic! 639
What Percentage? 661
Deadly Averages 666

Contents

Science can be very useful in the real world.
It is interesting to learn how scientific information is being used in the real world. You can see for yourself in the **Apply** features. You will also be asked to apply your own knowledge. This is a good way to learn!

Have Aliens Landed? 13		
Are Computers Alive? 39		
A Pet Paramecium 65		
Fantasy Island 91		
Curly Eared Cats 113		
Pedigree and Punnett Squares. 140		
A Breed All Their Own ... 163	Do Worms Make Good Neighbors? 355	Balloons Aloft 504
Classify This! 212	Ecological Indicators 385	Blood Delivery 552
Ingenious Engineering! ... 231	Bats and Submarines 418	Beverage Ban 578
A Mushroom Omelet ... 259	Coevolution in Australia .. 449	Fight or Flight? 601
The Accidental Garden... 279	The Pollution Cycle 461	Two Types of Twins 618
Can Trees Tell Time? 310	A Trip to Lake Superior ... 488	Cold Calamity 639
Jet Lag 331		Stress SOS 671

Connections

One science leads to another.
You may not realize it at first, but different areas of science are related to each other in many ways. Each **Connection** explores a topic from the viewpoint of another science discipline. In this way, areas of science merge to improve your understanding of the world around you.

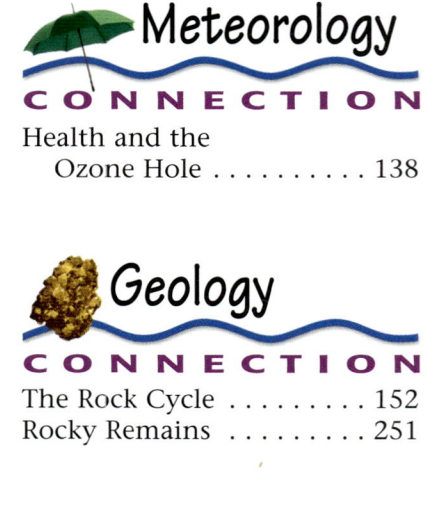

Oceanography CONNECTION
Antifreeze Fish 37
Eating Seaweed 658

Chemistry CONNECTION
Cellular ID Cards 58
Oxygen and Photosynthesis 89
Crystal Viruses 234
Glowing Protists 248
The Ozone Layer 500
Don't Sweat the Small Stuff 532
Breathing in the Mountains 557
Hormone Horrors 619

Meteorology CONNECTION
Health and the Ozone Hole 138

Geology CONNECTION
The Rock Cycle 152
Rocky Remains 251

Astronomy CONNECTION
Seasons and the Sun 309

Environment CONNECTION
Ozone Depletion 184
Ancient, Rare Sequoias ... 211
Animals and Seeds 279
Damaged Coral Reefs 349
Endangered Elephants 421
Global Warming 459
Drinkable Water 574

Physics CONNECTION
Magnetic Migration 331
Fish Eyes 378
Too High to Hear 598
Steamy Sterilization 638

Feature Articles

Feature articles for any appetite!
Science and technology affect us all in many ways. The following articles will give you an idea of just how interesting, strange, helpful, and action-packed science and technology are. At the end of each chapter, you will find two feature articles. Read them and you will be surprised at what you learn.

CAREERS

Zoologist	32
Paleobotanist	199
Ethnobotanist	297
Ecologist	495
Biologist	516
Naturopathic Physician	652

ACROSS THE SCIENCES

Battling Cancer with Pigs' Blood and Laser Light	80
Electrifying News About Microbes	100
Windows into the Past	198
It's Alive!	267
Robot Fish	396
The Aerodynamics of Flight	428
Ocean Vents	494
Quench Your Thirst!	584
Acne	630

Science, Technology, and Society

Mapping the Human Genome	124
Edible Vaccines	240
Moldy Bandages	266
Supersquash or Frankenfruit?	296
Engineered Skin	542
Light on Lenses	608
Technology in Its Infant Stages	631
Bacteria at Your Service	678

EYE ON THE ENVIRONMENT

Saving at the Seed Bank	172
A Rainbow of Cotton	317
Do Not Disturb!	340
Sizable Squid	371
Alien Invasion	455
The Mysterious Dead Zone	471

Eureka!

Hairy Oil Spills	543
Pathway to a Cure	609

Health

The Scrape of the Future	81
Lab Rats with Wings	125
Helpful Viruses	241
An Unusual Guest	454
Goats to the Rescue	565
A Voiceless Companion	585
Frogs in the Medicine Cabinet?	653
Meatless Munching	679

SCIENTIFIC DEBATE

Life on Mars?	50
DNA on Trial	146
It's a Bird, It's a Plane, It's a *Dinosaur*?	218
Where Should the Wolves Roam?	517

Science Fiction

"The Homesick Chicken"	33
"They're Made Out of Meat"	51
"Contagion"	101
"Moby James"	147
"The Anatomy Lesson"	173

Lobster-Lip Life-form	219
Mutant Mustard	316
Animal Cannibals	341
Water Bears	370
Warm Brains in Cold Water	397
Naked Mole-rats	429
Weather from Fire	470
Catching a Light Sneeze	564

How to Use Your Textbook

Your Roadmap for Success with *Holt Science & Technology*

Study the Terms to Learn
Key Terms are listed for each section. Learn the definitions of these terms because you will most likely be tested on them. Use the glossary to locate definitions quickly.

STUDY TIP If you don't understand a definition, reread the page where the term is introduced. The surrounding text should help make the definition easier to understand.

Read What You'll Do
Objectives tell you what you'll need to know.

STUDY TIP Reread the objectives when studying for a test to be sure you know the material.

Take Notes and Get Organized
Keep a science notebook so that you are ready to take notes when your teacher reviews the material in class. Keep your assignments in this notebook so that you can review them when studying for the chapter test. In addition, you will be asked to keep a *ScienceLog,* in which you will write your answers to certain questions. Your *ScienceLog* may be a section of your science notebook.

Be Resourceful, Use the Web

Internet Connect boxes in your textbook take you to resources that you can use for science projects, reports, and research papers. Go to **scilinks.org** and type in the SciLinks code to get information on a topic.

Visit go.hrw.com Find worksheets and other materials that go with your textbook at **go.hrw.com**. Click on the textbook icon and the table of contents to see all of the resources for each chapter.

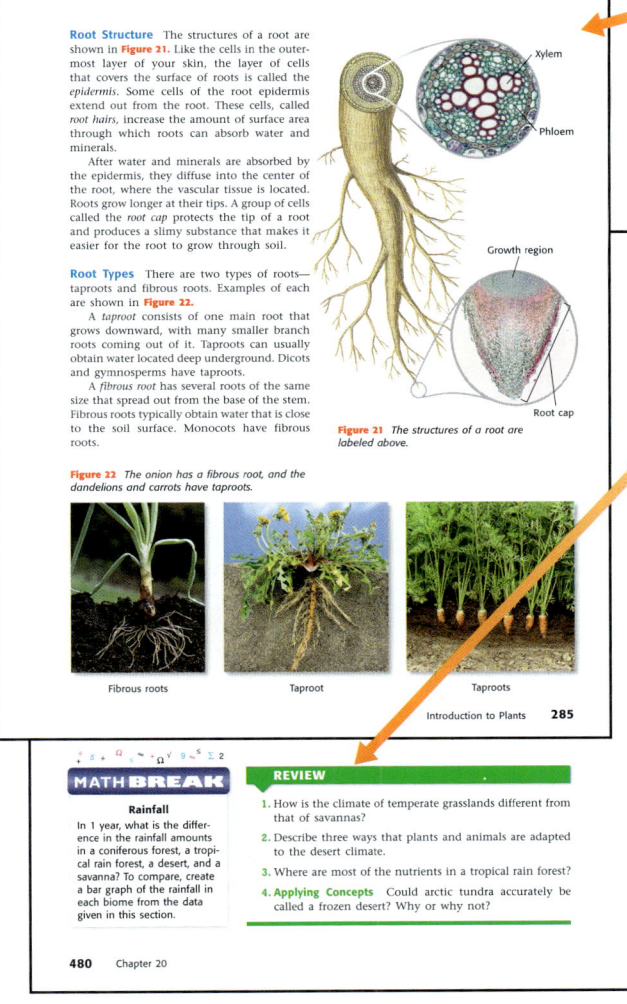

Use the Illustrations and Photos
Art shows complex ideas and processes. Learn to analyze the art so that you better understand the material you read in the text.

Tables and graphs display important information in an organized way to help you see relationships.

A picture is worth a thousand words. Look at the photographs to see relevant examples of science concepts you are reading about.

Answer the Section Reviews
Section Reviews test your knowledge over the main points of the section. Critical Thinking items challenge you to think about the material in greater depth and to find connections that you infer from the text.

STUDY TIP When you can't answer a question, reread the section. The answer is usually there.

Do Your Homework
Your teacher may assign worksheets to help you understand and remember the material in the chapter.

STUDY TIP Don't try to answer the questions without reading the text and reviewing your class notes. A little preparation up front will make your homework assignments a lot easier. Answering the items in the Chapter Review will help prepare you for the chapter test.

Visit Holt Online Learning
If your teacher gives you a special password to log onto the **Holt Online Learning** site, you'll find your complete textbook on the Web. In addition, you'll find some great learning tools and practice quizzes. You'll be able to see how well you know the material from your textbook.

Visit CNN Student News
You'll find up-to-date events in science at **cnnstudentnews.com**.

Master Materials List

The following chart provides a comprehensive list of all the materials you would need in order to teach all of the labs and investigations in *Holt Science and Technology, Life Science*.

For added convenience, Science Kit® provides materials-ordering software on CD-ROM designed specifically for *Holt Science and Technology*. This software allows you to create an electronic materials list, complete with item numbers. Using this software, you can order complete kits or individual items quickly and efficiently.

For more information about this software, contact your HRW representative, call Science Kit® directly at 1-800-828-7777, or visit the Web site: www.sciencekit.com.

As you can see from the listings, *Holt Science and Technology* is designed around readily available materials and equipment, with an emphasis on economy. More specific materials lists and information can be found with the lab or investigation in this *Annotated Teacher's Edition*.

MATERIALS AND EQUIPMENT CONSUMABLE	AMOUNT*	QuickLab PAGE NO.	START-UP Activity PAGE NO.	LabBook PAGE NO.
Agar, nutrient	30 mL		223, 635	781
Algae	1 sample			696
Aluminum foil	1 sheet	43	269	737
Animal, aquatic	5		457	
Apple	1		641	737
Bag, heavy-plastic, sealable, 9 × 12 in.	2			737
Bag, plastic, sealable	1	257		
Bag, plastic, sealable	2		567	744, 774
Bag, plastic, trash	1			766
Baking soda	10 g			728
Balloon, round	2		373	
Balloon, slender	1			740
Balloon, small	1			766
Beef, 1 cm cubes	3			768
Birdseed	$\frac{1}{8}$ lb			744
Bone, chicken	1	527		
Bottle, soda, 2 L	1		299, 473	766
Box, large	3		105	
Bread, slice	1	257		
Can, coffee	1		5	
Candle	1	460		
Candy, hard	2 pieces	569		
Card, index, 3 × 5 in.	1			727
Card, index, 3 × 5 in.	5		433	
Card, index, 3 × 5 in.	20	487		
Cardboard, 2 × 2 ft	1	308		
Carton, egg	2	161		
Celery leaves	1			732
Chalk	1 stick			690
Charcoal briquette	1		127	

*Amount is for one group of students.

MATERIALS AND EQUIPMENT CONSUMABLE (CONTINUED)	AMOUNT*	QuickLab PAGE NO.	START-UP Activity PAGE NO.	LabBook PAGE NO.
Chocolate, candy-coated	75			711
Clay, modeling	1 stick	460		
Clay, modeling	2 sticks		149	
Clay, water-resistant, modeling	2 sticks			766
Coat hanger, wire	1			722
Cotton ball	6	66		
Cotton ball	30			774
Cricket	2			737
Cricket, small, live	4			742
Cup, paper, 300 mL	1		149	
Cup, plastic	3	569	83	692, 698
Cup, plastic	6			698
Earthworm	1			732
Egg, chicken	1		373	
Egg, chicken, soft-boiled	3–5			774
Elodea sprig	1	55		
Elodea sprig, 20 cm long	3			728
Fertilizer	$\frac{1}{4}$ cup			756
Flour	$\frac{1}{2}$ cup			692
Flour	200 mL		567	
Food coloring, various colors	1 box	641		
Food sample, various types	5	43		
Fruit-juice agar plate	1			723
Gloves, protective	1 pair		635	686, 690, 720, 724, 728, 742, 750, 752, 756, 767, 768, 770, 774, 778
Gravel	6 oz		473	744
Gumdrop, black	10			702
Gumdrop, green	10			702
Hydrochloric acid, 0.1 M	10 mL			768
Hydrogen peroxide, diluted	4 mL			770
Iodine solution	20 mL	43		
Isopod	4			690
Leaf, fresh	1		149	
Leaf, fresh, various kinds	5			724
Liver, beef, 1 cm cubes	3			770
Magazine	2			746, 760
Marker, black, nonpermanent	1			686
Marker, black, permanent	1		201	730, 748, 763, 768
Marker, fine-point, washable	1			772
Marker, various colors	1 pack			614, 697, 712, 721, 722, 732, 745, 746
Marshmallow, large	15			702
Marshmallow, small, colored	50			710
Marshmallow, small, white	50			710

* Amount is for one group of students.

Master Materials List

Master Materials List

MATERIALS AND EQUIPMENT		QuickLab	Start-Up Activity	LabBook
CONSUMABLE (CONTINUED)	AMOUNT*	PAGE NO.	PAGE NO.	PAGE NO.
Meat tenderizer with bromelain	1 bottle			768
Meat tenderizer with papain	1 bottle			768
Moss, dry sphagnum	1 sample	275		
Mushroom	1	259		723
Newspaper	1		497	689, 760
Oil, cooking	70 mL		373	
Oil, cooking	100 mL		567	
Oil, cooking	1 cup	360		774
Paper, adding-machine	1 roll		175	
Paper, construction, various colors	5 sheets			721, 776
Paper, filter	2 pieces			750
Paper, graph	1 sheet	435		688, 730, 763, 772
Paper, graph	2 sheets			775
Paper, pH	1 piece			750
Paper, tracing	1 sheet	404	127	
Paper, wax, 15 × 15 cm	1 sheet	559		
Paper, white	1 sheet		5, 127, 243, 343	780
Paper, white	2 sheets		365, 373, 399	697, 723
Paper towel	1 roll			732, 767
Pencil, assorted colored	4			775
Pencil, wax	1	302		756, 781
Petroleum jelly	1 oz		149	
Phenol red indicator solution	4 drops			767
Phenolphthalein solution	10 mL			778
Pipe cleaner	3			702, 721, 727, 776
Plant, potted	3	308		
Plant, stem cutting	1			730
Plant, various species	5		457	724
Plaster of Paris	300 mL		149	
Plastic wrap, clear, 3 × 10 cm	1			689
Plastic wrap, clear, approx. 1 × 2 ft	1 sheet	84	641	721, 737, 752, 756
Plate, paper	1		149	
Pond water with living organisms	300 mL		243	756
Poster board	1			614, 694, 712, 732, 746
Poster board, 3 × 10 cm	1			689
Poster board, colored	1			706, 722
Poster board, white	1			706, 745
Potato	3			698
Potato, small slice	1			690
ProtoSlo™	5 drops		243	
Rice	¼ lb	161		
Rubbing alcohol	50 mL			686
Salt	1 box			698
Seed, bean	1			726
Seed, bean	12	302		

* Amount is for one group of students.

MATERIALS AND EQUIPMENT		QuickLab	START-UP Activity	LabBook
CONSUMABLE (CONTINUED)	AMOUNT*	PAGE NO.	PAGE NO.	PAGE NO.
Seed, corn	6		299	
Seed, kidney bean	4		269	
Shell	1		149	
Shoe box	1			690, 732
Soap, liquid, antibacterial	1 bottle		635	781
Sodium hydroxide	15 g			778
Soil	8 oz	223	473	732, 690
Soil	500 g			752
Soil, potting	4 cups		269	750
Stain, Lugol's iodine solution	1 drop		55	
Straw, drinking	1	404		744, 766, 767
String (or yarn)	3 m	487		721, 722, 744
Sugar, granulated	$\frac{1}{4}$ cup		83	692
Swab, cotton	1	66	55	
Tape, duct	1 m	308		
Tape, masking	25 cm	112		723, 737, 768
Tape, transparent	4 cm	360	127	689
Tape, transparent	1 roll		223, 635	694, 721, 722, 723, 744, 766, 776, 781
Toothpick, green	6			702
Toothpick, red	6			702
Vinegar	2 cups	527		
Yeast, active, dry-baking	1 packet		83	692
Yeast, active or inactive, dry-baking	1 packet			692
Yeast, inactive, dry-baking	1 packet			692
Yogurt	1 cup	66		

MATERIALS AND EQUIPMENT		QuickLab	START-UP Activity	LabBook
NONCONSUMABLE	AMOUNT*	PAGE NO.	PAGE NO.	PAGE NO.
Aquarium	1		457	752
Bag, large, paper	1			706
Bag, medium, paper or plastic	14			702
Bag, small, paper	1			748
Bead, set of 3 different colors	5 sets	84		
Beaker, 50 mL	1			750
Beaker, 250 mL	1			692, 778
Beaker, 400 mL	1		275, 497	688
Beaker, 600 mL	1			728, 737, 742
Beaker, 600 mL	2			736
Bean, pinto	4–12 oz			748
Binoculars	1		321	
Blender	1		497	
Board, flat, 0.5 × 0.5 m	1		497	

* Amount is for one group of students.

Master Materials List

Master Materials List

MATERIALS AND EQUIPMENT NONCONSUMABLE (CONTINUED)	AMOUNT*	QuickLab PAGE NO.	START-UP Activity PAGE NO.	LabBook PAGE NO.
Bottle, spray	1			732
Bowl, large, plastic	1	84	373, 521	736
Box, sand, 2 × 3 m	1			708
Calculator	1	625		612, 736, 748
Cloth, colored, 50 × 50 cm	1			710
Container, plastic with lid	1			690, 715, 740
Cork, small	1			740, 772
Coverslip, plastic	1	66	55, 243	696, 756
Eyedropper, plastic	1	43	243, 641	689, 696, 756, 767, 768, 772, 778
Fishbowl, medium-sized	1			740, 742
Flashlight	1		35	732
Flask, Erlenmeyer	150 mL			767
Frog, live	1			742
Funnel, glass	1			728, 750
Gloves, heat-resistant	1 pair	460		688, 692
Gloves, various styles	5 pairs		105	
Graduated cylinder, 10 mL	1			770
Graduated cylinder, 25 mL	1			750, 768
Graduated cylinder, 50 mL	5			686
Graduated cylinder, 100 mL	1			692, 736, 756, 767
Graduated cylinder, 250 mL	1			752
Hammer	1	569		
Hat, various styles	5		105	
Hole punch	1			689
Hot plate	1			688, 692
Incubator	1			781
Insect, large, dead	5			750
Jar, 1 pt	1			750
Jar, 1 qt	3			756
Jar, glass, with lid	1	460		
Jar, wide-mouthed	1	527	473	
Knife, plastic	1	259	373	
Lamp, goose-neck	1			737
Marble	2		635	
Magnifying lens	1	20, 259	127, 321	692, 723, 737
Measuring spoons	1 set			768
Meterstick	1		587, 611	
Microscope, compound	1	66, 226	55, 243	696, 756
Microscope slide, plastic	1	66	55, 243	696, 756
Mortar and pestle	1			770
Pan, dissecting	1			732
Pan, square	1		497	
Penny	100			715
Petri dish, plastic	2	302	635	

*Amount is for one group of students.

MATERIALS AND EQUIPMENT NONCONSUMABLE *(continued)*	AMOUNT*	QuickLab PAGE NO.	START-UP Activity PAGE NO.	LabBook PAGE NO.
Petri dish, plastic	3		223	781
Pin, dissecting	1			772
Pin, map	15			702
Pin, straight	1	404		
Pipe, PVC, $\frac{3}{4}$ in. diam., 12 cm	1			740
Plant guidebook	1			724
Plate, small	1		521	770
Probe	1			732
Pushpin, blue	10			702
Pushpin, green	10			702
Rock, large, approx. 3 lb	1			742
Rubber band	1			740
Rubber band	2			766
Ruler, metric	1	625	83, 175	689, 690, 708, 728, 730, 732, 763, 766, 772
Sand	approx. 20 lb			708
Sand, fine	1 lb			694
Scarf, various styles	5		105	
Scale (or balance)	1			694, 736, 750, 752, 754
Scale, bathroom	1			700
Scissors	1		399	614, 694, 702, 706, 721, 722, 726, 727, 744, 746, 776
Sock	1		5	
Scoopula	1			692
Scrub brush, new	1			781
Shoe, various styles	10		201	
Slide, prepared, bacteria	3	226		
Spatula	1		497	770
Sponge	2			754
Sponge, natural	1			736
Stirring rod	1		83	730, 756
Stirring stick, wooden	3			692
Stopwatch	1	330	545	688, 690, 710, 762, 767
Tape measure	1		611	700
Test tube	1			728
Test tube	2		83	730
Test tube	3			692, 770
Test tube	4			768
Test-tube rack	1		83	692, 730, 768, 770
Thermometer, Celsius	1			686, 688, 692, 762
Thermometer clip	1			688, 692
Towel	1	569		
Tweezers	1		55	723, 770
Wire screen, approx. 2 × 2 ft	1		497	

* Amount is for one group of students.

Master Materials List xxxiii

Science & Math Skills Worksheets

The *Holt Science and Technology* program helps you meet the needs of a wide variety of students, regardless of their skill level. The following pages provide examples of the worksheets available to improve your students' science and math skills whether they already have a strong science and math background or are weak in these areas. Samples of assessment checklists and rubrics are also provided.

In addition to the skills worksheets represented here, *Holt Science and Technology* provides a variety of worksheets that are correlated directly with each chapter of the program. Representations of these worksheets are found at the beginning of each chapter in this Annotated Teacher's Edition.

Many worksheets are also available on the HRW Web site. The address is **go.hrw.com**.

Science Skills Worksheets: Thinking Skills

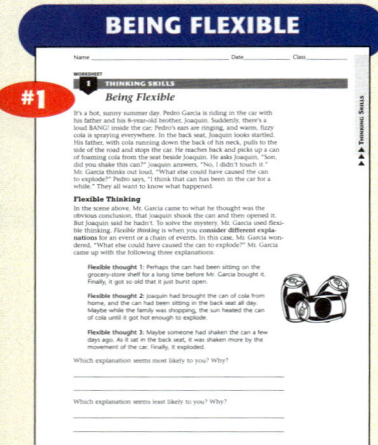
#1 BEING FLEXIBLE — Being Flexible

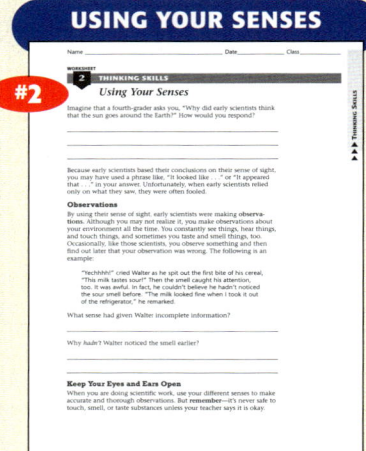
#2 USING YOUR SENSES — Using Your Senses

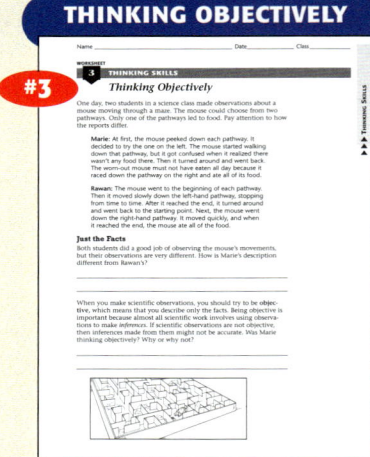
#3 THINKING OBJECTIVELY — Thinking Objectively

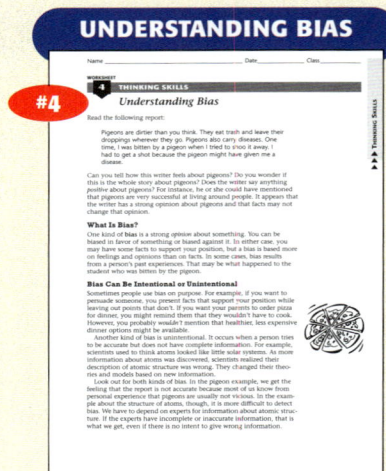
#4 UNDERSTANDING BIAS — Understanding Bias

#5 USING LOGIC — Using Logic

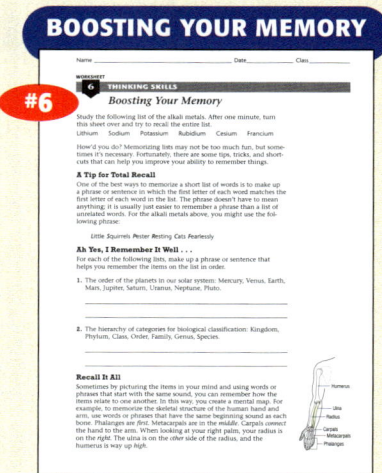
#6 BOOSTING YOUR MEMORY — Boosting Your Memory

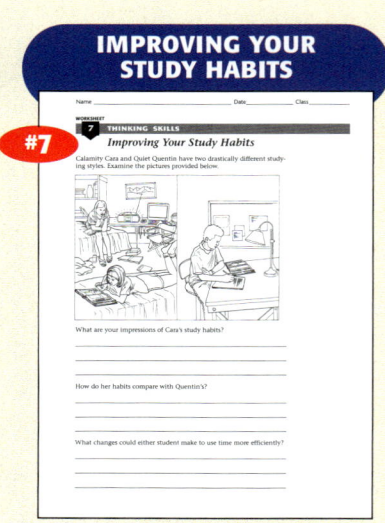
#7 IMPROVING YOUR STUDY HABITS — Improving Your Study Habits

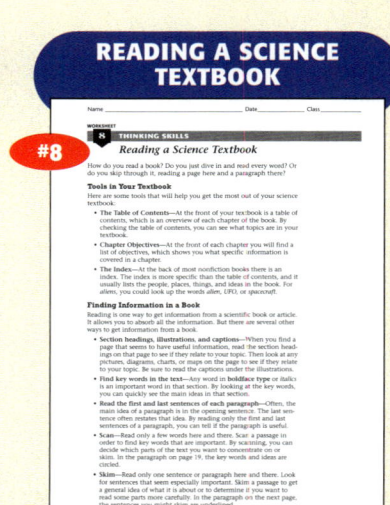
#8 READING A SCIENCE TEXTBOOK — Reading a Science Textbook

Science Skills Worksheets: Experimenting Skills

SAFETY RULES!

#9

DOING A LAB WRITE-UP

#10

UNDERSTANDING VARIABLES
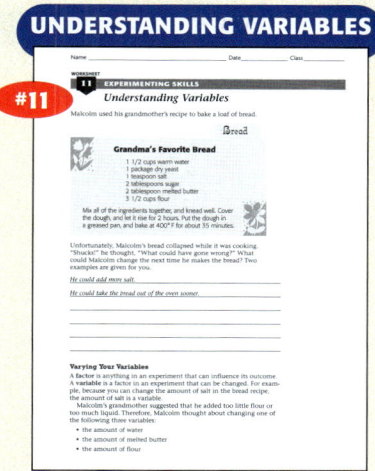
#11

WORKING WITH HYPOTHESES
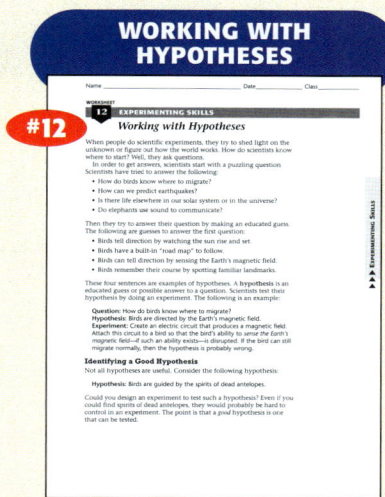
#12

DESIGNING AN EXPERIMENT
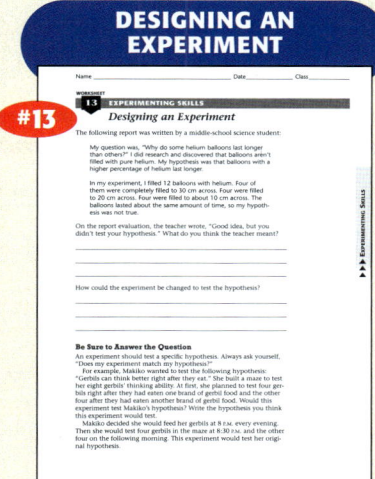
#13

USING THE INTERNATIONAL SYSTEM OF UNITS (SI)

#14

MEASURING
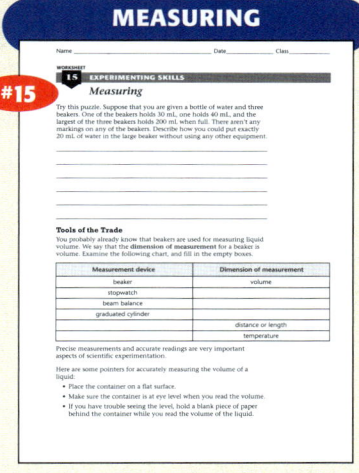
#15

Science Skills Worksheets: Researching Skills

CHOOSING YOUR TOPIC
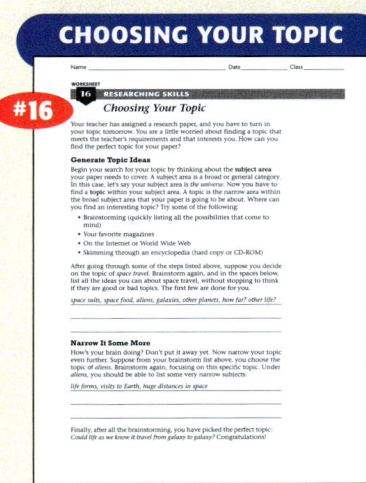
#16

ORGANIZING YOUR RESEARCH
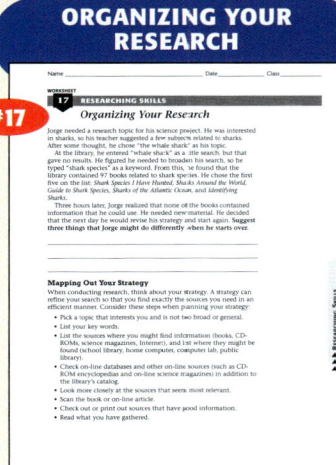
#17

FINDING USEFUL SOURCES
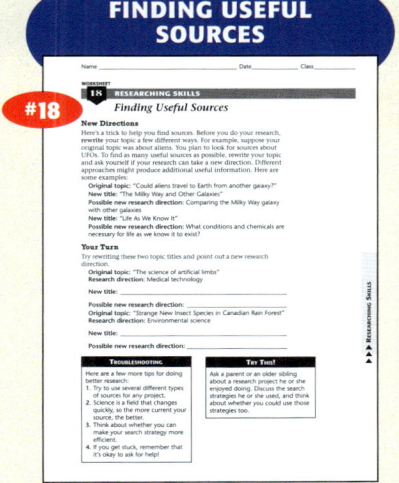
#18

RESEARCHING ON THE WEB

#19

Science & Math Skills Worksheets

Science & Math Skills Worksheets (continued)

Science Skills Worksheets: Researching Skills (continued)

IDENTIFYING BIAS

#20

TAKING NOTES

#21

SCIENCE WRITING
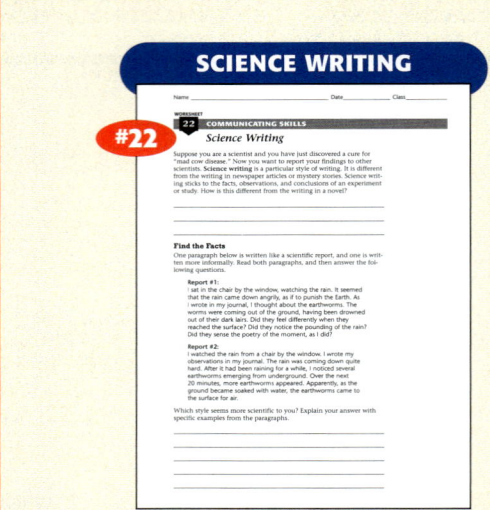
#22

Science Skills Worksheets: Communicating Skills

SCIENCE DRAWING
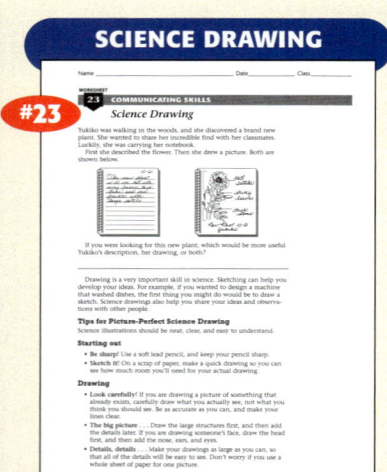
#23

USING MODELS TO COMMUNICATE

#24

INTRODUCTION TO GRAPHS

#25

GRASPING GRAPHING

#26

INTERPRETING YOUR DATA
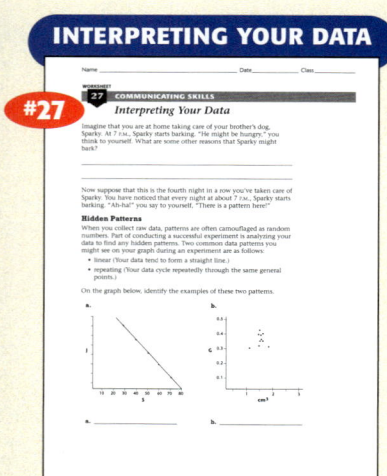
#27

RECOGNIZING BIAS IN GRAPHS
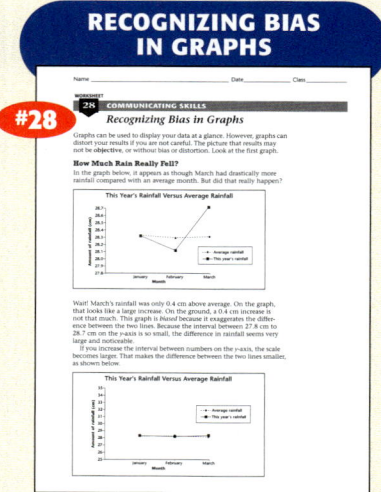
#28

MAKING DATA MEANINGFUL
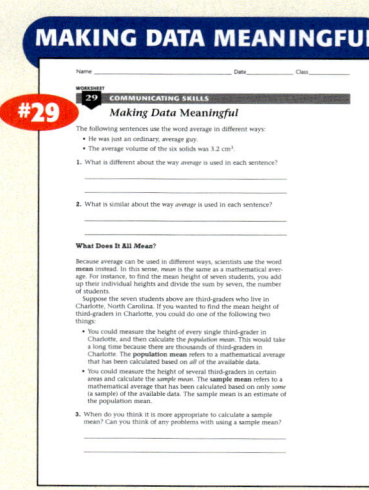
#29

HINTS FOR ORAL PRESENTATIONS
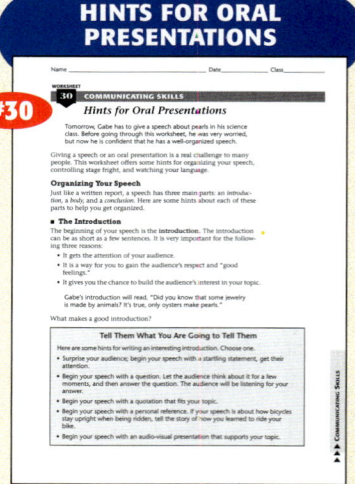
#30

Math Skills for Science

ADDITION AND SUBTRACTION

MULTIPLICATION

DIVISION

AVERAGES

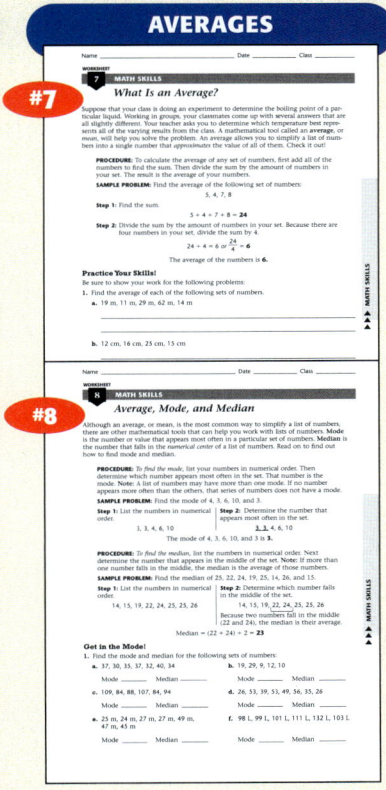

POSITIVE AND NEGATIVE NUMBERS

FRACTIONS

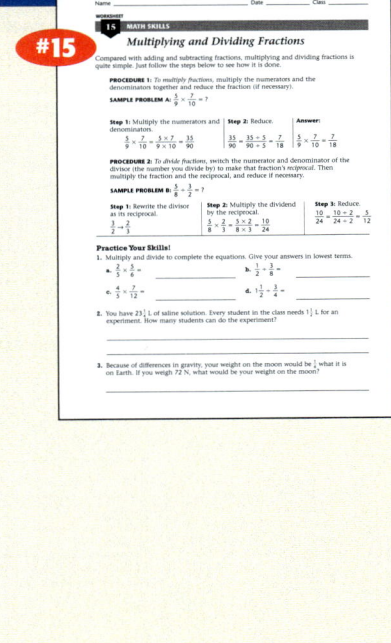

Science & Math Skills Worksheets

Science & Math Skills Worksheets (continued)

Math Skills for Science (continued)

RATIOS AND PROPORTIONS

DECIMALS

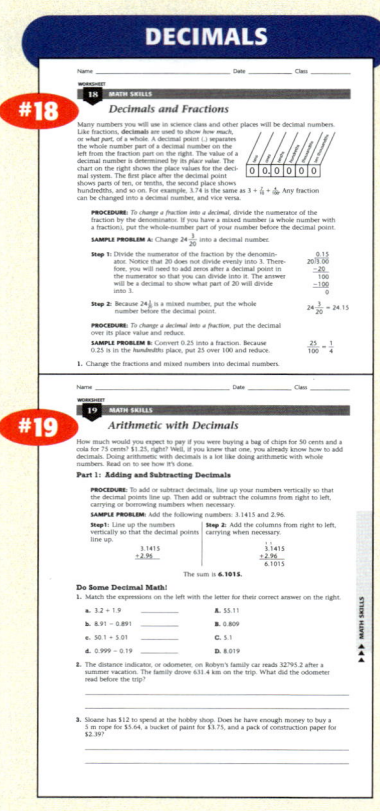

PERCENTAGES
SI MEASUREMENT AND CONVERSION

POWERS OF 10

SCIENTIFIC NOTATION

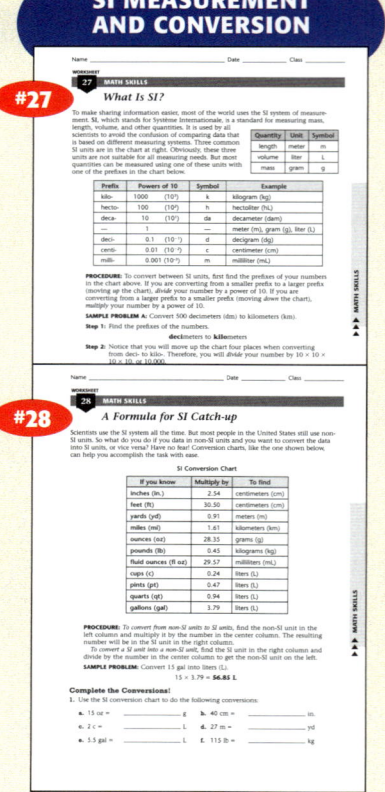

Math Skills for Science (continued)

GEOMETRY

THE UNIT FACTOR AND DIMENSIONAL ANALYSIS

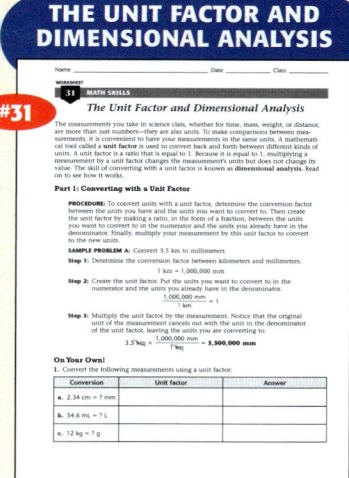

MATH IN SCIENCE: INTEGRATED SCIENCE

Science & Math Skills Worksheets

Science & Math Skills Worksheets (continued)

Math Skills for Science (continued)

MATH IN SCIENCE: LIFE SCIENCE

MATH IN SCIENCE: EARTH SCIENCE

Math Skills for Science (continued)

MATH IN SCIENCE: PHYSICAL SCIENCE

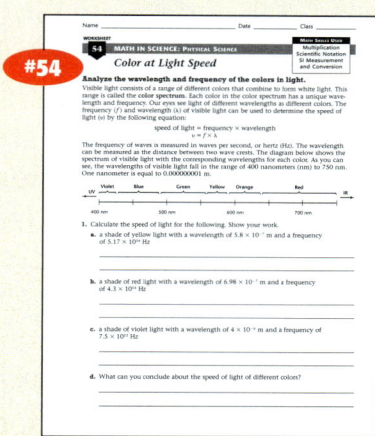

Assessment Checklist & Rubrics

The following is just a sample of over 50 checklists and rubrics contained in this booklet.

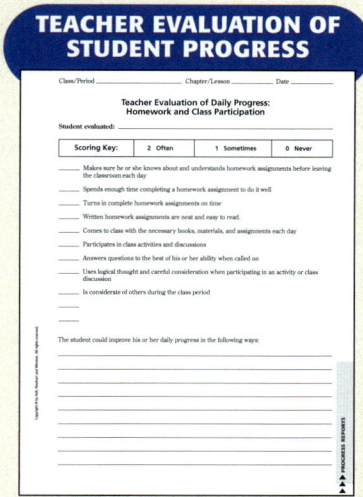

Science & Math Skills Worksheets

UNIT 1

TIMELINE
The Study of Living Things

Life science is the study of living things—from the tiniest bacterium to the largest tree! In this unit, you will discover the similarities of all living things. You will learn about the tools life scientists use, and you'll learn to ask your own questions about the living world around you.

People have always searched for answers about life. This timeline includes a few of the many people who have studied living things through the centuries. And there's always more to be learned, so keep your eyes open.

2640 B.C.
Si Ling-Chi, Empress of China, observes silkworms in her garden and develops a process to cultivate them and make silk.

1944
Oswald T. Avery proposes that DNA is the material that carries genetic properties in living organisms.

1946
ENIAC, the first entirely electronic computer, is built. It weighs 30 tons and takes up 450 m².

1967
The first successful human heart transplant is performed by Dr. Christiaan Barnard.

1970
Floppy disks for computer data storage are introduced.

1010
Arab physicist Ibn al Haytham discovers that vision is caused by the reflection of light from objects into the eye.

1590
Zacharius Jansen constructs the first microscope. It contains two lenses and a tube.

1685
Improvements to microscopes allow the first observation of red blood cells.

1914
George Washington Carver's studies on agriculture and soil conservation lead to research on peanuts.

1934
Dorothy Crowfoot Hodgkin uses X-ray techniques to determine protein structure.

1931
The first electron microscope is developed.

1983
Dian Fossey writes *Gorillas in the Mist,* a book about her research on mountain gorillas in Africa and her efforts to save them from poachers.

1984
A process known as DNA fingerprinting is developed by Alec Jeffries.

1998
In China, scientists discover a fossil of a dinosaur with feathers.

The Study of Living Things

Chapter Organizer

CHAPTER ORGANIZATION	TIME MINUTES	OBJECTIVES	LABS, INVESTIGATIONS, AND DEMONSTRATIONS
Chapter Opener pp. 4–5	45	National Standards: SAI 1	**Start-Up Activity** A Little Bit of Science, p. 5
Section 1 Asking About Life	45	▶ Explain the importance of asking questions in life science. ▶ Give three reasons why life science is beneficial to living things. UPC 1, SAI 1, 2, SPSP 3, HNS 1–3	**Long-Term Projects & Research Ideas,** Project 1 ADVANCED
Section 2 Thinking Like a Life Scientist	90	▶ Describe the scientific method. ▶ Evaluate the designs of experiments. ▶ Interpret the information in tables and graphs. ▶ Explain how scientific knowledge can change. UPC 3, SAI 1, 2, SPSP 5, HNS 1; LabBook SAI 1, 2, HNS 1, 3	**Demonstration,** Frog Call, p. 12 in ATE BASIC **Skill Builder,** Does It All Add Up? p. 686 GENERAL **Datasheets for LabBook,** Does It All Add Up? Datasheet 1 GENERAL **Skill Builder,** Graphing Data, p. 688 BASIC **Datasheets for LabBook,** Graphing Data, Datasheet 2 BASIC **Inquiry Labs,** One Side or Two? Lab 1 BASIC **Whiz-Bang Demonstrations,** Air Ball, Demo 1 GENERAL **Whiz-Bang Demonstrations,** Getting to the Point, Demo 2 GENERAL
Section 3 Tools of Life Scientists	90	▶ Describe the tools life scientists use for seeing. ▶ Explain how life scientists use computers. ▶ Explain the importance of the International System of Units. UPC 3, SAI 1, ST 2, SPSP 5, HNS 1; LabBook SAI 1, HNS 1, 3	**Demonstration,** p. 19 in ATE BASIC **QuickLab,** See for Yourself, p. 20 GENERAL **Demonstration,** p. 20 in ATE GENERAL **Demonstration,** Relative Size, p. 22 in ATE GENERAL **Demonstration,** Displacement, p. 24 in ATE BASIC **Interactive Explorations CD-ROM,** Something's Fishy! GENERAL A **Worksheet** is also available in the **Interactive Explorations Teacher's Guide.** **Making Models,** A Window to a Hidden World, p. 689 BASIC **Datasheets for LabBook,** A Window to a Hidden World, Datasheet 3 BASIC

*See page **T20** for a complete correlation of this book with the* **NATIONAL SCIENCE EDUCATION STANDARDS.**

TECHNOLOGY RESOURCES

 Guided Reading Audio CD English or Spanish, Chapter 1

 One-Stop Planner CD-ROM with Test Generator

 Interactive Explorations CD-ROM CD 1, Exploration 1, Something's Fishy!

 Multicultural Connections, Hopi Science, Segment 1

Scientists in Action, A Biologist's Dolphin Investigation, Segment 1

3A Chapter 1 • The World of Life Science

Chapter 1 • The World of Life Science

CLASSROOM WORKSHEETS, TRANSPARENCIES, AND RESOURCES	SCIENCE INTEGRATION AND CONNECTIONS	REVIEW AND ASSESSMENT
Directed Reading Worksheet 1 BASIC **Science Puzzlers, Twisters & Teasers,** Worksheet 1 ADVANCED **Science Skills Worksheet 8,** Reading a Science Textbook ADVANCED		
Directed Reading Worksheet 1, Section 1 BASIC	**Multicultural Connection,** p. 8 in ATE **Real-World Connection,** p. 8 in ATE **Connect to Environmental Science,** p. 8 in ATE BASIC **Career:** Zoologist—Eric Pianka, p. 32 GENERAL	**Review,** p. 9 GENERAL **Quiz,** p. 9 in ATE GENERAL **Alternative Assessment,** p. 9 in ATE GENERAL
Transparency 1, The Scientific Method **Directed Reading Worksheet 1,** Section 2 BASIC **Math Skills for Science Worksheet 7,** What Is an Average? GENERAL **Reinforcement Worksheet 1,** The Mystery of the Bubbling Top GENERAL **Problem Solving Worksheet 1,** The Case of the Bulge ADVANCED	**Cross-Disciplinary Focus,** p. 11 in ATE GENERAL **Apply,** p. 13 GENERAL **MathBreak,** Averages, p. 16 GENERAL **Cross-Disciplinary Focus,** p. 16 in ATE **Real-World Connection,** p. 17 in ATE	**Self-Check,** p. 12 **Homework,** p. 12 in ATE GENERAL **Homework,** p. 13 in ATE ADVANCED **Homework,** p. 15 in ATE GENERAL **Self-Check,** p. 15 **Homework,** p. 16 in ATE GENERAL **Review,** p. 18 GENERAL **Quiz,** p. 18 in ATE GENERAL **Alternative Assessment,** p. 18 in ATE GENERAL
Directed Reading Worksheet 1, Section 3 BASIC **Math Skills Worksheet 19,** Arithmetic with Decimals GENERAL **Transparency 2,** Compound Light Microscope **Transparency 3,** Common SI Units **Math Skills Worksheet 28,** A Formula for SI Catch-up GENERAL **Math Skills Worksheet 27,** What Is SI? GENERAL **Transparency 4,** Scale of Sizes **Math Skills Worksheet 29,** Finding Perimeter and Area GENERAL **Math Skills Worksheet 30,** Finding Volume GENERAL **Transparency 238,** Three Temperature Scales **Science Skills Worksheet 9,** Safety Rules! GENERAL	**Multicultural Connection,** p. 20 in ATE ADVANCED **Multicultural Connection,** p. 21 in ATE GENERAL **Math and More,** p. 23 in ATE BASIC **MathBreak,** Finding Area, p. 24 GENERAL **Math and More,** p. 25 in ATE GENERAL **Real-World Connection,** p. 26 in ATE **Connect to Physical Science,** p. 26 in ATE **Holt Anthology of Science Fiction,** *The Homesick Chicken* GENERAL	**Homework,** p. 25 in ATE GENERAL **Review,** p. 27 GENERAL **Quiz,** p. 27 in ATE GENERAL **Alternative Assessment,** p. 27 in ATE GENERAL

END-OF-CHAPTER REVIEW AND ASSESSMENT

Chapter Review in Study Guide
Vocabulary and Notes in Study Guide
Chapter Tests with Performance-Based Assessment, Chapter 1 Test
Chapter Tests with Performance-Based Assessment, Performance-Based Assessment 1
Concept Mapping Transparency 1

 Holt, Rinehart and Winston On-line Resources
go.hrw.com
For worksheets and other teaching aids related to this chapter, visit the HRW Web site and type in the keyword: **HSTLIV**

 National Science Teachers Association
www.scilinks.org
Encourage students to use the *sci*LINKS numbers listed in the internet connect boxes to access information and resources on the **NSTA** Web site.

Chapter Resources & Worksheets

Visual Resources

TEACHING TRANSPARENCIES

TEACHING TRANSPARENCIES

CONCEPT MAPPING TRANSPARENCY

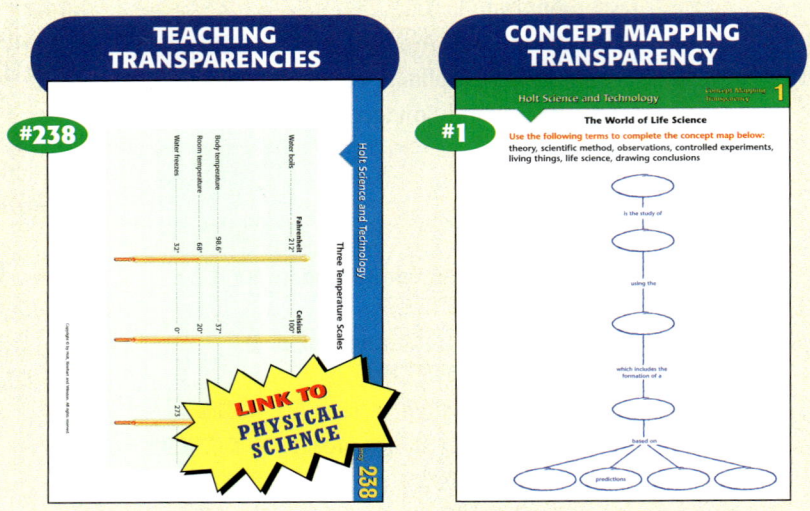

Meeting Individual Needs

DIRECTED READING

REINFORCEMENT & VOCABULARY REVIEW

SCIENCE PUZZLERS, TWISTERS & TEASERS

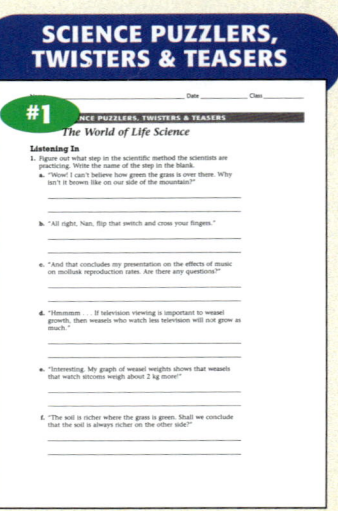

Chapter 1 • The World of Life Science

Review & Assessment

STUDY GUIDE

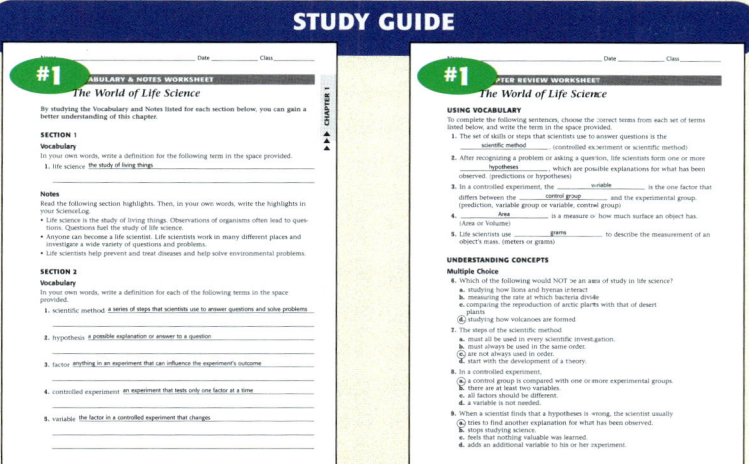

CHAPTER TESTS WITH PERFORMANCE-BASED ASSESSMENT

Lab Worksheets

INQUIRY LABS

WHIZ-BANG DEMONSTRATIONS

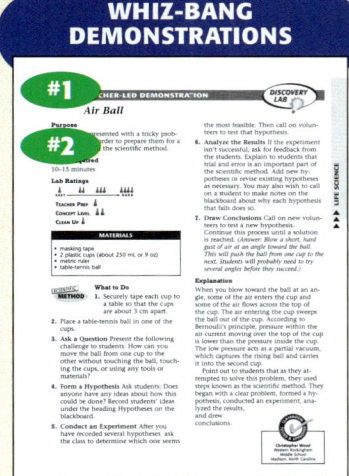

LONG-TERM PROJECTS & RESEARCH IDEAS

DATASHEETS FOR LABBOOK

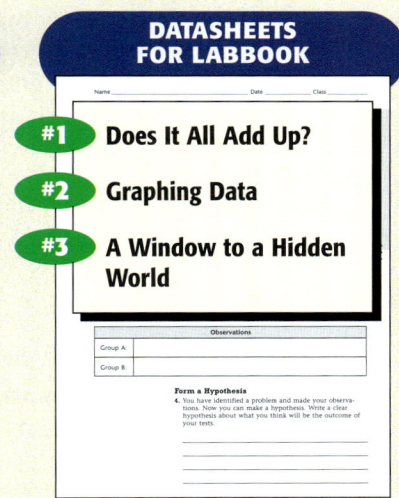

Applications & Extensions

CRITICAL THINKING & PROBLEM SOLVING

MULTICULTURAL CONNECTIONS

SCIENTISTS IN ACTION

INTERACTIVE EXPLORATIONS

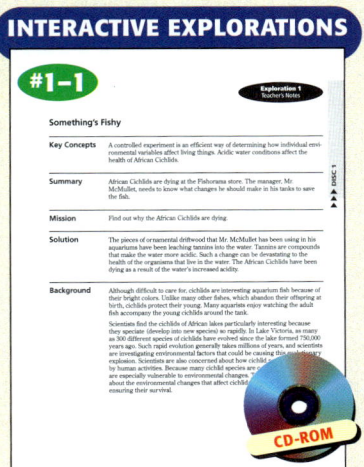

Chapter 1 • Chapter Resources & Worksheets   **3D**

Chapter Background

SECTION 1

Asking About Life

▶ **Deformed Frogs**

The discovery of deformed frogs by Minnesota middle-school students in 1995 sparked much attention around the country. Since that summer, reports of amphibian malformations have poured into agencies from many parts of the continent.

- Besides northern leopard frogs, the type of frog found in Minnesota by the students, other deformed amphibians have been reported, including deformed wood frogs, bullfrogs, green frogs, mink frogs, gray tree frogs, American toads, spring peepers, Pacific tree frogs, and several types of salamanders.

- Despite a recent surge of research, little solid data exists on the causes of the malformations. The problem's extent is also not known.

▶ **Dr. Pepperberg's Studies on Parrot Intelligence**

Parrots, or psittacids, are rarely mentioned during discussions of animal intelligence, but recent studies indicate that they are intelligent animals. Dr. Irene Pepperberg, an associate professor at the University of Arizona's Department of Ecology and Evolutionary Biology, has demonstrated that African grey parrots can process information and make decisions.

- Pepperberg has studied Alex, an African grey parrot, for more than 20 years. Pepperberg says that she has used a variety of techniques to establish a form of interspecies communication with Alex. "The existence of such behavior," she says, "demonstrates that at least one avian species is capable of interactive, referential communication."

- Alex can count and identify more than 35 objects, such as paper, a key, wood, and grain; recognize seven colors; identify five different shapes; and combine names to identify, request, refuse, and categorize more than 100 objects; and even learned to boss around lab assistants in order to modify his environment.

- Pepperberg and her assistants are busy teaching Alex phonics, and evidence suggests that Alex's communications skills will improve to the point that he may one day be able to read.

▶ **Scientists Seek to Improve Polio Vaccines**

The Salk and Sabin polio vaccines have nearly eliminated from the Americas the virus that causes poliomyelitis. Although the disease persists in some corners of the world, the World Health Organization is working to ensure that poliomyelitis is eventually eradicated. This would make polio the second disease in history to be erased by vaccination. The first was smallpox.

IS THAT A FACT!

- Only about 430 Siberian, or Amur, tigers still exist in the wild. Most of them can be found in eastern Russia. Another 490 or so Siberian tigers live in captivity.

Chapter 1 • The World of Life Science

SECTION 2
Thinking Like a Life Scientist

▶ **Vanishing Amphibians**

Scientists are perplexed by the steady decline in the world's amphibian population since the mid-1980s. Although population reductions or eliminations in the past were easily explained by the activities of people in specific areas, populations have been dropping even in protected wilderness areas. What's the cause?

- Some scientists point to the thinning of the ozone layer, which has resulted in an increase of ionizing radiation (UV-B). A second possible cause is pollution by chemicals, either by acid rain or by fertilizers and pesticides. Two other possible causes are the introduction of nonnative competitors and predators into amphibian environments and attacks from new or existing pathogens.

- Frog populations in Australia and Central America have been decimated by outbreaks of chytrid skin fungi. Recent studies have suggested that the fungus may be responsible for mysterious frog deaths in the United States also.

▶ **Neanderthal DNA Study**

Some scientists believe that Neanderthals are our ancestors; some don't. Researchers who analyzed DNA extracted from a Neanderthal tooth discovered a significant difference between the mitochondrial DNA of *Homo sapiens* and that of Neanderthals. This supports the hypothesis that Neanderthals are not our ancestors. Some scientists, however, believe that the conclusion is a bit premature. They point out that the DNA findings were based on a very small sequence of DNA from one individual and that the data are still compatible with what is known about Neanderthal ancestry. The debate goes on.

SECTION 3
Tools of Life Scientists

▶ **The Amazing Electron**

The electron microscope, particle accelerators, nuclear energy, radar, and lasers are technological developments that resulted from the discovery of the electron by physicist Joseph John Thomson in 1897. Around the home, technological marvels, such as the microwave oven and the television, owe their beginnings to Thomson.

- Scientists still do not understand why the electron appears not to take up any space, even though it has mass.

▶ **How Does MRI Work?**

Magnetic resonance imaging (MRI) utilizes large magnets, radio-frequency signals, and computers to capture images of internal human structures. When a body is placed in a magnet, hydrogen protons in the body (the body is mostly water) align themselves with the magnetic field. A radio-frequency signal is then transmitted through the body. An interaction between the newly aligned protons and the radio-frequency signal produces a new signal, which is then received by a computer. The computer uses the data to produce detailed magnetic resonance images.

For background information about teaching strategies and issues, refer to the *Professional Reference for Teachers*.

CHAPTER 1

The World of Life Science

Pre-Reading Questions

Students may not know the answers to these questions before reading the chapter, so accept any reasonable response.

Sample Answers

1. Scientific methods are the ways in which scientists answer questions and solve problems.
2. A model is a representation of an object or system. The limitations of models include that they do not look or act exactly like the things they model.
3. A balance is used to measure mass, and a graduated cylinder is used to measure volume.

Directed Reading Worksheet 1

Science Puzzlers, Twisters & Teasers Worksheet 1

Guided Reading Audio CD
English or Spanish, Chapter 1

Science Skills Worksheet 8
"Reading a Science Textbook"

CHAPTER 1

The World of Life Science

Sections

1. Asking About Life....... 6
   Internet Connect 9
2. Thinking Like a
   Life Scientist......... 10
   Apply 13
   MathBreak 16
3. Tools of Life Scientists.. 19
   QuickLab 20
   MathBreak 24
   Internet Connect 27

Chapter Review 30
Feature Articles 32, 33
LabBook 686–689

Pre-Reading Questions

1. What are scientific methods?
2. What is a model, and what are the limitations of models?
3. What tools are used to measure mass and volume?

How Many Legs Do Frogs Have?

It's not a trick question. In parts of the northern United States and southern Canada, deformed frogs, like the ones shown here, have been found. What's happening to these frogs? Many people have been searching for clues to help answer this question. In this chapter, you will learn about science. You will also learn about the process used to help people find answers to questions such as, How many legs do frogs have?

internetconnect

HRW On-line Resources
go.hrw.com
For worksheets and other teaching aids, visit the HRW Web site and type in the keyword: **HSTLIV**

www.scilinks.com
Use the *sci*LINKS numbers at the end of each chapter for additional resources on the **NSTA** Web site.

www.cnnfyi.com
Visit the CNN Web site for current events coverage and classroom resources.

This teacher and student are searching for frogs—and answers!

START-UP Activity

A LITTLE BIT OF SCIENCE

In this activity, you'll find out that you can learn about the unknown without having to see it.

Procedure

1. Your teacher will give you a **coffee can** to which a **sock** has been attached. Do not look into the can.
2. Reach your hand through the opening in the sock. You will feel **several objects** inside the can.
3. Record observations you make about the objects by feeling them, moving them, shaking the can, etc.
4. Infer what is in the can. In your ScienceLog, record your list of items. State some reasons for your decisions.
5. Pour the contents of the can onto your desk. Compare your list with what was in the can.

Analysis

6. Were you correct in figuring out what was in the can? Which items confused you? Explain your answer.
7. What characteristics of the objects were you not able to identify while they were in the can? Which of your five senses was needed to identify each of these characteristics?

A LITTLE BIT OF SCIENCE

MATERIALS

FOR EACH STUDENT:
- coffee can
- sock
- various small objects, such as nuts, washers, pencils, and paper clips

Teacher's Notes: You must prepare this activity ahead of time. Fill the cans with four or five small objects. Try to choose some common and some uncommon objects that would require more than one of the five senses to identify. To assemble each setup, cut the toe out of a sport sock, stretch the open toe around the open end of the coffee can, and use duct tape to secure the sock to the can.

Answers to START-UP Activity

6. Answers will vary.
7. Answers will vary. Unidentifiable characteristics will most likely be characteristics that can be detected only by sight or smell.

Section 1 • The World of Life Science

SECTION 1

Focus

Asking About Life

This section provides students with an introduction to the life sciences. Students discover that the first step in learning about the living world around us is to ask plenty of questions. Students also learn about various areas of study in the life sciences and meet several scientists who are conducting important studies in their fields.

🔔 Bellringer

Have students write five questions about the natural world in their ScienceLog. *(Examples might be: How do homing pigeons find their way home? How do plants grow new leaves? Why are dinosaurs extinct?)*

Ask several students to share their questions with the class.

1) Motivate

COOPERATIVE LEARNING

Divide the class into groups of four or five. Have the groups brainstorm about what types of life scientists (botanists, bacteriologists, physiologists, etc.) might be working in their community. Have each group choose a professional in the Life Sciences field to interview by phone or E-mail. Encourage them to consider health-care workers, physicians, professors, environmentalists, science teachers, and agricultural experts, as well as the more traditional zoologists, botanists, microbiologists, and so on. Students can present reports and perhaps invite a scientist to visit the class.

Section 1

Terms to Learn
life science

What You'll Do
- Explain the importance of asking questions in life science.
- Give three reasons why life science is beneficial to living things.

Asking About Life

It's summer. You are lying in the grass at the park, casually observing your surroundings. Three dogs are playing on your left. A few bumblebees are visiting nearby flowers. An ant makes off with a crumb from your sandwich. Suddenly a question pops into your head. "Why don't ants grow as big as people?" Then you think of another question. "Why do the bumblebees visit the purple flowers but not the white ones?"

Congratulations! You have just taken the first steps toward becoming a life scientist. How did you do it? You observed the living world around you. You were curious, and you asked questions about your observations. After all, that's what science is all about. **Life science** is the study of living things.

It All Starts with a Question

The world around you is full of an amazing diversity of life. Single-celled algae float unseen in ponds. Giant redwood trees seem to touch the sky. Forty-ton whales swim through the oceans. For every living thing, or *organism*, that has ever lived, you could ask many questions, such as "How does it obtain food?" "Where does it live?" and "Why does it behave in a particular way?"

In Your Own Backyard Questions are easy to find. Take a look around your room, around your home, and around your neighborhood. What questions about life science come to mind? The student at left didn't have to look far to realize that he had questions about some very familiar organisms. Do you know the answer to any of his questions?

Touring the World Your neighborhood gives you just a taste of the questions that the world holds. The world is made up of many different places to live, such as deserts, forests, coral reefs, and tide pools. Just about anywhere you go, you will find some kind of living organism.

Q: What's the difference between a friendly dog and a marine biologist?

A: One's a tail wagger; the other's a whale tagger.

---

6 Chapter 1 • The World of Life Science

Looking for Answers

Close your eyes for a moment, and imagine a life scientist. What do you see? Is it someone in a laboratory, peering into a microscope? Which of the people in **Figure 1** do you think are scientists?

Figure 1 *Life scientists are people who ask many different kinds of questions.*

Irene Duhart Long asks, "How does the human body respond to space travel?"

Geerat Vermeij asks, "How have shells changed over time?"

Irene Pepperberg asks, "Are parrots smart enough to learn a language?"

Who? If you guessed that all of the people in Figure 1 are scientists, then you are right. Anyone can investigate the world around us. Women and men from any cultural or ethnic background can become life scientists.

Where? Doing investigations in a laboratory is an important part of life science, but life science can be studied in many other places too. Life scientists carry out investigations on farms, in forests, on the ocean floor—even in space. They work for businesses, hospitals, government agencies, and universities. Many are also teachers.

What? What a life scientist studies is determined by one thing—his or her curiosity. Life scientists specialize in many different areas of life science. They study how organisms function and behave and how organisms interact with each other and with their environment. Life scientists explore how organisms reproduce and how organisms pass traits from one generation to the next. Some life scientists investigate the origins of organisms and how organisms change over time.

Would you like to make a career out of learning about lizards? Turn to page 32 to read about someone who has.

IS THAT A FACT!

Although the word *science* has been used in English since the 1300s, the term *scientist* wasn't coined until about 1840. Investigators such as Benjamin Franklin and Chevalier de Lamarck, therefore, were not known as scientists until long after their deaths.

2 Teach, continued

Multicultural CONNECTION

Shisaburo Kitasato, born in 1852, was a Japanese life scientist who searched for bacteria and found ways to fight diseases. Kitasato was one of the first scientists to discover the bacteria for tetanus, diphtheria, and the bubonic plague. A graduate of the University of Tokyo Medical School, Kitasato accomplished what many thought was impossible: He developed a procedure to grow pure tetanus bacteria. This enabled him to develop effective treatments for tetanus infections and led him to discover the techniques and materials he would use to fight diphtheria and the plague.

REAL-WORLD CONNECTION

Dr. Neal Haskell is a forensic entomologist—a scientist trained in getting information about crimes from insects. Insects develop and grow at very regular rates. When Dr. Haskell finds particular larvae on a corpse, he can calculate exactly how long ago a person must have died. When a man was murdered and left in a junk pile in Oklahoma, Dr. Haskell was asked to establish the time of death using photographs, case reports, and a few vials of fly larvae. Using this information, Dr. Haskell determined exactly when the murder took place. This information was crucial to the team that solved the crime.

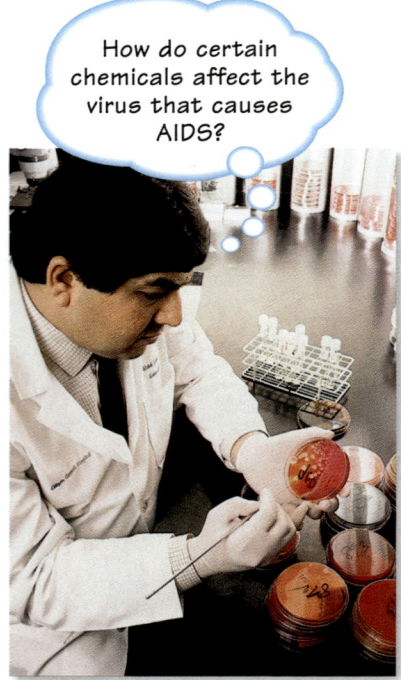

Figure 2 *Abdul Lakhani studies AIDS to find a cure for the disease.*

Why Ask Why?

What is the point of asking all these questions? Life scientists might find some interesting answers, but do any of the answers really matter? Will the answers affect *your* life? Absolutely! As you study life science, you will see how it affects you and all the living things around you.

Combating Disease Polio is a disease that affects the brain and nerves, causing paralysis. Do you know anyone who has had polio? Probably not. The polio virus has been eliminated from most of the world. But at one time it was much more common. Before life scientists discovered ways to prevent the spread of the polio virus, it infected 1 in every 3,000 Americans.

Today scientists continue to search for ways to fight diseases such as tuberculosis and acquired immune deficiency syndrome (AIDS). The scientist in **Figure 2** is trying to learn more about AIDS, which now kills thousands of people every year. Life scientists have discovered how the virus that causes AIDS is carried from one person to another and how it affects the body. By learning more about the virus, scientists may find a cure for this deadly disease.

Inherited Diseases Some diseases, such as cystic fibrosis, are inherited. They are passed from parents to children. Susumu Tonegawa, shown in **Figure 3**, is one of the many scientists worldwide who are studying the human genome. An organism's genome is inherited from its parents. The genome is the information in an organism's cells that controls the cells' activities. Changes in small parts of an organism's genome may cause the organism to be born with or to develop certain diseases. By learning about the human genome, scientists hope to find ways to cure or prevent inherited diseases.

Figure 3 *Susumu Tonegawa's work may help in the battle to fight inherited diseases.*

CONNECT TO ENVIRONMENTAL SCIENCE

To help students understand how pollution is spread from one area to the next, squeeze or peel a lemon or an orange in front of the class. Tell students to raise their hand when they can smell the fragrance.
Sheltered English

Protecting the Environment If you were to make a list of environmental problems, it would probably be long. Many environmental problems are caused by people's misuse and improper disposal of natural resources. Understanding how we affect the world around us is the first step in finding solutions to problems such as pollution and the extinction of wildlife.

Why should we try to decrease air and water pollution? Pollution can harm our health and the health of other organisms. Water pollution may be a cause of the frog deformities seen in Minnesota and other states. Pollution in oceans kills marine mammals, birds, and fish. By finding ways to produce less pollution, we can help make the world a healthier place.

When we cut down trees to clear land for crops or to get lumber to build houses, we alter and sometimes destroy habitats. Dale Miquelle, shown in **Figure 4,** is part of a team of Russian and American scientists studying the Siberian tiger. Hunting and deforestation have almost caused the tigers to become extinct. By learning about the tigers' food and habitat needs, the scientists hope to develop a conservation plan that will ensure their survival.

Figure 4 *To learn how much territory a Siberian tiger covers, Dale Miquelle tracks a tiger that is wearing a radio-transmitting collar.*

REVIEW

1. Define life science.
2. What benefits can life science provide?
3. Where do life scientists work? What do life scientists study?
4. Do you agree with the following statement? *The information learned by life scientists isn't very important.* Explain your answer.
5. **Applying Concepts** Look at the scene below, and list five questions about the organisms. See if any of your classmates have the answers.

TOPIC: Careers in Life Science
GO TO: www.scilinks.org
sciLINKS NUMBER: HSTL010

---

3) Extend

GOING FURTHER

Writing Have students create an imaginary animal and an environment in which it can live. Then have them write a story about it. Students should consider what the animal will eat, which other animals and plants will live there, and how the life-forms will coexist.

4) Close

Quiz

1. Who can be a life scientist?
 (Anyone from any background can learn to be a life scientist.)
2. Why is polio no longer a significant health concern?
 (Life scientists developed a vaccine.)

ALTERNATIVE ASSESSMENT

Writing Encourage students to develop ideas about what they can do to help preserve animal habitats. Encourage them to contact local nature organizations to find out if there are specific things they can do to promote animal preservation in their area. Have the students write a report and prepare a brief presentation on what they learned.

▼ Answers to Review

1. Life science is the study of living things and their relationships to each other and to their environment.
2. Sample answer: combating disease and protecting the environment
3. Life scientists work in laboratories and offices, outdoors, underwater, and in space. Life scientists study anything dealing with living things.
4. Answers may vary but should reflect an understanding that knowledge of living things has a direct impact on the students' own lives.
5. Questions and answers will vary.

SECTION 2

Focus

Thinking Like a Life Scientist

This section introduces the scientific method. Students see how the method's six steps are used in an actual investigation of deformed frogs. Students will also discover how new technologies lead to new answers about old questions.

Bellringer

As an exercise in observation, write 15–20 words on the overhead projector. Allow the students to look at the words for 10 seconds. Turn the projector off, and have the students spend a few minutes writing down as many of the words as they can remember in their ScienceLog.

1 Motivate

DEBATE

Write this question on the board:

"Which is more important, imagination or knowledge?"

Ask students to debate this question. Stress to them that creativity, flexible and original thinking, and openness to new and even wild ideas are important qualities for a good scientist to possess.

Teaching Transparency 1
"The Scientific Method"

Directed Reading Worksheet 1 Section 2

Section 2

Terms to Learn
scientific method
hypothesis
controlled experiment
variable
theory
technology

What You'll Do
- Describe the scientific method.
- Evaluate the designs of experiments.
- Interpret the information in tables and graphs.
- Explain how scientific knowledge can change.

Thinking Like a Life Scientist

No matter where life scientists work or what questions they try to answer, all life scientists have two things in common. They are curious about the natural world, and they use similar methods to investigate it. Imagine that you are one of the students who discovered the deformed frogs discussed at the beginning of this chapter. If you wanted to investigate the cause of the frogs' deformities, where would you begin? Actually, you've already taken the first steps in the scientific process. You've made observations, and you've asked questions. What's next?

The Scientific Method

Most life scientists use the scientific method as the basis of their investigations. The **scientific method** is often described as a series of steps that is used to answer a question or solve a problem. **Figure 5** outlines the six steps of the scientific method. Take a moment to read each step.

- **Ask a question** based on observations.
- **Form a hypothesis,** which is a possible explanation for what you have observed.
- **Test the hypothesis** by conducting experiments.
- **Analyze the results** collected from experiments.
- **Draw conclusions** from the results of your experiment.
- **Communicate results** to other scientists.

Figure 5 Life scientists often use the scientific method to solve problems and answer questions.

Science Is a Creative Process You may think that following each step in order will automatically produce the correct answer to your question or problem. But many questions cannot be answered that easily. Life scientists must use their imaginations to explain what they have observed. They must also be creative when designing experiments to test their explanations. Scientists may have to repeat steps of the scientific method or do them in a different order. In addition, every question doesn't necessarily require an experiment. Sometimes only observations are needed to find an answer. And sometimes an answer cannot be found.

In the next few pages, you will see how the six steps of the scientific method were used in a real-life investigation.

IS THAT A FACT!

North American bullfrogs use an amazing method to make their distinctive call. The sound travels up their throat and blasts out from their large, flat eardrum.

Ask a Question

Have you ever observed something out of the ordinary or difficult to explain? The observation usually raises questions. Looking for answers often involves making more observations.

A Real-World Question Once the students from Le Sueur realized there was something wrong with the frogs, they decided to continue their observations by collecting some data, as shown in **Figure 6.** They counted the number of deformed and normal frogs they caught. The students also photographed the frogs, took measurements, and wrote a thorough description of each frog.

In addition, the students collected data on other organisms living in the pond. They also conducted many tests on the pond water, measuring things such as the level of acidity. The students carefully recorded their data and observations.

Figure 6 Collecting data was the first step in the students' investigation.

Make Accurate Observations Observations can take many forms. They may be measurements of length, volume, time, or speed. They may describe how loud or soft a sound is or indicate the color or shape of an organism. Observations may reveal the number of organisms in an area or patterns of their behavior. The range of observations a scientist can make is endless. But no matter what observations reveal, they are useful only if they are accurately made and recorded. A few of the tools that scientists use to make observations are shown in **Figure 7.**

Figure 7 Microscopes, rulers, and thermometers are some of the many tools scientists use to collect information.

2) Teach

READING STRATEGY

Mnemonics Have students develop a mnemonic device that will remind them of the six steps in the scientific method: **A**sk a question, **H**ypothesize, **T**est, **A**nalyze results, **D**raw conclusions, and **C**ommunicate results. An example is, "**A**nn **H**as **T**wenty **A**dorable **D**ogs and **C**ats."

CROSS-DISCIPLINARY FOCUS

Social Studies To help students become aware of how science and technology affect their lives, have them work together to develop a timeline of discoveries that have occurred during their lifetime. Divide the class into small groups, and assign each group a year. Have them use library resources to research their year. Each student will be responsible for selecting two events and preparing a note card for each event. The cards should include the year, what the discovery was, and a few descriptive sentences about the discovery and its significance. Have several volunteers assemble the timeline on a bulletin board. Several other volunteers could then be called on to illustrate the timeline.

LabBook PG 686
Does It All Add Up?

In 1786, Luigi Galvani noted that frog legs jerked when he touched them with a metal probe. When he touched a nerve with the probe, the nerve, the metal, and the liquid around the nerve created a small electrical current, which stimulated the nerve. The nerve in turn stimulated the muscle. By observing the physiological result of an electrical current, Galvani helped to establish the study of neurophysiology and clinical neurology.

2) Teach, continued

ACTIVITY

Investigate Your Area Have students observe the daily activities in and around a local pond over a period of several weeks. Tell them to record their observations in a journal.

MEETING INDIVIDUAL NEEDS

Advanced Learners Encourage students to come up with a hypothesis and test it themselves. Questions that might lead to hypotheses they can test include:

- Does soda pop help plants grow?
- Does soft music help plants grow?
- Which degrades faster in compost—natural or human-made fibers?

Students should check the design of their experiment with their teacher before they begin.

DEMONSTRATION

Frog Call The northern leopard frog, which inhabits the pond that was studied by the Minnesota students, has quite a peculiar call—a mixture of grunts, snores, and squeaks that sound like a wet palm being rubbed across an inflated balloon. Ask a volunteer to demonstrate the frog's call for the class.
<mark>Sheltered English</mark>

Answer to Self-Check

2. Insecticides caused the frog deformities.

Why did the chicken cross the highway? See page 33 to find out about "The Homesick Chicken," a science-fiction mystery.

Form a Hypothesis

After making observations, scientists form one or more hypotheses. A **hypothesis** is a possible explanation or answer to a question. When scientists form hypotheses, they think logically and creatively and consider what they already know.

A hypothesis must be testable by experimentation. A hypothesis is not testable if no observations or information can be gathered or no experiment can be designed to test the hypothesis. Just because a hypothesis is not testable does not mean that it is wrong. It just means that there is no way to support or disprove the hypothesis.

Different scientists may have different hypotheses for the same problem. In the case of the frogs, the hypotheses shown below were formed. Which, if any, of these explanations was correct? To find out, each hypothesis would have to be tested.

> **Hypothesis 1:** The deformities were caused by one or more chemical pollutants in the water.
>
> **Hypothesis 2:** The deformities were caused by attacks from parasites or other frogs.
>
> **Hypothesis 3:** The deformities were caused by an increase in exposure to ultraviolet light from the sun.

✓ Self-Check

Which of the following statements is a hypothesis?
1. Deformed frogs have been found in the United States and Canada.
2. Insecticides caused the frog deformities.
3. The frogs in Le Sueur were deformed.

(See page 782 to check your answers.)

Homework

Testing Hypotheses Answers to questions in many areas of life can be found by forming and testing a hypothesis. Write a hypothesis based on the following observation:

The blacktop feels hotter than the sidewalk.

Ask students how such a hypothesis might be tested.

Predictions

Before scientists can test a hypothesis, they must first make predictions. A prediction is a statement of cause and effect that can be used to set up a test for a hypothesis. Predictions are usually stated in an "If . . ., then . . ." format.

More than one prediction may be made for each hypothesis. For each of the hypotheses on the previous page, the following predictions were made:

Hypothesis 2
Prediction: If a parasite is causing the deformities, then this parasite will be found more often in frogs that have deformities.

Hypothesis 1
Prediction: If a substance in the pond water is causing the deformities, then the water from ponds with deformed frogs will be different from the water from ponds in which no abnormal frogs have been found.
Prediction: If a substance in the pond water is causing the deformities, then some tadpoles will develop deformities when they are raised in pond water collected from ponds with deformed frogs.

Hypothesis 3
Prediction: If an increase in exposure to ultraviolet light is causing the deformities, then some frog eggs exposed to ultraviolet light in a laboratory will develop into deformed frogs.

Once predictions are made, scientists can conduct experiments to see which predictions, if any, prove to be true and support the hypotheses.

Have Aliens Landed?

You and a friend are walking through a heavily wooded park. Suddenly, you come upon a small area where all of the trees are lying on the ground. What knocked them down or caused them to fall over? Your friend thinks that extraterrestrials caused the trees to fall. Is your friend's hypothesis testable? In your ScienceLog, explain your answer. What other hypothesis can you come up with?

Answer to APPLY
The hypothesis that extraterrestrials caused the trees to fall is not testable because there is no way to support or disprove the hypothesis. A viable hypothesis is that a volcanic eruption knocked the trees down.

MEETING INDIVIDUAL NEEDS

Learners Having Difficulty
Have students use a dictionary to find the definitions and origins of the words *thesis* and *hypothesis*. Have volunteers write on the board the information they find. As an alternative or additional activity, small groups of students could then compile lists of words that contain *hypo-* or *-thesis*—for example, *hypodermic*, *synthesis*, and *photosynthesis*.

Homework

Researching Galileo
The Italian astronomer and physicist Galileo (1564–1642) was the first scientist to be credited with using a scientific method to solve problems. He recognized the importance of carefully controlled experiments in developing scientific theories. The steps that he followed became the foundation of the scientific method used by scientists today. Have students research some of Galileo's discoveries and present their findings in an oral report to the class.

MISCONCEPTION ALERT

Students may believe that an experiment is a failure if their hypothesis is not supported by the data gathered. Remind them that the point of conducting experiments is to investigate the hypothesis and to learn from the data. Often, more can be learned from experiments that do not support a hypothesis than from experiments that do.

Section 2 • Thinking Like a Life Scientist

2) Teach, continued

RETEACHING

Have students propose other possible experiments that scientists could use to test the effect of UV light on frogs. Ask them if conducting the experiments in the frogs' natural environment would be a good idea. Discuss how such an experiment might be set up.

USING THE TABLE

Have students study the table on this page. Ask them the following questions:

What is the only factor that differs between the control group and the experimental groups? (the variable, which is UV light exposure time)

What would happen if the number of eggs was different for each of the groups? (The experiment would not be controlled; the results would be invalid.)

BRAIN FOOD

At the forefront of the deformed-frog situation is this concern:

Is human health at risk? Do the malformed frogs signal a widespread environmental problem?

Discuss this concern with students, and pose this question: What steps can scientists take to find out whether humans are also at risk?

Test the Hypothesis

After scientists make a prediction, they test the hypothesis. Scientists try to design experiments that will clearly show whether a particular factor caused an observed outcome. A *factor* is anything in an experiment that can influence the experiment's outcome. Factors can be anything from temperature to the type of organism being studied.

Under Control Scientists strive to perform controlled experiments. A **controlled experiment** tests only one factor at a time. There is a control group and one or more experimental groups. All of the factors for the control group and the experimental groups are the same except for one. The one factor that differs is called the **variable.** Because the variable differs between the control group and the experimental groups, scientists can be more certain that differences in the variable are causing any differences observed in the outcome of the experiment.

Designing an Experiment Designing a good experiment requires a lot of planning. Let's examine the prediction for Hypothesis 3: *If an increase in exposure to ultraviolet light is causing the deformities,* **then** *some frog eggs exposed to ultraviolet light in a laboratory will develop into deformed frogs.*

To test a hypothesis, a scientist must first identify the variable. In this case, the variable is the amount of ultraviolet (UV) light exposure. This is shown in the table at left. All other factors, such as the kind of frog, the number of frog eggs in each aquarium, and the temperature of the water, should be the same in the control group and the experimental groups.

Design of Experiment to Test the Effect of UV Light on Frogs

Group	Factors			
	Kind of frog	Number of eggs	Temperature of water	Variable: UV light exposure
#1 Control	leopard frog	100	25°C	0 days
#2 Experimental	leopard frog	100	25°C	15 days
#3 Experimental	leopard frog	100	25°C	24 days

MISCONCEPTION ALERT

Students often assume that worthwhile experiments should be dazzling—something must explode or change color or sizzle with electricity. However, as the frog-egg example shows, most good experiments are not so dramatic. In addition, they often take awhile to yield results. The upside is that anyone can perform experiments; they aren't just for "mad scientists."

Collect Data As you can see from the table on the previous page, each group in the experiment contains 100 eggs. Scientists always try to test many individuals. The more organisms tested, the more certain scientists can be that differences in the outcome of an experiment are actually caused by differences in the variable and not by natural differences between individuals. Scientists also support their conclusions by repeating their experiments. If an experiment produces the same results again and again, scientists can be more certain about the effect the variable has on the outcome of the experiment. The experimental setup to test Hypothesis 3 is illustrated in **Figure 8.**

Figure 8 *This controlled experiment was designed to test whether UV light can cause frog deformities.*

Control Group
#1 No UV light exposure

Experimental Groups
#2 UV light exposure for 15 days
#3 UV light exposure for 24 days

 Self-Check

Henry is testing the effects of different antibacterial soaps on the growth of bacteria. His experiment contains several jars of the same strain of bacteria. Which of the jars described below is the control group?

1. To Jar A, Henry adds two drops of Supersoap.
2. To Jar B, Henry adds two drops of Anti-B Suds.
3. To Jar C, Henry adds no soap.

(See page 782 to check your answer.)

2) Teach, continued

USING THE FIGURE

Table and Bar Graph Have students carefully compare the data presented in both graphics. Ask students which method of organizing the data is clearer to them? Does one have an advantage over the other? Ask if there are other ways that the scientists could have presented their findings. If students have not already done so, point out that the data could also have been presented in paragraph form. Ask what the possible advantages and disadvantages of a written summary might be.

Homework

Interpreting Data Point out to students that according to the data in **Figure 9,** the deformities began quite abruptly after 24 days of exposure to UV light. Ask students to speculate why there were no deformities found before then. Shouldn't a shorter period of exposure have resulted in at least a few mutations? (Some scientists have determined that the end of the 24-day period of exposure corresponds to the same period that leg buds begin to form in tadpoles. No deformities are seen before then because the tadpoles don't form legs until approximately the 24th day.)

Answer to MATHBREAK

$$\frac{(6 + 5 + 4)}{3} = \frac{15}{3} = 5 \text{ days}$$

 Math Skills Worksheet 7 "What Is an Average?"

Experimental Results

Group	Length of UV light exposure	Number of deformed frogs
#1	0 days	0
#2	15 days	0
#3	24 days	47

Figure 9 *The table and the bar graph show that some frog eggs exposed to UV light for 24 days developed into frogs with deformities.*

Analyze the Results

A scientist's work does not end when an experiment is finished. Scientists must organize the data so that they can be analyzed. For example, they may put the data into a table or a graph. The data collected from the UV light experiment are shown in **Figure 9.**

MATH BREAK

Averages

Finding the average of a group of numbers is one way to analyze data. Three seeds kept at 25°C sprouted in 8, 8, and 5 days. To find the average number of days that it took the seeds to sprout, add 8, 8, and 5 and divide the sum by 3, the number of subjects (seeds).

$$\frac{(8 + 8 + 5)}{3} = \frac{21}{3} = 7 \text{ days}$$

Three seeds kept at 30°C sprouted in 6, 5, and 4 days. What's the average number of days that it took these seeds to sprout?

Draw Conclusions

After scientists have analyzed the data from several experiments, they can draw conclusions. They decide whether the results of the experiments support a hypothesis.

When scientists find that a hypothesis is not supported by the tests, they must try to find another explanation for what they have observed. Proving that a hypothesis is wrong is just as helpful as supporting it. Why? Either way, the scientist has learned something, which is the purpose of using the scientific method to investigate or answer a question.

Is It the Answer? The UV light experiment supports the hypothesis that the frog deformities can be caused by exposure to UV light. Does this mean that UV light definitely caused the frogs living in the Minnesota wetland to be deformed? No, the only thing this experiment shows is that UV light may be a cause of the deformities. Tests performed in a laboratory may have different results than tests performed in the wild. In addition, the experiment did not investigate the effects of parasites or some other substance on the frogs. In fact, many scientists think that more than one factor could be involved.

Graphing Data

CROSS-DISCIPLINARY FOCUS

Statistics Scientists often use mathematical techniques and formulas to determine whether their data are meaningful or are just the result of chance or coincidence. The discipline called statistics deals with the development of techniques to analyze and interpret data.

Puzzles as complex as the deformed-frog mystery are rarely solved with a single experiment. The quest for a solution may continue for years. Finding an answer doesn't always end an investigation. Often that answer begins another investigation.

Communicate Results

Scientists form a global community. After scientists complete their investigations, they communicate their results to other scientists, as the student in **Figure 10** is doing. Other scientists may repeat the experiments to see if they get the same results. The information can also help scientists discover new questions and answers. New answers may strengthen scientific hypotheses or show that the hypotheses need to be altered. The paths from observations and questions to communicating results are shown in **Figure 11.**

Figure 10 *This student scientist is communicating the results of his investigation at a science fair.*

Figure 11 *Scientific investigations do not always proceed from one step to the next. Sometimes steps can be skipped, and sometimes they must be repeated.*

IS THAT A FACT!

Evidence suggests that UV light levels are highest in late spring and early summer, the time of year when Minnesota's frog population is laying eggs. Such evidence points to a need for UV experiments in natural environments at various times of the year.

3) Extend

GOING FURTHER

Have students read articles in scientific or nature magazines and find experiments that illustrate the scientific method. Students might notice that scientists don't always rigidly employ the steps in the same order. Have them outline as many steps as they can in each experiment and copy them into their ScienceLog.

REAL-WORLD CONNECTION

Suggest that students find out what it takes to become a data collector. Some scientific studies require massive collections of data over a huge area or over long time periods. Have students investigate organizations that are searching for sightings or facts about animals in their community. As a result of the Le Sueur students' discovery, a program called "A Thousand Friends of Frogs" was started to encourage students and other citizens to collect data about frogs and toads. The data collected can then be used to help scientists in their research.

MISCONCEPTION ALERT

Students should be reminded about the difference between a scientific theory and a hypothesis. Emphasize that theories need to be supported by a convincing body of evidence. Explain that it often takes many years to develop enough evidence to push a set of hypotheses into the realm of theory.

Section 2 • Thinking Like a Life Scientist

4 Close

Quiz

1. Why is proving a hypothesis wrong just as helpful as supporting it? (You learn something either way.)
2. What was the variable in the frog experiment? (the amount of UV light exposure)

ALTERNATIVE ASSESSMENT

Classifying is an important element in any scientific investigation. Have small groups of students practice categorizing and differentiating between random items based on shared characteristics. Provide students with items such as buttons, paper clips, screws, rubber bands, and so on, and have them group them in as many ways as possible. Afterward, you might like to introduce students to dichotomous keys and explain how they can use them to help differentiate items.

Reinforcement Worksheet 1
"The Mystery of the Bubbling Top"

Problem Solving Worksheet 1
"The Case of the Bulge"

Scientific Knowledge Changes

As you read earlier, there can be more than one prediction for a hypothesis. Each time a prediction is proven true, the hypothesis gains more support. A unifying explanation for a broad range of hypotheses and observations that have been supported by testing is a **theory**.

However, when scientists reexamine data or experimental results, they may draw different conclusions. Other times, new observations show that the old conclusions are wrong. Or, new observations just show that more research is needed.

Life scientists are always asking new questions or looking at old questions from a different angle. As they find new answers, scientific knowledge continues to grow and change.

New Tools New technology allows scientists to get information that wasn't available previously. **Technology** is the use of knowledge, tools, and materials to solve problems and accomplish tasks. For example, scientists have long wondered whether Neanderthals are the ancestors of humans. Neither Neanderthal fossils, which show what they looked like, nor dating techniques, which reveal when Neanderthals lived, provided enough data to answer the question. The technology for comparing genetic information was developed recently. The scientist shown in **Figure 12** is using this technology to look for the answer.

Figure 12 Dr. Mark Stoneking is using modern techniques to find out if Neanderthals are our ancestors.

Temperature (°C)	Time to double (minutes)
10	130
20	60
25	40
30	29
37	17
40	19
45	32
50	no growth

REVIEW

1. What are the six basic steps of the scientific method?
2. What causes scientific knowledge to change and grow?
3. **Graphing Data** The table at left shows how long it takes for one bacterium to divide and become two bacteria. Plot this information on a graph, with temperature on the x-axis and the time to double on the y-axis. What temperature allows the bacteria to multiply most quickly?

Answers to Review

1. Ask a question, form a hypothesis, test the hypothesis, analyze the results, draw conclusions, and communicate results.
2. the discovery of new information, the use of new technologies, the asking of new questions, and the reexamination of old questions and ideas
3. The graph will slope down and to the right and then rise up again; 37°C.

Section 3

Tools of Life Scientists

Terms to Learn

compound light microscope
electron microscope
area
volume
mass
temperature

What You'll Do

- Describe the tools life scientists use for seeing.
- Explain how life scientists use computers.
- Explain the importance of the International System of Units.

Life scientists use various tools to aid them in their work. These tools are used to make observations and to gather, store, and analyze information.

Tools for Seeing

If you look at a jar of pond water, you may see some scum and a few creatures swimming around. But examine that same water under a microscope or with a magnifying lens, and presto!—a complex community of organisms suddenly appears.

To make accurate observations of organisms and parts of organisms that are too small to be seen with the naked eye, life scientists use tools that can magnify. People have used glass as a magnifier for almost 3,000 years. Today life scientists use magnifying lenses and microscopes.

Compound Light Microscope One type of microscope commonly used today is the compound microscope, shown in **Figure 13**. The **compound light microscope** is made up of three main parts—a tube with lenses, a stage, and a light. Specimens viewed through a compound microscope are sometimes stained with special dyes, which enable the specimens to be seen more clearly.

Specimens are placed on the stage so that the light passes through them. The lenses at each end of the tube magnify the image, making it appear larger than it actually is.

Figure 13 A compound light microscope can produce an image that is 1,000 times (1,000×) larger than the actual specimen. The paramecium shown here has been magnified 200×.

SCIENCE HUMOR

Q: What is the only thing that you can put in a bucket that will make it lighter?

A: a hole

SECTION 3

Focus

Tools of Life Scientists

In this section students will explore the variety of tools that scientists use in their jobs. They will discover how scientists use computers to help them solve complex problems. Students will also learn why scientists use the International System of Units (SI).

Bellringer

As you are taking attendance, tell students that researchers recently built the world's smallest guitar—about 10 micrometers long, the size of a single cell—to demonstrate a new technology for making small mechanical devices. Ask students to think of everyday devices that they regularly use that might be better if they were smaller. Have them write these answers in their ScienceLog.

1) Motivate

DEMONSTRATION

Bring to class a collection of microscopic images of ordinary objects. On an overhead projector, show students the images. Ask students to identify the objects. Sheltered English

Teaching Transparency 2
"Compound Light Microscope"

Math Skills Worksheet 19
"Arithmetic with Decimals"

Directed Reading Worksheet 1 Section 3

Section 3 • Tools of Life Scientists **19**

2) Teach

  PG 689
A Window to a Hidden World

DEMONSTRATION

Using a Microscope Help students become familiar with the parts of a compound microscope and its functions. Encourage students to ask questions as you are demonstrating. Then prepare a wet-mount slide with a drop of pond water. Allow each student to view the slide through the microscope and turn the focus knob to view the water at different depths of focus. Discuss what the students observed.

MATERIALS

FOR EACH STUDENT:
• magnifying lens

Safety Caution: Tell the students to be careful with the lens. It is a delicate piece of scientific equipment and can break. Remind them not to use the lens to focus sunlight.

Have students note five new observations they can make using the lens.

Answers to QuickLab
The lens magnifies objects. Student drawings will vary.

---

internetconnect

SCLINKS NSTA

TOPIC: Tools of Life Science
GO TO: www.scilinks.org
sciLINKS NUMBER: HSTL015

A hidden world all around you? See what it means on page 689 of your LabBook.

Electron Microscope In **electron microscopes,** tiny particles of matter called electrons are used to produce magnified images. Living specimens cannot be examined with an electron microscope because the process that prepares specimens for viewing kills them. There are two kinds of electron microscopes used in life science—the transmission electron microscope and the scanning electron microscope.

Transmission electron microscopes can magnify specimens up to 200,000 times (200,000×) their actual size. The scanning electron microscope can produce images that are up to 100,000 times their actual size. The images that electron microscopes produce are clearer and more detailed than those made by compound microscopes. **Figure 14** shows each kind of electron microscope, with a description of its specialized purpose and an example of the image that it can produce.

Figure 14 *The transmission electron microscope produces a greatly magnified image. The scanning electron microscope provides a clear view of surface features.*

Transmission Electron Microscope	Scanning Electron Microscope
• Electrons pass through the specimen. • A flat image is produced.	• Electrons bounce off the surface of the specimen. • A three-dimensional (3-D) image is produced.
	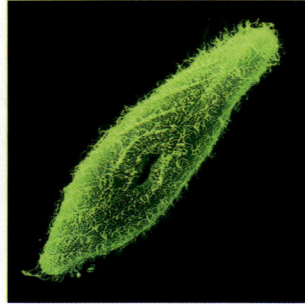
Paramecium (15,000×)	*Paramecium* (1,500×)

See for Yourself
Take a look at one of your fingernails. In your ScienceLog, draw and describe what you see. Then, look at your nail with a **magnifying lens.** How does this affect what you can see? Draw and describe how your nail looks when it is magnified.

Multicultural CONNECTION

Writing Have students research and write reports about Alhazen, who was born in A.D. 965 in what is now Iraq and who is considered one of the greatest scientists of the medieval period. In his book, *Optics,* he challenged Euclid's and Ptolemy's doctrines on visual rays and formulated his own.

20 Chapter 1 • The World of Life Science

X Rays Life scientists also use several tools to help them see internal structures of organisms. For almost a century, X rays have provided pictures of internal body structures such as the bones, heart, and lungs. If you have ever broken a bone, you have had an X ray, such as the one shown in **Figure 15.** X rays have also been used to help life scientists learn about the structures of proteins, which are important to the life processes of every organism.

Figure 15 This X ray shows a broken arm.

CT Scans and MRI CT (computed tomography) scans and MRI (magnetic resonance imaging) usually provide clearer, more detailed images of internal tissues than do X rays. In a CT scan, such as the one shown in **Figure 16,** low-dosage X-ray beams are passed through the body at different angles. Often a dye is injected to help highlight the tissues. MRI uses short bursts of a magnetic field and produces images like the one shown in **Figure 17**. With CT scans and MRI, data are transferred to a computer that creates an image that an expert can interpret. Both of these techniques are especially useful for studying the brain and spinal tissue.

Computers

Since the first electronic computer was built in 1946, improvements in technology have made computers more powerful and easier to use. The amount of information that a computer can collect, store, organize, and analyze is enormous. Modern computers can complete billions of calculations in the same amount of time that it took early computers to do thousands. With the help of computers, life scientists are able to solve problems that they were not able to solve in the past.

Computers can be used to create graphs, solve complex mathematical problems, and analyze data. Computers also help scientists share data and ideas with each other and prepare reports and articles about their research.

Figure 16 The internal tissues of the brain are shown in this CT scan.

Figure 17 This image, showing blood circulation through the lungs, was produced with MRI.

WEIRD SCIENCE

Back in the 1940s and 1950s, many shoe stores had a shoe-fitting X-ray unit. Customers inserted their feet into the device and then peeked into a port to glimpse the fluorescent image of their toes. Although the machine was popular, it leaked radiation like a sieve! Bans and heavy regulations removed most of the machines by 1970. A few might still be in existence. One was discovered in a department store in 1981 and was promptly removed.

② Teach, continued

Demonstration

Relative Size Show students just how small a nanometer is! Draw a 1 m line on the chalkboard. Tell students that a nanometer is one-billionth of that meter. Ask a student to try to draw a 1 nm line beneath the 1 m line. (Any length drawn will be too long.) Then ask a student volunteer to give you a strand of hair. As you hold the strand of hair, tell students that the diameter of the hair is about 200,000 nm—huge compared with a single nanometer!

Using the Chart

Writing Tell students to note the prefixes for the common SI units. Ask students what they think each of the prefixes mean. *(kilo-* means 1,000; *centi-* means 0.01; *milli-* means 0.001; and so on)

Have students use their dictionaries to discover more words that use each of these prefixes. Students could then write the definitions of these words and record them in their ScienceLog.

Teaching Transparency 3
"Common SI Units"

Math Skills Worksheet 28
"A Formula for SI Catch-up"

---

internetconnect

SC*i*LINKS
NSTA

TOPIC: SI Units
GO TO: www.scilinks.org
***sci*LINKS NUMBER:** HSTL020

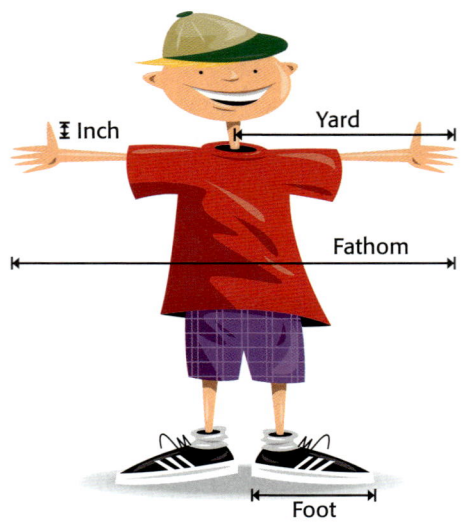

Figure 18 *The modern English system is widely used in the United States. The units were once based on parts of the human body.*

Systems of Measurement

The ability to make accurate and reliable measurements is an important tool in science. There are many different systems of measurement used throughout the world. At one time in England, the standard for 1 inch was three grains of barley arranged end to end. Even modern standardized units were once based on parts of the body, as shown in **Figure 18.** Such systems were not very reliable because they were based on objects that varied in size.

In the late 1700s, the French Academy of Sciences began to develop a global measurement system now known as the International System of Units, or SI. Today most scientists and almost all countries use this system. Using SI measurements helps scientists share and compare their observations and results.

The table below contains commonly used SI units for length, volume, mass, and temperature. Prefixes are used with these units to change them to larger or smaller units. For example, *kilo* means 1,000 times and *milli* indicates 1/1,000 times. All units are based on the number 10, which makes conversions from one unit to another easier.

Common SI Units

Length	meter (m)	
	kilometer (km)	1 km = 1,000 m
	decimeter (dm)	1 dm = 0.1 m
	centimeter (cm)	1 cm = 0.01 m
	millimeter (mm)	1 mm = 0.001 m
	micrometer (μm)	1 μm = 0.000 001 m
	nanometer (nm)	1 nm = 0.000 000 001 m
Volume	cubic meter (m^3)	
	cubic centimeter (cm^3)	1 cm^3 = 0.000 001 m^3
	liter (L)	1 L = 1 dm^3 = 0.001 m^3
	milliliter (mL)	1 mL = 0.001 L = 1 cm^3
Mass	kilogram (kg)	
	gram (g)	1 g = 0.001 kg
	milligram (mg)	1 mg = 0.000 001 kg
Temperature	Kelvin (K)	
	Celsius (°C)	0°C = 273 K
		100°C = 373 K

SCIENCE HUMOR

There are three kinds of mathematicians: those who can count and those who cannot.

The Long and the Short of It How long is a lizard? A life scientist, like the one in **Figure 19,** would probably use millimeters (mm) to describe a small lizard's length. If you divide 1 m into 1,000 parts, each part equals 1 mm. This means that 1 mm is one-thousandth of a meter. Although that seems pretty small, some organisms and structures are so tiny that even smaller units must be used. To describe the length of microscopic objects, scientists use micrometers (μm) or nanometers (nm). The scale in **Figure 20** compares the sizes of different organisms.

Figure 19 *This scientist is measuring a lizard's length using a metric ruler.*

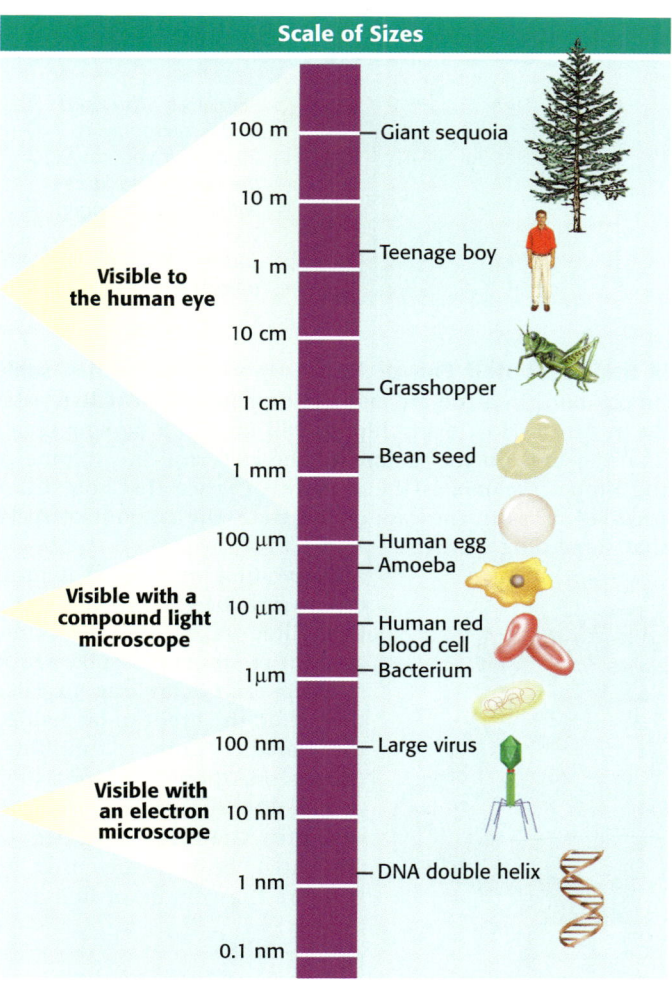

Figure 20 *This scale compares organisms that can be seen with the naked eye with organisms and structures that are microscopic.*

Activity

Measure the width of your desk, but do not use a ruler. Pick an object to use as your unit of measurement. It could be a pencil, your hand, or anything else. Use that unit to determine how wide your desk is, and compare your measurement with those of your classmates. Explain why it is important to use standard units of measurement.

TRY at HOME

IS THAT A FACT!
The International System of Units is abbreviated SI because it stands for the French *Système International d'Unités.*

Answer to Activity
Standard units allow people to communicate data to each other easily.

MATH and MORE

International System of Units Write the following chart on the board:

1 km = 1 m × 10 × 10 × 10
1 hm = 1 m × 10 × 10
1 dam = 1 m × 10
1 m = 1 m
1 dm = 1 m ÷ 10
1 cm = 1 m ÷ 10 ÷ 10
1 mm = 1 m ÷ 10 ÷ 10 ÷ 10

Have students copy this chart in their ScienceLog, and then ask them to describe any patterns they see. (All units are structured in multiples of 10, using meters as the base unit.)

To help students understand SI conversions, have them answer the following questions:

1. How many meters are there in a kilometer? (1,000 m)
2. How many centimeters are in a meter? (100 cm)
3. What is 20 hm in millimeters? (2,000,000 mm)

Math Skills Worksheet 27 "What Is SI?"

Teaching Transparency 4 "Scale of Sizes"

Section 3 • Tools of Life Scientists

2) Teach, continued

Answers to MATHBREAK

1. 25 m²
2. Answers will vary.
3. 4 cm

DEMONSTRATION

Displacement Use a graduated beaker or cylinder to demonstrate to students that a piece of clay will always displace the same amount of water, no matter how the clay is shaped. (Be sure to keep your piece of clay constant. Any additions, losses, or air pockets will change your results.)

ACTIVITY

Calculating Volume Have students bring in empty cereal boxes and fill them with dried beans, rice, or other inexpensive material. Have them predict the volume of the box. Then have them pour the contents into a large graduated cylinder or small square box of predetermined volume, and note the volume of the box itself. Ask the students why cereal manufacturers might use tall, narrow boxes for their packaging. **(Tall, thin boxes appear to hold more than small square ones, they offer a large front space for eye-catching graphics, and they are easier to pour from.)**

 Math Skills Worksheet 29 "Finding Perimeter and Area"

MATH BREAK

Finding Area

You can use the equation at right to find the area of any rectangular surface.

1. What is the area of a square with sides measuring 5 m?
2. What is the area of the top of your desk?
3. A rectangle has an area of 36 cm² and a length of 9 cm. What does its width measure?

Area How much carpet would it take to cover the floor of your classroom? Answering this question involves finding the area of the floor. **Area** is a measure of how much surface an object has.

Some quantities, such as area, can't be expressed with one measurement. That is, they are formed from combinations of two or more measurements. To calculate area, first measure the length and width, and then use the following equation:

$$\text{Area} = \text{length} \times \text{width}$$

The units for area are called square units, such as m², cm², and km². **Figure 21** will help you understand square units.

Figure 21 The area of this rectangle is 20 cm². If you count the smaller squares within the rectangle, you'll count 20 squares that each measure 1 cm².

Is the Glass Half Full or Half Empty? Suppose that some hippos born in a zoo are being relocated to their native habitat in Africa. How many hippos will fit into a moving crate? That depends on the volume of the crate and the volume of the hippos. **Volume** is the amount of space that something occupies or, as in the case of the crate, the amount of space that something contains.

The volume of a liquid is most often described using liters (L). One liter takes up the same amount of space as a cube whose sides are each 1 dm long. Just like the meter, the liter can be divided into smaller units. A milliliter (mL) is one-thousandth of a liter. A microliter (µL) is one-millionth of a liter. Graduated cylinders or graduated beakers are used to measure the volume of liquids.

Q: What has holes but holds water?

A: a sponge

IS THAT A FACT!

While he was taking a bath, Archimedes, a famous Greek mathematician, discovered that an object's volume can be calculated by measuring the amount of water that the object displaces. In this case, the object was himself!

The volume of a solid object, such as a crate, is described using cubic meters (m³). Smaller objects can be measured in cubic centimeters (cm³) or cubic millimeters (mm³). One cm³ is equal to one mL. To calculate the volume of a cube (or any other rectangular shape), multiply the length by the width by the height. Find the volume of the aquarium in **Figure 22.**

An object like a hippo or a rock has an irregular shape. If you multiplied its length, width, and height, you would not get a very accurate measure of its volume. One way to figure out the volume of an irregularly shaped object is to measure how much fluid the object displaces.

The girl in **Figure 23** is measuring the volume of a rock by placing it in a graduated cylinder that contains a known quantity of water. The rock displaces some water, which causes the level of the water to rise. The girl can figure out the volume of the rock by subtracting the volume of the water alone from the volume of the water and the rock. Then the volume of water in milliliters displaced by the rock must be converted to cm³.

Figure 22 *The volume of this aquarium is found by multiplying its length, width, and height. What is its volume?*

Figure 23 *This graduated cylinder contains 70 mL of water. After the rock was added, the water level moved to 80 mL. Because the rock displaced 10 mL of water and because 1 mL = 1 cm³, the volume of the rock is 10 cm³.*

IS THAT A FACT!

As long as a boat and its contents weigh less than the water that the boat displaces, it will float. Joseph-Louis Lambot patented boats made of wire and concrete in 1847, and during World War II, when steel was in short supply, ships made of concrete were common.

RESEARCH

Explain to students that the United States is the only industrialized nation in the world that does not officially use the SI system. Talk about some of the reasons why the country has had such a hard time changing. Then have students research the history of the English and SI systems of measurement. Suggest that they also investigate English measurements such as the furlong and the stone.

MATH and MORE

Have students answer the question in the caption for **Figure 22:**

What is the volume of the aquarium? (The volume of the aquarium is 1.5 m × 1 m × 0.3 m = 0.45 m³. To find the liquid volume, calculate 0.45 m³ × 1000 $\frac{\text{liters}}{\text{m}^3}$ = 450 L.)

Math Skills Worksheet 30 "Finding Volume"

Homework

Writing Because dense materials, such as rock, tend to sink, it is easy to forget that huge, seaworthy ships are often made of very dense materials, such as steel. Ships have even been made of concrete. Have students conduct library and computer research on any of the following topics:

- why ships float
- what materials have been used in the history of ship building
- how ships are designed
- how ships are constructed
- concrete-canoe competitions (held at many universities)

Section 3 • Tools of Life Scientists

3) Extend

REAL-WORLD CONNECTION

The carat is a unit of measure used only for expressing the mass of diamonds and other precious gems. It was originally based on the weight of local grains or seeds and varied widely from place to place. The carat is now a standard unit, with one metric carat equal to 0.200 g. The masses of diamonds, rubies, emeralds, sapphires, aquamarines, zircon, spinel, opals, and pearls are all properly expressed in carats. Ask students:

Why is it important for the mass of a diamond to be expressed in a universally understood measurement?

CONNECT TO PHYSICAL SCIENCE

If temperature can be defined as a measure of the energy, or movement, of atoms, then atoms that are very still must be very cold. Using this logic, physicist Steven Chu chilled sodium atoms to nearly absolute zero (–273°C, or –523°F) by using laser beams aimed at different angles to restrict the atoms' movement. The result was a glowing pea-sized blob of chilled atoms that seemed to hang in the air at the intersection of the laser beams. Use the following Teaching Transparency to demonstrate the difference between absolute zero and the freezing point of water.

Teaching Transparency 238 "Three Temperature Scales" *LINK TO PHYSICAL SCIENCE*

A Massive Undertaking Mass is the amount of matter that makes up an object. The kilogram (kg) is the basic unit for mass. The mass of a very large object is described using kilograms (kg) or metric tons. A kilogram equals 1,000 g; therefore, a gram is one-thousandth of a kilogram. A metric ton equals 1,000 kg. Grams are used to describe the mass of small objects. A medium-sized apple has a mass of about 100 g. As shown in **Figure 24**, mass can be measured with a balance.

Figure 24 The mass of the apple equals the mass of the weights.

Is It Hot Enough for You? How hot does it need to be to kill bacteria? To answer this question, a life scientist would measure the temperature at which bacteria die. **Temperature** is a measure of how hot or cold something is. You may not realize it, but the molecules that make up all matter are constantly moving. When energy is transferred to these molecules, they move even more, which causes the temperature to increase. Temperature, then, can also be defined as a measure of the average energy of the molecules of a substance.

You are probably used to describing temperature using degrees Fahrenheit (°F). Scientists commonly use degrees Celsius (°C), although Kelvins are the official SI units for temperature. You will use °C in this book. The thermometer in **Figure 25** shows the relationship between °F and °C.

Figure 25 Water freezes at 0°C and boils at 100°C. Your normal body temperature is 37°C, which is equal to 98.6°F.

MISCONCEPTION ALERT

The terms *mass* and *weight* do not mean the same thing. Mass is a fundamental property of an object, while weight is a relative property—a measure of the gravitational force experienced by an object.

For example, a rocket has the same mass whether it is standing on Earth or on the moon, but it will weigh less on the moon because the moon exerts a smaller gravitational force on it.

Safety Rules!

Life science is exciting and fun, but it can also be dangerous. So don't take any chances! Always follow your teacher's instructions, and don't take shortcuts—even when you think there is little or no danger.

Before starting an experiment, get your teacher's permission and read the lab procedures carefully. Pay particular attention to safety information and caution statements. The diagram below shows the safety symbols used in this book. Get to know these symbols and what they mean. Do this by reading the safety information starting on page 682. **This is important!** If you are still unsure about what a safety symbol means, ask your teacher.

Stay on the safe side by reading the safety information on page 682.
This is a must before doing an experiment!

Safety Symbols

 Eye Protection
 Clothing Protection
 Hand Safety
 Heating Safety
 Electric Safety
 Sharp Object
 Chemical Safety
 Animal Safety
 Plant Safety

REVIEW

1. How is temperature related to energy?
2. If you were going to measure the mass of a fly, which metric unit would be most appropriate?
3. What are two benefits of using the International System of Units?
4. **Understanding Technology** What tool was used to produce the image at right? How can you tell?

internetconnect

SCLINKS NSTA

TOPIC: Tools of Life Science, SI Units
GO TO: www.scilinks.org
sciLINKS NUMBER: HSTL015, HSTL020

---

4) Close

  PG 682
Safety First!

Quiz

1. What are the three main parts of a compound microscope? (tube with lenses, stage, and light)
2. What are CT scans and MRI especially useful for studying? (brain and spinal tissue)

ALTERNATIVE ASSESSMENT

Writing Have students create an illustrated dictionary of vocabulary terms that were used in this chapter. Students can share their dictionaries with the rest of the class.
Sheltered English

ACTIVITY

Writing Have students provide written answers to the Review. Answers are provided at the bottom of this page. Then have students write a letter to a scientist, dated well into the future, that describes some of the tools that scientists use today.

 Science Skills Worksheet 9 "Safety Rules!"

 Interactive Explorations CD-ROM "Something's Fishy!"

Answers to Review

1. The higher the temperature is, the greater the energy.
2. milligram
3. All scientists use the International System of Units so that they can share and compare their results. Another benefit is that calculations are easier because SI units are based on powers of 10.
4. a scanning electron microscope; the image is three-dimensional.

Chapter Highlights

Vocabulary Definitions

Section 1
life science the study of living things

Section 2
scientific method a series of steps that scientists use to answer questions and solve problems

hypothesis a possible explanation or answer to a question

controlled experiment an experiment that tests only one factor at a time

variable the factor in a controlled experiment that changes

theory a unifying explanation for a broad range of hypotheses and observations that have been supported by testing

technology the application of knowledge, tools, and materials to solve problems and accomplish tasks; technology can also refer to the objects used to accomplish tasks

Chapter Highlights

SECTION 1

Vocabulary
life science *(p. 6)*

Section Notes
- Life science is the study of living things. Observations often lead to questions. Questions fuel the study of life science.
- Anyone can become a life scientist. Life scientists work in many different places and investigate a wide variety of questions and problems.
- Life scientists help prevent and treat diseases and help solve environmental problems.

SECTION 2

Vocabulary
scientific method *(p. 10)*
hypothesis *(p. 12)*
controlled experiment *(p. 14)*
variable *(p. 14)*
theory *(p. 18)*
technology *(p. 18)*

Section Notes
- The scientific method is a series of steps that scientists use to answer a question or solve a problem.
- The parts of the scientific method are not always completed in the same order. Steps are sometimes skipped or repeated.
- Scientists perform controlled experiments to test the effects of one factor at a time.
- Scientists must make careful observations, record data accurately, and be creative in finding answers and designing experiments.
- A hypothesis, which is a possible explanation for what has been observed, must be testable.

✓ Skills Check

Math Concepts
UNIT CONVERSIONS Imagine that you are writing a paper on the Empire State Building, in New York City. One source in the library lists the height of the building as 381,000,000 μm. This is a very large number, so you'll probably want to convert it to a more manageable number by using meters instead of micrometers. As you can see in the table on page 22, 1 μm = 0.000 001 m. To convert micrometers to meters, you multiply by 0.000 001.

$$381{,}000{,}000 \times 0.000\,001 = 381 \text{ m}$$

Visual Understanding
HOW BIG? To review what can be seen with different types of microscopes, turn to pages 19 and 20. The Scale of Sizes, on page 23, will also help you visualize sizes decribed using the metric system.

SAFETY FIRST! Make sure that you know and understand the different safety symbols shown on page 27.

Lab and Activity Highlights

Does It All Add Up? PG 686

Graphing Data PG 688

A Window to a Hidden World PG 689

Datasheets for LabBook
(blackline masters for these labs)

28 Chapter 1 • The World of Life Science

VOCABULARY DEFINITIONS, continued

SECTION 3

compound light microscope a microscope that consists of a tube with lenses, a stage, and a light source

electron microscope a microscope that uses tiny particles of matter to produce magnified images

area the measure of how much surface an object has

volume the amount of space that something occupies or the amount of space that something contains

mass the amount of matter that something is made of; its value does not change with the object's location

temperature a measure of how hot (or cold) something is; specifically, a measure of the average energy of the molecules of a substance

SECTION 2

- A theory is a unifying explanation for a broad range of hypotheses and observations that have been supported by testing.
- Scientific knowledge is constantly changing and growing as scientists ask new questions, find different answers to the same questions, and use tools that allow them to gather information in new ways.

Labs
Does It All Add Up? (p. 686)
Graphing Data (p. 688)

SECTION 3

Vocabulary
compound light microscope (p. 19)
electron microscope (p. 20)
area (p. 24)
volume (p. 24)
mass (p. 26)
temperature (p. 26)

Section Notes
- Life scientists commonly use compound light microscopes and electron microscopes to make observations of organisms or parts of organisms that are too small to be seen with the naked eye.
- X rays, CT scans, and MRI are used to view internal structures of organisms.
- Life scientists use computers to collect, store, organize, analyze, and share data.
- The International System of Units (SI), which is a simple and reliable system of measurement, is used by most scientists.

Labs
A Window to a Hidden World (p. 689)

 Vocabulary Review Worksheet 1

 Blackline masters of these Chapter Highlights can be found in the **Study Guide**.

---

internetconnect

GO TO: go.hrw.com

Visit the **HRW** Web site for a variety of learning tools related to this chapter. Just type in the keyword:

KEYWORD: HSTLIV

GO TO: www.scilinks.org

Visit the **National Science Teachers Association** on-line Web site for Internet resources related to this chapter. Just type in the sciLINKS number for more information about the topic:

TOPIC:	sciLINKS NUMBER:
Scientific Method	HSTL004
Deformed Frogs	HSTL005
Careers in Life Science	HSTL010
Tools of Life Science	HSTL015
SI Units	HSTL020

Lab and Activity Highlights

LabBank

Whiz-Bang Demonstrations
- Air Ball, Demo 1
- Getting to the Point, Demo 2

Inquiry Labs, One Side or Two? Lab 1

Long-Term Projects & Research Ideas,
The Length of a Fethel, Project 1

Interactive Explorations CD-ROM

 CD 1, Exploration 1, "Something's Fishy!"

Chapter 1 • Chapter Highlights

Chapter Review Answers

USING VOCABULARY

1. scientific method
2. hypotheses
3. variable; control group
4. Area
5. grams

UNDERSTANDING CONCEPTS

Multiple Choice

6. d
7. c
8. a
9. a
10. c
11. b

Short Answer

12. A hypothesis must be testable by experimentation in order for scientists to disprove the hypothesis or support it.
13. A prediction is a statement of cause and effect used to set up an experiment.
14. The SI units for measuring volume are liters (L), units based on the liter, and units based on the cubic meter (m^3, cm^3, mm^3). The mass of an object is measured in kilograms (grams, milligrams, etc.).

Science Skills Worksheet 7
"Improving Your Study Habits"

Chapter Review

USING VOCABULARY

To complete the following sentences, choose the correct term from each pair of terms listed below:

1. The set of skills or steps that scientists use to answer questions is the __?__. (*controlled experiment* or *scientific method*)

2. After recognizing a problem or asking a question, life scientists form one or more __?__, which are possible explanations for what has been observed. (*predictions* or *hypotheses*)

3. In a controlled experiment, the __?__ is the one factor that differs between the __?__ and the experimental group. (*prediction, variable group* or *variable, control group*)

4. __?__ is a measure of how much surface an object has. (*Area* or *Volume*)

5. Life scientists use __?__ to describe the measurement of an object's mass. (*meters* or *grams*)

UNDERSTANDING CONCEPTS

Multiple Choice

6. Which of the following would *not* be an area of study in life science?
   a. studying how lions and hyenas interact
   b. measuring the rate at which bacteria divide
   c. comparing the reproduction of arctic plants with that of desert plants
   d. studying how volcanoes are formed

7. The steps of the scientific method
   a. must all be used in every scientific investigation.
   b. must always be used in the same order.
   c. are not always used in order.
   d. start with the development of a theory.

8. In a controlled experiment,
   a. a control group is compared with one or more experimental groups.
   b. there are at least two variables.
   c. all factors should be different.
   d. a variable is not needed.

9. When a scientist finds that a hypothesis is wrong, the scientist usually
   a. tries to find another explanation for what has been observed.
   b. stops studying science.
   c. feels that nothing valuable was learned.
   d. adds an additional variable to his or her experiment.

10. What tool would a life scientist use to get a three-dimensional image of a microscopic organism?
    a. CT scan
    b. X ray
    c. scanning electron microscope
    d. magnifying lens

11. The International System of Units
    a. is based on standardized body measurements.
    b. contains units that are based on the number 10.
    c. is useful only for measuring lengths.
    d. is a device used to measure volume.

Short Answer

12. Why do hypotheses need to be testable?

13. What is a prediction?

14. Which SI units can be used to describe the measurement of volume? Which SI units can be used to describe the mass of an object?

Concept Mapping

15. Use the following terms to create a concept map: observations, predictions, questions, controlled experiments, variable, hypothesis.

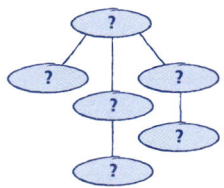

CRITICAL THINKING AND PROBLEM SOLVING

Write one or two sentences to answer the following questions:

16. In a controlled experiment, why should there be several individuals in the control group and several in each of the experimental groups?

17. A scientist who studies mice observes that on the day he feeds the mice vitamins with their meals, they perform better in mazes. What hypothesis would you form to explain this phenomenon?

18. The volume of an egg and water in a graduated beaker is 200 mL. After the egg is removed, the volume of the water is found to be 125 mL. What is the volume of the egg in cm³?

200 mL   125 mL

MATH IN SCIENCE

19. If you magnified a 5 µm long organism 1,000 ×, how long would that organism appear in millimeters (mm)?

INTERPRETING GRAPHICS

Examine the illustration below of an experiment set up to test the following prediction: **If** bees are more attracted to yellow flowers than to red flowers, **then** bees will visit yellow flowers more often than they will visit red flowers.

11 visits   3 visits   11 visits

2 visits   9 visits   4 visits

20. How many total visits did the yellow flowers receive? How many total visits did the red flowers receive?

21. What is the average number of visits for yellow flowers? What is the average number of visits for red flowers?

22. In what ways might the experimental setup be an unreliable test of the prediction?

Reading Check-up Take a minute to review your answers to the Pre-Reading Questions found at the bottom of page 4. Have your answers changed? If necessary, revise your answers based on what you have learned since you began this chapter.

Concept Mapping

15. An answer to this exercise can be found at the end of this book.

CRITICAL THINKING AND PROBLEM SOLVING

16. The more individuals there are in the groups, the more confident scientists can be that differences between the groups were caused by the variable and not by natural differences between individual organisms.

17. Possible answer: Vitamins increase the mice's spatial reasoning capabilities.

18. 75 mL = 75 cm³

MATH IN SCIENCE

19. 5 mm

INTERPRETING GRAPHICS

20. 20; 20
21. 10; 5
22. There is more than one variable. There are different kinds of flowers used in the experiment. If flower color is being tested, then flower color should be the only difference between the flowers. There should also be the same number of flowers of each color.

Concept Mapping Transparency 1

Blackline masters of this Chapter Review can be found in the **Study Guide**.

CAREERS

Zoologist—Eric Pianka

Background

Zoology dates back more than 2,300 years, to ancient Greece, where the philosopher Aristotle observed and theorized about animal behavior. About 200 years later, Galen, a Greek physician, began dissecting and experimenting with animals. However, there were few advances in zoology until the 1700s and 1800s. During this period, the Swedish naturalist Carolus Linnaeus developed a classification system for animals, and Charles Darwin published his theory on natural selection and evolution.

Today, zoology is divided into many specialized areas. These areas include comparative anatomy (the study of anatomical structures among many different animals), physiology (the study of how bodies function), genetics (the study of heredity), embryology (the study of embryo development), entomology (the study of insects), ichthyology (the study of fish), and herpetology (the study of reptiles and amphibians).

CAREERS

ZOOLOGIST

Eric Pianka became interested in lizards when he was 6 years old. "On a trip across the country with my family, I saw a big green lizard at a roadside park," Pianka explains. "I tried to catch it, but all I got was the tail. At that moment, I knew I had to find out everything I could about the kind of life it led." Pianka is now a world-famous professor of zoology at the University of Texas, in Austin, Texas.

One of the things Eric Pianka likes best about his job is being in the wilderness and seeing things that few people have ever seen. "I've been almost everywhere! I've spent a lot of time studying deserts in the western United States. I've been to deserts in southern Africa, India, and Chile. My most current (and oldest) interest is in the deserts of Australia. I haven't had a chance to study the Brazilian Amazon yet, but that's a goal for the future!"

The Ecology of Desert Lizards

In his research as a zoologist, Pianka has focused on the ecology of desert lizards. He goes to a desert, collects lizards, and examines and classifies them. Then he compiles data and interprets them in books or papers. As Pianka puts it, "I try to answer questions like, Why are there more lizards in one place than in another? How do they react with each other and other species? How have they adapted to their environment?"

Recently, Pianka conducted a study to learn about the effects of wildfires on the ecology and diversity of lizard species. He hopes this work will show how lizard species adapted to the large-scale wildfires that at one time occurred regularly in desert areas but that today are usually controlled by humans.

▼ *The collared lizard lives in rocky regions of the southwestern United States.*

Learning from Wildlife

Pianka believes that doing research on lizards and other animals may help us protect our environment. "Everyone always asks, 'Why lizards?' I turn the question around and say, 'Why you?' The general attitude is that everything on Earth has to somehow serve humans. By looking at how other species have lived and died and changed over millions of years, we can gain a better understanding of the world we live in."

Be a Zoologist for a Day

▶ Select a common animal that lives in your area and that can be easily observed. Spend a few hours watching it carefully. Document everything you observe. Did you discover anything you did not already know? Present your findings to the class.

Answer to Be a Zoologist for a Day

Student observations will vary according to the choice of animal and the duration of observation. However, students should demonstrate clear observational skills and organize the records of what they observed.

Science Fiction

"The Homesick Chicken"
by Edward D. Hoch

OK, OK, why *did* the chicken cross the road? Oh sure, you know the answer to this old riddle, don't you? Or maybe you just think you do! But "The Homesick Chicken," by Edward D. Hoch, may surprise you. That old chicken may not be exactly what it seems…

You see, one of the chickens at Tangaway Research Farms has escaped—not just flown the coop, mind you, but really escaped. It pecked a hole in a super-strength security fence and then crossed an eight-lane highway to get away. But after all that effort, it just stopped! It was found in a vacant lot across the highway from Tangaway, pecking away contentedly.

Barnabus Rex, a specialist in solving scientific riddles, is called in to work on the mystery. He is intrigued by this escaping chicken. Why would it go to all the trouble to peck through the tough security fence, risk being flattened on the superhighway, and then just stop when it got to the other side?

There are a few clues in the story. As you read it, maybe you can see what Mr. Rex sees. If you know anything about chickens, you might be able to solve the mystery. Escape to the *Holt Anthology of Science Fiction* and read "The Homesick Chicken."

SCIENCE FICTION
"The Homesick Chicken"
by Edward D. Hoch

So why DID the chicken cross the road, anyway? It's a mystery, but it's not one Detective Barnabus Rex can't handle!

Teaching Strategy

Reading Level This is a relatively short story that should not be difficult for the average student to read and comprehend.

Background

About the Author Known for his exciting mystery stories, Edward D. Hoch occasionally writes other forms of literature. "The Homesick Chicken" is a delightful story because it blends science fiction with elements of a detective story or mystery. Hoch has published more than 200 mystery stories in *Ellery Queen's Mystery Magazine*. He has worked as a professional writer since 1968. Before that, he worked in libraries and advertising and served in the U.S. Army. In 1967, he won the Edgar Allan Poe Award of Mystery Writers for his story "The Oblong Room." Currently, he lives in Rochester, New York, where he continues to write. His most recent work, a mystery novel called, *Diagnosis: Impossible*, was published in 1996.

Further Reading If students liked "The Homesick Chicken," you can recommend more mystery stories by Edward D. Hoch. Some of these works include the following:

The Monkey's Clue, Grosset, 1978

The Stolen Sapphire, Grosset, 1978

The Night, My Friend: Stories of Crime & Suspense, Ohio University Press, 1992

Chapter Organizer

CHAPTER ORGANIZATION	TIME MINUTES	OBJECTIVES	LABS, INVESTIGATIONS, AND DEMONSTRATIONS
Chapter Opener pp. 34–35	45	National Standards: UCP 5, SAI 1, LS 3c, 4c	**Start-up Activity** Lights On! p. 35
Section 1 Characteristics of Living Things	90	▶ List the characteristics of living things. ▶ Distinguish between asexual reproduction and sexual reproduction. ▶ Define and describe homeostasis. UCP 1, 2, LS 1b–1d, 2a–2c, 3a–3c, 5a	**Discovery Lab,** Roly-Poly Races, p. 690 `GENERAL` **Datasheets for LabBook,** Roly-Poly Races, Datasheet 4 `GENERAL`
Section 2 The Simple Bare Necessities of Life	90	▶ Explain why organisms need food, water, air, and living space. ▶ Discuss how living things obtain what they need to live. UCP 2, SAI 2, HNS 1, 2, LS 1c, 3a, 3d, 4b–4d	**Demonstration,** Fire and Life, p. 41 in ATE `GENERAL`
Section 3 The Chemistry of Life	90	▶ Compare and contrast the chemical building blocks of cells. ▶ Explain the importance of ATP. UCP 2, 5, SAI 1, LS 1a, 1c, 2c; LabBook UCP 2, SAI 1, HNS 1, LS 3c	**Demonstration,** Protein Model, p. 42 in ATE `BASIC` **QuickLab,** Starch Search, p. 43 `GENERAL` **Discovery Lab,** The Best-Bread Bakery Dilemma, p. 692 `ADVANCED` **Datasheets for LabBook,** The Best-Bread Bakery Dilemma, Datasheet 5 `ADVANCED` **Labs You Can Eat,** Say Cheese! Lab 1 `GENERAL` **Long-Term Projects & Research Ideas,** Project 2 `ADVANCED`

*See page **T20** for a complete correlation of this book with the*

NATIONAL SCIENCE EDUCATION STANDARDS.

TECHNOLOGY RESOURCES

 Guided Reading Audio CD English or Spanish, Chapter 2

 One-Stop Planner CD-ROM with Test Generator

  Science, Technology & Society, Tapping into Yellowstone's Hot Springs, Segment 1

Chapter 2 • It's Alive!! Or, Is It?

CLASSROOM WORKSHEETS, TRANSPARENCIES, AND RESOURCES	SCIENCE INTEGRATION AND CONNECTIONS	REVIEW AND ASSESSMENT
Directed Reading Worksheet 2 BASIC **Science Puzzlers, Twisters & Teasers,** Worksheet 2 ADVANCED		
Directed Reading Worksheet 2, Section 1 BASIC **Math Skills for Science Worksheet 4,** A Shortcut for Multiplying Large Numbers GENERAL **Math Skills for Science Worksheet 26,** Multiplying and Dividing in Scientific Notation GENERAL **Critical Thinking Worksheet 2,** Intergalactic Planetary Mission ADVANCED **Math Skills for Science Worksheet 18,** Decimals and Fractions GENERAL **Math Skills for Science Worksheet 21,** Percentages, Fractions, and Decimals GENERAL	**Oceanography Connection,** p. 37 **Math and More,** p. 37 in ATE GENERAL **Math and More,** p. 38 in ATE GENERAL **Apply,** p. 39 GENERAL	**Self-Check,** p. 37 **Review,** p. 39 GENERAL **Quiz,** p. 39 in ATE GENERAL **Alternative Assessment,** p. 39 in ATE ADVANCED
Directed Reading Worksheet 2, Section 2 BASIC **Transparency 178,** Climate Zones of the Earth **Reinforcement Worksheet 2,** Amazing Discovery BASIC	**Connect to Earth Science,** p. 40 in ATE **MathBreak,** How Much Oxygen? p. 43 GENERAL **Scientific Debate:** Life on Mars? p. 50 ADVANCED	**Review,** p. 41 GENERAL **Quiz,** p. 41 in ATE GENERAL **Alternative Assessment,** p. 41 in ATE ADVANCED
Directed Reading Worksheet 2, Section 3 BASIC **Transparency 5,** Phospholipid Molecule and Cell Membrane **Transparency 6,** Energy for Cells **Reinforcement Worksheet 2,** Building Blocks BASIC	**Multicultural Connection,** p. 42 in ATE GENERAL **Holt Anthology of Science Fiction,** They're Made Out of Meat GENERAL	**Homework,** p. 44 in ATE GENERAL **Review,** p. 45 GENERAL **Quiz,** p. 45 in ATE GENERAL **Alternative Assessment,** p. 45 in ATE GENERAL

END-OF-CHAPTER REVIEW AND ASSESSMENT

Chapter Review in Study Guide
Vocabulary and Notes in Study Guide
Chapter Tests with Performance-Based Assessment, Chapter 2 Test
Chapter Tests with Performance-Based Assessment, Performance-Based Assessment 2
Concept Mapping Transparency 2

 Holt, Rinehart and Winston On-line Resources
go.hrw.com
For worksheets and other teaching aids related to this chapter, visit the HRW Web site and type in the keyword: **HSTALV**

 National Science Teachers Association
www.scilinks.org
Encourage students to use the sciLINKS numbers listed in the internet connect boxes to access information and resources on the **NSTA** Web site.

Chapter 2 • Chapter Organizer

Chapter Resources & Worksheets

Visual Resources

Meeting Individual Needs

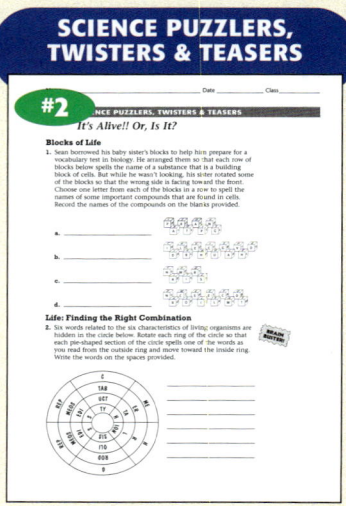

Chapter 2 • It's Alive!! Or, Is It?

Review & Assessment

STUDY GUIDE

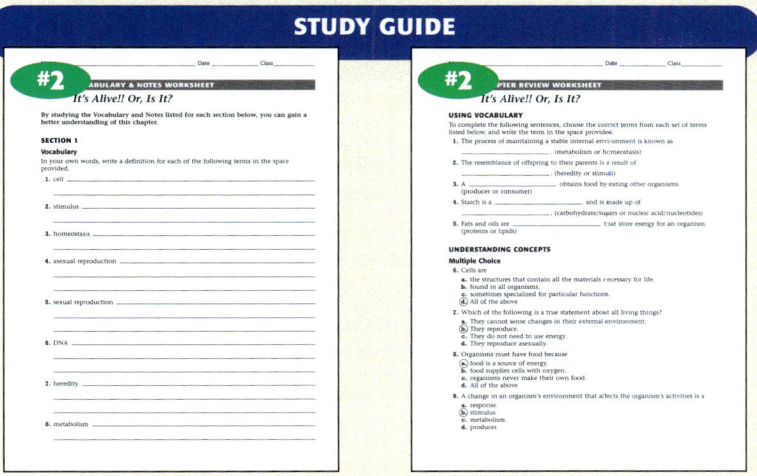

CHAPTER TESTS WITH PERFORMANCE-BASED ASSESSMENT

Lab Worksheets

LABS YOU CAN EAT

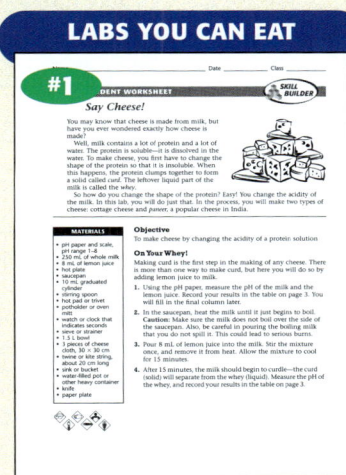

LONG-TERM PROJECTS & RESEARCH IDEAS

DATASHEETS FOR LABBOOK

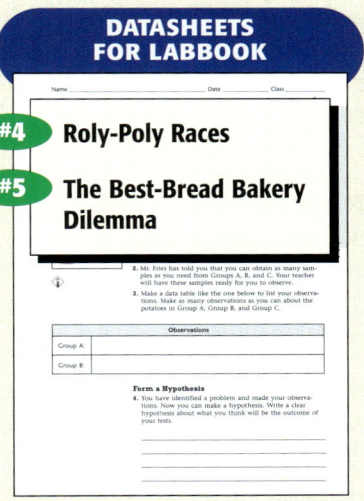

#4 Roly-Poly Races

#5 The Best-Bread Bakery Dilemma

Applications & Extensions

CRITICAL THINKING & PROBLEM SOLVING

SCIENCE TECHNOLOGY

Chapter 2 • Chapter Resources & Worksheets

Chapter Background

SECTION 1
Characteristics of Living Things

▶ **Biogenesis**
The theory of biogenesis states that living things come only from other living things. However, until the late 1600s, people generally believed in spontaneous generation, the theory that lower forms of life, such as insects, come from nonliving things. The first evidence to disprove spontaneous generation came from controlled experiments conducted in 1667 by Italian Francesco Redi.

- Redi showed that maggots will appear on meat in an uncovered jar but not on meat in a closed container. Why? The maggots came from eggs laid by flies that had access to the uncovered meat.

▶ **Robert Hooke**
Robert Hooke was one of the greatest scientists of his time. In addition to his studies in biology with the compound microscope, he was also involved in physics, astronomy, chemistry, geology, and architecture.

- Hooke applied his discovery of the law of elasticity (that the stretching of a solid material is proportional to the force applied to it) to the design of balance springs for watches and clocks. His sketches of Mars were used 200 years later to determine that planet's rate of rotation. He studied the crystal structure of snowflakes. In 1672, he developed the wave theory of light to explain diffraction, which he had also discovered. Hooke was the first person to examine fossils with a microscope and to recognize, 200 years before Charles Darwin was born, that fossils are evidence of changes in organisms on Earth over millions of years.

IS THAT A FACT!

- Different cells in the human body have different life spans, ranging from a few days for intestinal cells to about 120 days for red blood cells and years for brain cells. Scientists have recently discovered that the brain does make new cells.

However, they only mature in the hippocampus, which is responsible for learning and memory.

▶ **Anton van Leeuwenhoek**
Anton van Leeuwenhoek was born in 1632 into a family of tradespeople in Delft, Holland. He was poor and received no advanced education. In 1648, he was apprenticed to a fabric merchant to learn this trade. On his own initiative, he began to grind lenses to experiment with magnification. Historians think he may have been inspired by Robert Hooke's book, *Micrographia* (Small Drawings).

SECTION 2
The Simple Bare Necessities of Life

▶ **A Place to Call Home**
Every organism needs a place to live, and the places where some organisms thrive are surprising.

- Antarctica is a harsh and unforgiving environment. Most of the subantarctic islands are solid rock, and 98 percent of the continent is covered with ice. But it is home to more than 400 types of lichens and 85 mosses. Lichens, a symbiotic association of algae and fungi, can tolerate low temperatures and minimal moisture. Green algae thrive near penguin colonies. Moss grows on the few small patches of soil that exist.

- In Death Valley National Park, summertime temperatures routinely reach 50°C, and rainfall averages 3.8 cm per year. Yet more than 900 types of plants live there. More than 400 animal species also live in this region, including bats, kangaroo rats, gophers, bighorn sheep, lizards, tortoises, snakes, spiders, scorpions, beetles, turkey vultures, and roadrunners.

- Three to four kilometers deep in the ocean, where the pressure is 275 times that at sea level and it is cold and dark, lurk huge yellow jellyfish, giant clams, blind fish, and red worms that are 2 m long. These animals

Chapter 2 • It's Alive!! Or, Is It?

live near deep-sea vents. Water that is trapped beneath the ocean floor and is heated by volcanic activity to as much as 300°C escapes through these vents. The cold ocean cools the water around the vents to about 13°C. Because there is no sunlight at this depth, the animals use the chemicals in the water for energy through a process called chemosynthesis. However, the amount of energy available through chemosynthesis is far less than that obtained through photosynthesis on Earth's surface.

IS THAT A FACT!

- The sand grouse of Chad, in northern Africa, builds its nest many miles from a water source. When the chicks hatch, the parents fly to Lake Chad, where they soak their breast feathers before flying back to their chicks. The chicks then drink the water from their parents' feathers; this both feeds and cools them.

- Some animals that hunt at night, such as cats and some dogs, have a special eye structure that helps them see in the dark. The *tapetum lucidum*, or "bright carpet," a mirrorlike layer of cells, enhances the eye's ability to see in low light. It makes a cat's eyes appear to glow in the dark.

SECTION 3
The Chemistry of Life

▶ "Chemical" Menu
Our bodies need certain kinds of chemicals to live.

- Carbohydrates are the body's primary source of energy. Simple carbohydrates, or sugars, are found in fruits, some vegetables, and milk. Complex carbohydrates, which include starches, are obtained from pasta, seeds, nuts, and vegetables such as peas, beans, and potatoes.

- Lipids include saturated and polyunsaturated fats. Saturated fats are present in greater amounts in animal products. Vegetable-based oils have more polyunsaturated fats.

- Nucleic acids, which may contain thousands of components called nucleotides, contain essential information for the construction of proteins.

- Proteins are made of 20 different amino acids. Our cells arrange these amino acids in different combinations to make all the proteins in our body.

IS THAT A FACT!

- If stretched out end to end, the DNA in an average human body would measure 20 billion kilometers.

- For about 100 years, beginning in the late 1700s, sperm whales were a major source of oil for lubricants and fuel for lamps. These huge animals grow to 18 m long. Sperm oil came from the whale's blubber and unusually large head. Whaling nearly made sperm whales extinct.

▶ Metabolism
Biochemical reactions that take place within a cell are collectively known as metabolism. Enzymes, which are themselves proteins, catalyze or accelerate most of the chemical reactions within a cell. Each type of reaction is catalyzed by a specific enzyme.

- A metabolic pathway is the sequence of chemical reactions needed to make a particular biological molecule. If a disruption occurs somewhere along the pathway, then the organism might develop an illness or suffer a deficiency.

IS THAT A FACT!

- When bears sleep in their dens during winter, their body temperature decreases several degrees. We know this because scientists crawled into the dens and took their temperatures. The lower body temperature reduces energy requirements, so bears can sleep for weeks or months without eating.

For background information about teaching strategies and issues, refer to the *Professional Reference for Teachers*.

Chapter 2

It's Alive!! Or, Is It?

 Pre-Reading Questions

Students may not know the answers to these questions before reading the chapter, so accept any reasonable response.

Suggested Answers

1. All living things have cells, reproduce, sense and respond to change, have DNA, use energy, and grow and develop.
2. All organisms need food, water, air, and a place to live.

 Directed Reading Worksheet 2

 Science Puzzlers, Twisters & Teasers Worksheet 2

 Guided Reading Audio CD English or Spanish, Chapter 2

Chapter 2

It's Alive!! Or, Is It?

Sections

1. Characteristics of Living Things.......... 36
   Oceanography Connection 37
   Apply 39
   Internet Connect 39
2. The Simple Bare Necessities of Life................ 40
   Internet Connect 41
3. The Chemistry of Life.... 42
   MathBreak 43
   QuickLab 43

Chapter Review 48
Feature Articles 50, 51
LabBook 690–693

 Pre-Reading Questions

1. What characteristics do all living things have in common?
2. What do organisms need in order to stay alive?

Robot Bugs!

What does it mean to say something is *alive*? Machines have some of the characteristics of living things, but they do not have all of them. This amazing robot insect can respond to changes in its environment. It can walk over obstacles. It can perform some tasks. But it is still not alive. How is it like and unlike the living insect pictured here? In this chapter, you'll learn about the characteristics that all living things share.

---

 internet connect

 HRW On-line Resources
go.hrw.com
For worksheets and other teaching aids, visit the HRW Web site and type in the keyword: **HSTALV**

 sciLINKS NSTA
www.scilinks.com
Use the *sci*LINKS numbers at the end of each chapter for additional resources on the **NSTA** Web site.

 CNNfyi.com
www.cnnfyi.com
Visit the CNN Web site for current events coverage and classroom resources.

START-UP Activity

LIGHTS ON!

Living things respond to change. In this activity, you will work with a partner to see how eyes react to changes in light.

Procedure

1. Observe a classmate's eyes in a room with normal light. Find the pupil, which is the black area in the center of the colored part of the eye, and note its size.

2. Have your partner keep both eyes open, and have him or her cover each one with a cupped hand. Wait about 1 minute.

3. Instruct your partner to pull away both hands quickly. Immediately look at your partner's pupils. Record what happens.

4. Now briefly shine a **flashlight** into your partner's eyes. In your ScienceLog, record how this affects the pupils.

   Caution: Do not use the sun as the source of the light.

5. Change places with your partner, and repeat steps 1–4 so that your partner can observe your eyes.

Analysis

6. How did your partner's eyes respond to changes in the level of light?

7. How did changes in the size of your pupils affect your vision? What does this tell you about why pupils change size?

START-UP Activity

LIGHTS ON!

MATERIALS
FOR EACH GROUP: • flashlight

Safety Caution

Students must not use the sun as a source of light.

Answers to START-UP Activity

3. The pupils were enlarged.
4. The pupils became smaller.
6. The pupils enlarged when there was little light and became smaller when there was a lot of light.
7. The larger the pupils were, the brighter things appeared. In a dark environment, pupils become larger, so more light can enter the eye. The surroundings appear brighter and can be more easily seen. In a bright environment, the pupils become smaller and less light enters the eye. Students may infer that pupils change size in response to the amount of light available to the eye. This response helps us see clearly when light conditions change.

SECTION 1

Focus

Characteristics of Living Things

This section explains the characteristics that describe living things. Students will learn that living things have cells; that they sense and respond to stimuli; that they reproduce, have DNA, and use energy; and that they grow and develop. Based on this information, students will be able to identify things as either living or nonliving.

🔔 Bellringer

Display this question on the board or an overhead projector:

What are four living and four nonliving things that you interact with or see everyday? (Sample answer: living: family members, pets, house plants and trees, birds, insects; nonliving: clothes, books, automobile, furniture, radio, sidewalk)
Sheltered English

1) Motivate

DISCUSSION

Stimuli Ask students what they do when they go outside and it is cold. (They put on a jacket or go back inside, where it is warmer.)

Explain that feeling cold is a stimulus and that their reaction to the cold is a response. Ask students how people use technology to improve their ability to respond to environmental stimuli. (Examples are furnaces and wood stoves to heat buildings, air conditioners to cool buildings, sunglasses to shield eyes from bright sunlight, greenhouses to extend plant growing seasons.)

Section 1

Terms to Learn
cell
stimulus
homeostasis
asexual reproduction
sexual reproduction
DNA
heredity
metabolism

What You'll Do
- List the characteristics of living things.
- Distinguish between asexual reproduction and sexual reproduction.
- Define and describe homeostasis.

Characteristics of Living Things

While out in your yard one day, you notice something strange in the grass. It's slimy, bright yellow, and about the size of a dime. You have no idea what it is. Is it a plant part that fell from a tree? Is it alive? How can you tell?

Even though an amazing variety of living things exist on Earth, they are all alike in several ways. What does a dog have in common with a tree? What does a fish have in common with a mushroom? And what do *you* have in common with a slimy blob (also known as a slime mold)? Read on to find out about the six characteristics that all organisms share.

Slime mold

1 Living Things Have Cells

Every living thing is composed of one or more cells. A **cell** is a membrane-covered structure that contains all of the materials necessary for life. The membrane that surrounds a cell separates the contents of the cell from the cell's environment.

Many organisms, such as those in **Figure 1**, are made up of only one cell. Other organisms, such as the monkeys and trees in **Figure 2**, are made up of trillions of cells. Most cells are too small to be seen with the naked eye.

In an organism with many cells, cells perform specialized functions. For example, your nerve cells are specialized to transport signals, and your muscle cells are specialized for movement.

Figure 1 Each of these organisms is made of only one cell.

Figure 2 Trillions of cells make up these organisms.

36

Directed Reading Worksheet 2 Section 1

 internetconnect
SCILINKS **NSTA**
TOPIC: Characteristics of Living Things
GO TO: www.scilinks.org
*sci*LINKS NUMBER: HSTL030

Science Bloopers

Leonardo da Vinci made many scientific discoveries and observations in the fifteenth and sixteenth centuries, but he mistakenly believed that the eye emitted a ray that struck and then rebounded from the observed object.

---

36 Chapter 2 • It's Alive!! Or, Is It?

2 Living Things Sense and Respond to Change

All organisms have the ability to sense change in their environment and to respond to that change. When your pupils are exposed to light, they respond by becoming smaller. A change in an organism's environment that affects the activity of the organism is called a **stimulus** (plural, *stimuli*).

Stimuli can be chemicals, gravity, darkness, light, sounds, tastes, or anything that causes organisms to respond in some way. A gentle touch causes a response in the plant shown in **Figure 3.**

> **Self-Check**
>
> Is your alarm clock a stimulus? Explain. *(See page 782 to check your answer.)*

Figure 3 The touch of an insect triggers the Venus' flytrap to quickly close its leaves.

Homeostasis Even though an organism's external environment may change, the organism must maintain a stable internal environment to survive. This is because the life processes of organisms involve many different kinds of chemical reactions that can occur only in delicately balanced environments. The maintenance of a stable internal environment is called **homeostasis** (HOH mee OH STAY sis).

Your body maintains a temperature of about 37°C. When you get hot, your body responds by sweating. When you get cold, your muscles twitch in an attempt to generate heat. This causes you to shiver. Whether you are sweating or shivering, your body is trying to return things to normal. Another example of homeostasis is your body's ability to maintain a stable amount of sugar in your blood.

Fish that live in the ice-cold waters off Antarctica make a natural antifreeze that keeps them from freezing.

WEIRD SCIENCE

The first indication that the pancreas was the organ that secreted insulin, the compound that removes sugar from the blood, came when flies were noticed swarming over the urine of a dog whose pancreas was damaged. The flies were attracted to the excess sugar in the urine.

Critical Thinking Worksheet 2 "Intergalactic Planetary Mission"

2 Teach

GUIDED PRACTICE

Writing Have students list stimuli that they experience in their lives. Write them on the board. (Sample answers: heat, cold, a red traffic light)

Ask each student to write this list on a sheet of paper and then to write how a person would respond to each stimulus. **Sheltered English**

Answer to Self-Check

Your alarm clock is a stimulus. It rings, and you respond by shutting it off and getting out of bed.

MEETING INDIVIDUAL NEEDS

Learners Having Difficulty Have students use pictures from magazines to create a poster that shows three living and three nonliving things. Underneath each picture, have students write a brief paragraph explaining the characteristics that identify each thing as either living or nonliving. **Sheltered English**

MATH and MORE

Red blood cells are very small. Healthy humans have about 5 million red blood cells per microliter (µL) of blood. If there are 1,000 µL per mL, how many cells are there in a mL? (5 million × 1,000 = 5 billion, or 5,000,000,000)

Math Skills Worksheet 4 "A Shortcut for Multiplying Large Numbers"

Math Skills Worksheet 26 "Multiplying and Dividing in Scientific Notation"

Section 1 • Characteristics of Living Things

3 Extend

Roly-Poly Races

DEBATE

Nature Versus Nurture
Scientists have proven that we inherit our physical characteristics from our parents (nature). They continue to research whether we inherit our personalities from our parents. Some scientists say that where we live and how we are raised are more important (nurture). What do students think is the critical factor, nurture (care) or nature (heredity)? Why?

MATH and MORE

The red kangaroo can cover 12 m in a single jump. The African sharp-nosed frog can leap 5.35 m. What percentage of the kangaroo's jump is the frog's leap?

(5.35 ÷ 12 = 0.4458, or 0.45
0.45 × 100 = 45%)

The common flea can leap 19 cm. What percentage of the frog's leap is the flea's?

(5.35 × 100 = 535 cm
19 ÷ 535 = 0.0355, or 0.04
0.04 × 100 = 4%)

 Math Skills Worksheet 18 "Decimals and Fractions"

 Math Skills Worksheet 21 "Percentages, Fractions, and Decimals"

Figure 4 The hydra can reproduce asexually by forming buds that will break off and grow into new individuals.

3 Living Things Reproduce

Organisms make other organisms like themselves. This is accomplished in one of two ways: by asexual reproduction or by sexual reproduction. In **asexual reproduction,** a single parent produces offspring that are identical to the parent. **Figure 4** shows an organism that reproduces asexually. Most single-celled organisms reproduce in this way. **Sexual reproduction,** however, almost always requires two parents to produce offspring that will share characteristics of both parents. Most animals and plants reproduce in this way. The bear cubs in **Figure 5** were produced sexually by their parents.

Figure 5 Like most animals, bears produce offspring by sexual reproduction.

4 Living Things Have DNA

The cells of all living things contain a special molecule called **DNA** (**d**eoxyribo**n**ucleic **a**cid). DNA provides instructions for making molecules called *proteins*. Proteins take part in almost all of the activities of an organism's cells. Proteins also determine many of an organism's characteristics.

When organisms reproduce, they pass on copies of their DNA to their offspring. The transmission of characteristics from one generation to the next is called **heredity.** Offspring, such as the children in **Figure 6,** resemble their parents because of heredity.

Figure 6 Children resemble their parents because of heredity.

5 Living Things Use Energy

Organisms use energy to carry out the activities of life. These activities include such things as making food, breaking down food, moving materials into and out of cells, and building cells. An organism's **metabolism** (muh TAB uh LIZ uhm) is the total of all of the chemical activities that it performs.

MISCONCEPTION ALERT

Though very much alive, mules and most other hybrids cannot reproduce. Hybrids are the result of mating organisms from different species. A mule is the offspring of a mare (a female horse) and a jack (a male donkey). Mules often live long, healthy lives, but they never have babies.

IS THAT A FACT!

Lichens, which dominate the flora of Antarctica, have an extremely slow growth rate. Certain species grow only 1 mm every 100 years. Scientists estimate that some lichens may be more than 5,000 years old.

Are Computers Alive?
Computers can do all kinds of things, such as storing information and doing complex calculations. Some computers have even been programmed to learn, that is, to get better and faster at solving problems over time. Do you think computers could become so advanced that they should be considered alive? Why or why not?

6 Living Things Grow and Develop

All living things, whether they are made of one cell or many cells, grow during periods of their lives. Growth in single-celled organisms occurs as the cell gets larger. Organisms made of many cells grow mainly by increasing their number of cells.

In addition to getting larger, living things may develop and change as they grow. Just like the organisms in **Figure 7**, you will pass through different stages in your life as you develop into an adult.

Figure 7 Over time, acorns develop into oak seedlings, which become oak trees.

REVIEW

1. What characteristics of living things does a river have? Is a river alive?
2. What does the fur coat of a bear have to do with homeostasis?
3. How is reproduction related to heredity?
4. **Applying Concepts** What are some stimuli in your environment? How do you respond to these stimuli?

internet connect

SC_**LINKS**_
NSTA

TOPIC: Characteristics of Living Things
GO TO: www.scilinks.org
sciLINKS NUMBER: HSTL030

4 Close

Answer to APPLY
Answers will vary. Students should include the six characteristics of living things in their answer and explain why a computer could or could not do those things and be considered alive.

Quiz

1. An apple tree is a living thing. Can it make oranges? Why or why not? (No; living things reproduce only themselves, not different living things.)
2. What is the difference between growth and development? (Growth is an increase in size. Development is the change of form of an organism.)
3. Name three activities of an organism that require energy. (Organisms need energy to make food, to break down food, to move materials into and out of cells, and to build cell parts.)

ALTERNATIVE ASSESSMENT

Writing Have students read a story of their choice and find five examples of stimuli and responses. Then have students write an explanation of why it is important to be able to respond to all of these stimuli.

Answers to Review

1. A river has energy (it moves) and can grow larger (after rain, or when snow melts). But it is not alive because it is not made of cells, cannot respond to stimuli, has no DNA, and cannot reproduce.
2. Homeostasis is the maintenance of a stable internal environment. The fur coat of a bear helps it keep a stable body temperature.
3. Heredity is the passing of characteristics from parents to offspring. When organisms reproduce, offspring inherit copies of their parents' DNA.
4. Answers will vary. Examples can include such things as the way something tasted, smelled, felt, sounded, or looked. Responses to the stimuli should describe the action or effect the stimuli produced in the student.

SECTION 2

Focus

The Simple Bare Necessities of Life

This section identifies the things that an organism needs to live. Students will learn the roles that food, water, and air play in an organism's survival. They will also learn that where an organism lives is related to its ability to obtain the necessities of life.

Bellringer

Pose the following question to students:

What do you think your mass would be if there were no water in your body? Write your answer in your ScienceLog. **(The human body is approximately 70 percent water. If a student has a mass of 40 kg, the water's mass is 40 kg × 0.70 = 28 kg. The student's mass without water would be 40 kg − 28 kg = 12 kg.)**

1 Motivate

DISCUSSION

Adaptation Show students pictures of a desert, the canopy of a rain forest, the Arctic, and seaside cliffs. Ask students to describe animals that could live in these places and to explain how each is adapted to obtain its necessities.

 Directed Reading Worksheet 2 Section 2

Section 2

Terms to Learn

producer
consumer
decomposer

What You'll Do

- Explain why organisms need food, water, air, and living space.
- Discuss how living things obtain what they need to live.

The Simple Bare Necessities of Life

Would it surprise you to learn that you have the same basic needs as a tree, a frog, or a fly? In fact, almost every organism has the same basic needs: food, water, air, and living space.

Food

All living things need food. Food provides organisms with the energy and raw materials needed to carry on life processes and to build and repair cells and body parts. But not all organisms get food in the same way. In fact, organisms can be grouped into three different categories based on how they get their food.

Making Food Some organisms, such as plants, are called **producers** because they can produce their own food. Like most producers, plants use energy from the sun to make food from water and carbon dioxide. Some producers, like the microorganisms in Movile Cave, obtain energy and food from the chemicals in their environment.

Getting Food Other organisms are called **consumers** because they must eat (consume) other organisms to get food. The salamander in **Figure 8** is an example of a consumer. It gets the energy it needs by eating insects and other organisms.

Some consumers are decomposers. **Decomposers** are organisms that get their food by breaking down the nutrients in dead organisms or animal wastes.

Figure 8 *The salamander is a consumer. The fungus is a decomposer, and the plants are producers.*

Water

You may have heard that your body is made mostly of water. In fact, your cells and the cells of almost all living organisms are approximately 70 percent water—even the cells of a cactus and a camel. Most of the chemical reactions involved in metabolism require water.

Organisms differ greatly in terms of how much water they need and how they obtain it. You could survive for only about 3 days without water. You obtain water from the fluids you drink and the food you eat. The desert-dwelling kangaroo rat never drinks. It gets all of its water from its food.

40

CONNECT TO EARTH SCIENCE

Use Teaching Transparency 178 to encourage student discussion of how animals thrive in so many different climates and biomes.

 Teaching Transparency 178 "Climate Zones of the Earth"

internetconnect

TOPIC: The Necessities of Life
GO TO: www.scilinks.org
sciLINKS NUMBER: HSTL035

Air

Air is a mixture of several different gases, including oxygen and carbon dioxide. Animals, plants, and most other living things use oxygen in the chemical process that releases energy from food. Organisms that live on land get oxygen from the air. Organisms living in fresh water and salt water either take in dissolved oxygen from the water or come to the water's surface to get oxygen from the air. Some organisms, such as the European diving spider in **Figure 9,** go to great lengths to get oxygen.

Green plants, algae, and some bacteria need carbon dioxide gas in addition to oxygen. The food these organisms produce is made from carbon dioxide and water by *photosynthesis* (FOHT oh SIN thuh sis), the process that converts the energy in sunlight to energy stored in food.

Figure 9 This spider surrounds itself with an air bubble so that it can obtain oxygen underwater.

A Place to Live

All organisms must have somewhere to live that contains all of the things they need to survive. Some organisms, such as elephants, require a large amount of space. Other organisms, such as bacteria, may live their entire life in a single pore on the tip of your nose.

Because the amount of space on Earth is limited, organisms often compete with each other for food, water, and other necessities. Many animals, including the warbler in **Figure 10,** will claim a particular space and try to keep other animals away. Plants also compete with each other for living space and for access to water and sunlight.

Figure 10 A warbler's song is more than just a pretty tune. The warbler is protecting its home by telling other warblers to stay out of its territory.

REVIEW

1. Why are decomposers categorized as consumers? How do they differ from producers?
2. Why are most cells 70 percent water?
3. **Making Inferences** Could life as we know it exist on Earth if air contained only oxygen? Explain.
4. **Identifying Relationships** How might a cave, an ant, and a lake meet the needs of an organism?

TOPIC: The Necessities of Life
GO TO: www.scilinks.org
*sci*LINKS NUMBER: HSTL035

SECTION 3

Focus

The Chemistry of Life
In this section, students will learn about life on a cellular level. They will learn about proteins, carbohydrates, lipids, phospholipids, nucleic acids, and ATP and why they are essential to sustain life. Students will learn how these substances are alike and how they are different in both form and function.

Bellringer
Have students unscramble the following words and then use all four of them in a single sentence.

cdporesru (producers)
gnreey (energy)
dofo (food)
rwtea (water)

(Sample sentence: Producers use energy from the sun to make food from carbon dioxide and water.)

1 Motivate

DEMONSTRATION

Protein Model On each of 10–15 small self-adhesive notes, write a single letter of the alphabet. The letters should spell a few simple words when placed side by side. Place the note papers on two or three of the colored papers. Tell students that the binder contents represent proteins. The letters are the "amino acids." Each word is a "protein." Dismantle the "proteins," and use some of the "amino acids" to assemble a new "protein." <mark>Sheltered English</mark>

Section 3

Terms to Learn
protein   phospholipid
carbohydrate   nucleic acid
lipid   ATP

What You'll Do
◆ Compare and contrast the chemical building blocks of cells.
◆ Explain the importance of ATP.

The Chemistry of Life

All living things are made of cells, but what are cells made of? Everything, whether it is living or not, is made up of tiny building blocks called *atoms*. There are about 100 different kinds of atoms.

A substance made up of one type of atom is called an *element*. When two or more atoms join together, they form what's called a *molecule*. Molecules found in living things are usually made of different combinations of six elements: carbon, hydrogen, nitrogen, oxygen, phosphorous, and sulfur. These elements combine to form proteins, carbohydrates, lipids, nucleic acids, and ATP.

Proteins

Almost all of the life processes of a cell involve proteins. After water, proteins are the most abundant materials in cells. **Proteins** are large molecules that are made up of subunits called *amino acids*.

Organisms break down the proteins in food to supply their cells with amino acids. These amino acids are then linked together to form new proteins. Some proteins are made up of only a few amino acids, while others contain more than 10,000 amino acids.

Proteins in Action Proteins have many different functions. Some proteins form structures that are easy to see, such as those in **Figure 11.** Other proteins are at work at the cellular level. The protein *hemoglobin* (HEE moh GLOH bin) in red blood cells attaches to oxygen so that oxygen can be delivered throughout the body. Some proteins help protect cells from foreign materials. And special proteins called *enzymes* make many different chemical reactions in a cell occur quickly.

Figure 11 *Feathers, spider webs, and hair are all made of proteins.*

Multicultural CONNECTION
Hunters and gatherers of all races historically required very large areas of land to sustain them. Most cultures later developed farming and herding techniques that made possible higher population densities. Staple crops vary around the world, but the millet and sorghum grains of Africans, the wheat and barley of Europeans, the corn and squash of Native Americans, and the rice and soybeans of Asians, in correct amounts and supplemented with other foods, all are equally nutritious.

42 Chapter 2 • It's Alive!! Or, Is It?

Carbohydrates

Carbohydrates are a group of compounds made of sugars. Cells use carbohydrates as a source of energy and for energy storage. When an organism needs energy, its cells break down carbohydrates to release the energy stored in the carbohydrates.

There are two types of carbohydrates, simple carbohydrates and complex carbohydrates. Simple carbohydrates are made of one sugar molecule or a few sugar molecules linked together. Table sugar and the sugar in fruits are examples of simple carbohydrates.

Too Much Sugar! When an organism has more sugar than it needs, its extra sugar may be stored in the form of complex carbohydrates. Complex carbohydrates are made of hundreds of sugar molecules linked together. Your body makes some complex carbohydrates and stores them in your liver. Plants make a complex carbohydrate called *starch*. A potato plant, such as the one in **Figure 12,** stores its extra sugar as starch. When you eat mashed potatoes or French fries, you are eating a potato plant's stored starch. Your body can then break down this complex carbohydrate to release the energy stored in it.

MATH BREAK

How Much Oxygen?
Each red blood cell carries about 250 million molecules of hemoglobin. How many molecules of oxygen could a single red blood cell deliver throughout the body if every hemoglobin molecule attached to four oxygen molecules?

Figure 12 Most sugars are simple carbohydrates. The extra sugar in a potato plant is stored in the potato as starch, a complex carbohydrate.

QuickLab

Starch Search

When **iodine** comes into contact with starch, the iodine turns black. Use this handy trait to find out which **food samples** supplied by your teacher contain starch.

Caution: Iodine can stain clothing. Wear goggles, protective gloves, and an apron.

WEIRD SCIENCE

Fireflies produce their flashing light by a chemical reaction. The enzyme luciferase acts on the chemical luciferin in the presence of ATP to create the light. Scientists now use luciferase in the laboratory to study everything from heart disease to muscular dystrophy.

internet connect

SC_{LINKS} NSTA
TOPIC: The Chemistry of Life
GO TO: www.scilinks.org
*sci*LINKS NUMBER: HSTL040

Section 3 • The Chemistry of Life

3) Extend

 PG 692
The Best-Bread Bakery Dilemma

MEETING INDIVIDUAL NEEDS

Writing | Advanced Learners When the human body is unable to make a necessary protein, the result is often a disease. Hemophilia and diabetes are two conditions caused by missing or defective proteins. Have students prepare a report on the cause of and the treatment for one of these conditions. Their information should include the specific protein that is lacking, a brief description of how the condition affects the body, and the role of DNA in the disease.

Homework

Concept Mapping Have students collect the nutrition labels from five food items in their home and examine the number of grams of carbohydrates, fats, and proteins in each item. Tell students to construct a concept map that best relates the food items with the headings "Carbohydrates," "Lipids," and "Proteins," based on the nutrient content. If an item belongs in two categories, the map should reflect that information.

 Teaching Transparency 5 "Phospholipid Molecule and Cell Membrane"

Yeast cells get energy the same way other cells do. See for yourself on page 692 of the LabBook.

Lipids

Lipids are compounds that cannot mix with water. Lipids have many important functions in the cell. Like carbohydrates, some lipids store energy. Other lipids form the membranes of cells.

Fats and Oils Fats and oils are lipids that store energy. When an organism has used up most of its carbohydrates, it can obtain energy from these lipids. The structures of fats and oils are almost identical, but at room temperature most fats are solid and oils are liquid. Most of the lipids stored in plants are oils, while most of the lipids stored in animals are fats.

Phospholipids All cells are surrounded by a structure called a *cell membrane*. **Phospholipids** are the molecules that form much of the cell membrane. As you read earlier, water is the most abundant material in a cell. When phospholipids are in water, the tails come together and the heads face out into the water. This happens because the head of a phospholipid molecule is attracted to water, while the tail is not. **Figure 13** shows how phospholipid molecules form two layers when they are in water.

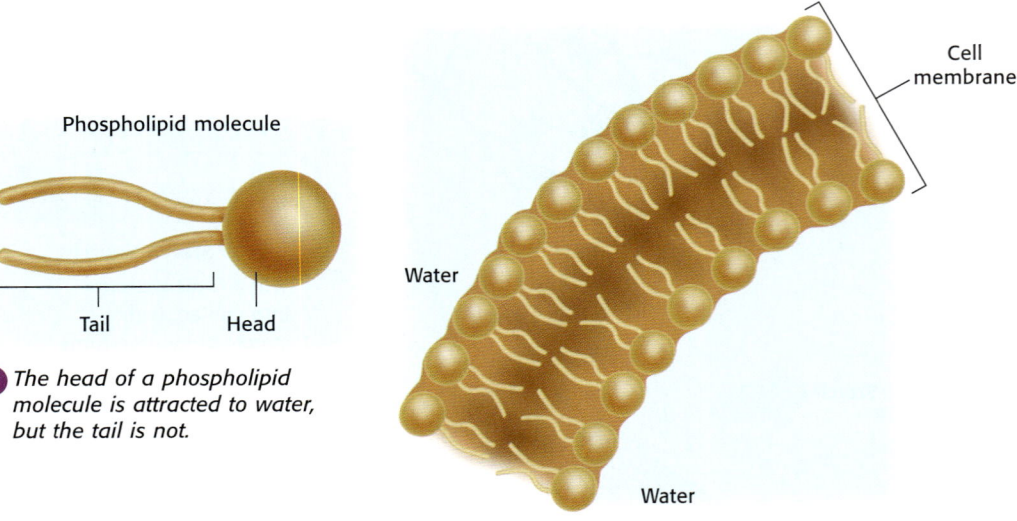

Figure 13 The contents of a cell are surrounded by a membrane of phospholipid molecules.

a The head of a phospholipid molecule is attracted to water, but the tail is not.

b When phospholipid molecules come together in water, they form two layers.

IS THAT A FACT!

Fats and lipids are also vital to nerve tissue formation and function. Fat acts as an insulator on the nerve, speeding up the electrical impulse that the nerve is carrying.

Nucleic Acids

Nucleic acids are compounds made up of subunits called *nucleotides*. A nucleic acid may contain thousands of nucleotides. Nucleic acids are sometimes called the blueprints of life because they contain all the information needed for the cell to make all of its proteins.

DNA is a nucleic acid. A DNA molecule is like a recipe book titled *How to Make Proteins*. When a cell needs to make a certain protein, it gets information from DNA to direct how amino acids are hooked together to make that protein. You will learn more about DNA later.

The Cell's Fuel

Another molecule that is important to cells is ATP (**a**denosine **tri**phosphate). **ATP** is the major fuel used for all cell activities that require energy.

When food molecules, such as carbohydrates and fats, are broken down, some of the released energy is transferred to ATP molecules, as shown in **Figure 14.** The energy in carbohydrates and lipids must be transferred to ATP before the stored energy can be used by cells to fuel their life processes.

REVIEW

1. What are the subunits of proteins? of starch? of DNA?
2. What do carbohydrates, fats, and oils have in common?
3. Are all proteins enzymes? Explain your answer.
4. **Making Predictions** What would happen to the supply of ATP in your cells if you did not eat enough carbohydrates? How would this affect your cells?

Figure 14 The energy in the carbohydrates and lipids in food must be transferred to ATP molecules before cells can use the energy.

4) Close

Quiz

1. Explain the difference between simple and complex carbohydrates. (Simple carbohydrates are made of one or two sugar molecules. Complex carbohydrates are made of many sugar molecules that are linked together.)
2. Name two functions of lipids. (Some lipids store energy, and others form the cell membrane.)
3. How are proteins used by an organism? (An organism breaks down proteins and uses their amino acids to build other proteins that are used to carry out chemical reactions in cells, transport materials, and protect the cell.)

ALTERNATIVE ASSESSMENT

Writing Have students write a job description for the cell's basic chemical building blocks. Tell students to write a classified ad that describes the required job responsibilities and physical qualifications. Have them include a description of the expected workload by explaining whether the building block will have to work constantly or sporadically. Finally, they should indicate whether the building block will work independently or with other cell components.

Answers to Review

1. The subunits of proteins are amino acids. Sugar molecules are the subunits of starch, and nucleotides are the subunits of DNA.
2. All three compounds store energy.
3. Not all proteins are enzymes. Enzymes are a special type of protein that speeds up certain chemical reactions in the cell.
4. The supply of ATP would decrease. A decrease in ATP would cause a cell to have less energy than it needs to carry out its activities. Your body would have to get ATP from other sources, like lipids.

Teaching Transparency 6
"Energy for Cells"

Reinforcement Worksheet 2
"Building Blocks"

Chapter Highlights

Vocabulary Definitions

Section 1

cell a membrane-covered structure that contains all of the materials necessary for life

stimulus anything that affects the activity of an organism, organ, or tissue

homeostasis the maintenance of a stable internal environment

asexual reproduction reproduction in which a single parent produces offspring that are genetically identical to the parent

sexual reproduction reproduction in which two parents are required to produce offspring that will share characteristics of both parents

DNA deoxyribonucleic acid; hereditary material that controls all the activities of a cell, contains the information to make new cells, and provides instructions for making proteins

heredity the passing of traits from parent to offspring

metabolism the combined chemical processes that occur in a cell or living organism

Section 2

producer an organism that uses sunlight directly to make sugar

consumer an organism that eats producers or other organisms for energy

decomposer an organism that gets energy by breaking down the remains of dead organisms and consuming or absorbing the nutrients

Chapter Highlights

SECTION 1

Vocabulary
cell (p. 36)
stimulus (p. 37)
homeostasis (p. 37)
asexual reproduction (p. 38)
sexual reproduction (p. 38)
DNA (p. 38)
heredity (p. 38)
metabolism (p. 38)

Section Notes
- All living things share the six characteristics of life.
- Organisms are made of one or more cells.
- Organisms detect and respond to stimuli in their environment.
- Organisms work to keep their internal environment stable so that the chemical activities of their cells are not disrupted. The maintenance of a stable internal environment is called homeostasis.
- Organisms reproduce and make more organisms like themselves. Offspring can be produced asexually or sexually.
- Offspring resemble their parents. The passing of characteristics from parent to offspring is called heredity.
- Organisms grow and may change during their lifetime.
- Organisms use energy to carry out the chemical activities of life. Metabolism is the sum of an organism's chemical activities.

Labs
Roly-Poly Races (p. 690)

SECTION 2

Vocabulary
producer (p. 40)
consumer (p. 40)
decomposer (p. 40)

Section Notes
- Organisms must have food. Producers make their own food. Consumers eat other organisms for food. Decomposers break down the nutrients in dead organisms and animal wastes.

✓ Skills Check

Math Concepts

HOW MANY? In the MathBreak on page 43, you determined how many molecules of oxygen a single red blood cell could carry.

$$\frac{250{,}000{,}000 \text{ molecules of hemoglobin}}{1 \text{ red blood cell}} \times \frac{4 \text{ molecules of oxygen}}{1 \text{ molecule of hemoglobin}}$$

$= 1{,}000{,}000{,}000$ molecules of oxygen

Visual Understanding

PHOSPHOLIPIDS Look at the illustrations of phospholipids and the cell membrane on page 44. Notice that the fluid inside and outside of the cell contains a lot of water. The head of the phospholipid molecule is attracted to water. Therefore, the phospholipid molecules that form the cell membrane line up with their tails facing away from the water.

Lab and Activity Highlights

Roly-Poly Races PG 690

The Best-Bread Bakery Dilemma PG 692

Datasheets for LabBook
(blackline masters for these labs)

SECTION 2

- Organisms depend on water. Water is necessary for maintaining metabolism.
- Organisms need oxygen to release the energy contained in their food. Plants, algae, and some bacteria also need carbon dioxide.
- Organisms must have a place to live where they can obtain the things they need.

SECTION 3

Vocabulary
protein (p. 42)
carbohydrate (p. 43)
lipid (p. 44)
phospholipid (p. 44)
nucleic acid (p. 45)
ATP (p. 45)

Section Notes
- Proteins, carbohydrates, lipids, nucleic acids, and ATP are important to life.
- Cells use carbohydrates for energy storage. Carbohydrates are made of sugars.
- Fats and oils store energy. Phospholipids make cell membranes.
- Proteins are made up of amino acids and have many important functions. Enzymes are proteins that help chemical reactions occur quickly.
- Nucleic acids are made up of nucleotides. DNA is a nucleic acid that contains the information for making proteins.
- Cells use molecules of ATP to fuel their activities.

Labs
The Best-Bread Bakery Dilemma (p. 692)

VOCABULARY DEFINITIONS, continued

SECTION 3

protein a biochemical that is composed of amino acids; its functions include regulating chemical reactions, transporting and storing materials, and providing support

carbohydrate a biochemical composed of one or more simple sugars bonded together that is used as a source of energy and to store energy

lipid a type of biochemical that does not dissolve in water, including fats and oils; lipids store energy and make up cell membranes

phospholipid a molecule that forms much of a cell membrane

nucleic acid a biochemical that stores information needed to build proteins and other nucleic acids; made up of subunits called nucleotides

ATP adenosine triphosphate; molecule that provides energy for a cell's activities

 Vocabulary Review Worksheet 2

 Blackline masters of these Chapter Highlights can be found in the **Study Guide**.

---

internet connect

 GO TO: go.hrw.com

Visit the **HRW** Web site for a variety of learning tools related to this chapter. Just type in the keyword:

KEYWORD: HSTALV

 GO TO: www.scilinks.org

Visit the **National Science Teachers Association** on-line Web site for Internet resources related to this chapter. Just type in the *sci*LINKS number for more information about the topic:

TOPIC: Characteristics of Living Things — *sci*LINKS NUMBER: HSTL030
TOPIC: The Necessities of Life — *sci*LINKS NUMBER: HSTL035
TOPIC: The Chemistry of Life — *sci*LINKS NUMBER: HSTL040
TOPIC: Is There Life on Other Planets? — *sci*LINKS NUMBER: HSTL045

Lab and Activity Highlights

LabBank

Labs You Can Eat, Say Cheese! Lab 1

Long-Term Projects & Research Ideas,
I Think, Therefore I Live, Project 2

Chapter Review

USING VOCABULARY

To complete the following sentences, choose the correct term from each pair of terms listed below:

1. The process of maintaining a stable internal environment is known as __?__. (*metabolism* or *homeostasis*)

2. The resemblance of offspring to their parents is a result of __?__. (*heredity* or *stimuli*)

3. A __?__ obtains food by eating other organisms. (*producer* or *consumer*)

4. Starch is a __?__ and is made up of __?__. (*carbohydrate/sugars* or *nucleic acid/nucleotides*)

5. Fats and oils are __?__ that store energy for an organism. (*proteins* or *lipids*)

UNDERSTANDING CONCEPTS

Multiple Choice

6. Cells are
   a. the structures that contain all of the materials necessary for life.
   b. found in all organisms.
   c. sometimes specialized for particular functions.
   d. All of the above

7. Which of the following is a true statement about all living things?
   a. They cannot sense changes in their external environment.
   b. They have one or more cells.
   c. They do not need to use energy.
   d. They reproduce asexually.

8. Organisms must have food because
   a. food is a source of energy.
   b. food supplies cells with oxygen.
   c. organisms never make their own food.
   d. All of the above

9. A change in an organism's environment that affects the organism's activities is a
   a. response.   c. metabolism.
   b. stimulus.   d. producer.

10. Organisms store energy in
    a. nucleic acids.   c. lipids.
    b. phospholipids.   d. water.

11. The molecule that contains the information on how to make proteins is
    a. ATP.
    b. a carbohydrate.
    c. DNA.
    d. a phospholipid.

12. The subunits of nucleic acids are
    a. nucleotides.   c. sugars.
    b. oils.   d. amino acids.

Short Answer

13. What is the difference between asexual reproduction and sexual reproduction?

14. In one or two sentences, explain why living things must have air.

15. What is ATP, and why is it important to a cell?

48 Chapter 2 • It's Alive!! Or, Is It?

Concept Mapping

16. Use the following terms to create a concept map: cell, carbohydrates, protein, enzymes, DNA, sugars, lipids, nucleotides, amino acids, nucleic acid.

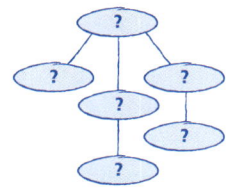

CRITICAL THINKING AND PROBLEM SOLVING

Write one or two sentences to answer the following questions:

17. A flame can move, grow larger, and give off heat. Is a flame alive? Explain.

18. Based on what you know about carbohydrates, lipids, and proteins, why is it important for you to eat a balanced diet?

19. Your friend tells you that the stimulus of music makes his goldfish swim faster. How would you design a controlled experiment to test your friend's claim?

MATH IN SCIENCE

20. An elephant has a mass of 3,900 kg. If 70 percent of the elephant's mass comes from water, how many kilograms of water does the elephant contain?

INTERPRETING GRAPHICS

Take a look at the pictures below, which show the same plant over a time span of 3 days.

Day 1

Day 2

Day 3

21. What is the plant doing?

22. What characteristic(s) of living things is the plant exhibiting?

Reading Check-up Take a minute to review your answers to the Pre-Reading Questions found at the bottom of page 34. Have your answers changed? If necessary, revise your answers based on what you have learned since you began this chapter.

CRITICAL THINKING AND PROBLEM SOLVING

17. The flame is not alive. Although a flame can move, grow, and give off heat, it does not have all of the characteristics of an organism. For example, a flame is not made up of cells and does not contain DNA.

18. You get the raw materials to make the carbohydrates, lipids, and proteins that your body needs from the foods you eat. Carbohydrates and lipids provide energy for cells, and proteins provide amino acids to make the proteins your cells need. You need all three for the body to function efficiently.

19. A controlled experiment to test your friend's claim would consist of goldfish in a control group and goldfish in an experimental group. The control group would not be exposed to music, but the goldfish in the experimental group would be exposed to music. The goldfish in both groups would need to be of the same age and kind. They would have to be fed the same type and amount of food. The environments of the fish would have to be identical in such things as temperature and water quality.

MATH IN SCIENCE

20. The elephant contains 2,730 kg of water.

INTERPRETING GRAPHICS

21. The plant is bending toward the light coming through the window.

22. The plant is sensing a stimulus (the light) and responding to it.

Chapter 2 • Chapter Review

SCIENTIFIC DEBATE
Life on Mars?

Background

Scientists have always been intrigued by the possibility of life on other planets. Only recently have advanced biological and chemical techniques been sufficient to begin to investigate such claims. Science is not always black and white, and scientists often have heated debates over scientific evidence. Students should appreciate that scientists often have very different ways of interpreting the same evidence and that science does not always provide a clear-cut answer.

The scientists who question the studies of the ALH84001 meteorite argue that each component of the evidence can be accounted for by an inorganic explanation. Supporters argue that if all of the evidence is considered collectively, they point toward an organic explanation. One point of debate is whether Mars was cool enough to support life. Many scientists believe that Mars was much cooler at the time the meteorite left Mars. Although the Martian crust appears very dry, research has indicated that water, a necessity for life, was present in low concentrations. Scientists believe that the Martian atmosphere was much thicker at one time and that many of the atmospheric components necessary for life, including carbon dioxide and oxygen, were probably much more abundant then.

SCIENTIFIC DEBATE

Life on Mars?

In late 1996 the headlines read, "Evidence of Life on Mars." What kind of life? Aliens similar to those that we see in sci-fi movies? Some creature completely unlike any we've seen before? Not quite, but the story behind the headlines is no less fascinating!

An Unusual Spaceship

In 1996, a group of researchers led by NASA scientists studied a 3.8-billion-year-old meteorite named ALH84001. These scientists agree that ALH84001 is a potato-sized piece of the planet Mars. They also agree that it fell to Earth about 13,000 years ago. It was discovered in Antarctica in 1984. And according to the NASA team, ALH84001 brought with it evidence that life once existed on Mars.

Life-Form Leftovers

On the surface of ALH84001, scientists found certain kinds of *organic molecules* (molecules containing carbon). These molecules are similar to those left behind when living things break down substances for food. And when these scientists examined the interior of the meteorite, they found the same organic

▲ *This scanning electron micrograph image of a tube-like structure found within meteorite ALH84001 is thought to be evidence of life on Mars.*

molecules throughout. Because these molecules were spread throughout the meteorite, scientists concluded the molecules were not contamination from Earth. The NASA team believes these organic leftovers are strong evidence that tiny organisms similar to bacteria lived, ate, and died on Mars millions of years ago.

Dirty Water or Star Dust

Many scientists disagree that ALH84001 contains evidence of Martian life. Some of them argue that the organic compounds are contaminants from Antarctic meltwater that seeped into the meteorite.

Others argue that the molecules were created by processes involving very high temperatures. These scientists think the compounds were formed during star formation and ended up on Mars when it became a planet. Other supporters of this theory believe that the compounds were created during the formation of rocks on Mars. In either case, they argue that no life-forms could exist at such high temperatures and that these compounds could not be the result of living things.

The Debate Continues

Scientists continue to debate the evidence of ALH84001. They are looking for evidence specific to biological life, such as proteins, nucleic acids, and cellular walls. Other scientists are looking to Mars itself for more evidence. Some hope to find underground water that might have supported life. Others hope to gather soil and rock samples that might hold evidence that Mars was once a living planet. Until scientists have more evidence, the debate will continue.

Think About It

▶ If you went to Mars, what kinds of evidence would you look for to prove that life once existed there? How could the discovery of nucleic or amino acids prove life existed on Mars?

Answer to Think About It
Answers will vary. The discovery of nucleic acids, amino acids, and cell walls would be strong evidence of life on Mars because they are components of living organisms.

internet connect

TOPIC: Is There Life on Other Planets?
GO TO: www.scilinks.org
sciLINKS NUMBER: HSTL045

Science Fiction

"They're Made Out of Meat"
by Terry Bisson

Two space travelers millions of light-years from home are visiting an uncharted sector of the universe to find signs of life. Their mission is to contact, welcome, and log any and all beings in this quadrant of the universe. Once they discover a living being, they must find a way to communicate with it.

During their mission they encounter a life-form quite unlike anything they have ever seen before. These unusual beings can think and communicate. They have even built a few simple machines, so they aren't exactly pond scum.

Nevertheless, the explorers have very strong doubts about adding this new species to the list of known life-forms in the universe. The creatures are just too strange and, well, disgusting. They just don't fit on the list. Besides, with their limited abilities, it is unlikely they will make contact with any of the other life-forms that dwell elsewhere in the universe.

Perhaps it might be better if the explorers agreed to pretend that they never encountered these beings at all. But the travelers' official duty is to contact and welcome all life-forms, no matter how ugly they are or what they are made of. Can they bring themselves to perform their official duty? Will anyone believe their story if they do?

You'll find out by reading Terry Bisson's short story "They're Made Out of Meat." This story is in the *Holt Anthology of Science Fiction*.

SCIENCE FICTION
"They're Made Out of Meat"
by Terry Bisson

A remarkable and intelligent life-form has been discovered at the far reaches of the universe, but it's tough to get excited about this find . . .

Teaching Strategy

Reading Level This is a relatively short story that should not be difficult for the average student to read and comprehend.

Background

About the Author Terry Bisson has written everything from comic books to short stories, novels, plays, how-to articles about writing, and news editorials. He has taken the scripts of several popular movies and converted them to novels. Some of Bisson's works have appeared in digital-audio format on the World Wide Web. "They're Made Out of Meat" is just one of several stories featured in the SciFi Channel's *Seeing Ear Theater*. In 1991, Bisson's short story "Bears Discover Fire" received the highest honors possible for science fiction writers—both the Nebula Award and the Hugo Award.

In addition to being a writer, Bisson has been an automobile mechanic, an editor, a publisher's consultant, and a teacher. Bisson teaches writing at Clarion University, in Pennsylvania, and at the New School for Social Research, in New York City. He also maintains a personal Web site full of interesting information, works by guest writers, and excerpts from his novels and stories.

Further Reading If students like Terry Bisson's style, suggest more of his stories to students. Some of his works include the following:

Bears Discover Fire and Other Stories, Tor Books, New York City, 1993

"10:07:24," *Absolute Magazine,* 1995

"First Fire," *Science Fiction Age,* Sept 1998

"The Player," *Fantasy and Science Fiction Magazine,* Oct/Nov 1997

UNIT 2

TIMELINE
Cells

Cells are everywhere. Even though most can't be seen with the naked eye, they make up every living thing. Your body alone contains trillions of cells.

In this unit, you will learn about cells. You will learn the difference between animal cells, plant cells, and bacterial cells. You'll learn about the different parts of a cell and see how they work together.

Cells were discovered in 1665, and since then we have learned a lot about cells and the way they work. This timeline shows some of the discoveries that have been made along the way, but there is still a lot to learn about the fascinating world of cells!

1620
The Pilgrims settle Plymouth Colony.

1665
Robert Hooke discovers cells after observing a thin piece of cork under a microscope.

1873
Anton Schneider observes and accurately describes mitosis.

1937
The Golden Gate Bridge opens in San Francisco.

1941
George Beadle and Edward Tatum discover that genes control the chemical reactions in cells by directing protein production.

1952
Martha Chase and Alfred Hershey demonstrate that DNA, found in the nucleus of cells, is the hereditary material.

1831 Robert Brown discovers the nucleus in a plant cell.

1838 Matthias Schleiden discovers that all plant tissue is made up of cells.

1839 Theodor Schwann shows that all animal tissue is made up of cells.

1861 The American Civil War begins.

1858 Rudolf Virchow determines that all cells are produced from cells.

1971 Lynn Margulis proposes a theory about the origin of cell organelles.

1956 The manufacture of protein in the cell is found to occur in ribosomes.

1997 A sheep named Dolly becomes the first animal to be cloned from a single cell.

Cells

Chapter Organizer

CHAPTER ORGANIZATION	TIME MINUTES	OBJECTIVES	LABS, INVESTIGATIONS, AND DEMONSTRATIONS
Chapter Opener pp. 54–55	45	National Standards: UCP 4, HNS 1, LS 1b, 5b	**Start-Up Activity** What Are Plants Made Of? p. 55
Section 1 Organization of Life	90	▶ Explain how life is organized, from a single cell to an ecosystem. ▶ Describe the difference between unicellular organisms and multicellular organisms. UCP 1, 2, 5, LS 1a–1e, 4a	
Section 2 The Discovery of Cells	90	▶ State the parts of the cell theory. ▶ Explain why cells are so small. ▶ Calculate a cell's surface-to-volume ratio. ▶ List the advantages of being multicellular. ▶ Explain the difference between prokaryotic cells and eukaryotic cells. UCP 3–5, SAI 1, 2, ST 2, SPSP 5, HNS 1–3, LS 1a–1d, 2c, 3b, 5a; LabBook UCP 2, 3, SAI 1	**Demonstration,** Membranes, p. 63 in ATE **ADVANCED** **QuickLab,** Do Bacteria Taste Good? p. 66 **GENERAL** **Making Models,** Elephant-Sized Amoebas? p. 694 **GENERAL** **Datasheets for LabBook,** Elephant-Sized Amoebas? Datasheet 6 **GENERAL**
Section 3 Eukaryotic Cells: The Inside Story	90	▶ Explain the function of each part of a eukaryotic cell. ▶ Describe the differences between animal cells and plant cells. UCP 2–5, ST 2, SPSP 4, 5, HNS 1, 3, LS 1a, 1c, 3a, 5a, 5b; LabBook UCP 1, SAI 1	**Demonstration,** Cell Walls, p. 69 in ATE **BASIC** **Discovery Lab,** Cells Alive! p. 696 **BASIC** **Datasheets for LabBook,** Cells Alive! Datasheet 7 **BASIC** **Skill Builder,** Name That Part! p. 697 **BASIC** **Datasheets for LabBook,** Name That Part! Datasheet 8 **BASIC** **Labs You Can Eat,** The Incredible Edible Cell, Lab 2 **ADVANCED** **Whiz-Bang Demonstrations,** Grand Strand, Demo 3 **ADVANCED** **Long-Term Projects & Research Ideas,** Project 3 **ADVANCED**

*See page **T20** for a complete correlation of this book with the*

NATIONAL SCIENCE EDUCATION STANDARDS.

TECHNOLOGY RESOURCES

 Guided Reading Audio CD English or Spanish, Chapter 3

 One-Stop Planner CD-ROM with Test Generator

 CNN. Science, Technology & Society, Flavor Cells, Segment 3
Treating Pets with Laser Light, Segment 4

Chapter 3 • Cells: The Basic Units of Life

CLASSROOM WORKSHEETS, TRANSPARENCIES, AND RESOURCES	SCIENCE INTEGRATION AND CONNECTIONS	REVIEW AND ASSESSMENT
Directed Reading Worksheet 3 `BASIC` **Science Puzzlers, Twisters & Teasers,** Worksheet 3 `ADVANCED`		
Directed Reading Worksheet 3, Section 1 `BASIC` **Transparency 7,** From Cell to Organism **Reinforcement Worksheet 3,** An Ecosystem `GENERAL`	**Chemistry Connection,** p. 58 **Real-World Connection,** p. 59 in ATE **Connect to Earth Science,** p. 59 in ATE	**Homework,** p. 57 in ATE `GENERAL` **Review,** p. 60 `GENERAL` **Quiz,** p. 60 in ATE `GENERAL` **Alternative Assessment,** p. 60 in ATE `GENERAL`
Directed Reading Worksheet 3, Section 2 `BASIC` **Transparency 8,** Surface-to-Volume Ratio **Math Skills for Science Worksheet 16,** What Is a Ratio? `GENERAL` **Math Skills for Science Worksheet 29,** Finding Perimeter and Area `GENERAL` **Math Skills for Science Worksheet 30,** Finding Volume `GENERAL`	**Connect to Astronomy,** p. 62 in ATE **Real-World Connection,** p. 62 in ATE **Math and More,** Surface Area, p. 64 in ATE `GENERAL` **MathBreak,** Surface-to-Volume Ratio, p. 65 **Apply,** p. 65 `GENERAL` **Connect to Earth Science,** p. 65 in ATE **Connect to Earth Science,** p. 66 in ATE **Health Watch:** The Scrape of the Future, p. 81 `GENERAL`	**Self-Check,** p. 63 **Self-Check,** p. 66 **Review,** p. 67 `GENERAL` **Quiz,** p. 67 in ATE `GENERAL` **Alternative Assessment,** p. 67 in ATE `GENERAL`
Directed Reading Worksheet 3, Section 3 `BASIC` **Transparency 260,** Structural Formulas **Critical Thinking Worksheet 3,** Cellular Construction `ADVANCED` **Transparency 9,** Organelles and Their Functions **Transparency 10,** Comparing Animal and Plant Cells **Reinforcement Worksheet 3,** Building a Eukaryotic Cell `BASIC`	**Connect to Physical Science,** p. 70 in ATE `BASIC` **Multicultural Connection,** p. 72 in ATE **Multicultural Connection,** p. 73 in ATE **Across the Sciences:** Battling Cancer with Pigs' Blood and Laser Light, p. 80 `ADVANCED`	**Homework,** p. 69 in ATE `GENERAL` **Self-Check,** p. 70 **Homework,** p. 71 in ATE `GENERAL` **Homework,** p. 74 in ATE `ADVANCED` **Review,** p. 75 `GENERAL` **Quiz,** p. 75 in ATE `GENERAL` **Alternative Assessment,** p. 75 in ATE `GENERAL`

END-OF-CHAPTER REVIEW AND ASSESSMENT

Chapter Review in Study Guide
Vocabulary and Notes in Study Guide
Chapter Tests with Performance-Based Assessment, Chapter 3 Test
Chapter Tests with Performance-Based Assessment, Performance-Based Assessment 3
Concept Mapping Transparency 3

Holt, Rinehart and Winston On-line Resources
go.hrw.com
For worksheets and other teaching aids related to this chapter, visit the HRW Web site and type in the keyword: **HSTCEL**

National Science Teachers Association
www.scilinks.org
Encourage students to use the *sci*LINKS numbers listed in the internet connect boxes to access information and resources on the **NSTA** Web Site.

Chapter 3 • Chapter Organizer   **53B**

Chapter Resources & Worksheets

Visual Resources

TEACHING TRANSPARENCIES

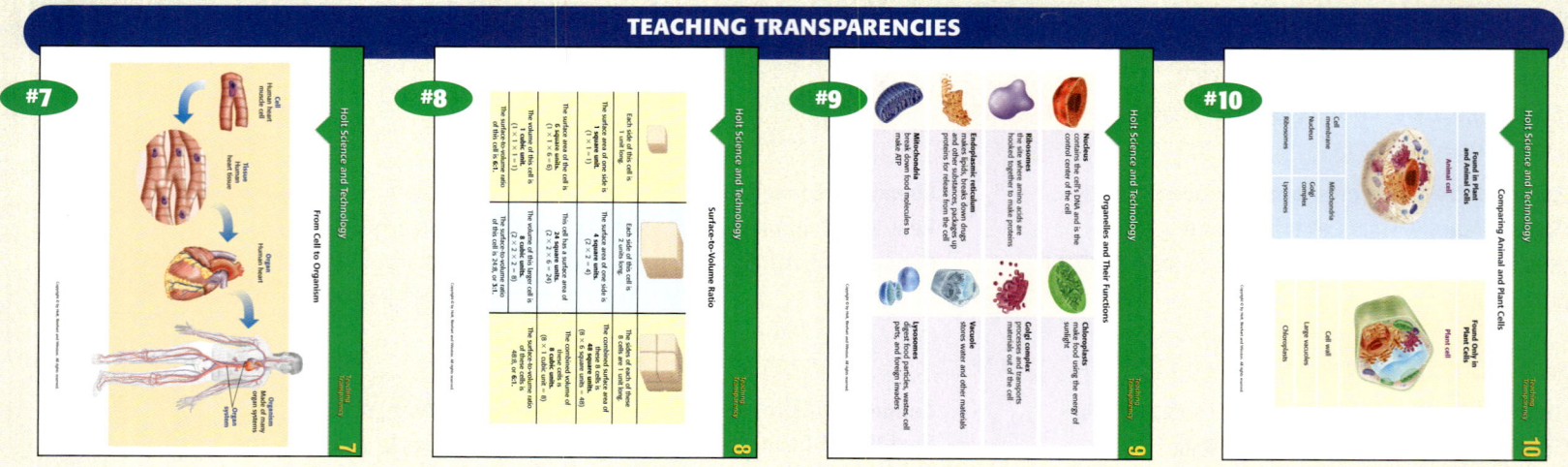

TEACHING TRANSPARENCIES

CONCEPT MAPPING TRANSPARENCY

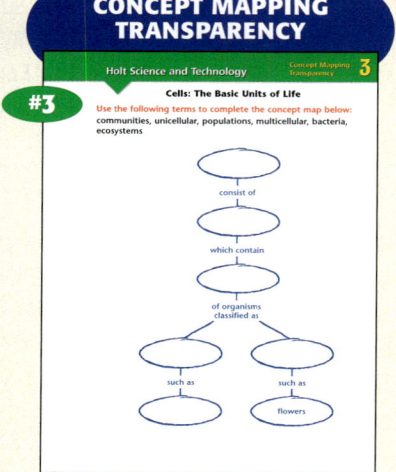

Meeting Individual Needs

DIRECTED READING

REINFORCEMENT & VOCABULARY REVIEW

SCIENCE PUZZLERS, TWISTERS & TEASERS

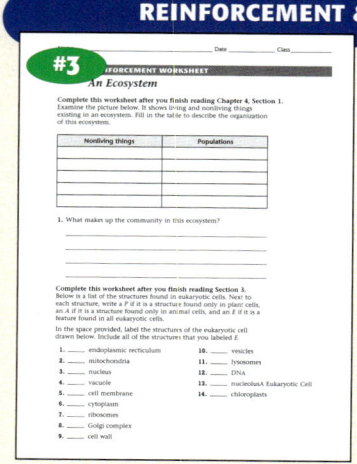

Chapter 3 • Cells: The Basic Units of Life

Chapter 3 • Cells: The Basic Units of Life

Review & Assessment

STUDY GUIDE

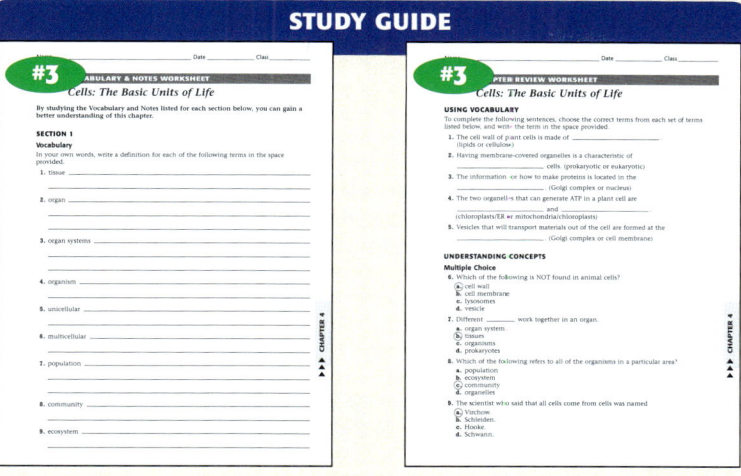

CHAPTER TESTS WITH PERFORMANCE-BASED ASSESSMENT

Lab Worksheets

LABS YOU CAN EAT

WHIZ-BANG DEMONSTRATIONS

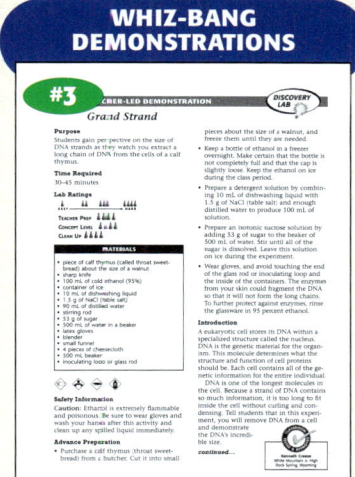

LONG-TERM PROJECTS & RESEARCH IDEAS

DATASHEETS FOR LABBOOK

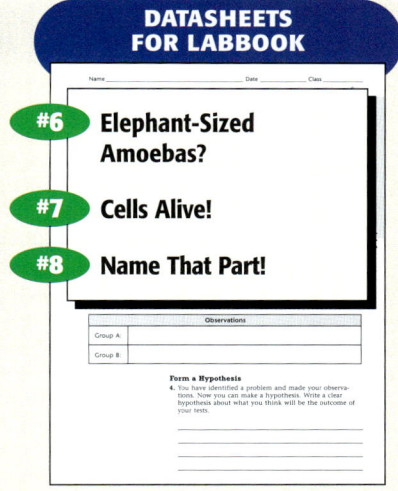

Applications & Extensions

CRITICAL THINKING & PROBLEM SOLVING

SCIENCE TECHNOLOGY

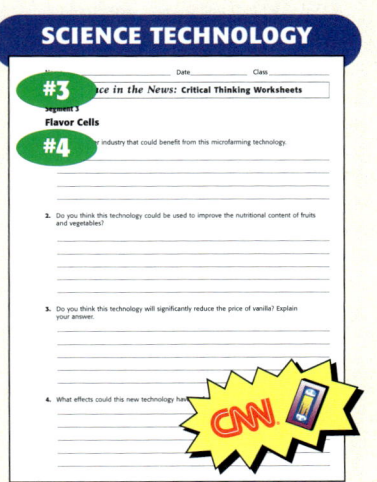

Chapter 3 • Chapter Resources & Worksheets   53D

Chapter Background

SECTION 1

Organization of Life

▶ **In a Heartbeat**
The heart will function properly only if the cells that form the connective tissue and muscle perform their jobs in coordination. Scientists can use an enzyme to dissolve an embryonic heart into its individual cells. When placed in a dish, these cells, called myocytes, will continue to beat, although out of sync with each other. After a couple of days, sheets of interconnected cells form and they beat in unison. Why? Openings develop between cells that touch, and their cytoplasms connect, allowing the cells to communicate directly with each other.

▶ **Organs: Delicate Workhorses**
The most frequently transplanted organ is the kidney, followed by the liver, heart, and lung. Most transplants must be done within a few hours after the organ is removed from a donor because organs are too delicate to survive current long-term storage procedures.

- Cryobiologists, scientists who study how life systems tolerate low temperatures, are studying the possibility of storing organs and organ systems at subfreezing temperatures. They are investigating the fluids that keep insects alive during subfreezing temperatures, hoping this knowledge can be applied to human organs.

IS THAT A FACT!

▶ In 1931, a doctor removed a patient's parathyroid glands in error. These glands control the amount of calcium in the blood, which in turn regulates the heart. As a last-ditch effort to save the patient, a cow's parathyroid glands were ground up and injected into the patient. The patient recuperated and lived another 30 years with similar treatments.

▶ Researchers are studying hypnosis as a weapon against cancer. Individuals with cancer are hypnotized to help them manage their pain. Data suggest that this treatment also helps patients live considerably longer.

SECTION 2

The Discovery of Cells

▶ **Microtomy**
The development of high-magnification microscopes required that the preparation of specimens for viewing also become more sophisticated. Microtomy used to refer only to specimen cutting because a microtome is the instrument used to slice tissue sections. Today microtomy refers collectively to the art of preparing specimens by any number of techniques. When microscopic organisms are viewed as whole-mounts, they are preserved, stained, dried (alcohol removes the water), and made transparent with clove or cedar oil. Then the organism is mounted in a drop of resin on a glass slide and covered with a piece of glass only 0.005 mm thick.

▶ **Physiology and the Cell Theory**
The development of the cell theory aided research in other fields. In the mid-1800s, French physiologist Claude Bernard proposed that plants and animals are composed of sets of control mechanisms that work to maintain the internal conditions necessary for life. He recognized that a mammal can sustain a constant body temperature regardless of the outside temperature. Today we recognize this ability as homeostasis. But at the time no one knew what the

53E Chapter 3 • Cells: The Basic Units of Life

Chapter 3 • Cells: The Basic Units of Life

"organized sets of control mechanisms" were. The discovery of cells, and how their many components function to sustain life in an organism, gave credence to Bernard's position.

IS THAT A FACT!

- Aeolid nudibranchs are mollusks that eat hydroids, small polyps that have protective stinging cells. The nudibranchs' digestive systems carefully sort out the hydroids' stinging cells and send them to the protective tentacles on their own backs.

SECTION 3

Eukaryotic Cells: The Inside Story

▶ **"Protein" Therapy**
As scientists delved deeper into the cell, they moved past the initial stages of merely identifying its structures to asking, "What do these organelles do?" and "How do they do it?" Decades of investigation have produced "gene therapy," which refers to the use of a cell's genetic material to cure disease. It might be more appropriate to call this rapidly expanding field of science "protein therapy."

- The gene can be thought of as a blueprint for the proteins essential to life. People with Duchenne's muscular dystrophy lack dystrophin, an essential muscle protein that maintains the structure of muscle cells. Researchers have been able to remove the harmful genetic components of a virus and replace them with the gene for dystrophin. Their plan is to inject the dystrophin gene (the gene that codes for the dystrophin protein) directly into the muscles of Duchenne's patients and trick the body into maintaining healthy muscle.

▶ **Cell Scientists**
Microbiologists study the characteristics of bacteria and other microorganisms to understand how they interact with people, plants, and animals. Virologists investigate viruses, which are active only inside a living cell. Mycologists study fungi, which include molds, and yeast. Environmental microbiologists inspect the water in rivers and lakes. Those in agriculture are concerned with organisms that affect soil quality.

▶ **Mitochondrial Diseases**
Mitochondrial diseases are a group of illnesses caused by malfunctioning mitochondria. The problem can be with either the genes of the mitochondria or the genes of the cell. Any activity or organ that requires energy is affected by these diseases. Because the brain requires huge amounts of energy to function, it often suffers in people who have a mitochondrial disease. Other commonly affected areas are muscles, including the heart; organs, such as the kidneys; and bone marrow.

▶ **Cell Walls**
Every culture in the world relies in some way on the cell walls of dead organisms. Materials such as thatch, reed, and wood are composed of cell walls that remain after an organism has died.

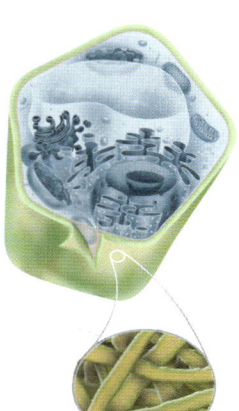

For background information about teaching strategies and issues, refer to the *Professional Reference for Teachers.*

CHAPTER 3

Cells: The Basic Units of Life

Pre-Reading Questions

Students may not know the answers to these questions before reading the chapter, so accept any reasonable response.

Suggested Answers

1. A cell is a membrane-covered structure that contains the items necessary to carry out life processes. Cells are found in all living things.

2. Cells allow life processes to occur. Cells are small because a large surface-to-volume ratio allows them to easily exchange food and wastes with the environment.

Directed Reading Worksheet 3

Science Puzzlers, Twisters & Teasers Worksheet 3

Guided Reading Audio CD
English or Spanish, Chapter 3

CHAPTER 3

Cells: The Basic Units of Life

Sections

1. **Organization of Life** ... 56
   - Chemistry Connection 58
   - Internet Connect 60

2. **The Discovery of Cells** 61
   - Apply 65
   - MathBreak 65
   - QuickLab 66
   - Internet Connect 67

3. **Eukaryotic Cells: The Inside Story** 68
   - Internet Connect 75

   Chapter Review 78
   Feature Articles 80, 81
   LabBook 694–697

Pre-Reading Questions

1. What is a cell, and where are cells found?
2. Why are there cells, and why are they so small?

TINY DEFENDERS

Invading bacteria have entered your body. These foreign cells are about to make you sick. But wait—your white blood cells come to the rescue! In this microscopic image, a white blood cell is reaching out its "arm" (called a *pseudopod*) to destroy a bacterium. In this chapter, you will learn about bacteria, blood cells, and other cells in your body.

---

internet connect

HRW On-line Resources
go.hrw.com
For worksheets and other teaching aids, visit the HRW Web site and type in the keyword: **HSTCEL**

sciLINKS NSTA
www.scilinks.com
Use the *sci*LINKS numbers at the end of each chapter for additional resources on the **NSTA** Web site.

CNNfyi.com
www.cnnfyi.com
Visit the CNN Web site for current events coverage and classroom resources.

START-UP Activity

WHAT ARE PLANTS MADE OF?

All living things, including plants, are made of cells. What do plant cells look like? Do this activity to find out.

Procedure

1. Tear off a small leaf near the tip of an *Elodea* sprig.
2. Using **tweezers,** place the whole leaf in a drop of **water** on a **microscope slide.**
3. Place a **coverslip** on top of the water drop. Put one edge on the slide, then slowly lower the coverslip over the drop to prevent air bubbles.
4. Place the slide on your **microscope.** Find the cells. You may have to use the highest powered lens to see them.
5. Draw a picture of what you see.

Analysis

6. Describe the shape of the *Elodea* cells. Are they all the same?
7. Do you think your cells look like *Elodea* cells? Explain your answer.

START-UP Activity

WHAT ARE PLANTS MADE OF?

MATERIALS

FOR EACH STUDENT:
- water
- plastic microscope slide
- *Elodea* sprig
- tweezers
- plastic coverslip
- microscope

Safety Caution

Remind students to review all safety cautions and icons before beginning this lab activity.

Answers to START-UP Activity

6. Students should see that all the cells share similar structures but may not be exactly the same.
7. Accept all reasonable responses. Plant cells differ from human body cells, but they share many similar structures.

Chapter 3 • Cells: The Basic Units of Life

SECTION 1

Focus

Organization of Life

In this section, students will learn that a cell is the smallest unit of life. In most multicellular organisms, groups of cells form tissues that compose organs. Two or more organs can interact to form an organ system. Students will also learn that organisms can be further organized into populations, communities, and ecosystems.

Bellringer

On the board or overhead viewer, write the following questions:

Why can't you use your teeth to breathe? Why can't you use your arm muscles to digest food?

Have students answer these questions in their ScienceLog.

1 Motivate

ACTIVITY

Concept Mapping Divide the class into small groups. Provide each group with pictures of tissues, organs, and organ systems. Have the students arrange the pictures into concept maps. Encourage them to notice unusual relationships between organs. For example, the stomach and the heart may seem very different, but both are made of muscle tissue, and both function by holding and moving substances through their cavities.

Section 1

Terms to Learn

tissue
organ
organ system
organism
unicellular

multicellular
population
community
ecosystem

What You'll Do

- Explain how life is organized, from a single cell to an ecosystem.
- Describe the difference between unicellular organisms and multicellular organisms.

Figure 1 The first cell of a chicken is one of the largest cells in the world.

Organization of Life

Imagine that you are going on a trip to Mars. In your suitcase, you should pack everything you will need in order to survive. What would you pack? To start, you'd need food, oxygen, and water. And that's just the beginning. You would probably need a pretty big suitcase, wouldn't you? Actually, you have all of these items inside your body's cells. A cell is smaller than the period at the end of this sentence, yet a single cell has all the items necessary to carry out life's activities.

Every living thing has at least one cell. Many living things exist as a single cell, while others have trillions of cells. To get an idea of what a living thing with nearly 100 trillion cells looks like, just look in the mirror!

Cells: Starting Out Small

Most cells are too small to be seen without a microscope, but you might have one of the world's largest cells in your refrigerator. To find out what it is, see **Figure 1.** The first cell of a chicken is yellow with a tiny white dot in it, and it is surrounded by clear, jellylike fluid called egg white. The white dot divides over and over again to form a chick. The yellow yolk (from the first cell) and the egg white provide nutrients for the developing chick's cells. Like a chicken, you too began as a single egg cell. Look at **Figure 2** to see some of the early stages of your development.

Not all of your cells look or act the same. You have about 200 different kinds of cells, and each type is specialized to do a particular job. Some are bone cells, some are blood cells, and others are skin cells. When someone looks at all of those cells together, they see you.

Figure 2 You began as a single cell. But after many cell divisions, you are now made of about 100 trillion cells.

24 hours   40 hours   6 days   4 months

56

 Directed Reading Worksheet 3 Section 1

SCIENCE HUMOR

Q: Why did the chicken cross the playground?

A: to get to the other slide

56   Chapter 3 • Cells: The Basic Units of Life

Tissues: Cells Working in Teams

When you look closely at your clothes, you can see that threads have been grouped together (woven) to make cloth that has a function. In the same way, cells are grouped together to make a tissue that has a function. A **tissue** is a group of cells that work together to perform a specific job in the body. The material around and between the cells is also part of the tissue. Some examples of tissues in your body are shown in **Figure 3**.

Organs: Teams Working Together

When two or more tissues work together to perform a specific job, the group of tissues is called an **organ**. Some examples of organs are your stomach, intestines, heart, lungs, and skin. That's right; even your skin is an organ because it contains different kinds of tissues. To get a closer look, see **Figure 4**.

Plants also have different kinds of tissues that work together. A leaf is a plant organ that contains tissue that traps light energy to make food. Other examples of plant organs are stems and roots.

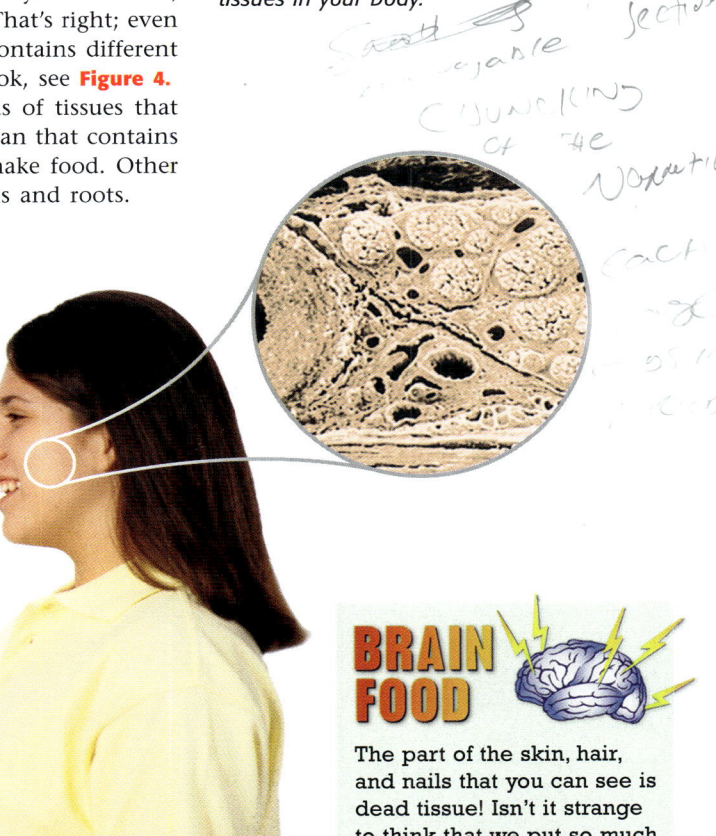

Figure 3 Blood, fat, and muscle cells are just a few of the many cells that make tissues in your body.

Figure 4 The skin is the body's largest organ. An average-sized person's skin has a mass of about 4.5 kg.

BRAIN FOOD

The part of the skin, hair, and nails that you can see is dead tissue! Isn't it strange to think that we put so much effort into making sure our dead cells look nice?

IS THAT A FACT!

In your lifetime you will shed about 18 kg (almost 40 lb) of dead skin.

---

2) Teach

DISCUSSION

Muscles Ask students to list all the ways they use their muscles. Responses will probably include walking, riding a bike, swimming, and throwing or kicking a ball. Explain that muscles are also involved in swallowing food (tongue), digestion (stomach), and blinking eyes (eyelids). Sometimes muscles act voluntarily (jumping), and sometimes they act involuntarily (the heart beating).

MISCONCEPTION ALERT

Hair and fingernails grow out of specialized skin cells. Even though they grow continuously, both are composed of dead cells along with a protein called *keratin*. If they were alive and contained nerve cells, like the deep skin layers, haircuts and manicures would be quite painful.

Homework

Writing Not all living things have the same kinds of tissues and organs. Yet all must perform similar life processes. Have students research and compare the structures a fish uses to breathe with those that a human uses. Their report should also answer the question, "What parts of the human and fish respiratory systems are similar?" (Even though a fish has gills and a human has lungs, both have cells that exchange and transport oxygen and carbon dioxide.)

2) Teach, continued

MEETING INDIVIDUAL NEEDS

Learners Having Difficulty
To help students understand the levels of organization within an organism, instruct them to write the following headings on the board:

    Cell, Tissue, Organ, Organ system

Tell students to write these headings across the top of their paper and list at least two examples of each under the headings. Then ask students to share their information with their classmates.

USING THE FIGURE

Writing Have students write an expanded caption for **Figure 5**. They should read additional references for information describing the functions of the leaf, stem, and root organ systems. Then have them identify systems in the human body, if any, that perform similar functions.

RETEACHING

Writing A great way to learn something is to teach it to someone else. Have students write a letter to a friend explaining how cells, tissues, organs, and organ systems are all related.

Answer to Activity
Accept all reasonable responses.

Chemistry CONNECTION

On the surface of every person's cells are special proteins that act like identification cards. When a person gets an organ transplant, the cells of the new organ must have most of the same "ID cards" as the person's cells. If too many are different, the person's body will try to reject the new organ.

Activity

A school system's job is to educate students at all levels. The different schools (elementary, middle, and high school) are like the different organs within an organ system. Groups of teachers at each school work together to teach a specific grade level. If each group of teachers can be thought of as tissue, what would that make each individual teacher? What other examples can you use to represent the parts of an organ system? Explain your answer.

 TRY at HOME

58

internetconnect

SC_{LINKS} NSTA

TOPIC: Organization of Life
GO TO: www.scilinks.org
***sci*LINKS NUMBER:** HSTL055

Organ Systems: A Great Combination

Organs work together in groups to perform particular jobs. These groups are called **organ systems**. Each system has a specific job to do in the body. For example, your digestive system's job is to break down food into very small particles so it can be used by all of your body's cells. Your nervous system's job is to transmit information back and forth between your brain and the other parts of your body. Organ systems in plants include leaf systems, root systems, and stem systems.

Your body has several organ systems. The digestive system is shown in **Figure 5**. Each organ in the digestive system has a job to do. A particular organ is able to do its job because of the different tissues within it.

The organs in an organ system depend on each other. If any part of the system fails, the whole system is affected. And failure of one organ system can affect other organ systems. Just think of what would happen if your digestive system stopped converting food to energy. None of the other organ systems would have energy to function.

Figure 5 The digestive system is one of the 11 main organ systems. It is made of different organs, which in turn are made of different tissues.

IS THAT A FACT!

An elephant's trunk is constructed of 135 kg (300 lb) of hair, skin, connective tissue, nerves, and muscles. The muscle tissue is composed of 150,000 tiny subunits of muscle, each coordinated with the others to enable an elephant to drink, breathe, grab, and greet its friends.

Chapter 3 • Cells: The Basic Units of Life

Organisms: Independent Living

Anything that can live on its own is called an **organism.** All organisms are made up of at least one cell. If a single cell is living on its own, it is called a **unicellular** organism. Most unicellular organisms are so small that you need to use a microscope to see them. Some different kinds of unicellular organisms are shown in **Figure 6.**

You are a **multicellular** organism. This means that you can exist only as a group of cells and that most of your cells can survive only if they remain a part of your body. When you fall down on a sidewalk and scrape your knee, the cells you leave behind on the sidewalk are not able to live on their own. **Figure 7** shows how your cells work together to make a multicellular organism.

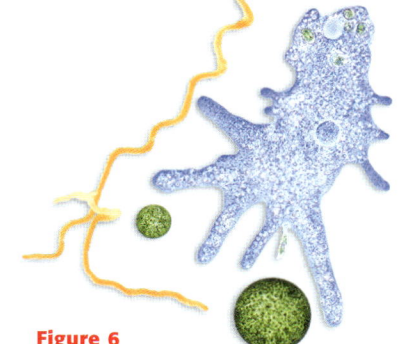

Figure 6 Unicellular organisms come in a wide variety of shapes and sizes.

Figure 7 Multicellular organisms are made of many cells that work together in tissues and organs.

The Big Picture

Although unicellular organisms and multicellular organisms can live on their own, they usually do not live alone. Organisms interact with each other in many different ways.

Populations A group of organisms that are of the same kind and that live in the same area make up a **population.** All of the ladybird beetles living in the forest shown in **Figure 8** make up the ladybird beetle population of that forest. All of the red oak trees make up the forest's red oak population.

Figure 8 A population is made up of all of the individuals of the same kind that live in the same area.

REAL-WORLD CONNECTION

Your skin cells depend on other body cells for nutrients and oxygen, which is why they cannot live independently of your body. When someone suffers a serious burn and no longer has a protective covering of skin cells, scientists can grow skin for them in a laboratory. They take healthy skin cells, mix them with collagen proteins from cow skin, and suspend them in a nutrient solution. These new cells are applied to the burned skin as a bandage while the damaged skin heals.

CONNECT TO EARTH SCIENCE

Populations are sometimes joined or divided by Earth's physical features, such as mountains, rivers, and islands. The islands of Madagascar and Comoro, off the east coast of Africa, are home to 50 species of lemurs, a type of primate. The lemurs are geographically isolated, so while they are quite diverse on Madagascar and Comoro, there are no other wild populations of lemurs anywhere else in the world. Speciation as a result of geographic isolation is not limited to islands. Species can form when populations are divided for thousands of years by mountains, rivers, and other barriers.

WEIRD SCIENCE

Living on your own doesn't mean you can't cooperate with others. On coral reefs, a group of striped fish called cleaner wrasses attract fish that are infested with parasites to an area on the reef. The infested fish lie still while wrasses eat the parasites and fungi off their body.

TOPIC: Populations, Communities, and Ecosystems
GO TO: www.scilinks.org
sciLINKS NUMBER: HSTL060

Teaching Transparency 7
"From Cell to Organism"

Reinforcement Worksheet 3
"An Ecosystem"

Section 1 • Organization of Life

3) Extend

GOING FURTHER

Writing Have students write promotional materials that encourage cells to join an organ or organ system or to remain a single cell. For example, a single cell might have independence but lack the help it needs to do its work. A tissue provides a cell with helpers that have similar interests, but it requires cooperation and good "intercellular skills."

4) Close

Quiz

1. What is the relationship between your digestive system, stomach, and intestines? (The digestive system is an organ system. The stomach and intestines are organs that are parts of the digestive system.)

2. The blood cells in your body are alive, are genetically similar to each other, and can be found in the same location (inside your body). Are these cells a population? (No. A population consists of organisms that are capable of living independently. Blood cells cannot live outside the body.)

ALTERNATIVE ASSESSMENT

Concept Mapping Have students choose a human organ system and identify its component organs. Then ask students to describe the function of these organs and their relationship to one another in a concept map.

Figure 9 *The fox, flowers, and trees are all part of a forest community.*

Communities Two or more different populations living in the same area make up a **community**. The populations of foxes, oak trees, lizards, flowers, and other organisms in a forest are all part of a forest community, as shown in **Figure 9.** Your hometown is a community that includes all of the people, dogs, cats, and other organisms living there.

Ecosystems The community and all of the nonliving things that affect it, such as water, soil, rocks, temperature, and light, make up an **ecosystem**. Ecosystems on land are called *terrestrial* ecosystems, and they include forests, deserts, prairies, and your own backyard. Ecosystems in water are called *aquatic* ecosystems, and they include rivers, ponds, lakes, oceans, and even aquariums. The community in Figure 9 lives in a terrestrial ecosystem.

REVIEW

1. Complete the following sentence: *Cells* are related to ? in the same way that ? are related to *organ systems*.

2. How do the cells of unicellular organisms differ from the cells of multicellular organisms?

3. **Applying Concepts** Use the picture of an aquarium below to answer the following questions:
   a. How many *different* kinds of organisms are visible?
   b. How many populations are visible?
   c. How many communities are visible?

TOPIC: Organization of Life & Populations, Communities, and Ecosystems
GO TO: www.scilinks.org
sciLINKS NUMBER: HSTL055, HSTL060

60   Chapter 3 • Cells: The Basic Units of Life

Answers to Review

1. tissues, organs
2. The cells of unicellular organisms can survive on their own, but the cells of multicellular organisms must remain a part of the organism's body to survive.
3. a. 8; don't forget to count the plants.
   b. 8
   c. 1; the community includes all the living things in the aquarium.

Section 2

The Discovery of Cells

Terms to Learn

cell membrane
organelles
cytoplasm
nucleus
prokaryotic
eukaryotic
bacteria

What You'll Do

- State the parts of the cell theory.
- Explain why cells are so small.
- Calculate a cell's surface-to-volume ratio.
- List the advantages of being multicellular.
- Explain the difference between prokaryotic cells and eukaryotic cells.

Most cells are so tiny that they are not visible to the naked eye. So how did we find out that cells are the basic unit of all living things? What would make someone think that a rabbit or a tree or a person is made up of tiny parts that cannot be seen? Actually, the first person to see cells was not even looking for them.

Seeing the First Cells

In 1665, a British scientist named Robert Hooke was trying to find something interesting that he could show to other scientists at a meeting. Earlier, he had built a crude microscope that allowed him to look at very tiny objects. One day he decided to look at a thin slice of cork, a soft plant tissue found in the bark of trees like the ones shown in **Figure 10.** To his amazement, the cork looked like hundreds of little boxes, which he described as looking like a honeycomb. He named these tiny boxes *cells,* which means "little rooms" in Latin.

Although Hooke did not realize it, these boxes were actually the outer layers of the cork cells that were left behind after the cells died. Later, he looked at thin slices of plants and saw that they too were made of tiny cells. Some of them were even filled with "juice" (those were living cells). Hooke's microscope and drawings of cork cells are shown in **Figure 11.**

Hooke also used his microscope to look at feathers, fish scales, and the eyes of house flies, but he spent most of his time looking at plants and fungi. Since plant and fungal cells had walls that were easier to see, Hooke thought that cells were found only in those types of organisms and not in animals.

Figure 10 *Cork is a soft material found in trees. Cork cells were the first cells seen with a microscope.*

Figure 11 *This is the compound microscope that Hooke used to see the first cells. Hooke made a drawing of the cork cells that he saw.*

Q: What did Robert Hooke say to his stockbroker?

A: Cell! Cell!

2) Teach

CONNECT TO ASTRONOMY

Both biologists and astronomers use magnifiers. Biologists use microscopes to see things that are too small to see with the unaided eye. Astronomers use telescopes to see planets, moons, and stars that are huge but too far away to view otherwise. The first telescope was made by a Dutchman named Hans Lipperhey in 1608. In 1609, the Italian scientist Galileo became the first to use a telescope for astronomy. He discovered four moons orbiting the planet Jupiter. Ask students to write a list of words that have the prefixes *micro-* and *tele-* and to use those examples to define those prefixes. **Sheltered English**

REAL-WORLD CONNECTION

The yeast used in baking is a relative of single-celled eukaryotes living among lots of other organisms in the air around us. It was probably an accidental discovery that wheat dough exposed to air for a length of time would rise and, when baked, produce bread. Sourdough breads require the right combination of yeast and bacteria in the dough, and strains of native yeast vary regionally the same way many other organisms do. Sourdough from San Francisco has its own characteristic taste because bakers there use a yeast that is most common in the air around that city.

 PG 694
Elephant-Sized Amoebas?

Figure 12 Leeuwenhoek saw unicellular organisms similar to these, which are found in pond scum.

Elephant-sized "animalcules"? Find out for yourself on LabBook page 694!

Seeing Cells in Other Life-Forms

In 1673, a few years after Hooke made his observations, a Dutch merchant named Anton van Leeuwenhoek (LAY vuhn hook) used one of his own handmade microscopes to get a closer look at pond scum, similar to that shown in **Figure 12.** He was amazed to see many small creatures swimming around in the slimy ooze; he named the creatures *animalcules,* which means "little animals."

Leeuwenhoek also looked at blood he took from different animals and tartar he scraped off their teeth and his own. He observed that blood cells in fish, birds, and frogs are oval-shaped, while those in humans and dogs are flatter. He was the first person to see bacteria, and he discovered that the yeasts used to make bread dough rise are actually unicellular organisms.

The Cell Theory

After Hooke first saw the cork cells, almost two centuries passed before anyone realized that cells are present in *all* living things. Matthias Schleiden, a German scientist, looked at many slides of plant tissues and read about what other scientists had seen under the microscope. In 1838, he concluded that all plant parts are made of cells.

The next year, Theodor Schwann, a German scientist who studied animals, stated that all animal tissues are made of cells. Not long after that, Schwann wrote the first two parts of what is now known as the *cell theory:*

- **All organisms are composed of one or more cells.**
- **The cell is the basic unit of life in all living things.**

About 20 years later, in 1858, Rudolf Virchow, a German doctor, saw that cells could not develop from anything except other cells. He then wrote the third part of the cell theory:

- **All cells come from existing cells.**

 SCIENCE

Scientists have discovered that enzymes in spinach cells can decompose explosives and reduce them to less-toxic byproducts. The process can be done at room temperature and does not require any special equipment. If field tests of this technique are successful, the tiny proteins of these microscopic cells will help safely eliminate a 500,000-ton stockpile of explosives around the country.

62 Chapter 3 • Cells: The Basic Units of Life

Cell Similarities

Cells come in many different shapes and sizes and perform a wide variety of functions, but they all have the following things in common:

Cell Membrane All cells are surrounded by a **cell membrane.** This membrane acts as a barrier between the inside of the cell and the cell's environment. It also controls the passage of materials into and out of the cell. **Figure 13** shows the outside of a cell.

Figure 13 The cell membrane holds the contents of the cell together.

Hereditary Material Part of the cell theory states that all cells are made from existing cells. When new cells are made, they receive a copy of the hereditary material of the original cells. This material is *DNA* (deoxyribonucleic acid). It controls all of the activities of a cell and contains the information needed for that cell to make new cells.

Cytoplasm and Organelles All cells have chemicals and structures that enable the cell to live, grow, and reproduce. The structures are called **organelles.** Although all cells have organelles, they don't all have the same kind. Some organelles are surrounded by membranes, but others are not. The cell in **Figure 14** has membrane-covered organelles. The chemicals and structures of a cell are surrounded by fluid. This fluid and almost everything in it are collectively called the **cytoplasm** (SIET oh PLAZ uhm).

Small Size Almost all cells are too small to be seen with the naked eye. You are made up of 100 trillion cells, and it would take 50 of these cells just to cover up the dot on the letter *i*.

Figure 14 This cell has many organelles. These organelles are surrounded by membranes.

Self-Check

Why do all cells need DNA? *(See page 782 to check your answer.)*

Answer to Self-Check

Cells need DNA to control cell processes and to make new cells.

IS THAT A FACT!

The largest cell in the world is the yolk of an ostrich egg. It's the size of a baseball.

② Teach, continued

READING STRATEGY

Prediction Guide Before reading this page, ask students to choose one of the following reasons for why they think cells are so small:

1. There isn't enough microscopic food available for them.
2. There isn't enough room in a multicellular organism.
3. another reason (ask for suggestions)

Have students evaluate their answer after they read the page.

MATH and MORE

Surface Area The following problem simplifies the principle of surface-to-volume ratio because it concerns a two-dimensional figure. Give each student a sheet of $\frac{1}{4}$ in. grid paper. Tell them to outline a rectangle 4 squares wide and 5 squares long. What is the area of this rectangle? **(4 × 5 = 20 squares)**

Now tell students to outline another rectangle that is twice as big, 8 squares wide and 10 squares long. What is the area of the second rectangle? **(8 × 10 = 80 squares)**

Next ask students to calculate the perimeter of each rectangle. **(5 + 5 + 4 + 4 = 18)** **(10 + 10 + 8 + 8 = 36)**

How did doubling the size of the rectangle affect its internal area? How did it affect its perimeter? **(The internal area quadrupled: 80 ÷ 20 = 4. The perimeter only doubled: 36 ÷ 18 = 2.)**

Giant Amoeba Eats New York City

This is not a headline you are likely to ever see. Why not? Amoebas consist of only a single cell. Most amoebas can't even grow large enough to be seen without a microscope. That's because as a cell gets larger, it needs more food and produces more waste. Therefore, more materials must be able to move into and out of the cell through the cell membrane.

Surface-to-Volume Ratio To keep up with these demands, a growing cell needs a larger surface area through which to exchange materials. As the cell's volume increases, its outer surface grows too. But the volume of a cell (the amount a cell will hold) increases at a faster rate than the area of its outer surface. If a cell gets too large, its surface will have too few openings to allow enough materials into and out of it.

To understand why the volume of a cell increases faster than its surface area, look at the table below. The *surface-to-volume ratio* is the area of a cell's outer surface in relation to its volume. The surface-to-volume ratio decreases as cell size increases. Increasing the number of cells but not their size maintains a high surface-to-volume ratio.

Surface-to-Volume Ratio

Each side of this cell is **1 unit long.**	Each side of this cell is **2 units long.**	The sides of each of these **8 cells are 1 unit long.**
The surface area of one side is **1 square unit.** (1 × 1 = 1)	The surface area of one side is **4 square units.** (2 × 2 = 4)	The combined surface area of these 8 cells is **48 square units.** (8 × 6 square units = 48)
The surface area of the cell is **6 square units.** (1 × 1 × 6 = 6)	This cell has a surface area of **24 square units.** (2 × 2 × 6 = 24)	The combined volume of these cells is **8 cubic units.** (8 × 1 cubic unit = 8)
The volume of this cell is **1 cubic unit.** (1 × 1 × 1 = 1)	The volume of this larger cell is **8 cubic units.** (2 × 2 × 2 = 8)	The surface-to-volume ratio of the combined cells is 48:8, or **6:1.**
The surface-to-volume ratio of this cell is **6:1.**	The surface-to-volume ratio of this cell is 24:8, or **3:1.**	

 Teaching Transparency 8 "Surface-to-Volume Ratio"

Q: Define *bacteria*.

A: the rear entrance to a cafeteria

The Benefits of Being Multicellular Do you know now why you are made up of many tiny cells instead of one large cell? A single cell as big as you are would have an incredibly small surface-to-volume ratio. The cell could not survive because its outer surface would be too small to allow in the materials it would need. Multicellular organisms grow by producing more small cells, not larger cells. The elephant in **Figure 15** has cells that are the same size as yours.

Many Kinds of Cells In addition to being able to grow larger, multicellular organisms are able to do lots of other things because they are made up of different kinds of cells. Just as there are teachers who are specialized to teach and mechanics who are specialized to work on cars, different cells are specialized to perform different jobs. A single cell cannot do all the things that many different cells can do. Having many different cells that are specialized for specific jobs allows multicellular organisms to perform more functions than unicellular organisms.

The different kinds of cells can form tissues and organs with different functions. People have specialized cells, such as muscle cells, eye cells, and brain cells, so they can walk, run, watch a movie, think, and do many other activities. If you enjoy doing many different things, be glad you are not a single cell.

Figure 15 *An elephant is larger than a human because it has more cells, not larger cells.*

A Pet *Paramecium*
Imagine that you have a pet *Paramecium*, a type of unicellular organism. In order to properly care for your pet, you have to figure out how much you need to feed it. The dimensions of your *Paramecium* are roughly 125 μm × 50 μm × 20 μm. If seven food molecules can enter through each square micrometer of surface every minute, how many molecules can it eat in 1 minute? If your pet needs one food molecule per cubic micrometer of volume every minute to survive, how much would you have to feed it every minute?

MATH BREAK

Surface-to-Volume Ratio
The shape of a cell can affect its surface-to-volume ratio. Examine the cells below, and answer the questions that follow:

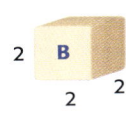

1. What is the surface area of Cell A? of Cell B?
2. What is the volume of Cell A? of Cell B?
3. Which of the two cells pictured here has the greater surface-to-volume ratio?

CONNECT TO
EARTH SCIENCE

The work of paleontologists helps us understand the antiquity of unicellular and multicellular life on Earth. Part of their work includes determining the ages of the rocks that contain fossils. But paleontologists can also learn about Earth's past climate by asking questions about life-forms, such as, "Was the organism a marine plant or an animal?"

Answers to MATHBREAK

1. 28 square units; 24 square units
2. 8 cubic units; 8 cubic units
3. Cell *A*'s surface-to-volume ratio is the largest, at 28:8. (Even though Cell *A* has a larger surface area, the two cells have the same volume.)

Math Skills Worksheet 16
"What Is a Ratio?"

Math Skills Worksheet 29
"Finding Perimeter and Area"

Math Skills Worksheet 30
"Finding Volume"

Answers to APPLY

- The surface area of the pet is 19,500 μm², so it can eat 136,500 molecules of food every minute.
- The volume of the pet is 125,000 μm³. If it needs one food molecule for every cubic micrometer, then it needs to be fed 125,000 food molecules every minute to survive.

2) Teach, continued

Answers to Self-Check
1. The surface-to-volume ratio decreases as the cell size increases.
2. A eukaryotic cell has a nucleus and membrane-covered organelles.

CONNECT TO EARTH SCIENCE

Astronomers are interested in the work of scientists who investigate bacteria and other microscopic organisms in Earth's crust. Microbiologists have drilled deep into the crust and found microbes nearly 3 km below the surface, where the temperature is 75°C (167°F). Because other planets have surface conditions similar to the harsh environment within the Earth's crust, astronomers believe it may be possible for microbes to live elsewhere in the solar system. Have students research and write a brief report on the conditions in Earth's crust and learn about the organisms that live there.

QuickLab

MATERIALS

FOR EACH STUDENT:
- cotton swab
- yogurt with active culture
- plastic microscope slide
- water
- plastic coverslip
- microscope

Answer to QuickLab
Drawings should depict rod-shaped bacteria.

TOPIC: Prokaryotic Cells
GO TO: www.scilinks.org
sciLINKS NUMBER: HSTL065

Self-Check

1. As a cell grows larger, what happens to its surface-to-volume ratio?
2. What does a eukaryotic cell have that a prokaryotic cell does not?

(See page 782 to check your answer.)

QuickLab

Do Bacteria Taste Good?
If they're the kind found in yogurt, they taste great! Using a **cotton swab**, put a small dot of **yogurt** on a **plastic microscope slide**. Add a drop of **water**, and use the cotton swab to stir. Add a **plastic coverslip**, and examine the slide using a **microscope**. Draw what you see.

The masses of rod-shaped bacteria feed on the sugar in milk (lactose) and convert it into lactic acid. Lactic acid causes milk to thicken, which makes yogurt!

Two Types of Cells

The many different kinds of cells that exist can be divided into two groups. As you have already learned, all cells have DNA. In one group, cells have a **nucleus,** which is a membrane-covered organelle that holds the cells' DNA. In the other group, the cells' DNA is not contained in a nucleus. Cells that do not have a nucleus are **prokaryotic** (proh KAR ee AH tik), and cells that have a nucleus are **eukaryotic** (yoo KAR ee AH tik).

Prokaryotic Cells Prokaryotic cells are also called **bacteria.** They are the world's smallest cells, and they do not have a nucleus. A prokaryotic cell's DNA is one long, circular molecule shaped sort of like a rubber band.

Bacteria do not have any membrane-covered organelles, but they do have tiny, round organelles called *ribosomes*. These organelles work like little factories to make proteins.

Most bacteria are covered by a hard cell wall outside a softer cell membrane. Think of the membrane pressing against the wall as an inflated balloon pressing against the inside of a glass jar. But unlike the balloon and jar, the membrane and the wall allow food and waste molecules to pass through. **Figure 16** shows a generalized view of a prokaryotic cell.

Bacteria were probably the first type of cells on Earth. The oldest fossils ever found are of prokaryotic cells. Scientists have estimated these fossils to be 3.5 billion years old.

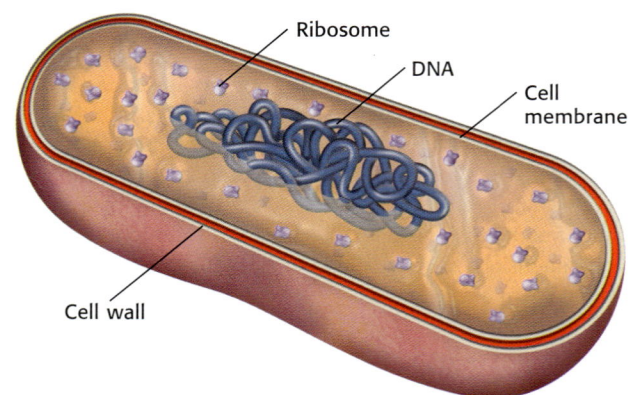

Figure 16 *Prokaryotic cells do not have a nucleus or any other membrane-covered organelles. The circular DNA is bunched up in the cytoplasm.*

WEIRD SCIENCE

In 1969, the *Apollo 12* crew retrieved a space probe from the moon that had been launched nearly three years earlier. In the probe's camera, NASA scientists found a stowaway. The bacterium *Streptococcus mitis* had traveled to the moon and back. Despite the rigors of space travel, more than two and a half years of radiation exposure, and freezing temperatures, the *Streptococcus mitis* was successfully reconstituted.

---

66 Chapter 3 • Cells: The Basic Units of Life

Eukaryotic Cells Eukaryotic cells are more complex than prokaryotic cells. Although most eukaryotic cells are about 10 times larger than prokaryotic cells, they still have a high enough surface-to-volume ratio to survive. Fossil evidence suggests that eukaryotic cells first appeared about 2 billion years ago. All living things that are not bacteria are made of one or more eukaryotic cells. This includes plants, animals, fungi, and protists.

Eukaryotic cells have a nucleus and many other membrane-covered organelles. An advantage of having the cell divided into compartments is that it allows many different chemical processes to occur at the same time. A generalized eukaryotic cell is shown in **Figure 17**.

There is more DNA in eukaryotic cells than in prokaryotic cells, and it is stored in the nucleus. Instead of being circular, the DNA molecules in eukaryotic cells are linear.

All eukaryotic cells have a cell membrane, and some of them have a cell wall. Those that have cell walls are found in plants, fungi, and some unicellular organisms. The tables below summarize the differences between eukaryotic and prokaryotic cells.

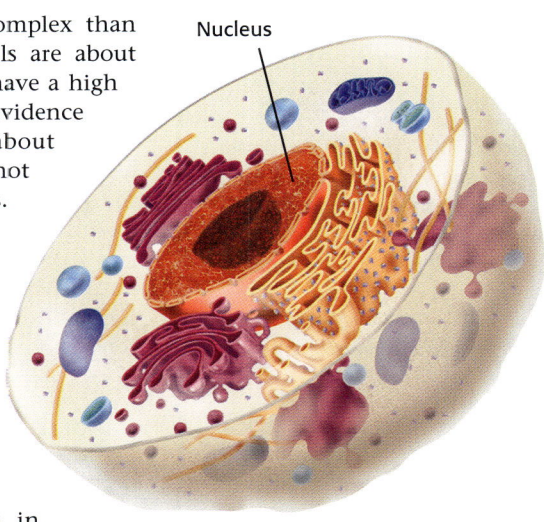

Figure 17 Eukaryotic cells contain a nucleus and many other organelles.

Prokaryotic Cells	Eukaryotic Cells
No nucleus	Nucleus
No membrane-covered organelles	Membrane-covered organelles
Circular DNA	Linear DNA
Bacteria	All other cells

Science CONNECTION

A new way to cure sick cells? See page 80.

REVIEW

1. What are the three parts of the cell theory?
2. What do all cells have in common?
3. What are two advantages of being multicellular?
4. If a unicellular organism has a cell wall, ribosomes, and circular DNA, is it eukaryotic or prokaryotic?
5. **Applying Concepts** Which has the greater surface-to-volume ratio, a tennis ball or a basketball? Explain your answer. What could be done to increase the surface-to-volume ratio of both?

internetconnect

TOPIC: Prokaryotic Cells
GO TO: www.scilinks.org
sciLINKS NUMBER: HSTL065

SECTION 3

Focus

Eukaryotic Cells: The Inside Story

In this section, students will learn the names and functions of organelles in a eukaryotic cell. They will learn which organelles enable a cell to make proteins, produce energy, transport and store materials, and prepare to divide. Finally, they will learn the difference between plant and animal cells.

Bellringer

On the board or overhead projector, write the following:

List three differences between prokaryotic and eukaryotic cells. (Prokaryotic cells have circular DNA, no nucleus, and no membrane-covered organelles. Eukaryotic cells have linear DNA, a nucleus, and membrane-covered organelles.)

1 Motivate

DISCUSSION

Cellular Activity Ask students if they can feel the flurry of activity within their cells that keeps them alive. (No.)

Ask how they know their cells are working. (They can breathe, digest food, and move.)

Explain that there is a tendency to consider life processes as activities performed only by whole organisms. What we sometimes forget is that the plant or animal can do these things only because its *cells* are doing these things.

Section 3

Terms to Learn

cell wall
ribosome
endoplasmic reticulum
mitochondria
chloroplast
Golgi complex
vesicle
vacuole
lysosome

What You'll Do

◆ Explain the function of each part of a eukaryotic cell.
◆ Describe the differences between animal cells and plant cells.

Eukaryotic Cells: The Inside Story

For a long time after the discovery of cells, scientists did not really know what cells were made of. Cells are so small that the details of their structure could not be seen until better methods of magnifying and staining were developed. We now know that cells are very complex, especially eukaryotic cells. Everything, from the structures covering the cells to the organelles inside them, performs a task that helps to keep the cells alive.

Holding It All Together

All cells have outer coverings that separate what is inside the cell from what is outside. One kind of covering, called the cell membrane, surrounds all cells. Some cells have an additional layer outside the cell membrane called the cell wall.

Cell Membrane All cells are covered by a cell membrane. The job of the cell membrane is to keep the cytoplasm inside, to allow nutrients in and waste products out, and to interact with things outside the cell. In **Figure 18,** you can see a close-up view of the cell membrane of a cell that has had its top half cut away.

Figure 18 *A cell membrane surrounds all cells. Phospholipid molecules form the cell membrane.*

MISCONCEPTION ALERT

Students often think of cells as flat. Pictures, and even viewing cells in a microscope, can reinforce that misconception. The fact that cells are three-dimensional is often overlooked. **Sheltered English**

Cell Wall The cells of plants and algae have a hard cell wall made of cellulose. The **cell wall** provides strength and support to the cell membrane. When too much water enters or leaves a plant cell, the cell wall can prevent the membrane from tearing. The strength of billions of cell walls in plants enables a tree to stand tall and its limbs to defy gravity. When you are looking at dried hay, sticks, and wooden boards, you are seeing the cell walls of dead plant cells. The cells of fungi, such as mushrooms, toadstools, mold, and yeasts, have cell walls made of a chemical similar to that found in the hard covering of insects. **Figure 19** shows a cross section of a generalized plant cell and a close-up view of the cell wall.

The Cell's Library

The largest and most visible organelle in a eukaryotic cell is the nucleus. The word *nucleus* means "kernel" or "nut" (maybe it does look sort of like a nut inside a piece of candy). As you can see in **Figure 20,** the nucleus is covered by a membrane through which materials can pass.

The nucleus has often been called the control center of the cell. As you know, it stores the DNA that has information on how to make all of the cell's proteins. Almost every chemical reaction that is important to the cell's life involves some kind of protein. Sometimes a dark spot can be seen inside the nucleus. This spot is called a *nucleolus,* and it looks like a small nucleus inside the big nucleus. The nucleolus stores the materials that will be used later to make ribosomes in the cytoplasm.

Figure 19 The cell wall surrounds the cell membrane. In plant cells, the cell wall is made of cellulose fibers.

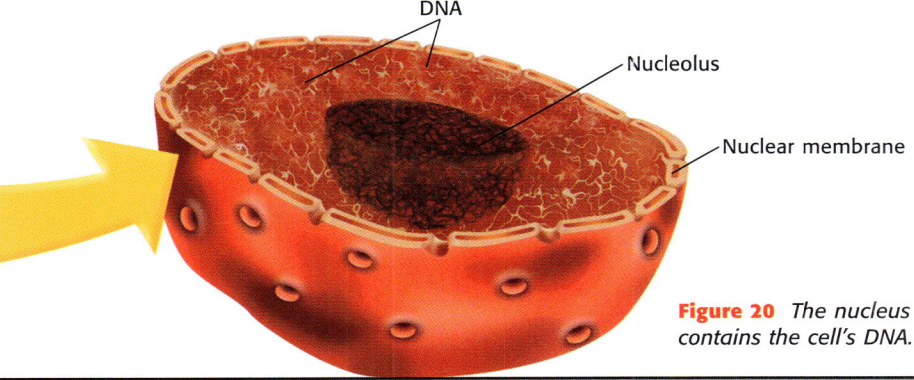

Figure 20 The nucleus contains the cell's DNA.

2) Teach

DEMONSTRATION

Cell Walls With a stick, a mushroom, and your own hand, you can illustrate the difference between a rigid cell wall and a flexible cell membrane like that found in human skin cells. Bend the stick, and it will break. Bend the mushroom, and it will come apart. Make a fist, and your skin stretches to accommodate the flexing of muscles and bone joints. If we had rigid cell walls like plants, we would find it extremely difficult to move.
Sheltered English

MEETING INDIVIDUAL NEEDS

Advanced Learners Because all multicellular plants and animals are composed of eukaryotic cells, stress that the eukaryotic cell can be an entity in itself, not just a component of a larger organism. Have students research one-celled eukaryotic organisms, like a yeast or a one-celled protist, and compare them with eukaryotic cells that are part of a multicellular plant or animal. Students should include drawings, and record their findings in their ScienceLog.

Directed Reading Worksheet 3 Section 3

Homework

Poster Project Have students investigate red blood cells and create a poster comparing the red blood cell with the cheek skin cell. (RBCs are the only cells in the human body that do not have a nucleus or mitochondria. Without a nucleus they cannot divide and reproduce. They live for only about 120 days, but new ones are made by bone marrow at the rate of up to 200 billion per day.)

Section 3 • Eukaryotic Cells: The Inside Story

② Teach, continued

MEETING INDIVIDUAL NEEDS

Writing | Advanced Learners
Have students write a science fiction story about an animal whose cells are invaded by chloroplasts. Students should describe how that animal's life processes would be affected and how that animal would use this unusual occurrence to its advantage. Encourage students to write about an animal other than a mammal.

Answer to Self-Check

Cell walls surround the cell membranes of some cells. All cells have cell membranes, but not all cells have cell walls. Cell walls give structure to some cells.

CONNECT TO PHYSICAL SCIENCE

Biophysics uses tools and techniques of physics to study the life processes of cells. Biophysicists are interested in the relationship between a molecule's structure and its function. Sophisticated techniques, such as electron microscopy, X-ray diffraction, magnetic resonance spectroscopy, and electrophoresis, allow them to study the structure of proteins, nucleic acids, and even parts of cells, such as ribosomes. Use the following Teaching Transparency to illustrate molecular structure.

Teaching Transparency 260 "Structural Formulas" *LINK TO PHYSICAL SCIENCE*

Protein Factories

Proteins, the building blocks of all cells, are made up of chemicals known as *amino acids*. These amino acids are hooked together to make proteins at very small organelles called **ribosomes.** Ribosomes are the smallest but most abundant organelles. *All* cells have ribosomes because all cells need protein to live. Unlike most other organelles, ribosomes are not covered with a membrane.

The Cell's Delivery System

Eukaryotic cells have an organelle called the endoplasmic (EN doh PLAZ mik) reticulum (ri TIK yuh luhm), which is shown in **Figure 21.** The **endoplasmic reticulum,** or ER, is a membrane-covered compartment that makes lipids and other materials for use inside and outside the cell. It is also the organelle that breaks down drugs and certain other chemicals that could damage the cell. The ER is the internal delivery system of a cell. Substances in the ER can move from one place to another through its many tubular connections, sort of like cars moving through tunnels.

The ER looks like flattened sacks stacked side by side or a cloth folded back and forth. Some ER may be covered with ribosomes that make its surface look rough. The proteins made at those ribosomes pass into the ER. Later the proteins are released from the ER for use elsewhere.

> **Self-Check**
> What is the difference between a cell wall and a cell membrane? *(See page 782 to check your answer.)*

Figure 21 The ER is made up of flattened compartments and tubes. Ribosomes are attached to some of the ER.

Scientists at the University of New Mexico have created artificial muscles that are twice as strong as the real thing. Pending government approval, these artificial muscles may be implanted to replace paralyzed tissue in people with serious injuries.

Chapter 3 • Cells: The Basic Units of Life

The Cell's Power Plants

In today's world, we use many sources of energy, such as oil, gas, and nuclear power. We need this energy to heat our homes, fuel our cars, and cook our food. Cells also need energy to function. Where do they get it?

Mitochondria Inside all cells, food molecules are "burned" (broken down) to release energy. The energy is transferred to a special molecule that the cell uses to get work done. As you learned earlier, this molecule is called ATP.

ATP can be made at several locations in eukaryotic cells, but most of it is produced at bean-shaped organelles called **mitochondria** (MIET oh KAHN dree uh), shown in **Figure 22**. These organelles are surrounded by two membranes. The inner membrane, which has many folds in it, is where most of the ATP is made.

Figure 22 Mitochondria have two membranes. The inner membrane has many folds.

Mitochondria can work only if they have oxygen. The reason you breathe air is to make sure your mitochondria have the oxygen they need to make ATP. Highly active cells, such as those in the heart and liver, may have thousands of mitochondria, while other cells may have only a few.

Chloroplasts Plants and algae have an additional kind of energy-converting organelle, called a **chloroplast,** which is shown in **Figure 23**. Chloroplasts have two membranes and structures that look like stacks of coins. These are flattened, membrane-covered sacs that contain an important chemical called chlorophyll. Chlorophyll is what makes chloroplasts green. The energy of sunlight is trapped by chlorophyll and used to make sugar. This process is called *photosynthesis*. The sugar that is produced is used by mitochondria to make ATP. You will learn more about photosynthesis in a later chapter.

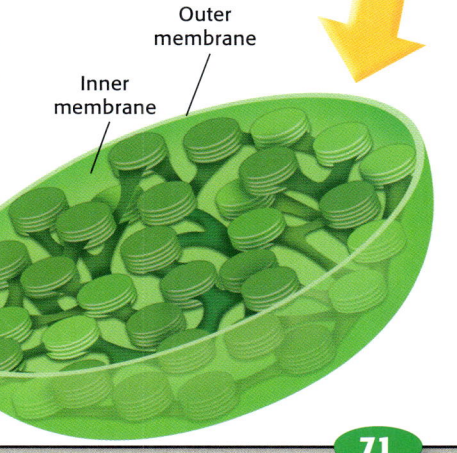

Figure 23 Chloroplasts, found in plant cells, also have two membranes. The inner membrane forms stacks of flattened sacs.

MEETING INDIVIDUAL NEEDS

Learners Having Difficulty Arrange students in pairs. Tell each pair to draw a plant or animal eukaryotic cell based on information presented in the text. Instruct them not to label the cell's parts. Then have them exchange drawings with another pair and put the proper labels on their classmates' picture. Finally, have each group of two pairs compare and discuss their work.

Homework

Making Models Invite the class to make edible cells at home and bring them to class. They can decorate a muffin, a cracker, a piece of pita bread, an English muffin, a pizza, or any other base they like and decorate their choice with edible organelles. Before they eat their creations, they should show them to the rest of the class and explain the way they've represented the cell's structure in food. Pictures of the edible cells can be displayed in the classroom. Sheltered English

IS THAT A FACT!

Nerve cells, called *neurons,* are the longest cells in the human body. They can be more than 1 m long.

Section 3 • Eukaryotic Cells: The Inside Story

2) Teach, continued

ACTIVITY

Making Models Have the students create a cell using a shoe box for the cell wall. Any material readily available can be used for the cell parts. Parts can be hung on a string, glued to the box, or attached by any method the student chooses. The boxes can be displayed in the classroom. Sheltered English

Camillo Golgi was born in 1843 in a small town called Corteno, in the northern Italian province of Lombardy. He received a medical degree in 1865. Although he was a psychiatrist, he was interested in the microscopic nature of the nervous system. He discovered the "black reaction," which is a method of staining tissue with silver nitrate so it can be viewed clearly with a microscope. In 1897, using this method, he saw the cellular structures we know today as the Golgi complex. Golgi died at the age of 83.

 PG 697

Name That Part!

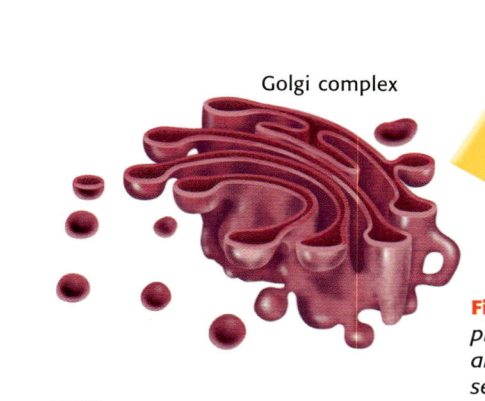

Figure 24 Mitochondria and chloroplasts may have originated from energy-producing ancestors that were engulfed by larger cells.

Where Did They Come From? Many scientists believe that mitochondria and chloroplasts originated as prokaryotic cells that were "eaten" by larger cells. Instead of being digested, the bacteria survived. **Figure 24** shows how bacteria might have become the ancestors of mitochondria and chloroplasts.

What evidence do scientists have that this theory is correct? The first piece of evidence is that mitochondria and chloroplasts are about the same size as bacteria. The second is that both are surrounded by *two membranes*. If the theory is correct, the outer membrane was created when the bacteria were engulfed by the larger cells. Other evidence supports this theory. Mitochondria and chloroplasts have the same kind of ribosomes and circular DNA as bacteria. They also divide like bacteria.

The Cell's Packaging Center

When proteins and other materials need to be processed and shipped out of a eukaryotic cell, the job goes to an organelle called the **Golgi complex.** This structure is named after Camillo Golgi, the Italian scientist who first identified it.

The Golgi complex looks like the ER, but it is located closer to the cell membrane. The Golgi complex of a cell is shown in **Figure 25.** Lipids and proteins from the ER are delivered to the Golgi complex, where they are modified for different functions. The final products are enclosed in a piece of the Golgi complex's membrane that pinches off to form a small compartment. This small compartment transports its contents to other parts of the cell or outside of the cell.

Figure 25 The Golgi complex processes, packages, and transports materials sent to it from the ER.

SCIENTISTS AT ODDS

Many scientists did not believe Golgi's claims about the Golgi complex. They thought he just saw tiny globs of the staining material. The existence of the Golgi complex was finally confirmed in the mid-1950s with the aid of the electron microscope.

Chapter 3 • Cells: The Basic Units of Life

The Cell's Storage Centers

All eukaryotic cells have membrane-covered compartments called **vesicles.** Some of them form when part of the membrane pinches off the ER or Golgi complex. Others are formed when part of the cell membrane surrounds an object outside the cell. This is how white blood cells engulf other cells in your body, as shown in **Figure 26.**

Vacuoles Most plant cells have a very large membrane-covered chamber called a **vacuole,** as shown in **Figure 27.** In plants, large central vacuoles store water and other liquids. Vacuoles that are full of water help support the cell. Some plants wilt when their cell vacuoles lose water. If you want crispy lettuce for a salad, all you need to do is fill up the vacuoles by leaving the lettuce in water overnight. Have you ever wondered what makes roses red and violets blue? It is a colorful liquid stored inside vacuoles. Vacuoles also contain the juices you associate with oranges and other fruits.

Some unicellular organisms that live in freshwater environments have a problem with too much water entering the cell. They have a special structure called a contractile vacuole that can squeeze excess water out of the cell. It works in much the same way that a pump removes water from inside a boat.

Figure 26 The smaller cell is a yeast cell that is being engulfed by a white blood cell.

Figure 27 This plant cell's vacuole is the large structure in the middle of the cell shown in blue. Vacuoles are usually the largest organelles in a plant cell.

Multicultural CONNECTION

Dr. Jewell Plummer Cobb, a cell biologist, was the first African American woman to be named president of a university in the California university system. Before she was named president of California State University at Fullerton in 1981, Dr. Cobb researched and helped explain how pigment cells normally function and how they change when they become cancerous. Dr. Cobb also taught at Sarah Lawrence College in New York and later at Rutgers University in New Jersey, where she also served as Dean. Throughout her career as a research biologist and university administrator, Dr. Cobb has demonstrated a deep commitment to research and education.

MEETING INDIVIDUAL NEEDS

Learners Having Difficulty
You can make a demonstration model of a vacuole within a cell by filling a balloon with water or air and putting it inside a clear-plastic storage bag. Show that the vacuole is part of the cell and is distinct within the cell. You can demonstrate that cells are full of motion and activity by moving the balloon around inside the bag.
Sheltered English

Critical Thinking Worksheet 3 "Cellular Construction"

IS THAT A FACT!

The vacuoles in grapes hold so much juice that they must dry in the sun for several weeks before they become raisins. A grape loses about three-fourths of its original weight in the process.

Section 3 • Eukaryotic Cells: The Inside Story

3) Extend

USING THE FIGURE

Have students refer to **Figure 29** and the chart below it to create their own drawing of a cell. But instead of drawing realistic images, tell them to draw an object that provides a visual clue about the organelle's job. For example, the Golgi complex, which transports materials, might be a car or a bus. **Sheltered English**

Homework

 The organelles in a cell are rebelling against the nucleus. They all think they work too hard and want to take a vacation. Have students write a dialog between the nucleus and the other organelles. Tell them to help each organelle present a case for why it needs a rest and then have the nucleus explain what would happen if even one of them took two weeks off.

 Teaching Transparency 9
"Organelles and Their Functions"

 Teaching Transparency 10
"Comparing Animal and Plant Cells"

 Reinforcement Worksheet 3
"Building a Eukaryotic Cell"

Packages of Destruction

What causes most of the cells of a caterpillar to dissolve into ooze inside a cocoon? What causes the tail of a tadpole to shrink and then disappear? Lysosomes, that's what!

Lysosomes are special vesicles in animal cells that contain enzymes. When a cell engulfs a particle and encloses it in a vesicle, lysosomes bump into these vesicles and pour enzymes into them. This is illustrated in **Figure 28**. The particles in the vesicles are digested by the enzymes.

Lysosomes destroy worn-out or damaged organelles. They also get rid of waste materials and protect the cell from foreign invaders.

Sometimes lysosome membranes break, and the enzymes spill into the cytoplasm, killing the cell. This is what must happen for a tadpole to become a frog. Lysosomes cause the cells in a tadpole's tail to die and dissolve as the tadpole becomes a frog. Lysosomes played a similar role in your development! Before you were born, lysosomes caused the destruction of cells that formed the webbing between your fingers. Lysosome destruction of cells may also be one of the factors that contribute to the aging process in humans.

Figure 28 This lysosome is pouring enzymes into a vesicle that contains food particles. The digested food molecules are released into the cytoplasm for use by the cell.

Organelles and Their Functions

	Nucleus contains the cell's DNA and is the control center of the cell		**Chloroplasts** make food using the energy of sunlight
	Ribosomes the site where amino acids are hooked together to make proteins		**Golgi complex** processes and transports materials out of the cell
	Endoplasmic reticulum makes lipids, breaks down drugs and other substances, packages up proteins for release from the cell		**Vacuole** stores water and other materials
	Mitochondria break down food molecules to make ATP		**Lysosomes** digest food particles, wastes, cell parts, and foreign invaders

TOPIC: Eukaryotic Cells
GO TO: www.scilinks.org
sciLINKS NUMBER: HSTL070

IS THAT A FACT!

Some tadpoles are three years old before they become frogs. The tadpole of the American bullfrog may take as long as 36 months before leaping to adulthood.

74 Chapter 3 • Cells: The Basic Units of Life

Plant or Animal?

How can you tell the difference between a plant cell and an animal cell? They both have a cell membrane, and they both have nuclei, ribosomes, mitochondria, endoplasmic reticula, Golgi complexes, and lysosomes. But plant cells have things that animal cells do not have: a cell wall, chloroplasts, and a large vacuole. You can see the differences between plant and animal cells in **Figure 29.**

Found in Plant and Animal Cells
- Nucleus
- Golgi complex
- Mitochondrion
- Lysosome
- Ribosome
- Cell membrane
- Endoplasmic reticulum

Found Only in Plant Cells
- Chloroplast
- Large vacuole
- Cell wall

Figure 29 *Animal and plant cells have some structures in common, but they also have some that are unique.*

REVIEW

1. How does the nucleus control the cell's activities?
2. Which of the following would not be found in an animal cell: mitochondria, cell wall, chloroplast, ribosome, endoplasmic reticulum, Golgi complex, large vacuole, DNA, chlorophyll?
3. Use the following words in a sentence: oxygen, ATP, breathing, and mitochondria.
4. **Applying Concepts** You have the job of giving new names to different things in a city. The new names have to be parts of a eukaryotic cell. Write down some things you would see in a city. Assign the name of a cell part that is most appropriate to their function. Explain your choices.

internet connect
SCILINKS NSTA
TOPIC: Eukaryotic Cells
GO TO: www.scilinks.org
sciLINKS NUMBER: HSTL070

Chapter Highlights

VOCABULARY DEFINITIONS

SECTION 1

tissue a group of similar cells that work together to perform a specific job in the body

organ a combination of two or more tissues that work together to perform a specific function in the body

organ system a group of organs working together to perform body functions

organism anything that can independently carry out life processes

unicellular made of a single cell

multicellular made of many cells

population a group of individuals of the same species that live together in the same area at the same time

community all of the populations of different species that live and interact in an area

ecosystem a community of organisms and their nonliving environment

SECTION 2

cell membrane a phospholipid layer that covers a cell's surface and acts as a barrier between the inside of a cell and the cell's environment

organelles structures within a cell, sometimes surrounded by a membrane

cytoplasm cellular fluid surrounding a cell's organelles

nucleus membrane-covered organelle found in eukaryotic cells that contains a cell's DNA and serves as a control center for the cell

prokaryotic describes a cell that does not have a nucleus or any other membrane-covered organelles; also called bacteria

eukaryotic describes a cell that has a nucleus

bacteria extremely small single-celled organisms without a nucleus; prokaryotic cells

Chapter Highlights

SECTION 1

Vocabulary
- **tissue** (p. 57)
- **organ** (p. 57)
- **organ system** (p. 58)
- **organism** (p. 59)
- **unicellular** (p. 59)
- **multicellular** (p. 59)
- **population** (p. 59)
- **community** (p. 60)
- **ecosystem** (p. 60)

Section Notes
- The cell is the smallest unit of life on Earth. Organisms can be made up of one or more cells.
- In multicellular organisms, groups of cells can work together to form tissue. Organs are formed from different tissues and work together with other organs in organ systems.
- The same kind of organisms living together in the same place at the same time make up a population. Different populations living together in the same area make up a community. An ecosystem includes the community and an area's nonliving parts, such as the water and soil.

SECTION 2

Vocabulary
- **cell membrane** (p. 63)
- **organelles** (p. 63)
- **cytoplasm** (p. 63)
- **nucleus** (p. 66)
- **prokaryotic** (p. 66)
- **eukaryotic** (p. 66)
- **bacteria** (p. 66)

Section Notes
- The cell theory states that all organisms are made of cells, the cell is the basic unit of life, and all cells come from other cells.
- All cells have a cell membrane, DNA, cytoplasm, and organelles. Most cells are too small to be seen with the naked eye.

✓ Skills Check

Math Concepts

SURFACE-TO-VOLUME RATIO You can determine the surface-to-volume ratio of a cell or other object by dividing surface area by the volume. To determine the surface-to-volume ratio of the rectangle at left, you must first determine the surface area. Surface area is the total area of all the sides. This rectangle has two sides with an area of 6 cm × 3 cm, two sides with an area of 3 cm × 2 cm, and two sides with an area of 6 cm × 2 cm.

surface area = 2(6 cm × 3 cm) + 2(3 cm × 2 cm) + 2(6 cm × 2 cm) = 72 cm^2

Next you need to find the volume. The volume is determined by multiplying the length of the three sides.

volume = 6 cm × 3 cm × 2 cm = 36 cm^3

To find surface-to-volume ratio, you divide the surface area by the volume:

$$\frac{72}{36} = 2$$

So the surface-to-volume ratio of this rectangle is 2:1.

Lab and Activity Highlights

Elephant-Sized Amoebas? PG 694

Name That Part! PG 697

Cells Alive! PG 696

Datasheets for LabBook (blackline masters for these labs)

SECTION 2

- Materials that cells need to take in or release must pass through the cell membrane.
- The surface-to-volume ratio is a comparison of the cell's outer surface to the cell's volume. A cell's surface-to-volume ratio decreases as the cell grows.
- Eukaryotes have linear DNA enclosed in a nucleus and membrane-covered organelles. Prokaryotic cells have circular DNA and organelles that are not covered by membranes.

Labs
Elephant-Sized Amoebas? *(p. 694)*

SECTION 3

Vocabulary
cell wall *(p. 69)*
ribosome *(p. 70)*
endoplasmic reticulum *(p. 70)*
mitochondria *(p. 71)*
chloroplast *(p. 71)*
Golgi complex *(p. 72)*
vesicle *(p. 73)*
vacuole *(p. 73)*
lysosome *(p. 74)*

Section Notes
- All cells have a cell membrane that surrounds the contents of the cell. Some cells have a cell wall outside their membrane.
- The nucleus is the control center of the eukaryotic cell. It contains the cell's DNA.
- Ribosomes are the sites where amino acids are strung together to form proteins. Ribosomes are not covered by a membrane.
- The endoplasmic reticulum (ER) and the Golgi complex are membrane-covered compartments in which materials are made and processed before they are transported to other parts of the cell or out of the cell.
- Mitochondria and chloroplasts are energy-producing organelles.
- Vesicles and vacuoles are membrane-covered compartments that store material. Large, central vacuoles are found in plant cells. Lysosomes are vesicles found in animal cells.

Labs
Cells Alive! *(p. 696)*
Name That Part! *(p. 697)*

VOCABULARY DEFINITIONS, continued

SECTION 3
cell wall a structure that surrounds the cell membrane of some cells and provides strength and support to the cell membrane

ribosome a small organelle in cells where proteins are made from amino acids

endoplasmic reticulum a membrane-covered cell organelle that produces lipids, breaks down drugs and other substances, and packages proteins for delivery out of the cell

mitochondria cell organelles surrounded by two membranes that break down food molecules to make ATP

chloroplast an organelle found in plant and algae cells where photosynthesis occurs

Golgi complex the cell organelle that modifies, packages, and transports materials out of the cell

vesicle a membrane-covered compartment in a eukaryotic cell that forms when part of the cell membrane surrounds an object and pinches off

vacuole a large membrane-covered structure that serves as storage containers for water and other liquids

lysosome a special vesicle in cells that digests food particles, wastes, and foreign invaders

---

internet connect

 GO TO: go.hrw.com

 GO TO: www.scilinks.org

Visit the **HRW** Web site for a variety of learning tools related to this chapter. Just type in the keyword:

KEYWORD: HSTCEL

Visit the **National Science Teachers Association** on-line Web site for Internet resources related to this chapter. Just type in the sciLINKS number for more information about the topic:

TOPIC: Organization of Life   **sciLINKS NUMBER:** HSTL055
TOPIC: Populations, Communities, and Ecosystems   **sciLINKS NUMBER:** HSTL060
TOPIC: Prokaryotic Cells   **sciLINKS NUMBER:** HSTL065
TOPIC: Eukaryotic Cells   **sciLINKS NUMBER:** HSTL070

77

Lab and Activity Highlights

LabBank

 Labs You Can Eat, The Incredible Edible Cell

Whiz-Bang Demonstrations, Grand Strand

 Long-Term Projects & Research Ideas, Ewe Again, Dolly?

 Vocabulary Review Worksheet

 Blackline masters of these Chapter Highlights can be found in the **Study Guide.**

Chapter 3 • Chapter Highlights   **77**

Chapter Review Answers

USING VOCABULARY

1. cellulose
2. eukaryotic
3. nucleus
4. mitochondria/chloroplasts
5. Golgi complex

UNDERSTANDING CONCEPTS

Multiple Choice

6. a
7. b
8. c
9. a
10. c
11. c

Short Answer

12. Cells must be small to have a large surface-to-volume ratio.
13. Mitochondria have a double membrane, possess their own ribosomes, contain circular DNA, divide like bacteria, and are about the same size as bacteria.
14. Answers should paraphrase the following points: all organisms are composed of one or more cells; the cell is the basic unit of life in all living things; all cells come from existing cells.

Concept Mapping Transparency 3

Chapter Review

USING VOCABULARY

To complete the following sentences, choose the correct term from each pair of terms listed below:

1. The cell wall of plant cells is made of __?__. *(lipids* or *cellulose)*
2. Having membrane-covered organelles is a characteristic of __?__ cells. *(prokaryotic* or *eukaryotic)*
3. The information for how to make proteins is located in the __?__. *(Golgi complex* or *nucleus)*
4. The two organelles that can generate ATP in a plant cell are __?__ and __?__. *(chloroplasts/ER* or *mitochondria/chloroplasts)*
5. Vesicles that will transport materials out of the cell are formed at the __?__. *(Golgi complex* or *cell membrane)*

UNDERSTANDING CONCEPTS

Multiple Choice

6. Which of the following is *not* found in animal cells?
   a. cell wall
   b. cell membrane
   c. lysosomes
   d. vesicle

7. Different __?__ work together in an organ.
   a. organ systems
   b. tissues
   c. organisms
   d. prokaryotes

8. Which of the following refers to all of the organisms in a particular area?
   a. population
   b. ecosystem
   c. community
   d. organelles

9. The scientist who said that all cells come from cells was named
   a. Virchow.
   b. Schleiden.
   c. Hooke.
   d. Schwann.

10. Which of the following are *not* covered by a membrane?
    a. Golgi complex
    b. mitochondria
    c. ribosomes
    d. none of the above

11. Which of the following contain enzymes that can break down particles in vesicles?
    a. mitochondria
    b. endoplasmic reticulum
    c. lysosomes
    d. none of the above

Short Answer

12. Why are most cells so small?
13. What five characteristics of mitochondria suggest that they may have originated as bacteria?
14. In your own words, list the three parts of the cell theory.

78 Chapter 3 • Cells: The Basic Units of Life

Concept Mapping

15. Use the following terms to create a concept map: ecosystem, cells, organisms, Golgi complex, organ systems, community, organs, endoplasmic reticulum, nucleus, population, tissues.

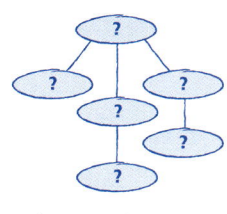

CRITICAL THINKING AND PROBLEM SOLVING

Write one or two sentences to answer the following questions:

16. Explain how the nucleus can control what happens in a lysosome.

17. Even though cellulose is not made at ribosomes, explain how ribosomes in a plant cell are important to the formation of a cell wall.

MATH IN SCIENCE

18. Assume that three food molecules per cubic unit of volume per minute is required for the cell below to survive. If one molecule can enter through each square unit of surface per minute, this cell is
    a. too big and would starve.
    b. too small and would starve.
    c. at a size that would allow it to survive.

INTERPRETING GRAPHICS

Look at the cell diagrams below, and answer the questions that follow:

Cell A

Cell B

19. Name the organelle labeled "19" in Cell A.

20. Is Cell A a bacterial cell, a plant cell, or an animal cell? Explain your answer.

21. What is the name and function of the organelle labeled "21" in Cell B?

22. Is Cell B a prokaryotic cell or a eukaryotic cell? Explain your answer.

 Take a minute to review your answers to the Pre-Reading Questions found at the bottom of page 54. Have your answers changed? If necessary, revise your answers based on what you have learned since you began this chapter.

Concept Mapping

15. 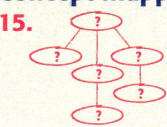 An answer to this exercise can be found at the end of this book.

CRITICAL THINKING AND PROBLEM SOLVING

16. The nucleus controls the production of proteins. The enzymes needed to break down materials in a lysosome are proteins.

17. Enzymes are used to make cellulose, and enzymes are proteins. All proteins are made at ribosomes.

MATH IN SCIENCE

18. a. too big and would starve

INTERPRETING GRAPHICS

19. mitochondrion
20. Animal; it is not a bacteria because it has a nucleus, and it is not a plant because it has no cell wall.
21. vacuole; storage of water and other materials
22. eukaryotic, because it has a nucleus

 Blackline masters of this Chapter Review can be found in the **Study Guide**.

ACROSS THE SCIENCES
Battling Cancer With Pigs' Blood and Laser Light

Background
Students may want to know more about the traditional forms of cancer treatment. Some common therapies are chemotherapy, radiation treatment, and surgery. These are often used in combination to combat a single cancer. Although these treatments are highly effective on many forms of cancer, there are side effects that accompany them. For instance, chemotherapy and radiation treatments are generally toxic to the human body, causing side effects that can even be life threatening. Side effects include nausea, diarrhea, hair loss, organ failure, and bone marrow toxicity. Also, many cancer treatments lower a patient's ability to fight other diseases.

Chemotherapy is usually administered intravenously and is designed to interrupt the growth of cancer cells at different points in their development. For instance, one drug is effective on cancer cells during their division stage, while another attacks the cancer in its growth phase. Radiation treatments use high-energy beams of X rays and gamma rays to destroy cancerous tissues. The radiation impairs the cells' ability to multiply. Unfortunately, many forms of cancer are resistant to these treatments, and doctors continually seek new and better ways to cure cancer.

ACROSS THE SCIENCES

LIFE SCIENCE • PHYSICAL SCIENCE

Battling Cancer with Pigs' Blood and Laser Light

What do you get when you cross pigs' blood and laser beams? Would you believe a treatment for cancer? Medical researchers have developed an effective new cancer treatment called *photodynamic therapy,* or PDT. It combines high-energy laser beams with a light-sensitive drug derived from pigs' blood to combat the deadly disease.

▲ *Blood from pigs provides substances used to help treat cancer.*

Pigs' Blood to the Rescue
The first step in PDT involves a light-sensitive substance called *porphyrin*. Porphyrins are natural chemicals found in red blood cells that bind to lipoproteins, which carry cholesterol in our blood. All cells use lipoproteins in their cell membranes. But cells that divide quickly, like cancer cells, make membranes faster than normal cells. Since they use more lipoproteins, they also accumulate more porphyrins.

Scientists have developed a synthetic porphyrin, called Photofrin®, made from natural porphyrins found in pigs' blood. Photofrin can absorb energy from light. When Photofrin is injected into a patient's bloodstream, it acts the same way natural porphyrins do—it becomes part of the cell membranes formed by cancer cells. A short time later, the patient visits a surgeon's office for step two of PDT, zapping the diseased tissue with a laser beam.

Hitting the Target
A surgeon threads a long, thin laser-tipped tube into the cancerous area where the Photofrin has accumulated. When the laser beam hits the cancerous tissue, Photofrin absorbs the light energy. Then, in a process similar to photosynthesis, Photofrin releases oxygen. The type of oxygen released damages the proteins, lipids, nucleic acids, and other components of cancer cells. This damage kills off cancer cells in the treated area but doesn't kill healthy cells. Photofrin is more sensitive to certain wavelengths of light than are natural porphyrins. And the intense beam of laser light can be precisely focused on the cancerous tissue without affecting nearby healthy tissue.

An Alternative?
PDT is an important medical development because it kills cancer cells without many of the harmful side effects caused by other cancer therapies, such as chemotherapy. However, PDT does have some side effects. Until the drug wears off, in about 30 days, the patient is susceptible to severe sunburn. Researchers are working to develop a second-generation drug, called BPD (benzoporphyrin derivative), that will have fewer side effects and respond to different wavelengths of lasers. BPD is also being tested for use in certain eye diseases and as a treatment for psoriasis.

Find Out for Yourself
▶ Do some research to find out why scientists used pigs' blood to create Photofrin.

Answer to Find Out for Yourself
Researchers used pigs' blood because it is similar to human blood and is available in the large quantities necessary for research.

Health Watch

The Scrape of the Future

What did you do the last time you scraped your knee? You probably put a bandage on it, and before you realized it your knee was as good as new. Bandages serve as barriers that help prevent infection and further injury. But what if there were such a thing as a living bandage that actually helped your body heal? It sounds like science fiction, but it's not!

▲ *Dr. Daniel Smith holds the GEBB that he designed.*

The Main Factor

An injury to the skin, such as a scraped knee, triggers skin cells to produce and release a steady stream of proteins that heal the injury. These naturally occurring proteins are called *human growth factors,* or just *growth factors.* Growth factors specialize in rebuilding the body. Some reconstruct connective tissue that provides structure for new skin, some help rebuild blood vessels in a wounded area, and still others stimulate the body's immune system. Thanks to growth factors, scraped skin usually heals in just a few days.

Help from a Living Bandage

Unfortunately, healing isn't always an easy, natural process. Someone with a weakened immune system may be unable to produce enough growth factors to heal a wound properly. For example, someone with severe burns may have lost the ability in the burned area to produce the proteins necessary to rebuild healthy tissues. In these cases, using manufactured human growth factors can greatly assist the healing process.

Recent advances in bioengineering can help people whose immune system prevents them from healing naturally. The Genetically Engineered Biological Bandage (GEBB) is a special bandage that is actually a bag of living skin cells taken from donors. The cells' DNA is manipulated to produce human growth factors. The GEBB is about 1 cm thick and consists of three layers: a thin gauze layer; a thin, permeable membrane; and a dome-shaped silicone bag containing the growth factors. The bandage is applied to the wound just as a normal bandage is, with the gauze layer closest to the injury. The growth factors leave the silicone bag through the membrane and pass through the gauze into the wound. There they act on the wound just as the body's own growth factors would.

Time-Release Formula

The GEBB also helps heal wounds more quickly. It maximizes the effectiveness of growth hormones by releasing them at a constant rate over 3 to 5 days.

Because the GEBB imitates the body's own healing processes, other versions of the living bandage will likely be used in the future to treat a variety of wounds and skin conditions, such as severe acne.

Think About It

▶ Can you think of other advances in medical technology, such as eyeglasses or a hearing aid, that mimic or enhance what the human body does naturally?

HEALTH WATCH

The Scrape of the Future

Background

Skin is a naturally healing tissue helped by growth factors. Bones, muscles, blood, and many major organs, including the liver and lungs, can also heal and repair major damage with the help of the body's own growth factors. Nerve cells, including those in the spinal cord and brain, are less able to recover from damage.

Scientists are studying how nerves grow and what growth factors are involved in hopes of discovering a way to promote healing in people who suffer from nerve cell damage.

Answers to Think About It

Answers will vary, but there are mechanical voices; artificial muscles; wheelchairs that respond to breath commands; hearing aids; glasses; and artificial hips, hands, legs, and even hearts.

Chapter Organizer

CHAPTER ORGANIZATION	TIME MINUTES	OBJECTIVES	LABS, INVESTIGATIONS, AND DEMONSTRATIONS
Chapter Opener pp. 82–83	45	National Correlations: UCP 3, SAI 1, SPSP 5, LS 1b	**Start-Up Activity** Cells in Action, p. 83
Section 1 Exchange with the Environment	120	▶ Explain the process of diffusion. ▶ Describe how osmosis occurs. ▶ Compare passive transport with active transport. ▶ Explain how large particles get into and out of cells. UCP 1–4, LS 1c; LabBook UCP 2, SAI 1	**QuickLab,** Bead Diffusion, p. 84 `GENERAL` **Demonstration,** Membrane Model, p. 84 in ATE `GENERAL` **Demonstration,** Crossing Membranes, p. 85 in ATE `GENERAL` **Interactive Explorations CD-ROM,** The Nose Knows `GENERAL` A **Worksheet** is also available in the **Interactive Explorations Teacher's Edition.** **Design Your Own,** The Perfect Taters Mystery, p. 698 `GENERAL` **Datasheets for LabBook,** The Perfect Taters Mystery, Datasheet 9 `GENERAL` **Inquiry Labs,** Fish Farms in Space, Lab 2 `GENERAL` **Whiz-Bang Demonstrations,** It's in the Bag! Demo 5 `BASIC`
Section 2 Cell Energy	120	▶ Describe photosynthesis and cellular respiration. ▶ Compare cellular respiration with fermentation. UCP 1, 3–5, SAI 2, ST 2, SPSP 4–5, LS 1c, 4c; LabBook SAI 1, SPSP 1, LS 1c	**Demonstration,** Light Response, p. 88 in ATE `BASIC` **Skill Builder,** Stayin' Alive! p. 700 `BASIC` **Datasheets for LabBook,** Stayin' Alive! Datasheet 10 `BASIC`
Section 3 The Cell Cycle	120	▶ Explain how cells produce more cells. ▶ Discuss the importance of mitosis. ▶ Explain how cell division differs in animals and plants. SAI 1, LS 1c, 2d	**Labs You Can Eat,** The Mystery of the Runny Gelatin, Lab 3 `GENERAL` **Whiz-Bang Demonstration,** Stop Picking on My Enzyme, Demo 4 `BASIC` **Long-Term Projects & Research Ideas,** Project 4 `ADVANCED`

See page T20 for a complete correlation of this book with the **NATIONAL SCIENCE EDUCATION STANDARDS.**

TECHNOLOGY RESOURCES

 Guided Reading Audio CD English or Spanish, Chapter 4

 One-Stop Planner CD-ROM with Test Generator

 CNN Science, Technology & Society, Radioactive Medicine, Segment 5

 Interactive Explorations CD-ROM CD 3, Exploration 1, The Nose Knows

Chapter 4 • The Cell in Action

CLASSROOM WORKSHEETS, TRANSPARENCIES, AND RESOURCES	SCIENCE INTEGRATION AND CONNECTIONS	REVIEW AND ASSESSMENT
Directed Reading Worksheet 4 BASIC **Science Puzzlers, Twisters & Teasers,** Worksheet 4 ADVANCED		
Directed Reading Worksheet 4, Section 1 BASIC **Transparency 11,** Passive and Active Transport **Transparency 12,** Endocytosis **Transparency 12,** Exocytosis **Reinforcement Worksheet 4,** Into and Out of the Cell BASIC	**Math and More,** p. 85 in ATE GENERAL	**Self-Check,** p. 85 **Homework,** p. 86 in ATE GENERAL **Review,** p. 87 GENERAL **Quiz,** p. 87 in ATE GENERAL **Alternative Assessment,** p. 87 in ATE GENERAL
Directed Reading Worksheet 4, Section 2 BASIC **Transparency 243,** Solar Heating Systems **Transparency 13,** Photosynthesis and Respiration: What's the Connection? **Reinforcement Worksheet 4,** Activities of the Cell BASIC **Critical Thinking Worksheet 4,** A Celluloid Thriller ADVANCED	**Connect to Physical Science,** p. 89 in ATE **Connect to Physical Science,** p. 90 in ATE **Apply,** p. 91 GENERAL **Chemistry Connection,** p. 89 **Across the Sciences:** Electrifying News About Microbes, p. 100 ADVANCED	**Homework,** p. 90 in ATE ADVANCED **Review,** p. 91 GENERAL **Quiz,** p. 91 in ATE GENERAL **Alternative Assessment,** p. 91 in ATE GENERAL
Directed Reading Worksheet 4, Section 3 BASIC **Math Skills for Science Worksheet 24,** Creating Exponents GENERAL **Science Skills Worksheet 24,** Using Models to Communicate GENERAL **Transparency 14,** The Cell Cycle: Phases of Mitosis **Reinforcement Worksheet 4,** This Is Radio KCEL BASIC	**MathBreak,** Cell Multiplication, p. 92 GENERAL **Math and More,** p. 93 in ATE GENERAL **Holt Anthology of Science Fiction,** Contagion ADVANCED	**Self-Check,** p. 93 **Homework,** p. 94 in ATE ADVANCED **Review,** p. 95 GENERAL **Quiz,** p. 95 in ATE GENERAL **Alternative Assessment,** p. 95 in ATE ADVANCED

END-OF-CHAPTER REVIEW AND ASSESSMENT

Chapter Review in Study Guide
Vocabulary and Notes in Study Guide
Chapter Tests with Performance-Based Assessment, Chapter 4 Test
Chapter Tests with Performance-Based Assessment, Performance-Based Assessment 4
Concept Mapping Transparency 4

internetconnect

Holt, Rinehart and Winston On-line Resources
go.hrw.com
For worksheets and other teaching aids related to this chapter, visit the HRW Web site and type in the keyword: **HSTACT**

National Science Teachers Association
www.scilinks.org
Encourage students to use the *sci*LINKS numbers listed in the internet connect boxes to access information and resources on the **NSTA** Web site.

Chapter 4 • Chapter Organizer **81B**

Chapter Resources & Worksheets

Visual Resources

TEACHING TRANSPARENCIES

TEACHING TRANSPARENCIES

CONCEPT MAPPING TRANSPARENCY

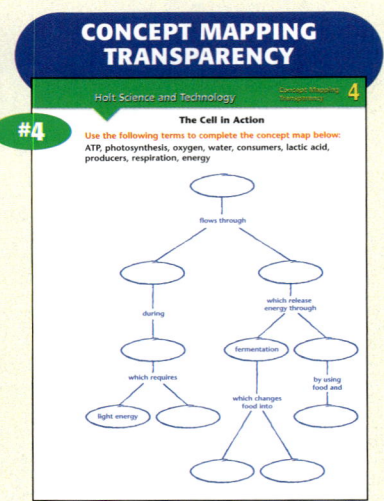

Meeting Individual Needs

DIRECTED READING

REINFORCEMENT & VOCABULARY REVIEW

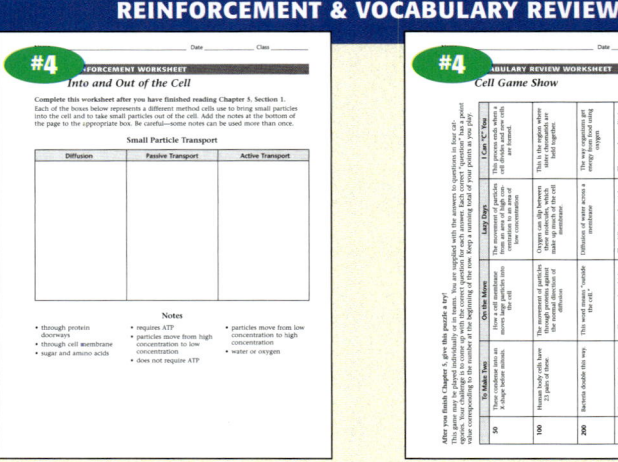

SCIENCE PUZZLERS, TWISTERS & TEASERS

Chapter 4 • The Cell in Action

Review & Assessment

STUDY GUIDE
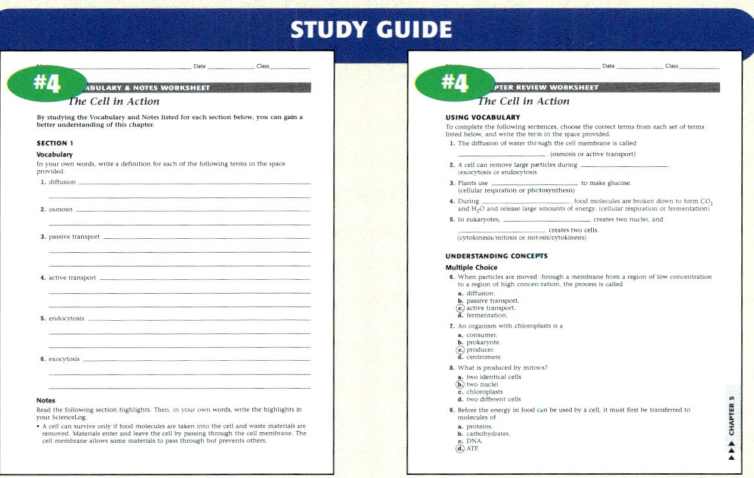

CHAPTER TESTS WITH PERFORMANCE-BASED ASSESSMENT

Lab Worksheets

INQUIRY LABS / LONG-TERM PROJECTS & RESEARCH IDEAS

LABS YOU CAN EAT

WHIZ-BANG DEMONSTRATIONS

DATASHEETS FOR LABBOOK
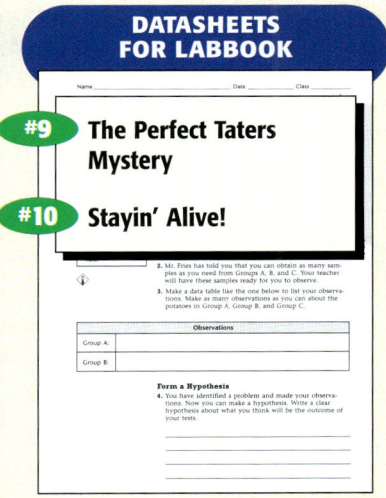

Applications & Extensions

CRITICAL THINKING & PROBLEM SOLVING

SCIENCE TECHNOLOGY

INTERACTIVE EXPLORATIONS

Chapter 4 • Chapter Resources & Worksheets

Chapter Background

SECTION 1

Exchange with the Environment

▶ **Endocytosis**
There are three different mechanisms of endocytosis: pinocytosis, phagocytosis, and receptor-mediated endocytosis. These processes allow a substance to enter a cell without passing through the cell membrane. The type of material involved determines which method is used.

- Large particles such as bacteria enter the cell by phagocytosis. The host cell changes shape, and the membrane sends out projections called pseudopods, meaning "false feet," which surround the particle, bringing it inside the cell.

- In receptor-mediated endocytosis, receptors on the membrane that are specific for a given substance bind to the substance before the endocytotic process begins. This method is used during cholesterol metabolism.

- In pinocytosis, the cell membrane surrounds the substance and forms a vesicle to bring the material into the cell. Pinocytosis usually involves material that is dissolved in water.

▶ **Reverse Osmosis**
Reverse osmosis is a process that forces water across semipermeable membranes under high pressure. The high pressure reverses the natural tendency of the solutes on the concentrated side of the membrane to pass through to the less-concentrated side. In this way water passing through the membrane is purified.

IS THAT A FACT!

▶ The largest single-celled organism that ever lived was a protozoa that measured 20 cm in diameter. It is now extinct.

SECTION 2

Cell Energy

▶ **Jan Baptista van Helmont (1580–1644)**
Van Helmont was a Belgian chemist, physiologist, and physician who coined the word *gas*. He was the first scientist to comprehend the existence of gases separate from the atmospheric air. Although he didn't know that it was carbon dioxide, van Helmont stated that the *spiritus sylvestre,* or "wild spirit," emitted by burning charcoal was the same as that given off by fermenting grape juice. He applied chemistry to the study of physiological processes, and for this he is known as the "father of biochemistry."

- Joseph Priestly (1733–1804) was an English clergyman and physical scientist who was one of the discoverers of oxygen. He also observed that light was vital for plant growth and that green leaves released oxygen.

- Jan Ingenhousz (1730–1799), a Dutch-born British physician and scientist, discovered photosynthesis.

▶ **Carotenoids and Photosynthesis**
Carotenoids are responsible for the orange colors in plants. Their presence is usually masked by chlorophyll. They are sensitive to wavelengths of light to which chlorophyll cannot respond. Carotenoids can absorb the light waves and transfer the energy to chlorophyll, which then incorporates that energy into the photosynthetic pathway.

Chapter 4 • The Cell in Action

IS THAT A FACT!

- Cellular respiration was discovered in 1937 by German biochemist Hans Krebs (1900–1981). The Krebs cycle is a series of chemical reactions that are essential to metabolic activities in all living organisms.

SECTION 3

The Cell Cycle

▶ Cytogenetics

Cytogeneticists study the role of human chromosomes in health and disease. Chromosome studies can reveal abnormalities such as whether a person is carrying the genetic material for a genetically linked disease.

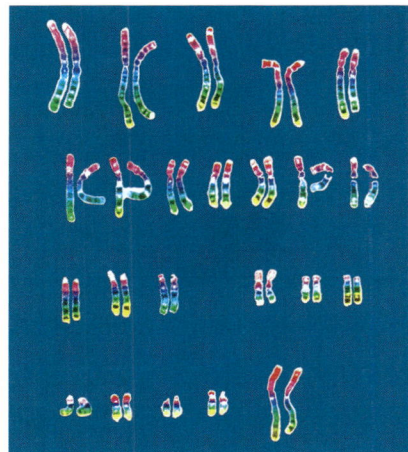

▶ Cell Division

The frequency of cell division varies a great deal. Fruit-fly embryo cells divide about every 8 minutes. Human liver cells may not divide for up to 1 year. Scientists are still trying to determine what orchestrates growth and regulates cell division. This information would help scientists understand diseases of unregulated cell division, such as cancer.

IS THAT A FACT!

- Cell division occurs at least 10 million times every second in an adult human body.

- DNA and chromosomes are related but are not the same thing. A chromosome is made up of DNA that has been wound up and organized with proteins that hold it all together. For much of the cell cycle, DNA is loose and not very visible.

▶ Cell Adhesion

Blood cells exist individually in the body, but most other cells are connected to each other. Usually this involves special adhesion proteins, such as adherins, cadherins, catenins, and integrins. These proteins connect adjoining cells by physically locking the cells together, fastening one cell to the next. Sometimes these junctions are outside the cell, and sometimes they are inside. Adherence proteins can span the cell membranes and connect the inside of one cell to the inside of its neighbor cell.

IS THAT A FACT!

- In a healthy body, cells reproduce at exactly the same rate at which they die. However, some agents make cells reproduce uncontrollably, causing a disease known as cancer. One of these carcinogenic agents is ultraviolet radiation, which is emitted by the sun and ultraviolet lamps. People who spend excessive amounts of time in the sun run the risk of developing skin cancer.

For background information about teaching strategies and issues, refer to the *Professional Reference for Teachers*.

Chapter 4

The Cell in Action

 Pre-Reading Questions

Students may not know the answers to these questions before reading the chapter, so accept any reasonable response.

Suggested Answers

1. Answers will vary but should reflect knowledge of diffusion, osmosis, endocytosis, active transport, and exocytosis.
2. Cells use food to make energy through respiration and fermentation.
3. Eukaryotic cells divide using mitosis and cytokinesis. Prokaryotic cells divide by binary fission. Every division doubles the number of cells.

 Directed Reading Worksheet 4

 Science Puzzlers, Twisters & Teasers Worksheet 4

 Guided Reading Audio CD
English or Spanish, Chapter 4

Chapter 4
The Cell in Action

Sections

1. **Exchange with the Environment** 84
   - QuickLab 84
   - Internet Connect 87
2. **Cell Energy** 88
   - Chemistry Connection.. 89
   - Apply............ 91
   - Internet Connect 91
3. **The Cell Cycle**........ 92
   - MathBreak 92
   - Internet Connect..... 95

   Chapter Review.......... 98
   Feature Articles 100, 101
   LabBook 698–701

1. How do water, food, and wastes get into and out of a cell?
2. How do cells use food molecules?
3. How does one cell produce many cells?

A Copier Machine

These cells are from the growing tip of a plant root. In order to grow, the plant is producing many new cells. When plant cells divide, the cell copies its genetic material. The cell then undergoes mitosis. Mitosis is the process that ensures that each new cell ends up with the correct complement of chromosomes. All the different stages of mitosis can be seen in this tissue.

 HRW On-line Resources
go.hrw.com
For worksheets and other teaching aids, visit the HRW Web site and type in the keyword: **HSTACT**

 www.scilinks.com
Use the *sci*LINKS numbers at the end of each chapter for additional resources on the **NSTA** Web site.

 www.cnnfyi.com
Visit the CNN Web site for current events coverage and classroom resources.

START-UP Activity

CELLS IN ACTION

Yeasts are fungi that are used in baking. Yeast cells break down sugar molecules to release energy. In the process, a gas called carbon dioxide (CO_2) is produced. Bubbles of CO_2 cause the bread dough to rise. The amount of CO_2 produced depends on how much sugar is broken down.

Procedure

1. Pour **4 mL of a sugar solution** into **a cup** that contains **10 mL** of a **yeast-and-water mixture.** Mix the two liquids with a **stirring rod.**
2. Pour the contents into a **small test tube.**
3. Place a slightly **larger test tube** over the small test tube. The top of the small test tube should touch the bottom of the larger test tube. Quickly turn both test tubes over. Use a **ruler** to measure the height of the fluid in the large test tube.
4. Place the test tubes in a **test-tube rack** and do not disturb them. After 20 minutes, measure the height of the liquid in the larger test tube again.

Analysis

5. What is the difference between the first height measurement and the second?
6. What do you think caused the change in the height of the fluid?

START-UP Activity

CELLS IN ACTION

MATERIALS
FOR EACH STUDENT: • small plastic cup • yeast-and-water mixture • small plastic test tube • sugar solution • stirring rod • large plastic test tube • test-tube rack • ruler

Safety Caution

Remind students to review all safety cautions and icons before beginning this lab activity. Students should wear safety goggles at all times and wash their hands when they are finished. Students should not taste the solutions.

Teacher's Notes

The yeast suspension is prepared by mixing one package of dry yeast in 250 mL of water. The sugar solution is prepared by dissolving 30 mL (2 tbsp) of sugar in 100 mL of water. Some students can put their vials on ice and others can put them in a warm place, and others can leave them in a warm place overnight. In this way, students can see how temperature can affect the metabolism of yeast cells.

Answers to START-UP Activity

5. Answers will vary. Students should subtract the first measurement from the second measurement.
6. When the yeast cells released the energy in sugar, the CO_2 that the cells produced increased the volume of air in the smaller tube and pushed more yeast-and-sugar mixture into the larger tube, increasing the height of the liquid in the larger tube.

SECTION 1

Focus

Exchange with the Environment

This section explains the processes involved in the exchange of materials between a cell and its environment. Students will learn about diffusion and osmosis, which is the diffusion of water across the cell membrane. Finally, students will compare and contrast active and passive transport and learn how large particles move into and out of cells.

Write the following on the board or the overhead projector:

Which of the following best describes a living cell:

a. a building block
b. a living organism
c. a complex factory
d. all of the above

Have students write a paragraph in their ScienceLog defending their choice.

1) Motivate

DEMONSTRATION

Membrane Model Blow soap bubbles in front of the class. Explain that soap bubbles have several properties that are similar to biological membranes. One property is flexibility. The components of soap film and the cell membrane move around freely. Both soap bubbles and membranes are self-sealing. If two bubbles or membranes collide, they fuse. If one is cut in half, two smaller but whole bubbles or membranes form.

Sheltered English

Section 1

Terms to Learn

diffusion   active transport
osmosis   endocytosis
passive transport exocytosis

What You'll Do

- Explain the process of diffusion.
- Describe how osmosis occurs.
- Compare passive transport with active transport.
- Explain how large particles get into and out of cells.

QuickLab

Bead Diffusion

Arrange three groups of **colored beads** on the bottom of a **plastic bowl.** Each group should have five beads of the same color. Stretch some **clear plastic wrap** tightly over the top of the bowl. Gently shake the bowl for 10 seconds while watching the beads. How is the scattering of the beads like the diffusion of particles? How is it different from the diffusion of particles?

QuickLab

MATERIALS

FOR EACH GROUP:
- three groups of colored beads
- plastic bowl
- clear plastic wrap

Exchange with the Environment

What would happen to a factory if its power were shut off or its supply of raw materials never arrived? What if it couldn't get rid of its garbage? The factory would stop functioning. Like a factory, a cell must be able to obtain energy and raw materials and get rid of wastes.

The exchange of materials between a cell and its environment takes place at the cell's membrane. To understand how materials move into and out of the cell, you need to know about diffusion, a process that affects the movement of particles.

What Is Diffusion?

What happens if you pour dye into a container of solid gelatin? At first, it is easy to see where the gelatin ends and the dye begins. But over time the line between the two layers will become blurry, as shown in **Figure 1.** Why? Dye and gelatin, like all matter, are made up of tiny particles. The particles are always moving and colliding with each other. The mixing of the different particles causes the layers to blur. This occurs whether matter is in the form of a gas, liquid, or solid.

Figure 1 *The particles of the dye and the gelatin slowly begin to mix because of diffusion.*

Particles naturally travel from areas where they are crowded to areas where they are less crowded. **Diffusion** is the movement of particles from an area where their concentration is high to an area where their concentration is low. This movement can occur across cell membranes or outside of cells. Cells do not need to use any energy for diffusion of particles to occur.

Answers to QuickLab

The beads moved from areas where the colors were more concentrated to areas where they were less concentrated. Eventually, the different-colored beads were mixed somewhat evenly. The mixing of the beads required the use of the students' energy and also occurred much more quickly than diffusion normally occurs.

Diffusion of Water All organisms need water to live. The cells of living organisms are surrounded by and filled with fluids that are made mostly of water. The diffusion of water through the cell membrane is so important to life processes that it has been given a special name—**osmosis**.

Water, like all matter, is made up of small particles. Pure water has the highest possible concentration of water particles. To lower this concentration, you simply mix water with something else, such as food coloring, sugar, or salt. **Figure 2** shows what happens when osmosis occurs between two different concentrations of water.

Figure 2 This container is divided by a barrier. Particles of water are small enough to pass through the barrier, but the particles of food coloring are not.

1. The side of the container with pure water has the higher concentration of water.
2. During osmosis, water particles move to where they are less concentrated.

The Cell and Osmosis As you have learned, water particles will move from areas of high concentration to areas of lower concentration. This concept is especially important when you look at it in relation to your cells.

For example, **Figure 3** shows the effects of different concentrations of water on a red blood cell. As you can see, osmosis takes place in different directions depending on the concentration of water surrounding the cell. Fortunately for you, your red blood cells are normally surrounded by blood plasma, which is made up of water, salts, sugars, and other particles in the same concentration as they exist inside the red blood cells.

The cells of plants also take in and release water by osmosis. This is why a wilted plant or even a wilted stalk of celery will become firm again if given water.

This cell has a normal shape because the concentration of water in the cell is the same as the concentration outside the cell.

This cell is in pure water. It is gaining water because the concentration of water particles is lower inside the cell than outside.

Figure 3 The shape of these red blood cells is affected by the concentration of water outside the cell.

✓ Self-Check

What would happen to a grape if you placed it in a dish of pure water? in water mixed with a large amount of sugar? *(See page 782 to check your answer.)*

2) Teach

MATH and MORE

Gases diffuse approximately 10,000 times faster in air than in water. If a gas diffuses to fill a room completely in 6 minutes, how long would it take the gas to fill a similar volume of still water? **(60,000 minutes)** How many hours would that be? **(1,000 hours)** How many days? **(41.67 days)**

DEMONSTRATION

Crossing Membranes

MATERIALS
• plastic sandwich bag
• twist tie
• tincture of iodine
• cornstarch
• 500 mL beakers (2)
• eyedropper
• graduated cylinder

Fill one beaker with 250 mL of water. Add 20 drops of iodine. Fill a second beaker with 250 mL water, and stir in 15 mL (1 tbsp) of cornstarch. Pour one-half of the starch-and-water mixture into the plastic bag. Secure the top of the bag with the twist tie. If any starch-and-water mixture spills onto the outside of the bag, rinse it off. Place the bag in the iodine-water mixture. Check immediately for any changes. Look again after 30 minutes. Iodine is used to test for the presence of starch and will turn the starch-and-water mixture black. The iodine particles are small enough to move through the tiny holes in the plastic bag, but the starch molecules are too large. **Sheltered English**

Directed Reading Worksheet 4 Section 1

---

internetconnect

TOPIC: Osmosis
GO TO: www.scilinks.org
sciLINKS NUMBER: HSTL075

Answers to Self-Check

In pure water, the grape would absorb water and swell up. In water mixed with a large amount of sugar, the grape would lose water and shrink.

Section 1 • Exchange with the Environment

2) Teach, continued

The Perfect Taters Mystery — PG 698

ACTIVITY

Odor Diffusion One day prior to doing this activity, prepare the following:

MATERIALS

FOR EACH GROUP:
- small container with tight-fitting lid (one per pair of students)
- cotton ball for each container
- several strong-smelling liquids, such as vanilla, garlic oil, and eucalyptus

Soak a cotton ball in one of the liquids. Place the cotton ball in a container, and cover the container with a lid. Repeat until all containers have a soaked cotton ball.

Ask students if they can detect what is inside. If not, instruct students how to safely investigate the odors in the bottle. Have them hold the container 30 cm in front of their face and waft the air above the container toward their nose. Instruct them never to sniff directly from a container. Tell them to remove the lids, and ask them what they smell.

Explain that the cotton balls were soaked in aromatic fluids and that those fluids vaporized and diffused from the area of greatest concentration (the cotton ball) and moved to the area of lesser concentration (the air). **Sheltered English**

Teaching Transparency 11 "Passive and Active Transport"

Help solve The Perfect Taters Mystery on page 698 of the LabBook!

Moving Small Particles

Many particles, such as water and oxygen, can diffuse directly through the cell membrane, which is made of phospholipid molecules. These particles can slip through the molecules of the membrane in part because of their small size. However, not all of the particles a cell needs can pass through the membrane in this way. For example, sugar and amino acids aren't small enough to squeeze between the phospholipid molecules, and they are also repelled by the phospholipids in the membrane. They must travel through protein "doorways" located in the cell membrane in order to enter or leave the cell.

Particles can travel through these proteins either by passive transport or by active transport. **Passive transport,** shown in **Figure 4,** is the diffusion of particles through the proteins. The particles move from an area of high concentration to an area of low concentration. The cell does not need to use any energy to make this happen.

Active transport, shown in **Figure 5,** is the movement of particles through proteins against the normal direction of diffusion. In other words, particles are moved from an area of low concentration to an area of high concentration. The cell must use energy to make this happen. This energy comes from the molecule ATP, which stores energy in a form that cells can use.

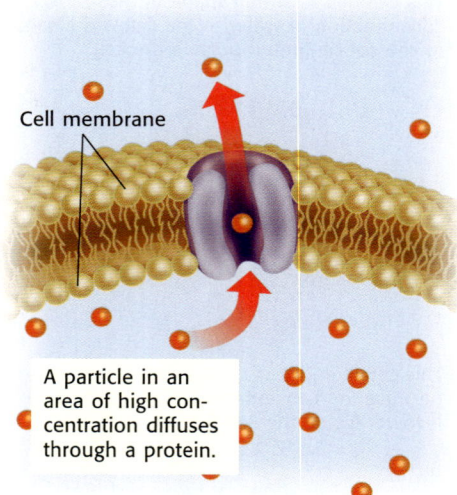

Figure 4 In passive transport, particles travel through proteins from areas of high concentration to areas of low concentration.

Figure 5 In active transport, cells use energy to move particles from areas of low concentration to areas of high concentration.

Homework

Writing Ask students to describe how each of the following materials would get through a cell membrane and into a cell. Which of the materials require active transport?

a. pure water
b. sugar entering a cell that already contains a high concentration of particles
c. sugar entering a cell that has a low concentration of particles
d. a large protein

(b, d)

Moving Large Particles

Diffusion, passive transport, and active transport are good methods of moving small particles into and out of cells, but what about moving large particles? The cell membrane has two ways of accomplishing this task: *endocytosis* and *exocytosis*.

Endocytosis In **endocytosis**, the cell membrane surrounds a particle and encloses it in a vesicle. This is how large particles, such as other cells, can be brought into a cell, as shown in **Figure 6**.

❶ The cell comes into contact with a particle.
❷ The cell membrane begins to wrap around the particle.
❸ Once the particle is completely surrounded, a vesicle pinches off.

Figure 6 Endocytosis *means "within the cell."*

Exocytosis When a large particle must be removed from the cell, the cell uses a different process. In **exocytosis**, vesicles are formed at the endoplasmic reticulum or Golgi complex and carry the particles to the cell membrane, as shown in **Figure 7**.

❶ Large particles that must leave the cell are packaged in vesicles.
❷ The vesicle travels to the cell membrane and fuses with it.
❸ The cell releases the particles into its environment.

Figure 7 Exocytosis *means "outside the cell."*

REVIEW

1. During diffusion, how do particles move?
2. How does a cell take in large particles? How does a cell expel large particles?
3. **Making Inferences** The transfer of glucose into a cell does not require ATP. What type of transport supplies a cell with glucose? Explain your answer.

internet connect
sciLINKS NSTA
TOPIC: Osmosis
GO TO: www.scilinks.org
sciLINKS NUMBER: HSTL075

3 Extend

RESEARCH

Writing — Have students write a brief biography of Albert Claude (1898–1983), who used the electron microscope to study cells. (He shared the 1974 Nobel Prize for physiology or medicine with his student George Palade and with Christian de Duve.)

4 Close

Quiz

1. What part of the cell do materials pass through to get into and out of the cell? (the cell membrane)
2. What is osmosis? (the diffusion of water through the cell membrane)

ALTERNATIVE ASSESSMENT

Writing — Have students write an instruction manual that tells a cell how to transport both a large molecule and a small molecule through the cell membrane.

 Teaching Transparency 12 "Endocytosis" "Exocytosis"

 Reinforcement Worksheet 4 "Into and Out of the Cell"

 Interactive Explorations CD-ROM "The Nose Knows"

Answers to Review

1. During diffusion, particles move from areas of high concentration to areas of low concentration.
2. Large particles are taken in by endocytosis and expelled by exocytosis.
3. Passive transport supplies a cell with glucose. Passive transport doesn't require the use of energy. Inform students who have trouble answering the question that glucose is a type of sugar.

Section 1 • Exchange with the Environment

SECTION 2

Focus

Cell Energy

This section introduces energy and the cell. Students learn about solar energy and the process of photosynthesis. Finally, students learn about cellular respiration and fermentation.

Ask students to make a list in their ScienceLog of all the reasons why a cell might need energy. Remind students that there are many types of cells doing many different jobs.

1 Motivate

DEMONSTRATION

Light Response Cut out a square from black construction paper. Fold the square over a plant leaf of a common houseplant, such as a geranium. Affix the square with a paper clip. Be sure the leaf does not receive any sunlight. Leave the leaf covered for about 1 week. Remove the black square. The leaf will be much paler than the other leaves. In the absence of sunlight, chlorophyll is depleted and not replenished. Thus, the leaf's green color will have faded. **Sheltered English**

Directed Reading Worksheet 4 Section 2

Section 2

Terms to Learn

photosynthesis
cellular respiration
fermentation

What You'll Do

- Describe photosynthesis and cellular respiration.
- Compare cellular respiration with fermentation.

Cell Energy

Why do you get hungry? Feeling hungry is your body's way of telling you that your cells need energy. Your cells and the cells of all organisms use energy to carry out the chemical activities that allow them to live, grow, and reproduce.

From Sun to Cell

Nearly all of the energy that fuels life comes from the sun. Plants are able to capture light energy from the sun and change it into food through a process called **photosynthesis.** The food that plants make supplies them with energy and also becomes a source of energy for the organisms that eat the plants. Without plants and other producers, consumers would not be able to live.

Photosynthesis Plants have molecules in their cells that absorb the energy of light. These molecules are called *pigments.* Chlorophyll, the main pigment used in photosynthesis, gives plants their green color. In the cells of plants, chlorophyll is found in chloroplasts, which are shown in **Figure 8.**

Plants use the energy captured by chlorophyll to change carbon dioxide (CO_2) and water (H_2O) into food, the simple sugar glucose ($C_6H_{12}O_6$). Glucose is a carbohydrate. When plants make glucose, they are converting the sun's energy into a form of energy that can be stored. The energy in glucose is used by the plant's cells, and some of it may be stored in the form of other carbohydrates or lipids. Photosynthesis also produces oxygen (O_2). Photosynthesis can be summarized by the following equation:

Plant Cell

Chloroplast

$$6CO_2 + 6H_2O + \text{light energy} \rightarrow C_6H_{12}O_6 + 6O_2$$

Carbon dioxide — Water — Glucose — Oxygen

Figure 8 *During photosynthesis, plant cells use the energy in sunlight to make food (glucose) from carbon dioxide and water. Photosynthesis takes place in chloroplasts.*

MISCONCEPTION ALERT

The processes of photosynthesis and respiration involve many chemical reactions. The equations shown for respiration and photosynthesis in this chapter are the *net* equations for those reactions.

88   Chapter 4 • The Cell in Action

Getting Energy from Food

The food you eat has to be broken down so that the energy it contains can be converted into a form your cells can use. In fact, all organisms must break down food molecules in order to release the stored energy. There are two ways to do this. One way uses oxygen and is called **cellular respiration.** The other way does not use oxygen and is called **fermentation.**

Cellular Respiration The word *respiration* means "breathing," but cellular respiration is not the same thing as breathing. Breathing supplies your cells with the oxygen they need to perform cellular respiration. Breathing also rids your body of carbon dioxide, which is a waste product of cellular respiration.

Most organisms, such as the cow in **Figure 9,** use cellular respiration to obtain energy from food. During cellular respiration, food (glucose) is broken down into CO_2 and H_2O, and energy is released. A lot of the energy is stored in the form of ATP. ATP is the molecule that supplies energy to fuel the activities of cells. Most of the energy released, however, is in the form of heat. In some organisms, including yourself, this heat helps to maintain the body's temperature.

In the cells of eukaryotes, cellular respiration takes place in mitochondria. The process of cellular respiration is summarized in the equation below. Does this equation remind you of the equation for photosynthesis? The diagram on the next page shows how photosynthesis and respiration are related.

Chemistry CONNECTION

When the Earth was young, its atmosphere lacked oxygen. The first forms of life used fermentation to gain energy. After organisms evolved the ability to photosynthesize, about 3 billion years ago, the oxygen they produced was added to the atmosphere.

$$C_6H_{12}O_6 + 6O_2 \rightarrow 6CO_2 + 6H_2O + \text{energy (ATP)}$$

Glucose — Oxygen — Carbon dioxide — Water

Animal Cell — Mitochondria

Figure 9 The mitochondria in the cells of this cow will use cellular respiration to release the energy stored in the grass.

Q: How do cells communicate with each other?

A: by cellular phone

---

2) Teach

GROUP ACTIVITY

Writing Divide the class into groups of three or four. Have each group write the story of a carbon atom as it is used throughout time. Stories should begin with a molecule of carbon dioxide. What plant uses it for photosynthesis? What animals swallow it and use it to fuel respiration? Have students share their stories if time allows.

 PG 700

Stayin' Alive!

CONNECT TO PHYSICAL SCIENCE

Conventional solar heating is a much simpler process than photosynthesis. The sun's energy heats either the house itself, or it heats water, which then circulates through the house. If students have ever felt the warm water from a hose that has been left in the sun, they have felt stored solar energy. Use Teaching Transparency 243 to illustrate how solar energy can be used to heat a home.

 Teaching Transparency 243 "Solar Heating Systems"

TOPIC: Cell Energy
GO TO: www.scilinks.org
sciLINKS NUMBER: HSTL080

Section 2 • Cell Energy

2) Teach, continued

USING THE FIGURE

Refer students to the diagram on this page. Ask students to answer the following questions: What happens to the ATP? Where does the ATP go? How is ATP used by the cell? How is the cell's use of CO_2 and H_2O analogous to people's recycling of paper and glass bottles?

CONNECT TO PHYSICAL SCIENCE

Scientists have developed new solar cells that simulate photosynthesis more closely than traditional solar cells do. Just as plant cells use energy from the sun to change water and carbon dioxide into energy-rich sugars, these new solar cells use the sun's energy to convert water into energy-rich hydrogen gas, which can be used as fuel. As in plants, the byproduct of this process is clean oxygen.

Teaching Transparency 13
"Photosynthesis and Respiration: What's the Connection?"

Reinforcement Worksheet 4
"Activities of the Cell"

Critical Thinking Worksheet 4
"A Celluloid Thriller"

Photosynthesis and Respiration: What's the Connection?

Photosynthesis
Light energy, carbon dioxide, and water are used to make glucose in chloroplasts. Oxygen is released.

Light Energy

$CO_2 + H_2O$

Chloroplast

Mitochondrion

$C_6H_{12}O_6 + O_2$

ATP

Cellular Respiration
Oxygen and the energy in glucose are used to make ATP. ATP is a molecule that stores energy in a form that cells can use. ATP is produced by mitochondria. Carbon dioxide and water are also released. Cellular respiration occurs in both plant and animal cells.

internet connect
TOPIC: Photosynthesis
GO TO: www.scilinks.org
sciLINKS NUMBER: HSTL085

Homework

Comparing Cell Processes Have students compare and contrast photosynthesis and respiration. Ask students to use diagrams to display their comparisons. Encourage students to share their diagrams with their classmates.

90 Chapter 4 • The Cell in Action

Fermentation Have you ever run so far that you started to feel a burning sensation in your muscles? Well, sometimes your muscle cells can't get the oxygen they need to produce ATP by cellular respiration. When this happens, they use the process of fermentation. Fermentation leads to the production of a small amount of ATP and products from the partial breakdown of glucose.

There are two major types of fermentation. The first type occurs in your muscles. It produces lactic acid, which contributes to muscle fatigue after strenuous activity. This type of fermentation also occurs in the muscle cells of other animals and in some types of fungi and bacteria. The second type of fermentation occurs in certain types of bacteria and in yeast. This type of fermentation is described in **Figure 10**.

Figure 10 Yeast cells make carbon dioxide and alcohol during the fermentation of sugar. The carbon dioxide causes bubbles to form in bread.

Fantasy Island

You have been given the assignment of restoring life to a barren island. What types of organisms would you put on the island? If you want to have animals on the island, what other organisms must be on the island as well? Explain your answer.

REVIEW

1. Why are producers important to the survival of all other organisms?
2. How do the processes of photosynthesis and cellular respiration relate to each other?
3. What does breathing have to do with cellular respiration?
4. How are respiration and fermentation similar? How are they different?
5. **Identifying Relationships** In which cells would you expect to find the greater number of mitochondria: cells that are very active or cells that are not very active? Why?

internet connect

SC_**i**_**LINKS**
NSTA

TOPIC: Cell Energy, Photosynthesis
GO TO: www.scilinks.org
sciLINKS NUMBER: HSTL080, HSTL085

---

3) Extend

GOING FURTHER

Tell students that plants are often referred to as the "lungs of the Earth." Ask students to reflect on this idea and to prepare a presentation for the class. Suggest that students research rain forests as an example of Earth's "lungs" and explain their contribution to the health of the planet.

Answer to APPLY

Answers will vary. Plants must be on the island in order to provide a source of food and energy for the animals.

4) Close

Quiz

Ask students whether the following statements are true or false.

1. Plants and animals capture their energy from the sun. (false)
2. Cellular respiration describes how a cell breathes. (false)
3. Fermentation produces ATP and lactic acid. (true)

ALTERNATIVE ASSESSMENT

Concept Mapping Have students draw a concept map of energy transfer using the following images:

sunshine; tree, for firewood; sugar cane; yeast consuming sugar, making bread rise; person chopping firewood, for baking oven; person eating bread

Students should note on their map which organisms use photosynthesis, which use respiration, and which use fermentation. **Sheltered English**

Answers to Review

1. Producers harness energy in sunlight to produce food (glucose). This food becomes an energy source for producers and for the organisms that consume them.
2. Photosynthesis uses light energy, carbon dioxide, and water to produce glucose and oxygen. Respiration uses the products of photosynthesis to make ATP, carbon dioxide, and water.
3. Breathing supplies the oxygen that cells need for cellular respiration.
4. Both processes release the energy stored in food. Respiration requires oxygen, but fermentation does not.
5. Active cells would have more mitochondria because they have a greater need for energy.

SECTION 3

Focus

The Cell Cycle

This section introduces the life cycle of a cell. Students will learn how cells reproduce and the importance of mitosis. Finally, students will learn how cell division differs in plants and animals.

 Bellringer

On the board or an overhead projector, write the following:

> Biology is the only science in which multiplication means the same thing as division.

Have students explain this sentence in their ScienceLog. *(When cells divide, they are multiplying.)*

Answer to MATHBREAK

After 24 hours, 16 cells will have formed from Cell A, and 8 cells will have formed from Cell B. Cell A will have formed 8 more cells than Cell B.

1) Motivate

ACTIVITY

Making Models Have pairs of students use string for the cell membrane and pieces of pipe cleaners for chromosomes to demonstrate the basic steps of mitosis, as described in this section. Sheltered English

 Directed Reading Worksheet 4 Section 3

Section 3

Terms to Learn

cell cycle
chromosome
binary fission
homologous chromosomes
chromatids
centromere
mitosis
cytokinesis

What You'll Do

◆ Explain how cells produce more cells.
◆ Discuss the importance of mitosis.
◆ Explain how cell division differs in animals and plants.

MATH BREAK

Cell Multiplication

It takes Cell A 6 hours to complete its cell cycle and produce two cells. The cell cycle of Cell B takes 8 hours. How many more cells would be formed from Cell A than from Cell B in 24 hours?

The Cell Cycle

In the time that it takes you to read this sentence, your body will have produced millions of new cells! Producing new cells allows you to grow and replace cells that have died. For example, the environment in your stomach is so acidic that the cells lining it must be replaced every few days!

The Life of a Cell

As you grow, you pass through different stages in life. Similarly, your cells pass through different stages in their life cycle. The life cycle of a cell is known as the **cell cycle.**

The cell cycle begins when the cell is formed and ends when the cell divides and forms new cells. Before a cell divides, it must make a copy of its DNA. DNA contains the information that tells a cell how to make proteins. The DNA of a cell is organized into structures called **chromosomes.** In some organisms, chromosomes also contain protein. Copying chromosomes ensures that each new cell will be able to survive.

How does a cell make more cells? Well, that depends on whether the cell is prokaryotic or eukaryotic.

Making More Prokaryotic Cells Prokaryotic cells (bacteria) and their DNA are not very complex. Bacteria have ribosomes and a single, circular molecule of DNA, but they don't have any membrane-covered organelles. Because of this, cell division in bacteria is fairly simple. It is called **binary fission,** which means "splitting into two parts." Each of the resulting cells contains one copy of the DNA. Some of the bacteria in **Figure 11** are undergoing binary fission.

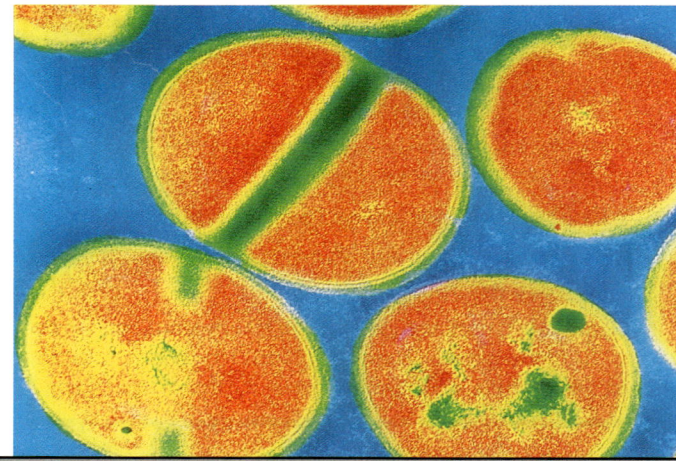

Figure 11 Bacteria reproduce by pinching in two.

---

internet connect

TOPIC: Microbes
GO TO: www.scilinks.org
sciLINKS NUMBER: HSTL095

IS THAT A FACT!

Before sophisticated microscopes were available, scientists could not see cells pinching and dividing. Many believed that cells came into existence spontaneously—as though crystallizing out of bodily fluids.

---

92 Chapter 4 • The Cell in Action

Eukaryotic Cells and Their DNA Eukaryotic cells are usually much larger and more complex than prokaryotic cells. Because of this, eukaryotic cells have a lot more DNA. The chromosomes of eukaryotes contain DNA and proteins.

The number of chromosomes in the cells of eukaryotes differs from one kind of organism to the next and has nothing to do with the complexity of an organism. For example, fruit flies have 8 chromosomes, potatoes have 48, and humans have 46. **Figure 12** shows the 46 chromosomes of a human body cell lined up in pairs. These pairs are made up of similar chromosomes known as **homologous** (hoh MAHL uh guhs) **chromosomes.**

Making More Eukaryotic Cells The eukaryotic cell cycle includes three main stages. In the first stage, the cell grows and copies its organelles and chromosomes. During this time, the strands of DNA and proteins are like loosely coiled pieces of thread. After each chromosome is duplicated, the two copies are called **chromatids.** Chromatids are held together at a region called the **centromere.** The chromatids each twist and coil and condense into an X shape, as shown in **Figure 13.** After this happens, the cell enters the second stage of the cell cycle.

In the second stage, the chromatids separate. The complicated process of chromosome separation is **mitosis.** Mitosis ensures that each new cell receives a copy of each chromosome. Mitosis can be divided into four phases, as shown on the following pages.

In the third stage of the cell cycle, the cell divides and produces two cells that are identical to the original cell. Cell division will be discussed after mitosis has been described.

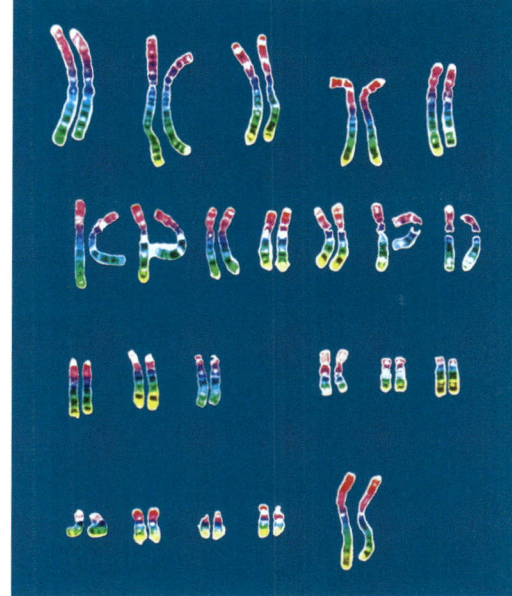

Figure 12 *Human body cells have 46 chromosomes, or 23 pairs of homologous chromosomes.*

Chromatids

Centromere

Figure 13 *Two strands of DNA and protein coiled together to form this duplicated chromosome, which consists of two chromatids.*

Self-Check

After duplication, how many chromatids are there in a pair of homologous chromosomes? *(See page 782 to check your answer.)*

WEIRD SCIENCE

A fern called *Ophioglossum reticulatum* has 1,260 chromosomes per cell, more than any other organism.

2) Teach

READING STRATEGY

Prediction Guide Have students guess whether the following statement is true or false before reading this page:

The number of chromosomes in eukaryotic cells differs because some organisms are more complex than others. (false)

Have students evaluate their answer after they read the page.

MATH and MORE

Have students make a bar graph to represent the following information:

Cell Type A divides every 3 hours; Cell Type B divides every 6 hours; and Cell Type C divides every 8 hours. If you start with one cell of each type, how many A, B, and C cells will be produced in a 24-hour period? On a graph, compare the number of cells produced by each type. (Cell A, 256; Cell B, 16; Cell C, 8)

Math Skills Worksheet 24 "Creating Exponents"

Answer to Self-Check

After duplication, there are four chromatids—two from each of the homologous chromosomes.

TOPIC: The Cell Cycle
GO TO: www.scilinks.org
sciLINKS NUMBER: HSTL090

2) Teach, continued

ACTIVITY

Making Models To help students visualize cells, have them work in small groups to make three-dimensional models of plant and animal cells. Have students use different colors of clay to represent the nucleus, the chloroplasts, the mitochondria, and the cytoplasm. Students can use aluminum foil for cell walls and can use plastic wrap as cell membranes.

Next have students model mitosis. Tell them to base their model on the illustrations on pages 94 and 95. Students could use curly noodles or packaging "popcorn" to represent the four chromosomes. <mark>Sheltered English</mark>

MEETING INDIVIDUAL NEEDS

Advanced Learners Have students research in high school or college texts to find the names of the four phases of mitosis **(prophase, metaphase, anaphase, and telophase)** and the name of the time between cell divisions **(interphase).** Students should put this information on a circular diagram illustrating the cell cycle. <mark>Sheltered English</mark>

Homework

Cells and Diseases Most human diseases can be examined at the cellular level. Viruses take over cellular functions. Bacteria can cause infections and produce toxins that irritate or destroy our cells. Other diseases affect cellular function. Have students research and prepare an oral presentation on a disease that interests them, noting the kinds of cells affected by the disease.

Mitosis and the Cell Cycle

The diagram below shows the cell cycle and the phases of mitosis in an animal cell. Although mitosis is a continuous process, it can be divided into the four phases that are shown and described. As you know, different types of living things have different numbers of chromosomes. In this diagram, only four chromosomes are shown to make it easier to see what's happening.

Before mitosis begins, the chromosomes and other cell materials are copied. The pair of *centrioles*, which are two cylindrical structures, are also copied. Each chromosome now consists of two chromatids.

Mitosis Phase 1
Mitosis begins. The nuclear membrane breaks apart. Chromosomes condense into rodlike structures. The two pairs of centrioles move to opposite sides of the cell. Fibers form between the two pairs of centrioles and attach to the centromeres.

Mitosis Phase 2
The chromosomes line up along the equator of the cell.

Mitosis Phase 3
The chromatids separate and are pulled to opposite sides of the cell by the fibers attached to the centrioles.

Science Skills Worksheet 24 "Using Models to Communicate"

IS THAT A FACT!
About 1 trillion mitoses occur in an adult human every 24 hours.

94 Chapter 4 • The Cell in Action

Mitosis Phase 4
The nuclear membrane forms around the two sets of chromosomes, and they unwind. The fibers disappear. Mitosis is completed.

Once mitosis is completed, the cytoplasm splits in two. This process is called **cytokinesis.** The result is two identical cells that are also identical to the original cell from which they were formed. After cytokinesis, the cell cycle is complete, and the new cells are at the beginning of their next cell cycle.

More About Cytokinesis In animal cells and other eukaryotes that do not have cell walls, division of the cytoplasm begins at the cell membrane. The cell membrane begins to pinch inward to form a groove, which eventually pinches all the way through the cell, and two daughter cells are formed. Cytokinesis in an animal cell is shown above.

Eukaryotic cells that have a cell wall, such as the cells of plants, algae, and fungi, do things a little differently. In these organisms, a *cell plate* forms in the middle of the cell and becomes the new cell membranes that will separate the two new cells. After the cell is split in two, a new cell wall forms between the two membranes. Cytokinesis in a plant cell is shown in **Figure 14.**

Figure 14 When plant cells divide, a cell plate forms and the cell is split in two.

REVIEW

1. How are binary fission and mitosis similar? How are they different?
2. Why is it important for chromosomes to be copied before cell division?
3. How does cytokinesis differ in animals and plants?
4. **Applying Concepts** What would happen if cytokinesis occurred without mitosis?

internetconnect

SCLINKS NSTA

TOPIC: The Cell Cycle
GO TO: www.scilinks.org
sciLINKS NUMBER: HSTL090

Answers to Review

1. Both processes lead to the production of two identical cells. Mitosis is the division of the nucleus in a eukaryotic cell. Binary fission is the division of a prokaryotic (bacterial) cell, which does not possess a nucleus.
2. Two copies of the chromosomes must be present before cell division because each of the two new cells needs to have a copy.
3. Animal cells pinch in two, and plant cells form a cell plate to divide into two cells.
4. One of the new cells would not have a set of chromosomes.

---

3) Extend

GOING FURTHER

Writing Have students research the role of mitosis in cancer and write a report based on their research. Their reports should include a discussion of the goals of various cancer treatments, such as radiation, chemotherapy, and surgery.

4) Close

Quiz

1. What is cell division? (It is the process by which cells reproduce themselves.)
2. How do prokaryotic cells make more cells? (binary fission)
3. How do eukaryotic cells make more cells? (mitosis and cytokinesis)

ALTERNATIVE ASSESSMENT

Writing Have students write and illustrate the biography of a cell. It can be humorous or serious, but it should include accurate descriptions of how materials are transported in and out of the cell and of the processes involved in cell reproduction.

Teaching Transparency 14
"The Cell Cycle: Phases of Mitosis"

Reinforcement Worksheet 4
"This Is Radio KCEL"

Section 3 • The Cell Cycle

Chapter Highlights

Vocabulary Definitions

Section 1

diffusion the movement of particles from an area where their concentration is high to an area where their concentration is low

osmosis the diffusion of water across a cell membrane

passive transport the diffusion of particles through proteins in the cell membrane from areas where the concentration of particles is high to areas where the concentration of particles is low

active transport the movement of particles through proteins in the cell membrane against the direction of diffusion; requires cells to use energy

endocytosis the process in which a cell membrane surrounds a particle and encloses it in a vesicle to bring it into the cell

exocytosis the process used to remove large particles from a cell; during exocytosis, a vesicle containing the particles fuses with the cell membrane

Section 2

photosynthesis the process by which plants capture light energy from the sun and convert it into sugar

cellular respiration the process of producing ATP from oxygen and glucose; releases carbon dioxide as a waste product

fermentation the breakdown of sugars to make ATP in the absence of oxygen

Chapter Highlights

SECTION 1

Vocabulary
- **diffusion** (p. 84)
- **osmosis** (p. 85)
- **passive transport** (p. 86)
- **active transport** (p. 86)
- **endocytosis** (p. 87)
- **exocytosis** (p. 87)

Section Notes

- A cell can survive only if food molecules are taken into the cell and waste materials are removed. Materials enter and leave the cell by passing through the cell membrane. The cell membrane allows some materials to pass through but prevents others.

- A cell does not need to use energy to move particles from regions of high concentration to regions of low concentration. This type of movement is called diffusion.

- Osmosis is the diffusion of water through a membrane.

- Some substances enter and leave a cell by passing through proteins. During passive transport, substances diffuse through proteins. During active transport, substances are moved from areas of low concentration to areas of high concentration. The cell must supply energy for active transport to occur.

- Particles that are too large to pass easily through the membrane can enter a cell by a process called endocytosis. Large particles can leave a cell by exocytosis.

Labs
The Perfect Taters Mystery (p. 698)

✓ Skills Check

Math Concepts

CELL CYCLE It takes 4 hours for a cell to complete its cell cycle and produce 2 cells. How many cells can be produced from this cell in 12 hours? First you must determine how many cell cycles will occur in 12 hours:

12 hours/4 hours = 3

The number of cells doubles after each cycle:

Cycle 1   1 cell × 2 = 2 cells
Cycle 2   2 cells × 2 = 4 cells
Cycle 3   4 cells × 2 = 8 cells

Therefore, after 3 cell cycles (12 hours), 8 cells will have been produced from the original cell.

Visual Understanding

MITOSIS The process of mitosis can be confusing, but looking at illustrations can help. Look at the illustrations of the cell cycle on pp. 94 and 95. Read the label for each phase, and look at the illustrations and photographs for each. Look for the cell structures that are described in the label. Trace the movement of chromosomes through each step. By carefully studying the labels and pictures, you can better understand mitosis.

Lab and Activity Highlights

The Perfect Taters Mystery `PG 698`

Stayin' Alive! `PG 700`

Datasheets for LabBook
(blackline masters for these labs)

96   Chapter 4 • The Cell in Action

SECTION 2

Vocabulary
photosynthesis *(p. 88)*
cellular respiration *(p. 89)*
fermentation *(p. 89)*

Section Notes
- The sun is the ultimate source of almost all energy needed to fuel the chemical activities of organisms. Most producers use energy from sunlight to make food during the process known as photosynthesis. This food then becomes a source of energy for the producers and for the consumers that eat the producers.
- Cells use cellular respiration or fermentation to release the energy from food to make ATP. Cellular respiration requires oxygen, but fermentation does not.

Labs
Stayin' Alive! *(p. 700)*

SECTION 3

Vocabulary
cell cycle *(p. 92)*
chromosome *(p. 92)*
binary fission *(p. 92)*
homologous chromosomes *(p. 93)*
chromatids *(p. 93)*
centromere *(p. 93)*
mitosis *(p. 93)*
cytokinesis *(p. 95)*

Section Notes
- The life cycle of a cell is called the cell cycle. The cell cycle begins when the cell is formed and ends when the cell divides to produce two new cells. Prokaryotic cells produce new cells by binary fission. Eukaryotic cells produce new cells by mitosis and cytokinesis.

- Before mitosis, the chromosomes are copied. During mitosis, chromatids separate, and two new nuclei are formed. During cytokinesis, the cell divides.

VOCABULARY DEFINITIONS, continued

SECTION 3

cell cycle the life cycle of a cell; in eukaryotes it consists of chromosome duplication, mitosis, and cytokinesis

chromosome coiled structure of DNA and protein that forms in the cell nucleus during cell division

binary fission the simple cell division in which one cell splits into two; used by bacteria

homologous chromosomes chromosomes with matching information

chromatids identical copies of a chromosome

centromere the region that holds chromatids together when a chromosome is duplicated

mitosis nuclear division in eukaryotic cells in which each cell receives a copy of the original chromosomes

cytokinesis the process in which cytoplasm divides after mitosis

 Vocabulary Review Worksheet 4

 Blackline masters of these Chapter Highlights can be found in the **Study Guide**.

GO TO: go.hrw.com

Visit the **HRW** Web site for a variety of learning tools related to this chapter. Just type in the keyword:

KEYWORD: HSTACT

GO TO: www.scilinks.org

Visit the **National Science Teachers Association** on-line Web site for Internet resources related to this chapter. Just type in the *sci*LINKS number for more information about the topic:

TOPIC:	Osmosis	*sci*LINKS NUMBER:	HSTL075
TOPIC:	Cell Energy	*sci*LINKS NUMBER:	HSTL080
TOPIC:	Photosynthesis	*sci*LINKS NUMBER:	HSTL085
TOPIC:	The Cell Cycle	*sci*LINKS NUMBER:	HSTL090
TOPIC:	Microbes	*sci*LINKS NUMBER:	HSTL095

Lab and Activity Highlights

LabBank

 Inquiry Labs, Fish Farms in Space, Lab 2

Whiz-Bang Demonstrations
- It's in the Bag! Demo 5
- Stop Picking on My Enzyme, Demo 4

Labs You Can Eat, The Mystery of the Runny Gelatin, Lab 3

 Long-Term Projects & Research Ideas, Taming the Wild Yeast, Project 4

Interactive Explorations CD-ROM

 CD 3, Exploration 1, "The Nose Knows"

Chapter Review Answers

UNDERSTANDING VOCABULARY

1. osmosis
2. exocytosis
3. photosynthesis
4. cellular respiration
5. mitosis, cytokinesis

UNDERSTANDING CONCEPTS

Multiple Choice

6. c
7. c
8. b
9. d
10. a
11. c

Short Answer

12. Cells need chloroplasts for photosynthesis and need mitochondria for respiration.
13. At the beginning of mitosis, each chromosome consists of two chromatids.
14. The first stage is cell growth and copying of DNA (duplication). The second stage is mitosis, and the third stage is cytokinesis (cell division).

Chapter Review

USING VOCABULARY

To complete the following sentences, choose the correct term from each pair of terms listed below:

1. The diffusion of water through the cell membrane is called __?__. (*osmosis* or *active transport*)

2. A cell can remove large particles during __?__. (*exocytosis* or *endocytosis*)

3. Plants use __?__ to make glucose. (*cellular respiration* or *photosynthesis*)

4. During __?__, food molecules are broken down to form CO_2 and H_2O and release large amounts of energy. (*cellular respiration* or *fermentation*)

5. In eukaryotes, __?__ creates two nuclei, and __?__ creates two cells. (*cytokinesis* or *mitosis*)

UNDERSTANDING CONCEPTS

Multiple Choice

6. When particles are moved through a membrane from a region of low concentration to a region of high concentration, the process is called
   a. diffusion.
   b. passive transport.
   c. active transport.
   d. fermentation.

7. An organism with chloroplasts is a
   a. consumer.   c. producer.
   b. prokaryote.   d. centromere.

8. What is produced by mitosis?
   a. two identical cells
   b. two nuclei
   c. chloroplasts
   d. two different cells

9. Before the energy in food can be used by a cell, it must first be transferred to molecules of
   a. proteins.
   b. carbohydrates.
   c. DNA.
   d. ATP.

10. Which one of the following does not perform mitosis?
    a. prokaryotic cell
    b. human body cell
    c. eukaryotic cell
    d. plant cell

11. Which of the following would form a cell plate during the cell cycle?
    a. human cell
    b. prokaryotic cell
    c. plant cell
    d. all of the above

Short Answer

12. What cell structures are needed for photosynthesis? for respiration?

13. How many chromatids are present in a chromosome at the beginning of mitosis?

14. What are the three stages of the cell cycle in a eukaryotic cell?

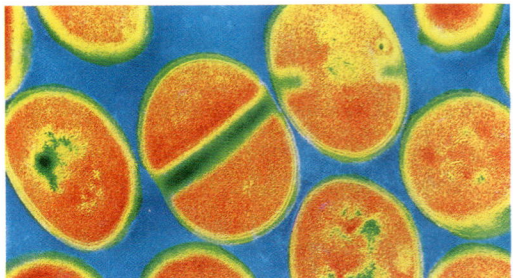

Concept Mapping

15. Use the following terms to create a concept map: chromosome duplication, cytokinesis, prokaryote, mitosis, cell cycle, binary fission, eukaryote.

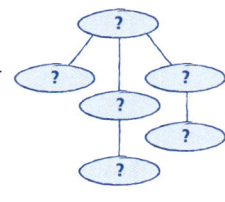

CRITICAL THINKING AND PROBLEM SOLVING

Write one or two sentences to answer the following questions:

16. Which one of the plants below was given water mixed with salt, and which one was given pure water? Explain how you know, and be sure to use the word *osmosis* in your answer.

17. Why would your muscle cells need to be supplied with more food when there is a lack of oxygen than when there is plenty of oxygen present?

18. A parent cell has 10 chromosomes before dividing.
    a. Will the cell go through binary fission or mitosis and cytokinesis to produce new cells?
    b. How many chromosomes will each new cell have after the parent cell divides?

MATH IN SCIENCE

19. A cell has six chromosomes at the beginning of its cell cycle. How many chromatids will line up at the equator of the cell during mitosis?

INTERPRETING GRAPHICS

Look at the cell below to answer the following questions:

20. Is the cell prokaryotic or eukaryotic?
21. In what stage of the cell cycle is this cell?
22. How many chromatids are present? How many pairs of homologous chromosomes are present?
23. How many chromosomes will be present in each of the new cells after the cell divides?

Take a minute to review your answers to the Pre-Reading Questions found at the bottom of page 82. Have your answers changed? If necessary, revise your answers based on what you have learned since you began this chapter.

99

Concept Mapping Transparency 4

Blackline masters of this Chapter Review can be found in the **Study Guide.**

Concept Mapping

15. An answer to this exercise can be found at the end of this book.

CRITICAL THINKING AND PROBLEM SOLVING

16. The wilted plant on the right was given salt water. Osmosis occurred, and water in the plant moved into the soil, where the concentration of water was lower.
17. When there is plenty of oxygen, the cells can get energy from cellular respiration. When there is a lack of oxygen, the cell must use fermentation, which doesn't produce as much energy. For fermentation to produce more energy, more food would be required.
18. a. The cell is a eukaryotic cell and will go through mitosis and cytokinesis. Prokaryotic cells have only one chromosome.
    b. Each new cell will receive a copy of each chromosome, so each will have 10 chromosomes.

MATH IN SCIENCE

19. Each chromosome will duplicate before mitosis, so $6 \times 2 = 12$ chromatids.

INTERPRETING GRAPHICS

20. The cell is eukaryotic because it shows sister chromatids linked at centromeres.
21. The cell is in mitosis because the chromosomes have already duplicated.
22. There are 12 chromatids. There are three pairs of homologous chromosomes.
23. There will be six chromosomes in each new cell.

Chapter 4 • Chapter Review 99

ACROSS THE SCIENCES
Electrifying News About Microbes

Background
The release of energy from food is called *cellular respiration*. Cellular respiration takes place in two stages, resulting in the storage of energy in ATP *(adenosine triphosphate)* molecules.

In the microbial battery, scientists harvest some of this energy and transfer it into electricity that can be readily used.

One of the benefits of the microbial battery is its ability to make use of waste products. Ask students to consider the effect this might have on the energy demands of nations that have limited access to fossil fuels.

ACROSS THE SCIENCES

LIFE SCIENCE • PHYSICAL SCIENCE

Electrifying News About Microbes

Your car is out of fuel, and there isn't a service station in sight. No problem! Your car's motor runs on electricity supplied by trillions of microorganisms—and they're hungry. You pop a handful of sugar cubes into the tank along with some fresh water, and you're on your way. The microbes devour the food and produce enough electricity to get you home safely.

A "Living" Battery
Sound far-fetched? Peter Bennetto and his team of scientists at King's College, in London, don't think so. Chemists there envision "living" batteries that will someday operate everything from wristwatches to entire towns. Although cars won't be using batteries powered by bacteria anytime soon, the London scientists have demonstrated that microorganisms can convert food into usable electrical energy. One test battery that is smaller than 0.5 cm^2 kept a digital clock operating for a day.

Freeing Electrons
For nearly a century, scientists have known that living things produce and use electric charges. But only in the last few decades have they figured out the chemical processes that produce these tiny electric charges. As part of their normal activities, living cells break down starches and sugars, and these chemical reactions release electrons. Scientists produce electricity by harvesting these free electrons from single-celled organisms, such as bacteria.

Bennetto and his colleagues have developed a list of foods that matches the carbohydrates, such as table sugar and molasses, with the microorganisms that digest them the most efficiently. Bennetto explains that there are lazy bacteria and efficient bacteria. An efficient microbe can convert more than 90 percent of its food into compounds that will fuel an

▲ *Bacteria like this can convert carbohydrates to electrical energy.*

electric reaction. A less efficient microbe converts 50 percent or less of its food into electron-yielding compounds.

Feed Them Leftovers
One advantage that batteries powered by microbes have over generators is that microbes do not require nonrenewable resources, such as coal or oil. Microbes can produce electricity by consuming pollutants, such as certain byproducts from the milk and sugar industries. And since the microorganisms reproduce constantly, no battery charging is necessary; just give the battery a bacteria change from time to time. For now, the London scientists are content to speculate on the battery's potential. Other specialists, such as electrical engineers, are needed to make this technology practical.

Project Idea
▶ Imagine that you manage a government agency and you are asked to provide funds for research on batteries powered by microbes. Think of some of the benefits of developing "living batteries." Are there any problems you can think of? As a class, decide whether you would fund the research.

Answer to Project Idea
Answers will vary, but students should recognize the two sides to investing in new discoveries. New technologies are risky, but solutions to scientific problems often begin as far-fetched ideas.

"Contagion"
by Katherine MacLean

A quarter mile from their spaceship, the *Explorer*, a team of doctors walk carefully along a narrow forest trail. Around them, the forest looks like an Earth forest in the fall—the leaves are green, copper, purple, and fiery red. But it isn't fall. And the team is not on Earth.

Minos is enough like Earth to be the home of another colony of humans. But Minos might also be home to unknown organisms that could cause severe illness or death among the *Explorer*'s crew. These diseases might be enough like Earth diseases to be contagious, yet just different enough to be extremely difficult to treat.

Something large moves among the shadows —it looks like a man. When he suddenly steps out onto the trail, he is taller than any of them, lean and muscled, and darkly tanned with bright red hair. Even more amazing, he speaks.

"Welcome to Minos. The mayor sends greetings from Alexandria."

And so we, and the crew of the *Explorer*, meet red-haired Patrick Mead. According to Patrick, there was once a colony of humans on Minos. About two years after the colony arrived, a terrible plague swept through the colony and killed everyone except the Mead family. But, Patrick tells them, the plague has never come back and there are no other contagions on Minos.

Or are there? What has Patrick hidden from the crew of the *Explorer*? Read Katherine MacLean's "Contagion" in the *Holt Anthology of Science Fiction* to find out.

Further Reading If students enjoyed this story, suggest some of Katherine MacLean's other works, such as the following:

The Missing Man (novella), Bart Books, 1988

The Diploids (short story collection), Gregg Press, 1981

The Man in the Bird Cage (novel), Ace Books, 1971

SCIENCE FICTION
"Contagion"
by Katherine MacLean

When they arrive on the previously unknown planet Minos, the crew of the Earth ship Explorer *immediately admire their friendly, strong, healthy, and handsome host. But could he carry a deadly disease?*

Teaching Strategy

Reading Level This is a relatively long story, containing quite a few medical terms. Students may find it challenging.

Background

About the Author Katherine MacLean's desire to write science fiction comes from an interest in combining her lifelong interests in psychology, biology, and history. In her short story collection, *The Diploids,* she applies the methods of experimentation used in physics and chemistry to anthropology and psychology. Much like "Contagion," many of these stories suggest that scientists have a choice; if they pursue science correctly, their discoveries and insights will change human interactions for the better. In one of her most famous stories, "The Snowball Effect," MacLean warns against the dangers of amateurs delving into science where only experts should venture.

MacLean's stories have appeared in many anthologies and magazines. In addition, MacLean has written several novels. In 1971 MacLean's unique blending of the sciences won her a Nebula Award for her novella *The Missing Man.*

Chapter 4 • Science Fiction

UNIT 3

TIMELINE

Heredity, Evolution, and Classification

The differences and similarities among living things are the subject of this unit. You will learn how characteristics are passed from one generation to another, how living things are classified based on their characteristics, and how these characteristics help living things survive.

Scientists have not always understood these topics, and there is still much to be learned. This timeline will give you an idea of some things that have been learned so far.

1753
Carolus Linnaeus publishes the first of two volumes containing the classification of all known species.

1951
Rosalind Franklin photographs DNA.

1953
James Watson and Francis Crick figure out the structure of DNA.

1960
Louis and Mary Leakey discover fossil bones of the human ancestor *Homo habilis* in Olduvai Gorge, Tanzania.

1969
Apollo 11 lands on the moon. Neil Armstrong becomes the first person to walk on the lunar surface.

1859
Charles Darwin suggests that natural selection is a mechanism of evolution.

1860
Abraham Lincoln is elected the 16th president of the United States.

1865
Gregor Mendel publishes the results of his studies of genetic inheritance in pea plants.

1930
The planet Pluto is discovered.

1905
Nettie Stevens describes how sex is determined by the X and Y chromosomes.

1974
Donald Johanson discovers a fossilized skeleton of one of the first hominids.

1990
Ashanti DeSilva is given genetically engineered white blood cells to combat disease.

2000
The Human Genome Project has identified thousands of human genes and is scheduled to decode the entire human genome by 2003.

Heredity, Evolution, and Classification **103**

Chapter Organizer

CHAPTER ORGANIZATION	TIME MINUTES	OBJECTIVES	LABS, INVESTIGATIONS, AND DEMONSTRATIONS
Chapter Opener pp. 104–105	45	National Standards: UCP 2, 4, LS 1d, 2c	**Start-Up Activity** Clothing Combos, p. 105
Section 1 Mendel and His Peas	90	▶ Explain the experiments of Gregor Mendel. ▶ Explain how genes and alleles are related to genotypes and phenotypes. ▶ Use the information in a Punnett square. UCP 1, 2, SAI 1, 2, ST 1, 2, SPSP 1, 5, HNS 2, 3, LS 1f, 2b–2e; LabBook UCP 2, SAI 1, HNS 2, LS 2b, 2c, 2e	**Demonstration,** Flower Dissection, p. 109 in ATE `BASIC` **QuickLab,** Take Your Chances, p. 112 `GENERAL` **Making Models,** Bug Builders, Inc., p. 702 `GENERAL` **Datasheets for LabBook,** Bug Builders, Inc., Datasheet 11 `GENERAL` **Design Your Own,** Tracing Traits, p. 704 `GENERAL` **Datasheets for LabBook,** Tracing Traits, Datasheet 12 `GENERAL`
Section 2 Meiosis	90	▶ Explain the difference between mitosis and meiosis. ▶ Describe how Mendel's ideas are supported by the process of meiosis. ▶ Explain the difference between male and female sex chromosomes. UCP 2, SAI 1, SPSP 5, HNS 2, 3, LS 1c, 1d, 2a–2d	**Demonstration,** Modeling Meiosis, p. 116 in ATE `BASIC` **Long-Term Projects & Research Ideas,** Project 5 `ADVANCED`

See page **T20** for a complete correlation of this book with the

NATIONAL SCIENCE EDUCATION STANDARDS.

TECHNOLOGY RESOURCES

 Guided Reading Audio CD English or Spanish, Chapter 5

 One-Stop Planner CD-ROM with Test Generator

 CNN Science, Technology & Society, BioDiesel, Segment 6 Bioengineered Plants, Segment 8

Chapter 5 • Heredity

Chapter 5 • Heredity

CLASSROOM WORKSHEETS, TRANSPARENCIES, AND RESOURCES	SCIENCE INTEGRATION AND CONNECTIONS	REVIEW AND ASSESSMENT
Directed Reading Worksheet 5 BASIC **Science Puzzlers, Twisters & Teasers,** Worksheet 5 ADVANCED		
Directed Reading Worksheet 5, Section 1 BASIC **Transparency 293,** White Light Is Separated by a Prism **Science Skills Worksheet 18,** Finding Useful Sources GENERAL **Math Skills for Science Worksheet 16,** What Is a Ratio? GENERAL **Math Skills for Science Worksheet 40,** Punnett Square Popcorn GENERAL **Transparency 15,** Punnett Square: *PP* × *pp* Cross **Transparency 15,** Punnett Square: *Pp* × *Pp* Cross **Reinforcement Worksheet 5,** Dimples and DNA BASIC **Critical Thinking Worksheet 5,** A Bittersweet Solution ADVANCED	**Connect to Physical Science,** p. 108 in ATE **Multicultural Connection,** p. 108 in ATE **MathBreak,** Understanding Ratios, p. 110 GENERAL **Math and More,** p. 110 in ATE BASIC **Apply,** p. 113 GENERAL **Science, Technology, and Society:** Mapping the Human Genome, p. 124 GENERAL	**Homework,** p. 106 in ATE ADVANCED **Homework,** p. 109 in ATE GENERAL **Homework,** p. 112 in ATE GENERAL **Review,** p. 113 GENERAL **Quiz,** p. 113 in ATE GENERAL **Alternative Assessment,** p. 113 in ATE GENERAL
Directed Reading Worksheet 5, Section 2 BASIC **Transparency 16,** Meiosis in Eight Easy Steps: A **Transparency 17,** Meiosis in Eight Easy Steps: B **Transparency 18,** Meiosis and Mendel	**Cross-Disciplinary Focus,** p. 116 in ATE **Health Watch:** Lab Rats with Wings, p. 125 ADVANCED	**Self-Check,** p. 117 **Homework,** p. 118 in ATE GENERAL **Review,** p. 119 GENERAL **Quiz,** p. 119 in ATE GENERAL **Alternative Assessment,** p. 119 in ATE GENERAL

 Holt, Rinehart and Winston On-line Resources
go.hrw.com
For worksheets and other teaching aids related to this chapter, visit the HRW Web site and type in the keyword: **HSTHER**

 National Science Teachers Association
www.scilinks.org
Encourage students to use the *sci*LINKS numbers listed in the internet connect boxes to access information and resources on the **NSTA** Web site.

END-OF-CHAPTER REVIEW AND ASSESSMENT

Chapter Review in Study Guide
Vocabulary and Notes in Study Guide
Chapter Tests with Performance-Based Assessment, Chapter 5 Test
Chapter Tests with Performance-Based Assessment, Performance-Based Assessment 5
Concept Mapping Transparency 5

Chapter Resources & Worksheets

Visual Resources

TEACHING TRANSPARENCIES

TEACHING TRANSPARENCIES

CONCEPT MAPPING TRANSPARENCY

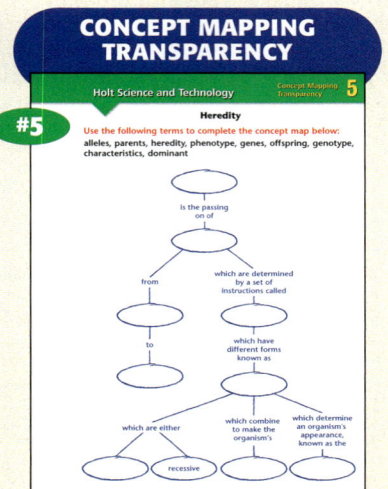

Meeting Individual Needs

DIRECTED READING

REINFORCEMENT & VOCABULARY REVIEW

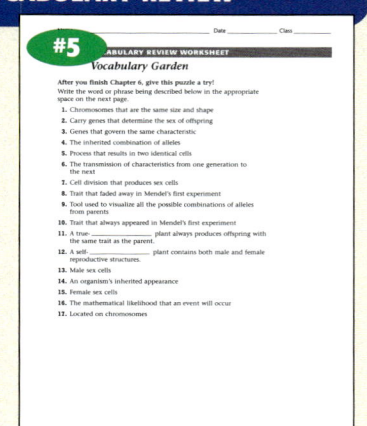

SCIENCE PUZZLERS, TWISTERS & TEASERS

Chapter 5 • Heredity

Chapter 5 • Heredity

Review & Assessment

STUDY GUIDE

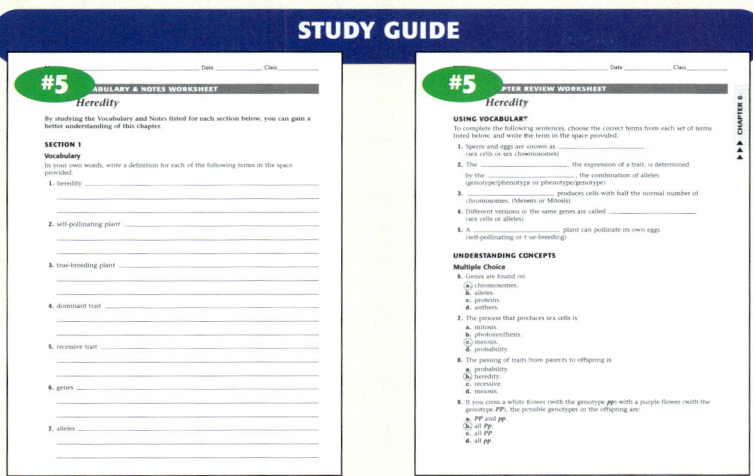

CHAPTER TESTS WITH PERFORMANCE-BASED ASSESSMENT

Lab Worksheets

LONG-TERM PROJECTS & RESEARCH IDEAS

DATASHEETS FOR LABBOOK

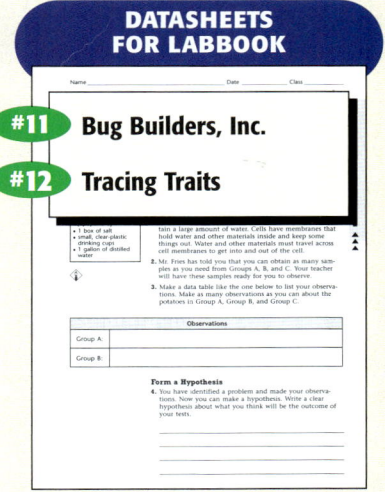

#11 Bug Builders, Inc.

#12 Tracing Traits

Applications & Extensions

CRITICAL THINKING & PROBLEM SOLVING

SCIENCE TECHNOLOGY

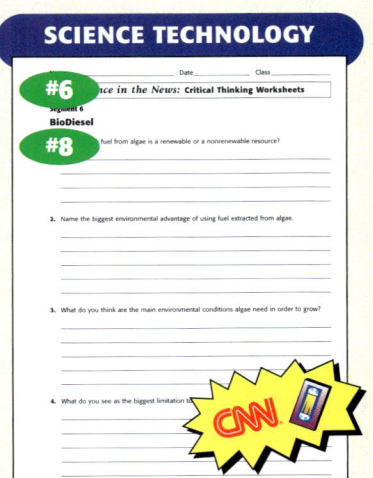

Chapter 5 • Chapter Resources & Worksheets   103D

Chapter Background

SECTION 1

Mendel and His Peas

▶ **Gregor Mendel**
In 1843, in the city of Brünn, Austria (which is now Brno, a city in the Czech Republic), Gregor Mendel (1822–1884) entered a monastery. In 1865, Mendel published the results of his garden-pea experiments. Although Mendel's ideas are widespread today, few scientists took notice of his work during his lifetime. Mendel presented his findings in two lectures, and he had only 40 copies of his work made. Because there were no computers or photocopy machines during Mendel's time, his findings were not distributed to many scientists.

- When Mendel was elected abbot of the monastery in 1868, his duties prevented him from visiting scientists and attending conferences where he could have discussed his results. It was not until 1900, when Mendel's work was rediscovered by scientists in Holland, Germany, and Austria-Hungary, that his theories gained general acceptance in the scientific community.

- Mendel's observations were used to justify Darwin's theory of evolution by natural selection. Mendel's ideas are considered to be the foundation of modern genetics.

IS THAT A FACT!

◆ From 1856 to 1863, while studying inheritance, Mendel grew almost 30,000 pea plants!

◆ Mendel also made contributions to beekeeping, horticulture, and meteorology. In 1877, Mendel became interested in weather and began issuing weather reports to local farmers.

◆ Punnett squares are named after their inventor, R. C. Punnett. Punnett explored inheritance by crossing different breeds of chickens in the early 1900s, soon after Mendel's work was rediscovered.

▶ **Pollination**
Pollen can be transferred between plants by wind, insects, and a variety of animals. Some common pollinators are bees, butterflies, moths, flies, bats, and birds. Animals are attracted to the color of the flower, the patterns found on the petals, or the flower's fragrance. Pollen is an excellent food for some animals.

SECTION 2

Meiosis

▶ **Chromosomes**
Chromosomes are composed of genes, the sequences of DNA that provide the instructions for making all the proteins in an organism. During cell division, the duplicated chromosomes separate so that one copy of each chromosome is present in the two new cells.

IS THAT A FACT!

◆ Male bees have only half the number of chromosomes that female bees have.

▶ **Walther Flemming**
Walther Flemming (1843–1905), a German physician and anatomist, was the first to use a microscope and

special dyes to study cell division. Flemming used the term *mitosis* to describe the process he observed.

▶ Mitosis

In mitosis, a cell divides to form two identical cells. The steps of the process are similar in almost all living organisms. In addition to enabling growth, mitosis allows organisms to replace cells that have died or malfunctioned. Mitosis can take anywhere from a few minutes to a few hours, and it may be affected by characteristics of the environment, such as light and temperature.

▶ Meiosis

In humans, meiosis is very different in males and females. In males, meiosis results in four similar sperm cells. In females, however, only one functional egg is produced. The other three resulting cells, which are known as *polar bodies,* contain the same amount of genetic material as the functional egg but do not mature.

▶ Genetic Disorders

A genetic disorder results from an inherited disruption in an organism's DNA. These inherited disruptions can take several forms, including a change in the number of chromosomes and the deletion or duplication of entire chromosomes or parts of chromosomes. Often the change responsible for a disorder is the alteration of a single specific gene. However, some genetic disorders result from several of these genetic alterations occurring simultaneously. Diseases resulting from these alterations cause a wide variety of physical malfunctions and developmental problems.

- Hemophilia is an inherited blood disorder affecting about one person in 10,000. People with hemophilia are genetically unable to produce the blood proteins necessary to form blood clots. As a result, cuts and bruises considered unthreatening to anyone else can be dangerous for hemophiliacs. The clotting factors missing in people with hemophilia are now widely available and can be self-administered.

- Cystic fibrosis (CF) is a disease for which one in 31 Americans carries a recessive trait. If two of these people have children together, there is a 25 percent chance that any child born to them will have the disease. CF affects the intestinal, bronchial, and sweat glands. In people with CF, these glands secrete thick, sticky fluids that are difficult for the body to process, impeding breathing and digestion. Modern medical treatment has extended the median age for people with CF to about 30 years, an enormous improvement in just a few decades.

- Rubinstein-Taybi syndrome (RTS) is a complex genetic disorder whose characteristics include broad thumbs and toes, mental retardation, and distinctive facial features. This wide range of characteristics is believed to be linked to any one of a number of mutations in a gene responsible for providing the body with a protein called CBP. CBP is thought to be vital to the body's delicate metabolism. Because CBP greatly influences body processes, people with a problem producing CBP have a wide range of difficulties. Children with RTS can benefit from proper nutrition and early intervention with therapies and special education.

For background information about teaching strategies and issues, refer to the *Professional Reference for Teachers.*

Heredity

 Pre-Reading Questions

Students may not know the answers to these questions before reading the chapter, so accept any reasonable response.

Suggested Answers

1. Humans do not all look alike because we have a huge variety of genes that are combined differently in each of us.
2. A baby will be a boy if he has one X sex chromosome and one Y sex chromosome. A baby will be a girl if she has two X sex chromosomes.

 Directed Reading Worksheet 5

 Science Puzzlers, Twisters & Teasers Worksheet 5

 Guided Reading Audio CD English or Spanish, Chapter 5

Heredity

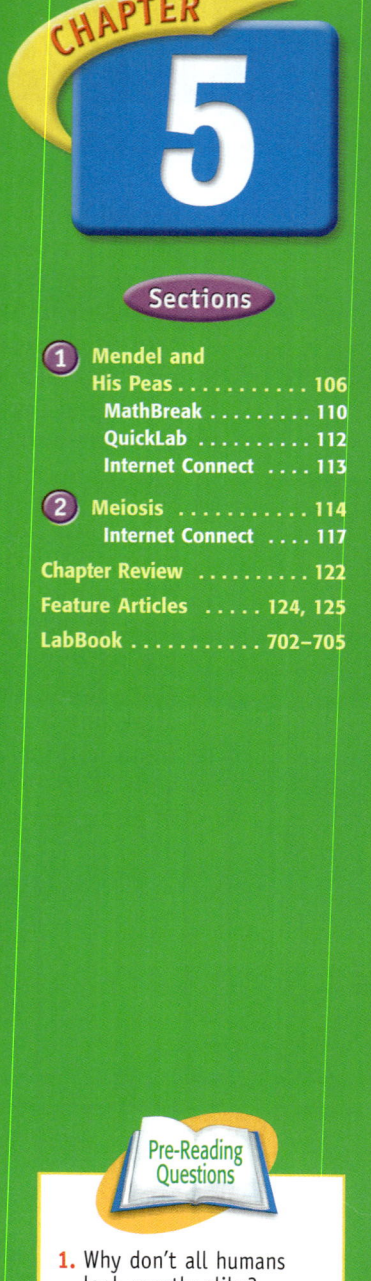

Sections

1. Mendel and His Peas 106
    MathBreak 110
    QuickLab 112
    Internet Connect 113
2. Meiosis 114
    Internet Connect 117

Chapter Review 122
Feature Articles 124, 125
LabBook 702–705

Pre-Reading Questions

1. Why don't all humans look exactly alike?
2. What determines whether a human baby will be a boy or a girl?

INDIAN PAINTBRUSHES

What do you notice about the red and yellow flowers in this photo? Besides their color, these flowers look very much alike. This similarity is because the flowers are of the same kind of plant, called Indian Paintbrush. Many things about the way a plant looks, including flower color, is determined by the plant's genes. These plants have different genes for flower color. In this chapter, you will learn about genes and about how differences in genes are important to evolution.

 internet connect

 HRW On-line Resources
go.hrw.com
For worksheets and other teaching aids, visit the HRW Web site and type in the keyword: **HSTHER**

 SCLINKS NSTA
www.scilinks.com
Use the sciLINKS numbers at the end of each chapter for additional resources on the **NSTA** Web site.

 CNNfyi.com
www.cnnfyi.com
Visit the CNN Web site for current events coverage and classroom resources.

START-UP Activity

CLOTHING COMBOS

In this activity, your class will investigate how traits from parents can be joined to make so many different combinations in children.

Procedure

1. The entire class should use **three boxes.** One box contains **five hats.** One box contains **five gloves,** and one box contains **five scarves.**
2. Without looking in the boxes, five of your classmates will select one item from each box. Lay the items on the table. Repeat this process, five students at a time, until the entire class has picked "an outfit." Record what hat, scarf, and glove each student chose.

Analysis

3. Were any two outfits exactly alike? Do you think you saw all of the possible combinations? Explain your answer.
4. Choose a partner. Using the pieces of clothing you and your partner selected from the box, how many different combinations could you make by giving a third person one hat, one glove, and one scarf?
5. How is step 4 like parents passing traits to their children?
6. Based on this activity, why do you think parents often have children who look very different from each other?

START-UP Activity

CLOTHING COMBOS

MATERIALS
FOR EACH GROUP: • box with 5 hats • box with 5 scarves • box with 5 gloves

Safety Caution

Infestations of head lice are a common problem in schools. Sharing hats would, of course, be inadvisable during such a period. Jackets or sweatshirts could be substituted for hats in this exercise.

Answers to START-UP Activity

3. Answers will vary. There should be many different combinations. It is unlikely that students will see all of the possible combinations.
4. 8
5. You are choosing hats, scarves, and gloves randomly. Traits are passed from parent to offspring randomly as well. By combining the traits of two parents, there are many possible combinations of traits in the offspring.
6. Answers will vary. The number of possible genetic combinations is huge because we have so many genes.

Chapter 5 • Heredity

SECTION 1

Focus

Mendel and His Peas

This section introduces the genetic experiments of Gregor Mendel. Students explore how flowering plants are fertilized and how the offspring are affected by different crosses. Students also learn to use a Punnett square to predict the results of genetic crosses.

Pose the following questions to your students:

Some people have brown eyes, some have blue, and some have green. Some people have earlobes attached directly to their head, while others have earlobes that hang loose. Where do people get these different traits? How are they passed from one generation to the next? Write your thoughts in your ScienceLog.

1 Motivate

ACTIVITY

Creating Tables Ask students to notice the differences in eye color, hair color, and earlobes among their classmates. Have them count the number of students with each trait and make a data table for each trait. The tables for eye color and earlobes will each have two columns. Have students calculate the ratios of attached to unattached earlobes and brown to blue eyes. Students may have eyes that are a color other than blue or brown, and this could be noted in a third column. (Note: A class of students is not a scientific sample and may not yield statistically significant results.)

106 Chapter 5 • Heredity

Section 1

Terms to Learn

heredity   alleles
dominant trait   genotype
recessive trait   phenotype
genes   probability

What You'll Do

- Explain the experiments of Gregor Mendel.
- Explain how genes and alleles are related to genotypes and phenotypes.
- Use the information in a Punnett square.

Imagine that you are planning to meet your pen pal at the airport, but you have never met. How would you describe yourself? Would you say that you are tall or short, have curly hair or straight hair, have brown eyes or green eyes? Make a list. Put a check mark next to traits you think you inherited.

106

Mendel and His Peas

There is no one else in the world exactly like you. You are unique. But what sets you apart? If you look around your classroom, you'll see that you share many physical characteristics with your classmates. For example, you all have skin instead of scales and a noticeable lack of antennae. You are a human being very much like all of your fellow human beings.

Yet you are different from everyone else in many ways. The people you most resemble are your parents and your brothers and sisters. But you probably don't look exactly like them either. Read on to find out why this is so.

Why Don't You Look Like a Rhinoceros?

The answer to this question seems simple: Neither of your parents is a rhinoceros. But there's more to this answer than meets the eye. As it turns out, **heredity,** or the passing of traits from parents to offspring, is a very complicated subject. For example, you might have curly hair, while both of your parents have straight hair. You might have blue eyes, even though both of your parents have brown eyes. How does this happen? People have investigated this question for a long time. About 150 years ago, some very important experiments were performed that helped scientists begin to find some answers. The person who performed these experiments was Gregor Mendel.

Who Was Gregor Mendel?

Gregor Mendel was born in 1822 in Heinzendorf, Austria. Growing up on his family's farm, Mendel learned a lot about cultivating flowers and fruit trees. After completing his studies at a university, he entered a monastery. He worked in the monastery garden, where he was able to use plants to study the way traits are passed from parents to offspring. **Figure 1** shows an illustration of Mendel in the monastery garden.

Figure 1 Gregor Mendel

Homework

Writing What rhinoceroses look like is also genetically determined and varied. There are five species of rhinoceros, ranging in length from 2.5 m (8 ft) to 4.3 m (almost 14 ft). Have interested students research and give a written report on the rhinos alive today and the ones we know about from fossils.

Unraveling the Mystery

From his experiences breeding plants, Mendel knew that sometimes the patterns of inheritance seemed simple and sometimes they did not. Mendel wanted to find out why.

Mendel was interested in the way traits are passed from parents to offspring. For example, sometimes a trait that appeared in one generation did not show up in any of the offspring in the next generation. In the third generation, though, the trait showed up again. Mendel noticed similar patterns in people, plants, and many other living things.

To simplify his investigation, Mendel decided to study only one kind of organism. He had already done studies using the garden pea plant, so he chose this as his subject.

Figure 2 *This photograph of a flower shows the male and female reproductive structures.*

How Do You Like Your Peas? Garden peas were a good choice for several reasons. These plants grow quickly, they are usually self-pollinating, and they come in many varieties. A *self-pollinating plant* contains both male and female reproductive structures, like the flower in **Figure 2.** Therefore, pollen from one flower or plant can fertilize the eggs of the same flower or the eggs of another flower on the same plant. **Figure 3** illustrates the parts of a flower and how fertilization takes place in plants.

Figure 3 *During pollination, pollen from the anthers (male) is transferred to the stigma (female). Fertilization occurs when a sperm from the pollen travels through the stigma and enters the egg in an ovule.*

2) Teach

USING THE FIGURES
Discuss the physical processes involved in the fertilization of the flowers illustrated in **Figure 3.** The flower on the right can be fertilized by another flower or can fertilize itself. Compare this figure with **Figure 5,** and point out that removing the anthers from the flower makes it impossible for the plant to self-pollinate. <mark>Sheltered English</mark>

DISCUSSION
Scientific Method Have students identify the steps of the scientific method in Mendel's work.

- **Ask a question**—How are traits inherited?
- **Form a hypothesis**—Inheritance has a pattern.
- **Test the hypothesis**—Cross true-breeding plants and offspring.
- **Analyze the results**—Identify patterns in inherited traits.
- **Draw conclusions**—Traits are inherited in predictable patterns.

What step did Mendel omit? (Hint: Why was his work overlooked for so long?) (communicate the results)

Directed Reading Worksheet 5 Section 1

TOPIC: Gregor Mendel
GO TO: www.scilinks.org
sciLINKS NUMBER: HSTL105

IS THAT A FACT!
Although Mendel was brilliant, he had difficulty learning from scientific texts. In the monastery gardens, Mendel explored the scientific ideas he had trouble with in school. While trying to grow better peas, he discovered genetics, an entirely new field of science!

Section 1 • Mendel and His Peas

2) Teach, continued

MEETING INDIVIDUAL NEEDS

Learners Having Difficulty
Ask students the following questions: What other traits might vary among flowers of the same species? Why do traits vary among individuals of the same species? Can any traits of a plant's offspring be predicted? Sheltered English

CONNECT TO PHYSICAL SCIENCE

Flower colors vary widely, from white to nearly black. White flowers reflect the entire visible spectrum of light. Flowers displaying other colors absorb all the visible wavelengths except for the colors that we see on them. A red rose absorbs all the visible wavelengths of light except red, which is why it appears red to us. Use the following Teaching Transparency to illustrate how white light is composed of all the colors of the rainbow.

Teaching Transparency 293
"White Light Is Separated by a Prism"
LINK TO PHYSICAL SCIENCE

Multicultural CONNECTION

 Writing
Throughout history, cultures have developed different interpretations of how traits are inherited between generations. Social prohibitions have helped cultures avoid genetic interbreeding. Have interested students write a research report to share with the class.

Science Skills Worksheet 18
"Finding Useful Sources"

108   Chapter 5 • Heredity

Seed Shape
Round   Wrinkled

Plant Height
Tall   Short

Flower Color
Purple   White

Figure 4 These are some of the plant characteristics that Mendel studied.

Peas Be My Podner

Mendel chose to study only one characteristic, such as plant height or pea color, at a time. That way, he could understand the results. Mendel chose plants that had two forms for each of the characteristics he studied. For example, for the characteristic of plant height, one form always produced tall plants, and the other form always produced short plants. Some of the characteristics investigated by Mendel are shown in **Figure 4**. The two different traits of each characteristic are also shown.

True-Breeding Plants Mendel was very careful to use plants that were true breeding for each of the traits he was studying. When a *true-breeding plant* self-pollinates, it will always produce offspring with the same trait the parent plant has. For example, a tall true-breeding plant will always produce offspring that are tall.

Mendel decided to find out what would happen if he crossed two plants that had different forms of a single trait. To do this, he used a method known as *cross-pollination*. In cross-pollination, the anthers of one plant are removed so that the plant cannot self-pollinate. Then pollen from another plant is used to fertilize the plant without anthers. This way, Mendel could select which pollen would fertilize which plant. This technique is illustrated in **Figure 5**.

Figure 5 Mendel removed the anthers from a plant that produced round seeds. Then he used pollen from a plant that produced wrinkled seeds to fertilize the plant that produced round seeds.

108

TOPIC: Heredity
GO TO: www.scilinks.org
sciLINKS NUMBER: HSTL110

WEIRD SCIENCE

Environmental stimuli can sometimes affect flower color. Hydrangeas growing in acidic soil produce blue flowers. If the soil is made alkaline, the same plants will produce pink flowers.

Mendel's First Experiment

In his first experiment, Mendel performed crosses to study seven different characteristics. Each of the crosses was between the two traits of each characteristic. The results of the cross between plants that produce round seeds and plants that produce wrinkled seeds are shown in **Figure 6.** The offspring from this cross are known as the *first generation.* Do the results surprise you? What do you think happened to the trait for wrinkled seeds?

Mendel got similar results for each of the crosses that he made. One trait always appeared, and the other trait seemed to vanish. Mendel chose to call the trait that appeared the **dominant trait.** The other trait seemed to recede into the background, so Mendel called this the **recessive trait.** To find out what might have happened to the recessive trait, Mendel decided to perform another experiment.

Mendel's Second Experiment

Mendel allowed the first generation from each of the seven crosses to self-pollinate. This is also illustrated in Figure 6. This time the plant with the dominant trait for seed shape (which is round) was allowed to self-pollinate. As you can see, the recessive trait for wrinkled seeds showed up again.

Mendel performed this same experiment on the two traits of each of the seven characteristics. No matter which characteristic Mendel investigated, when the first generation was allowed to self-pollinate, the recessive trait reappeared.

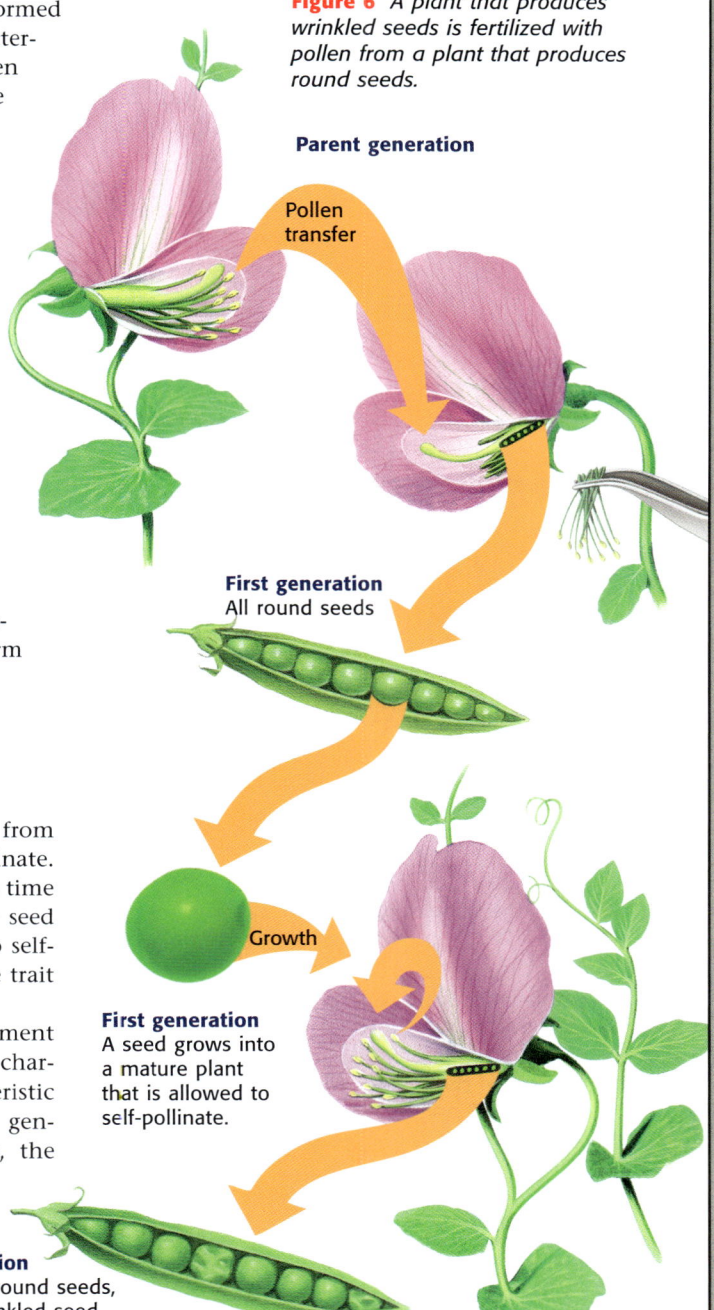

Figure 6 *A plant that produces wrinkled seeds is fertilized with pollen from a plant that produces round seeds.*

Parent generation

Pollen transfer

First generation
All round seeds

Growth

First generation
A seed grows into a mature plant that is allowed to self-pollinate.

Second generation
For every three round seeds, there is one wrinkled seed.

GROUP ACTIVITY

Mendelian Crosses Give each student a purple bead and a white bead, and ask them to perform a Mendelian cross. Tell students to begin with the first generation with the allele combination *Pp.* Have students randomly "pollinate" with 10 other members of the class. To "pollinate," students should pair up and shake all four beads together. Without looking, each student should choose one bead. The two beads selected will determine the genotype of the offspring. Have them do this 10 times. Students should record the genotype for each pollination. Have students tally the results and determine the ratio of white-flowering plants to purple-flowering plants resulting from the matches.

DEMONSTRATION

Flower Dissection Obtain a flower that has anthers and a stigma, such as a pea flower, a tulip, or a lily. Be careful: Pollen can stain clothing and cause allergic reactions. Dissect the flower, and show students the anthers and the stigma. Could this flower self-pollinate? (Yes; it has both anthers and a stigma.)

Demonstrate how Mendel removed the anthers of his flowers and then used a small brush to transfer pollen from plant to plant. Sheltered English

TOPIC: Dominant and Recessive Traits
GO TO: www.scilinks.org
*sci*LINKS NUMBER: HSTL115

Homework

Poster Project Have students create posters to illustrate Mendel's first and second experiments. Have each student demonstrate one of the seven traits Mendel studied. Encourage students to use materials such as flowers, yellow and green seeds, or wrinkled and round peas. Each project should clearly identify the parents, the first generation, and the second generation. (This activity can also be done with seven groups, one for each trait.) Sheltered English

Section 1 • Mendel and His Peas

2) Teach, continued

Bug Builders, Inc. PG 702

USING THE TABLE

As seen in the table on this page, Mendel used at least 580 plants for each trait he studied. Why did Mendel work with such large samples? **(Because Mendel was studying probability, larger samples increased the accuracy of his results.)**

Would his data have been different if he had used much smaller samples? **(Yes; the data would probably have been less accurate.)**

MATH and MORE

Ratios are commonly used to compare two values. For instance, ratios are often used to express speeds, such as 55 km/h, and prices, such as 79 cents/kg. In these examples, the ratios are 55:1 and 79:1.

 Math Skills Worksheet 16 "What Is a Ratio?"

Answer to MATHBREAK

The ratio of nougat-filled chocolates to caramel-filled chocolates is 18:6, or $\frac{18}{6}$, which can be reduced to $\frac{3}{1}$. This can be rewritten as 3:1 or 3 to 1.

 Math Skills Worksheet 40 "Punnett Square Popcorn"

Bug Builders, Inc. needs your help to design some new bugs. Turn to page 702 of the LabBook.

MATH BREAK

Understanding Ratios

A ratio is a way to compare two numbers by using division. The ratio of plants with purple flowers to plants with white flowers can be written as 705 to 224 or 705:224. This ratio can be reduced, or simplified, by dividing the first number by the second as follows:

$$\frac{705}{224} = \frac{3.15}{1}$$

which is the same thing as a ratio of 3.15:1.

For every three plants with purple flowers, there will be roughly one plant with white flowers. Try this problem:

In a box of chocolates, there are 18 nougat-filled chocolates and 6 caramel-filled chocolates. What is the ratio of nougat-filled chocolates to caramel-filled chocolates?

Ratios for Mendel's Results

The reduced ratios of dominant to recessive traits in Mendel's specimens are as follows:

Flower color	3.15:1
Seed color	3.00:1
Seed shape	2.96:1
Pod color	2.82:1
Pod shape	2.95:1
Flower position	3.14:1
Plant height	2.84:1

A Different Point of View

Mendel then did something that no one else had done before: He decided to count the number of plants with each trait that turned up in the second generation. He hoped that this might help him explain his results. Take a look at Mendel's actual results, shown in the table below.

Mendel's Results

Characteristic	Dominant trait	Recessive trait	Ratio
Flower color	705 purple	224 white	3.15:1
Seed color	6,002 yellow	2,001 green	?
Seed shape	5,474 round	1,850 wrinkled	?
Pod color	428 green	152 yellow	?
Pod shape	882 smooth	299 bumpy	?
Flower position	651 along stem	207 at tip	?
Plant height	787 tall	277 short	?

As you can see, the recessive trait showed up again, but not as often as the dominant trait showed up. Mendel decided to calculate the *ratio* of dominant traits to recessive traits for each characteristic. Follow in Mendel's footsteps by calculating the dominant-to-recessive ratio for each characteristic. (If you need help, check out the MathBreak at left.) Can you find a pattern among the ratios?

Answer to the question at the bottom of the student page

All the ratios can be rounded off to 3:1.

A Brilliant Idea

Mendel realized that his results could be explained only if each plant had two sets of instructions for each characteristic. Each parent donates one set of instructions, now known as **genes,** to the offspring. The fertilized egg would then have two forms of the same gene for every characteristic—one from each parent. The two forms of a gene are known as **alleles.**

The Proof Is in the Punnett Square To understand Mendel's conclusions, we'll use a diagram called a Punnett square. A *Punnett square* is used to visualize all the possible combinations of alleles from the parents. Dominant alleles are symbolized with capital letters, and recessive alleles are symbolized with lowercase letters. Therefore, the alleles for a true-breeding purple-flowered plant are written as *PP*. The alleles for a true-breeding white-flowered plant are written as *pp*. The cross between these two parent plants, as shown in **Figure 7,** is then written as *PP × pp*. The squares contain the allele combinations that could occur in the offspring. The inherited combination of alleles is known as the offspring's **genotype.**

Figure 7 shows that all of the offspring will have the same genotype: *Pp*. The dominant allele, *P*, in each genotype ensures that all of the offspring will be purple-flowered plants. An organism's appearance is known as its **phenotype.** The recessive allele, *p*, may be passed on to the next generation.

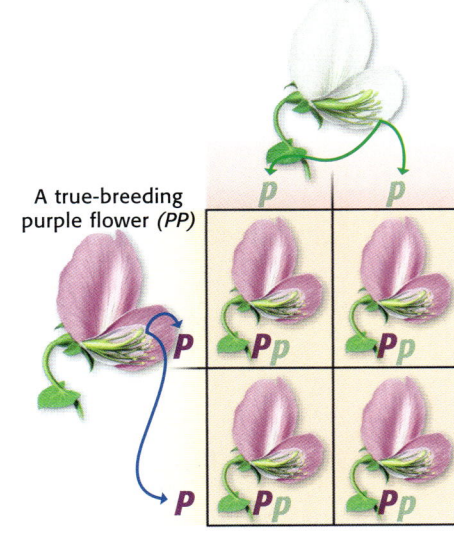

Figure 7 *The possible allele combinations in the offspring for this cross are all the same:* **Pp.**

How to Make a Punnett Square

Draw a square, and divide it into four sections. Next, write the letters that represent alleles from one parent along the top of the box. Write the letters that represent alleles from the other parent along the side of the box.

The cross shown at right is between a plant that produces only round seeds, *RR,* and a plant that produces only wrinkled seeds, *rr.* Follow the arrows to see how the inside of the box was filled. The resulting alleles inside the box show all the possible genotypes for the offspring from this cross. What would the phenotypes for these offspring be?

Answer to How to Make a Punnett Square

All the phenotypes would be round.

Q: What do you get when you cross a bridge with a bicycle?

A: to the other side

3) Extend

RETEACHING

Ratios If students have difficulty calculating ratios, review fractions using this demonstration. Display three pennies and one nickel, and ask students the following questions:

How many coins are there in all? (four) What fraction of the coins are pennies? ($\frac{3}{4}$)

What fraction of the coins are nickels? ($\frac{1}{4}$)

How many pennies and nickels are there? (three pennies and one nickel)

What is the ratio of pennies to nickels? (3 to 1)

Sheltered English

MISCONCEPTION ALERT

Not all inherited traits follow the examples studied by Mendel. For instance, a cross between a red horse and a white horse can produce a horse with both red and white hair. Such a horse is said to have a roan coat. This is an example of codominance. In this and similar cases, both alleles are equally dominant, so the model developed by Mendel does not apply.

 Teaching Transparency 15 "Punnett Square: *PP × pp* Cross"

Section 1 • Mendel and His Peas

3) Extend, continued

Homework

Punnett Squares Have students create Punnett squares for the different crosses in Mendel's experiments. Students should include the phenotype and genotype of the parents and offspring.

MATERIALS

For Each Group:
- masking tape
- 2 quarters

Answers to QuickLab

Students should find that they get the *bb* combination about $\frac{1}{4}$, or 25 percent, of the time. The more trials there are, the closer the probability will be to 25 percent. Note that each coin represents one parent's alleles. For example, the female parent has the alleles *B* and *b*. The probability that the offspring will inherit either of these alleles from the female parent is $\frac{1}{2}$, or 50 percent. The same is true for the male parent. The probability of throwing two *b* alleles in a row is calculated as follows: $\frac{1}{2} \times \frac{1}{2} = \frac{1}{4}$, and $\frac{1}{4} \times 100 = 25$ percent.

Teaching Transparency 15
"Punnett Square: *Pp* × *Pp* Cross"

Reinforcement Worksheet 5
"Dimples and DNA"

Critical Thinking Worksheet 5
"A Bittersweet Solution"

Figure 8 This Punnett square shows the possible results from the cross **Pp** × **Pp**.

Take Your Chances

You have two guinea pigs you would like to breed. Each has brown fur and the genotype **Bb.** What are the chances that their offspring will have white fur with the genotype **bb?** Try this to find out. Stick a piece of **masking tape** on both sides of **two quarters.** Label one side of each quarter with a capital **B** and the other side with a lowercase **b.** Toss both coins 50 times, making note of your results each time. How many times did you get the **bb** combination? What is the probability that the next toss will result in **bb?**

More Evidence In Mendel's second experiment, he allowed the first-generation plants to self-pollinate. **Figure 8** shows a self-pollination cross of a first-generation plant with the genotype **Pp.** The parental alleles in the cross indicate that the egg and sperm can contain either a *P* allele or a *p* allele.

What might the genotypes of the offspring be? Notice that one square shows the *Pp* combination, while another shows the *pP* combination. These are exactly the same genotype, even though the letters are written in a different order. The other possible genotypes in the offspring are *PP* and *pp*. The combinations *PP*, *Pp*, and *pP* have the same phenotype—purple flowers—because they each contain at least one dominant allele (*P*). Only one combination, *pp*, produces plants with white flowers. The ratio of dominant to recessive is 3:1, just as Mendel calculated from his data.

What Are the Chances?

It's important to understand that offspring are equally likely to inherit either allele from either parent. Think of a coin toss. There's a 50 percent chance you'll get heads and a 50 percent chance you'll get tails. Like the toss of a coin, the chance of inheriting one allele or another is completely random.

Probability The mathematical chance that an event will occur is known as **probability.** Probability is usually expressed as a fraction or percentage. If you toss a coin, the probability of tossing tails is $\frac{1}{2}$. This means that half the number of times you toss a coin, you will get tails. To express probability as a percentage, divide the numerator of the fraction by the denominator, and then multiply the answer by 100.

$$\frac{1}{2} \times 100 = 50\%$$

To find the probability that you will toss two heads in a row, multiply the probability of the two events.

$$\frac{1}{2} \times \frac{1}{2} = \frac{1}{4}$$

The percentage would be $1 \div 4 \times 100$, which equals 25 percent.

Many ordinary fruits and vegetables carry recessive genes for bizarre traits. For instance, a recessive gene in tomatoes causes the skin to be covered with fuzzy hair!

Curly Eared Cats

A curly eared cat, like the one at right, mated with a cat that had normal ears. If half the kittens had the genotype *Cc* and curly ears, and the other half had the genotype *cc* and normal ears, which was the allele for curly ears?

What was the genotype of each parent? (**Hint:** Use a Punnett square to fill in the genotypes of the offspring, and then work backward.)

Genotype Probability The same method is used to calculate the probability that an offspring will inherit a certain genotype. For a pea plant to inherit the white flower trait, it must receive a *p* allele from each parent. There is a 50 percent chance of inheriting either allele from either parent. So the probability of inheriting two *p* alleles from a *Pp* × *Pp* cross is $\frac{1}{2} \times \frac{1}{2}$. This equals $\frac{1}{4}$ or 25 percent.

Gregor Mendel—Gone but Not Forgotten Good ideas are often overlooked or misunderstood when they first appear. This was the fate of Gregor Mendel's ideas. In 1865, he published his findings for the scientific community. Unfortunately, his work didn't get much attention. It wasn't until after his death, more than 30 years later, that Mendel finally got the recognition he deserved. Once Mendel's ideas were rediscovered and understood, the door was opened to modern genetics.

REVIEW

1. The allele for a cleft chin, *C*, is dominant among humans. What would be the results from a cross between a woman with the genotype *Cc* and a man with the genotype *cc*? Create a Punnett square showing this cross.

2. Of the possible combinations you found in question 1, what is the ratio of offspring with a cleft chin to offspring without a cleft chin?

3. **Applying Concepts** The Punnett square at right shows the possible combinations of alleles for fur color in rabbits. Black fur, *B*, is dominant over white fur, *b*. Given the combinations shown, what are the genotypes of the parents?

internet connect

TOPIC: Heredity, Dominant and Recessive Traits
GO TO: www.scilinks.org
*sci*LINKS NUMBER: HSTL110, HSTL115

Section 1 • Mendel and His Peas   113

SECTION 2

Focus

Meiosis

This section discusses chromosomes, describes the process of meiosis, and explains the difference between meiosis and mitosis. The section explains how meiosis supports Mendel's findings and concludes with a discussion of sex chromosomes and how sex is determined.

Bellringer

Ask students to write a sentence for each of the following terms:

heredity, genotype, and phenotype

(**Heredity** is the passing on of traits from parents to offspring.

The combination of an organism's alleles is its **genotype**.

The way that an organism looks is known as its **phenotype**.)

1 Motivate

DISCUSSION

Inherited Traits Lead a class discussion about traits that are passed from parents to their children. Have the students list examples of traits that "run in families" and that could be genetically determined. (Answers may include traits such as hair color; a tendency to develop diseases, such as diabetes and some forms of cancer; or personality traits, such as shyness.)

Ask students to think about how traits are inherited. For example, some traits are carried by one sex, and some diseases are said to "skip a generation." Explain that this section will introduce the physical processes that determine genetic inheritance.

114 Chapter 5 • Heredity

SECTION 2

Terms to Learn

sex cells
homologous chromosomes
meiosis
sex chromosomes

What You'll Do

◆ Explain the difference between mitosis and meiosis.
◆ Describe how Mendel's ideas are supported by the process of meiosis.
◆ Explain the difference between male and female sex chromosomes.

Figure 9 Human body cells have 46 chromosomes, or 23 pairs of chromosomes. One member of a pair of homologous chromosomes is shown at right.

internetconnect

TOPIC: Cell Division
GO TO: www.scilinks.org
sciLINKS NUMBER: HSTL120

Meiosis

In the early 1900s, scientists began doing experiments similar to those done by Gregor Mendel. Excited by their findings, they searched for similar results obtained by others. They came across Mendel's forgotten paper and realized that their discoveries were not new; Mendel had made the same observation 35 years earlier. However, genes were still a mystery. Where were they located, and how did they pass information from one cell to another? Understanding reproduction was the first step in finding the answers to these questions.

Two Kinds of Reproduction

You know that there are two types of reproduction: asexual reproduction and sexual reproduction.

One Makes Two In *asexual reproduction*, only one parent cell is needed for reproduction. First, the internal structures of the cell are copied by a process known as mitosis. The parent cell then divides, producing new cells that are exact copies of the parent cell. Most single-celled organisms reproduce in this way. Most of the cells in your body also divide this way.

Two Make One A different type of reproduction is used to make a new human being or a new pea plant. In *sexual reproduction*, two parent cells join together to form a new individual. The parent cells, known as **sex cells**, are different from ordinary body cells. Human body cells, for example, have 46 chromosomes (or 23 pairs), as shown in **Figure 9**. The chromosomes in each pair are called **homologous** (hoh MAHL uh guhs) **chromosomes**. But human sex cells have only 23 chromosomes—half the usual number. Male sex cells are called *sperm*. Female sex cells are called *eggs*, or ova. Each sperm and each egg has only one of the chromosomes from each homologous pair.

Science Bloopers

In 1918, a prominent scientist miscounted the number of chromosomes in a human cell. He counted 48. For almost 40 years, scientists thought this number was correct. In fact, it wasn't until 1956 that chromosomes were correctly counted and found to be only 46.

Less Is More Why is it important that sex cells have half the usual number of chromosomes? When an egg and a sperm join to form a new individual, each parent donates one half of a homologous pair of chromosomes. This ensures that the offspring will receive a normal number of chromosomes in each body cell. Each body cell must have an entire set of 46 chromosomes in order to grow and function properly.

Meiosis to the Rescue Sex cells are made during meiosis, a copying process that is different from mitosis. **Meiosis** (mie OH sis) produces new cells with half the usual number of chromosomes. When the sex cells are made, the chromosomes are copied once, and then the nucleus divides twice. The resulting sperm and eggs have half the number of chromosomes found in a normal body cell.

Meanwhile, Back at the Lab

What does all of this have to do with the location of genes? Not long after Mendel's paper was rediscovered, a young graduate student named Walter Sutton made an important observation. Sutton was studying sperm cells in grasshoppers. Sutton knew of Mendel's studies, which showed that the egg and sperm must each contribute the same amount of information to the offspring. That was the only way the 3:1 ratio found in the second generation could be explained. Sutton also knew from his own studies that although eggs and sperm were different, they did have something in common: their chromosomes were located inside a nucleus. Using his observations of meiosis, his understanding of Mendel's work, and some creative thinking, Sutton proposed something very important:

Genes are located on chromosomes!

And Sutton was correct, as it turned out. The steps of meiosis are outlined on the next two pages. But first, let's review mitosis so that you can compare the two processes.

Mitosis Revisited

1. Inside a typical cell: each of the long strands (chromosomes) makes a copy of itself.

2. Each chromosome consists of two identical copies called chromatids. The chromosomes thicken and shorten.

3. The nuclear membrane dissolves. The chromosomes line up along the equator (center) of the cell.

4. The chromatids pull apart.

5. The nuclear membrane forms around the separated chromatids. The chromosomes unwind, and the cell divides.

6. The result: two identical copies of the original cell.

2) Teach

READING STRATEGY

Prediction Guide Before students read the passage about meiosis, ask them whether the following statements are true or false. Students will discover the answers as they explore Section 2.

- Mitosis is the only type of cell division. (false)
- Only sex cells undergo meiosis. (true)
- Sex cells contain half the number of chromosomes as other body cells. (true)

USING THE FIGURES

Use the graphical representations of mitosis and meiosis in this section to describe what happens in each type of division. On the board, draw two identical cells, each containing four chromosomes. Label one cell "Mitosis," and label the other "Meiosis." Have students describe what happens in each stage of mitosis and illustrate the stages on the board. (Using colored chalk might help distinguish between the dividing chromosomes.) Repeat the process for meiosis. Point out that in this case mitosis results in two identical cells, each containing four chromosomes, while meiosis results in four cells, each containing two chromosomes. **Sheltered English**

 Directed Reading Worksheet 5 Section 2

IS THAT A FACT!

In human males, meiosis and sperm production take about 9 weeks. It's a continuous process that begins at puberty. In females, meiosis and egg production begin before birth. The process stops abruptly, however, and does not begin again until a girl enters puberty. Until a woman reaches menopause, one egg each month resumes meiosis and finishes its development. Therefore, the meiosis of a single egg may take up to 50 years to complete!

Section 2 • Meiosis   115

2 Teach, continued

DEMONSTRATION

Modeling Meiosis Select all cards that are the same color, and shuffle them. Each card will represent one chromosome. Tell students that two cards of the same number or face—for example, a queen of spades and a queen of clubs—represent homologous chromosomes. Next pair up the cards according to face or number. Make two piles; each pile should contain one of a pair. Ask students what this division represents. (the separation of homologous chromosomes into two cells)

Emphasize that this activity models only the first cell division of meiosis. Stress that after the second cell division of meiosis, each new cell will have half the number of chromosomes. **Sheltered English**

CROSS-DISCIPLINARY FOCUS

Theater Students may enjoy watching a choreographed dance or skit that walks them methodically through the steps of meiosis. Have interested students design the skit or dance, and allow them time to perform it. This can be a very effective way to present this difficult material. **Sheltered English**

Teaching Transparency 16
"Meiosis in Eight Easy Steps: A"

Meiosis in Eight Easy Steps

The diagram on these two pages shows each stage of meiosis. Read about each step as you look at the diagram. Different types of living things have different numbers of chromosomes. In this diagram, only four chromosomes are shown.

1 Before meiosis begins, the chromosomes are in a threadlike form. Each chromosome makes an identical copy of itself, forming two exact halves called *chromatids*. The chromosomes then thicken and shorten into a form that is visible under a microscope. The nuclear membrane disappears.

One pair of homologous chromosomes

Two chromatids

2 Each chromosome is now made up of two chromatids, the original and an exact copy. Similar chromosomes pair with one another, forming *homologous chromosome pairs*. The paired homologous chromosomes line up at the equator of the cell.

3 The chromosomes separate from their homologous partners and move to opposite ends of the cell.

4 The nuclear membrane re-forms, and the cell divides. The paired chromatids are still joined.

116

Q: If human sex cells are created by meiosis, how are cat sex cells produced?

A: by meowsis

In some species of animals, there is only one gender! For instance, all desert whiptail lizards *(Cnemidophorus neomexicanus)* are female. Eggs are produced through parthenogenesis, and the unfertilized eggs develop into females that are genetically identical to their mother.

5 Each cell contains one member of each homologous chromosome pair. The chromosomes are not copied again between the two cell divisions.

6 The chromosomes line up at the equator of each cell.

7 The chromatids pull apart and move to opposite ends of the cell. The nuclear membrane forms around the separated chromosomes, and the cells divide.

8 The result: Four new cells have formed from the original single cell. Each new cell has half the number of chromosomes present in the original cell.

✓ Self-Check

1. How many chromosomes are in the original single cell in the diagram on page 116?
2. How many homologous pairs are shown in the original cell?
3. How many times do the chromosomes make copies of themselves during meiosis? How many times do cells divide during meiosis?
4. How many chromosomes are present in each cell at the end of meiosis? at the end of mitosis?

(See page 782 to check your answers.)

internet connect

SC*LINKS*
NSTA
TOPIC: Cell Division
GO TO: www.scilinks.org
***sci*LINKS NUMBER:** HSTL120

Scientists have bred watermelons that have an extra set of chromosomes. These watermelons are sterile, and their seeds do not develop. The result is seedless watermelons.

MEETING INDIVIDUAL NEEDS

Advanced Learners
Using high school or college texts, have students find the names of each stage of meiosis. Students should use this information to make a poster of meiosis. They can also compare the process of meiosis and mitosis.

ACTIVITY

Concept Mapping Have students use the new terms in this section to create a concept map.

Teaching Transparency 17
"Meiosis in Eight Easy Steps: B"

Answers to Self-Check

1. four
2. two
3. They make copies of themselves once. They divide twice.
4. Two, or half the number of chromosomes in the parent are present at the end of meiosis. After mitosis, there would be four chromosomes, the same number as in the parent cell.

Section 2 • Meiosis   **117**

Meiosis and Mendel

As Walter Sutton realized, the steps in meiosis explain Mendel's findings. **Figure 10** illustrates what happens to a pair of homologous chromosomes during meiosis and fertilization. The cross is between a plant that is true breeding for round seeds and a plant that is true breeding for wrinkled seeds.

Figure 10 *Meiosis helps explain Mendel's findings.*

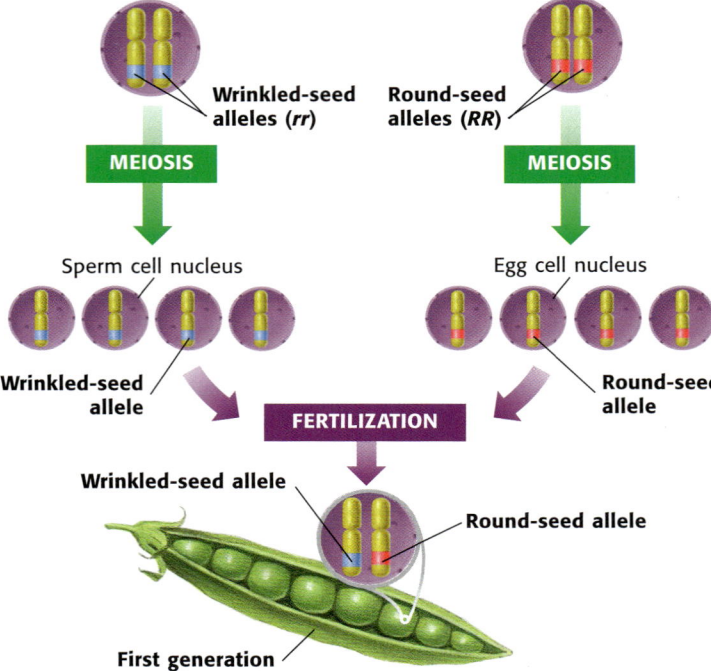

Following **meiosis**, each sperm cell contains a recessive allele for wrinkled seeds and each egg cell contains a dominant allele for round seeds.

Fertilization of any egg by any sperm results in the same genotype (*Rr*) and the same phenotype (round). This is exactly what Mendel found in his studies.

Each fertilized egg in the first generation contained one dominant allele and one recessive allele for seed type. Only one genotype was possible because all sperm formed during meiosis contained the wrinkled-seed allele and all eggs contained the round-seed allele. When the first generation was allowed to self-pollinate, the possible genotypes changed. There are three genotype possibilities for this cross: **RR**, **Rr**, and **rr**.

Teaching Transparency 18 "Meiosis and Mendel"

Male or Female?

There are many ways that different organisms become male or female. To see how this happens in humans, examine **Figure 11.** Then look back at Figure 9, on page 114. Each figure shows the chromosomes in human body cells. Which chromosome photograph is from a female, and which is from a male? Here's a hint: Females have 23 matched pairs, while males have 22 matched pairs and one unmatched pair.

Sex Chromosomes The chromosomes in Figure 11 are from a male, and the chromosomes in Figure 9 are from a female. **Sex chromosomes** carry genes that determine whether the offspring is male or female. In humans, females have two X chromosomes (the matching pair), and males have one X chromosome and one Y chromosome (the unmatched pair).

During meiosis, one of each of the chromosome pairs ends up in a sex cell. This is also true of the sex chromosomes. Females have two X chromosomes in each body cell. When meiosis produces the egg cells, each egg contains one X chromosome. Males have both an X chromosome and a Y chromosome in each body cell. During meiosis, these chromosomes separate, so each sperm cell contains either an X or a Y chromosome. An egg fertilized by a sperm with an X chromosome will produce a female. If the sperm contains a Y chromosome, the offspring will be male. This is illustrated in **Figure 12.**

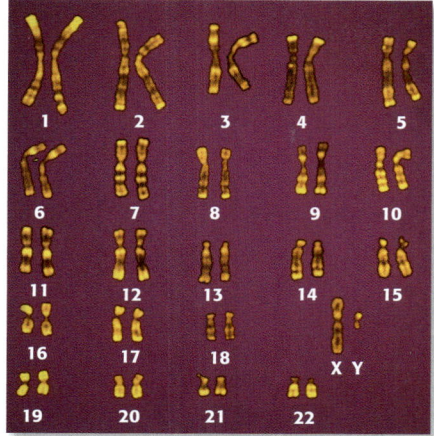

Figure 11 Are these chromosomes from a male or female? How can you tell?

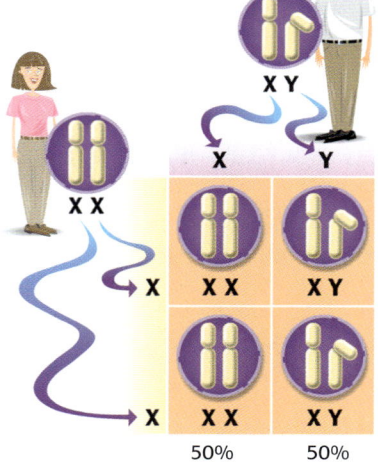

Figure 12 Egg and sperm combine to form either the XX or XY combination.

REVIEW

1. Explain the difference between sex cells and sex chromosomes.

2. If there are 14 chromosomes in pea plant cells, how many chromosomes are present in a sex cell of a pea?

3. **Interpreting Illustrations** Examine the illustration at right. Does it show a stage of mitosis or meiosis? How can you tell?

Chapter Highlights

Vocabulary Definitions

Section 1

heredity the passing of traits from parent to offspring

dominant trait a trait observed when at least one dominant allele for a characteristic is inherited

recessive trait a trait that is apparent only when two recessive alleles for the characteristic are inherited

genes segments of DNA that carry hereditary instructions located on chromosomes and passed from parent to offspring

alleles alternative forms of a gene that govern the same characteristics

genotype the inherited combination of alleles

phenotype an organism's inherited appearance

probability the mathematical chance that an event will occur

Chapter Highlights

SECTION 1

Vocabulary
- heredity (p. 106)
- dominant trait (p. 109)
- recessive trait (p. 109)
- genes (p. 111)
- alleles (p. 111)
- genotype (p. 111)
- phenotype (p. 111)
- probability (p. 112)

Section Notes
- Heredity is the passing of traits from parents to offspring.
- Traits are inherited forms of characteristics.
- Gregor Mendel used pea plants to study heredity.
- Mendel's pea plants were self-pollinating. They contained both male and female reproductive structures. They were also true breeding, always producing offspring with the same traits as the parents.
- Offspring inherit two sets of instructions for each characteristic, one set from each parent.
- The sets of instructions are known as genes.
- Different versions of the same gene are known as alleles.
- If both the dominant allele and the recessive allele are inherited for a characteristic, only the dominant allele is expressed.
- Recessive traits are apparent only when two recessive alleles for the characteristic are inherited.
- A genotype is the combination of alleles for a particular trait.
- A phenotype is the physical expression of the genotype.
- Probability is the mathematical chance that an event will occur. It is usually expressed as a fraction or as a percentage.

Labs
Bug Builders, Inc. (p. 702)
Tracing Traits (p. 704)

✓ Skills Check

Math Concepts

RATIOS A jar contains 24 green marbles and 96 red marbles. There are 4 red marbles for every 1 green marble.

$$\frac{96}{24} = \frac{4}{1}$$

This can also be written as follows:

4:1

Visual Understanding

PUNNETT SQUARES A Punnett square can help you visualize all the possible combinations of alleles passed from parents to offspring. See page 111 to review how Punnett squares are made.

Lab and Activity Highlights

Tracing Traits PG 704

Bug Builders, Inc. PG 702

Datasheets for LabBook
(blackline masters for these labs)

SECTION 2

Vocabulary
- sex cells *(p. 114)*
- homologous chromosomes *(p. 114)*
- meiosis *(p. 115)*
- sex chromosomes *(p. 119)*

Section Notes
- Genes are located on chromosomes.
- Most human cells contain 46 chromosomes, or 23 pairs.
- Each pair contains one chromosome donated by the mother and one donated by the father. These pairs are known as homologous chromosomes.
- Meiosis produces sex cells, eggs and sperm.
- Sex cells have half the usual number of chromosomes.
- Sex chromosomes contain genes that determine an offspring's sex.
- Human females have two X chromosomes, and males have one X chromosome and one Y chromosome.

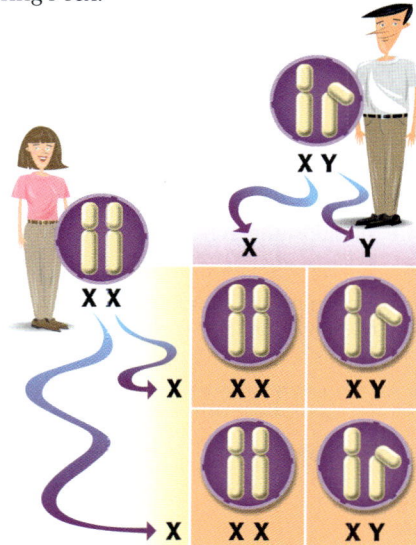

VOCABULARY DEFINITIONS, continued

SECTION 2

sex cells eggs or sperm; a sex cell carries half the number of chromosomes found in other body cells

homologous chromosomes chromosomes with matching information

meiosis cell division that produces sex cells

sex chromosomes chromosomes that carry genes that determine the sex of offspring

 Vocabulary Review Worksheet 5

 Blackline masters of these Chapter Highlights can be found in the **Study Guide.**

---

internetconnect

GO TO: go.hrw.com

Visit the **HRW** Web site for a variety of learning tools related to this chapter. Just type in the keyword:

KEYWORD: HSTHER

GO TO: www.scilinks.org

Visit the **National Science Teachers Association** on-line Web site for Internet resources related to this chapter. Just type in the *sci*LINKS number for more information about the topic:

TOPIC	*sci*LINKS NUMBER
Gregor Mendel	HSTL105
Heredity	HSTL110
Dominant and Recessive Traits	HSTL115
Cell Division	HSTL120

Lab and Activity Highlights

LabBank

 Long-Term Projects & Research Ideas,
Portrait of a Dog, Project 5

Chapter 5 • Chapter Highlights

Chapter Review Answers

USING VOCABULARY
1. sex cells
2. phenotype, genotype
3. Meiosis
4. alleles
5. self-pollinating

UNDERSTANDING CONCEPTS
Multiple Choice
6. a
7. c
8. b
9. b
10. c
11. c
12. c

Short Answer
13. Females have two X chromosomes. Males have one X and one Y chromosome.
14. Sample answer: A recessive trait is a genetic trait that is expressed only if there are two recessive alleles for the gene. A recessive trait is not expressed if an allele for a dominant trait is present.
15. Sex cells have half the number of chromosomes as other body cells.

Concept Mapping
16. An answer to this exercise can be found at the end of this book.

CRITICAL THINKING AND PROBLEM SOLVING
17. The trait for blue eyes must be determined by a recessive allele. Brown must be dominant to blue. So both parents must carry the blue recessive allele, and a blue recessive allele must have been passed on to the child from both parents.
18. Meiosis is important for reproduction because it ensures that the characteristic number of chromosomes will not be doubled when an egg and a sperm come together.

122 Chapter 5 • Heredity

Chapter Review

USING VOCABULARY

To complete the following sentences, choose the correct term from each pair of terms listed below:

1. Sperm and eggs are known as __?__. (*sex cells* or *sex chromosomes*)

2. The __?__, the expression of a trait, is determined by the __?__, the combination of alleles. (*genotype* or *phenotype*)

3. __?__ produces cells with half the normal number of chromosomes. (*Meiosis* or *Mitosis*)

4. Different versions of the same genes are called __?__. (*sex cells* or *alleles*)

5. A __?__ plant can pollinate its own eggs. (*self-pollinating* or *true-breeding*)

UNDERSTANDING CONCEPTS

Multiple Choice

6. Genes are found on
   a. chromosomes.
   b. alleles.
   c. proteins.
   d. anthers.

7. The process that produces sex cells is
   a. mitosis.
   b. photosynthesis.
   c. meiosis.
   d. probability.

8. The passing of traits from parents to offspring is
   a. probability.
   b. heredity.
   c. recessive.
   d. meiosis.

9. If you cross a white flower (with the genotype *pp*) with a purple flower (with the genotype *PP*), the possible genotypes in the offspring are:
   a. *PP* and *pp*.
   b. all *Pp*.
   c. all *PP*.
   d. all *pp*.

10. For the above cross, what would the phenotypes be?
    a. all white
    b. all tall
    c. all purple
    d. $\frac{1}{2}$ white, $\frac{1}{2}$ purple

11. In meiosis,
    a. the chromosomes are copied twice.
    b. the nucleus divides once.
    c. four cells are produced from a single cell.
    d. All of the above

12. Probability is
    a. always expressed as a ratio.
    b. a 50% chance that an event will occur.
    c. the mathematical chance that an event will occur.
    d. a 3:1 chance that an event will occur.

Short Answer

13. Which sex chromosomes do females have? Which do males have?

14. In your own words, give a one- or two-sentence definition of the term *recessive trait*.

15. How are sex cells different from other body cells?

122

19. No; true-breeding plants always produce the same trait. If Mendel had not used true-breeding plants, then he would have seen much more variation in traits. He would not have been able to tell whether traits were dominant or recessive because there would not have been reproducible ratios of dominant to recessive traits.

Concept Mapping Transparency 5

Concept Mapping

16. Use the following terms to create a concept map: meiosis, eggs, cell division, X chromosome, sex cells, sperm, mitosis, Y chromosome.

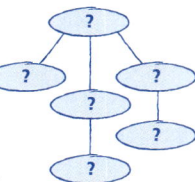

CRITICAL THINKING AND PROBLEM SOLVING

Write one or two sentences to answer the following questions:

17. If a child has blue eyes and both her parents have brown eyes, what does that tell you about the trait for blue eyes? Explain your answer.

18. Why is meiosis important for sexual reproduction?

19. Gregor Mendel used only true-breeding plants. If he had used plants that were not true breeding, do you think he would have discovered dominant and recessive traits? Why or why not?

MATH IN SCIENCE

20. Assume that **Y** is the dominant allele for yellow seeds and **y** is the recessive allele for green seeds. What is the probability that a pea plant with the genotype **Yy** crossed with a pea plant with the genotype **yy** will have offspring with the genotype **yy**?

INTERPRETING GRAPHICS

Examine the Punnett square below, and then answer the following questions:

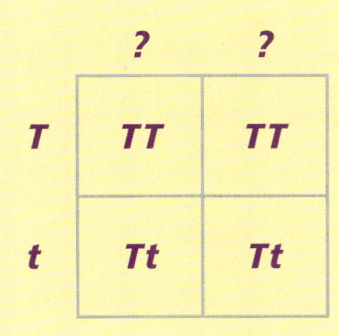

21. What is the unknown genotype?

22. If **T** represents the allele for tall pea plants, and **t** represents the allele for short pea plants, what is the phenotype of each parent and of the offspring?

23. If each of the offspring were allowed to self-fertilize, what are the possible genotypes in the next generation?

24. What is the probability of each genotype in item 23?

 Take a minute to review your answers to the Pre-Reading Questions found at the bottom of page 104. Have your answers changed? If necessary, revise your answers based on what you have learned since you began this chapter.

MATH IN SCIENCE

20. The probability of inheriting a **y** allele from the **Yy** plant is $\frac{1}{2}$. The probability of inheriting a **y** allele for the **yy** plant is $\frac{1}{1}$. Therefore, the probability that the offspring will inherit the **yy** genotype is $\frac{1}{1} \times \frac{1}{2}$, or 50 percent. These results can be visualized by using a Punnett square.

INTERPRETING GRAPHICS

21. *TT*
22. All the parents and offspring are tall pea plants.
23. Students should make two new Punnett squares. Self fertilization of *TT (TT × TT)* will yield offspring of all *TT*. Self fertilization of *Tt (Tt × Tt)* will yield offspring of *TT, Tt,* and *tt*.
24. *TT* has a 100 percent probability with a *TT* parent and a 25 percent probability with a *Tt* parent. *Tt* has a 50 percent probability with a *Tt* parent, and a 0 percent probability with a *TT* parent. The genotype *tt* has a 25 percent probability with a *Tt* parent, and a 0 percent probability with a *TT* parent.

 Blackline masters of this Chapter Review can be found in the **Study Guide.**

SCIENCE, TECHNOLOGY, AND SOCIETY

Mapping the Human Genome

Answer to What Do You Think?
The Human Genome Project has spawned a flurry of debate over ethical, social, and legal issues surrounding the use of genetic information. Students have been asked to further investigate these issues. Some issues students may wish to consider include the following:

1. **Genetic privacy** Insurance companies may require genetic testing before offering health insurance. Should insurance companies be allowed to see a person's genetic profile when deciding to provide an otherwise healthy person medical insurance? Employers may choose not to hire people who may become sick. Are people entitled to keep their genetic profiles private?

2. **Ownership of genetic information** Many researchers are rushing to sequence and patent genes. Sometimes scientists patent genes even when they do not know what proteins these genes code for. When researchers patent and claim rights to genetic information, they limit its use by other scientists. Patenting genetic information, however, encourages competition and more-frequent discoveries. Should scientists be able to patent genetic information?

Science, Technology, and Society

Mapping the Human Genome

Scientists with the United States Department of Energy and National Institutes of Health are in the midst of what may be the most ambitious scientific research project ever—the Human Genome Project (HGP). These researchers want to create a map of all the genes found on human chromosomes. The body's complete set of genetic instructions is called the genome. Scientists hope this project will provide valuable information that may help prevent or even cure many genetic diseases.

Whose Genes Are These?
You might be wondering whose genome the scientists are decoding. Actually, it doesn't matter because each person is unique in only about 1 percent of his or her genetic material. The scientists' goal is to identify how tiny differences in that 1 percent of DNA make each of us who we are, and to understand how some changes can cause disease.

Genetic Medicine
The tiny changes that can cause disease, called mutations, are often inherited. Once scientists determine the normal order of our genes, doctors may be able to use this information to help detect mutations in patients. Then doctors would be able to warn patients of an increased risk of a disease before any symptoms appear! For example, a doctor's early warning about a genetic risk of high cholesterol would give a person a chance to eat healthier and exercise more before any serious symptoms were detectable.

Advancing Technology
Scientists organizing the HGP hope to have a complete and accurate sequence of the human

▲ *This scientist is performing one of the many steps involved in the research for the Human Genome Project.*

genome—estimated to have between 50,000 and 100,000 genes—by 2003. One day in the future, scientists may even be able to provide people with a healthy gene to replace a mutated one. This technique, called gene therapy, may eventually be the cure for many genetic diseases.

What Do You Think?
▶ Despite the medical advancements the Human Genome Project will bring, many people continue to debate ethical, social, and legal issues surrounding this controversial project. Look into these issues, and discuss them with your classmates!

3. **Perfect babies** Doctors can test developing fetuses for some genetic problems. Should they be able to replace bad genes? Should parents be able to manipulate the genetic information so their children will have a desired eye color or hair color? When should physicians be allowed to change a baby's genetic information, and when shouldn't they?

Health Watch

Lab Rats with Wings

What's less than 1 mm in length, can be extremely annoying when buzzing around your kitchen, and sometimes grows legs out of its eyes? The answer is *Drosophila melanogaster*—better known as the fruit fly because it feeds on fruit. This tiny insect has played a big role in helping us understand many illnesses, especially those that occur at certain stages of human development. Scientists use fruit flies to find out more about diseases and disorders such as cancer, Alzheimer's disease, muscular dystrophy, and Down's syndrome.

Why a Fly?

Fruit flies are some scientists' favorite research animal. Scientists can raise several generations of fruit flies in just a few months. Because fruit flies have only a two-week life cycle, scientists can alter a fruit-fly gene as part of an experiment and then see the results very quickly.

Another advantage to using these tiny animals is their small size. Thousands of fruit flies can be raised in a relatively small space.

▲ *This is what a normal fruit fly looks like under a scanning electron microscope.*

▲ *This fruit fly has legs growing out of its eyes!*

Researchers can afford to buy and maintain a variety of fruit fly strains to use in experiments.

Comparing Codes

Another important reason for using these "lab rats with wings" is that their genetic code is relatively simple and well understood. Fruit flies have 12,000 genes, whereas humans have more than 70,000. Nonetheless, many fruit-fly genes are similar in function to human genes, and scientists have learned to manipulate them to produce genetic mutations. Scientists who study these mutations gain valuable information about genetic mutations in humans. Without fruit flies, some human genetic problems that we now have important information about—such as basal cell carcinoma cancer—might have taken many more years and many more dollars to study.

Where Do You Draw the Line?

▶ Do you think it is acceptable for scientists to perform research on fruit flies? What about on rats, mice, and rabbits? Have a debate with your classmates about conducting scientific experiments on other species.

HEALTH WATCH
Lab Rats with Wings

Teaching Strategy

This activity has two objectives. First, it will allow the students to obtain a better grasp of the relationship a gene has to other body structures, such as cells or organs. Second, it will give students a better understanding of what is meant by the word *mutation* in the fruit-fly article.

For this activity to work, students must understand what blueprints are. Explain that blueprints are sheets of paper that have sketches of all the aspects of the house to be built. These plans are followed precisely in order to build the house. Show students sample blueprints, and point out all the dimensional information they contain.

Next present an analogy to the students using the following representations:

body = city
organ = neighborhood
cell of organ = house in neighborhood
chromosomes in cell = blueprints for house in neighborhood
gene on chromosome = part of blueprints that gives instructions for certain aspect of house (like dimensions of the master bedroom or direction in which a door will open)

Answers to Where Do You Draw The Line?

Answers will vary, but students should be aware that animals are used in biological research. Scientists have learned a great deal using animal models. Many scientists who work with animals take great care to minimize animal suffering during the experiments. In recent years, other models—such as computer models and cultured cells—have become available and can be used as substitutes for animals in some experiments.

Chapter Organizer

CHAPTER ORGANIZATION	TIME MINUTES	OBJECTIVES	LABS, INVESTIGATIONS, AND DEMONSTRATIONS
Chapter Opener pp. 126–127	45	National Standards: UCP 2, SAI 1, LS 1f, 2c–2e	**Start-Up Activity** Fingerprint Your Friends, p. 127
Section 1 What Do Genes Look Like?	90	▶ Describe the basic structure of the DNA molecule. ▶ Explain how DNA molecules can be copied. ▶ Explain some of the exceptions to Mendel's heredity principles. UCP 2, 5, SAI 1, 2, ST 1, 2, SPSP 4, 5, HNS 1–3, LS 1a, 2c–2e, 5a; LabBook UCP 2, 5, HNS 1, LS 1a	**Demonstration,** p. 133 in ATE `BASIC` **Making Models,** Base-Pair Basics, p. 706 `BASIC` **Datasheets for LabBook,** Base-Pair Basics, Datasheet 13 `BASIC`
Section 2 How DNA Works	90	▶ Explain the relationship between genes and proteins. ▶ Outline the basic steps in making a protein. ▶ Define *mutation,* and give an example. ▶ Evaluate the information in a pedigree. UCP 1, 2, SAI 1, 2, ST 2, SPSP 5, LS 1f, 2b–2e, 5b	**QuickLab,** Mutations, p. 139 `GENERAL` **Interactive Explorations CD-ROM,** DNA Pawprints `GENERAL` A **Worksheet** is also available in the **Interactive Explorations Teacher's Edition.** **Long-Term Projects & Research Ideas,** Project 6 `ADVANCED`

*See page **T20** for a complete correlation of this book with the*

NATIONAL SCIENCE EDUCATION STANDARDS.

TECHNOLOGY RESOURCES

 Guided Reading Audio CD
English or Spanish, Chapter 6

 One-Stop Planner CD-ROM with Test Generator

 CNN Science, Technology & Society, Developing the Perfect Pepper, Segment 9

 Interactive Explorations CD-ROM
CD 3, Exploration 8, DNA Pawprints

Chapter 6 • Genes and Gene Technology

Chapter 6 • Genes and Gene Technology

CLASSROOM WORKSHEETS, TRANSPARENCIES, AND RESOURCES	SCIENCE INTEGRATION AND CONNECTIONS	REVIEW AND ASSESSMENT
Directed Reading Worksheet 6 BASIC **Science Puzzlers, Twisters & Teasers,** Worksheet 6 ADVANCED		
Directed Reading Worksheet 6, Section 1 BASIC **Transparency 19,** DNA Structure **Math Skills for Science Worksheet 4,** A Shortcut for Multiplying Large Numbers GENERAL **Science Skills Worksheet 23,** Science Drawing GENERAL **Transparency 20,** Incomplete Dominance	**Real-World Connection,** p. 129 in ATE **MathBreak,** Genes and Bases, p. 131 GENERAL **Math and More,** p. 131 in ATE GENERAL **Cross-Disciplinary Focus,** p. 132 in ATE **Scientific Debate:** DNA on Trial, p. 148 GENERAL	**Homework,** p. 128 in ATE ADVANCED **Self-Check,** p. 131 **Homework,** p. 133 in ATE GENERAL **Review,** p. 135 GENERAL **Quiz,** p. 135 in ATE GENERAL **Alternative Assessment,** p. 135 in ATE GENERAL
Directed Reading Worksheet 6, Section 2 BASIC **Transparency 21,** The Making of a Protein **Transparency 167,** The Formation of Smog **Transparency 22,** An Example of Substitution **Transparency 23,** Pedigree **Reinforcement Worksheet 6,** DNA Mutations BASIC **Critical Thinking Worksheet 6,** The Perfect Parrot ADVANCED	**Math and More,** p. 137 in ATE GENERAL **Meteorology Connection,** p. 138 **Connect to Earth Science,** p. 138 in ATE **Cross-Disciplinary Focus,** p. 139 in ATE ADVANCED **Apply,** p. 140 GENERAL **Cross-Disciplinary Focus,** p. 140 in ATE **Holt Anthology of Science Fiction,** *Moby James* BASIC	**Self-Check,** p. 137 **Review,** p. 141 GENERAL **Quiz,** p. 141 in ATE GENERAL **Alternative Assessment,** p. 141 in ATE GENERAL

END-OF-CHAPTER REVIEW AND ASSESSMENT

Chapter Review in Study Guide
Vocabulary and Notes in Study Guide
Chapter Tests with Performance-Based Assessment, Chapter 6 Test
Chapter Tests with Performance-Based Assessment, Performance-Based Assessment 6
Concept Mapping Transparency 6

 Holt, Rinehart and Winston On-line Resources
go.hrw.com

For worksheets and other teaching aids related to this chapter, visit the HRW Web site and type in the keyword: **HSTDNA**

 National Science Teachers Association
www.scilinks.org

Encourage students to use the *sci*LINKS numbers listed in the internet connect boxes to access information and resources on the **NSTA** Web site.

Chapter Resources & Worksheets

Visual Resources

TEACHING TRANSPARENCIES

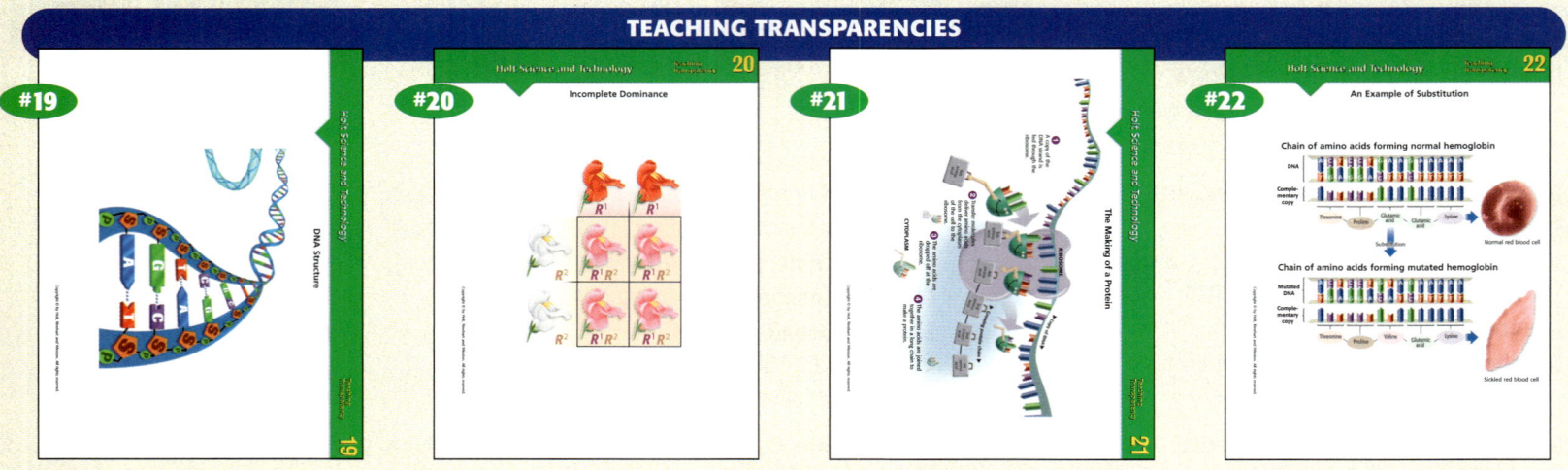

TEACHING TRANSPARENCIES

CONCEPT MAPPING TRANSPARENCY

Meeting Individual Needs

DIRECTED READING

REINFORCEMENT & VOCABULARY REVIEW

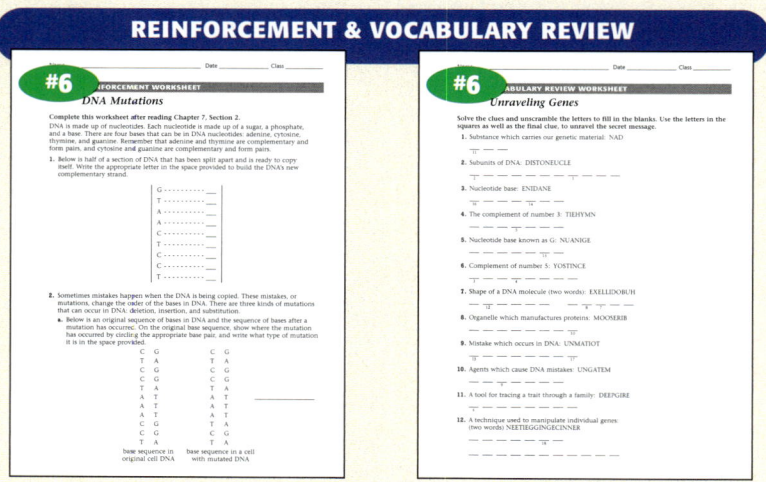

SCIENCE PUZZLERS, TWISTERS & TEASERS

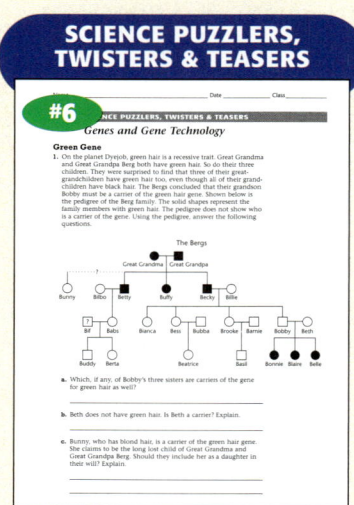

Chapter 6 • Genes and Gene Technology

Chapter 6 • Genes and Gene Technology

Review & Assessment

STUDY GUIDE

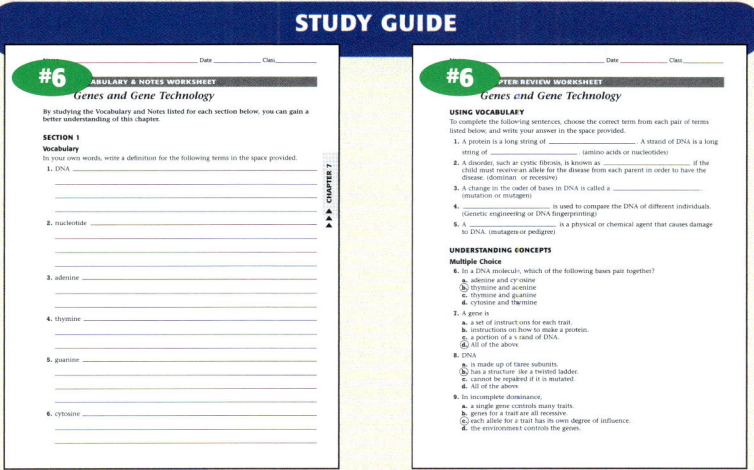

CHAPTER TESTS WITH PERFORMANCE-BASED ASSESSMENT

Lab Worksheets

LONG-TERM PROJECTS & RESEARCH IDEAS

DATASHEETS FOR LABBOOK

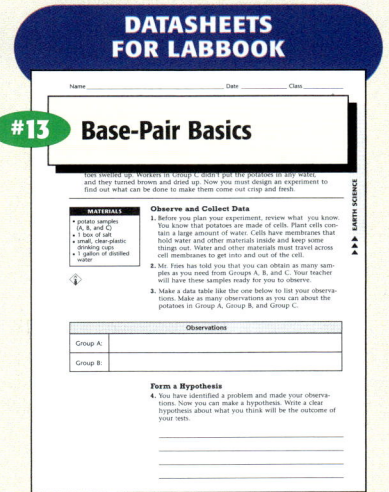

Applications & Extensions

CRITICAL THINKING & PROBLEM SOLVING

SCIENCE TECHNOLOGY

INTERACTIVE EXPLORATIONS

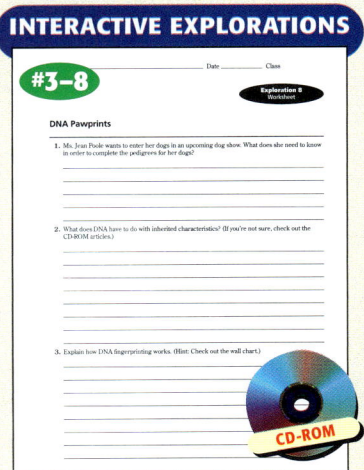

Chapter 6 • Chapter Resources & Worksheets 125D

Chapter Background

SECTION 1

What Do Genes Look Like?

▶ **DNA**

In 1869, long before the time of Watson and Crick, a 22-year-old Swiss scientist isolated DNA from a cell nucleus. Unfortunately, he had no idea of its function, much less of its role in inheritance. It was not until 75 years later, in 1944, that an American geneticist named Oswald T. Avery found evidence that DNA is the carrier of genetic information.

IS THAT A FACT!

- Human DNA consists of about 3 billion base pairs.

- If you could print a book with all the genetic information carried in just one human cell, it would be 500,000 pages long.

- The uncoiled DNA in the nucleus of a human body cell is about 2 m long. The DNA in chromosomes is so tightly coiled that the 46 chromosomes from a human body cell would be only about 0.00032 cm long if they were lined up end to end!

▶ **Eye Color**

Eye color is a trait that is influenced by the presence of melanin, a dark pigment, in the iris. People whose eyes have the least pigment have blue eyes, and people whose eyes have the most pigment have brown eyes. Scientists think that the number of alleles present for eye pigment control eye color. For example, one allele is thought to contribute to a medium blue eye color, while as many as eight alleles may contribute to dark brown eye color.

SECTION 2

How DNA Works

▶ **Cracking the Genetic Code**

In the 1960s, scientists cracked the genetic code—the translation between codons, the three base sequences and amino acids. They have found that the genetic code is universal in almost all living organisms. If a codon aligns with a particular amino acid in humans, the same codon aligns with the same amino acid in bacteria. This similarity suggests that all life-forms have a common evolutionary ancestor.

▶ **Mutations and Natural Selection**

The discovery that changes in DNA can lead to new traits supports Darwin's theory of evolution by natural selection. When an environment changes, mutations may enhance an organism's chances of survival in the new conditions. For example, a certain mutation makes houseflies resistant to DDT but also reduces their growth rate. Originally, this mutation was harmful, but after DDT became part of the environment of many houseflies, the mutation helped the flies survive. By the process of natural selection, the mutation was spread throughout the fly population.

▶ **Amino Acids**

Of the known amino acids, 20 are necessary for human growth and metabolism. The human body can manufacture 10 of these. The other 10, which are called the essential amino acids, must be obtained from plant or animal proteins in the diet. Foods containing all the essential amino acids include eggs, milk, seafood, and meat. Legumes, grains, nuts, and seeds contain many of the essential amino acids.

▶ **Protein Synthesis**

It took many years for scientists to determine how protein is synthesized in the cell. The discovery that DNA's nucleotide sequence corresponds to a certain

Chapter 6 • Genes and Gene Technology

amino acid sequence was a key step in unlocking this mystery. This link was conclusively proven by Charles Yanofsky and Sydney Brenner in 1964.

- The genetic sequences used to make proteins can be compared to sentences. Where each three-letter "word" in the genetic "sentence" starts and stops is very important for constructing a protein. For example, suppose the sentence to code for a particular protein read "PAT SAW THE FAT CAT." If you start just one base pair too late, the sentence would read "ATS AWT HEF ATC AT," which is meaningless.

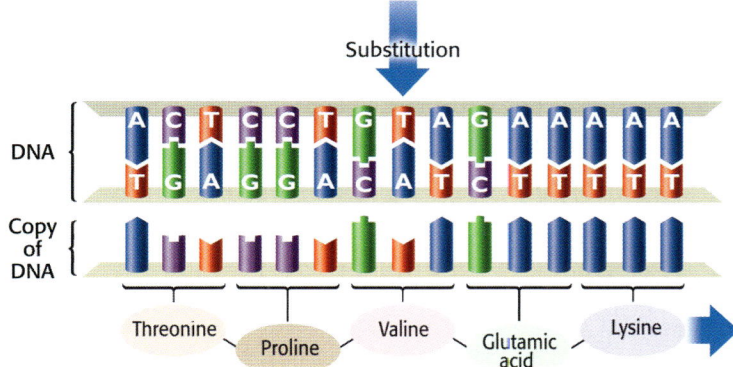

▶ Huntington's Disease
Huntington's disease is a hereditary degenerative brain disease caused by a dominant allele. People affected by Huntington's often display peculiar, dancelike movements. In the United States, many cases of Huntington's disease can be traced back to two brothers. The two men immigrated to North America from England in the 1600s because their family was accused of witchcraft. Apparently, they were persecuted because of their strange behaviors, which are now understood to be symptoms of Huntington's disease.

▶ Chimeras
Genetically engineered hybrid creatures are often called chimeras. The word *chimera* comes from Greek mythology; the Chimera was a fire-breathing she-monster, usually depicted as a composite of a lion, a goat, and a serpent.

▶ Ethical Issues
Scientists disagree about both the ethics of genetic engineering and the safety risks involved.

- Dr. Maxine Frank Singer was one of the first scientists to alert the National Academy of Science to the potential hazards of genetic engineering. Due to the efforts of Dr. Singer and her colleagues, the National Institute of Health developed specific guidelines for genetic research in 1973. These guidelines regulate the production and use of genetically engineered DNA and organisms.

▶ Worm Work
Caenorhabditis elegans, a tiny worm used in genetic experiments, has many genes in common with humans. In fact, scientists have given these worms human antidepressants to study the genetic causes of depression.

▶ DNA Fingerprints
DNA fingerprints are frequently used in criminal investigations. The DNA can come from hair, skin cells, blood, or other body fluids left at the crime scene by the perpetrator. Scientists use enzymes to make many copies of the DNA and then use other enzymes to cut the DNA into fragments. The fragments are separated by size and other characteristics on a specially treated plate. A photograph of the plate is taken, showing a unique set of dark bands. This set of bands is known as a DNA fingerprint. The fingerprint is then compared with the DNA fingerprint of the suspect to help determine innocence or guilt.

For background information about teaching strategies and issues, refer to the *Professional Reference for Teachers.*

Genes and Gene Technology

 Pre-Reading Questions

Students may not know the answers to these questions before reading the chapter, so accept any reasonable response.

Suggested Answers

1. Proteins act as chemical messengers, and they help determine how tall you will grow, what colors you can see, and whether your hair is curly or straight.

2. Genes are the inherited genetic information that code for the proteins in all living things. They are found on chromosomes.

3. Sometimes diseases are caused by problems in the DNA. Scientists are learning ways of using gene therapy to correct or replace problematic DNA.

 Directed Reading Worksheet 6

 Science Puzzlers, Twisters & Teasers Worksheet 6

 Guided Reading Audio CD English or Spanish, Chapter 6

Sections

1. **What Do Genes Look Like?** 128
   MathBreak 131
   Internet Connect 135

2. **How DNA Works** 136
   Meteorology Connection 138
   QuickLab 139
   Apply 140
   Internet Connect 141

Chapter Review 144
Feature Articles 146, 147
LabBook 706–707

1. How are proteins related to the way you look?
2. What are genes? Where are they found?
3. How does knowing about DNA help scientists treat diseases?

Genes and Gene Technology

Unlocking Life's Master Codes

Did you know that each one of your cells has a 2-meter-long strand of DNA? This computer-generated DNA model hints at just how complex a DNA molecule is. Like a giant puzzle, the patterns in the spiraling DNA strands contain the codes for the growth of all cells and processes in living things. Human DNA has about 3 billion individual codes, or puzzle pieces. As of the year 2000, gene scientists mapped them all. In this chapter, you will learn about the structure of DNA and the genetic information it contains.

---

internet connect

 HRW On-line Resources
go.hrw.com
For worksheets and other teaching aids, visit the HRW Web site and type in the keyword: **HSTDNA**

 sciLINKS NSTA
www.scilinks.com
Use the *sci*LINKS numbers at the end of each chapter for additional resources on the **NSTA** Web site.

 CNNfyi.com
www.cnnfyi.com
Visit the CNN Web site for current events coverage and classroom resources.

START-UP Activity

FINGERPRINT YOUR FRIENDS

One common method of identification is fingerprinting. Does it really work? Are everyone's fingerprints different? Try this activity to find out.

Procedure

1. Rub a **piece of charcoal** back and forth across a **piece of tracing paper**. Rub the tip of one of your fingers on the charcoal mark. Then place a **small piece of transparent tape** over the charcoal on your finger. Remove the tape, and stick it on a **piece of white paper**. Do the same for the rest of your fingers.

2. Observe the patterns with a **magnifying lens**. What kinds of patterns do you see? The fingerprint patterns shown below are the most common found among humans.

Analysis

3. Compare your fingerprints with those of your classmates. How many of each type do you see? Do any two people in your class have the same prints? Try to explain your findings.

Whorl   **Arch**   **Loop**

START-UP Activity

FINGERPRINT YOUR FRIENDS

MATERIALS
FOR EACH GROUP: • piece of charcoal • sheet of tracing paper • transparent tape • white paper • magnifying lens

Safety Caution

Remind students to review all safety cautions and icons before beginning this lab activity. Charcoal is nontoxic, but it can stain clothes.

Teacher's Notes

The loop pattern is found in about 65 percent of the population, the whorl in about 30 percent, and the arch in about 5 percent.

Answer to START-UP Activity

3. The number of fingerprint types will vary for each class. No two students should have the same fingerprint (unless there are identical twins in the class). Any logical, reasonable explanation for this is acceptable, but students should discuss genetic variety in their explanation.

Chapter 6 • Genes and Gene Technology

SECTION 1

Focus

What Do Genes Look Like?

This section introduces students to the structure and function of DNA, the process of DNA replication, and the relationship of DNA to traits. The section concludes with a discussion of some exceptions to Mendelian genetics.

Bellringer

Have students unscramble the following words and use them in a sentence:

NDA (DNA)

etcutsurr (structure)

(Sample sentence: DNA has a complex structure.)

1) Motivate

ACTIVITY

Modeling Genetic Code
Create a code by pairing each letter of the alphabet with a numeral. For example, the numeral 1 could represent the letter *a*. Have students encode a brief message. Then have students exchange and decode the message. Compare the process of encoding messages with the encoding of genetic information in DNA. Explain that the genetic code is based on the sequence of the four nucleotide bases.

 Directed Reading Worksheet 6 Section 1

Section 1

Terms to Learn

DNA
nucleotide
adenine
thymine
guanine
cytosine

What You'll Do

◆ Describe the basic structure of the DNA molecule.
◆ Explain how DNA molecules can be copied.
◆ Explain some of the exceptions to Mendel's heredity principles.

What Do Genes Look Like?

Scientists know that traits are determined by genes and that genes are passed from one generation to another. Scientists also know that genes are located on chromosomes, structures in the nucleus of most cells. Chromosomes are made of protein and **DNA**, short for deoxyribonucleic (dee AHKS ee RIE boh noo KLEE ik) acid. But which type of material makes the genes?

The Pieces of the Puzzle

The gene material must be able to do two things. First it must be able to supply instructions for cell processes and for building cell structures. Second it must be able to be copied each time a cell divides, so that each cell contains an identical set of genes. Early studies of DNA suggested that DNA was a very simple molecule. Because of this, most scientists thought protein probably carried hereditary information. After all, proteins are complex molecules.

In the 1940s, however, scientists discovered that genes of bacteria are made of DNA. How could something so simple hold the key to an organism's characteristics? To find the answer, let's take a closer look at the subunits of a DNA molecule.

Nucleotides—The Subunits of DNA DNA is made of only four subunits, which are known as **nucleotides.** Each nucleotide consists of three different types of material: a sugar, a phosphate, and a base. Nucleotides are identical except for the base. The four bases are **adenine, thymine, guanine,** and **cytosine,** and they each have a slightly different shape. The bases are usually referred to by the first letters in their names, A, T, G, and C. **Figure 1** shows diagrams of the four nucleotides.

Adenine (A)

Nucleotide

Thymine (T) Guanine (G) Cytosine (C)

Figure 1 *Can you imagine how the nucleotides might fit together?*

Homework

Research Have students collect information on the use of amino acids to gain muscle. Suggest that they look at ads for amino acid supplements in health-food or fitness magazines or at labels of amino acid powdered drinks at the supermarket. Use these materials to discuss issues such as the expense of such supplements and how they might be used by the body. Discuss how amino acids might be acquired in a balanced diet.

128 Chapter 6 • Genes and Gene Technology

Chargaff's Rules In the 1950s, a biochemist named Erwin Chargaff found that the amount of adenine in DNA always equals the amount of thymine, and the amount of guanine always equals the amount of cytosine. His findings are known as Chargaff's rules.

At the time, no one knew quite what to make of Chargaff's findings. How could Chargaff's rules help solve the mysteries of DNA's structure? Read on to find out.

A Picture of DNA

More clues came from the laboratory of British scientist Maurice Wilkins. There, chemist Rosalind Franklin, shown in **Figure 2,** was able to create images of DNA molecules. The process that she used to create these images is known as X-ray diffraction. In this process, X rays bombard the DNA molecule. When the X ray hits a particle within the molecule, the ray bounces off the particle. This creates a pattern that is captured on film. The images that Franklin created suggested that DNA has a spiral shape.

Figure 2 Rosalind Franklin, 1920–1958

Eureka!

Two other young scientists, James Watson and Francis Crick, shown in **Figure 3,** were also investigating the mystery of DNA's structure. Based on the work of others, Watson and Crick built models of DNA using simple materials, such as labeled pieces of cardboard. After seeing the X-ray images of DNA made by Rosalind Franklin, Watson and Crick concluded that DNA resembles a twisted ladder shape known as a *double helix*. Watson and Crick used their DNA model to predict how DNA is copied. Upon making the discovery, Crick is said to have exclaimed, "We have discovered the secret of life!"

Figure 3 This photo shows James Watson, on the left, and Francis Crick, on the right, with their model of DNA.

SCIENTISTS AT ODDS

In 1951, Rosalind Franklin began working with Maurice Wilkins in the lab at King's College, in London, but she and Wilkins never got along. Both Wilkins and James Watson belittled Franklin's abilities and accomplishments. Francis Crick, however, respected her work. Franklin's study suggesting the helical structure of DNA was instrumental in Watson and Crick's discovery of DNA's double-stranded shape. If Franklin had not died in 1958, she almost certainly would have shared the Nobel Prize awarded to Watson, Crick, and Wilkins in 1962 for their discovery of the structure of the DNA molecule.

② Teach, continued

ACTIVITY
Making a DNA Model

MATERIALS

FOR EACH GROUP:
- 2 licorice whips (60 cm long)
- 50–60 toothpicks
- 50–60 gumdrops in four different colors

Have students work in groups to construct a candy model of DNA. The licorice represents the sides of the DNA molecule, and the gumdrops represent the base pairs. Each group should stretch out two licorice whips parallel to each other. Tell them to slide two gumdrops onto the middle of a toothpick to resemble a complementary base pair and to then insert each end of the toothpick into the licorice whips, connecting them the way rungs connect the two sides of a ladder. After the ladder of toothpicks grows to 20–30 base pairs, have students shape the helix by spiraling it around a tube or pole. **Sheltered English**

MEETING INDIVIDUAL NEEDS
Learners Having Difficulty
To help students better understand how the term *complementary* relates to the structure of DNA, point out that the term means "completing." Using **Figure 5**, explain that complementary base pairs join together to *complete* each rung on the spiral-staircase structure of DNA. Then point out that complementary strands of DNA join together to complete one DNA molecule. **Sheltered English**

 Teaching Transparency 19 "DNA Structure"

DNA Structure

The twisted ladder, or double helix, shape is represented in **Figure 4.** As you can see in **Figure 5,** the two sides of the ladder are made of alternating sugar molecules and phosphate molecules. The rungs of the ladder are composed of a pair of nucleotide bases. Adenine on one side always pairs up with thymine on the other side. Guanine always pairs up with cytosine in the same way. How might this structure explain Chargaff's findings?

Figure 4 The structure of DNA can be compared to a twisted ladder.

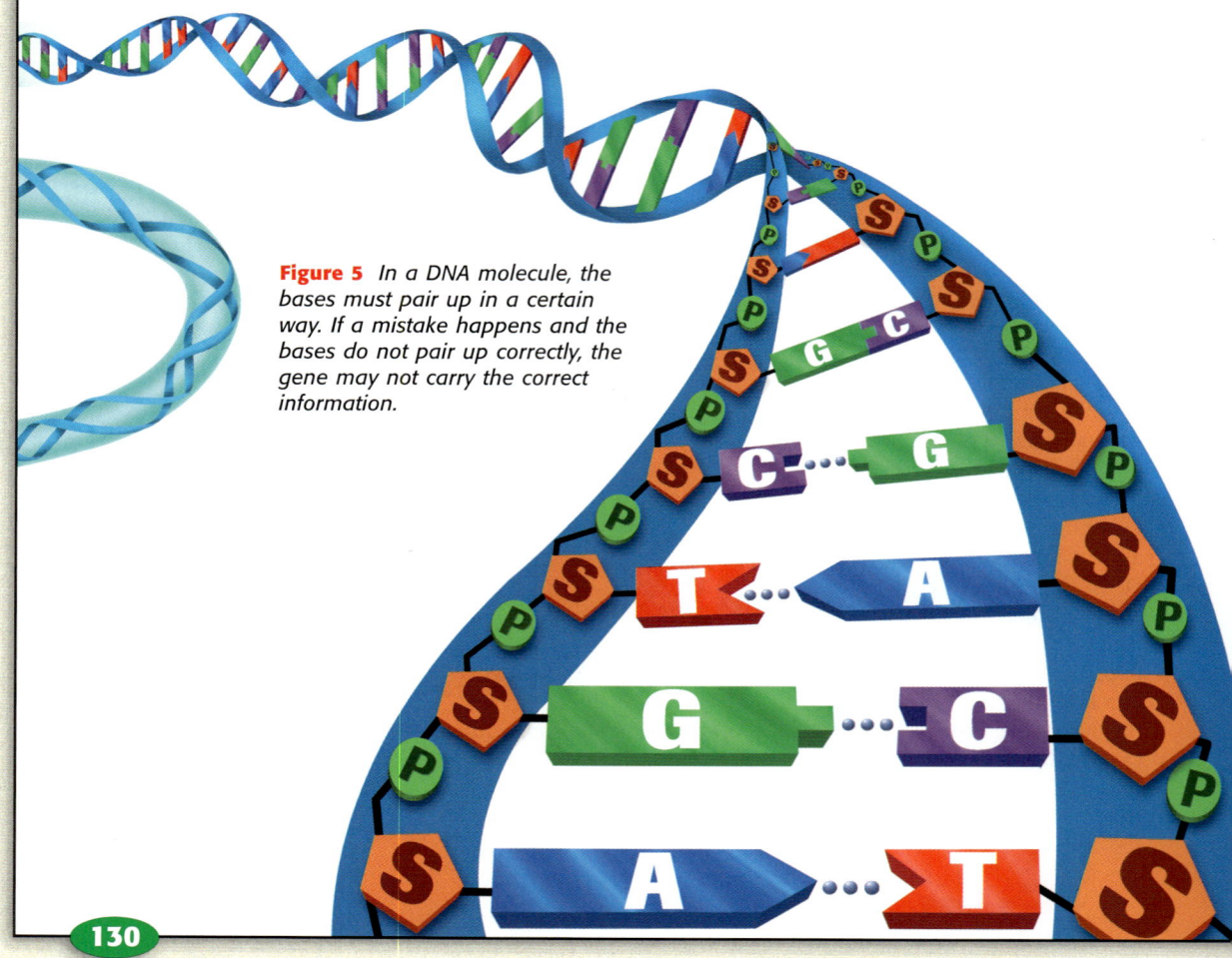

Figure 5 In a DNA molecule, the bases must pair up in a certain way. If a mistake happens and the bases do not pair up correctly, the gene may not carry the correct information.

 SCIENCE

Do werewolves really exist? No, but there is a gene believed to be located on the X chromosome that causes thick and abundant hair to grow on the upper body and face, including the ears, nose, cheeks, forehead, and even eyelids of affected males. This condition is sometimes called the werewolf syndrome because people with this gene resemble werewolves depicted in movies. This condition only affects people's appearance, however, not their behavior.

Making Copies of DNA

What's so great about DNA? Because adenine always bonds with thymine and guanine always bonds with cytosine, one side of a DNA molecule is *complementary* to the other. For example, a sequence such as ACCG always binds to the sequence TGGC. This allows DNA to make a copy of itself, or *replicate*.

As illustrated in **Figure 6,** a DNA molecule replicates by splitting down the middle where the two bases meet. The bases on each side of the molecule can be used as a template, or pattern, for a new complementary side. This creates two identical molecules of DNA.

MATH BREAK

Genes and Bases

A human being has about 100,000 genes. If there are about 30,000 bases in each human gene, about how many bases are in all the genes?

Figure 6 *The illustration shows DNA separating down the middle in order to make a copy of itself. Each half of the original molecule serves as a template along which a new complementary strand forms. The photograph shows a DNA molecule that has separated. It is magnified about 1 million times.*

Old   New   New   Old

Self-Check

What would the complementary strand of DNA be for the following sequence of bases? ACCTAGTTG
(See page 782 to check your answer.)

BRAIN FOOD

If you took all the DNA in your body from all of your cells and stretched it out end to end, it would extend about 610 million kilometers. That's long enough to stretch from Earth to the sun and back—twice!

Answer to MATHBREAK
3,000,000,000

USING THE FIGURE

Have students compare the illustration with the photograph of DNA replication in **Figure 6.** Have them identify the fork, or upside-down V, in both images. Point out that this is the point where the two strands of DNA have separated. Ask the following question:

How many molecules of DNA will there be when the process is complete? (two)

Are the new DNA molecules complementary or identical to the original DNA molecule? (identical)

Answer to Self-Check
TGGATCAAC

MATH and MORE

By causing DNA to replicate in a test tube, scientists can make as many as a billion copies of the original DNA template in very little time. This is a chain reaction in which DNA multiplies **exponentially** with time. This process is extremely important in biotechnology and in genetic research. To help students understand the concept of exponential growth, calculate how much money you will have in 30 days if you start with a penny on day 1 and the amount of money you have doubles every day. Using a calculator, write the products of each multiplication on the board.

(In 30 days you will have $5,368,709.12!)

 Math Skills Worksheet 4 "A Shortcut for Multiplying Large Numbers"

MISCONCEPTION ALERT

Can ancient DNA be used to produce dinosaurs as seen in the movies *Jurassic Park* and *The Lost World*? In these movies, scientists make dinosaurs by combining fragments of ancient DNA with DNA from modern-day frogs. In reality, fragments of ancient DNA have indeed been found, but a fragment of DNA does not provide enough information to make an entire organism. Moreover, there is no way to know whether the DNA fragments are even from a dinosaur. In addition, a frog's DNA will grow a frog, which is an amphibian, not a reptile. Most scientists agree that dinosaurs were reptiles.

Section 1 • What Do Genes Look Like?

2) Teach, continued

CROSS-DISCIPLINARY FOCUS

Music Researchers at the University of California, San Francisco, are trying to find out if a gene is responsible for "perfect pitch," the ability to immediately determine any musical note upon hearing it. It is a rare ability—possessed by perhaps only one in every 2,000 people—found most often among musicians. People with perfect pitch can easily determine the musical note of a dial tone, the hum of a refrigerator, or any sound they hear. Preliminary findings indicate that people with perfect pitch may inherit the ability, but that an early education in music may also be necessary for the trait to be fully expressed.

MISCONCEPTION ALERT

Recessive traits are sometimes referred to in a negative way, as if having a recessive trait is a bad thing. Emphasize that some recessive traits are beautiful, such as the light blue eyes of the white tiger.

TOPIC: Genes and Traits
GO TO: www.scilinks.org
*sci*LINKS NUMBER: HSTL135

From Trait to Gene

The Watson-Crick model also explains how DNA can contain so much information. The bases on one side of the molecule can be put in any order, allowing for an enormous variety of genes. Each gene consists of a string of bases. The order of the bases gives the cell information about how to make each trait.

Putting It All Together DNA functions in the same way for all organisms, from bacteria to mosquitoes to whales to humans. DNA unites us all, and at the same time, it makes each of us unique. The journey from trait to DNA base is illustrated in the diagram on these two pages.

1 The skin of your forehead . . .

2 . . . magnified 10 times

3 A cross section of your skin reveals many different types of cells.

4 A typical skin cell is about 0.0025 cm in diameter.

132

Science Bloopers

James Watson disliked Rosalind Franklin so much that at a 1951 lecture where she gave information about the size and possible shape of the DNA molecule, Watson refused to take notes. It took Watson and Crick 2 more years to discover some of the same information on their own. When they did, their great discovery of the shape of the DNA molecule came within 2 weeks!

8 A single loop of DNA...

7 Each chromosome contains an enormous amount of DNA.

9 ...contains even more coils.

6 Each chromosome is made of protein and DNA.

10 Each molecule of DNA contains two halves that are connected down the center and twisted like a spiral staircase.

5 Each skin cell contains 46 chromosomes.

IS THAT A FACT!
Genetic disorders are a serious health problem for humans. Scientists know that faulty or missing genes cause diseases such as cystic fibrosis and sickle cell anemia. Scientists hope to be able to treat genetic disorders someday by altering genes within body cells.

3) Extend

DEMONSTRATION
To illustrate the difficulty of fitting all of the DNA into a cell, challenge one or more students to stuff 2 m of embroidery floss into a size "0" Vegicap™. Vegicaps are available at most health-food stores. **Sheltered English**

GROUP ACTIVITY
Have students imagine that they have just discovered the structure of DNA and must present their findings to a group of scientists. Have small groups of students use a model of DNA, a poster, or another visual aid to briefly describe the structure of DNA to their classmates. **Sheltered English**

Homework
Poster Project Have students use colored pencils to draw a portion of a DNA molecule. The drawing should reflect the correct structure of DNA and should contain a legend for identifying the subunits. You may also want students to outline the steps involved in copying DNA.

Science Skills Worksheet 23 "Science Drawing"

internet connect
TOPIC: DNA
GO TO: www.scilinks.org
sciLINKS NUMBER: HSTL130

Section 1 • What Do Genes Look Like? **133**

3) Extend, continued

READING STRATEGY

Prediction Guide Before students read this page, ask them if they agree with the following three statements. Students will discover the answers as they explore Section 1.

- Tigers with white fur are likely to have blue eyes. (true)
- There are four possible shades of blue among people with blue eyes. (false)
- If a person inherits genes for tallness, that person will grow tall no matter what. (false)

USING THE FIGURE

Emphasize that not all phenotypes result from completely dominant or completely recessive genes. Ask students what the flowers in **Figure 7** would look like if the gene for red flower color were completely dominant over the gene for white flower color. (All the offspring would be red.)

RETEACHING

  Have students describe three exceptions to Mendel's heredity principles in their ScienceLog.

Base-Pair Basics

Teaching Transparency 20 "Incomplete Dominance"

DNA on trial? Read all about it on page 146.

Figure 7 The snapdragon provides a good example of incomplete dominance.

A C G T
Learn the DNA alphabet on page 706.

More News About Traits

As you may have already discovered, things are often more complicated than they first appear to be. Gregor Mendel uncovered the basic principles of how genes are passed from one generation to the next. But as scientists learned more about heredity, they began to find exceptions to Mendel's principles. A few of these exceptions are explained in the following paragraphs.

Incomplete Dominance In his studies with peas, Mendel found that different traits did not blend together to produce an in-between form. Since then, researchers have found that sometimes one trait is not completely dominant over another. These traits do not blend together, but each allele has its own degree of influence. This is known as *incomplete dominance*. One example of this is the snapdragon flower. **Figure 7** shows a cross between a true-breeding red snapdragon (R^1R^1) and a true-breeding white snapdragon (R^2R^2). As you can see, all of the possible phenotypes for their offspring are pink because both alleles of the gene have some degree of influence.

One Gene Can Influence Many Traits Sometimes one gene influences more than one trait. An example of this phenomenon is shown by the white tiger at right. The white fur is caused by a single gene, but this gene influences more than just fur color. Do you see anything else unusual about the tiger? If you look closely, you'll see that the tiger has blue eyes. Here the gene that controls fur color also influences eye color.

IS THAT A FACT!

One of the many traits Mendel studied in pea plants was seed shape. He found that round seeds were dominant over wrinkled seeds. Seen under a microscope, the *RR* seeds have many starch grains that give them a full, round shape. The *rr* seeds have few starch grains, so they have a wrinkled shape. *Rr* seeds have an intermediate number of starch grains; they have enough starch to be full and round, but they have fewer starch grains than *RR* seeds. This is an example of incomplete dominance.

134   Chapter 6 • Genes and Gene Technology

Many Genes Can Influence a Single Trait Some traits, such as the color of your skin, hair, and eyes, are the result of several genes acting together. That's why it's difficult to tell if a trait is the result of a dominant or recessive gene. As shown in **Figure 8,** you may have blue eyes, but they are probably a slightly different shade of blue than the blue eyes of a classmate. Different combinations of alleles result in slight differences in the amount of pigment present.

The Importance of Environment It's important to remember that genes aren't the only influences on your development. Many things in your environment also influence how you grow and develop. Consider the importance of a healthy diet, exercise, and examples set by family and friends. For example, your genes may determine that you can grow to be tall, but you must receive the proper nutrients as you grow in order to reach your full potential height. You may have inherited a special talent, but you need to practice.

Figure 8 *At least two genes determine human eye color. That's why so many shades of a single color are possible.*

REVIEW

1. List and describe the parts of a nucleotide.
2. Which bases pair together in a DNA molecule?
3. What shape was suggested by Rosalind Franklin's X-ray images?
4. Explain what is meant by the statement, "DNA unites all organisms."
5. **Doing Calculations** If a sample of DNA were found to contain 20 percent cytosine, what percentage of guanine would be in this sample? Why?

internet connect

SCILINKS
NSTA

TOPIC: DNA, Genes and Traits
GO TO: www.scilinks.org
***sci*LINKS NUMBER:** HSTL130, HSTL135

4) Close

Quiz

1. Why did scientists believe that proteins, instead of DNA, carried genetic information? (because proteins are much more complex than DNA)
2. Name the three parts of every nucleotide. (a phosphate, a sugar, and a base)
3. What is incomplete dominance? (In incomplete dominance, each of the two alleles that determine a trait has its own degree of influence.)

ALTERNATIVE ASSESSMENT

Making Models Have students work independently or in pairs to make a model of DNA. Provide a variety of materials, including construction paper, pipe cleaners, scissors, glue, ribbon, and paper clips. Encourage students to use their model to demonstrate base pairing and DNA replication.
Sheltered English

▼ Answers to Review

1. Phosphate and sugar combine to form a backbone. One of the four bases is attached to the backbone, forming a nucleotide.
2. Adenine pairs with thymine, and guanine pairs with cytosine.
3. Franklin's X-ray diffraction suggested a spiral or coiled shape.
4. The statement means that the genetic code contained in DNA is the same for virtually all living things.
5. Cytosine always pairs with guanine, so the percentage of guanine would also be 20 percent.

SECTION 2

Focus

How DNA Works

This section shows how DNA is used as a template for making proteins and how errors in DNA can lead to mutations and genetic disorders. Finally, students learn about pedigrees and how they are interpreted.

Have students unscramble the following words and use them both in a sentence:

tpsoneir (proteins)

neesg (genes)

(Genes contain instructions for making proteins.)

1) Motivate

GROUP ACTIVITY

Ask students to work in small groups to come up with as many different three-letter codes as possible using the four different bases. Give each group four pieces of paper, with one of the following four letters printed on each piece: *A*, *T*, *C*, or *G*. Tell students that each piece of paper represents a different amino acid. (There are 64 possible three-letter codes—the number of codons in the genetic code responsible for making proteins.) **Sheltered English**

Directed Reading Worksheet 6 Section 2

Section 2

Terms to Learn
ribosome   mutagen
mutation   pedigree

What You'll Do
- Explain the relationship between genes and proteins.
- Outline the basic steps in making a protein.
- Define *mutation,* and give an example.
- Evaluate the information in a pedigree.

How DNA Works

Scientists knew that the order of the bases formed a code that somehow told each cell what to do. The next step in understanding DNA involved breaking this code.

Genes and Proteins

Scientists discovered that the bases in DNA read like a book, from one end to the other and in one direction only. The bases **A**, **T**, **G**, and **C** form the alphabet of the code. Groups of three bases code for a specific amino acid. For example, the three bases **CCA** code for the amino acid proline. The bases **AGC** code for the amino acid serine. As you know, proteins are made up of long strings of amino acids. The order of the bases determines the order of amino acids in a protein. Each gene is a set of instructions for making a protein. This is illustrated in **Figure 9**.

NUCLEUS — A copy of a portion of the DNA molecule where a particular gene is located is made and transferred outside of the cell nucleus.

This single strand is a copy of one strand of the original DNA.

Base — Each group of three bases codes for one amino acid.

Figure 9 *A gene is a section of DNA that contains instructions for stringing together amino acids to make a protein.*

Why Proteins? You may be wondering, "What do proteins have to do with who I am or what I look like?" Proteins are found throughout cells. They act as chemical messengers, and they help determine how tall you will grow, what colors you can see, and whether your hair is curly or straight. Human cells contain about 100,000 genes, and each gene spells out sequences of amino acids for specific proteins. Proteins exist in an almost limitless variety. The human body contains about 50,000 different kinds of proteins. Proteins are the reason for the multitude of different shapes, sizes, colors, and textures found in living things, such as antlers, claws, hair, and skin.

Q: Why did the mutant chromosome go to the tailor?

A: because it had a hole in its genes

---

136   Chapter 6 • Genes and Gene Technology

The Making of a Protein

As explained in Figure 9, the first step in making a protein is to copy the section of the DNA strand containing a gene. A copy of this section is made with the help of copier enzymes. Messenger molecules take the genetic information from the sections of DNA in the nucleus out into the cytoplasm.

In the cytoplasm, the copy of DNA is fed through a kind of protein assembly line. The "factory" where this assembly line exists is known as a **ribosome**. The copy is fed through the ribosome three bases at a time. Transfer molecules act as translators of the message contained in the copy of DNA. Each transfer molecule picks up a specific amino acid from the cytoplasm. The amino acid is determined by the order of the bases the transfer molecule contains. Like pieces of a puzzle, bases on the transfer molecule then match up with bases on the copy of DNA inside the ribosome. The transfer molecules then drop off their amino acid "suitcases," which are strung together to form a protein. This process is illustrated in **Figure 10**.

Self-Check

1. How many amino acids are present in a protein that requires 3,000 bases in its code?
2. Explain how proteins influence how you look.

(See page 782 to check your answers.)

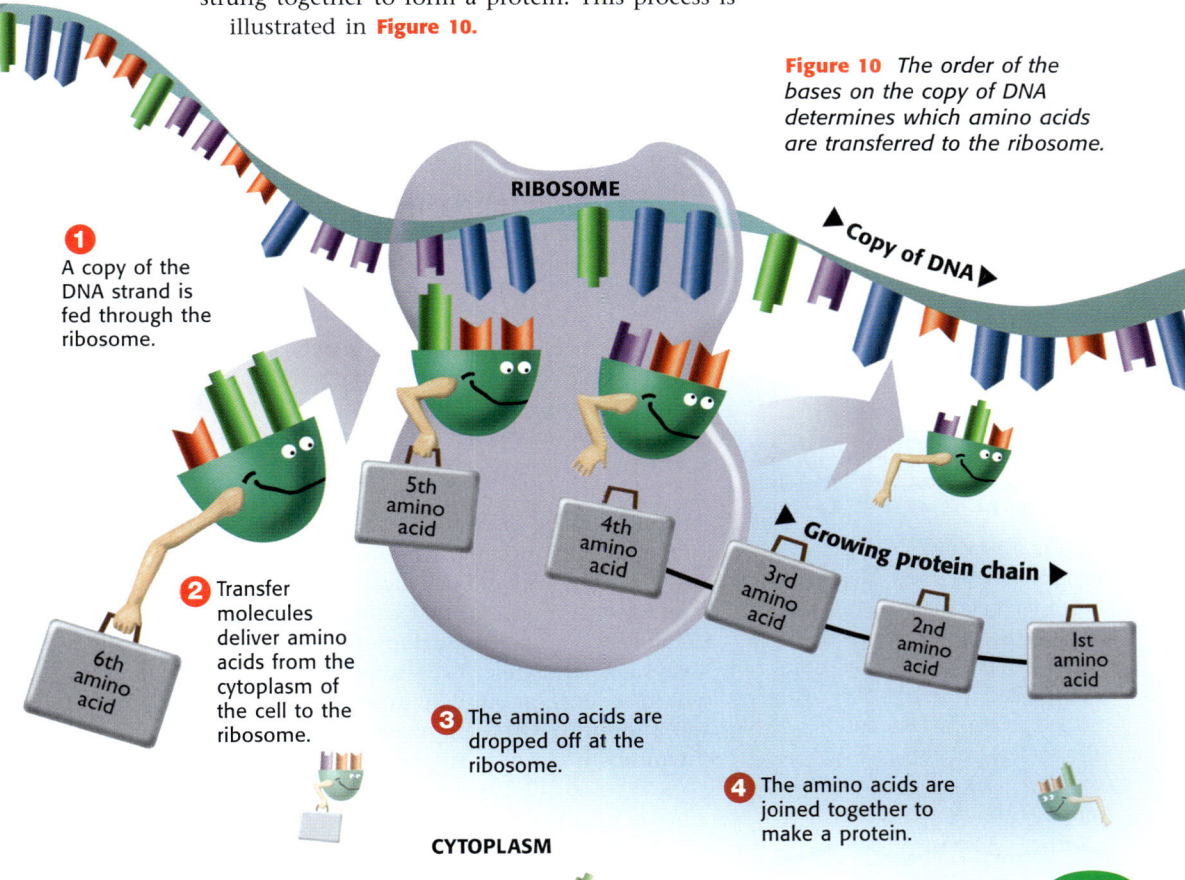

Figure 10 The order of the bases on the copy of DNA determines which amino acids are transferred to the ribosome.

① A copy of the DNA strand is fed through the ribosome.

② Transfer molecules deliver amino acids from the cytoplasm of the cell to the ribosome.

③ The amino acids are dropped off at the ribosome.

④ The amino acids are joined together to make a protein.

2) Teach

Answers to Self-Check

1. 1,000
2. DNA codes for proteins. Your flesh is composed of proteins, and the way those proteins are constructed and combined influences much about the way you look.

MATH and MORE

Use mathematics to discuss how DNA codes for amino acids. With four possible nucleotides in three possible positions, there are $4 \times 4 \times 4$, or 64, possible combinations. (for example, AAA, AAT, AAG, and AAC)

These combinations are called codons. DNA produces only 20 amino acids; thus, most amino acids have several corresponding codons.

COOPERATIVE LEARNING

Skit Have groups of students write and perform a short skit to demonstrate the formation of a protein. For instance, students could play the roles of a ribosome, an amino acid, a transfer enzyme, and a DNA copy.

Teaching Transparency 21
"The Making of a Protein"

Q: What happens when an amateur-tein gets paid?

A: It becomes a pro-tein.

Section 2 • How DNA Works

2 Teach, continued

GUIDED PRACTICE

Write a sequence of DNA, such as AACTACGGT, on the chalkboard. Ask students to write the sequence for a copy of the DNA using base-pairing rules. (TTGATGCCA)

Then ask students to give examples of deletion, insertion, and substitution mutations to the DNA.

MISCONCEPTION ALERT

Are mutations rare? Scientists estimate that we inherit hundreds of mutations from our parents. In addition, new mutations can happen due to environmental factors and mistakes made during DNA replication and cell division. Mistakes are made during DNA replication in approximately one out of every 1,000 base pairs. But thanks to repair enzymes and other proofing mechanisms, the final error rate is much lower—somewhere between one in a million and one in a billion.

CONNECT TO EARTH SCIENCE

Ozone is a gas made of three oxygen atoms. High in the atmosphere, ozone absorbs dangerous ultraviolet radiation (the high-energy light that can cause cancer). When produced near the surface of the Earth, however, ozone is a pollutant that affects plant growth and makes breathing more difficult. Use Teaching Transparency 167 to illustrate the process of ozone production.

Teaching Transparency 167 "The Formation of Smog"

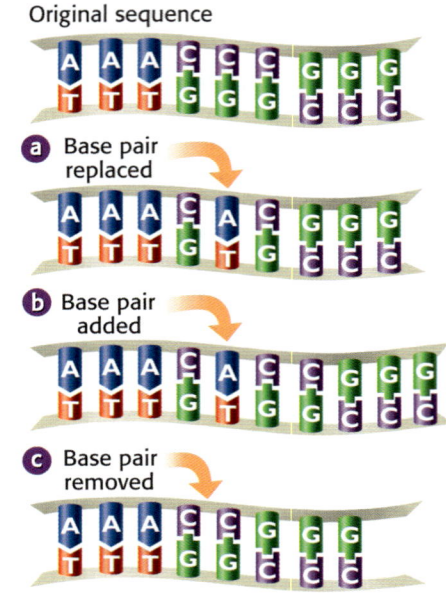

Figure 11 The original base-pair sequence at the top has been changed to illustrate (a) substitution, (b) insertion, and (c) deletion.

Meteorology CONNECTION

The layer of ozone in the Earth's atmosphere helps shield the planet's surface from ultraviolet (UV) radiation. UV radiation can cause mutations in skin cells that can lead to cancer. Each year more than 750,000 people get skin cancer. Scientists fear that damage to the ozone layer may greatly increase the number of skin cancers each year.

Changes in Genes

Imagine that you've been invited to ride on a brand-new roller coaster at the state fair. Just before you climb into the front car, you are informed that some of the metal parts on the coaster have been replaced by parts made of a different substance. Would you still want to ride this roller coaster?

Perhaps a stronger metal was substituted. Or perhaps a material not suited to the job was used. Imagine what would happen if cardboard were used instead of metal!

Mutant Molecules Substitutions like this can occur in DNA. They are known as **mutations.** Mutations occur when there is a change in the order of bases in an organism's DNA. Sometimes a base is left out; this is known as a *deletion*. Or an extra base might be added; this is known as an *insertion*. The most common error occurs when an incorrect base replaces a correct base. This is known as a *substitution*. **Figure 11** illustrates these three types of mutations.

Mistakes Happen Fortunately, repair enzymes are continuously on the job, patrolling the DNA molecule for errors. When an error is found, it is usually repaired. But occasionally the repairs are not completely accurate, and the mistakes become part of the genetic message. There are three possible consequences to changes in DNA: an improvement, no change at all, or a harmful change. If the mutation occurs in the sex cells, it can be passed from one generation to the next.

How Can DNA Become Damaged? In addition to random errors that occur when DNA is copied, damage can be caused by physical and chemical agents known as mutagens. A **mutagen** is anything that can cause a mutation in DNA. Examples of mutagens include high-energy radiation from X rays and ultraviolet radiation. Ultraviolet radiation is the type of energy in sunlight that is responsible for suntans and sunburns. Other mutagens include asbestos and the chemicals in cigarette smoke.

WEIRD SCIENCE

A human cell contains between 50,000 and 100,000 genes. Human DNA is about 3 billion base pairs long. Only about 3 percent of those base pairs are used in making proteins; the other 97 percent are regulatory sequences and nonfunctioning genes.

138 Chapter 6 • Genes and Gene Technology

An Example of a Substitution

Consider the DNA sequence containing the three bases **GAA**. GAA are the three letters that give the instructions: "Put the amino acid glutamic acid here." If a mistake occurs and the sequence is changed to **GTA**, a completely different message is sent: "Put valine here."

This simple change just described can cause the disease *sickle cell anemia*. Sickle cell anemia is a disease that affects red blood cells. When valine is substituted for glutamic acid in a blood protein, as shown in **Figure 12**, the red blood cells become distorted into a sickle shape.

The sickled cells are not as good as normal red blood cells at carrying oxygen. They are also more likely to get stuck in blood vessels, causing painful and dangerous clots.

QuickLab

Mutations

The sentence below contains all three-letter words but has experienced a mutation. Can you find the mutation?

THE IGR EDC ATA TET HEB IGB ADR AT

What kind of mutation did you find? Now what does the sentence say?

TRY at HOME

Figure 12 The simple change of one base leads to the disease called sickle cell anemia.

Science Bloopers

A person who carries a single allele for sickle cell anemia is said to have *sickle cell trait*. In the past, many people did not understand that people who have sickle cell trait do not pose a risk to the community. In some areas, children with the trait were banned from public schools because people feared the condition was contagious.

3) Extend

Answers to QuickLab

The mutation is a deletion.
THE BIG RED CAT ATE THE BIG BAD RAT

RETEACHING

Write a sequence of DNA on the chalkboard, and invite students to come up to the board and change the sequence. Then ask the class to discuss the possible consequences of such a mutation in DNA. (It might cause a different amino acid to be substituted. This could result in a genetic disorder, an improvement, or no change at all.)

Ask how the mutation could be corrected. (Enzymes may find and repair the error.)

Finally, ask what could have caused the mutation. (Mutations are caused by random errors in the copying of DNA, by physical and chemical damage to the DNA, or by X rays and other mutagens.)

Sheltered English

CROSS-DISCIPLINARY FOCUS

Writing — **History** Have students conduct Internet or library research and write a report on the history of Queen Victoria and her descendants. The queen was a carrier of hemophilia, a recessive disorder in which a person lacks a protein needed to form blood clots. The hemophilia gene passed from Queen Victoria to her daughters and from them to the Russian, Spanish, and German families they married into.

Teaching Transparency 22 "An Example of Substitution"

Section 2 • How DNA Works

3) Extend, continued

CROSS-DISCIPLINARY FOCUS

Social Studies Czar Nicholas II ruled Russia from 1894 to 1917. Nicholas, his wife, and their children were shot to death by the Bolsheviks in 1918 in the aftermath of the Russian Revolution. Their bodies were not found until 1991, when Russian anthropologists discovered their bones. To be certain of the identity of the remains, DNA samples were taken from the remains and from living members of the family. The DNA fingerprints of the deceased were similar to those of the surviving family members. The remains were determined to be Czar Nicholas II and his family.

Answer to APPLY

Individuals I_2 and III_2 are nearsighted. Both of Jane's parents are *Nn*. Jane's genotype can be either *NN* or *Nn*. It can't be *nn* because Jane is not nearsighted.

Jane's Fiancé

	N	n
Jane N	NN	Nn
N	NN	Nn

Jane's Fiancé

	N	n
Jane N	NN	Nn
n	Nn	nn

Genetic Counseling

Most hereditary disorders, such as sickle cell anemia, are recessive disorders. This means that the disease occurs only when a child inherits a defective gene from both parents. Some people, called carriers, have only one allele for the disease. Carriers of the gene may pass it along to their children without knowing that they have the mutated gene.

Genetic counseling provides information and counseling to couples who wish to have children but are worried that they might pass a disease to their children. Genetic counselors often make use of a diagram known as a **pedigree,** which is a tool for tracing a trait through generations of a family. By making a pedigree, it is often possible to predict whether a person is a carrier of a hereditary disease. In **Figure 13,** the trait for the disease cystic fibrosis is tracked through four generations. Each generation is numbered with Roman numerals, and each individual is numbered with Arabic numerals.

Figure 13 Cystic fibrosis is a recessive hereditary disease that affects the respiratory system. A pedigree for cystic fibrosis is shown below.

☐ Males   ○ Females

 Vertical lines connect children to their parents.

■ or ● A solid square or circle indicates that the person has a certain trait.

◨ or ◐ A half-filled square or circle indicates that the person is a carrier of the trait.

Pedigree and Punnett Squares

The pedigree at right shows the recessive trait of nearsightedness in Jane's family. Jane, her parents, and her brother all have normal vision. Which individuals in the pedigree are nearsighted? What are the possible genotypes of Jane's parents? Jane has two possible genotypes. What are they? Jane is planning to marry a person who has normal vision but carries the trait for nearsightedness. Work two Punnett squares to show the possible genotypes of Jane's future children.

Teaching Transparency 23
"Pedigree"

Reinforcement Worksheet 6
"DNA Mutations"

WEIRD SCIENCE

Gene therapy is an experimental field of medical research in which defective genes are replaced with healthy genes. One way to insert healthy genes involves using a delivery system called a gene gun to inject microscopic gold bullets coated with genetic material.

Designer Genes

For thousands of years, humans have been aware of the benefits of selective breeding. In *selective breeding,* organisms with certain desirable characteristics are mated to produce a new breed. You probably have enjoyed the benefits of selective breeding, although you may not have realized it. For example, you may have eaten an egg from a chicken that was bred to produce a large number of eggs. Your pet dog might even be a result of selective breeding. Some kinds of dogs, for example, have a thick coat so that they can retrieve game in icy waters.

Engineering Organisms Scientists now have the ability to produce desired characteristics in some organisms without breeding. They can manipulate individual genes using a technique known as genetic engineering. Like all types of engineering, genetic engineering puts scientific knowledge to practical use. Basically, *genetic engineering* allows scientists to transfer genes from one organism to another. Genetic engineering is already used to manufacture proteins, repair damaged genes, and identify individuals who may carry an allele for a disease. Some other uses are shown in **Figures 14** and **15.**

Figure 14 Scientists added a gene found in fireflies to this tobacco plant. The plant now produces an enzyme that causes the plant to glow.

Figure 15 A sheep called Dolly was the first successfully cloned mammal.

REVIEW

1. List the three types of mutations. How do they differ?
2. What type of mutation causes sickle cell anemia?
3. How is genetic engineering different from selective breeding?
4. **Applying Concepts** Mutations can occur in sex cells or in body cells. In which cell type might a mutation be passed from generation to generation? Explain.

internetconnect

NSTA

TOPIC: Genetic Engineering
GO TO: www.scilinks.org
***sci*LINKS NUMBER:** HSTL140

---

4) Close

Quiz

1. What is the function of the ribosome? (In the ribosome, the DNA code is translated into proteins.)
2. List some causes of DNA mutations. (UV radiation, cigarette smoke, or X rays)

ALTERNATIVE ASSESSMENT

Writing Have students prepare an instruction manual for their DNA. The manual should include instructions for copying their DNA and translating it into proteins. It should also include information about protecting their DNA from mutations by avoiding mutagens and correcting any mutations that occur.

Critical Thinking Worksheet 6
"The Perfect Parrot"

Interactive Explorations CD-ROM "DNA Pawprints"

internetconnect

TOPIC: Genetic Engineering
GO TO: www.scilinks.org
***sci*LINKS NUMBER:** HSTL140

▼ Answers to Review

1. insertion: an extra base is inserted; deletion: a base is deleted; substitution: one base is substituted for another
2. substitution
3. Selective breeding involves choosing desired traits and breeding organisms that have those traits. Genetic engineering involves altering the DNA at the molecular level, thereby changing an organism's genome.
4. Mutations can only be passed from generation to generation if they occur in sex cells. This is because the genes in an individual's sex cells are used to reproduce a new individual.

Chapter Highlights

VOCABULARY DEFINITIONS

SECTION 1

DNA deoxyribonucleic acid; hereditary material that controls all the activities of a cell, contains the information to make new cells, and provides instructions for making proteins

nucleotide a subunit of DNA consisting of a sugar, a phosphate, and one of four nitrogenous bases

adenine one of the four bases that combine with sugar and phosphate to form a nucleotide subunit of DNA; adenine pairs with thymine

thymine one of the four bases that combine with sugar and phosphate to form a nucleotide subunit of DNA; thymine pairs with adenine

guanine one of the four bases that combine with sugar and phosphate to form a nucleotide subunit of DNA; guanine pairs with cytosine

cytosine one of the four bases that combine with sugar and phosphate to form a nucleotide subunit of DNA; cytosine pairs with guanine

Chapter Highlights

SECTION 1

Vocabulary
- **DNA** (p. 128)
- **nucleotide** (p. 128)
- **adenine** (p. 128)
- **thymine** (p. 128)
- **guanine** (p. 128)
- **cytosine** (p. 128)

Section Notes
- Proteins are made of long strings of amino acids.
- DNA is made of long strings of nucleotides.
- Chromosomes are made of protein and DNA.
- The DNA molecule looks like a twisted ladder. The rungs of the ladder are made of base pairs, either adenine and thymine, or cytosine and guanine.
- DNA carries genetic information in the order of the nucleotide bases.
- DNA can be copied because one strand of the molecule serves as a template for the other side.

Labs
Base-Pair Basics (p. 706)

✓ Skills Check

Math Concepts

THE GENETIC CODE The MathBreak on page 131 asks you to calculate the number of bases in all of your genes. If there are about 30,000 bases in each gene and there are 100,000 genes, then multiply to find the answer.

$$30{,}000 \times 100{,}000 = 3{,}000{,}000{,}000$$

So, there are about 3 billion bases in all of your genes.

Visual Understanding

COPIES OF DNA Look at Figure 9 on page 136. You can see the nucleus and the pores in its membrane. The copy of DNA emerges through these pores on its way to deliver its coded message to the ribosomes. Why does DNA send a copy out of the nucleus to relay its message? The answer is that DNA is much more protected from factors that might cause a mutation if it stays inside the nucleus. The messenger copy may encounter bad luck, but the master DNA usually stays very safe!

Lab and Activity Highlights

Base-Pair Basics PG 706

Datasheets for LabBook
(blackline masters for this lab)

SECTION 2

Vocabulary
- **ribosome** *(p. 137)*
- **mutation** *(p. 138)*
- **mutagen** *(p. 138)*
- **pedigree** *(p. 140)*

Section Notes
- A gene is a set of instructions for assembling a protein.
- Each group of three bases in a gene codes for a particular amino acid.
- Genes can become mutated when the order of the bases is changed.

VOCABULARY DEFINITIONS, continued

SECTION 2

ribosome a small organelle in cells where proteins are made from amino acids

mutation a change in the order of the bases in an organism's DNA; deletion, insertion, or substitution

mutagen anything that can damage or cause changes in DNA

pedigree a diagram of family history used for tracing a trait through several generations

 Vocabulary Review Worksheet 6

 Blackline masters of these Chapter Highlights can be found in the **Study Guide.**

---

internet connect

 GO TO: go.hrw.com

Visit the **HRW** Web site for a variety of learning tools related to this chapter. Just type in the keyword:

KEYWORD: HSTDNA

 GO TO: www.scilinks.org

Visit the **National Science Teachers Association** on-line Web site for Internet resources related to this chapter. Just type in the *sci*LINKS number for more information about the topic:

TOPIC: DNA   *sci***LINKS NUMBER:** HSTL130
TOPIC: Genes and Traits   *sci***LINKS NUMBER:** HSTL135
TOPIC: Genetic Engineering   *sci***LINKS NUMBER:** HSTL140
TOPIC: DNA Fingerprinting   *sci***LINKS NUMBER:** HSTL145

Lab and Activity Highlights

LabBank

 Long-Term Projects & Research Ideas, The Antifreeze Protein, Project 6

Interactive Explorations CD-ROM

 CD 3, Exploration 8, "DNA Pawprints"

Chapter Review
Answers

USING VOCABULARY
1. amino acids; nucleotides
2. recessive
3. mutation
4. mutagen

UNDERSTANDING CONCEPTS

Multiple Choice
5. b
6. d
7. b
8. c
9. c
10. b

Short Answer
11. GAATCCGAATGGT
12. DNA molecules split down the middle, then each side of the molecule pairs up with an additional nucleotide. (Picture should resemble a zipper being zipped up.)
13. insertion

Chapter Review

USING VOCABULARY

To complete the following sentences, choose the correct term from each pair of terms listed below:

1. A protein is a long string of __?__. A strand of DNA is a long string of __?__. (*amino acids* or *nucleotides*)

2. A disorder, such as cystic fibrosis, is known as __?__ if the child must receive an allele for the disease from each parent in order to have the disease. (*dominant* or *recessive*)

3. A change in the order of bases in DNA is called a __?__. (*mutation* or *mutagen*)

4. A __?__ is a physical or chemical agent that causes damage to DNA. (*mutagen* or *pedigree*)

UNDERSTANDING CONCEPTS

Multiple Choice

5. In a DNA molecule, which of the following bases pair together?
   a. adenine and cytosine
   b. thymine and adenine
   c. thymine and guanine
   d. cytosine and thymine

6. A gene is
   a. a set of instructions for each trait.
   b. instructions on how to make a protein.
   c. a portion of a strand of DNA.
   d. All of the above

7. DNA
   a. is made up of three subunits.
   b. has a structure like a twisted ladder.
   c. cannot be repaired if it is mutated.
   d. All of the above

8. In incomplete dominance,
   a. a single gene controls many traits.
   b. genes for a trait are all recessive.
   c. each allele for a trait has its own degree of influence.
   d. the environment controls the genes.

9. Watson and Crick
   a. studied the amounts of each base in DNA.
   b. took X-ray pictures of DNA.
   c. made models to determine DNA structure.
   d. discovered that genes were located on chromosomes.

10. Which of the following is NOT a step in making a protein?
    a. Copies of DNA are taken to the cytoplasm.
    b. Transfer molecules deliver amino acids to the nucleus.
    c. Amino acids are joined together at the ribosome to make a protein.
    d. A copy of the DNA is fed through the ribosome.

Short Answer

11. What would the complementary strand of DNA be for the following sequence of bases?

    C T T A G G C T T A C C A

12. How does DNA copy itself? Draw a picture to help explain your answer.

13. If the DNA sequence TGAGCCATGA is changed to TGAGCACATGA, what kind of mutation has occurred?

Concept Mapping

14. Use the following terms to create a concept map: bases, adenine, thymine, nucleotides, guanine, DNA, cytosine.

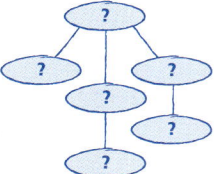

CRITICAL THINKING AND PROBLEM SOLVING

Write one or two sentences to answer the following questions:

15. If neither parent shows signs of having sickle cell anemia, does this fact guarantee that their children will not contract the disease? Explain.

16. How many amino acids does this DNA sequence code for?

    T C A G C C A C C T A T G G A

MATH IN SCIENCE

17. The goal of a project called the Human Genome Project is to discover the location and DNA sequence of all human genes. Scientists estimate that there are 100,000 human genes. In 1998, 38,000 genes had been discovered. How many more genes must the Human Genome Project discover?

18. If scientists find 6,000 genes each year, how many years will it take to finish the project?

19. Of the 38,000 genes discovered, 7,000 have been mapped to their chromosome location. What percentage of the discovered genes have been mapped?

INTERPRETING GRAPHICS

Examine the pedigree for albinism shown below, and then answer the following questions. You may need to use a Punnett square to answer some of these questions. (Albinism is a trait among individuals who produce no pigment in their skin, hair, or eyes.)

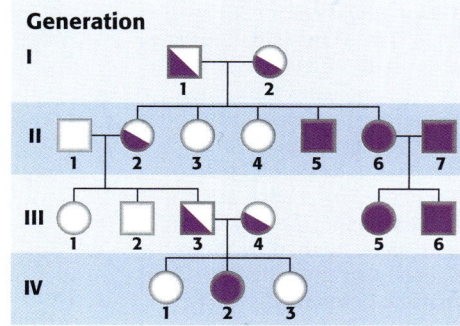

20. How many males are represented on this pedigree? How many females?

21. How many individuals in Generation II had albinism? How many were carriers of the trait?

22. Do you think albinism is a dominant trait or a recessive trait? Explain.

Take a minute to review your answers to the Pre-Reading Questions found at the bottom of page 126. Have your answers changed? If necessary, revise your answers based on what you have learned since you began this chapter.

Concept Mapping

14. An answer to this exercise can be found at the end of this book.

CRITICAL THINKING AND PROBLEM SOLVING

15. No; it does not. The trait for sickle cell anemia is recessive. Both parents could be carrying it and could transfer it to their child. If their child inherits the recessive gene from both parents, he or she will have the disease.

16. This sequence codes for five amino acids.

MATH IN SCIENCE

17. approximately 62,000
18. more than 10 years
19. about 18.4 percent

INTERPRETING GRAPHICS

20. 7 males, 11 females
21. 3, 1
22. recessive, because offspring have to inherit the albinism allele from each parent to display albinism as in III_5, III_6, and IV_2, for example

Concept Mapping Transparency 6

Blackline masters of this Chapter Review can be found in the **Study Guide**.

SCIENTIFIC DEBATE

DNA on Trial

The tension in the courtroom was so thick you could cut it with a knife. The prosecuting attorney presented the evidence: "DNA analysis indicates that blood found on the defendant's shoes matches the blood of the victim. The odds of this match happening by chance are one in 20 million." The jury members were stunned by these figures. Can there be any doubt that the defendant is guilty?

Next Defendant: DNA

Court battles involving DNA fingerprinting are becoming more and more common. Traditional fingerprinting has been used for more than 100 years, and it has been an extremely important identification tool. Recently, many people have claimed that DNA fingerprinting, also called DNA profiling, will replace the traditional technique. The DNA profiling technique has been used to clear thousands of wrongly accused or convicted individuals. However, the controversy begins when the evidence is used to try to prove a suspect's guilt.

Room for Reasonable Doubt

Critics claim that the DNA fingerprinting process allows too much room for human error.

▲ *This forensic scientist is gathering dead skin cells from an article of clothing in hopes of collecting samples of DNA.*

Handling samples from a crime scene can be tricky—a sample may have been removed from a small area beneath a victim's fingernail or scraped off a dirty sidewalk. Contamination by salt, chemicals, denim, or even a lab person's sneeze can affect the accuracy of the results.

Much of the controversy about DNA fingerprinting surrounds the interpretation of the results. The question becomes, "How likely is it that someone else also has that same DNA profile?" Answers can range from one in three to one in 20 million, depending on the person doing the interpreting, the sample size, and the process used.

Critics also point out that the results may be calculated without regard for certain factors. For instance, individuals belonging to certain ethnic groups are likely to share more characteristics of their DNA with others in their group than with people outside the group.

Beyond a Reasonable Doubt

Those who support DNA evidence point out that the analysis is totally objective because the labs that do the DNA analysis receive samples labeled in code. The data either clear or incriminate a suspect. Moreover, DNA evidence alone is rarely used to convict a person. It is one of several forms of evidence, including motive and access to the crime scene, used to reach a verdict.

Supporters of DNA fingerprinting say that checks and balances in laboratories help prevent human errors. In addition, recent efforts to standardize both evidence gathering and interpretation of samples have further improved results.

What Do You Think?

▶ Should DNA fingerprinting be admitted as evidence in the courtroom? Do some additional research, and decide for yourself.

Science Fiction

"Moby James"
by Patricia A. McKillip

Rob Trask has a problem. It's his older brother, James. Rob is convinced that James is not his real brother. Rob and his family live on a space station, and he just knows that his real brother was sent back to Earth. This person who claims to be James is really either some sort of mutant, irradiated plant life or a mutant pair of dirty sweat socks.

Now Rob has another problem—his class is reading Herman Melville's novel *Moby Dick*. At first, Rob just can't get interested in the story. But as he reads more and more, Rob becomes entranced by the story of Captain Ahab and his quest for revenge against the great white whale Moby Dick. Moby Dick had taken something from Ahab—his leg—and Ahab wants to make the whale pay!

Suddenly Rob realizes that his brother is a great white mutant whale—Moby James. As Rob follows Ahab on his search for Moby Dick, Rob begins to understand what he must do to get his real brother back again. So he watches Moby James, trying to catch James in some mistake that will reveal him for the mutant he is. Once Rob catches the fake James, he will be able to get the real James back again.

To find out if Rob is successful in his quest to find his real brother, read "Moby James" in the *Holt Anthology of Science Fiction*.

Further Reading If students liked this story, encourage them to read more of Patricia McKillip's stories, such as the following:

Fool's Run, Warner, 1987
Something Rich and Strange, Bantam, 1994
Winter Rose, Ace, 1996

SCIENCE FICTION
"Moby James"
by Patricia A. McKillip

Rob's brother is changing—but into what? a mutant robot? an evil irradiated skunk cabbage? a great white mutant whale? Whatever it is, it's making Rob very nervous . . .

Teaching Strategy

Reading Level This is a relatively short story that should not be difficult for students to read and comprehend.

Background

About the Author Patricia Anne McKillip (1948–) began her career not as a writer, but as a storyteller. As the second of six children, she often found herself in charge of looking after her younger brothers and sisters. She can't remember exactly when she first began telling her siblings stories. She does remember, however, her first attempt at writing. At age 14 she wrote a 30-page fairy tale.

Today McKillip is a full-time writer of science fiction and fantasy. In 1975, she won the World Fantasy Award for her novel *The Forgotten Beasts of Eld*. A few years later she was nominated for a Hugo Award for *Harpist in the Wind*. McKillip has written a number of other novels, and her short stories have appeared in various periodicals, including the *Science Fiction and Fantasy Review*, the *Los Angeles Times*, and the *New York Times Book Review*.

Chapter Organizer

CHAPTER ORGANIZATION	TIME MINUTES	OBJECTIVES	LABS, INVESTIGATIONS, AND DEMONSTRATIONS
Chapter Opener pp. 174–175	45	National Standards: UCP 2, LS 5c	**Start-Up Activity** Making a Fossil, p. 149
Section 1 Change Over Time	90	▶ Explain how fossils provide evidence that organisms have evolved over time. ▶ Identify three ways that organisms can be compared to support the theory of evolution. UCP 2–5, SAI 2, LS 2, 3a, 3d, 5a–5c; LabBook UCP 2, SAI 1, HNS 2	**Design Your Own,** Mystery Footprints, p. 708 **ADVANCED** **Datasheets for LabBook,** Mystery Footprints, Datasheet 14 **ADVANCED**
Section 2 How Does Evolution Happen?	90	▶ Describe the four steps of Darwin's theory of evolution by natural selection. ▶ Explain how mutations are important to evolution. UCP 2–5, SAI 1, 2, ST 2, SPSP 2, 5, HNS 1–3, LS 2c, 3a, 3d, 5b, 5c; LabBook SAI 1, HNS 2, LS 5b	**Demonstration,** Form and Function, p. 159 in ATE **BASIC** **QuickLab,** Could We Run Out of Food? p. 161 **GENERAL** **Design Your Own,** Survival of the Chocolates, p. 711 **GENERAL** **Datasheets for LabBook,** Survival of the Chocolates, Datasheet 16 **GENERAL**
Section 3 Natural Selection in Action	90	▶ Give two examples of natural selection in action. ▶ Outline the process of speciation. UCP 2, 3, LS 2c, 3d, 5b; LabBook UCP 2, SAI 1, HNS 2, LS 5b, 5c	**Demonstration,** Natural Selection, p. 164 in ATE **GENERAL** **Discovery Lab,** Out-of-Sight Marshmallows, p. 710 **BASIC** **Datasheets for LabBook,** Out-of-Sight Marshmallows, Datasheet 15 **BASIC** **Whiz-Bang Demonstrations,** Adaptation Behooves You, Demo 6 **GENERAL** **Long-Term Projects & Research Ideas,** Project 7 **ADVANCED**

See page **T20** for a complete correlation of this book with the

NATIONAL SCIENCE EDUCATION STANDARDS.

TECHNOLOGY RESOURCES

 Guided Reading Audio CD English or Spanish, Chapter 7

 One-Stop Planner CD-ROM with Test Generator

 CNN Multicultural Connections, A Thailand Fossil Discovery, Segment 4

Science, Technology & Society, Deciphering Dog DNA, Segment 10

Chapter 7 • The Evolution of Living Things

CLASSROOM WORKSHEETS, TRANSPARENCIES, AND RESOURCES	SCIENCE INTEGRATION AND CONNECTIONS	REVIEW AND ASSESSMENT
Directed Reading Worksheet 7 BASIC **Science Puzzlers, Twisters & Teasers,** Worksheet 7 ADVANCED		
Directed Reading Worksheet 7, Section 1 BASIC **Transparency 24,** Changes in Life Over Earth's History **Transparency 113,** A Sedimentary Rock Cycle **Transparency 25,** Comparative Skeletal Structures **Transparency 26,** Vertebrate Embryos	**Geology Connection,** p. 152 **Multicultural Connection,** p. 152 in ATE **Connect to Earth Science,** p. 152 in ATE GENERAL **Math and More,** p. 153 in ATE GENERAL **Cross-Disciplinary Focus,** p. 154 in ATE	**Homework,** p. 153 in ATE ADVANCED **Review,** p. 157 GENERAL **Quiz,** p. 157 in ATE GENERAL **Alternative Assessment,** p. 157 in ATE GENERAL
Directed Reading Worksheet 7, Section 2 BASIC **Math Skills for Science Worksheet 3,** Multiplying Whole Numbers GENERAL **Transparency 27,** Natural Selection in Four Steps **Reinforcement Worksheet 7,** Bicentennial Celebration GENERAL	**Connect to Geography,** p. 159 in ATE **Apply,** p. 163 GENERAL **Eye on the Environment:** Saving at the Seed Bank, p. 172 ADVANCED	**Homework,** p. 162 in ATE ADVANCED **Review,** p. 163 GENERAL **Quiz,** p. 163 in ATE GENERAL **Alternative Assessment,** p. 163 in ATE GENERAL
Directed Reading Worksheet 7, Section 3 BASIC **Transparency 28,** Evolution of the Galápagos Finches **Critical Thinking Worksheet 7,** Taking the Earth's Pulse ADVANCED	**Real-World Connection,** p. 165 in ATE **Holt Anthology of Science Fiction,** *The Anatomy Lesson* GENERAL	**Self-Check,** p. 165 **Review,** p. 167 GENERAL **Quiz,** p. 167 in ATE GENERAL **Alternative Assessment,** p. 167 in ATE ADVANCED

internet connect

 Holt, Rinehart and Winston On-line Resources
go.hrw.com

For worksheets and other teaching aids related to this chapter, visit the HRW Web site and type in the keyword: **HSTEVO**

 National Science Teachers Association
www.scilinks.org

Encourage students to use the *sci*LINKS numbers listed in the internet connect boxes to access information and resources on the **NSTA** Web site.

END-OF-CHAPTER REVIEW AND ASSESSMENT

Chapter Review in Study Guide
Vocabulary and Notes in Study Guide
Chapter Tests with Performance-Based Assessment, Chapter 7 Test
Chapter Tests with Performance-Based Assessment, Performance-Based Assessment 7
Concept Mapping Transparency 7

Chapter 7 • Chapter Organizer

Chapter Resources & Worksheets

Visual Resources

TEACHING TRANSPARENCIES

TEACHING TRANSPARENCIES

CONCEPT MAPPING TRANSPARENCY

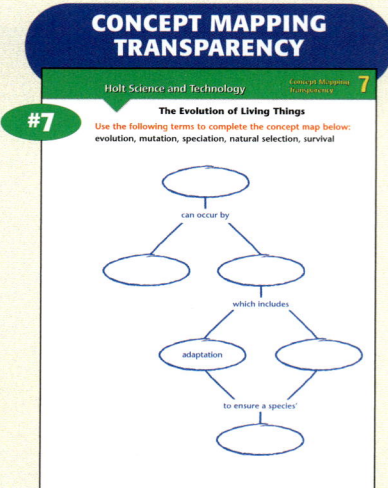

Meeting Individual Needs

DIRECTED READING

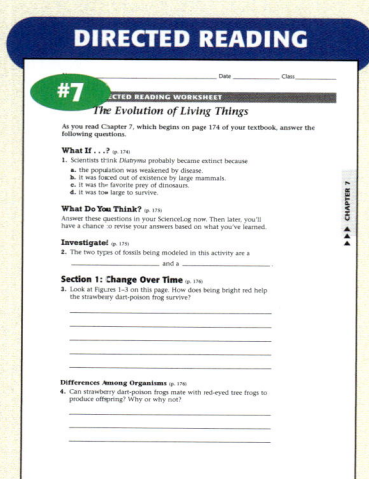

REINFORCEMENT & VOCABULARY REVIEW

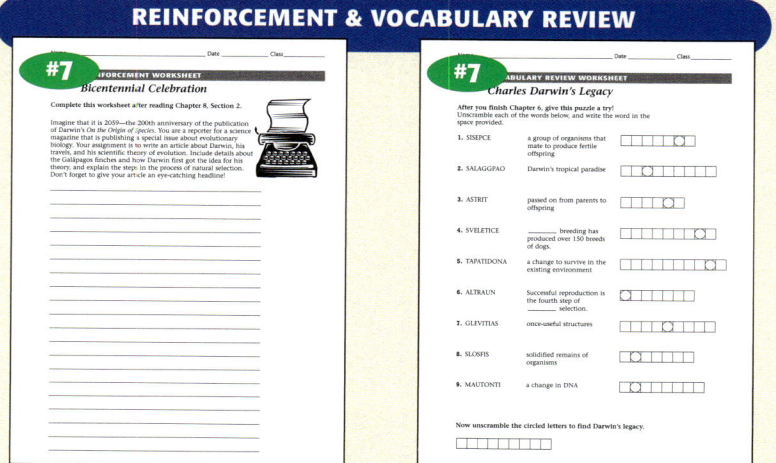

SCIENCE PUZZLERS, TWISTERS & TEASERS

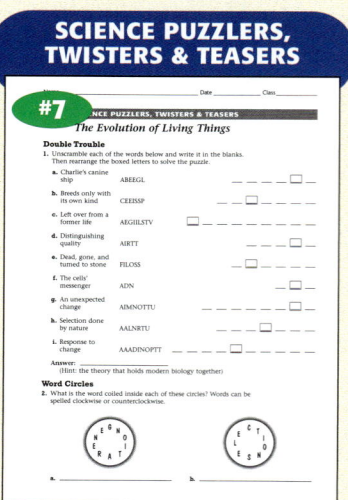

Chapter 7 • The Evolution of Living Things

Chapter 7 • The Evolution of Living Things

Review & Assessment

STUDY GUIDE
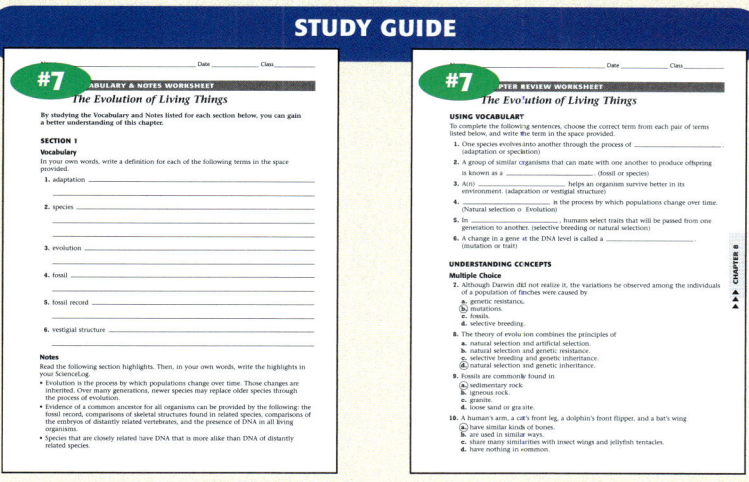

CHAPTER TESTS WITH PERFORMANCE-BASED ASSESSMENT

Lab Worksheets

WHIZ-BANG DEMONSTRATIONS

LONG-TERM PROJECTS & RESEARCH IDEAS

DATASHEETS FOR LABBOOK
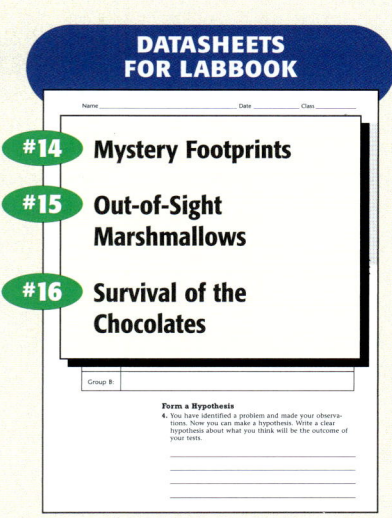

- #14 Mystery Footprints
- #15 Out-of-Sight Marshmallows
- #16 Survival of the Chocolates

Applications & Extensions

CRITICAL THINKING & PROBLEM SOLVING

MULTICULTURAL CONNECTIONS

SCIENCE TECHNOLOGY

Chapter 7 • Chapter Resources & Worksheets   147D

Chapter Background

SECTION 1
Change Over Time

▶ **Homologous Versus Analogous Structures**

Homologous structures have similar origins and exhibit similar anatomical patterns. Bird wings, human arms, whale flippers, and deer forelimbs, for example, are similar in skeletal structure.

- In the early 1800s, French naturalist Etienne Geoffroy Saint-Hilaire studied embryos and recognized the importance of homologous structures for identifying evolutionary relationships among species.

- Today, scientists can study homologies among cellular components. Hemoglobin molecules from different vertebrate species have similar amino acid sequences and are therefore homologous. But hemocyanin, which transports oxygen in crabs, has a very different sequence and is analogous to hemoglobin; that is, the two molecules have a similar function but different structure.

- Bird wings and butterfly wings are another example of analogous structures.

▶ **Convergent Evolution**

When scientists study the fossils, skeletons, and DNA of species thought to be related, they sometimes find that the organisms are not related at all. For example, the jerboa and the kangaroo rat look almost identical, but they have different ancestors. Cases like this illustrate convergent evolution. The two species developed similar adaptations because they were subjected to the same environmental influences.

IS THAT A FACT!

▸ The human appendix is a vestigial organ. It's a narrow tube attached to the large intestine. It performs no function but can become infected and require surgical removal. In chimpanzees, gorillas, and orangutans the appendix is an intestinal sac that helps them digest tough plant material.

▶ **Frozen Fossils**

In some cases scientists can obtain DNA from ancient tissues that have not completely decomposed or fossilized. Two Japanese geneticists hope to create a mammoth-elephant hybrid by using frozen tissue from a Siberian mammoth. Critics of the project remain highly skeptical. The chances of finding intact DNA are remote, and the genetic structures of mammoths and elephants are not 100 percent compatible.

SECTION 2
How Does Evolution Happen?

▶ **Alfred Russel Wallace**

Alfred Wallace (1823–1913) was born in England. He came from a poor family and had no formal scientific education. Though originally interested in botany, he began to study insects with the encouragement of British naturalist Henry Walter Bates, whom he met when he was about 20 years old. Bates and Wallace explored the Amazon from 1848 to 1852 and found much evidence to support the theory of evolution.

- From 1854 to 1862 Wallace traveled in the Malay Archipelago to find more evidence of evolution. In 1855, he published a preliminary essay, "On the Law Which Has Regulated the Introduction of New Species." Meanwhile, nearly 20 years after his voyage on the HMS *Beagle,* Charles Darwin was still mulling over his data. In 1858, Wallace mailed an essay to Darwin that explained Wallace's theory that natural selection pressures species to change.

Chapter 7 • The Evolution of Living Things

- In July 1858, Wallace's essay was presented along with a paper by Darwin at a meeting of the Linnean Society in London. In the following year, after nearly two decades of delay (because of his doubts and repeated analyses of the data), Darwin published *On the Origin of Species by Means of Natural Selection*.

▶ Charles Lyell

Charles Lyell (1797–1875), the eldest of 10 children, was born in Scotland and raised in England. His father was a naturalist who traveled with him to collect butterflies and aquatic insects, informal research that Charles continued throughout college.

- Lyell's research led him to the belief that natural processes occurring over millions of years have shaped the Earth's features. This idea was known as uniformitarianism. Lyell's work influenced Darwin's formulation of his theory of natural selection. Darwin's proposed mechanism for evolution was plausible only if the Earth was ancient and if organisms had the requisite time for adaptation and change.

SECTION 3

Natural Selection in Action

▶ Adaptive Coloration

Penguins, puffins, killer whales, and blue sharks are just some of the ocean animals that have white bellies and black or dark blue dorsal surfaces. This type of coloration is called countershading. When seen from below, the white underside helps the animal blend into the lighter sky above the water. When viewed from above, the dark coloration makes the animal difficult to see against the ocean depths.

IS THAT A FACT!

- Ptarmigans (chickenlike birds), Arctic foxes, and ermines change their color twice a year! All three are white in winter to blend with the snow of their northern habitat. The ptarmigan is mottled brown in summer, the fox is grayish brown, and the ermine is white below and brown on top.

- Octopuses and squid can change their color in a second. They have special cells called chromatophores that enable them to blend in with different-colored rocks and varied light conditions.

▶ The Fruitful Fruit Fly

In the mid-1800s a fruit fly that parasitized the hawthorn tree and its fruit infested apple trees in the Hudson River Valley area of New York. During the past 150 years, the apple tree variety of these flies has spread across the United States. Biologists have observed that the flies that attack apple trees do not also infest the hawthorns. Recent DNA studies revealed that the two groups are becoming isolated genetically. Scientists have concluded that speciation is occurring in these flies.

- Since the first step in speciation is separation, how did this process begin? Scientists classify this example as sympatric speciation. The flies began specializing on new host plants without geographic isolation. Separate trees were the extent of their separation.

IS THAT A FACT!

- The largest flying bird that ever lived had a wing span of more than 7 m. It was a New World vulture, and its fossil was discovered in Argentina. These birds were known as teratorns.

For background information about teaching strategies and issues, refer to the *Professional Reference for Teachers*.

CHAPTER 7

The Evolution of Living Things

 Pre-Reading Questions

Students may not know the answers to these questions before reading the chapter, so accept any reasonable response.

Suggested Answers

1. Evolution is the process by which species change over time.
2. An organism's environment provides the selective pressures that enable some organisms to thrive and reproduce.

 Directed Reading Worksheet 7

 Science Puzzlers, Twisters & Teasers Worksheet 7

 Guided Reading Audio CD English or Spanish, Chapter 7

CHAPTER 7

The Evolution of Living Things

Sections

1. **Change Over Time** 150
   Geology Connection 152
2. **How Does Evolution Happen?** 158
   QuickLab 161
   Apply 163
   Internet Connect 163
3. **Natural Selection in Action** 164
   Internet Connect 167

Chapter Review 170
Feature Articles 172, 173
LabBook 708–711

Pre-Reading Questions

1. What is evolution?
2. What role does the environment play in the survival of an organism?

Hidden Treasure

Can you see the fish in this picture? Look closer. The fish are coral blennies, and they are hard to see against the background of coral. Their coloring makes them likely to live longer and to have more offspring than blennies that don't blend in as well. In this chapter, you will learn how some characteristics help organisms survive and reproduce. You will also learn how these characteristics are passed from parents to their offspring.

148

---

internet connect

 HRW On-line Resources
go.hrw.com
For worksheets and other teaching aids, visit the HRW Web site and type in the keyword: **HSTEVO**

 sciLINKS NSTA
www.scilinks.com
Use the sciLINKS numbers at the end of each chapter for additional resources on the NSTA Web site.

 CNNfyi.com
www.cnnfyi.com
Visit the CNN Web site for current events coverage and classroom resources.

START-UP Activity

MAKING A FOSSIL

In this activity, you will make a model of a fossil.

Procedure

1. Get a **paper plate**, some **modeling clay,** and a **leaf** or a **shell** from your teacher.

2. Flatten some of the modeling clay on the paper plate. Push the leaf or shell into the clay. Be sure that your leaf or shell has made a mark in the clay. Remove the leaf or shell carefully.

3. Ask your teacher to cover the clay completely with some **plaster of Paris.** Allow the plaster to dry overnight.

4. Carefully remove the paper plate and the clay from the plaster the next day.

Analysis

5. Which of the following do you think would make good fossils—a clam, a jellyfish, a crab, or a mushroom? Explain your answer.

6. Real fossils usually are formed when a dead organism is covered in tiny bits of sand or dirt. Oxygen cannot be present when fossils are forming. What are some limitations of your fossil model?

START-UP Activity

MAKING A FOSSIL

MATERIALS
FOR EACH GROUP: • paper plate • modeling clay • leaf or shell • plaster of Paris

Teacher's Notes

Some of the most famous fossilized molds are in the Laetoli region of northern Tanzania, in East Africa. In 1976, a paleontologist working with archaeologist Mary Leakey discovered thousands of animal tracks. Two years later, a team discovered human footprints. These tracks were made about 3.6 million years ago. After ash from a nearby volcano was dampened by rain, elephants, giraffes, people, and some now-extinct mammals walked across this area. Ash from another eruption of the volcano in turn covered the tracks and fossilized them.

Answers to START-UP Activity

5. The crab and clam will make the best fossils because they have hard body parts that decay slowly and leave impressions. The softer organisms—the jellyfish and mushroom—are less likely to make impressions in the sediment, and so they are less likely to make fossils.

6. This model does not show why the formation of fossils requires tiny sediment and lack of oxygen.

SECTION 1

Focus

Change Over Time
This section introduces students to the theory of evolution. They will see how organisms change at the population level through adaptations. Students will learn about the evidence of evolution, including the fossil record and comparisons of organisms' physical structures, DNA, and embryonic structures.

Bellringer
Have the following information displayed on the chalkboard or an overhead projector when students enter:

The cockroach originated on Earth more than 250 million years ago and is thriving today all over the world. A giant deer that stood 2.1 m and had antlers up to 3.6 m evolved less than one million years ago and became extinct around 11,000 years ago.

Why do you think one animal thrived and the other perished? *(Accept all reasonable answers.)*

Directed Reading Worksheet 7 Section 1

Section 1

Terms to Learn
adaptation
species
evolution
fossil
fossil record
vestigial structure

What You'll Do
- Explain how fossils provide evidence that organisms have evolved over time.
- Identify three ways that organisms can be compared to support the theory of evolution.

BRAIN FOOD

Native tribes in Central America rub the poison from the strawberry dart-poison frog on their arrow tips before hunting. The poison helps to paralyze their prey.

Change Over Time

If someone asked you to describe a frog, you might say that a frog has long hind legs, eyes that bulge, and a habit of croaking from time to time. Then you might start to think about some of the differences among frogs—differences that set one kind of frog apart from another. Take a look at **Figures 1, 2,** and **3** on this page. These frogs look different from each other, yet they all inhabit a tropical rain forest.

Figure 1 *The red-eyed tree frog hides among a tree's leaves during the day and comes out at night.*

Figure 2 *The smoky jungle frog blends into the forest floor.*

Figure 3 *The strawberry dart-poison frog's bright coloring warns predators that it is poisonous.*

Differences Among Organisms

As you can see, these three frogs have different adaptations that enable them to survive. An **adaptation** is a characteristic that helps an organism survive and reproduce in its environment. Adaptations can include structures and behaviors for finding food, for protection, and for moving from place to place.

Living things that share the same characteristics and adaptations may be members of the same species. A **species** is a group of organisms that can mate with one another to produce fertile offspring. For example, all red-eyed tree frogs are members of the same species and can mate with one another to produce more red-eyed tree frogs.

The gastric brooding frogs of Australia, now extinct, incubated their tadpoles in their stomachs and gave birth to their young through their mouths!

Do Species Change over Time? These frogs are just a few of the millions of different species that share the Earth with us. The species on Earth today range from bacteria that lack cell nuclei to multicellular fungi, plants, and animals. Have these same species always existed on Earth?

Earth is a very old planet. Scientists estimate that it is 4.6 billion years old. The planet itself has changed a great deal during that long period of time. Fossil evidence shows that living things have changed as well. Since life first appeared on Earth, a great number of species have died out and have been replaced by newer species. **Figure 4** shows some of the different life-forms that have existed during Earth's history.

What causes species to change? Scientists think that newer species have descended from older species through the process of evolution. **Evolution** is the process by which populations accumulate inherited changes over time. Because of evolution, scientists think that all living things, from daisies to crocodiles to humans, share a common ancestor.

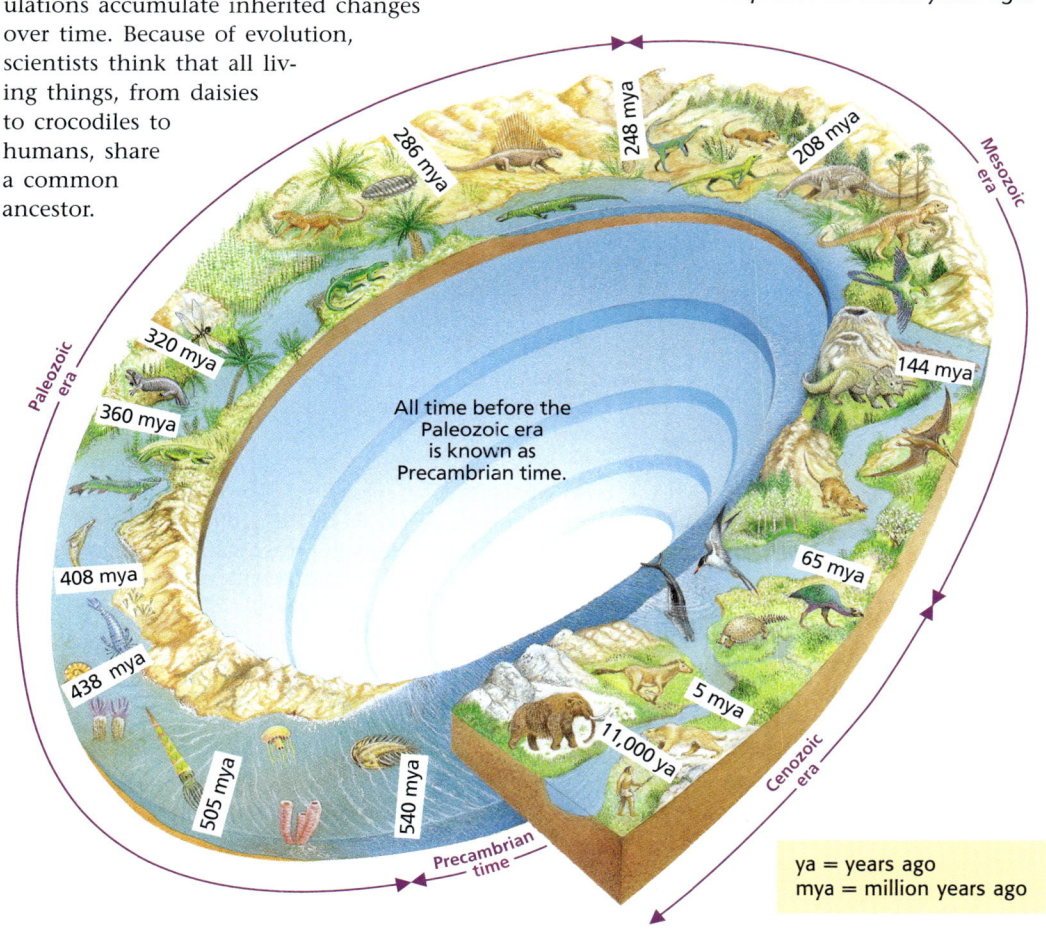

Figure 4 This spiral diagram represents many changes in life on Earth since the formation of the planet 4.6 billion years ago.

1 Motivate

DISCUSSION

Adaptation Ask students if a polar bear could live comfortably in Hawaii. Ask if a fish could survive in a forest. Why or why not? Help students understand that each animal has characteristics that make it well-suited for its home environment. The polar bear has a thick layer of fat and dense fur to keep it warm. The fish's gills allow it to obtain oxygen from water. These are physical adaptations to specific environments.

2 Teach

USING THE FIGURE

Direct students to review **Figure 4** and explain why there are more fossils from the Cenozoic era than the earlier eras. (Sample answer: Fossils from earlier eras are usually deeper in the Earth and harder to find.)

Ask students how they think changes in the planet could have affected the appearance and disappearance of various life-forms over time. (Sample answer: Temperature fluctuations due to ice ages and other climactic changes would have affected which plants and animals could survive. Climate changes caused changes in the vegetation and in the availability of food for animals. Until the planet was able to support a lot of vegetation, there wouldn't have been much food for animals to eat.)

 Teaching Transparency 24 "Changes in Life over Earth's History"

IS THAT A FACT!

There are more than 100,000 living mollusk species, and at least 35,000 extinct forms are known from the fossil record. As a group, mollusks are very successful—there have been mollusks on Earth for nearly 600 million years.

Evidence of Evolution: The Fossil Record

Evidence that living things evolve comes from many different sources. This evidence includes fossils as well as comparisons among different groups of organisms.

To date, scientists have described and named about 300,000 fossil species.

Fossils The Earth's crust is arranged in layers, with different kinds of rock and soil stacked on top of one another. These layers are formed when sediments, particles of sand, dust, or soil are carried by wind and water and are deposited in an orderly fashion. Older layers are deposited before newer layers and are buried deeper within the Earth. **Fossils,** the solidified remains or imprints of once-living organisms, are found in these layers. Fossils, like those pictured in **Figure 5,** can be of complete organisms, parts of organisms, or just a set of footprints.

Figure 5 *The fossil on the left is of a trilobite, an ancient aquatic animal. The fossils on the right are of seed ferns.*

Geology CONNECTION

Fossils are usually found in layered rock called sedimentary rock. Sedimentary rock usually forms when rock is broken into sediment by wind, water, and other means. The wind and water move the sediment around and deposit it. Over time, layers of sediment pile up. Lower layers are compressed and changed into rock.

Fossils are usually formed when a dead organism is covered by a layer of sediment. Over time, more sediment settles on top of the organism. Minerals in the sediment may seep into the organism, gradually replacing the organism with stone. Or the organism may rot away completely after being covered, leaving a hole in the rock called a *mold*.

Reading the Fossil Record Fossils provide a historical sequence of life known as the **fossil record.** The fossil record supplies evidence about the order in which evolutionary changes have occurred. Fossils found in the upper, or newer, layers of the Earth's crust tend to resemble present-day organisms. This similarity indicates that the fossilized organisms were close relatives of present-day organisms. The deeper in the Earth's crust fossils are found, the less they tend to look like present-day organisms. These fossils are of earlier forms of life that may now be extinct.

TOPIC: The Fossil Record
GO TO: www.scilinks.org
sciLINKS NUMBER: HSTL160

Gaps in the Fossil Record If every organism that lived left an imprint behind, the fossil record would resemble a very large evolutionary family tree. **Figure 6** shows a hypothetical fossil record in which all relationships between organisms are clearly mapped.

Although scientists have collected thousands of fossils, gaps remain in the current fossil record, as shown in **Figure 7.** This is because specific conditions are necessary for fossils to form. The organism must be buried in very fine sediment. Also, oxygen—which promotes decay—cannot be present. However, very few places are free of oxygen. Because the conditions needed for fossils to form are rare, fossils are often difficult to find. Nevertheless, scientists have identified some fossils that complete sections of the fossil record.

Vestigial Structures Whales are similar in shape to fish. Yet whales are *mammals*—animals that breathe air, give birth to live young, and produce milk. Although modern whales do not have hind limbs, there are remnants of hind-limb bones inside their bodies, as shown in **Figure 8.** These remnants of once-useful structures are known as **vestigial** (ves TIJ ee uhl) **structures.** Scientists think that over millions of years, whales evolved from doglike land dwellers into sea-dwelling organisms. But scientists have not had the fossil evidence to support their ideas—until now. Read the following case study to learn the story of whale evolution.

Figure 6 *This is the way the fossil record might appear if fossils from every species had been found.*

Figure 7 *This diagram illustrates the many gaps in the existing fossil record.*

Figure 8 *Remnants of hind-limb bones are embedded deep inside the whale's body.*

IS THAT A FACT!

Indricotherium, a giant land mammal that was about 4 m tall and was up to 6 m long, lived in Asia between 18 million and 32 million years ago.

MATH and MORE

Say to students: Imagine that you are a scientific time traveler assigned to count the life-forms in what will become your home state 1 million years from now. You know that at present your home state contains 1,200 insect species, 550 animal species, and 600 plant species. Only 24 percent of these species are expected to survive the next million years. How many species existing now should you expect to find in 1 million years?
(insects: 1,200 × 0.24 = 288
animals: 550 × 0.24 = 132
plants: 600 × 0.24 = 144)

Homework

Writing | Research the Horse Have students check additional resources to find the four main ancestors of the horse as revealed through the fossil record. (*Eohippus, Mesohippus, Merychippus, Pliohippus*)

Ask students to make a poster that shows each ancestral horse in order of appearance and to write a paragraph about each one explaining its unique physical characteristics. Students should conclude their reports by answering the following question:

Are the wild horses in North America direct descendants of fossil horses found on this continent? (No; the fossil record shows that horses native to North America disappeared. Today's wild horses are descendants of horses introduced to this continent by Spanish explorers in the early 1500s.)

2) Teach, continued

CROSS-DISCIPLINARY FOCUS

Art The role of a scientific illustrator is to make accurate pictures of organisms and things that scientists study. In the case of long-extinct species, such as dinosaurs, artists must sometimes fill in where science leaves off. Have students look for examples of illustrations of extinct animals and compare them with other illustrations of the same animal. Have students try to identify areas where artistic interpretation is used. You may wish to provide students with examples of similar illustrations from hundreds of years ago, when much less was known about these animals. **Sheltered English**

ACTIVITY

Making Posters
Have students create pictures of their own imaginary animal that is evolving from an ocean-dwelling species into a terrestrial one. Tell them to draw at least three stages of the progression and to label each significant body part with a description of how the animals of that species use that part. **Sheltered English**

TOPIC: Species and Adaptation
GO TO: www.scilinks.org
sciLINKS NUMBER: HSTL155

Case Study: Evolution of the Whale

Scientists hypothesize that whales evolved from land-dwelling mammals like *Mesonychid* (muh ZOH ni kid), shown below, which returned to the ocean about 55 million years ago. During the 1980s and 1990s, several fossils of whale ancestors were discovered. These discoveries support a theory of whale evolution.

55 million years ago
Mesonychid

Ambulocetus (AM byoo loh SEE tuhs), pictured below, lived in coastal waters. *Ambulocetus* had shorter legs than *Mesonychid*, but it still had feet and toes that could support its weight on land. Although *Ambulocetus* had a tail, scientists think it kicked its legs like an otter in order to swim and used its tail for balance.

50 million years ago
Ambulocetus

WEIRD SCIENCE

In 1938, some fishermen caught a live coelacanth, a primitive type of fish that was thought to have been extinct for about 65 million years.

46 million years ago
Rodhocetus

Forty-six million years ago, *Rodhocetus* (roh doh SEE tuhs) appeared in the fossil record. This animal more closely resembled modern whales, but it had hind limbs and feet that it retained from its land-dwelling ancestor. Because of its short legs, *Rodhocetus* was restricted to a crocodile-like waddle while on land. Unlike the legs of *Ambulocetus*, these legs were not necessary for swimming. Instead, *Rodhocetus* depended on its massive tail to propel it through the water. While *Ambulocetus* probably pulled itself onto land every night, *Rodhocetus* probably spent most of its time in the water.

Prozeuglodon (pro ZOO gloh dahn), which appeared in the fossil record 6 million years after *Rodhocetus*, was well adapted for life at sea. Although it still had a pair of very small legs, *Prozeuglodon* lived only in the water.

BRAIN FOOD

During their early development, modern whale embryos have four limbs. The rear limbs disappear before birth, and the front limbs develop into flippers.

40 million years ago
Prozeuglodon

IS THAT A FACT!
Baby blue whales can weigh 9,000 kg (about 20,000 lb) at birth.

DISCUSSION

Inland Whales Explain to students that in 1849 workers constructing a railroad near the town of Charlotte, Vermont, discovered bones that were later identified as those of a beluga whale. Ask students to locate Charlotte on a map and explain why this discovery is so unusual. (It is more than 150 miles from the nearest ocean.)

Ask students what these bones tell us about the history of the land around Charlotte. (It used to be part of an ocean.)

Explain that the Champlain Sea, an extension of the ocean, existed for 2,500 years after the last glaciers retreated 12,500 years ago.

MISCONCEPTION ALERT

It is easy for students to confuse adaptation with acclimation or intentional change or adjustment. For example, a student might write that over many years, a species learned to adapt to its new environment. Explain to students that adaptation is something that happens to a species over many generations and not an activity that a species learns or chooses to do.

Acclimation is an adjustment to a condition that is within an organism's range of tolerance, such as seasonal adjustment to climate changes. This, too, is a part of an organism's evolutionary adaptations and is not something it learns to do.

Section 1 • Change Over Time

3) Extend

Over the years, some bacteria have become resistant to antibiotics that doctors use to treat or prevent diseases. Some scientists suggest that as bacteria become more and more resistant, people will be increasingly susceptible to microbes that cannot be stopped. Scientists are concerned that by using antibiotics, we are creating a larger problem for the future.

Research

Scientists study animal skeletons and DNA to determine evolutionary relationships and development because merely looking at the outward appearance of a species can be misleading. The giant panda and red panda illustrate this problem. Their common names indicate that the two pandas seem closely related, but scientists now believe that the red panda is the only member of the subfamily Ailurinae of the raccoon family Procyonidae, which is quite separate from the giant panda. Have students investigate and write a report based on recent studies on the classification of these two pandas.

Teaching Transparency 25 "Comparative Skeletal Structures"

Evidence of Evolution: Comparing Organisms

Evidence that life has evolved also comes from comparisons of different groups of organisms. On the following pages, the different kinds of evidence that support the theory of evolution are discussed in greater detail.

Human arm

Cat leg

Dolphin flipper

Bat wing

Figure 9 *The bones in the front limbs of these animals are similar, even though the limbs are used in different ways. Similar bones are shown in the same color.*

Comparing Skeletal Structures
What does your arm have in common with the front leg of a cat, the front flipper of a dolphin, or the wing of a bat? At first glance, you might think that they have little in common. After all, these structures don't look very much alike and are not used in the same way. If you look under the surface, however, the structure and order of the bones in the front limbs of these different animals, shown in **Figure 9,** are actually similar to the structure and order of the bones found in your arm.

The similarities indicate that animals as different as a cat, a dolphin, a bat, and a human are all related by a common ancestor. The evolutionary process has modified these bones over millions of years to perform specific functions.

Comparing DNA from Different Species
Scientists hypothesize that if all organisms living today evolved from a common ancestor, they should all have the same kind of genetic material. And in fact they do. From microscopic bacteria to giant polar bears, all organisms share the same genetic material—DNA.

In addition, scientists hypothesize that species appearing to be close relatives should have greater similarities in their DNA than species appearing to be distant relatives. For example, chimpanzees and gorillas appear to be close relatives. Chimpanzees and toucans appear to be distant relatives. The DNA of chimpanzees is, in fact, more similar to the DNA of gorillas than to the DNA of toucans.

156

Mystery Footprints PG 708

It seems as though the knee joints of birds bend backward, but they bend just like a human's knees. Birds walk on their toes. The long bone just above the toes is the foot! The first big joint above that (the one people often think is the knee) is actually a bird's ankle.

Comparing Embryonic Structures Can you tell the difference between a chicken, a rabbit, and a human? It's pretty easy when you compare adults from each species. But what about comparing members of these species before they are born? Look at the left side of **Figure 10,** which depicts the very early embryos of a chicken, a rabbit, and a human.

All the organisms shown in the figure are *vertebrates,* or animals that have a backbone. Early in development, human embryos and the embryos of all other vertebrates are similar. These early similarities are evidence that all vertebrates share a common ancestor. Although the embryos look similar to each other in very early stages, none of them look like their adult forms. Embryo development has evolved over millions of years, causing the embryonic structures to grow into many different species of vertebrates. The changes in the process of embryo development therefore produce animals as different as a chicken and a human.

Figure 10 The embryos of different vertebrates are very similar during the earliest stages of development.

REVIEW

1. How does the fossil record suggest that species have changed over time?

2. How do the similarities in the fore-limb bones of humans, cats, dolphins, and bats support the theory of evolution?

3. **Interpreting Graphics** The photograph at right shows the layers of sedimentary rock exposed during the construction of a road. Imagine that a species which lived 200 million years ago is found in the layer designated as **b.** Its ancestor, which lived 250 million years ago, would most likely be found in which layer, **a** or **c**? Explain your answer.

---

4) Close

Quiz

1. Use the words *adaptations, population,* and *evolution* together in a sentence. (Sample answer: Evolution is the process by which a population accumulates inherited adaptations over time.)

2. List two reasons why gaps exist in the fossil record. (Fossilization requires precise and sometimes rare conditions, including the absence of oxygen and burial in very fine sediment.)

ALTERNATIVE ASSESSMENT

Writing Charles Darwin's journals contain notes and records from his travels. Ask students to imagine that they are traveling with Darwin and keeping their own journals. Their notes and drawings should reflect what they see, the questions that arise from their observations, and the hypotheses that they form. Encourage students to write journal entries about other animals on the Galápagos Islands besides the finches, such as the Galápagos tortoise and marine iguanas.

MISCONCEPTION ALERT

Explain to students that the embryonic figures shown in **Figure 10** are not all at the same stage of development. The similarities are fleeting, but they are shown here to indicate that the vertebrate body plan is evident in early development.

Teaching Transparency 26 "Vertebrate Embryos"

▼ **Answers to Review**

1. Fossils provide a historical sequence of life. The fossils found in the upper, or newer, layers of the Earth's crust tend to resemble present-day organisms. The deeper in the Earth's crust fossils are found, the less they look like present-day organisms; these are fossils of earlier forms of life that are now extinct.

2. The similarities indicate that animals as different as a cat, a dolphin, a bat, and a human are all descendants of a common ancestor. They have been modified over millions of years to perform different functions.

3. c

Section 1 • Change Over Time

SECTION 2

Focus

How Does Evolution Happen?

This section introduces students to Charles Darwin and his voyage to the Galápagos Islands. Students will learn how artificial selection, geology, and the writings of Thomas Malthus and Charles Lyell helped Darwin formulate his theory of natural selection. Finally, students will learn that twentieth-century biologists used their knowledge of genetics to explain that species change through genetic mutation.

Bellringer

On the board or on an overhead projector write the following list:

upright walking, hair, fingerprints, binocular vision, speech

These are traits that almost all humans have in common. Ask students to list the advantages and disadvantages of each trait.

1 Motivate

DISCUSSION

Dinosaurs Ask students to describe a dinosaur. Ask them to explain why there are no dinosaurs alive today. Ask them, finally, if they think dinosaurs became extinct because they were not "evolved" enough to survive until the present. **(Explain that dinosaurs were well adapted to their environment and lived over 150 million years on Earth. But a catastrophic event changed the environment faster than the dinosaurs could adapt, and they became extinct.)**

Section 2

Terms to Learn

trait
selective breeding
natural selection
mutation

What You'll Do

◆ Describe the four steps of Darwin's theory of evolution by natural selection.
◆ Explain how mutations are important to evolution.

 Directed Reading Worksheet 7 Section 2

TOPIC: The Galápagos Islands
GO TO: www.scilinks.org
sciLINKS NUMBER: HSTL165

How Does Evolution Happen?

The early 1800s was a time of great scientific discovery. Geologists realized that the Earth is much older than anyone had previously thought. Evidence showed that gradual processes had shaped the Earth's surface over millions of years. Fossilized remains of bizarre organisms were found. Fossils of familiar things were also found, but some of them were in unusual places. For example, fish fossils and shells were found on the tops of mountains. The Earth suddenly seemed to be a place where great change was possible. Many people thought that evolution occurs, but no one had been able to determine *how* it happens—until Charles Darwin.

Charles Darwin

In 1831, 21-year-old Charles Darwin, shown in **Figure 11**, had just graduated from college. Like many young people just out of college, Darwin didn't know what he wanted to do with his life. His father wanted him to become a doctor. However, Darwin was sickened by watching surgery. Although he eventually earned a degree in theology, he was *really* interested in the study of plants and animals.

Darwin was able to talk his father into letting him sign on for a 5-year voyage around the world. He served as the naturalist (a scientist who studies nature) on a British naval ship, the HMS *Beagle*. During this voyage, Darwin made observations that later became the foundation for his theory of evolution by natural selection.

Figure 11 *Charles Darwin, shown at far left, sailed around the world on a ship very similar to this one.*

The tailbone in humans is a vestigial structure that is a remnant of the tails of ancestor species.

Darwin's Excellent Adventure

As the HMS *Beagle* made its way around the world, Darwin collected thousands of plant and animal samples and kept detailed notes of his observations. The *Beagle*'s journey is charted in **Figure 12.** During the journey, the ship visited the Galápagos Islands, shown below, which are 965 km (600 mi) west of Ecuador, a country in South America.

Figure 12 The course of the HMS *Beagle* is noted by the red line.

Darwin's Finches

Darwin observed that the animals and plants on the Galápagos Islands were very similar, yet not identical, to the animals and plants on the nearby South American mainland. For example, he noted that the finches living on the Galápagos Islands differed slightly from the finches in Ecuador. The finches on the islands were different not only from the mainland finches but also from each other. As you can see in **Figure 13,** the birds differed from each other mainly in the shape of their beaks and in the food they ate.

Figure 13 The beaks of these three species of finches are adapted to the different ways the finches obtain food.

The **large ground finch** has a heavy, strong beak adapted for cracking big, hard seeds. This finch's beak works like a nutcracker.

The **cactus finch** has a tough beak that is good for eating cactus and its nectar. It works like a pair of needle-nosed pliers.

The **warbler finch's** small, pointed beak is adapted for probing into cracks and crevices to obtain small insects. This beak works like a pair of tweezers.

IS THAT A FACT!

The giant tortoises of the Galápagos Islands weigh up to 270 kg and can live for over 150 years.

Survival of the Chocolates

2 Teach

DEMONSTRATION

Form and Function Present and identify to students the following pieces of clothing:

sneaker, dress pump, loafer, necktie, scarf, anklet, knee sock

Explain that all these items are pieces of clothing but some are more closely related than others. Within each group (shoes, neckwear, socks), every item is best suited for one particular function. This relationship of similarities and differences is what Charles Darwin observed in many animal and plant species.

MEETING INDIVIDUAL NEEDS

Advanced Learners Encourage interested students to investigate Darwin's voyage and similar long-distance travel by explorers in the 1800s in greater detail. Topics for reports include the types of ships used for travel in that era, the kinds of food eaten by the explorers, and the sophistication and thoroughness of maps in the 1800s.

CONNECT TO GEOGRAPHY

The Galápagos Islands are administratively part of the country of Equador, though they are 1,000 km west of the mainland. They are a group of 19 volcanically formed islands. Though they have a land area of only 8,000 km², they are dispersed over almost 60,000 km² of the Pacific Ocean. It is easy to imagine how new species could arise in such a place.

Section 2 • How Does Evolution Happen?

2 Teach, continued

READING STRATEGY

Prediction Guide Before reading this page, have students answer the following questions:

- Why did the finches Darwin saw on the Galápagos Islands look similar to those he saw in South America?
- Why did they look a little different?

Have students evaluate their answers after they read the page.

MEETING INDIVIDUAL NEEDS

Advanced Learners Biogeography is the study of where animals and plants are found and how they came to live in their particular location. It uses information from the fossil record and integrates ideas from biology, geology, paleontology, and chemistry. Encourage interested students to write a report about island biogeography. Have them include information about how it is used to design and manage terrestrial wildlife refuges.

RETEACHING

To help students understand the process of speciation, have them write a brief paragraph about each new term in this chapter. Each paragraph should begin with a definition. Then have students write sample sentences using the term.

Have you ever heard of a bank that has no money, only seeds? Read about it on page 172.

Darwin Does Some Thinking

Darwin's observations raised questions that he couldn't easily answer, such as, "Why are the finches on the islands similar but not identical to the finches on the mainland?" and "Why do the finches from different islands differ from one another?" Darwin thought that perhaps all the finches on the Galápagos Islands descended from finches on the South American mainland. The original population of finches may have been blown from South America to the Galápagos Islands by a storm. Over many generations, the finches that survived may have adapted to various ways of living on the Galápagos Islands.

After Darwin returned to England, he spent many years working on his theory of how evolution happens. During this period, he gathered many ideas from a variety of sources.

Darwin Learned from Farmers and Animal and Plant Breeders

In Darwin's time, many varieties of farm animals and plants had been selectively produced. Farmers chose certain **traits,** distinguishing qualities such as plump corn kernels, and bred only the individuals that had the desired traits. This procedure is called **selective breeding** because humans, not nature, select which traits will be passed along to the next generation. Selective breeding in dogs, shown in **Figure 14,** has exaggerated certain traits to produce more than 150 different breeds.

In your studies of genetics and heredity, you learned that a great variety of traits exists among individuals in a species. Darwin was impressed that farmers and breeders could direct and shape these traits and make such dramatic changes in animals and plants in just a few short generations. He thought that wild animals and plants could change in a similar way but that the process would take much longer because variations would be due to chance.

Figure 14 Dogs are a good example of how selective breeding works. Over the past 12,000 years, dogs have been selectively bred to produce more than 150 different breeds.

IS THAT A FACT!

As a result of selective breeding, the smallest horse is the Falabella, which is only about 76 cm tall. The largest is the Shire, originally bred in England. It can grow more than 1.73 m high at the shoulder and weigh as much as 910 kg.

Darwin Learned from Geologists

Geologists told Darwin that they had evidence that the Earth was much older than anyone had imagined. He learned from reading *Principles of Geology*, by Charles Lyell, that Earth had been formed by natural processes over a long period of time. Lyell's data were important because Darwin thought that populations of organisms changed very slowly, requiring a lot of time.

Darwin Learned from the Work of Thomas Malthus

In his *Essay on the Principle of Population*, Malthus proposed that humans have the potential to reproduce beyond the capacity of their food supplies. However, he also recognized that death caused by starvation, disease, and war affects the size of human populations. Malthus's thoughts are represented in **Figure 15**.

Darwin realized that other animal species are also capable of producing too many offspring. For these animal species, starvation, disease, and predators affect the size of their populations. Only a limited number survive to reproduce. Thus, there must be something special about the survivors. What traits make them better equipped to survive and reproduce? Darwin reasoned that the offspring of the survivors inherit traits that help them survive in their environment.

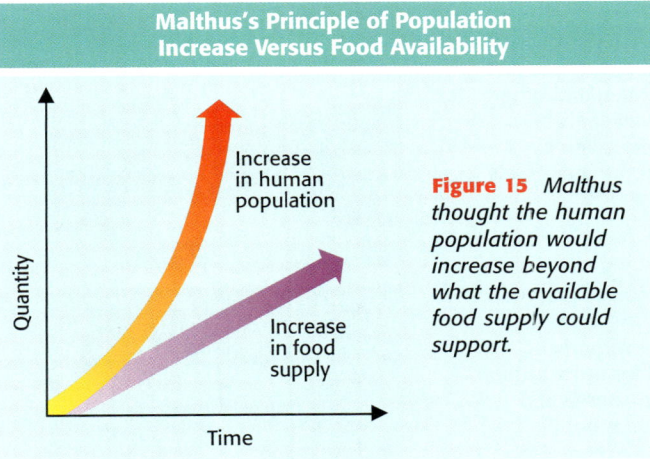

Figure 15 Malthus thought the human population would increase beyond what the available food supply could support.

QuickLab

Could We Run out of Food?

Malthus thought we could. Do the following activity to better understand Malthus's hypothesis. Get **2 empty egg cartons** and a **bag of rice**. Label one carton "Food supply" and the second carton "Population growth." In the food supply carton, place one grain of rice in the first cup. Increase the amount by one in each subsequent cup. Each grain represents a unit of food. In the population growth carton, place one grain of rice in the first cup, and double the number of grains of rice in each subsequent cup. This rice represents people.

1. How many "people" are there in the last cup?
2. How many units of food are there in the last cup?
3. What conclusion can you draw?

QuickLab

MATERIALS

FOR EACH STUDENT:
• 2 empty 12-egg cartons
• bag of rice

In a balanced system organisms interact so that there is maximum diversity, and population increase equals population decrease. The QuickLab demonstrates an unbalanced system. There is nothing to slow the rapid increase of the rice grain population.

Answers to QuickLab

1. There are 2,048 "people."
2. There are 12 grains of rice.
3. There is not enough food to support the population.

Students should work this out mathematically before each step. They should also divide the task of counting after the first 6 cups.

SCIENTISTS AT ODDS

Not all scientists who study evolution agree on how the process takes place. Gradualism, the theory that Darwin supported, is based on the principle that changes in species occur slowly and steadily over thousands of years. In the 1970s, Stephen Jay Gould and others proposed the theory of punctuated equilibrium, which holds that species can remain unchanged for millions of years and then, due to dramatic environmental changes, undergo relatively rapid changes. The fossil record provides evidence that supports both sides of this debate.

SCIENCE HUMOR

Q: How did the dinosaurs listen to music?

A: on their fossil records

Math Skills Worksheet 3
"Multiplying Whole Numbers"

3) Extend

INDEPENDENT PRACTICE

Concept Mapping Have students make a concept map in their ScienceLog that outlines the process of change for a population of squirrels (each of which is black, red, grey, or white) marooned on a treeless island of black sand that is also home to squirrel-eating foxes. Sheltered English

Homework

Poster Project Have students research the natural history and current status of sea turtles (or a specific sea turtle species) to find examples for each of the four steps of natural selection. Have them construct a display to present their findings. For example, cotton balls glued to the poster board can represent eggs, and a dark plastic bag can symbolize a polluted ocean. Present the following questions as guides for their research:

1. On average, how many offspring does a sea turtle produce each year?
2. What physical adaptations have helped sea turtles survive in their environment?
3. What specific environmental factors affect their ability to survive?
4. What natural and man-made factors may be affecting their ability to survive long enough to reproduce successfully?

Teaching Transparency 27 "Natural Selection in Four Steps"

Natural Selection

In 1858, about 20 years after he returned from his voyage on the HMS *Beagle*, Darwin received a letter from a naturalist named Alfred Russel Wallace. Wallace had independently arrived at the same theory of evolution that Darwin had been working on for so many years. Darwin and Wallace discussed their research and made plans to present their findings at a meeting later in the year. Then, in 1859, Darwin published his own results in his book called *On the Origin of Species by Means of Natural Selection*. Darwin theorized that evolution occurs through a process he called **natural selection.** This process, examined below, is divided into four parts.

Natural Selection in Four Steps

1 Overproduction Each species produces more offspring than will survive to maturity.

2 Genetic Variation The individuals in a population are slightly different from one another. Each individual has a unique combination of traits, such as size, color, and the ability to find food. Some traits increase the chances that the individual will survive and reproduce. Other traits decrease the chances of survival. These variations are genetic and can be inherited.

3 Struggle to Survive A natural environment does not have enough food, water, and other resources to support all the individuals born. In addition, many individuals are killed by other organisms. Only some of the individuals in a population survive to adulthood.

4 Successful Reproduction Successful reproduction is the key to natural selection. The individuals that are well adapted to their environment, that is, those that have better traits for living in their environment, are more likely to survive and reproduce. The individuals that are not well adapted to their environment are more likely to die early or produce few offspring.

IS THAT A FACT!

In 1809 French naturalist Jean Baptiste Lamarck's theory of evolution stated that if an animal changed a body part through use or nonuse, that change would be inherited by its offspring. For example, larger or stronger leg muscles as a result of extensive running would be passed on to the next generation. Genetic studies in the 1930s and 1940s, however, disproved Lamarck's mechanism for inherited traits.

162 Chapter 7 • The Evolution of Living Things

A Breed All Their Own

Imagine that your grandfather has owned a kennel for more than 50 years but has never sold a dog. He cares for the dogs and keeps them in one large pen. Originally there were six labs, six terriers, and six pointers. There are now 76 dogs, and you are surprised that only a few look like pointers, labs, and terriers. The other dogs look similar to each other but not to any of the specific breeds. Your grandfather says that over the past 50 years each generation has looked less like the generation that preceded it.

By the time you visited the kennel, what may have happened to make most of the dogs look similar to each other but not to any specific original breed? Base your answer on what you've learned about selective breeding in this section.

More Evidence of Evolution

One of the observations on which Darwin based his theory of evolution by natural selection is that parents pass traits to their offspring. But Darwin did not know *how* inheritance occurs or *why* individuals vary within a population.

During the 1930s and 1940s, biologists combined the principles of genetic inheritance with Darwin's theory of evolution by natural selection. This combination of principles explained that the variations Darwin observed within a species are caused by **mutation**, or changes in a gene.

Since Darwin's time, new evidence has been collected from many fields of science. Although scientists recognize that other mechanisms may also play a part in the evolution of a species, the theory of evolution by natural selection provides the most thorough explanation for the diversity of life on Earth.

REVIEW

1. Why are some animals more likely to survive to adulthood than other animals?
2. **Summarizing Data** What did Darwin think happened to the first small population of finches that reached the Galápagos Islands from South America?
3. **Doing Calculations** A female cockroach can produce 80 offspring at a time. If half of the offspring were female, and each female produced 80 offspring, how many cockroaches would there be in 3 generations?

internet connect

TOPIC: The Galápagos Islands, Darwin and Natural Selection
GO TO: www.scilinks.org
***sci*LINKS NUMBER:** HSTL165, HSTL170

Section 2 • How Does Evolution Happen? **163**

SECTION 3

Focus

Natural Selection in Action

In this section students will learn that natural selection is occurring constantly and is not just a historical relic. They will learn how a species' generation time affects its ability to adapt. Finally, students will learn the three steps of speciation: separation, adaptation, and division.

Bellringer

Display on the board or the overhead projector these instructions to students:

Write the four steps of natural selection, and create a mnemonic device to remember each step by using the first letter of each step.

1) Motivate

DEMONSTRATION

Natural Selection Place 20 black jellybeans and 20 red jellybeans on a piece of black paper, and call the display *Generation 1*. Tell students to pretend the candies are fish and ask which would most likely be eaten first by the jellybean shark. Then add 5 black jellybeans and take away 5 red ones. Call this group *Generation 2*. Ask students how many fish in this generation might survive the jellybean shark. Have students offer explanations for what happened between *Generation 1* and *Generation 2*.

Directed Reading Worksheet 7 Section 3

Section 3

Terms to Learn
generation time
speciation

What You'll Do
- Give two examples of natural selection in action.
- Outline the process of speciation.

Natural Selection in Action

The theory of natural selection explains how a population changes over many generations in response to its environment. In fact, members of a population tend to be well adapted to their environment because natural selection is continuously taking place.

Insecticide Resistance To keep crops safe from certain insects, some farmers use a wide variety of chemical insecticides. However, some insecticides that worked well in the past are no longer as effective. In the 50 years that insecticides have been widely used, more than 500 species of insects have developed resistance to certain insecticides.

Insects quickly develop resistance to insecticides because they produce many offspring and usually have short generation times. A **generation time** is the period between the birth of one generation and the birth of the next generation. Look at **Figure 16** to see how a common household pest, the cockroach, has adapted to become resistant to certain insecticides.

1. An insecticide will kill most insects, but a few may survive. These survivors have genes that make them resistant to the insecticide.

2. The survivors then reproduce, passing the insecticide-resistance genes to their offspring.

3. In time, the replacement population of insects is made up mostly of individuals that have the insecticide-resistance genes.

4. When the same kind of insecticide is used on the insects, only a few are killed because most of them are resistant to that insecticide.

Figure 16 *Variety in a population's characteristics helps ensure that some individuals will be able to survive a change in the environment.*

We're off to hunt the marshmallows! Look on page 710 to find out why.

 PG 710
Out-of-Sight Marshmallows

Q: What do you get when you cross a crocodile with an abalone?

A: a crocabaloney

Adaptation to Pollution There are two color variations among European peppered moths, as shown in **Figure 17.** Before 1850, the dark peppered moth was considered rare. The pale peppered moth was much more common. After the 1850s, however, dark peppered moths became more abundant in heavily industrialized areas.

Figure 17 *Against a dark tree trunk (above), the pale peppered moth stands out. Against a light tree trunk (right), the dark peppered moth stands out.*

What caused this change in the peppered moth population? Several species of birds eat peppered moths that rest on tree trunks. Before the 1850s, the trees had a gray appearance, and pale peppered moths blended into their surroundings. Dark peppered moths were easier for the birds to see and were eaten more frequently. After the 1850s, soot and smoke from newly developing industrial areas blackened nearby trees. The dark peppered moths became less visible on the dark tree trunks. The pale peppered moths stood out against the dark background and became easy prey for the birds. More dark moths survived and produced more dark offspring. Thus, the population changed from mostly light-colored moths to mostly dark-colored moths.

> **Self-Check**
>
> If the air pollution in Europe were cleaned up, what do you think would happen to the population of light-colored peppered moths? *(See page 782 to check your answers.)*

2) Teach, continued

GOING FURTHER

Ask students if they can define *subspecies*. (A subspecies is a population within a species that is different enough to be given its own name.)

Because subspecies can breed with one another, all are still members of the same species. Then tell them that all seven subspecies of a particular salamander can be found in California. Each one gradually integrates into the next subspecies. But in two locations, two of the subspecies interbreed rarely if at all. Ask students if they should be considered different species. Why or why not? (They are not yet different species because they can still interbreed.)

Ask how they would research this question. Then tell them that early DNA studies indicate that the single salamander species is becoming two different species, possibly more.

SCIENTISTS AT ODDS

Scientists at the American Ornithologists' Union are responsible for the official list of scientific bird names used in the United States. They used to recognize the Eastern towhee and the spotted towhee. Then they decided to make them one species, the rufous-sided towhee. Then they changed their minds (based on further study) and "split" the classification again. Stay tuned.

Formation of New Species

The process of natural selection can explain how a species can evolve into a new species. A portion of a species' population can become separated from the original population. Over time, the two populations can become so different that they can no longer interbreed. This process is called **speciation.** One way that speciation can occur is shown in the following three steps:

1. Separation The process of speciation often begins when a portion of a population becomes isolated. **Figure 18** shows some of the ways this can happen. A newly formed canyon, mountain range, and lake are a few of the ways that populations can be divided.

Figure 18 *Populations can become separated in a variety of ways.*

2. Adaptation If a population has been divided by one of the changes illustrated above, the environment may also change. This is where natural selection comes in. As the environment changes, so may the population that lives there. Over many generations, the separated groups may adapt to better fit their environment, as shown in **Figure 19.** If the environmental conditions are different for each of the groups, the adaptations in the groups may also be different.

Figure 19 *When a single population becomes divided, the groups may evolve separately and may form separate species.*

IS THAT A FACT!

Some species that have adapted to live in total darkness no longer even have eyes! Just as whales have evolved into legless forms, these species have completely adapted to life without light, and some have evolved forms lacking eyes altogether. There are blind cave fish, eels, salamanders, worms, shrimp, crayfish, spiders, beetles, and crickets.

166 Chapter 7 • The Evolution of Living Things

3. Division Over many hundreds, thousands, or even millions of generations, the two groups of a population may become so different that they can no longer interbreed, even if the geographical barrier is removed. At this point, the two groups are no longer the same species. Scientists think that the finches on the Galápagos Islands evolved by these three basic steps. **Figure 20** illustrates how this might have happened.

Figure 20 *The finches on the Galápagos Islands might have evolved into different species by the process depicted below.*

❶ Some finches left the mainland and reached one of the islands (separation).

❷ The finches reproduced and adapted to the environment (adaptation).

❸ Some finches flew to a second island (separation).

❹ The finches reproduced and adapted to the different environment (adaptation).

❺ Some finches flew back to the first island but could no longer interbreed with the finches there (division).

❻ This process may have occurred over and over again as the finches flew to the other islands.

REVIEW

1. Why did the number of dark peppered moths increase after the 1850s?
2. What factor indicates that a population has evolved into two separate species?
3. **Applying Concepts** Most cactuses have spines, which are leaves modified to protect the plant. The spines cover a juicy stem that stores water. Explain how cactus leaves and stems might have changed through the process of natural selection.

internet connect

SCLINKS
NSTA

TOPIC: Species and Adaptation
GO TO: www.scilinks.org
sciLINKS NUMBER: HSTL155

Chapter Highlights

VOCABULARY DEFINITIONS

SECTION 1

adaptation a hereditary characteristic that helps an organism survive and reproduce in its environment

species the most specific of the seven levels of classification; characterized by a group of organisms that can mate with one another to produce fertile offspring

evolution the process by which populations accumulate inherited changes over time

fossil the solidified remains or imprints of once-living organisms

fossil record a historical sequence of life indicated by fossils found in layers of the Earth's crust

vestigial structure the remnant of a once-useful anatomical structure

SECTION 2

trait distinguishing qualities that can be passed from one generation to another

selective breeding breeding of organisms that have a certain desired trait

natural selection the process by which organisms with favorable traits survive and reproduce at a higher rate than organisms without the favorable trait

mutation a change in the order of the bases in an organism's DNA; deletion, insertion, or substitution

Chapter Highlights

SECTION 1

Vocabulary
- **adaptation** (p. 150)
- **species** (p. 150)
- **evolution** (p. 151)
- **fossil** (p. 152)
- **fossil record** (p. 152)
- **vestigial structure** (p. 153)

Section Notes
- Evolution is the process by which populations change over time. Those changes are inherited.
- Evidence of a common ancestor for all organisms is provided by the following: the fossil record, comparisons of skeletal structures found in related species, comparisons of the embryos of distantly related vertebrates, and the presence of DNA in all living organisms.
- Species that are closely related have DNA that is more alike than DNA of distantly related species.

Labs
Mystery Footprints (p. 708)

SECTION 2

Vocabulary
- **trait** (p. 160)
- **selective breeding** (p. 160)
- **natural selection** (p. 162)
- **mutation** (p. 163)

Section Notes
- Charles Darwin developed an explanation for evolution after years of studying the organisms he observed on the voyage of the *Beagle*.
- Darwin's study was influenced by the concepts of selective breeding, the age of the Earth, and the idea that some organisms are better equipped to survive than others.

✓ Skills Check

Math Concepts

MALTHUS'S PRINCIPLE The graph on page 161 shows two types of growth. The straight line represents an increase in which the same number is added to the previous number, as in 3, 4, 5, 6, . . . , where 1 is added to each number.

The curved line represents an increase in which each number is multiplied by the same factor, as in 2, 4, 8, 16, . . . , where each number is multiplied by 2. As you can see on the graph, the curved line increases at a much faster rate than the straight line.

Visual Understanding

SKELETAL STRUCTURE Figure 9 on page 156 illustrates skeletal evidence for evolution. By looking at the same-colored bones, you can see how the early mammalian skeletal structure has evolved in certain species to help with specialized tasks such as flying and swimming.

Lab and Activity Highlights

Survival of the Chocolates PG 711

Mystery Footprints PG 708

Out-of-Sight Marshmallows PG 710

Datasheets for LabBook
(blackline masters for these labs)

SECTION 2

- Darwin explained that evolution occurs through natural selection. Natural selection can be divided into four parts:
  (1) Each species produces more offspring than will survive to reproduce.
  (2) Individuals within a population are slightly different from one another.
  (3) Individuals within a population compete with one another for limited resources.
  (4) Individuals that are better equipped to live in an environment are more likely to survive and reproduce.

- Evolution is explained today by combining the principles of natural selection with the principles of genetic inheritance.

Labs
Survival of the Chocolates (p. 711)

SECTION 3

Vocabulary
generation time (p. 164)
speciation (p. 166)

Section Notes

- Natural selection allows a population to adapt to changes in environmental conditions.

- Evidence of natural selection can be seen by studying generations of organisms that have developed resistance to an insecticide or antibiotic.

- Natural selection also explains how one species may evolve into another through the process of speciation.

Labs
Out-of-Sight Marshmallows (p. 710)

VOCABULARY DEFINITIONS, continued

SECTION 3

generation time the period between the birth of one generation and the birth of the next generation

speciation the process by which two populations of the same species become so different that they can no longer interbreed

Vocabulary Review Worksheet 7

Blackline masters of these Chapter Highlights can be found in the **Study Guide.**

---

internet connect

GO TO: go.hrw.com

Visit the **HRW** Web site for a variety of learning tools related to this chapter. Just type in the keyword:

KEYWORD: HSTEVO

GO TO: www.scilinks.org

Visit the **National Science Teachers Association** on-line Web site for Internet resources related to this chapter. Just type in the sciLINKS number for more information about the topic:

TOPIC: Species and Adaptation   **sciLINKS NUMBER:** HSTL155
TOPIC: The Fossil Record   **sciLINKS NUMBER:** HSTL160
TOPIC: The Galápagos Islands   **sciLINKS NUMBER:** HSTL165
TOPIC: Darwin and Natural Selection   **sciLINKS NUMBER:** HSTL170

Lab and Activity Highlights

LabBank

Whiz-Bang Demonstrations, Adaptation Behooves You, Demo 6

Long-Term Projects & Research Ideas, Evolution's Explosion, Project 7

Chapter Review

USING VOCABULARY

To complete the following sentences, choose the correct term from each pair of terms listed below:

1. One species evolves into another through the process of __?__. *(adaptation or speciation)*

2. A group of similar organisms that can mate with one another to produce offspring is known as a __?__. *(fossil or species)*

3. A(n) __?__ helps an organism survive better in its environment. *(adaptation or vestigial structure)*

4. __?__ is the process by which populations change over time. *(Natural selection or Evolution)*

5. In __?__, humans select traits that will be passed from one generation to another. *(selective breeding or natural selection)*

6. A change in a gene at the DNA level is called a __?__. *(mutation or trait)*

UNDERSTANDING CONCEPTS

Multiple Choice

7. Although Darwin did not realize it, the variations he observed among the individuals of a population of finches were caused by
   a. genetic resistance.
   b. mutations.
   c. fossils.
   d. selective breeding.

8. The theory of evolution combines the principles of
   a. natural selection and artificial selection.
   b. natural selection and genetic resistance.
   c. selective breeding and genetic inheritance.
   d. natural selection and genetic inheritance.

9. Fossils are commonly found in
   a. sedimentary rock.
   b. igneous rock.
   c. granite.
   d. loose sand or granite.

10. A human's arm, a cat's front leg, a dolphin's front flipper, and a bat's wing
    a. have similar kinds of bones.
    b. are used in similar ways.
    c. share many similarities with insect wings and jellyfish tentacles.
    d. have nothing in common.

11. The fact that all organisms have DNA as their genetic material is evidence that
    a. natural selection occurred.
    b. all organisms descended from a common ancestor.
    c. selective breeding takes place every day.
    d. genetic resistance rarely occurs.

12. What body part of the Galápagos finches appears to have been most modified by natural selection?
    a. their webbed feet
    b. their beaks
    c. the bone structure of their wings
    d. the color of their eyes

Short Answer

13. Describe the four parts of Darwin's theory of evolution by natural selection.

14. How do the fossils of whales provide evidence that whales have evolved over millions of years?

15. What might account for gaps in the fossil record?

Concept Mapping

16. An answer to this exercise can be found at the end of this book.

Concept Mapping Transparency 7

Chapter Review Answers

USING VOCABULARY

1. speciation
2. species
3. adaptation
4. Evolution
5. selective breeding
6. mutation

UNDERSTANDING CONCEPTS

Multiple Choice

7. b
8. d
9. a
10. a
11. b
12. b

Short Answer

13. 1. overproduction: Each species produces more offspring than will survive.
    2. genetic variation: Each individual has a unique combination of traits. Some traits increase the chances that the individual will survive and reproduce.
    3. struggle to survive: Individuals compete for limited resources. Some will not compete successfully and will not survive to adulthood.
    4. successful reproduction: Those individuals that are well-adapted and have traits that help them survive in their environment are more likely to survive and reproduce.

14. Fossils of the stages of whale evolution have been discovered that clearly indicate their sequence of change from land-dwelling carnivores to sea-dwelling mammals.

15. The required conditions for fossil formation are rare. The shell or bones must be completely covered in sediment in an anaerobic environment.

170   Chapter 7 • The Evolution of Living Things

Concept Mapping

16. Use the following terms to create a concept map: struggle to survive, genetic variation, Darwin, overpopulation, natural selection, successful reproduction.

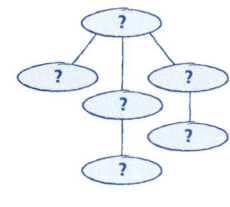

CRITICAL THINKING AND PROBLEM SOLVING

Write one or two sentences to answer the following questions:

17. In selective breeding, humans influence the course of evolution. What determines the course of evolution in natural selection?

18. Many forms of bacteria evolve resistance to antibiotics, drugs that kill bacteria. Based on what you know about how insects evolve to resist insecticides, suggest how bacteria might evolve to resist antibiotics.

19. The two species of squirrels shown below live on opposite sides of the Grand Canyon, in Arizona. The two squirrels look very similar, but they cannot interbreed to produce fertile offspring. Explain how a single species of squirrel might have become two species.

INTERPRETING GRAPHICS

Use the following graphs to answer questions 20, 21, and 22:

20. What is the most common birth weight?

21. What birth weight has the highest survival rate?

22. How do the principles of natural selection help explain why there are more deaths among babies with low birth weights than among babies of average birth weights?

 Take a minute to review your answers to the Pre-Reading Questions found at the bottom of page 148. Have your answers changed? If necessary, revise your answers based on what you have learned since you began this chapter.

CRITICAL THINKING AND PROBLEM SOLVING

17. Conditions in the environment to which organisms must be adapted are part of the selection process in nature. Natural selection is the process of adaptation over time to changes in environmental conditions. The genetic changes that bring about adaptations in a species are thought to determine the course of evolution through natural selection.

18. A course of antibiotics may leave behind bacteria that have traits that help them survive. The survivors may reproduce, producing more individuals that have the survival trait. In this way, a strain of bacteria may become immune to an antibiotic.

19. Individual organisms in a population have their own unique set of traits. When a population becomes separated over time, each separate group may evolve in a different direction. Eventually, the groups may become different genetically and they are no longer able to interbreed. Even though they may retain a similar appearance, they have become separate species.

INTERPRETING GRAPHICS

20. 7 lb
21. 7 lb
22. Human babies are best adapted to survive at a birth weight of about 7 lb.

Blackline masters of this Chapter Review can be found in the **Study Guide.**

EYE ON THE ENVIRONMENT

Saving at the Seed Bank

Teaching Strategy

In order to help students understand the changes in agriculture, you may wish to create a table that contrasts "traditional" and "industrial" farming practices. Under the heading *Traditional*, list words or phrases that describe traditional farming practices, such as *smaller scale, few machines or manual labor, more plant varieties,* and *mainly for sustenance.* Under the heading *Industrial*, list words or phrases that describe industrial farming practices, such as *larger scale, more mechanized, fewer plant varieties,* and *primarily for profit.* Encourage students to add their own words or phrases to contrast the types of farming practices.

In addition, point out to students that farmers in some areas, including many developing countries, practice some form of traditional agriculture. Consequently, scientists at seed banks try to visit those areas as often as necessary to obtain samples of those seeds.

EYE ON THE ENVIRONMENT

Saving at the Seed Bank

A very unusual laboratory can be found in Fort Collins, Colorado. There, sealed in test tubes, locked in specialized drawers, and even frozen in liquid nitrogen at –196°C, are hundreds of thousands of seeds and plants. Although in storage for now, these organisms may hold the keys to preventing worldwide famine or medicine shortage in the future. Sound serious? Well, it is.

This laboratory is called the National Seed Storage Lab, and it is the largest of a worldwide network of seed banks. The seeds and plant cuttings stored within these seed banks represent almost every plant grown for food, clothing, and medicine.

▲ *To protect tomorrow's wheat fields, we need the genetic diversity of crops stored in seed banks.*

No More Pizza!

Imagine heading out for pizza only to discover a sign on the door that says, "Closed today due to flour shortage." Flour shortage? How can that be? What about burritos? When you get to the burrito stand, the sign is the same, "Closed due to flour shortage." Think this sounds far-fetched? Well, it really isn't.

If wheat crops around the world are ruined by a disease, we could have a flour shortage. And the best way to fight such devastation, and even prevent it, is by breeding new varieties. Through the process of selective breeding, many plants have been improved to increase their yields and their resistance to disease and insects. But to breed new crops, plant breeders need lots of different genetic material. Where do they get this genetic material? At the seed bank, of course!

Why We'll Never Know

But what if some plants never make it to the seed bank? We have the new and improved varieties, so why does it matter if we keep the old ones? It matters because these lost varieties often have important traits, like resistance to disease and drought, that might come in handy in the future. Once a variety of plant is improved, demand for the old variety can dwindle to nothing. If an old variety is no longer grown, it may become extinct if it is not placed in the seed bank. In fact, many varieties of plants have already been lost forever. We'll never know if one of those lost varieties was capable of resisting a severe drought.

It's All in the Bank

Fortunately, seed banks have collected seeds and plants for more than a century. They preserve the genetic diversity of crop plants while allowing farmers to grow the most productive varieties in their fields. As long as there are seed banks across the globe, it is unlikely that there will be a flour shortage. Let's go out for pizza!

Going Further

▶ Many seed banks are in jeopardy. Why? Find out by doing research to learn more about the complicated and costly process of operating a seed bank.

Answer to Going Further
Answers will vary.

Science Fiction

"The Anatomy Lesson"

by Scott Sanders

You know what it's like. You have an important test tomorrow, or your semester project is due, and you've forgotten your book or just run out of clay. Suddenly things seem very serious.

That's the situation a certain medical student faces in Scott Sanders's "The Anatomy Lesson." The student needs to learn the bones of the human body for an anatomy exam the next day. After arriving at the anatomy library to check out a skeleton-in-a-box, the student finds that all the skeletons have been checked out. Without bones to assemble as practice, the student knows passing the exam will be impossible. So the student asks the librarian to look again. Sure enough, the librarian finds one last box. And that's when things start to get strange.

There are too many bones. They are the wrong shape. They don't fit together just right. Somebody must be playing a joke! The bones fit together, sort of—but not in any way that helps the medical student get ready for the exam. When the student complains to the librarian, the librarian isn't very sympathetic. It seems she has other things on her mind. Now the student is really worried.

Find out what this medical student and a quiet librarian have in common. And find out how they will never be the same after "The Anatomy Lesson." You can read it in the *Holt Anthology of Science Fiction*.

Further Reading If students enjoy this story, you may wish to recommend some of Sanders's other works, such as the following:

Terrarium, Indiana University Press, 1996

The Engineer of Beasts, Orchard Books, 1988

Hear the Wind Blow: American Folksongs Retold, Simon & Shuster Children's, 1985

SCIENCE FICTION
"The Anatomy Lesson"
by Scott Sanders

While studying for an exam, a medical student attempts to assemble a very unusual skeleton that may drastically change the student's future.

Teaching Strategy

Reading Level This is a relatively short story and should not be difficult for the average student to read and comprehend.

Background

About the Author Scott Sanders (1945–) writes many different kinds of stories—from folktales to science fiction. Early in life, he chose to become a writer rather than a scientist, though he has a keen interest in both writing and science. Sanders has written about a range of subjects, including folklore, physics, the naturalist John James Audubon, and settlers of Indiana. Much of his work is nonfiction. His writing has been published in many different newspapers and magazines, including the *Chicago Sun-Times*, *Harper's*, and *Omni*. Currently, Sanders lives and teaches in Indiana, where he belongs to writers' groups and to groups such as the Sierra Club and Friends of the Earth.

Chapter Organizer

CHAPTER ORGANIZATION	TIME MINUTES	OBJECTIVES	LABS, INVESTIGATIONS, AND DEMONSTRATIONS
Chapter Opener pp. 174–175	45	National Standards: UCP 2, HNS 3	**Start-Up Activity** Earth's Timeline, p. 175
Section 1 Evidence of the Past	90	▶ Explain how fossils are dated. ▶ Describe the geologic time scale and the information it provides scientists. ▶ Describe the possible causes of mass extinctions. ▶ Explain the theory of plate tectonics. UCP 1–4, SAI 1, 2, SPSP 3, HNS 1–3, LS 3a, 5c; LabBook UCP 1, 3, SAI 1, LS 5c	**Skill Builder,** Dating the Fossil Record, p. 712 GENERAL **Datasheets for LabBook,** Dating the Fossil Record, Datasheet 17 GENERAL **Skill Builder,** The Half-life of Pennies, p. 715 GENERAL **Datasheets for LabBook,** The Half-life of Pennies, Datasheet 18 GENERAL
Section 2 Eras of the Geologic Time Scale	90	▶ Outline the major developments that allowed for the existence of life on Earth. ▶ Describe the different types of organisms that arose during the four eras of the geologic time scale. UCP 1, 3, SPSP 3, LS 1b, 3a, 5c	**Interactive Explorations CD-ROM,** Rock On! GENERAL A **Worksheet** is also available in the **Interactive Explorations Teacher's Guide.**
Section 3 Human Evolution	90	▶ Discuss the shared characteristics of primates. ▶ Describe what is known about the differences between hominids. UCP 2, 5, SAI 2, HNS 2, 3, LS 1a, 5a	**QuickLab,** Thumb Through This, p. 189 GENERAL **Long-Term Projects & Research Ideas,** Project 8 ADVANCED

See page **T20** *for a complete correlation of this book with the*

NATIONAL SCIENCE EDUCATION STANDARDS.

TECHNOLOGY RESOURCES

 Guided Reading Audio CD
English or Spanish, Chapter 8

 One-Stop Planner CD-ROM with Test Generator

 Interactive Explorations CD-ROM
CD 2, Exploration 6, Rock On!

 CNN. Multicultural Connections, Protecting New Mexico's Petroglyphs, Segment 6
Scientists in Action, Creating Digital Dinos, Segment 12
Ice Age Discoveries, Segment 23

Chapter 8 • The History of Life on Earth

Chapter 8 • The History of Life on Earth

CLASSROOM WORKSHEETS, TRANSPARENCIES, AND RESOURCES	SCIENCE INTEGRATION AND CONNECTIONS	REVIEW AND ASSESSMENT
Directed Reading Worksheet 8 BASIC **Science Puzzlers, Twisters & Teasers,** Worksheet 8 ADVANCED		
Directed Reading Worksheet 8, Section 1 BASIC **Transparency 110,** The Rock Cycle **Transparency 29,** Unstable Atoms and the Half-life **Math Skills for Science Worksheet 36,** Radioactive Decay and the Half-life GENERAL **Transparency 30,** The Geologic Time Scale and Representative Organisms **Critical Thinking Worksheet 8,** Fossil Revelations ADVANCED **Math Skills for Science Worksheet 45,** Geologic Time Scale GENERAL **Transparency 31,** Formation of the Modern Continents **Transparency 32,** The Tectonic Plates **Reinforcement Worksheet 8,** Earth Timeline BASIC	**Connect to Earth Science,** p. 177 in ATE **Connect to Earth Science,** p. 180 in ATE GENERAL **Multicultural Connection,** p. 180 in ATE GENERAL **Careers:** Paleobotanist—Bonnie Jacobs, p. 199 GENERAL	**Homework,** p. 177 in ATE GENERAL **Self-Check,** p. 179 **Review,** p. 181 GENERAL **Quiz,** p. 181 in ATE GENERAL **Alternative Assessment,** p. 181 in ATE GENERAL
Directed Reading Worksheet 8, Section 2 BASIC **Math Skills for Science Worksheet 2,** Subtraction Review GENERAL **Reinforcement Worksheet 8,** Condensed History GENERAL	**Connect to Earth Science,** p. 183 in ATE ADVANCED **Environment Connection,** p. 184 **Math and More,** p. 185 in ATE GENERAL **Real-World Connection,** p. 185 in ATE GENERAL **Multicultural Connection,** p. 186 in ATE **Across the Sciences:** Windows into the Past, p. 198 GENERAL	**Self-Check,** p. 185 **Homework,** p. 185 in ATE GENERAL **Review,** p. 187 GENERAL **Quiz,** p. 187 in ATE GENERAL **Alternative Assessment,** p. 187 in ATE BASIC
Transparency 33, Primate Skeletal Structures **Directed Reading Worksheet 8,** Section 3 BASIC	**Cross-Disciplinary Focus,** p. 189 in ATE **Cross-Disciplinary Focus,** p. 190 in ATE **Cross-Disciplinary Focus,** p. 191 in ATE GENERAL	**Review,** p. 193 GENERAL **Quiz,** p. 193 in ATE GENERAL **Alternative Assessment,** p. 193 in ATE GENERAL

END-OF-CHAPTER REVIEW AND ASSESSMENT

Chapter Review in Study Guide
Vocabulary and Notes in Study Guide
Chapter Tests with Performance-Based Assessment, Chapter 8 Test
Chapter Tests with Performance-Based Assessment, Performance-Based Assessment 8
Concept Mapping Transparency 8

internet connect

Holt, Rinehart and Winston On-line Resources
go.hrw.com

For worksheets and other teaching aids related to this chapter, visit the HRW Web site and type in the keyword: **HSTHIS**

National Science Teachers Association
www.scilinks.org

Encourage students to use the sciLINKS numbers listed in the internet connect boxes to access information and resources on the **NSTA** Web site.

Chapter 8 • Chapter Organizer

Chapter Resources & Worksheets

Visual Resources

TEACHING TRANSPARENCIES

TEACHING TRANSPARENCIES

CONCEPT MAPPING TRANSPARENCY

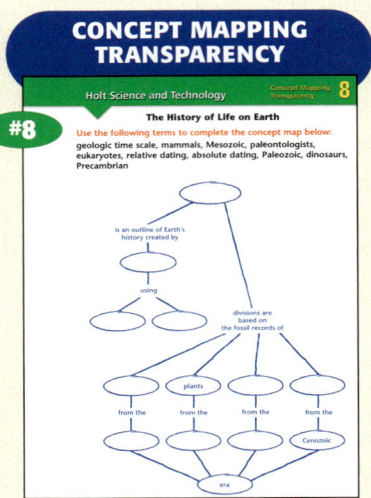

Meeting Individual Needs

DIRECTED READING

REINFORCEMENT & VOCABULARY REVIEW

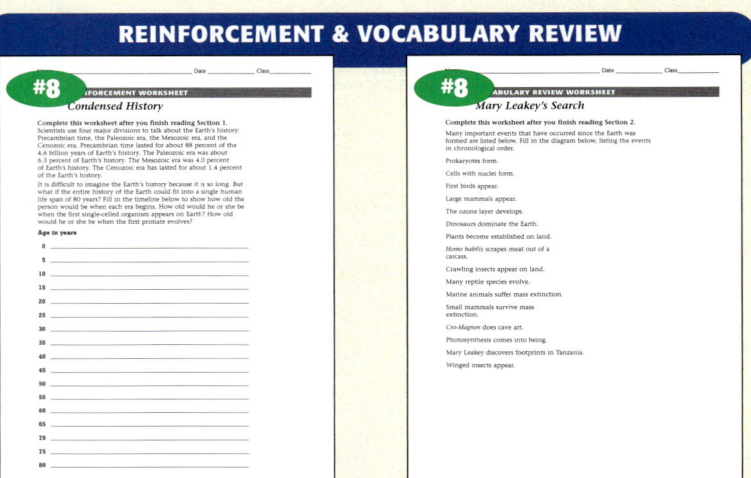

SCIENCE PUZZLERS, TWISTERS & TEASERS

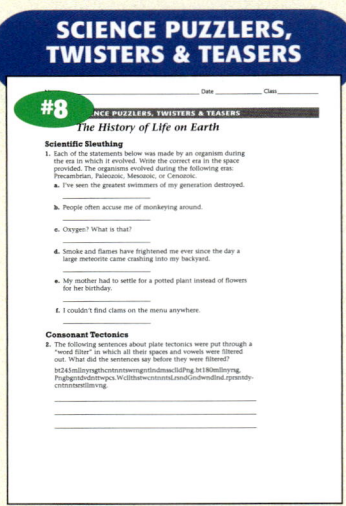

173C Chapter 8 • The History of Life on Earth

Chapter 8 • The History of Life on Earth

Review & Assessment

STUDY GUIDE

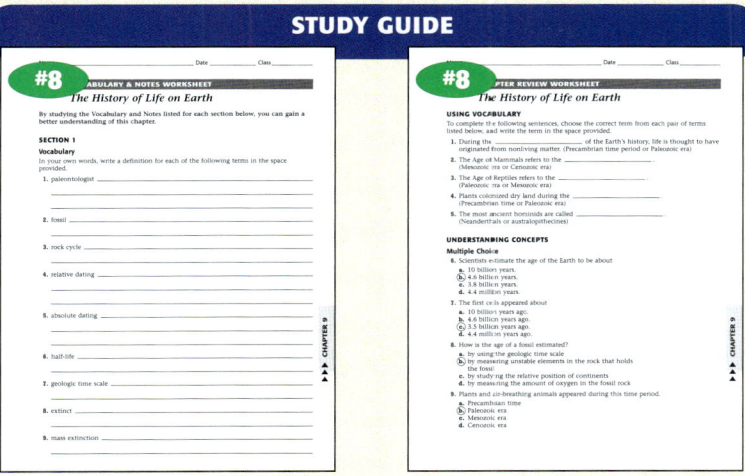

CHAPTER TESTS WITH PERFORMANCE-BASED ASSESSMENT

Lab Worksheets

LONG-TERM PROJECTS & RESEARCH IDEAS

DATASHEETS FOR LABBOOK

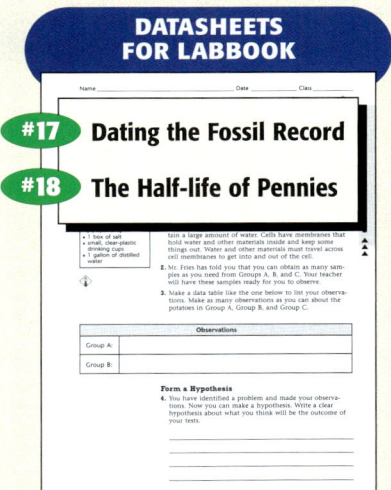

Applications & Extensions

CRITICAL THINKING & PROBLEM SOLVING

MULTICULTURAL CONNECTIONS

SCIENTISTS IN ACTION

INTERACTIVE EXPLORATIONS

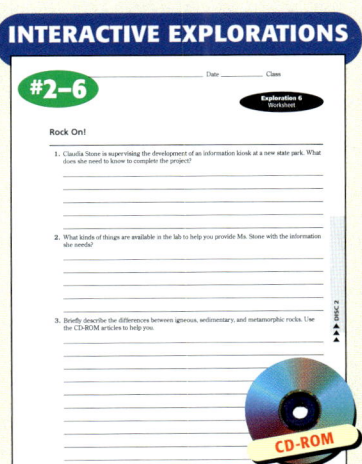

Chapter 8 • Chapter Resources & Worksheets 173D

Chapter Background

SECTION 1

Evidence of the Past

▶ **Fossils**
Fossils are not only preserved plants and animals but also traces of plants and animals. Preserved footprints, feces, gnaw marks, and root holes can all be considered fossils.

- Despite what many people think, fossils are not particularly difficult to find. Nearly every state in the United States contains an abundance of fossils. However, scientists think that only a tiny fraction of the countless organisms that lived on Earth have been preserved as fossils. Many organisms have lived and died without leaving evidence of their existence in the fossil record.

IS THAT A FACT!
▬ The oldest fossils are of prokaryotes that are more than 3 billion years old.

▶ **Law of Superposition**
The law of superposition states that in a series of sedimentary rock layers, each layer is older than the one above it and younger than the one below it. This law is based on an observation made by Nicolaus Steno, a Danish physician, in 1669.

▶ **Methods of Absolute Dating**
Absolute dating determines a fossil's age in years. Radioisotope dating is the most widely used method for dating a fossil. This method gives only a range of probable ages. A newly developed method uses a particle accelerator and can date fossils up to 60,000 years old.

▶ **Modern Mass Extinction**
Many scientists believe that our planet has entered another era of mass extinction and that human activities are mainly responsible for these extinctions. Urban sprawl and pollution threaten many species. During the last 200 years, more than 50 species of birds, more than 75 species of mammals, and perhaps hundreds of other species of animals and plants have become extinct.

IS THAT A FACT!
▬ Dinosaurs are not the biggest animals ever to live on Earth. Blue whales are bigger than the largest known dinosaur.

SECTION 2

Eras of the Geologic Time Scale

▶ **Probing into Earth's Past and Beyond**
In an effort to gain insights into Earth's past, a huge machine called an *ion microprobe* is closely examining tiny clusters of atoms in ancient rocks. When a flake of rock is placed in the machine, isotopes of certain elements in the flake can be sorted and counted. Using this technique to study the apatite from an island off Greenland, scientists were able to learn that the first signs of life on Earth came 400 million years earlier than previously thought. There weren't any fossils in the apatite, but there was chemical evidence that the 3.85-billion-year-old apatite had an organic origin.

Chapter 8 • The History of Life on Earth

▶ **Experiment About the Origin of Life**

In 1953, American scientist Stanley Miller devised an experiment to simulate life-forming conditions in the early environment. He mixed together hydrogen, ammonia, and methane (to represent the early air) and water (to represent the early oceans) in a flask. Then he applied electricity to the mixture and produced amino acids. His experiment demonstrated that the building blocks of life could be created on Earth chemically. Scientists have since found amino acids in meteorites, confirming that conditions favorable for their formation exist elsewhere and not just on primeval Earth.

IS THAT A FACT!

◆ Bristlecone pines are the oldest living trees. Some Colorado bristlecones have lived over 2,500 years. But they're young compared with the Sierra bristlecones, which have been dated as old as 4,765 years!

SECTION 3

Human Evolution

▶ **Clues to Migration Route**

Scientists believe that people passed through the Nile Valley of Egypt when they migrated from Africa, beginning about 100,000 years ago. Up until recently, no evidence supporting this idea existed. Now Pierre Vermeersch, an archaeologist from the Catholic University of Louvain, in Belgium, and some colleagues have found the skeleton of a child at Taramsa Hill, in the Nile Valley of southern Egypt. The skeleton of the child may be 80,000 years old

and is clearly that of a modern human. Similarities between its skull and teeth and those of equally old human remains found in East Africa and the Middle East suggest a relationship between the two populations.

▶ **Dawn of Language**

Scientists Matt Cartmill and Richard Kay examined fossil hominid skulls and measured the hole through which the hypoglossal nerve passes in its course from the brain to the tongue. The hypoglossal nerve enables precise control over the tongue movements needed for speech. A large hole suggests a larger nerve. Chimpanzees have much smaller holes in their skulls than do modern humans. Because australopithecine skulls have small holes, like the skulls of chimpanzees, Cartmill and Kay think that australopithecines were unable to form words, as modern humans do.

For background information about teaching strategies and issues, refer to the *Professional Reference for Teachers*.

Chapter 8 • Chapter Background   **173F**

The History of Life on Earth

Pre-Reading Questions

Students may not know the answers to these questions before reading the chapter, so accept any reasonable response.

Suggested Answers

1. by finding out where it was in relation to other fossils and by measuring the percentage of radioactive atoms in the sample
2. 150 million years

 Directed Reading Worksheet 8

 Science Puzzlers, Twisters & Teasers Worksheet 8

 Guided Reading Audio CD English or Spanish, Chapter 8

CHAPTER 8

The History of Life on Earth

Sections

1. Evidence of the Past .. 176
2. Eras of the Geologic Time Scale 182
   Environment Connection 184
   Internet Connect 187
3. Human Evolution 188
   QuickLab 189
   Internet Connect 193

Chapter Review 196
Feature Articles 198, 199
LabBook 712–715

Mammoth Discovery

What is 23,000 years old, nine feet tall, and nicknamed "Zharkov"? Give up? It is the partial remains of a woolly mammoth—including huge tusks, bones, skin, and hair—dug up from the frozen ground in Siberia in late 1999. Its gigantic tusks appear in the photo. Scientists have determined that woolly mammoths roamed the frozen arctic until about 3,000 years ago. In this chapter, you will learn how scientists determine the age of fossils and about the history of life on Earth.

Pre-Reading Questions

1. How can you tell how old a fossil is?
2. How long did dinosaurs roam the Earth?

 HRW On-line Resources
go.hrw.com
For worksheets and other teaching aids, visit the HRW Web site and type in the keyword: **HSTHIS**

 www.scilinks.com
Use the sciLINKS numbers at the end of each chapter for additional resources on the **NSTA** Web site.

 www.cnnfyi.com
Visit the CNN Web site for current events coverage and classroom resources.

START-UP Activity

EARTH'S TIMELINE

To help you understand Earth's history, make a timeline.

Procedure

1. Mark off 10 cm sections on a **strip of adding machine paper** that is 46 cm long. Divide each 10 cm section into ten 1 cm sections. (Each 1 cm represents 100 million years.)

2. Label each 10 cm section in order from top to bottom as follows: 1 bya (billion years ago), 2 bya, 3 bya, and 4 bya. The timeline begins at 4.6 bya.

3. At the appropriate place on your timeline, mark these important events of Earth's history:

    a. Earth began about 4.6 billion years ago.

    b. The earliest cells appeared about 3.5 billion years ago.

    c. Dinosaurs first appeared on Earth about 215 million years ago. Then about 65 million years ago, they became extinct.

    d. About 100,000 years ago, humans with modern features appeared.

4. Continue to mark events on your timeline as you learn about them in this chapter.

Analysis

5. Compare the length of time dinosaurs roamed the Earth with the length of time humans have existed.

START-UP Activity

EARTH'S TIMELINE

MATERIALS

FOR EACH GROUP:
- pencil
- metric ruler
- strip of adding machine paper, 46 cm long

Teacher's Notes

Suggest that students tape the full length of the strip of paper securely to a flat surface before they begin to record measurements.

Make sure students can relate distance to a time scale.

Answer to START-UP Activity

5. Dinosaurs roamed for approximately 150 million years, and humans have existed for about 5 million years. Dinosaurs existed 30 times longer than humans have so far.

SECTION 1

Focus

Evidence of the Past

This section introduces students to fossils and how they provide clues to Earth's past. Students learn how fossils form in sedimentary rock. They explore the methods scientists use to determine the age of fossils. Finally, students learn how scientists place events in the Earth's history in the correct order and what they think might have caused mass extinctions.

🔔 Bellringer

Ask students to imagine that they didn't clean their room for 30 years. After 30 years, they finally decide to sort through the 2 m pile of stuff on their floor. Ask:

What might you find on the top of the pile? in the middle? on the bottom?

1 Motivate

ACTIVITY

Photo Analysis Have students bring in copies (*not* originals, since they may be irreplaceable) of old photos of themselves, and tack the copies on the bulletin board. Ask students to describe how they have changed during the years since the pictures were taken. Point out that scientists use traces or imprints of living things preserved in rock in a similar way to observe how life on Earth has changed over time.

Directed Reading Worksheet 8 Section 1

176 Chapter 8 • The History of Life on Earth

Section 1

Evidence of the Past

Terms to Learn

fossil
relative dating
absolute dating
geologic time scale
extinct
plate tectonics

What You'll Do

◆ Explain how fossils are dated.
◆ Describe the geologic time scale and the information it provides scientists.
◆ Describe the possible causes of mass extinctions.
◆ Explain the theory of plate tectonics.

Some scientists look for clues to help them reconstruct what happened in the past. These scientists are called paleontologists. *Paleontologists,* like the man in **Figure 1,** use fossils to reconstruct the history of life millions of years before humans existed. Fossils show us that life on Earth has changed a great deal. They also provide us with clues to how those changes occurred.

Figure 1 *In 1995, Paul Sereno found this dinosaur fossil in the Sahara Desert. The dinosaur may have been the largest land predator that has ever existed!*

Fossils

Fossils are traces or imprints of living things—such as animals, plants, bacteria, and fungi—that are preserved in rock. Fossils are usually formed when a dead organism is covered by a layer of sediment. These sediments may later be pressed together to form sedimentary rock. **Figure 2** shows one way fossils can be formed in this type of rock.

Figure 2 *The pictures below show one way fossils can form.*

❶ An organism dies and becomes buried in sediment.

❷ The organism gradually dissolves, leaving a hollow impression, or mold, in the sediment.

❸ Over time, the mold fills with sediment that forms a cast of the original organism.

SCIENTISTS AT ODDS

In the 1870s, two American scientists, Edward Drinker Cope and Othniel Charles Marsh, studied dinosaur fossils. They became bitter rivals and often argued. In 1878, Marsh and Cope were both excavating fossils near Como Bluff, Wyoming. They had separate excavations and didn't want to share their findings. Both groups found more fossils than they could carry. To prevent the other group from taking their fossils, each group smashed all the fossils that couldn't be carried away.

The Age of Fossils

When paleontologists find a fossil, how do they determine its age? They can use one of two methods: relative dating or absolute dating.

Relative Dating A cross section of sedimentary rock shows many layers. The oldest layers are on the bottom, and the newer layers are on the top. If fossils are found in the rock, a scientist could start at the bottom and work upward to examine a sequence of fossils in the order that the organisms existed. This method of ordering fossils to estimate their age is known as **relative dating**.

Bananabana bobana is a rare fossil! Turn to page 712 in your LabBook to see it.

Absolute Dating How can scientists determine the age of a fossil? The answer lies in particles called *atoms* that make up all matter. Atoms, in turn, are made of smaller particles. These particles are held together by strong forces. If there isn't enough force to hold them together, the atom is said to be unstable. Unstable atoms decay by releasing either energy or particles or both. That way, the atom becomes stable, but it also becomes a different kind of atom.

Each kind of unstable atom decays at its own rate. As shown in **Figure 3,** the time it takes for half of the unstable atoms in a sample to decay is its *half-life*. Half-lives range from fractions of a second to billions of years. By measuring the ratio of unstable atoms to stable atoms, scientists can determine the approximate age of a rock sample and the fossil it contains. This method is called **absolute dating**.

Figure 3 Sometimes volcanic rock will cover a dead organism. By finding the age of the rock, scientists can get a good idea about the age of the fossil.

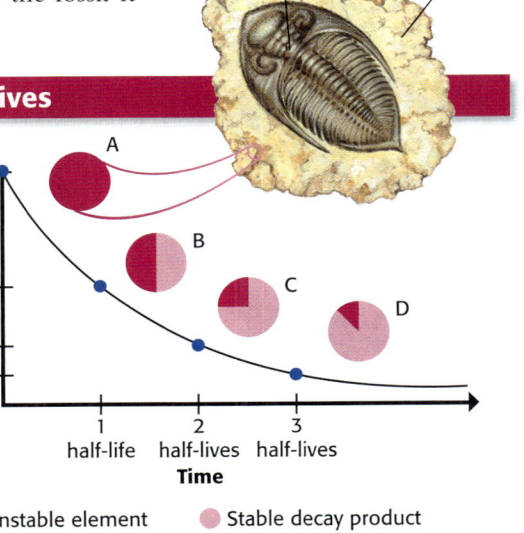

Half-lives

A. The unstable atoms in the sample of volcanic rock have a half-life of 1.3 billion years. The sample contained 4 mg of unstable atoms when the rock formed.

B. After 1.3 billion years, or one half-life, only 2 mg of the unstable atoms will be left in the rock, and 2 mg of its stable decay product will have formed.

C. After another 1.3 billion years (two half-lives), there will only be 1 mg of the unstable atoms and 3 mg of the decay atoms.

D. How many milligrams of unstable atoms are left after 3 half-lives?

● Unstable element   ● Stable decay product

2) Teach, continued

MEETING INDIVIDUAL NEEDS

Advanced Learners Geologic time is the period of time that Earth has been in existence. Geologic time is divided into eras. Eras are broken into smaller divisions called periods. Periods can be divided into epochs. Challenge students to construct a geologic time line that identifies all of these divisions. Tell them they can research in the library or on the Internet for information.

RESEARCH

Students could research plant and animal species that have become extinct within the last 200 years. Many of the extinctions were caused by human activities. Extinct birds include the dodo, great auk, Labrador duck, moa, and passenger pigeon. Extinct mammals include the Steller's sea cow and the quagga.

DISCUSSION

Explain to students that *mya* means "million years ago." Likewise, *my* means "million years" and *bya* means "billion years ago." Ask students why they think geologists use this form of dating.

The Half-life of Pennies PG 715

Teaching Transparency 30 "The Geologic Time Scale and Representative Organisms"

The Geologic Time Scale

When you consider important events that have happened during your lifetime, you usually recall each event in terms of the day, month, or year in which it occurred. These divisions of time make it easier to recall when you were born, when you kicked the winning soccer goal, or when you started the fifth grade. Because the span of time is so great from the formation of the Earth to now, scientists also use a type of calendar to divide the Earth's long history into very long units of time.

The calendar scientists use to outline the history of life on Earth is called the **geologic time scale**, shown in the table at left. After a fossil is dated using relative and absolute dating techniques, a paleontologist can place the fossil in chronological order with other fossils. This forms a picture of the past that shows how organisms have changed over time.

The Geologic Time Scale

Era	Period	MYA	Representative Organisms
CENOZOIC	Quaternary	1.8	
CENOZOIC	Tertiary	65	
MESOZOIC	Cretaceous	144	
MESOZOIC	Jurassic	206	
MESOZOIC	Triassic	248	
PALEOZOIC	Permian	290	
PALEOZOIC	Carboniferous	354	
PALEOZOIC	Devonian	417	
PALEOZOIC	Silurian	443	
PALEOZOIC	Ordovician	490	
PALEOZOIC	Cambrian	540	
PRECAMBRIAN		4,600	

Divisions in the Geologic Time Scale Paleontologists have divided the time scale into large blocks of time called *eras*. Each era has been subdivided into smaller blocks of time as paleontologists have continued to find more fossil information.

Eras are characterized by the type of animal that dominated the Earth at the time. For instance, the Mesozoic era—dominated by dinosaurs and other reptiles—is referred to as the Age of Reptiles. The end of each era is marked by the extinction of certain organisms. The next section analyzes the different eras of the geologic time scale in greater detail.

BRAIN FOOD

In 1997, the most complete skeleton of a *Tyrannosaurus rex* ever found was auctioned. The winning bid was $8.36 million, made by the Field Museum of Natural History in Chicago. Scientists were relieved that a museum-led consortium was the highest bidder; their fear was that a private collector would buy the skeleton fossil, and scientists and the public would not be allowed to view it. Ask students how they feel about nonscientists owning and controlling access to fossils.

Figure 4 A meteorite hit Earth about 65 million years ago, perhaps leading to major climatic changes.

Mass Extinctions Some of the important divisions in the geologic time scale are marked by events that caused many animal and plant species to die out completely, or become **extinct.** Once a species is extinct, it does not reappear. There have been several periods in the Earth's history when a large number of species died out at the same time. These periods of large-scale extinction are called *mass extinctions*.

Scientists are not sure what causes mass extinctions. Mass extinctions may result from major changes in the Earth's climate or atmosphere. Some scientists think the mass extinction of the dinosaurs occurred when a meteorite collided with Earth and caused catastrophic climate changes. An artist's depiction of this event is shown in **Figure 4.** Changes in the climate may have also been caused by the movement of continents. Read on to find out how this is possible.

Scientists estimate that only a small fraction (1/20 of 1 percent) of all the species that have ever existed on Earth are living today. All the other species existed in the past and then became extinct.

Self-Check

Ten grams of an unstable atom were present in a rock when the rock solidified. In grams, how much of these atoms will be present after one half-life? What amount of the unstable atoms will be present after two half-lives? *(See page 782 to check your answers.)*

3) Extend

GOING FURTHER

 Poster Project Have students research what their area was like millions of years ago. They can develop a written report and a poster describing the climate, living things, and landforms at different points in time.

INDEPENDENT PRACTICE

If any students have rock collections, ask them to share these collections with the class. Allow students time to observe the different collections and to ask questions about them.
<mark>Sheltered English</mark>

Answer to Self-Check

5 g, 2.5 g

 Critical Thinking Worksheet 8 "Fossil Revelations"

 Math Skills Worksheet 45 "Geologic Time Scale"

 TOPIC: Mass Extinctions
GO TO: www.scilinks.org
*sci*LINKS NUMBER: HSTL185

TOPIC: The Geologic Time Scale
GO TO: www.scilinks.org
*sci*LINKS NUMBER: HSTL190

WEIRD SCIENCE

One species that became extinct during the time of the dinosaurs was the insect having the largest wingspan on record. The insect belonged to the order Protodonata, and it measured an astonishing 76 cm (30 in.) from wingtip to wingtip. Its body was 46 cm (18 in.) long. It died out about 200 million years ago. Fossils of this insect have been found in Kansas.

3) Extend, continued

RETEACHING
Ask students to draw a picture in their ScienceLog illustrating how future plate movements might change the geography of the world. (Some predictions might include a wider Atlantic Ocean and a shift northward of Africa, Australia, and South America.)

MEETING INDIVIDUAL NEEDS
Advanced Learners Ask students: What might have happened to the animals inhabiting Pangea as it broke up? How might the changing landscape influence the evolution of living things? Have students explain how the breakup might have affected the distribution of animal species. Encourage students to use diagrams or other visual effects when sharing their ideas with the class. (Student responses should demonstrate an understanding that changes within the environment affect the ability of certain organisms to survive.)

CONNECT TO EARTH SCIENCE

The Great Rift Valley of Africa marks a spreading center that is found on a continent. Have students identify the rift valley on a map. Ask: What kind of features mark this location? (deep valleys and lakes)

What do you think will become of this rift valley in a few million years? (It will probably continue to widen and eventually become an inland sea.)

Teaching Transparency 31 "Formation of the Modern Continents"

180 Chapter 8 • The History of Life on Earth

The Changing Earth

Do you know that dinosaur fossils have been found on Antarctica? Antarctica, now frozen, must have once had a warm climate to support these large reptiles. How could this be? Antarctica and the other continents have not always been in their present position. Antarctica was once located nearer the equator!

Pangaea If you take a look at a map of the world, you might notice that the shapes of the continents seem to resemble pieces of a puzzle. If you could move the pieces around, you might find that some of them almost fit together. A similar thought occurred to the German scientist Alfred Wegener in the early 1900s. He proposed that long ago the continents were part of one great landmass surrounded by a single gigantic ocean. Wegener called that single landmass *Pangaea* (pan JEE uh), meaning "all Earth."

Wegener thought our present continents were once part of one great supercontinent for three reasons. First, the shapes of the continents seemed to "fit" together. Second, fossils of plants and animals discovered on either side of the Atlantic Ocean were very similar. Third, Wegener noticed that glaciers had existed in places that now have very warm climates. **Figure 5** shows how the continents may have formed from Pangaea.

About **245 million years ago**, the continents were one giant landmass called Pangaea. The grey outlines indicate where the continents are today.

About **180 million years ago**, Pangaea began to divide into two pieces: Laurasia and Gondwanaland.

Even as recently as **65 million years ago**, the location of Earth's continents was very different from their current location.

Figure 5 Because the continents are moving 1–10 cm per year, the continents will be arranged very differently in 150 million years.

Multicultural CONNECTION

Tell the class that the Mid-Atlantic Ridge rises above water at only one place, Iceland. Point to Iceland on a map, and indicate the Arctic Circle, which includes the northern part of the island. Tell students that these two features suggest that Iceland is a place of both extreme cold and extreme heat. Ask students to do some research on what life is like in Iceland. Have them focus on how geologic processes, such as glaciers, geysers, and volcanic activity, affect the lifestyle of the people who live there.

Do the Continents Move? In the mid-1960s, J. Tuzo Wilson of Canada came up with the idea that it wasn't the continents that were moving. Wilson thought that huge pieces of the Earth's crust are driven back and forth by forces within the planet. Each huge piece of crust is called a *tectonic plate*. Wilson's theory of how these huge pieces of crust move around the globe is called **plate tectonics.**

According to Wilson, the outer crust of the Earth is broken into seven large, rigid plates and several smaller ones, shown in **Figure 6.** The continents and oceans ride on top of these plates. It is the motion of the plates that causes continents to move.

Figure 6 Scientists think that the tectonic plates, outlined above, have been slowly rearranging the continents since the crust cooled billions of years ago.

Adaptation in Slow Motion Although tectonic plates move very slowly, the motion of continents affects living organisms. Living things usually have time to adapt, through evolution, to the changes brought about by moving continents. That is why you are able to see living things that are well adapted to the environment they live in. In the same location, however, you may find fossil evidence of very different organisms that could not survive the changes.

> ### REVIEW
> 1. What information does the geologic time scale provide, and what are the major divisions of time?
> 2. What is one possible cause of mass extinctions?
> 3. Explain one way that geological changes in the Earth can cause plants and animals to change.
> 4. What is the difference between relative dating and absolute dating of fossils?
> 5. **Understanding Concepts** Fossils of *Mesosaurus*, a small aquatic lizard, shown at right, have been found only in Africa and South America. Using what you know about plate tectonics, how would you explain this finding?

4) Close

Quiz

1. What is a fossil? How are fossils usually formed? (Fossils are traces or imprints of living things that are preserved in rock. Fossils are usually formed when an organism is buried in sediments that harden into rock.)
2. What can scientists learn about Earth's past from fossils? (Fossils provide evidence that life on Earth has changed and show how those changes occurred.)
3. Why would fossils found in rock layers near Earth's surface probably be younger than those found in rock layers at the bottom of a deep canyon? (The upper layers were deposited more recently than the lower layers.)

ALTERNATIVE ASSESSMENT

Each student in a group receives three blank cards. The group looks at the geologic time scale on page 178 and thinks of questions that could be answered using information presented on the time scale. Students write a question on one side of a card. They stack the cards with the blank sides up. In turn, each student draws a card, reads the question on it, and attempts to answer the question. Group members determine if the answer is correct by consulting the geologic time scale.

Answers to Review
1. The geologic time scale provides classification of geologic time; Precambrian time, Paleozoic, Mesozoic, Cenozoic
2. perhaps a drastic change in the environment
3. Geologic changes cause animals of a single species to become separated and new species to form.
4. Relative dating is determining when a fossil was formed by examining where the fossil appears in the layers of rock. Absolute dating is measuring the percentage of radioactive material left in the rock surrounding a fossil.
5. Perhaps *Mesosaurus* evolved after Laurasia and Gondwanaland separated but before South America and Africa separated.

 Teaching Transparency 32 "The Tectonic Plates"

 Reinforcement Worksheet 8 "Earth Timeline"

Section 1 • Evidence of the Past

SECTION 2

Focus

Eras of the Geologic Time Scale

This section discusses current theories regarding the origin of life. Students are introduced to the four eras of geological time in chronological order: the Precambrian, the Paleozoic, the Mesozoic, and the Cenozoic. They learn about the life-forms that characterize each era.

Bellringer

Write the following supposition on the board or on an overhead projector for students to address in their ScienceLog:

Suppose that electric energy was never developed. How would your life differ from what it is like now?

Discuss with students the consequences of great changes over time.

1) Motivate

DISCUSSION

Historical Perspective Have students pretend that they are in a time-travel machine. What scientifically significant events would they witness as they travel back in time to Earth's origin? List the events on the board in the order that they are suggested. Ask students how they can determine whether the events are in chronological order. (They can consult the geologic time scale or other scientific materials.)

Directed Reading Worksheet 8 Section 2

Section 2

Terms to Learn
Precambrian time
Paleozoic era
Mesozoic era
Cenozoic era

What You'll Do
- Outline the major developments that allowed for the existence of life on Earth.
- Describe the different types of organisms that arose during the four eras of the geologic time scale.

Eras of the Geologic Time Scale

Look at the photograph of the Grand Canyon shown in **Figure 7.** If you look closely, you will notice that the walls of the canyon are layered with different kinds and colors of rocks. The deeper you go down into the canyon, the older the layer of rocks. It may surprise you to learn that each layer of the Grand Canyon was once the top layer. Billions of years ago the bottom layer was on top!

Each layer tells a story about what was happening on Earth when that layer was on top. The story is told mainly by the types of rocks and fossils found in the layer. In studying these different rocks and fossils, scientists have divided geologic history into four eras: Precambrian time, the Paleozoic era, the Mesozoic era, and the Cenozoic era.

Precambrian Time

If you journey to the bottom of the Grand Canyon, you can see layers of Earth that are over 1 billion years old. These layers are from Precambrian time. **Precambrian time** began when the Earth originated 4.6 billion years ago, and continued until about 540 million years ago. During this time life began and transformed the planet.

Figure 7 Each rock layer of the Grand Canyon is like a page in the "history book of the Earth."

IS THAT A FACT!

Throughout Earth's history, the forces of erosion have been altering the planet's surface, making it almost impossible to find rocks older than 3.5 billion years. However, a number of rocks dating from about 3.5 to 3.9 billion years ago have been found in Canada and Greenland. The oldest of the rocks was found in the Northwest Territories of Canada in 1989.

The Early Earth Scientists hypothesize that life began when conditions were quite different from Earth's current environment. These conditions included an atmosphere that lacked oxygen but was rich in other gases, such as carbon monoxide, carbon dioxide, hydrogen, and nitrogen. Also, the early Earth, as illustrated in **Figure 8,** was a place of great turmoil. Meteorites crashed into the Earth's surface. Violent thunderstorms and volcanic eruptions were constant on the young planet. Intense radiation, including ultraviolet radiation from the sun, bombarded Earth's surface.

Figure 8 *The early Earth was a violent place.*

How Did Life Begin? Scientists hypothesize that under these conditions, life developed from nonliving matter. In other words, life started from the chemicals that already existed in the environment. These chemicals included water, clay, dissolved minerals in the oceans, and the gases present in the atmosphere. The energy present in the early Earth caused these chemicals to react with one another, forming the complex molecules that made life possible.

Some scientists further hypothesize that for millions of years these small, complex molecules floated in the ancient oceans and joined together to form larger molecules. These larger molecules combined into more-complicated structures. As time passed, complicated structures developed into cell-like structures that eventually became the first true cells, called prokaryotes. *Prokaryotes* are cells that lack a nucleus. Early prokaryotic cells, like the one shown in **Figure 9,** were *anaerobic*, which means they did not require oxygen to survive. Many varieties of anaerobic organisms still live on Earth today. Organisms that need oxygen could not have survived on early Earth because there was no free oxygen in the atmosphere.

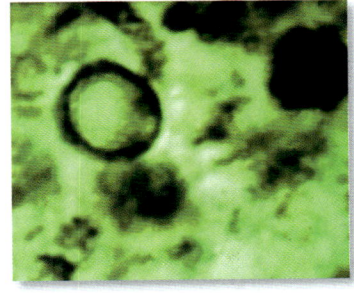

Figure 9 *Fossilized prokaryotes (such as the circular structure in the photograph) suggest that life first appeared on Earth more than 3.5 billion years ago.*

2) Teach

ACTIVITY

Using Maps Have students locate the three earthquake and volcano zones on a world map. One zone extends nearly all the way around the edge of the Pacific Ocean. A second zone is located near the Mediterranean Sea and extends across Asia into India. The third zone extends through Iceland to the middle of the Atlantic Ocean. Sheltered English

GUIDED PRACTICE

Concept Mapping Have students construct a concept map that shows how life on Earth developed from nonliving matter. They should base their map on information presented in the last two paragraphs on this page. The primary subject headings should refer to the chemicals that already exist in the environment. The final part of the concept map should identify prokaryotes as the first life-forms to appear on Earth.

USING THE FIGURE

Tell students that fossils can indicate how the Earth's surface has evolved. Ask them what they think scientists could infer if they found a fossil, such as the one shown in **Figure 9,** in rocks high above sea level. (The area was once covered by water.)

CONNECT TO EARTH SCIENCE

Have students research mountain ranges that formed during the different geologic eras and locate them on a world map. Paleozoic era: Caledonian Mountains of Scandinavia, Acadian Mountains of New York, Appalachian Mountains of North America, and the Ural Mountains of Russia; Mesozoic era: Palisades Mountains of New Jersey and the Rocky Mountains of North America; Cenozoic era: Andes Mountains of South America, Alps of Central Europe, and the Himalayas of Central Asia.

2) Teach, continued

DISCUSSION

Ask students how they think the emergence of cyanobacteria and their ability to photosynthesize affected the evolution of organisms on Earth. (Organisms that use oxygen were able to evolve.)

USING THE FIGURE

The organisms in **Figure 10** are cyanobacteria. These organisms can photosynthesize, making their own food from sunlight and carbon dioxide. Unlike plants, however, many species also can take in nitrogen from the atmosphere and convert it to a form that plants can use. Plants rely on other organisms to "fix" nitrogen gas into a form plants can use. Ask students: How might this ability to fix nitrogen make cyanobacteria useful to rice farmers? (Rice is grown in "paddies," which are wet, warm areas. The plants actually grow in the shallow water of the paddies. Cyanobacteria in the water make nitrogen compounds and excrete them, fertilizing the rice plants.)

MEETING INDIVIDUAL NEEDS

Learners Having Difficulty
Help students understand the importance of photosynthesis in the evolution of life on Earth. Ask them what kind of organisms were living before the development of photosynthesis. (anaerobic prokaryotes)

Then ask them how life on Earth changed after photosynthesis. (Many aerobic organisms evolved.)

Have students write answers to the questions and accompany their answers with illustrations.

Figure 10 Cyanobacteria are the simplest living organisms that photosynthesize.

Ozone depletion in the upper atmosphere is a serious problem. Chemicals, such as those used in refrigerators and air conditioners, are slowly destroying the ozone layer in the Earth's atmosphere. Because of ozone depletion, all living things are exposed to higher levels of radiation, which can cause skin cancer. Some countries have outlawed ozone-depleting chemicals.

Most of us think of Earth as an oxygen-rich planet. In actuality, only about 20 percent of Earth's present atmosphere is oxygen. The rest is made up mostly of nitrogen.

The Earth's First Pollution—Oxygen! As indicated by the fossil record, prokaryotic organisms called cyanobacteria appeared more than 3 billion years ago. Cyanobacteria, pictured in **Figure 10,** are photosynthetic organisms, which means that they use sunlight to produce food. One of the byproducts of this process is oxygen. As cyanobacteria carried out photosynthesis, they released oxygen gas into the oceans. The oxygen then escaped out into the air, changing Earth's atmosphere forever. Over the next several million years, more and more oxygen was added to the atmosphere.

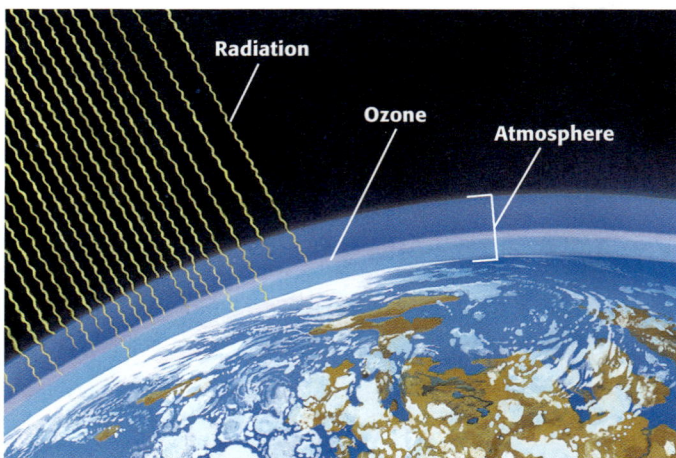

Figure 11 Oxygen from photosynthesis formed ozone, which helps to absorb ultraviolet radiation.

Radiation Shield As the atmosphere filled with oxygen, some of the oxygen formed a layer of ozone in the upper atmosphere, as shown in **Figure 11.** *Ozone* is a gas that absorbs ultraviolet (UV) radiation from the sun. UV radiation damages DNA but is absorbed by water. Before ozone formed, therefore, life was restricted to the oceans and underground. But the new ozone blocked out most of the UV radiation. This brought radiation on Earth's surface down to a level that allowed life to move onto dry land.

Life's So Complex The fossil record tells us that after a long period of time, about 1 billion years, more-complex life-forms appeared. These organisms, known as *eukaryotes,* are much larger than prokaryotes. They contain a central nucleus and a complicated internal structure. Scientists think that over the past 2.5 billion years, eukaryotic cells have evolved together to form organisms that are composed of many cells.

The Paleozoic Era

The **Paleozoic era** began about 540 million years ago and ended about 248 million years ago. *Paleozoic* comes from the Greek words meaning "ancient life." Considering how long Precambrian time lasted, the Paleozoic era was relatively recent. Rocks from the Paleozoic era are rich in fossils of animals such as sponges, corals, snails, clams, squids, and trilobites. Fishes, the earliest animals with backbones, also appeared during this era, and ancient sharks became abundant. Some Paleozoic organisms are shown in **Figure 12**.

The Greening of the Earth During the Paleozoic era, plants, fungi, and air-breathing animals colonized dry land over a period of 30 million years. Plants provided the first land animals with food and shelter. By the end of the Paleozoic era, forests of giant ferns, club mosses, horsetails, and conifers covered much of the Earth. All major plant groups except for flowering plants appeared during this era.

Creepers Crawl onto Land Fossils indicate that crawling insects were some of the first animals to appear on land. They were followed by large salamanderlike animals. Near the end of the Paleozoic era, reptiles, winged insects, cockroaches, and dragonflies appeared.

The largest mass extinction known occurred at the end of the Paleozoic era, about 248 million years ago. As many as 90 percent of all marine species died out.

Self-Check

Place the following events in chronological order:
a. The ozone layer formed, and living things moved onto dry land.
b. Gases in the atmosphere and minerals in the oceans combined to form small molecules.
c. The first prokaryotic, anaerobic cells appeared.
d. Cyanobacteria appeared.

(See page 782 to check your answer.)

Figure 12 Organisms that appeared in the Paleozoic era include the first reptiles, amphibians, fishes, worms, and ferns.

Homework

Comparing Organisms Have students compare the characteristics of each of the Paleozoic organisms pictured on this page with those of a descendant living today. Students can organize the information in the form of a chart.

READING STRATEGY

Have students read the text on this page. Have them write in their ScienceLog new headings for the first three paragraphs. For example, the heading for the first paragraph might be *Life Is Abundant in the Seas;* the heading for the second paragraph might be *Huge Forests of Ferns and Other Plants Develop;* and the heading for the third paragraph might be *Animals That Live on Land All the Time Appear.*

MATH and MORE

Using the premise that the Earth is 4.6 billion years old, have students calculate the length of the Earth's Precambrian and Paleozoic eras. They should use the information presented in the first paragraph on this page to determine the length of each of the eras (in millions of years). (Precambrian: $4,600-540 = 4,060$, Paleozoic: $540-248 = 292$)

Math Skills Worksheet 2 "Subtraction Review"

Answer to Self-Check
b, c, d, a

REAL-WORLD CONNECTION

The huge plants that grew in forests during the Paleozoic era later became coal. Ask students to research the locations of the world's coal deposits and mark them on a world map. (Most of the known coal reserves are in Australia, China, Germany, Poland, Great Britain, India, Russia, South Africa, the United States, and Canada.)

3) Extend

READING STRATEGY

Prediction Guide Before students read the text on these pages, ask them whether the following events occurred in the Mesozoic era, which began about 248 million years ago, or in the Cenozoic era, which began about 65 million years ago and continues today:

- Dinosaurs dominated Earth and then died out by the end of this era. **(Mesozoic)**
- Mammals appeared. **(Mesozoic)**
- Rock layers close to Earth's surface contain fossils from this era. **(Cenozoic)**
- The first birds appeared. **(Mesozoic)**
- Humans appeared. **(Cenozoic)**

RESEARCH

Writing Have students research reptiles and list their distinctive characteristics. **(Reptiles are ectothermic; they have a distinctive type of heart; most reptiles have scales; many reptiles have claws; and most reptiles lay their eggs on land.)**

Tell students that all living reptiles fall into four orders—turtles, lizards and snakes, crocodiles and related forms, and the tuatara. Have students investigate these orders and list examples of each.

---

internetconnect
SCILINKS TOPIC: Birds and Dinosaurs
NSTA GO TO: www.scilinks.org
sciLINKS NUMBER: HSTL200

The Mesozoic Era

The **Mesozoic era** began about 248 million years ago and lasted about 183 million years. *Mesozoic* comes from the Greek words meaning "middle life." Scientists think that, after the extinctions of the Paleozoic era, a burst of evolution occurred among the surviving reptiles, resulting in many different species. Therefore, the Mesozoic era is commonly referred to as the Age of Reptiles.

Life in the Mesozoic Era Dinosaurs are the most well known of the reptiles that evolved during the Mesozoic era. Dinosaurs dominated the Earth for about 150 million years. (Consider that humans and their ancestors have been around for only about 4 million years.) Dinosaurs had a great variety of physical characteristics, such as duck bills and projecting spines. In addition to dinosaurs, there were giant marine lizards that swam in the ocean. The first birds also appeared during the Mesozoic era. The most important plants during the early part of the Mesozoic era were cone-bearing seed plants, which formed large forests. Flowering plants appeared later in the Mesozoic era. Some of the organisms that appeared during the Mesozoic era are shown in **Figure 13.**

A Bad Time for Dinosaurs At the end of the Mesozoic era, 65 million years ago, dinosaurs and many other animal and plant species became extinct. What happened to the dinosaurs? According to one hypothesis, a large meteorite hit the Earth and generated giant dust clouds and enough heat to cause worldwide fires. The dust and smoke from these fires blocked out much of the sunlight, causing many plants to die out. Without enough plants to eat, the plant-eating dinosaurs died out. As a result, the meat-eating dinosaurs that fed on the plant-eating dinosaurs died. Global temperatures may have dropped for many years. Only a few organisms, including some small mammals, were able to survive.

Figure 13 The Mesozoic era ended with the mass extinction of most of the large animals. Survivors included small mammals and *Archaeopteryx*.

Multicultural CONNECTION

Recently, a fossil plesiosaur was found in a riverside cliff in Hokkaido, Japan, with shellfish remains in its stomach. Scientists had long suspected that plesiosaurs were predators, but they had no proof. Geologist Tamaki Sato thinks that the plesiosaur swallowed its tiny prey whole because its long, sharp teeth were unsuitable for crushing hard outer shells.

The Cenozoic Era

The **Cenozoic era** began about 65 million years ago and continues today. *Cenozoic* comes from the Greek words meaning "recent life." Scientists have more information about the Cenozoic era than about any of the previous eras because fossils from the Cenozoic era are embedded in rock layers that are close to the Earth's surface. This makes them easier to find. During the Cenozoic era, many kinds of mammals, birds, insects, and flowering plants appeared. Some organisms that appeared in the Cenozoic era are shown in **Figure 14.**

A Good Time for Large Mammals

The Cenozoic era is sometimes referred to as the Age of Mammals. Mammals came to dominate the Cenozoic era much as reptiles dominated the Mesozoic era. Early Cenozoic mammals were small forest dwellers. Larger mammals appeared later. Some of these larger mammals had long legs for running, teeth that were specialized for eating different kinds of food, and large brains. Cenozoic mammals include mastodons, saber-toothed cats, camels, giant ground sloths, and small horses.

Figure 14 *Many types of mammals evolved during the Cenozoic era.*

REVIEW

1. What is the main difference between the atmosphere 3.5 billion years ago and the atmosphere today?
2. How do prokaryotic cells and eukaryotic cells differ?
3. Explain why cyanobacteria are so important to the development of new life-forms.
4. **Identifying Relationships** Match the organisms to the time period in which they first appeared.

   1. eukaryotes
   2. dinosaurs
   3. fishes
   4. flowering plants
   5. birds

   a. Precambrian time
   b. Paleozoic era
   c. Mesozoic era
   d. Cenozoic era

TOPIC: Mass Extinctions, The Geologic Time Scale
GO TO: www.scilinks.org
sciLINKS NUMBER: HSTL185, HSTL190

Section 3

Focus

Human Evolution

In this section, students will learn that scientists think humans share a common ancestor and common characteristics with other primates, such as apes and monkeys. This section describes the characteristics of hominids and explains how trends in their evolution gave rise to modern humans.

Bellringer

On the board or an overhead projector, pose the following question to your students at the beginning of class:

What makes you unique among your family members? Please write the answer in your ScienceLog. **(Responses might include references to food preferences, physical appearances, and talents.)**

Point out that understanding evolution requires recognizing similarities and differences, like those seen in families.

1) Motivate

DISCUSSION

Comparing Primates Display a picture of an ape and a picture of a human for students to compare. Have students identify characteristics that the two animals have in common. **(Most likely answers will include references to common physical characteristics.)** Then ask students how the two animals are different from each other. **(Most likely answers will include references to differences in intellectual ability.)**

Section 3

Human Evolution

Terms to Learn
primate   australopithecine
hominid   Neanderthal

What You'll Do
- Discuss the shared characteristics of primates.
- Describe what is known about the differences between hominids.

After studying thousands of fossilized skeletons and other evidence, scientists theorize that humans evolved over millions of years from a distant ancestor that is also common to apes and monkeys. This common ancestor is thought to have lived more than 30 million years ago. How did we get from that distant ancestor to who we are today? This section presents some of the evidence that has been gathered so far.

Primates

To understand human evolution, we must first understand the characteristics that make us human beings. Humans are classified as primates. **Primates** are a group of mammals that includes humans, apes, monkeys, and prosimians. Primates have the characteristics illustrated below and in **Figure 15.**

Figure 15 The gorilla (left) and these orangutans (right) have characteristics that make them nonhuman primates, including opposable big toes!

Characteristics of Primates

Most primates have five flexible fingers—four fingers plus an opposable thumb.

This opposable thumb enables primates to grip objects.

Both eyes are located at the front of the head, providing **binocular,** or three-dimensional, vision. Each eye sees a slightly different image of the same scene. The brain merges these two images to create one three-dimensional image.

Although the skulls of a human and a chimpanzee appear to be very similar, there are significant differences. The cranium of a human skull is domed, whereas the chimpanzee's cranium is flatter. Also, the canine teeth in the human skull do not overlap, as they do in the chimpanzee skull. Ask students what conclusions they might make about the brain and the chewing ability of a human and of a chimpanzee based on these differences. **(A human brain is larger than a chimp's brain. A chimp can't easily move its jaws from side to side when chewing.)**

Based on physical and genetic similarities, the closest living relative of humans is thought to be the chimpanzee. This conclusion does not mean that humans descended from chimpanzees. Rather, it means that humans and chimpanzees share a common ancestor. The ancestor of humans is thought to have diverged from the ancestor of the chimpanzee about 7 million years ago. Since then, humans and chimpanzees have evolved along different paths.

Hominids Humans are assigned to a family separate from other primates, called **hominids**. The word *hominid* refers specifically to humans and their human-like ancestors. The main characteristic that distinguishes hominids from other primates is walking upright on two legs as their main way of moving around. Walking on two legs is called *bipedalism*. Examine **Figure 16** to see some skeletal similarities and differences between a hominid and an ape. Except for present-day humans, all hominid species are now extinct.

Figure 16 *The bones of a gorilla and a human are basically the same in form, but the human pelvis is suited for walking upright.*

The **gorilla pelvis** tilts the large rib cage and heavy neck and head forward. The arms are long to provide balance on the ground while the ape looks forward.

The **human pelvis** is vertical and helps hold the entire skeleton upright.

QuickLab

Thumb Through This

Tape your thumbs to the side of your hands so they cannot be used. Attempt each of the tasks listed below.

- Sharpen a pencil.
- Cut a circle out of a piece of paper using scissors.
- Tie your shoelaces.
- Button several buttons.

After each attempt, answer the following questions:

1. Is the task more difficult with or without an opposable thumb?
2. Without an opposable thumb, do you think you would carry out this task on a regular basis?

CROSS-DISCIPLINARY FOCUS

Anthropology The ability to walk fully upright distinguishes us from the apes. So do our large rear ends. But are they a prerequisite or a consequence of upright posture? Thomas Greiner, a physical anthropologist, believes the latter is true. Greiner developed a computer model that shows how muscle action changes in response to changes in bone shape. By means of his model, Greiner concluded that having both a smaller gluteus maximus and a larger ilium than a human hinders an ape's ability to walk upright.

2) Teach

ACTIVITY

Exploring Vision Students can explore the utility of binocular vision by making a dot on a sheet of paper and placing the paper on a desktop. Have them stand about half a meter away from the desk and close their right eye. Then have them try to touch the dot on the paper with the tip of a pencil. Have them repeat the action with their left eye closed and then with both eyes open. (Students should find that it is easier to touch the dot with a pencil when they have both eyes open than when they have one eye closed.) Sheltered English

Answers to QuickLab

1. without
2. Probably not; it would be too difficult.

USING THE FIGURE

Discuss with students how binocular vision, illustrated at the bottom of page 188, is important. How is it useful to humans? (Answers should reflect an understanding that binocular vision enables humans to perceive depth and to judge distances, to hunt, use tools, drive vehicles, and play sports.)

 Teaching Transparency 33 "Primate Skeletal Structures"

 Directed Reading Worksheet 8 Section 3

Section 3 • Human Evolution

2) Teach, continued

CROSS-DISCIPLINARY FOCUS

History Many cartoons in the nineteenth century satirized humans' relationship to apes. In one such cartoon, Henry Bergh, the founder of the Society for the Prevention of Cruelty to Animals, chides Charles Darwin for insulting apes by suggesting that they are related to humans.

USING THE FIGURE

Discuss the characteristics of the lemur shown in **Figure 17.** How might each characteristic help the lemur survive in its environment? (Students might suggest that the lemur's fur helps keep it warm, that its tail aids in balance, and so on.) **Sheltered English**

MEETING INDIVIDUAL NEEDS

Learners Having Difficulty Help students identify the characteristics that distinguish primates from other mammal groups. Show them pictures of primate and nonprimate mammals. Ask how the primates are different from the other animals. Help students determine that primates generally have flatter faces than nonprimates. Their eyes are located at the front of the head rather than at the sides, their snouts are small, and their fingers are flexible.

Hominid Evolution

The first primate ancestors appeared during the Cenozoic era, 55 million years ago, and evolved in several directions. These ancestors are thought to have been mouse-like mammals that were active during the night, lived in trees, and ate insects. When the dinosaurs died out, these mammals survived and gave rise to the first primates called *prosimians*, which means "before monkeys." Only a few species, such as the one pictured in **Figure 17,** survive today. How long after prosimians appeared did the first hominid appear? No one has been able to answer that question, but scientists have discovered fossil bones of hominids that date back to 4.4 million years ago.

Figure 17 Prosimians, such as this lemur, hunt in trees for insects and small animals.

Australopithecines Scientists think hominid evolution began in Africa. Among the oldest hominids are **australopithecines** (ah STRA loh PITH uh seens). The word *Australopithecus* means "southern man ape." These early hominids had long arms, short legs, and small brains. Fossil evidence shows that the australopithecines differed from apes in several important ways. For example, they were bipedal. Also, australopithecine brains were generally larger than ape brains, although they were still much smaller than the brains of present-day humans.

In 1976, paleoanthropologist Mary Leakey discovered a series of footprints in Tanzania. Mary Leakey and the footprints are pictured in **Figure 18.** By determining the age of the rock containing the prints, she learned that the footprints were more than 3.6 million years old. The footprints indicated that a group of three hominids had walked in an upright position across the wet volcanic ash-covered plain.

Figure 18 Mary Leakey is shown here with the 3.6-million-year-old footprints.

SCIENTISTS AT ODDS

In 1975, fossils of 13 hominids were found in Ethiopia. These fossils differed in body size and jaw shape. Some anthropologists think that the larger fossils represent the males and the smaller fossils represent the females of a particular species. Other anthropologists, including Mary Leakey, believe that the differences indicate that the fossils are of two distinct species.

190 Chapter 8 • The History of Life on Earth

Lucy In 1979, a group of fossils was discovered in Ethiopia. Included in this group was the most complete skeleton of an australopithecine ever found. Nicknamed Lucy, this australopithecine lived about 2 million years ago. Lucy had a sturdy body and stood upright, but her brain was about the size of a chimpanzee's. Fossil discoveries like this one demonstrate that upright posture evolved long before the brain enlarged.

A Face Like Ours Hominids with more humanlike facial features appeared approximately 2.3 million years ago, probably evolving from australopithecine ancestors. This species is known as *Homo habilis*. Its skull is shown in **Figure 19**. Fossils of *Homo habilis* have been found along with crude stone tools. About 2 million years ago, *Homo habilis* was replaced by its larger-brained descendant, *Homo erectus*, pictured in **Figure 20**. *Homo erectus* was larger than *Homo habilis* and had a smaller jaw.

Hominids Go Global Fossil evidence shows that *Homo erectus* may have lived in caves, built fires, and wore clothing. They successfully hunted large animals and butchered them using tools made of flint and bone. The appearance of *Homo erectus* marks the beginning of the expansion of human populations across the globe. *Homo erectus* survived for more than 1 million years, which is longer than any other species of hominid has lived. *Homo erectus* disappeared about 200,000 years ago. This is about the time present-day humans, called *Homo sapiens*, first appear in the fossil record.

Although *Homo erectus* migrated across the globe, it is thought that *Homo sapiens* evolved in Africa and then migrated to Asia and Europe.

Figure 19 *Homo habilis* is called handy man because this group of hominids made stone tools.

Figure 20 *Homo erectus* lived about 2 million years ago and may have looked like the sculpture above.

IS THAT A FACT!
Lucy's nickname came from the Beatles's hit song "Lucy in the Sky with Diamonds."

RETEACHING
Help students complete an outline describing the most important characteristics of *Australopithecus*, *Homo habilis*, and *Homo erectus*. Then have students identify characteristics common to two or more of the hominid species; for example, all of the species walked in an upright position, and both *Homo habilis* and *Homo erectus* made and used tools. Students could also identify characteristics unique to a species, such as that *Homo erectus* built fires. **Sheltered English**

DISCUSSION
Analyzing Tools *Homo habilis* is thought to have made one of the oldest recognizable stone tools. The tool was a pebble with some sharp edges. Ask students how they think the tool was made. (Answers should express the idea that flakes were chipped off the pebble to sharpen it.)

CROSS-DISCIPLINARY FOCUS
Art Sculptors probably helped paleoanthropologists determine the physical appearance of the hominid shown in **Figure 20**. Sculptors can apply their knowledge of anatomy to reconstruct body features. Have students use clay to sculpt a model of the head of *Homo erectus*.

TOPIC: Human Evolution
GO TO: www.scilinks.org
*sci*LINKS NUMBER: HSTL195

Section 3 • Human Evolution

3) Extend

GOING FURTHER

 Have students use the description of Cro-Magnons on this page as a guide for drawing the head of a Cro-Magnon with facial features. **Sheltered English**

GROUP ACTIVITY

Writing Small groups of students can work together to write a play about hunting and killing a mammoth. Tell students that Cro-Magnons hunted together and that a mammoth kill was a group endeavor. How did they do it? What weapons might they have used? How did they carve the meat? What did they do with the skin, tusks, and bones? Did the hunt include women? Have each group present its play to the class.

INDEPENDENT PRACTICE

 Poster Project Provide students with markers and poster board. Have them construct evolutionary trees of humans with whole-body sketches.

Answer to Activity

Answers should include spearpoints, arrowheads, choppers, skinners, or scrapers.

Neanderthals In the Neander Valley, in Germany, fossils were discovered that belonged to a group of hominids referred to as **Neanderthals** (nee AN duhr TAHLS). They lived in Europe and western Asia beginning about 230,000 years ago.

Neanderthals hunted large animals, made fires, and wore clothing. There is evidence that they also cared for the sick and elderly and buried their dead, sometimes placing food, weapons, and even flowers with the dead bodies. Pictured in **Figure 21** is an artist's idea of how a Neanderthal might have looked. About 30,000 years ago, Neanderthals disappeared; nobody knows what caused their extinction.

Some scientists think the Neanderthals are a separate species, *Homo neanderthalensis*, from present-day humans, *Homo sapiens*. Other scientists think Neanderthals are a race of *Homo sapiens*. There is not yet enough evidence to fully answer this question.

Figure 21 Neanderthals had heavy brow ridges, like *Homo erectus, but a larger brain than modern humans.*

Cro-Magnons In 1868, fossil skulls were found in caves in southwestern France. The skulls were about 35,000 years old, and they belonged to a group of *Homo sapiens* with modern features, called *Cro-Magnons*. Cro-Magnons may have existed in Africa 100,000 years ago and migrated from Africa about 40,000 years ago, coexisting with Neanderthals. Compared with Neanderthals, Cro-Magnons had a smaller and flatter face, and their skulls were higher and more rounded, like an artist has modeled in **Figure 22.** The only significant physical difference between Cro-Magnons and present-day humans is that Cro-Magnons had thicker and heavier bones.

Activity

Neanderthals made sophisticated spear points and other stone tools. Examine the Neanderthal tools below. Each of these tools was specialized for a particular task. Can you suggest what each stone tool was used for?

Figure 22 *This is an artist's idea of how a Cro-Magnon woman may have looked.*

Science Bloopers

A skull of a *Homo sapiens* who had bad teeth was found in Zambia. There was a hole in one side and signs of a partially healed abscess. This skull was made famous by a writer who imagined the hole was caused by a bullet shot from an interplanetary visitor's gun 120,000 years ago.

The chapter introduction discussed the cave paintings made by Cro-Magnons. These paintings are the earliest known examples of human art. In fact, Cro-Magnon culture is marked by an amazing diversity of artistic efforts, including cave paintings, sculptures, and carvings, like the one shown in **Figure 23.** The preserved villages and burial grounds of Cro-Magnon groups also show that they had a complex social organization.

Figure 23 *Cro-Magnons left many kinds of paintings, sculptures, and carvings, such as this carving of a bull.*

New Evidence of Human Evolution Although we know a great deal about our hominid ancestors, much remains to be understood. Each fossil discovery causes great excitement and raises new questions, such as, "Where did *Homo sapiens* evolve?" Current evidence suggests that *Homo sapiens* evolved in Africa. "Which australopithecine gave rise to humans?" Some scientists think *Australopithecus afarensis* is the ancestor of all hominids, including present-day humans. But recent fossil discoveries indicate another australopithecine species gave rise to human ancestors. There is still much to be learned about the evolution of humans.

REVIEW

1. Identify three characteristics of primates.
2. Compare *Homo habilis* with *Homo erectus*. What made the two species different from one another?
3. What evidence suggests Neanderthals were like present-day humans?
4. **Inferring Conclusions** Imagine you are a scientist excavating an ancient campsite. What might you conclude about the people who used the site if you found the charred bones of large animals and various stone blades among human fossils?

internetconnect

SC*i*LINKS
NSTA
TOPIC: Human Evolution
GO TO: www.scilinks.org
***sci*LINKS NUMBER:** HSTL195

Chapter Highlights

Vocabulary Definitions

SECTION 1

fossil the solidified remains or imprints of once living organisms

relative dating determining whether an event or object, such as a fossil, is older or younger than other events or objects

absolute dating estimating the age of a sample or event in years, usually by measuring the ratio of unstable atoms to stable atoms in the sample

geologic time scale the division of Earth's 4.6-billion-year history into distinct intervals of time

extinct a species of organism that has died out completely

plate tectonics the study of the forces that drive the movement of pieces of the Earth's crust around the surface of the planet

SECTION 2

Precambrian time the period in the geologic time scale beginning when the Earth originated 4.6 billion years ago and continuing until complex organisms appear about 540 million years ago

Chapter Highlights

SECTION 1

Vocabulary
fossil (p. 176)
relative dating (p. 177)
absolute dating (p. 177)
geologic time scale (p. 178)
extinct (p. 179)
plate tectonics (p. 181)

Section Notes
- Paleontologists are scientists who study fossils.
- The age of a fossil can be determined using relative dating and absolute dating. Relative dating is an estimate based on the known age of the sediment layer in which the fossil is found. Absolute dating usually involves the measurement of the rate of decay of the unstable atoms found in the rock surrounding the fossil.
- The geologic time scale is a calendar scientists use to outline the history of Earth and life on Earth.
- Many species existed for a few million years and then became extinct. Mass extinctions have occurred several times in Earth's history.

Labs
Dating the Fossil Record (p. 712)
The Half-life of Pennies (p. 715)

SECTION 2

Vocabulary
Precambrian time (p. 182)
Paleozoic era (p. 185)
Mesozoic era (p. 186)
Cenozoic era (p. 187)

Section Notes
- Precambrian time includes the formation of the Earth, the beginning of life, and the evolution of simple multi-cellular organisms.

✓ Skills Check

Math Concepts

HALF-LIFE To understand half-life better, imagine that you have $10.00 in your pocket. You determine that you are going to spend half of all the money you have in your possession every 30 minutes. How much will you have after 30 minutes? ($5.00) How much will you have after another 30 minutes? ($2.50) How much will you have after 3 hours? (a little more than 15¢)

Visual Understanding

THE GEOLOGIC TIME SCALE You have probably seen old movies or cartoons that show humans and dinosaurs inhabiting the same environment. Can this be possible? Dinosaurs and humans did not exist at the same time. Dinosaurs became extinct 65 million years ago. Humans and their ancestors have been around for less than 4 million years. Review the Geologic Time Scale on page 178.

Lab and Activity Highlights

Dating the Fossil Record `PG 712`

The Half-life of Pennies `PG 715`

 Datasheets for LabBook (blackline masters for these labs)

SECTION 2

- The Earth is about 4.6 billion years old. Life formed from nonliving matter on the turbulent early Earth.
- The first cells, prokaryotes, were anaerobic. Later, photosynthetic cyanobacteria evolved and caused oxygen to enter the atmosphere.
- During the Paleozoic era, animals appeared in the oceans, and plants and animals colonized the land.
- Dinosaurs and other reptiles roamed the Earth during the Mesozoic era. Flowering plants, birds, and primitive mammals also appeared.
- Primates evolved during the Cenozoic era, which extends to the present day.

SECTION 3

Vocabulary
primate (p. 188)
hominid (p. 189)
australopithecine (p. 190)
Neanderthal (p. 192)

Section Notes

- Humans, apes, and monkeys are primates. Primates are distinguished from other mammals by their opposable thumbs and binocular vision.
- Hominids, a subgroup of primates, include humans and their human-like ancestors. The oldest known hominids are australopithecines.
- Neanderthals were a species of humans that disappeared about 30,000 years ago.
- Cro-Magnons did not differ very much from present-day humans.

VOCABULARY DEFINITIONS, continued

Paleozoic era the period in the geologic time scale beginning about 570 million years ago and ending about 248 million years ago

Mesozoic era the period in the geologic time scale beginning about 248 million years ago and ending about 65 million years ago

Cenozoic era the period in the geologic time scale beginning about 65 million years ago and continuing until the present day

SECTION 3

primate a group of mammals that includes humans, apes, and monkeys; distinguished by opposable thumbs and binocular vision

hominid a family of humans and several extinct humanlike species, some of which were human ancestors

australopithecine an early hominid that evolved more than 3.6 million years ago

Neanderthal a species of hominid that lived in Europe and western Asia from 230,000 years ago to about 30,000 years ago, when they mysteriously went extinct

---

internetconnect

GO TO: go.hrw.com

Visit the **HRW** Web site for a variety of learning tools related to this chapter. Just type in the keyword:

KEYWORD: HSTHIS

SCILINKS NSTA

GO TO: www.scilinks.org

Visit the **National Science Teachers Association** on-line Web site for Internet resources related to this chapter. Just type in the sciLINKS number for more information about the topic:

TOPIC: Evidence of the Past	sciLINKS NUMBER: HSTL180
TOPIC: Mass Extinctions	sciLINKS NUMBER: HSTL185
TOPIC: The Geologic Time Scale	sciLINKS NUMBER: HSTL190
TOPIC: Human Evolution	sciLINKS NUMBER: HSTL195
TOPIC: Birds and Dinosaurs	sciLINKS NUMBER: HSTL200

 Vocabulary Review Worksheet 8

 Blackline masters of these Chapter Highlights can be found in the **Study Guide**.

Lab and Activity Highlights

LabBank

 Long-Term Projects & Research Ideas, A Horse Is a Horse, Project 8

Interactive Explorations CD-ROM

 CD 2, Exploration 6, "Rock On!"

Chapter Review Answers

USING VOCABULARY

1. Precambrian time period
2. Cenozoic era
3. Mesozoic era
4. Paleozoic era
5. australopithecines

UNDERSTANDING CONCEPTS

Multiple Choice

6. b
7. c
8. b
9. b
10. c

Short Answer

11. Fossils tell us about the kinds of organisms that existed and how they changed over time.
12. Precambrian: life begins, prokaryotes and eukaryotes appear; Paleozoic: multicellular organisms, plants, insects, and amphibians appear; Mesozoic: dinosaurs and other reptiles, birds, and small mammals appear; Cenozoic: large mammals, including humans, and more-diverse birds and insects appear
13. Fossils in the Cenozoic era are closer to the surface of Earth and thus are easier to find.

Chapter Review

USING VOCABULARY

To complete the following sentences, choose the correct term from each pair of terms listed below:

1. During the __?__ of the Earth's history, life is thought to have originated from nonliving matter. (*Precambrian time period* or *Paleozoic era*)

2. The Age of Mammals refers to the __?__. (*Mesozoic era* or *Cenozoic era*)

3. The Age of Reptiles refers to the __?__. (*Paleozoic era* or *Mesozoic era*)

4. Plants colonized dry land during the __?__. (*Precambrian time* or *Paleozoic era*)

5. The most ancient hominids are called __?__. (*Neanderthals* or *australopithecines*)

UNDERSTANDING CONCEPTS

Multiple Choice

6. Scientists estimate the age of the Earth to be about
   a. 10 billion years.
   b. 4.6 billion years.
   c. 3.8 billion years.
   d. 4.4 million years.

7. The first cells probably appeared about
   a. 10 billion years ago.
   b. 4.6 billion years ago.
   c. 3.5 billion years ago.
   d. 4.4 million years ago.

8. How is the age of a fossil estimated?
   a. by using the geologic time scale
   b. by measuring unstable elements in the rock that holds the fossil
   c. by studying the relative position of continents
   d. by measuring the amount of oxygen in the fossil rock

9. Plants and air-breathing animals appeared during this time period.
   a. Precambrian time
   b. Paleozoic era
   c. Mesozoic era
   d. Cenozoic era

10. These hominids made sophisticated tools, hunted large animals, wore clothing, and cared for the sick and elderly. Their extinction is a mystery.
    a. australopithecines
    b. hominids in the genus *Homo*
    c. Neanderthals
    d. Cro-Magnons

Short Answer

11. What kinds of information do fossils provide about the evolutionary history of life?

12. Name at least one important biological event that occurred during each of the following geologic eras: Precambrian time, Paleozoic era, Mesozoic era, and Cenozoic era.

13. Why are there usually more fossils from the Cenozoic era than from other geologic eras?

Concept Mapping

14. Use the following terms to create a concept map: Earth's history, humans, Paleozoic era, dinosaurs, Precambrian time, cyanobacteria, Mesozoic era, land plants, Cenozoic era.

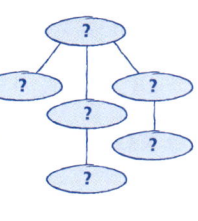

CRITICAL THINKING AND PROBLEM SOLVING

Write one or two sentences to answer the following questions:

15. Why do scientists think the first cells were anaerobic?

16. List three evolutionary changes in early hominids that led to the rise of modern humans.

MATH IN SCIENCE

17. A rock containing a newly discovered fossil is found to contain 5 mg of an unstable form of potassium and 5 mg of the stable element formed from its decay. If the half-life of the unstable form of potassium is 1.3 billion years, how old is the rock? What can you infer about the age of the fossil?

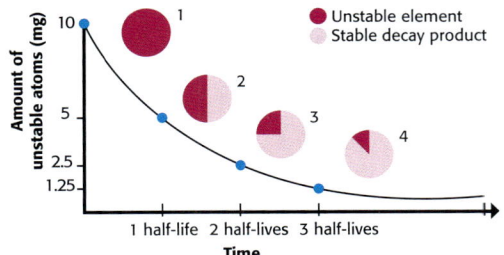

INTERPRETING GRAPHICS

The figure below illustrates the evolutionary relationships between some primates. Examine the figure, and answer the questions.

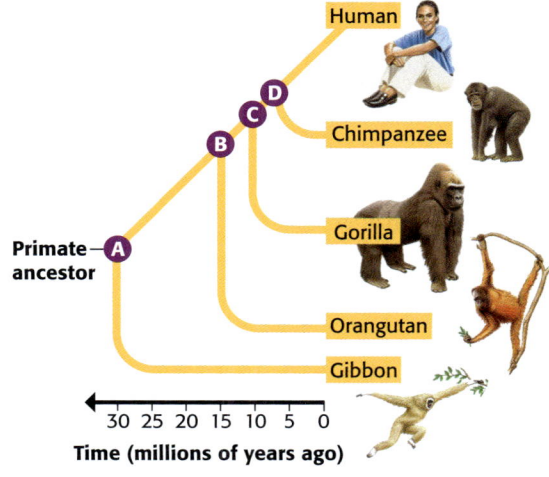

18. Which letter represents when gorillas took a different evolutionary path?

19. About how long ago did orangutan diverge from the human evolutionary line?

20. Which group has been separated from the human line of evolution the longest?

Take a minute to review your answers to the Pre-Reading Questions found at the bottom of page 174. Have your answers changed? If necessary, revise your answers based on what you have learned since you began this chapter.

Concept Mapping

14. An answer to this exercise can be found at the end of this book.

CRITICAL THINKING AND PROBLEM SOLVING

15. There was no oxygen available when they developed.
16. larger brains, longer legs, shorter arms

MATH IN SCIENCE

17. 1.3 billion years old; the fossil is also about 1.3 billion years old.

INTERPRETING GRAPHICS

18. point C
19. 15 million years ago
20. the gibbons

Concept Mapping Transparency 8

Blackline masters of this Chapter Review can be found in the **Study Guide.**

ACROSS THE SCIENCES
Windows into the Past

Background

Unlike the sun and the giant gas planets of the outer solar system, Earth and its three nearest planetary neighbors, Mercury, Venus, and Mars, are solid bodies with surfaces of rock. For this reason they are known as terrestrial planets. But even though the Earth has a solid, durable surface, it is constantly changing because of forces acting at and below its surface.

Rock is any naturally occurring solid mixture of minerals and other materials. Minerals, in turn, are any naturally occurring, inorganic chemical compound found in the Earth. Because there are so many minerals in the Earth's crust, there are also many types of rock. Rocks are broadly classified according to how they are formed.

Although all three rock types are found on the Earth's surface, most of the Earth's crust consists of igneous rock. We don't often see these igneous rocks because most of the continents are covered by a relatively thin layer of sedimentary rock. Only in a few places have natural processes brought the "basement rocks" to the Earth's surface, where we can see them.

LIFE SCIENCE • EARTH SCIENCE

Windows into the Past

When you think about the history of life on Earth, you may not think of rocks. After all, rocks are nonliving! What can they tell you about life? It may surprise you to learn that a great deal of what we know about life on Earth has been provided by rocks. How? It just so happens that life-forms have been fossilized between layers of rock for million of years—maybe even since life first appeared on Earth. And finding these fossils is like finding an old snapshot of ancient life-forms.

Layers of Rock

Fossils are most likely to be found in sedimentary rock. This is a type of rock that forms as exposed rock surfaces are worn away by wind, rain, and ice. The particles from these rock surfaces then collect in low-lying areas. As these layers build up, their combined weight compacts the particles, and chemical reactions cement them together. After thousands of years, the layers of particles become solid rock—and so do parts of any organism that has been trapped in the layers.

The Rock Cycle

The illustration at right shows how sedimentary rock forms. It also shows how igneous rock and metamorphic rock form. Notice that sedimentary and metamorphic rock can melt and become igneous rock; this happens deep underground. Can you see why fossils would not normally be found in igneous rock?

The rock cycle is a continuous process. All three kinds of rock eventually become another type of rock. Fortunately for life scientists, this process can take millions of years. If this process happened more quickly—and sedimentary rock became either metamorphic or igneous rock at a faster pace—our fossil record would be much shorter. We may not have found out about the dinosaurs!

Cycle This!

▶ Suppose you found several fossils of the same organism. You found some fossils in very deep layers of sedimentary rock and some fossils in very shallow layers of sedimentary rock. What does this say about the organism?

▼ *The Rock Cycle*

Answer to Cycle This!
If fossils of the same type of organism are found in both deep and shallow layers of sedimentary rock, this probably indicates that the organism existed for the time span that the sedimentary rock containing the fossils was forming.

CAREERS

PALEOBOTANIST

In school **Bonnie Jacobs** was fascinated by fossils, ancient cultures, and geology. "I have always had an interest in ancient things," she says. To pursue her interests, Jacobs became a paleobotanist. "A paleobotanist is someone who studies fossil plants," she explains. "That means you study fossilized leaves, wood, pollen, flower parts, or anything else that comes from a plant."

Bonnie Jacobs teaches and does research at Southern Methodist University, in Dallas, Texas. As a paleobotanist, she uses special "snapshots" that let her "see" back in time. If you look at these snapshots, you might see an ancient grassland, desert, or rain forest. Jacobs's snapshots might even give you a glimpse of the place where our human family may have started.

Fossil Plants and Ancient Climates

Jacobs and other paleobotanists study present-day plant species and how they grow in different climates. Plants that grow in warm, wet climates today probably grew in the same kind of climate millions of years ago. So when Jacobs finds ancient plant fossils that are similar to plants that exist today, she can determine what the ancient climate was like. But her fossils give more than just a climate report.

Plants and . . . Ancient Bones

Because some of these same plant fossils are found in rocks that also contain bits of bone—some from human ancestors—they may hold clues to human history. "Ideas about the causes of human evolution have a lot to do with changes in the landscape," Jacobs explains. "For instance, many scientists who study human evolution assumed that there was a big change from forested to more-open environments just before the origin of the human family. That assumption needs to be tested. The best way to do that is to go back to the plants themselves."

It's an Adventure!

In doing her research, Jacobs has traveled to many different places and worked with a wide variety of people. "Kiptalam Chepboi, a colleague we worked with in Kenya, grew up in the area where we do fieldwork. He took me to a sweat-bee hive. Sweat bees don't sting. You can take a honeycomb out from under a rock ledge, pop the whole thing in your mouth, and suck out the honey without worrying about getting stung. That was one of the neatest things I did out there."

Making a Modern Record

▶ Make your own plant fossil. Press a leaf part into a piece of clay. Fill the depression with plaster of Paris. Then write a report describing what the fossil tells you about the environment it came from.

▲ *Fossilized leaves*

CAREERS
Paleobotanist— Bonnie Jacobs

Background

Paleobotanists study the fossils of plants not only to learn about the plants themselves but also to search for clues about ancient climates, ecosystems, and the evolution of species.

Jacobs is one of a group of experts from all over the world who have studied in the Lake Baringo region of Kenya. Researchers studying the evolution of humans and of a wide variety of plants, mammals, fish, and microorganisms have joined forces with specialists in geology and dating techniques to gather information from the area. Human fossils from this area are among the oldest human remains ever found.

Answer to Making a Modern Record
The fossils that the students make will be representative of the environment in which the students live. Their descriptions should reflect that.

Chapter Organizer

CHAPTER ORGANIZATION	TIME MINUTES	OBJECTIVES	LABS, INVESTIGATIONS, AND DEMONSTRATIONS
Chapter Opener pp. 226–227	45	National Standards: UCP 1	**Start-Up Activity** Classifying Shoes, p. 201
Section 1 Classification: Sorting It All Out	90	▶ List the seven levels of classification. ▶ Explain the importance of having scientific names for species. ▶ Explain how scientific names are written. ▶ Describe how dichotomous keys help in identifying organisms. UCP 1, SAI 2, HNS 1–3, LS 5a; LabBook UCP 1, SAI 1	**Demonstration,** Classifying Objects, p. 202 in ATE **BASIC** **QuickLab,** Evolutionary Diagrams, p. 205 **GENERAL** **Skill Builder,** Shape Island, p. 716 **BASIC** **Datasheets for LabBook,** Shape Island, Datasheet 19 **BASIC** **Discovery Lab,** Voyage of the USS *Adventure*, p. 718 **BASIC** **Datasheets for LabBook,** Voyage of the USS *Adventure*, Datasheet 20 **BASIC** **EcoLabs & Field Activities,** Water Wigglers, Field Activity 1 **GENERAL**
Section 2 The Six Kingdoms	90	▶ Explain how classification schemes for kingdoms developed as greater numbers of different organisms became known. ▶ List the six kingdoms, and provide two characteristics of each. UCP 5, SAI 1, HNS 1, 2, LS 1b, 1f, 2a, 2c, 4b, 4c, 5b	**Long-Term Projects & Research Ideas,** Project 9 **ADVANCED**

See page **T20** for a complete correlation of this book with the

NATIONAL SCIENCE EDUCATION STANDARDS.

TECHNOLOGY RESOURCES

 Guided Reading Audio CD English or Spanish, Chapter 9

 One-Stop Planner CD-ROM with Test Generator

Chapter 9 • Classification

CLASSROOM WORKSHEETS, TRANSPARENCIES, AND RESOURCES	SCIENCE INTEGRATION AND CONNECTIONS	REVIEW AND ASSESSMENT
Directed Reading Worksheet 9 BASIC **Science Puzzlers, Twisters & Teasers,** Worksheet 9 ADVANCED		
Directed Reading Worksheet 9, Section 1 BASIC **Transparency 34,** Levels of Classification **Science Skills Worksheet 6,** Boosting Your Memory GENERAL **Math Skills for Science Worksheet 4,** A Shortcut for Multiplying Large Numbers GENERAL **Transparency 35,** Evolutionary Relationships Among Four Mammals **Transparency 35,** Evolutionary Relationships Among Four Plants **Transparency 36,** Dichotomous Key to 10 Common Mammals in the Eastern United States **Problem Solving Worksheet 9,** A Breach on Planet Biome ADVANCED	**Connect to Environmental Science,** p. 202 in ATE **Math and More,** p. 204 in ATE BASIC **Multicultural Connection,** p. 206 in ATE **Scientific Debate:** It's a Bird, It's a Plane, It's a *Dinosaur*? p. 218 ADVANCED	**Review,** p. 207 GENERAL **Quiz,** p. 207 in ATE GENERAL **Alternative Assessment,** p. 207 in ATE GENERAL
Transparency 112, Intrusive Igneous Rock Formations **Directed Reading Worksheet 9,** Section 2 BASIC **Math Skills for Science Worksheet 19,** Arithmetic with Decimals GENERAL **Reinforcement Worksheet 9,** Keys to the Kingdoms GENERAL	**Connect to Environmental Science,** p. 208 in ATE **Connect to Earth Science,** p. 209 in ATE **Real-World Connection,** p. 210 in ATE **MathBreak,** Building a Human Chain Around a Giant Sequoia, p. 211 GENERAL **Environment Connection,** p. 211 **Multicultural Connection,** p. 211 in ATE **Apply,** p. 212 GENERAL **Weird Science:** Lobster-Lip Life-Form, p. 219 GENERAL	**Homework,** pp. 209, 210 in ATE ADVANCED **Self-Check,** p. 210 **Review,** p. 213 GENERAL **Quiz,** p. 213 in ATE GENERAL **Alternative Assessment,** p. 213 in ATE GENERAL

 Holt, Rinehart and Winston On-line Resources
go.hrw.com

For worksheets and other teaching aids related to this chapter, visit the HRW Web site and type in the keyword: **HSTCLS**

 National Science Teachers Association
www.scilinks.org

Encourage students to use the *sci*LINKS numbers listed in the internet connect boxes to access information and resources on the **NSTA** Web site.

END-OF-CHAPTER REVIEW AND ASSESSMENT

Chapter Review in Study Guide
Vocabulary and Notes in Study Guide
Chapter Tests with Performance-Based Assessment, Chapter 9 Test
Chapter Tests with Performance-Based Assessment, Performance-Based Assessment 9
Concept Mapping Transparency 9

Chapter Resources & Worksheets

Visual Resources

Meeting Individual Needs

Chapter 9 • Classification

Review & Assessment

STUDY GUIDE

CHAPTER TESTS WITH PERFORMANCE-BASED ASSESSMENT

Lab Worksheets

ECOLABS & FIELD ACTIVITIES

LONG-TERM PROJECTS & RESEARCH IDEAS

DATASHEETS FOR LABBOOK

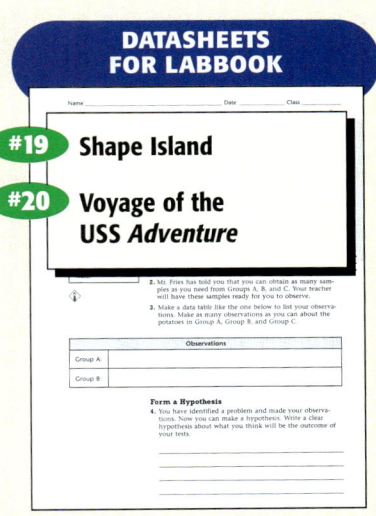

Applications & Extensions

CRITICAL THINKING & PROBLEM SOLVING

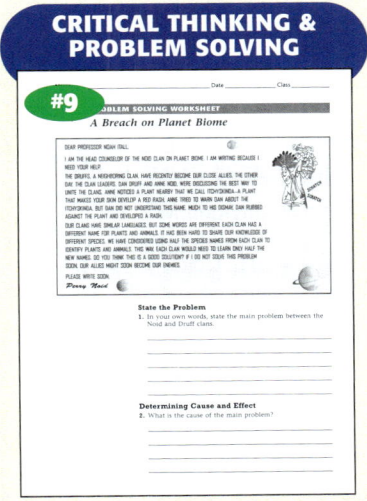

Chapter 9 • Chapter Resources & Worksheets

Chapter Background

SECTION 1

Classification: Sorting It All Out

▶ **Aristotle's Classification System**
The great Greek philosopher and scientist Aristotle (384–322 B.C.) began classifying animals into logical groupings more than 2,000 years ago. Although Aristotle did not view different kinds of organisms as being related by descent, he arranged all living things in an ascending ladder with humans at the top.

- Animals were separated into two major groups—those with red blood and those without red blood—which correspond very closely with our modern classification of vertebrates and invertebrates.

- Animals were further classified according to their way of life, their actions, and their body parts.

- Aristotle grouped plants as herbs, shrubs, or trees, based on their size and appearance.

▶ **Species in Classification**
In the late 1600s, the English scientist John Ray established the species as the basic unit of classification.

▶ **Basis for Modern Classification System**
Our modern system of classification was introduced by Swedish scientist Carolus Linnaeus. He published a book on plant classification in 1753 and a book on animal classification in 1758.

- Organisms were classified according to their structure.

- Plants and animals were arranged into genus and species, and the categories of class and order were introduced.

- Species were given distinctive two-word names. Linnaeus's system is still in use today, although with many changes.

- Carolus Linnaeus is the Latin translation of the Swedish scientist's given name, Carl von Linné.

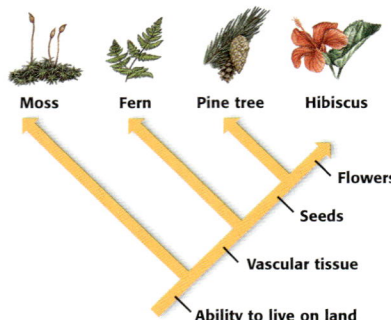

▶ **Subgroups in the Animal Kingdom**
Baron Cuvier Georges first divided the animal kingdom into subgroups, such as Vertebrata, Mollusca, Articulata, and Radiata, in 1817.

IS THAT A FACT!

◆ The legs of birds are covered in scales very similar to the scales that cover many reptiles.

199E Chapter 9 • Classification

Chapter 9 • Classification

SECTION 2

The Six Kingdoms

▶ **Variations of the Classification System**
Variations of the five-kingdom system introduced by R. H. Whittaker in 1969 are used by some modern scientists. Whittaker's system classifies organisms according to whether they are prokaryotic or eukaryotic, whether they are unicellular or multicellular, and whether they obtain food by photosynthesis, ingestion, or absorption of nutrients from their environment.

- Because studies of DNA indicate that there are significant differences between archaebacteria and eubacteria, many scientists place archaebacteria in a sixth kingdom.

▶ **Different Classification Methods**
Branches of biology use different methods of classification.

- The classification method microbiologists use is organized by volume, section, family, and genus.

- Botanists used to use the term *division* instead of *phylum* for plants and fungi.

▶ **The Planet Within**
When we organize life on Earth into categories, it is important to remember that organisms are not equally distributed throughout our classification system. Even though we often think of the Earth's living things in terms of plants and animals—organisms living above the Earth's surface—the largest kingdoms in terms of the number of species, number of individuals,

and total biomass are bacteria. And their most common home may be deep within the Earth's crust.

- Scientists have known for some time that bacteria exist all around us and that some have the ability to live in extreme environments. Some live in hot geysers, others in water with salt concentrations so high no other organisms can survive in it. Scientists have also known that many archaebacteria can thrive in anaerobic and high-pressure environments, such as those found underground. But only recently have scientists learned just how far underground they are and just how many bacteria live there.

- In 1987, scientists were drilling in the rock beneath the Savannah River in South Carolina, investigating the safety of the drinking water. The cores of the rock they investigated at a depth of 500 m harbored bacteria. Other scientists found bacteria in the ocean at 750 m. A South African gold mine, as far down as 5 km, yielded other bacteria.

- Once scientists knew to look deep in the Earth for life-forms, they began looking in the sediment under the ocean and found more organisms. That sediment is 15 km deep in places, and some speculate that organisms could inhabit the sediment even to that depth. If that is the case, then the total biomass of these astonishing organisms beneath the surface of the Earth may exceed the total biomass of all the living things on the Earth's surface.

- No one knows exactly how these creatures tolerate the tremendous pressures and temperatures of their environment, but scientists have learned that these organisms are meeting their nutritional needs in a variety of ways. Some live on oxidized forms of sulfur; others on bits of organic matter found in the sediment. Some bacteria have even been found in igneous rocks, apparently subsisting on the carbon dioxide and hydrogen gas trapped in the rock.

For background information about teaching strategies and issues, refer to the *Professional Reference for Teachers.*

Chapter 9

Classification

Pre-Reading Questions

Students may not know the answers to these questions before reading the chapter, so accept any reasonable response.

Suggested Answers

1. Classification is systematically organizing things or ideas.
2. People classify many things that are important in their everyday lives, such as food, addresses, and clothing.
3. Scientists classify things in order to find similarities that help us understand our world.

Directed Reading Worksheet 9

Science Puzzlers, Twisters & Teasers Worksheet 9

Guided Reading Audio CD
English or Spanish, Chapter 9

Chapter 9 Classification

Sections

1. **Classification: Sorting It All Out** 202
   QuickLab 205
2. **The Six Kingdoms** 208
   MathBreak 211
   Environment Connection 211
   Apply 212
   Internet Connect 213

Chapter Review 216
Feature Articles 218, 219
LabBook 716–719

Pre-Reading Questions

1. What is classification?
2. How do people use classification in their everyday lives?
3. Why do scientists classify living things?

All Sorts of Insects!

Look at the katydids, grasshoppers, and other insects on this page. Every insect has a label that bears the insect's name and other information. Suppose you discovered a new insect. How would you name, sort, and identify—or classify—the new insect? Where would you start? In this chapter, you will learn how scientists classify living things. You will also learn about the six kingdoms into which all living things are classified.

---

internet connect

HRW On-line Resources
go.hrw.com
For worksheets and other teaching aids, visit the HRW Web site and type in the keyword: **HSTCLS**

www.scilinks.com
Use the *sci*LINKS numbers at the end of each chapter for additional resources on the **NSTA** Web site.

www.cnnfyi.com
Visit the CNN Web site for current events coverage and classroom resources.

CLASSIFYING SHOES

In this activity, you will develop a system of classification for shoes.

Procedure

1. Gather **10 different shoes.** Use **masking tape** to label each sole with a number (1–10).

2. Make a list of shoe features, such as left or right, color, size, and laces or no laces. In your ScienceLog, make a table with a column for each feature. Complete the table by describing each shoe.

3. Use the data in the table to make a shoe identification key. The key should be a list of steps. Each step should have two statements about the shoes. The statements will lead you to two more statements. For example, step 1 might be:
   1a. This is a red sandal.
       Shoe 4
   1b. This isn't a red sandal.
       Go to step 2.

4. Each step should eliminate more shoes until only one shoe fits the description, such as in 1a, above. Check the number on the sole of the shoe to see if you are correct.

5. Trade keys with another group. How did their key help you to identify the shoes?

Analysis

6. How helpful was it to list the shoe features before making the key?

7. Could you identify the shoes using another group's key? Explain.

START-UP Activity

CLASSIFYING SHOES

MATERIALS

FOR EACH GROUP:
- 10 different shoes (from class members, a second-hand store, or a garage sale)
- masking tape

Teacher's Notes

Make certain students understand that the list of shoe characteristics should be unique to a particular set of 10 shoes.

Characteristics of shoes listed should be those that can easily be observed. For example, whether a shoe belongs to a boy or to a girl is not always obvious to an observer.

Answers to START-UP Activity

6. Making a list of characteristics is important to help you decide on the series of descriptive statements.

7. Each group may describe the shoes differently, but their descriptions should be clear enough to lead the other groups to the same conclusion.

SECTION 1

Focus

Classification: Sorting It All Out

In this section, students learn about the modern biological classification system. The section explains how organisms are classified based on their evolutionary relationships and how their scientific names are determined. Finally, students learn how to identify animals using a dichotomous key.

Ask students to think about the different ways humans classify things. Ask them to list in their ScienceLog at least five groups of things that humans classify. You may want to give them examples, such as library books, department-store merchandise, and addresses.

1) Motivate

DEMONSTRATION

Classifying Objects Display a variety of small solid objects. Ask students for their ideas on ways to put the objects into groups. For each grouping, record the defining characteristic and the objects that belong in the group. Identify objects that fit in more than one grouping. Discuss how putting objects into groups can be helpful.

Directed Reading Worksheet 9 Section 1

Section 1

Terms to Learn
classification   family
kingdom   genus
phylum   species
class   taxonomy
order   dichotomous key

What You'll Do
- List the seven levels of classification.
- Explain the importance of having scientific names for species.
- Explain how scientific names are written.
- Describe how dichotomous keys help in identifying organisms.

Classification: Sorting It All Out

Imagine that you live in a tropical rain forest and are responsible for getting your own food, shelter, and clothing from the forest. If you are going to survive, you will need to know which plants you can eat and which are poisonous. You will need to know which animals to eat and which may eat you. You will need to organize the living things around you into categories, or classify them. **Classification** is the arrangement of organisms into orderly groups based on their similarities.

Why Classify?

For thousands of years, humans have classified different kinds of organisms based on their usefulness. For example, the Chácabo people of Bolivia, like the family shown in **Figure 1,** know of 360 species of plants in the forest where they live, and they have uses for 305 of those plants. How many plants can you name that are useful in your life?

Biologists also classify organisms—both living and extinct. Why? There are millions of different living things in the world. Making sense of the sheer number and diversity of living things requires classification. Classifying living things makes it easier for biologists to find the answers to many important questions, including the following:

- How many known species are there?
- What are the characteristics of each?
- What are the relationships between these species?

In order to classify an organism, a biologist must use a system that groups organisms according to shared characteristics and their relationships between one another. There are seven levels of classification used by biologists—kingdom, phylum, class, order, family, genus, and species.

Figure 1 The Chácabo people have a great amount of knowledge about their environment.

CONNECT TO ENVIRONMENTAL SCIENCE

Some tropical rain forests are being cut down and converted into farms to feed native populations. Scientists suspect that the forests we are losing may be pharmaceutical treasure troves. One-fifth of all the world's known plant species live in tropical rain forests. Only a small percentage of the species have been studied. These plants might be sources of medicines that can be used to treat diseases. Ask students what they think could be done to ensure that rain-forest species are preserved while food needs are also met.

Levels of Classification

Each organism is classified into one of several **kingdoms,** which are the largest, most general groups. All the organisms in a kingdom are then sorted into several *phyla* (singular, **phylum**). The members of one phylum are more like each other than they are like members of another phylum. Then all the organisms in a given phylum are further sorted into **classes.** Each class is subdivided into one or more **orders,** orders are separated into **families,** families are sorted into *genera* (singular, **genus**), and genera are sorted into **species.**

Examine **Figure 2** to follow the classification of the ordinary house cat from kingdom Animalia to species *Felis domesticus*.

Kingdom Animalia contains all the different phyla of animals.

Phylum Chordata contains animals with a hollow nerve cord.

Figure 2 *Kingdom Animalia contains all species of animals, while species* Felis domesticus *contains only one.*

Class Mammalia contains only animals that have a backbone and nurse their young.

Order Carnivora contains animals with a backbone that nurse their young and whose ancestors had special teeth for tearing meat.

Family Felidae contains animals with a backbone that nurse their young, have well-developed claws and special teeth for tearing meat, and are cats.

Genus *Felis* contains animals that have characteristics of the previous classifications, but they can't roar; they can only purr.

Species *Felis domesticus* contains only one kind of animal, the common house cat. It has characteristics of all the levels above it, but it has other unique characteristics.

Activity

A mnemonic device is a tool to help you remember something. One way to remember the levels of classification is to use a mnemonic device like this sentence:
King **P**hillip **C**ame **O**ver **F**or **G**rape **S**oda.
Invent your own mnemonic device for the levels of classification using words that are meaningful to you.

TRY at HOME

IS THAT A FACT!

The term *dinosaur* wasn't coined until the nineteenth century. Until then, as dinosaur bones were uncovered all over the world, the most widely accepted view was that they belonged to dragons.

Teaching Transparency 34
"Levels of Classification"

Science Skills Worksheet 6
"Boosting Your Memory"

2 Teach

MEETING INDIVIDUAL NEEDS

Learners Having Difficulty To help students understand what constitutes a species, genus, family, order, class, phylum, and kingdom, ask them the following questions:

What does a species contain? (organisms that have the same characteristics)

What does a genus contain? (similar species)

What does a family contain? (similar genera)

What does an order contain? (similar families)

What does a class contain? (similar orders)

What does a phylum contain? (similar classes)

What does a kingdom contain? (similar phyla) **Sheltered English**

USING THE FIGURE

Concept Mapping Refer students to **Figure 2**. Have them answer these questions to enhance their understanding of the sorting process used to classify the common house cat. What animals are pictured at the kingdom level? (lion, bird, human, bear, lynx, house cat, worm, whale)

Which of these pictured animals do not fit the description of a chordate? (the worm)

Which of the animals pictured at the chordate level do not fit the description of a mammal? (the bird)

Continue this questioning pattern for the remaining levels of classification. Have students put the information expressed in the diagram into a concept map.

Section 1 • Classification: Sorting It All Out **203**

2 Teach, continued

ACTIVITY

Evolutionary Diagrams Fossils show that one difference between ancestral genera of the modern horse, *Equus*, is the number of toes:

Eohippus (55 mya*) 4 toes
Mesohippus (35 mya) 3 toes
Merychippus (26 mya) 1 large toe, 2 small toes
Pliohippus (3 mya) 1 large toe surrounded by a hoof
Equus (modern) 1 large toe, more broad and flat, surrounded by a hoof

(*mya = million years ago)

Have students use this information to construct their own evolutionary diagram. Use the diagram on this page as a model.

Shape Island

MATH and MORE

Give students the following information:

There are more than 700,000 known species of insects in the world. The number of insect species accounts for about half of all known species. Have students calculate the approximate total number of Earth's known species. (over 1.4 million)

Math Skills Worksheet 4
"A Shortcut for Multiplying Large Numbers"

Teaching Transparency 35
"Evolutionary Relationships Among Four Mammals"

What Is the Basis for Classification?

Carolus Linnaeus (lin AY uhs), pictured in **Figure 3**, was a Swedish physician and botanist who lived in the 1700s. Linnaeus founded **taxonomy**, the science of identifying, classifying, and naming living things.

Linnaeus attempted to classify all known organisms only by their shared characteristics. Later, scientists began to recognize that evolutionary changes form a line of descent from a common ancestor. Taxonomy changed to include these new ideas about evolutionary relationships.

Modern Classification Today's taxonomists still classify organisms based on presumed evolutionary relationships. Species with a recent common ancestor can be classified together. For example, the platypus, brown bear, lion, and house cat are related because they are thought to have an ancestor in common—an ancient mammal. Because of this relationship, all four animals are grouped into the same class—Mammalia.

A brown bear, lion, and house cat are more closely related to each other than to the platypus. They are all mammals, but only the platypus lays eggs. Brown bears, lions, and house cats share a different common ancestor—an ancient carnivore. Thus, they are classified into the same order—Carnivora.

Figure 3 Carolus Linnaeus classified more than 7,000 species of plants.

Branching Diagrams The close evolutionary relationship between lions and house cats is shown by the branching diagram in **Figure 4**. The characteristics listed on the arrow pointing to the right are the characteristics that make the next animal unique. The house cat and the platypus share the characteristics of hair and mammary glands. But they are different in many ways. The branch that leads to lions is closest to the branch that leads to house cats. The lion and the house cat are closely related because they share the most recent common ancestor—an ancient cat.

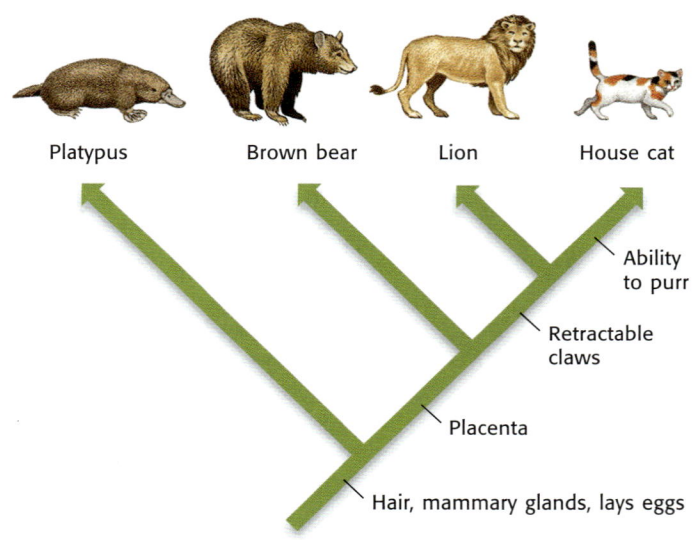

Figure 4 This branching diagram shows the evolutionary relationships between four mammals.

SCIENTISTS AT ODDS

Chinese paleontologists have found a 121-million-year-old fossil of a dinosaur that appeared to have feathers. This, say some scientists, is further proof that birds evolved directly from dinosaurs. Other scientists refute that hypothesis because of the lack of a relationship between dinosaurs' fossilized "finger" bones and the corresponding bones in bird embryos. Additional studies by zoologists dispute the bird-dinosaur connection with comparisons of the respiratory structures of modern birds, mammals, and crocodiles and those of early bird fossils and theropod dinosaurs.

Naming Names

By classifying organisms, biologists are also able to give them scientific names. A scientific name is always the same for a specific organism no matter how many common names it might have.

Before Linnaeus's time, scholars used Latin names up to 12 words long to identify species. Linnaeus simplified the naming of organisms by giving each species a two-part scientific name. The first part of the name identifies the genus, and the second part identifies the species. The scientific name for the Indian elephant, for example, is *Elephas maximus*. No other species has this name, and all scientists know that *Elephas maximus* refers to the Indian elephant.

It's All Greek (or Latin) to Me Scientific names might seem difficult to understand because they are in Latin or Greek. Most scientific names, however, are actually full of meaning. Take a look at **Figure 5**. You probably already know this animal's scientific name. It's *Tyrannosaurus rex*! The first word is a combination of two Greek words meaning "tyrant lizard," and the second word is Latin for "king." The genus name always begins with a capital letter, and the species name begins with a lowercase letter. Both words are underlined or italicized. You may have heard *Tyrannosaurus rex* called *T. rex*. This is acceptable in science as long as the genus name is spelled out the first time it is used. The species name is incomplete without the genus name or its abbreviation.

Come aboard the starship USS *Adventure*! Turn to page 718 in your LabBook.

Evolutionary Diagrams

A branching evolutionary diagram can be used to show evolutionary relationships between different organisms.

Construct a diagram similar to the one on page 204. Use a frog, a snake, a kangaroo, and a rabbit. What do you think is one major evolutionary change between one organism and the next? Write them on your diagram.

Voyage of the USS Adventure

PG 718

Answer to QuickLab

BRAIN FOOD

Have students consider the importance of classification to human thought. Ask students to try to think of something that cannot be classified in some way. Suggest that they test any item or concept they come up with by placing it in the following sentence:

(A) _____ is a type of _____.

For example, if the word is *speech*, the sentence could be filled in as follows:

<u>Speech</u> is a type of <u>communication</u>.

You may wish to hold a contest or have students share their examples in class.

Figure 5
You would never call *Tyrannosaurus rex* just *rex*!

IS THAT A FACT!

If you put all the insects in the world together, they would weigh more than all the people and the rest of the animals combined.

TOPIC: The Basis for Classification
GO TO: www.scilinks.org
*sci*LINKS NUMBER: HSTL205

Section 1 • Classification: Sorting It All Out

3 Extend

GROUP ACTIVITY
Have small groups of students work together to create an identification key that would identify common mammals in your area.

Point out to students that some of the common names we have for animals came from other languages. For example, *burro* came from Spanish, *grebe* came from French, *macaw* came from Portuguese, and *orangutan* came from Malay. Encourage interested students to look in a dictionary for the language source of other common animal names.

RETEACHING
Display a picture of a bird whose common name is not well-known to your students. Without providing any additional information about the bird, ask them to give the bird a name. Then list all the given names on the chalkboard. Help students understand that scientists around the world would have difficulty sharing information about the bird if they used more than one name for it. **Sheltered English**

---

internet**connect**

SC**LINKS**
NSTA

TOPIC: Levels of Classification
GO TO: www.scilinks.org
*sci*LINKS NUMBER: HSTL210

TOPIC: Dichotomous Keys
GO TO: www.scilinks.org
*sci*LINKS NUMBER: HSTL215

Why Are Scientific Names So Important? Examine the cartoon in **Figure 6**. What name do you have for the small black and white and sometimes smelly animal pictured? The skunk is called by several common names in English and has even more names—at least one name in every language! All of these common names can cause quite a bit of confusion for biologists who want to discuss the skunk. Biologists from different parts of the world who are interested in skunks need to know that they are all talking about the same animal, so they use its scientific name, *Mephitis mephitis*. All known living things have a two-part scientific name.

Figure 6 Using an organism's two-part scientific name is a sure way for scientists to know they are discussing the same organism.

When and where did the first bird live? Find out about the debate on page 218.

Dichotomous Keys
Taxonomists have developed special guides known as **dichotomous keys** to aid in identifying unknown organisms. A dichotomous key consists of several pairs of descriptive statements that have only two alternative responses. From each pair of statements, the person trying to identify the unknown organism chooses the appropriate statement. From there, the person is directed to another pair of statements. By working through the statements in the key, the person can eventually identify the organism. Using the simple dichotomous key on the next page, try to identify the two animals shown.

206

WEIRD SCIENCE
It's exciting when scientists find new species of plants or insects that have gone unnoticed, but it is rare when scientists find a new mammal. Between 1992 and 1998, scientists in Vietnam discovered three new species of deerlike mammals. The most recent was discovered in August 1997. This newly discovered mammal, the Truong Son muntjac, is about one-third of a meter (14 in.) tall, weighs 15.5 kg (34 lb), has a black coat and very short antlers, and barks like a dog. These mammals stay well hidden in the thick Vietnamese forest. The two other mammal species discovered recently are the Vu Quang ox and the giant muntjac.

Dichotomous Key to 10 Common Mammals in the Eastern United States

1. **a.** This mammal flies. Its hand is formed into a wing. — **Little brown bat**
   b. This mammal does not fly. — Go to step 2

2. **a.** This mammal has a naked (no fur) tail. — Go to step 3
   b. This mammal doesn't have a naked tail. — Go to step 4

3. **a.** This mammal has a short, naked tail. — **Eastern mole**
   b. This mammal has a long, naked tail. — Go to step 5

4. **a.** This mammal has a black mask across its face. — **Raccoon**
   b. This mammal does not have a black mask across its face. — Go to step 6

5. **a.** This mammal has a tail that is flattened and shaped like a paddle. — **Beaver**
   b. This mammal has a tail that is not flattened or shaped like a paddle. — **Opossum**

6. **a.** This mammal is brown with a white underbelly. — Go to step 7
   b. This mammal is not brown with a white underbelly. — Go to step 8

7. **a.** This mammal has a long, furry tail that is black on the tip. — **Longtail weasel**
   b. This mammal has a long tail without much fur. — **White-footed mouse**

8. **a.** This mammal is black with a narrow white stripe on its forehead and broad white stripes on its back. — **Striped skunk**
   b. This mammal is not black with white stripes. — Go to step 9

9. **a.** This mammal has long ears and a short, cottony tail. — **Eastern cottontail**
   b. This mammal has short ears and a medium-length tail. — **Woodchuck**

REVIEW

1. Why do scientists use scientific names for organisms?
2. Explain the two parts of a scientific name.
3. List the seven levels of classification.
4. Describe how a dichotomous key helps to identify unknown organisms.
5. **Interpreting Illustrations** Study the figure at right. Which plant is the closest relative of the hibiscus? Which plant is most distantly related to the hibiscus? Which plants have seeds?

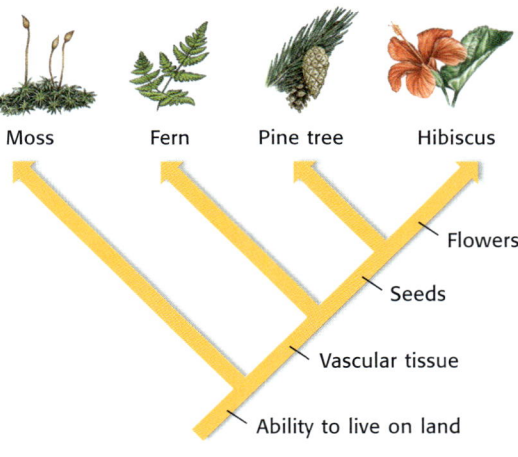

Moss — Fern — Pine tree — Hibiscus
Flowers
Seeds
Vascular tissue
Ability to live on land

4) Close

Quiz

1. Why do scientists classify animals? (to facilitate studying them)
2. What was the basis for classification systems in the past? (shared characteristics)
3. What is the basis of modern classification systems? (evolutionary relationships)

ALTERNATIVE ASSESSMENT

 Have students create a cartoon that shows how using different common names for an animal instead of its scientific name creates confusion. Students must include authentic common names and scientific names in their cartoon. Sheltered English

Answer to Dichotomous Key

Mammal on the top left:
1b, 2b, 4b, 6a, 7a, longtail weasel

Mammal on the top right:
1b, 2b, 4b, 6b, 8b, 9b, woodchuck

 Teaching Transparency 35
"Evolutionary Relationships Among Four Plants"

 Teaching Transparency 36
"Dichotomous Key to 10 Common Mammals in the Eastern United States"

 Problem Solving Worksheet 9
"A Breach on Planet Biome"

Answers to Review

1. Scientists use scientific names for organisms to be clear and precise.
2. genus and species; The genus is a broader classification, and the species name is more specific and is often given by the species' discoverer.
3. Kingdom, Phylum, Class, Order, Family, Genus, Species
4. A dichotomous key is organized into a series of pairs of questions. By working through the statements in the key, unknown organisms can be identified.
5. pine tree; moss; pine tree and hibiscus

SECTION 2

Focus

The Six Kingdoms

This section explains how improved understanding of organisms leads to revisions in our system of biological classification. Students are introduced to the six kingdoms: Archaebacteria, Eubacteria, Protista, Plantae, Fungi, and Animalia. They learn how organisms belonging in each kingdom are distinguished.

Bellringer

Have students list seven musical artists, bands, or acts. Have them categorize the names on their lists by style of music. Ask them to describe in their ScienceLog the categories they chose and also explain which bands might fit into more than one category.

1) Motivate

DISCUSSION

Grouping Animals Ask students how zoos group animals. (Answers may include by type, by climate preferences, and by natural habitats.)

Encourage knowledgeable students to describe the layout of zoos with which they are familiar.

Have students write letters to zoos all around the country requesting a copy of the map they issue to visitors. Students could then compare the layouts of many zoos. Be sure to have students include a stamped, self-addressed envelope with their letter describing the project.

Section 2

Terms to Learn

Archaebacteria Plantae
Eubacteria Fungi
Protista Animalia

What You'll Do

◆ Explain how classification schemes for kingdoms developed as greater numbers of different organisms became known.
◆ List the six kingdoms, and provide two characteristics of each.

Figure 7 How would you classify this organism? *Euglena*, shown here magnified 1,000 times, has characteristics of both plants and animals.

BRAIN FOOD

If *Euglena*'s chloroplasts are shaded from light or removed, it will begin to hunt for food like an animal. If the chloroplasts are shaded long enough, the chloroplasts degenerate and never come back.

The Six Kingdoms

For hundreds of years, all living things were classified as either plants or animals. These two kingdoms, Plantae and Animalia, worked just fine until organisms like the species *Euglena*, shown in **Figure 7**, were discovered. If you were a taxonomist, how would you classify such an organism?

What Is It?

As you know, organisms are classified by their characteristics. Being the excellent taxonomist that you are, you decide to list the characteristics of *Euglena*:

■ *Euglena* are a species of single-celled organisms that live in pond water.

■ *Euglena* are green and, like most plants, can make their own food through photosynthesis.

"This is easy!" you think to yourself. "*Euglena* are plants." Not so fast! There are other important characteristics to consider:

■ *Euglena* can move about from place to place by whipping their "tails," called flagella.

■ Sometimes *Euglena* use food obtained from other organisms.

Plants don't move around and usually do not eat other organisms. Does this mean that *Euglena* are animals? As you can see, neither category seems to fit. Scientists ran into the same problem, so they decided to add another kingdom for classifying organisms such as *Euglena*. This kingdom is known as Protista.

More Kingdoms As scientists continued to learn more about living things, they added kingdoms in order to account for the differences and similarities between organisms. Currently, most scientists agree that the six-kingdom classification system works best. There is still some disagreement, however, and still more to be learned. In the following pages, you will learn more about each of the kingdoms.

CONNECT TO ENVIRONMENTAL SCIENCE

Recently, signs of salmonella infection were found in the droppings of an Antarctic gentoo penguin. The bacteria were most likely introduced from outside the Antarctic. The bacterium, *Salmonella enteritidis*, is not endemic to penguins. Scientists think that sewage dumped from passing ships or visiting albatrosses that feed on waste-contaminated squid in the oceans surrounding South America might be the sources of the bacteria. The bacteria could become infectious and pathogenic and kill the penguin chicks.

208 Chapter 9 • Classification

The Two Kingdoms of Bacteria

Bacteria are extremely small single-celled organisms. Bacteria are different from all other living things in that they are *prokaryotes*, organisms that do not have nuclei. Many biologists divide bacteria into two kingdoms, **Archaebacteria** (AHR kee bak TEER ee uh) and **Eubacteria** (YOO bak TEER ee uh).

Archaebacteria have been on Earth at least 3 billion years. The prefix *archae* comes from a Greek word meaning "ancient." Today you can find archaebacteria living in places where most organisms could not survive. **Figure 8** shows a hot spring in Yellowstone National Park. The yellow and orange rings around the edge of the hot spring are formed by the billions of archaebacteria that live there.

Most of the other thousands of kinds of bacteria are eubacteria. These microscopic organisms live in the soil, in water, and even on and inside the human body! For example, the eubacterium *Escherichia coli*, pictured in **Figure 9,** is present in great numbers in human intestines, where it produces vitamin K. Another kind of eubacterium converts milk to yogurt, and yet another species causes ear and sinus infections and pneumonia.

Figure 8 *The Grand Prismatic Spring, in Yellowstone National Park, contains water that is about 90°C (194°F). The spring is home to archaebacteria that thrive in its hot water.*

Figure 9 *E. coli, shown on the point of a pin, are seen with a scanning electron microscope. These eubacteria live in the intestines of animals, where they decompose undigested food.*

Homework

Researching Sanitation Have students research and write reports on measures that protect against harmful bacteria. How can bacteria be killed? How can bacteria be prevented from growing on living tissues? When harmful bacteria get inside the body, how does the body defend itself?

TOPIC: The Six Kingdoms
GO TO: www.scilinks.org
sciLINKS NUMBER: HSTL220

② Teach

REAL-WORLD CONNECTION
People in China, Japan, and other Asian countries have been practicing mariculture for thousands of years. Seaweed, shrimp, and mussels are commonly grown and harvested for food. In western countries, mariculture has experienced steady growth since the 1960s. Farmers grow kelp, fish, and shellfish for food in special farms near ocean shores or in ponds.

Answers to Self-Check
1. The two kingdoms of bacteria are different from all other kingdoms because bacteria are prokaryotes—single-celled organisms that have no nucleus.
2. The organisms in the kingdom Protista are all eukaryotes.

Homework

Writing — Researching Protists
Have students research the protists shown in the pictures in **Figures 10, 11,** and **12** (*Paramecium*, slime mold, and giant kelp, respectively). Have them write descriptions about each of the protists, including information about its size, form, method of obtaining nutrients, method of reproduction, and in the case of the giant kelp, its commercial uses.

Figure 10 *Paramecium* usually moves about rapidly.

Figure 11 A slime mold spreads over a fallen log on the forest floor.

Figure 12 This giant kelp is a multicellular protist.

Kingdom Protista
Members of the kingdom **Protista,** commonly called protists, are single-celled or simple multicellular organisms. Unlike bacteria, protists are *eukaryotes,* organisms that have cells with a nucleus and membrane-bound organelles. Kingdom Protista contains all eukaryotes that are not plants, animals, or fungi. Scientists think the first protists evolved from ancient bacteria about 2 billion years ago. Much later, protists gave rise to plants, fungi, and animals as well as to modern protists.

As you can see, kingdom Protista contains many different kinds of organisms. Protists include protozoa, which are animal-like protists; algae, which are plantlike protists; and slime molds and water molds, which are funguslike protists. *Euglena,* which were discussed earlier, are also members of kingdom Protista, as are the *Paramecium* and the slime mold pictured in **Figures 10** and **11.** Most protists are single-celled organisms, but some are multicellular, such as the giant kelp shown in **Figure 12.**

✓ Self-Check
1. How are the two kingdoms of bacteria different from all other kingdoms?
2. How would you distinguish Protista from the two kingdoms of bacteria?

(See page 782 to check your answers.)

SCIENTISTS AT ODDS
Is a slime mold a fungus? They were traditionally classified as Fungi because despite other differences they exhibit a similar life cycle, including the formation of spores on sporangia. But critics point out that some bacteria (myxobacteria) do this also, and those organisms are not reclassified as Fungi.

IS THAT A FACT!
Farmers on the Orkney Islands of Scotland have historically used seaweed as fertilizer and food for their sheep.

Kingdom Plantae

Although plants vary remarkably in size and form, most people easily recognize the members of kingdom **Plantae**. Plants are complex multicellular organisms that are usually green and use the sun's energy to make sugar by a process called *photosynthesis*. The giant sequoias and flowering plants shown in **Figures 13** and **14** are examples of the different organisms classified in the kingdom Plantae.

MATH BREAK

Building a Human Chain Around a Giant Sequoia

How many students would it take to join hands and form a human chain around a giant sequoia that is 30 m in circumference? Assume for this calculation that the average student can extend his or her arms about 1.3 m. NOTE: You can't have a fraction of a student, so be sure to round up your answer to the nearest whole number.

Environment CONNECTION

Giant sequoia trees are very rare. They grow only in California and are a protected species. Some of them are over 3,000 years old.

Figure 13 *A giant sequoia can measure 30 m around its base and can grow to more than 91.5 m tall.*

Figure 14 *Plants such as these are common in the rain forest.*

Multicultural CONNECTION

The name sequoia comes from *Sequoya*, the name of a Cherokee who is credited with developing the Cherokee written language during the 1820s.

3) Extend

GOING FURTHER

Writing Tell students that Pennsylvania, which has many caves, is one of the major mushroom-growing regions of the United States. Caves are ideal places in which to grow some kinds of mushrooms. Ask students to research and write a report on mushroom farming in the United States. What kinds of mushrooms are grown commercially, and what special conditions does each species require? Inexpensive kits are available for growing mushrooms, and interested students might enjoy the experience of raising their own.

RESEARCH

 Students can research members of the six kingdoms that are prevalent in your immediate area. They can draw pictures of the organisms accompanied by descriptive paragraphs.

Answers to APPLY

Students are likely to think this plant is a fungus related to mushrooms because of its color and texture, but it is a plant. They will probably suggest that they need to know how it makes food because it obviously is not a green plant with leaves. Indian pipe, or *Monotropa uniflora*, is actually a wildflower member of the wintergreen family. It is a saprophyte living on the decayed roots of other plants. It gets all of its nutrients from other plants and needs neither leaves nor chlorophyll.

Kingdom Fungi

Molds and mushrooms are examples of the complex multicellular members of the kingdom **Fungi**. Fungi (singular, *fungus*) were originally classified as plants, but fungi do not obtain nutrients by photosynthesis. Moreover, fungi do not have many animal characteristics. Because of their unusual combination of characteristics, fungi are classified in a separate kingdom.

Fungi do not perform photosynthesis, as plants do, and they do not eat food, as animals do. Instead, fungi absorb nutrients from their surroundings after breaking them down with digestive juices. **Figure 15** shows a pretty but deadly mushroom, and **Figure 16** shows black bread mold (a fungus) growing on a piece of bread. Have you ever seen this type of mold on bread?

Figure 15 *This beautiful mushroom of the genus* Amanita *is poisonous.*

Figure 16 *This black bread mold can be dangerous if you inhale the spores. Some molds are dangerous, and others produce life-saving antibiotics.*

Classify This!

You and a friend are walking through the forest and you come upon the organism shown at right. You think it is a plant, but you are not sure. It has a flower and seeds, very small leaves, and roots that are growing into a rotting log. But this organism is white from its roots to its petals. To which kingdom do you think this organism belongs? What characteristic is your answer based on? What additional information would you need in order to give a more accurate answer?

IS THAT A FACT!

About 3,000 mushroom species grow in North America. Worldwide, about 70–80 species are poisonous.

Kingdom Animalia

Animals are complex multicellular organisms that belong to the kingdom **Animalia.** Most animals can move about from place to place and have nervous systems that help them sense and react to their surroundings. At the microscopic level, animal cells differ from those of fungi, plants, most protists, and bacteria because animal cells lack cell walls. **Figure 17** shows some members of the kingdom Animalia.

Figure 17 The kingdom Animalia contains many different organisms, such as eagles, tortoises, beetles, and dolphins.

REVIEW

1. Name the six kingdoms.
2. Which of the six kingdoms include prokaryotes, and which include eukaryotes?
3. Explain the different ways plants, fungi, and animals obtain nutrients.
4. Why are protists placed in their own kingdom?
5. **Applying Concepts** To which kingdom do humans belong? What characteristics place humans in this kingdom?

internetconnect

TOPIC: The Basis for Classification, The Six Kingdoms
GO TO: www.scilinks.org
sciLINKS NUMBER: HSTL205, HSTL220

Answers to Review

1. Plantae, Animalia, Protista, Eubacteria, Archaebacteria, Fungi
2. Eubacteria and Archaebacteria contain the prokaryotes. Plantae, Animalia, Protista, and Fungi are all eukaryotes.
3. Plants make food in their tissues from CO_2, water, and the energy in sunlight. Fungi absorb nutrients from their surroundings after breaking them down with digestive juices. Animals eat plants and other animals to obtain food.
4. Protists are organisms that don't fit in the other kingdoms.
5. Animalia; we move, have a nervous system, and lack cell walls.

Chapter Highlights

VOCABULARY DEFINITIONS

SECTION 1

classification the arrangement of organisms into orderly groups based on their similarities and presumed evolutionary relationships

kingdom the most general of the seven levels of classification

phylum the level of classification after kingdom; the organisms from all the kingdoms are sorted into several phyla

class the level of classification after phylum; the organisms in all phyla are sorted into classes

order the level of classification after class; the organisms in all the classes are sorted into orders

family the level of classification after order; the organisms in all orders are sorted into families

genus the level of classification after family; the organisms in all families are sorted into genera

species the most specific of the seven levels of classification; characterized by a group of organisms that can mate with one another to produce fertile offspring

taxonomy the science of identifying, classifying, and naming living things

dichotomous key an aid to identifying unknown organisms that consists of several pairs of descriptive statements; of each pair of statements, only one will apply to the unknown organism, and that will lead to another set of statements, and so on, until the unknown organism can be identified

Chapter Highlights

SECTION 1

Vocabulary
classification (p. 202)
kingdom (p. 203)
phylum (p. 203)
class (p. 203)
order (p. 203)
family (p. 203)
genus (p. 203)
species (p. 203)
taxonomy (p. 204)
dichotomous key (p. 206)

Section Notes
- Classification refers to the arrangement of organisms into orderly groups based on their similarities and evolutionary relationships.
- Biologists classify organisms in order to organize the number and diversity of living things and to give them scientific names.
- The classification scheme used today is based on the work of Carolus Linnaeus. Linnaeus founded the science of taxonomy, in which organisms are described, named, and classified.
- Modern classification schemes include evolutionary relationships.
- Today organisms are classified using a seven-level system of organization. The seven levels are kingdom, phylum, class, order, family, genus, and species. The genus and species of an organism compose its two-part scientific name.
- A scientific name is always the same for a specific organism, no matter how many common names it has.
- Dichotomous keys help to identify organisms.

Labs
Shape Island (p. 716)
Voyage of the USS Adventure (p. 718)

✓ Skills Check

Math Concepts
LARGE ORGANISMS The rounding-off rule states: If the number you wish to round is greater than or equal to the midpoint, round the number to the next greater number.

Sometimes when you are working with objects instead of numbers, you have to use a different rule! The MathBreak on page 211 asks you to round up your answer even though the answer includes a fraction that is less than halfway to the next number. Why is that? The answer is that if you don't round up, you won't have enough students to encircle the tree.

Visual Understanding
LEVELS OF CLASSIFICATION If you are still a little unsure about how organisms are grouped into levels of classification, turn back to page 203. Review Figure 2. Notice that the broadest, most inclusive level is kingdom. For example, all animals are grouped into kingdom Animalia. From there, the groups become more and more specific until only one animal is included under the level of species. Working from species up, notice that more and more animals are included in the group as you move toward the level of kingdom.

Lab and Activity Highlights

Shape Island PG 716

Voyage of the USS Adventure PG 718

 Datasheets for LabBook (blackline masters for these labs)

SECTION 2

Vocabulary
Archaebacteria (p. 209)
Eubacteria (p. 209)
Protista (p. 210)
Plantae (p. 211)
Fungi (p. 212)
Animalia (p. 213)

Section Notes
- At first, living things were classified as either plants or animals. As scientists discovered more about living things and discovered more organisms, new kingdoms were added that were more descriptive than the old two-kingdom system.

- Most biologists recognize six kingdoms—Archaebacteria, Eubacteria, Protista, Plantae, Fungi, and Animalia.

- Bacteria are prokaryotes, single-celled organisms that do not contain nuclei. The organisms of all other kingdoms are eukaryotes, organisms that have cells with nuclei.

- Archaebacteria have been on Earth for about 3 billion years and can live where most other organisms cannot survive.

- Most bacteria are eubacteria and live almost everywhere. Some are harmful, and some are beneficial.

- Plants, most fungi, and animals are complex multicellular organisms. Plants perform photosynthesis. Fungi break down material outside their body and then absorb the nutrients. Animals eat food, which is digested inside their body.

VOCABULARY DEFINITIONS, continued

SECTION 2

Archaebacteria a classification kingdom that contains ancient bacteria that thrive in extreme environments

Eubacteria a classification kingdom containing mostly free-living bacteria found in many varied environments

Protista a kingdom of eukaryotic single-celled or simple, multicellular organisms; kingdom Protista contains all eukaryotes that are not plants, animals, or fungi

Plantae the kingdom that contains plants—complex, multicellular organisms that are usually green and use the sun's energy to make sugar by photosynthesis

Fungi a kingdom of complex organisms that obtain food by breaking down other substances in their surroundings and absorbing the nutrients

Animalia the classification kingdom containing complex, multicellular organisms that lack cell walls, are usually able to move about, and possess nervous systems that help them be aware of and react to their surroundings

internetconnect

GO TO: go.hrw.com

Visit the **HRW** Web site for a variety of learning tools related to this chapter. Just type in the keyword:

KEYWORD: HSTCLS

GO TO: www.scilinks.org

Visit the **National Science Teachers Association** on-line Web site for Internet resources related to this chapter. Just type in the *sci*LINKS number for more information about the topic:

TOPIC: The Basis for Classification   *sci*LINKS NUMBER: HSTL205
TOPIC: Levels of Classification   *sci*LINKS NUMBER: HSTL210
TOPIC: Dichotomous Keys   *sci*LINKS NUMBER: HSTL215
TOPIC: The Six Kingdoms   *sci*LINKS NUMBER: HSTL220

 Vocabulary Review Worksheet 9

 Blackline masters of these Chapter Highlights can be found in the **Study Guide.**

Lab and Activity Highlights

LabBank

 EcoLabs & Field Activities, Water Wigglers, Field Activity 1

 Long-Term Projects & Research Ideas, The Panda Mystery, Project 9

Chapter 9 • Chapter Highlights   **215**

Chapter Review

USING VOCABULARY

To complete the following sentences, choose the correct term from each pair of terms listed below:

1. Linnaeus founded the science of __?__. (*DNA analysis* or *taxonomy*)

2. All of the organisms classified into a single kingdom are then divided into one of several __?__. (*phyla* or *classes*)

3. The narrowest level of classification is the __?__. (*genus* or *species*)

4. Linnaeus began naming organisms using __?__. (*two-part scientific names* or *evolutionary relationships*)

5. Archaebacteria and eubacteria are __?__. (*prokaryotes* or *eukaryotes*)

UNDERSTANDING CONCEPTS

Multiple Choice

6. When scientists classify organisms, they
   a. arrange them in orderly groups.
   b. give them many common names.
   c. decide whether they are useful.
   d. ignore evolutionary relationships.

7. When the seven levels of classification are listed from broadest to narrowest, which level is in the fifth position?
   a. class
   b. order
   c. genus
   d. family

8. The scientific name for the European white water lily is *Nymphaea alba*. What is the genus to which this plant belongs?
   a. *Nymphaea*
   b. *alba*
   c. water lily
   d. alba lily

9. "Kings Play Chess On Fine-Grained Sand" is a mnemonic device that helps one remember
   a. the scientific names of different organisms.
   b. the six kingdoms.
   c. the seven levels of classification.
   d. the difference between prokaryotic and eukaryotic cells.

10. Most bacteria are classified in which kingdom?
    a. Archaebacteria
    b. Eubacteria
    c. Protista
    d. Fungi

11. What kind of organism thrives in hot springs and other extreme environments?
    a. archaebacteria
    b. eubacteria
    c. protists
    d. fungi

Short Answer

12. Why is the use of scientific names so important in biology?

13. List two kinds of evidence used by modern taxonomists to classify organisms based on evolutionary relationships.

14. Is a eubacterium a type of eukaryote? Explain your answer.

Concept Map

15. Use the following terms to create a concept map: kingdom, fern, lizard, Animalia, Fungi, algae, Protista, Plantae, mushroom.

CRITICAL THINKING AND PROBLEM SOLVING

Write one or two sentences to answer the following questions:

16. How are the levels of classification related to evolutionary relationships among organisms?

17. Explain why two species that belong to the same genus, such as white oak *(Quercus alba)* and cork oak *(Quercus suber)*, also belong to the same family.

18. What characteristic do the members of all six kingdoms have in common?

MATH IN SCIENCE

19. Scientists estimate that millions of species are yet to be discovered and classified. If only 1.5 million, or 10 percent, of species have been discovered and classified, how many species do scientists think exist on Earth?

20. Sequoia trees can grow to more than 90 m in height. There are 3.28 ft per meter. How many feet are in 90 m?

INTERPRETING GRAPHICS

The diagram below illustrates the evolutionary relationships among several primates.

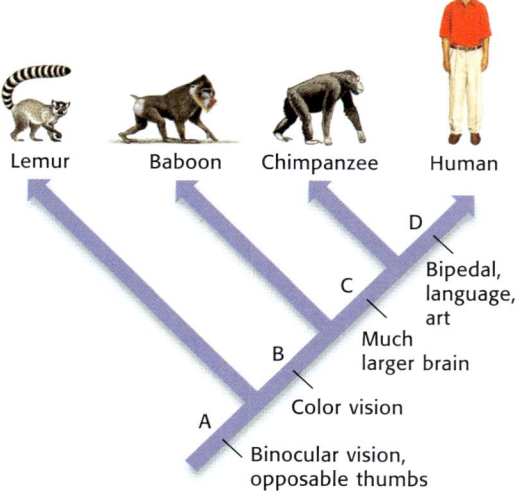

21. Which primate is the closest relative to the common ancestor of all primates?

22. Which primate shares the most traits with humans?

23. Do lemurs share the characteristics listed at point D with humans? Explain your answer.

24. What characteristic do baboons have that lemurs do not have? Explain your answer.

Take a minute to review your answers to the Pre-Reading Questions found at the bottom of page 200. Have your answers changed? If necessary, revise your answers based on what you have learned since you began this chapter.

Concept Mapping

15. An answer to this exercise can be found at the end of this book.

CRITICAL THINKING AND PROBLEM SOLVING

16. Each level of classification groups organisms according to characteristics they share. Starting at the kingdom level, each level contains fewer organisms with characteristics in common until there is only one species at the species level.

17. The family level of classification contains genuses and all the species in those genuses. All of the *Quercus* genera are in the same family because of shared characteristics.

18. All members of all six kingdoms are or once were living organisms. All living things share a common ancestor. They also have the genetic code in common, which means they all have DNA.

MATH IN SCIENCE

19. 15 million; Some scientists think that there may be as many as 15 million species on Earth today, most of which are undiscovered and unnamed.

20. 295.2 ft

INTERPRETING GRAPHICS

21. lemur
22. chimpanzee
23. No; lemurs branched off between points A and B.
24. Color vision; color vision appears on the diagram after lemurs have branched off.

 Concept Mapping Transparency 9

 Blackline masters of this Chapter Review can be found in the **Study Guide.**

SCIENTIFIC DEBATE

It's a Bird, It's a Plane, It's a *Dinosaur*?

Background

Scientists have identified many physical traits of birds that appear similar to those of dinosaurs. For example, some dinosaur skeletons contain a birdlike wishbone. Also, the two-legged upright stance of certain dinosaurs suggests that they were endothermic (birds are endothermic). All ectothermic animals are "sprawlers," meaning that they move around on all four feet.

The *Sinosauropteryx* found in northern China was first thought to support the birds-from-dinosaurs hypothesis because the fossil has featherlike features. But other paleontologists contend that rather than feathers, the structures are bristly fibers of collagen. Still other scientists believe these "feathers" are made of the same material as modern feathers but lack the organization of true feathers.

A 1997 find in Argentina gives some support to the proponents of the birds-from-dinosaurs hypothesis. A 6 ft long fossil found in Argentina shows the most birdlike dinosaur ever discovered. Its skeletal structure indicates it had arms that could flap and fold like wings. It had a birdlike pelvis as well. The sediments the dinosaur was found in suggest it is 90 million years old. But this fossil, too, has fueled the debate. Some experts say the dinosaur existed long after the development of modern birds. Birds, they argue, evolved from another line of reptiles.

SCIENTIFIC DEBATE

It's a Bird, It's a Plane, It's a *Dinosaur*?

Think about birds. Parrots, pigeons, buzzards, emus . . . they're everywhere! But once there were no birds. So where did they come from? When did birds evolve? Was it 225 million years ago, just 115 million years ago, or somewhere in between? No one really knows for sure, but the topic has fueled a long-standing debate among scientists.

The debate began when the fossil remains of a 150-million-year-old dinosaur with wings and feathers—*Archaeopteryx*—were found in Germany in 1860 and 1861.

▲ *Archaeopteryx was the first true bird.*

Birds Are Dinosaurs!

Some scientists think that birds evolved from small, carnivorous dinosaurs like *Velociraptor* about 115 million to 150 million years ago. Their idea relies on similarities between modern birds and these small dinosaurs. Particularly important are the size, shape, and number of toes and "fingers"; the location and shape of the breastbone and shoulder; the presence of a hollow bone structure; and the development of wrist bones that "flap" for flight. To many scientists, all this evidence is overwhelming. It can lead to only one conclusion: Modern birds are descendants of dinosaurs.

No They Aren't!

"Not so fast!" say a smaller but equally determined group of scientists who think that birds developed 100 million years before *Velociraptor* and its relatives. They point out that all these dinosaurs were ground dwellers and were the wrong shape and size for flying. They would never get off the ground! Further, these dinosaurs lacked at least one of the bones necessary for flight in today's birds.

This "birds came before dinosaurs" idea rests on fossils of *thecodonts*, small tree-dwelling reptiles that lived about 225 million years ago. One thecodont, a small, four-legged tree dweller called *Megalancosaurus*, had the right bones and body shape—and the right center of gravity—for flight. The evidence is clear, say these scientists, that birds flew long before dinosaurs even existed!

▲ *This small tree-dwelling reptile, Megalancosaurus, may have evolved into the birds we know today.*

So Who Is Right?

Both sides are debating fossils 65 million years to 225 million years old. Some species left many fossils, while some left just a few. In the last few years, new fossils discovered in China, Mongolia, and Argentina have just added fuel to the fire. So scientists will continue to study the available evidence and provide their educated guesses. Meanwhile, the debate rages on!

Compare for Yourself

▶ Find photographs of *Sinosauropteryx* and *Archaeopteryx* fossils, and compare them. How are they similar? How are they different? Do you think birds could be modern dinosaurs? Debate your idea with someone who holds the opposite view.

Answer to Compare for Yourself

All reasonable answers should be accepted. These are some possible responses. Similarities between *Sinosauropteryx* and *Archeopteryx* include: a reptilian skeleton, a long tail, sharp teeth, and claws of approximately the same size. The most noticeable difference between *Archeopteryx* and *Sinosauropteryx* is that *Archeopteryx* had wings and feathers and *Sinosauropteryx* had short front limbs without feathers.

WEIRD SCIENCE

LOBSTER-LIP LIFE-FORM

Have you ever stopped to think about lobsters' lips? Did you even know that lobsters have lips? Oddly enough, they do. And even stranger, scientists have found a tiny animal living on lobsters' lips. Surprised? Although scientists noticed this little critter about 30 years ago, they had never studied it closely. When they finally did, they were astounded! This tiny organism is different from anything else in the world. Meet *Symbion pandora*.

▲ Although scientists knew of *Symbion pandora's* existence for 30 years, they did not realize how unusual it was.

A Little Weird

What makes *Symbion pandora* so unusual? As if spending most of its life on lobster lips isn't strange enough, *S. pandora* also seems to combine the traits of very different animals. Here are some of its strange characteristics:

- **Life stages:** *S. pandora's* life cycle involves many different *stages,* or body forms. The stages are very different from each other. For instance, at certain times in its life, *S. pandora* can swim around, while at other times, it can exist only by attaching to a lobster's mouth.
- **Dwarf males:** Male *S. pandora* are much smaller than the females. Thus, they are called *dwarf males.*
- **Feeding habits:** Dwarf males don't eat; they can only find a female, reproduce, and then die!
- **Budding:** Many individuals are neither male nor female. These animals reproduce through a process called *budding.* In budding, a new, complete animal can sprout out of the adult. In turn, the new offspring can reproduce in the same way.
- **Disappearing guts:** When an adult starts to form a new bud, its digestive and nervous systems disappear! Part of these guts help make the new bud. Then the adult forms new digestive and nervous systems to replace the old ones.

How Unusual Is It?

When scientists discover a new plant or animal, they may conclude that it represents a new species within an existing genus. In that case scientists make up a name for the new species. Usually, the person who finds the new organism gets to name it. If the new organism is *very* unusual, scientists may place it not only in a new species but also in a new genus.

S. pandora is so unusual that it was placed not only in a new species and a new genus, but also in a new family, a new order, a new class, and even a new phylum! Such a scientific discovery is extremely rare. In fact, when this discovery was made, in 1995, it was announced in newspapers all over the world!

Where Would You Look?

▶ *S. pandora* was first noticed more than 30 years ago, but no one realized how unusual it was until scientists studied it. Scientists estimate that we've identified less than 10 percent of Earth's organisms. Find out about other new animal species that have been discovered within the last 10 years. Where are some places you would look for new species?

Answer to Where Would You Look?
Answers will vary. On page 320 of this book, students can read the story of the discovery of a barking bird.

WEIRD SCIENCE
Lobster-Lip Life-Form

Background

When *Symbion pandora* was proposed as a new species, the scientists who described it decided that it didn't fit into any existing phyla. Thus, they made up a new phylum, Cycliophora.

When someone proposes a new phylum, it usually takes some time before other scientists decide whether they agree that a new phylum designation is warranted. Even after debate, scientists often disagree. As a result, there are between 30 and 40 existing animal phyla, depending on whom you ask. Most biologists agree that there are at least 34 living phyla of animals. Before Cycliophora, no new phyla had been proposed since 1983.

The name *Symbion pandora* was deliberately chosen. *Symbion* refers to the organism's close association with lobsters. (The relationship is an example of commensalism, because *S. pandora* benefits and the lobster is largely unaffected.) *Pandora* was chosen because the bud-within-bud structure of the animal reminded the researchers of the Greek myth of Pandora's box. You may wish to have a group of students learn about this myth and share their results with the class.

Chapter 9 • Weird Science

UNIT 4

TIMELINE
Simple Organisms, Fungi, and Plants

You are probably familiar with plants. But do you know how important plants are? When plants make food for themselves, they provide oxygen and food for other living things.

Throughout history, people have been trying to understand plants, and in this unit you will join them.

You'll also learn about fascinating organisms that you may not know about—bacteria, protists, and fungi. Although many of these organisms are too small to see, they are just as important as plants. Some cause disease, but others provide food and medicines. Read on, and be amazed!

250 B.C.
Mayan farmers build terraces to control the flow of water to their crops.

1580
Prospero Alpini discovers that plants have both male and female structures.

1898
Martinus Beijerinck gives the name *virus* to infectious material that is smaller than bacteria.

1928
Alexander Fleming observes that certain molds can eliminate bacterial growth, and he discovers penicillin.

1955
Jonas Salk develops a vaccine for the polio virus.

▶ 1683
Anton van Leeuwenhoek is the first to describe bacteria.

1763
Joseph Kölreuter studies pollination in plants.

1897 ◀
Beatrix Potter, the author of *The Tale of Peter Rabbit*, completes her collection of 270 watercolors of fungi. She is now considered an expert in mycology, the study of fungi.

1864
Louis Pasteur uses heat to eliminate microbes. This process is later called pasteurization.

▶ 1983
HIV, the virus responsible for AIDS, is isolated.

▶ 1995
An outbreak of the deadly Ebola virus occurs in Zaire.

▶ 1972
Ananda Chakrabarty uses genetics to design bacteria that can break down oil in oil spills.

Simple Organisms, Fungi, and Plants

Chapter Organizer

CHAPTER ORGANIZATION	TIME MINUTES	OBJECTIVES	LABS, INVESTIGATIONS, AND DEMONSTRATIONS
Chapter Opener pp. 222–223	45	National Standards: SAI 1	**Start-Up Activity** Your Constant Companions, p. 223
Section 1 Bacteria	90	▶ Describe the characteristics of a prokaryotic cell. ▶ Explain how bacteria reproduce. ▶ Compare and contrast eubacteria and archaebacteria. UCP 1, 3, 5, SAI 1, LS 1b, 1c, 2a, 3a, 3b, 4b	**QuickLab,** Spying on Spirilla, p. 226 GENERAL **Demonstration,** Bacterial Shapes, p. 226 in ATE BASIC
Section 2 Bacteria's Role in the World	90	▶ Explain why life on Earth depends on bacteria. ▶ List five ways bacteria are useful to people. ▶ Describe why some bacteria are harmful to people. UCP 4, ST 1, SPSP 5, HNS 1, 3, LS 1f; LabBook UCP 2, 3, 5, SAI 1, LS 1c	**Design Your Own Lab,** Aunt Flossie and the Intruder, p. 720 ADVANCED **Datasheets for LabBook,** Aunt Flossie and the Intruder, Datasheet 21 ADVANCED **Ecolabs & Field Activities,** Ditch's Brew, Field Activity 2 GENERAL **Labs You Can Eat,** Bacterial Buddies, Lab 4 GENERAL **Inquiry Lab,** It's an Invasion! Lab 3 GENERAL **Interactive Explorations CD-ROM,** Scope it Out! GENERAL A **Worksheet** is also available in the **Interactive Explorations Teacher's Guide.**
Section 3 Viruses	90	▶ Explain how viruses are similar to and different from living things. ▶ List the four major virus shapes. ▶ Describe the two kinds of viral reproduction. UCP 1, SAI 1, 2, SPSP 1, 4, 5, LS 1b, 1f, 2a; LabBook UCP 2, 5	**Demonstration,** Flame Tulips, p. 233 in ATE GENERAL **Making Models,** Viral Decorations, p. 721 ADVANCED **Datasheets for LabBook,** Viral Decorations, Datasheet 22 ADVANCED **Long-Term Projects & Research Ideas,** Project 10 ADVANCED

See page T20 for a complete correlation of this book with the

NATIONAL SCIENCE EDUCATION STANDARDS.

TECHNOLOGY RESOURCES

 Guided Reading Audio CD
English or Spanish, Chapter 10

 **One-Stop Planner CD-ROM with Test Generator**

 Science, Technology, & Society, Fingerprinting *E. coli*, Segment 15

 Interactive Explorations CD-ROM
CD 1, Exploration 3, Scope It Out!

Chapter 10 • Bacteria and Viruses

CLASSROOM WORKSHEETS, TRANSPARENCIES, AND RESOURCES	SCIENCE INTEGRATION AND CONNECTIONS	REVIEW AND ASSESSMENT
Directed Reading Worksheet 10 `BASIC` **Science Puzzlers, Twisters & Teasers,** Worksheet 10 `ADVANCED`		
Directed Reading Worksheet 10, Section 1 `BASIC` **Transparency 37,** Bacterial Reproduction: Binary Fission **Transparency 38,** The Most Common Shapes of Bacteria **Reinforcement Worksheet 10,** Bacteria Bonanza `GENERAL`	**MathBreak,** Airborne Organisms, p. 224 `GENERAL` **Math and More,** p. 225 in ATE `GENERAL` **Connect to Physical Science,** p. 225 in ATE `GENERAL`	**Homework,** p. 226 in ATE `ADVANCED` **Homework,** p. 227 in ATE `GENERAL` **Self-Check,** p. 227 **Review,** p. 228 `GENERAL` **Quiz,** p. 228 in ATE `GENERAL` **Alternative Assessment,** p. 228 in ATE `GENERAL`
Directed Reading Worksheet 10, Section 2 `BASIC` **Critical Thinking Worksheet 10,** Bacterial Blastoff `ADVANCED`	**Real-World Connection,** p. 230 in ATE **Multicultural Connection,** p. 230 in ATE **Apply,** p. 231 `GENERAL`	**Homework,** p. 231 in ATE `ADVANCED` **Review,** p. 232 `GENERAL` **Quiz,** p. 232 in ATE `GENERAL` **Alternative Assessment,** p. 232 in ATE `BASIC`
Directed Reading Worksheet 10, Section 3 `BASIC` **Transparency 107,** Gold Crystal Structure **Transparency 39,** The Basic Shapes of Viruses **Transparency 40,** The Lytic Cycle **Math Skills for Science Worksheet 3,** Multiplying Whole Numbers `GENERAL` **Reinforcement Worksheet 10,** The Lytic Cycle `BASIC`	**MathBreak,** Sizing Up a Virus, p. 233 `GENERAL` **Chemistry Connection,** p. 234 **Connect to Earth Science,** p. 234 in ATE **Science, Technology, and Society:** Edible Vaccines, p. 240 `ADVANCED` **Health Watch:** Helpful Viruses, p. 241 `GENERAL`	**Review,** p. 235 `GENERAL` **Quiz,** p. 235 in ATE `GENERAL` **Alternative Assessment,** p. 235 in ATE `ADVANCED`

END-OF-CHAPTER REVIEW AND ASSESSMENT

Chapter Review in Study Guide
Vocabulary and Notes in Study Guide
Chapter Tests with Performance-Based Assessment, Chapter 10 Test
Chapter Tests with Performance-Based Assessment, Performance-Based Assessment 10
Concept Mapping Transparency 10

 Holt, Rinehart and Winston On-line Resources
go.hrw.com

For worksheets and other teaching aids related to this chapter, visit the HRW Web site and type in the keyword: **HSTVIR**

 National Science Teachers Association
www.scilinks.org

Encourage students to use the *sci*LINKS numbers listed in the internet connect boxes to access information and resources on the **NSTA** Web site.

Chapter 10 • Chapter Organizer   **221B**

Chapter Resources & Worksheets

Visual Resources

TEACHING TRANSPARENCIES

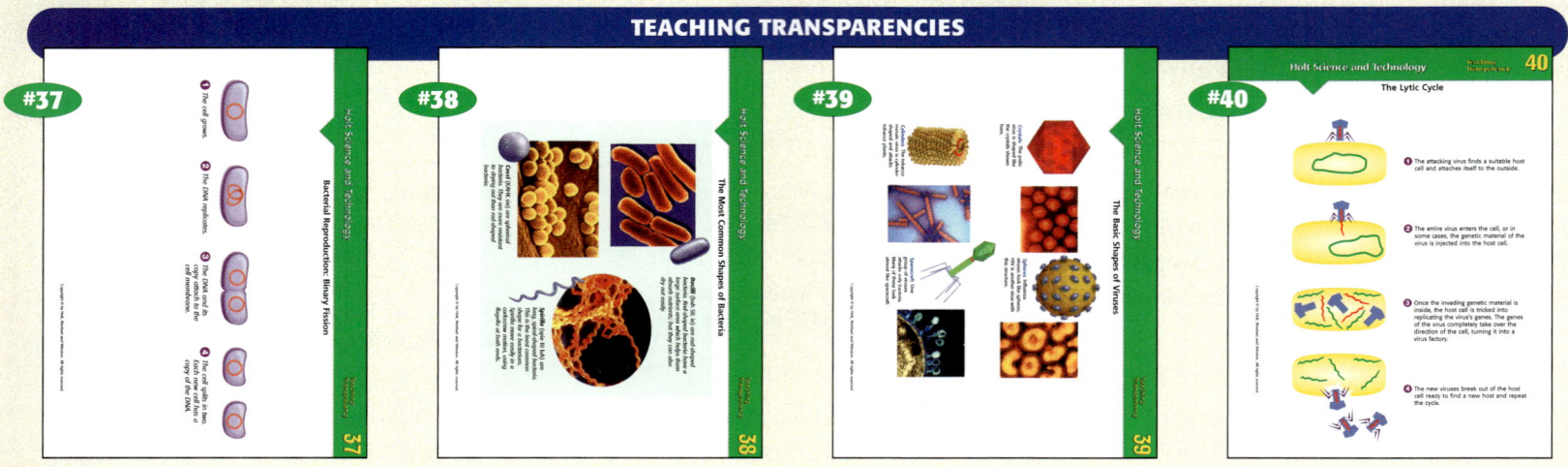

TEACHING TRANSPARENCIES   **CONCEPT MAPPING TRANSPARENCY**

 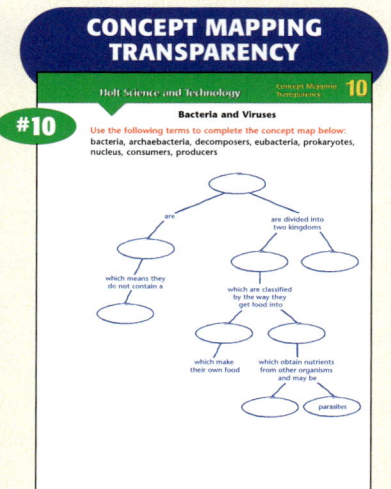

Meeting Individual Needs

DIRECTED READING   **REINFORCEMENT & VOCABULARY REVIEW**   **SCIENCE PUZZLERS, TWISTERS & TEASERS**

   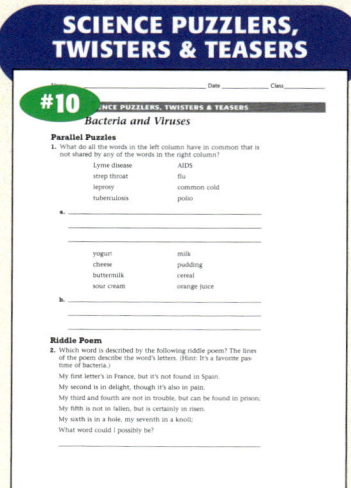

Chapter 10 • Bacteria and Viruses

Chapter 10 • Bacteria and Viruses

Review & Assessment

STUDY GUIDE

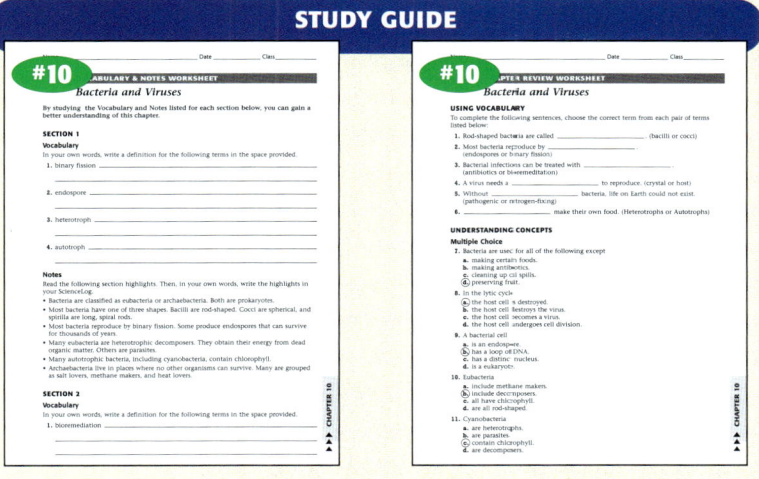

CHAPTER TESTS WITH PERFORMANCE-BASED ASSESSMENT

Lab Worksheets

INQUIRY LABS

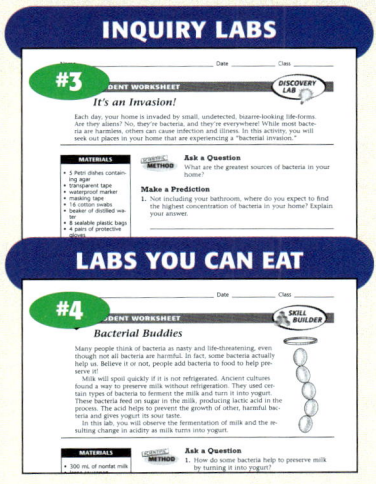

ECOLABS & FIELD ACTIVITIES

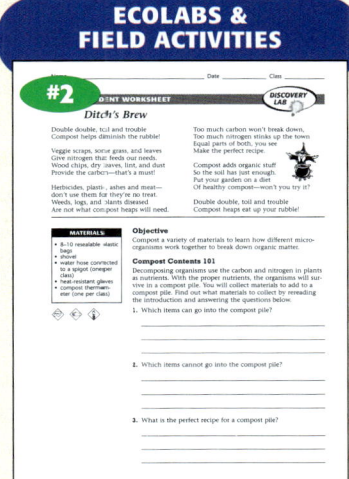

LONG-TERM PROJECTS & RESEARCH IDEAS

DATASHEETS FOR LABBOOK

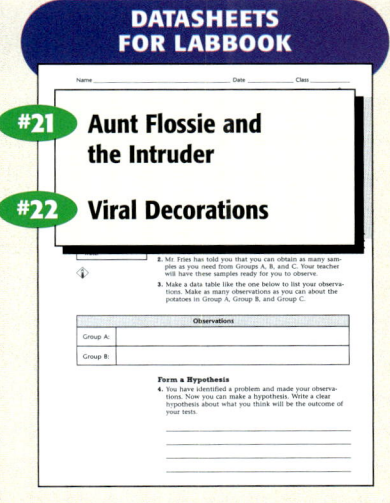

Applications & Extensions

CRITICAL THINKING & PROBLEM SOLVING

SCIENCE TECHNOLOGY

INTERACTIVE EXPLORATIONS

Chapter 10 • Chapter Resources & Worksheets

Chapter Background

SECTION 1

Bacteria

▶ **Kingdoms of Bacteria**
The classification of living things is an ongoing, ever-changing process. This book utilizes a six-kingdom system of classification in which bacteria are divided into two separate kingdoms: Eubacteria and Archaebacteria. In five-kingdom systems of classification, all bacteria are classified in the kingdom Monera.

- In addition to being classified by shape, many eubacteria also are classified as Gram-positive or Gram-negative. Gram-positive bacteria have a thick peptidoglycan cell wall that appears purple when stained with crystal violet, iodine, and safranine. Gram-negative bacteria have a much thinner peptidoglycan cell wall, as well as additional layers of lipids and polysaccharides that are not found in Gram-positive cells. Gram-negative bacteria appear red when stained with the same combination of dyes.

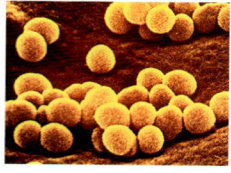

▶ **Mistaken Identity**
Cyanobacteria were once classified as blue-green algae because they sometimes grow together in long filaments that resemble algae and undergo photosynthesis. This classification was incorrect because cyanobacteria are prokaryotes and do not have nuclei or membrane-bound organelles. Blue-green algae, in contrast, are eukaryotes and have nuclei and membrane-bound organelles.

IS THAT A FACT!
- ◆ While some cyanobacteria are blue-green in color, cyanobacteria can also be yellow, red, brown, green, or black.

SECTION 2

Bacteria's Role in the World

▶ **Bacteria and Plants**
When the nitrogen-fixing bacteria *Rhizobium* enters a plant's roots, it forms a nodule. *Rhizobium* inhabits only the roots of legumes, which include beans, peas, soybeans, alfalfa, clover, peanuts, and vetch.

- One example of the effective biological control of insects involves the bacteria *Bacillus thunguriensis*. When sprayed or dusted onto a plant's leaves, the bacteria are an effective destroyer of leaf-eating insects, such as the tomato hornworm. When ingested by the insect, the bacteria begin to secrete enzymes that dissolve the insect's digestive system. Within 24 hours after ingestion, the insect stops eating and dies.

IS THAT A FACT!
- ◆ Bacteria are used in a number of industrial applications. They can peel and eat the paint off old aircraft. They can be used as biosensors to help determine the health of a specific habitat. Bacteria are even being used to remove the sulfur from coal before it is burned, which helps reduce acid rain.

▶ **A Taste of Their Own Medicine**
Common antibiotics produced by bacteria include streptomycin and tetracycline. A fungus produces penicillin, one of the most common antibiotics.

▶ **Poison Producers**
Botulism, a type of food poisoning, is caused by a toxin produced by the bacteria *Clostridium botulinum*. Consumption of very small amounts—sometimes as little as one-millionth of a gram—can cause paralysis and eventually death. *C. botulinum* grows in foods that have been improperly canned and sterilized.

- The intestinal disorder that many travelers refer to as traveler's diarrhea is frequently caused by a strain of the common intestinal bacteria *Escherichia coli*, commonly called *E. coli*. In many countries, contraction of the disease can be avoided by not drinking tap water and by not eating uncooked fruits and vegetables.

Chapter 10 • Bacteria and Viruses

IS THAT A FACT!

▰ The water droplets in the air produced in a sneeze can carry between 10,000 and 100 million bacteria. The bacteria that cause whooping cough, tuberculosis, diphtheria, and scarlet fever can be carried through the air on droplets such as these.

SECTION 3

Viruses

▶ The Discovery of Viruses

Viruses were first discovered when scientists were trying to find the cause of tobacco mosaic disease, a disease in which the leaves of tobacco plants become wrinkled, blotchy, and yellow and have stunted growth.

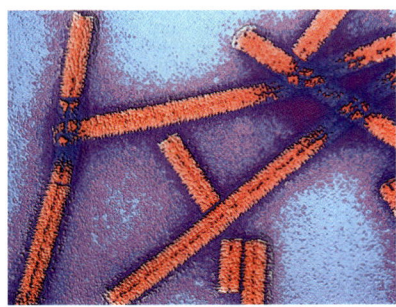

- In 1883, a German scientist named Adolf Mayer discovered that tobacco mosaic disease was contagious, and he suspected that "very small" bacteria caused the disease. Mayer's hypothesis was tested in 1892 by the Russian biologist Dmitri Ivanovsky, who passed the liquid from a diseased plant through extremely fine filters to isolate the small bacteria. He found no bacteria but discovered that the filtered sap from an infected plant caused the disease in a healthy plant. He concluded that "poison" from the bacteria was the cause of the disease. In 1897, a Dutch biologist named Martinus Beijernick discovered that the disease-causing agent was something smaller and simpler than bacteria. In 1898, Beijernick used the word *virus* to describe these tiny disease-causing agents.

- An American biochemist named Wendell Stanley (1904–1971) first isolated the tobacco mosaic virus in 1935. He treated the sap from infected plants in such a way that the viruses formed needle-shaped crystals. When Stanley spread the crystals from the diseased plant onto the leaves of a healthy plant, the healthy plant developed the disease.

- Even though Stanley isolated and chemically analyzed viruses in 1935, viruses were not seen until 1940, when the electron microscope was invented.

IS THAT A FACT!

▰ Most viruses are named for the disease they cause; for example, the cause of tobacco mosaic disease is tobacco mosaic virus.

▰ All viruses are parasitic, that is, they must have a host to reproduce. Because of this trait, viruses could not have been the first organisms on Earth.

▶ Vaccines

One of the greatest medical uses of vaccines was the elimination of smallpox infections from the world. Smallpox is a disease in which small pustules form on the victim's skin, causing permanent disfigurement and, in half the cases, death. In 1798, an English doctor named Edward Jenner (1749–1823) developed the first effective vaccine for smallpox. The use of smallpox vaccines rapidly spread in industrialized countries around the world. The last reported case in the United States occurred in 1949.

- Jonas Salk (1914–1995) developed a vaccine for the paralyzing disease polio in 1952.

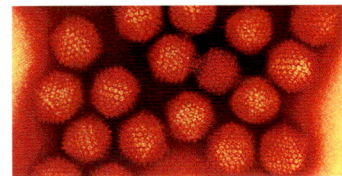

IS THAT A FACT!

▰ A 23-year-old man named Ali Maow Maalin, of Merka, Somalia, contracted the last known case of smallpox in the world in 1977.

For background information about teaching strategies and issues, refer to the *Professional Reference for Teachers*.

Bacteria and Viruses

 Pre-Reading Questions

Students may not know the answers to these questions before reading the chapter, so accept any reasonable response.

Suggested Answers
1. One cell makes up a bacterium.
2. Bacteria are used to make cheese and yogurt.
3. Sample answer: A virus is not alive because it cannot reproduce on its own.

 Directed Reading Worksheet 10

 Science Puzzlers, Twisters & Teasers Worksheet 10

 Guided Reading Audio CD
English or Spanish, Chapter 10

CHAPTER 10

Bacteria and Viruses

Sections

1. Bacteria 224
   MathBreak 224
   QuickLab 226
   Internet Connect..... 228
2. Bacteria's Role in the World 229
   Apply 231
3. Viruses 233
   MathBreak 233
   Chemistry Connection 234
   Internet Connect 235

Chapter Review 238
Feature Articles 240, 241
LabBook 720–721

1. How many cells make up a bacterium?
2. What do cheese and yogurt have to do with bacteria?
3. Do you think a virus is alive? Explain your answer.

Bacteria: Friend and Foe!!

Bacteria are everywhere. Some provide us with medicines and some make foods we eat. Others, like the one pictured here, can cause illnesses. This bacterium is a kind of *Salmonella*, and it can cause food poisoning. *Salmonella* can live inside chickens and other birds. Cooking eggs and chicken properly helps make sure that you don't get sick from *Salmonella*. In this chapter, you will learn more about bacteria and viruses.

---

internet connect

HRW On-line Resources
go.hrw.com
For worksheets and other teaching aids, visit the HRW Web site and type in the keyword: **HSTVIR**

www.scilinks.com
Use the *sci*LINKS numbers at the end of each chapter for additional resources on the **NSTA** Web site.

www.cnnfyi.com
Visit the CNN Web site for current events coverage and classroom resources.

START-UP Activity

OUR CONSTANT COMPANIONS

Bacteria are everywhere. They are in the soil, in the air, and even inside you. When grown in a laboratory, microscopic bacteria form colonies that you can see. In this activity, you will see some of the bacteria that share your world.

Procedure

1. Get **three plastic Petri dishes** containing **nutrient agar** from your teacher. Label one dish "Hand," another "Breath," and another "Soil." Wipe your finger across the inside of the first dish. Breathe into the second dish. Place a small amount of **soil** into the third dish.

2. Secure the Petri dish lids with **transparent tape.** Wash your hands. Place the dishes in a warm, dark place for about 1 week. **Caution:** Do not open the Petri dishes after they are sealed.

3. Observe the Petri dishes each day. What do you see? Record your observations in your ScienceLog.

Analysis

4. How does the appearance of the agar in each dish differ?

5. Which source had the most bacterial growth—your hand, your breath, or the soil? Why do you think this might be?

START-UP Activity

OUR CONSTANT COMPANIONS

MATERIALS

For Each Group:
- 3 plastic Petri dishes filled with nutrient agar
- soil
- transparent tape

Safety Caution

When students breathe on the dishes, they should be careful not to breathe on each other. Plastic dishes are safer than glass dishes.

Teacher's Notes

Prepoured agar plates can be purchased from a biological supply house.

To minimize the risk of contamination from airborne bacteria, students should only lift the Petri dish lids slightly when treating the agar.

Do not allow students to open the Petri dishes after they have been inoculated and sealed.

If moisture collects on the plates in step 2, try storing the plates upside down.

Answers to START-UP Activity

4. Answers will vary, but students should mention color differences, variations in colony shapes and sizes, and differing amounts of growth.

5. Answers will vary. Most likely, the Petri dish that is exposed to soil will have the most bacterial growth. All logical conclusions should be accepted.

SECTION 1

Focus

Bacteria

This section introduces students to the characteristics of a prokaryotic cell. Students will compare and contrast eubacteria and archaebacteria. Students will distinguish between bacterial producers and consumers and will describe the three main groups of archaebacteria.

Bellringer

Pose the following question to your students, and have them write their answers in their ScienceLog:

If you can't see bacteria without a microscope, how do you know when you have come in contact with them? (Sample answer: Bacteria sometimes cause infected sores, and sometimes cause food to spoil.)

1) Motivate

DISCUSSION

Types of Cells Review with students the differences between prokaryotic cells and eukaryotic cells. Prokaryotic cells do not have nuclei, and their genetic material is not separated from the rest of the cell by a membrane. Eukaryotic cells have nuclei, and their genetic material is separated from the rest of the cell by the nuclear membrane. Remind students that prokaryotic cells are usually much smaller than eukaryotic cells.

Answers to MATHBREAK

30 × 4,000 = 120,000 bacteria

The answers to the second question will vary and depend on the size of the classroom.

224   Chapter 10 • Bacteria and Viruses

Section 1

Terms to Learn
binary fission
endospore

What You'll Do
- Describe the characteristics of a prokaryotic cell.
- Explain how bacteria reproduce.
- Compare and contrast eubacteria and archaebacteria.

MATH BREAK
Airborne Organisms
Air typically has around 4,000 bacteria per cubic meter. Cindy's bedroom is 3 m long and 4 m wide. Her ceiling is 2.5 m high. That means there are 30 m³ in her bedroom (3 m × 4 m × 2.5 m). About how many bacteria are in her bedroom's air? About how many bacteria are in the air of your classroom?

internetconnect
TOPIC: Bacteria
GO TO: www.scilinks.org
sciLINKS NUMBER: HSTL230

Bacteria

Bacteria are the smallest and simplest organisms on the planet. They are also the most abundant. A single gram of soil (which is about equal to the mass of your pencil eraser) can contain over 2.5 billion bacteria!

Not all bacteria are that small. The largest known bacteria are a thousand times larger than the *average* bacterium. Can you imagine an animal a thousand times larger than you? The first giant bacteria ever identified were found in the intestines of a surgeonfish like the one in **Figure 1.**

Figure 1 The giant bacteria inside this fish are 0.6 mm long. That's big enough to be seen with the naked eye.

Classifying Bacteria

All organisms fit into one of the six kingdoms: Protista, Plantae, Fungi, Animalia, Eubacteria, and Archaebacteria. Bacteria make up the kingdoms Eubacteria (yoo bak TIR ee uh) and Archaebacteria (AHR kee bak TIR ee uh). These two kingdoms contain the oldest forms of life on Earth. In fact, for over 2 billion years, they were the *only* forms of life on Earth.

Look, Mom! No Nucleus! Bacteria are single-celled organisms that do not have nuclei. A cell with no nucleus is called a *prokaryote*. A prokaryote is able to use cellular respiration, move around, and reproduce. Because a prokaryote has these abilities, it can function as an independent organism.

IS THAT A FACT!

Bacteria are small, but viruses are even smaller. Millions of viruses can fit inside a single bacterium.

Bacterial Reproduction

Most bacteria reproduce by a type of simple cell division known as **binary fission,** illustrated in **Figures 2** and **3.** In binary fission, a prokaryote's DNA is replicated before cell division. The DNA and its copy attach to the inside of the cell membrane. As the cell grows and the membrane grows longer, the loops of DNA become separated. When the cell is about double in size, the membrane pinches inward. A new cell wall forms, separating the two new cells and their DNA.

Figure 2 Binary Fission

❶ The cell grows.

❷ The DNA replicates and attaches to the cell membrane.

❸ The DNA and its copy separate as the cell grows even larger.

❹ The cell splits in two. Each new cell has a copy of the DNA.

Figure 3 This bacterium is about to complete binary fission.

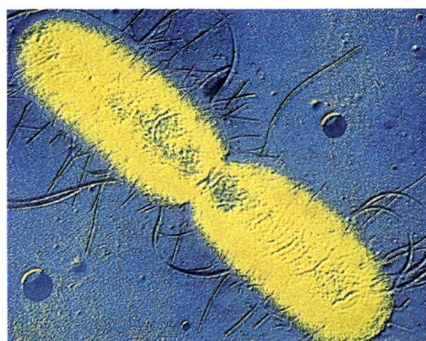

Endospores Each species of bacteria reproduces best at a certain temperature and with a certain amount of moisture. Most species thrive in warm, moist environments. If the environment is unfavorable, some species will be unable to survive. Others will survive by growing a thick protective membrane. These bacteria are then called **endospores.**

Many endospores can survive boiling, freezing, and extremely dry environments. When conditions become favorable again, the endospores will break open, and the bacteria will become active. Scientists have found endospores in the digestive tract of an insect that had been preserved in amber for 30 million years. A similar piece of amber can be seen in **Figure 4.** When the endospores were moistened in a laboratory, the bacteria began to grow!

Figure 4 Endospores found in a preserved insect indicate that bacteria can survive for millions of years.

CONNECT TO PHYSICAL SCIENCE

Have students look up the term *fission* in a dictionary. Students should recognize at least two definitions:

- biological definition (cell division)
- physical science definition (the splitting of an atomic nucleus)

2) Teach

READING STRATEGY

Prediction Guide Before students read this page, ask the following question:

What do you think happens to the DNA inside a bacterium before it reproduces? (Accept all reasonable answers. Students should infer that, as with mitosis in eukaryotic cells, the DNA replicates before the cell divides.)

Have students evaluate their answer after they read about bacterial reproduction.

MATH and MORE

Some species of bacteria undergo binary fission every 30 minutes. For such bacteria, have students calculate how many bacteria there would then be after 1 hour, beginning with a single bacterium (4), after 2 hours (16), after 3 hours (64), after 4 hours (256), and after 5 hours (1,024).

USING THE FIGURE

Discuss the stages of bacterial cell division by binary fission, shown in **Figure 2.** Point out to students what takes place during each step of this process. As you review each step, point out the key structures involved.

Sheltered English

 Teaching Transparency 37 "Bacterial Reproduction: Binary Fission"

 Directed Reading Worksheet 10 Section 1

2) Teach, continued

QuickLab

MATERIALS

FOR EACH GROUP:
• microscope
• prepared slides of bacteria

Safety Caution: Caution students to be careful when handling microscope slides.

Answers to QuickLab
Students should see rod-shaped, spherical, and spiral-shaped bacteria. These are called bacilli, cocci, and spirilla, respectively. The drawings in the ScienceLog should resemble each of these shapes.

DEMONSTRATION

Bacterial Shapes On an overhead projector, display objects that resemble the three shapes of eubacteria, such as a marble, a grain of rice, and a piece of rotini pasta. Ask students to compare the three shapes with the three shapes of eubacteria, illustrated in **Figure 6.** Sheltered English

Homework

Research Types of Bacteria
Have students use the library or the Internet to research the differences in the structure of the cell wall between Gram-positive and Gram-negative bacteria. Students should discover that when bacteria are stained with a specific purple dye and iodine and then rinsed with alcohol and counterstained with safranine, a red dye, some bacteria are stained purple (Gram-positive) and others are stained red (Gram-negative).

Teaching Transparency 38
"The Most Common Shapes of Bacteria"

Spying on Spirilla
Use a **microscope** to observe prepared **slides of bacteria**. What shapes can you see? What are these shapes called? Draw and label the bacteria in your ScienceLog.

The Shape of Bacteria

Almost all bacteria have a rigid cell wall that gives the organism its characteristic shape. Bacteria have a great variety of shapes. The three most common shapes are illustrated below. Each shape provides a different advantage. Can you guess what the advantage of each shape might be?

Whipping Something Up Some bacteria have hairlike structures called flagella (singular, *flagellum*) that help them move around. *Flagellum* means "whip" in Latin. A flagellum spins like a corkscrew, propelling a bacterium through liquid.

The Most Common Shapes of Bacteria

◀ **Bacilli** (buh SIL ie) *are rod-shaped bacteria. Rod-shaped bacteria have a large surface area, which helps them absorb nutrients, but they can also dry out easily.*

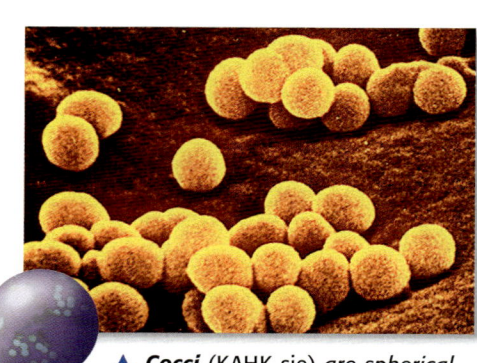

▲ **Cocci** (KAHK sie) *are spherical bacteria. They are more resistant to drying out than rod-shaped bacteria.*

▲ **Spirilla** (spie RI luh) *are long, spiral-shaped bacteria. This is the least common shape for a bacterium. Spirilla move easily in a corkscrew motion, using flagella at both ends.*

Bacteria are used to mine copper. Copper ore contains metal sulfides. The bacteria *Thiobacillus ferrooxidans* take in the sulfides—molecules made of copper and sulfur—and separate the two elements. The bacteria then excrete the purified copper as a waste product.

Kingdom Eubacteria

Most bacteria are eubacteria. The kingdom Eubacteria has more individual organisms than any of the other five kingdoms. Eubacteria have existed for over 3.5 billion years.

Eu Are What Eu Eat Eubacteria are classified by the way they get food. *Consumers* obtain nutrients from other organisms. Most eubacteria, like those helping to decay the leaf in **Figure 5,** are consumers. Many consumers are *decomposers,* which feed on dead organic matter. Other consumers are *parasitic,* which means they invade the body of another organism to obtain food.

Eubacteria that make their own food are *producers*. Some producers are photosynthetic. Like green plants, they convert the energy of the sun into food. These bacteria contain the green pigment *chlorophyll* that is needed for photosynthesis.

Plant Predecessor? Some bacterial producers are *cyanobacteria* (SIE uh noh bak TIR ee uh). Cyanobacteria live in many different types of water environments, such as the one shown in **Figure 6.** It may be that billions of years ago photosynthetic bacteria similar to these began to live inside certain cells with nuclei. The photosynthetic bacteria made food, and the host provided a protected environment for the bacteria. This might be how the first plants came to be.

Figure 5 Decomposers, like the ones helping to decay this leaf, return nutrients to the ecosystem.

Self-Check

Cyanobacteria were once classified as plants. Can you explain why? *(See page 782 to check your answer.)*

Figure 6 Cyanobacteria in this hot spring excrete chemicals that help form the chalky terraces.

Thiomargarita namibiensis is a species of bacteria so large, an individual bacterium is visible to the naked eye. It is the largest known bacterium, about 750 microns (0.030 in.) wide. Even large bacteria are single-celled organisms, and their surface-area-to-volume ratio is far less than that of smaller bacteria. What problems might this cause an organism? *(A small surface-area-to-volume ratio makes it difficult to take in a sufficient quantity of nutrients and eliminate wastes efficiently.)*

---

3) Extend

RESEARCH

Bacterial Environments Ask students to use the library or the Internet to research the extreme habitats of archaebacteria. Encourage students to make posters of their findings to share with the class.

Homework

Concept Mapping After students read this section, have them create a concept map in their ScienceLog that includes the following terms:

bacteria, Eubacteria, Archaebacteria, prokaryotes, nucleus, cells, eukaryotes, harsh environments

Answers to Self-Check

Cyanobacteria were once classified as plants because they use photosynthesis to make food.

4 Close

Quiz

1. What functions must a prokaryotic cell perform? (Prokaryotic cells must respire, make or consume food, move around on their own, and reproduce.)
2. What are the three main types of archaebacteria? (methane makers, heat lovers, and salt lovers)

ALTERNATIVE ASSESSMENT

Divide the class into two teams, and provide each team with 10 large index cards. Have each team look through this section and write 10 questions about the characteristics of bacteria, one question per index card. Bring the teams together to play a trivia game about bacteria.

Reinforcement Worksheet 10 "Bacteria Bonanza"

TOPIC: Archaebacteria
GO TO: www.scilinks.org
*sci*LINKS NUMBER: HSTL235

Kingdom Archaebacteria

Archaebacteria thrive in places where no other living things are found. Scientists have found archaebacteria in the hot springs at Yellowstone National Park and beneath 430 m of ice in Antarctica. They have even been found living 8 km below the Earth's surface!

Archaebacteria are genetically different from eubacteria. Not all archaebacteria have cell walls. The cell walls of archaebacteria—when they do have them—are chemically different from those of all other organisms.

Pass the Salt There are three main types of archaebacteria: methane makers, heat lovers, and salt lovers. Methane makers excrete methane gas. They are found in many places including swamps. Heat lovers live in places like ocean rift vents where temperatures are over 360°C. Salt lovers live in places where the concentration of salt is very high, such as the Dead Sea, shown in **Figure 7**.

Figure 7 The Dead Sea is so salty that only archaebacteria can survive in it. Fish carried into the Dead Sea by the Jordan River die instantly.

TOPIC: Bacteria, Archaebacteria
GO TO: www.scilinks.org
*sci*LINKS NUMBER: HSTL230, HSTL235

REVIEW

1. Draw and label the three main shapes of bacteria.
2. Describe the four steps of binary fission.
3. How do eubacteria and archaebacteria differ?
4. **Analyzing Concepts** Many bacteria cannot reproduce in cooler temperatures and are destroyed at high temperatures. How do humans take advantage of this when preparing and storing food?

▼ Answers to Review

1. The drawings should resemble the pictures on page 226.
2. The cell grows, the DNA replicates, the DNA molecules separate as the cell grows, and the cell splits in two.
3. Eubacteria and archaebacteria are genetically different. Their cell walls are also chemically different.
4. Humans store food in refrigerators and freezers to slow bacterial growth. Humans also cook food at high temperatures, which helps kill many bacteria.

Section 2

Terms to Learn
bioremediation
antibiotic
pathogenic bacteria

What You'll Do
- Explain why life on Earth depends on bacteria.
- List five ways bacteria are useful to people.
- Describe why some bacteria are harmful to people.

Bacteria's Role in the World

Bacteria may be invisible to us, but their effects on the planet are not. Because many types of bacteria cause disease, bacteria have gotten a bad reputation. However, they also do many things that are important to humans.

Good for the Environment

Life as we know it could not exist without bacteria. They are vital to our environment, and we benefit from them in several ways.

Nitrogen-Fixing Nitrogen is an essential chemical for all organisms because it is a component of proteins and DNA. Plants must have nitrogen in order to grow properly. You might think getting nitrogen would be easy because nitrogen gas makes up more than 75 percent of the air. But most plants cannot use nitrogen from the air. They need to take in a different form of nitrogen. *Nitrogen-fixing bacteria* consume nitrogen in the air and change it into a form that plants can use. This process is described in **Figure 8.**

Figure 8 Bacteria's Role in the Nitrogen Cycle.

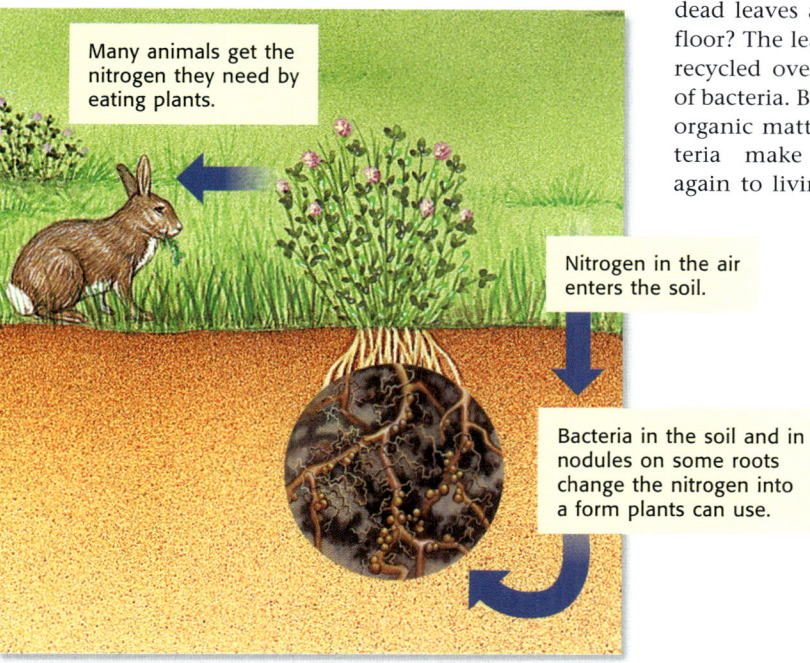

Many animals get the nitrogen they need by eating plants.

Nitrogen in the air enters the soil.

Bacteria in the soil and in nodules on some roots change the nitrogen into a form plants can use.

Recycling Have you ever seen dead leaves and twigs on a forest floor? The leaves and twigs will be recycled over time with the help of bacteria. By breaking down dead organic matter, decomposing bacteria make nutrients available again to living things.

IS THAT A FACT!
Food crops use nitrogen very rapidly. To make sure that crops receive all the nitrogen they need, farmers worldwide applied more than 65 million metric tons of nitrogen fertilizer in 1990.

 PG 720
Aunt Flossie and the Intruder

SECTION 2

Focus
Bacteria's Role in the World

This section explains why life on Earth depends on bacteria. Students learn how bacteria are both harmful and beneficial to people.

🔔 Bellringer

Display the following question on the board or an overhead projector:

Are harmful bacteria more of a problem or less of a problem to people now than they were 200 years ago? (Students should infer that harmful bacteria generally cause fewer problems because people understand that maintaining hygienic conditions eliminates many bacteria. The discovery of antibiotics has also helped us overcome some of the health problems posed by bacteria.)

1) Motivate

DISCUSSION

Bacterial Products Ask students to name products they use that are made using bacteria. (Answers might include yogurt, cheese, sauerkraut, and other foods.)

Ask students what products exist because of the scientific discovery that bacteria can cause disease. (Answers might include sterile bandages, antiseptic creams and soaps, antibacterial cleansers, canned food, antibiotics, and water filters.)

Directed Reading Worksheet 10 Section 2

Section 2 • Bacteria's Role in the World

2) Teach

SCIENTISTS AT ODDS

Joseph Lister (1827–1912), a professor of surgery at Glasgow University, in Scotland, pioneered using antiseptics in surgery. Surgeons of the day were critical of Lister. But the surgeons who followed Lister's techniques immediately had greater success in surgery; the death rate fell from 1 in 3 to 1 in 20. In time, all surgeons were educated about the importance of using antiseptics in surgery and hospital care. Operations today are much safer because of one man's determination to save his patients.

REAL-WORLD CONNECTION

Fresh foods are susceptible to bacteria, but canning food enables us to keep food year-round. It also makes food more convenient. In 1795, Napoleon offered a prize for the most practical method of preserving food for soldiers. In 1804, a chef named Nicolas Appert discovered that liquids, such as soups, and small fruits, like cherries, could be preserved by packing them into champagne bottles and plunging the sealed bottles into a bath of boiling water. Although he didn't know why at the time, he was sterilizing bacteria that would have otherwise spoiled the food.

Interactive Explorations CD-ROM "Scope It Out!"

TOPIC: Antibiotics
GO TO: www.scilinks.org
sciLINKS NUMBER: HSTL240

Figure 9 Bioremediating bacteria are added to soil to consume pollutants and excrete them as harmless chemicals.

Cleaning Up Recently bacteria have been used to combat pollution. **Bioremediation** (BIE oh ri MEE dee AY shuhn) is the use of bacteria and other microorganisms to change pollutants into harmless chemicals. Bioremediation is used to clean up industrial, agricultural, and municipal wastes, as well as oil spills. The workers in **Figure 9** are using bioremediation to remove toxins from the soil.

Figure 10 Genes from the Xenopus frog were used to produce the first genetically engineered bacteria.

Good for People

Scientists are constantly searching for new ways to use bacteria to better the lives of humans. People have been able to genetically engineer bacteria since 1973. It was then that researchers inserted genes from a frog like the one in **Figure 10** into the bacterium *Escherichia coli* (ES uhr RI shee uh COHL ie). The bacterium started reproducing the frog genes. Never before had such a genetically altered organism existed.

Now scientists can genetically engineer bacteria for many purposes, including the production of medicines, insecticides, cleansers, adhesives, foods, and many other products.

Fighting Bacteria with Bacteria Although some bacteria cause diseases, others make chemicals that treat diseases. **Antibiotics** are medicines used to kill bacteria and other microoganisms. Many bacteria have been genetically engineered to make antibiotics in large quantities.

Alexander Fleming, the Scottish scientist who discovered antibiotics, created a microbial growth shaped like the British flag in honor of the queen's visit to his lab. She was *not* amused.

Multicultural CONNECTION

One of the first people to describe the importance of composting dead plant material was African-American agricultural chemist George Washington Carver (1864–1903). While teaching at Tuskegee Institute, Carver and his students added leaves, weeds, and potato peelings to the soil. Once these materials were incorporated, bacteria in the soil broke down the plant material into nutrients that plants could use.

Ingenious Engineering!

Ralph specializes in genetically engineering bacteria. He has engineered many different types of bacteria to help solve medical and environmental problems, but today he is completely out of ideas. He needs you to help him think of a design for a new bacterium that will either treat a disease or help the environment. What would you want this new bacterium to do? What kinds of traits would you give it?

Insulin Scientists have created genetically engineered bacteria that can produce other medicines, such as insulin. Insulin is a substance needed by the body to properly use sugars and other carbohydrates. People who have *diabetes* cannot produce the insulin they need. They must take insulin daily. In the late 1970s, scientists put genes carrying the genetic code for human insulin into *E. coli* bacteria. The bacteria produced human insulin, which can be separated from the bacteria and given to diabetics.

Feeding Time! Believe it or not, people breed bacteria for food! Every time you eat cheese, yogurt, buttermilk, or sour cream, you also eat a lot of lactic-acid bacteria. *Lactic-acid bacteria* digest the milk sugar lactose and convert it into lactic acid. The lactic acid acts as a preservative and adds flavor to the food. The foods in **Figure 11** could not be made without bacteria.

Activity

Create a week's meal plan without any foods made with bacteria. What would your diet be like without prokaryotes?

TRY at HOME

Figure 11 Bacteria are used to make many different types of food, including sauerkraut, sourdough bread, some kinds of sausages, pickles, and dairy products.

IS THAT A FACT!

A bulging can of food is a dangerous object! The bulge could be indicative of the presence of the *Clostridium botulinum* bacteria, which can cause a severe type of food poisoning called botulism. Caution students never to eat food from a can with a bulging lid or sides.

4 Close

Quiz

1. Explain the role of bacteria in recycling. (Bacteria act as decomposers of dead organisms. They break down the materials in the dead organisms so that nutrients will be available for use by other living things.)
2. Explain why bacteria are important in helping plants obtain nitrogen. (Nitrogen-fixing bacteria that live in nodules on a plant's roots consume nitrogen gas and change it into a form that can be used by plants.)

ALTERNATIVE ASSESSMENT

Writing On the board, write the headings "Helpful Bacteria" and "Harmful Bacteria." Have student volunteers go to the board one at a time and write an example of how bacteria can be either helpful or harmful. Review the list as a class.

MISCONCEPTION ALERT

The man in the bed in **Figure 12** is depicted in blue. This is to symbolize that he had the bubonic plague. People with the plague do not actually appear blue.

Critical Thinking Worksheet 10 "Bacterial Blastoff"

Figure 12 Between the years 1346 and 1350, the bubonic plague killed 25 million people. That was one-third of Europe's population at the time.

Figure 13 This branch of a pear tree has fire blight, a bacterial disease.

Harmful Bacteria

We couldn't survive without bacteria, but they are also capable of doing incredible damage. Scientists realized in the mid-1800s that some bacteria are pathogenic. **Pathogenic bacteria** cause diseases, such as the one illustrated in **Figure 12**. These bacteria invade a host organism and obtain nutrients from the host's cells. In the process, they cause damage to the host. Today, almost all bacterial diseases can be treated with antibiotics. Many can also be prevented with vaccines. Some diseases caused by bacteria are shown in the table below.

Bacterial Diseases

- Dental cavities
- Ulcers
- Strep throat
- Food poisoning
- Bacterial pneumonia
- Lyme disease
- Tuberculosis
- Leprosy
- Typhoid fever
- Bubonic plague

Enough Diseases to Go Around Bacteria cause diseases in other organisms as well as in people. Have you ever seen a plant with discolored spots or soft rot? If so, you've seen bacterial damage to another organism.

Pathogenic bacteria attack plants, animals, protists, fungi, and even other bacteria. They can cause considerable damage to grain, fruit, and vegetable crops. The branch of a pear tree in **Figure 13** shows the effects of pathogenic bacteria.

REVIEW

1. List three different products bacteria are used to make.
2. What are two ways that bacteria affect plants?
3. How can bacteria both cause and cure diseases?
4. **Analyzing Relationships** Describe some of the problems humans would face if there were no bacteria.

Answers to Review

1. Sample answer: insulin, pickles, adhesives
2. Bacteria affect plants by providing them with nitrogen (nitrogen-fixing bacteria) and by providing them with nutrients from decayed organic matter (decomposers).
3. Pathogenic bacteria cause disease by obtaining nutrition from their host's cells. Other bacteria can be used to make antibiotics that help kill pathogenic bacteria. Many types of bacteria also make medicines, such as insulin.
4. Answers can vary. Sample answer: If there were no bacteria, we would not have pickles, cheese, or yogurt. Also, nothing would decompose, and plants wouldn't be able to grow because they wouldn't be able to process nitrogen.

Section 3

Terms to Learn
virus
host

What You'll Do
- Explain how viruses are similar to and different from living things.
- List the four major virus shapes.
- Describe the two kinds of viral reproduction.

Viruses

Viruses have been called the greatest threat to the survival of humanity. But what are they? A **virus** is a microscopic particle that invades a cell and often destroys it. They are everywhere, and for humans they are mostly one big headache. That's because many diseases are caused by viruses, including the common cold, flu, and acquired immune deficiency syndrome (AIDS). AIDS is caused by the human immunodeficiency virus (HIV).

It's a Small World

Viruses are incredibly tiny. They are even smaller than the smallest bacteria. About 5 billion of them can fit into a single drop of blood. Because of viruses' small size and ever-changing nature, scientists don't know how many types of viruses exist. The number may be in the billions or higher!

Are They Living?

Like living things, viruses contain protein and nucleic acids. But viruses, such as the ones shown in **Figure 14,** don't eat, grow, breathe, or perform other biological functions. A virus cannot "live" on its own, although it can reproduce inside a living organism that serves as its host. A **host** is an organism that supports a parasite. Using a host's cell as a miniature factory, viruses instruct the cell to produce viruses rather than healthy new cells.

MATH BREAK

Sizing Up a Virus

If you enlarged an average virus 600,000 times, it would be about the size of a small pea. How tall would you be if you were enlarged 600,000 times?

Get a leg up on viruses. Turn to page 721 in your LabBook.

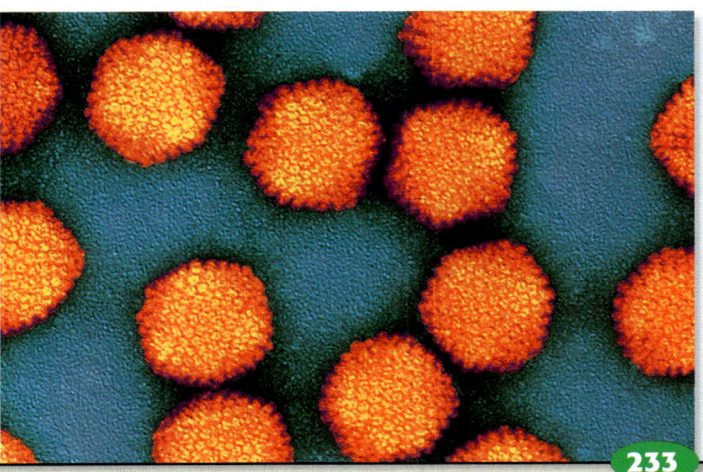

Figure 14 Viruses are not cells. They do not have cytoplasm or organelles.

PG 721
Viral Decorations

Answer to MATHBREAK
This answer will vary depending on the student's height. Example: If the student is 1.6 m (5 ft 2 in.), he or she would be 960,000 m (3,100,000 ft) tall if enlarged 600,000 times.

Section 3

Focus

Viruses

This section describes the characteristics that viruses and living things share, and those they do not. Students will learn that viruses are classified by the disease they cause, what they do inside host cells, or by their shape. Students will learn how viruses reproduce.

Bellringer

Asks students to answer the following question in their ScienceLog:

What are the characteristics of living things? (In Chapter 2, students learned that all living things have cells, sense and respond to change, reproduce, have DNA, use energy, and grow and develop.)

1) Motivate

DEMONSTRATION

Flame Tulips Show students a flame tulip or pictures of a flame tulip. Its name is due to the distinctive contrasting colors in its petals. (Photos of these beautiful tulips can be found in bulb and seed catalogs.) Explain to students that a virus that infects the flower causes the distinctive colors. These mutant plants were hybridized by plant breeders and are grown in gardens around the world. Sheltered English

 Directed Reading Worksheet 10 Section 3

② Teach

RESEARCH

Viral Diseases After students read this section, have them conduct library or Internet research to find out about a virus that causes the disease, the symptoms of the disease, and the treatment for the disease. Have students prepare an oral report about their findings to share with the class.

CONNECT TO EARTH SCIENCE

Crystallography is a branch of chemistry in which scientists study the specific form and structure of crystals. Like specific viruses that always form the same type of crystals, other materials also form crystals that have a distinct size, shape, and number of facets. For example, NaCl, table salt, forms crystals visible with a magnifying glass. Use the following Teaching Transparency to illustrate the crystalline structure of gold.

 Teaching Transparency 107 "Gold Crystal Structure"

 Teaching Transparency 39 "The Basic Shapes of Viruses"

Many viruses can form crystalline structures. This is a property of chemicals, not cellular organisms.

Classifying Viruses

Viruses can be grouped by the type of disease they cause, their life cycle, or the type of genetic material they contain. Viruses can also be classified by their basic shape, as illustrated below. No matter what its structure is, every virus is basically some form of genetic material enclosed in a protein coat.

The Basic Shapes of Viruses

▲ **Crystals** The polio virus is shaped like the crystals shown here.

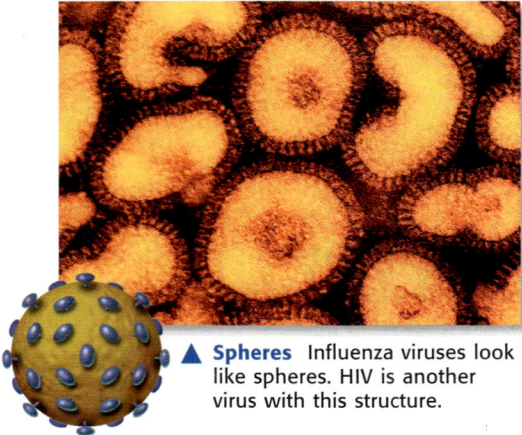
▲ **Spheres** Influenza viruses look like spheres. HIV is another virus with this structure.

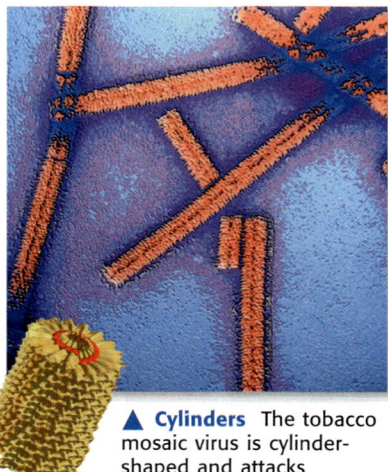
▲ **Cylinders** The tobacco mosaic virus is cylinder-shaped and attacks tobacco plants.

▲ **Spacecraft** One group of viruses attacks only bacteria. Many of these look almost like spacecraft.

A Destructive House Guest

The one function that viruses share with living things is that they reproduce. They do this by infecting living cells and turning them into virus factories. This is called the *lytic cycle*, as shown in **Figure 15.**

Figure 15 The Lytic Cycle

❶ The virus finds a host cell.

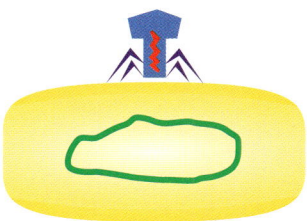

❷ The virus enters the cell, or in some cases, the virus's genes are injected into the cell.

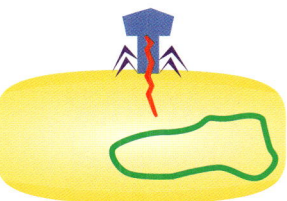

❸ Once the virus's genes are inside, they take over the direction of the host cell, turning it into a virus factory.

❹ The new viruses break out of the host cell ready to find a new host and repeat the cycle.

A Ticking Time Bomb Some viruses don't go straight into the lytic cycle. These viruses insert their genes into the host cell, but no new viruses are made immediately. When the host cell divides, each new cell has a copy of the virus's genes. This is called the *lysogenic cycle*. The viral genes can remain inactive for long periods of time until a change in the environment or stress to the organism causes the genes to launch into the lytic cycle.

REVIEW

1. What would happen if one generation of measles viruses never found a host?
2. Describe the four steps in the lytic cycle.
3. **Analyzing Relationships** Do you think modern transportation has had an effect on the way viruses are spread? Explain your answer.

internetconnect

SCILINKS
NSTA

TOPIC: Viruses
GO TO: www.scilinks.org
sciLINKS NUMBER: HSTL245

---

4) Close

Quiz

1. Describe three shapes of viruses, and give an example of each. (Sample answer: crystals—polio virus; spheres—influenza virus; rods—tobacco mosaic virus)

2. How are viruses like and unlike living things? (Like living things, viruses contain protein and nucleic acids. But unlike living things, viruses don't eat, grow, breathe, or perform other functions.)

ALTERNATIVE ASSESSMENT

Writing Have students write a short story in which they discover a new type of disease-causing virus. Ask students to include specific details about the structure of the new virus and how it reproduces. Ask student volunteers to read their stories to the class.

Teaching Transparency 40
"The Lytic Cycle"

Reinforcement Worksheet 10
"The Lytic Cycle"

▼ Answers to Review

1. If a generation of measles viruses never found a host, measles would die out; viruses can't reproduce themselves without a host.

2. First, the virus enters the host cell. Second, the virus releases its genes into the host cell. Third, the host cell is directed to make more viral genes, and new proteins are made to make coats for the new viruses. Fourth, the host cell is destroyed and the viruses move to infect other cells.

3. Answers can vary but should be logical. People and livestock are much more mobile now, and thus able to bring viruses to new places.

Section 3 • Viruses   235

Chapter Highlights

VOCABULARY DEFINITIONS

SECTION 1

endospore a membrane containing inactive cell material

binary fission the simple cell division in which one cell splits into two; used by bacteria

Chapter Highlights

SECTION 1

Vocabulary
binary fission (p. 225)
endospore (p. 225)

Section Notes
- Bacteria are classified as eubacteria or archaebacteria. Both are prokaryotes.
- Most bacteria have one of three shapes. Bacilli are rod-shaped. Cocci are spherical, and spirilla are long, spiral rods.
- Most bacteria reproduce by binary fission. Some produce endospores that can survive for thousands of years.
- Many eubacteria are decomposers. They obtain their energy from dead organic matter. Others are parasites.
- Many bacterial producers, including cyanobacteria, contain chlorophyll.
- Archaebacteria live in places where no other organisms can survive. Many are grouped as salt lovers, methane makers, and heat lovers.

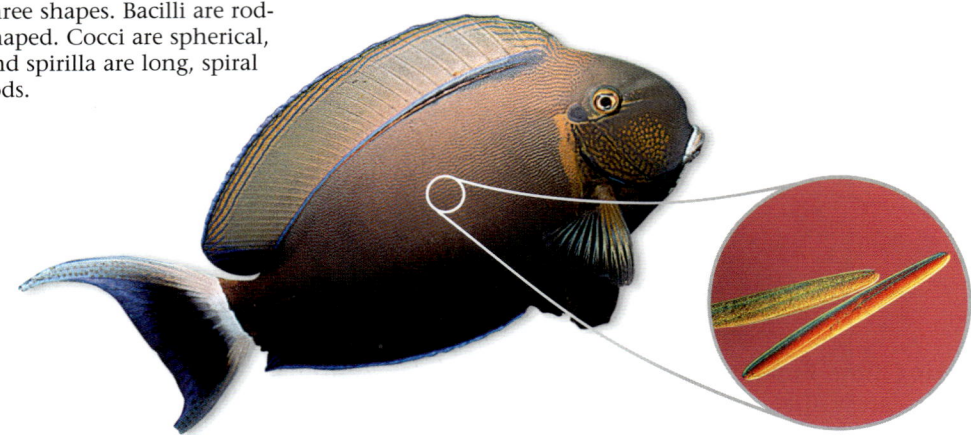

✓ Skills Check

Math Concepts

MULTIPLYING MICROORGANISMS Some bacteria can divide every 20 minutes in an ideal growing environment. That means that if you start out with just one bacterium, in an hour there will be eight bacteria. There will be 512 bacteria in 3 hours, 32,768 in 5 hours, and 1,073,741,824 bacteria in 10 hours!

Visual Understanding

BACTERIA VERSUS VIRUSES The diagrams on pp. 225 and 235 illustrate the way some bacteria and viruses reproduce. Make sure you understand how each process works. Viruses use their hosts' cells to reproduce. Think about how this is different from the way pathogenic bacteria use a host's cell.

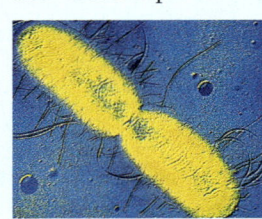

Lab and Activity Highlights

Aunt Flossie and the Intruder — PG 720

Viral Decorations — PG 721

Datasheets for LabBook
(blackline masters for these labs)

236 Chapter 10 • Bacteria and Viruses

SECTION 2

Vocabulary
bioremediation *(p. 230)*
antibiotic *(p. 230)*
pathogenic bacteria *(p. 232)*

Section Notes
- Bacteria are important to the planet. Some act as decomposers. Others convert nitrogen gas to a form that plants can use.
- Bacteria are used in making a variety of foods, medicines, and pesticides. They are also used to clean up pollution.
- Pathogenic bacteria cause diseases in humans as well as other organisms.

Labs
Aunt Flossie and the Intruder *(p. 720)*

SECTION 3

Vocabulary
virus *(p. 233)*
host *(p. 233)*

Section Notes
- Viruses have characteristics of both living and nonliving things. They can reproduce only inside a living cell.
- Viruses may be classified by their structure, the kind of disease they cause, or their life cycle.

- In order for a virus to reproduce, it must enter a cell, reproduce itself, and then break open the cell. This is called the lytic cycle.
- The genes of a virus are incorporated into the genes of the host cell in the lysogenic cycle. The virus's genes may remain inactive for years.

Labs
Viral Decorations *(p. 721)*

VOCABULARY DEFINITIONS, continued

SECTION 2
bioremediation the use of bacteria and other microorganisms to change pollutants in soil and water into harmless chemicals

antibiotic substance used to kill bacteria or slow the growth of bacteria

pathogenic bacteria bacteria that invade a host organism and obtain the food they need for growth and reproduction from the host's cells

SECTION 3
virus a microscopic particle that invades a cell and often destroys it

host an organism on which a parasite lives

 Vocabulary Review Worksheet 10

 Blackline masters of these Chapter Highlights can be found in the **Study Guide.**

---

internet connect

GO TO: go.hrw.com

Visit the **HRW** Web site for a variety of learning tools related to this chapter. Just type in the keyword:

KEYWORD: HSTVIR

GO TO: www.scilinks.org

Visit the **National Science Teachers Association** on-line Web site for Internet resources related to this chapter. Just type in the *sci*LINKS number for more information about the topic:

TOPIC:	Bacteria	*sci*LINKS NUMBER:	HSTL230
TOPIC:	Archaebacteria	*sci*LINKS NUMBER:	HSTL235
TOPIC:	Antibiotics	*sci*LINKS NUMBER:	HSTL240
TOPIC:	Viruses	*sci*LINKS NUMBER:	HSTL245

237

Lab and Activity Highlights

LabBank

Labs You Can Eat, Bacterial Buddies, Lab 4

Inquiry Labs, It's an Invasion! Lab 3

EcoLabs & Field Activities, Ditch's Brew, Lab 2

Long-Term Projects & Research Ideas, Bacteria to the Rescue! Project 10

Interactive Explorations CD-ROM

 CD 1, Exploration 3, "Scope It Out!"

Chapter Review Answers

USING VOCABULARY

1. bacilli
2. binary fission
3. antibiotics
4. host
5. nitrogen-fixing
6. Producers

UNDERSTANDING CONCEPTS

Multiple Choice

7. d
8. a
9. b
10. b
11. c
12. d
13. c
14. d

Short Answer

15. Both forms of bacteria help plants grow. Nitrogen-fixing bacteria supply plants with nitrogen, and decomposers supply plants with nutrients.
16. In the lytic cycle, the virus immediately reproduces after infecting the host. In the lysogenic cycle, the virus inserts its genes into the host cell. The host cell divides several times before viruses begin their lytic cycle.

Chapter Review

USING VOCABULARY

To complete the following sentences, choose the correct term from each pair of terms listed below:

1. Rod-shaped bacteria are called __?__. *(bacilli* or *cocci)*
2. Most bacteria reproduce by __?__. *(endospores* or *binary fission)*
3. Bacterial infections can be treated with __?__. *(antibiotics* or *bioremediation)*
4. A virus needs a __?__ to reproduce. *(crystal* or *host)*
5. Without __?__ bacteria, life on Earth could not exist. *(pathogenic* or *nitrogen-fixing)*
6. __?__ make their own food. *(Consumers* or *Producers)*

UNDERSTANDING CONCEPTS

Multiple Choice

7. Bacteria are used for all of the following except
   a. making certain foods.
   b. making antibiotics.
   c. cleaning up oil spills.
   d. preserving fruit.

8. In the lytic cycle
   a. the host cell is destroyed.
   b. the host cell destroys the virus.
   c. the host cell becomes a virus.
   d. the host cell undergoes cell division.

9. A bacterial cell
   a. is an endospore.
   b. has a loop of DNA.
   c. has a distinct nucleus.
   d. is a eukaryote.

10. Eubacteria
    a. include methane makers.
    b. include decomposers.
    c. all have chlorophyll.
    d. are all rod-shaped.

11. Cyanobacteria
    a. are consumers.
    b. are parasites.
    c. contain chlorophyll.
    d. are decomposers.

12. Archaebacteria
    a. are a special type of eubacteria.
    b. live only in places without oxygen.
    c. are primarily lactic-acid bacteria.
    d. can live in hostile environments.

13. Viruses
    a. are about the same size as bacteria.
    b. have nuclei.
    c. can reproduce only within a host cell.
    d. don't infect plants.

14. Bacteria are important to the planet as
    a. decomposers of dead organic matter.
    b. processors of nitrogen.
    c. makers of medicine.
    d. All of the above

Short Answer

15. How are the functions of nitrogen-fixing bacteria and decomposers similar?
16. What is the difference between the lytic cycle and the lysogenic cycle?

Concept Mapping

17. Use the following terms to create a concept map: eubacteria, bacilli, cocci, spirilla, parasites, consumers, producers, cyanobacteria.

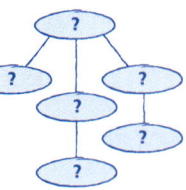

CRITICAL THINKING AND PROBLEM SOLVING

Write one or two sentences to answer the following questions:

18. Describe some of the problems you think bacteria might face if there were no humans.

19. A nuclear power plant explodes and wipes out every living thing within a 30 km radius. What kind of organism do you think might colonize the radioactive area first? Why?

MATH IN SCIENCE

20. An ounce is equal to about 28 g. If 1 g of soil contains 2.5 billion bacteria, how many bacteria are in 1 oz?

21. A bacterial cell infected by a virus divides every 20 minutes. After 10,000 divisions, the virus breaks loose from its host cell. About how many weeks will this take?

INTERPRETING GRAPHICS

The following diagram illustrates the stages of binary fission. Match each statement with the correct stage.

❶

❷

❸

❹

22. The DNA loops separate.
23. The DNA loop replicates.
24. The parent cell starts to expand.
25. The DNA attaches to the cell membrane.

 Take a minute to review your answers to the Pre-Reading Questions found at the bottom of page 222. Have your answers changed? If necessary, revise your answers based on what you have learned since you began this chapter.

Concept Mapping

17. An answer to this exercise can be found at the end of this book.

CRITICAL THINKING AND PROBLEM SOLVING

18. Sample answer: Most bacteria would face no problems at all. The only bacteria that might have a problem are pathogenic bacteria that only infect humans.
19. Sample answer: Perhaps archaebacteria would colonize first because they can live in hostile environments.

MATH IN SCIENCE

20. about 70 billion bacteria
21. about 20 weeks:
    200,000 min × $\frac{1 \text{ hr}}{60 \text{ min}}$ × $\frac{1 \text{ day}}{24 \text{ hr}}$ × $\frac{1 \text{ week}}{7 \text{ days}}$ = 19.8 or 20 weeks

INTERPRETING GRAPHICS

22. stage 3
23. stage 2
24. stage 1
25. stage 2

Concept Mapping Transparency 10

Blackline masters of this Chapter Review can be found in the **Study Guide**.

SCIENCE, TECHNOLOGY, AND SOCIETY
Edible Vaccines

Background

During the 1970s, molecular biologists developed techniques to manipulate the genetic information of plants and animals. Scientists use enzymes called restriction enzymes to "cut out" and isolate certain genes. These genes are then incorporated into the DNA of other organisms. Human growth hormone and insulin, formerly collected from human cadavers, were among the first medicinal products to be produced using these techniques.

Genes contain sets of instructions that tell the body how to make specific proteins. In the case of transgenic organisms, the new genes instruct the molecular machinery of the organisms to produce new proteins. Encourage students to consider any ethical issues that may surround the production of transgenic animals. Is using animals to produce drugs and organs different from using them to produce food? Are there genes we should not transfer into animals? How many genes does it take before an animal might be considered human?

Science, Technology, and Society
Edible Vaccines

No one likes getting a shot, right? Unfortunately, though, shots are a necessary part of life. This is because people in this country are protected from life-threatening diseases by vaccinations. But vaccination shots are expensive, may require refrigeration, and require trained medical professionals to administer them. These facts often keep people in developing countries from getting vaccinated.

▲ *Banana vaccines may soon replace a shot in the arm!*

Pass the Banana, Please
Edible vaccines would have several important advantages over traditional injected vaccines. First of all, they wouldn't require a painful shot! But more important, these vaccines will be cheaper to produce and may not require refrigeration or trained medical professionals. Plants like bananas are easily grown in fields and greenhouses in many Third World countries. One banana could even carry vaccines for several diseases at one time! But just how could a banana do this?

Add Some DNA
Scientists have made DNA that closely resembles the "fingerprints" of specific disease particles. They can insert this DNA into banana genes that code for proteins. Scientists hope they can trick the human immune system into recognizing these proteins as invaders and producing the necessary antibodies to fight diseases. Unlike traditional vaccines, these transgenic bananas (bananas containing foreign DNA) do not carry the risk of infection because they do not contain any viral particles.

Transgenic plants aren't all that new. Agricultural scientists make transgenic plants to improve crops. Scientists have introduced new DNA into fruits and vegetables so that they are more resistant to pests and drought; have larger, sweeter, and more colorful fruit; and ripen more quickly.

Important Questions
Unfortunately, edible vaccines will not be available for several years. Some safety concerns must still be addressed before these vaccines can be given to people. Do edible vaccines have side effects? How long will the resistance last? What happens if someone eats too many bananas? Research labs are testing the vaccines to answer these questions.

Check It Out!
▶ The milk of transgenic animals is also being tested as a potential vaccine carrier. Scientists hope that goat's milk containing malarialike proteins will prevent as many as 3 million deaths each year. Investigate for yourself how the malaria vaccine will work.

Answer to Check It Out!
Scientists put the genes for the proteins in the goat's genome. When the mammary cells express the proteins into the milk, the scientists can then milk the goats and isolate the malarialike proteins. The scientists then can use the proteins to make a vaccine.

Health Watch
Helpful Viruses

Less than 100 years ago, people had no way to treat bacterial infections. If you became ill from contact with pathogenic bacteria, you could only hope that your immune system would be able to defeat the invaders. But in 1928 a Scottish scientist named Alexander Fleming discovered the first antibiotic, or bacteria-killing drug. This first antibiotic was called penicillin.

Using Viruses to Fight Bacteria

Since Fleming's discovery, people have used antibiotics to treat infections and to purify water supplies. But scientists are now realizing that many bacteria are becoming resistant to existing antibiotics. It is quite possible that the overuse of antibiotics will make all current antibiotics ineffective in the near future. So what will people use to fight bacterial infections? Some scientists think viruses might be the answer! You might be thinking that viruses can only cause diseases, not cure them, but there is a particular type of virus, called a bacteriophage, that attacks only bacteria.

How Do They Do This?

Bacteriophages destroy bacteria cells in the same way other viruses can destroy animal or plant cells. Each kind of bacteriophage can only infect a particular species of bacteria. This can make an extremely effective antibiotic. Existing antibiotics kill not only harmful bacteria but also bacteria that people need to stay healthy. This can make people treated with antibiotics very sick, causing a breakdown in their immune system or digestive process. Because bacteriophages would kill only specific harmful bacteria, using bacteriophages could eliminate antibiotics' damaging side effects.

Current Uses

Bacteriophages are not yet used as antibiotics because the immune system destroys the viruses before they can infect the pathogenic bacteria. Scientists are still researching ways to use bacteriophages effectively.

Bacteriophages are currently used to diagnose bacterial infections quickly. Diagnoses can be made by injecting many different types of bacteriophages into a patient. Blood tests then indicate which virus was able to reproduce, in turn determining the type of bacterial infection the patient has. Scientists are also able to use bacteriophages in the same way to detect bacterial contamination of food and water supplies. Perhaps one day in the future, your doctor will give you a helpful virus instead of an antibiotic to fight the harmful bacteria that make you sick!

◀ Some bacteriophages look more like machines than living organisms.

Going Further

▶ Bacteriophages aren't always so helpful. Sometimes they can do more harm than good. Can you think of ways bacteriophages can cause trouble for humans?

HEALTH WATCH
Helpful Viruses

Background

Bacteriophages were described first by F. W. Twort in 1915. It was immediately hoped that the bacteriophages could be used to combat pathogenic bacteria, but no one has discovered a way to do that successfully.

In the 1920s, bacteriophages were used to identify particular strains of bacteria. In the 1940s, Max Delbruck, Salvadore Luria, and other scientists began to discover the intricacies of bacteriophage reproduction. This precipitated the study of bacteriophage genetics. Scientists are now investigating how to use viruses as the vehicles to carry replacement copies of genes used for gene therapy.

Teaching Strategy

Have students research the structure of a bacteriophage. They should draw a bacteriophage and label its parts. They should then write a sentence or two describing the function of each part.

Answer to Going Further

Bacteriaphages can kill beneficial bacteria such as bacteria that help make food (lactic-acid bacteria), bacteria that supply plants with nitrogen (nitrogen-fixing bacteria), and bacteria that make medicine.

Chapter Organizer

CHAPTER ORGANIZATION	TIME MINUTES	OBJECTIVES	LABS, INVESTIGATIONS, AND DEMONSTRATIONS
Chapter Opener pp. 242–243	45	National Standards: SAI 1, SPSP 1, LS 1c, 1f, 4b	**Start-Up Activity** A Microscopic World, p. 243
Section 1 Protists	90	▶ Describe the characteristics of protists. ▶ Name the three groups of protists, and give examples of each. ▶ Explain how protists reproduce. UCP 5, SPSP 1, LS 1b, 1c, 1f, 2a, 3a, 4b, 4c, 5a; LabBook UCP 2	**Demonstration,** Algin and Carrageenan, p. 247 in ATE `BASIC` **Making Models,** Making a Protist Mobile, p. 722 `GENERAL` **Datasheets for LabBook,** Making a Protist Mobile, Datasheet 23 `GENERAL`
Section 2 Fungi	90	▶ Describe the characteristics of fungi. ▶ Distinguish between the four main groups of fungi. ▶ Describe how fungi can be helpful or harmful. ▶ Define *lichen*. UCP 5, SAI 1, SPSP 5, HNS 1, LS 1b–1d, 1f, 2a, 4b, 4c; LabBook SAI 1	**QuickLab,** Moldy Bread, p. 257 `GENERAL` **QuickLab,** Observe a Mushroom, p. 259 `GENERAL` **Skill Builder,** There's a Fungus Among Us! p. 723 `GENERAL` **Datasheets for LabBook,** There's a Fungus Among Us! Datasheet 24 `GENERAL` **Labs You Can Eat,** Knot Your Average Yeast Lab, Lab 5 `BASIC` **Whiz-Bang Demonstrations,** Unleash the Yeast! Demo 7 `GENERAL` **Long-Term Projects & Research Ideas,** Project 11 `ADVANCED`

See page **T20** *for a complete correlation of this book with the*

NATIONAL SCIENCE EDUCATION STANDARDS.

TECHNOLOGY RESOURCES

 Guided Reading Audio CD
English or Spanish, Chapter 11

 One-Stop Planner CD-ROM with Test Generator

 CNN. **Eye on the Environment,** The Fire Ants and the Fungus, Segment 18

Chapter 11 • Protists and Fungi

CLASSROOM WORKSHEETS, TRANSPARENCIES, AND RESOURCES	SCIENCE INTEGRATION AND CONNECTIONS	REVIEW AND ASSESSMENT
Directed Reading Worksheet 11 BASIC **Science Puzzlers, Twisters & Teasers,** Worksheet 11 ADVANCED	**Across the Sciences,** It's Alive! p. 267 GENERAL	
Directed Reading Worksheet 11, Section 1 BASIC **Transparency 41,** *Euglena* **Transparency 121,** The Geologic Time Scale **Transparency 41,** *Paramecium* **Transparency 42,** The Life Cycle of *Plasmodium vivax* **Science Skills Worksheet 17,** Organizing Your Research GENERAL **Math Skills for Science Worksheet 4,** A Shortcut for Multiplying Large Numbers GENERAL **Critical Thinking Worksheet 11,** Protist Pop Culture ADVANCED **Reinforcement Worksheet 11,** Protists on Parade BASIC	**Multicultural Connection,** p. 246 in ATE **Cross-Disciplinary Focus,** p. 246 in ATE ADVANCED **Chemistry Connection,** p. 248 **Connect to Earth Science,** p. 248 in ATE **Geology Connection,** p. 251 **Connect to Earth Science,** p. 251 in ATE **Math and More,** Multiplying Protists, p. 253 in ATE GENERAL	**Self-Check,** p. 246 **Review,** p. 249 GENERAL **Self-Check,** p. 252 **Homework,** p. 253 in ATE ADVANCED **Review,** p. 254 GENERAL **Quiz,** p. 254 in ATE GENERAL **Alternative Assessment,** p. 254 in ATE ADVANCED
Directed Reading Worksheet 11, Section 2 BASIC **Reinforcement Worksheet 11,** An Ode to a Fungus BASIC	**Multicultural Connection,** p. 257 in ATE **MathBreak,** Multiplying Yeasts, p. 258 GENERAL **Math and More,** The Price of Truffles, p. 258 in ATE ADVANCED **Apply,** p. 259 GENERAL **Cross-Disciplinary Focus,** p. 260 in ATE ADVANCED **Real-World Connection,** p. 260 in ATE **Science, Technology, and Society:** Moldy Bandages, p. 266 ADVANCED	**Self-Check,** p. 256 **Self-Check,** p. 257 **Review,** p. 261 GENERAL **Quiz,** p. 261 in ATE GENERAL **Alternative Assessment,** p. 261 in ATE GENERAL

internet connect

 Holt, Rinehart and Winston On-line Resources
go.hrw.com

For worksheets and other teaching aids related to this chapter, visit the HRW Web site and type in the keyword: **HSTPRO**

 National Science Teachers Association
www.scilinks.org

Encourage students to use the *sci*LINKS numbers listed in the internet connect boxes to access information and resources on the **NSTA** Web site.

END-OF-CHAPTER REVIEW AND ASSESSMENT

Chapter Review in Study Guide
Vocabulary and Notes in Study Guide
Chapter Tests with Performance-Based Assessment, Chapter 11 Test
Chapter Tests with Performance-Based Assessment, Performance-Based Assessment 11
Concept Mapping Transparency 11

Chapter Resources & Worksheets

Visual Resources

Meeting Individual Needs

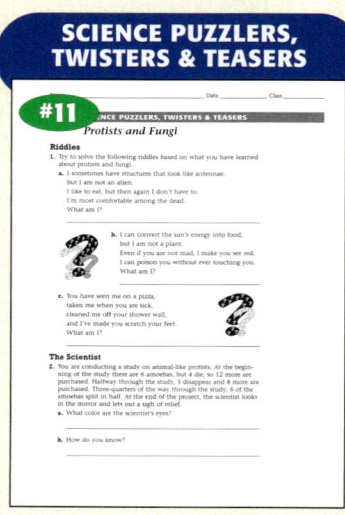

Chapter 11 • Protists and Fungi

Review & Assessment

STUDY GUIDE

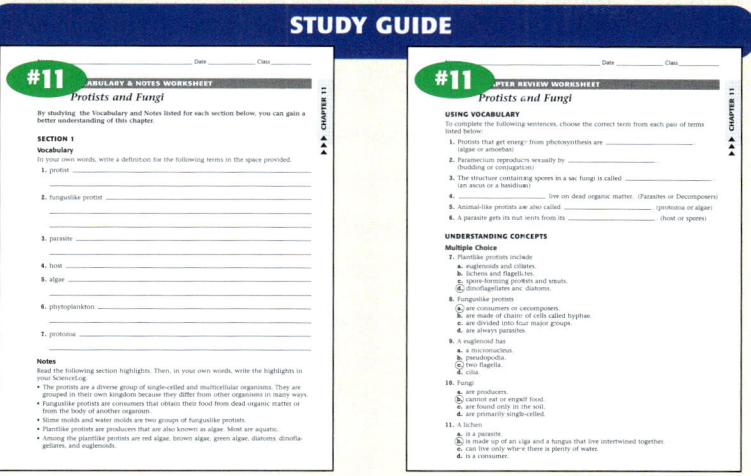

CHAPTER TESTS WITH PERFORMANCE-BASED ASSESSMENT

Lab Worksheets

LABS YOU CAN EAT

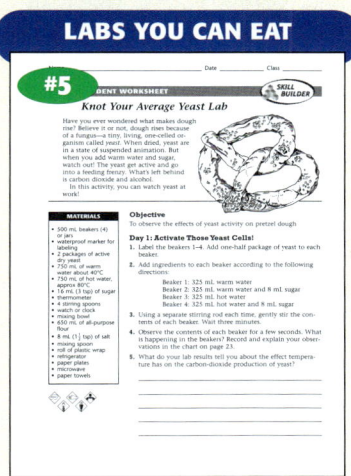

LONG-TERM PROJECTS & RESEARCH IDEAS

WHIZ-BANG DEMONSTRATIONS

DATASHEETS FOR LABBOOK

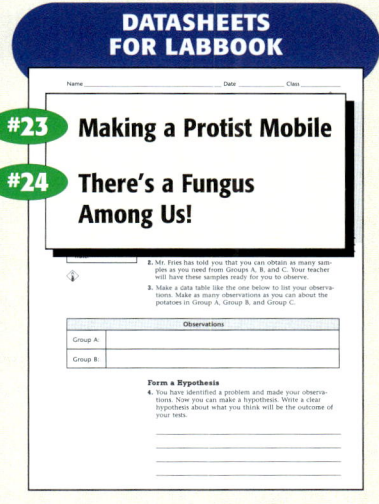

Applications & Extensions

CRITICAL THINKING & PROBLEM SOLVING

EYE ON THE ENVIRONMENT

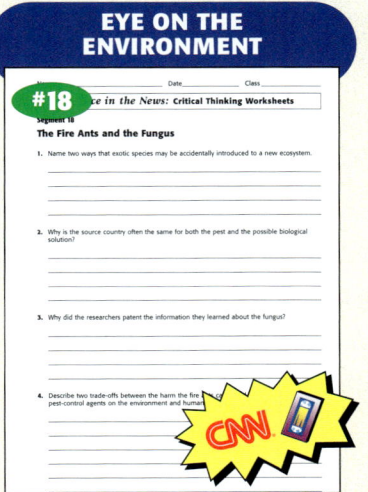

Chapter 11 • Chapter Resources & Worksheets   **241D**

Chapter Background

SECTION 1
Protists

▶ **Protists, Protists, Everywhere**
Most protists are aquatic. Some live in marine environments; others live in fresh water or in the water that surrounds soil particles. Still other protists live in the body fluids of other organisms.

▶ **Products from Algae**
The cell walls of red algae contain a mucous substance that gives the algae a slippery texture. Agar, which is derived from this substance, has the consistency of gelatin and is used worldwide as a culture medium for growing bacteria.

- Giant kelp and other brown algae are the source of algin, which has hundreds of uses. For example, it is used as a thickening and stabilizing agent in ice cream, milkshakes, pie fillings, and weight-control drinks; as an additive in paper and a coating on frozen food packages; as a smoothing agent in lotions and creams; and as an ingredient in latex paints and adhesives.

IS THAT A FACT!
- During the Irish potato famine of 1846, people ate a red alga called dulse as a substitute for potatoes. Another red alga, commonly called purple laver or nori, is used extensively in food today, especially in Asia.

▶ **Slime Molds**
There are two types of slime molds: cellular slime molds (about 70 species in the phylum Acrasiomycota) and plasmodial or acellular slime molds (roughly 500 species in the phylum Myxomycota).

- Plasmodial slime molds are named for their slimy, often large and colorful plasmodia. A plasmodium is the feeding phase of the slime mold, and it engulfs bacteria, yeast, and bits of organic matter in its path. A plasmodium can flow around obstacles and will even flow through the meshwork of a piece of cloth.

IS THAT A FACT!
- Many students who have kept fish in an aquarium have seen the common water mold *Saprolegnia,* which forms a fuzzy white mass as it grows over the surface of a dead or injured fish.

▶ **Diatoms**
The word *diatom* comes from the Greek *diatomos,* which means "cut in two." It refers to the glassy, two-part shells (called frustules) that enclose these single-celled organisms.

- The frustules of diatoms have complex and strikingly beautiful markings that are different for each species and are therefore important in diatom identification.

- One liter of sea water may contain almost a million diatoms.

IS THAT A FACT!
- A harmless species of symbiotic amoeba called *Entamoeba gingivalis* lives in the mouths of many people, where it feeds on loose cells and organic debris.

▶ **The Need to Conjugate**
Laboratory experiments have shown that some species of *Paramecium* must conjugate periodically to survive. If they are not allowed to conjugate, these *Paramecium* have the capacity for only a limited number of asexual divisions (about 350) before they die.

Chapter 11 • Protists and Fungi

SECTION 2

Fungi

▶ Fungi Functions

About 50,000 species of fungi have been identified. Fungi are extremely important as decomposers; they break down complex organic material to simple organic compounds and inorganic molecules, making carbon, nitrogen, phosphorus, and other essential elements available to living things.

- Fungi are also essential in the making of bread, cheeses, wine, beer, and soy sauce; in the production of many antibiotics; and as research organisms for geneticists, biochemists, cytologists, and microbiologists.

- On the other hand, fungi are the major cause of plant diseases. There are at least 5,000 different kinds of fungi that attack crops, garden plants, and wild plants. Some fungi also cause disease in animals, such as ringworm.

▶ Sac Fungi

There are more than 30,000 known species of sac fungi (class Ascomycota), about 500 of which are single-celled yeasts.

- Morels and truffles are multicellular sac fungi. For hundreds of years, the only way to enjoy truffles, which grow underground on the roots of oak and hazelnut trees, was to unearth wild ones with the help of specially trained "truffle-hunting" pigs and dogs. Truffles are now cultivated commercially in France, but they remain a very expensive delicacy.

▶ True Mushrooms

Club fungi include the true mushrooms. There are about 25,000 known species of club fungi.

IS THAT A FACT!

- One mycelium of the club fungus *Armillaria bulbosa*, is among of the world's oldest and largest organisms. Found in a Michigan forest, this particular mycelium is estimated to be more than 1,500 years old, to weigh more than 10,000 kg, and to cover an area of 150,000 m^2.

▶ A Predatory Fungus

One of the imperfect fungi *(Arthrobotrys dactyloides)* preys on tiny roundworms (nematodes) in soil. The filaments of the fungi produce minute "nooses" that swell rapidly when nematodes try to crawl through them. The nooses hold the nematodes tightly while hyphae grow into their bodies and kill them.

▶ Lichens

Approximately 15,000 species of lichens have been identified. Lichens are a symbiotic association between a fungus—in most cases a sac fungus, or ascomycete—and a species of photosynthetic algae or cyanobacteria.

- In severe growing conditions, lichens grow extremely slowly; even small lichens may be hundreds or even thousands of years old.

IS THAT A FACT!

- Lichens are one of the most important foods eaten by caribou. During winter on the tundra, when other foods are not available, caribou survive almost exclusively on a diet of lichens.

For background information about teaching strategies and issues, refer to the *Professional Reference for Teachers*.

CHAPTER 11

Protists and Fungi

Pre-Reading Questions

Students may not know the answers to these questions before reading the chapter, so accept any reasonable response.

Suggested Answers
1. Seaweed is a type of alga.
2. A fungus is a eukaryotic consumer.
3. Mushrooms do not have roots. They grow from hyphae.

Directed Reading Worksheet 11

Science Puzzlers, Twisters & Teasers Worksheet 11

Guided Reading Audio CD
English or Spanish, Chapter 11

CHAPTER 11

Protists and Fungi

Sections

1. **Protists** 244
   Chemistry Connection . 248
   Geology Connection .. 251
   Internet Connect 254
2. **Fungi** 255
   QuickLab 257
   MathBreak 258
   QuickLab 259
   Apply 259
   Internet Connect 261

Chapter Review 264
Feature Articles 266, 267
LabBook 722–723

Pre-Reading Questions

1. What is seaweed?
2. What is a fungus?
3. Do mushrooms have roots?

Hardworking Mushrooms!

The kingdoms Protista and Fungi (FUHN JIE) contain many fascinating and beneficial organisms. Protists make most of Earth's oxygen. Many trees and other plants need the help of fungi to get nutrients from the soil. The mushrooms on these pages are fungi that help break down dead plant matter on the forest floor. This process helps recycle the nutrients of the forest. In this chapter, you will learn more about protists and fungi.

---

internet connect

 HRW On-line Resources
go.hrw.com
For worksheets and other teaching aids, visit the HRW Web site and type in the keyword: **HSTPRO**

 sciLINKS NSTA
www.scilinks.com
Use the sciLINKS numbers at the end of each chapter for additional resources on the **NSTA** Web site.

 CNNfyi.com
www.cnnfyi.com
Visit the CNN Web site for current events coverage and classroom resources.

START-UP Activity

A MICROSCOPIC WORLD

In this activity, you will observe some common protists in pond water or in a solution called a *hay infusion*.

Procedure

1. Using a **plastic eyedropper**, place one drop of **pond water** or **hay infusion** onto a **microscope slide**.
2. Add one drop of **ProtoSlo™** to the drop on the slide.
3. Add a **plastic coverslip** by putting one edge on the slide and then slowly lowering it over the drop to prevent air bubbles.
4. Observe the slide under low power of a **microscope**. Once you've located an organism, try high power for a closer look.
5. In your ScienceLog, sketch the organisms you see under high power.

Analysis

6. How many different organisms do you see?
7. Are the organisms alive? Support your answer with evidence.
8. How many cells does each organism appear to have?

START-UP Activity

A MICROSCOPIC WORLD

MATERIALS
For Each Student: • plastic dropper • pond water or hay infusion • ProtoSlo™ • microscope slide • plastic coverslip • microscope

Safety Caution

Tell students not to taste the solution. Care should be taken handling microscope slides and coverslips. check for known mold or fungi reactions among students before conducting this lab. Have an eyewash available in the even of a splash to the eye. Instruct students to wipe up all spills immediately.

Teacher's Notes

Pond water may contain plant-like protists, such as *Spirogyra* and *Volvox*, and animal-like protists, such as *Stentor*, *Vorticella*, *Euglena*, *Paramecium*, and amoebas. Students may also see nematode worms and small fast-moving multicellular animals called rotifers.

Answers to START-UP Activity

6. Answers will vary.
7. The organisms are moving, which suggests that they are alive.
8. Answers may vary, but most, if not all, are single-celled organisms.

Chapter 11 • Protists and Fungi

SECTION 1

Focus

Protists

This section introduces students to organisms that make up the kingdom Protista. Students learn that protists are commonly grouped into three categories—funguslike protists, plantlike protists, and animal-like protists—based on the way in which they obtain nutrients. Students are introduced to representatives of each protist group and also learn about reproduction in protists.

Bellringer

Ask students to imagine that an organism needs to transport itself without the use of arms, fins, wings or legs. How would the organism do it? What environments could the organism live in?

Have students write their answers in their ScienceLog. Encourage students to illustrate their answers whenever possible. (Accept all reasonable responses. Tell students that many protists live in water and move with the help of flagella and cilia.)

Directed Reading Worksheet 11 Section 1

Section 1

Terms to Learn

protist
funguslike protist
parasite
host
algae
phytoplankton
protozoa

What You'll Do

- Describe the characteristics of protists.
- Name the three groups of protists, and give examples of each.
- Explain how protists reproduce.

Figure 1 Protists have many different shapes and sizes.

Pretzel slime mold

Protists

Some are so tiny they cannot be seen without a microscope, and others grow many meters long. Some are poisonous, and others provide food. Some are like plants. Some are like animals. And some are nothing like plants or animals. Despite their differences, all of these organisms are related. What are they? They are all members of the kingdom Protista and are called **protists**. Look at **Figure 1** to see some of the variety of protists.

Zooflagellate

Paramecium

Ulva

General Characteristics

All protists are *eukaryotic*. That means their cells have a nucleus. Most protists are single-celled organisms, but some are multicellular. Scientists generally agree that the more complex eukaryotic organisms—plants, animals, and fungi—all originated from primitive protists.

Some protists are *producers*. Like plants, they get their energy from the sun through *photosynthesis*. Others are *consumers*. They cannot obtain energy from sunlight and must get food from their environment. Protists are often classified by the way they obtain energy. This method groups these organisms into funguslike protists, plantlike protists, or animal-like protists.

IS THAT A FACT!

The glassy "shells" of many kinds of diatoms are perforated by tiny holes. Although most diatoms contain chlorophyll and carry out photosynthesis, many also are able to absorb minerals through these perforations.

244   Chapter 11 • Protists and Fungi

Funguslike Protists

A fungus is an organism that obtains its food from dead organic matter or from the body of another organism. You will learn more about fungi in the next section. The protists that get food this way are called **funguslike protists.** The funguslike protists are consumers that secrete digestive juices into the food source and then absorb the digested nutrients. These protists also reproduce like fungi. Two types of funguslike protists will be discussed in this chapter—slime molds and water molds.

It's Slime! *Slime molds* are thin masses of living matter. They look like colorful, shapeless globs of slime. Many slime molds live as single-celled organisms. But during times of environmental stress, these single organisms come together to form a group of cells with many nuclei and a single cytoplasm. Slime molds live in cool, shady, moist places in the woods and in fresh water. **Figure 2** shows a slime mold growing over a log.

Slime molds eat bacteria, yeast, and small bits of decaying plant and animal matter. They surround food particles and digest them. As long as food and water are available, a slime mold will continue to grow. It may cover an area more than 1 m across!

When growth conditions are unfavorable, a slime mold develops stalklike structures with rounded knobs at the top. You can see this in **Figure 3.** The knobs contain *spores*. The spores can survive for a long time without water or nutrients. When conditions improve, the spores will develop into new slime molds.

Figure 2 Slime molds, like this scrambled egg slime mold, are consumers.

Figure 3 The spore-containing knobs of a slime mold are called sporangia.

WEIRD SCIENCE

At the 1933 Chicago World's Fair, an exhibit of "hair growing on wood" was displayed in the Believe It or Not pavilion. Although the "hair" amazed many fair-goers, it was actually the clustered fruiting bodies of a slime mold.

1) Motivate

MAKING MODELS

Slime Mold For this activity, students should wear safety goggles, an apron, and protective gloves. They should not put any of the materials in their mouth. Food coloring is nontoxic but can stain skin and clothing.

Students can make a substance that behaves very much like a slime mold. Divide the class into groups of 4–5 students. Each group should have a 25 × 25 cm (9 × 9 in.) pan, cornstarch, food coloring, a small container of water, a measuring cup, and a tablespoon. Instruct the students to place 240 mL (1 cup) of cornstarch in the pan. Then have them add 15 mL (1 tbsp) of water at a time to the cornstarch until the mixture has the consistency of a slime that flows slowly. If they add too much water, have them add a little more cornstarch to get the right consistency. Then mix a few drops of food coloring into the mixture and allow students to explore moving the slime around in the pan. They can put small objects, such as paper clips, in the path of the slime and let the substance surround the objects.
Sheltered English

Section 1 • Protists 245

② Teach

READING STRATEGY

Prediction Guide Before students read about algae, ask them the following question:

Knowing that algae carry out photosynthesis, what substance would you expect to find in their cells? (the green pigment chlorophyll)

ACTIVITY

  Concept Mapping
Have students construct a concept map using the following words and phrases:

funguslike protists, water mold, slime mold, protists, bacteria, producers, consumers

Answers to Self-Check

No; some funguslike protists are parasites or consumers.

Multicultural CONNECTION

Native Hawaiians have historically used a species of brown algae, a type of *Sargassum*, to heal cuts caused by corals. The algae was chopped up and applied to cuts as a poultice.

Other seaweeds contain compounds that may have medicinal value as well. About 20 different seaweeds are used in preparations for treating diseases, including intestinal parasite infections and cancer.

Moldy Water? Another type of funguslike protist is the *water mold*. Most water molds are small, single-celled organisms. Water molds live in water, moist soil, or other organisms.

Some water molds are *decomposers* and eat dead organic matter. But many water molds are parasites. **Parasites** invade the body of another organism to obtain the nutrients they need. The organism a parasite invades is called a **host**. Hosts can be living plants, animals, algae, or fungi. A parasitic water mold is shown in **Figure 4.**

Some parasitic water molds cause diseases. A water mold causes "late blight" of potatoes, the disease that led to the Great Potato Famine. Another water mold attacks grapes and threatened the French wine industry in the late 1800s. These protists still endanger crops today, but fortunately methods now exist to control them.

Figure 4 *Parasitic water molds attack various organisms, including fish.*

Plantlike Protists: Algae

A second group of protists are producers. Like plants, they use the sun's energy to make food through photosynthesis. These plantlike protists are also known as **algae** (AL JEE). All algae (singular, *alga*) have the green pigment chlorophyll, which is used for photosynthesis. But most algae also have other pigments that give them a specific color. Almost all algae live in water. You can see some examples of algae in **Figure 5.**

Some algae are multicellular. These algae generally live in shallow water along the shore. You may know these as *seaweed* or *kelp*. Some of these algae can grow to many meters in length.

Self-Check

Are all funguslike protists decomposers? Explain. *(See page 782 to check your answers.)*

Figure 5 *Algae range in size from giant seaweeds to single-celled organisms.*

Spirogyra

Kelp

CROSS-DISCIPLINARY FOCUS

Art Anna Atkins (1799–1871) was an amateur botanist. Atkins specialized in making photographic blueprints called cyanotypes, or sunprints. Over a 10-year period, Atkins created hundreds of cyanotypes of algae from the British Isles. Her book, *British Algae: Cyanotype Impressions*, was published in 1843 and is thought to be the first book illustrated with photographic images. Interested students may wish to create their own cyanotypes of algae (or leaves, fern fronds, or other plant parts if algae are not available) to accompany their reports. Cyanotype paper can be obtained from biological supply houses.

Single-celled algae cannot be seen without a microscope. They usually float near the water's surface. The single-celled algae make up **phytoplankton** (FITE oh PLANK tuhn). Phytoplankton are producers that provide food for most other water-dwelling organisms. They also produce most of the world's oxygen.

The plantlike protists are divided into phyla based on their color and cell structure. We will discuss six of the phyla here: red algae, brown algae, green algae, diatoms, dinoflagellates, and euglenoids.

Red Algae Most of the world's seaweeds are red algae. They contain chlorophyll and a red pigment that gives them their color. These multicellular protists live mainly in tropical marine waters, attached to rocks or other algae. Their red pigment allows them to absorb the light that filters deep into the clear water of the Tropics. Red algae can grow as much as 260 m below the surface of the water but are usually less than 1 m in length.

Brown Algae Most of the seaweeds found in cool climates are brown algae. They attach to rocks or form large floating beds in ocean waters. Brown algae have chlorophyll and a yellow-brown pigment. Many are very large—some grow 60 m in just one growing season! The tops of these gigantic algae are exposed to sunlight. The food made here by photosynthesis is transported to the parts of the algae that are too deep in the water to receive sunlight. An example of a brown alga can be seen in **Figure 6**.

Figure 6 Laminaria *is a brown alga.*

Green Algae The green algae are the most diverse group of plantlike protists. They are green because chlorophyll is the main pigment they contain. Most live in water or moist soil, but others are found in melting snow, on tree trunks, and even inside other organisms.

Many green algae are single-celled, microscopic organisms. Others are multicellular. These species may grow up to 8 m long. Individual cells of some species of green algae live in groups called colonies. **Figure 7** shows colonies of *Volvox*.

Figure 7 Volvox *is a green alga that grows in round colonies.*

IS THAT A FACT!

Giant kelp, a type of brown algae, is anchored to the ocean bottom. It has air bladders in its stems that help keep the stem floating upward, toward the water's surface, where the sunlight is the strongest.

MEETING INDIVIDUAL NEEDS

Writing **Learners Having Difficulty** To help students organize information about the three types of algae described on page 247, have them create a chart with three columns, one for each type of algae. Each column should have three rows: one describing the size of the algae, one describing where the algae can be found, and one describing how the algae get their food. Then have students reread page 247 and record information about the different kinds of algae in the appropriate spaces on their charts. **Sheltered English**

DEMONSTRATION

Algin and Carrageenan
Display the following products (or product packages) on a table in the classroom:

> ice cream, salad dressing, jelly beans, chocolate milk or eggnog, instant pudding, dry gravy mix or canned gravy, marshmallows, and a nondairy dessert topping

Tell students that two substances extracted from algae—algin and carrageenan—are common ingredients in many foods. Algin comes from giant kelp and other brown algae, while carrageenan is extracted from a red alga. Both are used as food thickeners, stabilizers, and emulsifiers. Have students read the ingredients on the packages and discuss how widespread the use of algin and carrageenan is in commercially prepared foods. **Sheltered English**

TOPIC: Algae
GO TO: www.scilinks.org
*sci*LINKS NUMBER: HSTL255

Section 1 • Protists **247**

2) Teach, continued

READING STRATEGY

Mnemonics Tell students that the word *phytoplankton* comes from the Greek words *phyto,* which means "plant," and *planktos,* which means "wandering." (Remind students that phytoplankton are now classified as protists, not as plants.) Tell students that plankton also contains tiny animals that as a group are referred to as *zooplankton;* the Greek root word *zoion* means "animal." An easy way to remember the difference is that both *phytoplankton* and *plant* begin with the letter *p,* while *zooplankton* contains the word *zoo,* which is a place where animals are kept.

CONNECT TO EARTH SCIENCE

Diatomaceous earth is a sedimentary rock composed mainly of the glass shells of diatoms. It has many commercial uses. It is used as a filter for oils, chemicals, and even some beverages; as an abrasive in many kinds of polishes; and in the manufacture of ceramics.

Diatomaceous earth is spread in gardens to kill slugs. When these 10-million-year-old diatoms are crushed, they become as sharp as glass and slice the slugs on contact.

Figure 8 *Although most diatoms are free floating, many cling to plants, shellfish, sea turtles, and whales.*

Some dinoflagellates give off light. A chemical reaction in the cells produces light that is similar to the light produced by fireflies. Water filled with these dinoflagellates glows like a twinkling neon light.

Figure 9 *Red tides occur throughout the world and are common in the Gulf of Mexico.*

Diatoms Diatoms (DIE e TAHMZ) are single-celled organisms. They are found in both salt water and fresh water. As with all algae, diatoms get their energy from photosynthesis. They make up a large percentage of phytoplankton. As you can see in **Figure 8,** many diatoms have unusual shapes. Their cell walls contain cellulose and silica, a rigid, glasslike substance. The cells are enclosed in a shell with two parts that fit neatly together. Piles of diatom shells deposited over millions of years form a fine, crumbly substance that is used in silver polish, toothpaste, filters, and insulation.

Dinoflagellates Most dinoflagellates (DIE noh FLAJ uh lits) are single-celled algae. They live primarily in salt water, although a few species live in fresh water, and some are even found in snow. Dinoflagellates have two whiplike strands called *flagella* (singular, *flagellum*). The beating of these flagella causes the cells to spin through the water. For this reason they are sometimes called spinning flagellates.

Most dinoflagellates get energy from photosynthesis, but a few are consumers, decomposers, or parasites. Some dinoflagellates are red and produce a strong poison. If these algae multiply rapidly, they can turn the water red, causing a dangerous condition known as *red tide*. When shellfish eat these algae, the poison is concentrated in their bodies. The shellfish are then toxic to humans and other vertebrates who eat them. A red tide is shown in **Figure 9.**

Knock, Knock!
Q: Who's there?
A: *Euglena.*
Q: *Euglena* who?
A: *Euglena* your room, or you're grounded!

248 Chapter 11 • Protists and Fungi

Euglenoids Euglenoids (yoo GLEE noydz) are single-celled protists that live primarily in fresh water. Most euglenoids have characteristics of both plants and animals. Like plants, they use photosynthesis. But when light is too low for photosynthesis, they can become consumers, like animals. Euglenoids can also move like animals. Flagella propel the organisms through the water. The structure of a euglenoid is shown in **Figure 10**.

Some euglenoids do not have chloroplasts for photosynthesis. These species either consume other small protists or absorb dissolved nutrients.

Chloroplasts are needed for photosynthesis. These structures contain the green pigment chlorophyll.

Nucleus

Most euglenoids have two **flagella**, one long and one short. The long flagellum is used to move the organism through water.

Euglenoids can't see, but they have **eyespots** that respond to light.

A special structure called a **contractile vacuole** collects excess water and removes it from the cell.

Figure 10 *Euglenoids have both plant and animal characteristics.*

REVIEW

1. How does a slime mold survive when food and water are limited?
2. Which plantlike protists move? How?
3. Add the following terms to the concept map at right: consumer, water mold, diatom, euglenoid.
4. Look at the picture of a euglenoid on this page. Which cell structures are plantlike? Which are animal-like?
5. **Analyzing Relationships** How do funguslike protists differ from plantlike protists?

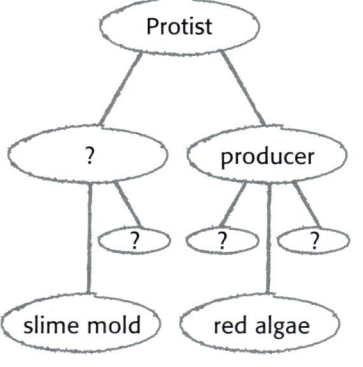

RETEACHING

Writing Have students read the description of a typical euglenoid on this page, and study **Figure 10.** Then ask students to imagine they are writing a letter to a friend describing a euglenoid and its animal-like and plantlike characteristics. Have students write their letters in their ScienceLog.
Sheltered English

SCIENTISTS AT ODDS

Euglenoids pose a special problem for taxonomists because they exhibit characteristics of both plants and animals. Most euglenoids have plastids containing pigments similar to those in green algae, and they can carry on photosynthesis in sunlight. These are characteristics of algae. But euglenoids do not have cell walls, and they use flagella to propel themselves through water or anchor themselves in place. When a euglenoid is kept in the dark, it loses its green color and begins to feed like an animal. In sunlight it photosynthesizes just like a plant. For these reasons biologists used to classify euglenoids as protozoa in the phylum Zoomastigophora. Now they are classified as euglenoids in the phylum Euglenophyta.

Teaching Transparency 41
"Euglena"

Answers to Review

1. Slime molds form spores when water and food are limited. These spores can survive poor growth conditions and will develop into new individuals when conditions improve.
2. Dinoflagellates and euglenoids move. Both organisms use flagella to move through the water.
3. Students might indicate a protist can be a consumer, such as a water mold or a slime mold. A protist can also be a producer, such as a diatom, a red algae, or a euglenoid.
4. In euglenoids, chloroplasts are plantlike. Eyespots and flagella are animal-like.
5. Funguslike protists are consumers. They get nutrients from other organisms. Plantlike protists are producers and can use photosynthesis.

2) Teach, continued

USING THE FIGURE

Tell students that the amoeba shown in **Figure 12** is engulfing prey. Ask students to make drawings in their ScienceLog that show all the stages in endocytosis—the amoeba's pseudopodia surrounding the prey, joining at their tips, and then forming a food vacuole around the engulfed organism. Then challenge students to create a similar series of drawings that illustrate the process of exocytosis (expelling a waste-filled vacuole) in an amoeba.
<mark>Sheltered English</mark>

ACTIVITY

Observing Live Amoebas
Obtain live amoebas from a biological supply house. Have students work in pairs to place an amoeba on a slide with a little water and observe it under a microscope. In their ScienceLog, have students describe how the amoeba moves. Students should also look for contractile vacuoles in their specimens.
<mark>Sheltered English</mark>

TOPIC: Protozoa
GO TO: www.scilinks.org
sciLINKS NUMBER: HSTL260

Animal-Like Protists: Protozoa

The animal-like protists are single-celled consumers. These protists are also known as **protozoa.** Some are parasites. Many can move. Scientists do not agree on how to group protozoa, but they are often divided into four phyla: amoebalike protists, flagellates, ciliates, and spore-forming protists.

Amoebalike Protists
An amoeba (uh MEE buh) is a soft, jellylike protozoan. Amoebas are found in both fresh and salt water, in soil, or as parasites in animals. Although an amoeba looks shapeless, it is actually a highly structured cell. Like euglenoids, amoebas have contractile vacuoles to get rid of excess water. Amoebas move with *pseudopodia* (soo doh POH dee uh). *Pseudopodia* means "false feet." You can see how an amoeba uses pseudopodia to move in **Figure 11.**

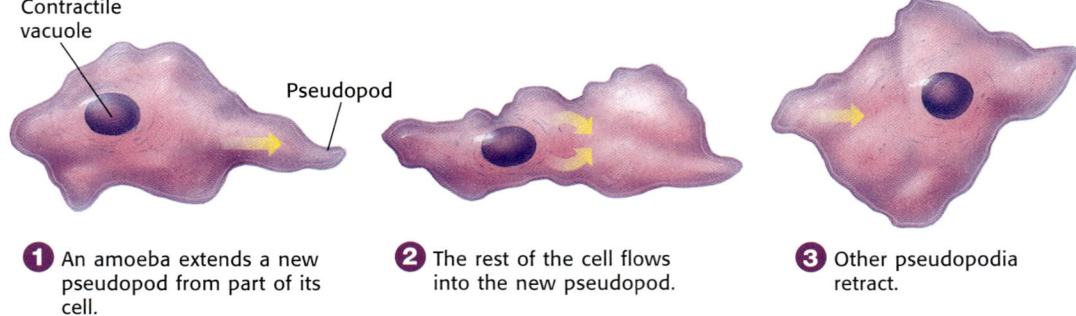

① An amoeba extends a new pseudopod from part of its cell.

② The rest of the cell flows into the new pseudopod.

③ Other pseudopodia retract.

Figure 11 *The shape of an amoeba changes constantly as new pseudopodia form.*

Feeding Amoebas
Like slime molds, amoebas feed by engulfing food. An amoeba senses the presence of another single-celled organism and moves toward it. It surrounds a bacterium or small protist with its pseudopodia, forming a *food vacuole*. Enzymes move into the vacuole to digest the food, and the digested food passes out of the vacuole into the cytoplasm of the amoeba. To get rid of wastes, an amoeba reverses the process. A waste-filled vacuole is moved to the edge of the cell and is released. **Figure 12** shows an amoeba feeding.

Some amoebas are parasites. Certain species live in the human intestine and cause amebic dysentery, a painful condition that can involve bleeding ulcers.

Figure 12 *An amoeba engulfs its prey with its pseudopodia.*

People may have more in common with amoebas than they think. Researchers have discovered that very similar contractile proteins are involved in both amoeboid movement and the movement of animal muscles. The cytoplasm of an amoeba contains thick and thin filaments that are almost identical to the thick myosin filaments and the thin actin filaments found in striated muscle.

Protozoa with Shells Not all amoebalike protozoa look like amoebas. Some have an outer shell. *Radiolarians* (RAY dee oh LER ee uhnz) have shells made of silica that look like glass ornaments. This type of protozoan is shown in **Figure 13.** *Foraminiferans* (fuh RAM uh NIF uhr uhnz) have snail-like shells made of calcium carbonate.

Flagellates Flagellates (FLAJ uh LITS) are protozoa that use flagella to move. The flagella wave back and forth to propel the organism forward. Some flagellates live in water. Others are parasites that can cause disease.

The flagellate parasite, *Giardia lamblia,* lives in the digestive tracts of humans and other vertebrates. This parasite is shown in **Figure 14.** In an inactive form, *Giardia* (JEE ar DEE uh) can survive in water. Hikers or others who drink water infected with *Giardia* can get diarrhea and severe stomach cramps, but the disease is usually not fatal.

Some flagellates live in symbiosis with vertebrates or invertebrates. In *symbiosis,* one organism lives closely with another organism, and each organism helps the other survive. One symbiotic flagellate lives in the guts of termites and digests the cellulose in the wood that the termites eat. Without the protozoa, the termites could not completely digest the cellulose.

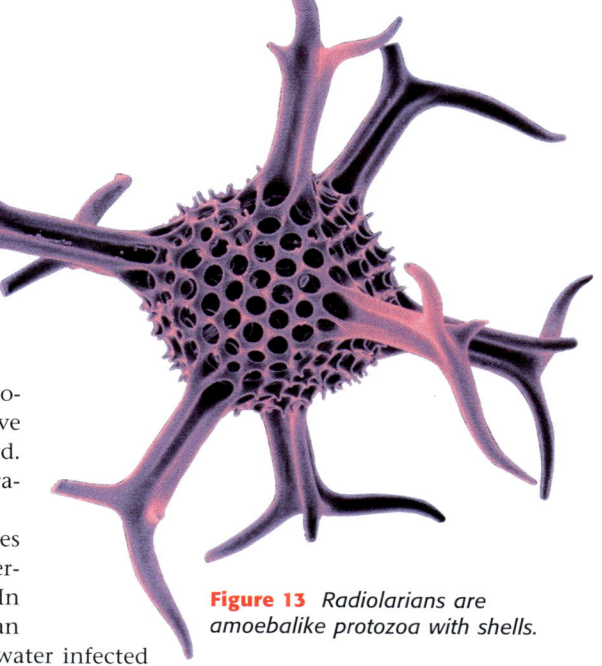

Figure 13 *Radiolarians are amoebalike protozoa with shells.*

Geology CONNECTION

Foraminiferans have existed for over 600 million years. During this time, the shells of dead foraminiferans have been sinking to the bottom of the ocean. Millions of years ago, foraminiferan shells formed a thick layer of sediment of limestone and chalk deposits. The chalk deposits known as the White Cliffs of Dover in England were formed this way.

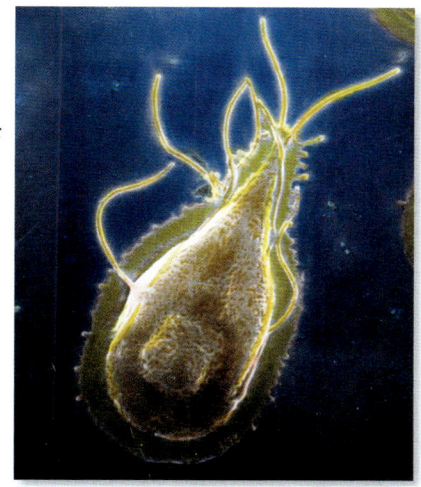

Figure 14 *The parasitic protist,* Giardia lamblia, *is a primitive cell. Can you see why it is a flagellate?*

IS THAT A FACT!

Deposits of foraminiferan shells on the sea floor are thousands of meters thick and cover millions of square kilometers. The sand of some beaches is also mostly from foraminiferan remains. There are nearly 50,000 foraminiferan shells in a gram of sand.

Section 1 • Protists   **251**

3) Extend

 PG 722
Making a Protist Mobile

Going Further

Anton van Leeuwenhoek (1632–1723) called the tiny, active organisms he viewed under his handmade microscopes *animalcules*. The ciliated protozoa undoubtedly are the most animal-like members of the kingdom Protista. Have students research a ciliate protozoan of their choice. Encourage students to make posters of their ciliate, complete with a large, detailed drawing of it and information about where it lives, what it eats, how it moves, and other interesting aspects of its biology. Ask permission to display students' posters in the school cafeteria or the library.

Answers to Self-Check

1. Cilia are used to move a ciliate through the water and to sweep food toward the organism.
2. Ciliates are classified as animal-like protists because they are consumers and they move.

Teaching Transparency 41 *"Paramecium"*

Explore the different shapes of protists on page 722 of your LabBook.

Ciliates Ciliates (SIL ee its) are the most complex protozoa. Ciliates have hundreds of tiny hairlike structures known as *cilia*. The cilia move a protozoan forward by beating back and forth. Cilia can beat up to 60 times a second! In some species, clumps of cilia form bristlelike structures used for movement. Cilia are also important for feeding. Ciliates use their cilia to sweep food through the water toward them. The best known ciliate is *Paramecium* (PAR uh MEE see uhm), shown in **Figure 15**.

Ciliates have two kinds of nuclei. A large nucleus called a *macronucleus* controls the functions of the cell. A smaller nucleus, the *micronucleus*, passes genetic material to another individual during sexual reproduction.

Figure 15 *Paramecium* is a complex protozoa with many cell structures.

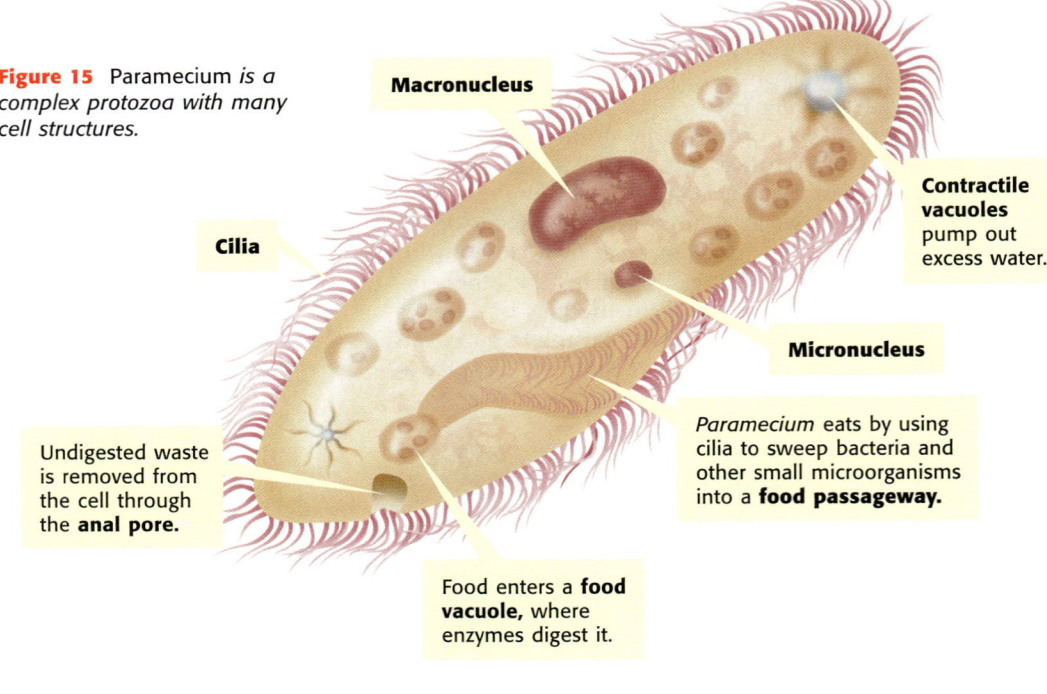

- **Macronucleus**
- **Cilia**
- **Contractile vacuoles** pump out excess water.
- **Micronucleus**
- *Paramecium* eats by using cilia to sweep bacteria and other small microorganisms into a **food passageway**.
- Undigested waste is removed from the cell through the **anal pore**.
- Food enters a **food vacuole**, where enzymes digest it.

✓ Self-Check

1. What are the functions of cilia?
2. Why are the ciliates classified as animal-like protists?

(See page 782 to check your answers.)

WEIRD SCIENCE

Not all ciliates feed on small prey. A barrel-shaped *Didinia* gobbles up protists that are much larger than itself. *Paramecium* is a common prey of *Didinia*, even though *Paramecium* is twice as large as *Didinia*. To accomplish this feat, *Didinia* essentially folds a paramecium in half and then engulfs it.

Spore-Forming Protists The spore-forming protozoa are all parasites that absorb nutrients from their hosts. They have no cilia or flagella, and they cannot move on their own. Spore-forming protozoa have complicated life cycles that usually involve two or more different hosts.

Plasmodium (plaz MOH dee uhm) *vivax* (VIE vaks) is the spore-forming protist that causes malaria. Malaria is a serious disease that is carried by mosquitoes in tropical areas. Although malaria can be treated with drugs, more than 2 million people die from malaria each year.

The Life Cycle of *Plasmodium vivax*

Plasmodium vivax is a parasite that has two different hosts, mosquitoes and humans. It needs both hosts to survive. Once a human is bitten by an infected mosquito, *Plasmodium* spores enter the liver. The spores multiply and change form. They then enter red blood cells and multiply, causing the red blood cells to burst. If the malaria victim is bitten by another mosquito, the disease can then be carried to another human.

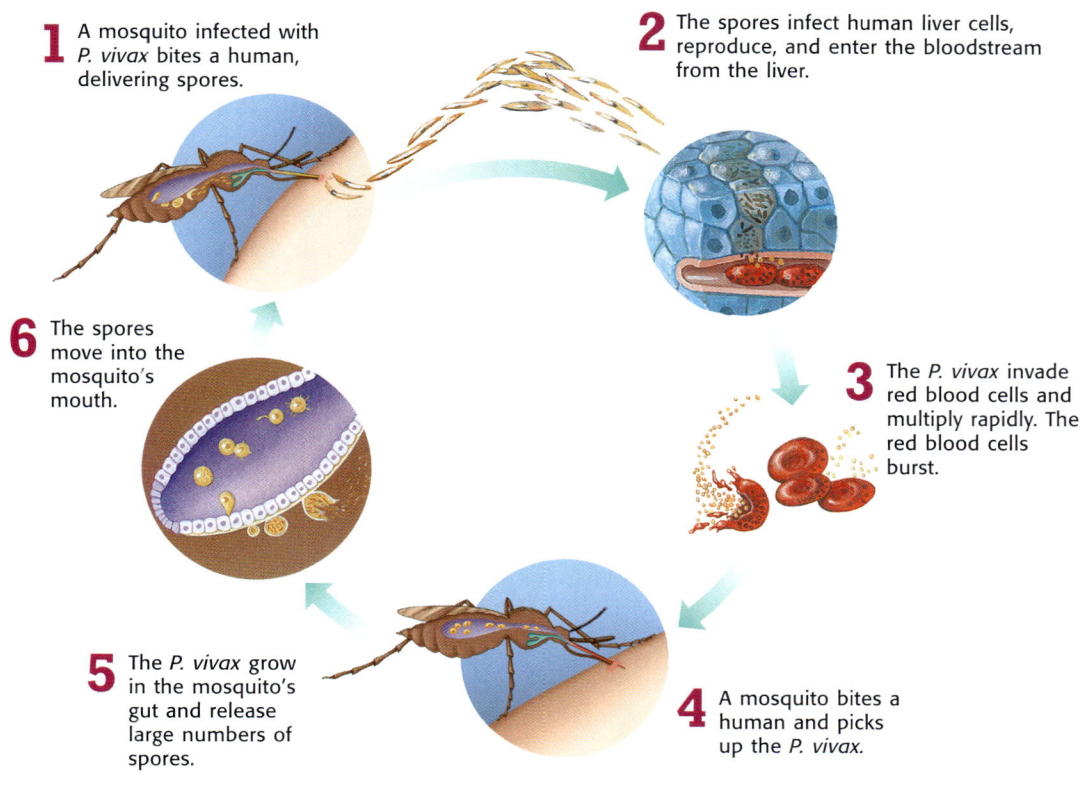

1 A mosquito infected with *P. vivax* bites a human, delivering spores.

2 The spores infect human liver cells, reproduce, and enter the bloodstream from the liver.

3 The *P. vivax* invade red blood cells and multiply rapidly. The red blood cells burst.

4 A mosquito bites a human and picks up the *P. vivax*.

5 The *P. vivax* grow in the mosquito's gut and release large numbers of spores.

6 The spores move into the mosquito's mouth.

IS THAT A FACT!

After a person is bitten by a malaria-carrying mosquito, he or she can get malaria even if only one *Plasmodium* spore successfully reaches the liver and reproduces.

Teaching Transparency 42 "The Life Cycle of *Plasmodium vivax*"

Science Skills Worksheet 17 "Organizing Your Research"

MATH and MORE

Many protists reproduce asexually simply by dividing in two, a process called fission. Students are probably familiar with this form of division, which can result in a population growing exponentially over time; that is, 1 cell divides to produce 2 cells, which in turn divide to produce 4 cells, then 8, 16, 32, 64, and so on. *Plasmodium* and some other parasitic, spore-forming protozoa can divide asexually by a process known as schizogony, or multiple fission. For example, a single spore (technically called a sporozoite) of malaria-causing strain called *Plasmodium vivax* can produce 40,000 offspring.

Researchers have determined that when a *Plasmodium*-infected mosquito inserts its proboscis into a human blood vessel, it injects about a thousand spores. Have students calculate how many *Plasmodium vivax* spores could be present in a person's body after just one division by multiple fission.

(1,000 spores × 40,000 offspring = 40,000,000 spores)

 Math Skills Worksheet 4 "A Shortcut for Multiplying Large Numbers"

Homework

 Research Encourage students to research and report on malaria and the work currently being done on developing malaria vaccines.

4) Close

Quiz

1. What important characteristic do funguslike protists have in common with true fungi? (Sample answer: Both fungi and funguslike protists are consumers that obtain their food from dead organic matter or from the bodies of other organisms.)

2. Give three examples of protists that are producers in ocean food chains. (red, brown, and green algae; diatoms; dinoflagellates)

ALTERNATIVE ASSESSMENT

Ask students to create an illustrated book of the kingdom Protista, in which they devote a chapter to each of the major protist groups: funguslike protists, plantlike protists, and animal-like protists. Encourage students to use reference books and their textbook to create illustrations and write text for their protist books.

Reinforcement Worksheet 11 "Protists on Parade"

Critical Thinking Worksheet 11 "Protist Pop Culture"

Reproduction of Protists

Some protists reproduce asexually. In asexual reproduction, the offspring come from just one parent. Both animal-like amoebas and plantlike *Euglena* reproduce asexually by fission, as shown in **Figure 16.**

Some protists can also reproduce sexually. Sexual reproduction requires two parents. Animal-like *Paramecium* sometimes reproduces sexually by a process called conjugation. During conjugation, two *Paramecium* join together and exchange genetic material using their micronuclei. Then they divide to produce four organisms with new combinations of genetic material. Conjugation is shown in **Figure 17.**

Many protists reproduce both asexually and sexually. In some algae, asexual reproduction and sexual reproduction alternate from one generation to the next.

Figure 16 During fission, *Euglena* divides lengthwise.

Figure 17 Conjugation in *Paramecium* is a type of sexual reproduction.

internet connect
SCLINKS
NSTA
TOPIC: Algae, Protozoa
GO TO: www.scilinks.org
sciLINKS NUMBER: HSTL255, HSTL260

REVIEW

1. Name the three main groups of protists, and give the characteristics of each.
2. What are three ways that flagella and cilia differ?
3. **Making Inferences** Killing mosquitoes is one method of controlling malaria. Using what you know about the organism that causes malaria, explain why this method works.

▼ Answers to Review

1. **Funguslike protists** get their food from dead organic matter or from the body of another organism. **Plantlike protists** are producers that carry out photosynthesis. **Animal-like protists** are single-celled consumers.

2. Flagella are whiplike structures, and cilia are tiny hair-like structures. Organisms have a small number of flagella at specific locations on their body. Organisms with cilia have hundreds of cilia all over their outer surface. Flagella are used only in moving the organism. Cilia are also used for feeding.

3. Malaria requires two hosts—mosquitoes and humans. Because it must have both hosts to survive, removing the mosquitoes will keep the protist from infecting additional humans.

Section 2

Fungi

Terms to Learn

fungus
hyphae
mycelium
spore
mold
lichen

What You'll Do

◆ Describe the characteristics of fungi.
◆ Distinguish between the four main groups of fungi.
◆ Describe how fungi can be helpful or harmful.
◆ Define *lichen*.

Have you ever heard someone say, "A fungus is among us"? This statement has more truth in it than you may realize. The mushrooms on pizza are a type of fungus (plural, *fungi*). The yeast used to make bread is a fungus. Fungi are also used to produce cheeses, antibiotics, and soy sauce. And if you've ever had athlete's foot, you can thank a fungus. Fungi are everywhere!

Characteristics of Fungi

Fungi are eukaryotic consumers, but they are so different from other organisms that they are placed in their own kingdom. As you can see in **Figure 18,** fungi come in a variety of shapes, sizes, and colors. But all fungi have similar ways of obtaining food and reproducing.

Straight coral fungus

Ascomycetus

Figure 18 *Fungi vary in their size and shape.*

Bird's nest fungus

Witch's hat fungus

Food for Fungi Fungi are consumers, but they cannot eat or engulf food. Fungi must live on or near their food supply. Most fungi obtain nutrients by secreting digestive juices onto a food source, then absorbing the dissolved substances. Many fungi are *decomposers*. This means that they feed on dead plant or animal matter. Other fungi are parasites.

Some fungi live in symbiotic relationships with other organisms. For example, many types of fungi grow on the roots of plants. They release an acid that changes minerals in the soil into forms that plants can use. The fungi also protect the plant from some disease-causing organisms.

255

IS THAT A FACT!

There are about 350 species of yeast. The most economically important yeast is *Saccharomyces cerevisiae*, which has been used by humans in the production of bread, beer, and wine for thousands of years.

Directed Reading Worksheet 11 Section 2

internetconnect

TOPIC: Fungi
GO TO: www.scilinks.org
sciLINKS NUMBER: HSTL265

Section 2

Focus

Fungi

In this section, students learn about fungi—eukaryotic consumers that obtain their food by absorbing nutrients from other organisms. Students are introduced to the four main groups of fungi: threadlike fungi, sac fungi, club fungi, and imperfect fungi. Finally, students learn about lichens, which are symbiotic associations between a fungus and an organism that can photosynthesize, usually an alga.

Bellringer

Ask students to answer the following questions in their ScienceLog:

What are mushrooms? What is the function of the cap of a button mushroom? (Accept all reasonable responses. The umbrella-shaped mushrooms that students may be most familiar with are club fungi. The aboveground portion of the mushroom is the spore-producing part of the organism.)

1) Motivate

DISCUSSION

Ask students to describe a world without fungi. (Accept all reasonable responses, but guide them to understand that without fungi there would be no leavened bread, no penicillin, no bleu cheese, no mushroom pizza. Tell them that fungi are decomposers and that huge amounts of dead organic matter might collect without fungi.)

Section 2 • Fungi   255

2 Teach

Answers to Self-Check

1. Both fungi and funguslike protists are consumers. Both form spores.
2. Hyphae are chains of fungal cells that grow together to form a large mass called the mycelium.

READING STRATEGY

Prediction Guide Before students read the rest of this section, ask them if the following three statements are true or false. Students will learn the answers as they explore Section 2.

- Unlike protists, fungi can reproduce only asexually. **(false)**
- Morels and truffles are highly prized mushrooms. **(true)**
- Lichens are a combination of a fungus and an alga. **(true)**

DISCUSSION

Allergies and Molds Ask students if they or people they know are allergic to molds. As a class, encourage students to discuss reasons why mold allergies are so common, and the types of environments or substances that mold-sensitive individuals might want to avoid and why. **(Sample answer: caves, damp basements, damp soil, leaf litter and other decaying organic matter, and so on; Molds flourish in such places and materials.)**

Self-Check

1. In what ways are fungi and funguslike protists alike?
2. How are hyphae and mycelia related?

(See page 782 to check your answer.)

Hidden from View All fungi are made of eukaryotic cells, which have nuclei. Some fungi are single-celled, but most fungi are multicellular. Multicellular fungi are made up of chains of cells called **hyphae** (HIE fee). Hyphae are fungal filaments that are similar to plant roots. These filaments are made of cells. But unlike plant root cells, the hyphae cells have openings in their cell walls that allow cytoplasm to move freely between the cells. The hyphae grow together to form a twisted mass called the **mycelium** (mie SEE lee uhm). The mycelium is the major part of the fungus, but it is often hidden from view underneath the ground. **Figure 19** shows the hyphae and mycelium of a fungus.

Figure 19 The mycelium of a fungus is formed by hyphae and is often underground.

Making More Fungi Reproduction in fungi may be either asexual or sexual. Asexual reproduction occurs in two ways. In one type of asexual reproduction, the hyphae break apart and each new piece becomes a new individual. Asexual reproduction can also occur by the production of spores. **Spores** are small reproductive cells protected by a thick cell wall. Spores are light and easily spread by the wind. See for yourself in **Figure 20**. If the growing conditions where it lands are right, a spore will produce a new fungus.

Sexual reproduction occurs in fungi when special structures form to make sex cells. The sex cells join to produce sexual spores that grow into a new fungus.

Figure 20 This puffball is releasing spores that can produce new fungi.

IS THAT A FACT!

Yeasts are widely used in genetic research. Yeasts were the first eukaryotic organisms to have their DNA manipulated through the techniques of genetic engineering; today they are the organisms of choice for many types of experiments in molecular and cell biology. Experiments on yeasts such as *Saccharomyces cerevisiae*, the common bread yeast, have provided enormous insight into the functioning of eukaryotic cells.

Kinds of Fungi

Fungi are divided into four main groups: threadlike fungi, sac fungi, club fungi, and imperfect fungi. A fungus is classified into a particular group based on its shape and the way it reproduces.

Threadlike Fungi Have you ever seen fuzzy black mold growing on bread? **Molds** are shapeless fuzzy fungi, as shown in **Figure 21**. This particular mold belongs to a group of fungi called *threadlike fungi*. Most of the fungi in this group live in the soil and are usually decomposers, although some are parasites.

Threadlike fungi can reproduce asexually. Extensions of the hyphae grow into the air and form round spore cases at the tips called *sporangia* (spoh RAN jee uh). These sporangia are shown in **Figure 22**. When the sporangia break open, many tiny spores are released into the air.

Threadlike fungi can also reproduce sexually. Two hyphae from different individuals join and develop into specialized sporangia. These sporangia can survive periods of cold or drought. When conditions become more favorable, these specialized sporangia release spores that can grow into new fungi.

Figure 21 Black bread mold is a soft, cottony mass that grows on bread and fruit.

Figure 22 Each of the round sporangia contains thousands of spores.

QuickLab

Moldy Bread

If you took a **slice of bread**, moistened it with a few drops of **water**, and then sealed it in a **plastic bag** for 1 week, what do you think would happen? Would the bread get moldy? Why or why not? Where would mold spores come from? How would these spores grow? Design an experiment to check your predictions. How many pieces of bread will you use? Will you treat them the same or differently? Why? If your teacher approves, try your experiment. Did it answer your questions? If not, what changes could you make to get the answers?

✓ Self-Check

What is the relationship between spores and sporangia? *(See page 782 to check your answers.)*

Multicultural CONNECTION

Centuries ago, Indonesians discovered that the bread mold *Rhizopus* can be used to produce a food called tempeh. Soybeans that have been stripped of their skins and boiled are inoculated with this mold and allowed to sit for 24 hours. A mycelium grows around the soybeans, holding them together in a mass and producing enzymes that increase the level of B vitamins in the mixture. Tempeh is very nutritious and is prepared daily in many Indonesian households, just as bread is in many other countries. Tempeh is usually served fried, baked, steamed, or roasted.

QuickLab

MATERIALS

FOR EACH GROUP:
- slice of bread
- water
- plastic bag

Answers to QuickLab

Answers will vary, but explanations and experimental designs should be logical. Students may suggest that the bread would become moldy. Mold spores would come from the air and grow using the nutrients in the bread and water. An experiment to test the hypothesis would have at least two groups—a plastic bag containing a dry piece of bread and a plastic bag containing a moistened slice of bread. Students may also suggest other variations, such as leaving one bag open and the other sealed.

Answer to Self-Check

Sporangia are round tips on hyphae extensions. Spores are found in the sporangia.

WEIRD SCIENCE

The mold *Pilobolus* grows on animal manure. The name comes from Greek words meaning "hat thrower." The name fits: *Pilobolus* produces little black sacs of spores on top of stalked structures that swell just beneath the sacs. As the spores mature, pressure builds up in the swollen parts of the stalks until spore-containing sacs are shot into the air, sometimes as much as 8 m! The sticky spore sacs adhere to grass and leaves. When animals eat the plants, *Pilobolus* spores pass unharmed through their digestive track and end up in their dung, where the spores germinate and begin the cycle again.

Section 2 • Fungi 257

2) Teach

MAKING MODELS

Encourage students to research a species of sac or club fungus in an encyclopedia, in books on fungi, or on the Internet. Provide students with colored modeling clay, and have them create lifelike models of the fungi they have investigated. Make a class display of the fungus models. **Sheltered English**

MATH and MORE

Truffles are called the black diamonds of French cooking. Tell students that, in western France an unusually dry summer produced a smaller than usual harvest. Prices of first quality truffles rose from $535 per kilogram to $625 per kilogram.

Ask students the following question:

> What percentage increase in the price of truffles does this represent? ($625 − $535 = $90; $90 ÷ 535 = 0.168, or a 17% increase)

Tell students to imagine they are chefs and are required to make a new dish with a recipe calling for 1 lb of truffles. How many kilograms of this high-priced fungi will they need to buy, and what will it cost at the new price? (1 kg = 2.2 lb, so students will need 0.45 kg for this recipe. The cost would be $625 × 0.45 = $281.25.)

Figure 23 Many people think truffles are delicious. Would you eat them?

MATH BREAK

Multiplying Yeasts

Under ideal conditions, a yeast will produce a new cell by budding in about 30 minutes. Suppose a beaker contains 100 yeast cells. How many cells will it contain after 30 minutes? after 1 hour? after 2 hours? Make a graph to show the increase in size of the yeast population over a period of 5 hours.

Figure 25 Dutch elm disease is a fungal disease that has killed thousands of elm trees in North America.

Answers to MATHBREAK

After 30 minutes, there will be 200 yeast cells. After 1 hour, there will be 400 cells, and after 2 hours, there will be 1,600 cells. The graph will show exponential growth to a point of 102,400 cells (5 hours).

Sac Fungi Sac fungi form the largest group of fungi. Sac fungi include yeasts, powdery mildews, truffles, and morels. Truffles are shown in **Figure 23**.

Sexual reproduction in these fungi involves the formation of a sac called an *ascus*. These sacs give the sac fungi their name. Sexually produced spores develop within the ascus. During their life cycles, sac fungi usually reproduce both sexually and asexually.

Most sac fungi are multicellular, but *yeasts* are single-celled sac fungi. Yeasts reproduce asexually by *budding*. In budding, a new cell pinches off from an existing cell. A yeast is budding in **Figure 24**. Yeasts are the only fungi to reproduce by budding.

Figure 24 Yeasts reproduce by budding. A round scar forms where a bud breaks off of a parent cell. How many times has the larger cell reproduced?

Some sac fungi are very useful to humans. One example is yeasts, which are used in making bread. Yeasts use sugar as food and produce carbon dioxide gas and alcohol as waste products. Trapped bubbles of carbon dioxide cause the dough to rise and make bread light and fluffy. Other sac fungi are sources of antibiotics and vitamins. Truffles and morels are prized edible fungi.

Many sac fungi are parasites. They cause plant diseases, such as chestnut blight and Dutch elm disease, shown in **Figure 25**.

IS THAT A FACT!

Some yeast produce an enzyme called invertase that is used by commercial candy makers to soften or liquefy the centers of chocolate candies after the coating has been applied.

Club Fungi The umbrella-shaped mushrooms are the most commonly known fungi. They belong to a group of fungi called *club fungi.* During sexual reproduction, special hyphae develop and produce clublike structures called *basidia* (buh SID ee uh), the Greek word for "clubs." Sexual spores develop inside the basidia.

What you think of as a mushroom is only the sexual spore-producing part of the organism. The mass of hyphae from which mushrooms are produced may grow 35 m across. Since mushrooms usually grow at the outer edges of the mass of hyphae, they often appear in circles, as shown in **Figure 26.**

The most familiar mushrooms are known as gill fungi because the basidia develop in the grooves, or *gills,* under the cap. Some varieties are grown commercially and sold in supermarkets, but not all gill fungi are edible. The white destroying angel is one type that is very poisonous. Simply a taste of this mushroom can be fatal. See if you can pick out the poisonous fungus in **Figure 27.**

Figure 26 *A ring of mushrooms can appear overnight. In European folk legends, these were known as "fairy rings."*

Figure 27 *Many poisonous mushrooms look good to eat. The mushrooms on the left are edible, but the ones on the right are poisonous.*

A Mushroom Omelet
A friend wants to make a mushroom omelet, but he has no mushrooms. He recently got a mushroom book that has pictures of all the poisonous and edible mushrooms. Using the book, he picks some mushrooms in the woods behind his house. He uses the wild mushrooms to make an omelet. Do you think he should eat the omelet? Why or why not?

Observe a Mushroom

1. Identify the stalk, cap, and gills on a **mushroom** that your teacher has provided.
2. Carefully twist or cut off the cap, and cut it open with a **knife.** Observe the gills with a **magnifying lens.** Look for spores.
3. Observe the other parts of the mushroom with the magnifying lens. The mycelium begins at the bottom of the stalk. Try to find individual hyphae.
4. Sketch the mushroom, and label the parts.

WEIRD SCIENCE

Mushrooms consist mostly of water (about 90 percent), and most edible species are low in nutritional value. An exception is the shiitake mushroom, which has been grown for centuries in Japan and China. In ancient China, people believed that eating shiitake mushrooms promoted good health. They were right—shiitake mushrooms are rich in iron, phosphorus, and calcium and in vitamins B, D, and C. They also have twice the protein content of most other commercially grown mushrooms.

3) Extend

CROSS-DISCIPLINARY FOCUS

 Literature Beatrix Potter (1866–1943) is best known for authoring and illustrating such famous stories as *The Tale of Peter Rabbit* and *The Tale of Mr. Toad*. She lived and worked in England and had a scholarly interest in fungi. Some of her papers were unfairly rejected, and she detailed this in her diaries. She was a shy person, easily dismissed by the scholars at the Royal Society and the Royal Botanical Gardens. After all, what could the inventor of Peter Rabbit know about fungi? She is now widely respected as a mycologist (a scientist who studies fungi) and is recognized for contributing many valuable papers on the subject. Her detailed drawings of more than 270 examples of fungi are displayed in a library in Ambleside, England. Encourage interested students to research and present a report on the life of Beatrix Potter.

 PG 723

There's a Fungus Among Us!

REAL-WORLD CONNECTION

Cyclosporin is a chemical compound that was discovered in an imperfect fungus in the 1980s. Cyclosporin suppresses immune reactions that lead to rejection of transplanted organs. This fungal drug has led to much greater success in organ transplants.

Figure 28 *Bracket fungi look like shelves on trees. Spores are found on the underside of the bracket.*

Figure 29 *This corn crop is infected with a club fungus called a smut.*

Mushrooms are not the only club fungi. Bracket fungi, puffballs, smuts, and rusts are also in this group of fungi. Bracket fungi grow outward from wood, forming small shelves or brackets, as shown in **Figure 28**. Smuts and rusts are common plant parasites. They often attack crops such as corn and wheat. This can be seen in **Figure 29**.

BRAIN FOOD

Did you know that stonewashed jeans aren't really washed with stones? They get their faded look from a fungus! Jeans are soaked in a solution containing the fungus *Trichoderma*. This fungus produces enzymes that partially digest the cotton fibers to give jeans a stone-washed appearance.

Imperfect Fungi The *imperfect fungi* group includes all the species of fungi that do not quite fit in the other groups. These fungi do not reproduce sexually. Most are parasites that cause diseases in plants and animals. One common human disease caused by these fungi is athlete's foot, a skin disease. Another fungus from this group produces a poison called *aflatoxin*, which can cause cancer.

Some imperfect fungi are useful. *Penicillium*, shown in **Figure 30**, is the source of the antibiotic penicillin. Other imperfect fungi are also used to produce medicines. Some imperfect fungi are used to produce cheeses, soy sauce, and the citric acid used in cola drinks.

Figure 30 *The fungus* Penicillium *produces a substance that kills certain bacteria.*

WEIRD SCIENCE

Near Seattle, Washington, a fungus was found that covered an area of 4 km^2 (2.5 mi^2) and weighed nearly 1,000 tons. When scientists took tissue samples of this honey mushroom fungus, they found it to be one organism! The fungus is estimated to be up to 1,000 years old.

IS THAT A FACT!

If you are allergic to penicillin, you will probably be allergic to Camembert and Roquefort cheeses too, because these cheeses get their flavor from *Penicillium* molds.

Lichens

A **lichen** is a combination of a fungus and an alga that grow intertwined. The alga actually lives inside the protective walls of the fungus. The resulting organism is different from either of the two organisms growing alone. The merging of the two organisms to form a lichen is so complete that scientists give lichens their own scientific names. **Figure 31** shows examples of lichens.

Unlike fungi, lichens are producers. The algae in the lichens produce food through photosynthesis. Unlike algae, lichens can withstand drying out because of the protective walls of the fungus. Lichens are found in almost every type of terrestrial environment. They can even grow in extreme environments like dry deserts and the Arctic.

Lichens need only air, light, and minerals to grow. This is why lichens can grow on rocks. They produce acids that break down the rock and cause cracks. Bits of rock and dead lichens fill the cracks, making soil that other organisms can grow on.

Lichens absorb water and minerals from the air. As a result, they are easily affected by air pollution. Thus, the presence or absence of lichens is a good measure of air quality in an area.

Jewel lichen

Fruticose lichen

British soldier lichen

Figure 31 These are some of the many types of lichens.

REVIEW

1. How are fungi able to withstand periods of cold or drought?
2. Why are fungi such an important part of the natural world?
3. What are the four main groups of fungi? Give a characteristic of each.
4. **Making Inferences** Why are lichens an example of symbiosis?

TOPIC: Fungi, Lichens
GO TO: www.scilinks.org
sciLINKS NUMBER: HSTL265, HSTL270

261

Chapter Highlights

VOCABULARY DEFINITIONS

SECTION 1

protist an organism that belongs to the kingdom Protista

funguslike protist describes a protist that obtains its food from dead organic matter or from the body of another organism

parasite an organism that feeds on another living creature, usually without killing it

host an organism on which a parasite lives

algae protists that convert the sun's energy into food through photosynthesis

phytoplankton a microscopic photosynthetic organism that floats near the surface of the ocean

protozoa animal-like protists that are single-celled consumers

Chapter Highlights

SECTION 1

Vocabulary
- protist (p. 244)
- funguslike protist (p. 245)
- parasite (p. 246)
- host (p. 246)
- algae (p. 246)
- phytoplankton (p. 247)
- protozoa (p. 250)

Section Notes
- The protists are a diverse group of single-celled and multicellular organisms. They are grouped in their own kingdom because they differ from other organisms in many ways.
- Funguslike protists are consumers that obtain their food from dead organic matter or from the body of another organism.
- Slime molds and water molds are two groups of funguslike protists.
- Plantlike protists are producers that are also known as algae. Most are aquatic.
- Among the plantlike protists are red algae, brown algae, green algae, diatoms, dinoflagellates, and euglenoids.
- The animal-like protists are single-celled consumers also known as protozoa. Most can move.
- The protozoa include amoebalike protists, flagellates, ciliates, and spore-forming protists.
- Some protists reproduce sexually, some asexually, and some both sexually and asexually.

Labs
Making a Protist Mobile (p. 722)

☑ Skills Check

Math Concepts
MICROBE MULTIPLICATION Suppose an amoeba can reproduce by fission once every 30 minutes. If you start with 50 amoebas, after 30 minutes you will have twice as many because each amoeba has divided.

$$2 \times 50 = 100 \text{ amoebas}$$

After 1 hour (30 minutes later) the number of amoebas will double again.

$$2 \times 100 = 200 \text{ amoebas}$$

Visual Understanding
PROTIST STRUCTURE Look at the illustration of *Paramecium* on page 252. Carefully read the labels, and look at each part described. Now do the same thing with the illustration of the euglenoid on page 249. Notice what the two cells have in common and how they differ.

Lab and Activity Highlights

Making a Protist Mobile PG 722

There's a Fungus Among Us! PG 723

 Datasheets for LabBook (blackline masters for these labs)

262 Chapter 11 • Protists and Fungi

SECTION 2

Vocabulary
- fungus *(p. 255)*
- hyphae *(p. 256)*
- mycelium *(p. 256)*
- spore *(p. 256)*
- mold *(p. 257)*
- lichen *(p. 261)*

Section Notes
- Fungi are consumers. They can be decomposers or parasites, or they can live in symbiotic relationships with other organisms.
- Most fungi are made up of chains of cells called hyphae. Many hyphae join together to form a mycelium.
- The four main groups of fungi are threadlike fungi, sac fungi, club fungi, and imperfect fungi.
- Threadlike fungi are primarily decomposers that form sporangia to hold spores.
- Molds are shapeless, fuzzy fungi.
- During sexual reproduction, sac fungi form little sacs in which sexual spores develop.
- Club fungi form structures called basidia during sexual reproduction.
- The imperfect fungi include all the species that do not quite fit anywhere else. Most are parasites that reproduce only by asexual reproduction.
- A lichen is a combination of a specific fungus and a specific alga that is different from either organism growing alone.

Labs
There's a Fungus Among Us! *(p. 723)*

VOCABULARY DEFINITIONS, continued

SECTION 2

fungus an organism in the kingdom Fungi

hyphae chains of cells that make up multicellular fungi

mycelium a twisted mass of fungal hyphae that have grown together

spore a small reproductive cell protected by a thick wall

mold a shapeless, fuzzy fungus

lichen combination of a fungus and an alga that grow intertwined and exist in a symbiotic relationship

 Vocabulary Review Worksheet 11

 Blackline masters of these Chapter Highlights can be found in the **Study Guide.**

---

internetconnect

 GO TO: go.hrw.com

Visit the **HRW** Web site for a variety of learning tools related to this chapter. Just type in the keyword:

KEYWORD: HSTPRO

 GO TO: www.scilinks.org

Visit the **National Science Teachers Association** on-line Web site for Internet resources related to this chapter. Just type in the *sci*LINKS number for more information about the topic:

TOPIC: Algae	*sci*LINKS NUMBER: HSTL255
TOPIC: Protozoa	*sci*LINKS NUMBER: HSTL260
TOPIC: Fungi	*sci*LINKS NUMBER: HSTL265
TOPIC: Lichens	*sci*LINKS NUMBER: HSTL270

Lab and Activity Highlights

LabBank

 Labs You Can Eat, Knot Your Average Yeast Lab, Lab 5

Whiz-Bang Demonstrations, Unleash the Yeast! Demo 7

 Long-Term Projects & Research Ideas, Algae for All! Project 11

Chapter 11 • Chapter Highlights

Chapter Review Answers

USING VOCABULARY

1. algae
2. conjugation
3. an ascus
4. Decomposers
5. protozoa
6. host

UNDERSTANDING CONCEPTS

Multiple Choice

7. d
8. a
9. c
10. b
11. b
12. d
13. b

Short Answer

14. Helpful fungi are decompsers that recycle nutrients. Some provide food for humans and are also used to make some medicines. Harmful fungi cause diseases in humans and damage crops.
15. *Paramecium* uses cilia to move and to get food.
16. A red tide is formed when red dinoflagellates multiply rapidly and form reddish brown water.
17. Both slime molds and amoebas are protists, and both feed by engulfing food.

Chapter Review

USING VOCABULARY

To complete the following sentences, choose the correct term from each pair of terms listed below:

1. Protists that get energy from photosynthesis are __?__. (*algae* or *amoebas*)
2. *Paramecium* reproduces sexually by __?__. (*budding* or *conjugation*)
3. The structure containing spores in a sac fungi is called __?__. (*an ascus* or *a basidium*)
4. __?__ live on dead organic matter. (*Parasites* or *Decomposers*)
5. Animal-like protists are also called __?__. (*protozoa* or *algae*)
6. A parasite gets its nutrients from its __?__. (*host* or *spores*)

UNDERSTANDING CONCEPTS

Multiple Choice

7. Plantlike protists include
   a. euglenoids and ciliates.
   b. lichens and flagellates.
   c. spore-forming protists and smuts.
   d. dinoflagellates and diatoms.

8. Funguslike protists
   a. are consumers or decomposers.
   b. are made of chains of cells called hyphae.
   c. are divided into four major groups.
   d. are always parasites.

9. A euglenoid has
   a. a micronucleus.
   b. pseudopodia.
   c. two flagella.
   d. cilia.

10. Fungi
    a. are producers.
    b. cannot eat or engulf food.
    c. are found only in the soil.
    d. are primarily single-celled.

11. A lichen
    a. is a parasite.
    b. is made up of an alga and a fungus that live intertwined together.
    c. can live only where there is plenty of water.
    d. is a consumer.

12. Animal-like protists
    a. are also known as protozoa.
    b. include amoebas and *Paramecium*.
    c. may be either free living or parasitic.
    d. All of the above

13. A contractile vacuole
    a. is a food passageway.
    b. pumps out excess water.
    c. is the location of food digestion.
    d. can be found in any animal-like protist.

Short Answer

14. How are fungi helpful to humans? How are they harmful?
15. What is the function of cilia in *Paramecium*?
16. What is a red tide?
17. How are slime molds and amoebas similar?

264 Chapter 11 • Protists and Fungi

Concept Mapping

18. Use the following terms to create a concept map: fungi, ascus, club fungi, basidia, bread mold, yeast, threadlike fungi, mushrooms.

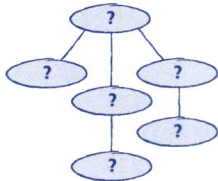

CRITICAL THINKING AND PROBLEM SOLVING

Write one or two sentences to answer the following questions:

19. What might happen if all the protists on Earth died?

20. Water can pass easily through a cell membrane, but too much water can cause a cell to burst. Single-celled amoebas and *Paramecium* have thin cell membranes, and they also live in water. Why don't these organisms burst?

21. You discover some mushrooms in your backyard one morning, and you pull them out of the ground. But the next day you find even more mushrooms. They seem to be growing in a line. Where did the new mushrooms come from?

MATH IN SCIENCE

22. You and your classmates are studying the growth of *Euglena*. Using a microscope, you count the number of organisms in a small container each day. Your teacher says you can expect the number of *Euglena* to double in 1.5 days. If you started out with five *Euglena*, how many *Euglena* do you think you will see on the third day?

INTERPRETING GRAPHICS

Look at the pictures of fungi below, and answer the following questions:

a   **b**

c   **d**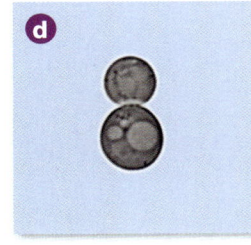

23. What kind of fungus is shown here?
24. What cellular process is shown in these pictures?
25. Which picture was taken first? last? Arrange the pictures in order.
26. Which is the original parent cell? How do you know?

Reading Check-up

Take a minute to review your answers to the Pre-Reading Questions found at the bottom of page 242. Have your answers changed? If necessary, revise your answers based on what you have learned since you began this chapter.

Concept Mapping

18. An answer to this exercise can be found at the end of this book.

CRITICAL THINKING AND PROBLEM SOLVING

19. Sample answer: If all the protists on Earth died, many larger organisms that depend on protists for food might also die. The oxygen supply on Earth might be severely limited if there were no plantlike protists.

20. Amoebas and *Paramecium* have contractile vacuoles that pump excess water outside of the cell.

21. The new mushrooms grew from mycelia that are hidden below the ground.

MATH IN SCIENCE

22. 20 *Euglena*

INTERPRETING GRAPHICS

23. yeast (sac fungus)
24. budding
25. b was first; c was last; b, d, a, c
26. The large cell in picture b is the parent cell because it is the first to bud.

 Concept Mapping Transparency 11

 Blackline masters of this Chapter Review can be found in the **Study Guide**.

Chapter 11 • Chapter Review

SCIENCE, TECHNOLOGY, AND SOCIETY
Moldy Bandages

Background
The research into fungi-based dressing is being done nearly exclusively by the British Textile Technology Group. More-detailed descriptions of the research can be found on the Internet.

Teaching Strategy
Have the students research a folk remedy and create a poster depicting the ailment and the treatment.

Science, Technology, and Society
Moldy Bandages

When you think of the word *fungus*, you probably think of moldy leftovers in the refrigerator or mushrooms growing at the base of a tree. You may even think of athlete's foot or some other ailment caused by a fungus. Someday you may also think of bandages when you think of fungi. At least that is the hope of Paul Hamlyn and his colleagues at the British Textile Technology Group (BTTG).

▲ *Would you believe that fungi like this may someday be used in surgical bandages?*

Fungi Versus Infection
The scientists at BTTG, along with scientists at the Welsh School of Pharmacy, have discovered that the cell walls of fungi contain polymers that promote the growth of the human cells responsible for rebuilding tissue around a wound. These human healing cells are called fibroblasts, and studies show that the fungal polymers attract and help bind the fibroblasts at a wound. Researchers believe that the polymers react with oxygen to produce hydrogen peroxide. The hydrogen peroxide activates white blood cells and promotes the growth of the fibroblasts. The white blood cells help fight infection around the wound.

From Crab Shells to Wound Healing
Until recently, the only sources of these polymers were crab and prawn shells. The quality and quantity of polymers found in the shells of crabs and prawns vary with weather conditions and with the seasons. Hamlyn's studies have shown that fungi can provide a more consistent product. For even more consistent results, scientists are able to grow fungi in the laboratory in a liquid growth medium.

Where Do We Go from Here?
Although his work is still in the research stage, Hamlyn is working toward a commercial application of the wound-healing fungi. He is researching the possibility of manufacturing two types of bandages from fungi. The first would be made by freeze-drying pieces of the fungi to create an absorbent dressing. This could be used for patients with deep wounds. The second type would be used to help patients with bed sores or diabetic skin ulcers. This bandage would involve a wet dressing of fungi that could be placed over sores or abrasions on the surface of the skin. The fungi would help accelerate the healing process.

Fungi Find the Cure
▶ Fungal products have long been used in the field of medicine. One modern use is cyclosporin. It is a drug used to help prevent the rejection of transplanted organs in humans. Other uses for fungi include a popular folk remedy—placing moldy bread on a wound to promote healing. Research these or other types of medicines that are made from fungi to discover how they work.

Answers to Fungi Find the Cure
Accept all reasonable answers. There are many books that provide lists of such home remedies. One such series is *Chicken Soup and Other Folk Remedies,* by Joan and Lydia Wilen.

ACROSS THE SCIENCES

LIFE SCIENCE • EARTH SCIENCE

It's Alive!

The Maya of Mexico and their descendants believe that Cueva de Villa Luz (the Cave of the Lighted House) is inhabited by powerful spirits. For centuries, they have walked past slimy globs that drip from the cave's ceiling without even thinking about them. When scientists decided to analyze these slime balls, they discovered that the formations are home to billions of microscopic organisms! They nicknamed these colonies "snot-tites" because they resemble mucus.

Life in Battery Acid

As people climb down into the pitch-dark passages of Cueva de Villa Luz, they are greeted by the stench of rotten eggs, an odor rarely found in caves and quickly recognized as potentially deadly hydrogen sulfide gas. This foul and dangerous gas is emitted by the snot-tites! Because it is not safe to remain inside the caverns if there is too much hydrogen sulfide, explorers must constantly monitor the level of the gas in the air.

A closer inspection of snot-tite drippings reveals that they contain sulfuric acid. When sulfuric acid dripped on some of the explorers' clothes, the clothes dissolved right off of their backs!

How do the organisms live in such harsh conditions? It turns out that snot-tites can actually get energy from sulfur, which is toxic to most organisms. And since snot-tites do not have to rely on photosynthesis for energy, they can live in absolute darkness.

A Unique Ecosystem

During dry seasons, the Mayan people feast on tiny fish called mollies that are abundant in the milky-white streams that flow through Cueva de Villa Luz. It's very rare to find so many fish in cave streams. Why are there fish in this cave?

Scientists have discovered that the snot-tites are part of a complex underground ecosystem, possibly unlike any other on Earth. When snot-tites use the sulfur found in the cave, they produce a nutritionally rich waste product. This waste drips into the streams below, where hungry fish can eat it.

Life on Mars?

Many scientists argue that conditions on Mars are too harsh to support any form of life. However, Martian rocks have a large amount of sulfur and scientists know that Mars has caves. Snot-tites have proven that life can exist in these harsh conditions. Someday a space traveler might find a similar organism on Mars!

Going to Extremes

▶ Snot-tites have adapted to extreme environmental conditions that would kill other organisms. Such organisms are called extremophiles. Investigate to find out about other extremophiles. Why are scientists so interested in extremophiles?

◀ Several billion sulfur-eating microbes can live in a single cubic centimeter of these slimy, gooey snot-tites!

ACROSS THE SCIENCES
It's Alive!

Teaching Strategy

Snot-tites, which are a mixture of fungi and bacteria, prove that life can exist in the most brutal environments. Scientists study extremophiles because they believe that the adaptations of organisms to tolerate harsh conditions may have practical applications. Most extremophiles have special enzymes or biological catalysts that allow them to survive in such extreme conditions. For example, enzymes allow snot-tites to convert sulfur, which kills most organisms, into cellular energy.

Heat-loving microorganisms, called thermophiles, can thrive in boiling temperatures of 212°F! Scientists are still trying to figure out how the enzymes of these organisms stay in one piece. Encourage students to investigate the thermophiles that live in the hot springs of Yellowstone National Park.

Answer to Going to Extremes

The enzymes of extremophiles are used industrially to produce sweeteners and to diagnose some diseases. Unfortunately, most enzymes fall apart and stop working when they are exposed to heat or harsh chemicals, such as acid. Scientists must take great steps to ensure that enzymes stay intact. Enzymes from extremophiles, nicknamed "extremozymes," may eliminate these difficult or costly steps.

Chapter Organizer

CHAPTER ORGANIZATION	TIME MINUTES	OBJECTIVES	LABS, INVESTIGATIONS, AND DEMONSTRATIONS
Chapter Opener pp. 268–269	45	National Standards: UCP 1, 2, 5, SPSP 5, LS 1a, 4c	**Start-Up Activity** Observing Plant Growth, p. 269
Section 1 What Makes a Plant a Plant?	90	▶ Identify the characteristics that all plants share. ▶ Discuss the origin of plants. ▶ Explain how the four main groups of plants differ. UCP 1, 2, 5, SAI 1, 2, ST 2, HNS 2, LS 1a, 1d, 2b, 4c, 5a	**Demonstration,** Water Travel in Plants, p. 270 in ATE GENERAL **Interactive Explorations CD-ROM,** Shut Your Trap! GENERAL A **Worksheet** is also available in the **Interactive Explorations Teacher's Guide.**
Section 2 Seedless Plants	90	▶ Describe the features of mosses and liverworts. ▶ Describe the features of ferns, horsetails, and club mosses. ▶ Explain how plants without seeds are important to humans and to the environment. UCP 1–3, 5, SAI 1, LS 1a, 1c, 2b, 5c	**QuickLab,** Moss Mass, p. 275 GENERAL
Section 3 Plants with Seeds	90	▶ Compare a seed with a spore. ▶ Describe the features of gymnosperms. ▶ Describe the features of angiosperms. ▶ List the economic and environmental importance of gymnosperms and angiosperms. UCP 1, 2, 5, SAI 1, SPSP 4, 5, LS 1a, 1d, 2b–2d, 4b–4d; LabBook UCP 2, 5, SAI 1, HNS 1, LS 1a, 5b	**Skill Builder,** Travelin' Seeds, p. 726 GENERAL **Datasheets for LabBook,** Travelin' Seeds, Datasheet 26 GENERAL **EcoLabs & Field Activities,** The Case of the Ravenous Radish, EcoLab 3 GENERAL
Section 4 The Structures of Seed Plants	90	▶ Describe the functions of roots. ▶ Describe the functions of stems. ▶ Explain how the structure of leaves is related to their function. ▶ Identify the parts of a flower and their functions. UCP 1, 2, 5, SAI 1, LS 1a, 1d, 2b, 3d, 4c, 5b; LabBook UCP 2, 5, SAI 1, HNS 1, LS 1a, 2b, 5b	**Demonstration,** Seed Transport, p. 284 in ATE GENERAL **Skill Builder,** Leaf Me Alone! p. 724 GENERAL **Datasheets for LabBook,** Leaf Me Alone! Datasheet 25 GENERAL **Making Models,** Build a Flower, p. 727 GENERAL **Datasheets for LabBook,** Build a Flower, Datasheet 27 GENERAL **Whiz-Bang Demonstrations,** Inner Life of a Leaf, Demo 8 BASIC **Long-Term Projects & Research Ideas,** Project 12 ADVANCED

---

*See page **T20** for a complete correlation of this book with the*

NATIONAL SCIENCE EDUCATION STANDARDS.

TECHNOLOGY RESOURCES

 Guided Reading Audio CD English or Spanish, Chapter 12

 One-Stop Planner CD-ROM with Test Generator

 CNN. Eye on the Environment, Prairie Restoration, Segment 16

 Interactive Explorations CD-ROM CD 1, Exploration 2, Shut Your Trap!

Chapter 12 • Introduction to Plants

Chapter 12 • Introduction to Plants

CLASSROOM WORKSHEETS, TRANSPARENCIES, AND RESOURCES	SCIENCE INTEGRATION AND CONNECTIONS	REVIEW AND ASSESSMENT
Science Puzzlers, Twisters & Teasers, Worksheet 12 `ADVANCED` **Directed Reading Worksheet 12** `BASIC`		
Directed Reading Worksheet 12, Section 1 `BASIC` **Transparency 43,** Plant Life Cycle **Transparency 44,** The Main Groups of Living Plants	**Multicultural Connection,** p. 272 in ATE **Math and More,** Percentages, p. 272 in ATE `GENERAL` **MathBreak,** Practice with Percents, p. 273 `GENERAL` **Careers:** Ethnobotanist–Paul Cox, p. 297 `GENERAL`	**Self-Check,** p. 272 **Review,** p. 273 `GENERAL` **Quiz,** p. 273 in ATE `GENERAL` **Alternative Assessment,** p. 273 in ATE `GENERAL`
Directed Reading Worksheet 12, Section 2 `BASIC`	**Cross-Disciplinary Focus,** p. 274 in ATE **Real-World Connection,** p. 275 in ATE	**Homework,** p. 276 in ATE `GENERAL` **Review,** p. 277 `GENERAL` **Quiz,** p. 277 in ATE `GENERAL` **Alternative Assessment,** p. 277 in ATE `ADVANCED`
Directed Reading Worksheet 12, Section 3 `BASIC` **Science Skills Worksheet 22,** Science Writing `GENERAL` **Transparency 45,** Two Classes of Angiosperms **Reinforcement Worksheet 12,** Classifying Plants `GENERAL` **Reinforcement Worksheet 12,** Drawing Dicots `GENERAL`	**Environment Connection,** p. 279 **Apply,** p. 279 `GENERAL` **Connect to Earth Science,** p. 280 in ATE **Cross-Disciplinary Focus,** p. 282 in ATE `ADVANCED` **Science, Technology, and Society:** Supersquash or Frankenfruit? p. 296 `GENERAL`	**Homework,** p. 281 in ATE `ADVANCED` **Review,** p. 283 `GENERAL` **Quiz,** p. 283 in ATE `GENERAL` **Alternative Assessment,** p. 283 in ATE `GENERAL`
Directed Reading Worksheet 12, Section 4 `BASIC` **Transparency 46,** Root Structure **Science Skills Worksheet 21,** Taking Notes `GENERAL` **Transparency 47,** Stem Structure **Transparency 48,** Leaf Structure **Transparency 235,** Photosynthesis **Transparency 48,** Flower Structure **Critical Thinking Worksheet 12,** The Voodoo Lily `ADVANCED`	**Cross-Disciplinary Focus,** p. 286 in ATE `ADVANCED` **Connect to Physical Science,** p. 289 in ATE	**Review,** p. 287 `GENERAL` **Self-Check,** p. 288 **Homework,** p. 288 in ATE `ADVANCED` **Review,** p. 291 `GENERAL` **Quiz,** p. 291 in ATE `GENERAL` **Alternative Assessment,** p. 291 in ATE `ADVANCED`

END-OF-CHAPTER REVIEW AND ASSESSMENT

Chapter Review in Study Guide
Vocabulary and Notes in Study Guide
Chapter Tests with Performance-Based Assessment, Chapter 12 Test
Chapter Tests with Performance-Based Assessment, Performance-Based Assessment 12
Concept Mapping Transparency 12

internet connect

Holt, Rinehart and Winston On-line Resources
go.hrw.com
For worksheets and other teaching aids related to this chapter, visit the HRW Web site and type in the keyword: **HSTPL1**

National Science Teachers Association
www.scilinks.org
Encourage students to use the *sci*LINKS numbers listed in the internet connect boxes to access information and resources on the **NSTA** Web site.

Chapter 12 • Chapter Organizer **267B**

Chapter Resources & Worksheets

Visual Resources

TEACHING TRANSPARENCIES

TEACHING TRANSPARENCIES

CONCEPT MAPPING TRANSPARENCY

Meeting Individual Needs

DIRECTED READING

REINFORCEMENT & VOCABULARY REVIEW

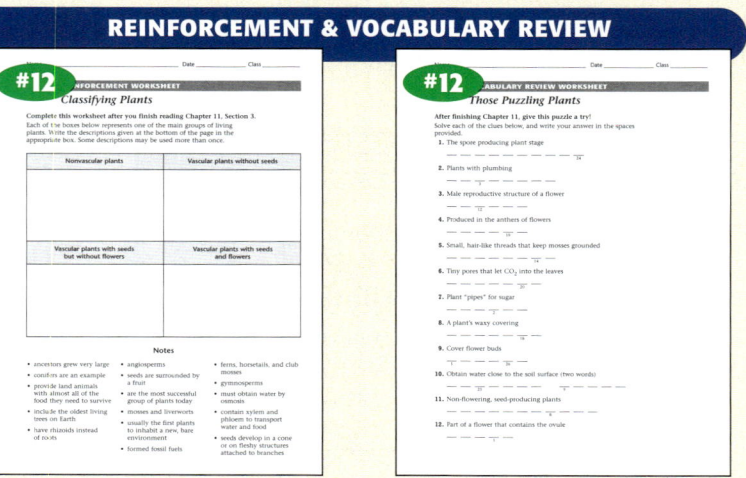

SCIENCE PUZZLERS, TWISTERS & TEASERS

267C Chapter 12 • Introduction to Plants

Chapter 12 • Introduction to Plants

Review & Assessment

STUDY GUIDE

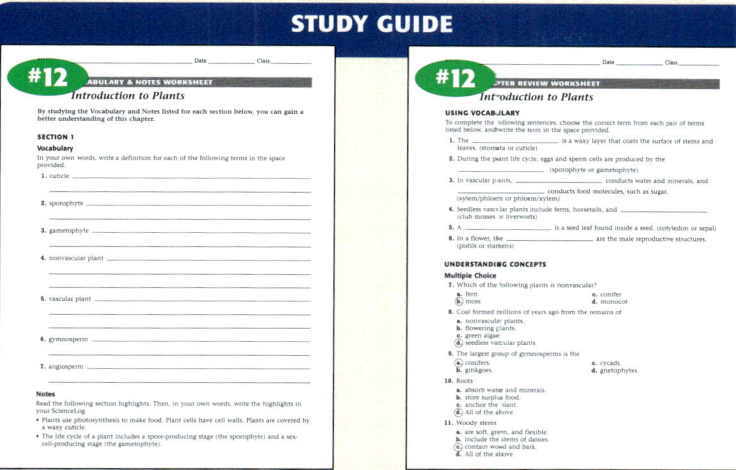

CHAPTER TESTS WITH PERFORMANCE-BASED ASSESSMENT

Lab Worksheets

ECOLABS & FIELD ACTIVITIES

WHIZ-BANG DEMONSTRATIONS

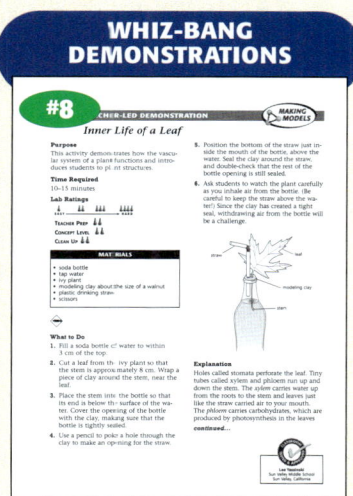

LONG-TERM PROJECTS & RESEARCH IDEAS

DATASHEETS FOR LABBOOK

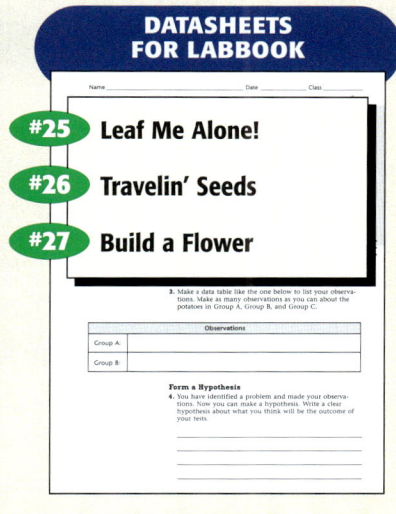

Applications & Extensions

CRITICAL THINKING & PROBLEM SOLVING

EYE ON THE ENVIRONMENT

INTERACTIVE EXPLORATIONS

Chapter 12 • Chapter Resources & Worksheets

Chapter Background

SECTION 1

What Makes a Plant a Plant?

▶ **Theophrastus**
Theophrastus (372–288 B.C.), Aristotle's student, was one of the first botanists. He wrote two books, *History of Plants* and *The Causes of Plants*. He described the morphology, uses, propagation, and pollination of 500 plants and described sexual reproduction in plants. Theophrastus directed the Lyceum (a school and center of learning), in Athens. The Lyceum housed the first botanical garden. Theophrastus's writings were the standard for botanical study until the sixteenth century.

IS THAT A FACT!

- The leaves of a pitcher plant form tall, narrow cups that hold rainwater. The tip of the plant is colorful and has nectar-secreting glands that attract insects. The insects follow a path of tiny hairs down into the cup, where the walls are smooth. The insects lose their grip and drown.

▶ **Carnivorous Plants**
Carnivorous plants photosynthesize and are true plants. They tend to grow in bogs and marshes, where the soil is waterlogged. Bacteria and fungi cannot thrive in these soils, so there is little decomposition of organic matter to provide nutrients to plants. The small invertebrates that carnivorous plants catch provide additional nutrients, especially nitrates. The insects are digested by juices secreted by the leaves or by bacteria and fungi living in the plant.

SECTION 2

Seedless Plants

▶ **Bryophytes: Good Things Come in Small Packages**
Bryophytes, which include mosses, hornworts, and liverworts, make up 15,000 described species worldwide. Various species tend to be restricted to particular environments because of sensitivities to temperature, light exposure, water availability, and chemical composition of the substrate. This makes them good indicator species for applied ecologists and conservation biologists; they can characterize an environment by identifying the bryophytes.

- Bryophytes are also useful for studies of evolution and population genetics. Their structures are complex enough to use as models for land-plant evolution but still simple enough for genetic studies. They are small and are easy to culture in the lab. Field biologists, however, can usually observe them year-round under natural conditions.

▶ **Evolution of Ferns**
Ferns are an ancient group of plants with fossil records dating to the Devonian period, 408 million years ago. Nearly all of those early fern groups are now extinct. Only one or two living genera can be traced directly to Carboniferous ancestors.

IS THAT A FACT!

- Before the invention of flashbulbs and strobe lights for indoor and low-light photography, photographers created an explosive flash of light with a powder. They spread the powder on a metal bar attached to a T-shaped device and ignited it. The powder contained millions of spores from club mosses (seedless, vascular plants that are related to ferns and horsetails and are not true mosses).

Chapter 12 • Introduction to Plants

SECTION 3

Plants with Seeds

▶ **The Millennium Seed Bank**
The Royal Botanic Gardens, in Kew, England, has launched a project to collect seeds from 25,000 plant species around the world. One-fourth of the world's plants might become extinct in the next 50 years, but the seed bank will ensure the survival of plants vital for stabilizing soil and providing food crops, medicine, and building materials. The collected seeds are dried and stored in subzero temperatures. Scientists believe the seeds will be viable even hundreds of years in the future.

▶ **The Economic and Social Importance of Plants**
Farming originated thousands of years ago. Three of the earliest cultivated crops—wheat, rice, and corn—today feed more than half of the people in the world.

- Herbs and spices were valued commodities on ancient trade routes. In medieval times, explorers and merchants brought spices to Europe by camel caravan from east Asia.

- Perfume makers use essential oils from a variety of flowers, including rose, orange, lavender, and jasmine.

- The ancient Egyptians made paper from papyrus reeds. Paper can also be made from nettles, bamboo, and other plants. Today, most paper is made from wood pulp.

IS THAT A FACT!

◆ Alder fruits rely on water to disperse their seeds. The fruits contain oil droplets to keep the seeds afloat.

SECTION 4

The Structures of Seed Plants

▶ **Inflorescence**
The cluster of flowers that develops on many plants is called an inflorescence, of which there are two types. In a determinate inflorescence, the peduncle (main axis) terminates in a flower bud that prevents the peduncle from continued growth. In indeterminate inflorescence, the lower buds open first. As the peduncle continues to grow, the youngest flowers are always at the top. There are several forms of indeterminate inflorescence, including the following:

- raceme: each flower of the cluster is on a pedicel (short stem) that extends from the peduncle (snapdragon)

- spike: resembles a raceme but has no pedicels (gladiolus)

- panicle: branched raceme in which each branch has multiple flowers (lilac)

- head: short, dense spike with flowers in a circular mass (dandelion)

- umbel: all the pedicels grow from the same point at the top of the peduncle (onion)

▶ **Can't Keep a Good Grass Down**
Grass is mowed, eaten, and trampled, and still it grows. Grass buds are not on the ends of the leaf blades but are at ground level. Grazing geese and rabbits, lawn mowers, and people walking do not destroy the buds.

- People eat the seeds of grasses when they consume rice, wheat, oats, barley, rye, corn, millet, and sorghum.

For background information about teaching strategies and issues, refer to the *Professional Reference for Teachers*.

CHAPTER 12

Introduction to Plants

 Pre-Reading Questions

Students may not know the answers to these questions before reading the chapter, so accept any reasonable response.

Suggested Answers

1. Answers will vary, but students should discuss the function of flowers and fruits in the reproductive cycle of flowering plants.

2. Answers may vary, but students should point out that plants make their own food and that animals have to eat the nutrients they need. Animal cells do not have chlorophyll or cell walls.

 Directed Reading Worksheet 12

 Science Puzzlers, Twisters & Teasers Worksheet 12

 Guided Reading Audio CD English or Spanish, Chapter 12

CHAPTER 12

Introduction to Plants

Sections

1. **What Makes a Plant a Plant?** 270
   MathBreak 273
   Internet Connect 273

2. **Seedless Plants** 274
   QuickLab 275
   Internet Connect 277

3. **Plants with Seeds** ... 278
   Environment Connection 279
   Apply 279
   Internet Connect 283

4. **The Structures of Seed Plants** 284
   Internet Connect 291

Chapter Review 294
Feature Articles 296, 297
LabBook 724–727

1. How do plants use flowers and fruits?
2. How are plants different from animals?

Green Aliens?

In Costa Rica's Monteverde cloud forest, a green pattern begins to unfold. It is hidden from all but the most careful observer. It looks alien, but it is very much of this Earth. It is part of a fern, a plant that grows in moist areas. How do we know this patterned mass is a fern? How do we know a fern is a plant? In this chapter, you will learn what plants are, how they differ from one another, and how they survive and reproduce.

These round clusters, called sori, contain structures that produce spores.

---

internet connect

 HRW On-line Resources
go.hrw.com
For worksheets and other teaching aids, visit the HRW Web site and type in the keyword: **HSTPL1**

 SCiLINKS NSTA
www.scilinks.com
Use the *sci*LINKS numbers at the end of each chapter for additional resources on the NSTA Web site.

 CNNfyi.com
www.cnnfyi.com
Visit the CNN Web site for current events coverage and classroom resources.

START-UP Activity

OBSERVING PLANT GROWTH

When planting a garden, you bury seeds in the ground, water them, and then wait for tiny sprouts to poke through the soil. What happens to the seeds while they're below the soil? How do seeds grow into plants?

Procedure

1. Fill a **clear 2 L bottle** to within 3 cm of the top with **potting soil.** Your teacher will have already cut off the neck of the bottle.
2. Press **three or four bean seeds** into the soil and against the wall of the bottle. Add an additional 5 cm of potting soil.
3. Cover the sides of the bottle with **aluminum foil** to keep out light. Leave the top uncovered.
4. Water the seeds with about **60 mL of water.** Add more water when the soil dries out.
5. Check on your seeds each day. Record your observations.

Analysis

6. How long did it take for the seeds to germinate?
7. How many seeds grew?
8. Where do the seeds get the energy to start growing?

START-UP Activity

OBSERVING PLANT GROWTH

MATERIALS
FOR EACH GROUP: • 2 L clear-plastic bottle (with top half cut off) • potting soil • bean seeds • aluminum foil • water (60 mL)

Safety Caution

Some students—particularly those who suffer from allergies—may wish to wear protective gloves while handling the soil and seeds. Have students wash their hands when they are finished with the activity.

Teacher's Notes

Cut off the neck of each bottle before distributing it to students.

Make sure students do not cover the seeds with more than 5 cm of potting soil. Doing so will delay the seedling from emerging from the surface.

Be sure students keep seeds evenly moist to ensure germination.

Answers to START-UP Activity

6. Answers will vary. Germination times vary depending on the seeds used. Soaking the seeds in advance will decrease the number of days to germination.
7. Students may report that not all of their seeds germinated.
8. The seed contains stored food molecules that are used for energy.

Chapter 12 • Introduction to Plants

SECTION 1

Focus

What Makes a Plant a Plant?

In this section students will learn the shared characteristics of plants, such as that all plants make their own food, have a cuticle, reproduce with spores and sex cells, and have cells with cell walls. Finally, students will learn that the four main plant groups are classified as either nonvascular or vascular, depending on how materials are transported within the plant.

🔔 Bellringer

Tell students there are four major types of plants. Ask them to try to identify those types and to give at least two examples for each one. Have them review their responses when they have finished reading this section. **(Students will likely respond with flowers, trees, weeds, and grasses. They might also list fruits and vegetables. They probably will not classify plants according to the chapter information.)**

1) Motivate

DEMONSTRATION

Water Travel in Plants Slice a stalk of celery lengthwise to just below the leaves. Place the two halves in separate beakers, each containing a different color of water. Red and blue food coloring work best. Students should be able to see the veins in the leaves change color after the colored liquids have traveled up the stalk. **Sheltered English**

Section 1

Terms to Learn

sporophyte
gametophyte
nonvascular plant
vascular plant
gymnosperm
angiosperm

What You'll Do

- Identify the characteristics that all plants share.
- Discuss the origin of plants.
- Explain how the four main groups of plants differ.

What Makes a Plant a Plant?

Imagine spending a day without anything made from plants. Not only would it be impossible to make chocolate chip cookies, it would be impossible to do many other things, too. You couldn't wear jeans or any clothes made of cotton or linen. You couldn't use any furniture constructed of wood. You couldn't write with wooden pencils or use paper in any form, including money. You couldn't eat anything because almost all food is made from plants or from animals that eat plants. Spending a day without plants would be very hard to do. In fact, life as we know it would be impossible if plants did not exist!

Fern

Sugar maple

Plant Characteristics

Plants come in many different shapes and sizes. What do cactuses, water lilies, ferns, and all other plants have in common? Although one plant may seem very different from another, all plants share certain characteristics.

Plants Make Their Own Food One thing that you have probably noticed about plants is that most of them are green. This is because plant cells have chloroplasts. As you learned earlier, chloroplasts are organelles that contain the green pigment *chlorophyll*. Chlorophyll absorbs light energy from the sun. Plants then use this energy to make food molecules, such as glucose. You may recall that this process is called *photosynthesis*.

Plants Have a Cuticle A *cuticle* is a waxy layer that coats the surface of stems, leaves, and other plant parts exposed to air. Most plants live on dry land, and the cuticle is an adaptation that helps keep plants from drying out.

Prickly pear cactus

270

Directed Reading Worksheet 12 Section 1

internetconnect
TOPIC: Plant Characteristics
GO TO: www.scilinks.org
sciLINKS NUMBER: HSTL280

Q: How many sides are there to a tree?

A: two; inside and outside

Chapter 12 • Introduction to Plants

Plant Cells Have Cell Walls Plant cells are surrounded by a cell membrane and a rigid cell wall. The cell wall lies outside the cell membrane, as shown in **Figure 1**. The cell wall helps support and protect the plant. Cell walls contain complex carbohydrates and proteins that form a hard material. When the cell reaches its full size, a tough secondary cell wall may develop. Once this wall is formed, a plant cell cannot grow any larger.

Plants Reproduce with Spores and Sex Cells A plant's life cycle can be divided into two parts. Plants spend one part of their lives in the stage that produces spores and the other part in the stage that produces sex cells (egg and sperm cells). The spore-producing stage is called a **sporophyte** (SPOH roh FIET). The stage that produces egg cells and sperm cells is called a **gametophyte** (guh MEET oh FIET). A diagram of the plant life cycle is shown in **Figure 2**.

Spores and sex cells are tiny reproductive cells. Spores that land in a suitable environment, such as damp soil, can grow into new plants. In contrast, sex cells cannot grow directly into new plants. Instead, a male sex cell (sperm cell) must join with a female sex cell (egg cell). The fertilized egg that results may grow into a new plant.

Figure 1 In addition to the cell membrane, a cell wall surrounds plant cells.

Figure 2 Plant Life Cycle

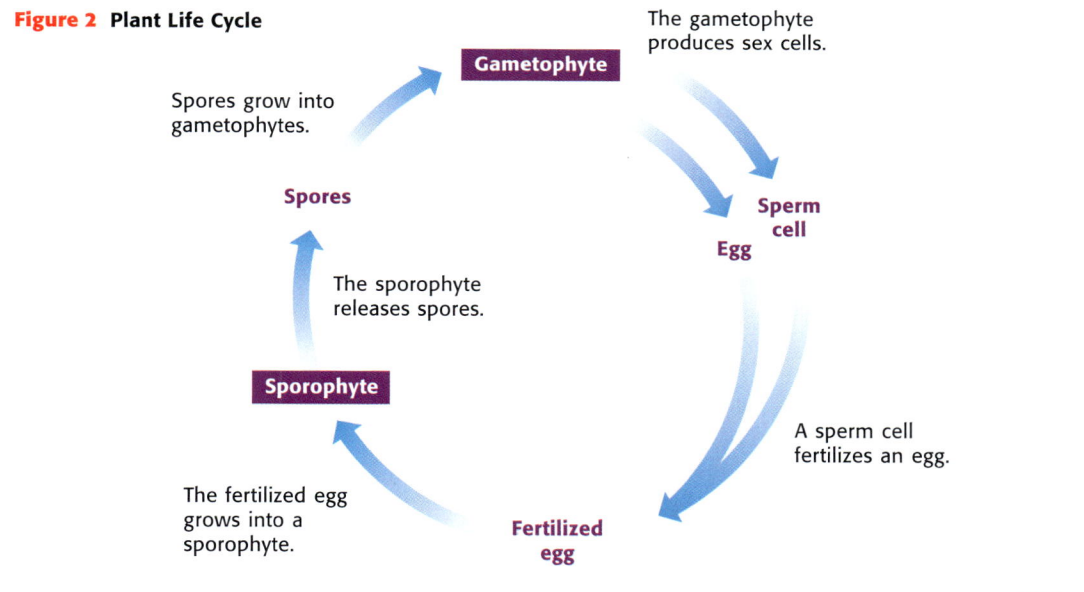

IS THAT A FACT!

Some flowering plants have a type of surface protector that functions much like sunscreen lotion. Alpine flowers at high elevations produce purple pigments in their leaves to shield them from the damaging effects of ultraviolet light. The pigment allows sunlight in that is needed for photosynthesis but filters out harmful UV rays.

2 Teach

GROUP ACTIVITY

MATERIALS

FOR EACH GROUP:
- baby powder
- water
- eyedroppers or spoons

Organize the class into groups of 3 or 4, and give each group one set of the materials listed above. Tell students that all but one member of the group should coat the palms of their hands with the powder. Instruct the remaining member of the group to release a few drops of water on his or her classmates' hands and to record his or her observations. Explain to students that a plant's cuticle forms a similar barrier to prevent a plant from losing moisture.

Students should wash their hands immediately following this exercise. **Sheltered English**

MEETING INDIVIDUAL NEEDS

Advanced Learners Have students compare and contrast the basic life cycle of a plant with that of bacteria and that of fungi. Tell them to create a series of illustrations that show how all three organism types reproduce and to include captions that explain similarities and differences.

Teaching Transparency 43 "Plant Life Cycle"

Section 1 • What Makes a Plant a Plant? **271**

2 Teach, continued

Multicultural CONNECTION

The ancient Maya and Aztec people made extensive use of the breadnut. It was boiled and eaten like potatoes or mashed into a gruel and sweetened. Breadnuts were ground, cooked, and mixed with corn to make tortillas. The diluted sap was fed to babies when their mother's milk was not available. The Maya and Aztecs also fed the leaves to female animals to increase their milk supply.

MATH and MORE

Percentages Ask students to suppose the dandelions in their backyard produce 58,791 seeds. The germination rate is 36 percent. How many seeds will germinate?

($58{,}791 \times 0.36 = 21{,}165$ seeds)

Answer to Self-Check

Plants need a cuticle to keep the leaves from drying out. Algae grow in a wet environment, so they do not need a cuticle.

Teaching Transparency 44 "The Main Groups of Living Plants"

Interactive Explorations CD-ROM "Shut Your Trap!"

TOPIC: How Are Plants Classified?
GO TO: www.scilinks.org
sciLINKS NUMBER: HSTL285

The Origin of Plants

If you were to travel back in time 440 million years, Earth would seem like a strange, bare, and unfriendly place. For one thing, no plants lived on land. Where did plants come from?

Take a look at the photographs in **Figure 3.** On the left is an organism called green algae. Plants and green algae are similar in color, but their similarities go beyond color. Green algae and plants contain the same kind of chlorophyll and have similar cell walls. They both store their energy in the form of starch. Like plants, green algae also have a two-part life cycle. These similarities suggest that ancient green algae that lived in the oceans were the ancestors of all plants.

Green algae

Plant

Figure 3 *The similarities between modern green algae and plants suggest that both may have originated from an ancient species of green algae.*

How Are Plants Classified?

There are more than 260,000 species of plants living on Earth today. Although all plants share the basic characteristics discussed earlier, they can be divided into two groups—vascular plants and nonvascular plants.

Plants Without "Plumbing" The nonvascular plants, mosses and liverworts, are shown in **Figure 4.** **Nonvascular plants** have no "pipes" to transport water and nutrients. They depend on diffusion and osmosis to move materials from one part of the plant to another. This is possible because nonvascular plants are small. If they were large—the size of trees, for example—there would be no way to deliver the needed materials to all the cells by diffusion and osmosis.

Figure 4 *Mosses and liverworts are examples of nonvascular plants.*

✓ Self-Check

Green algae cells do not have a cuticle surrounding them. Why do plants need a cuticle, while algae do not? *(See page 782 to check your answer.)*

IS THAT A FACT!

The coconut palm sends its seed not by air but by sea. Inside the hard-shelled seed, there are supplies for a long voyage, such as plenty of food and water. The shell's exterior has a fibrous coat that helps it float. This self-contained travel package has enabled the coconut to travel miles at sea and to colonize beaches throughout the tropics.

272 Chapter 12 • Introduction to Plants

Plants with "Plumbing" Vascular plants do not rely solely on diffusion and osmosis to deliver needed materials to their cells. **Vascular plants** have tissues that deliver needed materials throughout a plant, much as pipes deliver water to faucets in your home. These tissues are called *vascular tissues*. Because vascular tissues can carry needed materials long distances within the plant body, vascular plants can be almost any size.

Vascular plants can be divided into two groups—plants that produce seeds and plants that do not. Plants that do not produce seeds include ferns, horsetails, and club mosses. Plants that produce seeds also fall into two groups—those that produce flowers and those that do not. Nonflowering plants are called **gymnosperms** (JIM noh SPUHRMZ). Flowering plants are called **angiosperms** (AN jee oh SPUHRMZ). The four main groups of living plants are shown in **Figure 5.**

MATH BREAK

Practice with Percents

The following list gives an estimate of the number of species in each plant group:

Mosses and liverworts	15,000
Ferns, horsetails, and club mosses	12,000
Gymnosperms	760
Angiosperms	235,000

What percentage of plants do not produce seeds?

Figure 5 The Main Groups of Living Plants

Nonvascular: Mosses and liverworts
Vascular — No seeds: Ferns, horsetails, and club mosses
Vascular — Seeds, Nonflowering: Gymnosperms
Vascular — Seeds, Flowering: Angiosperms

REVIEW

1. What are two characteristics that all plants have in common?
2. What type of organism is thought to be the ancestor of all plants? Why?
3. How are ferns, horsetails, and club mosses different from angiosperms?
4. **Applying Concepts** How would you decide whether an unknown organism is a type of green algae or a plant?

internet connect

SCILINKS NSTA

TOPIC: Plant Characteristics, How Are Plants Classified?
GO TO: www.scilinks.org
sciLINKS NUMBER: HSTL280, HSTL285

273

Answers to Review

1. Plants make their own food, have rigid cell walls, have a cuticle, and reproduce with spores and sex cells.
2. green algae, because both green algae and plants share many traits including the same kind of chlorophyll
3. Ferns, horsetails, and club mosses do not produce seeds. Angiosperms do produce seeds.
4. You should determine whether or not the organism has a cuticle. If the organism does, then it is a plant. If the organism does not, then it may be a type of alga.

SECTION 2

Focus

Seedless Plants

In this section, students will learn that seedless plants include the nonvascular mosses and liverworts and the vascular ferns, horsetails, and club mosses. Students will learn about the features of each group and its life cycles. Finally, students will learn the importance of these plants to the environment and to humans.

 Bellringer

Use the board or an overhead projector to display this question:

If plants can make their own food, why do people add fertilizer to the soil? (Fertilizers add nutrients to the soil that plants cannot make for themselves, such as minerals and nitrogen compounds.)

1 Motivate

DISCUSSION

Dandelions Ask students to describe a young dandelion flower and a mature flower that has developed seeds. (The flower's yellow head becomes white and "downy" at summer's end.)

Ask what happens to the "downy" head. (It breaks apart in the wind.)

What is blown away? Explain that although this section is about seedless plants, students can use this visual imagery of the dandelion to understand the different phases of a seedless plant's life cycle.

Section 2

Terms to Learn
rhizoid
rhizome

What You'll Do
- Describe the features of mosses and liverworts.
- Describe the features of ferns, horsetails, and club mosses.
- Explain how plants without seeds are important to humans and to the environment.

Seedless Plants

Two groups of plants don't make seeds. One group of seedless plants is the nonvascular plants—mosses and liverworts. The other group is made up of several vascular plants—ferns, horsetails, and club mosses.

Mosses and Liverworts

Mosses and liverworts are small. They grow on soil, the bark of trees, and rocks. Because they lack a vascular system, these plants usually live in places that are always wet. Each cell of the plant must absorb water directly from the environment or from a neighboring cell.

Mosses and liverworts don't have true stems, roots, or leaves. They do, however, have structures that carry out the activities of stems, roots, and leaves.

Rock-to-Rock Carpeting Mosses typically live together in large groups, covering soil or rocks with a mat of tiny green plants. Each moss plant has slender, hairlike threads of cells called **rhizoids.** Like roots, rhizoids help hold the plant in place. Each moss plant also has a leafy stalk. The life cycle of the moss alternates between the gametophyte and the sporophyte, as shown in **Figure 6.**

Figure 6 Moss Life Cycle

CROSS-DISCIPLINARY FOCUS

History Elizabeth Knight Britton was a botanist when female scientists faced many obstacles in their careers. She worked as the unofficial curator of mosses at Columbia University, in New York, and published 346 scientific papers between 1881 and 1930. Britton is credited with being the first person to suggest the establishment of the New York Botanical Garden, located in the Bronx, and she was a founder of the Wild Flower Preservation Society of America. One of her later achievements included helping to enact important conservation laws for the state of New York.

Liverworts Like mosses, liverworts are small, nonvascular plants that usually live in damp or moist places. Liverworts have a life cycle similar to that of mosses. The gametophytes of liverworts can be leafy and mosslike or broad and flattened, like those shown in **Figure 7**. Rhizoids extend out of the lower side of the liverwort body and help anchor the plant.

The Importance of Mosses and Liverworts

Although nonvascular plants are small, they play an important role in the environment. They are usually the first plants to inhabit a new environment, such as newly exposed rock. When the mosses and liverworts die, they form a thin layer of soil in which new plants can grow. New mosses and liverworts cover the soil and help hold it in place. This reduces soil erosion. Mosses also provide nesting materials for birds.

Peat mosses are important to humans. Peat mosses grow in bogs and other wet places. In certain locations, such as Ireland, dead peat mosses have built up thick deposits in bogs. This peat can be taken from the bog, dried, and burned as a fuel.

Ferns, Horsetails, and Club Mosses

Unlike most of their modern descendants, ancient ferns, horsetails, and club mosses grew to be quite tall. The first forests were made up of 40 m high club mosses, 18 m high horsetails, and 8 m high ferns. **Figure 8** shows how these forests may have looked. These plants had vascular systems and could therefore grow taller than nonvascular plants.

Figure 7 *This liverwort has a broad, flattened gametophyte. The sporophyte looks like a tiny palm tree or umbrella.*

Figure 8 *Vascular tissue allowed the ancestors of modern ferns, horsetails, and club mosses to grow tall.*

QuickLab

Moss Mass

Determine the mass of a small sample of **dry sphagnum moss.** Place this sample in a **large beaker of water** for 10–15 minutes. What do you think the mass will be after soaking in water? Remove the wet moss from the beaker, and determine its mass. How much mass did the moss gain? Compare your findings with your predictions. What could this absorbent plant be used for? Do some research to find out.

WEIRD SCIENCE

Some of the same factors that encourage the development of peat—high acidity and low oxygen—have preserved the bodies of people who died in bogs. Preserved bodies have been recovered from bogs in Europe and in Florida. Some of the bodies are 2,000 years old.

internet connect

TOPIC: Seedless Plants
GO TO: www.scilinks.org
sciLINKS NUMBER: HSTL290

2) Teach, continued

READING STRATEGY

 Activity Refer students to the diagram of the fern life cycle. Have them expand the identification of each stage with information they have learned from the text. For example, students could write a physical description of the gametophyte and of the conditions necessary for the sperm cell to fertilize the egg.

ACTIVITY

Identifying Plant Parts Before students read this page, let them view a potted fern. Tell students to draw a picture of the fern and to label as many parts as they can. Ask students if they have drawn and labeled the stem. (Answers will vary. Some students may realize that no stem was visible. Some may label a part of the fronds as a stem.)

Then remove the fern from the soil, point to the rhizome, and ask students if they know what it is. Explain that this structure is an underground stem. Stress to students that the structure and function of a plant part, not its location, is evidence of that part's identity. **Sheltered English**

Homework

Fern Food Fiddleheads are a delicacy found in the forests of the northeastern United States during the spring. Edible fiddleheads are actually the tightly coiled, emerging fronds of the fern, *Matteuccia struthiopteris*. Have interested students research recipes for fiddleheads or prepare some dishes for the class.

Figure 9 This fern produces spores in spore cases on the underside of fronds. Fiddleheads grow into new fronds.

Ferns Ferns grow in many places, from the cold Arctic to warm, humid tropical forests. Although most ferns are relatively small plants, some tree ferns in the tropics grow as tall as 23 m.

Figure 9 shows a typical fern. Most ferns have an underground stem, called a **rhizome,** that produces leaves called *fronds* and wiry roots. Young fronds are tightly coiled. They are called *fiddleheads* because they look like the end of a violin, or fiddle.

Like the life cycles of all other plants, the life cycle of ferns, shown in **Figure 10,** is divided into two parts. You are probably most familiar with the sporophyte. The fern gametophyte is a tiny plant about the size of half of one of your fingernails. It is green and flat, and it is usually shaped like a tiny heart. The fern gametophyte has male structures that produce sperm cells and female structures that produce eggs. If a thin film of water is on the ground, the sperm cells can swim through it to an egg.

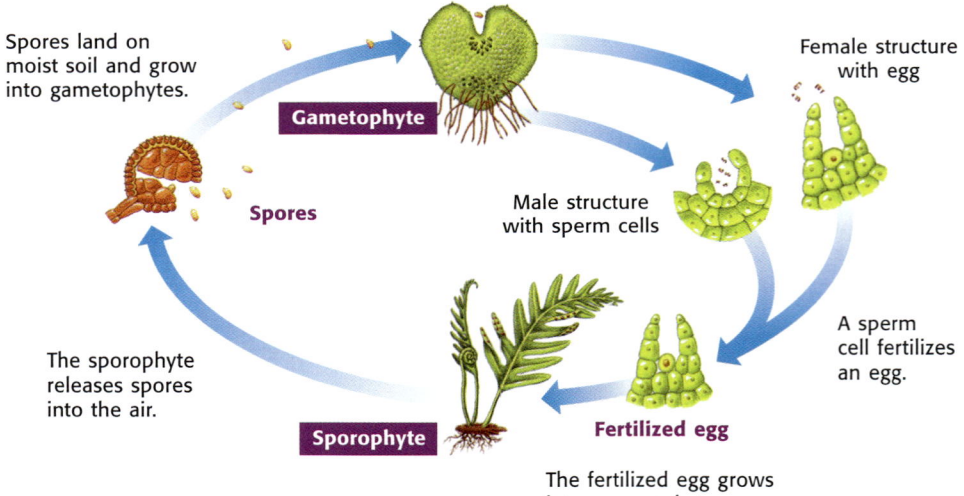

Figure 10 Fern Life Cycle

IS THAT A FACT!

The largest plant leaves in the world are those of the raffia plant of the Mascarene Islands, in the Indian Ocean, and of the bamboo palm of South America and Africa. These leaves can grow to nearly 20 m in length.

Chapter 12 • Introduction to Plants

Horsetails Horsetails were common plants millions of years ago, but only about 15 species have survived to the present. Modern horsetails, shown in **Figure 11,** are small vascular plants usually less than 1.3 m tall. They grow in wet, marshy places. Their stems are hollow and contain silica. Because of this, they feel gritty. In fact, pioneers of the early United States called horsetails "scouring rushes" and used them to scrub pots and pans. The life cycle of horsetails is similar to that of ferns.

Figure 11 *The conelike tips of horsetails contain spores.*

Club Mosses Club mosses, shown in **Figure 12,** are about 25 cm tall and grow in woodlands. Club mosses are not actually mosses. Unlike true mosses, club mosses have vascular tissue. Like horsetails, club mosses were common plants millions of years ago.

The Importance of Seedless Vascular Plants Seedless vascular plants play important roles in the environment. Like nonvascular plants, the ferns, horsetails, and club mosses help form soil. They also hold the soil in place, preventing soil erosion.

Ferns are popular as houseplants because of their beautiful leaves. The fiddleheads of some ferns are harvested in early spring, cooked, and eaten.

For humans, some of the most important seedless vascular plants lived and died about 300 million years ago. The remains of these ancient ferns, horsetails, and club mosses formed coal, a fossil fuel that we now extract from the Earth's crust.

Figure 12 *Club mosses release spores from their conelike tips.*

REVIEW

1. What is the connection between coal and seedless vascular plants?
2. How are horsetails and club mosses similar to ferns?
3. List two ways that seedless vascular plants are important to the environment.
4. **Applying Concepts** Why don't mosses ever grow as large as ferns?

internetconnect

SCLINKS NSTA

TOPIC: Seedless Plants
GO TO: www.scilinks.org
*sci*LINKS NUMBER: HSTL290

SECTION 3

Focus

Plants with Seeds

Students will learn the characteristics that differentiate plants with seeds from those without seeds and how to compare and contrast seeds and spores. Students will also learn about the physical and reproductive features of gymnosperms and angiosperms as well as the ecological and economic importance of those plants.

Bellringer

Use the board or an overhead projector to pose this question to students:

> If plants cannot move, how do they disperse their seeds?

1 Motivate

ACTIVITY

Seed Types

MATERIALS

FOR EACH CLASS:
- grey stripe sunflower seeds (not the small black oil variety)
- pumpkin seeds
- wildflower seed mix (available in nature stores and from catalogs)

Give students all of the seed varieties to examine. Tell students to compare and contrast the seeds in terms of size, shape, color, and texture. Ask students to compare this information with what they know about spores. Then ask students if they think it would be easier to introduce seed plants or seedless plants to a new plot of land. Why? Explain that this section will help them refine their answers. **Sheltered English**

Section 3

Terms to Learn
pollen
pollination
cotyledon

What You'll Do
- Compare a seed with a spore.
- Describe the features of gymnosperms.
- Describe the features of angiosperms.
- List the economic and environmental importance of gymnosperms and angiosperms.

Plants with Seeds

Do the plants on this page look familiar to you? They are all seed plants.

As you read earlier, there are two groups of vascular plants that produce seeds—the gymnosperms and the angiosperms. Gymnosperms are trees and shrubs that produce seeds in cones or fleshy structures on stems. Pine, spruce, fir, and ginkgo trees are examples of gymnosperms. Angiosperms, or flowering plants, produce their seeds within a fruit. Peach trees, grasses, oak trees, rose bushes, and buttercups are all examples of angiosperms.

Peaches

Characteristics of Seed Plants

Just like the life cycle of other plants, the life cycle of seed plants alternates between two stages. During part of the cycle, the seed plants are called sporophytes. During another stage, the seed plants are called gametophytes. Gametophytes produce sex cells. But seed plants differ from other plants in the following ways:

- Seed plants produce seeds, structures in which young sporophytes are nourished and protected.

- Unlike the gametophytes of seedless plants, the gametophytes of seed plants do not live independently of the sporophyte. Gametophytes of seed plants are tiny and are always found protected in the reproductive structures of the sporophyte.

- The male gametophytes of seed plants do not need water to travel to the female gametophytes. Male gametophytes develop inside tiny structures that can be transported by the wind or by animals. These dustlike structures are called **pollen**.

These characteristics allow seed plants to live just about anywhere. That is why seed plants are the most common plants on Earth today.

Desert yucca

English elm

IS THAT A FACT!

The smallest seeds in the world belong to an epiphytic orchid; 992.25 million of its seeds have a mass of 1 g.

What's So Great About Seeds?

A seed develops after fertilization takes place. Fertilization is the union of an egg and a sperm cell. A seed is made up of three parts: a young plant (the sporophyte), stored food, and a tough seed coat that surrounds and protects the young plant. These parts are shown in **Figure 13.**

Did you know that seeds like to travel far from home? See how on page 726 of your LabBook.

Figure 13 *A seed contains stored food and a young plant. A seed is surrounded and protected by a seed coat.*

Plants that reproduce by seeds have several advantages over spore-forming seedless plants. For example, when a seed *germinates,* or begins to grow, the young plant is nourished by the food stored in the seed. By the time the young plant uses up these food reserves, it is able to make all the food it needs by photosynthesis. In contrast, the gametophyte that develops from a spore must be in an environment where it can begin photosynthesis as soon as it begins to grow.

Environment CONNECTION

Animals need plants to live, but some plants need animals, too. These plants produce seeds with tough seed coats that can't begin to grow into new plants until they have been eaten by an animal. When the seed is exposed to the acids and enzymes of the animal's digestive system, the seed coat wears down. After the seed passes out of the animal's digestive tract, it is able to absorb water, germinate, and grow.

The Accidental Garden

During the summer, Patrick and his sister love to sit out on the porch munching away on juicy watermelon. One year they held a contest to see who could spit the seeds the farthest. The next spring, Patrick noticed some new plants growing in their yard. When he examined them closely, he realized little watermelons were growing on the plants. Patrick and his sister had no idea that they were starting a watermelon garden. Think about the eating habits of animals in the wild. How might they start a garden?

WEIRD SCIENCE

A large number of plants in the heathland of South Africa produce seeds with a very tasty covering called an elaiosome—tasty, that is, to ants, which carry seeds down into their underground colonies. The ants nibble off the outside covering and then leave the seed alone. The ants plant the seed at just the right depth for it to successfully germinate.

Section 3 • Plants with Seeds

2 Teach, continued

MEETING INDIVIDUAL NEEDS

Learners Having Difficulty
Many students are already familiar with conifers, such as pine trees, but may suddenly feel confused when the term *gymnosperm* is introduced. Encourage these students to list the characteristics they have observed in pine trees. (stay green all year; thin, needle- or toothpick-like leaves; pine cones)

Stress that while this section provides additional information about gymnosperms, students already know a great deal about them. **Sheltered English**

CONNECT TO EARTH SCIENCE

Geochronology, the interpretation and dating of the geologic record, includes dendrochronology, which is the study of trees' growth rings. Bristlecone pines have been particularly useful in this endeavor because many of them are very old. Using an increment borer, scientists extract a thin core sample and measure the growth rings from trees of known age. These values are plotted on a graph. Then scientists measure the rings of dead trees of unknown ages. They compare the measurement value of the outer ring of the undated tree with that of a ring in the living tree to find out when the undated tree died. By counting backward from that point, they can determine when the older tree began to grow. Scientists have used this technique to assemble a record that extends back nearly 10,000 years.

Gymnosperms: Seed Plants Without Flowers

The seeds of gymnosperms are not enclosed in a fruit. The word *gymnosperm* is Greek for "naked seed." There are four groups of gymnosperms: conifers, ginkgoes, cycads, and gnetophytes (NEE toh FIETS). Examples are shown in **Figure 14**.

Figure 14 *Gymnosperms do not produce flowers or fruits.*

▲ The **conifers,** with about 550 species, make up the largest group of gymnosperms. Most conifers are evergreen and keep their needle-shaped leaves all year. Conifer seeds develop in cones. Pines, spruces, firs, and hemlocks are examples of conifers.

◀ The **ginkgoes** contain only one living species, the ginkgo tree. Ginkgo seeds are produced in fleshy structures that are attached directly to branches.

▲ The **cycads** were more common millions of years ago. Today there are only about 140 species. These plants grow in the tropics. Like seeds of conifers, seeds of cycads develop in cones.

▲ The **gnetophytes** consist of about 70 species of very unusual plants. This gnetophyte is a shrub that grows in dry areas. Its seeds are formed in cones.

Science Bloopers

When scientists compared radiocarbon dates of bristlecone pines with those obtained from tree ring patterns, they discovered that their calibrations for carbon-14 analysis were incorrect.

The new data indicated that some artifacts found in Europe were 1,000 years older than had been previously thought. The bristlecone pines became known as the "trees that rewrote history."

Gymnosperm Life Cycle The gymnosperms that are most familiar to you are probably the conifers. The name *conifer* comes from Greek and Latin words that mean "carry cones." Conifers have two kinds of cones—male and female. These are shown in **Figure 15.** Male spores are produced in the male cones, and female spores are produced in the female cones. The spores develop into gametophytes. The male gametophytes are pollen, dustlike particles that produce sperm cells. The female gametophyte produces eggs. Wind carries pollen from the male cones to the female cones on the same plant or on different plants. The transfer of pollen is called **pollination.**

After the egg is fertilized, it develops into a seed within the female cone. When the seed is mature, it is released by the cone and falls to the ground. The seed then germinates and grows into a new tree. The life cycle of a pine tree is shown in **Figure 16.**

Figure 15 *A pine tree has male cones and female cones.*

The Importance of Gymnosperms Conifers are the most economically important group of gymnosperms. People harvest conifers and use the wood for building materials and paper products. Pine trees produce a sticky fluid called resin, which is used to make soap, turpentine, paint, and ink.

Figure 16 Pine Life Cycle

People who buy a lot of books on gardening become good weeders.

3) Extend

CROSS-DISCIPLINARY FOCUS

Writing — Art Before the development of artificial dyes, artists and textile workers used solutions made from berries, roots, bark, leaves, flowers, and seeds of various plants to create colored paints and fabrics. Some of the plants they used included buckthorn, dogwood, fennel, sandalwood, and milkweed. Have students research three natural dyes that are each obtained from a different plant part. Their report should include an illustration of the plant and an explanation of how the dye is processed.

GOING FURTHER

Seed Dispersal

MATERIALS
FOR EACH GROUP: • cotton balls • clear or masking tape • construction paper • scissors • fan • table

Have students shred the cotton balls and place the pieces on a table in front of the fan. Turn on the fan, and have students observe how far the cotton "seeds" travel. Have students wad a strip of tape into a marble-size ball and attach it to the table. How far does the ball move when subjected to the "wind"? Ask students how they think the seeds in this type of fruit might best be transported. (on an animal's fur)

Have students cut a "maple fruit" from construction paper. The rounded tips must be longer on one side than the other. Have students observe how this "fruit" behaves in the wind.

Sheltered English

Angiosperms: Seed Plants with Flowers

Flowering plants, or angiosperms, are the most abundant plants today. Angiosperms can be found in almost every environment on land. There are at least 235,000 species of flowering plants, many more than all other plant species combined. Angiosperms come in a wide variety of sizes and shapes, from dandelions and water lilies to prickly-pear cactuses and oak trees.

All angiosperms are vascular plants that produce flowers and fruits. Tulips and roses are examples of flowering plants with large flowers. Other flowering plants, such as grasses and maple trees, have small flowers. After fertilization, angiosperms produce seeds within fruits. Peaches, lemons, and grapes are fruits, as are tomatoes, cucumbers, and many other foods we think of as vegetables.

What Are Flowers For? Flowers help angiosperms reproduce. Some angiosperms depend on the wind for pollination, but others have flowers that attract animals. As shown in **Figure 17,** when animals visit different flowers, they may carry pollen from flower to flower.

Figure 17 This bee is on its way to another squash flower, where it will leave some of the pollen it is carrying.

What Are Fruits For? Fruits are also important structures for reproduction in angiosperms. They help to ensure that seeds survive as they are transported to areas where new plants can grow. Fruits surround and protect seeds. Some fruits and seeds, such as those shown in **Figure 18,** have structures that help the wind carry them short or long distances. Other fruits may attract animals that eat the fruits and discard the seeds some distance from the parent plant. Prickly burrs are fruits that are carried from place to place by sticking to the fur of animals or to the clothes and shoes of people.

Figure 18 Special structures allow some fruits and seeds to float or drift through the air.

Dandelion

Maple

Milkweed

IS THAT A FACT!

The giant fan palm, which is native to Seychelles, in Africa, produces a single seed in its fruit that weighs up to 20 kg and takes up to 10 years to develop.

Monocots and Dicots Angiosperms are divided into two classes—monocots and dicots. The two classes differ in the number of cotyledons in their seeds. A **cotyledon** (KAHT uh LEED uhn) is a seed leaf found inside a seed. Monocot seeds have one cotyledon, and dicot seeds have two cotyledons. Other differences between monocots and dicots are summarized in **Figure 19**. Monocots include grasses, orchids, onions, lilies, and palms. Dicots include roses, cactuses, sunflowers, peanuts, and peas.

The Importance of Angiosperms
Flowering plants provide animals that live on land with the food they need to survive. A deer nibbling on meadow grass is using flowering plants directly as food. An owl that consumes a field mouse is using flowering plants indirectly as food because the field mouse ate seeds and berries.

Humans depend on flowering plants and use them in many ways. All of our major food crops, such as corn, wheat, and rice, are flowering plants. Some flowering plants, such as oak trees, are used to make furniture and toys. Others, such as cotton and flax, supply fibers for clothing and rope. Flowering plants are used to make many medicines as well as cork, rubber, and perfume oils.

Figure 19 Two Classes of Angiosperms

REVIEW

1. What are two differences between a seed and a spore?
2. Briefly describe the four groups of gymnosperms. Which group is the largest and most economically important?
3. How do monocots and dicots differ from each other?
4. **Identifying Relationships** In what ways are flowers and fruits adaptations that help angiosperms reproduce?

internetconnect
SCLINKS. NSTA
TOPIC: Plants with Seeds
GO TO: www.scilinks.org
sciLINKS NUMBER: HSTL295

4) Close

Quiz

1. Give one reason why angiosperms greatly outnumber gymnosperms? (Angiosperms have adapted to almost every environment on land. In some cases, they are helped by animals that carry pollen and disperse seeds.)

2. Which plant group is more important to people, angiosperms or gymnosperms? (Angiosperms; most plant-derived foods for people and animals come from angiosperms.)

ALTERNATIVE ASSESSMENT

Concept Mapping Have students organize the following terms into a concept map:

plants, gymnosperm, angiosperm, flowers, fruits, maple trees, cucumbers, conifers, cycads, monocot, dicot, orchids, lilies, peanuts, saguaro cactus, dandelion

Teaching Transparency 45
"Two Classes of Angiosperms"

Reinforcement Worksheet 12
"Classifying Plants"

Reinforcement Worksheet 12
"Drawing Dicots"

▼ **Answers to Review**

1. Unlike seeds, spores have no stored food to nourish the new plant. Spores are single-celled. Seeds are made of many cells.
2. Conifers are the most economically important group of gymnosperms. Students should provide descriptions similar to those in **Figure 14**.
3. Students should discuss the differences illustrated in **Figure 19**.
4. The flowers help attract animals that are needed to deliver pollen to other plants. Animals eat the fruit and transport the seeds to areas where new plants can grow.

SECTION 4

Focus

The Structures of Seed Plants

In this section, students will learn about the physical structures and the functions of a plant's root and shoot systems. Students will also learn how those two factors are related. Finally, students will learn to identify a flower's parts and explain their functions.

Show students a cactus. Point out the spines, and ask students to identify them and explain their purpose in their ScienceLog. (Spines are modified leaves that help protect the plant from grazing animals.) `Sheltered English`

1) Motivate

DEMONSTRATION

Seed Transport Using a piece of Velcro™, demonstrate how some seeds become dispersed. The burdock plant served as inspiration to the inventor of Velcro. Burdocks are members of the thistle family, and they shed their seeds in burrs. These burrs are transported by animals or in people's clothing to new areas, where they take root. George de Mestral, a Swiss engineer, looked very closely at a burdock burr. He observed that the surface of a burr is covered with tiny hooks. Over the next 8 years, he worked with this design and developed a similar fastener out of nylon. `Sheltered English`

Section 4

The Structures of Seed Plants

Terms to Learn
xylem
phloem
sepal
petal
stamen
pistil
stigma
ovary

What You'll Do
- Describe the functions of roots.
- Describe the functions of stems.
- Explain how the structure of leaves is related to their function.
- Identify the parts of a flower and their functions.

You have different body systems that carry out a variety of functions. For example, your cardiovascular system transports materials throughout your body, and your skeletal system provides support and protection. Similarly, plants have systems too—a root system, a shoot system, and a reproductive system.

Plant Systems

A plant's root system and shoot system supply the plant with needed resources that are found underground and above ground. The root system is made up of roots. The shoot system is made up of stems and leaves.

The root system and the shoot system are dependent on each other. The vascular tissues of the two systems are connected, as shown in **Figure 20**. There are two kinds of vascular tissue—xylem (ZIE luhm) and phloem (FLOH em). **Xylem** transports water and minerals through the plant. **Phloem** transports sugar molecules. Xylem and phloem are found in all parts of vascular plants.

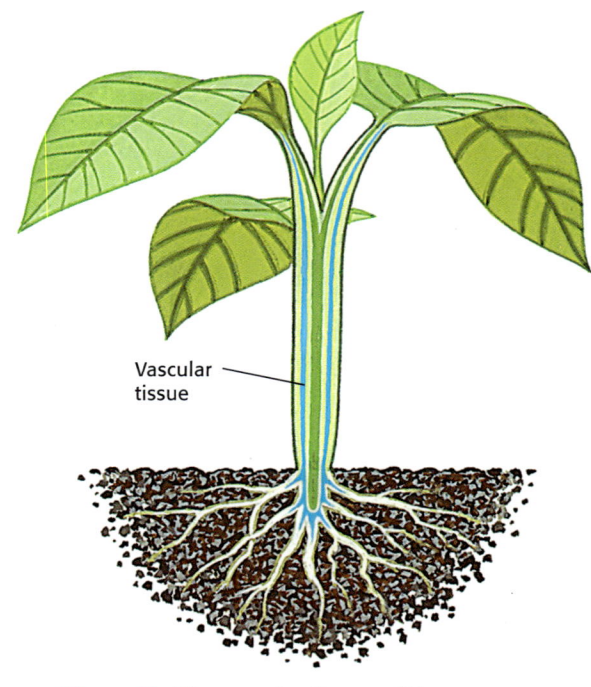

Figure 20 The vascular tissues of the roots and shoots are connected.

The Root of the Matter

Because most roots are underground, many people do not realize how extensive a plant's root system can be. For example, a 2.5 m tall corn plant can have roots that grow 2.5 m deep and 1.2 m out away from the stem!

Root Functions The main functions of roots are as follows:

- **Roots supply plants with water and dissolved minerals that have been absorbed from the soil.** These materials are transported throughout the plant in the xylem.

- **Roots support and anchor plants.** Roots hold plants securely in the soil.

- **Roots often store surplus food made during photosynthesis.** This food is produced in the leaves and transported as sugar in the phloem to the roots. There the surplus food is usually stored as sugar or starch.

 Directed Reading Worksheet 12 Section 4

IS THAT A FACT!

The deepest roots ever discovered belonged to a wild fig tree in South Africa. The roots had penetrated to a depth of 122 m.

284 Chapter 12 • Introduction to Plants

Root Structure The structures of a root are shown in **Figure 21.** Like the cells in the outermost layer of your skin, the layer of cells that covers the surface of roots is called the *epidermis*. Some cells of the root epidermis extend out from the root. These cells, called *root hairs,* increase the amount of surface area through which roots can absorb water and minerals.

After water and minerals are absorbed by the epidermis, they diffuse into the center of the root, where the vascular tissue is located. Roots grow longer at their tips. A group of cells called the *root cap* protects the tip of a root and produces a slimy substance that makes it easier for the root to grow through soil.

Root Types There are two types of roots—taproots and fibrous roots. Examples of each are shown in **Figure 22.**

A *taproot* consists of one main root that grows downward, with many smaller branch roots coming out of it. Taproots can usually obtain water located deep underground. Dicots and gymnosperms have taproots.

A *fibrous root* has several roots of the same size that spread out from the base of the stem. Fibrous roots typically obtain water that is close to the soil surface. Monocots have fibrous roots.

Figure 21 *The structures of a root are labeled above.*

Figure 22 *The onion has a fibrous root, and the dandelions and carrots have taproots.*

Fibrous roots

Taproot

Taproots

2 Teach

DISCUSSION

Attracting Pollinators Discuss in class that flowers serve an important purpose for plants. They are designed to attract pollinators. They also protect pollen and fruit. Ask students to read the section on flowers and to consider how the following factors make flowers successful in the plant world: color, shape, and smell. (The color of a flower may appeal to a certain insect. Bright colors are effective attractors. The shape of a flower may be specifically designed for a specific pollinator. The tubelike flower of a honeysuckle is perfect for the long beak of a hummingbird. The fragrance, or smell, of a flower is designed to attract pollinators; butterflies flock to sweet-smelling flowers, and flies are drawn to rancid-smelling flowers.)

Teaching Transparency 46
"Root Structure"

Science Skills Worksheet 21
"Taking Notes"

IS THAT A FACT!

Red mangrove trees grow in salt water along tropical coasts. Once the tree is established, additional roots grow down from the branches. After a while, it looks as if the tree's crown is supported by stilts.

Section 4 • The Structures of Seed Plants

2) Teach, continued

ACTIVITY

Have students draw pictures that illustrate the functions of stems listed on this page. Tell them to write captions for each illustration. **Sheltered English**

CROSS-DISCIPLINARY FOCUS

History The stems of many large aquatic grasses are called *reeds*. After reeds are harvested and dried, they can be used as a resource material to construct many useful products. For thousands of years, arrows, pens, baskets, musical instruments, furniture, and houses have been made out of reeds. Building boats from reeds is an ancient craft and is still practiced in some places where reeds are plentiful. Ancient Egyptian buildings include friezes of ocean-going ships made of reeds.

In the 1960s, a Norwegian explorer named Thor Heyerdahl wondered if a reed ship could have provided people with transportation across the Atlantic Ocean hundreds or even thousands of years ago. To demonstrate that such a journey was possible, he had Bolivian craftsmen build a traditional reed vessel, the *Ra II*, and in 1970, he sailed it across the Atlantic Ocean.

What's the Holdup?

As shown in **Figure 23,** stems vary greatly in shape and size. Stems are usually located above ground, although many plants have underground stems.

Stem Functions A stem connects a plant's roots to its leaves and flowers and performs these main functions:

- **Stems support the plant body.** Leaves are arranged on stems so that each leaf can absorb the sunlight it needs for photosynthesis. Stems hold up flowers and display them to pollinators.

- **Stems transport materials between the root system and the shoot system.** Xylem carries water and dissolved minerals upward from the roots to the leaves and other shoot parts. Phloem carries the glucose produced during photosynthesis to roots and other parts of the plant.

- **Some stems store materials.** For example, the stems of the plants in **Figure 24** are adapted for water storage.

Figure 23 *The stalks of daisies and the trunks of trees are stems.*

Valley oak

Daisy

BRAIN FOOD

Root or shoot? Even though potatoes grow in the ground, they're not roots. The white potato is an underground stem adapted to store starch.

Figure 24 *Baobab trees store large quantities of water and starch in their massive trunks. Cactuses store water in their thick, green stems.*

IS THAT A FACT!

Linen is a fabric woven from the long fibers harvested from the stems of flax plants.

WEIRD SCIENCE

Garlic bulbs are fleshy, nutrient-storing stems of garlic plants. Garlic has a pungent flavor and is often used to season foods and as a nutritional supplement. At the annual Garlic Festival, in Gilroy, California, visitors can purchase garlic ice cream and garlic candy.

Stem Structures

Herbaceous Stems

Phloem
Xylem

Woody Stems

Phloem
Xylem

The plants in this group have stems that are soft, thin, and flexible. These stems are called *herbaceous* stems. Examples of plants with herbaceous (her BAY shuhs) stems include wildflowers, such as clovers and poppies, and many vegetable crops, such as beans, tomatoes, and corn. Some plants with herbaceous stems live only 1 or 2 years. A cross section of one kind of herbaceous stem is shown above.

Trees and shrubs have rigid stems made of wood and bark. Their stems are called *woody* stems. If a tree or a shrub lives in an area with cold winters, the plant has a growing period and a dormant period.

At the beginning of each spring growing period, large xylem cells are produced. As fall approaches, the plants produce smaller xylem cells, which appear darker. In the fall and winter, the plants stop producing new cells. The cycle begins again when the spring growing season begins. A ring of dark cells surrounding a ring of light cells make up a growth ring.

REVIEW

1. What are three functions of roots?
2. What are three functions of stems?
3. **Applying Concepts** Suppose the cross section of a tree reveals 12 light-colored rings and 12 dark-colored rings. How many years of growth are represented?

Answers to Review

1. Roots supply plants with water and dissolved minerals absorbed from the soil, support and anchor plants, and store surplus food made during photosynthesis.
2. Stems support the plant body, transport materials between the root system and the shoot system, and store materials.
3. 12 years

MEETING INDIVIDUAL NEEDS

Learners Having Difficulty

MATERIALS

FOR EACH CLASS:
• 3 different-colored clays
• butter knife

Have students roll one clay into a thin sheet about 10 × 5 cm. Tell students to roll each of the remaining clays into a thin tube-shaped form about 4 cm long and 0.5 cm in diameter. Have students (1) lay out the clay sheet lengthwise, (2) roll up 3 cm of the sheet, (3) place the first tube on the sheet, (4) roll the sheet another 3 cm, (5) place the second tube on the sheet, and (6) roll the rest of the sheet. Then have students mold the ends of the rolled-up sheet until they form a solid cap at either end. Finally, have an adult cut the clay roll with the butter knife and have the students draw the cross section that is now visible. Sheltered English

ACTIVITY

Analyzing Tree Growth Rings

MATERIALS

FOR EACH GROUP:
• preserved cross sections of trees that clearly show growth rings

Have students identify the xylem and phloem rings. Ask students to measure the width of each ring and to interpret the measurements. Have them take into account the growing conditions in the spring and summer. Sheltered English

 Teaching Transparency 47 "Stem Structure"

Section 4 • The Structures of Seed Plants

A Plant's Food Factories

Leaves vary greatly in shape and size. They may be round, narrow, heart-shaped, or fan-shaped. The raffia palm, shown in **Figure 25,** has leaves that may be six times longer than you are tall. A leaf of the duckweed, a tiny aquatic plant also shown in Figure 25, is so small that several can fit on your fingernail.

Sweet gum

Leaf Function The main function of leaves is to make food for the plant. Leaves capture the energy in sunlight and absorb carbon dioxide from the air. Light energy, carbon dioxide, and water are needed to carry out photosynthesis. During photosynthesis, plants use light energy to make food (sugar) from carbon dioxide and water.

Figure 25 *Even though the leaves of these plants are very different, they serve the same purpose.*

Raffia palm

Mimosa

Duckweed

✓ Self-Check

How is the function of stems related to the function of leaves? *(See page 782 to check your answers.)*

IS THAT A FACT!

Duckweed plants, which live on the surfaces of calm ponds, are the smallest flowering plants in the world. They can be less than 1 mm long and have a mass of about 150 µg, or the equivalent of two grains of table salt. It's a good thing animals like to eat duckweed, because it reproduces exponentially. One species reproduces every 30–36 hours. Left unchecked, one plant could produce 1 nonillion plants (1 followed by 30 zeros) in 4 months!

Leaf Structure The structure of leaves is related to their main function—photosynthesis. **Figure 26** shows a cutaway view of a small block of leaf tissue. The top and bottom surfaces of the leaf are covered with a single layer of cells called the epidermis. Light can easily pass through the thin epidermis to the leaf's interior. Notice the tiny pores in the epidermis. These pores, called *stomata* (singular, *stoma*), allow carbon dioxide to enter the leaf. *Guard cells* open and close the stomata.

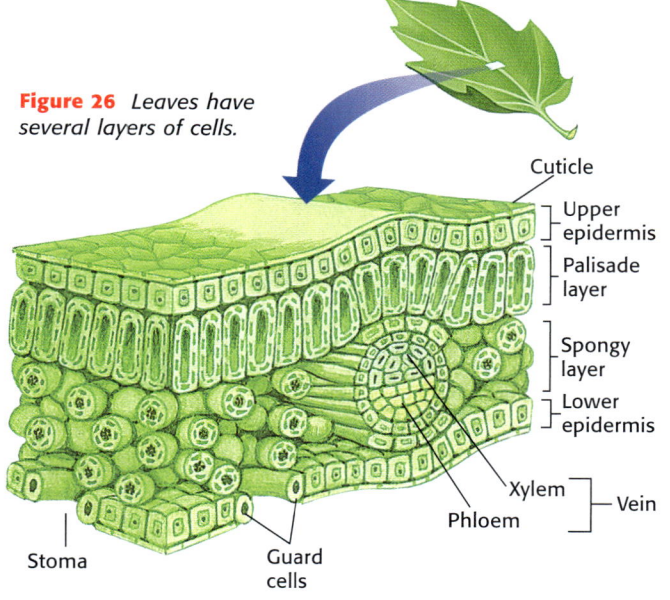

Figure 26 *Leaves have several layers of cells.*

The middle of a leaf, which is where photosynthesis takes place, has two layers. The upper layer is the *palisade layer*, and the lower layer is the *spongy layer*. Cells in the palisade layer contain many chloroplasts, the green organelles that carry out photosynthesis. Cells in the spongy layer are spread farther apart than cells in the palisade layer. The air spaces between these cells allow carbon dioxide to diffuse more freely throughout the leaf.

The veins of a leaf contain xylem and phloem surrounded by supporting tissue. Xylem transports water and minerals to the leaf. Phloem conducts the sugar made during photosynthesis from the leaf to the rest of the plant.

Leaf Adaptations Some leaves have functions other than photosynthesis. For example, the leaves on a cactus plant are modified as spines. These hard, pointed leaves discourage animals from eating the succulent cactus stem. **Figure 27** shows leaves with a most unusual function. The leaves of a sundew are modified to catch insects. Sundews grow in soil that does not contain enough nitrogen to meet the plants' needs. By catching and digesting insects, a sundew is able to meet its nitrogen requirement.

Figure 27 *This damselfly is trapped in the sticky fluid of a sundew flower.*

RETEACHING

Have students choose a type of plant from the groups presented in this chapter and draw simple illustrations that depict the development of that plant. Tell students to begin with fertilization of the egg by the sperm cell and to continue with germination; the growth of roots, stem, leaves, flowers, and fruits; and seed dispersal; depending on the plant chosen. **Sheltered English**

INDEPENDENT PRACTICE

Writing A cactus's spines are modified leaves. Other plants have sharp projections to protect them. Roses have thorns, as does the hawthorn tree. Have students research thorns and other "painful" plant parts. Their report should state whether the projection is a leaf modification or another physical structure.

CONNECT TO PHYSICAL SCIENCE

Photosynthesis is the chemical reaction that provides plants with food from sunlight. Use the following Teaching Transparency to illustrate photosynthesis.

Teaching Transparency 235 "Photosynthesis"

IS THAT A FACT!

The more water-repellent a leaf is, the healthier it may be, according to some scientists. Dirt, which contains disease-causing microbes, has a stronger attraction to water droplets than to a leaf's surface. When the water rolls off the leaf, so do the microbes. Water repellence thus helps prevent infection.

3) Extend

RESEARCH

Have students research the flower colors that are most attractive to specific pollinators, such as hummingbirds and bees. (red and yellow, respectively)

Tell students that some pollinators, such as bats, are active at night. Have them research what flower colors best attract nocturnal pollinators. (white)

GOING FURTHER

Writing | Life in a Dead Tree
Now that students have learned about live trees, encourage them to explore the life in and around a dead tree, called a snag. Once a snag has fallen down, it is called a log. Have students research the animals that use snags and logs as shelter, including songbirds, hawks, owls, snakes, bats, raccoons, and insects.

Build a Flower

Teaching Transparency 48
"Flower Structure"

TOPIC: The Structure of Seed Plants
GO TO: www.scilinks.org
sciLINKS NUMBER: HSTL300

Flowers

Most people admire the beauty of flowers, such as roses or lilies, without stopping to think about *why* plants have flowers. Flowers are adaptations for sexual reproduction. Flowers come in many different shapes, colors, and fragrances that attract pollinators or catch the wind. Flowers usually contain the following parts: sepals, petals, stamens, and one or more pistils. The flower parts are usually arranged in rings around the central pistil. **Figure 28** shows the parts of a typical flower.

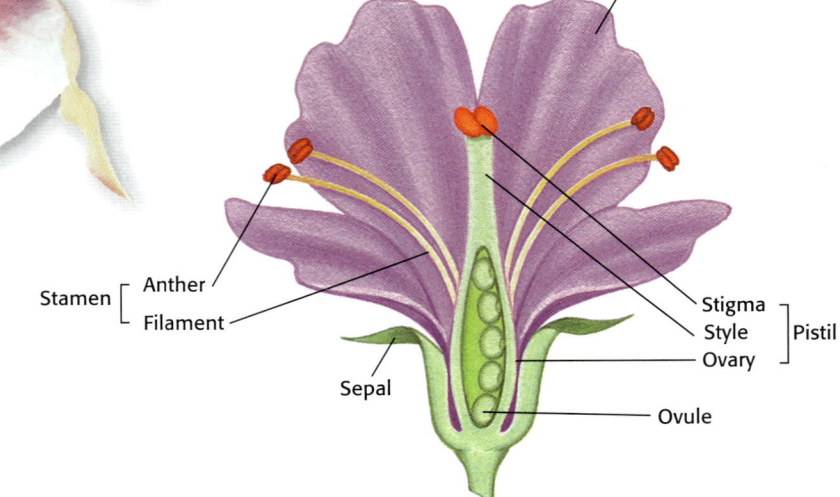

Figure 28 *The stamens, which produce pollen, and the pistil, which produces eggs, are surrounded by the petals and the sepals.*

Build a flower of your very own on page 727.

Sepals make up the bottom ring of flower parts. They are often green like leaves. The main function of sepals is to cover and protect the immature flower when it is a bud. As the blossom opens, the sepals fold back so that the petals can enlarge and become visible.

Petals are broad, flat, and thin, like sepals, but they vary in shape and color. Petals may attract insects or other animals to the flower. These animals help plants reproduce by transferring pollen from flower to flower.

IS THAT A FACT!

The heaviest flower in the world is a species of rafflesia from Malaysia, *Rafflesia arnoldii*. The flowers can weigh 11 kg and measure 1 m in diameter.

WEIRD SCIENCE

Carrion-eating flies are probably the pollinators of *Rafflesia arnoldii*. This would explain why the flowers emit a scent reminiscent of rotting meat.

Chapter 12 • Introduction to Plants

Just above the petals is a circle of **stamens,** which are the male reproductive structures. Each stamen consists of a thin stalk called a *filament,* and each stamen is topped by an *anther.* Anthers are saclike structures that produce pollen grains.

In the center of most flowers is one or more **pistils,** the female reproductive structures. The tip of the pistil is called the **stigma.** Pollen grains collect on stigmas, which are often sticky or feathery. The long, slender part of the pistil is the *style.* The rounded base of the pistil is called the **ovary.** As shown in **Figure 29,** the ovary contains one or more *ovules.* Each ovule contains an egg. If fertilization occurs, the ovule develops into a seed, and the ovary develops into a fruit.

Flowers that have brightly colored petals and aromas usually depend on animals for pollination. Plants without bright colors and aromas, such as the grass flowers shown in **Figure 30,** depend on wind to spread pollen.

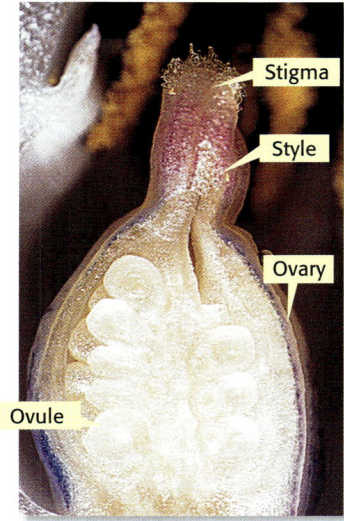

Figure 29 *This hyacinth ovary contains many ovules.*

Figure 30 *The tall stems of these pampas grass flowers allow their pollen to be picked up by the wind.*

REVIEW

1. Describe the internal structure of a typical leaf. How is a leaf's structure related to its function?
2. Which flower structure produces pollen?
3. **Identifying Relationships** Compare the functions of xylem and phloem in roots, stems, leaves, and flowers.

internetconnect

SCILINKS NSTA
TOPIC: The Structure of Seed Plants
GO TO: www.scilinks.org
sciLINKS NUMBER: HSTL300

4) Close

Quiz

1. Why is it that some plants have brightly colored flowers and other plants do not? (Plants with brightly colored flowers usually need to attract insects, birds, or mammals to ensure pollination. Plants without showy flowers usually rely on the wind to assist with pollination.)

2. Describe the two types of roots, and list at least one plant that has each type. (A taproot is one main root with smaller branch roots. Dandelions and carrots have a taproot. Fibrous roots are similar in size and grow from the base of the stem. Onions have fibrous roots.)

ALTERNATIVE ASSESSMENT

Writing Have students list ingredients for a salad. (lettuce, tomato, cucumber, carrot, mushroom, red onion, red cabbage, alfalfa sprouts)

Tell them to identify each item as a monocot, dicot, fruit, vegetable, or other. (The mushroom is a fungus.)

Then tell students to list the part of the plant that is eaten. (stem, root, leaves)

Critical Thinking Worksheet 12 "The Voodoo Lily"

Answers to Review

1. The epidermis is transparent to allow sunlight in. Stomata allow gases to enter and leave the leaf. The palisade layer in the leaf contains chloroplasts, which carry out photosynthesis. The spongy layer contains cells that are spread out to help the diffusion of carbon dioxide. The veins transport materials to and from the leaf.
2. The anthers produce pollen.
3. Water and nutrients travel through the xylem in the roots, stems, leaves, and flowers. Sugar molecules travel through the phloem from the leaves to other parts of the plant where the sugar is used or stored.

Chapter Highlights

VOCABULARY DEFINITIONS

SECTION 1

sporophyte a stage in a plant's life cycle during which spores are produced

gametophyte a stage in a plant's life cycle during which eggs and sperm are produced

nonvascular plant a plant that depends on the processes of diffusion and osmosis to move materials from one part of the plant to another

vascular plant a plant that has specialized tissues called xylem and phloem, which move materials from one part of the plant to another

gymnosperm a plant that produces seeds but does not produce flowers

angiosperm a plant that produces seeds in flowers

SECTION 2

rhizoids small hairlike threads of cells that help hold nonvascular plants in place

rhizome the underground stem of a fern

SECTION 3

pollen dustlike particles that carry the male gametophytes of seed plants

pollination the transfer of pollen to the female cone in conifers or to the stigma in angiosperms

cotyledon a seed leaf inside a seed

Chapter Highlights

SECTION 1

Vocabulary
- **sporophyte** (p. 271)
- **gametophyte** (p. 271)
- **nonvascular plant** (p. 272)
- **vascular plant** (p. 273)
- **gymnosperm** (p. 273)
- **angiosperm** (p. 273)

Section Notes
- Plants use photosynthesis to make food. Plant cells have cell walls. Plants are covered by a waxy cuticle.
- The life cycle of a plant includes a spore-producing stage (the sporophyte) and a sex-cell-producing stage (the gametophyte).
- Plants probably evolved from a type of ancient green algae.
- Vascular plants have tissues that carry materials throughout a plant. Nonvascular plants do not have vascular tissues and must depend on diffusion and osmosis to move materials.

SECTION 2

Vocabulary
- **rhizoid** (p. 274)
- **rhizome** (p. 276)

Section Notes
- There are two groups of plants that do not make seeds.
- Mosses and liverworts are small, nonvascular plants. They are small because they lack xylem and phloem. Mosses and liverworts need water to transport sperm cells to eggs.
- Ferns, horsetails, and club mosses are vascular plants. They can grow larger than nonvascular plants. Ferns, horsetails, and club mosses need water to transport sperm cells to eggs.

✓ Skills Check

Math Concepts

DO THE PERCENTAGES ADD UP? If 38 percent of the plants in a forest are flowering plants, what percentage of the plants are not flowering plants? The two groups together make up 100 percent. So subtract 38 percent from 100.

100 percent − 38 percent = 62 percent

Look again at the MathBreak on page 273. You can calculate the percentage of plants that do produce seeds by subtracting your MathBreak answer from 100 percent.

Visual Understanding

SEEDS This image shows the two cotyledons of a dicot seed. The seed has been split, and the two cotyledons laid open like two halves of a hamburger bun. You are looking at the inside surfaces of the two cotyledons. Open a peanut and see for yourself. In peanuts, the two cotyledons come apart very easily. You can even see the young delicate plant inside.

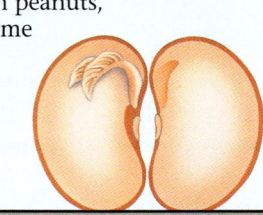

Lab and Activity Highlights

LabBook

Travelin' Seeds PG 726

Leaf Me Alone! PG 724

Build a Flower PG 727

Datasheets for LabBook
(blackline masters for these labs)

292   Chapter 12 • Introduction to Plants

VOCABULARY DEFINITIONS, continued

SECTION 4

xylem specialized plant tissue that transports water and minerals from one part of the plant to another

phloem specialized plant tissue that transports sugar molecules from one part of the plant to another

sepal a leaflike structure that covers and protects an immature flower

petal the often colorful structure on a flower that is usually involved in attracting pollinators

stamen the male reproductive structure in the flower that consists of a filament topped by a pollen-producing anther

pistil the female reproductive structure in a flower that consists of a stigma, style, and ovary

stigma the flower part that is the tip of the pistil

ovary in flowers, the structure that contains ovules and develops into fruit following fertilization

SECTION 3

Vocabulary
- **pollen** (p. 278)
- **pollination** (p. 281)
- **cotyledon** (p. 283)

Section Notes
- Seed plants are vascular plants that produce seeds. The sperm cells of seed plants develop inside pollen.
- Gymnosperms are seed plants that produce their seeds in cones or in fleshy structures attached to branches. The four groups of gymnosperms are conifers, ginkgoes, cycads, and gnetophytes.
- Angiosperms are seed plants that produce their seeds in flowers. The two groups of flowering plants are monocots and dicots.

Labs
Travelin' Seeds (p. 726)

SECTION 4

Vocabulary
- **xylem** (p. 284)
- **phloem** (p. 284)
- **sepal** (p. 290)
- **petal** (p. 290)
- **stamen** (p. 291)
- **pistil** (p. 291)
- **stigma** (p. 291)
- **ovary** (p. 291)

Section Notes
- Roots generally grow underground. Roots anchor the plant, absorb water and minerals, and store food.
- Stems connect roots and leaves. Stems support leaves and other structures; transport water, minerals, and food; and store water and food.
- The main function of leaves is photosynthesis. Leaf structure is related to this function.

- Flowers usually have four parts—sepals, petals, stamens, and pistils. Stamens produce sperm cells in pollen. The ovary in the pistil contains ovules. Each ovule contains an egg. Ovules become seeds after fertilization.

Labs
Leaf Me Alone! (p. 724)
Build a Flower (p. 727)

 Vocabulary Review Worksheet 12

 Blackline masters of these Chapter Highlights can be found in the **Study Guide**.

---

internet connect

 GO TO: go.hrw.com

Visit the **HRW** Web site for a variety of learning tools related to this chapter. Just type in the keyword:

KEYWORD: HSTPL1

 GO TO: www.scilinks.org

Visit the **National Science Teachers Association** on-line Web site for Internet resources related to this chapter. Just type in the *sci*LINKS number for more information about the topic:

TOPIC:	Plant Characteristics	*sci*LINKS NUMBER: HSTL280
TOPIC:	How Are Plants Classified?	*sci*LINKS NUMBER: HSTL285
TOPIC:	Seedless Plants	*sci*LINKS NUMBER: HSTL290
TOPIC:	Plants with Seeds	*sci*LINKS NUMBER: HSTL295
TOPIC:	The Structure of Seed Plants	*sci*LINKS NUMBER: HSTL300

293

Lab and Activity Highlights

LabBank

EcoLabs & Field Activities, The Case of the Ravenous Radish, EcoLab 3

Whiz-Bang Demonstrations, Inner Life of a Leaf, Demo 8

Long-Term Projects & Research Ideas, Plant Planet, Project 12

Interactive Explorations CD-ROM

 CD 1, Exploration 2, "Shut Your Trap!"

Chapter Review Answers

USING VOCABULARY

1. cuticle
2. gametophyte
3. xylem/phloem
4. club mosses
5. cotyledon
6. stamens

UNDERSTANDING CONCEPTS

Multiple Choice

7. b
8. d
9. a
10. d
11. c
12. a
13. b
14. c

Short Answer

15. The young plant in a seed is well developed and consists of many cells; a seed can survive in many environments; a seed has stored food for the new plant.
16. Water is necessary for sexual reproduction because sperm cells swim to the egg. Water also opens the spore.

Chapter Review

USING VOCABULARY

To complete the following sentences, choose the correct term from each pair of terms listed below:

1. The ___?___ is a waxy layer that coats the surface of stems and leaves. (*stomata* or *cuticle*)
2. During the plant life cycle, eggs and sperm cells are produced by the ___?___. (*sporophyte* or *gametophyte*)
3. In vascular plants, ___?___ transports water and minerals, and ___?___ transports food molecules, such as sugar. (*xylem/phloem* or *phloem/xylem*)
4. Seedless vascular plants include ferns, horsetails, and ___?___. (*club mosses* or *liverworts*)
5. A ___?___ is a seed leaf found inside a seed. (*cotyledon* or *sepal*)
6. In a flower, the ___?___ are the male reproductive structures. (*pistils* or *stamens*)

UNDERSTANDING CONCEPTS

Multiple Choice

7. Which of the following plants is nonvascular?
   a. fern
   b. moss
   c. conifer
   d. monocot

8. Coal formed millions of years ago from the remains of
   a. nonvascular plants.
   b. flowering plants.
   c. green algae.
   d. seedless vascular plants.

9. The largest group of gymnosperms is the
   a. conifers.
   b. ginkgoes.
   c. cycads.
   d. gnetophytes.

10. Roots
    a. absorb water and minerals.
    b. store surplus food.
    c. anchor the plant.
    d. All of the above

11. Woody stems
    a. are soft, green, and flexible.
    b. include the stems of daisies.
    c. contain wood and bark.
    d. All of the above

12. The veins of a leaf contain
    a. xylem and phloem.
    b. stomata.
    c. epidermis and cuticle.
    d. xylem only.

13. In a flower, petals function to
    a. produce ovules.
    b. attract pollinators.
    c. protect the flower bud.
    d. produce pollen.

14. Monocots have
    a. flower parts in fours or fives.
    b. two cotyledons in the seed.
    c. parallel veins in leaves.
    d. All of the above

Short Answer

15. What advantages does a seed have over a spore?
16. How is water important to the reproduction of mosses and ferns?

294 Chapter 12 • Introduction to Plants

Concept Map

17. Use the following terms to create a concept map: nonvascular plants, vascular plants, xylem, phloem, ferns, seeds in cones, plants, gymnosperms, spores, angiosperms, seeds in flowers.

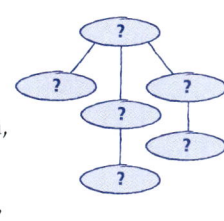

CRITICAL THINKING AND PROBLEM SOLVING

Write one or two sentences to answer the following questions:

18. Plants that are pollinated by wind produce much more pollen than plants that are pollinated by animals. Why do you suppose this is so?

19. If plants did not possess a cuticle, where would they have to live? Why?

20. Grasses do not have strong aromas or bright colors. How might this be related to the way these plants are pollinated?

21. Imagine that a seed and a spore are beginning to grow in a deep, dark crack in a rock. Which reproductive structure—the seed or the spore—is more likely to survive and develop into an adult plant after it begins to grow? Explain your answer.

MATH IN SCIENCE

22. One year a maple tree produced 1,056 seeds. If only 15 percent of those seeds germinated and grew into seedlings, how many seedlings would there be?

INTERPRETING GRAPHICS

23. Examine the cross section of the flower below to answer the following questions:
    a. Which letter corresponds to the structure in which pollen is produced? What is the name of this structure?
    b. Which letter corresponds to the structure that contains ovules? What is the name of this structure?

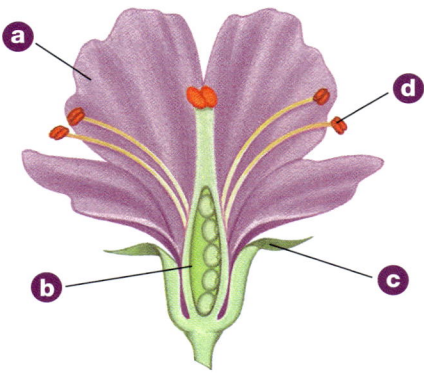

24. In a woody stem, a ring of dark cells and a ring of light cells represent 1 year of growth. Examine the cross section of a tree trunk below, and determine the age of the tree.

 Take a minute to review your answers to the Pre-Reading Questions found at the bottom of page 268. Have your answers changed? If necessary, revise your answers based on what you have learned since you began this chapter.

Concept Map

17. An answer to this exercise can be found at the end of this book.

CRITICAL THINKING AND PROBLEM SOLVING

18. Pollen carried by wind has a smaller probability of reaching another plant of the same species than pollen carried by an animal does. An animal is likely to revisit the same type of plant that it picked up the pollen from.

19. Without a cuticle, plants would lose too much moisture. They might, however, be able to survive in a wet environment.

20. Grasses are not pollinated by insects, so they do not need bright colors or a strong aroma. Their structure is suited to wind pollination.

21. A seed has a better chance of surviving and producing a plant because it has stored nutrients.

MATH IN SCIENCE

22. 158 seedlings

INTERPRETING GRAPHICS

23. a. Pollen is produced in structure *d*, the anther.
    b. Ovules are contained in structure *b*, the ovary.

24. 10 years

 Concept Mapping Transparency 12

Blackline masters of this Chapter Review can be found in the **Study Guide.**

SCIENCE, TECHNOLOGY, AND SOCIETY

Supersquash or Frankenfruit?

Background

The Flavr-Savr™ tomato was approved for consumer use by the Food and Drug Administration in 1994. By inserting an extra gene into the tomato, scientists were able to slow down a series of chemical reactions that cause tomatoes to rot. As a result, this genetically altered tomato can be left to ripen on the vine and can stay on the shelf much longer before becoming soft and spoiling. Many consumers think it also has a better flavor.

Consumer reaction to the tomato was not entirely positive, however. After the FDA's approval was announced, some consumer groups quickly began preparing a boycott of the product as well as planning public "tomato squashes," in which the tomatoes were crushed as a protest against genetically engineered foods.

The tomato marked a new era in commercial agriculture. Genetic engineering may eventually produce crops that can tolerate much harsher growing conditions, including the application of herbicides that are currently too strong to be used.

Science, Technology, and Society

Supersquash or Frankenfruit?

The fruits and vegetables you buy at the supermarket may not be exactly what they seem. Scientists may have genetically altered these foods to make them look and taste better, contain more nutrients, or have a longer shelf life.

From Bullets to Bacteria

Through genetic engineering, scientists are now able to duplicate one organism's DNA and place a certain gene from the DNA into the cells of another species of plant or animal. This technology enables scientists to give plants and animals a new trait. The new trait can then be passed along to the organism's offspring and future generations.

Scientists alter plants by inserting a gene with a certain property into a plant's cells. The DNA is usually inserted by one of two methods. In one method, new DNA is first placed inside a special bacterium, and the bacterium carries the DNA into the plant cell. In another method, microscopic particles of metal coated with the new DNA are fired into the plant cells with a special "gene gun."

High-tech Food

During the past decade, scientists have inserted genes into more than 50 different kinds of plants. In most cases, the new trait from the inserted gene makes the plants more disease resistant or more marketable in some way. For example, scientists have added genes from a caterpillar-attacking bacterium to cotton, tomato, and potato plants. The altered plants produce proteins that kill the crop-eating caterpillars. Scientists are also trying to develop genetically altered peas and red peppers that stay sweeter longer. A genetically altered tomato that lasts longer and tastes better is already in many supermarkets. One day it may even be possible to create a caffeine-free coffee bean.

Are We Ready?

As promising as these genetically engineered foods seem to be, they are not without controversy. Some scientists are afraid that genes introduced to crop plants could be released into the environment or that foods may be changed in ways that endanger human health. For example, could people who are allergic to peanuts become sick from eating a tomato plant that contains certain peanut genes? All of these concerns will have to be addressed before the genetically altered food products are widely accepted.

Find Out for Yourself

▶ Are genetically altered foods controversial in your area? Survey a few people to get their opinions about genetically altered foods. Do they think grocery stores should carry these foods? Why or why not?

◀ *A scientist uses a "gene gun" to insert DNA into plant cells.*

Answer to Find Out for Yourself

Discuss with the class the pros and cons of genetically altered foods. Then ask students to form an opinion about the genetic engineering of animals. Is this any different from that of plants? Why or why not? Accept all reasonable responses. You may wish to divide the class into two teams and organize a debate on the topic of genetically engineered organisms.

CAREERS

ETHNOBOTANIST

Paul Cox is an *ethnobotanist*. He travels to remote places to look for plants that can help cure diseases. He seeks the advice of shamans and other native healers in his search. In 1984, Cox made a trip to Samoa to observe healers. While there he met a 78-year-old Samoan healer named Epenesa. She was able to identify more than 200 medicinal plants, and she astounded Cox with her knowledge. Epenesa had an accurate understanding of human anatomy, and she dispensed medicines with great care and accuracy.

In Samoan culture, the healer is one of the most valued members of the community. After all, the healer has the knowledge to treat diseases. In some cases, Samoan healers know about ancient treatments that Western medicine has yet to discover. Recently, some researchers have turned to Samoan healers to ask them about their medical secrets.

Blending Polynesian and Western Medicine

After Cox spent months observing Epenesa as she treated patients, Epenesa gave him her treatment for yellow fever—a tea made from the wood of a rain-forest tree. Cox brought the yellow-fever remedy to the United States, and in 1986 researchers at the National Cancer Institute (NCI) began studying the plant. They found that the plant contains a virus-fighting chemical called *prostratin*. Further research by NCI indicates that prostratin may also have potential as a treatment for AIDS.

Another compound from Samoan healers treats inflammation. The healers apply the bark of a local tree to the inflamed skin. When a team of scientists evaluated the bark, they found that the healers were absolutely correct. The active compound in the bark, *flavanone,* is now being researched for its medicinal properties. Some day Western doctors may prescribe medicine containing flavanone.

Preserving Their Knowledge

When two of the healers Cox observed in Samoa died in 1993, generations of medical knowledge died with them. The healers' deaths point out the urgency of recording the ancient wisdom before all of the healers are gone. Cox and other ethnobotanists must work hard to gather information from healers as quickly as they can.

The Feel of Natural Healing

▶ The next time you have a mosquito bite or a mild sunburn, consider a treatment that comes from the experience of Native American healers. Aloe vera, another plant product, is found in a variety of lotions and ointments. Find out how well it works for you!

▶ *These plant parts from Samoa may one day be used in medicines to treat a variety of diseases.*

CAREERS
Ethnobotanist– Paul Cox

Background

Some biologists estimate that there are 235,000 species of flowering plants in the world. Of these, less than half of 1 percent have been studied for their potential medicinal qualities. Because there are so many species, efficient strategies are necessary to find the plants most likely to have medicinal value.

One strategy used by ethnobotanists is to assume that if native people use a local plant for medicine, then the plant probably has some medicinal value. Many ethnobotanists seek out native healers or shamans. Ethnobotanists hope to acquire the knowledge that has taken the shamans years to accumulate. With these insights, the researchers can then decide which plants they should collect and study.

Some of the most useful drugs developed from plants used by indigenous peoples include aspirin, for reducing pain and inflammation; codeine, for easing pain and suppressing coughs; and quinine, for combating malaria.

Teaching Strategy

Ethnobotanists, like Paul Cox, must be familiar with the names of plants and plant products from many different cultures. Ask students: From what languages have some of our modern English words for plant products been derived? (There are many examples. *Ginseng* and *tea* came from Chinese, *cinnamon* from Hebrew, *alcohol* and *coffee* from Arabic, *bamboo* from Malay, *pistachio* from Persian, *cashew* from Tupi, and *quinine* from Quechua.)

Chapter Organizer

CHAPTER ORGANIZATION	TIME MINUTES	OBJECTIVES	LABS, INVESTIGATIONS, AND DEMONSTRATIONS
Chapter Opener pp. 298–299	45	National Standards: UCP 3, SAI 1, SPSP 5, LS 3c, 4c	**Start-Up Activity** Which End Is Up? p. 299
Section 1 The Reproduction of Flowering Plants	90	▶ Describe the roles of pollination and fertilization in sexual reproduction. ▶ Describe how fruits are formed from flowers. ▶ Explain the difference between sexual and asexual reproduction in plants. UCP 2–5, SAI 1, 2, SPSP 4, HNS 1, LS 1a, 2a, 2b, 2d, 5b	**Demonstration,** Identify the Parts of a Flower, p. 300 in ATE `GENERAL` **QuickLab,** Thirsty Seeds, p. 302 `GENERAL` **Labs You Can Eat,** Not Just Another Nut, Lab 6 `GENERAL`
Section 2 The Ins and Outs of Making Food	90	▶ Describe the process of photosynthesis. ▶ Discuss the relationship between photosynthesis and cellular respiration. ▶ Explain the importance of stomata in the processes of photosynthesis and transpiration. UCP 1, 5, LS 1a, 1c, 3c, 4c; LabBook UCP 1–5, SAI 1, 2, SPSP 3, HNS 2, LS 1a, 4c	**Skill Builder,** Food Factory Waste, p. 728 `GENERAL` **Datasheets for LabBook,** Food Factory Waste, Datasheet 28 `GENERAL` **Skill Builder,** Weepy Weeds, p. 730 `GENERAL` **Datasheets for LabBook,** Weepy Weeds, Datasheet 29 `GENERAL`
Section 3 Plant Responses to the Environment	90	▶ Describe how plants may respond to light and gravity. ▶ Explain how some plants flower in response to night length. ▶ Describe how some plants are adapted to survive cold weather. UCP 1–3, SAI 1, 2, SPSP 2, 3, 5, HNS 1, 2, LS 2b, 2c, 3a, 3c, 3d, 5b	**QuickLab,** Which Way Is Up? p. 308 `GENERAL` **Interactive Explorations CD-ROM,** How's It Growing? `GENERAL` A **Worksheet** is also available in the **Interactive Explorations Teacher's Edition.** **EcoLabs & Field Activities,** Recycle! Make Your Own Paper, EcoLab 4 `BASIC` **Long-Term Projects & Research Ideas,** Project 13 `ADVANCED`

TECHNOLOGY RESOURCES

 Guided Reading Audio CD English or Spanish, Chapter 13

 One-Stop Planner CD-ROM with Test Generator

 Interactive Explorations CD-ROM CD 2, Exploration 8, How's It Growing?

  Eye on the Environment, Tropical Reforestation, Segment 15

Scientists in Action, Growing Plants in Space, Segment 16

*See page **T20** for a complete correlation of this book with the*

NATIONAL SCIENCE EDUCATION STANDARDS.

Chapter 13 • Plant Processes

CLASSROOM WORKSHEETS, TRANSPARENCIES, AND RESOURCES	SCIENCE INTEGRATION AND CONNECTIONS	REVIEW AND ASSESSMENT
Directed Reading Worksheet 13 BASIC **Science Puzzlers, Twisters & Teasers,** Worksheet 13 ADVANCED **Science Skills Worksheet 2,** Using Your Senses GENERAL		
Transparency 49, Pollination and Fertilization **Transparency 50,** From Flower to Fruit **Directed Reading Worksheet 13,** Section 1 BASIC **Reinforcement Worksheet 13,** Fertilizing Flowers GENERAL	**Cross-Disciplinary Focus,** p. 300 in ATE **Cross-Disciplinary Focus,** p. 302 in ATE **Weird Science:** Mutant Mustard, p. 318 GENERAL	**Self-Check,** p. 301 **Review,** p. 303 GENERAL **Quiz,** p. 303 in ATE GENERAL **Alternative Assessment,** p. 303 in ATE BASIC
Transparency 51, Photosynthesis **Directed Reading Worksheet 13,** Section 2 BASIC **Reinforcement Worksheet 13,** A Leaf's Work Is Never Done BASIC **Math Skills for Science Worksheet 50,** Balancing Chemical Equations GENERAL **Transparency 256,** Balancing a Chemical Equation **Transparency 52,** Transpiration	**Math and More,** p. 305 in ATE GENERAL **Connect to Physical Science,** p. 305 in ATE	**Self-Check,** p. 305 **Review,** p. 306 GENERAL **Quiz,** p. 306 in ATE GENERAL **Alternative Assessment,** p. 306 in ATE GENERAL
Directed Reading Worksheet 13, Section 3 BASIC **Transparency 53,** Night Length and Blooming Flowers **Transparency 53,** The Change of Seasons and Pigment Color **Reinforcement Worksheet 13,** How Plants Respond to Change GENERAL **Critical Thinking Worksheet 13,** Space Plants ADVANCED	**MathBreak,** Bending by Degrees, p. 307 GENERAL **Astronomy Connection,** p. 309 **Real-World Connection,** p. 309 in ATE GENERAL **Apply,** p. 310 GENERAL **Eye On The Environment:** Rainbow of Cotton, p. 319 GENERAL	**Self-Check,** p. 308 **Homework,** p. 309 in ATE GENERAL **Review,** p. 311 GENERAL **Quiz,** p. 311 in ATE GENERAL **Alternative Assessment,** p. 311 in ATE GENERAL

END-OF-CHAPTER REVIEW AND ASSESSMENT

Chapter Review in Study Guide
Vocabulary and Notes in Study Guide
Chapter Tests with Performance-Based Assessment, Chapter 13 Test
Chapter Tests with Performance-Based Assessment, Performance-Based Assessment 13
Concept Mapping Transparency 13

 Holt, Rinehart and Winston On-line Resources
go.hrw.com
For worksheets and other teaching aids related to this chapter, visit the HRW Web site and type in the keyword: **HSTPL2**

 National Science Teachers Association
www.scilinks.org
Encourage students to use the *sci*LINKS numbers listed in the internet connect boxes to access information and resources on the **NSTA** Web site.

Chapter Resources & Worksheets

Visual Resources

TEACHING TRANSPARENCIES

TEACHING TRANSPARENCIES

CONCEPT MAPPING TRANSPARENCY

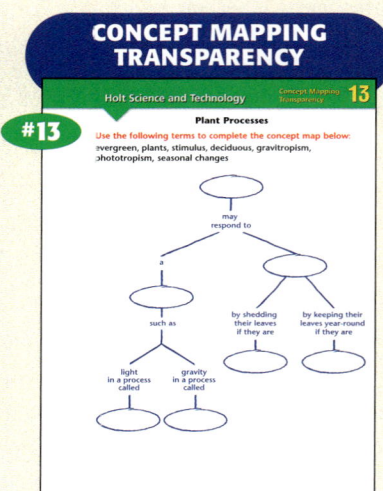

Meeting Individual Needs

DIRECTED READING

REINFORCEMENT & VOCABULARY REVIEW

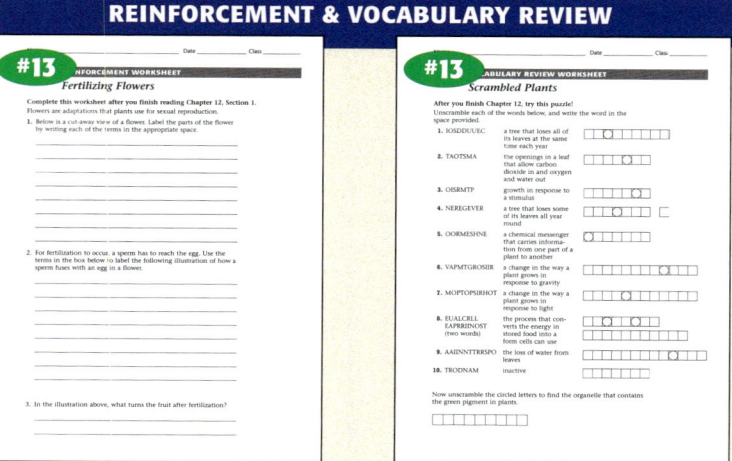

SCIENCE PUZZLERS, TWISTERS & TEASERS

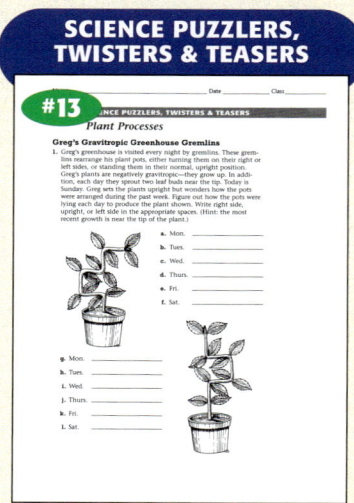

Chapter 13 • Plant Processes

Review & Assessment

STUDY GUIDE

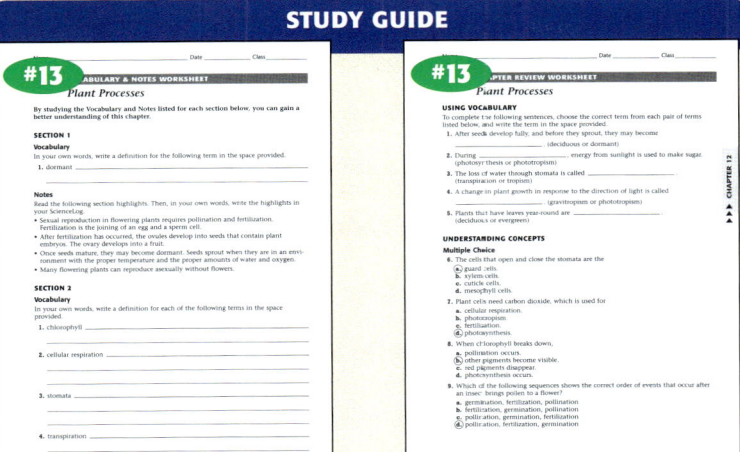

CHAPTER TESTS WITH PERFORMANCE-BASED ASSESSMENT

Lab Worksheets

LABS YOU CAN EAT

ECOLABS & FIELD ACTIVITIES

LONG-TERM PROJECTS & RESEARCH IDEAS

DATASHEETS FOR LABBOOK

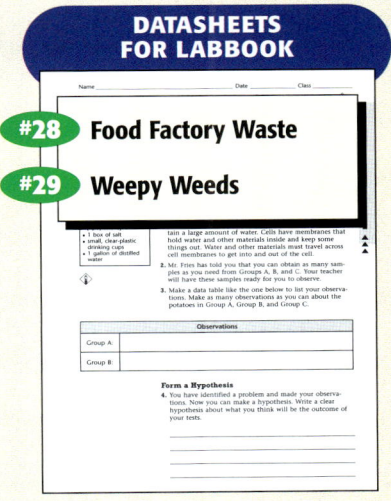

Applications & Extensions

CRITICAL THINKING & PROBLEM SOLVING

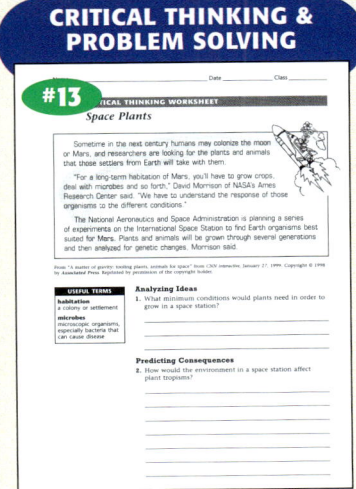

EYE ON THE ENVIRONMENT

SCIENTISTS IN ACTION

INTERACTIVE EXPLORATIONS

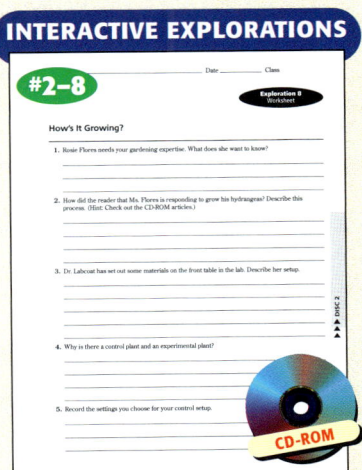

Chapter 13 • Chapter Resources & Worksheets **297D**

Chapter Background

SECTION 1

The Reproduction of Flowering Plants

▶ **Vegetative Reproduction**
Vegetative reproduction is another term for *asexual reproduction,* in which a piece of the plant grows into a complete plant. Tulip bulbs produce one or two new bulbs each year, which can be broken off the parent plant and used to produce new plants.

- Succulent plants, such as jade plants, have fleshy leaves full of water. This water sustains the leaves if they fall off the parent plant, often long enough for them to send down roots and develop into new plants.

▶ **The Perfect Flower?**
Flowers can be either perfect or imperfect. Perfect flowers have both male parts (stamens) and female parts (pistils). Imperfect flowers have one or the other—stamens or pistils—but not both.

IS THAT A FACT!

▸ Night-blooming flowers rely on nocturnal animals, such as bats and hawkmoths, to pollinate their flowers. The flowers are usually white for increased visibility and often have a strong fragrance to attract their pollinators.

▸ The oldest known fossil seeds are approximately 350 million years old, from the late Devonian period. They belong to plants called seed ferns.

SECTION 2

The Ins and Outs of Making Food

▶ **Water: A Basic Ingredient**
Water conservation is as important for alpine plants as it is for cactuses. At high altitudes there is little rainfall, but there are cold temperatures and high winds. In the Alps, the mountain aven and the mountain kidney vetch have hairlike coverings on their leaves to reduce water loss and provide insulation.

▶ **Sunlight**
Although sunlight is necessary for photosynthesis, too much sun—specifically, too much ultraviolet radiation—can damage a plant. The sun is more intense on mountains than at lower elevations. Hairlike coverings on leaves can protect some plants from excessive ultraviolet radiation. An example is the silversword, of Hawaii, which grows at altitudes up to 4,000 m.

▶ **Clean Air: A Byproduct of Photosynthesis**
A study sponsored by NASA has demonstrated that indoor plants in a controlled environment can extract pollutants from the air. The leaves remove low levels of pollutants, and the roots, assisted by activated carbon filters, can remove higher concentrations. The pollutants affected included formaldehyde and benzene gases.

- Scientists continue to study the effectiveness of plants at removing large particle pollutants, such as chemicals from detergents and cleaning fluids; fibers released from clothing, furniture, and insulation; and tobacco smoke.

- Photosynthesis also enables outdoor plants to cleanse the air of carbon emissions from cars and dwellings, nitrogen oxides, airborne ammonia, sulfur dioxide, and ozone.

IS THAT A FACT!

▸ One 80 ft beech tree can remove the daily carbon dioxide emissions produced by two single-family homes.

Chapter 13 • Plant Processes

SECTION 3

Plant Responses to the Environment

▶ Plant Pigments
In addition to containing the green pigment chlorophyll, plants contain other pigments that account for the colorful changes in autumn leaves. Xanthophylls are yellow, carotenes are yellowish orange, anthocyanins are red and purple, and tannins are golden yellow.

- In some years, the autumn colors of leaves—especially reds—are bright and colorful; in other years they are dull. Two factors contribute to the difference: warm, sunny days followed by cool nights (temperatures below 45°F) produce bright colors.

IS THAT A FACT!

- In 1997, the U.S. Department of Agriculture reported that nearly 60 million poinsettia *(Euphorbia pulcherrima)* plants were purchased in the United States, totaling about $222 million in sales. Poinsettias are the country's most popular potted plants.

▶ Discovery of Auxins
Charles Darwin (1809–1882) is credited with making the first recorded observations that led to the discovery of plant hormones. In 1881, Darwin and his son, Francis, described the occurrence of phototropism, the bending of a plant toward a light source. In an experiment, the Darwins placed lead caps on the growing tips of grass and oat seedlings and noted that the growing tips did not bend. When the lead caps were removed, the tips bent toward the light source. No additional work was done to follow up on the Darwins' experiments until the latter part of the nineteenth century.

▶ Germplasm
A plant's germplasm consists of the plant's genetic material and tissues, organs, and organisms that express the traits contained in the genetic material. The U.S. National Plant Germplasm System (NPGS) conserves and uses germplasm to improve crop plants by transferring disease resistance, improving yields, and adapting plants to grow under new conditions.

IS THAT A FACT!

- Plant hormones occur in very small quantities. In a pineapple plant, for example, only 6 μg of auxin are present for 1 kg of plant material. In terms of weight, this is equivalent to a needle in a 20-metric-ton truckload of hay.

For background information about teaching strategies and issues, refer to the *Professional Reference for Teachers*.

Plant Processes

 Pre-Reading Questions

Students may not know the answers to these questions before reading the chapter, so accept any reasonable response.

Suggested Answers

1. Answers will vary, but students may mention wilting, losing leaves, changing colors, and any other changes that show plants respond to the environment.
2. Answers will vary, but students may mention that plants need light in order to stay alive and make food.

 Directed Reading Worksheet 16

 Science Puzzlers, Twisters & Teasers Worksheet 16

 Guided Reading Audio CD English or Spanish, Chapter 16

 Science Skills Worksheet 2 "Using Your Senses"

CHAPTER 13

Plant Processes

Sections

1. **The Reproduction of Flowering Plants** 300
   - QuickLab 302
   - Internet Connect 303
2. **The Ins and Outs of Making Food** 304
   - Internet Connect 306
3. **Plant Responses to the Environment** 307
   - MathBreak 307
   - QuickLab 308
   - Astronomy Connection 309
   - Apply 310
   - Internet Connect 311

Chapter Review 314
Feature Articles 316, 317
LabBook 728–731

Pre-Reading Questions

1. How do plants respond to changes in their environment?
2. Why do plants need light?

298

VENUS'S-FLYTRAP

Look at the plant in the photo. Yes, those green spiny pads are its leaves. Why is the Venus's-flytrap such an unusual plant? Unlike most plants, the Venus's-flytrap eats meat. It obtains key nutrients by capturing and digesting insects and other small animals. The two green pads snap shut to trap the prey. In this chapter, you will learn how different types of plants reproduce themselves, respond to their environments, and take in nutrients. You will also learn how plants use sunlight to create food.

 go.hrw.com
HRW On-line Resources
For worksheets and other teaching aids, visit the HRW Web site and type in the keyword: **HSTPL2**

 www.scilinks.com
Use the sciLINKS numbers at the end of each chapter for additional resources on the **NSTA** Web site.

 www.cnnfyi.com
Visit the CNN Web site for current events coverage and classroom resources.

298 Chapter 13 • Plant Processes

START-UP Activity

WHICH END IS UP?

If you plant seeds with their "tops" facing in different directions, will their stems all grow upward? Do this activity to find out.

Procedure

1. Pack a **clear medium plastic cup** with slightly **moistened paper towels.**
2. Place **5 or 6 corn seeds,** equally spaced, around the cup between the cup and the paper towels. Point the tip of each seed in a different direction.
3. Use a **marker** to draw arrows on the outside of the cup to indicate the direction that each seed tip points.
4. Place the cup in a well-lit location for one week. Keep the seeds moist by adding **water** to the paper towels as needed.
5. After one week, observe the plant growth. Record the direction in which each plant grew.

Analysis

6. Compare the direction of growth for your seeds. What explanation can you give for the results?

START-UP Activity

WHICH END IS UP?

MATERIALS

For Each Group:
- clear plastic cup
- paper towels
- water
- corn seeds
- marker

Teacher's Notes

To minimize the effect of light on the growth of the stems, have students rotate the cups every day.

Be sure students keep the paper towels moist throughout the activity.

To further emphasize the effect of gravity on plant growth, have students turn their cups upside down after several days' growth.

Answer to START-UP Activity

6. Students should observe that the stems in all the germinating seeds grow away from the force of gravity.

Chapter 13 • Plant Processes

SECTION 1

Focus

The Reproduction of Flowering Plants

This section describes the roles of pollination and fertilization. Students will be able to explain how fruits are formed from flowers and differentiate between sexual and asexual reproduction in flowering plants.

Bellringer

Ask students to list the names of all the fruits and flowers they can think of in their ScienceLog.

1) Motivate

DEMONSTRATION

Identify the Parts of a Flower
Show students a variety of fresh flowers, and ask them to describe ways the flowers are similar and different. (Student answers should focus on size, structure, fragrance, and color.)

Refer students to **Figure 1.** Point out the anthers, stigmas, petals, and sepals in each flower. Remove the petals, and shake the flower over paper. (Note: Pollen can stain skin and clothing. You may wish to wear protective gloves.)

Ask students to identify the powder on the paper. (pollen)

Explain that pollen contains the flower's male reproductive cells. Sheltered English

 Teaching Transparency 49
"Pollination and Fertilization"

 Teaching Transparency 50
"From Flower to Fruit"

300 Chapter 13 • Plant Processes

Section 1

The Reproduction of Flowering Plants

Terms to Learn
dormant

What You'll Do
◆ Describe the roles of pollination and fertilization in sexual reproduction.
◆ Describe how fruits are formed from flowers.
◆ Explain the difference between sexual and asexual reproduction in plants.

If you went outside right now and made a list of all the different kinds of plants you could see, most of the plants on your list would probably be flowering plants. Flowering plants are the largest and the most diverse group of plants in the world. Their success is partly due to their flowers, which are adaptations for sexual reproduction. During sexual reproduction, an egg is fertilized by a sperm cell. In flowering plants, fertilization takes place within the flower and leads to the formation of one or more seeds within a fruit.

How Does Fertilization Occur?

In order for fertilization to occur, sperm cells must be able to reach eggs. The sperm cells of a flowering plant are contained in pollen grains. Pollination occurs when pollen grains are transported from anthers to stigmas. This is the beginning of fertilization, as shown in **Figure 1**. After the pollen lands on the stigma, a tube grows from the pollen grain through the style to the ovary. Inside the ovary are ovules. Each ovule contains an egg.

Sperm cells within the pollen grain move down the pollen tube and into an ovule. Fertilization occurs as one of the sperm cells fuses with the egg inside the ovule.

Figure 1 Fertilization occurs after pollination.

① Pollen grains land on the stigma and begin to grow pollen tubes.

② Sperm cells travel down pollen tubes and fertilize the eggs.

300

CROSS-DISCIPLINARY FOCUS

History In 1519, the explorer Hernando Cortez brought cacao beans and a recipe from Montezuma's court back to Spain. The recipe was for a new drink called chocolate made from the beans of the cacao plant. Served with honey and sugar, it greatly impressed the members of the Spanish court. In fact, they were so impressed that they kept this wonderful bean a secret for a hundred years. For the next century, Spanish monks were the only people in Europe who knew how to prepare chocolate.

From Flower to Fruit

After fertilization takes place, the ovule develops into a seed that contains a tiny, undeveloped plant. The ovary surrounding the ovule develops into a fruit. **Figure 2** shows how the ovary and ovules of a flower develop into a fruit and seeds.

Figure 2 *Fertilization leads to the development of fruit and seeds.*

Seed Production

A mature plant produces the flower. Pollination and fertilization take place.

Each ovule within the flower's ovary contains a fertilized egg.

Petals and stamens fall away.

The ovary becomes the fruit, and each ovule becomes a seed. When the fruit ripens, the seeds are dispersed.

Each seed contains a tiny plant. If a seed sprouts, or begins to grow, it will become a new plant.

✓ Self-Check

How many fruits and seeds could develop from a flower with one ovary containing six ovules? *(See page 782 to check your answer.)*

Will mutant mustard take over the world? Turn to page 316 to find out.

Directed Reading Worksheet 13 Section 1

TOPIC: Reproduction of Plants
GO TO: www.scilinks.org
sciLINKS NUMBER: HSTL305

Section 1 • The Reproduction of Flowering Plants **301**

2) Teach, continued

CROSS-DISCIPLINARY FOCUS

Art Have students use books from the library or from their home to find examples of how artists (painters, sculptors, photographers, and so on) throughout history have represented flowers and fruits in their work. You might want to show students reproductions of works by Claude Monet or Georgia O'Keeffe to encourage their interest in this activity. Interested students could create a drawing of a flower or a still life of fruit. Sheltered English

QuickLab

MATERIALS

FOR EACH GROUP:
- 12 bean seeds
- 2 Petri dishes
- marking pen or wax pencil
- water

Students should observe that the bean seeds that soaked in water increased in size. Students might also observe that the soaked seeds have begun to crack open.

Answer to QuickLab

5. The seeds swell because they are absorbing water. The stored water can then be used by the young plant.

Reinforcement Worksheet 13 "Fertilizing Flowers"

Familiar Fruits

While the ovules are developing into seeds, the ovary is developing into the fruit. As the fruit swells and ripens, it holds and protects the developing seeds. Look below to see which parts of the fruits developed from a flower's ovary and ovules.

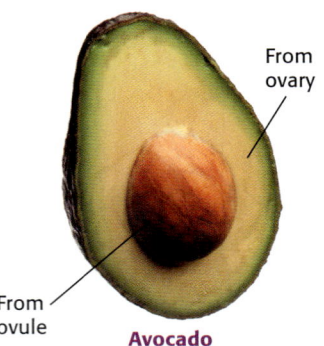

Tomato — From ovules / From ovary
Orange — From ovary / From ovules
Avocado — From ovary / From ovule

QuickLab

Thirsty Seeds

1. Obtain **12 dry bean seeds, 2 Petri dishes,** a **wax pencil,** and **water** from your teacher.
2. Fill one Petri dish two-thirds full of water and add six seeds. Label the dish "Water."
3. Add the remaining seeds to the dry Petri dish. Label this dish "Control."
4. The next day, compare the size of the two sets of seeds. Write your observations in your ScienceLog.
5. What caused the size of the seeds to change? Why might this be important to the seed's survival?

Seeds Become New Plants

Once a seed is fully developed, the young plant inside the seed stops growing. The seed may become dormant. When seeds are **dormant,** they are inactive. Dormant seeds can often survive long periods of drought or freezing temperatures. Some seeds need extreme conditions such as cold winters or even forest fires to break their dormancy.

When a seed is dropped or planted in an environment that has water, oxygen, and a suitable temperature, the seed sprouts. Each plant species has an ideal temperature at which most of its seeds will begin to grow. For most plants, the ideal temperature for growth is about 27°C (80.6°F). **Figure 3** shows the *germination,* or sprouting, of a bean seed and the early stages of growth in a young bean plant.

Figure 3 *Sexual reproduction produces seeds that grow into new plants.*

WEIRD SCIENCE

In 1967, the seeds of the arctic tundra lupine *(Lupinus arcticus)* were discovered by a mining engineer in a frozen animal burrow in the Yukon. Carbon dating showed the animal remains in the burrow to be at least 10,000 years old. Frozen seeds of the tundra lupine were found among the animal remains. When tested, these seeds germinated within 48 hours!

Other Methods of Reproduction

Many flowering plants can also reproduce asexually. Asexual reproduction in plants does not involve the formation of flowers, seeds, and fruits. In asexual reproduction, a part of a plant, such as a stem or root, produces a new plant. Several examples of asexual reproduction are shown below in **Figure 4.**

Figure 4 *Asexual reproduction can occur in several different ways. Some examples are shown here.*

▼ The strawberry plant produces runners, stems that run horizontally along the ground. Buds along runners grow into new plants.

▲ The "eyes" of potatoes are buds that can grow asexually into new plants.

▶ Kalanchoe plants produce plantlets, tiny plants along the margins of their leaves. Plantlets eventually fall off and root in the soil as separate plants.

REVIEW

1. How does pollination differ from fertilization?
2. Which part of a flower develops into a fruit?
3. **Relating Concepts** What do flowers and runners have in common? How are they different?
4. **Identifying Relationships** When might asexual reproduction be important for the survival of some flowering plants?

internetconnect

TOPIC: Reproduction of Plants
GO TO: www.scilinks.org
sciLINKS NUMBER: HSTL305

SECTION 2

Focus

The Ins and Outs of Making Food

This section describes photosynthesis. Students will learn about the relationship between photosynthesis and cellular respiration. In addition, they will learn about the importance of stomata in the processes of photosynthesis and transpiration.

 Bellringer

Write the following question on the board or overhead projector:

> Where do you get the energy you need to stay alive?

Have students write and explain their answer in their ScienceLog. (Students will probably answer that they get their energy from the foods they eat.)

Sheltered English

1) Motivate

DISCUSSION

Food and Energy Ask students the following questions before they begin reading this section.

- What kinds of foods do you eat? (Answers will vary.)
- Where do the animals you eat for food get their energy to survive? (Animals eat plants or other animals that eat plants.)
- Where do plants get their energy to survive? (Plants get their energy from sunlight.)

Explain to students that plants use energy from the sun to make their own food in a process called photosynthesis.

304 Chapter 13 • Plant Processes

Section 2

Terms to Learn

chlorophyll
cellular respiration
stomata
transpiration

What You'll Do

- Describe the process of photosynthesis.
- Discuss the relationship between photosynthesis and cellular respiration.
- Explain the importance of stomata in the processes of photosynthesis and transpiration.

 Teaching Transparency 51
"Photosynthesis"

 Directed Reading Worksheet 13 Section 2

 Reinforcement Worksheet 13
"A Leaf's Work Is Never Done"

The Ins and Outs of Making Food

Plants do not have lungs, but they need air just like you. Air is a mixture of oxygen, carbon dioxide, and other gases. Plants must have carbon dioxide to carry out photosynthesis, which is how they make their own food.

What Happens During Photosynthesis?

Plants need sunlight to produce food. During photosynthesis, the energy in sunlight is used to make food in the form of the sugar glucose ($C_6H_{12}O_6$) from carbon dioxide (CO_2) and water (H_2O). How does this happen?

Capturing Light Energy Plant cells have organelles called chloroplasts. Chloroplasts contain **chlorophyll**, a green pigment that absorbs light energy. You may not know it, but sunlight is actually a mixture of all the colors of the rainbow. **Figure 5** shows how light from the sun can be separated into different colors when passed through a triangular piece of glass called a prism. Chlorophyll absorbs all of the colors in light except green. Plants look green because chlorophyll reflects green light.

Figure 5 Plants look green to us because green is reflected by the leaves. The other colors of light are absorbed by the chlorophyll in plant cells.

Students may think that photosynthesis occurs only in the leaves of plants. In some plants, such as aspen trees and cactuses, photosynthesis occurs in the plants' trunks or stems.

Making Sugar The light energy absorbed by chlorophyll is used to break water (H_2O) down into hydrogen (H) and oxygen (O). The hydrogen is then combined with carbon dioxide (CO_2) from the air to make a sugar called glucose ($C_6H_{12}O_6$). Oxygen is given off as a byproduct. The process of photosynthesis is summarized in the following chemical equation:

$$6CO_2 + 6H_2O \xrightarrow{\text{light energy}} C_6H_{12}O_6 + 6O_2$$

The equation shows that it takes six molecules of carbon dioxide and six molecules of water to produce one molecule of glucose and six molecules of oxygen. The process is illustrated in **Figure 6**.

The energy stored in food molecules is used by plant cells to carry out their life processes. Within each living cell, glucose and other food molecules are broken down in a process called cellular respiration. **Cellular respiration** converts the energy stored in food into a form of energy that cells can use. During this process, the plant uses oxygen and releases carbon dioxide and water.

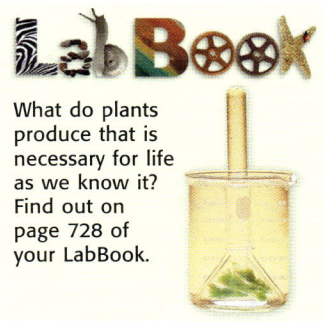

What do plants produce that is necessary for life as we know it? Find out on page 728 of your LabBook.

 Self-Check

What is the original source of the energy stored in the sugar produced by plant cells? (See page 782 to check your answer.)

Figure 6 *During photosynthesis, plants take in carbon dioxide and water and absorb light energy. They make sugar and release oxygen.*

TOPIC: Photosynthesis
GO TO: www.scilinks.org
sciLINKS NUMBER: HSTL310

3 Extend

Weepy Weeds

GROUP ACTIVITY

Divide students into groups of four. Provide each group with 6 black marbles representing carbon atoms, 18 white marbles representing oxygen, and 12 blue marbles representing hydrogen. Have students arrange the marbles to demonstrate that six molecules of carbon dioxide and six molecules of water are needed to produce one molecule of sugar and six molecules of oxygen gas. **Sheltered English**

4 Close

1. What molecules do plants use to make sugar? (carbon dioxide and water)
2. What substances enter and exit a leaf through the stomata? (enter: carbon dioxide; exit: oxygen and water)

ALTERNATIVE ASSESSMENT

Writing Have students write two paragraphs about stomata in their ScienceLog. The first paragraph should describe the appearance of stomata and the passage of materials through the stomata when light is available. The second paragraph should describe the same two events when it is dark.

Teaching Transparency 52
"Transpiration"

306 Chapter 13 • Plant Processes

Gas Exchange

All above ground plant surfaces are covered by a waxy cuticle. How does a plant obtain carbon dioxide through this barrier? Carbon dioxide enters the plant's leaves through the **stomata** (singular, *stoma*). A stoma is an opening in the leaf's epidermis and cuticle. Each stoma is surrounded by two *guard cells*, which act like double doors, opening and closing the gap. You can see open and closed stomata in **Figure 7**. The function of stomata is shown in **Figure 8.**

When the stomata are open, carbon dioxide diffuses into the leaf. The oxygen produced during photosynthesis diffuses out of the leaf cells and exits the leaf through the stomata.

When the stomata are open, water vapor also exits the leaf. The loss of water from leaves is called **transpiration**. Most of the water absorbed by a plant's roots is needed to replace water lost during transpiration. When a plant wilts, it is usually because more water is being lost through its leaves than is being absorbed by its roots.

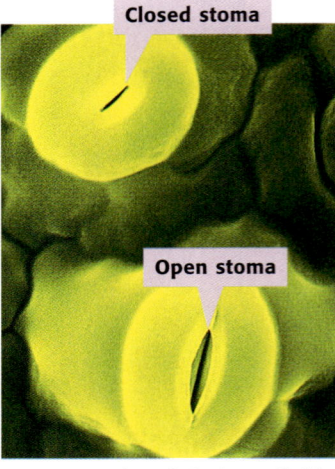

Figure 7 *When light is available for photosynthesis, the stomata are usually open. When it's dark, the stomata close to conserve water.*

Figure 8 *Plants take in carbon dioxide and release oxygen and water through the stomata in their leaves.*

TOPIC: Photosynthesis
GO TO: www.scilinks.org
sciLINKS NUMBER: HSTL310

REVIEW

1. What three things do plants need to carry out photosynthesis?
2. Why must plant cells carry out cellular respiration?
3. **Identifying Relationships** How are the opening and closing of stomata related to transpiration? When does transpiration occur?

▼ **Answers to Review**

1. Plants need light, water, and carbon dioxide for photosynthesis.
2. because the energy stored in food must be converted into a form of energy that cells can use
3. Transpiration occurs when water vapor exits the leaf through the stomata. It usually occurs when there is light available for photosynthesis and gas exchange is occurring.

Section 3

Plant Responses to the Environment

Terms to Learn

tropism
phototropism
gravitropism
evergreen
deciduous

What You'll Do

- Describe how plants may respond to light and gravity.
- Explain how some plants flower in response to night length.
- Describe how some plants are adapted to survive cold weather.

What happens when you get really cold? Do your teeth chatter as you shiver uncontrollably? If so, your brain is responding to the stimulus of cold by causing your muscles to twitch rapidly and generate warmth. Anything that causes a reaction in an organ or tissue is a stimulus. Do plant tissues respond to stimuli? They sure do! Examples of stimuli to which plants respond include light, gravity, and changing seasons.

Plant Tropisms

Some plants respond to an environmental stimulus, such as light or gravity, by growing in a particular direction. Growth in response to a stimulus is called a **tropism.** Tropisms are either positive or negative, depending on whether the plant grows toward or away from the stimulus. Plant growth toward a stimulus is a positive tropism. Plant growth away from a stimulus is a negative tropism. Two examples of tropisms are phototropism and gravitropism.

Sensing Light If you place a houseplant so that it gets light from only one direction, such as from a window, the shoot tips bend toward the light. A change in the growth of a plant that is caused by light is called **phototropism** (foh TAH troh PIZ uhm). As shown in **Figure 9,** the bending occurs when cells on one side of the shoot grow longer than cells on the other side of the shoot.

MATH BREAK

Bending by Degrees

Suppose a plant has a positive phototropism and bends toward the light at a rate of 0.3 degrees per minute. How many hours will it take the plant to bend 90 degrees?

Figure 9 The plant cells on the dark side of the shoot grow longer than the cells on the other side. This causes the shoot to bend toward the light.

IS THAT A FACT!

The tallest tree ever measured was found in Watts River, in Victoria, Australia. The tree—an Australian eucalyptus (*Eucalyptus regnans*)—was 132 m tall in 1872.

2) Teach

USING THE FIGURE

Have students look closely at **Figure 10**. Point out that after a few days the leaves of the plant grow upward and the roots grow downward. Explain that the plant growth is in response (positive or negative) to gravity. Ask students what other stimuli the stems might be growing in response to. (Students should reason that the stems grow upward in order for the leaves to reach sunlight and roots grow downward to reach water or moisture and to anchor the plant.)
Sheltered English

QuickLab

MATERIALS

FOR EACH GROUP:
- several potted plants
- duct tape
- cardboard

Answers to QuickLab

Observations may vary, but students should see that plant stems always try to grow perpendicular to the ground.

Gravity and light might have influenced the growth by causing the plant to grow upward.

Gravitropism benefits a plant because it directs the plant to grow so that the stems are aboveground and the roots grow downward.

---

internetconnect

SC_{INKS} **TOPIC:** Plant Tropisms
NSTA **GO TO:** www.scilinks.org
*sci*LINKS NUMBER: HSTL315

TOPIC: Plant Growth
GO TO: www.scilinks.org
*sci*LINKS NUMBER: HSTL320

Which Way Is Up? When the growth of a plant changes direction in response to the direction of gravity, the change is called **gravitropism** (GRAV i TROH piz uhm). The effect of gravitropism is demonstrated by the plants in **Figure 10.** A few days after a plant is placed on its side or turned upside down, the roots and shoots show a change in their direction of growth. Most shoot tips have negative gravitropism—they grow upward, away from the center of the Earth. In contrast, most root tips have positive gravitropism—they grow downward, toward the center of the Earth.

Figure 10 Gravity is a stimulus that causes plants to change their direction of growth.

▲ To grow away from the pull of gravity, this plant has grown upward.

This plant has recently been upside down. ▶

QuickLab

Which Way Is Up?

Will a potted plant grow sideways? You will need **several potted plants** to find out. Use **duct tape** to secure **cardboard** around the base of each plant so that the soil will not fall out. Turn the plants on their sides and observe what happens over the next few days. Describe two stimuli that might have influenced the direction of growth. How might gravitropism benefit a plant?

✓ Self-Check

1. Use the following terms to create a concept map: tropism, stimuli, light, gravity, phototropism, and gravitropism.
2. Imagine a plant in which light causes a negative phototropism. Will the plant bend to the left or to the right when light is shining only on the plant's right side?

(See page 782 to check your answers.)

Answers to Self-Check

1.
```
        Tropism
           |
  is a plant's response to
           |
        stimuli
          / \
       such as
        /     \
    gravity   light
       |         |
 which causes  which causes
       |         |
 gravitropism  phototropism
```

2. During negative phototropism, the plant would grow away from the stimulus (light), so it would be bending to the left.

Seasonal Responses

What would happen if a plant living in an area that has severe winters flowered in December? Would the plant be able to successfully produce seeds and fruits? If your answer is no, you're correct. If the plant produced any flowers at all, the flowers would probably freeze and die before they had the chance to produce mature seeds. Plants living in regions with cold winters can detect the change in seasons. How do plants do this?

As Different as Night and Day Think about what happens as the seasons change. For example, what happens to the length of the days and the nights? As autumn and winter approach, the days get shorter and the nights get longer. The opposite happens when spring and summer approach.

The difference between day length and night length is an important environmental stimulus for many plants. This stimulus can cause plants to begin reproducing. Some plants flower only in late summer or early autumn, when the night length is long. These plants are called short-day plants. Examples of short-day plants include poinsettias (shown in **Figure 11**), ragweed, and chrysanthemums. Other plants flower in spring or early summer, when night length is short. These plants are called long-day plants. Clover, spinach, and lettuce are examples of long-day plants.

Astronomy CONNECTION

The seasons are caused by Earth's tilt and its orbit around the sun. We have summer when the Northern Hemisphere is tilted toward the sun and the sun's energy falls more directly on the Northern Hemisphere. While the Northern Hemisphere experiences the warm season, the Southern Hemisphere experiences the cold season. The opposite of this occurs when the Northern Hemisphere is tilted away from the sun.

Figure 11 *Night length determines when poinsettias flower.*

Early summer

◀ In the early summer, night length is short. At this time, poinsettia leaves are all green, and there are no flowers.

Late fall

◀ Poinsettias flower in the fall, when nights are longer. The leaves surrounding the flower clusters turn red. Professional growers use artificial lighting to control the timing of the color change.

IS THAT A FACT!

Short-day plants are really "long-night" plants. The number of hours of darkness is actually more important to the plant than the number of hours of daylight. The poinsettias shown in **Figure 11,** for example, will not flower until the amount of darkness is 14 hours or longer. If that period of darkness is interrupted for any reason—for even a brief time—the plant will not flower.

② Teach, continued

Answer to APPLY
Sample answers include the following: experiments in which entire trees were covered for part of the day to prevent them from getting sunlight; experiments in which entire trees were exposed to artificial sunlight to determine if trees could be kept from losing their leaves; experiments in which some of the leaves were protected or given artificial sunlight to determine if some leaves could be kept on the tree, even when others fell off.

READING STRATEGY

Prediction Guide Before students read this page, ask the following questions:
- What kind of tree is an evergreen? Give two examples. (Evergreens are trees that have leaves adapted to survive throughout the year. Examples include conifers, such as pines and firs.)
- What are deciduous trees? (Deciduous trees lose all their leaves at the same time each year.)

MISCONCEPTION ALERT

The colored part of the poinsettia is not the flower, as most people think it is. The colored parts are really types of leaves called bracts. The flowers are the tiny berrylike structures at the center of the colored bracts.

Teaching Transparency 53
"The Change of Seasons and Pigment Color"

Reinforcement Worksheet 13
"How Plants Respond to Change"

310   Chapter 13 • Plant Processes

Can Trees Tell Time?
One fall afternoon, Holly looks into her backyard. She notices that a tree that was full of leaves the week before is now completely bare. What caused the tree to drop all its leaves? Holly came up with the following hypothesis:

Each leaf on the tree was able to sense day length. When the day length became short enough, each leaf responded by falling.

Design an experiment that would test Holly's hypothesis.

Seasonal Changes in Leaves All trees lose their leaves at some time. Some trees, such as pine and holly, shed some of their leaves year-round so that some leaves are always present on the tree. These trees are called **evergreen.** Evergreen trees have leaves adapted to survive throughout the year.

Other trees, such as the maple tree in **Figure 12,** are **deciduous** and lose all their leaves at the same time each year. Deciduous trees usually lose their leaves before winter begins. In tropical climates that have wet and dry seasons, deciduous trees lose their leaves before the dry season. Having bare branches during the winter or during the dry season may reduce the water lost by transpiration. The loss of leaves helps plants survive low temperatures or long periods without rain.

Figure 12 The leaves of some deciduous trees, like the maple shown here, change from green to orange in autumn. In winter, the maple is bare.

IS THAT A FACT!
When leaves change color in the fall, they make a beautiful display. Here are the autumn leaf colors of some common trees.
- flame red and orange—sugar maple, sumac
- dark red—dogwood, red maple, scarlet oak
- yellow—poplar, willow, birch
- plum purple—ash
- tan or brown—oak, beech, elm, hickory

The leaves of some trees, such as locusts, stay green until the leaves drop. The leaves of black walnut trees fall before they change color.

As shown in **Figure 13,** leaves often change color before they fall. As autumn approaches, chlorophyll, the green pigment used in photosynthesis, breaks down. As chlorophyll is lost from leaves, other yellow and orange pigments are revealed. These pigments were always present in the leaves but were hidden by the green chlorophyll. Some leaves also have red pigments, which also become visible when chlorophyll is broken down.

In autumn, trees growing near streetlights keep their leaves longer than their rural counterparts.

Figure 13 *The breakdown of chlorophyll in the autumn is a seasonal response in many trees. As the amount of chlorophyll in leaves decreases, other pigments become visible.*

REVIEW

1. What are the effects of the tropisms caused by light and gravity?
2. What is the difference between a short-day plant and a long-day plant?
3. How does the loss of leaves help a plant survive winter or long periods without rain?
4. **Applying Concepts** If a plant does not flower when exposed to 12 hours of daylight but does flower when exposed to 15 hours of daylight, is it a short-day plant or a long-day plant?

internet connect

SC_**i**_**LINKS**
NSTA

TOPIC: Plant Tropisms, Plant Growth
GO TO: www.scilinks.org
sciLINKS NUMBER: HSTL315, HSTL320

3) Extend

GOING FURTHER

Writing Have students explore other kinds of seasonal changes exhibited in plants. For example, encourage students to find out what conditions prompt bulbs to emerge in the spring and what conditions prompt seeds of flowering plants to germinate.

4) Close

Quiz

1. Why do some leaves change color in the fall? (Green chlorophyll in the leaves begins to break down, and other pigments become visible.)
2. What is the difference between an evergreen tree and a deciduous tree? (An evergreen tree has leaves adapted to survive throughout the year; they shed some of their leaves year-round. A deciduous tree loses all its leaves at the same time each year.)
3. What is a tropism in a plant? (A tropism is either a positive or negative response to an environmental stimulus, such as light or gravity.)

ALTERNATIVE ASSESSMENT

Have students make labeled drawings in their ScienceLog that illustrate plants showing positive and negative phototropism and positive and negative gravitropism. **Sheltered English**

Critical Thinking Worksheet 13 "Space Plants"

Answers to Review

1. Phototropism is caused by light. The cells on the dark side of the stem grow longer than the cells on the side facing the light, causing the stem to bend toward the light. Gravitropism is caused by gravity. Parts of the plant growing above the surface grow away from the pull of gravity. Parts below the surface grow toward it.
2. Plants that flower in only late summer or early autumn, when the night length is long, are called short-day plants. Plants that flower in the spring or early summer when night length is short, are called long-day plants.
3. Dropping its leaves prevents the tree from losing water through transpiration.
4. It is a long-day plant.

Chapter Highlights

Vocabulary Definitions

Section 1
dormant describes an inactive state of a seed

Section 2
chlorophyll a green pigment in chloroplasts that absorbs light energy for photosynthesis

cellular respiration the process of producing ATP in the cell from oxygen and glucose; releases carbon dioxide and water

stomata openings in the epidermis of a leaf that allow carbon dioxide to enter the leaf and allow water and oxygen to leave the leaf

transpiration the loss of water from plant leaves through openings called stomata

Chapter Highlights

SECTION 1

Vocabulary
dormant (p. 302)

Section Notes
- Sexual reproduction in flowering plants requires pollination and fertilization. Fertilization is the joining of an egg and a sperm cell.
- After fertilization has occurred, the ovules develop into seeds that contain plant embryos. The ovary develops into a fruit.
- Once seeds mature, they may become dormant. Seeds sprout when they are in an environment with the proper temperature and the proper amounts of water and oxygen.
- Many flowering plants can reproduce asexually without flowers.

SECTION 2

Vocabulary
chlorophyll (p. 304)
cellular respiration (p. 305)
stomata (p. 306)
transpiration (p. 306)

Section Notes
- During photosynthesis, leaves absorb sunlight and form glucose from carbon dioxide and water.
- During cellular respiration, a plant uses oxygen and releases carbon dioxide and water. Glucose is converted into a form of energy that cells can use.
- Plants take in carbon dioxide and release oxygen and water through stomata in their leaves.

Labs
Food Factory Waste (p. 728)
Weepy Weeds (p. 730)

✓ Skills Check

Visual Understanding

CIRCLE GRAPH A circle graph is a great visual for illustrating fractions without using numbers. Each circle graph on page 309 represents a 24-hour period. The blue area represents the fraction of time in which there is no sunlight, and the gold area represents the fraction of time in which there is light. As shown by the graph, early summer is about two-thirds day and one-third night.

BAR GRAPHS As shown on page 311, bar graphs are often used to compare numbers. The graph at right compares the success rate of flower seeds from five seed producers. As shown by the bar height, company D, at about 88 percent, had the highest rate of success.

Lab and Activity Highlights

Food Factory Waste PG 728

Weepy Weeds PG 730

Datasheets for LabBook (blackline masters for these labs)

312 Chapter 13 • Plant Processes

SECTION 3

Vocabulary
- **tropism** *(p. 307)*
- **phototropism** *(p. 307)*
- **gravitropism** *(p. 308)*
- **evergreen** *(p. 310)*
- **deciduous** *(p. 310)*

Section Notes
- A tropism is plant growth in response to an environmental stimulus, such as light or gravity. Plant growth toward a stimulus is a positive tropism. Plant growth away from a stimulus is a negative tropism.
- Phototropism is growth in response to the direction of light. Gravitropism is growth in response to the direction of gravity.
- The change in the amount of daylight and darkness that occurs with changing seasons often controls plant reproduction.
- Evergreen plants have leaves adapted to survive throughout the year. Deciduous plants lose their leaves before cold or dry seasons. The loss of leaves helps deciduous plants survive low temperatures and dry periods.

VOCABULARY DEFINITIONS, continued

SECTION 3

tropism a change in the growth of a plant in response to a stimulus

phototropism a change in the growth of a plant in response to light

gravitropism a change in the growth of a plant in response to gravity

evergreen describes trees that keep their leaves year-round

deciduous describes trees that have leaves that change color in autumn and fall off in winter

 Vocabulary Review Worksheet 13

 Blackline masters of these Chapter Highlights can be found in the **Study Guide.**

internet connect

GO TO: go.hrw.com

Visit the **HRW** Web site for a variety of learning tools related to this chapter. Just type in the keyword:

KEYWORD: HSTPL2

GO TO: www.scilinks.org

Visit the **National Science Teachers Association** on-line Web site for Internet resources related to this chapter. Just type in the *sci*LINKS number for more information about the topic:

TOPIC: Reproduction of Plants   *sci*LINKS NUMBER: HSTL305
TOPIC: Photosynthesis   *sci*LINKS NUMBER: HSTL310
TOPIC: Plant Tropisms   *sci*LINKS NUMBER: HSTL315
TOPIC: Plant Growth   *sci*LINKS NUMBER: HSTL320

Lab and Activity Highlights

LabBank

 Labs You Can Eat, Not Just Another Nut, Lab 6

Ecolabs & Field Activities, Recycle! Make Your Own Paper, EcoLab 4

Long-Term Projects & Research Ideas, Plant Partners, Project 13

Interactive Explorations CD-ROM

 CD 2, Exploration 8, "How's It Growing?"

Chapter 13 • Chapter Highlights

Chapter Review Answers

USING VOCABULARY

1. dormant
2. photosynthesis
3. transpiration
4. phototropism
5. evergreen

UNDERSTANDING CONCEPTS

Multiple Choice

6. a
7. d
8. b
9. d
10. c
11. d

Short Answer

12. The cuticle is the waxy covering that prevents the leaf from losing moisture. The stomata are openings in the epidermis of the leaf that open and close, allowing only a certain amount of moisture to escape the leaf. Transpiration is the process that occurs when moisture escapes through the stomata.
13. The stimulus is light. The cells on the dark side of the shoot grow longer than the cells on the other side. The shoot bends toward the light.
14. Phototropism is a positive tropism, and gravitropism in stems is a negative tropism.

Chapter Review

USING VOCABULARY

To complete the following sentences, choose the correct term from each pair of terms listed below:

1. After seeds develop fully, and before they sprout, they may become __?__. (*deciduous* or *dormant*)
2. During __?__, energy from sunlight is used to make sugar. (*photosynthesis* or *phototropism*)
3. The loss of water through stomata is called __?__. (*transpiration* or *tropism*)
4. A change in plant growth in response to the direction of light is called __?__. (*gravitropism* or *phototropism*)
5. Plants that have leaves year-round are __?__. (*deciduous* or *evergreen*)

UNDERSTANDING CONCEPTS

Multiple Choice

6. The cells that open and close the stomata are the
   a. guard cells.
   b. xylem cells.
   c. cuticle cells.
   d. mesophyll cells.
7. Plant cells need carbon dioxide, which is used for
   a. cellular respiration.   c. fertilization.
   b. phototropism.   d. photosynthesis.
8. When chlorophyll breaks down,
   a. pollination occurs.
   b. other pigments become visible.
   c. red pigments disappear.
   d. photosynthesis occurs.
9. Which of the following sequences shows the correct order of events that occur after an insect brings pollen to a flower?
   a. germination, fertilization, pollination
   b. fertilization, germination, pollination
   c. pollination, germination, fertilization
   d. pollination, fertilization, germination
10. When the amount of water transpired from a plant's leaves is greater than the amount absorbed by its roots,
    a. the cuticle conserves water.
    b. the stem exhibits positive gravitropism.
    c. the plant wilts.
    d. the plant recovers from wilting.
11. Ovules develop into
    a. fruits.   c. flowers.
    b. ovaries.   d. seeds.

Short Answer

12. What is the relationship between transpiration, the cuticle, and the stomata?
13. What is the stimulus in phototropism? What is the plant's response to the stimulus?
14. Give an example of a positive tropism and a negative tropism.

Concept Mapping

15. Use the following terms to create a concept map: plantlets, flower, seeds, ovules, plant reproduction, asexual, runners.

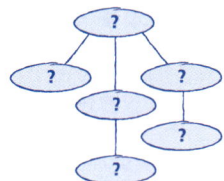

CRITICAL THINKING AND PROBLEM SOLVING

Write one or two sentences to answer the following questions:

16. Many plants that live in regions that experience severe winters have seeds that will not germinate at any temperature unless the seeds have been exposed first to a long period of cold. How might this characteristic help new plants survive?

17. If you wanted to make poinsettias bloom and turn red in the summer, what would you have to do?

18. What benefit is there for a plant's shoots to have positive phototropism? What benefit is there for its roots to have positive gravitropism?

MATH IN SCIENCE

19. If a particular leaf has a surface area of 8 cm², what is its surface area in square millimeters? (Hint: 1 cm² = 100 mm².)

20. Leaves have an average of 100 stomata per square millimeter of surface area. How many stomata would you expect the leaf in question 19 to possess?

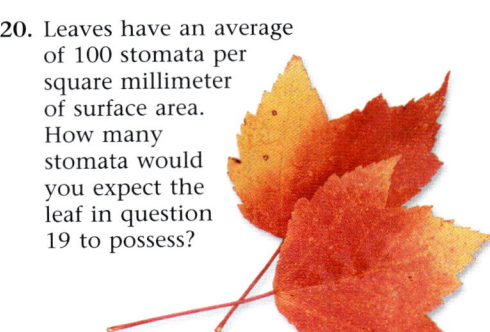

INTERPRETING GRAPHICS

Look at the illustrations below, and then answer the questions that follow. The illustration shows part of an experiment on phototropism in young plants. In part (1), the young plants have just been placed in the light after being in the dark. The shoot tip of one plant is cut off. The other tip is not cut. In part (2), the plants from part (1) are exposed to light from one direction.

Light rays

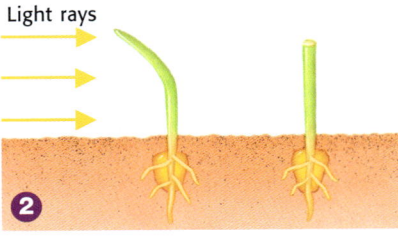

21. Why did the plant with the intact tip bend toward the light?

22. Why did the plant with the removed tip remain straight?

Reading Check-up Take a minute to review your answers to the Pre-Reading Questions found at the bottom of page 298. Have your answers changed? If necessary, revise your answers based on what you have learned since you began this chapter.

Concept Mapping

15. An answer to this exercise can be found at the end of this book.

CRITICAL THINKING AND PROBLEM SOLVING

16. Exposure to a long period of cold may prevent a seed from sprouting before winter. If a seed sprouted in the fall, it might not have time to produce more seeds before it dies.
17. You would have to use artificial means to provide a long period of darkness and a short period of light.
18. Positive phototropism helps the leaves get exposure to sunlight so that photosynthesis can occur. Gravitropism helps the roots grow in the correct direction so that they will have access to water and nutrients in the soil.

MATH IN SCIENCE

19. 800 mm²
20. 80,000 stomata

INTERPRETING GRAPHICS

21. The plant hormone auxin caused the shoot to bend toward the light.
22. The plant hormone auxin is produced in the shoot tip. If the tip is removed, the shoot will not bend toward the light.

Concept Mapping Transparency 13

Blackline masters of this Chapter Review can be found in the **Study Guide.**

Weird Science
Mutant Mustard

Teaching Strategy

To help your students understand how the parts of Meyerowitz's mustard flowers are all in the wrong places, you may wish to review with your students the appropriate locations of the parts of a flower. The parts of a flower are modified leaves, usually found in four successive whorls or rings. Create a diagram that shows four concentric circles. Label the innermost circle "Pistil." Label the next circle "Stamens." (Stamens produce pollen, and each stamen has two parts, the anther and the filament.) Label the third circle "Petals." (Petals are leaflike structures that surround the carpels and stamens. Their colors and shapes give many flowers a distinctive appearance.) Label the outermost circle "Sepals." (The sepals protect the flower when it is a bud.) Explain that the inner two circles mark the locations of the reproductive organs of the flower and that the petals and the sepals are called nonessential flower parts because they are not directly involved in reproduction.

MUTANT MUSTARD

The tiny mustard flowers grown by Elliot Meyerowitz are horribly deformed. You may think they are the result of a terrible accident, but Meyerowitz created these mutants on purpose. In fact, he is very proud of these flowers because they may help him solve an important biological mystery.

▲ *Elliot Meyerowitz, shown here in his laboratory, has raised about a million individual specimens of a mustard variety known as Arabidopsis thaliana.*

Normal and Abnormal Flowers

Normally, mustard flowers have four distinct parts that are arranged in a specific way. Many of the plants grown by Meyerowitz and his colleagues, however, are far from normal. Some have leaves in the center of their flowers. Others have seed-producing ovaries where the petals should be. At first glance, the arrangement of the parts seems random, but the structure of each flower has actually been determined by a small number of genes.

A Simple Model

After many years of careful studies, Meyerowitz and his colleagues have identified most of the genes that control the mustard flower's development. With this information, Meyerowitz has discovered patterns that have led to a surprisingly simple model. The model points to just three classes of genes that determine what happens to the various parts of a flower as it develops. He learned that if one or more of those gene classes is inactivated, a mutant mustard plant results.

Pieces of an Old Puzzle

By understanding how genes shape the growth of flowers, Meyerowitz hopes to add pieces to a long-standing puzzle involving the origin of flowering plants. Scientists estimate that flowering plants first appeared on Earth about 125 million years ago and that they quickly spread to become the dominant plants on Earth. By studying which genes produce flowers in present-day plants, Meyerowitz and his colleagues hope to learn how flowering plants evolved in the first place.

Meyerowitz's mutant plants are well qualified to add to our understanding of plant genetics. But don't look for these mustard plants in your local flower shop. These strange mutants won't win any prizes for beauty!

▲ *Meyerowitz alters the genes of a mustard plant so that it develops a mutant flower. The inset shows a normal flower.*

Think About It

▶ It is possible to genetically change a plant. What are some possible risks of such a practice?

Answer to Think About It

Accept all reasonable responses. Some students may point out that the process of growing many generations of plants may be quite lengthy. In addition, it often takes many unsuccessful tests to develop a successful hypothesis. Students may also point out that genetically altering a plant may have positive or negative repercussions in terms of the usefulness of the plant.

EYE ON THE ENVIRONMENT

A Rainbow of Cotton

Think about your favorite T-shirt. Chances are, it's made of cotton and brightly colored. The fibers in cotton plants, however, are naturally white. They must be dyed with chemicals—often toxic ones—to create the bright colors seen in T-shirts and other fabrics. To minimize the use of toxic chemicals, an ingenious woman named Sally Fox had an idea: What if you could grow the cotton *already colored*?

Learning from the Past

Cotton fibers come from the plant's seed pods, or *bolls*. Bolls are a little bigger than a golf ball and open at maturity to reveal a fuzzy mass of fibers and seeds. Once the seeds are removed, the fibers can be twisted into yarn and used to make many kinds of fabric. Sally Fox began her career as an *entomologist*, a scientist who studies insects. She first found out about colored cotton while studying pest resistance. Although most of the cotton grown for textiles is white, different shades of cotton have been harvested by Native Americans for centuries. These types of cotton showed some resistance to pests but had fibers too short to be used by the textile industry.

In 1982, Fox began the very slow process of crossbreeding different varieties of cotton to produce strains that were both colored *and* long-fibered. Her cotton is registered under the name FoxFibre® and has earned her high praise.

Solutions to Environmental Problems

The textile industry is the source of two major environmental hazards. The first hazard is the dyes used for cotton fabrics. The second is the pesticides that are required for growing cotton. These pesticides, like the dyes, can cause damage to both living things and natural resources, such as water and land.

Fox's cotton represents a solution to both of these problems. First, since the cotton is naturally colored, no dyes are necessary. Second, the native strains of cotton from which she bred her plants passed on their natural pest resistance. Thus, fewer pesticides are necessary to grow her cotton successfully.

Sally Fox's efforts demonstrate that with ingenuity and patience, science and agriculture can work together in new ways to offer solutions to environmental problems.

▲ *Sally Fox in a field of colored cotton*

Some Detective Work

▶ Like Fox's cotton, many types of plants and breeds of domesticated animals have been created through artificial selection. Research to find out where and when your favorite fruit or breed of dog was first established.

UNIT 5

TIMELINE
Animals

Have you ever been to a zoo or watched a wild-animal program on television? If so, you have some idea of the many different types of animals found on Earth—from tiny insects to massive whales.

Animals are fascinating, in part because of their variety in appearance and behavior. They also teach us about ourselves because we humans are also classified as animals. Humans have always observed and interacted with their fellow animals.

In this unit you will learn about many different types of animals, maybe even some that you never knew existed. So get ready for an animal adventure!

1610
Galileo uses a compound microscope to study insect anatomy.

1680
The dodo, a flightless bird, becomes extinct.

1960
Jane Goodall, an English zoologist, begins her research on chimpanzees in Tanzania.

1935
Francis B. Summer studies the protective coloration of fish.

1983
The U.S. Space Shuttle *Challenger* is launched with Sally Ride, the first American woman in space, on board.

1987
The last wild California condor is captured in an effort to save the species from extinction.

1693
John Ray correctly identifies whales as mammals.

1761
The first veterinary school is founded in Lyons, France.

1775
J. C. Fabricius develops a system for the classification of insects.

1882
Research on the ship *The Albatross* helps to increase our knowledge of marine life.

1827
John James Audubon publishes the first edition of *Birds of North America*.

1839
The first bicycle is constructed.

1995
Fourteen Canadian gray wolves are reintroduced to Yellowstone National Park.

1998
Keiko, the killer-whale star of the movie *Free Willy*, is taught to catch fish so that he can be released from captivity.

Animals

Chapter Organizer

CHAPTER ORGANIZATION	TIME MINUTES	OBJECTIVES	LABS, INVESTIGATIONS, AND DEMONSTRATIONS
Chapter Opener pp. 320–321	45	National Standards: UCP 1, 2, SAI 1, 2, HNS 1, 2, LS 3a, 3c	**Start-Up Activity** Go on a Safari! p. 321
Section 1 What Is an Animal?	45	▶ Describe the differences between vertebrates and invertebrates. ▶ Explain the characteristics of animals. UCP 1, SAI 1, HNS 3, LS 1a, 1b, 1d, 2b, 4b, 5a	
Section 2 Animal Behavior	90	▶ Explain the difference between learned and innate behavior. ▶ Explain the difference between hibernation and estivation. ▶ Give examples of how a biological clock influences behavior. ▶ Describe circadian rhythms. ▶ Explain how animals navigate. UCP 1, 3, 5, SAI 1, LS 3a, 3b–3d, 4d, 5b, 5c; LabBook UCP 2, 3, SAI 1, 2, HNS 2, LS 3c, 4a	**Demonstration,** Sign Language, p. 328 in ATE `BASIC` **QuickLab,** How Long Is a Minute? p. 330 `GENERAL` **Discovery Lab,** Wet, Wiggly Worms! p. 732 `GENERAL` **Datasheets for LabBook,** Wet, Wiggly Worms! Datasheet 30 `GENERAL` **Design Your Own,** Aunt Flossie and the Bumblebee, p. 734 `ADVANCED` **Datasheets for LabBook,** Aunt Flossie and the Bumblebee, Datasheet 31 `ADVANCED` **Inquiry Labs,** Follow the Leader, Lab 4 `GENERAL` **Whiz-Bang Demonstrations,** Six-Legged Thermometer, Demo 9 `ADVANCED`
Section 3 Living Together	90	▶ Discuss ways that animals communicate. ▶ List the advantages and disadvantages of living in groups. UCP 1, SAI 1, LS 1a, 2a, 3c, 3d, 4a, 4d	**Long-Term Projects & Research Ideas,** Project 14 `ADVANCED`

*See page **T20** for a complete correlation of this book with the*

NATIONAL SCIENCE EDUCATION STANDARDS.

TECHNOLOGY RESOURCES

 Guided Reading Audio CD English or Spanish, Chapter 14

 One-Stop Planner CD-ROM with Test Generator

 Eye on the Environment, Monarch Migrations, Segment 4

Scientists in Action, Studying Dolphin Behavior, Segment 18

Learning the Language of Animals, Segment 19

Chapter 14 • Animals and Behavior

CLASSROOM WORKSHEETS, TRANSPARENCIES, AND RESOURCES	SCIENCE INTEGRATION AND CONNECTIONS	REVIEW AND ASSESSMENT
Directed Reading Worksheet 14 BASIC **Science Puzzlers, Twisters & Teasers,** Worksheet 14 ADVANCED		
Transparency 54, The Animal Kingdom **Directed Reading Worksheet 14,** Section 1 BASIC **Science Skills Worksheet 25,** Introduction to Graphs GENERAL **Reinforcement Worksheet 14,** What Makes an Animal an Animal? BASIC		**Self-Check,** p. 324 **Homework,** pp. 324, 325 in ATE ADVANCED **Review,** p. 325 GENERAL **Quiz,** p. 325 in ATE GENERAL **Alternative Assessment,** p. 325 in ATE BASIC
Directed Reading Worksheet 14, Section 2 BASIC **Math Skills for Science Worksheet 21,** Percentages, Fractions, and Decimals GENERAL **Math Skills for Science Worksheet 8,** Average, Mode, and Median GENERAL **Transparency 104,** Finding Direction on Earth **Reinforcement Worksheet 14,** Animal Interviews BASIC **Critical Thinking Worksheet 14,** Masters of Navigation ADVANCED	**Math and More,** p. 327 in ATE GENERAL **Math and More,** p. 329 in ATE GENERAL **Connect to Earth Science,** p. 330 in ATE **Apply,** p. 331 GENERAL **Physics Connection,** p. 331 **Eye on the Environment:** Do Not Disturb! p. 340 GENERAL	**Review,** p. 328 GENERAL **Review,** p. 331 GENERAL **Quiz,** p. 331 in ATE GENERAL **Alternative Assessment,** p. 331 in ATE GENERAL
Directed Reading Worksheet 14, Section 3 BASIC **Transparency 55,** The Dance of the Bees	**Cross-Disciplinary Focus,** p. 333 in ATE GENERAL **Weird Science:** Animal Cannibals, p. 341 ADVANCED	**Homework,** p. 334 in ATE ADVANCED **Review,** p. 335 GENERAL **Quiz,** p. 335 in ATE GENERAL **Alternative Assessment,** p. 335 in ATE GENERAL

END-OF-CHAPTER REVIEW AND ASSESSMENT

Chapter Review in Study Guide
Vocabulary and Notes in Study Guide
Chapter Tests with Performance-Based Assessment, Chapter 14 Test
Chapter Tests with Performance-Based Assessment, Performance-Based Assessment 14
Concept Mapping Transparency 14

---

 internetconnect

 Holt, Rinehart and Winston On-line Resources
go.hrw.com
For worksheets and other teaching aids related to this chapter, visit the HRW Web site and type in the keyword: **HSTANM**

 National Science Teachers Association
www.scilinks.org
Encourage students to use the *sci*LINKS numbers listed in the internet connect boxes to access information and resources on the **NSTA** Web site.

Chapter Resources & Worksheets

Visual Resources

Meeting Individual Needs

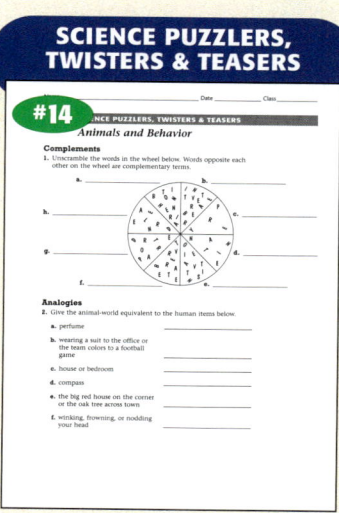

Chapter 14 • Animals and Behavior

Chapter 14 • Animals and Behavior

Review & Assessment

STUDY GUIDE
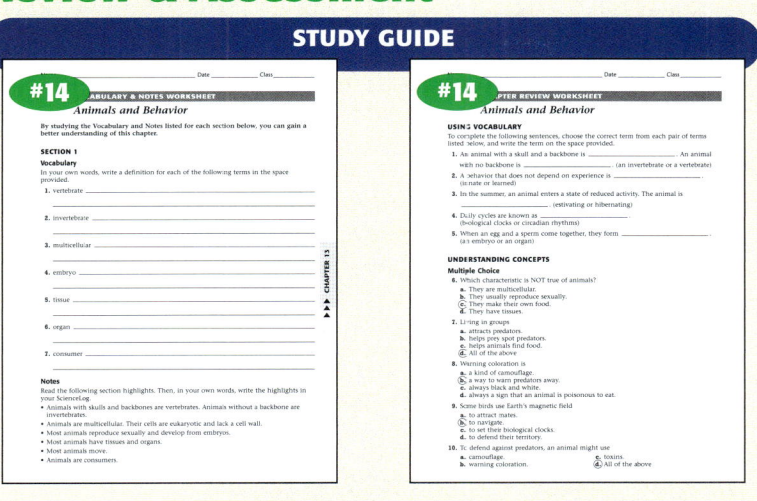

CHAPTER TESTS WITH PERFORMANCE-BASED ASSESSMENT

Lab Worksheets

INQUIRY LABS

WHIZ-BANG DEMONSTRATIONS
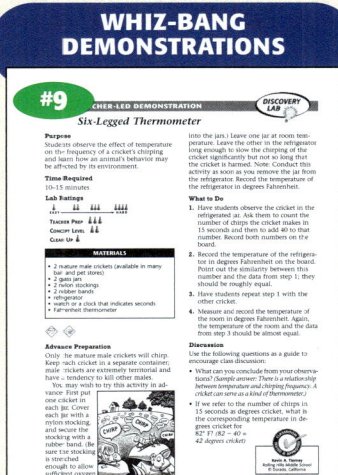

LONG-TERM PROJECTS & RESEARCH IDEAS

DATASHEETS FOR LABBOOK
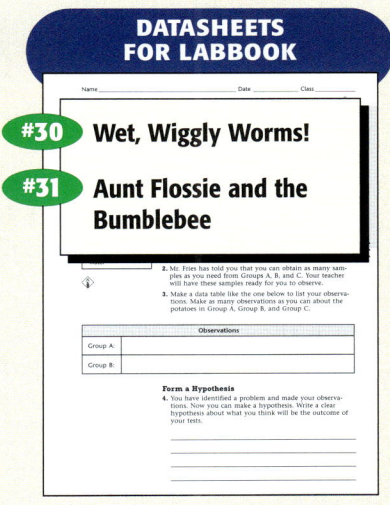

Applications & Extensions

CRITICAL THINKING & PROBLEM SOLVING
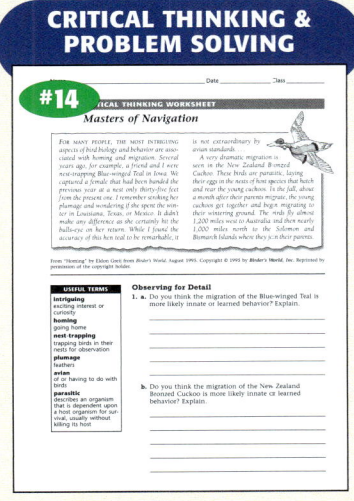

EYE ON THE ENVIRONMENT

SCIENTISTS IN ACTION
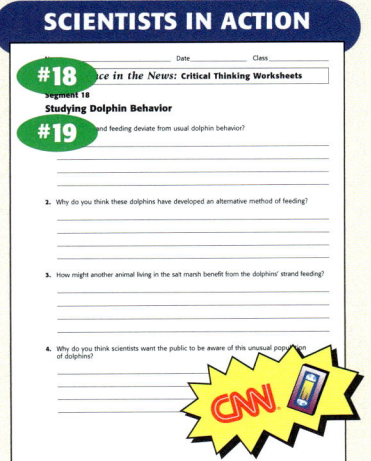

Chapter 14 • Chapter Resources & Worksheets

Chapter Background

SECTION 1

What Is an Animal?

▶ **Animal Classifications**
Zoologists classify the members of the animal kingdom on the basis of their similarities and differences. The animal kingdom has three subkingdoms (Protozoa, Parazoa, and Metazoa). The three subkingdoms are divided into phyla, and each phylum is divided into subphyla and other subgroups.

- The phylum Chordata (meaning "cord") has three subphyla, one of which is vertebrates. Vertebrates include amphibians, reptiles, birds, mammals, and three kinds of fish.

- The vast majority of animals are invertebrates. Significant invertebrate phyla include Arthropoda (meaning "jointed foot"), Porifera (meaning "hole bearers"), Nematoda (meaning "thread"), and Echinodermata (meaning "spiny skin"). Arthropoda, which includes crustaceans, spiders, millipedes, and insects, is by far the largest phylum. It includes more than 1 million living species.

▶ **Animal Reproduction**
Some animals can reproduce both sexually and asexually. The adult jellyfish, or medusa, releases sperm and eggs into the water, forming a planula. When the planula matures into a polyp, it reproduces asexually, duplicating itself and becoming ephyra. Ephyra then grow into adult jellyfish and start sexual reproduction once again.

▶ **Moving Around**
Animals use a variety of techniques to move from place to place.

- Cephalopods, which include the squid and the octopus, escape from predators by forcing a powerful jet of water from a siphon near their head. Squids have been known to swim as fast as 38 km/h (23 mph)!

- Kangaroo rats have powerful hind legs that help them quickly leap away from predators. Their tail, which acts like a rudder, enables them to change course while in midair.

SECTION 2

Animal Behavior

▶ **Animal Defense Strategies**
Animals use a variety of methods to defend themselves from predators. Many species inject or spray toxic chemicals. Other species have a foul odor or an unpleasant taste.

- Jellyfish eject poison-tipped barbs from nematocysts on their bodies. Although most jellyfish stings can't penetrate human skin, the stings of the Portuguese man-of-war and the box jellyfish are exceptions. Stings from both species can cause extreme pain, and in rare instances, even death. Don't ever step on a dead jellyfish. The nematocysts can still sting!

- Colorful ladybugs, also known as ladybirds, protect themselves from predators by virtue of their foul smell and terrible taste.

- A type of Chrysomelid beetle has such a toxic poison that the San, a tribe living mainly in Africa's Kalahari Desert, tip their arrows with it. The poison causes death by paralysis.

- Octopuses have beaks that are used to pierce the shells of crabs and lobsters. Once the prey is pierced, the octopus injects a poison that paralyzes its prey and helps soften the meat for easy removal.

Chapter 14 • Animals and Behavior

▶ Animal Migration
What mechanisms trigger animal migration? How are birds and other animals able to find their way to destinations often thousands of miles away?

- Studies performed during the 1960s produced experiments that indicated that birds use a "celestial compass" to guide them on their migratory travels.

- Ruby-throated hummingbirds, which live as far north as Canada during the summer, fly to Central America in the fall. Their route requires them to fly 833 km (500 mi) nonstop over the Gulf of Mexico.

- Topographical features such as mountain ranges emit low-frequency sounds that some scientists believe help birds such as pigeons navigate.

▶ Human Seasonal Rhythms
Seasonal affective disorder (SAD) is a form of depression that many people, especially those in northern countries, experience during the winter. Common symptoms include fatigue, sleeping more than usual, carbohydrate craving, increased appetite, and sudden weight gain. Researchers have found that many people with SAD improve when they undergo light therapy, or phototherapy.

▶ Learned and Innate Behaviors
All behaviors, innate or learned, represent an interplay of genes and the environment. We inherit the potential for innate behavior. An innate behavior is one that appears in its fully functional form the first time it is performed. Innate behavior expresses itself without prior experience. Learned behavior depends upon experience.

SECTION 3
Living Together

▶ Animal Communication
Some kinds of animals live together, and others maintain a solitary existence. Both situations offer advantages and disadvantages. Regardless of how animals live, they communicate with each other to protect themselves, to find food, to display dominance, to find mates, and for many other reasons.

- Although octopuses and squids are both cephalopods, their social habits are quite different. Whereas the octopus is a solitary creature, squids are frequently found in schools.

- Besides using a "waggle dance" to communicate the location of nectar, honeybees also communicate information about the taste and smell of food resources. They do this through the process of trophalaxis, or the regurgitation of food into the mouths of members of the colony.

IS THAT A FACT!
- Elephants have at least 25 distinct vocal calls, including the familiar trumpet that elephants make when they are excited. Elephants can also communicate dozens of messages through low-frequency, infrasonic rumbles. Such sounds can travel up to 9.5 km.

- Antelopes raise their tail and release a warning scent to communicate danger to the herd.

For background information about teaching strategies and issues, refer to the *Professional Reference for Teachers*.

Chapter 14 • Chapter Background

Chapter 14

Animals and Behavior

Pre-Reading Questions

Students may not know the answers to these questions before reading the chapter, so accept any reasonable response.

Suggested Answers

Possible answers include the following:

1. Animals are consumers, and plants are producers.
2. Biological clocks control seasonal migration. Animals also migrate when food is in short supply.

 Directed Reading Worksheet 14

 Science Puzzlers, Twisters & Teasers Worksheet 14

 Guided Reading Audio CD English or Spanish, Chapter 14

Chapter 14

Animals and Behavior

Sections

1. **What Is an Animal?** ... 322
   Internet Connect 325
2. **Animal Behavior** 326
   QuickLab 330
   Apply 331
   Physics Connection .. 331
   Internet Connect 331
3. **Living Together** 332
   Internet Connect 335

Chapter Review 338
Feature Articles 340, 341
LabBook 732–735

Pre-Reading Questions

1. What characteristics make an animal different from a plant?
2. How do animals know when to migrate?

---

internet connect

 HRW On-line Resources
go.hrw.com
For worksheets and other teaching aids, visit the HRW Web site and type in the keyword: **HSTANM**

 SCILINKS NSTA
www.scilinks.com
Use the *sci*LINKS numbers at the end of each chapter for additional resources on the **NSTA** Web site.

 CNNfyi.com
www.cnnfyi.com
Visit the CNN Web site for current events coverage and classroom resources.

Gotcha!

This spider needs to eat in order to survive. On the other hand, this hover fly needs to avoid being eaten. It has to escape in order to survive. How do the spider, the fly, and other animals get what they need in order to live? In this chapter you will learn what it means to be an animal. You will also learn how animals live, reproduce, and behave.

START-UP Activity

GO ON A SAFARI!

You don't have to travel far to see interesting animals. If you look closely, you are sure to find animals nearby.

Procedure

1. Go outside and find **two different animals** to observe.

2. Without disturbing the animals, sit quietly and watch them for a few minutes from a distance. You may want to use **binoculars** or a **magnifying lens**.

   Caution: Always be careful around animals that may bite or sting. Do not handle animals that are unfamiliar to you.

3. Write down everything you notice about each animal. What kind of animal is it? What does it look like? How big is it? What is it doing? You may want to draw a picture of it.

Analysis

4. Compare the animals that you studied. How are they similar? How are they different?

5. How do the animals move? Did you see them communicating with other animals or defending themselves?

6. Can you tell what each animal eats? What characteristics of each animal help it find or catch food?

START-UP Activity

GO ON A SAFARI!

MATERIALS

For Each Group:
- binoculars or magnifying glass

Safety Caution

Remind students to review all safety cautions and icons before beginning this lab activity. Students must be careful when handling the magnifying glass. Magnified sunlight should never be focused on people, animals, or flammable materials. Injuries or a fire could result. Students should observe animals from a distance and should be especially careful with animals that could bite or sting. Students allergic to insect bites or bee stings should avoid contact with these animals and receive immediate medical attention if stung.

Students should also avoid hazards, such as poisonous plants, holes, cliffs, water, cars, glass, and other dangers.

Teacher's Notes

This activity will work best with small groups. If possible, try to have your leading science students evenly dispersed among the groups.

Answers to START-UP Activity

4. Answers will vary, but students may refer to characteristics such as the way the animals moved, what they were eating, and their body type.
5. Answers will vary.
6. Answers will vary.

SECTION 1

Focus

What Is an Animal?

This section provides students with an introduction to the animal kingdom. Students will find out the difference between vertebrates and invertebrates and will learn how scientists classify animals. Students will also discover the characteristics that set animals apart from all other living things.

Bellringer

While you are taking attendance, ask students to ponder this question:

> What is the best material for washing a car—a cotton rag, a scratch pad, or an animal skeleton?

Have them take a few moments to record their answer in their ScienceLog. Before you begin the section, call on individual students to give their answer and reasoning. **(It may surprise some students to learn that genuine sponges–ones that some people use for washing cars–are animal skeletons. During the process of preparing sponges, all tissue is removed from the animals, leaving only skeletal remains. Although there are about 5,000 sponge species, fewer than 20 of them are of any commercial value.)**

 Teaching Transparency 54
"The Animal Kingdom"

 Directed Reading Worksheet 14 Section 1

Section 1

Terms to Learn

vertebrate   tissue
invertebrate organ
embryo   consumer

What You'll Do

- Describe the differences between vertebrates and invertebrates.
- Explain the characteristics of animals.

Figure 1 *This natural sponge used to be alive.*

What Is an Animal?

What do you think of when you hear the word *animal*? You may think of your dog or cat. You may think about giraffes or grizzly bears or other creatures you've seen in zoos or on television. But would you think about a sponge? Natural bath sponges, like the one in **Figure 1**, are the remains of an animal that lived in the ocean!

Animals come in many different shapes and sizes. Some have four legs and fur, but most do not. Some are too small to be seen without a microscope, and others are bigger than a car. But they are all part of the fascinating world of animals.

The Animal Kingdom

Scientists have named over 1 million species of animals. How many different kinds of animals do you see in **Figure 2**? It may surprise you to learn that in addition to sponges, sea anemones and corals are also animals. So are spiders, fish, birds, and dolphins. Slugs, whales, kangaroos, and humans are animals too. Scientists have divided all these animal species into about 35 phyla and classes.

Most animals look nothing like humans. However, we do share characteristics with a group of animals called vertebrates. Any animal with a skull and a backbone is a **vertebrate.** Vertebrates include fishes, amphibians, reptiles, birds, and mammals.

Figure 2 *All of the living things in this picture are classified as animals. Do they look like animals to you?*

A snail knocked on a man's door and asked for a donation to a snail charity. The man didn't like solicitors and kicked the snail off his porch. Ten years later, the snail knocked on the door again and said, "That wasn't a very nice thing to do!"

Even though you are probably most familiar with vertebrates, we are definitely the minority among living things. Less than five percent of known animal species are vertebrates. Take a look at **Figure 3.** As you can see, the great majority of known animal species are insects, snails, jellyfish, worms, and other **invertebrates,** animals without backbones. In fact, more than one-fourth of all animal species are beetles!

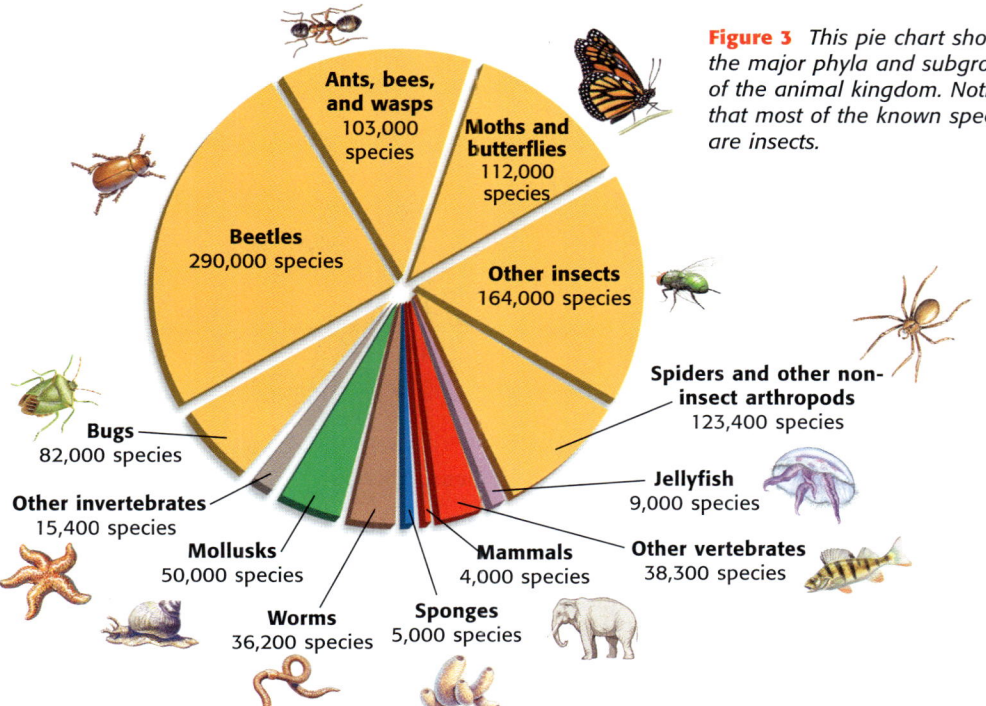

Figure 3 This pie chart shows the major phyla and subgroups of the animal kingdom. Notice that most of the known species are insects.

That's an Animal?

Sponges don't look like other animals. Indeed, until about 200 years ago, most people thought sponges were plants. Earthworms don't look anything like penguins, and no one would confuse a frog for a lion. So why do we say all these things are animals? What determines whether something is an animal, a plant, or something else?

There is no single answer. But all animals share characteristics that set them apart from all other living things.

Animals have many cells. All animals are *multicellular,* which means they are made of many cells. Your own body contains about 13 trillion cells. Animal cells are eukaryotic, and they do not have cell walls. Animal cells are surrounded by cell membranes only.

1) Motivate

GROUP ACTIVITY

Writing To explore the diversity of the animal kingdom, have students work in groups of four. Each group will write down examples for each of the following:

- 2 Arctic animals
  (penguin is incorrect)
- 2 Antarctic animals
  (polar bear is incorrect)
- 2 animals that crawl
- 2 animals that fly
- 2 animals with no bones
- 2 African animals
- 2 North American animals
- 2 animals that live in the soil
- 2 ocean animals
- 2 animals with more than four legs

Answers should be as specific as possible. For example, they should answer "garter snake," not "snake," or "praying mantis" instead of "insect." Have each group share its answers while other groups cross out matches on their own page. How many animals did the class think of? That's diversity!

Science Skills Worksheet 25 "Introduction to Graphs"

TOPIC: Vertebrates and Invertebrates
GO TO: www.scilinks.org
*sci*LINKS NUMBER: HSTL330

Science Bloopers

In 1798, when English scholars first observed the duck-billed platypus that had been sent to them by a scientist in Australia, they were convinced they were the victims of a joke. Surely, they thought, some prankster had pieced together parts of various animals. The English scholars cut and sliced the dead animal for signs of stitches holding the bill and webbed feet to its mammal-like body. It took a lot of convincing, but eventually they came to the conclusion that the animal was indeed real.

Section 1 • What Is an Animal?

② Teach

MEETING INDIVIDUAL NEEDS

Learners Having Difficulty
On the board, make a chart with column headings that list the shared animal characteristics here. Label the rows:

"Tree," "Slug," "Fungus," "Coati," "Snapdragon," "Kookaburra," "Serval"

Tell students to replicate this chart in their ScienceLog. Have students check off which characteristics are found in each of these organisms. Students will probably have to check additional resources to identify some of these organisms. **Sheltered English**

Homework

Research/ Presentation
Sometimes the specialized or differentiated cells of an animal develop into a unique characteristic. For example, all mammals have hair, but only the male lion has a large, bushy mane. Have students research unusual physical characteristics of animals that are exaggerated versions of ordinary characteristics. Tell students to prepare a poster with photographs or drawings of their research results. (Suggest that students investigate a peacock's feathers, an elephant's trunk, or the "suction pad" toes of various frogs.)

Animals usually reproduce by sexual reproduction. Animals make sex cells, eggs or sperm. When an egg and a sperm come together at fertilization, they form the first cell of a new individual. **Figure 4** shows an egg surrounded by sperm during fertilization. Some animals, like sponges and sea stars, can also reproduce asexually, by budding or fragmentation.

Animals develop from embryos. The fertilized egg cell divides into many different cells to form an embryo. An **embryo** is an organism in the earliest stage of development. A mouse embryo is shown in **Figure 5.**

Figure 4 Several sperm surround an egg. Only one sperm can fuse with the egg to form a new individual.

✓ Self-Check

Why are humans classified as vertebrates? (See page 782 to check your answer.)

Figure 5 A Mouse Embryo

Animals have many specialized parts. An animal's body has distinct parts that do different things. When a fertilized egg cell divides into many cells to form an embryo, the cells become different from each other. Some may become skin cells. Others may become muscle cells, nerve cells, or bone cells. These different kinds of cells arrange themselves to form **tissues,** which are collections of similar cells. For example, muscle cells form muscle tissue, and nerve cells form nerve tissue.

Most animals also have organs. An **organ** is a combination of two or more tissues. Your heart, lungs, and kidneys are all organs. All animals, including the shark shown in **Figure 6,** have different organs for different jobs.

Figure 6 Like most other animals, sharks have organs for digestion, circulation, and reproduction.

Answer to Self-Check
Like other vertebrates, humans have a skull and a backbone.

Q: What lies on the forest floor, 100 feet in the air?

A: a dead centipede

Animals move. Most animals can move from place to place. As shown in **Figure 7,** they fly, run, swim, and jump. While it's true that other organisms move, animals are more likely to move quickly in a single direction. Some animals do not move much, though. Sea anemones and clams, for example, attach to rocks or the ocean floor and wait for food to arrive. But most animals are active.

Figure 7 *Animals move in many different ways.*

Animals are consumers. Animals cannot make their own food. All animals survive by eating other organisms, parts of other organisms, or the products of other organisms. In other words, animals are consumers. A **consumer** is an organism that eats other organisms. This trait sets animals apart from plants. Except for the Venus' flytrap and a handful of other plants, plants do not eat other living things. Plants make their own food.

Animal food is as varied as animals themselves. Rabbits and caterpillars eat plants. Lions and spiders eat other animals. Reindeer eat lichens. Mosquitoes drink blood. Butterflies drink nectar from flowers.

internetconnect

SC/**INKS**
NSTA

TOPIC: Vertebrates and Invertebrates
GO TO: www.scilinks.org
sciLINKS NUMBER: HSTL330

REVIEW

1. What characteristics separate animals from plants?
2. How are tissues and organs related?
3. **Interpreting Illustrations** What characteristics of the chameleon shown at far right tell you it is an animal?

3) Extend

Homework

Writing **Research Invertebrates** Given that most of the animals in the world are invertebrates, encourage students to get to know them better. Have interested students choose any invertebrate and write a paragraph or two about it. Students should describe the invertebrate's range, habitat, and food sources. They should include how it obtains food, how it avoids predators, and how it affects people. Have students include one unusual fact about their subject.

PORTFOLIO

4) Close

Quiz

1. What do vertebrates have that invertebrates don't? (a skull and a backbone)
2. What are collections of similar cells called? (tissues)

ALTERNATIVE ASSESSMENT

Writing Have students write a summary of the characteristics shared by all animals. Tell them not to repeat the boldfaced paragraph headings in the text. Instead, students must explain each characteristic by first giving an example. (Sample answers: Monkeys run, climb, and swing in trees. Animals move.)

Reinforcement Worksheet 14 "What Makes an Animal an Animal?"

Answers to Review

1. Animals cannot make their own food; they are consumers. Plants are producers. Animal cells do not have cell walls. Plants do not usually move.
2. An organ is a combination of two or more tissues.
3. The chameleon is moving, and it is eating another organism.

SECTION 2

Focus

Animal Behavior

This section introduces students to animal behavior. Students will see how animals find food and defend themselves from predators. They will discover the difference between innate and learned behavior. Finally, they will learn some of the ways animals communicate, why animal behaviors change at different times of the year, and how an animal's biological clock controls its circadian rhythms and other cycles.

 Bellringer

Ask students to write a sentence for each of the following terms:

predator and *prey*

After each sentence have students list three animals that are predators and three that are prey.

- Predators hunt for their food. A list of predators might include alligators, sharks, spiders, lions, wolves, rattlesnakes, and eagles.
- Prey stay alert to avoid being eaten. A list of prey might include mice, rabbits, pigeons, flies, and deer. **Sheltered English**

Directed Reading Worksheet 14 Section 2

Section 2

Terms to Learn

predator   hibernation
prey   estivation
innate behavior   biological clock
learned behavior circadian rhythm

What You'll Do

- Explain the difference between learned and innate behavior.
- Explain the difference between hibernation and estivation.
- Give examples of how a biological clock influences behavior.
- Describe circadian rhythms.
- Explain how animals navigate.

Animal Behavior

In the last section, you learned the characteristics that help us recognize an animal. One characteristic of most animals is that they move. Animals jump, run, fly, dart, scurry, slither, and glide. But animals don't move just for the sake of moving. They move for a reason. They run from enemies. They climb for food. They build homes. Even the tiniest mite can actively stalk its dinner, battle for territory, or migrate. All of these activities are known as behavior.

Survival Behavior

In order to stay alive, an animal has to do many things. It must find food and water, avoid being eaten, and have a place to live. Animals have many behaviors that help them accomplish these tasks.

Looking for Lunch Animals use many different methods to find or catch food. Owls swoop down on unsuspecting mice. Bees fly from flower to flower collecting nectar. Koala bears climb trees to get eucalyptus leaves. Jellyfish harpoon and lasso their prey with their tentacles. Some animals, such as the chimpanzee shown in **Figure 8,** use tools to get dinner. Whatever the meal of choice, animals have adapted to their surroundings so that they can obtain the most food using the least amount of energy.

How to Avoid Being Eaten Animals that eat other animals are known as **predators.** The animal being eaten is the **prey.** At any given moment, an animal *diner* can become another animal's *dinner*. Therefore, animals looking for food often have to think about other things besides which food looks or tastes the best. Animals will pass up a good meal if it's too dangerous to get. But being careful is just one method of defense. Keep reading to find out what other things animals do to stay alive.

Figure 8 Chimpanzees make and use tools in order to get ants and other food out of hard-to-reach places.

IS THAT A FACT!

Zoo keepers and pet owners have found that when they challenge their animals to search for food, the animals' appetites improve and their activity level and alertness increases. In addition, the animals genuinely seem to enjoy the search. At one zoo, the polar bears appeared downright depressed until keepers began to hide their food and freeze their fish in big buckets of solid ice. Working for their food simulated the hunting the bears would do in the wild, perhaps alleviating some of the stress of captivity.

Hiding Out One way to avoid being eaten is to be hard to see. A rabbit often "freezes" so that its natural color blends into a background of shrubs or grass. Blending in with the background is called *camouflage*. Many animals mimic twigs, leaves, stones, bark, or other materials in their environment. The insect called a walking stick looks just like a twig. Some walking sticks even sway a bit, as though a breeze were blowing. See **Figure 9** for another example of camouflage.

In Your Face The horns of a bull and the spines of a porcupine clearly signal trouble to a potential predator, but other defenses may not be as obvious. For example, animals may defend themselves with chemicals. The skunk and the bombardier beetle both spray predators with irritating chemicals. Bees, ants, and wasps inject a powerful acid into their attackers. The skin of both the South American dart-poison frog and the hooded pitohui bird of New Guinea contains a deadly toxin. Any predator that eats, or even tries to eat, one of these animals will likely die.

Warning! Animals with a chemical defense need a way to warn predators that they should look elsewhere for a meal. Their chemical weapons are often advertised by the animal's outer covering, which has a bright design called *warning coloration*, as shown in **Figure 10.** Predators will avoid any animal with the colors and patterns they associate with pain, illness, or other unpleasant experiences. The most common warning colors are vivid shades of red, yellow, orange, black, and white.

Figure 9 This is a picture of a caterpillar camouflaged as a twig. Can you find the caterpillar?

Octopuses are camouflage experts. They can change the color of their entire body in less than 1 second.

Figure 10 The warning coloration of the hooded pitohui warns predators that it is poisonous. The yellow and black stripes of the stinging yellow jacket are another example.

The pitohui is one of the very few poisonous birds. This is not the only unusual thing about the colorful, foul-smelling bird, however. The poison that the bird emits—homobatrachotoxin—is the same poison made by the New World strawberry dart-poison frog. How can two species that are so different produce the same poison? Scientists are now exploring the mystery.

Section 2 • Animal Behavior   **327**

2) Teach, continued

DEMONSTRATION

Sign Language Learn five basic signs in Sign Language, and demonstrate them for the class. Choose words such as *hungry, sad, angry, tired,* and *happy.*

Tell students that because of our innate language ability, it's possible to learn another language, even a nonvocal one. But perhaps humans aren't the only species with this ability. Koko, a gorilla, learned more than 500 different signs while in captivity. She even created some of her own signs, such as "finger bracelet" for "ring." Once, her trainer became frustrated because Koko was not cooperating. The trainer signed "bad gorilla," and Koko corrected her by signing "funny gorilla." Koko fibbed at times to avoid getting in trouble and insulted trainers when she was angry. She even had her own kitten, a tiny tailless cat that she named All Ball. Sheltered English

 PG 734

Aunt Flossie and the Bumblebee

GUIDED PRACTICE

Writing Have students observe the eating habits of animals near their home over a period of a week or so. Have them record their observations in their ScienceLog.

Why Do They Behave That Way?

How do animals know when a situation is dangerous? How do predators know which warning coloration to avoid? Sometimes animals instinctively know what to do, but sometimes they have to learn. Biologists call these two kinds of animal behavior innate behavior and learned behavior.

What did the bumblebee do to Aunt Flossie? Find out on page 734.

It's in the Genes Behavior that doesn't depend on learning or experience is known as **innate behavior.** Innate behaviors are influenced by genes. Humans inherit genes that give us the ability to walk. Puppies inherit the tendency to chew, bees the tendency to fly, and earthworms the tendency to burrow.

Some innate behaviors are present at birth. Newborn whales all have the innate ability to swim. Other innate behaviors develop months or years after birth. For example, the tendency of a bird to sing is innate. But a bird does not sing until it is nearly grown.

Animal School Just because a behavior is innate does not mean that it cannot be modified. Learning can change innate behavior. **Learned behavior** is behavior that has been learned from experience or from observing other animals. Humans inherit the tendency to speak. But the language we speak is not inherited. We might learn English, Spanish, Chinese, or Tagalog.

Humans are not the only animals that modify inherited behaviors through learning. Nearly all animals can learn. For example, many young animals learn by watching their parents. **Figure 11** shows a monkey that learned a new behavior by observation.

Figure 11 *One Japanese macaque washed the sand off a sweet potato it found on the beach. Now all of the macaques on the island wash their potatoes.*

REVIEW

1. How do innate behavior and learned behavior differ?
2. **Applying Concepts** How does the effectiveness of warning coloration for protection depend on learning?

▼ **Answers to Review**

1. Innate behavior is influenced by genes and does not depend on experience. Learned behavior results from experience or observation.

2. Through experience or observation of other animals, predators learn which colors are associated with painful or undesirable consequences. Once a predator learns, it can avoid animals with these warning colors.

Seasonal Behavior

In many places, animals must deal with the winter hardships of little food and bitter cold. Some avoid winter by traveling to places that are warmer. Others collect and store food. Frogs bury themselves in mud, and insects burrow into the ground.

World Travelers When food is scarce because of winter or drought, many animals migrate. To *migrate* is to travel from one place to another. Animals migrate to find food, water, or safe nesting grounds. Whales, salmon, bats, and even chimpanzees migrate. Each winter, monarch butterflies, shown in **Figure 12,** gather in central Mexico from all over North America to wait for spring. And each year, birds in the Northern Hemisphere fly thousands of kilometers south. In the spring, they return north to nest.

Slowing Down Some animals deal with food and water shortages by hibernating. **Hibernation** is a period of inactivity and decreased body temperature that some animals experience in winter. Hibernating animals survive on stored body fat. Many animals hibernate, including mice, squirrels, and skunks. While an animal hibernates, its temperature, heart rate, and breathing rate drop. Some hibernating animals drop their body temperature to a few degrees above freezing and do not wake for weeks at a time. Other animals, like the polar bears in **Figure 13,** do not enter deep hibernation. Their body temperature does not drop as severely, and they sleep for shorter periods of time.

Winter is not the only time that resources can be scarce. Many desert squirrels and mice experience a similar internal slowdown in the hottest part of the summer, when they run low on water and food. This period of reduced activity in the summer is called **estivation.**

Figure 12 When the monarchs gather in Mexico, there can be as many as 4 million butterflies per acre!

Don't wake the bats!
Read about the effects of humans on bat hibernation on page 340.

Figure 13 Bears do not enter deep hibernation. However, they have periods of inactivity in which they do not eat, and their body functions slow down.

MEETING INDIVIDUAL NEEDS

Writing — Learners Having Difficulty In a given temperate region, different animals have different ways of surviving cold winters. Have students list as many behaviors or adaptations for winter survival that they can think of. **Sheltered English**

MATH and MORE

It's hard not to perceive sloths as lazy. However, their slow movement makes them almost invisible to predators and saves energy, too. You may envy the sleeping patterns of sloths; they sleep 15 to 18 hours a day!

Ask: What is the average number of hours a sloth spends asleep each day? (16.5 hours)

Ask: What percentage of the day does the sloth spend asleep? (69 percent)

Math Skills Worksheet 8 "Average, Mode, and Median"

internet connect

SCILINKS NSTA
TOPIC: Animal Behavior
GO TO: www.scilinks.org
sciLINKS NUMBER: HSTL335

WEIRD SCIENCE

Snakes are normally solitary creatures, but they will often group together in underground pits while hibernating. Hundreds or even thousands of snakes may spend the winter together in these hibernaculums. Why do they do it? Perhaps there is some protection from the cold in a group. (The protection would be limited, though, because snakes are ectotherms.) Or maybe it makes finding a mate much easier in the spring.

Section 2 • Animal Behavior

3 Extend

QuickLab

MATERIALS

FOR EACH PAIR:
• stopwatch

Answers to QuickLab

Answers will vary. Students should explain their answer using the concept of biological clocks.

GOING FURTHER

Writing **Maritime Navigation** Have students write a report about maritime navigation. Tell students to include a comparison of the instruments that were used 100 years ago and their modern counterparts. Their report should also explain how ancient people navigated.

CONNECT TO EARTH SCIENCE

Use the following Teaching Transparency to guide a student discussion about direction, mapping, and navigation.

Teaching Transparency 104 "Finding Direction on Earth" **LINK TO EARTH SCIENCE**

How Long Is a Minute?

Do you have an internal clock that helps you keep track of time? Pair up with a classmate. Your partner will start a **stopwatch** and say, "Go." When you think a minute has passed, say, "Stop!" Check the time. Try several times, and keep a record of your results. Then trade places and let your partner try. Were the recorded times close to a minute? Did your performance improve? Try again, using your pulse or your breathing as a guide. Were these times closer? Do you think you have an internal clock? Explain.

internetconnect

TOPIC: The Rhythms of Life
GO TO: www.scilinks.org
sciLINKS NUMBER: HSTL340

The Rhythms of Life

Humans need clocks and calendars to tell us when to get up and go to school, when a movie starts, and when it is someone's birthday. Other animals need to know when to store food and when to fly south for the winter. The internal clocks and calendars that animals use are called biological clocks. A **biological clock** is the internal control of natural cycles. Animals may use clues from their surroundings, such as the length of the day and the temperature, to set their clocks.

Some biological clocks keep track of very small amounts of time. Other biological clocks control daily cycles. These daily cycles are called **circadian rhythms.** *Circadian* means "around the day." Most animals wake up at about the same time each day and get sleepy at about the same time each night. This is an example of a circadian rhythm.

Some biological clocks control even longer cycles. Seasonal cycles are nearly universal among animals. Animals hibernate at certain times of the year and breed at other times. And every spring, migrating birds head north. Biological clocks control all of these cycles.

How Do Animals Find Their Way?

If you were planning a trip, you'd probably consult a map. If you were hiking, you might rely on a compass or trail markers to find your way. When it's time to migrate, how do animals, such as the arctic terns in **Figure 14,** know which way to go? They must *navigate,* or find their way from one place to another.

Figure 14 Each year, arctic terns make a 38,000 km round trip from the Northern Hemisphere to Antarctica.

MISCONCEPTION ALERT

Be sure that students understand that *hibernation* and *sleep* are not synonymous terms. Point out that animals do not hibernate continuously through the winter. They have periods that may last for days or weeks when their temperature rises to normal.

330 Chapter 14 • Animals and Behavior

Jet Lag

When people travel to places that are in a different time zone, they frequently suffer from "jet lag." Here's an example: New York time is 6 hours behind Paris time. A traveler from New York who is staying in Paris is suffering from jet lag. She goes to bed at 10 P.M., Paris time, but she wakes up at midnight, unable to fall back asleep. She lies awake all night and finally falls asleep at about 6 A.M., one hour before her alarm rings. How might circadian rhythms explain her jet lag? When it is 10 P.M. in Paris, what time is it in New York?

Take a Left at the Post Office For short trips, many animals, including humans, use landmarks to navigate. *Landmarks* are fixed objects that an animal uses to find its way. For example, once you see the corner gas station six blocks from your house, you know how to go the rest of the way. The gas station is a landmark for you.

Bees and pigeons have a kind of mental map of landmarks in their home territory. Birds use mountain ranges, rivers, and coastlines to find their way home. Humans and other animals also navigate short distances by using a mental image of an area. Not all landmarks are visual. Blind people can navigate precisely through a familiar house because they know where everything is and how long it takes to cross a room. Pigeons navigate in their home area based on smell as well as sight.

Compass Anyone? Like human sailors, animals use the position of the sun and stars as a map. But some animals, such as migratory birds, have other methods of finding their way. They navigate using the Earth's magnetic field. You can read about this in the Physics Connection at right.

Physics CONNECTION

Earth's core acts as a giant magnet, with magnetic north and south poles. The strength and direction of the Earth's magnetic field varies from place to place, and many birds use this variation as a map. Some migratory birds have tiny magnetic crystals of magnetite in their heads above their nostrils. Biologists think that the crystals somehow move or stimulate nerves so that a bird knows its position.

REVIEW

1. Why do animals migrate?
2. What are three methods animals use to navigate?
3. How are hibernation and estivation similar? How are they different?
4. **Applying Concepts** Some research suggests that jet lag can be overcome by getting plenty of exposure to sunlight in the new time zone. Why might this method work?

internet connect

SCILINKS
NSTA

TOPIC: Animal Behavior, The Rhythms of Life
GO TO: www.scilinks.org
sciLINKS NUMBER: HSTL335, HSTL340

SECTION 3

Focus

Living Together

In this section students will discover some of the ways that animals communicate with each other. They will explore how animals signal intentions and information to other animals through smell, sound, sight, and touch. Students will also learn about the advantages and disadvantages of living in a group.

Bellringer

As you are taking attendance, play a tape of humpback-whale songs. Ask students to offer suggestions related to what information the whales might be communicating. Your library might be a good source for whale tapes. Examples of whale songs can also be found on the Internet.

1 Motivate

ACTIVITY

Nonverbal Communication
Play a game of charades with students to demonstrate the importance of nonverbal communication among humans and other animals. Allow the class to provide feedback after a student guesses successfully.
<mark>Sheltered English</mark>

 Directed Reading Worksheet 14 Section 3

Section 3

Terms to Learn
social behavior
communication
territory
pheromone

What You'll Do
- Discuss ways that animals communicate.
- List the advantages and disadvantages of living in groups.

Living Together

Most animals do not live alone; they associate with other animals. When animals interact, it may be in large groups or one on one. Animals may work together, or they may compete with one another. All of this behavior is called social behavior. **Social behavior** is the interaction between animals of the same species. Whether friendly or hostile, all social behavior requires communication.

Communication

Imagine what life would be like if people could not talk or read. There would be no telephones, no televisions, no books, and no Internet. The world would certainly be a lot different! Language is an important way for humans to communicate. In **communication,** a signal must travel from one animal to another, and the receiver of the signal must respond in some way.

Communication helps animals live together, find food, avoid enemies, and protect their homes. Animals communicate to warn others of danger, to identify family members, to frighten predators, and to find mates. Some of the most dramatic uses of communication are courtship displays. *Courtship* is special behavior by animals of the same species that leads to mating. **Figure 15** shows two cranes performing a courtship display.

Animals also communicate to protect their living space. Many animals defend a **territory,** an area that is occupied by one animal or a group of animals and that other members of the species are excluded from. Many species, such as the wolves in **Figure 16,** use their territories for mating, finding food, and raising young.

Figure 15 *Japanese ground cranes perform an elaborate courtship dance.*

Figure 16 *These wolves are howling to discourage neighboring wolves from invading their territory.*

IS THAT A FACT!

Vampire bats are one of the few animals in the world that will share a meal with unrelated colony members—a truly altruistic behavior. These bats must consume 50–100 percent of their weight in blood each night (usually from cows or horses). If a bat misses a meal two nights in a row, it will die. As many as a third of the bats go without eating each night, yet few bats starve. A hungry bat will lick the wings of another bat, which in response usually regurgitates some of its meal to help the other bat survive.

How Do Animals Communicate?

Animals communicate by signaling intentions and information to other animals through smell, sound, vision, and touch. Most animal signals tend to be simple compared with those that we use. But no matter which signal is used, it must convey specific information.

Do You Smell Trouble? One method of communication is chemical. Even single-celled organisms communicate with one another by means of chemicals. In animals, these chemicals are called **pheromones** (FER uh MOHNZ).

Ants and other insects secrete a variety of pheromones. For example, alarm substances released into the air alert other members of the species to danger. Trail substances are left along a path so that others can follow to find food and return to the nest. Recognition odors on an ant's body announce which colony an ant is from. Such a message signals both friends and enemies, depending on who is receiving the message.

Many animals, including vertebrates, use pheromones to attract or influence members of the opposite sex. Amazingly, elephants and insects use some of the same pheromones to attract mates. Queen butterflies, like the one in **Figure 17**, use pheromones during their courtship displays.

Figure 17 Queen butterflies use pheromones as part of their courtship display.

Do You Hear What I Hear? Animals also communicate by making noises. Wolves howl. Dolphins and whales use whistles and complex clicking noises to communicate with others. Male birds may sing songs in the spring to claim their territory or attract a mate.

Sound is a signal that can reach a large number of animals over a large area. Elephants communicate with other elephants kilometers away using rumbles at a frequency too low for most humans to hear, as described in **Figure 18**. Humpback whales sing songs that can be heard for kilometers.

Figure 18 Elephants communicate with low-pitched sounds that humans cannot hear. When an elephant is communicating this way, the skin on its forehead flutters.

Research shows that baleen-whale sounds, which scientists believe are produced by the larynx, may be the loudest sounds produced by any animal on land or in the sea. Such sounds may carry hundreds of kilometers underwater.

internetconnect

TOPIC: Communication in the Animal Kingdom
GO TO: www.scilinks.org
sciLINKS NUMBER: HSTL345

Section 3 • Living Together **333**

2) Teach, continued

ACTIVITY

Investigate Grooming Tell students that grooming, or cleaning behavior, represents another way that animals communicate with each other through touch. Encourage students to do research about animals that communicate in this fashion. Examples include birds (preening), many mammals (mutual grooming), and certain fish (cleaning symbiosis). Students can use their research to create illustrated booklets that they can then share with the class.

GUIDED PRACTICE

Poster Project Tell students that wolves use body language called posturing to communicate with members of the pack. Have small groups of students research wolf posturing and then create illustrated charts showing various postures and what they mean. After posting the charts on the bulletin board, lead a discussion about wolf communication. Encourage students who have a pet dog to talk about the similarities and the differences between the body language used by their pet and the body language used by wolves. Sheltered English

Teaching Transparency 55 "The Dance of the Bees"

Figure 19 When dogs want to play, they drop down on their forelegs.

Showing Off Many forms of communication are visual. When we wink at a friend or frown at an opponent, we are communicating with *body language*. Other animals are no different. **Figure 19** shows one way dogs use body language.

An animal that wants to scare another animal may do something that makes it appear larger. It may ruffle its feathers or fur or open its mouth and show its teeth. Visual displays are also important in courtship. Fireflies blink complex signals in the dark to attract one another.

Getting in Touch An animal may also use touch to communicate, like the honeybee does. A honeybee that finds a patch of flowers rich in nectar returns to its hive to tell fellow workers where the flowers are. Inside the dark hive, the bee communicates by performing a complex figure-eight dance, as shown below, which the other bees learn by observation and touch.

The Dance of the Bees

Honeybees do a "waggle dance" to tell other bees where they've found nectar. As the bee goes through the middle of the figure eight, it communicates two things: the direction of the nectar and the distance to the nectar from the hive. Other worker bees gather closely around the dancing bee to learn the dance. By learning the dance, the bees learn the direction to the nectar.

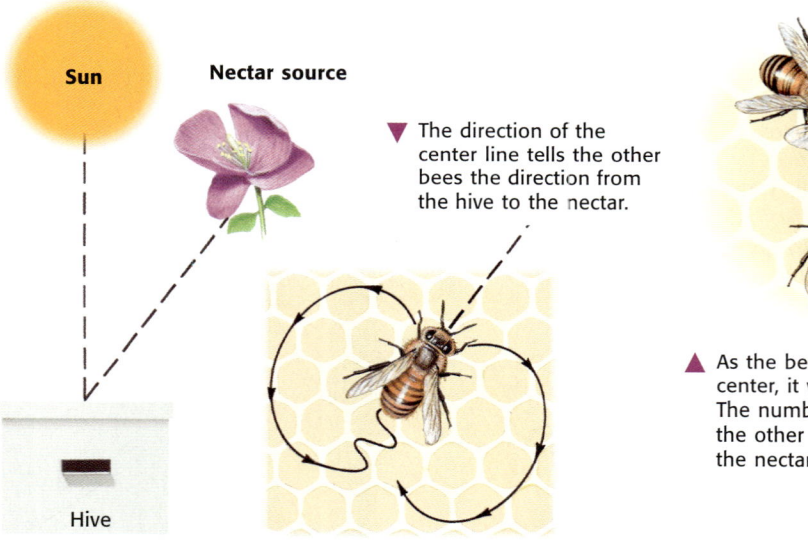

▼ The direction of the center line tells the other bees the direction from the hive to the nectar.

▲ As the bee goes through the center, it waggles its abdomen. The number of waggles tells the other bees how far away the nectar is.

Homework

Research Ant Behavior Have students research the behavior of ants. How do they organize the work of their colony? Several species of ants enslave other species. Have students investigate how one species of ant manages to capture and control another species.

Part of the Family

Tigers live alone. Except for the time a mother tiger spends with her cubs, a tiger meets other tigers rarely and for very short periods. Yet the tiger's closest relative, the lion, is rarely alone. Lions live in groups called prides. The members of a pride sleep together, hunt together, and raise their cubs together. **Figure 20** shows two lions at work. Why do some animals live in groups, while others live apart?

Figure 20 *This pair of lions cooperates to hunt a gazelle.*

The Benefits of Living in a Group Living with other animals is much safer than living alone. Large groups can spot a predator or other dangers quickly, and groups of animals can cooperate to defend themselves. For example, if a predator threatens them, a herd of musk oxen will circle their young with their horns pointed outward. Honeybees attack by the thousands when another animal tries to take their honey.

Living together can also help animals find food. Tigers and other animals that hunt alone can usually kill only animals that are smaller than themselves. In contrast, lions, wolves, hyenas, and other predators that hunt cooperatively can kill much larger prey.

The Downside of Living in a Group Living in groups causes problems as well. Animals living in groups attract predators, so they must always be on the lookout, as shown in **Figure 21**. Groups of animals need more food, and animals in groups compete with each other for food and for mates. Individuals in groups can also give each other diseases.

Figure 21 *A ground squirrel whistles a loud alarm to alert other ground squirrels that danger is near.*

REVIEW

1. Scientists have discovered pheromones in humans. Name three other types of animal communication used by humans.
2. Why is communication important? Name three reasons.
3. **Applying Concepts** Considering what you have learned about group living, list two advantages and two disadvantages to living in a group of humans.

internetconnect

TOPIC: Communication in the Animal Kingdom
GO TO: www.scilinks.org
sciLINKS NUMBER: HSTL345

Chapter Highlights

VOCABULARY DEFINITIONS

SECTION 1

vertebrate an animal with a skull and a backbone; examples include mammals, birds, reptiles, amphibians, and fish

invertebrate an animal without a backbone

embryo an organism in the earliest stage of development

tissue a group of similar cells that work together to perform a specific job in the body

organ a combination of two or more tissues that work together to perform a specific function in the body

consumer organisms that eat producers or other organisms for energy

SECTION 2

predator an animal that eats other animals

prey an organism that is eaten by another organism

innate behavior a behavior that is influenced by genes and does not depend on learning or experience

Chapter Highlights

SECTION 1

Vocabulary
- **vertebrate** (p. 322)
- **invertebrate** (p. 323)
- **embryo** (p. 324)
- **tissue** (p. 324)
- **organ** (p. 324)
- **consumer** (p. 325)

Section Notes
- Animals with a skull and a backbone are vertebrates. Animals without a backbone are invertebrates.
- Animals are multicellular. Their cells are eukaryotic and lack a cell wall.
- Most animals reproduce sexually and develop from embryos.
- Most animals have tissues and organs.
- Most animals move.
- Animals are consumers.

SECTION 2

Vocabulary
- **predator** (p. 326)
- **prey** (p. 326)
- **innate behavior** (p. 328)
- **learned behavior** (p. 328)
- **hibernation** (p. 329)
- **estivation** (p. 329)
- **biological clock** (p. 330)
- **circadian rhythm** (p. 330)

Section Notes
- Many animals use camouflage, chemicals, or both to defend themselves against predators.
- Behavior may be classified as innate or learned. The potential for innate behavior is inherited. Learned behavior depends on experience.
- Some animals migrate to find food, water, or safe nesting grounds.
- Some animals hibernate in the winter, and some estivate in the summer.

✓ Skills Check

Math Concepts

TIME DIFFERENCE In the Apply on page 331, you considered how the time difference between New York and Paris could explain jet lag. Paris time is 6 hours later than New York time. If it is 10 P.M. in Paris, subtract 6 hours to get New York time.

$$10 - 6 = 4$$

It is 4 P.M. in New York. Similarly, when it is 7 A.M. in Paris, it is 1 A.M. in New York.

Visual Understanding

THE DANCE OF THE BEES The illustration on page 334 shows how bees use the waggle dance to communicate the location of a nectar source. Notice the position of the sun in relation to the hive and the nectar source. The bee communicates this information by the direction of the center line in the dance.

Lab and Activity Highlights

Wet, Wiggly Worms! PG 732

Aunt Flossie and the Bumblebee PG 734

 Datasheets for LabBook (blackline masters for these labs)

SECTION 2

- Animals have internal biological clocks to control natural cycles.
- Daily cycles are called circadian rhythms.
- Some biological clocks are regulated by cues from an animal's environment.
- Animals navigate close to home using landmarks and a mental image of their home area.
- Some animals use the positions of the sun and stars or Earth's magnetic field to navigate.

Labs

Wet, Wiggly Worms! (p. 732)
Aunt Flossie and the Bumblebee (p. 734)

SECTION 3

Vocabulary

social behavior (p. 332)
communication (p. 332)
territory (p. 332)
pheromone (p. 333)

Section Notes

- Communication must include both a signal and a response.
- Two important kinds of communication are courtship and territorial displays.
- Animals communicate through sight, sound, touch, and smell.
- Group living allows animals to spot both prey and predators more easily.
- Groups of animals are more visible to predators than are individuals, and animals in groups must compete with one another for food and mates.

VOCABULARY DEFINITIONS, continued

learned behavior a behavior that has been learned from experience or observation

hibernation a period of inactivity that some animals experience in winter; allows them to survive on stored body fat

estivation a period of reduced activity that some animals experience in the summer

biological clock an internal control of natural cycles

circadian rhythm daily cycle

SECTION 3

social behavior the interaction between animals of the same species

communication a transfer of a signal from one animal to another that results in some type of response

territory an area occupied by one animal or a group of animals from which other members of the species are excluded

pheromone a chemical produced by animals for communication

---

internetconnect

 GO TO: go.hrw.com

Visit the **HRW** Web site for a variety of learning tools related to this chapter. Just type in the keyword:

KEYWORD: HSTANM

 GO TO: www.scilinks.org

Visit the **National Science Teachers Association** on-line Web site for Internet resources related to this chapter. Just type in the sciLINKS number for more information about the topic:

TOPIC: Vertebrates and Invertebrates sciLINKS NUMBER: HSTL330
TOPIC: Animal Behavior sciLINKS NUMBER: HSTL335
TOPIC: The Rhythms of Life sciLINKS NUMBER: HSTL340
TOPIC: Communication in the Animal Kingdom sciLINKS NUMBER: HSTL345

 Vocabulary Review Worksheet 14

 Blackline masters of these Chapter Highlights can be found in the **Study Guide**.

Lab and Activity Highlights

LabBank

Inquiry Labs, Follow the Leader, Lab 4

Whiz-Bang Demonstrations, Six-Legged Thermometer, Demo 9

Long-Term Projects & Research Ideas, Animal-Myth Behaviors, Project 14

Chapter Review Answers

USING VOCABULARY

1. a vertebrate, an invertebrate
2. innate
3. estivating
4. circadian rhythms
5. an embryo

UNDERSTANDING CONCEPTS

Multiple Choice

6. c
7. d
8. b
9. b
10. d

Short Answer

11. Pheromones are released by one animal to send a message to another animal.
12. A territory is an area occupied by one animal or a group of animals from which other members of the species are excluded. Examples will vary but may include a bedroom, a family house, or a school.
13. Answers will vary but should be unchanging objects, such as buildings or roads.
14. Both are seasonal behaviors controlled by biological clocks.

Concept Mapping

15. An answer to this exercise can be found at the end of this book.

Concept Mapping Transparency 14

Chapter Review

USING VOCABULARY

To complete the following sentences, choose the correct term from each pair of terms listed below:

1. An animal with a skull and a backbone is __?__. An animal with no backbone is __?__. (*an invertebrate* or *a vertebrate*)

2. A behavior that does not depend on experience is __?__. (*innate* or *learned*)

3. In the summer, an animal enters a state of reduced activity. The animal is __?__. (*estivating* or *hibernating*)

4. Daily cycles are known as __?__. (*biological clocks* or *circadian rhythms*)

5. When an egg and a sperm come together, they form __?__. (*an embryo* or *an organ*)

UNDERSTANDING CONCEPTS

Multiple Choice

6. Which characteristic is not true of animals?
   a. They are multicellular.
   b. They usually reproduce sexually.
   c. They make their own food.
   d. They have tissues.

7. Living in groups
   a. attracts predators.
   b. helps prey spot predators.
   c. helps animals find food.
   d. All of the above

8. Warning coloration is
   a. a kind of camouflage.
   b. a way to warn predators away.
   c. always black and white.
   d. always a sign that an animal is poisonous to eat.

9. Some birds use Earth's magnetic field
   a. to attract mates.
   b. to navigate.
   c. to set their biological clocks.
   d. to defend their territory.

10. To defend against predators, an animal might use
    a. camouflage.
    b. warning coloration.
    c. toxins.
    d. All of the above

Short Answer

11. How are pheromones used in communication?

12. What is a territory? Give an example of a territory from your own environment.

13. What landmarks help you navigate your way home from school?

14. What do migration and hibernation have in common?

Concept Mapping

15. Use the following terms to create a concept map: estivation, circadian rhythms, seasonal behaviors, hibernation, migration, biological clocks.

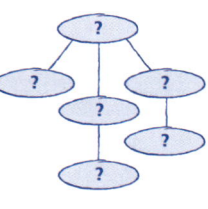

338 Chapter 14 • Animals and Behavior

CRITICAL THINKING AND PROBLEM SOLVING

Write one or two sentences to answer the following questions:

16. If you smell a skunk while riding in a car and you shut the car window, has the skunk communicated with you? Explain.

17. Flying is an innate behavior in birds. Is it an innate behavior or a learned behavior in humans? Why?

18. Ants depend on pheromones and touch for communication, but birds depend more on sight and sound. Why might these two types of animals communicate differently?

INTERPRETING GRAPHICS

The pie chart below shows the major phyla of the animal species on Earth. Use the chart to answer the questions that follow.

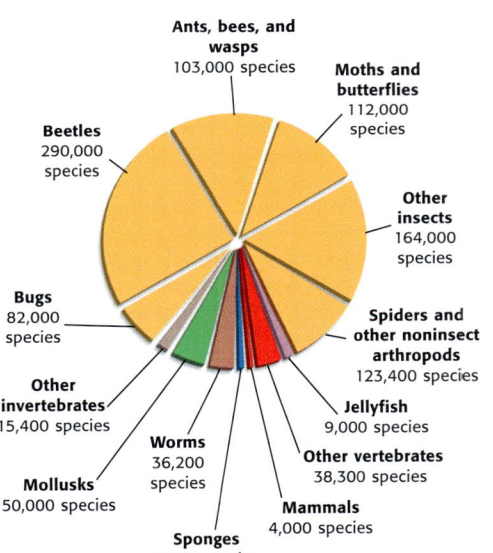

19. What group of animals has the most species? How is this shown on the chart?

20. How many species of beetles are on Earth? How does that compare with the number of mammal species?

21. How many species of vertebrates are known?

22. Scientists are still discovering new species. Which pie wedges are most likely to increase? Why do you think so?

MATH IN SCIENCE

Use the data from the pie chart to answer the following questions:

23. What is the total number of animal species on Earth?

24. How many different species of moths and butterflies are on Earth?

25. What percentage of all animal species are moths and butterflies?

26. What percentage of all animal species are vertebrates?

 Take a minute to review your answers to the Pre-Reading Questions found at the bottom of page 320. Have your answers changed? If necessary, revise your answers based on what you have learned since you began this chapter.

 Blackline masters of this Chapter Review can be found in the **Study Guide.**

CRITICAL THINKING AND PROBLEM SOLVING

16. Yes; even though you were not the intended recipient of the message, the skunk communicated with you. The skunk has sent a signal (its smell), and you have responded (by shutting the window).

17. It is a learned behavior. Humans are not born with the ability to fly, but we have learned to fly using airplanes.

18. Ants are much smaller and cannot see or hear over great distances, so they must depend on pheromones and touch for communication. Birds have better eyesight, and they can hear well and sing, so they can communicate by sound and sight.

INTERPRETING GRAPHICS

19. Beetles have the greatest number of species. Students may also list the group arthropods, which includes beetles, bugs, insects, and spiders—all of the wedges that are colored yellow. On the pie chart, this is shown by the largest wedge (or group of wedges) and by the label.

20. There are 290,00 species of beetles. There are only 4,000 species of mammals.

21. There are 42,300 vertebrate species (4,000 mammals + 38,300 other vertebrates).

22. Answers will vary, but students may suggest that new species of insects and beetles will be found. Because there are so many species in these groups, there is a greater chance that they have not all been found.

MATH IN SCIENCE

23. 1,032,300
24. 112,000
25. 10.9 percent
26. 4.1 percent

EYE ON THE ENVIRONMENT
Do Not Disturb!

Background

Bats make up the order Chiroptera, which means "hand wing." Bats are considered the best bug control around. For example, 20 million Mexican free-tail bats live in Bracken Cave, Texas. Each night they eat 250 tons of insects. Bats are also responsible for pollinating flowers and dispersing seeds for many plants. In Arizona, nectar-feeding bats pollinate giant cacti, such as the saguaro and organ pipe. In the rain forest, many trees and shrubs depend on bats to pollinate flowers and to disperse their seeds.

There are nearly 1,000 different species of bats. The smallest bat, the bumblebee bat of Thailand *(Craseonycteris thonglongyai)*, weighs less than a penny. The largest bat, the Indonesian flying fox *(Pteropus vampyrus)*, boasts a wingspan of nearly 1.8 m. Only three bats are considered vampire bats—the common vampire *(Desmodus rotundus)*, the hairy-legged vampire *(Diphylla ecaudata)*, and the white-winged vampire *(Diaemus youngi)*. All three are found in Latin America.

EYE ON THE ENVIRONMENT
Do Not Disturb!

Did you know that bats are the only mammals that can fly? Unlike many birds, most bat species in the northern and central parts of the United States don't fly south for the winter. Instead of migrating, many bat species go into hibernation. But if their sleep is disturbed too often, the bats may die.

Long Winter's Nap

Most bats eat insects, but winter is a time of food shortage. In late summer, many North American bats begin to store up extra fat. These fat reserves help them survive the winter. For the stored fat to last until spring, bats must hibernate. They travel to caves where winter temperatures are low enough—0°C to 9.5°C—and stable enough for the bats to hibernate comfortably.

Hibernating bats' body temperature drops to almost the same temperature as the surrounding cave. Their heart rate, normally about 400 beats per minute, slows to about 25 beats per minute. With these changes, the stored fat will usually last all winter, unless human visitors wake the bats from their deep sleep. If that happens, the bats may starve to death.

No Admittance!

Even with their slowed metabolism, bats must wake up occasionally. They still need to drink water every so often. Sometimes they move to a warmer or cooler spot in the cave. But bats usually have enough fat stored so that they can wake up a few times each winter and then go back to sleep.

People visiting the caves force the bats to wake up unnecessarily. This causes the bats to use up the fat they have stored faster than they can afford. For example, a little brown bat consumes 67 days worth of stored fat each time it awakes. And with no insects around to eat, it cannot build up its fat reserve again.

▲ *These little brown bats are roosting in a cave.*

Most species of hibernating bats can survive the winter after waking about three extra times. But frequent intrusions can lead to the death of a whole colony of bats. Thousands of these interesting and extremely beneficial mammals may die when people carelessly or deliberately disturb them as they hibernate.

Increase Your Knowledge

▶ Using the Internet or the library, find out more about bats. Learn how they are beneficial to the environment and what threatens their survival. Discuss with your classmates some ways to protect bats and their habitats.

Answer to Increase Your Knowledge

Answers will vary. Among other services, bats help keep insect populations under control, pollinate some plants, disperse seeds, and fertilize soil. Habitat destruction and human ignorance endanger bats. Solutions might include passing laws to protect bats and educating people about what bats do and don't do.

WEIRD SCIENCE

ANIMAL CANNIBALS

Competing, surviving, and reproducing are all part of life. And in some species, so is *cannibalism* (eating members of one's own species). But how does cannibalism relate to competing, surviving, and reproducing? It turns out that sometimes an animal's choice of food is a factor in whether its genes get passed on or not.

Picky Eaters

Tiger salamanders start life by eating zooplankton, aquatic insect larvae, and sometimes tadpoles. If conditions in their small pond include intense competition with members of their own species, some of the larger salamanders become cannibals!

Scientists are not sure why tiger salamanders become cannibals or why they usually eat nonrelatives. Scientists hypothesize that this behavior eliminates competition. By eating other salamanders, a tiger salamander reduces competition for food and improves the chances of its own survival. That increases the chances its genes will be passed on to the next generation. And eating nonrelatives helps to ensure that genes coming from the same family are more likely to be passed on to the next generation.

The Ultimate Sacrifice

Male Australian redback spiders take a different approach to making sure their genes are passed on. During mating, the male spider tumbles his body over, does a handstand, and waves his abdomen near the female's mouth, offering himself to her as a meal. The female accepts the dinner invitation if she is hungry. And it seems that about 65 percent of the time she is hungry!

▲ *During mating, male Australian redback spiders offer themselves as food to their mates.*

Male spiders want to pass on their genes, so they compete fiercely for the females. A female redback spider wants to make sure that as many of her eggs are fertilized as possible, so she often mates with two different males. If the female eats the first male, studies show that she will not mate with a second male as often as she would if she had not eaten the first suitor. Because eating the male takes some time, more eggs are fertilized by the mate who also becomes dinner. The male spider who offers himself as a meal may then have more of his genes passed to the next generation.

On Your Own

▶ Other animals devour members of their own species. Scientists believe there are a variety of reasons for the behavior. Using the Internet or the library, research cannibalism in different animals, such as praying mantises, blue crabs, stickleback fish, black widow spiders, spadefoot toad tadpoles, and lions. Present your findings to the class.

WEIRD SCIENCE
Animal Cannibals

Background

In a behavior related to cannibalism, some animals attempt to improve their chances of reproductive success by interfering with the reproductive cycle of their fellow species members. For example, consider a female stickleback fish that attacks the nest of a male (it is the male stickleback that tends the nest) and eats the embryos. She is more likely to have greater reproductive success because her own offspring will have less competition for food. When a lion takes over a pride, it kills the cubs so that it doesn't spend time raising and protecting young that don't carry its genes. The female lion, on the other hand, will try to protect the cubs in order to protect her genes.

Answer to On Your Own

Scientists think that cannibalism, a behavior that might appear to be detrimental to a species, may be part of a behavior adaptation called the "lifeboat strategy." Under adverse conditions, such as a scarcity of food, animals are more likely to practice cannibalism not only to feed themselves individually but also to reduce the population searching for food, which reduces competition. A good example is the blue crab, which feeds on soft-shell clams in normal circumstances. When the clams are in short supply, however, the crabs begin to eat one another. This reduces the number of crabs competing for clams and increases the chance that the species as a whole will survive.

Chapter Organizer

CHAPTER ORGANIZATION	TIME MINUTES	OBJECTIVES	LABS, INVESTIGATIONS, AND DEMONSTRATIONS
Chapter Opener pp. 342–343	45	National Standards: UCP 1, SAI 2, ST 2, SPSP 5	**Start-Up Activity** Classify It! p. 343
Section 1 Simple Invertebrates	90	▶ Describe the difference between radial and bilateral symmetry. ▶ Describe the function of a coelom. ▶ Explain how sponges are different from other animals. ▶ Describe the differences in the simple nervous systems of the cnidarians and the flatworms. UCP 1, 4, 5, SPSP 3, 4, LS 1a, 1d, 1f, 2a, 3a–3c, 4b, 5a; LabBook UCP 3, SAI 1	**Demonstration,** Sponges, p. 346 in ATE **BASIC** **Demonstration,** Stinging Cells, p. 349 in ATE **GENERAL** **Skill Builder,** Porifera's Porosity, p. 736 **BASIC** **Datasheets for LabBook,** Porifera's Porosity, Datasheet 32 **BASIC**
Section 2 Mollusks and Annelid Worms	90	▶ Describe the body parts of a mollusk. ▶ Explain the difference between an open circulatory system and a closed circulatory system. ▶ Describe segmentation. UCP 1–3, 5, SAI 2, SPSP 4, LS 1a, 2a, 3a, 4b, 5a;	**Inquiry Labs,** At a Snail's Pace, Lab 5 **ADVANCED** **Labs You Can Eat,** Here's Looking at You, Squid! Lab 7 **GENERAL**
Section 3 Arthropods	90	▶ List the four main characteristics of arthropods. ▶ Describe the different body parts of the four kinds of arthropods. ▶ Explain the two types of metamorphosis in insects. UCP 2, 3, 5, SAI 1, SPSP 4, LS 1a, 1d, 1f, 4b, 5a; LabBook SAI 1, LS 3c	**QuickLab,** Sticky Webs, p. 360 **GENERAL** **Discovery Lab,** The Cricket Caper, p. 737 **BASIC** **Datasheets for LabBook,** The Cricket Caper, Datasheet 33 **BASIC**
Section 4 Echinoderms	90	▶ Describe three main characteristics of echinoderms. ▶ Describe the water vascular system. UCP 5, LS 1a, 1d, 3a, 4b, 5a	**Long-Term Projects & Research Ideas,** Project 15 **ADVANCED**

See page T20 for a complete correlation of this book with the

NATIONAL SCIENCE EDUCATION STANDARDS.

TECHNOLOGY RESOURCES

 Guided Reading Audio CD English or Spanish, Chapter 15

 One-Stop Planner CD-ROM with Test Generator

 CNN Scientists in Action, Stopping the Termite Attack, Segment 21

Chapter 15 • Invertebrates

Chapter 15 • Invertebrates

CLASSROOM WORKSHEETS, TRANSPARENCIES, AND RESOURCES	SCIENCE INTEGRATION AND CONNECTIONS	REVIEW AND ASSESSMENT
Directed Reading Worksheet 15 BASIC **Science Puzzlers, Twisters & Teasers,** Worksheet 15 ADVANCED		
Directed Reading Worksheet 15, Section 1 BASIC **Critical Thinking Worksheet 15,** A New Form of Danger in the Deep ADVANCED **Reinforcement Worksheet 15,** Life Without a Backbone BASIC	**Multicultural Connection,** p. 344 in ATE ADVANCED **Real-World Connection,** p. 346 in ATE **Environment Connection,** p. 349 **Real-World Connection,** p. 350 in ATE **Weird Science:** Water Bears, p. 370 ADVANCED	**Review,** p. 347 GENERAL **Self-Check,** p. 349 **Homework,** p. 350 in ATE GENERAL **Review,** p. 351 GENERAL **Quiz,** p. 351 in ATE GENERAL **Alternative Assessment,** p. 351 in ATE ADVANCED
Directed Reading Worksheet 15, Section 2 BASIC	**MathBreak,** Speeding Squid, p. 352 GENERAL **Multicultural Connection,** p. 353 in ATE **Apply,** p. 355 GENERAL **Eye on the Environment:** Sizable Squid, p. 371 GENERAL	**Review,** p. 354 GENERAL **Review,** p. 356 GENERAL **Quiz,** p. 356 in ATE GENERAL **Alternative Assessment,** p. 356 in ATE GENERAL
Directed Reading Worksheet 15, Section 3 BASIC **Math Skills for Science Worksheet 5,** Dividing Whole Numbers with Long Division GENERAL **Math Skills for Science Worksheet 6,** Checking Division with Multiplication GENERAL **Transparency 56,** Incomplete Metamorphosis **Transparency 57,** Changing Form—Complete Metamorphosis	**Math and More,** p. 358 in ATE ADVANCED **Connect to Chemistry,** p. 359 in ATE	**Self-Check,** p. 359 **Review,** p. 362 GENERAL **Quiz,** p. 362 in ATE GENERAL **Alternative Assessment,** p. 362 in ATE GENERAL
Directed Reading Worksheet 15, Section 4 BASIC **Transparency 155,** The Three Groups of Marine Life **Transparency 58,** Water Vascular System **Reinforcement Worksheet 15,** Spineless Variety BASIC	**Connect to Earth Science,** p. 364 in ATE	**Review,** p. 365 GENERAL **Quiz,** p. 365 in ATE GENERAL **Alternative Assessment,** p. 365 in ATE GENERAL

END-OF-CHAPTER REVIEW AND ASSESSMENT

Chapter Review in Study Guide
Vocabulary and Notes in Study Guide
Chapter Tests with Performance-Based Assessment, Chapter 15 Test
Chapter Tests with Performance-Based Assessment, Performance-Based Assessment 15
Concept Mapping Transparency 15

 Holt, Rinehart and Winston On-line Resources
go.hrw.com

For worksheets and other teaching aids related to this chapter, visit the HRW Web site and type in the keyword: **HSTINV**

 National Science Teachers Association
www.scilinks.org

Encourage students to use the *sci*LINKS numbers listed in the internet connect boxes to access information and resources on the **NSTA** Web site.

Chapter 15 • Chapter Organizer   **341B**

Chapter Resources & Worksheets

Visual Resources

TEACHING TRANSPARENCIES

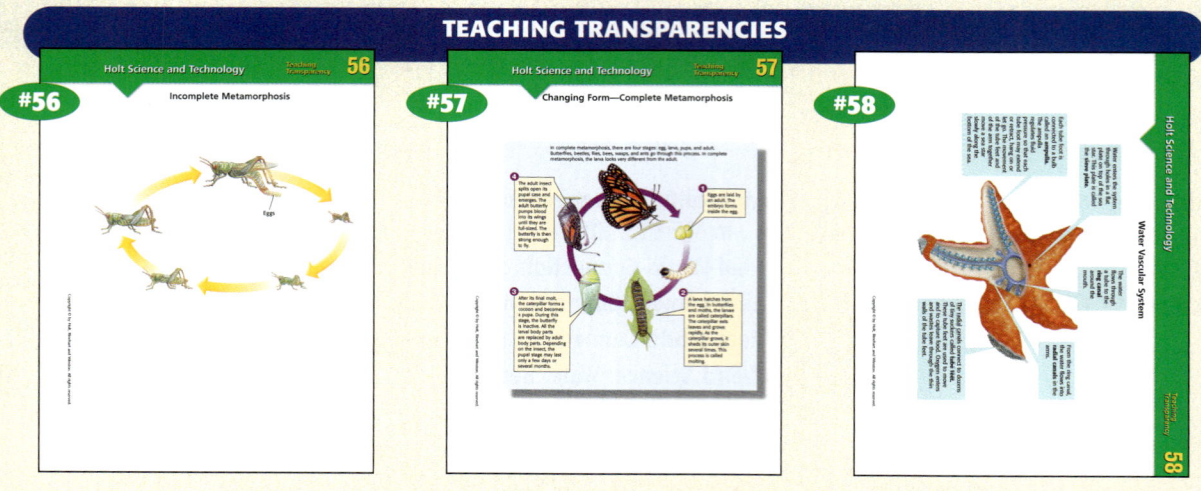

TEACHING TRANSPARENCIES — #155

CONCEPT MAPPING TRANSPARENCY — #15

Meeting Individual Needs

DIRECTED READING — #15

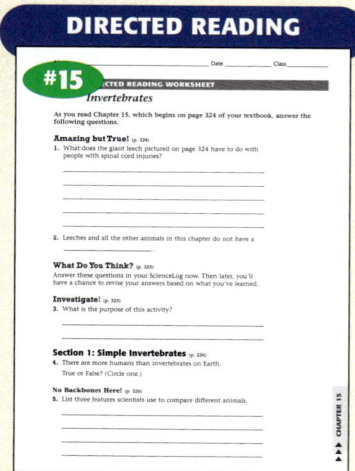

REINFORCEMENT & VOCABULARY REVIEW — #15

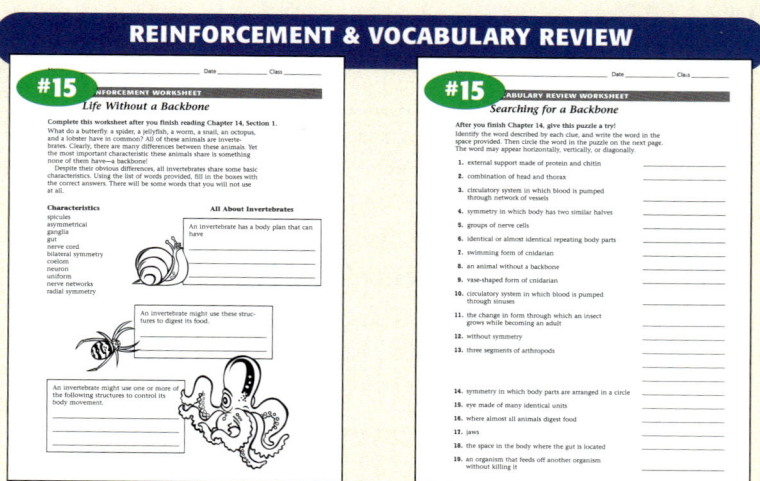

SCIENCE PUZZLERS, TWISTERS & TEASERS — #15

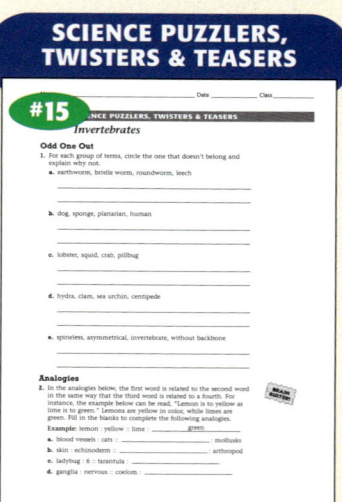

Chapter 15 • Invertebrates

Chapter 15 • Invertebrates

Review & Assessment

STUDY GUIDE
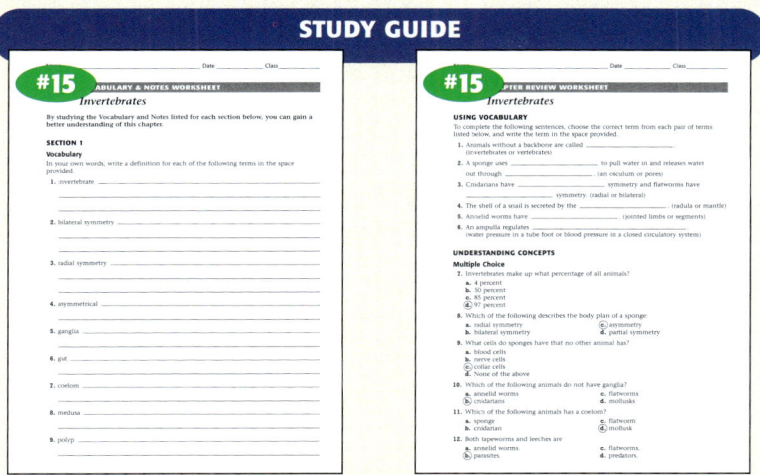

CHAPTER TESTS WITH PERFORMANCE-BASED ASSESSMENT

Lab Worksheets

INQUIRY LABS
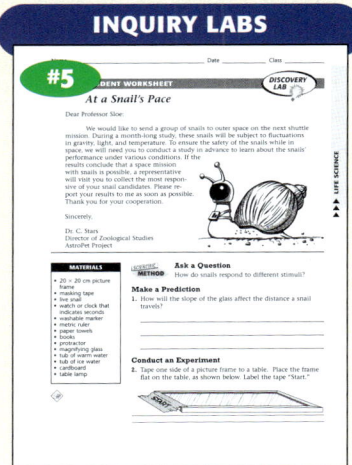

LABS YOU CAN EAT

LONG-TERM PROJECTS & RESEARCH IDEAS

DATASHEETS FOR LABBOOK
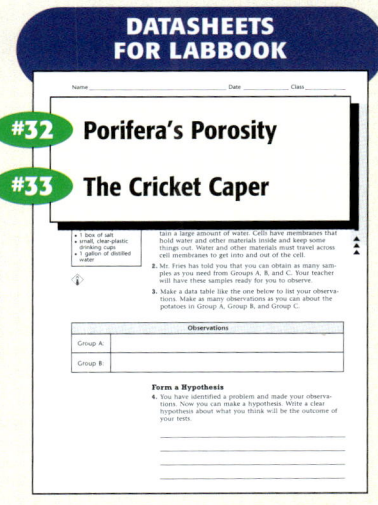

Applications & Extensions

CRITICAL THINKING & PROBLEM SOLVING

SCIENTISTS IN ACTION

Chapter Background

SECTION 1

Simple Invertebrates

▶ **Aristotle**
The Greek philosopher Aristotle (384–322 B.C.) made the first recorded distinctions between invertebrate and vertebrate animals. He even organized invertebrates into a number of different groups.

- Aristotle was particularly interested in marine invertebrates; he made detailed observations of sea stars, crustaceans, and mollusks—especially cuttlefish, which are related to squids.

▶ **Sponges as Animals**
Sponges were not completely accepted as animals until the early 1800s, when Scottish zoologist R. E. Grant conducted experiments in which he added fine, colored particles to the water around sponges. Grant watched under a microscope as the particles were taken into the sponges through microscopic pores and then "vomited forth" from the central cavity.

IS THAT A FACT!

🔶 Of roughly 5,000 living species of sponges, only about 150 species live in fresh water. All the rest live in marine habitats.

▶ **Medusa**
The tentacle-bearing medusa form of cnidarians gets its name from Medusa, a character in Greek mythology. Medusa was a monster whose long, curly "hair" was made up of snakes.

SECTION 2

Mollusks and Annelid Worms

▶ **Useful, Edible Mollusks**
Mollusks, more than any other invertebrates, are consumed as food by people worldwide. Oysters, mussels, clams, snails, squids, and octopuses are just a few edible mollusks.

IS THAT A FACT!

🔶 Giant clams are the largest living bivalves. Shells of the giant clam *Tridacna gigas* can be 1.5 m long and weigh more than 225 kg.

▶ **Earth-Movers**
Charles Darwin (1809–1882) spent many years studying earthworms and calculating their remarkable earth-moving abilities.

- Scientists estimate that the amount of soil brought to the surface by earthworms each year can be as much as 90 metric tons per hectare in temperate regions and considerably more in tropical regions. This activity helps aerate the soil and improve growing conditions for plants.

IS THAT A FACT!

🔶 Australia is home to the world's longest earthworms, which can exceed 3 m in length.

▶ **Terrestrial Leeches**
Most leeches are aquatic, but tropical rain forests are home to terrestrial leeches. The body heat of mammals attracts these tiny blood-sucking leeches. They will quickly move over vegetation to converge on any unlucky animal that stands in one place for more than a few minutes.

Chapter 15 • Invertebrates

SECTION 3
Arthropods

▶ **Diversity**
Nearly 1 million species of arthropods have been identified. Scientists estimate that between 2 million and 30 million species are yet to be named. As a group, arthropods are more densely and widely distributed than members of any other animal group.

- Arthropods are found in every imaginable type of environment, from mountain peaks to deep-sea trenches, from equatorial rain forests to polar regions. Some arthropods are adapted for life on land, others for life in the air, and still others in salty, brackish, or fresh water.

▶ **Beetles**
The order Coleoptera (meaning "sheathed wings"), containing beetles, fireflies, and weevils, is the largest order in the animal kingdom. There are at least 250,000 known species of beetles.

IS THAT A FACT!

- All known species of spiders are predators. Their chelicerae (anterior pair of appendages) end in fangs that inject venom that kills or paralyzes their prey. When spiders bite, they also pump digestive enzymes into their victims. A spider can then suck up the resulting predigested "broth" from its prey.

SECTION 4
Echinoderms

▶ **How Sea Stars Feed**
The mouth of a sea star is located on the underside of its body. A short esophagus leads to a large stomach that, in many species, can be pushed out, or everted, through the sea star's mouth.

- When a sea star, such as *Asterias,* comes upon a clam, for example, it uses its tube feet and muscular arms to pull the clam's shell apart just enough so that the sea star can push its everted stomach through the opening. The stomach then wraps around the soft parts of the clam's body, and digestion begins.

▶ **Class Crinoidea**
The fifth class of echinoderms, Crinoidea, is less familiar to most people than are the other classes in the phylum Echinodermata. Crinoids include sea lilies and feather stars.

- Sea lilies have a stalked body topped by feathery arms that are used to snare small plankton from the water. Most sea lilies live in deep water. Feather stars are colorful, free-moving animals with long, many-branched arms. Feather stars are common inhabitants of coral reefs.

IS THAT A FACT!

- When disturbed, many types of sea cucumbers will expel parts of their internal organs through the anus. This defense mechanism is quite effective in discouraging potential predators. The lost parts are quickly regenerated.

For background information about teaching strategies and issues, refer to the *Professional Reference for Teachers.*

Invertebrates

 Pre-Reading Questions

Students may not know the answers to these questions before reading the chapter, so accept any reasonable response.

Suggested Answers
1. Sponges have collar cells and asymmetry.
2. Humans are vertebrates, and octopuses are invertebrates. Both humans and octopuses have a brain and a closed circulatory system.

 Directed Reading Worksheet 15

 Science Puzzlers, Twisters & Teasers Worksheet 15

 Guided Reading Audio CD
English or Spanish, Chapter 15

Invertebrates

Sections

1. Simple Invertebrates .. 344
   Environment
      Connection 349
   Internet Connect 351
2. Mollusks and Annelid
   Worms 352
      MathBreak 352
      Apply 355
   Internet Connect 356
3. Arthropods 357
      QuickLab 360
   Internet Connect 362
4. Echinoderms 363
   Internet Connect 365

Chapter Review 368
Feature Articles 370, 371
LabBook 736–739

 **Pre-Reading Questions**

1. How are sponges different from other invertebrates?
2. How are you different from an octopus? How are you similar?

A Sci-Fi Slug?

No, this isn't an alien! It's a sea slug, a close relative of garden slugs and snails. This sea slug lives in the cold Pacific Ocean near the coast of California. Its bright coloring comes from the food that the slug eats. This animal doesn't breathe with lungs. Instead, it brings oxygen into its body through the spikes on its back.

Sea slugs don't have a backbone. In this chapter, you will discover many other animals that have no backbones. You will also learn about the structure and function of their bodies.

internet connect

 HRW On-line Resources
go.hrw.com
For worksheets and other teaching aids, visit the HRW Web site and type in the keyword: **HSTINV**

 sciLINKS NSTA
www.scilinks.com
Use the *sci*LINKS numbers at the end of each chapter for additional resources on the **NSTA** Web site.

 CNNfyi.com
www.cnnfyi.com
Visit the CNN Web site for current events coverage and classroom resources.

START-UP Activity

CLASSIFY IT!

Animals are classified according to their different characteristics, including their internal and external features. In this activity, you will try your hand at classification.

Procedure

1. Look at the **pictures** that your teacher has provided. Scientists group all of these animals together because these animals do not have a backbone.
2. Which animals are the most alike? Put them in the same group.
3. For each group, decide which animals within the group are the most alike. Put these animals into smaller groups inside of their larger group.
4. In your ScienceLog or using a computer, construct a table that organizes your classification groups.

Analysis

5. What features did you use to classify these animals into groups? Explain why you think these features are the most important.
6. What features did you use to place the animals in smaller groups? Explain your reasoning.
7. Compare your table with those of your classmates. What similarities or differences do you find?

START-UP Activity

CLASSIFY IT!

MATERIALS

FOR EACH STUDENT:
- pictures of invertebrates

Teacher's Notes

Biological classification, in which organisms are named and organized according to their relatedness, is also known as taxonomy. Researchers who specialize in this area of biology are called taxonomists.

Answers to START-UP Activity

2. Answers will vary according to the animals provided to students. Sample answer: The lobster, the spider, and the grasshopper are the most alike.
4. Look for logical grouping of animals. Animals within each group should share some characteristic(s) that is (are) not seen in other groups.
5. Answers will vary according to the animals provided to students. Students should explain the logic of their groupings. Sample answer: I grouped animals by their number of legs and wings, as well as their type of body covering.
6. Answers will vary according to the animals provided to students. Students should explain the logic of their groupings. Sample answer: I grouped animals by how many legs, antennae, wings, and eyes they have, as well as by where they live and what their body shape is.
7. Answers will vary. Look for logical, well-reasoned answers.

SECTION 1

Focus

Simple Invertebrates

This section introduces students to simple invertebrates—sponges, cnidarians, flatworms, and roundworms. Students learn about the different body plans of these animals and important characteristics of their sensory, nervous, and digestive systems.

🔔 Bellringer

Pose the following questions to your students:

- What is an invertebrate? (an animal without a backbone)
- What is your favorite invertebrate?
- What special features does this invertebrate have that help it survive in its environment?

Have students write their answers in their ScienceLog.

1 Motivate

ACTIVITY

Determining Symmetry Divide students into cooperative groups of three or four. Distribute to each group copies of simple, top-view drawings of a butterfly and a sea urchin and a small, rectangular hand mirror (mirrors without frames work best). Challenge students to use the mirror to demonstrate that the butterfly is bilaterally symmetrical and that the sea urchin is radially symmetrical. Encourage students to discuss their findings as a class.
Sheltered English

Section 1

Terms to Learn

invertebrate
bilateral symmetry
radial symmetry
asymmetrical
ganglia
gut
coelom

What You'll Do

- Describe the difference between radial and bilateral symmetry.
- Describe the function of a coelom.
- Explain how sponges are different from other animals.
- Describe the differences in the simple nervous systems of the cnidarians and the flatworms.

Simple Invertebrates

Animals without backbones, also known as **invertebrates,** make up an estimated 97 percent of all animal species. So far, more than 1 million invertebrates have been named. Most biologists think that millions more remain undiscovered.

Tiger beetle

No Backbones Here!

Invertebrates come in many different shapes and sizes. Grasshoppers, clams, earthworms, and jellyfish are all invertebrates, and they are all very different from each other. But one thing invertebrates have in common is that they don't have backbones.

The differences and similarities among all animals, including invertebrates, can be compared by looking at several characteristics. These characteristics include the type of body plan, the presence or absence of a head, and the way food is digested and absorbed.

Morpho butterfly

Horned flatworm

Harlequin shrimp

Body Plans Invertebrates have two basic body plans, or types of *symmetry*. Symmetry can be bilateral or radial. Animal body plans are shown on the next page.

Most animals have bilateral symmetry. An animal with **bilateral symmetry** has a body with two similar halves. For example, if you draw an imaginary line down the middle of an ant, you see the same features on each side of the line.

Some invertebrates have radial symmetry. In an animal with **radial symmetry,** the body parts are arranged in a circle around a central point. If you were to draw an imaginary line across the top of a sea anemone, you would see that both halves look the same. But you could draw the line in any direction and still see two similar halves.

The simplest invertebrates, the sponges, have no symmetry at all. Animals without symmetry are **asymmetrical.**

🌐 Multicultural CONNECTION

The silica spicules from many freshwater sponges are very sharp, abrasive, and strong. In Russia, dried freshwater sponges have long been used to polish silver, brass, and other metals. Indians who live along the Amazon River, in South America, add sponge spicules to clay to strengthen the pots they make from it. Have students research other uses of sponge spicules or entire sponges and create a poster based on their findings.

Animal Body Plans

This ant has **bilateral symmetry**. The two halves of its body mirror each other. On each side you see one eye, one antenna, and three legs.

This sea anemone has **radial symmetry**. Animals with radial symmetry have a body organized around the center, like spokes on a wheel.

This sponge is **asymmetrical**. You cannot draw a straight line so that its body is divided into two equal halves.

Getting a Head All animals except sponges have fibers called *nerves* that carry signals to control the movements of their body. Simple invertebrates have nerves arranged in networks or in nerve cords throughout their body. These simple animals have no brain or head.

In some invertebrates, dozens of nerve cells come together in groups called **ganglia** (singular, *ganglion*). Ganglia occur throughout the body, controlling different body parts. **Figure 1** shows one of the ganglia, the brain, and nerve cords of a leech.

More-complex animals have a brain and a head, where the brain is stored. The brain controls many different nerves in different parts of the body.

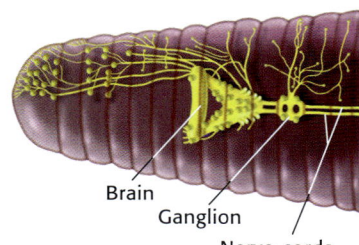

Figure 1 *Leeches have a simple brain and ganglia. A pair of nerve cords connects the brain and ganglia.*

Don't You Have Any Guts? Almost all animals digest food in a central gut. The **gut** is a pouch lined with cells that release powerful enzymes. These enzymes break down food into small particles that cells can then absorb. Your gut is your digestive tract.

Complex animals have a special space in the body for the gut. This space is the **coelom** (SEE luhm), shown in **Figure 2**. The coelom allows the gut to move food without interference from the movements of the body. Other organs, such as the heart and lungs, are also in the coelom, but they are separated from the gut.

Figure 2 *This is the coelom of an earthworm. The gut and organs are in this special cavity.*

IS THAT A FACT!

The discovery of a new species of carnivorous sponge in the Mediterranean Sea has amazed marine biologists and confused taxonomists. A typical sponge is a filter feeder, filtering out organic matter from the ocean water. This newly discovered sponge does not eat that way. Investigators discovered that it eats crustaceans by growing thin filaments that cover its prey. The prey is dissolved and digested by the sponge in a matter of days. Now scientists are rethinking the definition of *sponge*. This newly discovered creature resembles a sponge except in its feeding habits.

2) Teach, continued

REAL-WORLD CONNECTION

Sponges have few predators. The sharp spicules—or tough fibers—in their bodies discourage fish and other aquatic organisms from eating them. Many sponges also produce toxic chemicals that deter predators and keep other sponges from growing too close. A chemical isolated from a Caribbean sponge, *Cryptotethya crypta,* was one of the first marine compounds to be used in chemotherapy. Currently, many other chemical compounds produced by sponges are being tested as anticancer and antiviral drugs.

DEMONSTRATION

Sponges Place a thin, dry slice of a natural sponge under a microscope, and allow students to examine the spongin-fiber network. Next, add a few drops of water to the sponge, and have students examine the slice again. Students should be able to see clearly how the water is taken up by the fibers (the fibers will swell slightly) as well as into the spaces between the fibers.

Sheltered English

Porifera's Porosity

Sponges

Sponges are the simplest animals. They have no symmetry, no head or nerves, and no gut. Although sponges can move, they are so slow that their movement is very difficult to see. In fact, sponges were once thought to be plants. But sponges cannot make their own food and must eat other organisms. That's one reason they are classified as animals.

Kinds of Sponges All sponges live in water, and most are found in the ocean. As shown in **Figure 3,** they come in beautiful colors and a variety of shapes.

Most sponges have a skeleton made of needlelike splinters called *spicules,* as shown in **Figure 4.** Spicules come in many shapes, from simple, straight needles to curved rods and complex star shapes. The skeleton supports the body of the sponge and helps protect it from predators.

Sponges are divided into classes according to the type of spicules they have. The largest class of sponges contain spicules made of silicate, the material we use to make glass. Bath sponges are similar to silica sponges, but they lack spicules. Instead of spicules, they have a skeleton made of a protein called *spongin.* That is why they are soft. Another group of sponges have spicules made of calcium carbonate, the material that makes up the shells of shellfish.

Re-form and Replace If a sponge's body is broken apart by being forced through a sieve, the separate cells will come back together and re-form the same sponge. In addition, new sponges can form from pieces broken off another sponge. Unlike most animals, a sponge can also replace its body parts, or *regenerate.*

Giant barrel sponge

Tube sponge

Figure 3 *Sponges come in a variety of shapes, sizes, and colors.*

Figure 4 *This is the skeleton of a glass sponge.*

WEIRD SCIENCE

Nearly all sponges are sessile—they live attached to a surface and cannot move from place to place. *Tethya seychellensis,* which lives in the Red Sea, is an exception. Young sponges of this species can move very slowly—about 10 to 15 mm a day—by extending long, sticky projections from their body wall. The projections attach to the substrate and then contract, pulling the sponge forward.

How Do Sponges Eat? Sponges belong to the phylum Porifera. The name refers to the thousands of holes, or *pores*, on the outside of sponges. The sponge sweeps water into its body through these pores. Inside the body, cells called *collar cells* filter food particles and microorganisms from the water. The rest of the water flows into a central cavity and out a hole at the top of the sponge, like smoke going up a chimney. The hole at the top is called the *osculum*. **Figure 5** shows this process.

Sponges don't have a gut. Instead, each collar cell digests its own particles of food. No other animal has anything like collar cells.

Collar cells line the central cavity of a sponge. Each collar cell filters particles of food from the water and digests them.

Pore cells are used to pump water into a sponge.

Osculum

Water flow

Pores

Figure 5 *A sponge filters particles of food from water using collar cells and then pumps the water out the osculum. A sponge can filter up to 22 L of water a day.*

REVIEW

1. Why are collar cells important in classifying sponges as animals?
2. What is a coelom?
3. **Interpreting Graphics** Does the animal shown at right have radial symmetry, bilateral symmetry, or no symmetry? Explain your answer.

2 Teach, continued

READING STRATEGY

Mnemonics Write the words *medusa* and *polyp* on the chalkboard. Point out that *medusa* contains the letter **d** and that the medusa form of a cnidarian has tentacles that hang **d**own from the animal's body. By the same token, the word *polyp* contains the letter **p**, and the polyp form of a cnidarian has tentacles that project **up** from the animal's body. Tell students they can use this letter association to remember the different body forms.

GUIDED PRACTICE

Writing Have students research the jellyfish *Aurelia*. Then have students write a story about an *Aurelia* jellyfish in which they describe the jellyfish's life cycle, how it moves, what it eats, and how it senses its environment.

ACTIVITY

Observing Hydras Obtain live hydras and water fleas *(Daphnia)* from a biological supply house. Distribute the hydras in water-filled specimen dishes, and have students work in pairs to study the hydras under a dissecting microscope. Then add several water fleas to the water in each specimen dish, and have students observe how hydras use their nematocyst-equipped tentacles to capture and subdue prey. Encourage students to make drawings of the hydras and to record their observations about how hydras move and manipulate captured prey into their mouths. **Sheltered English**

Jellyfish

Hydra

Figure 6 *These three organisms are cnidarians. Why are they in the same phylum?*

Sea anemone

Cnidarians

Take a look at the organisms shown in **Figure 6**. They look very different, but all of these animals belong to the phylum Cnidaria (ni DER ee uh).

The word *cnidaria* comes from the Greek word for "nettle." Nettles are plants that release stinging barbs into the skin. Cnidarians do the same. All cnidarians have stinging cells. Do you know anyone who has been stung by a jellyfish? It is a very painful experience!

Cnidarians are more complex than sponges. Cnidarians have complex tissues, a gut for digesting food, and a nervous system. However, some species of cnidarians do share a characteristic with sponges. If the cells of the body are separated, they can come back together to form the cnidarian.

The Medusa and the Polyp Cnidarians come in two forms, the medusa and the polyp. They are shown in **Figure 7**. The *medusa* looks like a mushroom with tentacles streaming down from below. A well-known medusa is the jellyfish. As a medusa's body, or bell, contracts and relaxes, the medusa swims through the water.

The other cnidarian body form is the *polyp*. Polyps are shaped like vases and usually live attached to a surface.

Some cnidarians are polyps and medusas at different times in their life. But most cnidarians spend their life as a polyp.

Figure 7 *Both the medusa and the polyp have radial symmetry. Can you see why?*

WEIRD SCIENCE

The tentacles of some cnidarians are capable of stinging even if they are detached from the main body or after the animal itself is dead. *Physalia*, the Portuguese man-of-war, is a colonial cnidarian that frequently washes ashore along temperate and tropical beaches. Barefoot beachgoers who happen to step on these stranded cnidarians quickly discover that the stinging cells can still deliver a painful sting, even if the animals themselves have been dead for several days.

Kinds of Cnidarians There are three classes of cnidarians: hydras, jellyfish, and sea anemones and corals. Hydras are common cnidarians that live in fresh water. They spend their entire life in the polyp form. Jellyfish spend most of their life as a medusa.

Sea anemones and corals are polyps all their life. They look like brightly colored flowers. Corals are tiny cnidarians that live in colonies. These colonies build huge skeletons of calcium carbonate. Each new generation of corals builds on top of the last generation. Over thousands of years, these tiny animals build massive underwater reefs. Coral reefs can be found in warm tropical waters throughout the world.

Catching Lunch All cnidarians have long tentacles covered with special stinging cells. When a small fish or other organism brushes against the tentacles of a cnidarian, hundreds of stinging cells fire into the organism and release a paralyzing toxin. Each stinging cell uses water pressure to fire a tiny barbed spear called a *nematocyst* (ne MA toh sist). **Figure 8** shows a nematocyst before and after firing.

Environment CONNECTION

Coral reefs, some of which are more than 2.5 million years old, are home to one-fourth of all marine fish species. Unfortunately, living coral reefs are threatened by overfishing, pollution, mining, and accidental damage from swimmers and boats. Scientists are now looking for ways to help protect coral reefs.

Figure 8 *Each stinging cell contains a nematocyst.*

Before firing Coiled inside each stinging cell is a tiny barbed harpoon.

After firing When the nematocyst is fired, the long barbed strand ejects into the water. Larger barbs also cover the base of the strand.

You've Got Some Nerve Cnidarians have a simple network of nerve cells called a *nerve net*. The nerve net controls the movements of the body and the tentacles.

A medusa has a *nerve ring* in the center of its nerve net. This ring of nerve cells coordinates the swimming of a jellyfish in the same way that our spinal cord coordinates walking. The nerve ring is not a brain, however. Cnidarians do not think or plan in the way that more-complex animals do.

✓ Self-Check

Medusas have a nerve ring, but polyps do not. How does the way medusas move explain their more complex nervous system? *(See page 782 to check your answer.)*

Answer to Self-Check

Because medusas swim through the water by contracting their bodies, they must have a nervous system that can control these actions. Polyps move very little, so they don't need as complex a nervous system.

DEMONSTRATION

Stinging Cells After students have studied **Figure 8**, perform the following demonstration. Invert the fingers of a rubber glove, and use duct tape to attach the top of the glove securely to the head of a water faucet. Tell students that the inverted fingers of the glove represent nematocysts coiled within stinging cells. Scientists have discovered that nematocysts "fire" as a result of a sudden change in water pressure inside stinging cells. When a nematocyst is stimulated to discharge, the nematocyst membrane becomes highly permeable to water. As water rushes in, the sudden increase in water pressure pushes the nematocyst out with explosive force, turning it inside out in the process. Demonstrate this phenomenon by briefly turning on the faucet. The sudden pressure increase will cause the inverted fingers of the rubber glove to evert quickly and forcefully.
Sheltered English

BRAIN FOOD

Many jellyfish that capture and eat small fish have transparent or nearly transparent bodies and long, trailing tentacles that are very difficult to see in the water. Ask students to speculate about how these features are an advantage to jellyfish as predators.

Section 1 • Simple Invertebrates

3) Extend

REAL-WORLD CONNECTION

Schistosomiasis is an infectious disease caused by blood flukes of the genus *Schistosoma*. About 200 million people are afflicted by schistosomiasis worldwide, primarily in Africa, Latin America, tropical Asia, and the Middle East. Encourage students to research the *Schistosoma* blood fluke and, as a class, to create a bulletin-board display in which they describe and illustrate the fluke's complex life cycle, the symptoms of the disease, and steps that can be taken to reduce the chance of infection.

MISCONCEPTION ALERT

Students may think that tapeworm infections are relatively rare among people living in developed countries. Even in the United States, however, tapeworms from pigs and cattle can infect humans. Researchers estimate that about 1 percent of American cattle are infected with beef tapeworm. About 20 percent of all beef consumed in the United States is not federally inspected; lightly infected beef is frequently missed during inspections. As a result, if a person eats rare roast beef, hamburgers, or steaks, the chance of becoming infected with beef tapeworm is significant.

Critical Thinking Worksheet 15
"A New Form of Danger in the Deep"

Flatworms

When you think of worms, you probably think of earthworms. But there are many other types of worms, and most of them are too tiny to see. The simplest group of worms are the flatworms.

Look at the flatworm shown in **Figure 9.** Unlike the invertebrates you have studied so far, flatworms have bilateral symmetry. Most flatworms also have a clearly defined head and two large, unblinking eyespots. Even though the eyespots cannot focus, a flatworm knows the direction that light is coming from. A flatworm also has two bumps on each side of its head. These are *sensory lobes* and are used for detecting food.

Figure 9 *This flatworm is called a planarian. It has a head with eyespots and sensory lobes.*

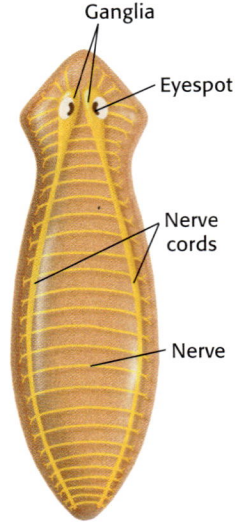

Planarians Flatworms are divided into three classes. The big-eyed flatworms we have been discussing are called *planarians*. Most of these flatworms are small; their length is less than the length of a fingernail. They live in water and on land. Most planarians are predators. They eat other animals or parts of other animals and digest food in their gut. The planarian's head, eyespots, and sensory lobes are clues that it has a brain for processing information. **Figure 10** shows a diagram of the nervous system of a planarian.

Flukes and Tapeworms The two other groups of flatworms are *flukes* and *tapeworms*. A fluke is shown in **Figure 11.** These animals are parasites. A *parasite* is an organism that feeds on another living creature, called the *host*. The host is usually not killed. Most flukes and all tapeworms find their way inside the bodies of other animals, where they live and reproduce. Fertilized eggs pass out of the host's body with the body's waste. If these fertilized eggs end up in drinking water or on food, they can be eaten by another host, where they will develop into a new fluke or tapeworm.

Figure 10 *The nervous system of a flatworm has nerves connecting two parallel nerve cords. Ganglia make up a primitive brain.*

Figure 11 *Flukes use suckers to attach to their host.*

Homework

Writing Have students research the life cycle of the roundworm parasite *Trichinella spiralis* and write a persuasive paragraph in their ScienceLog on the importance of cooking pork thoroughly to prevent contracting trichinosis.

IS THAT A FACT!

The adult broad-fish tapeworm, which can infect humans, grows 10 to 20 m in length and may consist of 3,000 to 4,000 sections. A mature fish tapeworm can shed a million eggs a day.

Flukes and tapeworms have tiny heads without eyespots or sensory lobes. They have special suckers and hooks for attaching to the host. Those flatworms that live inside the gut of their host have special skin that resists digestion by the stomach enzymes of the host. Tapeworms are so specialized that they have no gut at all. These creatures simply absorb nutrients from the intestines of their host. **Figure 12** shows a tapeworm that can infect humans.

Roundworms

Roundworms, or nematodes, are round when viewed in cross section and are long and slender. Like other worms, they have bilateral symmetry. Most species of roundworms are tiny. A single rotten apple lying on the ground in an orchard could contain 100,000 roundworms. These tiny creatures break down the dead tissues of plants and animals and help build rich soils. **Figure 13** shows a roundworm.

Roundworms have a simple nervous system. A ring of ganglia forms a primitive brain, and parallel nerve cords run the length of their body.

Most roundworms are parasites. Roundworms that infect humans include pinworms and hookworms. Another roundworm is passed from infected pork to humans and causes trichinosis (TRIK i NOH sis), a severe illness. Cooking pork thoroughly will kill the roundworms.

Figure 12 Tapeworms can reach enormous sizes. Some can grow longer than a school bus!

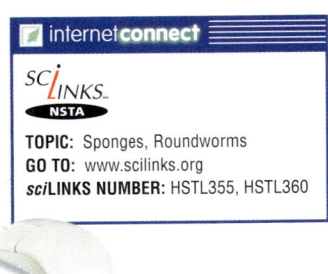

Figure 13 Roundworms have a fluid-filled body cavity.

REVIEW

1. What characteristic gives cnidarians their name?
2. What are two characteristics of flatworms that make them different from cnidarians?
3. **Analyzing Relationships** Both predators and parasites live off the tissues of other animals. Explain the difference between a predator and a parasite.

TOPIC: Sponges, Roundworms
GO TO: www.scilinks.org
sciLINKS NUMBER: HSTL355, HSTL360

Answers to Review

1. stinging cells
2. Flatworms have bilateral symmetry, and they have ganglia (and a brain). Cnidarians do not.
3. Both feed on other living organisms, but a predator kills its prey (or feeds on dead prey), and a parasite feeds on a host, usually without killing it.

SECTION 2

Focus

Mollusks and Annelid Worms

In this section, students are introduced to three major classes of the phylum Mollusca—gastropods, bivalves, and cephalopods. Students learn about the main parts of a mollusk's soft body, the way they feed, and the diversity in their circulatory and nervous systems. They will also explore annelid worms, including earthworms, bristle worms, and leeches.

Bellringer

Have students unscramble the following words, and write a sentence using them in their ScienceLog:

gluss (slugs)

isalns (snails)

sdusqi (squids)

klomssul (mollusks)

(Slugs, snails, and squids are all mollusks.)

1 Motivate

GROUP ACTIVITY

 Divide students into cooperative groups of four or five. Challenge each group to investigate how people in different countries use mollusks for food. Students can look for recipes on how to prepare and serve snails, clams, squids, and other mollusks. Ask each group to create a menu consisting of an appetizer and a main dish in which mollusks are the primary ingredient.

Answer to MATHBREAK

$\frac{30 \text{ km/h}}{60 \text{ min/h}} = 0.5 \text{ km/min}$

352 Chapter 15 • Invertebrates

Section 2

Terms to Learn

open circulatory system
closed circulatory system
segment

What You'll Do

- Describe the body parts of a mollusk.
- Explain the difference between an open circulatory system and a closed circulatory system.
- Describe segmentation.

Mollusks and Annelid Worms

Have you ever eaten clam chowder or calamari? Have you ever seen worms on the sidewalk after it rains? If you have, then you have encountered the invertebrates discussed in this section—mollusks and annelid worms. These invertebrates are more complex than the invertebrates you have read about so far. Mollusks and annelid worms have a coelom and a circulatory system. And they have more-complex nervous systems than those of the flatworms and roundworms.

Earthworm

Mollusks

The phylum Mollusca includes snails, slugs, clams, oysters, squids, and octopuses. The mollusks are the second largest phylum of animals. Most mollusks are in three classes: *gastropods* (slugs and snails), *bivalves* (clams and other two-shelled shellfish), and *cephalopods* (squids and octopuses). **Figure 14** shows some of the variety of mollusks.

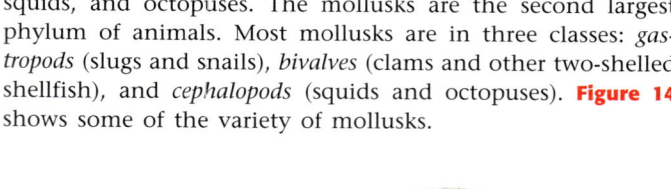

Snails

Squid

Clam

Figure 14 *A snail, a squid, and a clam are all mollusks. Snails are gastropods; squids are cephalopods; and clams are bivalves.*

MATH BREAK

Speeding Squid

If a squid is swimming at 30 km/h, how far can it go in 1 minute?

Most mollusks live in the ocean, but some live in freshwater habitats. Other mollusks, such as slugs and snails, have adapted to life on land.

Mollusks range in size from 1 mm long snails to the giant squid, which can reach up to 18 m in length. Most mollusks move slowly, but some squids can swim up to 40 km/h and leap more than 4 m above the water.

 SCIENCE

The blue-ringed octopus, found in the waters of the South Pacific, is deadly. When it is provoked, the blue rings on its skin turn so blue that they almost glow. The saliva in its bite contains a powerful toxin for which there is no known antidote! This toxin paralyzes the victim and shuts down all its life systems. If a person bitten by this octopus arrives at the hospital in time, he or she is put on a respirator for a few days until the toxin wears off.

How Do You Know a Mollusk When You See One? A snail, a clam, and a squid look quite different from one another. Yet on closer inspection, the bodies of all mollusks are almost the same. The body parts shared by mollusks are described in **Figure 15.**

Figure 15 *A mollusk has a soft body, usually covered by a shell. All mollusks also have a foot, a visceral mass, and a mantle.*

KEY
- Foot
- Visceral mass
- Mantle
- Shell

Clam   Squid   Snail

Foot The most obvious feature of a mollusk is a broad, muscular foot. A mollusk uses its foot to move. In gastropods, the foot secretes mucus that it slides along.

Visceral mass The visceral (VIS uhr uhl) mass contains the gills, gut, and other organs. It is located in a mollusk's coelom.

Mantle The visceral mass is covered by a layer of tissue called the mantle. The mantle protects the body of mollusks that do not have a shell.

Shell In most mollusks, the outside of the mantle secretes a shell. The shell protects the mollusk from predators and keeps land mollusks from drying out.

How Do Mollusks Eat? Each type of mollusk has its own way of eating. Clams and other bivalves sit in one place and filter tiny plants, bacteria, and other particles from the water around them. Snails and slugs eat with a ribbonlike tongue covered with curved teeth, called a *radula* (RAJ oo luh). **Figure 16** shows a close-up of a slug's radula. Slugs and snails use the radula to scrape algae off rocks, chunks of tissue from seaweed, or pieces from the leaves of plants. Predatory snails and slugs often have large teeth on their radula that they use to attack their prey. And parasitic snails pierce their victims much as a mosquito does. Octopuses and squids use tentacles to grab their prey and place it in their powerful jaws, just as we can use our fingers to eat.

Figure 16 *The rows of teeth on a slug's radula help to scrape food from surfaces.*

Science Bloopers

Nearly 30 cm long, the giant African snail, *Achatina fulica*, is native to east Africa, where it eats decaying vegetation. When these African snails were introduced to many Pacific islands, they munched crops instead and quickly became agricultural pests. In a misguided attempt to solve that problem, several kinds of predatory snails were released on the islands in the hope that they would kill off the African snails. Unfortunately, the predatory snails ignored the African snails and ate the islands' native snail species, some of which are now nearly extinct.

2) Teach

Multicultural CONNECTION

Giant clams live on coral reefs in warm tropical waters of the Pacific Ocean. They have long been a staple in the diet of many Pacific islanders and are a delicacy in many Asian countries. During the past 20 years, however, giant clams have been threatened with extinction due to overfishing. Scientists from Australia, Japan, Indonesia, and several other countries have been working to restore giant clam populations by raising thousands of these mollusks on giant clam "farms" along protected coasts. When farmed clams are large enough to be safe from predators, they are transplanted to coral reefs. As a result of these efforts, giant clams are once again common around many Pacific islands.

BRAIN FOOD

Giant clams as well as most corals contain mutualistic algae in their tissues. These photosynthetic algae, known as zooxanthellae, produce food for themselves and their hosts. In return, giant clams and corals provide the algae with a safe place to live. Ask students to hypothesize why giant clams and corals that contain zooxanthellae are found only in clear, relatively shallow ocean waters. (Clear, shallow water allows sunlight to reach the algae.)

Directed Reading Worksheet 15 Section 2

Section 2 • Mollusks and Annelid Worms

2) Teach, continued

MEETING INDIVIDUAL NEEDS

Learners Having Difficulty
Visual learners and students with limited English proficiency may have trouble understanding the difference between closed and open circulatory systems. Distribute copies of illustrations showing the closed circulatory system in a human and the open circulatory system in a clam. (A college-level biology textbook is a good source for illustrations of the clam circulatory system.) Encourage students to trace the path that blood takes in a clam. Call attention to the blood sinuses in the clam's body, and tell students that these irregular channels and spaces in the clam's tissues are filled and drained by blood vessels. Contrast this situation with the human circulatory system, in which blood is completely contained in vessels throughout the body. **Sheltered English**

COOPERATIVE LEARNING

Writing Have students work in pairs to research how cephalopods have been used in experimental studies of behavior and nerve function. Students may present their research in the form of a written report or as an oral interview, with one student acting as a magazine reporter who is gathering information for an article and the other student playing the role of a research scientist who has conducted experiments on cephalopods.

internetconnect
TOPIC: Mollusks and Annelid Worms
GO TO: www.scilinks.org
sciLINKS NUMBER: HSTL365

BRAIN FOOD

An octopus has three hearts! Two of them are near the gills and are called *gill hearts*.

Have a Heart Unlike simpler invertebrates, mollusks have a circulatory system. Most mollusks have an **open circulatory system.** In this system, a simple heart pumps blood through blood vessels that empty into spaces in the animal's body called *sinuses*. This is very different from our own circulatory system, which is a **closed circulatory system.** In a closed circulatory system, a heart circulates blood through a network of blood vessels that form a closed loop. Cephalopods (squids and octopuses) also have a closed circulatory system, although it is much simpler than ours.

It's a Brain! Mollusks have complex ganglia. In most mollusks, these ganglia occur throughout the body. Mollusks have ganglia that control breathing, ganglia that move the foot, and ganglia that control digestion.

Cephalopods, like the one in **Figure 17,** have a more complex nervous system than the other mollusks have. In fact, octopuses and squids have the most advanced nervous system of all invertebrates. They have a brain, where all of their ganglia are connected. Not surprisingly, these animals are the smartest of all invertebrates. Octopuses, for example, can learn to navigate a maze and can distinguish between different shapes and colors. If they are given bricks or stones, they will build a cave to hide in.

Figure 17 An octopus has a large brain. The brain coordinates the movement of its eight long arms.

REVIEW

1. What are the four main parts of a mollusk's body?
2. What is the difference between an open circulatory system and a closed circulatory system?
3. **Analyzing Relationships** What two features do cephalopods share with humans that other mollusks do not?

▼ **Answers to Review**
1. foot, visceral mass, mantle, and shell
2. In an open circulatory system, the heart pumps blood through vessels into sinuses. In a closed circulatory system, the blood is pumped through a closed network of vessels.
3. Like humans, cephalopods have a closed circulatory system and a brain.

Annelid Worms

You have probably seen earthworms, like the one in **Figure 18**. Earthworms belong to the phylum Annelida. Annelid worms are often called segmented worms because their body has segments. **Segments** are identical, or almost identical, repeating body parts.

These worms are much more complex than flatworms and roundworms. Annelid worms have a coelom and a closed circulatory system. They also have a nervous system that includes ganglia in each segment and a brain in the head. A nerve cord connects the brain and the ganglia.

Kinds of Annelid Worms The annelid worms include three classes: earthworms, bristle worms, and leeches. Annelid worms live in salt water, in fresh water, or on land. They may scavenge anything edible, or they may prey on other organisms as predators or as parasites.

More than Just Bait Earthworms are the most common annelid worms. An earthworm has 100 to 175 segments, most of which are identical. Some segments are specialized for eating and reproduction. Earthworms eat soil. They break down organic matter in the soil and excrete wastes called *castings*. Castings provide nutrients that plants can use. Earthworms also improve the soil by burrowing tunnels, which allow air and water to reach deep into the soil.

Earthworms have stiff bristles on the outside of their body to help them move. The bristles hold one part of the worm in place while the other part pushes through the soil.

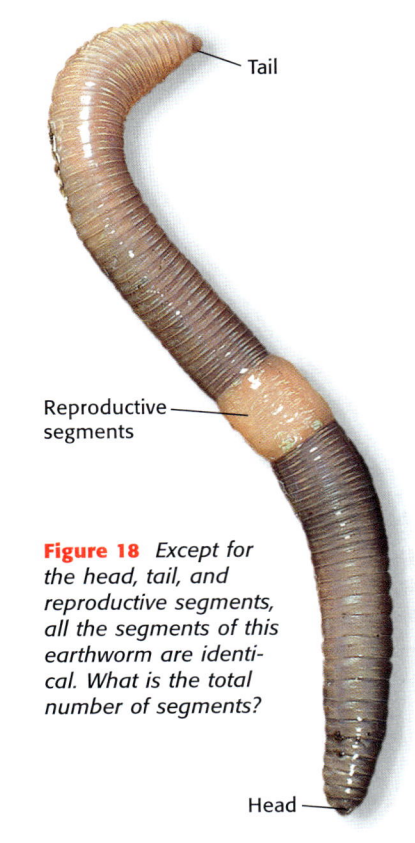

Figure 18 Except for the head, tail, and reproductive segments, all the segments of this earthworm are identical. What is the total number of segments?

Do Worms Make Good Neighbors?

A friend of yours is worried because his garden is full of earthworms. He wants to find a way to get rid of the worms. Do you think this is a good idea? Why? Write a letter to your friend explaining what you think he should do.

SCIENCE HUMOR

Q: What is worse than biting into an apple and finding a worm?

A: biting into an apple and finding half a worm

IS THAT A FACT!

The large fleshy lobe to the right of the octopus's eyes in **Figure 17** is not the head. It contains the visceral mass.

Section 2 • Mollusks and Annelid Worms

Figure 19 This bristle worm feeds by filtering particles from the water with its bristles. Can you see the segments on this worm?

Bristles Can Be Beautiful If there were a beauty contest for worms, bristle worms would win. These remarkable worms come in many varieties and in brilliant colors. **Figure 19** shows a bristle worm. All bristle worms live in water. Some burrow through soggy sand and mud, eating whatever small creatures and particles they meet. Others crawl along the bottom, eating mollusks and other small animals.

Blood Suckers and More Leeches are known mostly as parasites that suck other animals' blood. This is true of some leeches, but not all. Other leeches are scavengers that eat dead animals. Still others are predators that prey on insects, slugs, and snails. Leeches that are parasites feed on the blood of other animals.

But leeches aren't all bad. Until the twentieth century, doctors regularly used leeches in medical treatments. Doctors attached leeches to a sick person to drain "bad" blood from the body. Although this practice is not accepted today, leeches are still used in medicine. After surgery, doctors sometimes use leeches to prevent dangerous swelling near a wound, as shown in **Figure 20**. Leeches also make a chemical that keeps blood from forming clots. Modern doctors give heart attack patients medicines that contain this chemical to keep blood clots from blocking arteries.

Figure 20 Modern doctors sometimes use leeches to reduce swelling after surgery.

internetconnect

SC_i_**LINKS**_._
NSTA

TOPIC: Mollusks and Annelid Worms
GO TO: www.scilinks.org
sciLINKS NUMBER: HSTL365

REVIEW

1. Name the three types of annelid worms. How are they alike? How are they different?
2. **Making Inferences** Why would a chemical that keeps blood from clotting be beneficial to leeches?
3. **Analyzing Relationships** How are annelid worms different from flatworms and roundworms? What characteristics do all worms share?

Section 3

Arthropods

Terms to Learn
- exoskeleton
- compound eye
- antennae
- mandible
- metamorphosis

What You'll Do
- List the four main characteristics of arthropods.
- Describe the different body parts of the four kinds of arthropods.
- Explain the two types of metamorphosis in insects.

Fiddler crab

They have lived here for hundreds of millions of years and have adapted to nearly all environments. An acre of land contains millions of them. You know them by more common names, such as insects, spiders, crabs, and centipedes. They are *arthropods*, the largest group of animals on Earth.

Seventy-five percent of all animal species are arthropods. The world population of humans is about 6 billion. Biologists estimate the world population of arthropods to be about a billion billion.

Characteristics of Arthropods

All arthropods share four characteristics: jointed limbs, a segmented body with specialized parts, an exoskeleton, and a well-developed nervous system.

Jointed Limbs Jointed limbs give arthropods their name. *Arthro* means "joint," and *pod* means "foot." Jointed limbs are arms, legs, or other similar body parts that bend at joints. Jointed limbs allow arthropods to move easily.

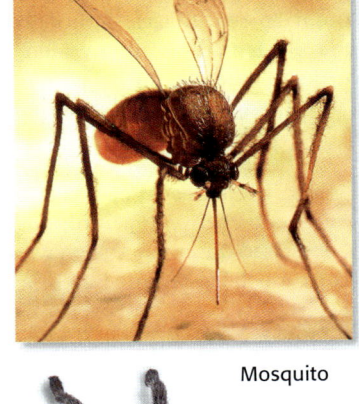
Mosquito

Segmented and Specialized Like annelid worms, arthropods are *segmented*. In some arthropods, such as the centipedes, nearly every segment is identical. Only the segments at the head and tail are different from the rest. Most other species of arthropods have segments that include very specialized parts, such as wings, antennae, gills, pincers, and claws. Many of these special parts form during the animal's development, when two or three segments grow together to form a *head*, a *thorax*, and an *abdomen*. These parts are labeled on the grasshopper pictured in **Figure 21.**

Tarantula

Figure 21 *The segments of this grasshopper fused together as the embryo grew to form a head, a thorax, and an abdomen.*

WEIRD SCIENCE

Mantis shrimp have powerful forelegs. They use them to smash the shells of prey such as snails and crabs. This "smasher" can deliver a blow with a force equal to that of a small-caliber bullet, which is enough to break through a glass tank!

Directed Reading Worksheet 15 Section 3

② Teach

MATH and MORE

The compound eyes of insects are made up of tiny bundles of light-sensitive cells called ommatidia (singular: ommatidium). The huge eyes of dragonflies contain about 28,000 ommatidia. The eyes of butterflies contain around 14,000, while those of houseflies have about 4,000. Ask students to calculate roughly how many times more ommatidia dragonflies have than butterflies or houseflies. **(Dragonflies have roughly twice as many ommatidia as butterflies and seven times as many as houseflies.)**

Then ask students to speculate on the relationship between the number of ommatidia and the ways these three types of arthropods get food. **(Possible answer: Dragonflies are fast-flying predators and need acute vision to spot potential prey and maneuver at high speeds; many butterflies feed on flowers and must distinguish between flower types (shapes and color); houseflies rely more on odor detection than vision to find their food, which often consists of dead or stationary organisms.)**

 Math Skills Worksheet 5 "Dividing Whole Numbers with Long Division"

 Math Skills Worksheet 6 "Checking Division with Multiplication"

Figure 22 *Compound eyes consist of many individual light-sensitive cells that work together.*

Knights in Shining . . . Chitin? Arthropods have a hard **exoskeleton,** an external skeleton made of protein and a special substance called *chitin* (KIE tin). The exoskeleton does some of the same things an internal skeleton does. It provides a stiff frame that supports the animal's body. The exoskeleton also allows the animal to move. All of the muscles attach to different parts of the skeleton. When the muscles contract, they move the exoskeleton, which moves the parts of the animal.

But the exoskeleton also does things that internal skeletons don't do well. The exoskeleton acts like a suit of armor to protect internal organs and muscles. It also allows arthropods to live on land without drying out.

They've Got Smarts All arthropods have a head and a well-developed brain. The brain coordinates information from many sense organs, including eyes and bristles on the exoskeleton. Bristles sense movement, vibration, pressure, and chemicals. The eyes of some arthropods are very simple; they can detect light but cannot form an image. But most arthropods have compound eyes, which allow them to see images, although not as well as we do. A **compound eye** is made of many identical light-sensitive cells, as shown in **Figure 22.**

Kinds of Arthropods

Arthropods are classified according to the kinds of body parts they have. You can also tell the difference between arthropods by looking at the number of legs, eyes, and antennae they have. **Antennae** are feelers that respond to touch, taste, and smell.

Centipedes and Millipedes Centipedes and millipedes have a single pair of antennae, jaws called **mandibles,** and a hard *head capsule*. The easiest way to tell a centipede from a millipede is to count the number of legs per segment. Centipedes have one pair of legs per segment. Millipedes have two pairs of legs per segment. Take a look at **Figure 23.** How many legs can you count?

Figure 23 *Centipedes have one pair of legs per segment. The number of legs can range from 30 to 354. Millipedes have two pairs of legs per segment. The record number of legs on a millipede is 752!*

WEIRD SCIENCE

Did you know that compass termites from the outback of Australia are able to air-condition their mounds? Their towers are up to 2.5 m long and 3 m high but are very narrow and tall. As many as 2 million termites may be living inside. When the nest becomes too hot, worker termites rush to open a valve made of dried mud at the top of the mound. Cooler air enters the nest and sinks to the bottom of the tower. By opening and closing the mud valve in their nest, the termites have complete control over the temperature of their mound!

Crustaceans Crustaceans include shrimps, barnacles, crabs, and lobsters. Nearly all crustaceans are aquatic and have *gills* for breathing underwater. All crustaceans have mandibles and two pairs of antennae. Crustaceans have two compound eyes, usually on the end of stalks. The lobster in **Figure 24** shows all of these traits. The double antennae of crustaceans set them apart from all other arthropods.

Self-Check

What is the difference between a segmented worm and a centipede? (See page 782 to check your answer.)

Figure 24 *A lobster is a crustacean. It has compound eyes on the end of eye stalks.*

Arachnids Spiders, scorpions, mites, ticks, and daddy longlegs are all arachnids. **Figure 25** shows that an arachnid has two main body parts, the cephalothorax (SEF uh loh THOR aks) and the abdomen. The *cephalothorax* consists of both a head and a thorax and usually has four pairs of walking legs. Arachnids have no antennae and no mandibles. Instead of mandibles, they have special mouthparts called *chelicerae* (kuh LIS uh ree), as illustrated in Figure 25. Some chelicerae look like pincers or fangs.

The eyes of arachnids are distinctive. While crustaceans and insects have compound eyes, arachnids do not. Spiders, for example, have eight simple eyes arranged in two rows at the front of the head. Count the eyes for yourself in **Figure 26**.

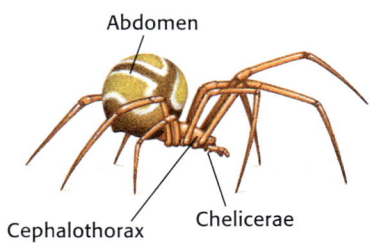

Figure 25 *Arachnids have two main body parts and special mouthparts called chelicerae.*

Figure 26 *In addition to eight legs, spiders have eight eyes!*

CONNECT TO CHEMISTRY

Chitin is a strong, flexible, waterproof polysaccharide (a polymer of glucose). Chitin molecules bond readily with proteins, such as those found in the exoskeletons of arthropods. A Japanese textile and fiber manufacturing company has exploited chitin's unique chemical properties to create chitin sutures for surgery and chitin-based artificial skin. Chitin sutures don't have to be removed because they dissolve in the body; they also bind so well with proteins that they may promote healing.

Section 3 • Arthropods **359**

② Teach, continued

Trapdoor spiders construct silk-lined burrows topped with a hinged lid that acts like a trapdoor. They lurk beneath the door, waiting for isopods, crickets, or other prey to pass by, then they bound up from below with remarkable speed. If the trapdoor is disturbed, the spiders pull their burrow doors shut with their chelicerae. Using a small spring scale, researchers have found that a trapdoor spider can exert an inward pull on its trapdoor that is 140 times its body weight. Calculate what your pulling strength would be if you could exert a force 140 times your weight.

(Example: 40 kg student × 140 = pulling strength of 5,600 kg)

MATERIALS

FOR EACH STUDENT:
- tape
- cooking oil

Answers to QuickLab

Fingers will not stick to tape when they have oil on them. Spiders secrete an oily substance in their legs that keeps them from sticking to their webs.

Figure 27 American Dog Tick

QuickLab

Sticky Webs

Some spiders spin webs of sticky silk to trap their prey. Why don't spiders stick to their own webs? This experiment will show you the answer. Place a piece of **tape** on your desk sticky side up. The tape represents a web. Your fingers will represent an insect. Holding the tape in place by the edges, "walk" your fingers across the tape. What happens? Dip your fingers in **cooking oil**, and "walk" them across the tape again. What happens this time? Why? How might this experiment explain why spiders don't get stuck in their webs?

360

internet connect

TOPIC: Arthropods
GO TO: www.scilinks.org
sciLINKS NUMBER: HSTL370

Spiders and Ticks Spiders do not carry diseases and are enormously useful to humans. They kill more insect pests than any other animal, including birds. Several arachnids have painful bites or stings. But the fangs of small garden spiders cannot pierce human skin. In the United States, just three species of spiders—the black widow and two species of brown spider—have bites poisonous enough to kill a person. However, with proper medical treatment, they are not fatal.

Ticks live in forests, brushy areas, and even country lawns. **Figure 27** shows an American dog tick. Ticks that bite humans sometimes carry Lyme disease, Rocky Mountain spotted fever, and other diseases. Many people wear long pants and hats when going into areas where ticks live, and they check themselves for ticks after being outdoors. Fortunately, most people who are bitten by ticks do not get sick.

Insects The largest group of arthropods is insects. If you put all of the insects in the world together, they would weigh more than all other animals combined! **Figure 28** shows some of the wide variety of insects.

Figure 28 These are a few of the many varieties of insects. Can you see what they have in common?

Atlas silk moth

Bumblebee

Praying mantis

Dragonfly

IS THAT A FACT!

The hind legs of the human flea, *Pulex irritans*, are especially adapted for jumping. How high can a flea jump? *Pulex* can leap 33 cm horizontally and 20 cm vertically—that's equal to an 85 m high jump for a human!

Chapter 15 • Invertebrates

Insects Are Everywhere (Almost) Insects live on land, in every freshwater environment, and at the edges of the sea. The only place on Earth insects do not live is in the ocean.

Many insects are beneficial. Most flowering plants depend on bees, butterflies, and other insects to carry pollen from one plant to another. Farmers depend on insects to pollinate hundreds of fruit crops, such as apples, cherries, tomatoes, and pumpkins.

Many insects are also pests. Fleas, lice, mosquitoes, and flies burrow into our flesh, suck our blood, or carry diseases. Plant-eating insects consume up to one-third of crops in this country, despite the application of pesticides.

Insect Bodies An insect's body has three parts: the head, the thorax, and the abdomen, as shown in **Figure 29.** On the head, insects have one pair of antennae and two compound eyes. They also have three pairs of mouthparts, including one pair of mandibles. The thorax is made of three segments, each with one pair of legs.

In many insects, the second and third segments of the thorax have a pair of wings. Some insects have no wings, and some have two pairs of wings.

Insect Development As an insect develops from an egg to an adult, it changes form. This process is called **metamorphosis.** There are two main types of metamorphosis, incomplete and complete. Primitive insects, such as grasshoppers and cockroaches, go through incomplete metamorphosis. In this metamorphosis there are only three stages: egg, nymph, and adult, as shown in **Figure 30.**

A cockroach can live for a week without its head! It finally dies of thirst because it has no mouth to drink water with.

Figure 29 *Wasps have the same body parts as all other insects.*

Head
Thorax
Abdomen

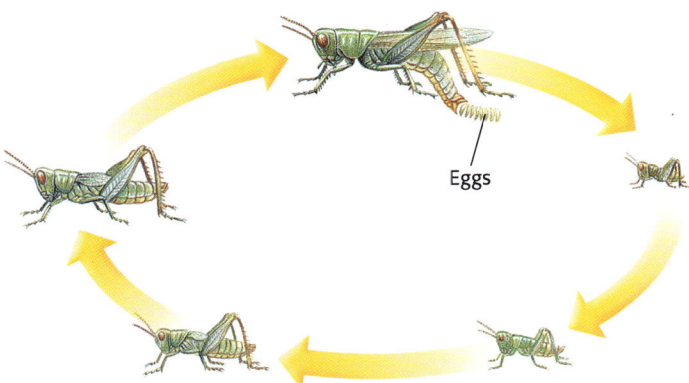

Eggs

Figure 30 *In incomplete metamorphosis, the larvae, called nymphs, look like smaller adults.*

Does a cricket like cold climates? Find out on page 737 of your LabBook.

3) Extend

ACTIVITY

Poster Project Insecticides are routinely sprayed on lawns and gardens to kill insect pests. Unfortunately, these chemicals also kill many beneficial insects, persist in the environment, and accumulate in the bodies of animals (including people) higher up the food chain. In recent years, a variety of biological controls for insect pests have been developed that are much more environmentally safe. Have students investigate different biological controls and create a poster on the topic that could be displayed at a local garden center.

GOING FURTHER

Encourage students with limited English proficiency to make flashcards of the vocabulary words in this chapter. You may wish to pair English-proficient students with ESL students for vocabulary practice. In addition, encourage students from other countries to share information about interesting arthropods that they remember seeing in their country. Sheltered English

 PG 737
The Cricket Caper

Teaching Transparency 56
"Incomplete Metamorphosis"

Science Bloopers

In 1869, the gypsy moth was introduced into the United States in an attempt to breed a better silkworm. The results were disastrous. Some moths escaped, and the species spread throughout the northeastern part of the country. Gypsy moth caterpillars eat the leaves of deciduous trees. In years when there are especially large numbers of caterpillars, millions of acres of forest can be stripped of their leaves.

Section 3 • Arthropods

4) Close

Quiz

Ask students whether the following statements are true or false:

1. The cephalothorax of a spider consists of both a head and a thorax. (true)
2. The legs of most insects arise from the abdomen. (false)
3. A few types of insects live in the ocean. (false)
4. The three stages of complete metamorphosis are egg, nymph or larva, and adult. (false)

Alternative Assessment

 Writing Have students write a narrative in which they describe a walk along a rocky ocean shore or through a tropical rain forest. Have them describe at least a dozen different arthropods that they are likely to encounter. Students should research the two different ecosystems before they begin writing. Some students may wish to create illustrations or collages to accompany their narratives.

Teaching Transparency 57 "Changing Form—Complete Metamorphosis"

Changing Form—Complete Metamorphosis

In complete metamorphosis, there are four stages: egg, larva, pupa, and adult. Butterflies, beetles, flies, bees, wasps, and ants go through this process. In complete metamorphosis, the larva looks very different from the adult.

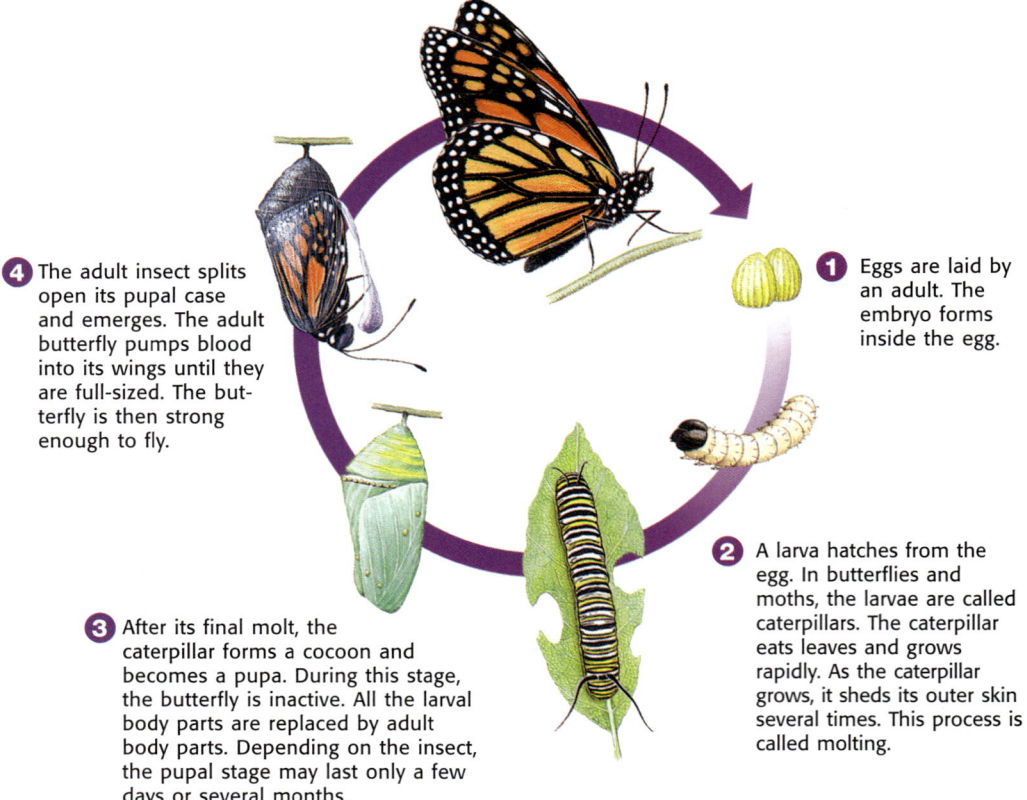

4 The adult insect splits open its pupal case and emerges. The adult butterfly pumps blood into its wings until they are full-sized. The butterfly is then strong enough to fly.

3 After its final molt, the caterpillar forms a cocoon and becomes a pupa. During this stage, the butterfly is inactive. All the larval body parts are replaced by adult body parts. Depending on the insect, the pupal stage may last only a few days or several months.

1 Eggs are laid by an adult. The embryo forms inside the egg.

2 A larva hatches from the egg. In butterflies and moths, the larvae are called caterpillars. The caterpillar eats leaves and grows rapidly. As the caterpillar grows, it sheds its outer skin several times. This process is called molting.

internet connect

sciLINKS
NSTA

TOPIC: Arthropods
GO TO: www.scilinks.org
sciLINKS NUMBER: HSTL370

REVIEW

1. Name the four kinds of arthropods. How are their bodies different?
2. What is the difference between complete metamorphosis and incomplete metamorphosis?
3. **Applying Concepts** Suppose you have found an arthropod in a swimming pool. The creature has compound eyes, antennae, and wings. Is it a crustacean? Why or why not?

362

▼ **Answers to Review**

1. **centipedes and millipedes**—one pair of antennae, mandibles, many segments, head capsules
   crustaceans—mandibles, compound eyes on stalks, two pairs of antennae
   arachnids—two main body parts: cephalothorax and abdomen, four pairs of legs, no antennae, no mandibles, chelicerae
   insects—one pair of antennae, three pairs of legs, head, thorax, abdomen; may or may not have wings

2. incomplete metamorphosis—three stages: egg, nymph, adult; larvae (nymphs) look like smaller adults
   complete metamorphosis—four stages: egg, larva, pupa, adult; larvae look much different than adults

3. No; crustaceans do not have wings.

Section 4

Echinoderms

Terms to Learn
endoskeleton
water vascular system

What You'll Do
◆ Describe three main characteristics of echinoderms.
◆ Describe the water vascular system.

The last major phylum of invertebrates is Echinodermata. All echinoderms (ee KI noh DUHRMS) are marine animals. They include sea stars (starfish), sea urchins, sea lilies, sea cucumbers, brittle stars, and sand dollars. The smallest echinoderms are only a few millimeters across. The largest is a sea star that grows to 1 m in diameter.

Brittle star

Echinoderms live on the sea floor in all parts of the world's oceans. Some echinoderms prey on oysters and other shellfish, some are scavengers, and others scrape algae off rocky surfaces.

Sea star

Feather star

Spiny Skinned

The name *echinoderm* means "spiny skinned." The surface of the animal is not the spiny part, however. The body of the echinoderm contains an **endoskeleton,** an internal skeleton similar to the kind that vertebrates have. The hard, bony skeleton is usually covered with spines. The spines may be no more than sharp bumps, as in many sea stars. Or they may be long and pointed, as in sea urchins. All of the spines are covered by the outer skin of the animal.

Bilateral or Radial?

Adult echinoderms have radial symmetry. But sea stars, sea urchins, sand dollars, and other echinoderms all develop from larvae with bilateral symmetry. **Figure 31** shows a sea urchin larva. Notice how the two sides are similar.

When echinoderm embryos first begin to develop, they form a mouth in the same way the embryos of vertebrates do. This is one of the reasons biologists think that vertebrates are more closely related to echinoderms than to other invertebrates.

Adult
Larva

Figure 31 *The sea urchin larva has bilateral symmetry. The adult sea urchin has radial symmetry.*

363

SECTION 4

Focus
Echinoderms

In this section, students are introduced to echinoderms—sea stars, brittle stars, sea urchins, sand dollars, and sea cucumbers. Students learn that echinoderms are characterized by an internal skeleton, spiny skin, radially symmetrical adults, bilaterally symmetrical larvae, a simple nervous system, and a water vascular system, which is unique to this phylum.

Bellringer

Pose the following question to your students:

Echinoderms include marine animals such as sea stars, sea urchins, and sea cucumbers. All these organisms are slow-moving bottom dwellers. How do you think they protect themselves from predators?

Have them write their thoughts in their ScienceLog.

1 Motivate

ACTIVITY

Sea Star Hypotheses Display an example of an echinoderm, such as a sea star. Have students draw it in their notebook and write a brief hypothesis describing (1) what it eats, (2) how it moves, (3) where it most likely lives. Discuss before beginning the section. Sheltered English

Directed Reading Worksheet 15 Section 4

BRAIN FOOD

Most adult echinoderms either are sessile (remain in one place) or move slowly over the sea floor. Echinoderm larvae, however, are able to swim, and with the help of ocean currents, they often travel great distances before they settle to the bottom and metamorphose into their adult form. Challenge students to speculate about why it is an advantage for echinoderm larvae to be bilaterally symmetrical and for echinoderm adults to be radially symmetrical.

Section 4 • Echinoderms   363

2 Teach

READING STRATEGY

Prediction Guide Before students read this page, ask the following question:

How does a starfish move from place to place?

a. It curls up its arms and rolls across the sea floor.
b. It uses suction-cup-like tube feet that systematically attach and release to move along.
c. It uses its spines to dig into the sea floor and pull itself forward.
d. With its long arms, a starfish can swim slowly through the water.

(b)

INDEPENDENT PRACTICE

Writing **Concept Mapping** Have students make a concept map in their ScienceLog using the terms that describe echinoderms' physical characteristics and nervous and water vascular systems. Students should connect at least 12 terms, and link them with meaningful phrases. Encourage students to share their concept maps with the class.

CONNECT TO EARTH SCIENCE

Echinoderms are members of the *benthos*, the organisms that live on the ocean floor. Use the following Teaching Transparency to illustrate the ocean context of echinoderms.

Teaching Transparency 155
"The Three Groups of Marine Life"
LINK TO EARTH SCIENCE

The Nervous System

All echinoderms have a simple nervous system similar to that of a jellyfish. Around the mouth is a circle of nerve fibers called the *nerve ring*. In sea stars, a *radial nerve* runs from the nerve ring to the tip of each arm, as shown in **Figure 32**. The radial nerves control the movements of the sea star's arms.

At the tip of each arm is a simple eye that senses light. The rest of the body is covered with cells that are sensitive to touch and to chemical signals in the water.

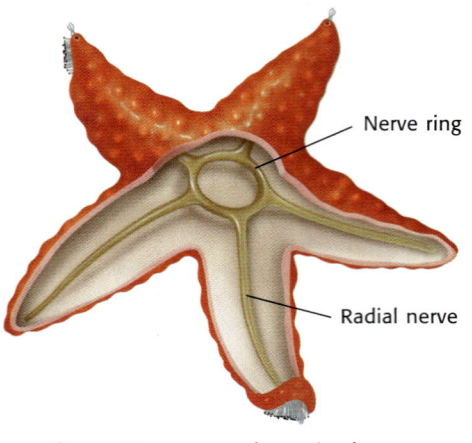
Figure 32 Sea stars have simple nervous systems.

Water Vascular System

One system that is unique to echinoderms is the **water vascular system.** This system uses water pumps to help the animal move, eat, breathe, and sense its environment. **Figure 33** shows the water vascular system of a sea star. Notice how water pressure from the water vascular system is used for a variety of functions.

Figure 33 A water vascular system allows sea stars and all echinoderms to move, eat, and breathe.

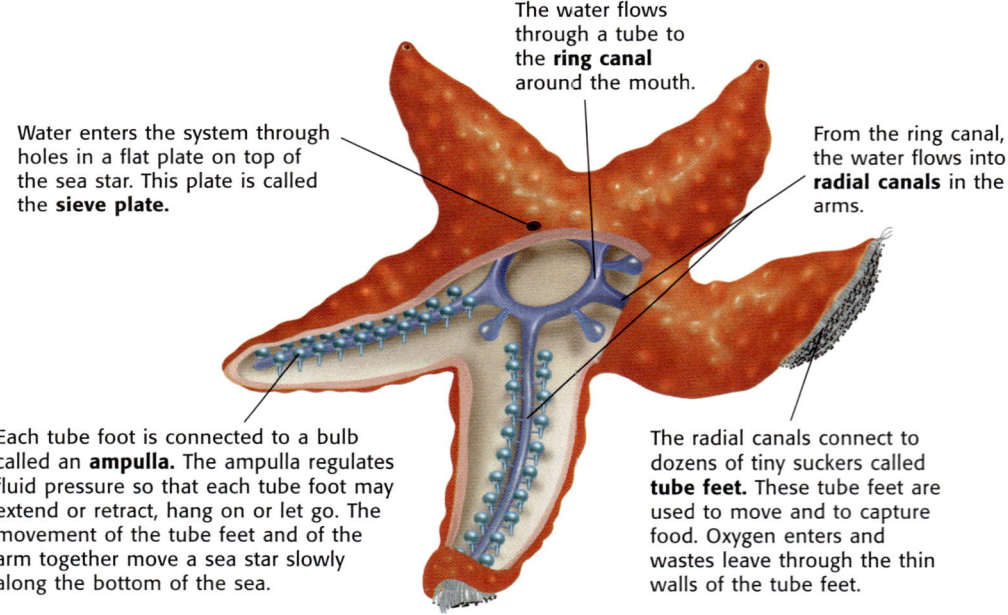

The water flows through a tube to the **ring canal** around the mouth.

Water enters the system through holes in a flat plate on top of the sea star. This plate is called the **sieve plate.**

From the ring canal, the water flows into **radial canals** in the arms.

Each tube foot is connected to a bulb called an **ampulla.** The ampulla regulates fluid pressure so that each tube foot may extend or retract, hang on or let go. The movement of the tube feet and of the arm together move a sea star slowly along the bottom of the sea.

The radial canals connect to dozens of tiny suckers called **tube feet.** These tube feet are used to move and to capture food. Oxygen enters and wastes leave through the thin walls of the tube feet.

Teaching Transparency 58
"Water Vascular System"

Reinforcement Worksheet 15
"Spineless Variety"

IS THAT A FACT!

Sea stars typically have five arms, but some species may have 40 or even 50 arms!

364 Chapter 15 • Invertebrates

Kinds of Echinoderms

Scientists divide echinoderms into several classes. Sea stars are the most familiar echinoderms, and they make up one class. But there are three classes of echinoderms that may not be as familiar to you.

Brittle Stars and Basket Stars The brittle stars and basket stars look like sea stars with long slender arms. These delicate creatures tend to be smaller than sea stars. **Figure 34** shows a basket star.

Sea Urchins and Sand Dollars Sea urchins and sand dollars are round, and their skeletons form a solid internal shell. They have no arms, but they use their tube feet to move in the same way as sea stars. Some sea urchins also walk on their spines. Sea urchins feed on algae they scrape from the surface of rocks and other objects and chew with special teeth. Sand dollars burrow into soft sand or mud, as shown in **Figure 35**, and eat tiny particles of food they find in the sand.

Sea Cucumbers Like sea urchins and sand dollars, sea cucumbers lack arms. A sea cucumber has a soft, leathery body. Unlike sea urchins, sea cucumbers are long and have a wormlike shape. **Figure 36** shows a sea cucumber.

Figure 34 Basket stars have longer arms than sea stars.

Figure 35 Sand dollars burrow in the sand.

Figure 36 Like other echinoderms, sea cucumbers move with tube feet.

REVIEW

1. How are sea cucumbers different from other echinoderms?
2. What is the path taken by water as it flows through the parts of the water vascular system?
3. **Applying Concepts** How are echinoderms different from other invertebrates?

internet**connect**

SC*L*INKS
NSTA

TOPIC: Echinoderms
GO TO: www.scilinks.org
*sci*LINKS NUMBER: HSTL375

Chapter Highlights

VOCABULARY DEFINITIONS

SECTION 1

invertebrate an animal without a backbone

bilateral symmetry a body plan in which two halves of an organism's body are mirror images of each other

radial symmetry a body plan in which the parts of a body are arranged in a circle around a central point

asymmetrical without symmetry

ganglia groups of nerve cells

gut the pouch where food is digested in animals

coelom a cavity in the body of some animals where the gut and organs are located

SECTION 2

open circulatory system a circulatory system consisting of a heart that pumps blood through spaces called sinuses

closed circulatory system a circulatory system in which a heart circulates blood through a network of vessels that forms a closed loop

segment one of many identical or almost identical repeating body parts

Chapter Highlights

SECTION 1

Vocabulary
- invertebrate (p. 344)
- bilateral symmetry (p. 344)
- radial symmetry (p. 344)
- asymmetrical (p. 344)
- ganglia (p. 345)
- gut (p. 345)
- coelom (p. 345)

Section Notes
- Invertebrates are animals without a backbone.
- Most animals have radial symmetry or bilateral symmetry.
- Unlike other animals, sponges have no symmetry.
- A coelom is a space inside the body. The gut hangs inside the coelom.
- Ganglia are clumps of nerves that help control the parts of the body.
- Sponges have special cells called collar cells to digest their food.
- Cnidarians have special stinging cells to catch their prey.
- Cnidarians have two body forms, the polyp and the medusa.
- Tapeworms and flukes are parasitic flatworms.

Labs
Porifera's Porosity (p. 736)

SECTION 2

Vocabulary
- open circulatory system (p. 354)
- closed circulatory system (p. 354)
- segment (p. 355)

Section Notes
- All mollusks have a foot, a visceral mass, and a mantle. Most mollusks also have a shell.
- Mollusks and annelid worms have both a coelom and a circulatory system.
- In an open circulatory system, the heart pumps blood through vessels into spaces called sinuses. In a closed circulatory system, the blood is pumped through a closed network of vessels.
- Segments are identical or nearly identical repeating body parts.

✓ Skills Check

Math Concepts

SPEED AND DISTANCE If a snail is moving at 30 cm/h, how far can it travel in 1 minute? There are 60 minutes in 1 hour:

$$\frac{30 \text{ cm}}{60 \text{ min}} = 0.5 \text{ cm/min}$$

In 1 minute the snail will travel 0.5 cm.

Visual Understanding

METAMORPHOSIS Some insects go through incomplete metamorphosis, and some go through complete metamorphosis. Look at the illustrations on pages 361 and 362 to see the difference between these two types of metamorphosis.

Lab and Activity Highlights

Porifera's Porosity PG 736

The Cricket Caper PG 737

Datasheets for LabBook (blackline masters for these labs)

366 Chapter 15 • Invertebrates

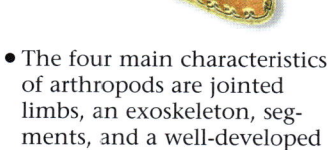

SECTION 3

Vocabulary
- **exoskeleton** *(p. 358)*
- **compound eye** *(p. 358)*
- **antennae** *(p. 358)*
- **mandible** *(p. 358)*
- **metamorphosis** *(p. 361)*

Section Notes
- Seventy-five percent of all animals are arthropods.

- The four main characteristics of arthropods are jointed limbs, an exoskeleton, segments, and a well-developed nervous system.
- Arthropods are classified by the type of body parts they have.
- The four kinds of arthropods are centipedes and millipedes, crustaceans, arachnids, and insects.
- Insects can undergo complete or incomplete metamorphosis.

Labs
The Cricket Caper *(p. 737)*

SECTION 4

Vocabulary
- **endoskeleton** *(p. 363)*
- **water vascular system** *(p. 364)*

Section Notes
- Echinoderms are marine animals that have an endoskeleton and a water vascular system.
- Most echinoderms have bilateral symmetry as larvae and radial symmetry as adults.
- The water vascular system allows echinoderms to move around by means of tube feet, which act like suction cups.
- Echinoderms have a simple nervous system consisting of a nerve ring and radial nerves.

VOCABULARY DEFINITIONS, continued

SECTION 3

exoskeleton an external skeleton made of protein and chitin found on arthropods

compound eye an eye that is made of many identical units, or eyes, that work together

antennae feelers on an arthropod's head that respond to touch or taste

mandible a jaw found on some arthropods

metamorphosis a process in which an insect or other animal changes form as it develops from an embryo or larva to an adult

SECTION 4

endoskeleton an internal skeleton

water vascular system a system of water pumps and canals found in all echinoderms that allows them to move, eat, and breathe

 Vocabulary Review Worksheet 15

 Blackline masters of these Chapter Highlights can be found in the **Study Guide**.

---

internetconnect

GO TO: go.hrw.com

Visit the **HRW** Web site for a variety of learning tools related to this chapter. Just type in the keyword:

KEYWORD: HSTINV

SCLINKS **NSTA**

GO TO: www.scilinks.org

Visit the **National Science Teachers Association** on-line Web site for Internet resources related to this chapter. Just type in the sciLINKS number for more information about the topic:

TOPIC:	sciLINKS NUMBER:
Sponges	HSTL355
Roundworms	HSTL360
Mollusks and Annelid Worms	HSTL365
Arthropods	HSTL370
Echinoderms	HSTL375

Lab and Activity Highlights

LabBank

 Labs You Can Eat, Here's Looking at You, Squid! Lab 7

Inquiry Labs, At a Snail's Pace, Lab 5

 Long-Term Projects & Research Ideas, Creepy, Crawly Food?, Project 15

Chapter Review Answers

USING VOCABULARY

1. invertebrates
2. pores, an osculum
3. radial, bilateral
4. mantle
5. segments
6. water pressure in a tube foot

UNDERSTANDING CONCEPTS

Multiple Choice
7. d
8. c
9. c
10. b
11. d
12. b
13. c
14. c
15. b
16. b

Chapter Review

USING VOCABULARY

To complete the following sentences, choose the correct term from each pair of terms listed below:

1. Animals without a backbone are called __?__. (*invertebrates* or *vertebrates*)

2. A sponge uses __?__ to pull water in and releases water out through __?__. (*an osculum* or *pores*)

3. Cnidarians have __?__ symmetry and flatworms have __?__ symmetry. (*radial* or *bilateral*)

4. The shell of a snail is secreted by the __?__. (*radula* or *mantle*)

5. Annelid worms have __?__. (*jointed limbs* or *segments*)

6. An ampulla regulates __?__. (*water pressure in a tube foot* or *blood pressure in a closed circulatory system*)

UNDERSTANDING CONCEPTS

Multiple Choice

7. Invertebrates make up what percentage of all animals?
   a. 4 percent   c. 85 percent
   b. 50 percent   d. 97 percent

8. Which of the following describes the body plan of a sponge:
   a. radial symmetry   c. asymmetry
   b. bilateral symmetry d. partial symmetry

9. What cells do sponges have that no other animal has?
   a. blood cells
   b. nerve cells
   c. collar cells
   d. none of the above

10. Which of the following animals do not have ganglia?
    a. annelid worms   c. flatworms
    b. cnidarians   d. mollusks

11. Which of the following animals has a coelom?
    a. sponge   c. flatworm
    b. cnidarian   d. mollusk

12. Both tapeworms and leeches are
    a. annelid worms.   c. flatworms.
    b. parasites.   d. predators.

13. Some arthropods do not have
    a. jointed limbs.
    b. an exoskeleton.
    c. antennae.
    d. segments.

14. Echinoderms live
    a. on land.   c. in salt water.
    b. in fresh water.   d. All of the above

15. *Echinoderm* means
    a. "jointed limbs."   c. "endoskeleton."
    b. "spiny skinned."   d. "shiny tube foot."

16. Echinoderm larvae have
    a. radial symmetry.
    b. bilateral symmetry.
    c. no symmetry.
    d. radial and bilateral symmetry.

Short Answer

17. What is a gut?
18. How are arachnids different from insects?
19. Which animal phylum contains the most species?
20. How does an echinoderm move?

Concept Mapping

21. Use the following terms to create a concept map: insect, sponges, sea anemone, invertebrates, arachnid, sea cucumber, crustacean, centipede, cnidarians, arthropods, echinoderms.

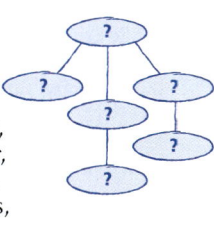

CRITICAL THINKING AND PROBLEM SOLVING

Write one or two sentences to answer the following questions:

22. You have discovered a strange new animal that has bilateral symmetry, a coelom, and nerves. Will this animal be classified in the Cnidaria phylum? Why or why not?
23. Unlike other mollusks, cephalopods can move rapidly. Based on what you know about the body parts of mollusks, why do you think cephalopods have this ability?
24. Roundworms, flatworms, and annelid worms belong to different phyla. Why aren't all the worms grouped in the same phylum?

MATH IN SCIENCE

25. If 75 percent of all animals are arthropods and 40 percent of all arthropods are beetles, what percentage of all animals are beetles?

INTERPRETING GRAPHICS

Below is an evolutionary tree showing how the different phyla of animals may be related to one another. The "trunk" of the tree is on the left. Use the tree to answer the questions that follow.

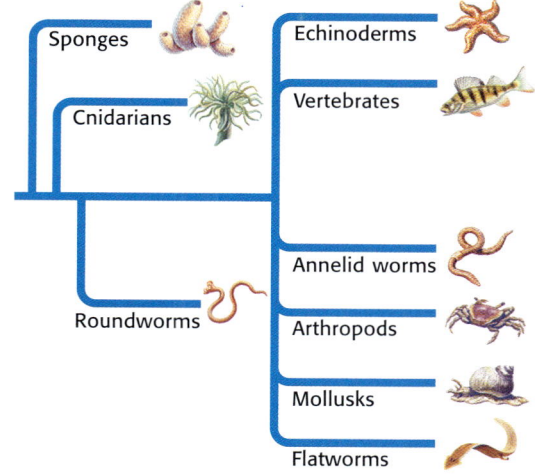

26. Which phylum is the oldest?
27. Are mollusks more closely related to roundworms or flatworms?
28. What phylum is most closely related to the vertebrates?

 Take a minute to review your answers to the Pre-Reading Questions found at the bottom of page 342. Have your answers changed? If necessary, revise your answers based on what you have learned since you began this chapter.

Short Answer

17. a pouch lined with cells that release enzymes to digest food
18. Arachnids have two body parts—a cephalothorax and abdomen—and eight legs. Insects have three body parts—a head, a thorax, an abdomen—and six legs. Arachnids have chelicerae. Insects have antennae.
19. arthropods
20. with tube feet and the water vascular system

Concept Mapping

21. An answer to this exercise can be found at the end of this book.

CRITICAL THINKING AND PROBLEM SOLVING

22. No; cnidarians have radial symmetry and do not have coeloms.
23. Because cephalopods do not have a shell, they need to move rapidly to avoid predators. They can move rapidly because they have a large brain.
24. All of the worms are not grouped in the same phylum because they have different characteristics. Annelid worms are segmented; the others are not. Annelid worms also have a coelom and a closed circulatory system. Roundworms have a round cross section, and flatworms do not. Roundworms have a more complex digestive system than flatworms. Flatworms are the only worms with eyespots and sensory lobes.

MATH IN SCIENCE

25. $0.75 \times 0.40 = 0.30 = 30$ percent

INTERPRETING GRAPHICS

26. the sponges
27. flatworms
28. the echinoderms

WEIRD SCIENCE
Water Bears

Background

Tardigrades are also known as moss piglets and can be placed in history by the fact that they were some of the first organisms Antony van Leeuwenhoek examined with his spectacular invention, the microscope.

This is of interest especially because these creatures are not well represented in the fossil record. And after Leeuwenhoek's initial study, tardigrades were largely ignored for the next three centuries, in large part because of their lack of economic importance.

Answer to On Your Own

Architect Eugene Tsui was inspired by the sturdiness of the tardigrade to build what he calls "the world's safest house."

The shape of Ojo de Sol, Tsui's house in Berkeley, California, mimics that of the water bear. He says he designed the house to be oval because "nature doesn't build boxes. They're among the weakest forms because stress is concentrated in corners and along flat surfaces, vulnerable to collapse."

Tsui hoped to design a house to withstand the earthquakes and wildfires, disasters that Northern California is prone to. Fires skirt curved walls instead of penetrating them, and the arches on the upper floor are wood, steel, and concrete. The structure might be safe from some natural events, but in regard to water bears, the question would be, "Can it resist drought?"

WEIRD SCIENCE
WATER BEARS

You're alive and you know it, but how? Well, eating, breathing, and moving around are all pretty sure signs of life. And once something stops eating or breathing, the end is near. Or is it? Oddly enough, this doesn't seem to be the case for one group of invertebrates–the water bears.

Grin and Bear It

When conditions get really rough—too hot, too cold, but mostly too dry to survive—a water bear will shut down its body processes. It's similar to a bear going into hibernation, but it is even more extreme. When a water bear can't find water, it dries itself out and forms a sugar that coats its cells. Scientists think this may keep the water bear's cells from breaking down, and it may be the key to its survival.

During this hibernation-like state, called *cryptobiosis* (CRIP toh bie OH sis), the water bear doesn't eat, move, or breathe. And amazingly, it doesn't die either. Once you add water, the water bear will come right back to normal life!

Water Bear

Hard to Put a Finger On

Officially called tardigrades (TAHR di graydz), water bears have been difficult to classify. But the 700 different species of water bears are probably most closely related to arthropods. Most make their homes on wet mosses and lichens. Some water bears feed on nematodes (a tiny, unsegmented worm) and rotifers (a tiny wormlike or spherical animal). Most feed on the fluids from mosses found near their homes.

From the tropics to the Arctic, the world is full of water bears. None are much larger than a grain of sand, but all have a slow, stomping walk. Some tardigrades live as deep as the bottom of the ocean, more than 4,700 m below sea level. Other water bears live at elevations of 6,600 m above sea level, well above the tree line. It is a wonder how water bears can withstand the range of temperatures found in these places, from 151°C to −270°C.

On Your Own

▶ What do you think people can learn from an organism like the water bear? Write down at least one reason why it is worthwhile to study these special creatures.

EYE ON THE ENVIRONMENT

Sizable Squid

"Before my eyes was a horrible monster... It swam crossways in the direction of the *Nautilus* with great speed, watching us with its enormous staring green eyes. The monster's mouth, a horned beak like a parrot's, opened and shut vertically." So wrote Jules Verne in his science-fiction story *Twenty Thousand Leagues Under the Sea*. But what was this horrible monster that was about to attack the submarine *Nautilus*? Believe it or not, it was a creature that actually exists—a giant squid!

Squid Facts

As the largest of all invertebrates, giant squids range from 8 m to 25 m long and weigh as much as 2,000 kg. It's hard to know for sure, though, because no one has ever studied a living giant squid. Scientists have studied only dead or dying giant squids that have washed ashore or have been trapped in fishing nets.

Giant squids are very similar to their much smaller relatives. They have a torpedo-shaped body, two tentacles, eight arms, a mantle, a funnel, and a beak. All their body parts are much larger, though! A giant squid's eyes, for instance, may be as large as a volleyball! And like adult squids of smaller species, giant squids feed not only on fish but also on smaller squids. Given the size of giant squids, it's hard to imagine that they have any enemies in the ocean, but they do.

A Hungry Enemy

Weighing in at 20 tons, toothed sperm whales eat giant squids. How do we know this? As many as 10,000 squid beaks have been found in the stomach of a single sperm whale. The hard beaks of giant squids are indigestible. It seems that giant squids are a regular meal for sperm whales. Yet this meal can result in some battle scars. Many whales bear ring marks on their forehead and fins that match the size of the suckers found on giant squids.

Fact or Fiction?

▶ Read Chapter 18 of Jules Verne's *Twenty Thousand Leagues Under the Sea*, and then try to find other stories about squids. Write your own story about a giant squid, and share it with the class.

▲ This giant squid was already dead when it was caught in a fishing net off the coast of New Zealand.

Answer to Fact or Fiction?
Answers will vary.

EYE ON THE ENVIRONMENT
Sizable Squid

Background

According to accounts, the giant squid can put up quite a fight against a whale.

Lighthouse keepers in South Africa claim to have seen a giant squid attack and subsequently drown a baby southern whale after an intense battle that lasted for more than an hour.

A Soviet whaler reported a deadly battle between an adult sperm whale and a giant squid. In that case, each did fatal damage to the other. The whale was finally strangled by the tentacles of the squid, but the squid's beak was found in the whale's stomach.

Researchers do know that squids have excellent eyesight—and some of the largest eyes in the animal kingdom—and one of the most highly developed brains of any invertebrate, two things that would contribute to making them difficult to catch.

They are also one of the most difficult mollusks to eat. Clyde Roper has a reputation for cooking and teaching courses on cephalopod cuisine; he was among the first to taste a portion of giant squid, but to his great dismay, the meat is bitter and has an ammonia flavor. It turns out that a profusion of ammonium ions, which are less dense than water, help the squid maneuver through the ocean.

Chapter Organizer

CHAPTER ORGANIZATION	TIME MINUTES	OBJECTIVES	LABS, INVESTIGATIONS, AND DEMONSTRATIONS
Chapter Opener pp. 372–373	45	National Standards: UCP 5, SAI 1, HNS 1, 3, LS 1a, 3a, 3b, 4d, 5b, 5c	**Start-Up Activity** Oil on Water, p. 373
Section 1 What Are Vertebrates?	90	▶ List the four characteristics of chordates. ▶ Describe the main characteristics of vertebrates. ▶ Explain the difference between an ectotherm and an endotherm. UCP 1–5, SAI 1, LS 1a, 1d, 3a–3d, 5a	**Demonstration,** Assembling Skeletons, p. 374 in ATE **BASIC** **QuickLab,** Body Temperature, p. 376 **GENERAL**
Section 2 Fishes	90	▶ Describe the three classes of living fishes, and give an example of each. ▶ Describe the function of a swim bladder and an oily liver. ▶ Explain the difference between internal fertilization and external fertilization. UCP 1–3, 5, SAI 1, ST 1, 2, SPSP 5, HNS 1, LS 1a, 1d, 2a, 2b, 3c, 3d, 5a, 5c; LabBook UCP 2, 5, SAI 1, 2, HNS 2, LS 1a, 3d	**QuickLab,** Oil on Troubled Waters, p. 381 **GENERAL** **Making Models,** Floating a Pipe Fish, p. 740 **GENERAL** **Datasheets for LabBook,** Floating a Pipe Fish, Datasheet 34 **GENERAL** **Whiz-Bang Demonstrations,** The Fish in the Abyss, Demo 10 **BASIC**
Section 3 Amphibians	90	▶ Describe the importance of amphibians in evolution. ▶ Explain how amphibians breathe. ▶ Describe metamorphosis in amphibians. UCP 1–5, SAI 1, LS 1a, 3c, 3d, 4d, 5b, 5c; LabBook UCP 2, 4, 5, SAI 1, LS 1a, 3c, 3d, 5b	**Demonstration,** Illustrating Fossilization, p. 382 in ATE **GENERAL** **Skill Builder,** A Prince of a Frog, p. 742 **BASIC** **Datasheets for LabBook,** A Prince of a Frog, Datasheet 35 **BASIC**
Section 4 Reptiles	90	▶ Explain the adaptations that allow reptiles to live on land. ▶ Name the three main groups of vertebrates that evolved from reptiles. ▶ Describe the characteristics of an amniotic egg. ▶ Name the three orders of modern reptiles. UCP 1, 2, 4, 5, LS 1a, 2a, 2b, 2e, 3a, 3c, 3d, 5a–5c	**Demonstration,** Reptile Exhibit, p. 389 in ATE **GENERAL** **Long-Term Projects & Research Ideas,** Project 16 **ADVANCED**

See page **T20** for a complete correlation of this book with the **NATIONAL SCIENCE EDUCATION STANDARDS.**

TECHNOLOGY RESOURCES

 Guided Reading Audio CD English or Spanish, Chapter 16

 One-Stop Planner CD-ROM with Test Generator

 CNN Science, Technology & Society, Salmon Sound Barriers, Segment 25

Eye on the Environment, Fish Farming, Segment 17

What's Slithering in Guam? Segment 19

371A Chapter 16 • Fishes, Amphibians, and Reptiles

Chapter 16 • Fishes, Amphibians, and Reptiles

CLASSROOM WORKSHEETS, TRANSPARENCIES, AND RESOURCES	SCIENCE INTEGRATION AND CONNECTIONS	REVIEW AND ASSESSMENT
Directed Reading Worksheet 16 BASIC **Science Puzzlers, Twisters & Teasers,** Worksheet 16 ADVANCED		
Directed Reading Worksheet 16, Section 1 BASIC **Science Skills Worksheet 26,** Grasping Graphing GENERAL **Transparency 59,** Chordates	**Multicultural Connection,** p. 374 in ATE GENERAL **Math and More,** p. 375 in ATE GENERAL **Real-World Connection,** p. 375 in ATE ADVANCED **Weird Science:** Warm Brains in Cold Water, p. 397 GENERAL	**Review,** p. 376 GENERAL **Quiz,** p. 376 in ATE GENERAL **Alternative Assessment,** p. 376 in ATE GENERAL
Directed Reading Worksheet 16, Section 2 BASIC **Transparency 269,** How a Cell Produces an Electric Current	**Physics Connection,** p. 378 **Real-World Connection,** p. 378 in ATE **Connect to Environmental Science,** p. 379 in ATE **MathBreak,** A Lot of Bones, p. 380 GENERAL **Math and More,** p. 380 in ATE ADVANCED **Connect to Physical Science,** p. 380 in ATE **Across the Sciences:** Robot Fish, p. 396 ADVANCED	**Homework,** p. 377 in ATE ADVANCED **Homework,** p. 379 in ATE GENERAL **Review,** p. 381 GENERAL **Quiz,** p. 381 in ATE GENERAL **Alternative Assessment,** p. 381 in ATE GENERAL
Directed Reading Worksheet 16, Section 3 BASIC **Transparency 60,** Metamorphosis of a Frog	**Connect to Physical Science,** p. 383 in ATE **Apply,** p. 385 GENERAL **Cross-Disciplinary Focus,** p. 385 in ATE BASIC **Multicultural Connection,** p. 385 in ATE	**Self-Check,** p. 383 **Homework,** p. 383 in ATE ADVANCED **Review,** p. 386 GENERAL **Quiz,** p. 386 in ATE GENERAL **Alternative Assessment,** p. 386 in ATE ADVANCED
Transparency 61, Reptile History **Directed Reading Worksheet 16,** Section 4 BASIC **Transparency 62,** Amniotic Egg **Math Skills for Science Worksheet 35,** Using Temperature Scales GENERAL **Reinforcement Worksheet 16,** Coldblooded Critters BASIC **Critical Thinking Worksheet 16,** Frogs Aren't Breathing Easy ADVANCED	**Math and More,** p. 389 in ATE GENERAL **Real-World Connection,** p. 390 in ATE **Multicultural Connection,** p. 390 in ATE	**Self-Check,** p. 389 **Homework,** p. 390 in ATE ADVANCED **Review,** p. 391 GENERAL **Quiz,** p. 391 in ATE GENERAL **Alternative Assessment,** p. 391 in ATE GENERAL

END-OF-CHAPTER REVIEW AND ASSESSMENT

Chapter Review in Study Guide
Vocabulary and Notes in Study Guide
Chapter Tests with Performance-Based Assessment, Chapter 16 Test
Chapter Tests with Performance-Based Assessment, Performance-Based Assessment 16
Concept Mapping Transparency 16

 Holt, Rinehart and Winston On-line Resources
go.hrw.com
For worksheets and other teaching aids related to this chapter, visit the HRW Web site and type in the keyword: **HSTVR1**

 National Science Teachers Association
www.scilinks.org
Encourage students to use the *sci*LINKS numbers listed in the internet connect boxes to access information and resources on the **NSTA** Web site.

Chapter Resources & Worksheets

Visual Resources

TEACHING TRANSPARENCIES

#59 Chordates
#60 Metamorphosis of a Frog
#61 Reptile History
#62 Amniotic Egg

TEACHING TRANSPARENCIES / CONCEPT MAPPING TRANSPARENCY

#269 How a Cell Produces an Electric Current — LINK TO PHYSICAL SCIENCE
#16 Fishes, Amphibians, and Reptiles

Meeting Individual Needs

DIRECTED READING

#16 Fishes, Amphibians, and Reptiles

REINFORCEMENT & VOCABULARY REVIEW

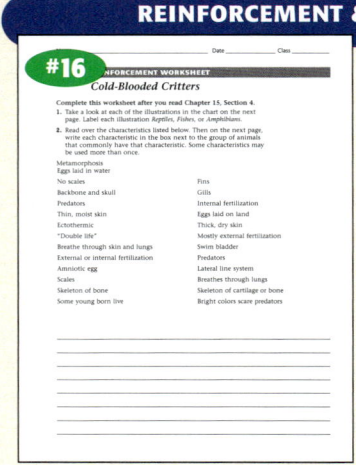

#16 Cold-Blooded Critters
#16 Fishin' for Vertebrates

SCIENCE PUZZLERS, TWISTERS & TEASERS

#16 Fishes, Amphibians, and Reptiles

371C Chapter 16 • Fishes, Amphibians, and Reptiles

Chapter 16 • Fishes, Amphibians, and Reptiles

Review & Assessment

STUDY GUIDE

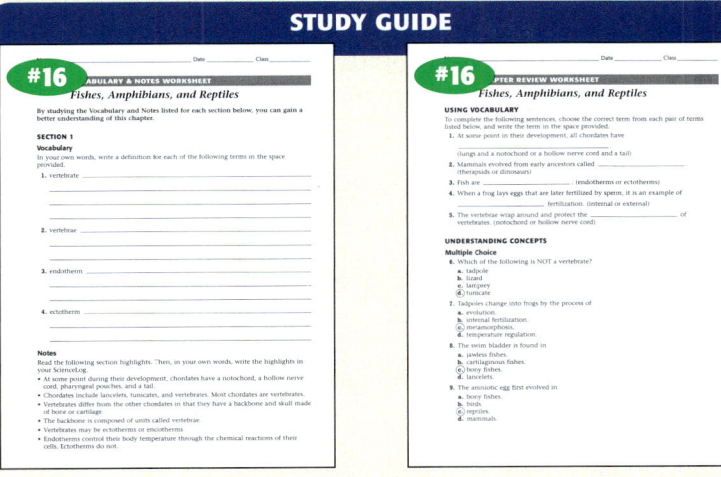

CHAPTER TESTS WITH PERFORMANCE-BASED ASSESSMENT

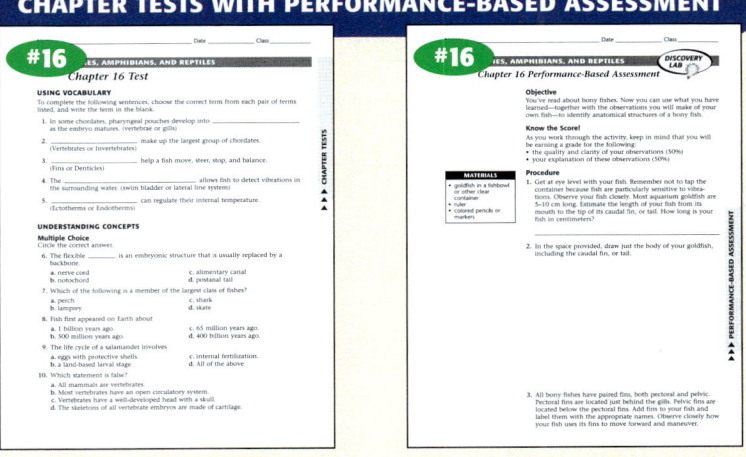

Lab Worksheets

WHIZ-BANG DEMONSTRATIONS

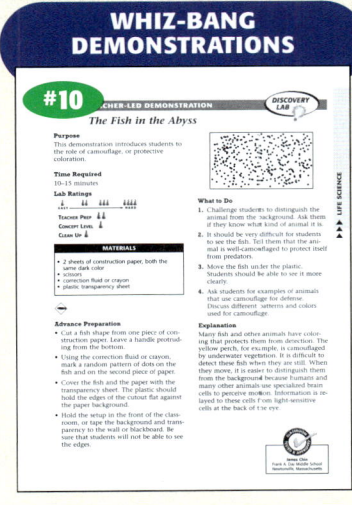

LONG-TERM PROJECTS & RESEARCH IDEAS

DATASHEETS FOR LABBOOK

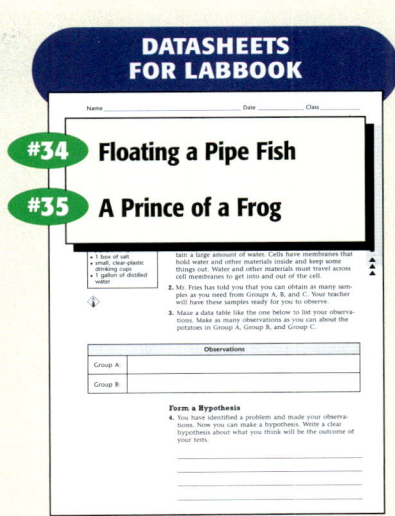

Applications & Extensions

CRITICAL THINKING & PROBLEM SOLVING

SCIENCE TECHNOLOGY

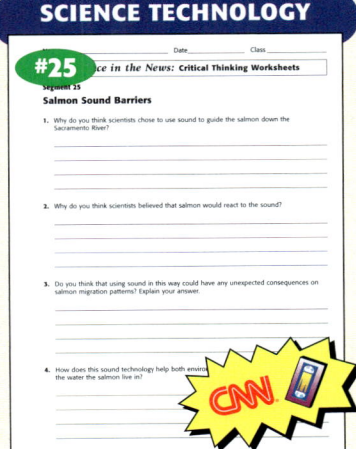

EYE ON THE ENVIRONMENT

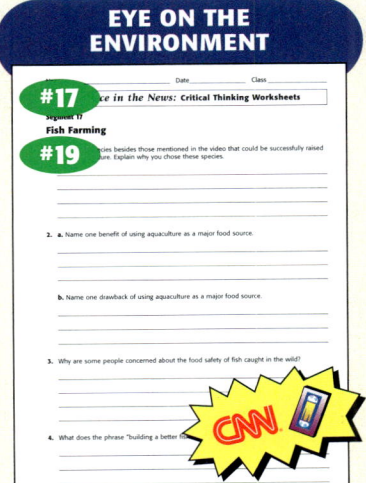

Chapter 16 • Chapter Resources & Worksheets

Chapter Background

Section 1

What Are Vertebrates?

▶ **Chordates**
Chordate embryos have four basic features that distinguish them from other animals. The first is the notochord, a semiflexible rod that runs along the length of the body. They also have a hollow dorsal nerve cord, with nerve fibers that make contact with the muscles; pharyngeal slits, which are openings between the pharynx and the outside of the animal; and a postanal tail, which is an extension of the notochord and dorsal nerve cord.

IS THAT A FACT!

- Cephalochordates (lancelets) have more than 100 pharyngeal slits that are used to strain food particles from water.

▶ **Vertebrates**
Vertebrates, which belong to the phylum Chordata, first appeared on Earth during the late Cambrian period, more than 500 million years ago. The first vertebrates were jawless creatures; jaws appeared about 100 million years later. Vertebrates include fishes, amphibians, reptiles, birds, and mammals.

Section 2

Fishes

▶ **Ray-Finned Fishes**
The actinopterygians, or ray-finned fishes, are the largest class of fishes. There are about 20,000 species of ray-finned fishes, making them by far the largest group of aquatic vertebrates as well.

- The first ray-finned fish appeared during the Devonian period.

▶ **Cartilaginous Fishes**
Sharks, skates, and rays are all Chondrichthyes, or cartilaginous fishes. About 800 species of cartilaginous fishes exist, compared with about 20,000 species of bony fishes. Cartilaginous fishes are an amazingly diverse group both behaviorally and physically. For example, sharks range in size from the 14 m (40 ft) whale shark to the 0.6 m (2 ft) dogfish shark. Shark diets differ greatly too. Although most eat other fish, great white sharks have been known to eat seals and other marine mammals. Some sharks, such as the gentle basking shark, eat nothing but plankton.

- Nurse sharks have special sensory organs beneath their nose called barbels that help them locate food on the bottom of the ocean.

IS THAT A FACT!

- Some ray-finned fishes have evolved special abilities. For example, Siamese fighting fish are capable of breathing air in addition to taking oxygen from water through their gills. Fish such as the walking catfish and mudskipper can even crawl on land!

- More people are killed in the United States each year by dogs than have been killed by great white sharks in the last century.

Chapter 16 • Fishes, Amphibians, and Reptiles

SECTION 3

Amphibians

▶ **Frogs and Toads**

What's the difference between toads and frogs? Toads are types of frogs that belong to the family Bufonidae. These "true toads" generally have stubby bodies, short hind legs, and dry and warty skin, and they tend to lay their eggs in long chains. "True frogs," which are members of the family Ranidae, generally have bulging eyes, strong and long webbed feet, and smooth skin, and they tend to lay their eggs in clusters. There are many exceptions to these rules, however; for example, there are some warty frogs and some smooth-skinned toads.

▶ **Salamanders**

Salamanders belong to the order Caudata. These carnivorous amphibians are distinguished from other amphibians by the presence of a tail, two pairs of legs of approximately the same size, ribs, teeth on both jaws, and other muscular and skeletal characteristics. Salamanders live in cool, moist habitats in almost all northern temperate areas of the world.

IS THAT A FACT!

▸ Some salamanders can extend their sticky, mucus-coated tongues as far as half their body length.

▸ Most salamanders can regenerate lost toes and even entire limbs. As a defense mechanism, they sometimes voluntarily shed their tail. Muscle contractions in the detached tail distract a predator long enough to enable the salamander to make a quick getaway.

SECTION 4

Reptiles

▶ **Reptile Characteristics**

Most of the 6,000 species of reptiles in existence today live in tropical areas. They include snakes, crocodiles, lizards, turtles, and tuatara, which are lizardlike animals that can be found only on some of the islets of New Zealand. Reptiles range in size from the tiny gecko lizard (3 cm) to the anaconda snake (up to 12 m).

▶ **Crocodiles and Alligators**

These two closely related carnivorous reptiles belong to the order Crocodylia. How do they differ from each other? Alligators have broader snouts than crocodiles. Also, the fourth tooth on either side of a crocodile's jaw protrudes when the crocodile's mouth is closed.

• Estuarine crocodiles can live to be over 100 years old.

IS THAT A FACT!

▸ The Chinese alligator, a relatively small animal found in China's Yangtze River region, is an endangered species and may indeed be extinct.

For background information about teaching strategies and issues, refer to the *Professional Reference for Teachers*.

Chapter 16 • Chapter Background   **371F**

Chapter 16
Fishes, Amphibians, and Reptiles

Pre-Reading Questions

Students may not know the answers to these questions before reading the chapter, so accept any reasonable response.

Suggested Answers

1. Ectotherms are sometimes called cold-blooded. They do not control their body temperature through the chemical reactions of their cells. Their body temperature depends on the temperature of the environment.
2. A reptile has thick, dry skin and lays amniotic eggs. An amphibian has thin, moist skin that it can breathe through, and it must live in or near water.

Directed Reading Worksheet 16

Science Puzzlers, Twisters & Teasers Worksheet 16

Guided Reading Audio CD
English or Spanish, Chapter 16

Chapter 16

Fishes, Amphibians, and Reptiles

Sections

1. **What Are Vertebrates?** .. 374
   QuickLab 376
   Internet Connect 376
2. **Fishes** 377
   Physics Connection .. 378
   MathBreak 380
3. **Amphibians** 382
   Apply 385
4. **Reptiles** 387
   Internet Connect 391

   Chapter Review 394
   Feature Articles 396, 397
   LabBook 740–743

Pre-Reading Questions

1. What does it mean to say an animal is cold-blooded?
2. What is the difference between a reptile and an amphibian?

372

---

internet connect

HRW On-line Resources

go.hrw.com
For worksheets and other teaching aids, visit the HRW Web site and type in the keyword: **HSTVR1**

www.scilinks.com
Use the *sci*LINKS numbers at the end of each chapter for additional resources on the **NSTA** Web site.

www.cnnfyi.com
Visit the CNN Web site for current events coverage and classroom resources.

A Blast from the Past!

In December 1938, Marjorie Courtenay Latimer made an amazing discovery. On a fishing dock in South Africa, she found a coelacanth (SEE luh kahnth). She sent a sketch of the fish to her friend J.L.B. Smith, an expert on fish. Smith recognized the fish right away. So what's so amazing about this giant fish? Scientists had thought that coelacanths became extinct about 70 million years ago! In this chapter, you will learn about other fishes as well as about amphibians and reptiles.

START-UP Activity

OIL ON WATER

To stay afloat, sharks store a lot of oil in their liver. In this activity, you will build a model of an oily liver to see how an oily liver can keep a shark afloat.

Procedure

1. Use a **beaker** to measure out equal amounts of **water** and **cooking oil**.
2. Fill **one balloon** with the water.
3. Fill a **second balloon** with the cooking oil.
4. Tie the balloons so that no air remains inside. Float each balloon in a **bowl half full of water**. Observe what happens to the balloons.

Analysis

5. Compare how the two balloons floated.
6. The function of an oily liver is to keep the fish from sinking. How does the structure of the liver complement its function?

START-UP Activity

OIL ON WATER

MATERIALS
For Each Group: • beaker • water • cooking oil • two balloons • bowl

Answers to START-UP Activity

5. The balloon filled with water will eventually settle about halfway to the bottom of the tank. The oil-filled balloon will float.
6. Sample answer: The oil in an oily liver is less dense than water. This property provides buoyancy to a cartilaginous fish and helps it stay afloat.

Chapter 16 • Fishes, Amphibians, and Reptiles

SECTION 1

Focus

What Are Vertebrates?

This section introduces students to vertebrates and other chordates. Students will learn about the characteristics of vertebrates and the traits that set them apart from other chordates. They will also discover the differences between ectotherms and endotherms.

While you are taking attendance, ask students to ponder this question:

> What are some of the physical characteristics shared by dinosaurs and people?

Have each student jot down two or three ideas. Then briefly discuss students' lists before beginning the section.

1) Motivate

DEMONSTRATION

Assembling Skeletons As an introduction to vertebrates, show students how to reassemble a small mammal skeleton. Obtain owl pellets (the bones of animals eaten by owls) from a nature center or biological supply company. Provide students with a simple illustration of a small mammal skeleton as a reference. In groups of two or three, have students break apart pellets and sort the bones, reconstructing an "exploded view" of whatever small mammal skeletons they find. `Sheltered English`

 Directed Reading Worksheet 16 Section 1

374   Chapter 16 • Fishes, Amphibians, and Reptiles

Section 1

Terms to Learn

vertebrate
vertebrae
endotherm
ectotherm

What You'll Do

- List the four characteristics of chordates.
- Describe the main characteristics of vertebrates.
- Explain the difference between an ectotherm and an endotherm.

What Are Vertebrates?

Have you ever seen a dinosaur skeleton at a museum? Fossilized dinosaur bones were put back together to show what the animal looked like. Most dinosaur skeletons are huge compared with the skeletons of the humans who view them. But humans have many of the same kinds of bones that dinosaurs had; ours are just smaller. Your backbone is very much like the one in a dinosaur skeleton, as shown in **Figure 1**. Animals with a backbone are called **vertebrates**.

Figure 1 Humans and dinosaurs are both vertebrates.

Chordates

Vertebrates belong to the phylum Chordata. Members of this phylum are called *chordates*. Vertebrates make up the largest group of chordates, but there are two other groups of chordates—lancelets and tunicates. These are shown in **Figure 2**. These chordates do not have a backbone or a well-developed head. They are very simple compared with vertebrates. But all three groups share chordate characteristics.

At some point in their life, all chordates have four special body parts: a *notochord*, a *hollow nerve cord*, *pharyngeal* (fuh RIN jee uhl) *pouches*, and a *tail*. These are shown in **Figure 3** on the next page.

Figure 2 Both tunicates, like the sea squirts at left, and the lancelet, shown above, are marine organisms.

Multicultural CONNECTION

In many parts of Asia, lancelets are commercially harvested and are an important food source. Have students research the use of lancelets as a food source, examining such things as taste, price per pound, and availability in the United States. Students could present their findings in an oral or written report or use the information they have gathered to develop recipes using lancelets.

A stiff but flexible rod called a **notochord** gives the body support. In most vertebrates, the embryo's notochord disappears and a backbone grows in its place.

A **hollow nerve cord** runs along the back and is full of fluid. In vertebrates, this nerve cord is called the *spinal cord*, and it is filled with *spinal fluid*.

Chordates have a **tail** that begins behind the anus. Some chordates have a tail in only the embryo stage.

Pharyngeal pouches are found in all chordate embryos. These develop into gills or other body parts as the embryo matures.

Figure 3 The chordate characteristics in a lancelet are shown here. All chordates have these four characteristics at some point in their life.

Getting a Backbone

Most chordates are vertebrates. Vertebrates have many traits that set them apart from the lancelets and tunicates. For example, vertebrates have a backbone. The backbone is a segmented column of bones. These bones are called **vertebrae** (VUHR tuh BRAY). You can see the vertebrae of a human in **Figure 4.** The vertebrae surround the nerve cord and protect it. Vertebrates also have a well-developed head protected by a skull. The skull and vertebrae are made of either cartilage or bone. *Cartilage* is the tough material that the flexible parts of our ears and nose are made of.

The skeletons of all vertebrate embryos are made of cartilage. But as most vertebrates grow, the cartilage is usually replaced by bone. Bone is much harder than cartilage.

Because bone is so hard, it can easily be fossilized. Many fossils of vertebrates have been discovered, and they have provided valuable information about relationships among organisms.

Vertebrae

Figure 4 The vertebrae interlock to form a strong but flexible column of bone. The backbone protects the spinal cord and supports the rest of the body.

⚛ WEIRD SCIENCE

Tunicates are actually more well developed as young larvae than they are when they "mature" into adults! As larvae, tunicates have many chordate features, look much like tadpoles, and are able to swim. As they reach adulthood, however, they lose their tail (and therefore their ability to swim), and their nervous system disintegrates.

---

2) Teach

MATH and MORE

Using the figures below, have students construct a pie graph to show the relative numbers of the species in the different classes of vertebrates.

Fish	25,000
Amphibians	4,600
Reptiles	6,000
Birds	9,000
Mammals	4,300

 Science Skills Worksheet 26 "Grasping Graphing"

REAL-WORLD CONNECTION

Paleontology Have students research the field of paleontology and report their findings to the class. The report could be part of a special "career day" on which students present reports on a variety of scientific fields. Suggest that students answer questions such as the following: What do paleontologists do? What type of education do they need? What types of career opportunities exist for paleontologists?

 Teaching Transparency 59 "Chordates"

TOPIC: Vertebrates
GO TO: www.scilinks.org
sciLINKS NUMBER: HSTL380

Section 1 • What Are Vertebrates?

3) Extend

QuickLab

MATERIALS

FOR EACH GROUP:
• fever thermometer

Answer to QuickLab

Human body temperature will not fluctuate more than a few tenths of a degree, even after exercise. An ectotherm's body temperature fluctuates more dramatically, depending on the temperature of its environment.

ACTIVITY

Invite a paleontologist or fossil enthusiast to speak with the class about fossil hunting in your area.

4) Close

Quiz

1. What is a segmented column of bones that supports the body of a vertebrate called? **(backbone)**

2. Of birds, fishes, mammals, reptiles, and amphibians, which are ectotherms and which are endotherms? **(Birds and mammals are endotherms. Fishes, amphibians, and reptiles are ectotherms.)**

ALTERNATIVE ASSESSMENT

Writing Have small groups of students compile lists of three or four questions related to the content in this section. Then have students use their questions to quiz each other.

QuickLab

Body Temperature

Use a nonglass **fever thermometer** for this experiment. Take your temperature every hour for at least 6 hours. Make a graph of your body temperature by placing the time of day on the *x*-axis and your temperature on the *y*-axis. Does your temperature change throughout the day? How much? Do you think your body temperature changes after exercise? How would your results be different if you were an ectotherm?

internet connect

SCILINKS
NSTA

TOPIC: Vertebrates
GO TO: www.scilinks.org
sciLINKS NUMBER: HSTL380

Are Vertebrates Warm or Cold?

Most animals need to stay warm. The chemical reactions that take place in their body cells occur only at certain temperatures. An animal's body temperature cannot be too high or too low. But some animals control their body temperature more than others.

Staying Warm Birds and mammals warm their body by capturing the energy released by the chemical reactions in their cells. Their body temperature stays nearly constant even as the temperature of their environment changes. Animals that maintain a constant body temperature are called **endotherms**. Endotherms are sometimes called *warmblooded* animals. Because of their constant body temperature, endotherms can live in cold environments.

Cold Blood? On sunny days, lizards, like the one in **Figure 5,** bask in the sun. As they become warm, they also become more active. They are able to hunt for food and escape predators. But when the temperature drops, lizards slow down.

Lizards and other animals that do not control their body temperature through the chemical reactions of their cells are called **ectotherms**. Their body temperature fluctuates with the temperature of their environment. Nearly all fishes, amphibians, and reptiles are ectotherms. Ectotherms are sometimes called *coldblooded* animals.

Figure 5 Lizards bask in the sun to absorb heat.

REVIEW

1. How are vertebrates the same as other chordates? How are they different?
2. How are endotherms and ectotherms different?
3. **Applying Concepts** Your pet lizard is not moving very much. The veterinarian tells you to put a heat lamp in the cage. Why might this help?

Answers to Review

1. Like other chordates, vertebrates have a notochord, a hollow nerve cord, pharyngeal pouches, and a tail at some point in their lives. Unlike other chordates, vertebrates have a backbone and a skull.

2. Endotherms regulate their body temperature by capturing the heat released by the chemical reactions in their cells. Ectotherms do not tightly control their body temperature through the chemical reactions of their cells. Their body temperature depends on the temperature of their environment.

3. A lizard is an ectotherm. The heat lamp will warm the cage and cause the body temperature of the lizard to rise. The lizard will become more active when its temperature rises.

Section 2

Fishes

Terms to Learn

fins
scales
lateral line system
gills
denticles
swim bladder

What You'll Do

- Describe the three classes of living fishes, and give an example of each.
- Describe the function of a swim bladder and an oily liver.
- Explain the difference between internal fertilization and external fertilization.

Find a body of water, and you'll probably find fish. Fishes live in almost every water environment, from shallow ponds and streams to the depths of the oceans. You can find fishes in cold arctic waters and in warm tropical seas. Fishes can be found in rivers, lakes, marshes, and even in water-filled caves.

Fish were the first vertebrates on Earth. Fossil evidence indicates that fish appeared about 500 million years ago. Today Earth's marine and freshwater fishes make up more species than all other vertebrates combined. There are more than 25,000 species of fishes, and more are being discovered. A few are shown in **Figure 6**.

Angelfish

Figure 6 These are just some of the many species of fishes. Do any look familiar?

Surgeonfish

Sea horse

Catfish

Wolf eel

Fish Characteristics

Although the fishes on this page look very different from each other, they share many characteristics that help them live in water.

Many fishes are predators of other animals. Others are herbivores. Because they must actively search for food, they need a strong body, well-developed senses, and a brain.

2) Teach

READING STRATEGY

Prediction Guide Before students read the passage about fishes, ask them whether the following statements are true or false.

1. Sharks are considered fish. (true)
2. Some fish will suffocate if they stop swimming. (true)
3. All fish need to swim to stay alive. (false)

Students will discover the answers as they explore Section 2.

DISCUSSION

Aquarium Presentations
Encourage students who have aquariums to share information about their fish with the class. Discuss the importance of providing oxygen-rich water and other care requirements.

REAL-WORLD CONNECTION

Minnows and carp make up the largest family of fishes, with 1,600 species. They are usually the most abundant freshwater fish in North America, Europe, Asia, and Africa. You may even have one in your own home; goldfish and tetras are carp, and in a large enough setting, they can grow to several inches in length. Under ideal conditions, fish continue to grow for their entire lives.

MISCONCEPTION ALERT

Fish remove oxygen gas that is dissolved in the water. They *do not* use the oxygen that is part of the water molecule itself. Each molecule of water contains one atom of oxygen, but it is unavailable to the fish.

Born to Swim Fishes have many body parts that help them swim. Strong muscles attached to the backbone allow fishes to swim vigorously after their prey. Fishes swim through the water by moving their fins. **Fins** are fanlike structures that help fish move, steer, stop, and balance. Many fishes have bodies covered by **scales,** which protect the body and reduce friction as they swim through the water. **Figure 7** shows some of the external features of a typical fish.

Figure 7 *Fishes come in a variety of shapes and sizes, but all have gills, fins, and a tail.*

Dorsal fin, Lateral line, Pelvic fin, Anal fin, Tail fin, Pectoral fins, Gills, Gill cover, Eye

When you look at an object through a magnifying glass, you have to move the lens back and forth in front of your eye to bring the object into focus. The same thing happens in fish eyes. Fish have special muscles to change the position of the lenses of their eyes. By moving the eye lenses, fish can bring objects into focus.

Making Sense of the World Fishes have well-developed vision, hearing, and sense of smell. Most fishes also have a lateral line system. The **lateral line system** is a row or rows of tiny sense organs along each side of the body that often extend onto the head. This system detects water vibrations, such as those caused by another fish swimming by. Fishes have a brain that keeps track of all the information coming in from these senses. A tough skull protects the brain.

Underwater Breathing Fishes breathe with gills. **Gills** are organs that remove oxygen from the water. Oxygen in the water passes through the thin membrane of the gills to the blood. The blood then carries oxygen throughout the body. Gills are also used to remove carbon dioxide from the blood.

Making More Fish Most fishes reproduce by *external fertilization*. The female lays unfertilized eggs in the water, and the male drops sperm on them. But some species of fish reproduce by internal fertilization. In *internal fertilization,* the male deposits sperm inside the female. In most cases the female then lays eggs that contain the developing embryos. Baby fish hatch from the eggs. But in some species, the embryos develop inside the mother, and the baby fish are born live.

TOPIC: Fishes
GO TO: www.scilinks.org
sciLINKS NUMBER: HSTL385

IS THAT A FACT!

Air has 26 times more oxygen than water at the same temperature. Consequently, fish expend much more energy breathing than most mammals do.

378   Chapter 16 • Fishes, Amphibians, and Reptiles

Types of Fishes

Fishes include five very different classes of animals. Two classes are now extinct. We know about them only because of fossils. The three classes of fishes living today are *jawless fishes, cartilaginous fishes,* and *bony fishes.*

Jawless Fishes The first fishes did not have jaws. You might think that having no jaws would make it hard to eat and would lead to extinction. But the jawless fishes have thrived for half a billion years. Today there are about 60 species of jawless fishes.

Modern jawless fishes include lampreys, as shown in **Figure 8,** and hagfish. These fishes are eel-like, and they have smooth, slimy skin and a round, jawless mouth. Their skeleton is made of cartilage, and they have a notochord but no backbone. These fishes have a skull, a brain, and eyes.

Figure 8 *Lampreys are parasites that live by attaching themselves to other fishes.*

Cartilaginous Fishes Did you know that a shark is a fish? Sharks, like the one in **Figure 9,** belong to a class of fishes called cartilaginous (KART'l AJ uh nuhs) fishes. In most vertebrates, soft cartilage in the embryo is gradually replaced by bone. In sharks, skates, and rays, however, the skeleton never changes from cartilage to bone. That is why they are called cartilaginous fishes.

Sharks are the most well-known cartilaginous fishes, but they are not the only ones. Another group includes skates and rays. A sting ray is shown in **Figure 10.**

As any shark lover knows, cartilaginous fishes have fully functional jaws. These fishes are strong swimmers and expert predators. Like most predators, they have keen senses. Many have excellent senses of sight and smell, and they have a lateral line system.

Figure 9 *Sharks, like this hammerhead, rarely prey on humans. They prefer to eat their regular food, which is fish.*

Figure 10 *Rays, like this sting ray, usually feed on shellfish and worms on the sea floor.*

READING STRATEGY

Prediction Guide Ask students: What are the three types of fishes alive in the world today?

(jawless, cartilaginous, and bony)

Sharks lack some of the features of bony fishes, such as a swim bladder. They also lack movable side fins. In bony fishes, the side fins behind the head can be swiveled so the fish can move backward and forward. Sharks can't do this. How would this affect the shark's movement through the water?

It is difficult or impossible for the shark to stop or to swim backward.

CONNECT TO ENVIRONMENTAL SCIENCE

Once home to 200–500 species of fishes, Lake Victoria, in East Africa, is now home to the Nile perch and little else. Most of the native fishes were small cichlids, with each species unique in appearance and habit. But they were relatively difficult to fish commercially. The Nile perch was being tested in a nearby lake for introduction into Lake Victoria for commercial fishing when it mysteriously appeared in the lake on its own. It has since nearly wiped out the native fishes in this huge lake, to the point that the Nile perch is now largely feeding on its own young and shrimp. As a commercial fishery, the introduction is considered a success. Ecologically, it is a disaster.

Homework

Have students indicate which class (or classes) of fishes have the following characteristics; *J* for jawless, *C* for cartilaginous, and *B* for bony.

gills (J, C, B)
denticles (C)
cartilage skeleton (J, C)
swim bladder (B)
scales (B)

Section 2 • Fishes

3 Extend

MATH and MORE

Carcharodon megalodon shark teeth are as much as 17.5 cm long. Based on its tooth length, scientists estimate the Miocene-era shark was probably 12 m long, which is about twice as long as today's great white shark. Have students imagine that they discovered some shark teeth with the following lengths: 35 cm, 70 cm, and 8.75 cm. Have them use ratios to estimate the sizes of the sharks these teeth came from. **(24 m, 48 m, and 6 m)**

 PG 740

Floating a Pipe Fish

Answer to MATHBREAK
There are 23,750 species of bony fishes (25,000 × 0.95 = 23,750).

CONNECT TO PHYSICAL SCIENCE

The electric eel is truly electric—more than half of its body is made up of electricity-producing cells. Found in shallow freshwater rivers in South America, it can reach 3 m in length and produces a prey-killing jolt of 600 V—enough to kill a person.

You can illustrate an electric current with the following Teaching Transparency.

 Teaching Transparency 269
"How a Cell Produces an Electric Current" **LINK TO PHYSICAL SCIENCE**

Figure 11 A shark's denticles and human teeth are made of the same materials.

Figure 12 A goldfish is a bony fish.

MATH BREAK

A Lot of Bones
If there are 25,000 species of fishes and 95 percent of all fishes are bony fishes, how many species of bony fishes are there?

The skin of cartilaginous fishes is covered with small tooth-like **denticles** that give it the feel of sandpaper. If you rub your hand on a shark's skin from head to tail, it feels smooth. But if you rub your hand from tail to head, you can get cut! Look at the magnified denticles in **Figure 11**.

To stay afloat, cartilaginous fishes store a lot of oil in their liver. See why in the QuickLab on the next page. Even with oily livers, these fishes are denser than water. They have to keep moving in order to stay afloat. Once they stop swimming, they gradually glide to the bottom.

Cartilaginous fishes do not swim just to keep from sinking, however. Some must swim to maintain the flow of water over their gills. If these fishes stop swimming, they will suffocate. Others do not have to swim. They can lie on the ocean floor and pump water across their gills.

Bony Fishes When you think of a fish, you probably think of something like the fish shown in **Figure 12**. Goldfish, tuna, trout, catfish, and cod are all bony fishes, the largest class of fishes. Ninety-five percent of all fishes are bony fishes. They range in size from 1 cm long to more than 6 m long.

As their name implies, bony fishes have a skeleton made of bone instead of cartilage. The body of a bony fish is covered by bony scales.

Unlike cartilaginous fishes, bony fishes can float in one place without swimming. This is because they have a swim bladder that keeps them from sinking. The **swim bladder** is a balloonlike organ that is filled with oxygen and other gases from the bloodstream. It gives fish *buoyancy*, or the ability to float in water. The swim bladder and other body parts of bony fishes are shown in **Figure 13**.

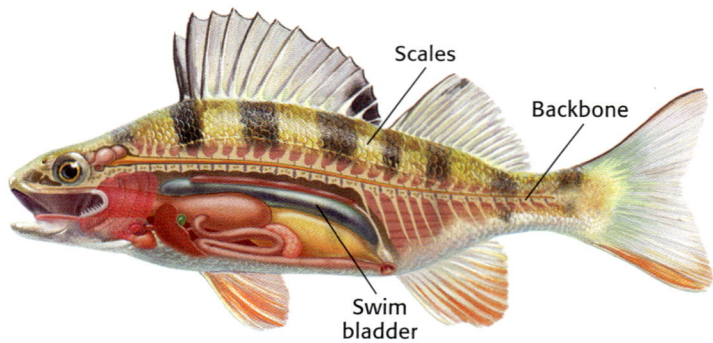

Figure 13 Bony fishes have a swim bladder, a bony skeleton, and scales.

IS THAT A FACT!

Basking sharks, which are the second largest fish, are hunted for the squalene oil in their liver. Although basking-shark livers are extremely large, the Basking Shark Society reports that 2,500–3,000 livers are needed to produce just 1 ton (0.91 metric tons) of squalene oil. Between 1987 and 1994, South Korea alone imported an average of 52 tons (47 metric tons) of the oil from Japan. Squalene oil is used as cooking oil, a skin moisturizer, and a lubricant.

There are two main groups of bony fishes. Almost all bony fishes are *ray-finned fishes*. Ray-finned fishes have paired fins supported by thin rays of bone. Ray-finned fishes include many familiar fishes, such as eels, herrings, trout, minnows, and perch. **Figure 14** shows a ray-finned fish.

Lobe-finned fishes and *lungfishes* make up a second group of bony fishes. Lobe-finned fishes have fins that are muscular and thick. The coelacanths, which were described at the beginning of the chapter, are lobe-finned fishes. There are six known species of modern lungfishes. You can see a lungfish in **Figure 15.** Scientists think that ancient fishes from this group were the ancestors of amphibians.

Figure 14 *Ray-finned fishes are some of the fastest swimmers in the world. A pike, like this one, can swim faster than the fastest human runners can run, about 48 km/h.*

Figure 15 *Lungfishes have air sacs, or lungs, and can gulp air. They are found in Africa, Australia, and South America and live in shallow waters that often dry up in the summer.*

REVIEW

1. What are the three types of fishes? Which type are the coelacanths?
2. Most bony fishes reproduce by external fertilization. What does this mean?
3. What is the lateral line system, and what is its function?
4. **Analyzing Relationships** Compare the ways that cartilaginous fishes and bony fishes maintain buoyancy.

4) Close

Quiz

1. Of the 25,000 species of fishes, about what percentage of them are bony fishes? (95 percent)
2. Sharks are a member of what class of fishes? (cartilaginous)

ALTERNATIVE ASSESSMENT

Concept Mapping Create a concept map using the following terms (students must also supply the connecting words linking the terms):

vertebrate, chordate, notochord, tail, hollow nervechord, pharyngeal pouches

Answers to Review

1. The three types of fishes are jawless fishes, cartilaginous fishes, and bony fishes. The coelacanth is a bony fish.
2. In external fertilization, the female lays unfertilized eggs, and sperm fertilize the egg outside the female's body.
3. The lateral line system is a row of sense organs along the side of a fish's body that detect water vibrations caused by other objects in the water.
4. Cartilaginous fishes have oily livers to help them stay afloat. Bony fishes have a swim bladder that helps them remain buoyant.

SECTION 3

Focus

Amphibians
In this section, students will discover when and how the first amphibians evolved from fishes. They will find out how amphibians breathe, reproduce, and develop through the process of metamorphosis. Students will also explore the three major groups of amphibians.

🔔 Bellringer
On the board or overhead projector, instruct the students to answer the following questions in their ScienceLog:

What is an advantage to the thin, moist skin of amphibians? What is the primary disadvantage to such skin? **(They can absorb oxygen and water right through their skin, but they also lose moisture through skin.)**

1) Motivate

DEMONSTRATION

Illustrating Fossilization Fill a small bucket halfway with sand. Place a kitchen sponge on top of the sand. Pour sand on top of the sponge until the bucket is nearly filled. Next, pour table salt in a small bucket of warm water, and stir until the salt no longer dissolves. Pour the solution over sand in the bucket, and leave overnight. On the next day, uncover the sponge. The water should have evaporated or drained to the bottom of the sand, and the salt should have hardened the sponge. Explain to students that fossils are formed in a similar manner. (Dissolved minerals enter openings or spaces in plant or animal material and harden.) `Sheltered English`

Section 3

Terms to Learn
lung   metamorphosis
tadpole

What You'll Do
- Describe the importance of amphibians in evolution.
- Explain how amphibians breathe.
- Describe metamorphosis in amphibians.

Figure 16 *Modern amphibians include frogs and salamanders.*

Barred leaf frog

Sierra Nevada salamander

internetconnect

SC$_{\text{LINKS}}$ **NSTA**
TOPIC: Amphibians
GO TO: www.scilinks.org
***sci*LINKS NUMBER:** HSTL390

Amphibians

By the end of the Devonian period, 350 million years ago, fishes lived wherever there was water. But none of these vertebrates could live on land. And the land was a wonderful place for a vertebrate. It had lush green forests, many tasty insects, and few predators. But for vertebrates to adapt to life on land, they needed lungs for breathing and legs for walking. How did these changes occur?

Moving to Land
Most of the amphibians living on Earth today are frogs or salamanders, like those in **Figure 16.** But the early amphibians looked much different. Fossil evidence indicates that the first amphibians evolved from ancient ancestors of modern lungfishes. These fishes developed lungs to get oxygen from the air. A **lung** is a saclike organ that takes oxygen from the air and delivers it to the blood. The fins of these ancient fishes became strong enough to support the fishes' body weight and eventually became legs.

Fossils show that the first amphibians looked like a cross between a fish and a salamander, as shown in **Figure 17.** The early amphibians were the first vertebrates to live most of their life on land, and they were very successful. Many were very large—up to 10 m long—and could stay on dry land longer than today's amphibians can. But early amphibians still had to return to the water to keep from drying out, to avoid overheating, and to lay their eggs.

Figure 17 *Ancient amphibians probably looked something like this.*

IS THAT A FACT!
- A group of frogs is called an army.
- A group of toads is called a knot.
- Fear of frogs is called ranidaphobia.
- Fear of toads is called bufonophobia.

Characteristics of Amphibians

Amphibian means "double life." Most amphibians have two parts to their life. Because amphibian eggs do not have a shell and a special membrane to prevent water loss, the embryos must develop in a very wet environment. After amphibians emerge from an egg, they live in the water, like fishes do. Later they develop into animals that can live on land. But even adult amphibians are only partly adapted to life on land, and they must always live near water.

Amphibians are ectotherms. Like the body of a fish, the body of an amphibian changes temperature according to the temperature of its environment.

Thin-Skinned Most amphibians do not have scales. Their skin is thin, smooth, and moist. They do not drink water. Instead, they absorb it through their skin. Amphibians can breathe by gulping air into their lungs. But many also absorb oxygen through their skin, which is full of blood vessels. Some salamanders, like the one in **Figure 18,** breathe only through their skin. Because amphibian skin is so thin and moist, these animals can lose water through their skin and become dehydrated. For this reason, most amphibians live in water or in damp habitats.

The skin of many amphibians is brilliantly colored. The colors are often a warning to predators because the skin of many amphibians contains poison glands. These poisons may simply be irritating or they may be deadly. The skin of the dart-poison frog, shown in **Figure 19,** contains one of the most deadly toxins known.

Figure 18 *The four-toed salamander has no lungs. It gets all of its oxygen through its skin.*

Figure 19 *The skin of this dart-poison frog is full of poison glands. In South America, hunters rub the tips of their arrows in the deadly toxin.*

 Self-Check

How is amphibian skin like a lung? *(See page 782 to check your answers.)*

Most toads are well adapted to life on land and leave their fertilized eggs to fend for themselves. The Surinam toad of South America is not like most toads. Highly aquatic, it cannot survive long out of the water. And in a strange mating encounter that involves somersaults, fertilized eggs are attached to the back of the female. The eggs grow into pockets for each developing embryo. Depending on the species, young emerge from the pockets either as tadpoles or as young toads.

② Teach, *continued*

ACTIVITY

Observing Development
Obtain frog or salamander eggs either locally or from a biological supply company. Set up an aquarium, and allow students to observe the metamorphosis that follows. Students should sketch the process each step of the way. Note: if the animals were not collected locally, they cannot be released into the wild. **Sheltered English**

RETEACHING

 Poster Project Have students create a poster with captions showing how a tadpole changes into a frog. **Sheltered English**

Some students may have the mistaken impression that they can get warts from touching frogs and toads. Tell them that warts are caused by human viruses.

 Teaching Transparency 60 "Metamorphosis of a Frog"

Leading a Double Life The amphibian embryo usually develops into an aquatic larva called a **tadpole**. The tadpole can live only in wet environments. It obtains oxygen through gills and uses its long tail to swim. Later the tadpole loses its gills and develops lungs and limbs. This change from a larval form to an adult form is called **metamorphosis** and is shown in **Figure 20**. Adult amphibians are capable of surviving on land.

Figure 20 *Most frogs and salamanders go through metamorphosis.*

- Adult frog
- The tail and gills disappear, and lungs become functional.
- Fertilized eggs
- A newly hatched tadpole feeds on yolk stored in its body and breathes with gills.
- The tadpole begins to feed and grow legs.

A few amphibians skip the aquatic stage and develop directly into adult frogs or salamanders. For example, one species of frog lays eggs on moist ground. Male adults guard the developing embryos. When an embryo begins to move, a male frog quickly takes it into its mouth and protects it inside its vocal sacs. When the embryo finishes developing, the adult frog opens its mouth, and a tiny frog jumps out. You can see this frog in **Figure 21**.

Figure 21 *Darwin frogs live in Chile and Argentina. A male frog may carry 5 to 15 embryos in its vocal sacs until the young are about 1.5 cm in length.*

WEIRD SCIENCE

Coast foam-nest tree frogs mate in trees that overhang ponds and streams. Then the females lay their eggs in large foamy, cocoonlike masses that cake over for protection from the sun. After a week or so of development, the tadpoles are ready to emerge, but only after a rain comes and moistens the foam. Once moistened, the foam drips into the water below, carrying with it the young tadpoles!

Kinds of Amphibians

It is estimated that there are 4,600 species of amphibians alive today. These belong to three groups: caecilians (see SIL yuhns), salamanders, and frogs and toads.

Caecilians Most people are not familiar with caecilians. These amphibians do not have legs and are shaped like worms or snakes, as shown in **Figure 22.** But they have the thin, moist skin of amphibians. Unlike other amphibians, some caecilians have bony scales. Many caecilians have very small eyes underneath their skin and are blind. Caecilians live in the tropical areas of Asia, Africa, and South America. About 160 species are known.

Figure 22 Caecilians are legless amphibians that live in damp soil in the tropics. Caecilians eat small invertebrates in the soil.

Salamanders Of modern amphibians, salamanders are the most like prehistoric amphibians. Although salamanders are much smaller than their ancient ancestors, they have a similar body shape, a long tail, and four strong legs. They range in size from a few centimeters long to 1.5 m long.

There are about 390 known species of salamanders. Most of them live under stones and logs in the damp woods of North America. They eat small invertebrates. A few, such as the axolotl (AK suh LAHT ′l), shown in **Figure 23,** do not go through metamorphosis. They live their entire life in the water.

Figure 23 This axolotl is an unusual salamander. It retains its gills and never leaves the water.

Ecological Indicators

Amphibians are often called ecological indicators. When large numbers of amphibians begin to die or show deformities, this may indicate a problem with the environment. Sometimes deformities are caused by parasites, but amphibians are also extremely sensitive to chemical changes in their environment. Based on what you know about amphibians, why do you think they are sensitive to water pollution and air pollution?

3) Extend

RESEARCH

Writing — Have interested students conduct research about the field of herpetology, the branch of zoology that deals with amphibians and reptiles. Students could prepare reports and present them to the class. As an alternative, invite a herpetologist or other zoologist from the area to speak with the class about herpetology.

4) Close

Quiz

1. Where do most amphibians start their lives? (in water)
2. What is the meaning of amphibian? (double life)
3. What is the largest group of amphibians? (frogs and toads)

ALTERNATIVE ASSESSMENT

Writing — Have students compose a song or poem accurately describing the life cycle of an amphibian of their choice.

 PG 742
A Prince of a Frog

Frogs and Toads Ninety percent of all amphibians are frogs or toads. They are found all over the world, from deserts to rain forests. Frogs and toads are very similar to each other, as you can see in **Figure 24**. In fact, toads are a type of frog.

Frog

Toad

Figure 24 *Frogs have smooth, moist skin. Toads spend less time in water than frogs do, and their skin is drier and bumpier.*

Frogs and toads are highly adapted for life on land. Adults have powerful leg muscles for jumping. They have well-developed ears for hearing, and they have vocal cords for calling. They also have extendible, sticky tongues. The tongue is attached to the front of the mouth so that it can be flipped out quickly to catch insects.

Singing Frogs Frogs are well known for their nighttime choruses, but many frogs sing in the daytime too. Like humans, they force air from their lungs across vocal cords in the throat. But frogs have something we lack. Surrounding their vocal cords is a thin sac of skin called the *vocal sac*. When frogs vocalize, the sac inflates with air, like a balloon does, and vibrates. You can see this in **Figure 25**. The vibrations of the sac increase the volume of the song so that it can be heard over long distances.

Figure 25 *Most frogs that sing are males, and their songs have different meanings.*

Examine the princely characteristics of a friendly frog on page 742 of your LabBook.

REVIEW

1. Describe metamorphosis in amphibians.
2. Why do amphibians have to be near water or in a very wet habitat?
3. What adaptations allow amphibians to live on land?
4. Name the three types of amphibians. How are they similar? How are they different?
5. **Analyzing Relationships** Describe the relationship between lungfishes and amphibians. What characteristics do they share? How do they differ?

▼ **Answers to Review**

1. After fertilization of an egg, the embryo develops into a tadpole that lives in water. The tadpole loses its gills and develops lungs and legs to become an adult.
2. Amphibians must live near water because they have very thin, moist skin and they can easily dehydrate.
3. lungs (instead of gills) and legs
4. Frogs and toads, salamanders, and caecilians all have a thin, moist skin; salamanders and frogs and toads have legs, but caecilians do not; caecilians have scales.
5. Both have lungs and can breathe air; amphibians have stronger legs and skin that absorbs oxygen; amphibians go through metamorphosis, but lungfish do not.

Section 4

Reptiles

Terms to Learn
therapsid
amniotic egg

What You'll Do
- Explain the adaptations that allow reptiles to live on land.
- Name the three main groups of vertebrates that evolved from reptiles.
- Describe the characteristics of an amniotic egg.
- Name the three orders of modern reptiles.

About 35 million years after the first amphibians colonized the land, some of them evolved special traits that prepared them for life in an even drier environment. These animals developed thick, dry skin that protected them from water loss. Their legs became stronger and more vertical, so they were better able to walk. And they evolved a special egg that could be laid on dry land. These animals were reptiles, the first animals to live completely out of the water.

Reptile History

Fossils show that soon after the first reptiles appeared, they split into groups. This can be shown in a family tree of the reptiles, as illustrated in **Figure 26.**

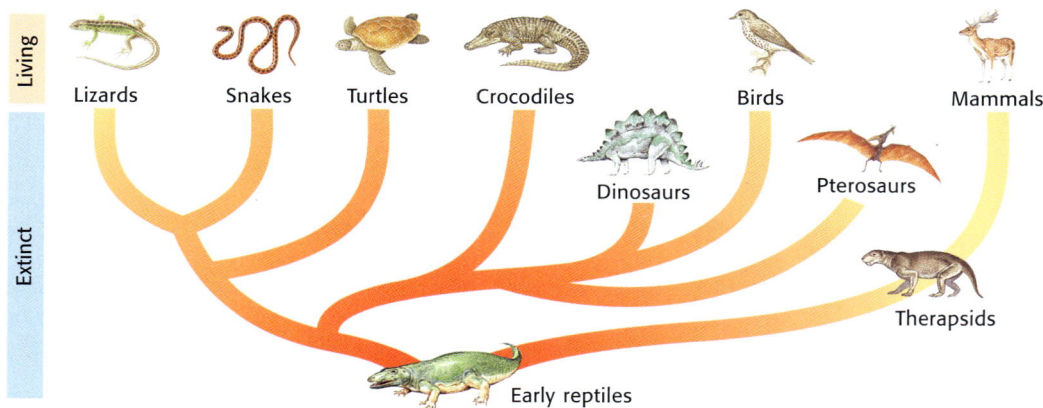

Figure 26 Early reptiles were the ancestors of modern reptiles, birds, and mammals.

Many of the most fascinating reptiles are now extinct. When we think of extinct reptiles, we usually think of dinosaurs. But only a fraction of the reptiles living in prehistoric times were land-dwelling dinosaurs. Many were swimming reptiles. A few were flying pterosaurs. And there were turtles, lizards, snakes, and crocodiles. In addition, there was a group of mammal-like reptiles called therapsids. As you can see in Figure 26, **therapsids** (thuh RAP sidz) were the ancestors of mammals.

IS THAT A FACT!
The pteranodon, a particularly large type of pterosaur, had a wingspan of more than 6.5 m (20 ft).

 Teaching Transparency 61 "Reptile History"

 Directed Reading Worksheet 16 Section 4

2) Teach

ACTIVITY

Organizing Reptiles Before reading about the types of reptiles, take a moment to try to put the following reptiles into their three orders. Match the animal on the left with its closest relative on the right. Check your answers after reading.

turtle	crocodile
snake	tortoise
alligator	lizard

(turtle, tortoise; snake, lizard; alligator, crocodile)

USING THE FIGURE

Encourage students to make comparisons between reptile eggs and amphibian eggs. *(Amphibian eggs don't have shells and must be laid in water or moist ground. Reptile eggs do have a shell and can be laid in the dry earth.)*

- Ask: How might these facts favor reptile reproduction over amphibian reproduction during a drought? *(Dehydration would kill off amphibian embryos, but reptile embryos would be more likely to survive.)*

Sheltered English

GUIDED PRACTICE

Writing Have students make a list of reasons why animals that internally regulate their temperatures have advantages over those that do not. Provide several examples to help students get started.

Teaching Transparency 62
"Amniotic Egg"

Characteristics of Reptiles

Reptiles are adapted for life on land. Although crocodiles, turtles, and a few species of snakes live in the water, all of these animals are descended from reptiles that lived on land. All reptiles use lungs to breathe air, just as you do.

Thick-Skinned A very important adaptation for life on land is thick, dry skin, which forms a watertight layer. This thick skin keeps cells from losing water by evaporation. Most reptiles cannot breathe through their skin the way amphibians can. Most depend entirely on their lungs for oxygen and carbon dioxide exchange. Check out the snake's skin in **Figure 27**.

Figure 27 Many people think snakes are slimy, but the skin of snakes and other reptiles is scaly and dry.

Coldblooded? Like fishes and amphibians, reptiles are ectotherms. That means that they usually cannot maintain a constant body temperature. Reptiles are active when their environment is warm, and they slow down when their environment is cool.

A few reptiles can generate some heat from their own body. For example, some lizards in the southwestern United States can keep their body temperature at about 34°C, even when the air temperature is cool. Still, modern reptiles are limited to mild climates. They cannot tolerate the cold polar regions, where many mammals and birds thrive.

The Amazing Amniotic Egg Among reptiles' many adaptations to land life, the most critical is the amniotic (AM nee AH tik) egg. The **amniotic egg** is surrounded by a shell, as shown in **Figure 28**. The shell protects the developing embryo and keeps the egg from drying out. An amniotic egg can be laid under rocks, in the ground, in forests, or even in the desert. The amniotic egg is so well adapted to a dry environment that even crocodiles and turtles return to land to lay their eggs.

Figure 28 Compare the amphibian eggs at left with the reptile eggs at right. What differences can you see?

WEIRD SCIENCE

The Texas horned toad of southwestern North America is actually a lizard with a bizarre defense mechanism. When threatened, the lizard puffs itself up, increasing its blood pressure until the capillaries around its eyes burst. The predator is stunned when it is then squirted with blood from up to 2.4 m (7 ft) away.

Parts of an Amniotic Egg The shell is just one important part of an amniotic egg. The other parts of an amniotic egg are illustrated in **Figure 29.** The egg protects the developing embryo from predators, bacterial infections, and dehydration.

Figure 29 An Amniotic Egg

The **shell** protects the egg from damage and keeps the egg from drying out. The shell has small pores that allow oxygen to pass through to the growing embryo and carbon dioxide to be removed.

The **albumen** (al BYOO muhn) provides water and protein to the embryo.

Embryo

The **amniotic sac** is filled with fluid. The amniotic fluid surrounds the embryo and protects it from injury.

Air space

The **yolk** provides a rich supply of food to the embryo.

The **allantois** (uh LAN toh wis) stores wastes from the embryo. It also passes oxygen to the embryo from the pores in the shell.

Reptile Reproduction The amniotic egg is fertilized inside the female. A shell then forms around the egg, and the female lays the egg. Because of the shell, most reptiles reproduce by internal fertilization.

Most reptiles lay their eggs in soil or sand. A few do not lay eggs. Instead the embryos develop inside the mother's reproductive passages, and the young are born live. In either case, the embryo develops into a tiny young reptile. Reptiles do not have a larval stage and do not undergo metamorphosis.

Types of Reptiles

In the age of the dinosaurs, from 300 million years ago until about 65 million years ago, most land vertebrates were reptiles. Today the 6,000 species of living reptiles represent only a handful of the many species of reptiles that once lived.

Modern reptiles include turtles and tortoises, crocodiles and alligators, and lizards and snakes.

 Self-Check

1. What adaptations of reptiles are important for living on dry land?
2. Why must animals that lay eggs with shells reproduce by internal fertilization?

(See page 782 to check your answers.)

IS THAT A FACT!

Like modern reptiles and birds, dinosaurs laid their eggs on land. There is a rich fossil record of these eggs. According to the National Geographic Society, eggs (some that contain embryos) and nests have been discovered at over 199 sites. Most of the sites—109—are in Asia. In North America, eggs have been found in 39 locations.

MATH and MORE

Tell students: Scientists use the Celsius scale when measuring temperature, while most Americans use the Fahrenheit scale in daily life. To convert Celsius to Fahrenheit, multiply the degrees Celsius by 1.8 (or $\frac{9}{5}$) and add 32. Try the following:

From the text you learned that some reptiles are able to keep their body at 34°C even when the environment is cool.

Convert 34°C to degrees Fahrenheit. **(93.2°F)**

Convert the following:

100°C **(212°F)**   8°C **(46.4°F)**
0°C **(32°F)**   72°C **(161.6°F)**

Math Skills Worksheet 35 "Using Temperature Scales"

DEMONSTRATION

Reptile Exhibit Invite a reptile expert from the local zoo or an amateur reptile enthusiast to bring several reptiles to the class for a hands-on presentation. Afterward, have students describe in their ScienceLog their impressions of the reptiles, including the reptiles' physical characteristics and the way the reptiles felt to the touch. Sheltered English

Answers to Self-Check

1. Thick, dry skin and amniotic eggs help reptiles live on dry land.
2. The hard shell prevents fertilization, so the egg must be fertilized before the shell is added.

2) Teach, continued

REAL-WORLD CONNECTION

Gerontologists—scientists who study aging in humans—are looking to the animal world to better understand the aging process. Why do some animals, such as turtles, live so long? And not only are turtles long-lived, they show almost no signs of aging until the very end. There is little difference between a 30-year-old tortoise and a 70-year-old tortoise.

People of Indonesia, Sri Lanka, the Philippines, and Southeast Asia have learned that they can use the water monitor—a carnivorous lizard nearly 2 m long—to find water. If the lizard is seen walking about, it is almost always heading for water.

Homework

 Reporting on Reptiles Have students choose their favorite reptile and write a brief report about the animal. Students should include the following information:

size, appearance, range (where is it found in the world?), habitat, diet, adaptations to its particular way of life (i.e., what tricks or methods does it use to survive?), relationship to people, and its status in the world (endangered? rare? common?)

MISCONCEPTION ALERT

Despite lingering urban legends, there has never been a confirmed sighting of an alligator living in the sewers of New York City.

Figure 30 The bottom shell of a box turtle is hinged on both ends so the turtle can pull it snug against the top shell.

Turtles and Tortoises The 250 species of turtles and tortoises are only distantly related to the rest of the reptiles.

The trait that makes turtles and tortoises unique is their shell. The shell makes a turtle slow and inflexible, so outrunning its predators is highly unlikely. On the other hand, many turtles can draw their head and limbs into the armorlike shell to protect themselves, as the box turtle shown in **Figure 30** is doing.

Most turtles spend some or all of their life in water. The front legs of sea turtles have evolved into flippers, as shown in **Figure 31.** Female sea turtles come ashore only to lay their eggs on sandy beaches. Desert tortoises are different from other turtles. They live only on land.

Figure 31 Sea turtles have a streamlined shell to help them swim and turn rapidly.

Crocodiles and Alligators The 22 species of crocodiles and alligators are all carnivores. They eat water bugs, fish, turtles, birds, and mammals. These reptiles spend most of their time in the water. Because their eyes and nostrils are on the top of their flat head, they can watch their surroundings while most of their body is hidden underwater. This gives them a great advantage over their prey. How can you tell the difference between an alligator and a crocodile? See for yourself in **Figure 32.**

Figure 32 An alligator has a broad head and a rounded snout. A crocodile has a narrow head and a pointed snout.

---

internet connect

TOPIC: Reptiles
GO TO: www.scilinks.org
sciLINKS NUMBER: HSTL395

SCIENCE HUMOR

Q: Why does a turtle live in a shell?

A: because it can't afford an apartment

390 Chapter 16 • Fishes, Amphibians, and Reptiles

Lizards Most of the species of modern reptiles are lizards and snakes. There are about 4,000 known species of lizards and about 1,600 known species of snakes.

Lizards live in deserts, forests, grasslands, and jungles. Chameleons, geckos, skinks, and iguanas are some of the amazing variety of lizards. Most lizards eat small invertebrates, but many are herbivores. The largest lizard is the 3 m long, 140 kg Komodo dragon of Indonesia, shown in **Figure 33**. But most lizards are less than 30 cm long.

Figure 33 Komodo dragons eat deer, pigs, and goats. They have even been known to eat humans in rare cases.

Snakes The most obvious characteristic of snakes is their lack of legs. Snakes move by contractions of their muscular body. On smooth surfaces, scales on their belly grip the surface and help pull the snake forward.

All snakes are carnivores. They eat small animals and eggs. Snakes swallow their prey whole, as shown in **Figure 34**. Snakes have special jaws with five joints that allow them to open their mouth wide and swallow very large prey. Some snakes, such as pythons and boas, kill their prey by squeezing it until it suffocates. Other snakes have poison glands and special fangs for injecting venom into their prey. The venom kills or stuns the prey and contains powerful enzymes that begin digesting it.

Snakes do not see or hear well, but they can smell extremely well. When a snake flicks its forked tongue out of its mouth, it is sampling the air. Tiny particles and molecules stick to the tongue. When the snake pulls its tongue inside its mouth, it places the tips of its tongue into two openings in the roof of its mouth, where the molecules are sensed.

Figure 34 This common egg eater snake is swallowing a bird's egg.

REVIEW

1. What characteristics set turtles apart from other reptiles?
2. What special adaptations do snakes have for eating?
3. **Applying Concepts** Like reptiles, mammals have an amniotic egg. But mammals give birth to live young. The embryo develops from a fertilized egg inside the female's body. Which parts of a reptilian amniotic egg do you think a mammal could do without? Explain your answer.

internet connect

SC/LINKS.
NSTA

TOPIC: Reptiles
GO TO: www.scilinks.org
sciLINKS NUMBER: HSTL395

3) Extend

RESEARCH

Writing Have students investigate and write a report on the differences between the diet of an alligator and that of a similarly sized carnivorous mammal (a lion or tiger). Which of these animals eats more? Why? (The mammal needs to eat more because mammals use a large amount of energy to keep themselves warm.)

4) Close

Quiz

1. What trait makes turtles stand out from other reptiles? (their shell)
2. What animals are the closest living relatives of dinosaurs? (crocodiles and alligators)

ALTERNATIVE ASSESSMENT

Writing Have students imagine that they are one of the reptiles in this section. They are also restaurateurs trying to attract other reptiles to their new restaurant. Have students prepare accurate menus containing delectables that will surely please their thick-skinned, ectothermic customers.

Answers to Review

1. Unlike other reptiles, turtles have a shell that they use for protection.
2. Snakes have special jaws so that they can open their mouth wide and swallow their prey whole. Some snakes have venom that begins digesting their prey.
3. Sample answer: Mammals do not need the shell of the amniotic egg because it does not need to be protected from the outside environment. Students might also suggest that mammals do not need the yolk because mammal embryos develop inside the mother and receive nutrients directly from her body.

Reinforcement Worksheet 16
"Coldblooded Critters"

Critical Thinking Worksheet 16
"Frogs Aren't Breathing Easy"

Chapter Highlights

VOCABULARY DEFINITIONS

SECTION 1

vertebrate an animal with a skull and a backbone; includes mammals, birds, reptiles, amphibians, and fish

vertebrae segments of bone or cartilage that interlock to form a backbone

endotherm an animal that maintains a constant body temperature despite temperature changes in its environment

ectotherm an animal whose body temperature fluctuates with the temperature of its environment

SECTION 2

fins fanlike structures that help fish move, turn, stop, and balance

scales bony structures that cover the skin of bony fishes

lateral line system row of tiny sense organs along the sides of a fish's body

gills organs that remove oxygen from the water and carbon dioxide from the blood

denticles small, sharp toothlike structures on the skin of cartilaginous fishes

swim bladder balloonlike organ that is filled with oxygen and other gases; gives bony fishes their buoyancy

Chapter Highlights

SECTION 1

Vocabulary
- vertebrate (p. 374)
- vertebrae (p. 375)
- endotherm (p. 376)
- ectotherm (p. 376)

Section Notes
- At some point during their development, chordates have a notochord, a hollow nerve cord, pharyngeal pouches, and a tail.
- Chordates include lancelets, tunicates, and vertebrates. Most chordates are vertebrates.
- Vertebrates differ from the other chordates in that they have a backbone and skull made of bone or cartilage.
- The backbone is composed of units called vertebrae.
- Vertebrates may be ectotherms or endotherms.
- Endotherms control their body temperature through the chemical reactions of their cells. Ectotherms do not.

SECTION 2

Vocabulary
- fins (p. 378)
- scales (p. 378)
- lateral line system (p. 378)
- gills (p. 378)
- denticles (p. 380)
- swim bladder (p. 380)

Section Notes
- There are three groups of living fishes: jawless fishes, cartilaginous fishes, and bony fishes.
- The cartilaginous fishes have an oily liver that helps them float.

✓ Skills Check

Math Concepts

HOW MANY SPECIES? If there are 6,000 species of reptiles and 67 percent of all reptiles are lizards, how many species of lizards are there?

Sixty-seven percent of 6,000 is:

$$6,000 \times 0.67 = 4,020$$

There are 4,020 species of lizards.

Visual Understanding

METAMORPHOSIS Most amphibians go through metamorphosis. They change form as they develop into an adult. Figure 20 on page 384 illustrates the metamorphosis of a frog. Follow the arrows to see how a frog develops from an egg to a tadpole to an adult.

Lab and Activity Highlights

Floating a Pipe Fish PG 740

A Prince of a Frog PG 742

Datasheets for LabBook
(blackline masters for these labs)

SECTION 2

- Most bony fishes have a swim bladder. The swim bladder is a balloonlike organ that gives bony fishes buoyancy.
- In external fertilization, eggs are fertilized outside the female's body. In internal fertilization, eggs are fertilized inside the female's body.

Labs
Floating a Pipe Fish (p. 740)

SECTION 3

Vocabulary
lung (p. 382)
tadpole (p. 384)
metamorphosis (p. 384)

Section Notes
- Amphibians were the first vertebrates to live on land.
- Amphibians breathe by gulping air into their lungs and by absorbing oxygen through their skin.
- Amphibians start life in water, where they breathe through gills. During metamorphosis, they lose their gills and develop lungs and legs that allow them to live on land.
- Modern amphibians include caecilians, salamanders, and frogs and toads.

Labs
A Prince of a Frog (p. 742)

SECTION 4

Vocabulary
therapsid (p. 387)
amniotic egg (p. 388)

Section Notes
- Reptiles evolved from amphibians by adapting to life on dry land.
- Reptiles have thick, scaly skin that protects them from drying out.
- A tough shell keeps the amniotic egg from drying out and protects the embryo.
- Amniotic fluid surrounds and protects the embryo in an amniotic egg.
- Vertebrates that evolved from early reptiles are reptiles, birds, and mammals.
- Modern reptiles include turtles and tortoises, lizards and snakes, and crocodiles and alligators.

VOCABULARY DEFINITIONS, continued

SECTION 3

lung a saclike organ that takes oxygen from the air and delivers it to the blood

tadpole aquatic larvae of an amphibian

metamorphosis process in which an insect or other animal changes form as it develops from an embryo or larva to an adult

SECTION 4

therapsid prehistoric, reptile ancestor of mammals

amniotic egg egg containing amniotic fluid to protect the developing embryo; usually surrounded by a hard shell

 Vocabulary Review Worksheet 16

 Blackline masters of these Chapter Highlights can be found in the **Study Guide.**

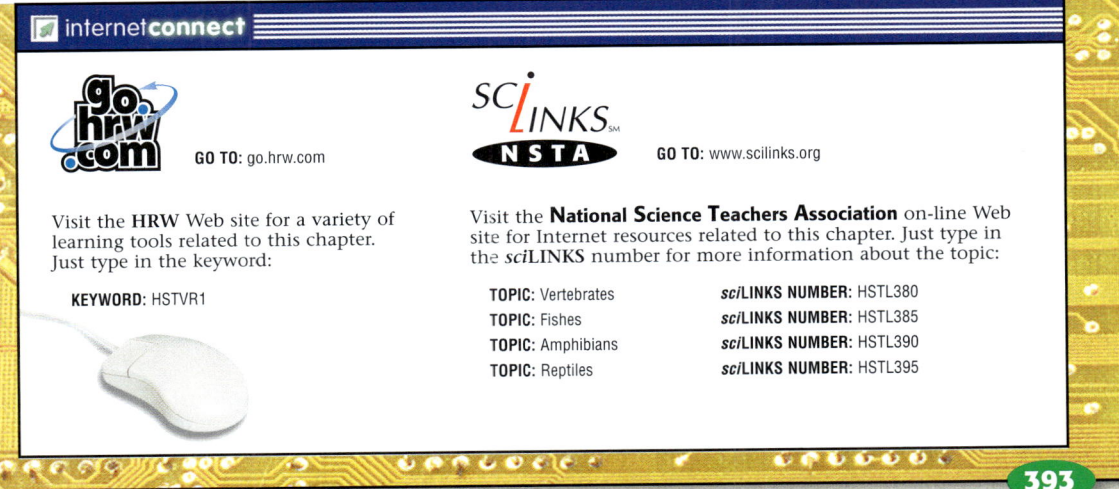

internetconnect

GO TO: go.hrw.com

GO TO: www.scilinks.org

Visit the **HRW** Web site for a variety of learning tools related to this chapter. Just type in the keyword:

KEYWORD: HSTVR1

Visit the **National Science Teachers Association** on-line Web site for Internet resources related to this chapter. Just type in the sciLINKS number for more information about the topic:

TOPIC: Vertebrates — sciLINKS NUMBER: HSTL380
TOPIC: Fishes — sciLINKS NUMBER: HSTL385
TOPIC: Amphibians — sciLINKS NUMBER: HSTL390
TOPIC: Reptiles — sciLINKS NUMBER: HSTL395

Lab and Activity Highlights

LabBank

 Whiz-Bang Demonstrations, The Fish in the Abyss, Demo 10

Long-Term Projects & Research Ideas, Go Fish!, Project 16

Chapter Review Answers

USING VOCABULARY

1. a hollow nerve cord and a tail
2. therapsids
3. ectotherms
4. external
5. hollow nerve cord

UNDERSTANDING CONCEPTS

Multiple Choice

6. d
7. c
8. c
9. c
10. a
11. b
12. d

Short Answer

13. Amphibians breathe through their skin, and some breathe with lungs.
14. They have gills to get oxygen from the water and fins and tails that allow them to swim.
15. Air passes through pores in the shell.

Concept Mapping

16. An answer to this exercise can be found at the end of this book.

Concept Mapping Transparency 16

Chapter Review

USING VOCABULARY

To complete the following sentences, choose the correct term from each pair of terms listed below:

1. At some point in their development, all chordates have __?__. *(lungs and a notochord* or *a hollow nerve cord and a tail)*

2. Mammals evolved from early ancestors called __?__. *(therapsids* or *dinosaurs)*

3. Fish are __?__. *(endotherms* or *ectotherms)*

4. When a frog lays eggs that are later fertilized by sperm, it is an example of __?__ fertilization. *(internal* or *external)*

5. The vertebrae wrap around and protect the __?__ of vertebrates. *(notochord* or *hollow nerve cord)*

UNDERSTANDING CONCEPTS

Multiple Choice

6. Which of the following is not a vertebrate?
   a. tadpole
   b. lizard
   c. lamprey
   d. tunicate

7. Tadpoles change into frogs by the process of
   a. evolution.
   b. internal fertilization.
   c. metamorphosis.
   d. temperature regulation.

8. The swim bladder is found in
   a. jawless fishes.
   b. cartilaginous fishes.
   c. bony fishes.
   d. lancelets.

9. The amniotic egg first evolved in
   a. bony fishes.   c. reptiles.
   b. birds.   d. mammals.

10. The yolk holds
    a. food for the embryo.
    b. amniotic fluid.
    c. wastes.
    d. oxygen.

11. Both bony fishes and cartilaginous fishes have
    a. denticles.
    b. fins.
    c. an oily liver.
    d. a swim bladder.

12. Reptiles are adapted to a life on land because
    a. they can breathe through their skin.
    b. they are ectotherms.
    c. they have thick, moist skin.
    d. they have an amniotic egg.

Short Answer

13. How do amphibians breathe?
14. What characteristics allow fish to live in the water?
15. How does an embryo in an amniotic egg get oxygen?

Concept Mapping

16. Use the following terms to create a concept map: dinosaur, turtle, reptiles, amphibians, fishes, shark, salamander, vertebrates.

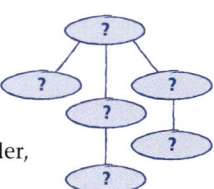

CRITICAL THINKING AND PROBLEM SOLVING

Write one or two sentences to answer the following questions:

17. Suppose you have found an animal that has a backbone and gills, but you can't find a notochord. Is it a chordate? How can you be sure?

18. Suppose you have found a shark that lacks the muscles needed to pump water over its gills. What does that tell you about the shark's lifestyle?

19. A rattlesnake does not see very well, but it can detect a temperature change of as little as three-thousandths of a degree Celsius. How is this ability useful to a rattlesnake?

20. It's 43°C outside, and the normal body temperature of a velociraptor is 38°C. Would you most likely find the raptor in the sun or in the shade? Explain.

MATH IN SCIENCE

21. A Costa Rican viper can eat a mouse that has one-third more mass than the viper. How much can you eat? Write down your mass in kilograms. To find your mass in kilograms, divide your mass in pounds by 2.2. If you were to eat a meal with a mass one-third larger than your mass, what would the mass of the meal be in kilograms?

INTERPRETING GRAPHICS

Examine the graph of body temperatures below, and answer the questions that follow.

22. How do the body temperatures of organism A and organism B change with the ground temperature?

23. Which of these organisms is most likely an ectotherm? Why?

24. Which of these organisms is most likely an endotherm? Why?

Take a minute to review your answers to the Pre-Reading Questions found at the bottom of page 372. Have your answers changed? If necessary, revise your answers based on what you have learned since you began this chapter.

CRITICAL THINKING AND PROBLEM SOLVING

17. Yes; animals with a backbone are vertebrates, and all vertebrates are chordates; the notochord is replaced by the backbone as a vertebrate develops.

18. The shark must swim constantly to pass water over its gills.

19. A snake could use such a skill to detect the warm body of a mouse or other prey.

20. The velociraptor would be in the shade. Because it is an ectotherm, its body temperature will respond to the environmental temperature. Since the outside temperature is already higher than the velociraptor's normal temperature, it will try to find a cool spot in the shade to cool its body down.

MATH IN SCIENCE

21. Answers will vary but can be determined by the following: mass (kg) + (mass (kg) × $\frac{1}{3}$) = mass of meal (kg).

INTERPRETING GRAPHICS

22. The body temperature of organism A increases as ground temperature increases. The body temperature of organism B does not change with ground temperature.

23. Organism A is probably an ectotherm. Its body temperature is dependent on the temperature of the environment.

24. Organism B is probably an endotherm. Its body temperature is constant even though the environmental temperature changes.

Blackline masters of this Chapter Review can be found in the **Study Guide**.

ACROSS THE SCIENCES
Robot Fish

Background

Fish can reverse their direction without slowing down at all. They can also turn with a turning radius as small as 10 to 30 percent of the length of their bodies. Yellowfin tuna have been reported to swim as fast as 73 km/h. Compare all of this with a typical human-made ship. A ship cruises at about 37 km/h, it must reduce its speed by about 50 percent to turn around, and it requires a circle with a radius of 10 times its hull length!

The mobility of a fish and a ship differ in other ways as well. A ship's motion is limited by the rigidity of its hull, while a fish's body is very smooth and flexible. Robotics technology is still too simple to accurately reproduce the flapping of a fish's tail. For this reason, fish-inspired mechanisms had performed rather poorly until the creation of RoboTuna.

Teaching Strategy

Lead a classroom discussion about swimming styles. Ask the students to comment on their own swimming technique. Do they swim more like a fish or a rowboat? How do they turn around? What kinds of swimming techniques have other animals adopted? You might also discuss the swimming methods of dogs, jellyfish, frogs, and whales.

ACROSS THE SCIENCES

LIFE SCIENCE • PHYSICAL SCIENCE

Robot Fish

When is a fish tail not a fish tail? When it's the tail of RoboTuna, a robotic fish designed by scientists at the Massachusetts Institute of Technology.

Something Fishy Going On

There's no doubt about it—fish are quicker and much more maneuverable than most ships and submarines. So why aren't ships and submarines built more like fish—with tails that flap back and forth? This question caught the imagination of some scientists at MIT and inspired them to build RoboTuna, a model of a bluefin tuna. This robot fish is 124 cm long and is composed of six motors, a skin of foam and Lycra™, and a skeleton of aluminum ribs and hinges connected by pulleys and strings.

A Tail of Force and Motion

The MIT scientists propose that if ships were designed to more closely resemble fish, the ships would use much less energy and thus save money. A ship moving through water leaves a trail of little whirlpools called *vortices*

behind it. These vortices increase the friction between the ship and the water. A fish, however, senses the vortices and responds by flapping its tail, creating vortices of its own. The fish's vortices counteract the effects of the original vortices, and the fish is propelled forward with much less effort.

RoboTuna has special sensors that measure changes in water pressure in much the same way that a living tuna senses vortices. Then the robot fish flaps its vortex-producing tail, allowing it to swim like a living fish. As strange as it may seem, RoboTuna may represent the beginning of a new era in nautical design.

Viewing Vortices

▶ Fill a roasting pan three-quarters full with water. Wait long enough for the water to stop moving. Then tie a 6 cm piece of yarn or ribbon to the end of a pencil. Drag the pencil through the water with the yarn or ribbon trailing behind it. How does the yarn or ribbon respond? Where are the vortices?

▶ *Inner Workings of MIT's RoboTuna*

1. A strut supports the robot, encloses the tendons, and conveys control and sensor information.
2. Ribs and flexible beams hold the skin in place while allowing the body to flex continuously.
3. A skin of foam and Lycra is smooth enough to eliminate wrinkles or bulges and prevent the stray turbulence they cause.

Answers to Viewing Vortices

The end of the ribbon or yarn should wiggle back and forth. This is caused in part by the creation of vortices, which trail behind the ribbon or yarn. You might want to put some sand on the bottom of the pan and have students observe how the sand grains move as the pencil passes over them.

WEIRD SCIENCE

WARM BRAINS IN COLD WATER

Of the world's 30,000 kinds of fish, only a few carry around their own brain heaters. *Brain heaters?* Why would a fish need a special heater just for its brain? Before you can answer that question, you have to think about how fish keep warm in the cold water of the ocean.

A Question of Temperature

Most fish and marine animals are ectotherms. An ectotherm's body temperature closely matches the temperature of its surroundings. Endotherms, on the other hand, maintain a steady body temperature regardless of the temperature of their surroundings. Humans are endotherms. Other mammals, such as dogs, elephants, whales, and birds, are also endotherms. But only a few kinds of fish—tuna, for example—are endotherms. These fish are still coldblooded, but they can heat certain parts of their bodies. Endothermic fish can hunt for prey in extremely chilly water. Yet these fish pay a high price for their ability to inhabit very cold areas—they use a lot of energy.

Being endothermic requires far more energy than being ectothermic. Some fish, such as swordfish, marlin, and sailfish, have adaptations that let them heat only part of their body. Instead of using large amounts of energy to warm the entire body, they warm only their eyes and brain. That's right—they have special brain heaters!

▶ Why do you think it is important to protect the brain and eyes from extreme cold?

Warming the Brain

In a "brain-warming" fish, a small mass of muscle attached to each eye acts as a thermostat. It adjusts the temperature of the brain and eyes as the fish swims through different temperature zones. These "heater muscles" help maintain delicate nerve functions that are important to finding prey.

Heater muscles allow the swordfish, for example, to swim in both warm surface waters of the ocean and depths of 485 m, where the temperature drops to near freezing. This adaptation has an obvious advantage: It gives the fish a large range of places to look for food.

Ectotherms in Action

▶ Contact a local pet store that sells various kinds of fish. Find out what water temperature is best for different fish from different regions of the Earth. For example, compare the ideal water temperatures for goldfish, discus fish, and angelfish. Why do you think fish-tank temperatures must be carefully controlled?

WEIRD SCIENCE
Warm Brains in Cold Water

Background

The body temperature of an ectothermic animal, commonly called "coldblooded," is about the same temperature as its surroundings. Amphibians, reptiles, and most fish are ectothermic. When the sun warms the body of an ectothermic animal, its body temperature can rise above that of an endothermic, or "warmblooded" animal.

Endothermic animals include all birds and mammals. The body of an endothermic animal produces most of its heat by metabolizing food. In many endothermic animals, a layer of fat beneath the skin and a covering of feathers, fur, or hair also help the animal maintain a constant body temperature. The principal means of reducing body heat are panting and sweating.

Many ectothermic animals partially control their body temperature through their behavior. For example, ectothermic land animals may bask in the sunlight to become warmer or move to the shade to cool down. Fish may swim closer to the surface of the water to warm themselves. If they become too warm, they may swim to deeper, cooler water.

Answer to Ectotherms in Action

Student answers will vary, depending on the fish they select. For instance, a Japanese goldfish is best suited for cool temperatures near 18°C (64°F), a South American discus requires warm temperatures of about 28°C (82°F), and a South American angelfish fares best in a temperature range of 24–26°C (75–79°F). The temperature in fish tanks must be controlled to ensure the fish's survival.

Chapter Organizer

CHAPTER ORGANIZATION	TIME MINUTES	OBJECTIVES	LABS, INVESTIGATIONS, AND DEMONSTRATIONS
Chapter Opener pp. 398–399	45	National Standards: UCP 2, 4, SAI 2, ST 1, 2, HNS 2, LS 5c	**Start-Up Activity** Let's Fly! p. 399
Section 1 Birds	90	▶ Name two characteristics that birds share with reptiles. ▶ Describe the characteristics of birds that make them well suited for flight. ▶ Explain *lift*. ▶ List some advantages of migration. UCP 1–3, 5, ST 2, SPSP 5, LS 1a, 1d, 3a–3c, 5a, 5b; LabBook UCP 2, 5, SAI 1, LS 1a, 1d	**Demonstration,** Observing Bird Bones, p. 403 in ATE **BASIC** **QuickLab,** Bernoulli Effect, p. 404 **GENERAL** **Making Models,** What? No Dentist Bills? p. 744 **BASIC** **Datasheets for LabBook,** What? No Dentist Bills? Datasheet 36 **BASIC** **Labs You Can Eat,** Why Birds of a Beak Eat Together, Lab 8 **GENERAL**
Section 2 Mammals	90	▶ Describe common characteristics of mammals. ▶ Explain the differences between monotremes, marsupials, and placental mammals. ▶ Give some examples of each type of mammal. UCP 1–5, SAI 1, HNS 2, LS 1a, 1d, 2a, 3a, 3c, 5a, 5c; LabBook SAI 1, LS 3a	**Demonstration,** Comparing Skulls, p. 412 in ATE **BASIC** **Discovery Lab,** Wanted: Mammals on Mars, p. 745 **BASIC** **Datasheets for LabBook,** Wanted: Mammals on Mars, Datasheet 37 **BASIC** **Long-Term Projects & Research Ideas,** Project 17 **ADVANCED**

See page **T20** for a complete correlation of this book with the

NATIONAL SCIENCE EDUCATION STANDARDS.

TECHNOLOGY RESOURCES

 Guided Reading Audio CD English or Spanish, Chapter 17

 CNN Eye on the Environment, Development and Preservation, Segment 2

 One-Stop Planner CD-ROM with Test Generator

Chapter 17 • Birds and Mammals

CLASSROOM WORKSHEETS, TRANSPARENCIES, AND RESOURCES	SCIENCE INTEGRATION AND CONNECTIONS	REVIEW AND ASSESSMENT
Directed Reading Worksheet 17 BASIC **Science Puzzlers, Twisters & Teasers,** Worksheet 17 ADVANCED		
Directed Reading Worksheet 17, Section 1 BASIC **Transparency 63,** The Digestive System of a Bird **Transparency 64,** Flight Adaptations of Birds **Transparency 227,** Wing Shape Creates Differences in Air Speed **Critical Thinking Worksheet 17,** A Puzzling Piece of Paleontology ADVANCED	**Multicultural Connection,** p. 401 in ATE **Connect to Physical Science,** p. 404 in ATE **Multicultural Connection,** p. 407 in ATE **Across the Sciences:** The Aerodynamics of Flight, p. 428 GENERAL	**Homework,** p. 400 in ATE ADVANCED **Self-Check,** p. 402 **Homework,** p. 403 in ATE ADVANCED **Homework,** p. 405 in ATE ADVANCED **Review,** p. 406 GENERAL **Review,** p. 409 GENERAL **Quiz,** p. 409 in ATE GENERAL **Alternative Assessment,** p. 409 in ATE GENERAL
Directed Reading Worksheet 17, Section 2 BASIC **Math Skills for Science Worksheet 31,** The Unit Factor and Dimensional Analysis GENERAL **Reinforcement Worksheet 17,** Mammals Are Us BASIC	**Multicultural Connection,** p. 412 in ATE **Connect to Physical Science,** p. 413 in ATE GENERAL **Cross-Disciplinary Focus,** p. 414 in ATE ADVANCED **Earth Science Connection,** p. 415 **Math and More,** p. 415 in ATE GENERAL **Connect to Earth Science,** p. 415 in ATE **MathBreak,** Ants for Dinner! p. 416 GENERAL **Cross-Disciplinary Focus,** p. 416 in ATE **Multicultural Connection,** p. 417 in ATE **Apply,** p. 418 GENERAL **Multicultural Connection,** p. 420 in ATE **Real-World Connection,** p. 420 in ATE **Environment Connection,** p. 421 **Weird Science:** Naked Mole-Rats, p. 429 ADVANCED	**Homework,** p. 411 in ATE GENERAL **Review,** p. 413 GENERAL **Homework,** p. 414 in ATE ADVANCED **Self-Check,** p. 416 **Self-Check,** p. 421 **Review,** p. 423 GENERAL **Quiz,** p. 423 in ATE GENERAL **Alternative Assessment,** p. 423 in ATE GENERAL

END-OF-CHAPTER REVIEW AND ASSESSMENT

Chapter Review in Study Guide
Vocabulary and Notes in Study Guide
Chapter Tests with Performance-Based Assessment, Chapter 17 Test
Chapter Tests with Performance-Based Assessment, Performance-Based Assessment 17
Concept Mapping Transparency 17

 Holt, Rinehart and Winston On-line Resources
go.hrw.com
For worksheets and other teaching aids related to this chapter, visit the HRW Web site and type in the keyword: **HSTVR2**

 National Science Teachers Association
www.scilinks.org
Encourage students to use the *sci*LINKS numbers listed in the internet connect boxes to access information and resources on the **NSTA** Web site.

Chapter 17 • Chapter Organizer

Chapter Resources & Worksheets

Visual Resources

TEACHING TRANSPARENCIES

#63 The Digestive System of a Bird

#64 Flight Adaptations of Birds

TEACHING TRANSPARENCIES

#227

CONCEPT MAPPING TRANSPARENCY

#17 Birds and Mammals

Meeting Individual Needs

DIRECTED READING

#17 Birds and Mammals

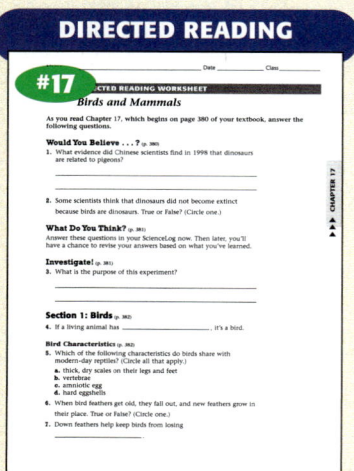

REINFORCEMENT & VOCABULARY REVIEW

#17 Mammals Are Us

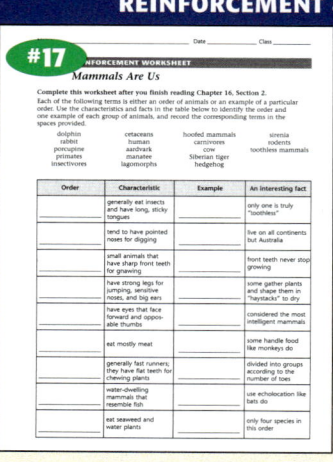

#17 Is It a Bird or a Mammal?

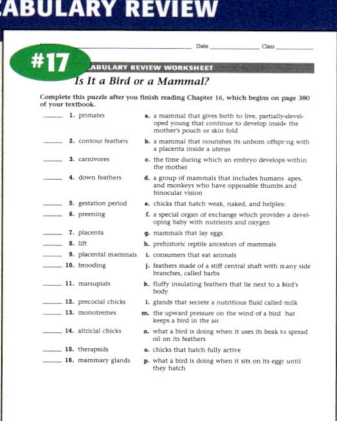

SCIENCE PUZZLERS, TWISTERS & TEASERS

#17 Birds and Mammals — Flying Without a Spare

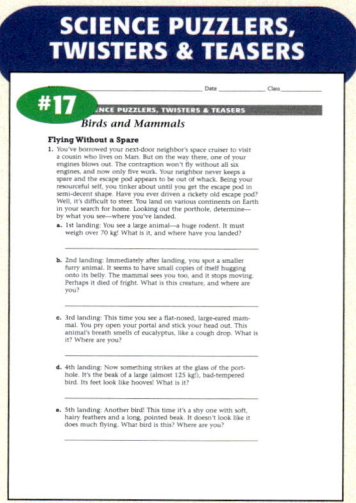

Chapter 17 • Birds and Mammals

Chapter 17 • Birds and Mammals

Review & Assessment

STUDY GUIDE

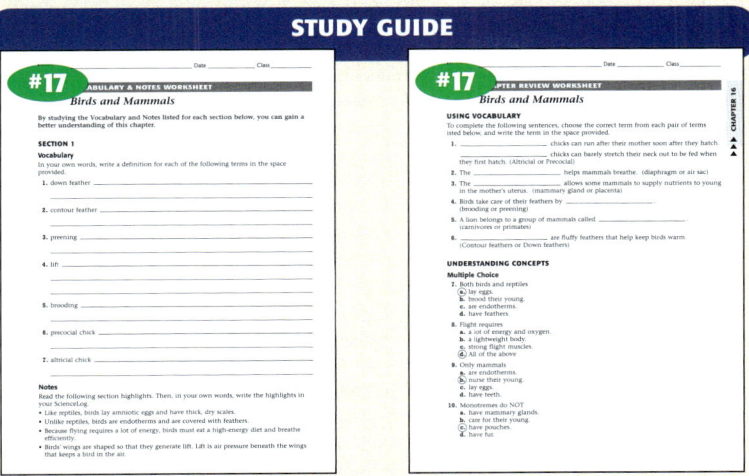

CHAPTER TESTS WITH PERFORMANCE-BASED ASSESSMENT

Lab Worksheets

LABS YOU CAN EAT

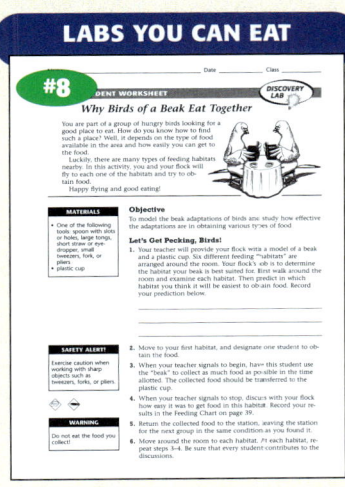

LONG-TERM PROJECTS & RESEARCH IDEAS

DATASHEETS FOR LABBOOK

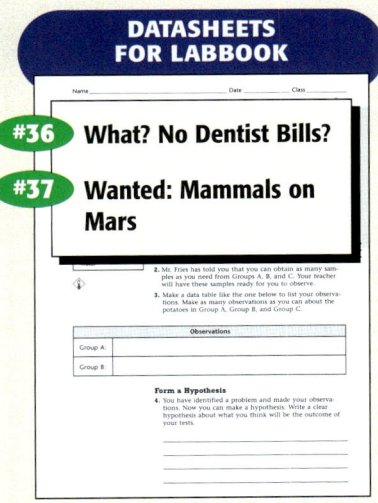

Applications & Extensions

CRITICAL THINKING & PROBLEM SOLVING

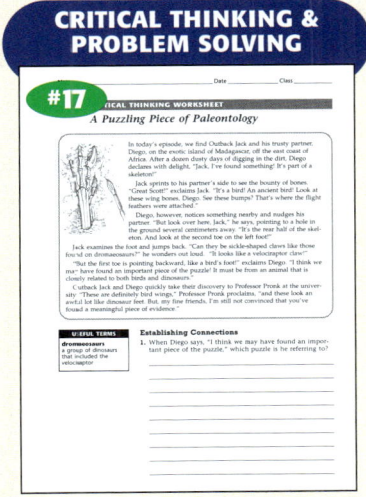

EYE ON THE ENVIRONMENT

Chapter 17 • Chapter Resources & Worksheets   397D

Chapter Background

SECTION 1

Birds

▶ **Birds of a Feather**
Ornithologists classify feathers based on their function and location on the bird's body. Contour feathers have a stiff shaft and firm barbs on the inner and outer vanes, although the base often is downy. Contour feathers include those on the outer surface of the body and the flight feathers of the wings (remiges) and the tail (rectrices). The auriculars, which cover the ears, are small, modified contour feathers.

- Semiplumes are small but have a relatively large shaft with downy vanes. They are hidden beneath the body feathers. Semiplumes fill in the spaces between the larger contour feathers, provide insulation, and increase buoyancy in water birds.

- Down feathers are tiny, completely fluffy, and have no shaft. In adult birds, down feathers remain hidden beneath contour feathers, but they are the sole body covering for many newly hatched birds. Down is important for insulation and is most abundant in water birds.

IS THAT A FACT!

- The ruby-throated hummingbird has about 940 feathers. The whistling swan has about 25,000. But per unit of body weight, the hummingbird has more feathers than the swan. This is because small birds have a greater need for efficient heat retention.

▶ **Stick Together**
Branching out from the shaft of a typical contour feather are thin, rather stiff barbs. On either side of the barbs grow even smaller barbules. There are several hundred on each barb. Each barbule has tiny hooks that wrap around the barbules of the adjacent barb so that all the parts of the feather are tightly attached to each other. This construction is what provides firmness to the feathers and increases their ability to insulate and waterproof a bird.

IS THAT A FACT!

- Cormorants and anhingas are fish-eating birds that must dive to catch their food. To decrease their buoyancy and enhance their ability to dive deep, they have unusually heavy bones (for a bird), reduced air sacs, and nonwaterproof plumage. After a dive, they must find a perch and spread their wings to dry off.

▶ **Forms of Flight**
During flapping flight, a bird's inner wing functions as an anchor for the outer portion and helps provide speed and power. At the bottom of the downstroke, which propels the bird, the "wrist" flexes and begins the upstroke.

- Soaring flight allows a bird to gain and maintain altitude without flapping its wings. Instead, the birds "ride" on warm air currents called thermals. Vultures, hawks, and eagles can use soaring flight because they fulfill the requirements of large size, maneuverability, and light wing load (the ratio of a bird's wing surface area to its weight).

- Kingfishers, kestrels, and some hawks are able to hover, but none match the hummingbird's ability to maintain a position in midair. Hummingbirds move their wings only from the shoulder, which provides unusual flexibility and maneuverability.

IS THAT A FACT!

- Hummingbirds are the only birds that can fly backward.

- A chimney swift that lived 9 years was estimated to have flown 2,000,000 km during its lifetime.

Chapter 17 • Birds and Mammals

SECTION 2

Mammals

▶ **Fur**

All mammals have hair, but not all "fur-bearing" mammals have true fur. True fur consists of two layers: a dense undergrowth of short ground hairs, which provide insulation, and longer guard hairs, which protect the skin and the ground hairs by repelling rain or snow.

▶ **Rodent Teeth**

Rodents, which include rats, mice, beavers, squirrels, guinea pigs, and capybaras, have evolved a unique jaw articulation to compensate for the huge incisors that grow throughout the animal's life. Both the upper and the lower pair are separated from the cheek teeth by a large gap. When the cheek teeth are engaged in chewing, the lower jaw is pulled back and the incisors do not meet. When the animal is gnawing with its incisors, the lower jaw is pulled forward and downward so the incisors can meet. Rodents spend a lot of time gnawing with their incisors to keep them worn down to a manageable level.

▶ **Beneficial Bats**

The insectivorous Mexican free-tailed bats in Texas eat an estimated 20,000 tons of insects each year. They provide a vital, chemical-free system of insect control.

- Guano from insectivorous bats is a valuable fertilizer in many countries because of its high nitrogen and phosphorous content. In some caves, the guano covers and helps preserve archaeologically valuable artifacts and fossils.

- Although some fruit-eating bats can reduce a farmer's harvest, many of them are essential to dispersing seeds that are responsible for new plant growth. Other bats eat only pollen and nectar and are the primary or exclusive pollinators of various plants.

IS THAT A FACT!

▶ Shrews and other small mammals have a high metabolic rate to compensate for large amounts of heat loss resulting from their large ratio of body surface to volume. A captive shrew (genus *Sorex*) consumed 3.3 times its body weight in a 24-hour period.

▶ From mid-April to mid-October, hundreds of thousands of Mexican free-tailed bats and thousands of several other species live in Carlsbad Caverns, in New Mexico. At night, the bats fly from the cave in great swarms that resemble clouds of smoke when seen from a distance. It is believed that early explorers of the southwest followed the "smoke" and discovered the cave.

▶ A three-toed sloth has nine cervical vertebrae and can turn its head 270°. Two-toed sloths and most mammals have seven neck vertebrae.

For background information about teaching strategies and issues, refer to the *Professional Reference for Teachers*.

CHAPTER 17

Birds and Mammals

 Pre-Reading Questions

Students may not know the answers to these questions before reading the chapter, so accept any reasonable response.

Suggested Answers

1. Planes and birds stay aloft because air traveling over the top of a wing moves faster than air traveling below it. This generates higher pressure beneath the wing than above it, causing lift.
2. Kangaroos are marsupial. Most mammals are placental.
3. Yes: monotremes are mammals that lay eggs. Bats are mammals that can fly.

 Directed Reading Worksheet 17

 Science Puzzlers, Twisters & Teasers Worksheet 17

 Guided Reading Audio CD English or Spanish, Chapter 17

CHAPTER 17

Birds and Mammals

Sections

1. Birds 400
   QuickLab 404
2. Mammals 410
   MathBreak 416
   Apply 418
   Environment
   Connection 421
   Internet Connect ... 423

Chapter Review 426
Feature Articles 428, 429
LabBook 744–745

Pre-Reading Questions

1. What holds a bird or plane up when it flies?
2. How do kangaroos differ from most other mammals?
3. Can mammals lay eggs? Can they fly?

Pest Control for Giraffes!

Why is this bird riding on this giraffe? Well, this tickbird is more than a passenger. In fact, the tickbird and the giraffe, a mammal, have a special relationship. The tickbird eats ticks and other pests off the giraffe. The tickbird also warns the giraffe if danger is near. In this chapter, you will learn what makes birds and mammals unique and about different kinds of birds and mammals.

---

internet connect

 HRW On-line Resources
go.hrw.com
For worksheets and other teaching aids, visit the HRW Web site and type in the keyword: **HSTVR2**

 www.scilinks.com
Use the *sci*LINKS numbers at the end of each chapter for additional resources on the **NSTA** Web site.

 www.cnnfyi.com
Visit the CNN Web site for current events coverage and classroom resources.

Down feathers are fluffy, insulating feathers that lie next to a bird's body. To keep from losing heat, birds fluff up their down feathers to form a layer of insulation. Air trapped in the feathers helps keep birds warm. **Contour feathers** are made of a stiff central *shaft* with many side branches, called *barbs*. The barbs link together to form a smooth surface, as can be seen in **Figure 3**. Contour feathers cover the body and wings of birds to form a streamlined flying surface.

Birds take good care of their feathers. They use their beaks to spread oil on their feathers in a process called **preening**. The oil is secreted by a gland near the bird's tail. The oil helps make the feathers water repellent and keeps them clean.

High-Energy Animals Birds need a lot of energy in order to fly. To get this energy, they have a high metabolism, which generates a lot of body heat. In fact, the average body temperature of a bird is 40°C, warmer than yours! If birds are too hot, they lay their feathers flat and pant like dogs do. Birds cannot sweat to cool their bodies.

Eat Like a Bird? Because of their high metabolism, birds eat large amounts of food in proportion to their body weight. Some small birds eat almost constantly to maintain their energy! Most birds eat a high-protein, high-fat diet of insects, nuts, seeds, or meat. This kind of diet requires only a small digestive tract. A few birds, such as geese, eat the leaves of plants.

Birds don't have teeth, so they can't chew their food. Instead, food goes directly from the mouth to the *crop*, where it is stored. Birds also have an organ called a *gizzard*, which often contains small stones. The stones in the gizzard grind up the food so that it can be easily digested by the intestine. A bird's digestive system is shown in **Figure 4**.

Figure 3 *The barbs of a contour feather have cross branches called barbules. Barbs and barbules give the feather strength and shape.*

Figure 4 *The digestive system of a bird allows food to be rapidly converted into usable energy.*

2) Teach

GUIDED PRACTICE
Making Models

MATERIALS

FOR EACH GROUP:
- pipe cleaners
- straws

Use the board to illustrate how a contour feather is constructed of a main shaft, projecting barbs, barbules, and barbule hooks.

Tell students to insert one or two pipe cleaners into a straw to make it stiff. Then tell them to follow the illustration to construct a model of a feather with at least three barbs and accompanying barbules and hooks.

Sheltered English

Multicultural CONNECTION

Bird myths and mythical birds are common cultural themes around the world. In the Hindu religion, the king of birds is a winged monster called Garuda that feeds on snakes. The fifteenth-century collection of stories *The Thousand and One Nights* presented the mythic roc, or *rukh*, that was so enormous it fed on elephants. And the folklore of the Athapascans, Inuit, and Hopi—three Native American cultures—features a huge eaglelike creature called a thunderbird.

Q: Why do seagulls fly over the open sea?

A: because if they flew over bays, they'd be bagels (bay-gulls)!

What? No Dentist Bills?

Teaching Transparency 63
"The Digestive System of a Bird"

2 Teach, continued

Answers to Self-Check

1. Down feathers are not stiff and smooth and could not give structure to the wings. They are adapted to keep the bird warm.
2. Birds need tremendous amounts of food for fuel because it takes a lot of energy to fly.

READING  STRATEGY

Prediction Guide Before students read these pages, ask them: Why are birds such successful flyers? (Birds possess feathers, a high metabolism, wings, lightweight bones, and air sacs.)

Have them review their answers after they read the text.

USING THE FIGURE

Writing Remind students that several bird species, including ostriches, kiwis, and emus, are flightless. Tell students to research the body and wing structure of flightless birds and to write another paragraph for each caption that explains any differences between the characteristics of flightless birds and birds that fly. **Sheltered English**

Teaching Transparency 64 "Flight Adaptations of Birds"

Up, Up, and Away

Most birds are flyers. Even flightless birds, such as ostriches, are descended from ancestors that could fly.

Birds have a long list of adaptations for flight. Birds must take in a large amount of energy from the food they eat and a large amount of oxygen from the air they breathe in order to fly. Feathers and wings are also important, as are strong muscles. Birds have lightweight bodies so that they can get off the ground. **Figure 5** on these two pages explains many of the bird characteristics that are important for flight.

Self-Check

1. Why don't birds have wings made of down feathers?
2. Why do birds eat large quantities of food?

(See page 782 to check your answers.)

Figure 5 Flight Adaptations of Birds

Most birds have **large eyes** and excellent eyesight. This allows them to see objects and food from a distance. Some birds, like hawks and eagles, can see eight times better than humans!

The **heart** of a bird beats rapidly. This ensures that the flight muscles get as much oxygen as the blood can carry. In small birds, the heart beats almost 1,000 times a minute! Your heart beats about 70 times a minute.

Birds have special organs called **air sacs** attached to their lungs. The air sacs increase the amount of oxygen that a bird can take in and allow air to flow constantly in one direction through the lungs.

 SCIENCE

Loons are heavy-bodied water birds. Their legs are set far back on their bodies for maximum streamlining while swimming. As a consequence, loons can barely walk on land. And because the ratio of their wing surface area to their body weight is so low, they have difficulty getting airborne. For comparison, think of a big-bodied plane with small wings. To get airborne, loons must "run" on the water while flapping their wings. They may have to taxi for half a kilometer to get aloft!

402 Chapter 17 • Birds and Mammals

The shape of a bird's **wings** is related to the kind of flying it does. Short, rounded wings allow rapid maneuvers, like the movements of a fighter plane. Long narrow wings are best for soaring, like the movement of a glider.

Bird skeletons are compact and strong. Some of the vertebrae, ribs, and hip bones are fused together. This makes the skeleton of birds more rigid than that of other vertebrates. The **rigid skeleton** lets a bird move its wings powerfully and efficiently.

Science CONNECTION

These characteristics help birds fly, but how do airplanes fly? Find out on page 428.

Birds that fly have powerful **flight muscles** attached to a large breastbone called a **keel**. These muscles move the wings.

Keel

Bone is a heavy material, but birds have much **lighter skeletons** than those of other vertebrates because their bones are hollow. But bird bones are still very strong because they have thin cross-supports that provide strength, much like the trusses of a bridge do.

DEMONSTRATION

Observing Bird Bones Obtain several bones from a chicken or a turkey, such as the lower leg bones (drumsticks) and thigh bones, that have been cooked and thoroughly cleaned. Carefully break open the bones so that students can examine the air spaces inside. Sheltered English

Homework

Researching Falconry
Falconry is an ancient sport that may date back to the eighth century B.C. in Assyria. It was immensely popular among the European upper classes in the Middle Ages. Today, the sport is tightly regulated by the United States Fish and Wildlife Service, which issues permits that allow individuals to trap and train hawks, falcons, and occasionally eagles. Have students research and write a report about the history of falconry. Their report should include information about the role of falconry in raptor conservation.

internetconnect
TOPIC: Bird Characteristics
GO TO: www.scilinks.org
sciLINKS NUMBER: HSTL405

Science Bloopers

The common name of a bird may be an accurate description of what it looks like, but it does not always accurately reflect what kind of bird it actually is. For example, the common nighthawk is not a hawk at all, although it appears hawklike in flight. The nighthawk belongs to the Caprimulgidae family, which are mostly insect eaters. Members of this family were called goatsuckers because Caprimulgidae comes from the Latin *caper*, "goat," and *mulgeo*, "to milk." According to legend, the birds sucked milk from goats at night!

Section 1 • Birds

2) Teach, continued

MEETING INDIVIDUAL NEEDS

Writing — Advanced Learners
Have students research and prepare a report on the parts and functions of an airplane's wing, comparing the information to the parts and functions of a bird's wing. For example, a bird spreads its primary wing feathers to slow down. Is there a movable piece on the plane's wing that helps slow down the plane when it is approaching the airstrip for a landing?

QuickLab

MATERIALS

FOR EACH STUDENT:
- drinking straw
- push or straight pin
- tissue paper (3 × 0.5 cm)

Safety Caution: Remind students to review all safety cautions and icons before beginning this lab activity. Students should be especially careful not to stick themselves with the pin when making the hole. They should not use any straw that another student has already used.

CONNECT TO PHYSICAL SCIENCE

For both birds and aircraft, the shape of the wing creates differences in maneuverability and air speed. Designing an airplane wing requires taking into account what kind of flying the plane will need to do. Selective pressures have generated a vast array of wing shapes in birds, enabling different species to fly in very different ways. Use Teaching Transparency 227 to illustrate the effect of wing shape on air speed and lift.

QuickLab

Bernoulli Effect

Is it true that fast-moving air creates low pressure? You bet. You can see this effect easily with a straw and a piece of paper. First find a partner. Use a **pin** to make a hole in one side of a **drinking straw.** Cut or tear a small strip of **paper** about 3 cm long and 0.5 cm wide. Hold the strip of paper as close to the hole as you can without letting the paper touch the straw. Ask your partner to blow into the straw. The fast-moving air will create low pressure in the straw. The higher air pressure in the room will push the paper against the hole. Try it!

Figure 7 The wandering albatross has a wingspan of 3.5 m, the largest of any living bird. Its large wings allow the albatross to glide for very long periods of time. An albatross comes ashore only to lay its eggs.

Teaching Transparency 227
"Wing Shape Creates Differences in Air Speed" — *LINK TO PHYSICAL SCIENCE*

Getting off the Ground

How do birds overcome gravity and fly? Birds flap their wings to get into the air and to push themselves through the air. Wings provide lift. **Lift** is the upward force on the wing that keeps a bird in the air.

When air flows past a wing, some of the air is forced over the top of the wing, and some is forced underneath. A bird's wing is curved on top, as shown in **Figure 6.** The curved shape forces the air on top to move *faster* than the air underneath. The fast-moving air on top creates low pressure in the air. This is called the *Bernoulli effect.* The air pressure under the wing is higher and pushes the wing up.

Figure 6 A bird's wing is shaped to produce lift. Air moving over the top of the wing moves faster than air moving underneath the wing. This creates a difference in air pressure that keeps a bird in the air.

Birds generate extra lift by flying faster. The faster a bird flies, the greater the lift. Another factor that affects lift is wing size. The larger the wing, the greater the lift. This is why birds with large wings can soar long distances without flapping their wings. An albatross, like the one in **Figure 7,** can glide over the ocean for many hours without flapping its wings.

IS THAT A FACT!

The wandering albatross's wings are 3–3.5 m long but are barely 23 cm wide. The wings are inefficient for flapping flight, but their unusual shape enables albatrosses to soar for months at a time, alighting only to nest and feed and when winds are too calm for soaring.

Fly Away

It is sometimes said that when the going gets tough, the tough get going. If that's true, birds must be some of the toughest animals in the world. For when times are hard, some birds get going faster and farther than any other animal. Because they are able to fly great distances, birds are able to migrate great distances.

Some birds have good reasons to migrate. By migrating, they can find better territories with more food. For example, in the far north in the summer, the Arctic sun is up nearly 24 hours a day. Plants, insects, and other organisms increase explosively, providing lots of food. It's a great place for birds to raise their young. However, the winters are long and harsh, and there is little to eat. So when winter comes, birds fly south to find better feeding grounds.

Bringing Up Baby

Like reptiles, birds reproduce by internal fertilization and lay amniotic eggs with the developing embryo inside. But unlike most reptiles, birds must keep their eggs warm for the embryo to develop.

Most birds build elaborate nests and lay their eggs inside them. **Figure 8** shows a few of the many different kinds of bird nests. Birds sit on their eggs until the eggs hatch, using their body heat to keep the eggs warm. This is called **brooding**. Some birds, such as gulls, share brooding duties equally between males and females. But among songbirds, the female is in charge of brooding the eggs, and the male brings her food.

Raising young birds is hard work. Some birds, such as cuckoos and cowbirds, have found a way to make other birds do their work for them. A cuckoo lays its eggs in the nest of another species of bird. When the cuckoo egg hatches, the young cuckoo is fed and protected by the foster parents.

Figure 8 *There are many different types of bird nests. Birds use grass, branches, mud, hair, feathers, and many other building materials.*

Homework

Migration Mapping Migratory birds fly over almost every part of North America. However, they generally follow one of four main migration routes. Have students research the primary migration corridors, or flyways, in North America (Pacific, Mississippi, Central, and Atlantic) and illustrate them on a map. Also have students list at least three species of birds that travel along each flyway, along with the time of year the birds travel. **Sheltered English**

COOPERATIVE LEARNING

Explain to students that many birds have elaborate courtship behaviors, or displays. Have students work in small groups to research the courtship behavior of a species of their choosing. Possibilities include golden eagles, mockingbirds, emperor penguins, and whooping cranes. Tell groups that they will be presenting their findings to the class. Have them divide tasks among group members; one person can do research, another can write the presentation, another can present the material, and another can make a poster.

MISCONCEPTION ALERT

There is more to flight than discussed in this chapter. Newton's Third law also plays a part— a tilted wing deflects horizontal airflow downward. In reaction the air exerts an upward force on the wing.

IS THAT A FACT!

Migrating takes a lot of energy. Small birds may lose as much as 40 percent of their body weight on a long migratory flight. Even though the costs are high, birds that migrate experience a payoff when they reach areas with good weather and abundant food.

 SCIENCE HUMOR

A hen is the only one who can lay down on the job and still get results.

Section 1 • Birds

2 Teach, continued

MEETING INDIVIDUAL NEEDS

Advanced Learners Konrad Lorenz (1903–1989), the man in **Figure 9,** was one of the founders of modern ethology, the study of animal behavior by comparative methods. Many of Lorenz's studies involved birds. In 1935, Lorenz observed behavior in young ducks and geese that we now know as *imprinting*. During a critical stage after hatching, young birds will follow the first moving object they see, even if it's not their biological parents. Have students research imprinting and summarize the results of Lorenz's classic bird studies. Have them compose their findings in a short report.

DISCUSSION

Precocial Versus Altricial After students have read this page, ask them to name the advantages and disadvantages of being a precocial chick. (Advantages are that precocial chicks can help find their own food and are not as vulnerable to the elements because their down protects them. A disadvantage is that they are especially vulnerable to predators.)

Ask them to name the advantages and disadvantages of being altricial chicks. (An advantage is that chicks are often safer in a nest. Disadvantages are that parents need to cover the chicks constantly to keep them warm until their feathers grow in, and parents must leave the chicks to find food for themselves and the chicks.)

Figure 9 *Precocial chicks learn to recognize their parents right after they hatch. But if their parents are not there, the chicks will follow the first moving thing they see, even a person.*

Ready to Go Some baby birds hatch from the egg ready to run around and eat bugs. Chicks that hatch fully active are *precocial* (pree KOH shuhl). Chickens, ducks, and shorebirds all hatch precocial chicks. Precocial chicks are covered with downy feathers and follow their parents as soon as they can stand up. You can see some precocial chicks following a stand-in parent in **Figure 9.** Precocial chicks depend on their mother for warmth and protection, but they can walk, swim, and feed themselves.

Help Wanted The chicks of hawks, songbirds, and many other birds hatch weak, naked, and helpless. These chicks are *altricial* (al TRISH uhl). Their eyes are closed when they are born. Newly hatched altricial chicks cannot walk or fly. Their parents must keep them warm and feed them for several weeks. **Figure 10** shows altricial chicks being fed by a parent.

When altricial chicks grow their first flight feathers, they begin learning to fly. This takes days, however, and the chicks often end up walking around on the ground. The parents must work feverishly to distract cats, weasels, and other predators and protect their young.

REVIEW

1. List three ways birds are similar to reptiles and three ways they are different.
2. Explain the difference between precocial chicks and altricial chicks.
3. People use the phrase "eats like a bird" to describe someone who eats very little. Is this saying appropriate? Why or why not?
4. Name some of the adaptations that make bird bodies lightweight.
5. **Understanding Technology** Would an airplane wing that is not curved on top generate lift? Draw a picture to illustrate your explanation.

Figure 10 *Both parents of altricial chicks leave the nest in search of food. They return to the nest with food every few minutes, sometimes making 1,000 trips a day between the two of them!*

▼ Answers to Review

1. Answers may vary. Both birds and reptiles have scales and amniotic eggs, and both are vertebrates. Unlike reptiles, birds are endotherms, have feathers, and have air sacs.
2. Precocial chicks are fully active after hatching and are covered with downy feathers. Newly hatched altricial chicks cannot walk or fly and do not have feathers.
3. No; birds eat a tremendous amount of food in relation to their mass.
4. Birds' skeletons are compact. Their bones are hollow. Their feathers are light. They even have less DNA than other vertebrates.
5. No; air moves faster over the top of the wing to create lower pressure. The higher pressure under the wing pushes the wing up, creating lift.

Kinds of Birds

There are almost 9,000 species of birds on Earth. Birds range in size from the 1.6 g bee hummingbird to the 125 kg North African ostrich. The bodies of birds have different characteristics too, depending on where they live and what they eat. Because of their great diversity, birds are classified into 29 different orders. That can be confusing, so birds are often grouped into four nonscientific categories: flightless birds, water birds, birds of prey, and perching birds. These categories don't include all birds, but they do show how different birds can be.

BRAIN FOOD

An ostrich egg has a mass of about 1.4 kg. A single ostrich egg is big enough to provide scrambled eggs for a family of four every morning for several days.

Flightless Birds

Ostriches, kiwis, emus, and other flightless birds do not have a large keel for flight. Though they cannot fly, many flightless birds are fast runners.

▲ The **kiwi,** of New Zealand, is a forest bird about the size of a chicken. Its feathers are soft and hairlike. Kiwis sleep during the day. At night, they hunt for worms, caterpillars, and berries.

▲ **Penguins** are unique flightless birds. They have a large keel and very strong flight muscles, but their wings have been modified into flippers. They flap these wings to swim underwater. Although penguins are graceful swimmers, they walk clumsily on land.

◀ The **ostrich** is the largest living bird. Ostriches can reach a height of 2.5 m and a mass of 125 kg. An ostrich's two-toed feet look almost like hoofs, and these birds can run up to 64 km/h (40 mi/h).

407

SCIENCE HUMOR

Q: What is the difference between *unlawful* and *illegal?*

A: An ill eagle is a sick bird.

MEETING INDIVIDUAL NEEDS

Learners Having Difficulty To reinforce the concept that feathers are the defining characteristic of birds, ask students whether or not the following animals are birds: hawk moth, penguin, eagle, bat, ostrich, flying squirrel. Have them justify their answers. Sheltered English

Multicultural CONNECTION

Throughout history eagles have represented power. An eagle was the emblem of the Babylonian god Ashur. An eagle adorned the staff of Zeus. In Norse myths, Odin, the king of the gods, often assumed the shape of an eagle. Native Americans of the plains decorated their war bonnets with eagle feathers. And of course, the bald eagle is the national symbol of the United States.

MISCONCEPTION ALERT

Be sure students understand that even though some birds look like they are covered with fur, they are actually covered with tiny feathers. The feathers of most birds grow in lines called *tracts*. Between the tracts are gaps. If you blow on a robin's belly, for example, the feathers will separate to reveal patches of bare skin. However, on penguins, ostriches, rheas, cassowaries, and emus, every part of the body is covered with feathers.

internetconnect

TOPIC: Kinds of Birds
GO TO: www.scilinks.org
sciLINKS NUMBER: HSTL410

Section 1 • Birds **407**

3 Extend

GOING FURTHER

Birds of prey such as eagles, owls, falcons and hawks are called *raptors*. There are raptor centers throughout the United States, many of which specialize in the care and rehabilitation of injured birds. The centers frequently serve as wildlife education centers, too. Many house and display for educational purposes birds that are too wounded or too accustomed to people to survive on their own. Have students research and contact these centers for more information about raptors and their care (remind them to include a stamped, self-addressed envelope if they expect a response by mail). If a raptor center is nearby, encourage students to work with the school administration to arrange a visit by a naturalist and a bird or two.

DEBATE

Destroy Wildlife to Save It?
The artist John James Audubon (1785–1851) painted pictures of birds that he shot. This was the only way he could get close enough to see the level of detail he needed in his paintings. Although modern cameras and binoculars provide researchers with excellent detail, scientists still sometimes kill birds for study and museum collections. This allows them to place the birds in proper evolutionary context. The results allow scientists to confirm the discovery of new species and develop specific conservation measures. Ask students to debate the pros and cons of this scientific technique.

Water Birds

Water birds are sometimes called *waterfowl*. These include cranes, ducks, geese, swans, pelicans, loons, and many other species. These birds usually have webbed feet for swimming, but they are also strong flyers.

▶ Male **wood ducks** have beautiful plumage to attract females. Like all ducks, they are strong swimmers and flyers.

◀ The **blue-footed booby** is a tropical water bird. These birds have an elaborate courtship dance that includes raising their feet one at a time.

▶ The **common loon** is the most primitive of modern birds. It can remain underwater for several minutes while searching for fish.

Birds of Prey

Eagles, hawks, falcons, and other birds of prey are meat eaters. They may eat mammals, fish, reptiles, birds, or other animals. The sharp claws on their feet and their sharp, curved beaks help these birds catch and eat their prey. They also have very good vision. Most birds of prey hunt during the day.

◀ Owls, like this **northern spotted owl,** are the only birds of prey that hunt at night. They have a keen sense of hearing to help them find their prey.

▲ **Ospreys** are fish eaters. They fly over the water and catch fish with their feet.

WEIRD SCIENCE

Some oceanic birds can eject a smelly oil from their stomachs. Fulmars can spew the foul-smelling liquid about 1 m as a defensive weapon. Elimination of the oil can also reduce a bird's weight before flight. The behavior is instinctive; newly hatched fulmars have been observed regurgitating the fluid while still emerging from the shell. The oil is also exchanged by adult fulmars during courtship. Eliminating the rich oil may help birds keep their metabolisms at the proper level.

Perching Birds

Songbirds, like robins, wrens, warblers, and sparrows, are perching birds. These birds have special adaptations for perching on a branch. When a perching bird lands on a branch, its feet automatically close around the branch. So even if the bird falls asleep, it will not fall off.

▲ **Parrots** are not songbirds, but they have special feet for perching and climbing. Their strong, hooked beak allows them to open seeds and slice fruit.

▲ **Chickadees** are lively little birds that frequently flock to garden feeders. They often dangle underneath a branch while hunting for insects, seeds, or fruits.

Most tanagers are tropical birds, ▶ but the **scarlet tanager** spends the summer in North America. The male is red, but the female is a yellow-green color that blends into the trees.

REVIEW

1. How did perching birds get their name?
2. Birds of prey have extremely good eyesight. Why is good vision important for these birds?
3. **Interpreting Illustrations** Look at the illustrations of bird feet at right. Which foot belongs to a water bird? a perching bird? Explain your answers.

409

▼ Answers to Review

1. Perching birds have special feet that allow them to perch easily on branches.
2. As birds of prey, they are flying high above the ground; they need to be able to spot their prey from great distances.
3. The foot in figure (c) belongs to a water bird. The foot in figure (b) belongs to a perching bird. The water bird has webbed feet. The perching bird has a foot adapted to grasping. (The foot in figure (a) belongs to a pheasant.)

4) Close

Quiz

1. What is the one characteristic that sets living birds apart from the rest of the animal kingdom? (feathers)
2. Why must birds eat a high-energy diet? (They need a lot of energy to maintain a constant body temperature and for flight.)
3. Trace the path of food from a bird's beak through the digestive system. (from the mouth, to the crop, then the gizzard, then the intestine)
4. How do perching birds differ from birds of prey? Give two examples of each kind of bird. (Perching birds, such as robins and sparrows, have special adaptations for perching on a branch; their feet automatically close around a branch when they land. Birds of prey, such as eagles and hawks, have sharp claws; sharp, hooked beaks; and good vision.)

ALTERNATIVE ASSESSMENT

Find pictures of birds in nature magazines, cut them out, number them, and display them for the class. Have students make charts with three columns. Tell them to put the number in the first column, the general type of bird (perching, water, etc.) in the second, and the reasons for their classification in the third.

Sheltered English

 Critical Thinking Worksheet 17 "A Puzzling Piece of Paleontology"

Section 1 • Birds **409**

SECTION 2

Focus

Mammals
This section introduces the mammals and describes their common characteristics. Students will learn the differences between monotremes, marsupials, and placental mammals and will provide examples of different kinds of mammals.

🔔 Bellringer
Write the following on the board or overhead transparency:

In the next 5 minutes, list as many characteristics of mammals as you can think of.

After the 5 minutes are up, ask students what characteristics they have listed, and put their answers on the board. Use their answers as a springboard for discussion about what mammals are and where they live.

1 Motivate

DISCUSSION
Domestication of Animals
Ask students to describe how humans have interacted with wild mammals over time. (Humans have hunted mammals and used their meat for food, their hides for clothing and shelter, and their bones for tools.)

Then ask students how the domestication of mammals, such as horses, cattle, pigs, and dogs, changed the lives of early humans. It became easier to obtain food (eggs, milk), to cultivate crops (oxen pulling plows), to catch wild game (hunting dogs), and to control pests (cats).

Section 2

Terms to Learn
mammary glands
diaphragm
monotreme
marsupial
placental mammal
gestation period

What You'll Do
- Describe common characteristics of mammals.
- Explain the differences between monotremes, marsupials, and placental mammals.
- Give some examples of each type of mammal.

Mandrill baboon

Figure 12 *Therapsids had characteristics of both reptiles and mammals and may have looked something like this.*

internetconnect

SC/LINKS NSTA

TOPIC: The Origin of Mammals
GO TO: www.scilinks.org
sciLINKS NUMBER: HSTL415

Mammals

Of all the vertebrates, we seem most interested in mammals. Maybe that's because we are mammals ourselves. But with about 4,500 species, mammals are actually a small class of animals. Mollusks, for example, include more than 90,000 species.

Mammals come in many different forms—from the tiniest bats, which weigh less than a cracker, to the largest whales. The blue whale, with a mass of more than 90,000 kg, is the largest animal—vertebrate or invertebrate—that has ever lived. You can find mammals in the coldest oceans, in the hottest deserts, and in every climate in between. You can see some of the variety of mammals in **Figure 11.**

Rhinoceros

Figure 11 *Even though they look very different, all of these animals are mammals.*

Beluga whale

The Origin of Mammals
Fossil evidence suggests that about 280 million years ago, mammal-like reptiles called therapsids appeared. *Therapsids* (thuh RAP sidz) were the early ancestors of mammals. An artist's rendition of a therapsid is shown in **Figure 12.**

About 200 million years ago, the first mammals appeared in the fossil record. These mammals were about the size of mice. The early mammals were endotherms. Because they did not depend on their surroundings for heat, they could forage at night and avoid their dinosaur predators during the day.

When the dinosaurs became extinct, there was more land and food available for the mammals. Mammals began to diversify and live in many different environments.

WEIRD SCIENCE
The world's smallest mammal is the Kitti's hog-nosed bat, which weighs only 2 g and is 33 mm long. This tiny bat lives in limestone caves in southwest Thailand.

Characteristics of Mammals

Dolphins and elephants are mammals, and so are monkeys, horses, and rabbits. You are a mammal, too! These animals are very different, but all mammals share many distinctive traits.

Mamma! All mammals have mammary glands; this sets them apart from other animals. **Mammary glands** secrete a nutritious fluid called milk. All female mammals supply milk to their young. Female mammals usually bear live young and care for their offspring, as illustrated in **Figure 13.** Although only mature female mammals make milk, male mammals also have small inactive mammary glands.

Lions and tigers and bears . . . on Mars?! Find out more on page 745 of your LabBook.

Figure 13 Like all mammals, this calf gets its first meals from its mother's milk.

All milk is made of water, protein, fat, and sugar. But the milk from different mammals has varying amounts of each nutrient. For example, human milk has half as much fat as cow's milk but twice as much sugar. The milk of seals may be more than one-half fat. At birth, elephant seals have a mass of 45 kg. After drinking this rich milk for just 3 weeks, their mass is 180 kg!

Cozy and Warm If you've ever had a dog fall asleep in your lap, you already know that mammals are really warm! All mammals are endotherms. Like birds, mammals require a lot of energy from the food they eat. Mammals quickly break down food in their bodies and use the energy released from their cells to keep their bodies warm. Usually a mammal keeps its body temperature constant. Only when a mammal is hibernating, estivating, or running a fever does its body temperature change.

Figure 14 Mammals feel warm to the touch because they are endotherms.

IS THAT A FACT!

Milk is more than food; it also contains antibodies that help the mother's offspring fight off infection.

2 Teach, continued

MEETING INDIVIDUAL NEEDS

Advanced Learners Explain to students that males and females of the same species often vary in size and coloration. Tell them this sex-related difference is called *sexual dimorphism*. Examples in mammals are the male lion's mane, the male deer's antlers, different facial coloration in mandrills (a species of baboon), and larger canine teeth in male baboons. Have students research and write a brief report on possible reasons for sexual dimorphism in mammals.

DEMONSTRATION

Comparing Skulls Display the skulls of several species for students to study. Ideally, include several mammal skulls, a reptile skull, a bird skull, and an amphibian skull. Tell students to carefully examine the skulls, paying close attention to the similarities and differences between classes (major groups) and within the mammal class. Ask them to describe differences in dentition (tooth structure and arrangement) and speculate about advantages and disadvantages of the arrangements they observe. Sheltered English

internetconnect
TOPIC: Characteristics of Mammals
GO TO: www.scilinks.org
sciLINKS NUMBER: HSTL420

Figure 15 The thick fur of this arctic fox keeps its body warm in even the coldest winters.

Figure 16 Mountain lions have sharp canine teeth for grabbing their prey. Donkeys have sharp incisors in front for cutting plants and flat grinding teeth in the back of their mouth.

Staying Warm Mammals have adaptations to help them keep warm. One way they stay warm is by having a thick coat, and many mammals have luxurious coats of fur. All mammals, even whales, have hair somewhere on their body. This is another trait that sets mammals apart from other animals. Mammals that live in cold climates usually have thick coats of hair, such as the fox in **Figure 15.** But large mammals that live in warm climates, like elephants, have less hair. Gorillas and humans have similar amounts of hair on their bodies, but human hair is finer and shorter.

Most mammals also have a layer of fat under the skin that acts as insulation. Whales and other mammals that live in cold oceans depend on a layer of fat called *blubber* to keep them warm.

Crunch! Another trait that sets mammals apart from other animals is their teeth. Birds don't even have teeth! And although fish and reptiles have teeth, their teeth tend to be all alike. In contrast, most mammals' teeth are specialized. They have different shapes and sizes for different functions.

Let's look at your teeth, for example. The teeth in the front of your mouth are cutting teeth, called *incisors*. Most people have four on top and four on the bottom. The next teeth are stabbing teeth, called *canines*. Canines help you grab food and hold onto it. Farther back in your mouth are flat teeth called *molars* that help grind up food.

The kinds of teeth a mammal has reflect its diet. Dogs, cats, wolves, foxes, and other meat-eating mammals have large canines. Molars are better developed in animals that eat plants. **Figure 16** shows the teeth of different mammals.

Unlike other vertebrates, mammals have two sets of teeth. A young mammal's first small teeth are called *milk teeth*. These are replaced by a set of permanent adult teeth after the mammal begins eating solid food and its jaw grows larger.

Multicultural CONNECTION

Native peoples of the Arctic region, such as the Inuit, have traditionally hunted marine mammals, such as seals, whales, and walruses. They use the seal's fur for water-repellent clothing and boots. They use seal blubber and whale blubber for lamp oil and for making soaps and lubricants. They even use marine mammal intestines to make waterproof outerwear.

Getting Oxygen Just as a fire needs oxygen in order to burn, all animals need oxygen to efficiently "burn," or break down, the food they eat. Like birds and reptiles, mammals use lungs to get oxygen from the air. But mammals also have a large muscle to help bring air into their lungs. This muscle is called the **diaphragm,** and it lies at the bottom of the rib cage.

Large Brains The brain of a mammal is much larger than the brain of another animal the same size. This allows mammals to learn, move, and think quickly. A mammal's highly developed brain also helps it keep track of what is going on in its environment and respond quickly.

Mammals depend on five major senses to provide them with information about their environment: vision, hearing, smell, touch, and taste. The importance of each sense for any given mammal often depends on the mammal's environment. For example, mammals that are active at night rely more heavily on their ability to hear than on their ability to see.

Mammal Parents All mammals reproduce sexually. Like birds and reptiles, mammals reproduce by internal fertilization. Most mammals give birth to live young, and all mammals nurse their young. Mammal parents are very protective, with one or both parents caring for their young until they are grown. **Figure 17** shows a brown bear caring for its young.

Activity

Like all mammals, you have a diaphragm. Place your hand underneath your rib cage. What happens as you breathe in and out? You are feeling the motion of your abdominal muscles, which are connected to your diaphragm. Contract and relax your abdominal muscles. What happens?

 TRY at HOME

Figure 17 *A mother bear will attack anything that threatens her cubs.*

REVIEW

1. Name three characteristics that are unique to mammals.
2. What is the purpose of a diaphragm?
3. **Making Inferences** Suppose you found a mammal skull on an archaeological dig. How would the teeth give you clues about the mammal's diet?

Answer to Explore
Contracting the abdominal muscles causes the diaphragm to contract and draw air into the lungs. Relaxing them allows air to leave the lungs.

CONNECT TO
PHYSICAL SCIENCE

MATERIALS
- 60 cc syringe (without needle)
- beaker of colored water

The diaphragm is a muscle that enables mammals to breathe. The diaphragm regulates the air pressure in the lungs. Tell students that in this simple model, the plunger of the syringe represents the diaphragm of a mammal. The barrel of the syringe represents the lungs. The colored water represents the air outside the body. Push the plunger all the way into the barrel. Place the tip of the syringe in the colored water. Pull the plunger back and fill the barrel with water. As you do this, explain that the barrel is filling because the pressure inside the barrel is decreasing as the space inside the barrel is increasing. Water is entering the barrel to equalize the pressure. This same principle enables the diaphragm to pull air into the lungs. **Sheltered English**

Answers to Review

1. Mammals have mammary glands, fur, and specialized teeth.
2. A diaphragm helps draw air into the lungs.
3. Large canine teeth would indicate that the animal was a meat eater. Flat molars, grinding teeth, and sharp incisors would suggest a plant eater.

2 Teach, continued

READING STRATEGY

Prediction Guide Before students read about marsupials, ask them to respond true or false to the following statement:

Marsupials are native only to Australia. (false)

Have them check their answer after they read the page.

CROSS-DISCIPLINARY FOCUS

Anthropology The artwork of Australia's Aborigines, an indigenous people, often depicts the country's unique and varied wildlife. Have students research the history of the tribes and the symbolism of the animals in their paintings. Students should bring their information to class to share their findings with their classmates.

Homework

Researching Mammals The platypus is an amphibious mammal. Tell students to find the word *amphibious* in a dictionary if they do not already know what it means. Then have them list examples of other amphibious mammals in their ScienceLog. (Examples include river otters, hippopotamuses, beavers, and muskrats.)

Kinds of Mammals

Mammals are divided into three groups based on the way their young develop. These groups are monotremes, marsupials, and placental mammals.

Monotremes Mammals that lay eggs are called **monotremes**. Monotremes are the only mammals that lay eggs, and early scientists called them "furred reptiles." But monotremes are not reptiles; they have all the mammal traits. They have mammary glands and a thick fur coat, and they are endotherms.

A female monotreme lays eggs with thick, leathery shells. Like bird and reptile eggs, monotreme eggs have a yolk and albumen to feed the developing embryo. The female incubates the eggs with her body heat. Newly hatched young are not fully developed. The mother protects her young and feeds them milk. Unlike other mammals, monotremes do not have nipples, and the babies cannot suck. Instead, the tiny monotremes nurse by licking milk from the skin and hair around their mother's mammary glands.

Figure 18 Echidnas are about the size of a house cat. They have large claws and long snouts that help them dig ants and termites out of their nests.

Two Kinds of Monotremes Monotremes are found only in Australia and New Guinea, and just three species of monotremes are alive today. Two are echidnas (ee KID nuhs), spine-covered animals with long snouts. Echidnas have long sticky tongues for catching ants and termites. You can see an echidna in **Figure 18**.

The third monotreme is the duckbilled platypus, shown in **Figure 19**. The duckbilled platypus is a swimming mammal that lives and feeds in rivers and ponds. It has webbed feet and a flat tail to help it move through the water. It also has a flat, rubbery bill that it uses to dig for food and to dig long tunnels in riverbanks to lay its eggs.

Figure 19 When underwater, a duckbilled platypus closes its eyes and ears. It uses its sensitive bill to find food.

IS THAT A FACT!

The platypus is one of the very few poisonous mammals.

WEIRD SCIENCE

Monotremes lack the glands that produce hydrochloric acid and peptic enzymes that help mammals digest protein. Scientists think that digestion in the echidnas is aided by the grinding action of the dirt they eat.

Marsupials You probably know that kangaroos, like those in **Figure 20,** have pouches. Kangaroos are **marsupials,** mammals with pouches. Like all mammals, marsupials are endotherms. They have mammary glands, fur, and teeth. Unlike the monotremes, marsupials do not lay eggs. They give birth to live young.

Like newly hatched monotremes, marsupial infants are not fully developed. At birth, the tiny embryos of a kangaroo are no larger than bumblebees. Shortly after birth, they drag themselves through their mother's fur until they reach a pouch on her abdomen. Inside the pouch are mammary glands. The young kangaroo climbs in, latches onto a nipple, and drinks milk until it is able to move around by itself and leave the pouch for short periods. Young kangaroos are called joeys.

There are about 280 species of marsupials. The only marsupial in North America north of Mexico is the opossum (uh PAHS suhm), shown in **Figure 21.** Other marsupials include koalas, shown in **Figure 22,** Tasmanian devils, and wallabies. Most marsupials live in Australia, New Guinea, and South America.

Figure 20 After birth, a kangaroo continues to develop in its mother's pouch. Older joeys leave the pouch but return if there is any sign of danger.

Figure 21 When in danger, an opossum will lie perfectly still and pretend to be dead so predators will tend to ignore it.

Figure 22 Koalas sleep in trees during the day and are active at night. They eat nothing but eucalyptus leaves.

BRAIN FOOD

When a kangaroo first climbs into its mother's pouch, the mother's milk is nonfat. Later, the milk is about 20 percent fat. A mother kangaroo with two babies that are different ages supplies nonfat milk to the baby and fat milk to the older one. Each youngster nurses from a different nipple.

MATH and MORE

Tell students: Red kangaroos can attain a maximum speed of 65 km/h and a stride of 7.5 m for short distances. How far could a red kangaroo travel in 2 minutes? How many strides would it take to travel that distance?

(65 km/h ÷ 60 min = 1.08 km/min
1.08 km/min × 2 min = 2.16 km
2.16 km × 1,000 m/km = 2,160 m
2,160 m ÷ 7.5 m/stride = 288 strides)

Math Skills Worksheet 31 "The Unit Factor and Dimensional Analysis"

CONNECT TO EARTH SCIENCE

About 50 million years ago, Australia and New Guinea began to separate from a larger continent into distinct land masses of their own. Placental mammals apparently did not reach Australia and New Guinea before the land masses separated from the other continents, although marsupials and monotremes were present then. Placental mammals found in Australia and New Guinea today are descendants of placental mammals that came to these regions only recently.

MISCONCEPTION ALERT

Be sure students understand that there is no guarantee that a newborn kangaroo or other marsupial will find its way to its mother's pouch. Despite being a tiny, blind embryo, the baby must crawl through the mother's fur with no assistance, climb into the pouch, and find a nipple. If the baby falls off, the mother will not pick it up.

2) Teach, continued

Answer to MATHBREAK

First calculate the number of ants per day, as follows:

$$\frac{50 \text{ ants}}{1 \text{ Calorie}} = \frac{x \text{ ants}}{1,800 \text{ Calories/day}}$$

$x = 90,000$ ants per day

at a rate of two ants per lick: 45,000 licks

The time will vary, but if the rate is 60 licks per minute, then

$$\frac{45,000 \text{ licks}}{60 \text{ licks/min}} = 750 \text{ minutes}$$

$$\frac{750 \text{ min}}{60 \text{ min/hour}} = 12.5 \text{ hours per day}$$

Answer to Self-Check

Monotremes are mammals that lay eggs. Marsupials bear live young but carry them in pouches or skin folds before they are able to live independently. Placentals develop inside the mother's body and are nourished through a placenta before birth.

Cross-Disciplinary Focus

Archaeology When archaeologists study the homes of prehistoric people, they usually look for traces of structures or fire circles, and they investigate caves. But scientists studying early South American Indians have learned that they used the shells of early armadillos to build roofs for their homes. These ancestors of modern armadillos had shells up to 3 m long.

Independent Practice

Concept Mapping Have students create a concept map that compares the development and life histories of monotremes, marsupials, and placental mammals. Some terms and concepts students can use include:

- type of egg with a shell, incubation, gestation, nest, uterus, mammary glands, method of nursing

416 Chapter 17 • Birds and Mammals

MATH BREAK

Ants for Dinner!

The giant anteater can stick its tongue out 150 times a minute. Count how many times you can stick out your tongue in a minute. Imagine that you are an anteater and you need 1,800 Calories a day. If you need to eat 50 ants to get 1 Calorie, how many ants would you have to eat per day? If you could catch two ants every time you stuck your tongue out, how many times a day would you have to stick out your tongue? How many hours a day would you have to eat?

Placental Mammals Most mammals are placental mammals. In **placental mammals**, the embryos stay inside the mother's body and develop in an organ called the *uterus*. Placental embryos form a special attachment to the uterus of their mother called a *placenta*. The placenta supplies food and oxygen from the mother's blood to the growing embryo. The placenta also removes wastes from the embryo.

The time during which an embryo develops within the mother is called the **gestation period**. Gestation (jeh STAY shuhn) periods in placental animals range from a few weeks in mice to as long as 23 months in elephants. Humans have a gestation period of about 9 months.

Self-Check

Explain the difference between a monotreme, a marsupial, and a placental mammal. *(See page 782 to check your answer.)*

Kinds of Placental Mammals

Over 90 percent of all the mammals on Earth are placental mammals. Living placental mammals are classified into 18 orders. The characteristics of the most common orders are given on the following pages.

Toothless Mammals

This group includes anteaters, armadillos, aardvarks, pangolins, and sloths. Although these mammals are called "toothless," only the anteaters are completely toothless. The others have small teeth. Most toothless mammals feed on insects they catch with their long sticky tongues.

▶ **Armadillos** eat insects, frogs, mushrooms, and roots. When threatened, an armadillo rolls up into a ball and is protected by its tough plates.

▲ The largest anteater is the 40 kg **giant anteater** of South America. Anteaters never destroy the nests of their prey. They open the nests, eat a few ants or termites, and then move on to another nest.

IS THAT A FACT!

Both placental mammals and marsupials have a placenta. So why do we call one group placental? The difference is that in marsupials, the placenta does not play a major role in nourishing the fetus, while in placental mammals, it does.

Insect Eaters

Insect eaters, or *insectivores,* live on every continent except Australia and Antarctica. Most insectivores are small, and most have long pointed noses to dig into the soil for food. Compared with other mammals, they have a very small brain and few specialized teeth. Insectivores include moles, shrews, and hedgehogs.

◄ The **star-nosed mole** has sensitive feelers on its nose to help it find insects and feel its way while burrowing underground. Although they have tiny eyes, moles cannot see.

▲ **Hedgehogs** live throughout Europe, Asia, and Africa. Their spines keep them safe from most predators.

Rodents

More than one-third of all mammalian species are rodents, and they can be found on every continent except Antarctica. Rodents include squirrels, mice, rats, guinea pigs, porcupines, and chinchillas. Most rodents are small animals with long, sensitive whiskers. Rodents are chewers and gnawers. All rodents have sharp front teeth for gnawing. Because rodents chew so much, their teeth wear down. So a rodent's incisors grow continuously, just like your fingernails do.

▲ The **capybaras** (KAP i BAH ruhs) of South America are the largest rodents in the world. A female can have a mass of 70 kg—as much as a grown man.

▲ Like all rodents, **beavers** have gnawing teeth. They use these teeth to cut down trees.

Multicultural CONNECTION

Shrews have been objects of fear and adoration. Some Native American lore holds that red-toothed shrews *(Sorex)* kill people by burrowing through the body to the heart. Some central Africans worship the hero shrew *(Scutisorex congicus).* The vertebrae in its backbone are arched and fused to protect it from being crushed. Some people believe that eating the shrew's heart will endow them with that same strength.

MISCONCEPTION ALERT

Though there are no true insectivores in Australia, there are mammals in Australia that eat insects. But they don't have a specialized insect diet or have familiar adaptations—such as long, narrow snouts, a highly developed sense of touch, and a good sense of smell—to help them obtain specific insects.

GOING FURTHER

Writing Not all orders of placental mammals are represented in this section. Have students research and draw a diagram depicting a hypothesis for the genetic relationships among all 18 orders of placental mammals.

Science Bloopers

Tree shrews are tiny animals that look like squirrels with long, cone-shaped noses. Though they are insectivores and have shrewlike noses, tree shrews are not actually shrews. Until late in the twentieth century, zoologists thought tree shrews were primates. Recently, taxonomists recognized their uniqueness and placed them in their own order, Scandentia.

2) Teach, continued

BRAIN FOOD

Tell students that if they were tracking lagomorphs in the snow, they would probably find all four footprints aligned or even prints from the back feet in front of those from the front feet! When moving quickly, lagomorphs rely on their powerful back legs to propel them forward. Their jump distance is increased when they swing their back legs forward until they touch down nearly in line with their front feet and then push off. Lagomorphs are one of the most efficient animals with this type of locomotion. Cheetahs can also do this.

DISCUSSION

Bat Fact and Fiction Ask students if the following statements are true or false:

1. Some bats have wing spans of more than 1.5 m. (True; the flying foxes of Indonesia are the largest bats.)
2. A single little brown bat can catch 1,200 mosquito-size insects in 1 hour. (true)
3. Bats present a serious disease threat to humans. (False; less than one-half of 1 percent of bats carry rabies. Most bite only when threatened.)

Lagomorphs

Rabbits, hares, and pikas belong to a group of placental mammals called lagomorphs. Like rodents, they have sharp gnawing teeth. But unlike rodents, they have two sets of incisors in their upper jaw and short tails. Rabbits and hares have long, powerful hind legs for jumping. To detect their many predators, they have sensitive noses and large ears and eyes.

◀ **Pikas** are small animals that live high in the mountains. Pikas gather plants and mound them in "haystacks" to dry. In the winter, they use the dry plants for food and insulation.

▲ The large ears of this **black-tailed jack rabbit** help it hear well.

Flying Mammals

Bats are the only mammals that can fly. Bats are active at night and sleep in sheltered areas during the day. Most bats eat insects. But some bats eat fruit, and three species of vampire bats drink the blood of other animals.

Most bats hunt for insects at night. They find their way using echolocation. Bats make clicking noises when they fly. Trees, rocks, insects, and other objects reflect the sound back to the bat, making an echo.

Echoes from a big, hard tree sound very different from those reflecting off a soft, tasty moth. Bats that echolocate often have enormous ears to help them hear the echoes of their own clicks.

In many Asian countries, **bats** ▶ are symbols of good luck, long life, and happiness.

Bats and Submarines

What do bats have in common with submarines? Submarines use a form of echolocation called sonar to find and avoid objects underwater. Based on what you know about echolocation, what kind of instruments do you think are needed to navigate a submarine with sonar?

418

Answer to APPLY

A submarine would need instruments to send signals and receive echoes and would need instruments to calculate distances using that information.

IS THAT A FACT!

Of the known mammal species, 25 percent are bats.

Carnivores

Carnivores are a group of mammals that have large canines and special teeth for slicing meat. The name *carnivore* means "meat eater"—the mammals in this group primarily eat meat. Carnivorous mammals include lions, wolves, weasels, otters, bears, raccoons, and hyenas. Carnivores also include a group of fish-eating marine mammals called *pinnipeds*. The pinnipeds include seals, sea lions, and walruses. Some carnivores also eat plants. For example, black bears eat grass, nuts, and berries and only rarely eat meat. But many carnivores eat nothing but other animals.

▲ **Coyotes** are members of the dog family. They live throughout North America and in parts of Central America.

▼ **Raccoons** have handlike paws that help them catch fish and hold their food. They can handle objects almost as well as monkeys can.

▲ Cats are divided into two groups, big cats and small cats. All the big cats can roar. The largest of the big cats is the **Siberian tiger,** with a mass of up to 300 kg.

◄ **Walruses** are pinnipeds. Unlike other carnivores, walruses do not use their canines for tearing food. Instead, they use them to defend themselves, to dig for food, and to climb on ice.

SCIENCE HUMOR

Q: Why did the lion cross the savanna?

A: to get to the other pride

ACTIVITY

Comparing Footprints Have students compare footprints or foot casts of two common carnivores, the domestic dog and the domestic cat. Students can make footprints by having a pet step on damp, claylike soil. They can make casts by pouring plaster of paris in a dried footprint. Have them study the casts and hypothesize about the reasons for the features and differences they notice. **Sheltered English**

DEBATE

Carnivore Conservation Explain to students that many carnivores are endangered because of habitat loss, hunting, and poaching. Historically, it has been difficult to persuade people to preserve animals that they considered dangerous to themselves and to livestock. Some carnivores are endangered because people hunt them for their fur or for body parts believed to have medicinal qualities. Have students debate the extent to which we should preserve large carnivores, such as wolves and tigers, and the steps that we should take to do so.

MISCONCEPTION ALERT

Not all Carnivora are strict carnivores. For example, pandas feed primarily on bamboo, and coatis eat mostly fruit. Tell students that, in this case, animals are classified according to ancestral relationships, not their actual diet.

2 Teach, continued

Multicultural CONNECTION

Hernando Cortéz reintroduced the horse into North America during the 1500s. Before then, Native Americans had to walk long distances on foot, carrying heavy loads on their backs. The arrival of the horse changed their lives forever. They were able to travel long distances more easily and were able to expand their trade routes. They were also able to hunt bison and other animals more efficiently. For plains tribes, such as the Kiowa, the horse became an important part of practical life and a key part of their culture.

REAL-WORLD CONNECTION

Water Buffaloes Many kinds of hoofed mammals are used for draft work. In the United States, thousands of farms still rely on horses or mules to pull some farm equipment. Oxen, llamas, goats, and camels are used in various parts of the world for pulling or carrying. But perhaps no animal is as widely used as the water buffalo. Water buffaloes are large, strong, and relatively docile animals. They are hardy and can survive eating rough, native vegetation. They were originally domesticated in Asia thousands of years ago and are still vital to the farms of southern China and Southeast Asia. The water buffalo was introduced to Africa about 1,400 years ago and is still used for draft work there. More recently, the water buffalo was introduced to Central and South America. Have interested students research and present to the class an oral report on the importance of water buffaloes or other draft animals to farmers around the world.

Hoofed Mammals

Horses, pigs, deer, and rhinoceroses are just a few of the many mammals that have thick hoofs. Most hoofed mammals are adapted for swift running. Because they are plant eaters, they have large, flat molars to help them grind plant material.

Hoofed mammals are divided into groups based on the number of toes they have. Odd-toed hoofed mammals have one or three toes. Horses and zebras have a single large hoof, or toe. Other odd-toed hoofed mammals include rhinoceroses and tapirs. Even-toed hoofed mammals have two or four toes. These mammals include pigs, cows, camels, deer, hippopotamuses, and giraffes.

▲ **Giraffes** are the tallest living mammals. They have long necks, long legs, and an even number of toes.

▲ **Tapirs** are large, three-toed mammals that live in forests. Tapirs can be found in Central America, South America, and Southeast Asia.

Camels are even-toed mammals. The hump of a camel is a large lump of fat that provides energy for the camel when food is scarce.

IS THAT A FACT!

The limbs of hoofed mammals are adapted for running and walking long distances over open terrain. These animals have between one and four toes and very long foot bones. In human terms, they are balancing on the tips of their toes.

Trunk-Nosed Mammals

Elephants are the only mammals with a trunk. The trunk is an elongated and muscular combination of the upper lip and nose. Elephants use their trunk the same way we use our hands, lips, and nose. The trunk is powerful enough to lift a tree yet agile enough to pick small fruits one at a time. Elephants use their trunk to place food in their mouth and to spray their back with water to cool off.

There are two species of elephants, African elephants and Asian elephants. African elephants are larger and have bigger ears and tusks than Asian elephants. Both species eat plants. Because they are so large, elephants eat up to 18 hours a day to get enough food.

Elephants are the largest land animals. Male African elephants can reach a mass of 7,500 kg! Elephants are very intelligent and may live more than 60 years.

▼ **Elephants** are social animals. They live in herds of related females and their offspring. The whole family helps take care of young.

Self-Check

1. Why are bats classified as mammals and not as birds?
2. How are rodents and lagomorphs similar? How are they different?

(See page 782 to check your answers.)

Environment CONNECTION

Both species of elephants are endangered. For centuries, humans have hunted elephants for their long teeth, called tusks. Elephant tusks are made of ivory, a hard material used for carving. Because of the high demand for ivory, much of the elephant population has been wiped out. Today elephant hunting is illegal.

SCIENCE HUMOR

Q: How do you make an elephant float?
A: Pour a glass of root beer, and add two elephants.

Answers to Self-Check

1. Bats bear live young, have fur, and do not have feathers.
2. Rodents and lagomorphs are small mammals with long, sensitive whiskers and gnawing teeth. Unlike rodents, lagomorphs have two sets of incisors and a short tail.

3) Extend

DEBATE

Elephants and People: Room for Both? As the human population in Africa has expanded, villages and ranches have spread into former elephant habitat. Fences prevent elephants from traveling traditional routes to forage and find water. In some areas elephants have raided crops, killed farmers who tried to defend their fields, and even destroyed their natural food sources because too many elephants were trying to live in too small an area. So although elephant populations have declined, current conditions have caused overcrowding among the ones that remain. Should "excess" elephants be killed? The meat from killed elephants is given to the local people, many of whom are in dire need of food. Have students debate the management of elephant populations.

GOING FURTHER

The ears of African and Asian elephants are the most noticeable difference between the two species. Have students explain the evolutionary significance of this difference by exploring how the ears differ and researching the environments in which the animals live. (The larger surface area of the African elephant's ears contains more blood vessels that can be exposed to a cooling breeze passing over the thin skin of the ears; the larger ears serve as "fans" for the animals in the searing African heat. Asian elephants spend a lot of time in the forest, shielded from the sun.)

3) Extend, continued

RESEARCH

Writing Have students research and write a short report about one aspect of whale biology. Possibilities include whale behavior, feeding habits, anatomy, and communication. Encourage interested students to do preliminary research to find an interesting subject to study. Have students present their findings to the class.

DEBATE

Whaling Have students research and debate the practice of hunting whales. Questions that they should be aware of include:

What is the history of whaling? What products do people obtain from whales? Are there other sources of these products? Why have some countries signed a treaty to cease commercial whaling? Why don't all countries sign the treaty? Are there any whale species with a population large enough to support an ongoing whaling industry?

Students should make a distinction between commercial whaling and small-scale whaling as it is practiced by people such as the Makah of Washington State.

Cetaceans

Whales, dolphins, and porpoises make up a group of water-dwelling mammals called cetaceans (see TAY shuhns). At first glance, whales and their relatives may look more like fish than mammals. But like all mammals, cetaceans are endotherms, have lungs, and nurse their young. Most of the largest whales are toothless whales that strain tiny, shrimp-like animals from sea water. But dolphins, porpoises, sperm whales, and killer whales have teeth, which they use to eat fish and other animals.

▲ **Spinner dolphins** spin like a football when they leap from the water. Like all dolphins, they are intelligent and highly social.

◀ Like bats, cetaceans use echolocation to "see" their surroundings. **Sperm whales,** like this one, use loud blasts of sound to stun fish, making them easier to catch.

Sirenia

The smallest group of water-dwelling mammals is called sirenia (sie REE nee uh). It includes just four species—three kinds of manatees and the dugong. These mammals are completely aquatic; they live along coasts and in large rivers. They are quiet animals that eat seaweed and water plants.

Manatees are also ▶ called sea cows.

422

WEIRD SCIENCE

Humpback whales have a fascinating fishing strategy. They make their own fishing nets out of bubbles! The bubble net can be up to 30 m (98 ft) in diameter, which is large enough for the whale to get inside. The whale creates this net by swimming around in a spiral directly underneath a school of fish. As the whale swims, it blows air out of its blowhole. This forms a bubble net entirely around the fish, trapping them. The whale then swims up through the net with its mouth wide open, scooping in fish as it goes.

Primates

Prosimians, monkeys, apes, and humans all belong to a group of mammals called *primates*. There are about 160 species of primates. All primates have the eyes facing forward, enabling both eyes to focus on a single point. Most primates have five fingers on each hand and five toes on each foot, with flat fingernails instead of claws. Primates' fingers and opposable thumbs are able to make complicated movements, like grasping objects. Primates have a large brain in proportion to their body size and are considered some of the most intelligent mammals.

Many primates live in trees. Their flexible shoulder joints and grasping hands and feet enable them to climb trees and swing from branch to branch. Most primates eat a diet of leaves and fruits, but some also eat animals.

▲ **Orangutans** and other apes frequently walk upright. Apes usually have larger brains and bodies than monkeys.

◀ **Spider monkeys,** like most monkeys, have grasping tails. Their long arms, legs, and tails help them move among the trees.

REVIEW

1. If you saw only the feet of a hippopotamus and a rhinoceros, could you tell the difference between the two animals? Explain your answer.
2. How are monotremes different from all other mammals? How are they similar?
3. To what group of placental mammals do dogs belong? How do you know?
4. **Making Inferences** What is a gestation period? Why do elephants have a longer gestation period than do mice?

internet connect

TOPIC: The Origin of Mammals, Characteristics of Mammals
GO TO: www.scilinks.org
sciLINKS NUMBER: HSTL415, HSTL420

▼ Answers to Review

1. Yes; the hippopotamus would be the one with two toes, and the rhinoceros would be the one with three toes.
2. Monotremes are the only mammals that lay eggs. Like other mammals, they have fur and nurse their young.
3. Dogs are carnivores, related to wolves. They have large canine teeth and hunt prey in the wild.
4. A gestation period is the length of time a developing fetus remains inside the mother. Elephants have larger bodies and need more time to develop.

4) Close

Quiz

1. Why did the mammal population increase when the dinosaurs became extinct? (There was more land and food available for the mammals.)
2. Where do mammals get the energy they need to keep their bodies warm? (Mammals quickly break down food in their bodies and use the energy released from their cells to keep their bodies warm.)
3. What are three characteristics of primates? (Possible answers: eyes that face forward, five fingers on each hand and five toes on each foot, flat fingernails and toenails instead of claws, fingers and thumbs that can make complicated movements, and a large brain)

ALTERNATIVE ASSESSMENT

Have students create a poster that visually summarizes the physiological information they have learned about birds and mammals and that provides examples of each of the animal categories discussed in the chapter. For example, a picture of a bird of prey catching its food would illustrate the grasping talons of raptors.

Sheltered English

 Reinforcement Worksheet 17 "Mammals Are Us"

Chapter Highlights

VOCABULARY DEFINITIONS

SECTION 1

down feather a fluffy insulating feather that lies next to a bird's body

contour feather a feather made of a stiff central shaft with many side branches` called barbs

preening activity in which a bird uses its beak to spread oil on its feathers

lift an upward force on an object (such as a wing) caused by differences in pressure above and below the object; opposes the downward pull of gravity

brooding when a bird sits on its eggs until they hatch

Chapter Highlights

SECTION 1

Vocabulary
down feather (p. 401)
contour feather (p. 401)
preening (p. 401)
lift (p. 404)
brooding (p. 405)

Section Notes
- Like reptiles, birds lay amniotic eggs and have thick, dry scales.
- Unlike reptiles, birds are endotherms and are covered with feathers.
- Because flying requires a lot of energy, birds must eat a high-energy diet and breathe efficiently.
- Birds' wings are shaped so that they generate lift. Lift helps keep a bird in the air during flight.
- Birds are lightweight. Their feathers are strong but lightweight, and their skeleton is relatively rigid, compact, and hollow.
- Because birds can fly, they can migrate great distances. They can nest in one habitat and winter in another. Migrating birds can take advantage of food supplies and avoid predators.

Labs
What? No Dentist Bills? (p. 744)

☑ Skills Check

Visual Understanding

LIFT The diagram on page 404 helps explain the concept of lift. The air above the curved wing moves faster than the air underneath the wing. Faster-moving air creates lower pressure above the wing. The higher pressure under the wing forces it up, creating lift.

Lab and Activity Highlights

What? No Dentist Bills? PG 744

Wanted: Mammals on Mars PG 745

 Datasheets for LabBook (blackline masters for these labs)

SECTION 2

Vocabulary
- **mammary glands** (p. 411)
- **diaphragm** (p. 413)
- **monotreme** (p. 414)
- **marsupial** (p. 415)
- **placental mammal** (p. 416)
- **gestation period** (p. 416)

Section Notes
- All mammals have mammary glands; in females, mammary glands produce milk. Milk is a highly nutritious fluid fed to the young.
- Like birds, mammals are endotherms.
- Mammals maintain their high metabolism by eating a lot of food and breathing efficiently.
- Mammals have a diaphragm that helps them draw air into their lungs.
- Mammals have highly specialized teeth for chewing different kinds of food. Mammals that eat plants have incisors and molars for cutting and grinding plants. Carnivores have canines for seizing and tearing their prey.
- Mammals are the only vertebrates that have mammary glands, fur, and two sets of teeth.
- Mammals are divided into three groups: monotremes, marsupials, and placental mammals.
- Monotremes lay eggs instead of bearing live young. Monotremes produce milk but do not have nipples or a placenta.
- Marsupials give birth to live young, but the young are born as embryos. The embryos climb into their mother's pouch, where they drink milk until they are more developed.
- Placental mammals develop inside of the mother for a period of time called a gestation period. Placental mothers nurse their young after birth.

Labs
Wanted: Mammals on Mars (p. 745)

VOCABULARY DEFINITIONS, continued

SECTION 2

mammary glands glands that secrete a nutritious fluid called milk

diaphragm the sheet of muscle underneath the lungs of mammals that helps draw air into the lungs

monotreme a mammal that lays eggs

marsupial a mammal that gives birth to live, partially developed young that continue to develop inside the mother's pouch or skin fold

placental mammal a mammal that nourishes unborn offspring with a placenta inside the uterus

gestation period the time during which an embryo develops within the mother

 Vocabulary Review Worksheet 17

 Blackline masters of these Chapter Highlights can be found in the **Study Guide**.

internetconnect

 GO TO: go.hrw.com

Visit the **HRW** Web site for a variety of learning tools related to this chapter. Just type in the keyword:

KEYWORD: HSTVR2

 GO TO: www.scilinks.org

Visit the **National Science Teachers Association** on-line Web site for Internet resources related to this chapter. Just type in the *sci*LINKS number for more information about the topic:

TOPIC	sciLINKS NUMBER
Bird Characteristics	HSTL405
Kinds of Birds	HSTL410
The Origin of Mammals	HSTL415
Characteristics of Mammals	HSTL420

Lab and Activity Highlights

LabBank

 Labs You Can Eat, Why Birds of a Beak Eat Together, Lab 8

 Long-Term Projects & Research Ideas, Look Who's Coming to Dinner, Project 17

Chapter Review Answers

USING VOCABULARY

1. Precocial, Altricial
2. diaphragm
3. placenta
4. preening
5. carnivores
6. Down feathers

UNDERSTANDING CONCEPTS

Multiple Choice

7. a
8. d
9. b
10. c
11. c
12. c

Short Answer

13. Marsupials bear live young that continue to develop in their mother's pouches. Like other mammals, they have fur, specialized teeth, and mammary glands.
14. Birds and mammals stay warm by converting food into energy for body heat. Mammals have fur, and birds have feathers, in part, to help retain body heat.
15. The Bernoulli effect is the vacuum created by fast-moving air.
16. Bats need large ears to hear echoes they use in locating food and other objects.

Chapter Review

USING VOCABULARY

To complete the following sentences, choose the correct term from each pair of terms listed below:

1. __?__ chicks can run after their mother soon after they hatch. __?__ chicks can barely stretch their neck out to be fed when they first hatch. (*Altricial* or *Precocial*)

2. The __?__ helps mammals breathe. (*diaphragm* or *air sac*)

3. The __?__ allows some mammals to supply nutrients to young in the mother's uterus. (*mammary gland* or *placenta*)

4. Birds take care of their feathers by __?__. (*brooding* or *preening*)

5. A lion belongs to a group of mammals called __?__. (*carnivores* or *primates*)

6. __?__ are fluffy feathers that help keep birds warm. (*Contour feathers* or *Down feathers*)

UNDERSTANDING CONCEPTS

Multiple Choice

7. Both birds and reptiles
   a. lay eggs.
   b. brood their young.
   c. have air sacs.
   d. have feathers.

8. Flight requires
   a. a lot of energy and oxygen.
   b. a lightweight body.
   c. strong flight muscles.
   d. All of the above

9. Only mammals
   a. have glands.
   b. nurse their young.
   c. lay eggs.
   d. have teeth.

10. Monotremes do not
    a. have mammary glands.
    b. care for their young.
    c. have pouches.
    d. have fur.

11. Lift
    a. is air that travels over the top of a wing.
    b. is provided by air sacs.
    c. is the upward force on a wing that keeps a bird in the air.
    d. is created by pressure from the diaphragm.

12. Which of the following is not a primate?
    a. a lemur   c. a pika
    b. a human   d. a chimpanzee

Short Answer

13. How are marsupials different from other mammals? How are they similar?

14. Both birds and mammals are endotherms. How do they stay warm?

15. What is the Bernoulli effect?

16. Why do some bats have large ears?

Concept Mapping

17. Use the following terms to create a concept map: monotremes, endotherms, birds, mammals, mammary glands, placental mammals, marsupials, feathers, hair.

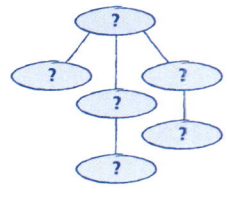

CRITICAL THINKING AND PROBLEM SOLVING

Write one or two sentences to answer the following questions:

18. Unlike bird and monotreme eggs, the eggs of placental mammals and marsupials do not have a yolk. How do developing embryos of marsupials and placental mammals get the nutrition they need?

19. Most bats and cetaceans use echolocation. Why don't these mammals rely solely on sight to find their prey and examine their surroundings?

20. Suppose you are working at a museum and are making a display of bird skeletons. Unfortunately, the skeletons have lost their labels. How can you separate the skeletons of flightless birds from those of birds that fly? Will you be able to tell which birds flew rapidly and which birds could soar? Explain your answer.

MATH IN SCIENCE

21. A bird is flying at a speed of 35 km/h. At this speed, its body consumes 60 Calories per gram of body mass per hour. If the bird has a mass of 50 g, how many Calories will it use if it flies for 30 minutes at this speed?

INTERPRETING GRAPHICS

Endotherms use a lot of energy when they run or fly. The graph below shows how many Calories a small dog uses while running at different speeds. Use this graph to answer the questions below.

22. As the dog runs faster, how does the amount of energy it consumes per hour change?

23. How much energy per hour will this dog consume if it is running at 4 km/h? at 9 km/h?

24. Energy consumed is given in Calories per kilogram of body mass per hour. If the dog has a mass of 6 kg and is running at 7 km/h, how many Calories per hour will it use?

Take a minute to review your answers to the Pre-Reading Questions found at the bottom of page 398. Have your answers changed? If necessary, revise your answers based on what you have learned since you began this chapter.

Concept Mapping

17. An answer to this exercise can be found at the end of this book.

CRITICAL THINKING AND PROBLEM SOLVING

18. Marsupials get their nutrition from their mother's milk. Placental mammals get their nutrition from their mother's body through the placenta.

19. Bats and cetaceans are both active in dark environments, where sound is more helpful than sight.

20. Birds that fly will have a large keel and larger wings. The birds with longer wings probably soared because longer wings are necessary to provide enough surface area for greater lift.

MATH IN SCIENCE

21. 1,500 Cal

INTERPRETING GRAPHICS

22. The faster the dog goes, the more energy it uses.

23. At 4 km/h, the dog consumes 9 Cal/kg/h. At 9 km/h, the dog consumes 16.5 Cal/kg/h.

24. At 7 km/h, the dog consumes 13.5 Cal/kg/h.
13.5 Cal/kg/h × 6 kg = 81 Cal/h.

Concept Mapping Transparency 17

Blackline masters of this Chapter Review can be found in the **Study Guide.**

ACROSS THE SCIENCES
The Aerodynamics of Flight

Background
The four aerodynamic forces described in this feature—lift, gravity, drag, and thrust—permit birds and planes to fly. Airplanes are designed differently to take advantage of these forces. Similarly, birds have particular adaptations that make them fast flyers or excellent gliders. Students should recognize how the physical features of airplanes and birds contribute to their ability to fly.

ACROSS THE SCIENCES

LIFE SCIENCE • PHYSICAL SCIENCE

The Aerodynamics of Flight

For centuries people have tried to imitate a spectacular feat that birds perfected millions of years ago—flight! It was not until 1903 that the Wright brothers were able to fly in a heavier-than-air flying machine. Their first flight lasted only 12 seconds, and they only traveled 37 m. Although modern airplanes are much more sophisticated, they still rely on the same principles of flight.

Fighting Gravity
The sleek body of a jet is shaped to battle drag, while the wings are shaped to battle Earth's gravity. In order to take off, airplanes must pull upward with a force greater than gravitational force. This upward force is called *lift*. Where does an airplane get lift? An airplane wing is designed so that as the wing moves through the air, air must travel faster above the wing than below it. This difference in air speed causes the pressure above the wing to be less than the pressure below the wing. The difference in pressure pulls the airplane upward.

Push and Pull
The design of its wing is not enough to get an airplane off the ground. Wings require air to flow past them in order to create lift. Airplanes also rely on *thrust*, the force that gives an airplane forward motion. Powerful engines and propellers provide airplanes with thrust. As airplanes move faster, more air rushes past the wings, and lift increases.

Airplanes usually take off into a head wind, which pushes against the airplane as it travels. Any force that pushes against an airplane's motion, like a head wind, is called *drag* and can slow an airplane down. The body of an airplane has smooth curves to minimize drag. A tail wind is an airflow that pushes the airplane from the rear and shortens travel time. In order to increase speed, engineers design airplanes with streamlined bodies to reduce drag. Wings can also be designed to increase lift. A rounded and longer wing provides greater lift, but it also produces more drag. Engineers must consider such trade-offs when they design airplanes. Athletes also consider drag when they choose equipment. For example, runners and cyclists wear tight-fitting clothing to reduce drag.

Think About It!
▶ Airplanes have a variety of shapes and sizes and are designed for many purposes, including transport, travel, and combat. Some planes are designed to fly fast, and others are designed to carry heavy loads. Do some research, and then describe how the aerodynamics differ.

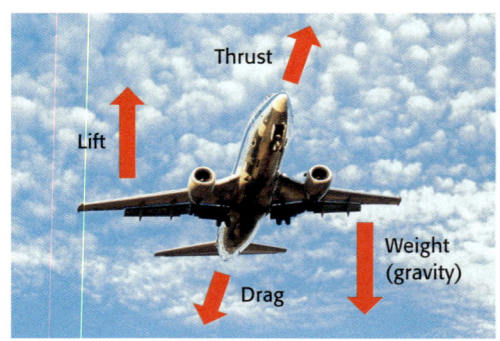

▲ *The design of airplanes got a boost from our feathered friends.*

Answer to Think About It!
Heavy cargo airplanes travel at much slower speeds than fighter jets. Cargo airplanes generally have thick wings to provide enough lift to get their massive contents off the ground. Fighter jets are much lighter and do not require as much lift. They often have thinner wings. Many fighter jets have powerful engines to give them more thrust and speed. The fastest fighter jets can travel over 2,000 mph! Fighter jets also have smooth, aerodynamic surfaces to minimize drag, which would slow them down. Short-distance flyers, such as many personal airplanes, do not have expensive, powerful engines but rely on propellers to provide thrust.

WEIRD SCIENCE

NAKED MOLE-RATS

What do you call a nearly blind rodent that is 7 cm long and looks like a hot dog that has been left in the microwave too long? A naked mole-rat. For more than 150 years, this mammal—which is native to hot, dry regions of Kenya, Ethiopia, and Somalia—has puzzled scientists by its strange appearance and peculiar habits.

What's Hair Got to Do with It?

Naked mole-rats have such strange characteristics that you might wonder whether they are really mammals at all. Their grayish pink skin hangs loosely, allowing them to maneuver through the narrow underground tunnel systems they call home. At first glance, the naked mole-rats appear to be hairless, and hair is a key characteristic of mammals. However, naked mole-rats are not hairless, but they do lack fur. In fact, they have whiskers to guide them through the dark passages and hair between their toes to sweep up loose dirt like tiny brooms. Believe it or not, they also have hair on their lips to prevent dirt from entering their mouth as their massive teeth dig new passages through the dirt!

Is It Cold in Here?

Naked mole-rats have the poorest endothermic capacity of any mammal. Their body temperature remains close to the temperature of the air in their tunnels—a cool 31°C (more than 5°C cooler than the body temperature of humans). At night these animals minimize heat loss by huddling close together. Fortunately, the temperature does not change very much in their native habitat.

Who's in Charge?

Naked mole-rats are the only mammals known to form communities similar to those formed by social insects, such as honey bees. A community of naked mole-rats is made up of between 20 and 300 individuals that divide up tasks much like bees, wasps, and termites do. Each community has one breeding female, called the queen, and up to three breeding males. All females are biologically capable of reproducing, but only one does. When a female becomes a queen, she actually grows longer!

Think About It!

▶ At first glance, naked mole-rats appear to be missing several key characteristics of mammals. Do further research to find out what characteristics they have that classifies them as mammals.

◀ Naked mole-rats are so unique that they have become a popular attraction at zoos.

WEIRD SCIENCE
Naked Mole-Rats

Answers to Think About It!

At first glance, the naked mole-rat *(Heterocephalus glaber)* may seem to not have all of the key characteristics of mammals. Encourage students to further investigate the naked mole-rat and discuss what features it has that qualify it as a mammal.

1. **Hair.** Although naked mole-rats appear hairless, closer inspection reveals that they do have specialized hairs on their face, feet, and lips.

2. **Mammary glands.** By definition, mammals feed their young with milk produced in the mammary glands. The queen has mammary glands, which she uses to feed her litter of 10 to 27 pups for about 4 weeks. All females are capable of reproducing and producing milk; however, only the queen does these activities.

3. **Placenta.** The young of all mammals except marsupials and monotremes develop in placentas. Naked mole-rat pups develop inside a placenta in the queen for 70 to 80 days.

4. **Endotherm.** Mammals have highly variable body temperatures. Despite their poor capacity to regulate internal body temperature, naked mole-rats are in fact endothermic.

UNIT 6

TIMELINE
Ecology

1661
John Evelyn publishes a book condemning air pollution in London, England.

1771
Joseph Priestley experiments with plants and finds that they use carbon dioxide and release oxygen.

1970
The Environmental Protection Agency (EPA) is formed to set and enforce pollution control standards in the United States.

1973
The U.S. Congress passes the Endangered Species Act.

1990
In order to save dolphins from being caught in fishing nets, United States tuna processors announce that they will not accept tuna caught in nets that can kill dolphins.

What did you have for breakfast this morning? Whatever you ate, your breakfast was a direct result of living things working together. For example, milk comes from a cow. The cow eats plants to gain energy. Bacteria help the plants obtain nutrients from the soil. And the soil has nutrients because fungi break down dead trees.

All living things on Earth are interconnected. Our actions have an impact on our environment, and our environment has an impact on us. In this unit you will study ecology, the interaction of Earth's living things. This timeline shows some of the ways humans have studied and affected the Earth.

1852
The United States imports sparrows from Germany to defend against crop-damaging caterpillars.

1854
Henry David Thoreau's *Walden* is published. In it, Thoreau asserts that people should live in harmony with nature.

1872
The first United States national park, Yellowstone, is established by Congress.

1933
The Civilian Conservation Corps is established. The corps plants trees, fights forest fires, and builds dams to control floods.

1962
Rachel Carson's book *Silent Spring*, which describes the wasteful use of pesticides and their destruction of the environment, is published.

1993
Americans recycle 59.5 billion aluminum cans (two out of every three cans).

1996
The Glen Canyon Dam is opened, purposefully flooding the Grand Canyon. The flooding helps maintain the ecological balance by restoring beaches and sandbars and rejuvenating marshes.

Ecology

Chapter Organizer

CHAPTER ORGANIZATION	TIME MINUTES	OBJECTIVES	LABS, INVESTIGATIONS, AND DEMONSTRATIONS
Chapter Opener pp. 432–433	45	National Standards: UCP 1, 5, SAI 1	**Start-Up Activity** Who Eats Whom? p. 433
Section 1 Everything Is Connected	90	▶ Distinguish between the biotic and abiotic environment. ▶ Explain how populations, communities, ecosystems, and the biosphere are related. ▶ Explain how the abiotic environment relates to communities. UCP 1, SAI 1, SPSP 2, LS 1a, 4a, 4c, 4d; LabBook SAI 2, LS 4d	**QuickLab,** The Human Population, p. 435 GENERAL **Skill Builder,** Capturing the Wild Bean, p. 748 GENERAL **Datasheets for LabBook,** Capturing the Wild Bean, Datasheet 39 GENERAL
Section 2 Living Things Need Energy	90	▶ Describe the functions of producers, consumers, and decomposers in an ecosystem. ▶ Distinguish between a food chain and a food web. ▶ Explain how energy flows through a food web. ▶ Distinguish between an organism's habitat and its niche. UCP 1, SAI 1, LS 1a, 4a–4d	**EcoLabs & Field Activities,** Survival Is Just a Roll of the Dice, EcoLab 5 GENERAL **Whiz-Bang Demonstrations,** Voracious Fly Catcher, Demo 11 BASIC
Section 3 Types of Interactions	135	▶ Distinguish between the two types of competition. ▶ Give examples of predators and prey. ▶ Distinguish between mutualism, commensalism, and parasitism. ▶ Define *coevolution,* and give an example. UCP 1, 4, LS 3a, 3c, 4a, 4d; LabBook UCP 1, 4, SAI 1, LS 1a, 3d	**Interactive Explorations CD-ROM,** What's Bugging You? GENERAL A **Worksheet** is also available in the **Interactive Explorations Teacher's Edition.** **Making Models,** Adaptation: It's a Way of Life, p. 746 GENERAL **Datasheets for LabBook,** Adaptation: It's a Way of Life, Datasheet 38 GENERAL **Long-Term Projects & Research Ideas,** Project 18 ADVANCED

See page T20 for a complete correlation of this book with the

NATIONAL SCIENCE EDUCATION STANDARDS.

TECHNOLOGY RESOURCES

 Guided Reading Audio CD English or Spanish, Chapter 18

 One-Stop Planner CD-ROM with Test Generator

 CNN. Eye on the Environment, Hummingbird Mites, Segment 3

 Interactive Explorations CD-ROM CD 2, Exploration 1, What's Bugging You?

Chapter 18 • Interactions of Living Things

CLASSROOM WORKSHEETS, TRANSPARENCIES, AND RESOURCES	SCIENCE INTEGRATION AND CONNECTIONS	REVIEW AND ASSESSMENT
Directed Reading Worksheet 18 BASIC **Science Puzzlers, Twisters & Teasers,** Worksheet 18 ADVANCED		
Transparency 65, The Five Levels of Environmental Organization **Directed Reading Worksheet 18,** Section 1 BASIC	**Multicultural Connection,** p. 435 in ATE **Multicultural Connection,** p. 436 in ATE **Connect to Environmental Science,** p. 436 in ATE **Eye on the Environment:** Alien Invasion, p. 455 GENERAL	**Review,** p. 437 GENERAL **Quiz,** p. 437 in ATE GENERAL **Alternative Assessment,** p. 437 in ATE GENERAL
Transparency 116, Formation of Coal **Directed Reading Worksheet 18,** Section 2 BASIC **Math Skills for Science Worksheet 22,** Working with Percentages and Proportions GENERAL **Transparency 66,** Energy Pyramid **Reinforcement Worksheet 18,** Weaving a Food Web GENERAL **Critical Thinking Worksheet 18,** A Struggle to Survive ADVANCED	**Connect to Earth Science,** p. 438 in ATE **Real-World Connection,** p. 439 in ATE **Math and More,** p. 440 in ATE BASIC **MathBreak,** Energy Pyramids, p. 441 GENERAL	**Self-Check,** p. 439 **Self-Check,** p. 440 **Review,** p. 443 GENERAL **Quiz,** p. 443 in ATE GENERAL **Alternative Assessment,** p. 443 in ATE GENERAL
Directed Reading Worksheet 18, Section 3 BASIC **Reinforcement Worksheet 18,** Symbiotic Relationships GENERAL	**Real-World Connection,** p. 447 in ATE **Multicultural Connection,** p. 448 in ATE **Apply,** p. 449 GENERAL **Health Watch:** An Unusual Guest, p. 454 GENERAL	**Self-Check,** p. 445 **Review,** p. 449 GENERAL **Quiz,** p. 449 in ATE GENERAL **Alternative Assessment,** p. 449 in ATE GENERAL

 Holt, Rinehart and Winston On-line Resources
go.hrw.com
For worksheets and other teaching aids related to this chapter, visit the HRW Web site and type in the keyword: **HSTINT**

 National Science Teacher's Association
www.scilinks.org
Encourage students to use the *sci*LINKS numbers listed in the internet connect boxes to access information and resources on the **NSTA** Web site.

END-OF-CHAPTER REVIEW AND ASSESSMENT

Chapter Review in Study Guide
Vocabulary and Notes in Study Guide
Chapter Tests with Performance-Based Assessment, Chapter 18 Test
Chapter Tests with Performance-Based Assessment, Performance-Based Assessment 18
Concept Mapping Transparency 18

Chapter 18 • Chapter Organizer **431B**

Chapter Resources & Worksheets

Visual Resources

TEACHING TRANSPARENCIES
- #65 — The Five Levels of Environmental Organization
- #66 — Energy Pyramid

TEACHING TRANSPARENCIES
- #116 — Formation of Coal — LINK TO EARTH SCIENCE

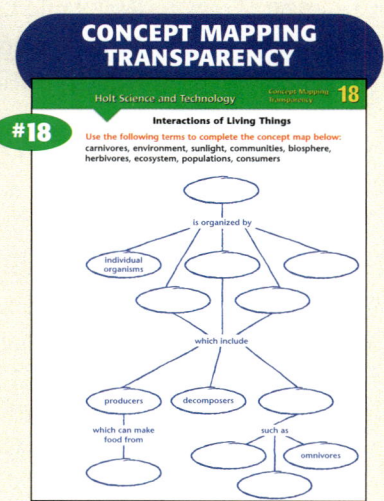

CONCEPT MAPPING TRANSPARENCY
- #18 — Interactions of Living Things

Meeting Individual Needs

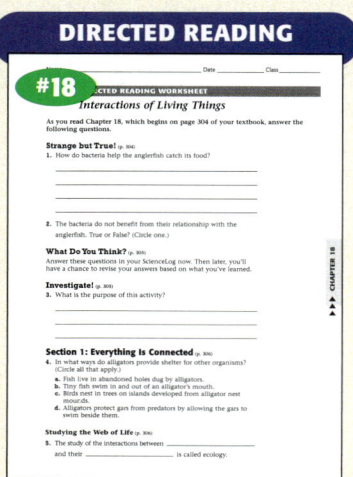

DIRECTED READING
- #18 — Interactions of Living Things

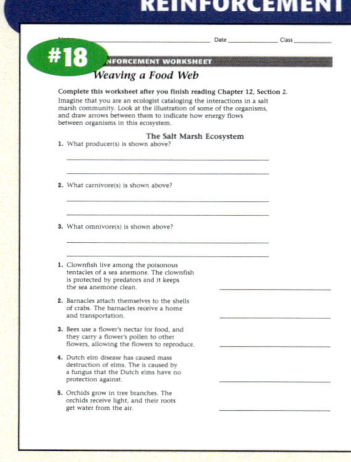

REINFORCEMENT & VOCABULARY REVIEW
- #18 Reinforcement — Weaving a Food Web
- #18 Vocabulary Review — Environmental Enigma

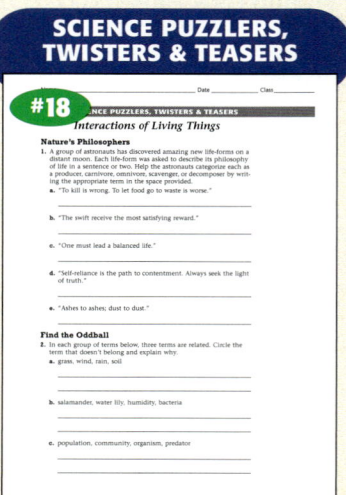

SCIENCE PUZZLERS, TWISTERS & TEASERS
- #18 — Interactions of Living Things

431C Chapter 18 • Interactions of Living Things

Chapter 18 • Interactions of Living Things

Review & Assessment

STUDY GUIDE

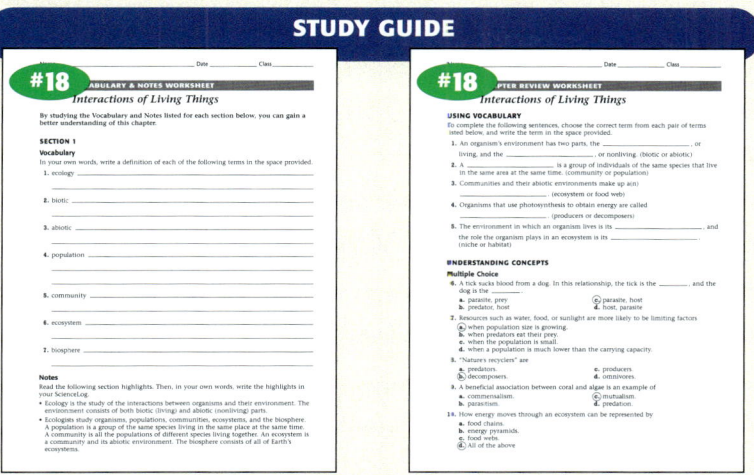

CHAPTER TESTS WITH PERFORMANCE-BASED ASSESSMENT

Lab Worksheets

ECOLABS & FIELD ACTIVITIES

WHIZ-BANG DEMONSTRATIONS

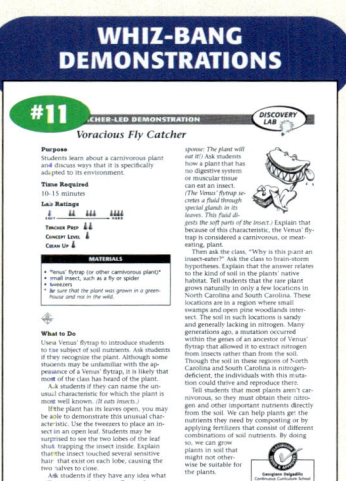

LONG-TERM PROJECTS & RESEARCH IDEAS

DATASHEETS FOR LABBOOK

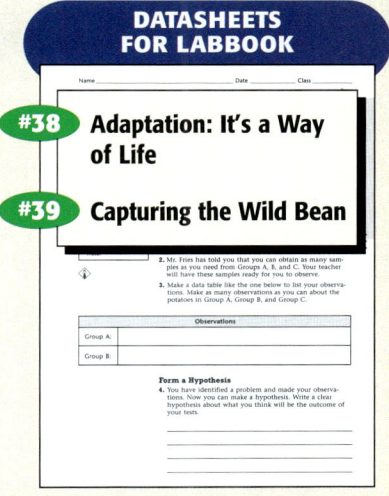

Applications & Extensions

CRITICAL THINKING & PROBLEM SOLVING

EYE ON THE ENVIRONMENT

INTERACTIVE EXPLORATIONS

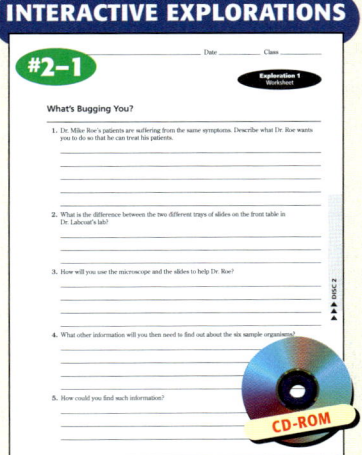

Chapter 18 • Chapter Resources & Worksheets   **431D**

Chapter Background

SECTION 1

Everything Is Connected

▶ **Indicator Species**
An indicator species is a plant or animal that, by its presence in a particular area, indicates the environmental conditions of the site. This information tells scientists what other species might thrive in the locale. For example, mosses usually indicate acidic soil, which would limit the types of plants that can survive in the same area. This, in turn, affects the variety of herbivores and other animals that can live there.

▶ **Ecology**
Ecology as an academic discipline can be traced to Theophrastus (c. 372–287 B.C.), a student of Aristotle (384–322 B.C.). Theophrastus offered the first descriptions of the relationships between organisms and the living and nonliving parts of their environment. The term *ecology* was coined in 1866 by Ernst Haeckel (1834–1919), a German zoologist. *Oekologie*, the German word for ecology, comes from the Greek *oikos*, which means "household, home, or place to live."

IS THAT A FACT!

- The Australian mallee fowl regulates the temperature of its nest mound with the help of other organisms. A healthy population of fungus and bacteria inhabit the leaf-and-twig mound built by the birds. As the bacteria decompose the leaves, they give off heat. When the temperature reaches 34°C (the birds can tell by sticking their beak into the mound), it's egg-laying time! The birds work hard to keep the mound and their eggs at a constant temperature by adding more material or digging ventilation shafts. They can also fight off potential predators while their eggs remain warm in the mound.

SECTION 2

Living Things Need Energy

▶ **Systems Ecology**
Some early ecologists focused on communities and populations, but others looked at the energy transfer between organisms. Today the study of energy transfer is called systems ecology. It involves analysis of the flow of energy and the recycling of nutrients within an ecosystem to answer the question, "How does the ecosystem function?" The use of modern materials and techniques, such as radioisotopes, computer science, and applied mathematics, has enabled scientists to quantify the movement of nutrients and energy through ecosystems.

IS THAT A FACT!

- The coral reef is the most productive habitat on Earth.

- Kelp is a marine alga, often called seaweed, anchored to the ocean floor. It is a primary producer. Sea urchins and many other organisms eat it. Kelp also provides shelter for animals such as bronze kelp perch. Sea otters sometimes wrap themselves in a blade of kelp to keep from drifting while they nap.

- Blades of the Pacific giant kelp can grow up to 60 m, taller than the Statue of Liberty.

- Some animals build a home within their habitat. The trapdoor spider digs a burrow in the ground and constructs a "trap door" of silk and mud with

Chapter 18 • Interactions of Living Things

silk hinges. It waits until an insect walks by, then quickly opens the door and grabs its prey. Trapdoor spiders inject venom into their prey, but they are harmless to people.

▰ Different habitats provide different materials for animals to use when constructing their home. These homes have different names. A squirrel's nest of leaves and sticks is called a drey. A badger's burrow is called a sett. A river otter's burrow in a river bank is called a holt.

Section 3

Types of Interactions

▶ Mimicry

Batesian mimicry was named for Henry Walter Bates (1825–1892), who described it in 1862. The mimic assumes the form of its model to take advantage of the model's defenses. For example, the viceroy butterfly looks just like the unappetizing monarch, which birds avoid. The snake caterpillar's movements resemble those of a real snake and thus help prevent attack by predators fearful of snakes.

- In 1878, Fritz Müller (1821–1897) described Müllerian mimicry, in which the resemblance of two species gives them mutual defense benefits. Both the sand wasp and the yellow jacket can sting. A predator that avoids one will avoid the other.

- Camouflage, a prey adaptation illustrated by the praying mantis's resemblance to a leaf, is a form of mimicry.

▶ Joke's on You: Prey Adaptations

The killdeer is a ground-nesting bird that will distract a predator from its nest or chicks with a "broken-wing" display. It will limp and drag a wing on the ground, making itself appear to be an easy catch. But because it is actually quite healthy, it always stays one step ahead of the predator.

▶ Plants and Ants

Symbiotic relationships between animals and plants are often a marvel to behold. There are epiphytes (plants that grow without soil) that have coevolved with ants. The plants provide knobby, chambered tubers in which the ants live. The excrement from the ants provides vital nutrition for the plant.

- Some tree-dwelling tropical ants collect and plant seeds in gardens they tend in their tree homes. The ants nourish the seeds with feces they collect and bring to the garden. The plants then grow and provide the ants with food.

- Other ants live inside the stems of rattan palms. When one of these palms, the ant-filled *Korthalsia*, is touched, the ants inside the plant begin smashing their mandibles (jaws) together, creating a hissing, whispering, or rattling noise. No one is quite sure of the function of this activity, but it may serve to deter interested animals from further disturbing the plant.

- In West Africa, stinging ants protect the *Barteria*, the small tree in which the ants live. The sting of this ant can numb a human for several days and can penetrate even the tough skin of an elephant.

▶ Mutualism

Coral animals live in a mutualistic relationship with the algae that live inside them. Humans benefit from the mutualistic relationship we have with the *Escherichia coli* that live inside of us. We provide the bacteria with food and comfortable growing conditions, and they help us digest our food and provide us with nutrients.

For background information about teaching strategies and issues, refer to the *Professional Reference for Teachers*.

CHAPTER 18

Interactions of Living Things

Pre-Reading Questions

Students may not know the answers to these questions before reading the chapter, so accept any reasonable response.

Suggested Answers
1. The deer eats the grass, tree leaves, and acorns. Wolves are common predators of deer. When the deer dies, it becomes food for scavengers and is eventually recycled back into the environment by decomposers.
2. the sun

Directed Reading Worksheet 18

Science Puzzlers, Twisters & Teasers Worksheet 18

Guided Reading Audio CD
English or Spanish, Chapter 18

CHAPTER 18

Interactions of Living Things

Sections

1. Everything Is Connected 434
   QuickLab 435
   Internet Connect 437
2. Living Things Need Energy 438
   MathBreak 441
3. Types of Interactions .. 444
   Apply 449
   Internet Connect 449

Chapter Review 452
Feature Articles 454, 455
LabBook 746–749

Pre-Reading Questions

1. Imagine a deer living in a meadow. What does the deer eat? What eats the deer? When the deer dies what happens to its remains?
2. What is the source of energy for plants?

What's for Dinner?

Look at the harsh, frozen environment surrounding this colony of penguins. What do you suppose the penguins eat? Penguin colonies sometimes number more than a million. They survive by swimming underwater to catch and eat krill, a type of tiny shellfish. Penguins compete with whales—and each other—for the supply of krill. In this chapter, you will learn how living things interact and how energy, in the form of food, travels in pathways through different organism groups.

---

internet connect

HRW On-line Resources
go.hrw.com
For worksheets and other teaching aids, visit the HRW Web site and type in the keyword: **HSTINT**

www.scilinks.com
Use the *sci*LINKS numbers at the end of each chapter for additional resources on the **NSTA** Web site.

www.cnnfyi.com
Visit the CNN Web site for current events coverage and classroom resources.

START-UP Activity

WHO EATS WHOM?

In this activity, you will learn how organisms interact when finding (or becoming) the next meal.

Procedure

1. On each of four **index cards**, print the name of one of the following organisms: white-tailed deer, turkey vulture, oak tree, and cougar

2. Arrange the cards on your desk in a chain to show who eats whom.

3. List the order of your cards in your ScienceLog.

4. In nature, would you expect to see more cougars, more deer, or more oak trees? Arrange the cards in order of most individuals to fewest.

Analysis

5. What might happen to the other organisms if the oak trees were removed from this group? What might happen if the cougars were removed?

6. Are there any organisms in this group that eat more than one kind of food? (Hint: What else might a deer, a cougar, or a turkey vulture eat?) How could you change the order of your cards to show this information? How could you use pieces of string to show these relationships?

START-UP Activity

WHO EATS WHOM?

MATERIALS

For Each Group:
- four 3 x 5 index cards

Answers to START-UP Activity

5. The other organisms might starve if the oak trees were removed. In this arrangement, the deer's only possible foods are oak tree leaves and acorns. And without the deer, the cougar and vulture would starve.

6. The deer, the cougar, and the vulture regularly eat more than one kind of food. But only the vulture would eat more than one of the organisms in this grouping: deer and cougar. Accept any arrangement of cards and string that indicates that deer eat oak, cougars eat deer, and vultures eat deer and cougars. Your best students may arrange the cards in trophic levels.

Section 1

Focus

Everything Is Connected

In this section, students will learn that ecology is the study of interactions between organisms and their environment. Students will also learn to identify the biotic and abiotic parts of an environment and how environments are organized into populations, communities, and ecosystems.

Use the board or an overhead projector to display these two sentences as students enter:

> People are a part of nature.
> People are not a part of nature.

Ask students to consider the meanings of these statements and explain them in their ScienceLog.

1) Motivate

DISCUSSION

The *fynbos* is a region in South Africa that contains more than 8,500 native plants, two-thirds of which live nowhere else. Non-native plants are now threatening the survival of the fynbos by out-competing the local plants for resources such as light, space, and water. Research has shown that there is a connection between the health of the fynbos and the well-being of the people nearby. Ask students the following question:

> Should the non-native plants be removed from the fynbos? That would be very expensive and difficult. What other options are there?

Section 1

Terms to Learn

ecology   community
biotic   ecosystem
abiotic   biosphere
population

What You'll Do

◆ Distinguish between the biotic and abiotic environment.
◆ Explain how populations, communities, ecosystems, and the biosphere are related.
◆ Explain how the abiotic environment relates to communities.

Everything Is Connected

Look at **Figure 1** below. An alligator drifts in a weedy Florida river, watching a long, thin fish called a gar. The gar swims too close to the alligator. Suddenly, in a rush of snapping jaws and splashing water, the gar becomes a meal for the alligator.

It is clear that these two organisms have just interacted with one another. But organisms have many interactions other than simply "who eats whom." For example, alligators dig underwater holes to escape from the heat. Later, after the alligators abandon these holes, fish and other aquatic organisms live in them when the water level gets low during a drought. Alligators also build nest mounds in which to lay their eggs, and they enlarge these mounds each year. Eventually, the mounds become small islands where trees and other plants grow. Herons, egrets, and other birds build their nests in the trees. It is easy to see that alligators affect many organisms, not just the gars that they eat.

Studying the Web of Life

All living things are connected in a web of life. Scientists who study the connections among living things specialize in the science of ecology. **Ecology** is the study of the interactions between organisms and their environment.

An Environment Has Two Parts An organism's environment is anything that affects the organism. An environment consists of two parts. The **biotic** part of the environment is all of the organisms that live together and interact with one another. The **abiotic** part of the environment includes all of the physical factors—such as water, soil, light, and temperature—that affect organisms living in a particular area. Take another look at Figure 1. How many biotic parts and abiotic parts can you see?

Figure 1 *The alligator affects, and is affected by, many organisms in its environment.*

 Teaching Transparency 65 "The Five Levels of Environmental Organization"

 Directed Reading Worksheet 18 Section 1

IS THAT A FACT!

Alligators often dig deep holes in the ground. These holes fill up with water and remain full, even during dry winters. Other animals rely heavily on these holes when fresh water is scarce. In Florida, cattle ranchers have used these water sources for their livestock during droughts.

434 Chapter 18 • Interactions of Living Things

Organization in the Environment At first glance, the environment may seem disorganized. To ecologists, however, the environment can be arranged into different levels, as shown in **Figure 2**. The first level contains the individual organism. The second level contains similar organisms, forming a population. The third contains different populations, forming a community. The fourth contains a community and its abiotic environment, forming an ecosystem. Finally, the fifth level contains all ecosystems, forming the biosphere. Turn the page and examine **Figure 3** to see these levels in a salt marsh.

Figure 2 The Five Levels of Environmental Organization

QuickLab

The Human Population

1. Using a **sheet of graph paper,** a **pencil,** and a **ruler,** draw and label a graph as shown below.

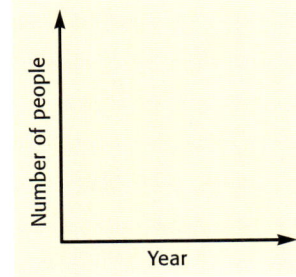

2. Plot the following points on your graph:
   - (1800, 1 billion people)
   - (1930, 2 billion people)
   - (1960, 3 billion people)
   - (1975, 4 billion people)
   - (1987, 5 billion people)
   - (1999, 6 billion people)

3. Draw a line connecting the points.

4. Answer the following questions in your ScienceLog.
   a. What does the curve that you have drawn indicate about human population growth?
   b. Do you think the human population can continue to grow indefinitely? Why or why not?

2) Teach

Answers to QuickLab

3. Students' drawings should look like this:

4. a. exponential growth
   b. Answers will vary but should indicate that the human population will run out of food, water, and other resources and will stop growing.

USING THE FIGURE

Have students redraw **Figure 2** using a field mouse as the base of the five levels of ecological organization. Tell students to include at least five different populations (field mice, worms, raccoons, meadow plants, owls, snakes, grasshoppers) in the community level. Have them divide the parts of the ecosystem into biotic and abiotic categories.

Capturing the Wild Bean

TOPIC: Biotic and Abiotic Factors
GO TO: www.scilinks.org
*sci*LINKS NUMBER: HSTL430

Multicultural CONNECTION

The Yanomami are a tribe living in remote rain-forest jungles of Venezuela and Brazil. The Yanomami in Venezuela have had very little contact with outsiders and are one of the few cultures remaining in the world in which people are still an integral part of an intact natural ecosystem. The Yanomami and their land in Venezuela are protected as an international biosphere reserve. Outsiders must get written permission to visit, but even these few visits have given the Yanomami a taste of the outside world. Many observers question how long the Yanomami hunting and gathering culture can last.

Section 1 • Everything Is Connected

2) Teach, continued

Multicultural CONNECTION

In Hawaii, officials of the Ethnobotanical Garden are working with scientists to develop wetland habitats that will support makaloa, a wetland sedge once used by Hawaiians to weave mats. The wetlands will be part of a waste-water treatment system and will support the resurgence of makaloa. Encourage interested students to research the weaving traditions of Hawaii and to present their findings to the class.

RETEACHING

Writing Ask students to list biotic and abiotic factors in their neighborhood. Write these factors on the board. Then ask students to describe how biotic factors change when abiotic factors change. (For example, if it rains a lot, plants grow more. If there is a drought, plants wither and leaves turn brown.) **Sheltered English**

TOPIC: Organization in the Environment
GO TO: www.scilinks.org
sciLINKS NUMBER: HSTL435

Figure 3 *Examine the picture of a salt marsh below. See if you can find examples of each level of organization in this environment.*

Populations A salt marsh is a coastal area where grasslike plants grow. A **population** is a group of individuals of the same species that live together in the same area at the same time. For example, all of the seaside sparrows that live together in a salt marsh are members of a population. The individuals in the population compete with one another for food, nesting space, and mates.

Communities A **community** consists of all of the populations of different species that live and interact in an area. The various animals and plants you see below form a salt-marsh community. The different populations in a community depend on each other for food, shelter, and many other things.

Ecosystems An **ecosystem** is made up of a community of organisms and its abiotic environment. An ecologist studying the salt-marsh ecosystem would examine how the ecosystem's organisms interact with each other and how temperature, precipitation, and soil characteristics affect the organisms. For example, the rivers and streams that empty into the salt marsh carry nutrients, such as nitrogen, from the land. These nutrients influence how the cordgrass and algae grow.

436

CONNECT TO ENVIRONMENTAL SCIENCE

Wetland communities are more than plant and animal habitats. Wetlands are also natural water-filtration systems that reduce levels of contaminants in municipal waste water. Wetlands also aid in soil formation, the replenishment of ground water, shoreline stabilization, and erosion prevention. In Arizona, California, Hawaii, New Mexico, and Nevada, engineers and biologists have constructed artificial wetlands to study these processes.

436 Chapter 18 • Interactions of Living Things

The Biosphere The **biosphere** is the part of Earth where life exists. It extends from the deepest parts of the ocean to very high in the atmosphere, where tiny insects and plant spores drift, and it includes every ecosystem. Ecologists study the biosphere to learn how organisms interact with the abiotic environment—Earth's gaseous atmosphere, water, soil, and rock. The water in the abiotic environment includes both fresh water and salt water as well as water that is frozen in polar icecaps and glaciers.

REVIEW

1. What is ecology?
2. Give two examples of biotic and abiotic factors in the salt-marsh ecosystem.
3. Using the salt-marsh example, distinguish between populations, communities, ecosystems, and the biosphere.
4. **Analyzing Relationships** What do you think would happen to the other organisms in the salt-marsh ecosystem if the cordgrass were to suddenly die?

internet connect

SCILINKS NSTA
TOPIC: Biotic and Abiotic Factors, Organization in the Environment
GO TO: www.scilinks.org
sciLINKS NUMBER: HSTL430, HSTL435

3) Extend

GOING FURTHER

Writing Have students write a brief report about the effects of temperature on alligator eggs; about the effects of rain, or the lack of rain, on the animals that live in Serengeti National Park, in Tanzania, and the Masai Mara, in Kenya; or about the salinity of the Dead Sea and its effects on organisms that live there.

4) Close

Quiz

1. A caterpillar, a deer, and a rabbit all want to drink from the same puddle, eat the same plant, and bask in the same spot of sunshine. Are they competing members of a population? Why or why not? (No; each is a different species. Therefore, they are competing members of a community.)

2. Using the salt marsh example, explain why ecologists state that saving a large animal, such as the heron or egret, can also save an ecosystem? (The heron and the egret can survive only if the salt marsh remains intact to provide shelter and food for the organisms that the birds need to eat.)

ALTERNATIVE ASSESSMENT

Have students find and draw pictures to create a poster that shows at least five biotic and five abiotic factors of either an aquatic or a terrestrial ecosystem. Sheltered English

▼ Answers to Review

1. Ecology is the study of the interactions of organisms with each other and with their environment.
2. Biotic factors include all living organisms in the salt marsh. Abiotic factors include all nonliving things in the salt marsh.
3. A population of seaside sparrows lives in a community, which includes all the populations around it. This community lives in a salt-marsh ecosystem, which is defined by a certain geographical location and a certain climate. This ecosystem exists within the biosphere, which is the part of Earth where life exists, including our atmosphere.
4. All the other organisms depend directly or indirectly on cordgrass for food. Without cordgrass, all of the other organisms would probably die out or move into other areas.

Section 1 • Everything Is Connected **437**

SECTION 2

Focus

Living Things Need Energy

In this section students will learn how producers, consumers, and decomposers obtain energy to survive. They will also learn the difference between a food chain and a food web and how energy is transferred among members of a food chain or a food web. Finally, students will learn to define *habitat* and *niche*.

Bellringer

Inform students that a plant called Indian pipe is completely white—it has no chlorophyll or chloroplasts. Can this plant still be a producer? If not, where does it get the energy it needs to survive? Have students write their answer in their ScienceLog. (This plant is a consumer. It lives off the roots of rotting trees with the help of a fungus.)

1) Motivate

ACTIVITY

Writing Before reading this section, students should define *producer* and *consumer* in their ScienceLog, using prior knowledge. They should also define *carnivore*, *omnivore*, and *herbivore* in their own words. After reading the section, students should revise their definitions.

TOPIC: Producers, Consumers, and Decomposers
GO TO: www.scilinks.org
sciLINKS NUMBER: HSTL440

Section 2

Terms to Learn
herbivore
carnivore
omnivore
scavenger
food chain
food web
energy pyramid
habitat
niche

What You'll Do
- Describe the functions of producers, consumers, and decomposers in an ecosystem.
- Distinguish between a food chain and a food web.
- Explain how energy flows through a food web.
- Distinguish between an organism's habitat and its niche.

Living Things Need Energy

All living things need energy to survive. For example, black-tailed prairie dogs, which live in the grasslands of North America, eat grass and seeds to get the energy they need. They use this energy to grow, move, heal injuries, and reproduce. In fact, everything a prairie dog does requires energy. The same is true for the plants that grow in the grasslands where the prairie dogs live. Coyotes that stalk prairie dogs, as well as the bacteria and fungi that live in the soil, all need energy.

The Energy Connection

Organisms in a prairie or any community can be divided into three groups based on how they obtain energy. These groups are producers, consumers, and decomposers. Examine **Figure 4** to see how energy passes through these groups in an ecosystem.

Producers Organisms that use sunlight directly to make food are called *producers*. They do this using a process called photosynthesis. Most producers are plants, but algae and some bacteria are also producers. Grasses are the main producers in a prairie ecosystem. Examples of producers in other ecosystems include cordgrass and algae in a salt marsh and trees in a forest. Algae are the main producers in the ocean.

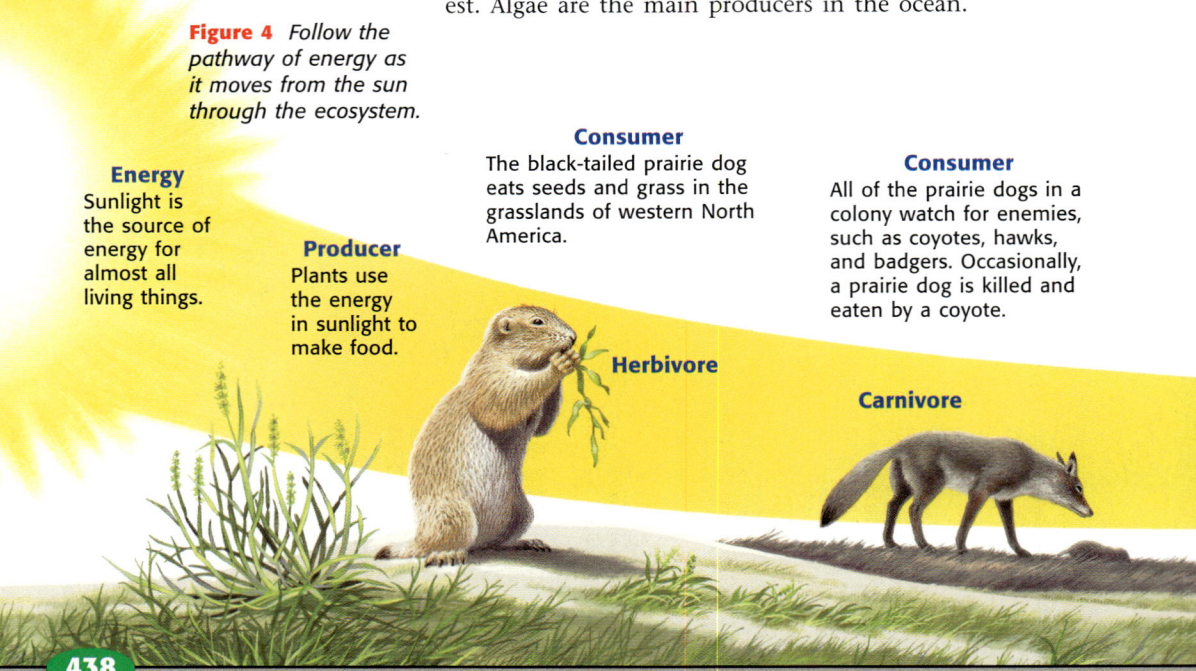

Figure 4 *Follow the pathway of energy as it moves from the sun through the ecosystem.*

Energy Sunlight is the source of energy for almost all living things.

Producer Plants use the energy in sunlight to make food.

Consumer The black-tailed prairie dog eats seeds and grass in the grasslands of western North America.

Consumer All of the prairie dogs in a colony watch for enemies, such as coyotes, hawks, and badgers. Occasionally, a prairie dog is killed and eaten by a coyote.

Herbivore

Carnivore

CONNECT TO EARTH SCIENCE

Fossil fuels store solar energy gathered by ancient plants. Use the following to illustrate the formation of coal.

Teaching Transparency 116 "Formation of Coal"

438 Chapter 18 • Interactions of Living Things

Consumers Organisms that eat producers or other organisms for energy are called *consumers.* They cannot use the sun's energy directly like producers can. Instead, consumers must eat producers or other animals to obtain energy. There are several kinds of consumers. A **herbivore** is a consumer that eats plants. Herbivores in the prairie ecosystem include grasshoppers, gophers, prairie dogs, bison, and pronghorn antelope. A **carnivore** is a consumer that eats animals. Carnivores in the prairie ecosystem include coyotes, hawks, badgers, and owls. Consumers known as **omnivores** eat a variety of organisms, both plants and animals. The grasshopper mouse is an example of an omnivore in the prairie ecosystem. It eats insects, scorpions, lizards, and grass seeds. **Scavengers** are animals that feed on the bodies of dead animals. The turkey vulture is a scavenger in the prairie ecosystem. Examples of scavengers in aquatic ecosystems include crayfish, snails, clams, worms, and crabs.

Prairie dogs are not really dogs. They are rodents. They are called dogs because their warning calls sound like the barking of dogs.

Decomposers Organisms that get energy by breaking down the remains of dead organisms are called *decomposers.* Bacteria and fungi are examples of decomposers. These organisms extract the last bit of energy from dead organisms and produce simpler materials, such as water and carbon dioxide. These materials can then be reused by plants and other living things. Decomposers are an essential part of any ecosystem because they are nature's recyclers.

Self-Check

Are you a herbivore, a carnivore, or an omnivore? Explain. *(See page 782 to check your answer.)*

Consumer
A turkey vulture may eat some of the coyote's leftovers. A scavenger can pick bones completely clean.

Decomposer
Any prairie dog remains not eaten by the coyote or the turkey vulture are broken down by bacteria and fungi that live in the soil.

Scavenger → Recycler

Turkey vultures have an acute sense of smell. A biologist once put decaying carcasses in metal containers, hid the containers in the California foothills, and used a fan to diffuse the odor. Turkey vultures were soon soaring overhead.

Engineers once pumped ethyl mercaptan, which smells like rotting flesh, into natural-gas lines. They located leaks by watching for turkey vultures attracted to the pipeline.

Section 2 • Living Things Need Energy   **439**

2) Teach, continued

Answer to Self-Check
A food chain shows how energy moves in one direction from one organism to the next. A food web shows that there are many energy pathways between organisms.

MATH and MORE

There are 12,000 units of the sun's energy available to grass at the base of an energy pyramid. Grass stores in its tissues 10 percent of the available energy, so that energy becomes available to the next consumer, a rabbit. The rabbit, a consumer of grass, stores 10 percent of the energy that was stored in the grass. A coyote, a consumer of rabbits, stores 10 percent of the energy that was stored in the rabbit. Calculate the units of food energy stored in the grass, the rabbit, and the coyote.

The grass stores 10 percent of the sun's energy:

$0.1 \times 12{,}000 = 1{,}200$ units of energy stored in the grass

The rabbit stores 10 percent of the grass' stored energy:

$0.1 \times 1{,}200 = 120$ units of energy stored in the rabbit

The coyote stores 10 percent of the rabbit's stored energy:

$0.1 \times 120 = 12$ units of energy stored in the coyote

 Math Skills Worksheet 22 "Working with Percentages and Proportions"

Self-Check
How is a food web different from a food chain? *(See page 782 to check your answer.)*

Figure 5 *Energy moves through an ecosystem in complex ways. Most consumers eat a variety of foods and can be eaten by a variety of other consumers.*

Food Chains and Food Webs

Figure 4, on pages 438–439, shows a **food chain,** which represents how the energy in food molecules flows from one organism to the next. But because few organisms eat just one kind of organism, simple food chains rarely occur in nature. The many energy pathways possible are more accurately shown by a **food web.** Figure 5 shows a simple food web for a woodland ecosystem.

Find the fox and the rabbit in the figure below. Notice that the arrow goes from the rabbit to the fox, showing that the rabbit is food for the fox. The rabbit is also food for the owl. Neither the fox nor the owl is ever food for the rabbit. Energy moves from one organism to the next in a one-way direction, even in a food web. Any energy not immediately used by an organism is stored in its tissues. Only the energy stored in an organism's tissues can be used by the next consumer.

---

 internet connect

TOPIC: Food Chains and Food Webs
GO TO: www.scilinks.org
sciLINKS NUMBER: HSTL445

SCIENCE HUMOR

Customer: Waiter! Waiter! There's a fly in my soup!

Waiter: Don't worry, sir, the spider in your salad will get it!

Energy Pyramids

A grass plant uses most of the energy it obtains from the sun for its own life processes. But some of the energy is stored in its tissues and is left over for prairie dogs and other animals that eat the grass. Prairie dogs need a lot of energy and have to eat a lot of grass. Each prairie dog uses most of the energy it obtains from eating grass and stores only a little of it in its tissues. Coyotes need even more energy than prairie dogs, so they must eat many prairie dogs to survive. There must be many more prairie dogs in the community than there are coyotes that eat prairie dogs.

The loss of energy at each level of the food chain can be represented by an **energy pyramid,** as shown in **Figure 6.** You can see that the energy pyramid has a large base and becomes smaller at the top. The amount of available energy is reduced at higher levels because most of the energy is either used by the organism or given off as heat. Only energy stored in the tissues of an organism can be transferred to the next level.

MATH BREAK

Energy Pyramids

Draw an energy pyramid for a river ecosystem that contains four levels—aquatic plants, insect larvae, bluegill fish, and a largemouth bass. The plants obtain 10,000 units of energy from the sun. If each level uses 90 percent of the energy it receives from the previous level, how many units of energy are available to the bass?

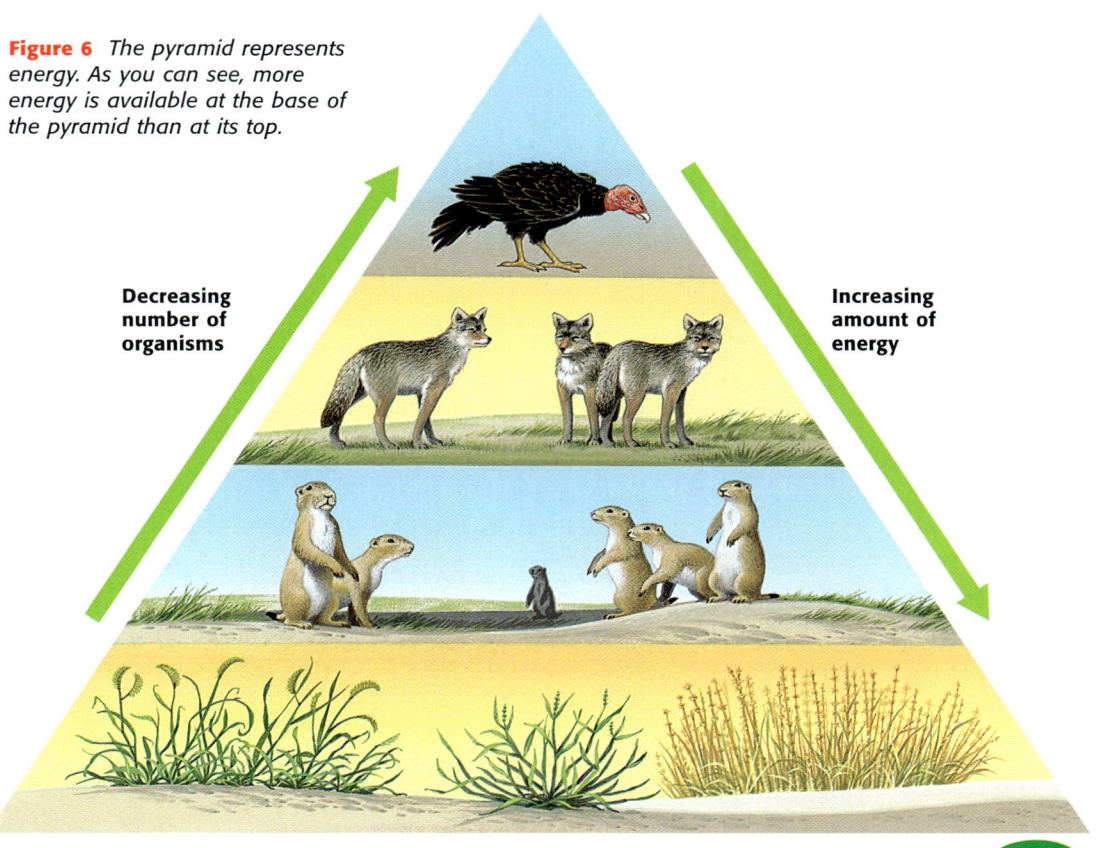

Figure 6 The pyramid represents energy. As you can see, more energy is available at the base of the pyramid than at its top.

Decreasing number of organisms

Increasing amount of energy

IS THAT A FACT!

In 1989, the Nature Conservancy purchased 30,000 acres of grassland in Oklahoma. The conservancy's goal is "the restoration of a functioning tall-grass prairie ecosystem." The land has been grazed by cattle but never plowed; the restoration will allow the more than 700 prairie plant species to reestablish themselves. A healthy prairie is also home to 300 bird species, 80 mammal species, and hundreds of thousands of insect species. Biologists have reintroduced bison, whose grazing is an integral part of the prairie food web.

Answer to MATHBREAK
10 units of energy

ACTIVITY

Writing | Inferring Information
Chipmunks, tree squirrels, and flying squirrels are all related animals that eat seeds. Yet each has its own niche, or way of life, that serves to limit the amount of competition between the species.

Have students describe in writing, to the best of their knowledge, the niche, or way of life, for each of these seed eaters.

(**Chipmunks** live underground, collect small seeds, and store these seeds in cheek pouches until depositing them in an underground storage area.

Tree squirrels live in trees, collect larger seeds and nuts one at a time, and bury them in the ground.

Flying squirrels are active only at night; live in trees; eat large and small seeds, fruits, and insects; and glide from tree to tree using flaps of skin.)

Teaching Transparency 66 "Energy Pyramid"

Section 2 • Living Things Need Energy

3) Extend

MEETING INDIVIDUAL NEEDS

Advanced Learners By 1970, peregrine falcon populations had been decimated by the effects of DDT. Professor Tom Cade of Cornell University established the Peregrine Fund for the captive breeding and release of peregrine falcons. Cade's release program and other programs placed the birds in urban environments, such as Chicago and Seattle. Have students investigate the peregrine falcon restoration programs and prepare a report that includes answers to the following questions: What is the peregrine falcon's natural habitat? What is its niche? How do cities provide a suitable habitat for the peregrine falcon?

ACTIVITY

Poster Project An organism's habitat may be large, as in the habitat of the gray wolf, or quite small, as in the habitat of planaria. For stationary animals, such as the mussel, the habitat can be as small as a group of rocks in the tidal zone of the ocean. The habitat of a blue whale may be nearly as large as the ocean itself. Have interested students make a poster depicting the components of four distinct habits of four very different animals. <mark>Sheltered English</mark>

Reinforcement Worksheet 18 "Weaving a Food Web"

Critical Thinking Worksheet 18 "A Struggle to Survive"

Wolves and the Energy Pyramid

A single species can be very important to the flow of energy in an environment. Gray wolves, for example, are a consumer species that can control the populations of many other species. The diet of gray wolves can include anything from a lizard to an elk.

Once common throughout much of the United States, gray wolves were almost wiped out as the wilderness was settled. You can see a pair of gray wolves in **Figure 7.** Without wolves, certain other species, such as elk, were no longer controlled. The overpopulation of elk in some areas led to overgrazing and starvation.

Gray wolves were recently restored to the United States at Yellowstone National Park, as shown in **Figure 8.** The U.S. Fish and Wildlife Service hopes this action will restore the natural energy flow in this wilderness area. Not everyone approves, however. Ranchers near Yellowstone are concerned about the safety of their livestock.

Figure 7 As the wilderness was settled, the gray wolf population in the United States declined.

Habitat and Niche

An organism's **habitat** is the environment in which it lives. The wolf's habitat was originally very extensive. It included forests, grasslands, deserts, and the northern tundra. Today the wolf's habitat in North America is much smaller. It includes wilderness areas in Montana, Washington, Minnesota, Michigan, Wisconsin, and Canada.

An organism's way of life within an ecosystem is its **niche.** An organism's niche includes its habitat, its food, its predators, and the organisms with which it competes. An organism's niche also includes how the organism affects and is affected by abiotic factors in its environment, such as temperature, light, and moisture.

Figure 8 Members of the U.S. Fish and Wildlife Service are moving a caged wolf to a location in Yellowstone National Park.

The Niche of the Gray Wolf

A complete description of a species' niche is very complex. To help you distinguish between habitat and niche, parts of the gray wolf niche are described on the next page.

WEIRD SCIENCE

In certain tropical areas, the dry season can last several months. Some frogs, such as the African bullfrog, burrow into the mud before the mud dries out. Then the frog sheds several intact layers of skin, which harden and form a protective covering. Only the frog's nostrils are exposed, so it can breathe. When the rains return, the frog breaks through the moist soil and returns to the surface.

442 Chapter 18 • Interactions of Living Things

Gray Wolves Are Consumers Wolves are carnivores. Their diet includes large animals, such as deer, moose, reindeer, sheep, and elk, as well as small animals, such as birds, lizards, snakes, and fish.

Gray Wolves Have a Social Structure Wolves live and hunt in packs, which are groups of about six animals that are usually members of the same family. Each member of the pack has a particular rank within the pack. The pack has two leaders that help defend the pack against enemies, such as other wolf packs or bears.

Gray Wolves Nurture and Teach Their Young A female wolf, shown in **Figure 9,** has five to seven pups and nurses her babies for about 2 months. The entire pack help bring the pups food and baby-sit when the parents are away from the den. It takes about 2 years for the young wolves to learn to hunt. At that time, some young wolves leave the pack to find mates and start their own pack.

Figure 9 *In small wolf packs, only one female has pups. They are well cared for, however, by all of the males and females in the pack.*

Gray Wolves Are Needed in the Food Web If wolves become reestablished at Yellowstone National Park, they will reduce the elk population by killing the old, injured, and diseased elk. This in turn will allow more plants to grow, which will allow animals that eat the plants, such as snowshoe hares, and the animals that eat the hares, such as foxes, to increase in number.

REVIEW

1. How are producers, consumers (herbivores, carnivores, and scavengers), and decomposers linked in a food chain?
2. How do food chains link together to form a food web?
3. Distinguish between an organism's habitat and its niche using the prairie dog as an example.
4. **Applying Concepts** Is it possible for an inverted energy pyramid to exist, as shown in the figure at right? Explain why or why not.

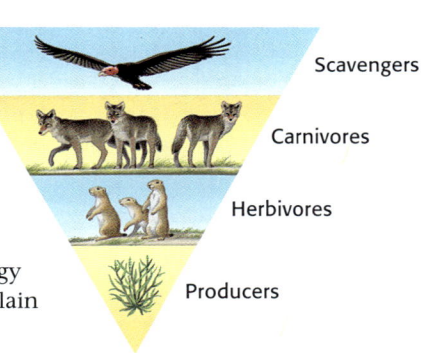

4) Close

Quiz

1. How might an omnivore be a link both at the beginning of a food web and near the end? (An omnivore can be at the beginning because it eats plants. It can be near the end because it also eats other consumers.)
2. Is your attendance at school a characteristic of your habitat or your niche? (Niche; being a student is one of the things I do within my habitat. It is part of my way of life.)

ALTERNATIVE ASSESSMENT

Writing Have students write an eight-step recipe for a decomposer's dinner. Tell students the first ingredient is sunlight.

TOPIC: Habitats and Niches
GO TO: www.scilinks.org
*sci*LINKS NUMBER: HSTL450

▼ Answers to Review

1. Producers convert sunlight into food. Herbivores and carnivores are both consumers. Herbivores eat producers, and carnivores eat herbivores and other consumers. Scavengers eat the bodies of dead animals. Decomposers break down the remains of dead animals and extract the last bit of energy from them.
2. Food chains show how energy is passed through an ecosystem from producers to decomposers. A food web shows how all the food chains of an ecosystem are connected.
3. The prairie is a prairie dog's habitat. What it affects and what affects it make up its niche.
4. No; the widest part of the pyramid has the most energy, and the pointed end has the least. An ecosystem cannot support the greatest energy level with the level that has the least energy.

SECTION 3

Focus

Types of Interactions

In this section, students will learn about the types of interactions that organisms have with each other and with their environment. Students will learn to distinguish the two types of competition and to identify predator and prey species. They will also learn to recognize mutualism, commensalism, and parasitism. Finally, students will learn to define *coevolution*.

Bellringer

On the board or overhead projector, write the following:

In your ScienceLog, make a list of predators that are also prey. (Answers may include salamanders, frogs, shrews, snakes, lizards, and weasels.) **Sheltered English**

1 Motivate

DISCUSSION

In India, the chital, a small deer, has trouble finding enough grass to eat during the dry season. The deer rely on help from a type of monkey to get enough to eat. Ask students:

Can you guess how the monkeys help the deer? (This particular monkey is a messy and finicky eater, dropping leaves as it feeds in the trees. The deer then gobble up the food.)

Which species benefit from this relationship? (It seems that only the deer benefit.)

Now tell students that the deer have keen eyesight, hearing, and sense of smell. They therefore help warn the monkeys of predators. Now which species do you think benefit? (Both species benefit.)

444 Chapter 18 • Interactions of Living Things

Section 3

Terms to Learn

carrying capacity
prey
predator
symbiosis
mutualism
commensalism
parasitism
coevolution

What You'll Do

◆ Distinguish between the two types of competition.
◆ Give examples of predators and prey.
◆ Distinguish between mutualism, commensalism, and parasitism.
◆ Define *coevolution*, and give an example.

Where on Earth could this bird live? Find out on page 746 of your LabBook.

Adaptation: It's a Way of Life

Types of Interactions

Look at the seaweed forest shown in **Figure 10** below. Notice that some types of organisms are more numerous than others. In natural communities, populations of different organisms vary greatly. The interactions between these populations affect the size of each population.

Figure 10 This seaweed forest is home to a large number of interacting species.

Interactions with the Environment

Most living things produce more offspring than will survive. A female frog, for example, might lay hundreds of eggs in a small pond. In a few months, the population of frogs in that pond will be about the same as it was the year before. Why won't the pond become overrun with frogs? An organism, such as a frog, interacts with biotic or abiotic factors in its environment that can control the size of its population.

Limiting Factors Populations cannot grow indefinitely because the environment contains only so much food, water, living space, and other needed resources. When one or more of those resources becomes scarce, it is said to be a *limiting factor*. For example, food becomes a limiting factor when a population becomes too large for the amount of food available. Any single resource can be a limiting factor to population size.

Green herons make interesting use of the biotic and abiotic parts of their environment in Japan. They will drop sticks and even bread crumbs into the water to attract fish. Sometimes they catch a fish just 2–3 seconds after they drop the bait.

Carrying Capacity The largest population that a given environment can support over a long period of time is known as the environment's **carrying capacity.** When a population grows larger than its carrying capacity, limiting factors in the environment cause the population to get smaller. For example, after a very rainy growing season in an environment, plants may produce a large crop of leaves and seeds. This may cause a herbivore population to grow large because of the unlimited food supply. If the next year has less rainfall than usual, there won't be enough food to support the large herbivore population. In this way, a population may temporarily exceed the carrying capacity. But a limiting factor will cause the population to die back. The population will return to a size that the environment can support over a long period of time.

Interactions Among Organisms

Populations contain interacting individuals of a single species, such as a group of rabbits feeding in the same area. Communities contain interacting populations of several species, such as a coral reef community with many species trying to find living space. Ecologists have described four main ways that species and individuals affect each other: competition, predators and prey, certain symbiotic relationships, and coevolution.

Competition

When two or more individuals or populations try to use the same limited resource, such as food, water, shelter, space, or sunlight, it is called *competition*. Because resources are in limited supply in the environment, their use by one individual or population decreases the amount available to other organisms.

Competition can occur among individuals *within* a population. The elks in Yellowstone National Park are herbivores that compete with each other for the same food plants in the park. This is a big problem for this species in winter. Competition can also occur *between* populations of different species. The different species of trees in **Figure 11** are competing with each other for sunlight and space.

Self-Check

1. Explain how water can limit the growth of a population.
2. Describe how the carrying capacity for deer in a forest ecosystem might be affected by weather.

(See page 782 to check your answers.)

Figure 11 Some of the trees in this forest grow tall in order to reach sunlight, reducing the amount of sunlight available to shorter trees nearby.

MISCONCEPTION ALERT

While it's true that all members of an ecosystem have important roles, some members are more important than others to the overall health of the ecosystem. Such species are called keystone species. Like removing the keystone that holds up the other stones in an arch, removing a keystone species can cause the whole system to collapse. This occurred when the sea otter was hunted to near extinction in the kelp forests of the Pacific Ocean. With the otters gone, nothing was left to eat the sea urchins, which multiplied and ate all the kelp. The kelp was home to dozens of animals, all of which disappeared, along with most of the sea urchins. When the otter was reintroduced, all these organisms returned!

---

2 Teach

Answers to Self-Check

1. If an area has only enough water to support 10 organisms, any additional organisms will cause some to go without water and move away or die.
2. Weather favorable for growing the food the deer eat will allow the forest to support more deer.

DISCUSSION

Examining Cycles The lynx relies primarily upon the snowshoe hare for food. Ask students:

How will an abundance of plant food affect the hare population? (The population will increase.)

What will then happen to the lynx population? (It will also increase.)

What will happen when the hares begin to run out of food? (Hares will grow weak from hunger and will be easily caught by lynxes. The lynx population will grow until so many hares are killed that the lynxes also begin to die off.)

How can the hare and lynx populations recover? (The plants must recover from the overbrowsing.)

Explain that observers have documented 10-year cycles of peaks and crashes in the lynx and snowshoe hare populations for the past 200 years. Studies have shown that snowshoe hares have the same population cycles when no lynxes are present. Lynx population cycles, however, are dependent on the availability of hares.

 Directed Reading Worksheet 18 Section 3

Section 3 • Types of Interactions **445**

2) Teach, continued

COOPERATIVE LEARNING

Divide students into six groups. Then divide each group into subgroups of two or three, and designate each subgroup as Predator or Prey. Instruct each Predator group to name a prey animal and the adaptation it uses to catch the prey. **(speed, talons, strength)**

Tell each Prey group to name a predator animal and its adaptations to evade capture. **(camouflage, speed, protective armor, flight)**

Have students write down the adaptations and share their information with the other groups. Sheltered English

Studies have shown that ducks can have one-half of their brain asleep while the other half is awake. The side that is awake can even have an eye open and respond to stimuli. The sides can also switch so that the half that was awake can rest and the rested half can become alert. Ask students why this ability might be helpful to ducks. **(Ducks need sleep, but when they sleep they are vulnerable to predators. Having the ability to keep an eye open and be alert to danger while part of their brain rests helps them avoid predators. Because they live in flocks, they can arrange themselves in a resting spot so that the ducks on the outside edge of the flock each have an open eye looking in a different direction.)**

Predators and Prey

Many interactions among species occur because one organism eats another. The organism that is eaten is called the **prey**. The organism that eats the prey is called the **predator**. When a bird eats a worm, the worm is the prey and the bird is the predator.

Predator Adaptations In order to survive, predators must be able to catch their prey. Predators have a wide variety of methods and abilities for doing this. The cheetah, for example, is able to run at great speed to catch its prey. Other predators, such as the goldenrod spider, shown in **Figure 12**, ambush their prey. The goldenrod spider blends in so well with the goldenrod flower that all it has to do is wait for its next insect meal to arrive.

Figure 12 *The goldenrod spider is difficult for its insect prey to see. Can you see it?*

Prey Adaptations Prey organisms have their own methods and abilities to keep from being eaten. Prey are able to run away, stay in groups, or camouflage themselves. Some prey organisms are poisonous to predators. They may advertise their poison with bright colors to warn predators to stay away. The fire salamander, shown in **Figure 13**, sprays a poison that burns. Predators quickly learn to recognize its warning coloration.

Many animals run away from predators. Prairie dogs run to their underground burrows when a predator approaches. Many small fishes, such as anchovies, swim in groups called schools. Antelopes and buffaloes stay in herds. All the eyes, ears, and noses of the individuals in the group are watching, listening, and smelling for predators. This behavior increases the likelihood of spotting a potential predator.

Some prey species hide from predators by using camouflage. Certain insects resemble leaves so closely that you would never guess they are animals.

Figure 13 *Experienced predators know better than to eat the fire salamander! This colorful animal will make an unlucky predator very sick.*

MISCONCEPTION ALERT

The phrase *balance of nature* does not imply that the components of an environment are static. Populations are in balance when their sizes are stable. That stability is the result of constant interactions between individuals of a population, between populations in a community, and between populations and environmental factors.

WEIRD SCIENCE

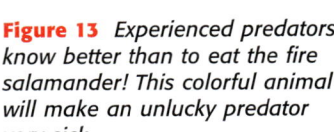

Pancake tortoises live on rocky hillsides in Africa. They are very flat and can wedge themselves into cracks in the rocks for protection from predators. Their bottom shells are pliable and can "inflate" so that a predator can't pry the tortoises out.

446 Chapter 18 • Interactions of Living Things

Symbiosis

Some species have very close interactions with other species. **Symbiosis** is a close, long-term association between two or more species. The individuals in a symbiotic relationship can benefit from, be unaffected by, or be harmed by the relationship. Often, one species lives in or on the other species. The thousands of symbiotic relationships that occur in nature are often classified into three groups: mutualism, commensalism, and parasitism.

Mutualism A symbiotic relationship in which both organisms benefit is called **mutualism.** For example, you and a species of bacteria that lives in your intestines benefit each other! The bacteria get a plentiful food supply from you, and in return you get vitamins that the bacteria produce.

Another example of mutualism occurs between coral and algae. The living corals near the surface of the water provide a home for the algae. The algae produce food through photosynthesis that is used by the corals. When a coral dies, its skeleton serves as a foundation for other corals. Over a long period of time, these skeletons build up large, rocklike formations that lie just beneath the surface of warm, sunny seas, as shown in **Figure 14.**

Figure 14 *In the smaller photo above, you can see the gold-colored algae inside the coral.*

Commensalism A symbiotic relationship in which one organism benefits and the other is unaffected is called **commensalism.** One example of commensalism is the relationship between sharks and remoras. **Figure 15** shows a shark with a remora attached to its body. Remoras "hitch a ride" and feed on scraps of food left by sharks. The remoras benefit from this relationship, while sharks are unaffected.

Figure 15 *The remora attached to the shark benefits from the relationship. The shark is neither benefited nor harmed.*

SCIENCE HUMOR

Q: What is a parasite's favorite party?

A: a louse-warming party

REAL-WORLD CONNECTION

As a simple exercise to help students understand the differences between mutualism, commensalism, and parasitism, ask students to think about their relationships with other species in the environment. Interactions with pets, livestock, backyard animals, or annoying insects shed light on these relationships. Are any of these interactions mutualism? parasitism? commensalism?

RETEACHING

The honey guide, a small African bird, lives up to its name. The bird sings in an attempt to lure all nearby creatures to a nest of honeybees it has found. Animals have learned to listen for this bird! Baboons, mongooses, ratels (or honey badgers), and even people will follow the bird to claim the honey. Out of harm's way, the bird waits for the leftovers: bee larvae. The bird's unique digestive system allows it to eat wax as well. Ask students the following questions:

Which animals in this story are in a mutualistic relationship? (The bird and the animals that eat the honey.)

Which animals are prey, and which are predators? (The bees are prey. All the other animals are predators.) **Sheltered English**

MISCONCEPTION ALERT

You will often hear the word *symbiosis* used when *mutualism* is meant. Mutualism is one type of symbiosis; commensalism and parasitism are the other two types.

Section 3 • Types of Interactions

3 Extend

MEETING INDIVIDUAL NEEDS

Learners Having Difficulty
Reinforce the concept of symbiosis by presenting the following examples and asking students to categorize the relationship:

1. Acacia ants live on the bullhorn acacia tree, which provides the ants' food and shelter. The ants deter browsing animals who want to eat the tree. (mutualism)

2. Plants called epiphytes, such as lianas and certain orchids, live on other plants, which provide only a substrate. Epiphytes absorb sunlight, water, and nutrients from their surroundings and make their own food. (commensalism)

3. There is a tiny wasp that lays its eggs in a variety of insects, such as caterpillars, spiders, aphids, and flies. The wasp larvae feed on the host insect, eventually killing it. (parasitism)
   Sheltered English

DEBATE

Bird Behavior The brown-headed cowbird is a parasite. It lays its eggs in the nests of other birds, which incubate the cowbird's eggs and raise the chicks. Some of the host species are smaller than the cowbird. Their own chicks cannot compete with the cowbird chicks for food and sometimes starve. Some people view the cowbird as a pest that harms other bird species. Others note that it has an adaptation that ensures its survival, no different from any other competitive advantage. Have students discuss these two points of view.

Figure 16 *The tomato hornworm is being parasitized by young wasps. Do you see their cocoons?*

Parasitism A symbiotic association in which one organism benefits while the other is harmed is called **parasitism**. The organism that benefits is called the *parasite*. The organism that is harmed is called the *host*. The parasite gets nourishment from its host, which is weakened in the process. Sometimes a host organism becomes so weak that it dies. Some parasites, such as ticks, live outside the host's body. Other parasites, such as tapeworms, live inside the host's body.

Figure 16 shows a bright green caterpillar called a tomato hornworm. A female wasp laid tiny eggs on the caterpillar. When the eggs hatch, each young wasp will burrow into the caterpillar's body. The young wasps will actually eat the caterpillar alive! In a short time, the caterpillar will be almost completely consumed and will die. When that occurs, the mature wasps will fly away.

In this example of parasitism, the host dies. Most parasites, however, do not kill their hosts. Can you think of reasons why?

Coevolution

Symbiotic relationships and other interactions among organisms in an ecosystem may cause coevolution. **Coevolution** is a long-term change that takes place in two species because of their close interactions with one another.

Coevolution sometimes occurs between herbivores and the plants on which they feed. For example, the ants shown in **Figure 17** have coevolved with a tropical tree called the acacia. The ants protect the tree on which they live by attacking any other herbivore that approaches the tree. The plant has coevolved special structures on its stems that produce food for the ants. The ants live in other structures also made by the tree.

Figure 17 *Ants collect food made by the acacia tree and store the food in their shelter, also made by the tree.*

Multicultural CONNECTION

In Africa, billions of dollars a year are spent to destroy a parasitic plant that lives off important crops such as sorghum. The parasite weakens the plant, preventing it from producing its much-needed grains. Recently, a sorghum plant that is resistant to the parasite was developed. Ethiopian farmers were so eager to get started again that they smuggled the new seeds in from Sudan before their own government approved the seeds.

Coevolution in Australia

In 1859, settlers released 12 rabbits in Australia. There were no predators or parasites to control the rabbit population, and there was plenty of food. The rabbit population increased so fast that the country was soon overrun by rabbits. To control the rabbit population, the Australian government introduced a virus that makes rabbits sick. The first time the virus was used, more than 99 percent of the rabbits died. The survivors reproduced, and the

rabbit population grew large again. The second time the virus was used, about 90 percent of the rabbits died. Once again, the rabbit population increased. The third time the virus was used, only about 50 percent of the rabbits died. Suggest what changes might have occurred in the rabbits and the virus.

Coevolution and Flowers Some of the most amazing examples of coevolution are between flowers and their pollinators. (An organism that carries pollen from flower to flower is called a *pollinator*.) When the pollinator travels to the next flower to feed, some of the pollen is left behind on the female part of the flower and more pollen is picked up. Because of pollination, reproduction can take place in the plant. Organisms such as bees, bats, and hummingbirds are attracted to a flower because of its colors, odors, and nectar.

During the course of evolution, hummingbird-pollinated flowers, for example, developed nectar with just the right amount of sugar for their pollinators. The hummingbird's long, thin tongue and beak coevolved to fit into the flowers so that they could reach the nectar. As the hummingbird, like the one shown in **Figure 18,** feeds on the nectar, its head and body become smeared with pollen.

Figure 18 *The bird is attracted to the flower's nectar and picks up the flower's pollen as it feeds.*

REVIEW

1. Briefly describe one example of a predator-prey relationship. Identify the predator and the prey.
2. Name and define the three kinds of symbiosis.
3. **Analyzing Relationships** Explain the probable relationship between the giant *Rafflesia* flower, which smells like rotting meat, and the carrion flies that buzz around it. HINT: *carrion* means "rotting flesh."

TOPIC: Producers, Consumers, and Decomposers
GO TO: www.scilinks.org
*sci*LINKS NUMBER: HSTL440

Chapter Highlights

VOCABULARY DEFINITIONS

SECTION 1

ecology the study of the interactions between organisms and their environment

biotic living factors in the environment

abiotic nonliving factors in the environment

population a group of individuals of the same species that live together in the same area at the same time

community all of the populations of different species that live and interact in an area

ecosystem a community of organisms and their nonliving environment

biosphere the part of the Earth where life exists

SECTION 2

herbivore a consumer that eats plants

carnivore a consumer that eats animals

omnivore a consumer that eats a variety of organisms

scavenger an animal that feeds on the bodies of dead animals

food chain a diagram that represents how the energy in food molecules flows from one organism to the next

food web a complex diagram representing the many energy pathways in a real ecosystem

energy pyramid a diagram shaped like a triangle showing the loss of energy at each level of the food chain

habitat the environment where an organism lives

niche an organism's way of life and its relationships with its abiotic and biotic environment

Chapter Highlights

SECTION 1

Vocabulary
ecology (p. 434)
biotic (p. 434)
abiotic (p. 434)
population (p. 436)
community (p. 436)
ecosystem (p. 436)
biosphere (p. 437)

Section Notes
- Ecology is the study of the interactions between organisms and their environment.
- The environment consists of both biotic (living) and abiotic (nonliving) parts.
- A population is a group of the same species living in the same place at the same time. A community is all of the populations of different species living together. An ecosystem is a community and its abiotic environment. The biosphere consists of all of Earth's ecosystems.

Labs
Capturing the Wild Bean (p. 748)

SECTION 2

Vocabulary
herbivore (p. 439)
carnivore (p. 439)
omnivore (p. 439)
scavenger (p. 439)
food chain (p. 440)
food web (p. 440)
energy pyramid (p. 441)
habitat (p. 442)
niche (p. 442)

Section Notes
- Organisms that use sunlight directly to make food are called producers. Consumers are organisms that eat other organisms to obtain energy. Decomposers are bacteria and fungi that break down the remains of dead organisms to obtain energy.

✓ Skills Check

Math Concepts

ENERGY PYRAMIDS Try calculating the MathBreak on page 441 as if each unit of energy were $1.00. If you have $10,000.00, but you spend 90 percent, how much do you have left to leave in your will? ($1,000.00) If your heir spends 90 percent of that, how much can your heir leave? ($100.00) After four generations, how much will the inheritance be? ($1.00) Not much, huh? That's why there are very few large organisms at the top of the energy pyramid.

Visual Understanding

FOOD WEBS Several food pathways are shown in the food web in Figure 5 on page 440. However, an actual food web in a woodland ecosystem is much more complex because hundreds of species live there. Find the mouse in Figure 5. How many organisms feed on the mouse? How many organisms feed on the butterfly? What might happen to this ecosystem if these animals were eliminated?

Lab and Activity Highlights

Capturing the Wild Bean PG 748

Adaptation: It's a Way of Life PG 746

 Datasheets for LabBook
(blackline masters for these labs)

SECTION 2

- A food chain shows how energy flows from one organism to the next.
- Because most organisms eat more than one kind of food, there are many energy pathways possible; these are represented by a food web.
- Energy pyramids demonstrate that most of the energy at each level of the food chain is used up at that level and is unavailable for organisms higher on the food chain.
- An organism's habitat is the environment in which it lives. An organism's niche is its role in the ecosystem.

SECTION 3

Vocabulary
carrying capacity (p. 445)
prey (p. 446)
predator (p. 446)
symbiosis (p. 447)
mutualism (p. 447)
commensalism (p. 447)
parasitism (p. 448)
coevolution (p. 448)

Section Notes
- Population size changes over time.
- Limiting factors slow the growth of a population. The largest population that an environment can support over a long period of time is called the carrying capacity.
- When one organism eats another, the organism that is eaten is the prey, and the organism that eats the prey is the predator.
- Symbiosis is a close, long-term association between two or more species. There are three general types of symbiosis: mutualism, commensalism, and parasitism.
- Coevolution involves the long-term changes that take place in two species because of their close interactions with one another.

Labs
Adaptation: It's a Way of Life (p. 746)

VOCABULARY DEFINITIONS, continued

SECTION 3
carrying capacity the largest population that a given environment can support over a long period of time

prey an organism that is eaten by another organism

predator an organism that eats other organisms

symbiosis a close, long-term association between two or more species

mutualism a symbiotic relationship in which both organisms benefit

commensalism a symbiotic relationship in which one organism benefits and the other is unaffected

parasitism a symbiotic association in which one organism benefits while the other is harmed

coevolution long-term changes that take place in two species because of their close interactions with one another

 Vocabulary Review Worksheet 18

 Blackline masters of these Chapter Highlights can be found in the **Study Guide.**

---

internet connect

GO TO: go.hrw.com

Visit the **HRW** Web site for a variety of learning tools related to this chapter. Just type in the keyword:

KEYWORD: HSTINT

sciLINKS — NSTA

GO TO: www.scilinks.org

Visit the **National Science Teachers Association** on-line Web site for Internet resources related to this chapter. Just type in the sciLINKS number for more information about the topic:

TOPIC: Biotic and Abiotic Factors	sciLINKS NUMBER: HSTL430
TOPIC: Organization in the Environment	sciLINKS NUMBER: HSTL435
TOPIC: Producers, Consumers, and Decomposers	sciLINKS NUMBER: HSTL440
TOPIC: Food Chains and Food Webs	sciLINKS NUMBER: HSTL445
TOPIC: Habitats and Niches	sciLINKS NUMBER: HSTL450

Lab and Activity Highlights

LabBank

 Whiz-Bang Demonstrations, Voracious Fly Catcher, Demo 11

EcoLabs & Field Activities, Survival Is Just a Roll of the Dice, EcoLab 5

Long-Term Projects & Research Ideas, Out of House and Home, Project 18

Interactive Explorations CD-ROM

 CD 2, Exploration 1, "What's Bugging You?"

Chapter 18 • Chapter Highlights

Chapter Review

USING VOCABULARY

To complete the following sentences, choose the correct term from each pair of terms listed below:

1. An organism's environment has two parts, the __?__, or living, and the __?__, or nonliving. (*biotic* or *abiotic*)

2. A __?__ is a group of individuals of the same species that live in the same area at the same time. (*community* or *population*)

3. A community and its abiotic environment make up a(n) __?__. (*ecosystem* or *food web*)

4. Organisms that use photosynthesis to obtain energy are called __?__. (*producers* or *decomposers*)

5. The environment in which an organism lives is its __?__, and the role the organism plays in an ecosystem is its __?__. (*niche* or *habitat*)

UNDERSTANDING CONCEPTS

Multiple Choice

6. A tick sucks blood from a dog. In this relationship, the tick is the __?__ and the dog is the __?__.
   a. parasite, prey
   b. predator, host
   c. parasite, host
   d. host, parasite

7. Resources such as water, food, or sunlight are more likely to be limiting factors
   a. when population size is decreasing.
   b. when predators eat their prey.
   c. when the population is small.
   d. when a population is approaching the carrying capacity.

8. "Nature's recyclers" are
   a. predators.
   b. decomposers.
   c. producers.
   d. omnivores.

9. A beneficial association between coral and algae is an example of
   a. commensalism.
   b. parasitism.
   c. mutualism.
   d. predation.

10. How energy moves through an ecosystem can be represented by
    a. food chains.
    b. energy pyramids.
    c. food webs.
    d. All of the above

11. The base of an energy pyramid represents which organisms in an ecosystem?
    a. producers
    b. carnivores
    c. herbivores
    d. scavengers

12. Which of the following is the correct order in a food chain?
    a. sun → producers → herbivores → scavengers → carnivores
    b. sun → consumers → predators → parasites → hosts
    c. sun → producers → decomposers → consumers → omnivores
    d. sun → producers → herbivores → carnivores → scavengers

13. Remoras and sharks have a relationship best described as
    a. mutualism.
    b. commensalism.
    c. predator and prey.
    d. parasitism.

Short Answer

14. Briefly describe the habitat and niche of the gray wolf.

15. What might different species of trees in a forest compete for?

16. How do limiting factors affect the carrying capacity of an environment?

17. What is coevolution?

Concept Mapping

18. An answer to this exercise can be found at the end of this book.

CRITICAL THINKING AND PROBLEM SOLVING

19. An ecosystem with no decomposers could not exist very long because the ecosystem would soon become buried under the bodies of its dead organisms. Decomposers recycle dead material back into the ecosystem.

Chapter Review Answers

USING VOCABULARY

1. biotic, abiotic
2. population
3. ecosystem
4. producers
5. habitat, niche

UNDERSTANDING CONCEPTS

Multiple Choice

6. c
7. d
8. b
9. c
10. d
11. a
12. d
13. b

Short Answer

14. The wolf's habitat includes wilderness areas in portions of Montana, Washington, Minnesota, Michigan, Wisconsin, and parts of Canada. Part of a wolf's niche is being a predator of large herbivores. Wolves remove the old and sick members of large herds of deer, moose, reindeer, sheep, and elk.

15. Trees might compete for sunlight, water, or space.

16. Limiting factors generally define an environment's carrying capacity. Populations cannot grow indefinitely because the environment contains a fixed amount of food, water, living space, and other needed resources. Each of these resources is a limiting factor. If only one of them is in short supply, the environment's carrying capacity is lowered for a specific species.

17. Coevolution is a long-term change that takes place in two species because of their close interactions with one another.

Concept Mapping

18. Use the following terms to create a concept map: individual organisms, producers, populations, ecosystems, consumers, herbivores, communities, carnivores, the biosphere.

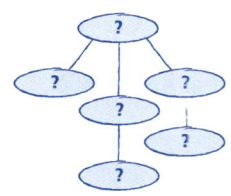

CRITICAL THINKING AND PROBLEM SOLVING

Write one or two sentences to answer the following questions:

19. Could a balanced ecosystem contain producers and consumers but no decomposers? Why or why not?

20. Some biologists think that certain species, such as alligators and wolves, help maintain biological diversity in their ecosystems. Predict what might happen to other species, such as gar fish or herons, if alligators were to become extinct in the Florida Everglades.

21. Does the Earth have a carrying capacity for humans? Explain your answer.

22. Explain why it is important to have a variety of organisms in a community of interacting species. Give an example.

MATH IN SCIENCE

23. The plants in each square meter of an ecosystem obtained 20,810 Calories of the sun's energy by photosynthesis per year. The herbivores in that ecosystem ate all of the plants, but they obtained only 3,370 Calories of energy. How much energy did the plants use for their own life processes?

INTERPRETING GRAPHICS

Examine the following graph, which shows the population growth of a species of *Paramecium,* a slipper-shaped, single-celled microorganism, over a period of 18 days. Food was occasionally added to the test tube in which the paramecia were grown. Answer the following questions:

24. What is the carrying capacity of the test tube as long as food is added?

25. Predict what will happen to the population if the researcher stops adding food to the test tube.

26. What keeps the number of *Paramecium* at a steady level?

27. Predict what might happen if the amount of water is doubled and the food supply stays the same.

Take a minute to review your answers to the Pre-Reading Questions found at the bottom of page 432. Have your answers changed? If necessary, revise your answers based on what you have learned since you began this chapter.

453

20. A predator, such as the alligator, removes the weak, old, or sick individuals from its prey population and contributes to the health of that population. If alligators became extinct in the Everglades, gars and herons might soon overpopulate. They would weaken their own food sources and possibly contribute to the extinction of other species.

21. The Earth does have a carrying capacity for humans. We have extended our carrying capacity by growing more crops and controlling our environments to make previously uninhabitable areas livable. But we will eventually reach a carrying capacity that we cannot exceed.

22. It is important to have a variety of organisms in a community of interacting species because most species depend on other species for survival. All consumers depend on producers for food. For example, rabbits depend on grasses for food. Mice eat seeds and berries. A hawk depends on small animals like rabbits and mice for food and on trees for resting and nesting. A variety of producers supports a variety of consumers.

MATH IN SCIENCE

23. 17,440 Cal

INTERPRETING GRAPHICS

24. about 65
25. The population will crash due to starvation.
26. The limiting factors, such as food supply, limit growth.
27. Any single factor can be limiting. Space may be increased, but unless food is increased, the carrying capacity is the same.

Concept Mapping Transparency 18

Blackline masters of this Chapter Review can be found in the **Study Guide.**

HEALTH WATCH
An Unusual Guest

Background

Follicle mites are harmless, but other kinds of mites are not benign guests. Mites are responsible for the devastation of honeybee populations in the United States. In the last few decades, tracheal mites and varroa mites have cut the number of domesticated colonies in half. There are almost no wild honeybees left in the United States.

The honeybee is a hardworking and important participant in agriculture. Apples and other orchard fruits require the honeybee for pollination. Domesticated honeybees annually enable the production of $10 billion worth of crops as well as produce $250 million worth of honey.

Scientists and beekeepers are trying various solutions to the mite infestations. Some chemicals seem to help. More promising solutions are found in new strains of honeybees bred to be resistant to mites, and in some honeybees that have developed the ability to groom mites off each other.

Health Watch
An Unusual Guest

What has a tiny tubelike body and short stumpy legs and lives upside down in your eyebrows and eyelashes? Would you believe a small animal? It's called a follicle mite, and humans are its host organism. Like all large animals, human beings are hosts to a variety of smaller creatures. They live in or on our bodies and share our bodies' resources. But none of our guests are stranger than follicle mites. They feed on oil and dead cells from your skin.

▲ *A follicle mite is smaller than the period at the end of this sentence.*

What Are They?
Follicle mites are arachnids—relatives of spiders. They are about 0.4 mm long, and they live in hair follicles all over your body. Usually they like to live in areas around the nose, cheek, forehead, chin, eyebrows, and eyelashes.

Follicle Mites Don't Bite
These tiny guests are almost always harmless, and they seldom live on children and adolescents. And you probably wouldn't even know they were there. Studies reveal that between 97 percent and 100 percent of all adults have these mites. Except in rare cases, follicle mites in adults are also pretty harmless.

Some Health Concerns
Although follicle mites rarely cause problems, they are sometimes responsible for an acnelike condition around the nose, eyebrows, and eyelashes. A large number of mites (up to 25) may live in the same follicle. This can cause an inflammation of the follicle. The follicle does not swell like acne; instead it becomes red and itchy.

Mites living in eyelashes and on eyelids can irritate those areas. The inflammation causes itchy eyelids or eyebrows. But such inflammations are rare, and the condition clears up very quickly when suitable medication is applied. So while follicle mites may be one of the strangest guests living on human skin, they are almost never a problem.

Other Companions
Many tiny organisms make their home in humans' bodies. Bacteria within the body may help maintain proper pH levels. Even *Escherichia coli,* a type of bacterium that can cause severe health problems, lives in the human colon. Without *E. coli,* a person would be unable to produce enough vitamin K or folic acid.

On Your Own
▶ Do some more research on follicle mites. Search for *Demodex folliculorum* or *Demodex brevis.* Find out more about some of the other strange organisms that rely on humans' bodies for food and shelter. Report on your findings, or write a story from the organism's point of view.

454

Answer to On Your Own
If you can find a copy of the book *Furtive Fauna: A Field Guide to the Creatures Who Live On You,* by Roger M. Knutson, you and your students will have more than enough information about follicle mites, tooth amoebas, bedbugs, ticks, and other organisms that find humans a wonderful place to live. There are a number of sites on the Internet that will provide additional information and links. (Use keywords such as follicle mites, Demodex, and human parasites.)

EYE ON THE ENVIRONMENT

Alien Invasion

A group of tiny aliens left their ship in Mobile, Alabama. Their bodies were red and shiny, and they walked on six legs. The aliens looked around and then quietly crawled off to make homes in the new land.

Westward Ho!

In 1918, fire ants were accidentally imported into the United States by a freighter ship from South America. In the United States, fire ants have no natural predators or competitors. In addition, these ants are extremely aggressive, and their colonies can harbor many queens, instead of just one queen, like many other ant species. With all these advantages, it is not surprising that the ants have spread like wildfire. By 1965, fire-ant mounds were popping up on the southeastern coast and as far west as Texas. Today they are found in at least 10 southern states and may soon reach as far west as California.

Jaws of Destruction

Imported fire ants have done a lot of damage as they have spread across the United States. Because they are attracted to electrical currents, they chew through wire insulation, causing shorts in electrical circuits. The invaders have also managed to disturb the natural balance of native ecosystems. In some areas, they have killed off 70 percent of the native ant species and 40 percent of other native insect species. Each year, about 25,000 people seek medical attention for painful fire-ant bites.

▶ Three types of fire ants are found in a colony: the queen, workers, and males. Notice how the queen ant dwarfs the worker ants.

Fighting Fire

Eighty years after the fire ants' introduction into the United States, the destructive ants continue to multiply. About 157 chemical products, including ammonia, gasoline, extracts from manure, and harsh pesticides, are registered for use against fire ants, but most have little or no success. Unfortunately, many of these remedies also harm the environment. By 1995, the government had approved only one fire-ant bait for large-scale use.

An Ant-Farm Census

▶ How many total offspring does a single fire-ant queen produce if she lives for 5 years and produces 1,000 eggs a day? If a mound contains 300,000 ants, how many mounds will her offspring fill?

EYE ON THE ENVIRONMENT
Alien Invasion

Background

In combating the spread of fire ants, people must be careful not to harm the environment. In the 1960s, ground-up corncobs and soybean oil were mixed with an ant poison and sprayed over huge areas of land. Studies have since shown that the poison used is toxic to many species. In addition, many researchers speculate that this strategy may have backfired because fire ants can recover from disasters much more quickly than other types of ants. After an area was treated with insecticides, the first ants that were able to reinhabit it were fire ants. Similar scenarios occurred in many different areas. As a result of these treatments, fire ants have become a serious ecological problem in many areas.

Discussion

Discuss with students some safe and natural ways that they can eliminate ants around their home. For instance, they can squeeze fresh lemon or lime juice into holes or cracks in their homes and then leave the peels where they have seen ants. They can also scatter aromatic substances, such as mint, red pepper, or paprika, around spots where ants enter homes. These substances repel ants.

Answers to An Ant-Farm Census

A typical queen may produce over 1.8 million eggs in her life:

1,000 eggs/day × 365 days/year × 5 years = 1,825,000 eggs.

Point out that a queen may not produce eggs every day.

You might also want to explain to the students that by dividing by 300,000 ants per mound, this number is equal to just over six mounds, or more than one new mound every year!

Chapter Organizer

CHAPTER ORGANIZATION	TIME MINUTES	OBJECTIVES	LABS, INVESTIGATIONS, AND DEMONSTRATIONS
Chapter Opener pp. 456–457	45	National Standards: UCP 2, 4, SAI 1, 2, HNS 2, 3	**Start-Up Activity** A Classroom Aquarium, p. 457
Section 1 The Cycles of Matter	90	▶ Trace the cycle of water between the atmosphere, land, and oceans. ▶ Diagram the carbon cycle, and explain its importance to living things. ▶ Diagram the nitrogen cycle, and explain its importance to living things. UCP 1–4, SAI 1, 2, SPSP 4, 5; LabBook UCP 1–3, SAI 1	**Demonstration,** The Water Cycle, p. 459 in ATE **GENERAL** **QuickLab,** Combustion, p. 460 **GENERAL** **Discovery Lab,** Nitrogen Needs, p. 750 **GENERAL** **Datasheets for LabBook,** Nitrogen Needs, Datasheet 40 **GENERAL**
Section 2 Ecological Succession	90	▶ Define *succession*. ▶ Contrast primary and secondary succession. UCP 1–4, SAI 1, SPSP 2; LabBook UCP 1–4, SAI 1	**Making Models,** A Passel o' Pioneers, p. 752 **GENERAL** **Datasheets for LabBook,** Passel o' Pioneers, Datasheet 41 **GENERAL** **Long-Term Projects & Research Ideas,** Project 19 **ADVANCED**

*See page **T20** for a complete correlation of this book with the*

NATIONAL SCIENCE EDUCATION STANDARDS.

TECHNOLOGY RESOURCES

 Guided Reading Audio CD English or Spanish, Chapter 19

 Science, Technology, & Society, Taking Earth's Pulse, Segment 21

 One-Stop Planner CD-ROM with Test Generator

Chapter 19 • Cycles in Nature

CLASSROOM WORKSHEETS, TRANSPARENCIES, AND RESOURCES	SCIENCE INTEGRATION AND CONNECTIONS	REVIEW AND ASSESSMENT
Directed Reading Worksheet 19 BASIC **Science Puzzlers, Twisters & Teasers,** Worksheet 19 ADVANCED		
Transparency 67, The Water Cycle **Directed Reading Worksheet 19,** Section 1 BASIC **Transparency 141,** The Water Cycle **Transparency 68,** The Carbon Cycle **Critical Thinking Worksheet 19,** Pass the Salt, Please ADVANCED **Transparency 69,** The Nitrogen Cycle **Reinforcement Worksheet 19,** What Goes Around.... GENERAL	**Environment Connection,** p. 459 **Connect to Earth Science,** p. 459 in ATE **MathBreak,** Gallons Galore, p. 461 GENERAL **Apply,** p. 461 GENERAL **Weird Science:** Weather From Fire, p. 470 GENERAL **Eye on the Environment:** The Mysterious Dead Zone, p. 471 GENERAL	**Review,** p. 461 GENERAL **Quiz,** p. 461 in ATE GENERAL **Alternative Assessment,** p. 461 in ATE BASIC
Directed Reading Worksheet 19, Section 2 BASIC **Transparency 70,** Primary Succession **Transparency 71,** Secondary Succession	**Math and More,** p. 463 in ATE GENERAL **Connect to Earth Science,** p. 463 in ATE **Multicultural Connection,** p. 463 in ATE	**Self-Check,** p. 464 **Homework,** p. 464 in ATE BASIC **Review,** p. 465 GENERAL **Quiz,** p. 465 in ATE GENERAL **Alternative Assessment,** p. 465 in ATE GENERAL

 Holt, Rinehart and Winston On-line Resources
go.hrw.com
For worksheets and other teaching aids related to this chapter, visit the HRW Web site and type in the keyword: **HSTCYC**

 National Science Teachers Association
www.scilinks.org
Encourage students to use the *sci*LINKS numbers listed in the internet connect boxes to access information and resources on the **NSTA** Web site.

END-OF-CHAPTER REVIEW AND ASSESSMENT

Chapter Review in Study Guide
Vocabulary and Notes in Study Guide
Chapter Tests with Performance-Based Assessment, Chapter 19 Test
Chapter Tests with Performance-Based Assessment, Performance-Based Assessment 19
Concept Mapping Transparency 19

Chapter Resources & Worksheets

Visual Resources

TEACHING TRANSPARENCIES

TEACHING TRANSPARENCIES

CONCEPT MAPPING TRANSPARENCY

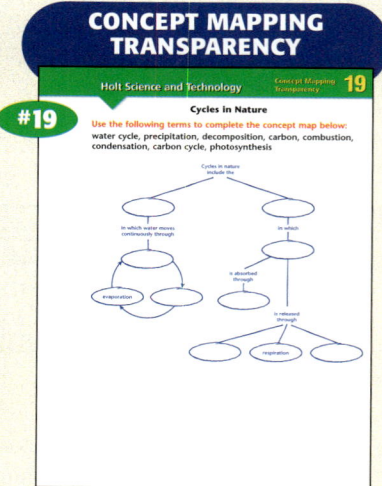

Meeting Individual Needs

DIRECTED READING

REINFORCEMENT & VOCABULARY REVIEW

SCIENCE PUZZLERS, TWISTERS & TEASERS

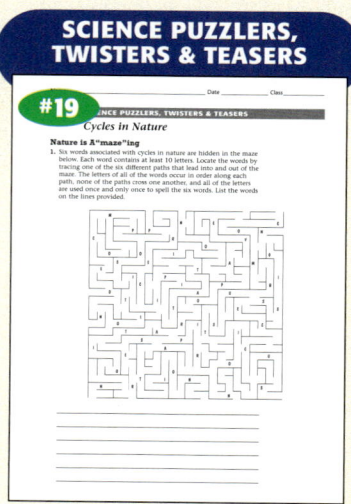

Chapter 19 • Cycles in Nature

Chapter 19 • Cycles in Nature

Review & Assessment

STUDY GUIDE

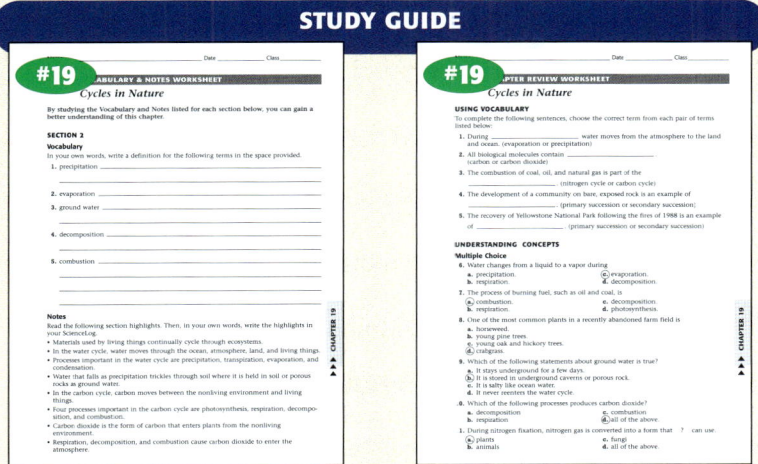

CHAPTER TESTS WITH PERFORMANCE-BASED ASSESSMENT

Lab Worksheets

LONG-TERM PROJECTS & RESEARCH IDEAS

DATASHEETS FOR LABBOOK

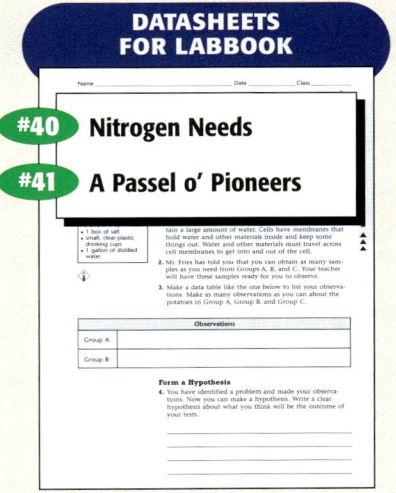

Applications & Extensions

CRITICAL THINKING & PROBLEM SOLVING

SCIENCE TECHNOLOGY

Chapter Background

SECTION 1

The Cycles of Matter

The Water Cycle

The water cycle, which is also known as the *hydrologic cycle,* is the continuous movement of water between the Earth and its atmosphere. There are about 1.4 billion cubic kilometers of water in the Earth system (a cubic kilometer is more than 264 billion gallons). Although that is an enormous volume of water, only a small fraction of it—13,000 km^3—exists in the atmosphere. In other words, if all of the water in the atmosphere fell to the Earth's surface at one time, the Earth would be covered with about 2.5 cm of water.

- The role of plants in the water cycle is often overlooked. But of the 1,200 km^3 of water that enters the atmosphere every day, as much as 120 km^3 is released by plants as they transpire. Plants take in water through their roots and release it through *stomates,* which are small pores located on the undersides of their leaves. Through this process, a one-acre cornfield can transpire as much as 15,000 liters of water every day.

- Not all water molecules are alike. There are six different isotopes of oxygen, but because of their relative abundance, drinking water primarily contains one. There are three isotopes of hydrogen. Known as protium (single-weight hydrogen), deuterium (double-weight hydrogen), and tritium (triple-weight hydrogen), these isotopes can be combined in many different ways to create water molecules of different weights. When combined with oxygen, protium forms light water, deuterium forms heavy water, and tritium forms superheavy water. In nature, most water is light.

IS THAT A FACT!

▶ A fully grown oak tree may transpire up to 380 L of water per day!

The Carbon Cycle

Like water, carbon is recycled in the natural world. Respiration among living things releases carbon dioxide, which is taken up by plants and converted to sugars. The carbon that accumulates in plants as carbohydrates circulates in nature in a number of ways. When plants are eaten, their carbon is transferred to animals. The waste products of the animals' metabolism—including carbon dioxide—are returned to nature. Finally, when living things die, their decomposition releases carbon.

- Human activities can alter the balance of the global carbon cycle. The burning of fossil fuels, for example, releases vast amounts of carbon dioxide into the atmosphere. The carbon contained in fossil fuels is formed very slowly, yet its combustion is rapid. As a result, the amount of carbon dioxide in the atmosphere is rising. This is of concern to some scientists because carbon dioxide is a greenhouse gas. Carbon dioxide, along with other greenhouse gases, traps heat and prevents it from radiating from Earth. Scientists are concerned that this phenomenon is causing the temperature on Earth to rise.

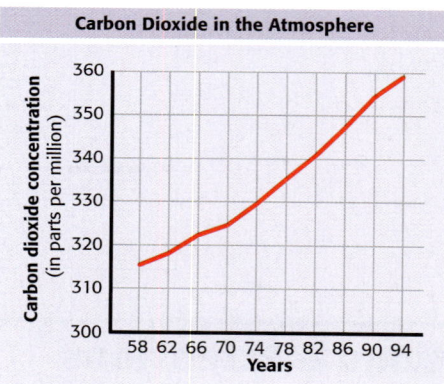

SECTION 2

Ecological Succession

The Nature of Ecosystems

Like living things, ecosystems are born, develop, and mature. Events such as fires, storms, and volcanic eruptions can disrupt ecosystems, setting into action a chain of events known as succession. Though discussions of succession generally center on forests, all ecosystems undergo the process.

Chapter 19 • Cycles in Nature

- Over the last several thousand years, the water level of the Great Lakes has gradually decreased. As the lake shores expanded, sand dunes formed. These dunes are ecosystems. Like a forest ecosystem, a sand dune ecosystem follows a pattern of succession.

Sand is unstable, infertile, and inhospitable. At first, only the hardiest plants can survive there. These pioneer plants stabilize the sand, enriching the soil as they decay. This makes a much more hospitable environment for other living things. Grasses move into the area, covering the dune. Their extensive root systems further stabilize the sand, holding the dune in place. Shrubs and pines then join the ecosystem, and the shade they produce eventually kills the grasses. A thick pine forest eventually replaces the grasses because the shade produced by the pines makes them unable to thrive. The pines create a more hospitable environment for deciduous trees. The pines are gradually replaced by trees such as oaks, maples, and elms. These trees are able to reproduce in the shady forest environment.

▶ Forest Management

The branch of forestry concerned with the life cycle of trees and the forest is known as forest management. Forest managers manage the forest for economic benefits and protect the ecosystem for wildlife. Balancing the two responsibilities is sometimes difficult.

- Forest managers perform some of the same functions carried out by nature. They plant trees, thin forest stands, and remove trees. Unmanaged trees burn or rot, so forest managers usually find ways to use the wood of managed forests.

- One controversial activity carried out by forest managers is known as prescribed burning. Though dangerous and often destructive, fire is a necessary component of the life cycle of forest communities. Its effects on wildlife are complex; fire can assist in the recycling of nutrients, regulate plant succession, help maintain biological diversity, reduce biomass, and help control insect and disease populations. In 1998, the U.S. Forest Service burned between 850,000 and 1 million acres.

▶ Forest Wildlife

As forests undergo succession, they attract different forms of wildlife. Piney forests attract different species than hardwood forests do. This is because the amount and type of resources in each favors certain animals but discourages others. For example, the southern pine beetle can survive only in pine forests. Other animals, known as browsers, can live in either hardwood or pine forest habitat. These animals, including deer and elk, rely upon the forest for shelter but often find food on its periphery.

▶ Plant Competition and Succession

Plant succession is affected by competition among plants for resources. Plants compete with one another for sunlight, water, and nitrogen, among other resources. As with other living things, plants that are able to efficiently use these resources are able to grow and reproduce more effectively than their competitors.

For background information about teaching strategies and issues, refer to the *Professional Reference for Teachers.*

Cycles in Nature

  Pre-Reading Questions

Students may not know the answers to these questions before reading the chapter, so accept any reasonable response.

Suggested Answers

1. Recycling means the process of making another product from a reprocessed product. Water, nitrogen, and carbon are three of the many substances essential to life on Earth that cycle from the physical environment, through living things, and back to the physical environment in different forms.

2. Rain falls to the Earth as precipitation. If it falls into the ocean, it may evaporate and fall as precipitation again. If rainwater falls on land, it may join a stream, river, or other body of water. It may also trickle down into the Earth to become ground water. It will eventually reenter the atmosphere through evaporation or transpiration.

 Directed Reading Worksheet 19

 Science Puzzlers, Twisters & Teasers Worksheet 19

 Guided Reading Audio CD English or Spanish, Chapter 19

Cycles in Nature

Sections

1. **The Cycles of Matter** . . 458
   Environment
      Connection 459
   QuickLab 460
   MathBreak 461
   Apply 461
   Internet Connect 461

2. **Ecological
   Succession** 462
   Internet Connect. 465

Chapter Review 468
Feature Articles 470, 471
LabBook 750–753

 **Pre-Reading Questions**

1. What is meant by *recycling*?
2. What happens to rainwater after it falls to Earth?

 internet connect

HRW On-line Resources
go.hrw.com
For worksheets and other teaching aids, visit the HRW Web site and type in the keyword: **HSTCYC**

www.scilinks.com
Use the *sci*LINKS numbers at the end of each chapter for additional resources on the **NSTA** Web site.

www.cnnfyi.com
Visit the CNN Web site for current events coverage and classroom resources.

Desert Post

Ever tried to send a desert to anyone? Thanks to the U.S. Postal Service, you can! Stamps were made from this picture of the Sonoran Desert. The stamps are intended to promote a greater appreciation of the diversity of the Sonoran Desert. The desert scene was the first of a series that commemorates America's natural environment. In this chapter, you will learn about the natural environment and how it works.

START-UP Activity

A CLASSROOM AQUARIUM

Did you know an aquarium is a small environment? In this activity, you will put an aquarium together. As you plan the aquarium, think about how all the parts are connected with each other.

Procedure

1. Get a **tank** from your teacher. Check the Internet, your library, or a pet store to find directions on the proper way to clean and prepare an aquarium.
2. Find out about the kinds of **plants** and **animals** that you can put in your aquarium.
3. Choose a place to put the tank, and tell your teacher your plans. Then set up the aquarium.

Analysis

4. How is the aquarium similar to and different from a natural body of water? Identify the limitations of your model.
5. After you read Section 1, take another look at the aquarium. See if you can name all the parts of this small ecosystem.

START-UP Activity

A CLASSROOM AQUARIUM

MATERIALS
For Each Group: • aquarium • various aquatic plants • aquatic animals

Answers to START-UP Activity

4. Sample answer: The aquarium is similar to a natural body of water because it is an aquatic environment that contains living things. It is different from a natural body of water in that it is confined by glass walls and may receive a different amount of sunlight. Some limitations of this model include the very limited number of organisms in the aquarium, the glass walls, the different nutrient inputs and outputs, and the lack of contact with other environments.

5. Sample answer: the water, the plants, the animals, the tank, the gravel (or stones), the filtration system, the air pump

SECTION 1

Focus

The Cycles of Matter

This section explains that matter is neither created nor destroyed. The water, carbon, and other materials in the environment are constantly recycled. The water cycle and the carbon cycle are used to illustrate how matter is recycled in nature.

Ask students to answer the following question in their ScienceLog:

What are the four major steps of the water cycle?
(transpiration, evaporation, condensation, and precipitation)

1) Motivate

DISCUSSION

Initiate a discussion with students about the properties of matter. Remind them that matter is anything that has mass and takes up space. Make sure that students understand that matter is always conserved. Illustrate this concept by telling them that the water they used to brush their teeth in the morning may have once been a dinosaur's bathwater!

Teaching Transparency 67
"The Water Cycle"

Directed Reading Worksheet 19 Section 1

TOPIC: The Water Cycle
GO TO: www.scilinks.org
sciLINKS NUMBER: HSTL455

458 Chapter 19 • Cycles in Nature

Section 1

Terms to Learn

precipitation decomposition
evaporation combustion
ground water

What You'll Do

- Trace the cycle of water between the atmosphere, land, and oceans.
- Diagram the carbon cycle, and explain its importance to living things.
- Diagram the nitrogen cycle, and explain its importance to living things.

The Cycles of Matter

The matter in your body has been on Earth since the planet was formed billions of years ago! *Matter,* which is anything that occupies space and has mass, is used over and over again. Each kind of matter has its own cycle. In these cycles, matter moves among the environment and living things.

The Water Cycle

The movement of water among the oceans, atmosphere, land, and living things is known as the *water cycle.* Locate each part of the water cycle in **Figure 1** as it is discussed.

Precipitation Water moves from the atmosphere to the land and oceans as **precipitation,** which includes rain, snow, sleet, and hail. About 91 percent of precipitation falls into the ocean. The rest falls on land, renewing the supply of fresh water.

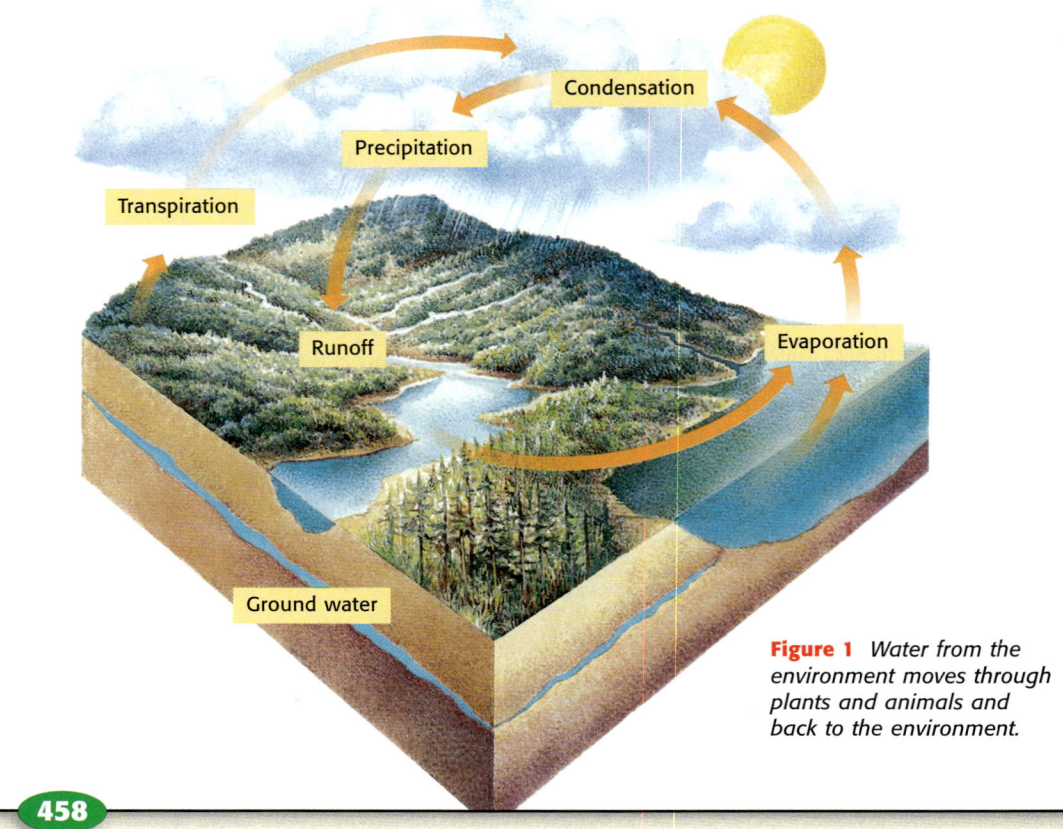

Figure 1 *Water from the environment moves through plants and animals and back to the environment.*

458

Converting ice to liquid requires thermal energy. When the process is reversed, some thermal energy is given off. Farmers use this principle when they spray crops with water during sudden cold weather. As the water freezes on the fruit, heat is given off, which prevents the fruit from freezing.

SCIENCE HUMOR

Q: If H_2O is water, what is H_2O_4?

A: Drinking!

Evaporation Water cycles back to the atmosphere through evaporation. During **evaporation,** the sun's heat causes water to change from liquid to vapor. When the water vapor cools during the process of *condensation,* it forms a liquid that can fall to the Earth as precipitation.

Ground Water Some precipitation seeps into the ground, where it is stored in underground caverns or in porous rock. This water, known as **ground water,** may stay in the ground for hundreds or even thousands of years. Ground water provides water to the soil, streams, rivers, and oceans.

Water and Life All organisms, from tiny bacteria to animals and plants, contain a lot of water. Your body is composed of about 70 percent water. Water carries waste products away from body tissues. Water also helps regulate body temperature through perspiration and evaporation, returning water to the environment in a process called *transpiration.* Without water, there would be no life on Earth.

Carbon dioxide is being released into the atmosphere in increasing quantities. Carbon dioxide causes the atmosphere to hold heat. The warmer atmosphere causes the temperatures of the land and ocean to rise. This is known as global warming.

The Carbon Cycle

Carbon is essential to living things because it is part of all biological molecules. The movement of carbon from the environment into living things and back into the environment is known as the *carbon cycle,* shown in **Figure 2.**

Figure 2 Carbon may remain in the environment for millions of years before becoming available to living things.

2 Teach

DEMONSTRATION
The Water Cycle

MATERIALS
• water
• hot plate
• saucepan
• heat-resistant glass saucepan
• ice cubes

Place a pan of water on the hot plate and bring it to a boil. Fill the glass saucepan with ice. As students watch, hold the ice-filled pan over the boiling water. Ask students to summarize their observations and relate them to the water cycle. (Heat causes the water in the pan to evaporate. The water vapor cools when it meets the saucepan of ice. The vapor condenses back into the pan.) **Sheltered English**

CONNECT TO
EARTH SCIENCE

Further illustrate the water cycle using Teaching Transparency 141.

Teaching Transparency 141
"The Water Cycle"

Teaching Transparency 68
"The Carbon Cycle"

Critical Thinking Worksheet 19
"Pass the Salt, Please"

TOPIC: The Carbon Cycle
GO TO: www.scilinks.org
*sci*LINKS NUMBER: HSTL460

IS THAT A FACT!

A lush oasis can exist in a desert that seldom receives rain. Water beneath the desert, called fossil water, slowly seeps to the surface at the oasis, allowing plants and animals to live in an otherwise dry place. Fossil water is water that was trapped underground, away from the water cycle, tens of thousands of years ago. When the fossil water is gone, the oasis it feeds will disappear.

Section 1 • The Cycles of Matter

3) Extend

QuickLab

MATERIALS
- candle
- glass jar with lid
- modeling clay

Safety Caution: Remind students to review all safety cautions and icons before beginning this lab activity. Students should stand several meters back from the candle flame.

Answers to QuickLab

- The substance on the side of the jar is water. The warm air contains moisture, which condenses when it contacts the cool glass. Therefore, some of the water comes from the warm air. Additionally, some of the water is from the combustion of the candle wax. Combustion releases carbon dioxide and water.

- The substance inside the jar is soot. Soot is carbon and is the product of the combustion of the candle wax and the wick.

 PG 750
Nitrogen Needs

Teaching Transparency 69
"The Nitrogen Cycle"

TOPIC: The Nitrogen Cycle
GO TO: www.scilinks.org
sciLINKS NUMBER: HSTL465

Combustion

Place a **candle** on a **jar lid** and secure it with **modeling clay.** Light the candle. Hold the **jar** very close to the candle flame. What is deposited on the jar? Where did the substance come from? Now place the jar over the candle. What is deposited inside the jar? Where did this substance come from?

Photosynthesis Photosynthesis is the process by which carbon cycles from the environment into living things. During photosynthesis, plants use carbon dioxide from the air to make sugars. Most animals get the carbon they need by eating plants.

Respiration How does carbon return to the environment? Animals and plants both respire. During *respiration,* sugar molecules are broken down to release energy. Carbon dioxide and water are released as byproducts.

Decomposition The breakdown of dead materials into carbon dioxide and water is called **decomposition.** When fungi and bacteria decompose organic matter, they return carbon to the environment.

Combustion The carbon in coal, oil, and natural gas returns to the atmosphere as carbon dioxide when these fuels are burned. The process of burning fuel is known as **combustion.** Combustion provides much of the fuel people need to drive cars, heat homes, and make electricity.

The Nitrogen Cycle

The movement of nitrogen from the environment to living things and back again is called the *nitrogen cycle,* shown in **Figure 3.**

Figure 3 Without bacteria, nitrogen could not enter living things or be returned to the atmosphere.

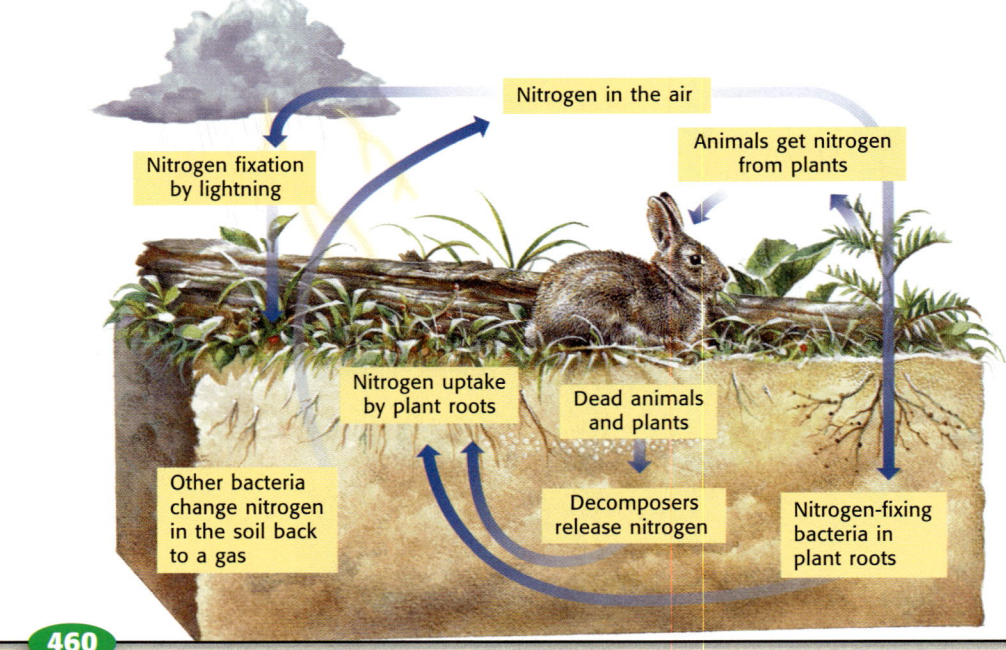

MISCONCEPTION ALERT

Students may believe that climate changes are caused solely by human activities that release carbon into the atmosphere. While it is important to be aware of our impact on the atmosphere, tell students most climate changes are not solely the result of human action. Scientists theorize that climate changes involve the complex interactions of natural phenomena, such as volcanic eruptions; changes in the output of the sun's energy; and continental drift. Deforestation and the burning of fossil fuels are just two possible factors affecting climates.

A Sea of Nitrogen About 78 percent of the Earth's atmosphere is nitrogen gas. However, most organisms cannot use nitrogen gas to obtain the nitrogen they need to build proteins and DNA. But bacteria in the soil are able to change nitrogen gas into forms that can be used by plants. This is called *nitrogen fixation*. Most animals get the nitrogen they need by eating plants.

Back to Gas The final step of the nitrogen cycle is also performed by bacteria in the soil. These bacteria are different species than the bacteria that fix nitrogen. The bacteria break down dead organisms and animal wastes. This process produces nitrogen gas, which is returned to the atmosphere.

Gallons Galore
An average person in the United States uses about 78 gal of water each day. How many liters is this? How many cubic centimeters? Remember: 1 gal = 3.79 L and 1 mL = 1 cm³.

The Pollution Cycle
Isabel read an article about how power plants near her home emit sulfur dioxide into the atmosphere. When sulfur dioxide mixes with water, it forms sulfuric acid, which is extremely toxic to living things. Isabel also learned that sulfur dioxide from these power plants has killed all the fish in a lake hundreds of kilometers away. Trees growing near the lake were also killed. Using what you know about the water cycle, write a letter to Isabel explaining how this could happen.

REVIEW

1. How are precipitation, evaporation, and ground water involved in the water cycle?
2. Draw a simple diagram of the nitrogen cycle. Make sure you include how animals get nitrogen.
3. **Analyzing Relationships** How is decomposition related to the carbon cycle?

TOPIC: The Water Cycle, The Nitrogen Cycle
GO TO: www.scilinks.org
sciLINKS NUMBER: HSTL455, HSTL465

Answers to Review

1. In the water cycle, water falls to Earth's surface as precipitation. Some water reenters the atmosphere by evaporation and by transpiration from plants. Water condenses and falls again as precipitation.
2. Student diagrams should resemble **Figure 3**.
3. Living organisms consume and store carbon. With the help of bacteria, dead organisms decompose and release that stored carbon back into the environment.

---

4) Close

Answer to MATHBREAK
78 gal = 295.6 L
78 gal = 295,620 cm³

Quiz

1. Compare the water cycle with the carbon cycle. What do both have in common? (Answers will vary but should reflect an understanding that, in each cycle, matter is used over and over again.)
2. Describe the role of living things in the carbon cycle. (Answers will vary. Students should note that plants obtain carbon from the atmosphere, using it to make sugars during photosynthesis. When animals eat the plants, they take in the carbon. Both plants and animals release carbon dioxide during cellular respiration.)

ALTERNATIVE ASSESSMENT

Concept Mapping Have students create a concept map using the new terms from this section, the section title, and any necessary additional terms. Remind them to include apt connecting words and phrases to link the terms of the map.

Answer to APPLY

The letter to Isabel should state that sulfur dioxide could be carried by wind to the area near the lake. Water vapor from evaporation, transpiration, and rain mix with sulfur dioxide and can form sulfuric acid. When the acidic water falls as rain or other precipitation, it can contaminate the lake and harm or kill trees.

Section 1 • The Cycles of Matter 461

SECTION 2

Focus
Ecological Succession
In this section, students are introduced to the development of communities by succession. Students will learn the difference between primary and secondary succession and the organisms characteristic of each. The gradual formation of a stable community is examined.

 Bellringer

Ask students to imagine that they have been hired to oversee the maintenance of a forest. Have them answer the following questions to describe how they would approach the task:

- How would you evaluate the health of the forest?
- What actions would you take to keep the forest healthy?
- What factors might pose a threat to the health of the forest? How would you prevent them from causing harm?

1 Motivate

DISCUSSION
Tell students that in deciduous forest areas, hardwood trees sometimes replace the pines that come before them. Point out that pine forests provide valuable resources. Encourage students to speculate about how forest managers might prevent hardwood trees from replacing pine trees in managed forests.

A Passel o' Pioneers PG 752

Section 2

Terms to Learn
succession
pioneer species

What You'll Do
- Define *succession*.
- Contrast primary and secondary succession.

Ecological Succession

Imagine you have a time machine that can take you back to the summer of 1988. If you had visited Yellowstone National Park during that year, you would have found large areas of the park burned to the ground. When the fires were put out, a layer of gray ash blanketed the forest floor. Most of the trees were dead, although many of them were still standing, as shown in **Figure 4**.

Figure 4 Parts of Yellowstone National Park burned in 1988.

Regrowth of a Forest

The following spring, the appearance of the "dead" forest began to change. In **Figure 5,** you can see that some of the dead trees are beginning to fall over, and small, green plants have begun to grow in large numbers. National Park foresters report that the number and kinds of plants growing in the recovering area have increased each year since the fire.

A gradual development of a community over time, such as the regrowth of the burned areas of Yellowstone National Park, is called **succession.** Succession takes place in all communities, not just those affected by disturbances such as forest fires. Succession occurs through predictable stages over time, as described on the following pages.

Figure 5 In the spring of 1989, regrowth was evident in the burned parts of Yellowstone National Park.

Directed Reading Worksheet 19 Section 2

TOPIC: Succession
GO TO: www.scilinks.org
*sci*LINKS NUMBER: HSTL470

462 Chapter 19 • Cycles in Nature

Primary Succession

Sometimes a small community of living things starts to live in an area that did not previously contain any plants or other organisms. There is no soil in this area, usually just bare rock. Over a very long time, a series of organisms live and die on the rock, and the rock is slowly transformed into soil. This process is called *primary succession.*

1 A slowly retreating glacier exposes bare rock where nothing lives, and primary succession begins.

2 Most primary succession begins with lichens. Acids from the lichens begin breaking the rocks into small particles. These particles mix with the remains of dead lichens to start forming soil. Because lichens are the first organisms to live on the rock, they are called **pioneer species.**

3 After many years, the soil is deep enough for mosses to grow. The mosses eventually replace the lichens. Other tiny organisms, such as insects, also make their home among the lichens and mosses. When they die, their remains add to the soil.

4 Over time, the soil layer thickens, and the moss community is replaced by ferns. The ferns in turn may be replaced by grasses and wildflowers. Once there is sufficient soil, shrubs and small trees come into the area.

5 After hundreds or even thousands of years, the soil may be deep enough to support a forest.

2) Teach

MATH and MORE

Point out to students that as succession proceeds, the number of species in an ecosystem may at first increase. Ask them to imagine the following scenario:

A pioneer plant makes the environment more hospitable for three other organisms. Each of these in turn allows for three additional organisms.

Challenge students to determine how many steps it would take to establish at least 100 species. *(One hundred species would be established in the fourth step from the pioneer plant.)*

CONNECT TO EARTH SCIENCE

Encourage students to use library or Internet resources to investigate where glaciers are located on Earth today as well as how they move. Have students use their findings to predict where new life communities are to appear in the future. Encourage them to share and discuss their predictions with one another.

Teaching Transparency 70
"Primary Succession"

Multicultural CONNECTION

Lichens contain unique chemicals that help them survive in harsh environments and deter bacteria, herbivores, and competing fungi from consuming the lichens. These chemicals have been used by cultures around the world, mostly as dyes and medicines. Scottish tweedmakers, Navaho weavers, and Chilkat Indians have historically used lichen for dyes. The wolf lichen was used by the Blackfoot tribe as a medicinal tea and to cure skin problems. Chemicals from the lichen genus *Usnea* have been extracted by cultures throughout the world to make medicinal teas and healing creams.

Section 2 • Ecological Succession

3 Extend

MEETING INDIVIDUAL NEEDS

Learners Having Difficulty
Help students distinguish between primary succession and secondary succession by preparing a table comparing the two. Encourage them to focus on how each type of succession starts, as well as on the organisms that are characteristic of each. Then have students write a sentence summarizing the differences between the two forms of succession. **Sheltered English**

GOING FURTHER

Writing Point out to students that while forest ecosystems are often used as an example to illustrate the process of succession, the process actually occurs in every ecosystem. Encourage students to select an ecosystem to investigate. Have them use library or Internet resources to find out how succession occurs in their chosen ecosystem. Have them prepare brief reports and encourage them to share their findings with the class.

Answer to Self-Check

The main difference between primary and secondary succession is that primary succession begins with the formation of soil. Secondary succession begins on preexisting soil, such as when an existing community is disrupted by a natural disaster or by farming. Pioneer species in primary succession are usually lichens, which begin the formation of soil. Pioneer species in secondary succession are usually seed plants, which germinate and take root in the soil.

Teaching Transparency 71
"Secondary Succession"

Secondary Succession

Sometimes an existing community is destroyed by a natural disaster, such as fire or flood. Or, a farmer might stop growing crops in an area that had been cleared. In either case, if soil is left intact, the original plant community may regrow through a series of stages called *secondary succession*.

1 The first year after a farmer stops growing crops, or after some other major disturbance, many weeds grow. Crabgrass is usually the most common weed during the first year.

2 By the second year, new weedy plants appear. Their seeds may have blown into the field by the wind, or insects may have carried them. One of the most common weeds during the second year is horseweed.

3 In 5 to 15 years, small pine trees may start growing among the weeds. The pines continue to grow, and, after about 100 years, a forest may form.

4 As older pines die, they may be replaced by hardwoods if the climate can support them.

✓ Self-Check

Describe the differences between primary succession and secondary succession. (See page 782 to check your answer.)

Homework

Have students identify each of the following examples as either primary succession (p) or secondary succession (s).

- a rock face exposed by a scraping glacier **(p)**
- a new shoreline in Hawaii created after a lava flow **(p)**
- a once forested area cleared by a tornado **(s)**
- an island appearing from the activity of an undersea volcano **(p)**
- the lawn of an abandoned farmhouse **(s)**

Chapter 19 • Cycles in Nature

Where Does It All End? In the early stages of succession only a few species grow in an area. These species grow fast and make many seeds that scatter easily. Because there are only a few species, they are open to invasion by other, longer-lasting species, disease, and other disturbances. In later stages of succession there are usually many more species present. Because of this, there are more pathways available to absorb disturbances. For example, in a mature forest, many species will survive an invasion by insects if these insects prefer to eat only one species of plant.

Eventually, if an area experiences no fires or other disturbances, it will reach a more or less stable stage. Communities change over time even though they are considered to be stable. A stable community may not always be a hardwood forest. Look at **Figure 6**. Why might a stable hardwood forest not develop there? The answer is that the area does not have the kind of climate that will support a stable hardwood forest. The climate in this area supports a desert community.

Activity

Make a diorama of the stages of primary succession. Use boxes, craft supplies, rocks, twigs, and other materials that you can find at home or at school. You can use one large box showing all the stages of primary succession, or you might use several small boxes, each showing a single stage of primary succession. Label and explain each stage.

TRY at HOME

Figure 6 *This is how a stable community in the Sonoran Desert in Arizona looks in spring.*

REVIEW

1. Define *succession*.
2. Describe succession in an abandoned field.
3. **Applying Concepts** Explain why soil formation is always the first stage of primary succession. Does soil formation stop when trees begin to grow? Why or why not?

internet connect

SC/**LINKS**
NSTA

TOPIC: Succession
GO TO: www.scilinks.org
*sci***LINKS NUMBER:** HSTL470

Chapter Highlights

VOCABULARY DEFINITIONS

SECTION 1

precipitation water in liquid or solid form that moves from the atmosphere to the land and ocean

evaporation the change from a liquid to a vapor

ground water water that is found in underground caverns or in porous rock below the Earth's surface

decomposition the breakdown of dead materials into water and carbon dioxide

combustion the burning of fuel; specifically, the process in which fuel combines with oxygen in a chemical change that produces thermal energy

Chapter Highlights

SECTION 1

Vocabulary
precipitation (p. 458)
evaporation (p. 459)
ground water (p. 459)
decomposition (p. 460)
combustion (p. 460)

Section Notes
- Materials used by living things continually cycle through ecosystems.
- In the water cycle, water moves through the ocean, atmosphere, land, and living things.
- Precipitation, evaporation, transpiration, and condensation are important processes in the water cycle.
- Water that falls is held in soil or porous rocks as ground water.
- Photosynthesis, respiration, decomposition, and combustion are important steps in the carbon cycle.
- Carbon enters plants from the nonliving environment as carbon dioxide.
- The process of changing nitrogen gas into forms that plants can use is called nitrogen fixation.

Labs
Nitrogen Needs (p. 750)

✓ Skills Check

Math Concepts

SAVING WATER Flushing the toilet accounts for almost half the water a person uses in a day. Some toilets use up to 6 gal per flush. More-efficient toilets use about 1.5 gal per flush. How many liters of water can you save using a more-efficient toilet if you flush five times a day?

$$6 \text{ gal} - 1.5 \text{ gal} = 4.5 \text{ gal}$$
$$4.5 \text{ gal} \times 5 \text{ flushes} = 22.5 \text{ gal}$$
$$1 \text{ gal is equal to } 3.79 \text{ L}$$
$$3.79 \text{ L} \times 22.5 \text{ gal} = 85.275 \text{ L of water saved}$$

Visual Understanding

SOIL FORMATION The formation of soil is part of every stage of primary succession. Look at page 463 to review how soil forms.

466

Lab and Activity Highlights

Nitrogen Needs PG 750

A Passel o' Pioneers PG 752

Datasheets for LabBook
(blackline masters for these labs)

466 Chapter 19 • Cycles in Nature

SECTION 2

Vocabulary
- succession *(p. 462)*
- pioneer species *(p. 463)*

Section Notes
- Ecological succession is the gradual development of communities over time. Often a series of stages is observed during succession.
- Primary succession occurs in an area that was not previously inhabited by living things; no soil is present.
- Secondary succession occurs in an area where an earlier community was disturbed by fire, landslides, floods, or plowing for crops; soil is present.

Labs
A Passel o' Pioneers *(p. 752)*

VOCABULARY DEFINITIONS, continued

SECTION 2

succession (ecological succession) the gradual regrowth or development of a community of organisms over time

pioneer species the first organisms to grow in an area undergoing ecological succession; usually lichens in primary succession and weedy plants in secondary succession

 Vocabulary Review Worksheet 19

 Blackline masters of these Chapter Highlights can be found in the **Study Guide**.

internet connect

GO TO: go.hrw.com

Visit the **HRW** Web site for a variety of learning tools related to this chapter. Just type in the keyword:

KEYWORD: HSTCYC

GO TO: www.scilinks.org

Visit the **National Science Teachers Association** on-line Web site for Internet resources related to this chapter. Just type in the *sci*LINKS number for more information about the topic:

TOPIC	*sci*LINKS NUMBER
The Water Cycle	HSTL455
The Carbon Cycle	HSTL460
The Nitrogen Cycle	HSTL465
Succession	HSTL470

467

Lab and Activity Highlights

LabBank

 Long-Term Projects & Research Ideas,
Smokey Says . . . , Project 19

Chapter 19 • Chapter Highlights   **467**

Chapter Review Answers

USING VOCABULARY

1. precipitation
2. carbon
3. carbon cycle
4. primary succession
5. secondary succession

UNDERSTANDING CONCEPTS

Multiple Choice

6. c
7. a
8. d
9. b
10. d
11. a
12. c
13. d

Short Answer

14. All water on Earth is part of the water cycle, even the water frozen in snow. This frozen water cycles by evaporation or by becoming liquid flowing into the ocean.
15. A scientist would probably require a life span of more than 100 years to observe all of the stages of secondary succession on an abandoned field. Scientists can photograph changes for future scientists to observe. We know about past changes in certain areas because of historical records of disturbances. One scientist is able to observe several stages but not all stages.

Chapter Review

USING VOCABULARY

To complete the following sentences, choose the correct term from each pair of terms listed below:

1. During __?__, water moves from the atmosphere to the land and ocean. (*evaporation* or *precipitation*)
2. All biological molecules contain __?__. (*carbon* or *carbon dioxide*)
3. The combustion of coal, oil, and natural gas is part of the __?__. (*nitrogen cycle* or *carbon cycle*)
4. The development of a community on bare, exposed rock is an example of __?__. (*primary succession* or *secondary succession*)
5. The recovery of Yellowstone National Park following the fires of 1988 is an example of __?__. (*primary succession* or *secondary succession*)

UNDERSTANDING CONCEPTS

Multiple Choice

6. Water changes from a liquid to a vapor during
   a. precipitation.
   b. respiration.
   c. evaporation.
   d. decomposition.

7. The process of burning fuel, such as oil and coal, is
   a. combustion.
   b. respiration.
   c. decomposition.
   d. photosynthesis.

8. One of the most common plants in a recently abandoned farm field is
   a. horseweed.
   b. young pine trees.
   c. young oak and hickory trees.
   d. crabgrass.

9. Which of the following statements about ground water is true?
   a. It stays underground for a few days.
   b. It is stored in underground caverns or porous rock.
   c. It is salty like ocean water.
   d. It never reenters the water cycle.

10. Which of the following processes produces carbon dioxide?
    a. decomposition
    b. respiration
    c. combustion
    d. all of the above

11. During nitrogen fixation, nitrogen gas is converted into a form that __?__ can use.
    a. plants
    b. animals
    c. fungi
    d. all of the above

12. Bacteria are essential to
    a. combustion.
    b. photosynthesis.
    c. nitrogen fixation.
    d. evaporation.

13. The pioneer species on bare rock are usually
    a. ferns.
    b. pine trees.
    c. mosses.
    d. lichens.

Short Answer

14. Is snow a part of the water cycle? Why or why not?
15. Can a single scientist observe all of the stages of secondary succession on an abandoned field? Explain your answer.

468 Chapter 19 • Cycles in Nature

Concept Mapping Transparency 19

Blackline masters of this Chapter Review can be found in the **Study Guide**.

Concept Mapping

16. Use the following terms to create a concept map: abandoned farmland, lichens, bare rock, soil formation, horseweed, succession, forest fire, primary succession, secondary succession, pioneer species.

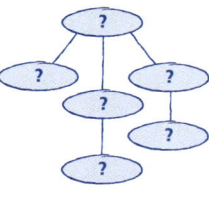

CRITICAL THINKING AND PROBLEM SOLVING

Write one or two sentences to answer the following questions:

17. Explain how living things would be affected if the water on our planet suddenly stopped evaporating.

18. How would living things be affected if there were no decomposers to cycle carbon back to the atmosphere?

19. Explain how living things would be affected if the bacteria responsible for nitrogen fixation were to die.

20. Describe why a lawn doesn't go through succession.

MATH IN SCIENCE

In 1996, 129 million metric tons of fertilizer were used world-wide. Use the following information to answer items 21, 22, and 23: 1996 world population = 5.7 billion; 1 metric ton = 1,000 kg; 1 kg = 2.2 lb.

21. Write out the number corresponding to 5.7 billion. How many zeros are in the number?

22. How many kilograms of fertilizer were used per person in 1996?

23. How many pounds of fertilizer were used per person?

INTERPRETING GRAPHICS

The following graph illustrates the concentration of carbon dioxide in the atmosphere from 1958 to 1994:

Carbon Dioxide in the Atmosphere

[Graph: Carbon dioxide concentration (in parts per million) vs. Years, showing values from about 315 ppm in 1958 rising to about 358 ppm in 1994]

24. What was the concentration of carbon dioxide in parts per million in 1960? in 1994?

25. Is the concentration of carbon dioxide increasing or decreasing? Explain.

26. If the level of carbon dioxide continues to change at the same steady rate, what might be the concentration in 2010?

Reading Check-up

Take a minute to review your answers to the Pre-Reading Questions found at the bottom of page 456. Have your answers changed? If necessary, revise your answers based on what you have learned since you began this chapter.

Concept Mapping

16. An answer to this exercise can be found at the end of this book.

CRITICAL THINKING AND PROBLEM SOLVING

17. Sample answer: The Earth would soon be covered with water. The water cycle would be interrupted. It would no longer rain. Land organisms would probably go extinct.

18. Sample answer: The carbon cycle would be interrupted. Dead organisms would remain unchanged. Plants could not perform photosynthesis, and there would be no food.

19. Sample answer: If the nitrogen cycle were interrupted, nitrogen might be locked in the atmosphere in an unusable form. Plants might not be able to obtain enough of the nitrogen needed for life. Living things might eventually run out of food.

20. A lawn does not go through the stages of succession because it is constantly being "disturbed" by mowing and other activities.

MATH IN SCIENCE

21. 5,700,000,000; 8 zeros
22. 22.6 kg
23. 22.6 kg × 2.2 lb = 49.7 lb

INTERPRETING GRAPHICS

24. 1960, 317 ppm; 1994, 359 ppm
25. Carbon dioxide in the atmosphere is showing a steady increase.
26. By extending the graph and drawing a straight line from coordinates (58, 315) through (92, 356), the concentration would be 378 ppm in 2010. There are other ways to estimate this figure.

ACROSS THE SCIENCES
Weather from Fire

Background
For massive plumes of flame and hot air to develop, a fire must have a wealth of fuel, such as very dry twigs and leaves, and there must be warm, rising currents of air. But wind is by far the most important factor in the creation of plumes. A strong crosswind can inhibit the formation of a plume.

Forest fires break out thousands of times a year around the world. In 1985, a total of 81,622 fires destroyed about 1.2 million hectares of forest in the United States alone. In 1871, fires in Wisconsin and Michigan killed 1,500 people and burned 1.7 million hectares of land—an area more than five times the size of Rhode Island!

Another type of interaction between fires and the weather occurs in confined regions, such as valleys. As the upper atmosphere cools after sunset, a temperature inversion occurs, causing warm air to be trapped beneath the denser, cooler air above it. A fire in the valley gradually uses up all of the oxygen in the trapped warm air and eventually starts to smolder, heating up the unburned material surrounding it. When the sun rises and heats the overlying cool air, the oxygen-depleted air escapes and is replaced with oxygen-rich air. The result can be an explosively renewed forest fire.

WEIRD SCIENCE
WEATHER FROM FIRE

As a wildfire burned near Santa Barbara, California, in 1993, huge storm clouds formed overhead. Fiery whirlwinds danced over the ground. The fire not only was destroying everything in its path—it was also creating its own weather!

Fire-Made Clouds
Hot air rising from a forest fire can create tremendous updrafts. Surrounding air rushes in underneath the rising air, stirring up columns of ash, smoke, hot air, and noxious gases. Cool, dry air normally sinks down and stops these columns from developing any further. But if the conditions are just right, a surprising thing happens.

If the upper atmosphere contains warm, moist air, the moisture begins to condense on the ash and smoke. These droplets can develop into clouds. As the clouds grow, the droplets begin to collide and combine until they are heavy enough to fall as rain. The result is an isolated rainstorm, complete with thunder and lightning.

Whirlwinds of Fire
Forest fires can also create whirlwinds. These small, tornado-like funnels can be extremely dangerous. Whirlwinds are similar to dust devils that dance across desert sands. Their circular motion is created by an updraft that is forced to turn after striking an obstacle, such as a cliff or hill. Whirlwinds move across the ground at 8–11 km/h, sometimes growing up to 120 m high and 15 m wide.

Most whirlwinds last less than a minute, but they can cause some big problems. Firefighters caught in the path of whirlwinds have been severely injured and even killed. Also, if a whirlwind is hot enough, it can suck up tremendous amounts of air. The resulting updraft can pull burning debris up through the whirlwind. In some cases, burning trees have been uprooted and shot into the air. When the debris lands, it often starts new fires hundreds of meters away.

▲ *This towering whirlwind is lifting burning debris from a forest fire in Idaho.*

Think About It
▶ Fires are a natural part of the growth of a forest. For example, some tree seeds are released only under the extreme temperatures of a fire. Some scientists believe that forest fires should be allowed to run their natural course. Others argue that forest fires cause too much damage and should be extinguished as soon as possible. Do some additional research and then decide what you think.

Answer to Think About It
Answers will vary. Make sure students support their answer with clear and logical reasoning. Students will probably agree that an approach between the two extremes, in which the largest fires are contained but smaller ones are allowed to burn themselves out, is best. Students may be interested to know that the policy of the U.S. Park Service is to let most naturally caused fires burn unless they pose a threat to human life or property.

EYE ON THE ENVIRONMENT

The Mysterious Dead Zone

Every summer, millions of fish are killed in an area in the Gulf of Mexico called a hypoxia region. Hypoxia is a condition that occurs when there is an unusually low level of oxygen in the water. The area is often referred to as the "dead zone" because almost every fish and crustacean in the area dies. In 1995, this zone covered more than 18,000 km², and almost 1 million fish were killed in a single week. Why does this happen? Can it be stopped?

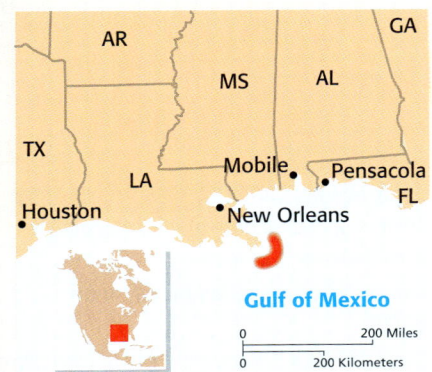

▲ The Gulf of Mexico hypoxia region grew to the size of New Jersey in 1995.

What's Going On?

When the oxygen levels in water drop drastically, the fish die. In the Gulf of Mexico hypoxia region, the water contains unusually high amounts of nitrogen and phosphorus. The nitrogen and phosphorus act as nutrients for the growth of algae. When the algae die, their bodies are decomposed by a large number of oxygen-consuming bacteria.

Scientists think the excess nitrogen and phosphate is from animal waste and runoff from farms and developments. The pollution may also be caused in part by the overfertilization of crops. The extra fertilizer runs into the rivers, which empty into the Gulf Coast.

Ecosystem Models Suggest Solutions

All along the Gulf Coast, marine scientists and Earth scientists are trying to find methods to reduce or eliminate the "dead zone." They have made physical and computer models of the Mississippi River ecosystem that have accurately predicted the data that has since been collected. The scientists have changed the models to see what happens. For example, wetlands are one of nature's best filters. They take up a lot of the chemicals present in water. Scientists predict that adding wetlands to the Mississippi River watershed could reduce the chemicals reaching the Gulf of Mexico. Although scientific models support this hypothesis, they also indicate that adding wetlands to the Mississippi River watershed would not be enough to completely prevent the "dead zone."

Find Some Solutions

▶ The Gulf of Mexico is not the only place that suffers from a hypoxia region. Research other bodies of water to find out how widespread the problem is. Have scientists found ways to reduce or eliminate the hypoxia regions elsewhere? How could this information be used to improve the situation in the Gulf of Mexico?

Chapter Organizer

CHAPTER ORGANIZATION	TIME MINUTES	OBJECTIVES	LABS, INVESTIGATIONS, AND DEMONSTRATIONS
Chapter Opener pp. 472–473	45	National Standards: SAI 1, ST 2, SPSP 2, 5, HNS 1, LS 3a, 3c, 4a, 4b	**Start-Up Activity** A Mini-Ecosystem, p. 473
Section 1 Land Ecosystems	90	▶ Define *biome*. ▶ Describe three different forest biomes. ▶ Distinguish between temperate grasslands and savannas. ▶ Describe the importance of permafrost to the arctic tundra biome. UCP 4, 5, SAI 1, SPSP 2, 3, LS 1a, 3a, 3c, 3d, 4b–4d, 5a, 5b; LabBook UCP 2, SAI 1, ST 1	**Design Your Own,** Life in the Desert, p. 754 BASIC **Datasheets for LabBook,** Life in the Desert, Datasheet 42 BASIC
Section 2 Marine Ecosystems	90	▶ Distinguish between the different areas of the ocean. ▶ Explain the importance of plankton in marine ecosystems. ▶ Describe coral reefs and intertidal areas. UCP 2, 3, SAI 2, SPSP 2, HNS 2, LS 1a, 3d, 4a–4d; LabBook SAI 1, LS 1a	**Interactive Explorations CD-ROM,** Sea Sick GENERAL A **Worksheet** is also available in the **Interactive Explorations Teacher's Edition.** **Design Your Own,** Discovering Mini-Ecosystems, p. 755 GENERAL **Datasheets for LabBook,** Discovering Mini-Ecosystems, Datasheet 43 GENERAL
Section 3 Freshwater Ecosystems	90	▶ List the characteristics of rivers and streams. ▶ Describe the littoral zone of a pond. ▶ Distinguish between two types of wetlands. UCP 2–4, LS 1a, 3d, 4a–4d; LabBook SAI 1, SPSP 2	**QuickLab,** Pond Food Connections, p. 487 GENERAL **Skill Builder,** Too Much of a Good Thing? p. 756 GENERAL **Datasheets for LabBook,** Too Much of a Good Thing? Datasheet 44 GENERAL **EcoLabs & Field Activities,** Biome Adventure Travel, EcoLab 7 GENERAL **Long-Term Projects & Research Ideas,** Project 20 ADVANCED

See page T20 for a complete correlation of this book with the

NATIONAL SCIENCE EDUCATION STANDARDS.

TECHNOLOGY RESOURCES

 Guided Reading Audio CD English or Spanish, Chapter 20

 One-Stop Planner CD-ROM with Test Generator

 Interactive Explorations CD-ROM CD 2, Exploration 2, Sea Sick

 CNN. Multicultural Connections, Saving Pacific Sea Horses, Segment 9

Eye on the Environment, Biosphere Pioneers, Segment 6

Chapter 20 • The Earth's Ecosystems

CLASSROOM WORKSHEETS, TRANSPARENCIES, AND RESOURCES	SCIENCE INTEGRATION AND CONNECTIONS	REVIEW AND ASSESSMENT
Directed Reading Worksheet 20 BASIC **Science Puzzlers, Twisters & Teasers,** Worksheet 20 ADVANCED	**Careers:** Ecologist—Alfonso Alonso-Mejía, p. 495 GENERAL	
Transparency 72, Earth's Biomes **Directed Reading Worksheet 20,** Section 1 BASIC **Math Skills for Science Worksheet 2,** Subtraction Review GENERAL **Transparency 73,** Coniferous Forest Biome **Transparency 74,** A Tropical Rain Forest Biome **Math Skills for Science Worksheet 37,** Rain-Forest Math GENERAL **Transparency 177,** An Example of the Rain Shadow Effect **Reinforcement Worksheet 20,** Know Your Biomes BASIC	**Cross-Disciplinary Focus,** p. 475 in ATE GENERAL **Math and More,** p. 476 in ATE GENERAL **Real-World Connection,** p. 477 in ATE ADVANCED **Multicultural Connection,** p. 477 in ATE **Multicultural Connection,** p. 478 in ATE **Connect to Earth Science,** p. 478 in ATE **MathBreak,** Rainfall, p. 480 GENERAL	**Self-Check,** p. 479 **Review,** p. 480 GENERAL **Quiz,** p. 480 in ATE GENERAL **Alternative Assessment,** p. 480 in ATE GENERAL
Directed Reading Worksheet 20, Section 2 BASIC **Science Skills Worksheet 1,** Being Flexible GENERAL	**Multicultural Connection,** p. 482 in ATE **Real-World Connection,** p. 483 in ATE **Connect to Physical Science,** p. 484 in ATE **Across the Sciences:** Ocean Vents, p. 494 GENERAL	**Self-Check,** p. 484 **Review,** p. 485 GENERAL **Quiz,** p. 485 in ATE GENERAL **Alternative Assessment,** p. 485 in ATE GENERAL
Transparency 75, River Features **Directed Reading Worksheet 20,** Section 3 BASIC **Transparency 76,** Lake Zones **Critical Thinking Worksheet 20,** Risky Development? ADVANCED	**Math and More,** p. 487 in ATE BASIC **Connect to Physical Science,** p. 487 in ATE ADVANCED **Apply,** p. 488 GENERAL	**Review,** p. 489 GENERAL **Quiz,** p. 489 in ATE GENERAL **Alternative Assessment,** p. 489 in ATE GENERAL

 Holt, Rinehart and Winston On-line Resources
go.hrw.com
For worksheets and other teaching aids related to this chapter, visit the HRW Web site and type in the keyword: **HSTECO**

 National Science Teachers Association
www.scilinks.org
Encourage students to use the *sci*LINKS numbers listed in the internet connect boxes to access information and resources on the **NSTA** Web site.

END-OF-CHAPTER REVIEW AND ASSESSMENT

Chapter Review in Study Guide
Vocabulary and Notes in Study Guide
Chapter Tests with Performance-Based Assessment, Chapter 20 Test
Chapter Tests with Performance-Based Assessment, Performance-Based Assessment 20
Concept Mapping Transparency 20

Chapter 20 • Chapter Organizer   **471B**

Chapter Resources & Worksheets

Visual Resources

TEACHING TRANSPARENCIES

TEACHING TRANSPARENCIES

CONCEPT MAPPING TRANSPARENCY

Meeting Individual Needs

DIRECTED READING

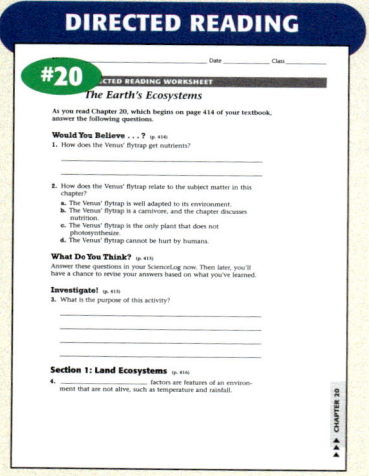

REINFORCEMENT & VOCABULARY REVIEW

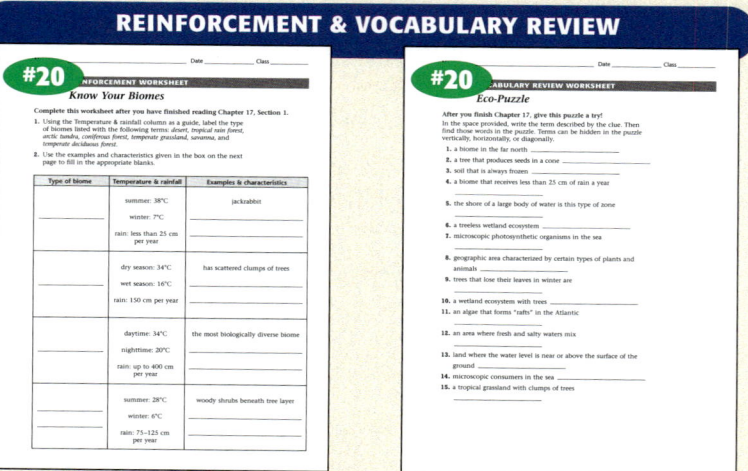

SCIENCE PUZZLERS, TWISTERS & TEASERS

Chapter 20 • The Earth's Ecosystems

Chapter 20 • The Earth's Ecosystems

Review & Assessment

STUDY GUIDE
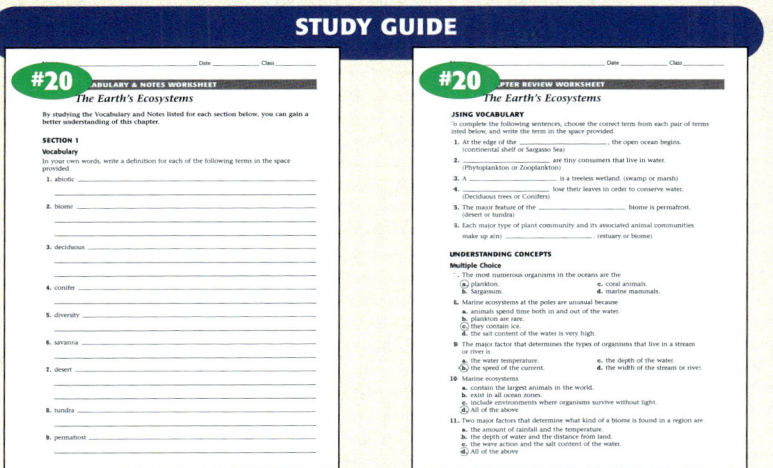

CHAPTER TESTS WITH PERFORMANCE-BASED ASSESSMENT

Lab Worksheets

ECOLABS & FIELD ACTIVITIES
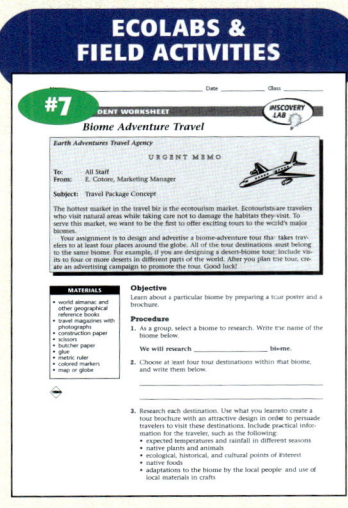

LONG-TERM PROJECTS & RESEARCH IDEAS

DATASHEETS FOR LABBOOK
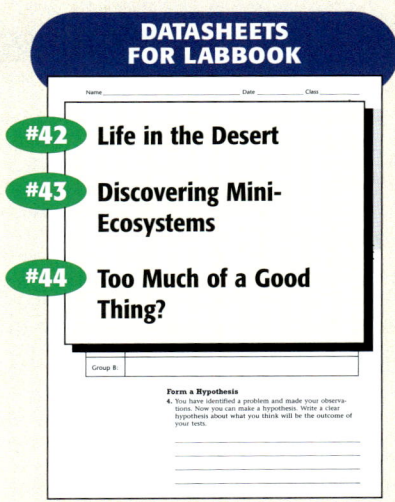

- #42 Life in the Desert
- #43 Discovering Mini-Ecosystems
- #44 Too Much of a Good Thing?

Applications & Extensions

CRITICAL THINKING & PROBLEM SOLVING

MULTICULTURAL CONNECTIONS
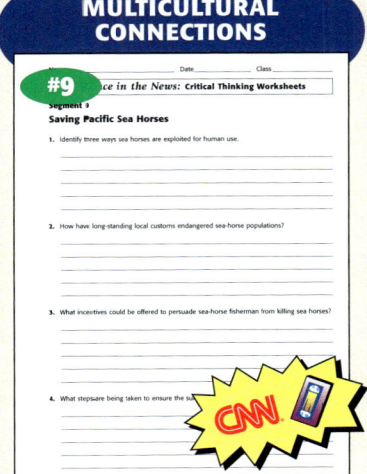

EYE ON THE ENVIRONMENT

INTERACTIVE EXPLORATIONS
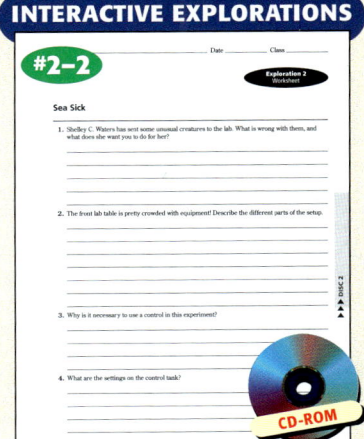

Chapter 20 • Chapter Resources & Worksheets 471D

Chapter Background

SECTION 1

Land Ecosystems

▶ The Biosphere
All parts of Earth that are inhabited by organisms make up the biosphere. The biosphere is a relatively thin layer encircling the planet.

- The Earth can be divided into gas, liquid, and solid parts. The atmosphere is the layer of gases that envelops Earth. The hydrosphere is the portion of Earth's surface that is covered by water. The lithosphere is the soil and rock on Earth's surface.

- Life began in the water and remained in the water for billions of years before migrating to land. Today, aquatic habitats continue to dominate the biosphere.

▶ Biotic and Abiotic Factors
An ecosystem encompasses all of the biotic and abiotic factors in a particular area. Ecology is the scientific study of how organisms interact with one another and with the abiotic factors in their environment. Biotic factors include all organisms—plants, animals, protists, fungi, and bacteria. Abiotic factors include temperature, water, sunlight, wind, rocks, soil, and nutrients.

- Almost all ecosystems are driven by energy from the sun. Thus, the amount of sunlight a region receives has a large effect on the number of producers and consumers that can be supported in the ecosystem.

- Just as chemical reactions are limited by a limiting reagent, populations within ecosystems are limited by limiting factors. The lack of any single abiotic factor can prevent the survival of a population. Limiting factors include the amount of light received, water, temperature, and nutrients in the soil.

IS THAT A FACT!
- One hectare of fertile soil can contain 6 million earthworms and over 2 billion bacteria!

▶ Tropical Rain Forests
Students may think that tropical rain forests are jungles. In fact, a jungle is an area of dense undergrowth within a tropical rain forest. Jungles grow in areas that receive large amounts of sunlight and are near rivers.

- The plants in a tropical rain forest can be divided into three layers. Some trees tower above the forest's canopy. A continuous layer of vegetation forms the upper canopy. Below the canopy is a mid-tree level and a shrubby understory. On the ground are grasses and ferns.

IS THAT A FACT!
- Tropical rain forests cover about 7 percent of Earth's surface. This small portion of Earth contains more than 50 percent of the species that inhabit the planet.

▶ Tundra
A tundra area may receive as little rainfall as a desert. But the soil in a tundra region remains wet due to permafrost, low temperatures, and the low rate of evaporation.

IS THAT A FACT!
- Antarctica has been accumulating ice for more than 25 million years. It contains about 90 percent of Earth's ice and about 70 percent of Earth's fresh water.

- In summer, when ice begins to melt and break off into icebergs, Antarctica shrinks. In winter, Antarctica expands to twice its summer size.

471E Chapter 20 • The Earth's Ecosystems

Chapter 20 • The Earth's Ecosystems

SECTION 2

Marine Ecosystems

▶ **Oceans**
The Earth's oceans include the Pacific Ocean, the Atlantic Ocean, the Indian Ocean, and the Arctic Ocean. Although these oceans have different names, they are all connected.

- Because the oceans are all connected, a change in one marine environment may eventually affect other marine environments.

IS THAT A FACT!

- Along Australia's northeastern coast is the Great Barrier Reef. It is the largest and most diverse reef system in the world.

▶ **Underwater Exploration**
New technology for remote-operated vehicles has broadened scientists' ability to explore ocean depths. Using vehicles equipped with cameras, mechanical arms, and remote sensors, scientists have discovered a watery new world that includes deep-sea animals, underwater volcanoes, thermal vents, and entire ecosystems that do not directly depend on light or photosynthesis for energy.

- Early diving suits consisted of a hard helmet, a canvas-and-rubber tunic, leather boots with lead-weighted soles, and additional 13 kg weights. Each boot weighed about 8 kg. Such a suit was called a standard diving suit and was invented by Augustus Siebe in the 1830s.

SECTION 3

Freshwater Ecosystems

▶ **Wetlands**
In the past, wetlands were underappreciated and even considered wastelands. People viewed wetlands as places that should be drained or filled in so that the land could be used for housing or other urban development. Because wetlands are a breeding ground for mosquitoes, they were also considered a health problem.

- Two types of wetlands are introduced in the text: the marsh and the swamp. However, there are many different kinds of wetlands, including inland freshwater wetlands, coastal freshwater wetlands, and coastal saltwater wetlands.

IS THAT A FACT!

- About 6 percent of Earth's surface is wetlands.

- Wetland areas in the contiguous United States have shrunk from 81 million hectares to 38 million hectares and continue to shrink each year.

- Ninety percent of the wetlands in the San Francisco Bay area have disappeared. In their place are airports, houses, industrial parks, and landfills.

For background information about teaching strategies and issues, refer to the *Professional Reference for Teachers.*

CHAPTER 20

The Earth's Ecosystems

Pre-Reading Questions

Students may not know the answers to these questions before reading the chapter, so accept any reasonable response.

Suggested Answers

1. There are many differences between a rain forest and a desert, such as water availability and average temperature.
2. Water in a lake is the endpoint of a river. The river may begin as snowmelt or may come from a spring, and it may grow from more and more tributaries joining it as it flows downstream to form a lake.
3. The open ocean contains few species, but some of them are quite large, such as the marine mammals. A swamp has many more species per unit area than does the open ocean.

Directed Reading Worksheet 20

Science Puzzlers, Twisters & Teasers Worksheet 20

Guided Reading Audio CD
English or Spanish, Chapter 20

CHAPTER 20

The Earth's Ecosystems

Sections

1. **Land Ecosystems**..... 474
   MathBreak 480
2. **Marine Ecosystems**... 481
   Internet Connect 485
3. **Freshwater Ecosystems**........ 486
   QuickLab 487
   Apply 488
   Internet Connect 489

Chapter Review 492
Feature Articles...... 494, 495
LabBook 754–757

Pre-Reading Questions

1. What are the main differences between a desert and a rain forest?
2. Where does the water in a lake come from?
3. Which has more species of plants and animals—the open ocean or a swamp? Why?

In Living Color

A flurry of orange fish swim through the sun-dappled crevices of a tropical coral reef. All around them other life exists—sea fans, eels, anemones, and living corals. Could this scene exist anywhere else? It could... if the place was underwater in a warm climate close to the shore. In this chapter, you will learn how the nonliving environment affects organisms and how they are adapted to where they live.

---

internet connect

HRW On-line Resources
go.hrw.com
For worksheets and other teaching aids, visit the HRW Web site and type in the keyword: **HSTECO**

sciLINKS NSTA
www.scilinks.com
Use the sciLINKS numbers at the end of each chapter for additional resources on the **NSTA** Web site.

www.cnnfyi.com
Visit the CNN Web site for current events coverage and classroom resources.

START-UP Activity

A MINI-ECOSYSTEM

In this activity, you will build and observe a miniature ecosystem.

Procedure

1. Place a layer of **gravel** in the bottom of a **large widemouth jar** or **2 L bottle** with the top cut off. Add a layer of **soil**.

2. Add a variety of **small plants** that require similar growing conditions. Choose plants that will not grow too quickly.

3. Spray **water** inside the jar to moisten the soil.

4. Cover the jar, and place it in indirect light. Describe the appearance of your ecosystem in your ScienceLog.

5. Observe your mini-ecosystem every week. Spray it with water to keep the soil moist. Record all of your observations.

Analysis

6. List all of the nonliving factors in the ecosystem you have created.

7. How is your mini-ecosystem similar to a real ecosystem? How is it different?

START-UP Activity

A MINI-ECOSYSTEM

MATERIALS
FOR EACH GROUP: • gravel • large widemouthed jar or 2 L soda bottle • soil • plants • water

Safety Caution

You may want to have students wear disposable gloves while handling plants. Plants and plant parts should be kept away from the face and eyes because they may scratch or otherwise cause irritation. Have students wash their hands after handling plants, seeds, and soil.

Answers to START-UP Activity

6. Answers to this question should include most of the nonliving factors one would find in nature, such as water, temperature, light, and air.

7. Answers will vary. In general, each mini-ecosystem is similar to a real ecosystem in that it contains various abiotic and biotic factors that interact and affect each other. It will differ from a real ecosystem in that it is enclosed, it was artificially assembled, and it did not naturally evolve to its present state.

Chapter 20 • The Earth's Ecosystems

SECTION 1

Focus

Land Ecosystems

This section introduces the concept of a *biome* and describes several land biomes. Students learn about different types of forest and grassland as well as about deserts and tundra.

Bellringer

Write the following on the board:

cactus	tropical rain forest
tree frog	polar ice
pine tree	desert
polar bear	mountain

Ask students to match the plant or animal in the first column with the environment in the second column where it would most likely be found. They should record their answers in their ScienceLog. **(Answer: cactus, desert; tree frog, tropical rain forest; pine tree, mountain; polar bear, polar ice)**

1) Motivate

ACTIVITY

Describing Ecosystems Pair up students and have them brainstorm about what distinguishes different land ecosystems—what makes a forest a forest, a desert a desert, and so on. Have the pairs write down their ideas and read them to the class. Write each idea on the board, and place marks next to an idea each time students suggest it. Tell students that they will learn how accurate this popularity contest was as they read this section.

Section 1

Land Ecosystems

Terms to Learn

abiotic
biome
savanna
desert
tundra
permafrost

What You'll Do

- Define *biome*.
- Describe three different forest biomes.
- Distinguish between temperate grasslands and savannas.
- Describe the importance of permafrost to the arctic tundra biome.

Imagine that you are planning a camping trip. You go to a travel agency, where you find a virtual-reality machine that can let you experience different places before you go. You put on the virtual-reality gear, and suddenly you are transported. At first your eyes hurt from the bright sunlight. The wind that hits your face is very hot and very dry. As your eyes grow accustomed to the light, you see a large cactus to your right and some small, bushy plants in the distance. A startled jack rabbit runs across the dry, dusty ground. A lizard basks on a rock. Where are you?

You may not be able to pinpoint your exact location, but you probably realize that you are in a desert. That's because most deserts are hot and dry. These **abiotic**, or nonliving, factors influence the types of plants and animals that live in the area.

The Earth's Biomes

A desert is one of Earth's biomes. A **biome** is a geographic area characterized by certain types of plant and animal communities. A biome contains a number of smaller but related ecosystems. For example, a tropical rain forest is a biome that contains river ecosystems, treetop ecosystems, forest-floor ecosystems, and many others. A biome is not a specific place. For example, a desert biome does not refer to a particular desert. A desert biome refers to any and all desert ecosystems on Earth. The major biomes of Earth are shown in **Figure 1**.

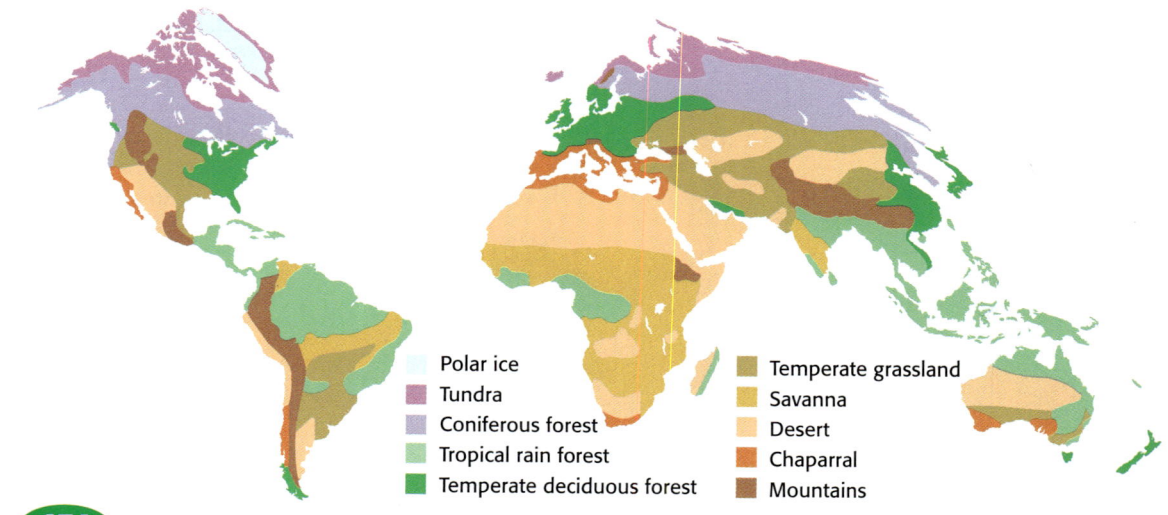

Figure 1 Rainfall and temperature are the main factors that determine what biome is found in a region. What kind of biome do you live in?

- Polar ice
- Tundra
- Coniferous forest
- Tropical rain forest
- Temperate deciduous forest
- Temperate grassland
- Savanna
- Desert
- Chaparral
- Mountains

Have students examine the map of biomes in **Figure 1.** Ask, "Does every continent include a biome?" and "Where on the map is Antarctica?" Encourage students to speculate about why Antarctica does not include a biome. Ask them what kinds of plants and animals live in Antarctica. **(Students may suggest seals, algae, bacteria, etc.)**

Point out that most organisms that inhabit Antarctica are part of an aquatic biome rather than a land biome.

474 Chapter 20 • The Earth's Ecosystems

Forests

Forest biomes develop where there is enough rain and where the temperature is not too hot in the summer or too cold in the winter. There are three main types of forest biomes—temperate deciduous forests, coniferous forests, and tropical rain forests. The type of forest that develops depends on the area's temperature and rainfall.

Temperate Deciduous Forests In the autumn, have you seen leaves that change colors and fall from trees? If so, you have seen trees that are *deciduous,* which comes from a Latin word meaning "to fall off." By losing their leaves in the fall, deciduous trees are able to conserve water during the winter. **Figure 2** shows a temperate deciduous forest. Most of these forests contain several different species of trees. Temperate deciduous forests also support a variety of animals, such as bears and woodpeckers.

Temperate Deciduous Forest
Average Yearly Rainfall
75–125 cm (29.5–49 in.)
Average Temperatures
Summer: 28°C (82.4°F)
Winter: 6°C (42.8°F)

Figure 2 *In a temperate deciduous forest, mammals, birds, and reptiles thrive on the abundance of leaves, seeds, nuts, and insects.*

In forests, plant growth occurs in layers. The leafy tops of the trees reach high above the forest floor, where they receive full sunlight.

Beneath the tree layer, woody shrubs and bushes catch the light that filters through the trees.

Grasses, herbs, ferns, and mosses are scattered across the forest floor. Most of the flowering plants bloom, and produce seeds in early spring, before the trees grow new leaves.

MISCONCEPTION ALERT

Students may think that the terms *biome* and *ecosystem* are synonyms. In fact, these terms are not used consistently even by scientists. You may want to point out that both biomes and ecosystems are determined by abiotic and biotic factors. However, a biome is a broader category than an ecosystem. A biome may contain several similar yet separate ecosystems.

2) Teach

MEETING INDIVIDUAL NEEDS

Learners Having Difficulty
Provide students with a concrete framework within which they can place the information in this chapter. First write the following hierarchy on the chalkboard or on a transparency:

biosphere, biome, ecosystem

Then provide groups of students with an assortment of craft materials and shoe boxes. Have students make a diorama of each level of the hierarchy. Display the dioramas around the room, and refer to the levels they represent as you teach this chapter.
Sheltered English

CROSS-DISCIPLINARY FOCUS

Language Arts Have students look up the words *temperate* and *tropical*. Then tell them to look again at the map in **Figure 1** and to examine a globe. Ask students to define a *temperate ecosystem* and a *tropical ecosystem*. Have them refer to and, if necessary, refine their definitions as they read on.

 Teaching Transparency 72 "Earth's Biomes"

 Directed Reading Worksheet 20 Section 1

TOPIC: Forests
GO TO: www.scilinks.org
*sci*LINKS NUMBER: HSTL480

Section 1 • Land Ecosystems **475**

2) Teach, continued

COOPERATIVE LEARNING

Provide small groups of students with an almanac and graph paper. Ask groups to find and graph the average monthly rainfall and average monthly temperature for their area. Some students can measure the temperature and rainfall for 1 month. If this is not practical, encourage students to obtain this information from a local weather station or news broadcast. Have other students graph and present the data. You may also want to have students compare the climate of the region in which you live with that of the different biomes discussed in this lesson.

MATH and MORE

Have students compare the amount of rainfall in each of the forest biomes described. Then ask:

Which forest biome receives the most rain? **(tropical rain forest)**

How much more rain does this biome usually receive than the forest biome that receives the least amount of rain? **(The coniferous forest receives a minimum of 35 cm per year. The tropical rain forest receives as much as 400 cm per year. The difference is 365 cm.)**

 Math Skills Worksheet 2 "Subtraction Review"

 Teaching Transparency 73 "Coniferous Forest Biome"

Coniferous Forest

Average Yearly Rainfall
35–75 cm (14–29.5 in.)

Average Temperatures
Summer: 14°C (57.2°F)
Winter: −10°C (14°F)

Figure 3 *Many animals that live in a coniferous forest survive the harsh winters by hibernating or migrating to a warmer climate for the winter.*

Coniferous Forests Coniferous forests do not change very much from summer to winter. They are found in areas with long, cold winters. These forests consist mainly of *evergreen* trees, which are trees that don't lose their leaves and stay green all year. Most of these trees are *conifers*, which means that they produce seeds in cones. You have probably seen a pine cone. Pine trees are common conifers.

Most conifers can also be identified by their compact, needlelike leaves. These leaves, or needles, have a thick waxy coating that prevents them from drying out and being damaged during winter.

Figure 3 shows a coniferous forest and some of the animals that live there. Notice that not many large plants grow beneath the conifers, partly because very little light reaches the ground.

A coniferous forest is home to many insects and to birds that eat them.

Herbivores that live in the coniferous forest include moose, deer, porcupines, and chipmunks.

These conifer leaves are adapted to conserve water.

Carnivores of the coniferous forest include foxes and lynxes.

476

IS THAT A FACT!

The coniferous forest is also known as a boreal forest or a taiga. More of Earth's land can be categorized under this biome than under any other biome.

476 Chapter 20 • The Earth's Ecosystems

Tropical Rain Forests The tropical rain forest has more biological *diversity* than any other biome on the planet; that is, it contains more species than any other biome. As many as 100 species of trees may live in an area about one-fourth the size of a football field. Although some animals live on the ground, the treetops, or *canopy*, are the preferred living site. A huge variety of animals live in the canopy. If you counted the birds in the canopy of a rain forest, you would find up to 1,400 species! **Figure 4** shows some of the diversity of the tropical rain forest biome.

Most of the nutrients in a tropical rain forest biome are in the vegetation. The topsoil is actually very thin and poor in nutrients. Farmers who cut down the forest to grow crops must move their crops to freshly cleared land after about 2 years.

Tropical Rain Forest

Average Yearly Rainfall
Up to 400 cm (157.5 in.)

Average Temperatures
Daytime: 34°C (93°F)
Nighttime: 20°C (68°F)

USING THE FIGURE

Have students compare **Figure 2**, **Figure 3**, and **Figure 4** and locate each type of forest on the biome map in **Figure 1**. Ask students to focus on the different kinds of trees and animals in each forest picture. Encourage students to relate the different plants and animals to the differences in temperature and rainfall for each area. **Sheltered English**

REAL-WORLD CONNECTION

Biological diversity is an important natural resource. Provide the following example for students. About 40 percent of prescription drugs sold in the United States are derivatives of chemicals found in wild plants. Thousands more helpful plant compounds probably lie undiscovered in forests throughout the world. However, less than 1 percent of known plants have been tested for their medicinal effectiveness. Have students discuss the consequences of losing tropical rain forests given these considerations.

Figure 4 A Tropical Rain Forest Biome

Trees of various heights form a continuous green roof, called the canopy, that may extend 60 m above the forest floor.

Woody vines climb the tree trunks to reach sunlight.

Little light reaches the ground. Low-growing plants of the rain forest don't require a lot of light.

 Teaching Transparency 67
"A Tropical Rain Forest Biome"

 Math Skills Worksheet 37
"Rain-Forest Math"

Multicultural CONNECTION

Scientist and Cornell University professor Eloy Rodriguez studies the chemical properties of plants to discover potentially useful compounds. One aspect of his research is learning about plants used by native cultures of tropical Africa, Asia, and Latin America. Using local knowledge may help Rodriguez find plant compounds with medicinal properties.

Section 1 • Land Ecosystems **477**

2) Teach, continued

Temperate grasslands provide almost ideal growing conditions for grain crops. For this reason, few temperate grasslands remain today. In fact, these areas, such as the American Midwest and Ukraine, are sometimes called the breadbaskets of the world because their temperate grasslands became farmland for grain crops.

USING SCIENCE FICTION

Encourage students to read "The Greatest Asset," by Isaac Asimov. It can be found in the *Holt Anthology of Science Fiction*.

CONNECT TO EARTH SCIENCE

Mountains can influence the climate of surrounding land, resulting in very different ecosystems existing in close proximity. Use the following Teaching Transparency to illustrate how a mountain can affect climate.

Teaching Transparency 177
"An Example of the Rain Shadow Effect"

LINK TO EARTH SCIENCE

TOPIC: Grasslands
GO TO: www.scilinks.org
sciLINKS NUMBER: HSTL485

Grasslands

Plains, steppes, savannas, prairies, pampas—these are names for regions where grasses are the major type of vegetation. Grasslands are found between forests and deserts. They exist on every continent. Most grasslands are flat or have gently rolling hills.

Temperate Grassland
Average Yearly Rainfall
25–75 cm (10–29.5 in.)

Average Temperatures
Summer: 30°C (86°F)
Winter: 0°C (32°F)

Temperate Grasslands Temperate grassland vegetation is mainly grasses mixed with a variety of flowering plants. There are few trees because fires prevent the growth of most slow-growing plants. The world's temperate grasslands support small, seed-eating mammals, such as prairie dogs and mice, and large herbivores, such as the bison of North America, shown in **Figure 5**.

Figure 5 Bison roamed the temperate grasslands in great herds before they were hunted nearly to extinction.

Savanna
Average Yearly Rainfall
150 cm (59 in.)

Average Temperatures
Dry season: 34°C (93°F)
Wet season: 16°C (61°F)

Savanna The **savanna** is a tropical grassland with scattered clumps of trees. During the dry season, the grasses die back, but the deep roots survive even through months of drought. During the wet season, the savanna may receive as much as 150 cm of rain. The savannas of Africa are inhabited by the most abundant and diverse groups of large herbivores in the world, like those shown in **Figure 6**. These include elephants, giraffes, zebras, gazelles, and wildebeests.

Figure 6 Carnivores, such as lions and leopards, prey on herbivores, such as these zebras and wildebeests. Hyenas and vultures usually "clean up" after the carnivores.

During the dry season, savanna plants survive as roots. Ask students to discuss how herds of large herbivores might survive when the vegetation dries up.

(Students may suggest that the animals migrate to an area where food and water are more plentiful. Point out that migration is a behavioral adaptation for survival.)

> ✓ **Self-Check**
>
> Use the map in Figure 1 to compare the locations of deciduous and coniferous forests. Explain the differences in location between the two biomes. (See page 782 to check your answers.)

How do animals survive in the heat of the desert? Quite nicely, thank you! See how on page 754 of your LabBook.

Deserts

Deserts are hot, dry regions that support a variety of plants and animals. In a desert, most of the water that falls to the ground evaporates. Organisms have evolved in specialized ways to survive extreme temperatures with very little water. For example, plants grow far apart to reduce competition for the limited water supply. Some plants have shallow, widespread roots that absorb water quickly during a storm, while others may have very deep roots that reach ground water.

Animals also have adaptations for survival in the desert. Most are active only at night, when temperatures are cooler. Tortoises eat the flowers or leaves of plants and store the water under their shells for months. **Figure 7** shows how some desert plants and animals survive in the heat with little water.

Desert
Average Yearly Rainfall Less than 25 cm (10 in.)
Average Temperatures Summer: 38°C (100°F) Winter: 7°C (45°F)

Figure 7 *There are many well-adapted residents of the desert biome.*

- Cactuses store water in their stems and roots.
- Deep-rooted plants can reach down to ground water as deep as 30 m.
- Some flowering plants bloom, bear seeds, and die within a few weeks after a heavy rain.
- Jack rabbits' huge ears help them get rid of body heat.
- Kangaroo rats never need to drink. They recycle water from the foods they eat.

Q: Which biome was Elvis's favorite?

A: Grassland

Answer to Self-Check

Deciduous forests tend to exist in mid-latitude, or temperate, regions, while coniferous forests tend to exist in colder, higher latitudes, closer to the poles.

3) Extend

"Life in the Desert"

GROUP ACTIVITY

Divide the class into groups of four or five students. Then have students play "What Biome Am I?" Each student chooses a land biome. Then students take turns describing their biome to the other members of the group. Members of the group try to guess which biome the student is describing. The successful guesser takes the next turn. Allow students to play the game until everyone has had a chance to describe a biome.

USING THE FIGURE

Have students locate the chaparral biome in **Figure 1.** Tell them that the chaparral has a Mediterranean climate. Ask students to hypothesize about what characteristics the chaparral might have. (It is located on the coast and has a mild climate.)

Explain that many chaparral plants are adapted to survive drought and fire. The plants grow back after fires from small bits of surviving tissue.

 Reinforcement Worksheet 20 "Know Your Biomes"

Section 1 • Land Ecosystems

4) Close

Quiz

Ask students whether these statements are true or false. Have students correct any false statements they find.

1. Permafrost thaws only briefly in the summer. (false)
2. Tropical rain forests have more species than any other biome. (true)
3. Grasslands have very poor soil. (false)

ALTERNATIVE ASSESSMENT

 Poster Project Have students choose one biome and make a poster to display facts and images of the biome. Posters should provide information about the uniqueness of the biome, indicate where the biome can be found, and compare the biome with other biomes.

Answer to MATHBREAK

Students should make a bar graph that includes the following data:

(The rainfall values below represent the top end of the average for each biome.)

Biome	Avg. yearly rainfall
Temp. deciduous forest	125 cm
Coniferous forest	75 cm
Tropical rain forest	400 cm
Temperate grassland	75 cm
Savanna	150 cm
Desert	25 cm
Tundra	50 cm

Tundra
Average Yearly Rainfall
30–50 cm (12–20 in.)

Average Temperatures
Summer: 12°C (53.6°F)
Winter: −26°C (−14°F)

Tundra

In the far north and on the tops of high mountains, the climate is so cold that no trees can grow. A biome called the **tundra** is found there.

Arctic Tundra

The major feature of the arctic tundra is permafrost. During the short growing season, only the surface of the soil thaws. The soil below the surface, the **permafrost,** stays frozen all the time. Even though there is little rainfall, water is not in short supply. That's because the permafrost prevents the rain that does fall from draining, and the surface soil stays wet and soggy. Lakes and ponds are common.

The layer of unfrozen soil above the permafrost is too shallow for deep-rooted plants to survive. Grasses, sedges, rushes, and small woody shrubs are common. A layer of mosses and lichens grows beneath these plants on the surface of the ground. Tundra animals, like the one shown in **Figure 8,** include large mammals such as caribous, musk oxen, and wolves, as well as smaller animals, such as lemmings, shrews, and hares. Migratory birds are abundant in summer.

Figure 8 *Caribou migrate to more plentiful grazing grounds during long, cold winters in the tundra.*

Alpine Tundra

Another tundra biome is found above the tree line of very high mountains. These areas, called alpine tundra, receive a lot of sunlight and precipitation, mostly in the form of snow.

MATH BREAK

Rainfall
In 1 year, what is the difference in the rainfall amounts in a coniferous forest, a tropical rain forest, a desert, and a savanna? To compare, create a bar graph of the rainfall in each biome from the data given in this section.

REVIEW

1. How is the climate of temperate grasslands different from that of savannas?
2. Describe three ways that plants and animals are adapted to the desert climate.
3. Where are most of the nutrients in a tropical rain forest?
4. **Applying Concepts** Could arctic tundra accurately be called a frozen desert? Why or why not?

Answers to Review

1. Savannas are hotter than temperate grasslands and receive twice as much annual rainfall. Also rain falls only during the wet season in the savanna.
2. Answers will vary. Sample responses: being active only at night, developing structures that help them get rid of heat, and recycling consumed water.
3. Most of the biome's nutrients are contained in the vegetation.
4. Accept any logical, well-argued response. Sample answer: Yes, it would be accurate because very little rain falls and because liquid water is only available during the short growing season.

480 Chapter 20 • The Earth's Ecosystems

Section 2

Marine Ecosystems

Terms to Learn

marine
phytoplankton
zooplankton
estuary

What You'll Do

- Distinguish between the different areas of the ocean.
- Explain the importance of plankton in marine ecosystems.
- Describe coral reefs and intertidal areas.

They cover almost three-quarters of Earth's surface and contain almost 97 percent of Earth's water supply. The largest animals on Earth inhabit them, along with billions of microscopic creatures, shown in **Figure 9.** Their habitats range from dark, cold, high-pressure depths to warm sandy beaches; from icy polar waters to rocky coastlines. They are oceans and seas. Wherever these salty waters are found, marine ecosystems are found. A **marine** ecosystem is one that is based on salty water. This abiotic factor has a strong influence on the ecosystems of oceans and seas.

Abiotic Factors Rule

Like terrestrial biomes, marine biomes are shaped by abiotic factors. These include temperature, the amount of sunlight penetrating the water, the distance from land, and the depth of the water. These abiotic factors are used to define certain areas of the ocean. As with terrestrial biomes, marine biomes occur all over Earth and can contain many ecosystems.

Sunny Waters Water absorbs light, so sunlight can penetrate only about 200 m below the ocean's surface, even in the clearest water. As you know, most producers use photosynthesis to make their own food. Because photosynthesis requires light, most producers are found only where light penetrates. The most abundant producers in the ocean are called **phytoplankton.** Phytoplankton are microscopic photosynthetic organisms that float near the surface of the water. Using the energy of sunlight, these organisms make their own food just as plants that live on land do. **Zooplankton** are the consumers that feed on the phytoplankton. They are small animals that, along with phytoplankton, form the base of the oceans' feeding relationships.

Figure 9 Marine ecosystems support a broad diversity of life, from the humpback whale to microscopic phytoplankton.

Directed Reading Worksheet 20 Section 2

IS THAT A FACT!

The sea kelp known as *Macrocystis* can grow as much as 60 m in one growing season. This organism can grow lengthwise faster than any other organism known! It grows along the coast of California.

SECTION 2

Focus

Marine Ecosystems

This section introduces different areas of the ocean as ecosystems. Students learn about the importance of abiotic factors in structuring oceanic life zones. The section also focuses on several unique marine ecosystems, including coral reefs and estuaries.

Bellringer

Write the following on the board or an overhead projector, and have students record their answers in their ScienceLog:

How much of the Earth's surface is covered by ocean?

$\frac{1}{4}$ $\frac{1}{2}$ $\frac{3}{4}$ $\frac{9}{10}$

(Answer: $\frac{3}{4}$)

What percentage of the Earth's water supply is found in the oceans?

37%   67%   77%   97%

(Answer: 97 percent)

1) Motivate

DISCUSSION

Oceans Students may not realize how connected their lives are to the oceans, especially if they live far from the coast. Ask students:

If all marine life were to die off, how would you be affected? How would others be affected?

Possible answers include: less food available (fish, crab, shrimp, shellfish, etc.), less oxygen in atmosphere (phytoplankton produce one-third to one-half of our oxygen), increased global warming (all that phytoplankton uses up huge amounts of carbon dioxide, the chief greenhouse gas), loss of jobs, and less enjoyment from ocean wildlife.

Section 2 • Marine Ecosystems   **481**

2 Teach

The Japanese and Koreans use brown seaweed to make *kombu* soup. Red algae is wrapped around rice to make a kind of sushi called *nori* rolls. Seaweed does provide iodine and other minerals, but it is used mostly for the taste and texture it adds to foods.

READING STRATEGY

Prediction Guide Before students read this page, ask them the following questions:

1. How do organisms in the dark depths of the ocean find food?
2. What kinds of organisms live on the ocean floor?
3. What is a thermal vent?
4. Which part of the ocean receives the most sunlight?

Have students evaluate their responses after they read about ocean biomes.

Discovering Mini-Ecosystems

Wonderful Watery Biomes

Unique and beautiful biomes exist in every part of oceans and seas. These biomes are home to many unusually adapted organisms. The major ocean areas and some of the organisms that live in them are shown below in **Figure 10**.

A **The Intertidal Zone** The intertidal zone is the area where the ocean meets the land. This area is above water part of the day, when the tide is out, and is often battered by waves. Mud flats, rocky shores, and sandy beaches are all in the intertidal area.

B **The Neritic Zone** Moving seaward, the water becomes gradually deeper toward the edge of the continental shelf. Water in this area is generally less than 200 m deep and usually receives a lot of sunlight. Diverse and colorful coral reefs exist in the waters over the continental shelf, where the water is warm, clear, and sunny.

Figure 10 *The life in a particular area depends on how much light the area receives, how far the area is from land, and how far the area is beneath the surface.*

A Sea grasses, periwinkle snails, and herons are common in a mud flat intertidal area. You will find sea stars and anemones on the rocky shores, while clams, crabs, and the shells of snails and conchs are common on the sandy beaches.

B Although phytoplankton are the major producers in this area, seaweeds are common too. Animals, such as sea turtles and dolphins, live in the area over the continental shelf. Corals, sponges, and colorful fish contribute to the vivid seascape.

Food is scarce in the benthic zone. As a result, organic matter that filters down from the surface is often quickly consumed. Scavengers, including relatives of the freshwater shrimp, will voraciously attack a dead fish that falls to the deep ocean floor, reducing the carcass to bones in just a few hours!

C **The Oceanic Zone** Past the continental shelf, the sea floor drops sharply. This is the deep water of the open ocean. To a depth of about 200 m, phytoplankton are the producers. At greater depths, no light penetrates, so most organisms obtain energy by consuming organic material that falls from the surface.

D **The Benthic Zone** The benthic zone is the sea floor. It extends from the upper edge of the intertidal zone to the bottom of the deepest ocean waters. Organisms that live on the deep-sea floor obtain food mostly by consuming material that filters from above. Some bacteria are *chemosynthetic*, which means they use chemicals in the water near thermal vents to make food. A thermal vent is a place on the ocean floor where heat escapes through a crack in the Earth's crust.

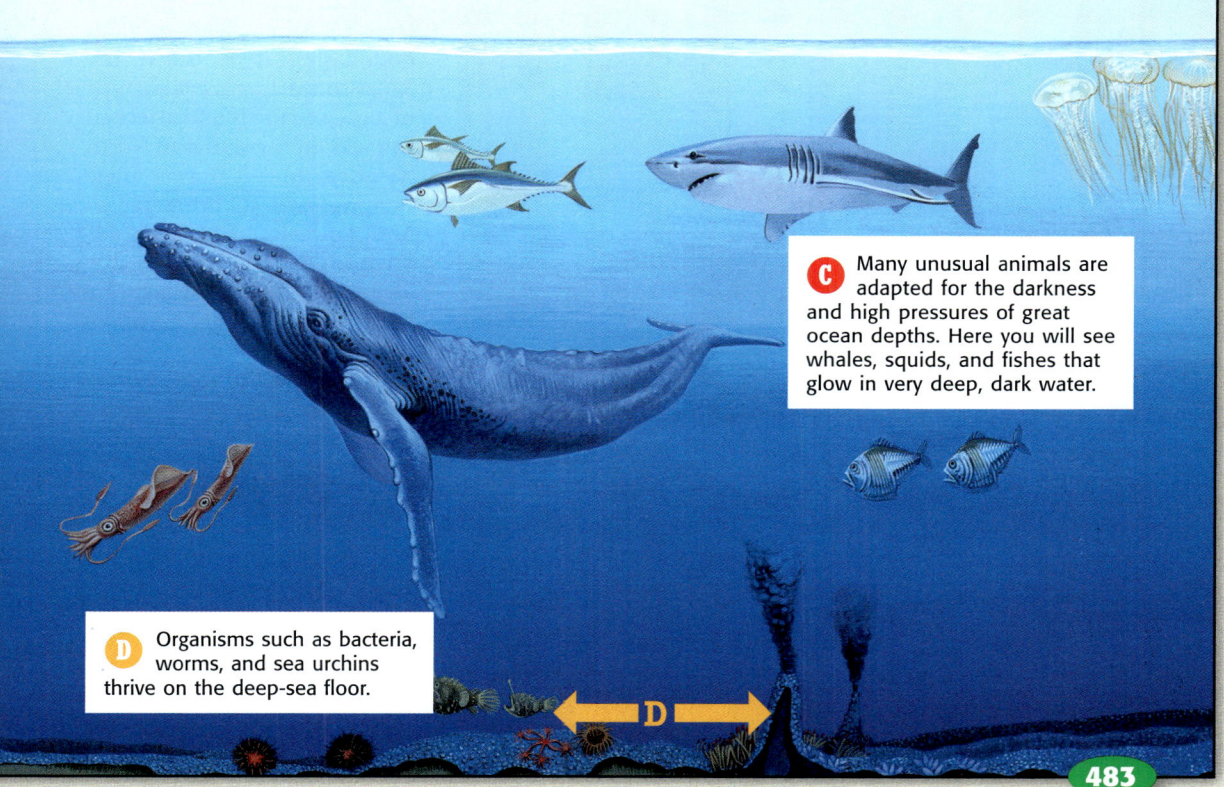

C Many unusual animals are adapted for the darkness and high pressures of great ocean depths. Here you will see whales, squids, and fishes that glow in very deep, dark water.

D Organisms such as bacteria, worms, and sea urchins thrive on the deep-sea floor.

IS THAT A FACT!
Deep-sea-vent ecosystems depend on neither sunlight nor photosynthesis for energy.

TOPIC: Marine Ecosystems
GO TO: www.scilinks.org
sciLINKS NUMBER: HSTL490

USING THE FIGURE
Help students understand the information in **Figure 10** by pointing out how it is organized. Make sure that students see the sequence of lettered captions above and below the water and link these letters to the letters indicating parts of the ocean. Also point out how the depth of the ocean changes as you go farther away from the shore. You may also want to help students interpret the magnified views of the ocean floor. Point out that these bubbles represent an up-close view of the area they extend from. **Sheltered English**

REAL-WORLD CONNECTION
A diving condition called the bends, or decompression sickness, can occur when a person dives very deeply, ascends to the surface too quickly, or stays under the water for a long period of time. The condition occurs when gas forms bubbles in body tissues. Divers suffering from decompression sickness need treatment in a pressure-decompression chamber.

CONNECT TO PHYSICAL SCIENCE
Red, orange, and yellow wavelengths of light striking the surface of the water are absorbed first. Blue and green wavelengths can penetrate the water more deeply. Thus, producers capable of using blue and green wavelengths of light for photosynthesis can live at greater depths.

Section 2 • Marine Ecosystems   **483**

3) Extend

GROUP ACTIVITY

Have students research and draw a coral reef. Provide reference materials, a large piece of butcher paper, markers, and map pencils. Encourage pairs of students to choose an organism that is part of a coral reef, to research the organism, and to draw it. Then students should place their organism in its habitat on the butcher-paper coral reef. You may want to have one coral reef per class or have all classes contribute to one large coral reef. **Sheltered English**

GOING FURTHER

Writing Tell students that Texas has started a "Rigs for Reefs" program in which oil companies are asked to donate oil-drilling equipment that would otherwise be dragged to shore and sold for scrap metal. The old oil rigs and platforms are easily converted to artificial reefs. Have students pretend that they are a member of the board for this or a similar organization. Then have students write a persuasive letter to an oil company explaining why the company should participate in the program.

Science Skills Worksheet 1 "Being Flexible"

Interactive Explorations CD-ROM "Sea Sick"

Figure 11 A coral reef is one of the most biologically diverse biomes.

Figure 12 The Sargasso Sea is a spawning place for eels and home to a rich diversity of organisms.

A Closer Look

Marine environments provide most of the water for Earth's rainfall through evaporation and precipitation. Ocean temperatures and currents have major effects on world climates and wind patterns. Humans harvest enormous amounts of food from the oceans and dump enormous amounts of waste into them. Let's take a closer look at some of the special environments that thrive in the ocean.

Coral Reefs In some sunny tropical waters, the sea floor contains coral reefs. Corals live in a close relationship with single-celled algae. The algae produce organic nutrients through photosynthesis. This provides food for the coral. The coral provide a place in the sun for the algae to live. The foundation of the reef is formed from coral skeletons that have built up over thousands of years. Coral reefs, like the one in **Figure 11,** are home to many marine species, including a large variety of brightly colored fish and organisms such as sponges and sea urchins.

The Sargasso Sea In the middle of the Atlantic Ocean is a large ecosystem with no land boundaries. It is called the Sargasso Sea. *Sargassum* is a type of algae usually found attached to rocks on the shores of North America, but it forms huge floating rafts in the Sargasso Sea. Animals adapted to this environment live among the algae. Most of the animals are the same color as the *Sargassum*. Some even look like it! Why do you think this is so? Can you find a fish in **Figure 12**?

> ### ✓ Self-Check
> 1. List three factors that characterize marine biomes.
> 2. Describe one way organisms obtain energy at great depths in the open ocean.
>
> (See page 782 to check your answers.)

Answers to Self-Check

1. Answers include: The amount of sunlight penetrating the water, the distance from land, the depth of the water, the salinity of the water, and the water's temperature.

2. There are several possible answers. Some organisms are adapted for catching prey at great depths; some feed on dead plankton and larger organisms that filter down from above; and some, such as the bacteria around thermal vents, make food from chemicals in the water.

Polar Ice The Arctic Ocean and the open waters surrounding Antarctica make up a very unusual marine biome—one that includes ice!

The icy waters are rich in nutrients from the surrounding landmasses. These nutrients support large populations of plankton. The plankton in turn support a great diversity of fish, birds, and mammals, as shown in **Figure 13.**

Figure 13 Sea lions and penguins are some of the animals found on the shores of Antarctica.

Estuaries An area where fresh water from streams and rivers spills into the ocean is called an **estuary.** The fresh water constantly mixes with the salt water of the sea. The amount of salt in an estuary changes frequently. When the tide rises, the salt content of the water rises. When the tide recedes, the water becomes fresher. The fresh water that spills into an estuary is rich in nutrients that are carried by water running off the land. Because estuaries are so nutrient-rich, they support large numbers of plankton, which provide food for many larger animals.

Intertidal Areas Intertidal areas include mudflats, sandy beaches, and rocky shores. Mud flats are home to many worms and crabs and the shorebirds that feed on them. Sandy beaches are also home to worms, clams, crabs, and plankton that live among the sand grains.

On rocky shores, organisms either have tough holdfasts or are able to cement themselves to a rock to avoid being swept away by crashing waves. **Figure 14** shows some of these animals.

Figure 14 Sea stars can wedge themselves under a rock to keep from being washed out to sea.

REVIEW

1. Explain how a coral reef is both living and dead.
2. Why do estuaries support such an abundance of life?
3. **Analyzing Relationships** Explain how the amount of light an area receives determines the kinds of organisms that live in the open ocean.

TOPIC: Marine Ecosystems
GO TO: www.scilinks.org
sciLINKS NUMBER: HSTL490

4) Close

Quiz
Ask students whether these statements are true or false. Have them rewrite any false statements so that they are true.

1. Although beautiful to look at, coral reefs are not very biologically diverse compared with other aquatic biomes. (false)
2. Ocean temperatures and currents have major effects on world climates. (true)
3. Phytoplankton are the most abundant consumers in the ocean. (false)
4. An intertidal area is one where the ocean meets the land. (true)
5. Marine ecosystems include those consisting of salt water or fresh water. (false)

ALTERNATIVE ASSESSMENT
Concept Mapping Have students create a concept map using the following terms:

marine biome, ocean, coral reef, polar ice, estuaries, intertidal areas, algae, phytoplankton, zooplankton

Remind students that they must supply words that show clear connections between the terms used in their maps.

Answers to Review

1. The foundation of a coral reef is made up of coral skeletons that have built up over thousands of years. Living coral animals are found at the outer edges of a reef near the surface.
2. Nutrients that run off from land into fresh water are deposited with the sediments in estuaries, making them nutrient-rich areas. They are also areas where juveniles can find shelter among the vegetation from rough water, tides, and predators.
3. Water absorbs light, so light does not travel into the deeper parts of the ocean. Therefore, the deeper an organism lives in the ocean, the less that organism is able to rely on the energy of sunlight. Phytoplankton, for example, must live in the photic zone.

SECTION 3

Focus

Freshwater Ecosystems

This section introduces freshwater ecosystems. Students learn about the characteristics of rivers, streams, and ponds. Students learn what happens to a pond as the seasons change. Students also learn how to distinguish between two types of wetlands.

🔔 Bellringer

Have students write an answer in their ScienceLog to the following question:

What are four different freshwater ecosystems? (Answers may include the following: stream, river, lake, marsh, pond, swamp, bog, creek.)

1 Motivate

ACTIVITY

Writing Have students write a short description of a personal freshwater experience (something they did at a stream, lake, or wetland). If they have not had such an experience, ask them to use their imagination, or perhaps a field trip can be arranged. Have the students focus on sensations they remember from the experience as well as on what they and others were doing at the time.

Section 3

Terms to Learn

tributary   wetland
littoral zone   marsh
open-water zone   swamp
deep-water zone

What You'll Do

- List the characteristics of rivers and streams.
- Describe the littoral zone of a pond.
- Distinguish between two types of wetlands.

Freshwater Ecosystems

A mountain brook bubbles over rocks down a mountainside. A mighty river thunders through a canyon. A small pond teems with life. A lake tosses boats during a heavy storm. A dense swamp echoes with the sounds of frogs and birds.

What do all of these places have in common? They are freshwater ecosystems. Like other ecosystems, freshwater ecosystems are characterized by abiotic factors, primarily the speed at which the water is moving.

Water on the Move

Brooks, streams, and rivers are ecosystems based on moving water. The water may begin flowing from melting ice or snow. Or it may come from a spring, where water flows up to the surface of the Earth. Each trickle or stream of water that joins a larger trickle or stream is a **tributary**.

Fast-Moving Water As more tributaries join a stream, the stream becomes larger and wider, forming a river. Aquatic plants line the edge of the river. Fishes live in the open waters. In the mud at the bottom, burrowers, such as freshwater clams and mussels, make their home.

Organisms that live in moving water require special adaptations to avoid being swept away with the current. Producers, such as algae and moss, cling to rocks. Consumers, such as insect larvae, live under rocks in the shallow water. Some consumers, such as tadpoles, use suction disks to hold themselves to rocks.

Slowing Down As a river grows wider and slower, it may *meander* back and forth across the landscape. Organic material and sediment may be deposited on the bottom, building *deltas*. Dragonflies, water striders, and other invertebrates live in and on slow-moving water. Eventually, the moving water empties into a lake or an ocean. **Figure 15** shows how a river can grow from melted snow.

Figure 15 This figure shows the features of a typical river. Where is the water moving rapidly? Where is it moving slowly?

Teaching Transparency 75
"River Features"

Directed Reading Worksheet 20 Section 3

IS THAT A FACT!

The Nile River in Africa is the longest river in the world, at 6,670 km long. The Amazon River in South America comes in a close second, at 6,275 km long.

486 Chapter 20 • The Earth's Ecosystems

Still Waters

Ponds and lakes have different ecosystems than streams and rivers have. Lake Superior, the largest lake in the world, has more in common with a small beaver pond than with a river. **Figure 16** shows a cross section of a typical lake. In looking at this illustration, you will notice that the lake has been divided into three zones. As you read on, you will learn about these zones and the ecosystems they contain.

Where Water Meets Land Look at Figure 16 again, and locate the **littoral zone.** It is the zone closest to the edge of the land. This zone has many inhabitants. Plants that grow in the water closest to the shore include cattails and rushes. Farther from the shore are floating leaf plants, such as water lilies. Still farther out are submerged pond weeds that grow beneath the surface of the water.

The plants of the littoral zone provide a home for small animals, such as snails, small arthropods, and insect larvae. Clams, worms, and other organisms burrow in the mud. Frogs, salamanders, water turtles, various kinds of fishes, and water snakes also live in this area.

Life at the Top Look again at Figure 16. This time locate the **open-water zone.** This zone extends from the littoral zone across the top of the water. The open-water zone only goes as deep as light can reach. This is the habitat of bass, blue gills, lake trout, and other fish. Phytoplankton are the most abundant photosynthetic organisms in the open-water zone of a lake.

Life at the Bottom Now look at Figure 16 and find the **deep-water zone.** This zone is below the open-water zone, where no light reaches. Catfish, carp, worms, insect larvae, crustaceans, fungi, and bacteria live here. These organisms feed on dead organic material that falls down from above.

QuickLab

Pond Food Connections

1. On **index cards**, write the names of the animals and plants that live in a typical freshwater pond or small lake. Write one type of organism on each card.
2. Use **yarn** or **string** to connect each organism to its food sources.
3. In your ScienceLog, describe the food relationships in the pond.

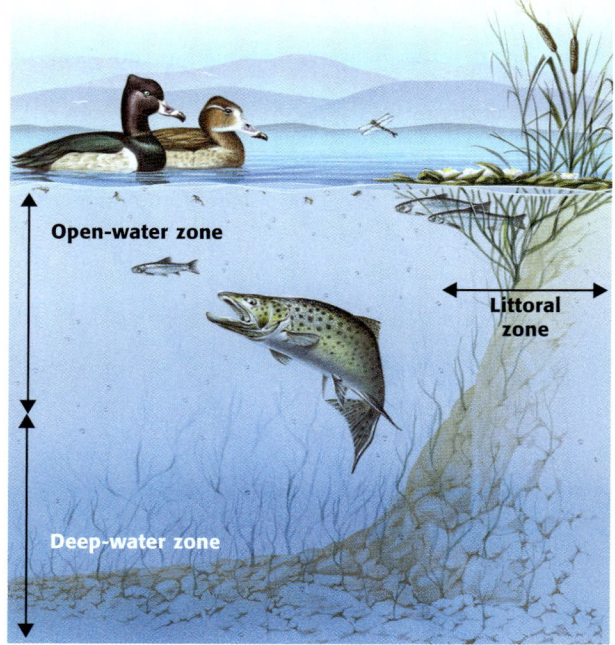

Figure 16 *Freshwater ecosystems are characterized by abiotic factors that determine which organisms live there.*

CONNECT TO PHYSICAL SCIENCE

Unlike most substances, solid water is less dense than liquid water. This is why ice floats. This property of water allows organisms to live beneath the frozen surface of the water. Ask students to consider what might happen if liquid water was less dense than frozen water. (Ice would sink, and entire bodies of water would freeze in winter, killing the organisms inhabiting the water.)

2) Teach

QuickLab

MATERIALS

For Each Student:
- index cards
- yarn or string

Answer to QuickLab

3. *Answers will vary. Accept any response that demonstrates a basic understanding of pond ecology.*

MATH and MORE

Tell students: Nearly all of the water of the world—97.6 percent—is found in the oceans. Where is the rest of the water? Construct a bar graph to show the relative amount of nonocean water in the world.

Ice and snow	29,000 km³
Ground water	4,000 km³
Lakes and reservoirs	125 km³
Atmosphere	113 km³
Salt lakes	104 km³
Surface soils	65 km³
Organisms	65 km³
Swamps, marshes	3.6 km³
Rivers and streams	1.7 km³

Teaching Transparency 69
"Lake Zones"

A Trip to Lake Superior
Suppose you are a life scientist who specializes in the plants that live in and near Lake Superior. You are preparing for a yearlong expedition to Thunder Bay, on the Canadian shore of Lake Superior. You will stay "in the wild." Based on what you have learned about ecosystems, answer the following questions: How will you live while you are there? What will you bring along? What problems will you encounter? How will you overcome them?

Wetlands

A **wetland** is an area of land where the water level is near or above the surface of the ground for most of the year. Wetlands support a variety of plant and animal life. They also play an important role in flood control. During heavy rains or spring snow melt, wetlands soak up large amounts of water. The water in wetlands also seeps into the ground, replenishing underground water supplies.

Marshes A **marsh** is a treeless wetland ecosystem where plants such as cattails and rushes grow. A freshwater marsh is shown in **Figure 17**. Freshwater marshes are found in shallow waters along the shores of lakes, ponds, rivers, and streams. The plants in a marsh vary depending on the depth of the water and the location of the marsh. Grasses, reeds, bulrushes, and wild rice are common marsh plants. Muskrats, turtles, frogs, and red-wing blackbirds can be found living in marshes.

While exploring in a wetland, you have discovered a new organism. In your ScienceLog, draw the organism. Describe what it looks like and how it is adapted to its environment. Trade with a partner. Is your partner's organism believable?

Figure 17 Turtles find a lot of places to escape from predators in a freshwater marsh. Many species raise their young in these protected areas.

IS THAT A FACT!
Fish living in streams with strong currents face a problem: how do they prevent themselves from being washed downstream? Some have developed suckers that hold them in place. Some stay in relatively calm waters behind rocks, and at least two—a kind of catfish in the Andes and a kind of loach in Borneo—have developed huge lips that they use to clamp on to river debris to hold their position.

Swamps A **swamp** is a wetland ecosystem where trees and vines grow. Swamps occur in low-lying areas and beside slow-moving rivers. Most swamps are flooded only part of the year, depending on the rainfall. Trees may include willows, bald cypresses, water tupelos, oaks, and elms. Vines such as poison ivy grow up trees, and Spanish moss hangs from the branches. Water lilies and other lake plants may grow in open-water areas. Swamps, like the one in **Figure 18,** provide a home for a variety of fish, snakes, and birds.

Figure 18 *The bases of the trunks of these trees are adapted to give the tree more support in the wet, soft sediment under the water in this swamp.*

From Lake to Forest

How can a lake or pond, like the one in **Figure 19,** disappear? Water entering a standing body of water usually carries nutrients and sediment along with it. These materials then settle to the bottom. Dead leaves from overhanging trees and decaying plant and animal life also settle to the bottom. Gradually, the pond or lake fills in. Plants grow in the newly filled areas, closer and closer toward the center. With time, the standing body of water becomes a marsh. Eventually, the marsh turns into a forest.

Figure 19 *Eventually decaying organic matter, along with sediment in the runoff from land, will fill in this pond.*

REVIEW

1. Describe some adaptations of organisms that live in moving water.
2. Compare the littoral zone with the open-water zone of a pond.
3. How is a swamp different from a marsh?
4. **Analyzing Concepts** The center of a pond is 10 m deep. Near the shore it is 0–1 m deep. Describe the types of organisms that might live in each zone.

TOPIC: Freshwater Ecosystems
GO TO: www.scilinks.org
sciLINKS NUMBER: HSTL495

Chapter Highlights

Vocabulary Definitions

Section 1

abiotic describes nonliving factors in the environment

biome a large region characterized by a specific type of climate and certain types of plant and animal communities

savanna a tropical grassland biome with scattered clumps of trees

desert a hot, dry biome inhabited by organisms adapted to survive high daytime temperatures and long periods without rain

tundra a far-northern biome characterized by long, cold winters, permafrost, and few trees

permafrost the permanently frozen ground just below the surface of the soil in the arctic tundra

Section 2

marine an ecosystem based on salty water

phytoplankton microscopic photosynthetic organisms that float near the surface of the ocean

zooplankton very small animals that, along with the phytoplankton they consume, form the base of the oceans' food web

estuary an area where fresh water from streams and rivers spills into the ocean

Chapter Highlights

SECTION 1

Vocabulary
- abiotic (p. 474)
- biome (p. 474)
- savanna (p. 478)
- desert (p. 479)
- tundra (p. 480)
- permafrost (p. 480)

Section Notes
- Rainfall and temperature are the main factors that determine what kind of biome is found in a region.
- The three main forest biomes are the temperate deciduous forest and the coniferous forest, which experience warm summers and cold winters, and the tropical rain forest, where temperatures stay warm.
- Grasslands receive more rain than deserts and receive less rain than forests. Temperate grasslands have hot summers and cold winters. Savannas have wet and dry seasons.
- Deserts receive less than 25 cm of rain a year. Plants and animals competing for the limited water supply have developed special adaptations for survival.
- The tundra biome is found mainly in the Arctic region. Arctic tundra is characterized by permafrost.

Labs
Life in the Desert (p. 754)

SECTION 2

Vocabulary
- marine (p. 481)
- phytoplankton (p. 481)
- zooplankton (p. 481)
- estuary (p. 485)

Section Notes
- The kinds of marine organisms that inhabit an area vary depending on the water depth, the temperature, the amount of light, and the distance from shore.
- The intertidal area is the area where sea and land meet.
- The sea floor is home to biomes as different as coral reefs and thermal vents.
- The open ocean includes unique biomes, including the Sargasso Sea and the cold water oceans around the poles.

✓ Skills Check

Math Concepts

RAINFALL Using a meterstick, measure 400 cm on the floor of your classroom. This distance represents the depth of rainfall a rain forest receives per year. Next measure 25 cm. This measurement represents the amount of rainfall a desert receives per year. Compare these two quantities. Express your comparison as a ratio.

$$\frac{25}{400} = \frac{1}{16}$$

In 1 year, a desert receives $\frac{1}{16}$ the rainfall that a rain forest receives.

Visual Understanding

RAIN FOREST Look at Figure 4, on page 477. There are three layers of a rain forest—the upper story, the middle story, and the ground story. The upper story is the canopy, where most rain forest species live and where there is the most sunlight. The middle story is under the canopy and above the ground. The ground story is dark in most parts of the forest. Most plants in the rain forest grow very tall to compete for light in the canopy. Growth of plants on the ground story is not very dense due to the lack of available light.

Lab and Activity Highlights

Life in the Desert PG 754

Discovering Mini-Ecosystems PG 755

Too Much of a Good Thing? PG 756

Datasheets for LabBook
(blackline masters for these labs)

490   Chapter 20 • The Earth's Ecosystems

SECTION 2

- An estuary is a region where fresh water from rivers spills into the ocean and the fresh and salt water mix with the rising and falling of the tides.

Labs
Discovering Mini-Ecosystems (p. 755)

SECTION 3

Vocabulary
- **tributary** (p. 486)
- **littoral zone** (p. 487)
- **open-water zone** (p. 487)
- **deep-water zone** (p. 487)
- **wetland** (p. 488)
- **marsh** (p. 488)
- **swamp** (p. 489)

Section Notes
- Freshwater ecosystems are classified according to whether they have running water or standing water. Brooks, rivers, and streams contain running water. Lakes and ponds contain standing water.
- As tributaries join a stream between its source and the ocean, the volume of water in the stream increases, the nutrient content increases, and the speed decreases.
- The types of organisms found in a stream or river are determined mainly by how quickly the current is moving.
- The littoral zone of a lake is inhabited by floating plants. These plants provide a home for a rich diversity of animal life.
- Wetlands include marshes, which are treeless, and swamps, where trees and vines grow.

Labs
Too Much of a Good Thing? (p. 756)

VOCABULARY DEFINITIONS, continued

SECTION 3
tributary a small stream or river that flows into a larger one

littoral zone the zone of a lake or pond closest to the edge of the land

open-water zone the zone of a lake or pond that extends from the littoral zone out across the top of the water and that is only as deep as light can reach through the water

deep-water zone the zone of a lake or pond below the open-water zone, where no light reaches

wetland an area of land where the water level is near or above the surface of the ground for most of the year

marsh a treeless wetland ecosystem where plants such as cattails and rushes grow

swamp a wetland ecosystem where trees and vines grow

 Vocabulary Review Worksheet 20

 Blackline masters of these Chapter Highlights can be found in the **Study Guide.**

---

internetconnect

 GO TO: go.hrw.com

Visit the **HRW** Web site for a variety of learning tools related to this chapter. Just type in the keyword:

KEYWORD: HSTECO

 GO TO: www.scilinks.org

Visit the **National Science Teachers Association** on-line Web site for Internet resources related to this chapter. Just type in the *sci*LINKS number for more information about the topic:

TOPIC: Forests	*sci*LINKS NUMBER: HSTL480
TOPIC: Grasslands	*sci*LINKS NUMBER: HSTL485
TOPIC: Marine Ecosystems	*sci*LINKS NUMBER: HSTL490
TOPIC: Freshwater Ecosystems	*sci*LINKS NUMBER: HSTL495

Lab and Activity Highlights

LabBank

 EcoLabs & Field Activities, Biome Adventure Travel, EcoLab 7

Long-Term Projects & Research Ideas, Tropical Medicine, Project 20

Interactive Explorations CD-ROM

 CD 2, Exploration 2, "Sea Sick"

Chapter 20 • Chapter Highlights

Chapter Review Answers

USING VOCABULARY
1. continental shelf
2. Zooplankton
3. marsh
4. Deciduous trees
5. tundra
6. biome

UNDERSTANDING CONCEPTS
Multiple Choice
7. a
8. c
9. b
10. d
11. d

Short Answer

12. Tributaries flow into it, increasing the volume of water. The salt and nutrient content of the water increases, as does the cloudiness. The speed of the water decreases.

13. Answers may vary; possible answer: being active only at night, and storing water in body tissue

14. No, wetlands are not *necessarily* always wet. However, wetlands have high water tables most of the year, so wetland soils are wet much of the time.

15. The salt content in the water of an estuary changes constantly as the tides rise and fall, moving water in and out of the estuary. The most important factor in the salinity of an estuary, however, is freshwater runoff from the land. After heavy rainfall, the salinity of the water in an estuary close to land will be very low because the salts will be diluted with additional fresh water.

Chapter Review

USING VOCABULARY

To complete the following sentences, choose the correct term from each pair of terms listed below:

1. At the edge of the __?__, the open ocean begins. *(continental shelf* or *Sargasso Sea)*

2. __?__ are tiny consumers that live in water. *(Phytoplankton* or *Zooplankton)*

3. A __?__ is a treeless wetland. *(swamp* or *marsh)*

4. __?__ lose their leaves in order to conserve water. *(Deciduous trees* or *Conifers)*

5. The major feature of the __?__ biome is permafrost. *(desert* or *tundra)*

6. Each major type of plant community and its associated animal communities make up a(n)__?__. *(estuary* or *biome)*

UNDERSTANDING CONCEPTS

Multiple Choice

7. The most numerous organisms in the oceans are the
   a. plankton.
   b. *Sargassum*.
   c. coral animals.
   d. marine mammals.

8. Marine ecosystems at the poles are unusual because
   a. animals spend time both in and out of the water.
   b. plankton are rare.
   c. they contain ice.
   d. the salt content of the water is very high.

9. The major factor that determines the types of organisms that live in a stream or river is
   a. the water temperature.
   b. the speed of the current.
   c. the depth of the water.
   d. the width of the stream or river.

10. Marine ecosystems
    a. contain the largest animals in the world.
    b. exist in all ocean zones.
    c. include environments where organisms survive without light.
    d. All of the above

11. Two major factors that determine what kind of a biome is found in a region are
    a. the amount of rainfall and the temperature.
    b. the depth of water and the distance from land.
    c. the wave action and the salt content of the water.
    d. All of the above

Short Answer

12. Describe how a stream changes as it moves from its source toward the ocean.

13. Describe two adaptations of animals to the desert environment.

14. Are wetlands always wet? Explain.

15. Explain how the salt content in an estuary changes constantly.

Concept Mapping

16. Use the following terms to create a concept map: tropical rain forest, deep-rooted plants, coral reef, canopy, biomes, permafrost, desert, continental shelf, tundra, ecosystems.

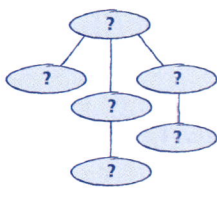

CRITICAL THINKING AND PROBLEM SOLVING

Write one or two sentences to answer the following questions:

17. While excavating a region now covered by grasslands, paleontologists discover the fossil remains of ancient fish and shellfish. What might they conclude?

18. In order to build a new shopping center, developers fill in a wetland. Afterward, flooding becomes a problem in this area. How can this be explained?

19. Explain why most desert flowering plants bloom, bear seeds, and die within a few weeks, while some tropical flowering plants remain in bloom for a much longer time.

MATH IN SCIENCE

20. What is the average difference in rainfall between a temperate deciduous forest and a coniferous forest?

21. An area of Brazilian rain forest received 347 cm of rain in one year. Using the following formula, calculate this amount of rainfall in inches.

    0.394 (the number of inches in a centimeter)
    × 347 cm
    _____?_____ in.

INTERPRETING GRAPHICS

The graphs below show the monthly temperatures and rainfall in a region during 1 year.

Average Monthly Precipitation

Average Monthly High Temperatures

22. What kind of biome is probably found in the region represented by these graphs?

23. Would you expect to find bulrushes in the region represented by these graphs? Why or why not?

Take a minute to review your answers to the Pre-Reading Questions found at the bottom of page 472. Have your answers changed? If necessary, revise your answers based on what you have learned since you began this chapter.

Concept Mapping

16. An answer to this exercise can be found at the end of this book.

CRITICAL THINKING AND PROBLEM SOLVING

17. At one time, this region was covered by water.
18. The wetland had soaked up large amounts of water. Because the water can no longer drain into the wetland, it now runs off the land, causing the flooding.
19. Rainfall is sparse in the desert. When rain does fall, flowering plants of the desert must bloom and bear seeds quickly, while there is still water in the ground.

MATH IN SCIENCE

20. about 45 cm
21. about 137 in.

INTERPRETING GRAPHICS

22. desert
23. No; The graph represents a typical hot, dry desert. Bulrushes grow in wetlands.

Concept Mapping Transparency 20

Blackline masters of this Chapter Review can be found in the **Study Guide**.

Chapter 20 • Chapter Review   **493**

ACROSS THE SCIENCES
Ocean Vents

Background
The first black smoker was found off the Galápagos Islands in 1977, and since then at least four have been found on the bottom of the Pacific Ocean floor 322 km (200 mi) off the coast of Canada. The heat generated by one of them was so intense that the surface of the ocean water was nearly boiling when the chimney was lifted out.

It seems almost impossible that creatures on our planet could survive under such conditions, but one of the species of tubeworms can withstand temperatures up to 80°C (176°F)!

Other recently discovered creatures on the bottom of the ocean thrive on frozen chunks of methane in the same way that these creatures thrive on sulfur. These discoveries of chemosynthetic life have been called a "biological revolution" by one scientist and have sparked debate about the possibilities for life on other planets.

LIFE SCIENCE • CHEMISTRY

Ocean Vents

▲ *"They're very slim, fuzzy, flattened-out worms. Really hairy,"* says scientist Bob Feldman about tubeworms.

Picture the extreme depths of the ocean. There is no light at all, and it is very cold. But in the cracks between the plates on the bottom of the ocean floor, sea water trickles deep into the Earth. On the way back up from these cracks, the heated water collects metals, sulfuric gases, and enough heat to raise the temperature of the chilly ocean to 360°C. That is hot enough to melt lead! This heated sea water blasts up into the ocean through volcanic vents. And when this hot and toxic brew collides with icy ocean waters, the metals and sulfuric gases *precipitate,* that is, settle out of the heated ocean water as solids.

These solids form tubes, called black smokers, that extend up through the ocean floor. To humans, this dark, cold, and toxic environment would be deadly. But to a community of 300 species, including certain bacteria, clams, mussels, and tube worms, it is home. For these species, black smokers make life possible.

Life Without Photosynthesis
For a long time, scientists believed that energy from sunlight was the basis for the Earth's food chains and for life itself. But in the last 15 years, researchers have discovered ecosystems that challenge this belief. We now know of organisms around black smokers that can live without sunlight. One type of bacteria uses toxic gases from a black smoker in the same way that plants use sunlight. In a process called *chemosynthesis,* these bacteria convert sulfur into energy.

These bacteria are producers, and the mussels and clams are the consumers in this deep-sea food web. The bacteria use the mussels and clams as a sturdy place to live. The mussels and clams, in turn, feed off the bacteria. This kind of relationship between organisms is called *symbiosis.* The closer to the vent the clams and mussels are, the more likely the bacteria are to grow. Because of this, the mussels and clams frequently move to find good spots near the black smokers.

What Do You Think?
▶ Conditions near black smokers are similar to conditions on other planets. Do some research on these extreme environments, both on Earth and elsewhere. Then discuss with your classmates where and how you think life on Earth may have started.

Answer to What Do You Think?
Answers will vary. Accept any response that is well researched, thoughtful, and well articulated.

CAREERS

CAREERS
Ecologist—
Alfonso Alonso-Mejía

ECOLOGIST

Most winters **Alfonso Alonso-Mejía** climbs up to the few remote sites in central Mexico where about 150 million monarch butterflies spend the winter. He is researching the monarchs because he wants to help preserve their habitat.

Monarch butterflies are famous for their long-distance migration. Those that eventually find their way to Mexico come from as far away as the northeastern United States and southern Canada. Some of them travel 3,200 km before reaching central Mexico.

Human Threats to Habitats
Unfortunately, the monarchs' habitat is increasingly threatened by logging and other human activities. Only nine of the monarchs' wintering sites remain. Five of the sites are set aside as sanctuaries for the butterflies, but even those are endangered by people who cut down fir trees for firewood or for commercial purposes.

Research to the Rescue
Alonso-Mejía's work is helping Mexican conservationists better understand and protect monarch butterflies. Especially important is his discovery that monarchs depend on bushlike vegetation that grows beneath the fir trees, called understory vegetation.

Alonso-Mejía's research showed that when the temperature dips below freezing, as it often does at the high-altitude sites where the monarchs winter, some monarchs depend on understory vegetation for survival. This is because low temperatures ($-1°C$ to $4°C$) limit the monarchs' movement—the butterflies are not even able to crawl. At extremely cold temperatures ($-7°C$ to $-1°C$), monarchs resting on the forest floor are in danger of freezing to death. But where there is understory vegetation, the monarchs can slowly climb the vegetation until they are at least 10 cm above the ground. This tiny difference in elevation can provide a microclimate that is warm enough to ensure the monarchs' survival.

The importance of understory vegetation was not known before Alonso-Mejía did his research. Now, thanks to his work, Mexican conservationists will better protect the understory vegetation.

Get Involved!
▶ If you are interested in a nationwide tagging program to help scientists learn more about the monarchs' migration route, write to Monarch Watch, Department of Entomology, 7005 Howorth Hall, University of Kansas, Lawrence, Kansas 66045.

Background
Why do animals migrate? Animals migrate, or move from one area to another area, to take advantage of different environmental conditions in different locations. Monarch butterflies, like many birds, migrate north in the summers, when the food supply and climate are favorable, and south in the winters, when the climate in the north is unfavorable.

Migrating animals often inhabit distinctly different biomes, as in the case of the monarch butterfly. Given their unique ecology, migrating animals can serve as indicators of the health of different ecosystems. Indeed, monarch butterflies face challenges in both their summer and winter homes: loss of habitat in Mexico and loss of their primary food source, milkweed, in Canada.

Discussion
Lead your students in a discussion about what Alfonso's research suggests about the organisms that inhabit Earth's ecosystems. Even common, broad-ranging organisms such as the monarch butterfly often have specific requirements for food and shelter. Monarch butterflies do not just need forests to winter in; they also need cool, humid forests covered with specific types of upperstory and understory vegetation. The monarch's tenuous situation illustrates the importance of both biotic (vegetation) and abiotic (temperature) factors for an organism's survival.

Chapter Organizer

CHAPTER ORGANIZATION	TIME MINUTES	OBJECTIVES	LABS, INVESTIGATIONS, AND DEMONSTRATIONS
Chapter Opener pp. 496–497	45	National Standards: ST 1, 2, SPSP 5, HNS 1, 2, LS 3a, 5c	**Start-Up Activity** Recycling Paper, p. 497
Section 1 First the Bad News	90	▶ Describe the major types of pollution. ▶ Distinguish between renewable and nonrenewable resources. ▶ Explain how habitat destruction affects organisms. ▶ Explain the impact of human population growth. UCP 3, SAI 1, SPSP 1–5, HNS 3, LS 3a, 4d	**Demonstration**, Crude Oil Spills and Seabird Eggs, p. 503 GENERAL
Section 2 The Good News: Solutions	90	▶ Explain the importance of conservation. ▶ Describe the three Rs and their importance. ▶ Explain how habitats can be protected. ▶ List ways you can help protect the Earth. UCP 3, 4, SAI 1, ST 2, SPSP 1, 2, 4, 5, HNS 2, LS 5c; LabBook SAI 1, 2, HNS 2, UCP 2, SPSP 4	**Demonstration**, Friendly Cleaner, p. 506 in ATE GENERAL **QuickLab**, Trash Check, p. 510 GENERAL **Interactive Explorations CD-ROM**, Moose Malady GENERAL A **Worksheet** is also available in the **Interactive Explorations Teacher's Edition.** **Discovery Lab**, Biodiversity—What a Disturbing Thought! p. 758 GENERAL **Datasheets for LabBook**, Biodiversity—What a Disturbing Thought! Datasheet 45 GENERAL **Skill Builder**, Deciding About Environmental Issues, p. 760 GENERAL **Datasheets for LabBook**, Deciding About Environmental Issues, Datasheet 46 GENERAL **EcoLabs & Field Activities**, A Filter with Culture, EcoLab 8 ADVANCED **Long-Term Projects & Research Ideas**, Project 21 ADVANCED

*See page **T20** for a complete correlation of this book with the*

NATIONAL SCIENCE EDUCATION STANDARDS.

TECHNOLOGY RESOURCES

 Guided Reading Audio CD English or Spanish, Chapter 21

 One-Stop Planner CD-ROM with Test Generator

  Interactive Explorations CD-ROM CD 2, Exploration 3, Moose Malady

 Multicultural Connections, Thailand Tire Furniture, Segment 12

Eye on the Environment, Smog Problems in Mexico, Segment 11

Scientists in Action, Forming the Future of Energy Efficiency, Segment 7 Tracking Mercury in the Everglades, Segment 15

495A Chapter 21 • Environmental Problems and Solutions

Chapter 21 • Environmental Problems and Solutions

CLASSROOM WORKSHEETS, TRANSPARENCIES, AND RESOURCES	SCIENCE INTEGRATION AND CONNECTIONS	REVIEW AND ASSESSMENT
Directed Reading Worksheet 21 BASIC **Science Puzzlers, Twisters & Teasers,** Worksheet 21 ADVANCED	**Multicultural Connection,** p. 497 in ATE **Careers:** Biologist—Dagmar Werner, p. 516 GENERAL	
Directed Reading Worksheet 21, Section 1 BASIC **Transparency 165,** The Greenhouse Effect **Math Skills for Science Worksheet 28,** A Formula for SI Catch-up GENERAL **Math Skills for Science Worksheet 37,** Rain-Forest Math GENERAL	**Cross-Disciplinary Focus,** p. 499 in ATE **Chemistry Connection,** p. 500 **Math and More,** p. 500 in ATE GENERAL **Connect to Earth Science,** p. 500 in ATE **MathBreak,** Water Depletion, p. 501 GENERAL **Math and More,** p. 502 in ATE GENERAL **Apply,** p. 504 GENERAL	**Review,** p. 500 GENERAL **Self-Check,** p. 501 **Review,** p. 504 GENERAL **Quiz,** p. 504 in ATE GENERAL **Alternative Assessment,** p. 504 in ATE GENERAL
Transparency 77, Practicing Conservation **Directed Reading Worksheet 21,** Section 2 BASIC **Reinforcement Worksheet 21,** It's "R" Planet! BASIC **Critical Thinking Worksheet 21,** Bud Kindfellow Has a Plan ADVANCED	**Math and More,** p. 506 in ATE BASIC **Connect to Chemistry,** p. 506 in ATE GENERAL **Multicultural Connection,** p. 509 in ATE **Cross-Disciplinary Focus,** p. 510 in ATE **Scientific Debate:** Where Should the Wolves Roam? p. 517 GENERAL	**Self-Check,** p. 507 **Review,** p. 508 GENERAL **Review,** p. 511 GENERAL **Quiz,** p. 511 in ATE GENERAL **Alternative Assessment,** p. 511 in ATE GENERAL

END-OF-CHAPTER REVIEW AND ASSESSMENT

Chapter Review in Study Guide
Vocabulary and Notes in Study Guide
Chapter Tests with Performance-Based Assessment, Chapter 21 Test
Chapter Tests with Performance-Based Assessment, Performance-Based Assessment 21
Concept Mapping Transparency 21

 Holt, Rinehart and Winston On-line Resources
go.hrw.com
For worksheets and other teaching aids related to this chapter, visit the HRW Web site and type in the keyword: **HSTENV**

 National Science Teachers Association
www.scilinks.org
Encourage students to use the sciLINKS numbers listed in the internet connect boxes to access information and resources on the **NSTA** Web site.

Chapter 21 • Chapter Organizer   **495B**

Chapter Resources & Worksheets

Visual Resources

TEACHING TRANSPARENCIES #77

TEACHING TRANSPARENCIES #165

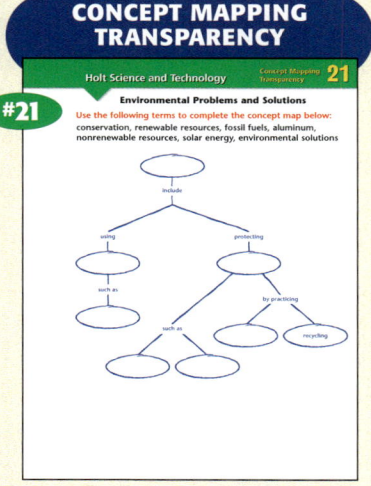

CONCEPT MAPPING TRANSPARENCY #21

Meeting Individual Needs

DIRECTED READING #21

REINFORCEMENT & VOCABULARY REVIEW #21

#21

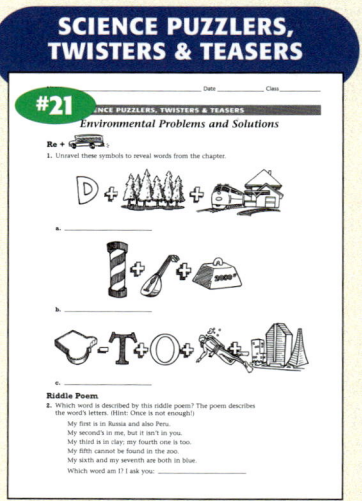

SCIENCE PUZZLERS, TWISTERS & TEASERS #21

Chapter 21 • Environmental Problems and Solutions

Chapter 21 • Environmental Problems and Solutions

Review & Assessment

STUDY GUIDE

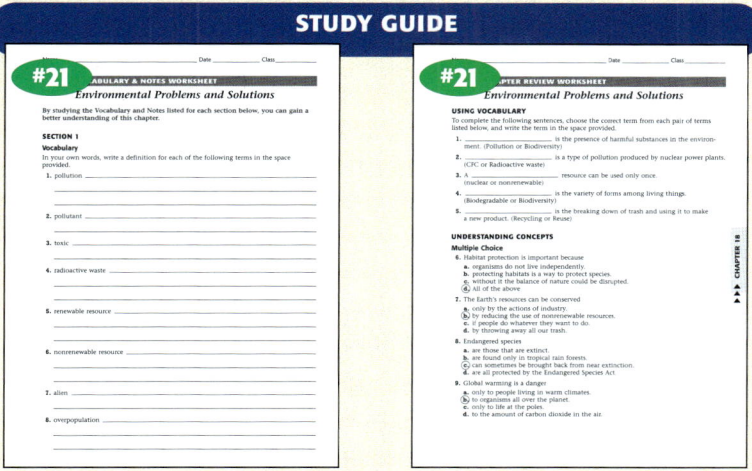

CHAPTER TESTS WITH PERFORMANCE-BASED ASSESSMENT

Lab Worksheets

ECOLABS & FIELD ACTIVITIES

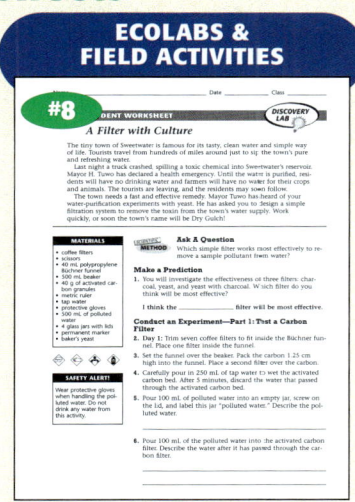

LONG-TERM PROJECTS & RESEARCH IDEAS

DATASHEETS FOR LABBOOK

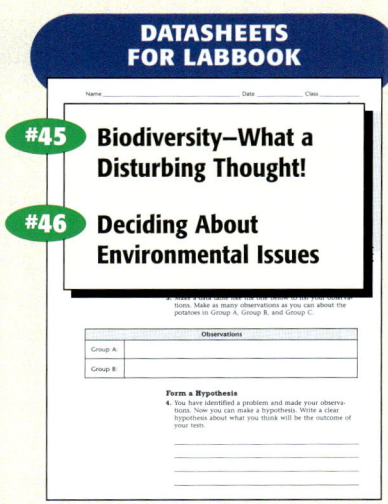

Applications & Extensions

CRITICAL THINKING & PROBLEM SOLVING

MULTICULTURAL CONNECTIONS

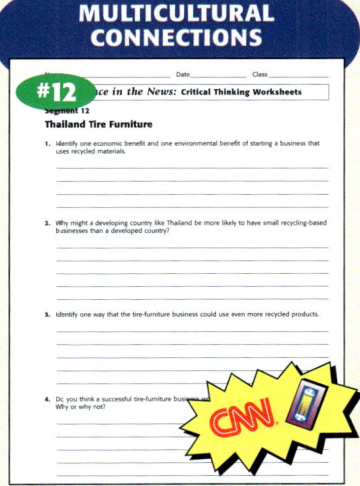

EYE ON THE ENVIRONMENT

SCIENTISTS IN ACTION

INTERACTIVE EXPLORATIONS

Chapter 21 • Chapter Resources & Worksheets   **495D**

Chapter Background

SECTION 1

First the Bad News

▶ **Rachel Carson (1907–1964)**

Rachel Carson was an American biologist and environmentalist. Her interest in nature and wildlife can be traced to her childhood in the western Pennsylvania countryside. In 1932, she received a masters degree from Johns Hopkins University and later obtained a job as an aquatic biologist with the U.S Bureau of Fisheries. She supplemented her income by writing articles about marine life. In 1941, she published her first book, *Under the Sea-Wind*—a vivid depiction of life in the oceans. Her second book, *The Sea Around Us,* was published in 1951 and was extremely well received. It became a best-seller, won the National Book Award, and established Carson as an outstanding science writer.

- Carson was apprehensive about the use of the pesticide DDT as early as 1945, but at that time few other people shared her concern. By the late 1950s, DDT use had increased enormously. It was routinely used on crops to control pests and (rather ineffectively) for mosquito control, but unfortunately it also killed nontargeted animals, such as birds, fish, crabs, grasshoppers, and bees.

- Carson began to research pesticides and turned up alarming evidence that pesticides contaminated soil, water, and air; became increasingly concentrated as they moved up the food chain; and that such chemicals are so stable that they persist as toxins for a very long time. In the meantime, chemical companies were zealously promoting the "miracles" worked by pesticides such as DDT. Carson compiled her evidence against chemical pesticides in her book *Silent Spring* (1962). The book's release sparked an immediate controversy. Chemical companies were Carson's most vociferous opponents.

- Many scientists, however, praised Carson's book. The American public took Carson's warnings to heart, and by the end of 1962, more than 40 bills concerning pesticide regulations had been introduced in state legislatures. The formation of the Environmental Protection Agency, in 1970, was due partly to Carson's efforts. The United States began to phase out the use of DDT in 1972.

IS THAT A FACT!

▪ Upon the release of *Silent Spring,* representatives of chemical manufacturers did not shrink from attacking Carson personally. Carson was accused of being a "high priestess of nature," and her book was said to be part of a "communist plot" to destroy the economies of noncommunist countries.

▶ **The Problems with Landfills**

Landfills take up valuable land, smell bad, and attract pests. They are responsible for a host of less-obvious but equally troublesome problems as well. Decades ago, little thought was given to landfills; they were established wherever cheap or seemingly "useless" land existed. For years, household trash—some of it containing toxic chemicals, such as those found in household cleaners, paints, bug sprays, plastics, motor oil, and batteries—was plowed into landfills.

- Over time, rainwater percolated through the mountains of garbage, picking up chemical and bacterial wastes and dissolved metals. The rainwater forms a poisonous concoction known as leachate. Leachate can seep into ground water and can eventually contaminate drinking water.

IS THAT A FACT!

▪ In March 1987, a tugboat hauling a barge loaded with more than 3,000 tons of garbage from New York City headed to North Carolina. Officials in North Carolina turned the boat away because they feared that the trash might be hazardous. The boat traveled from port to port along the Atlantic seaboard for 2 months, and all requests to dump its load were denied. It finally returned to New York. After a 3-month delay, the refuse was incinerated in Brooklyn.

Chapter 21 • Environmental Problems and Solutions

SECTION 2

The Good News: Solutions

▶ **John Muir (1838–1914)**
Scottish-born naturalist John Muir is often considered the father of the conservation movement in the United States. When Muir was 11, he and his family moved to the United States and settled on a farm in Wisconsin. Muir attended the University of Wisconsin for 2.5 years. In 1867, he set out to walk from Indianapolis to the Gulf of Mexico, an experience he described in his classic book, *A Thousand-Mile Walk to the Gulf* (1916). The walk was a turning point in Muir's life; he moved to Yosemite Valley, in California, and devoted himself to the study of the wilderness areas of the West.

- Muir wrote a number of natural-history articles for national magazines that opened the eyes of many to the wonders of nature. In 1876, he proposed to the federal government that it take measures to preserve forests. His efforts played a key role in the establishment of Sequoia and Yosemite National Parks in 1890.

- Two years later, Muir founded the Sierra Club, whose purpose was to "explore, enjoy, and render accessible the mountain regions of the Pacific Coast." Today the Sierra Club is a national organization with a much broader goal that includes the exploration and enjoyment of wilderness as well as the responsible use, protection, and restoration of the world's ecosystems.

▶ **A Heritage of Reuse and Recycling**
Before the 1950s in the United States, recycling and reuse were routine practices. Relatively few disposable items existed, and most products were not wrapped and sealed in multiple layers of packaging. A few items, such as sugar and flour, were packaged, but people either reused the large cotton sacks those items came in or made the sacks into clothing. Some of the sacks had decorative prints, encouraging their use as clothing.

IS THAT A FACT!

- In 1955, *Life* magazine published an article on the new "throwaway" lifestyle and how it liberated Americans from tedious cleanup chores. Among the noteworthy items the article highlighted were disposable curtains, hunting decoys, and barbecue grills.

- The conventional recycling of paper involves the use of harsh de-inking chemicals and requires that the paper be repulped and reprocessed into new paper. Most paper can be recycled only about three times before its cellulose fibers lose their integrity. Some paper is more suitable for recycling than others. In 1996, a mechanical engineer named Sameer Madanshetty devised a very gentle, chemical-free method that uses focused sound waves to "explode" ink off of paper. When paper is placed in water, tiny bubbles form around the inked portions of the paper. Sound waves directed at the bubbles blast the bubbles and remove the ink, which can then be filtered out of the water. The paper itself is undamaged and can be dried and reused repeatedly.

For background information about teaching strategies and issues, refer to the *Professional Reference for Teachers*.

Chapter 21

Environmental Problems and Solutions

Pre-Reading Questions

Students may not know the answers to these questions before reading the chapter, so accept any reasonable response.

Suggested Answers

1. Sample answer: People damage the Earth by creating harmful pollution and hazardous waste and releasing it into the environment. People reduce biodiversity by clearing forests and filling in wetlands. People also overuse nonrenewable resources and deplete the Earth of certain minerals and water sources.

2. Sample answer: People are trying to prevent further damage to the Earth by reducing human dependence on natural resources, by reusing many of the materials we would otherwise throw away, and by recycling materials that can be reprocessed for other purposes, such as aluminum, glass, plastic, and paper.

Directed Reading Worksheet 21

Science Puzzlers, Twisters & Teasers Worksheet 21

Guided Reading Audio CD
English or Spanish, Chapter 21

Environmental Problems and Solutions

Sections

1. **First the Bad News** .. 498
   - Chemistry Connection . 500
   - Internet Connection . . 500
   - MathBreak 501
   - Apply 504

2. **The Good News: Solutions** 505
   - QuickLab 510
   - Internet Connect 511

Chapter Review 514
Feature Articles 516, 517
LabBook 758–761

Pre-Reading Questions

1. Name three ways people damage the Earth.
2. Name three ways people are trying to prevent further damage to the Earth.

internet connect

 HRW On-line Resources
go.hrw.com
For worksheets and other teaching aids, visit the HRW Web site and type in the keyword: **HSTENV**

 sciLINKS NSTA
www.scilinks.com
Use the *sci*LINKS numbers at the end of each chapter for additional resources on the **NSTA** Web site.

 CNNfyi.com
www.cnnfyi.com
Visit the CNN Web site for current events coverage and classroom resources.

Sea of Red

On the shores of a tropical island, a chemical slick coats the clear water. Even though the environment may break down the chemical over time, preventing pollution is better for the environment. In this chapter, you will learn about the natural cycles that help break down substances and move them through the environment. You will also learn about problems facing the environment today and about some solutions, including actions you can take to help.

RECYCLING PAPER

In this activity, you will be making paper without cutting down trees. Instead you will be reusing paper that has already been made.

Procedure

1. Tear up **two sheets of old newspaper** into small pieces, and put them in a **blender**. Using a **beaker**, add **1 L of water**. Cover and blend until the mixture is soupy.
2. Cover the bottom of a **square pan** with **2-3 cm of water**. Place a **wire screen** in the pan. Pour 250 mL of the paper mixture onto the screen, and spread evenly.
3. Lift the screen out of the water with the paper on it. Drain excess water into the pan. Then place the screen inside a **section of newspaper.**
4. Close the newspaper, and turn it over so that the screen is on top of the paper mixture. Cover the newspaper with a **flat board.** Press on the board to squeeze out extra water.
5. Open the newspaper, and let your paper mixture dry. Use your recycled paper to write a note to a friend!

Analysis

6. In what ways is your paper like regular paper? How is it different?
7. What could you do to improve your papermaking methods?

RECYCLING PAPER

MATERIALS
For Each Group: • 2 sheets of old newspaper • blender • 1 L of water • square pan filled with water to a level of 2–3 cm • wire screen • section of newspaper • flat board

Safety Caution

Remind students to review all safety cautions and icons before beginning this lab activity. Cover all work surfaces, and have students wear aprons or smocks to protect their clothing.

The paper will have to dry at least overnight; the paper may need an additional day to dry, depending on how warm and moist the air is in your classroom. To ensure the quickest drying time, have students be sure they squeeze out as much excess water as they can.

Answers to START-UP Activity

6. Answers will vary, but students should note that their paper looks similar to regular paper, and both can be used for writing or drawing. The handmade paper is not as smooth, is easier to tear, and is thicker.

7. Answers will vary. Some students might mention using less water or squeezing more water out of the mixture.

SECTION 1

Focus

First the Bad News

In this section, students investigate the major types of pollutants and how pollution is generated. Students also distinguish between renewable and nonrenewable resources. Finally, they explore how increases in human population and human activities strain resources and threaten the habitats of other living things.

Bellringer

Ask students:

What is the difference between a renewable resource and a nonrenewable resource? Have them write two examples of each in their ScienceLog. (Renewable resources, such as pine trees, that are used at the proper rate will last forever because they grow back or replenish themselves. Nonrenewable resources, such as oil, do not replenish themselves or grow back, or they would take thousands or millions of years to replenish.)

1 Motivate

GROUP ACTIVITY

Writing In groups of four, have students come up with a list of challenges to the environment. From that list, have each group pick the four that they feel are most important and explain why they should be priorities. Afterward, have groups share their top four challenges, and write them on the board or overhead. This list could be used to generate topics for discussion, research, or action.

Section 1

Terms to Learn

pollution
renewable resource
nonrenewable resource
overpopulation
biodiversity
biodegradable

What You'll Do

- Describe the major types of pollution.
- Distinguish between renewable and nonrenewable resources.
- Explain how habitat destruction affects organisms.
- Explain the impact of human population growth.

Figure 1 The water poured into the river by this factory is polluted with chemicals and heat. The smoke contains harmful chemicals that pollute the air.

Figure 2 Every year, we throw away 150 million metric tons of garbage.

First the Bad News

You've probably heard it before. The air is unhealthy to breathe. The water is harmful to drink. The soil is filled with poisons. The message is that Earth is sick and in great danger.

Pollution

Pollution is the presence of harmful substances in the environment. These harmful substances, known as *pollutants*, take many forms. They may be solid materials, chemicals, noise, or even heat. Often, pollutants damage or kill the plants and animals living in the affected habitat, as shown in **Figure 1**. Pollutants may also harm humans.

Piles of Garbage Americans produce more household waste than any other nation. If stacked up, the beverage cans we use in one year could reach the moon 17 times! The average American throws away 12 kg of trash a week, which usually winds up in a landfill like the one in **Figure 2**. Businesses, mines, and industries also produce large amounts of wastes.

Billions of kilograms of this waste are classified as *hazardous waste*, which means it's harmful to humans and the environment. Many industries produce hazardous wastes, including paper mills, nuclear power plants, oil refineries, and plastic and metal processing plants. Hospitals and laboratories produce hazardous medical wastes. But industry shouldn't get all the blame. Hazardous wastes also come from homes. Old cars, paints, batteries, medical wastes, and detergents all pollute the environment.

IS THAT A FACT!

The U.S. Environmental Protection Agency defines hazardous waste as "by-products of society that can pose a substantial or potential hazard to human health or the environment when improperly managed." This includes material that is toxic, corrosive, reactive, or ignitable. Examples include many waste chemicals and radioactive waste from nuclear power plants.

Where Does It All Go? Most of our household waste goes into giant landfills. Hazardous wastes are buried in landfills specially designed to contain them. However, some companies illegally dispose of their hazardous wastes by dumping them into rivers and lakes. Some wastes are burned in incinerators designed to reduce the amount of pollutants that enter the atmosphere. But if wastes are burned improperly, they add to the pollution of the air.

Chemicals Are Everywhere Chemicals are used to treat diseases. They are also used in plastics, thermometers, paints, hair sprays, and preserved foods. In fact, chemicals are everywhere. We can't get along without chemicals. Sometimes, though, we cannot get along *with* them. Chemical pesticides used to kill crop-destroying insects also pollute the soil and water. Rachel Carson, shown in **Figure 3,** wrote about the dangers of pesticides more than three decades ago.

A class of chemicals called CFCs was once used in aerosol sprays, refrigerators, and plastics. These uses of CFCs have been banned. CFCs rise high into the atmosphere and can cause the destruction of ozone. Ozone protects the Earth from harmful ultraviolet light.

Another class of chemicals, called PCBs, was once used as insulation as well as in paints, household appliances, and other products. Then scientists learned that PCBs are *toxic,* or poisonous. PCBs are now banned, but they have not gone away. They break down very slowly in the environment, and they still pollute even the most remote areas on Earth, as shown in **Figure 4.**

Figure 3 Rachel Carson's book Silent Spring, *published in 1962, made people aware of the environmental dangers of pesticides, especially to birds.*

High-Powered Wastes Nuclear power plants produce electricity for millions of homes and businesses. They also produce *radioactive wastes,* special kinds of hazardous wastes that take hundreds or thousands of years to become harmless. These "hot" wastes can cause cancer, leukemia, and birth defects in humans. Radioactive wastes can have harmful effects on all living things.

Figure 4 PCBs and other pollutants have even been found in remote parts of the Arctic.

2 Teach

READING STRATEGY

Prediction Guide Before students begin to read the section, ask them to state whether the following statements are true or false.

- The United States produces more garbage than any other nation in the world. (true)
- Noise can be a form of pollution. (true)
- All natural resources can be reused. (false)
- The destruction of animal habitats has a negative effect on animals but does not affect humans. (false)

CROSS-DISCIPLINARY FOCUS

History Rules about garbage disposal have been on the books since at least 320 B.C., when residents of Athens, Greece, were prohibited from disposing of their garbage within city limits. During the Middle Ages, people in Europe commonly tossed their garbage into the streets, which attracted rodents and pests that often carried disease, such as bubonic plague.

Directed Reading Worksheet 21 Section 1

Science Bloopers

Can you imagine children going to school on top of a hazardous waste site? That's what happened in Niagara Falls, New York, in 1954 when a school and neighborhood were built on land covering an old dumping site for a chemical company. Kids played in and around pools of black muck. Parents noticed that their children were burned by the chemicals. Dogs lost their fur. Dark, smelly substances seeped into homes after rainfalls. In 1978, the state ordered the evacuation of 235 families living near the toxic site.

Section 1 • First the Bad News

2) Teach, continued

MATH and MORE

On average, for each mile (1.6 km) a car travels, 0.36 kg of carbon dioxide is added to the atmosphere.

For 2 weeks, have students keep a log of how many miles their family travels by car. At the end of 2 weeks, have students figure out how many total kilograms of carbon dioxide their family added to the atmosphere.

CONNECT TO EARTH SCIENCE

Only 20 percent of the radiation that enters the Earth's atmosphere is absorbed by gases in the atmosphere and transferred in the form of heat. But these gases capture heat in other ways. When land and water absorb radiation, their molecules move faster, increasing their temperature. This energy is transferred to gas molecules in the atmosphere before it can escape into space. As a result, the atmosphere warms up. The Earth's heating process, in which the gases in the atmosphere absorb radiation and transfer the energy in the form of heat, is known as the greenhouse effect. The Earth's atmosphere works much like a greenhouse, as shown in Teaching Transparency 165, "The Greenhouse Effect."

Teaching Transparency 165 "The Greenhouse Effect"
LINK TO EARTH SCIENCE

Chemistry CONNECTION

Ozone in the stratosphere absorbs most of the ultraviolet light that comes from the sun. Ozone is destroyed by CFCs. This image of the hole in the ozone layer (the gray area in the center) was taken in 1998.

Exposure to high levels of ultraviolet light can lead to blindness, rapid skin aging, skin cancer, and a weakened immune system.

Too Much Heat The Earth is surrounded by a mixture of gases, including carbon dioxide, that make up the atmosphere. The atmosphere acts as a protective blanket, keeping the Earth warm enough for life to exist. Since the late 1800s, however, the amount of carbon dioxide in the air has increased by 25 percent. Carbon dioxide and certain pollutants in the air act like a greenhouse. Most scientists think the increase in carbon dioxide and other pollutants has caused a significant increase in global temperatures. If the temperatures continue to rise, the polar icecaps could melt, raising the level of the world's oceans. Some scientists think the sea level could rise 10 cm to 1.2 m by the year 2100. A 1 m rise would flood coastal areas, pollute underground water supplies, and cause present shorelines to disappear.

It's Way Too Noisy! Some pollutants affect the senses. These include bad odors and loud noises. Too much noise is not just annoying; it affects the ability to hear and think. If construction workers and others who work in noisy environments do not protect their ears, they can slowly lose their hearing. The students shown in **Figure 5** are listening to music at a sensible volume so that their hearing will not be damaged.

Figure 5 *Listening to music at a sensible volume will help prevent hearing loss.*

internet connect

SCILINKS NSTA
TOPIC: Air Pollution
GO TO: www.scilinks.org
*sci*LINKS NUMBER: HSTL505

REVIEW

1. Describe two ways pollution can be harmful.
2. Explain how loud noise can be considered pollution.
3. **Applying Concepts** Explain how each of the following can help people but harm the environment: hospitals, refrigerators, and road construction.

▼ Answers to Review

1. Some pollutants are eyesores, such as open landfills. Some pollutants are poisonous to the environment and to living things.
2. Loud noise affects the ability to hear and think and can even permanently damage hearing.
3. hospitals: provide health care and generate medical waste; refrigerators: keep our food fresh and use a polluting chemical as a refrigerant; road construction: helps people travel easily from place to place and destroys habitat

Resource Depletion

Another problem for our environment is that we are using up, or depleting, natural resources. Some of the Earth's resources are renewable, but others are nonrenewable. A **renewable resource** is one that can be used again and again or has an unlimited supply. Fresh water and solar energy are renewable resources, as are some kinds of trees. A **nonrenewable resource** is one that can be used only once. Most minerals are nonrenewable. Fossil fuels, such as oil and coal, are also nonrenewable resources.

Some nonrenewable resources, such as petroleum, are probably not in danger of running out in your lifetime. But we use more and more nonrenewable resources every year, and they cannot last forever. Plus, the removal of some materials from the Earth carries a high price tag in the form of oil spills, loss of habitat, and damage from mining, as shown in **Figure 6**.

MATH BREAK

Water Depletion

An underground water supply has a depth of 200 m of water. Water seeps in at the rate of 4 cm/year. Water is pumped out at the rate of 1 m/year. How long will this water supply last?

To find the net water loss from an underground water supply, subtract the amount that seeps into the water supply from the amount removed from the water supply.

How long will the water supply last if water seeps in at the rate of 10 cm/year and is removed at the rate of 10 cm/year?

Figure 6 *This area has been mined for coal using a method called strip mining.*

Nonrenewable or Renewable? Some resources once thought to be renewable are becoming nonrenewable. Ecosystems, such as tropical rain forests, are being polluted and destroyed, resulting in huge losses of habitat. Around the world, rich soil is being eroded away and polluted. A few centimeters of soil takes thousands of years to form and can be washed away in less than a year. Underground water needed for drinking and irrigation is used faster than it is replaced. Several centimeters of water may seep into an underground source each year, but in the same amount of time, *meters* of water are being pumped out.

✓ Self-Check

1. In what ways do you use nonrenewable resources?
2. Why would it not be a good idea to use up a nonrenewable resource?

(See page 782 to check your answers.)

GUIDED PRACTICE

Write the following headings on the board: "Renewable," "Nonrenewable." Then write the names of the following resources on the board: soil, air, natural gas, coal, iron, fresh water, trees. Work with students to categorize each resource correctly. *(renewable: soil, air, fresh water, trees; nonrenewable: natural gas, coal, iron)*

Then write the heading "Renewable but could become nonrenewable." Suggest to students that all of the resources under the "Renewable" heading could be placed under this heading, and challenge them to explain why. *(All of the renewable resources could become so polluted or over-used that they would no longer be useful or available.)*

Answers to MATHBREAK

208.3 years; forever

Math Skills Worksheet 28 "A Formula for SI Catch-up"

TOPIC: Resource Depletion
GO TO: www.scilinks.org
*sci*LINKS NUMBER: HSTL510

Answers to Self-Check

1. We use nonrenewable resources when we burn fossil fuels while driving or riding in a car or burning coal for heat. When we use minerals that are mined, we are using a nonrenewable resource. Pumping ground water is another use of a nonrenewable resource, if the water is used faster than it is replenished.

2. If a nonrenewable resource is used up, we can no longer rely on that resource. Certain oil and coal deposits have been building since life began on the planet. It may take hundreds of years to replace a mature forest that can be cut in a day.

Section 1 • First the Bad News   **501**

2) Teach, continued

MATH and MORE

While Earth's human population is expected to continue to grow rapidly, not every country in the world is expected to grow at the same rate. The growth rates of some countries, such as Japan and Sweden, are expected to shrink. In 1998, there were 5.9 billion people in the world. If current trends continue, there will be 9.4 billion in 2050, almost double. You can quickly estimate the number of years it will take for a population to double by dividing 70 by the population's current growth rate (GR). Have students find the doubling time for the following regions:

Northern Europe, GR = 0.2
North America, GR = 0.7
Africa, GR = 2.9
Asia, GR = 1.8
Latin America, GR = 2.2

Northern Europe
70 ÷ 0.2 GR = 350 years

North America
70 ÷ 0.7 GR = 100 years

Africa 70 ÷ 2.9 GR = 24 years

Asia 70 ÷ 1.8 GR = 39 years

Latin America
70 ÷ 2.2 GR = 32 years

internetconnect
TOPIC: Population Growth
GO TO: www.scilinks.org
sciLINKS NUMBER: HSTL515

Figure 7 *The zebra mussel is an alien invader that is clogging water treatment plants in the Great Lakes region.*

Figure 8 *The purple loosestrife from Europe is choking out natural vegetation in North America.*

Alien Species

People are constantly on the move. Without knowing it, we take along passengers. Boats, airplanes, and cars carry plant seeds, animal eggs, and adult organisms from one part of the world to another. An organism that makes a home for itself in a new place is an *alien.* One reason alien species often thrive in foreign lands is that they are free from the predators in their native habitats.

Alien species often become pests and drive out native species. The zebra mussel, shown in **Figure 7,** hitched a ride on ships sailing from Europe to the United States in the 1980s. The purple loosestrife, shown in **Figure 8,** arrived long ago from Europe. Today it is crowding out native vegetation and threatening rare plant species in much of North America. Many organisms, such as the dandelion, are so common and have been here so long that it is easy to forget they don't belong.

Human Population Growth

In 1800, there were 1 billion people on Earth. In 1990, there were 5.2 billion. By 2100, there may be 14 billion. Today, one out of ten people goes to bed hungry every night, and millions die each year from hunger-related causes. Some people believe that the human population is already too high for the Earth to support.

More people require more resources, and the human population is growing rapidly. **Overpopulation** occurs when the number of individuals becomes so large that they can't get all the food, water, and other resources they need on an ongoing basis.

Figure 9 shows that it took most of human history for the human population to reach 1 billion. Will the planet be able to support 14 billion people?

Figure 9 *The Earth's human population is now doubling every few decades.*

Science Bloopers

During the 1930s, sometimes called the Dust Bowl years, soil conservation scientists in the southern United States recommended planting kudzu to hold soil in place. This fast-growing vine is native to China and Japan and can grow 18 m per season. Frosts kill kudzu in Asia, keeping its growth in check. In the South, where heavy frosts are infrequent, kudzu can grow all year. By the 1960s, kudzu had spread over trees and other plants throughout the South. Eradicating the vine is difficult because a single plant may have 50 or more vines attached to a giant root, which can weigh as much as 181 kg!

502 Chapter 21 • Environmental Problems and Solutions

Habitat Destruction

The term **biodiversity** means "variety of life." It refers to the many different species found in a particular habitat all across the planet.

Every habitat has its own diverse combination of occupants. Every time a bulldozer digs or a chainsaw buzzes, every time hazardous wastes are dumped, a habitat is damaged, changed, or destroyed. And every time a habitat is destroyed, biodiversity is lost.

Forests Trees give us oxygen, furniture, fuel, fruits and nuts, rubber, alcohol, paper, turpentine, pencils, and telephone poles. Once trees covered twice as much land as they do today. *Deforestation,* such as that in **Figure 10,** is the clearing of forest lands. Tropical forests are cut for mines, dams, and roads. They are also cleared for paper, fuel, and building materials. But after tropical rain forests are cleared, little can grow on the land. Tropical soil doesn't have many nutrients, so it cannot be used for farming and is often abandoned.

Figure 10 *Temperate forests are destroyed for many of the same reasons that tropical rain forests are destroyed.*

Wetlands Wetlands were once considered unimportant. But as you know, that's not true. Wetlands help control flooding by soaking up the water from overflowing rivers. They filter pollutants from flowing water and provide breeding grounds for animals. They help prevent soil erosion and restore underground water supplies. Yet wetlands are often drained and filled to provide land for farms, homes, and shopping malls. They are dredged to keep passages open for ships and boats. Wetland habitats can also be destroyed by pollution.

Activity

Look around the room. How many objects can you find that are made of wood? List them in your ScienceLog. Add all the products you can think of that come from trees.

TRY at HOME

Marine Habitats Oil is a major contributor to marine habitat loss. Oil from cities and industries is sometimes dumped into the ocean. Accidental spills and waste from oil tankers add more oil to the oceans. Spilled oil contaminates both open waters and coastal habitats, as shown in **Figure 11.** All the oceans are connected, so pollutants from one ocean can be carried around the world.

Figure 11 *Oil from the* Exxon Valdez *damaged more than 2,300 km² of the Alaskan coast.*

3) Extend

DEMONSTRATION

Oil Spills and Seabird Eggs (This activity can be done as a demonstration or as a group activity.) Have groups do the following activity to investigate how oil can seep through eggshells. Give each group four hardboiled eggs and a bowl filled with 250 mL of vegetable oil that has been dyed with oil-soluble red food coloring. Students will place all the eggs in the bowl, remove one egg every 5 minutes, and shell it. Have them record how much time elapses before a shelled egg shows red coloring, indicating that the oil has permeated the shell. Have students draw some conclusions about how crude oil seeping through the shells of developing seabirds might affect the unborn birds and how it might affect future seabird populations. (The oil might kill the developing birds, or it might interfere with their proper development such that if they are born, their chance of survival would be compromised. With fewer birds born or surviving to reproduce, the species' existence could be threatened.) **Sheltered English**

Math Skills Worksheet 37 "Rain-Forest Math"

IS THAT A FACT!

The destruction of coral reef habitats, which tend to be very high in biodiversity, threatens the existence of many marine organisms. Threats to coral reef habitats include the development of coastal land and damage to reefs by boat anchors.

MISCONCEPTION ALERT

Though rain forests are lush, the soil contains very few nutrients. When organisms die in a rain forest, they decompose quickly and the nutrients that are released are quickly taken up by other organisms.

Section 1 • First the Bad News **503**

4) Close

Answer to APPLY

It is not a good idea to release 1,000 balloons because the balloons will eventually burst and fall to Earth. The plastic material of the balloons will not degrade and will be a threat to wildlife.

Quiz

1. Why is it dangerous to dispose of hazardous waste by burying it? *(Buried hazardous waste can exude harmful chemicals that pollute drinking water.)*
2. Why is coal considered a nonrenewable resource? *(Coal is nonrenewable because it can be used only once and there is a limited supply of it.)*
3. What are two ways pollution can harm people? *(Possible answer: Exposure to some chemicals may cause cancer and other health problems; drinking polluted water and breathing polluted air may cause lung damage.)*

ALTERNATIVE ASSESSMENT

Have groups of students paint a mural of what the neighborhood near your school might look like in the year 2100 if pollution, resource depletion, and habitat destruction continue at a rapid rate. Sheltered English

Balloons Aloft

Your town is about to celebrate its 200th birthday. A giant birthday party is planned. As part of the celebration, the town plans to release 1,000 helium balloons that say "Happy Birthday to Our Town." Why is this not a good idea? What can you do to convince town officials to change their plans?

Figure 12 *This sea bird has become entangled in a plastic six-pack holder.*

BRAIN FOOD

If humans became extinct, other organisms would go on living. But if all the insects became extinct, many plants could not reproduce. Animals would lose their food supply. The organisms we depend on, and eventually all of us, would disappear from the face of the Earth.

Plastics are often dumped into marine habitats. They are lightweight and float on the surface. They are not **biodegradable**, so they are not broken down by the environment. Animals, such as the bird in **Figure 12**, try to eat them and often get tangled in them and die. Dumping plastics into the ocean is against the law, but it is difficult to enforce.

Effects on Humans

Trees and sea creatures are not the only organisms affected by pollution, global warming, and habitat destruction. The damage we do to the Earth affects us too. Sometimes the effect is immediate. If you drink polluted water, you may immediately get sick or even die. But sometimes the damage is not apparent right away. Some chemicals cause cancers 20 or 30 years after a person is exposed to them. Your children or grandchildren may have to deal with depleted resources.

Anything that endangers other organisms will eventually endanger us too. Taking good care of the environment requires being concerned about what is happening right now. It also requires looking ahead to the future.

REVIEW

1. Why do alien species often thrive?
2. Explain how human population growth is related to pollution problems.
3. **Applying Concepts** How can the destruction of wetland habitats affect humans?

Answers to Review

1. Alien species often thrive in foreign lands because they have no natural predators.
2. The larger the human population is, the more energy and materials that are needed and the more waste that is produced. Pollution problems happen when there is more waste being produced than we can dispose of without spoiling the environment.
3. Wetlands help control flooding, filter pollutants, prevent erosion, and help restore underground water supplies.

504 Chapter 21 • Environmental Problems and Solutions

Section 2

Terms to Learn
conservation
recycling
resource recovery

What You'll Do
- Explain the importance of conservation.
- Describe the three Rs and their importance.
- Explain how habitats can be protected.
- List ways you can help protect the Earth.

The Good News: Solutions

As you've seen, the news is bad. But it isn't *all* bad. In fact, there is plenty of good news. The good news is about what people can do—and are doing—to save the Earth. It is about what *you* can do to save the Earth. Just as people are responsible for damaging the Earth, people can also take responsiblity for helping to heal and preserve the Earth.

Conservation

One major way to help save the Earth is conservation. **Conservation** is the wise use of and the preservation of natural resources. If you ride your bike to your friend's house, you conserve fuel. At the same time, you prevent air pollution. If you use organic compost instead of chemical fertilizer on your garden, you conserve the resources needed to make the fertilizer. You also prevent soil and water pollution.

Practicing conservation means using fewer natural resources. It also means reducing waste. The three Rs, shown in **Figure 13,** describe three ways to conserve resources and reduce damage to the Earth: **R**educe, **R**euse, and **R**ecycle.

Figure 13 *These teenagers are observing the three Rs by using a cloth shopping bag, donating outgrown clothing to be reused, and recycling plastic.*

Dan and Ed made a great plan,
to recycle all that they can.
They reduced lots of waste
with a bit too much haste,
and recycled their mother's new van.

 Teaching Transparency 77
"Practicing Conservation"

 Directed Reading Worksheet 21 Section 2

2) Teach

DEMONSTRATION

Friendly Cleaner The following recipe is for safe, all-purpose cleaner. Write it on the chalkboard so that students may copy it if they wish.

- 3.78 L (1 gal) hot water
- 59 mL ($\frac{1}{4}$ cup) borax
- 59 mL ($\frac{1}{4}$ cup) vinegar
- 30 mL (2 tbsp) phosphate-free liquid soap

As you prepare the solution, share the following information with students. Borax (sodium tetraborate decahydrate) is a naturally occurring mineral that consists primarily of sodium and boron and works well as a cleanser, a disinfectant, and a deodorizer. Vinegar is a weak acid and is a good degreaser. The liquid soap removes dirt and grease. All the ingredients are nontoxic and are easy on the environment. When the solution is mixed, try it out in the classroom by using it on several surfaces. **Sheltered English**

MATH and MORE

Poster Project A faucet that drips at a rate of one drop per second wastes about 4 L of water per day. Have pairs of students incorporate this fact into a poster reminding people to turn off taps completely.

Reduce

The most obvious way to conserve the Earth's resources is to use less. This will also help reduce pollution and wastes. Some companies have started using a variety of strategies to conserve resources. They often save money in the process.

Reducing Waste and Pollution One-third of the waste from cities and towns is packaging. To conserve resources and reduce waste, products can be wrapped in less paper and plastic. Fast foods can be wrapped in thin paper instead of large plastic containers that are not biodegradable. You can choose to take your purchases without a sack if you don't need one. Scientists, such as the ones in **Figure 14**, are working to make better biodegradable plastics.

Some companies are searching for less hazardous materials to use in making products. For example, some farmers refuse to use pesticides and chemical fertilizers. They practice organic farming. They use mulch, compost, manure, and natural pesticides. Agricultural specialists are also developing new farming techniques that are better for the environment.

Figure 14 These scientists are studying ways to use waste products to make biodegradable plastics.

Reducing Use of Nonrenewable Resources Scientists are searching for alternative sources of energy. They want to avoid burning fuels and using nuclear energy. In some parts of the world solar energy heats water and powers homes, such as those shown in **Figure 15**. Engineers are working to make solar-powered cars practical. Other scientists are investigating the use of alternative power sources, such as wind, tides, and falling water.

It's Everyone's Responsibility Using fewer resources and reducing waste is not the job of industry and agriculture alone. Individuals use plenty of manufactured products and plenty of energy. They also produce large quantities of waste. Each United States citizen produces 40 times more waste than a citizen of a developing country. Why do you think this is so? What could you do to reduce the amount of trash that you produce? Everyone can take responsibility for helping to conserve the Earth's resources.

Figure 15 Rooftop solar panels provide most of the energy used in this neighborhood in Rotterdam, Holland.

CONNECT TO CHEMISTRY

Biodegradable plastics contain substances that can be broken down by microbes, such as starch. Suggest that students imagine that they work for a company that uses nondegradable plastic in the packaging of their products. Have them write a persuasive letter to the company's directors advocating a changeover to biodegradable plastics.

---

506 Chapter 21 • Environmental Problems and Solutions

Reuse

Do you get hand-me-down clothes from an older sibling? Do you try to fix broken sports equipment instead of throwing it away? If so, you are helping preserve the Earth by *reusing* products.

Reusing Products Every time someone reuses a plastic bag, one less bag needs to be made, and one less bag pollutes the Earth. Every time someone uses a rechargeable battery, one less battery needs to be made, and one less battery will pollute the Earth. Reusing is an important way to conserve resources and prevent pollution.

Reusing Water About 85 percent of the water used in homes goes down the drain. Communities with water shortages are experimenting with reclaiming and reusing this waste water. Some use green plants or filter-feeding animals such as clams to clean the water. The water isn't pure enough to drink, but it is fine for watering lawns and golf courses, such as the one shown in **Figure 16.**

Figure 16 *This golf course is being watered with reclaimed water.*

Recycle

Recycling is a form of reuse. **Recycling** requires breaking down trash and using it again. Sometimes recycled products are used to make the same kind of products. Sometimes they are made into different products. The park bench in **Figure 17** was made from plastic foam cups, hamburger boxes, and plastic bottles that once held detergent, yogurt, and margarine. All of the containers pictured in **Figure 18** can be easily recycled.

Figure 17 *This park bench is made of melted, remolded, and reused plastic.*

Figure 18 *These containers are examples of common household trash that can be recycled.*

Self-Check

1. How can you reduce the amount of electricity you use?
2. List five products that can be reused easily.

(See page 782 to check your answers.)

Meeting Individual Needs

Learners Having Difficulty To help students distinguish the difference between the words *reuse* and *recycle*, point out that *reuse* refers to using a particular item again and again. You might indicate this graphically by drawing a series of horizontal arrows and drawing a lunchbox (or other reusable item) between each of the arrows to indicate that it can be used many times. Then draw the triangular, three-arrowed recycling symbol on the board. Explain that the word *recycle* usually indicates that an item undergoes a process that transforms it into another item or another version of the same item. To depict recycling, you might draw three different items made from the same material (such as a newspaper, a piece of writing paper, and a cardboard box) at the three corners of the recycling symbol. Sheltered English

Research

Writing — Find out what specific materials are recycled in your town and county. For example, many areas recycle some types of plastics but not others. If you have curbside pickup, find out where you would need to take items not picked up, such as scrap metal or compost. Share your findings with the class.

Answers to Self-Check

1. Turn off lights, CD players, radios, and computers when leaving a room. Set thermostats a little lower in the winter (wear sweaters). Don't leave the refrigerator door open while deciding what you want.

2. Sample answers: plastic bags, rechargeable batteries, water, clothing, and toys. The difference between a reused and a recycled object is that a reused article may be cleaned but is basically unchanged. A recycled article has been broken down and re-formed into another useable product.

2) Teach, continued

READING STRATEGY

Prediction guide Ask students: What is "resource recovery"? (Hint: It's not the same as recycling.) (Resource recovery is the process of burning garbage to create electricity.)

Provide students with the following data about the time it takes various wastes to break down naturally.

- paper, 2–12 months
- plastic bags, 20–30 years
- aluminum cans, 200–500 years
- plastic rings from soft-drink six-packs, 450 years
- plastic-foam, never

Have students apply the reduce or reuse strategies to the above items. Ask if it is better to reduce the use of some of these items rather than reuse them. Why or why not?

TOPIC: Recycling
GO TO: www.scilinks.org
*sci*LINKS NUMBER: HSTL520

Figure 19 Each kind of recycled material is sorted into its own bin and then delivered to a recycling plant for processing.

Recycling Trash Plastics, paper, aluminum cans, waste wood, glass, and cardboard are some examples of materials that can be recycled. Every week, half a million trees are needed to make Sunday newspapers. Recycling newspapers could save many trees. Recycling aluminum foil and cans saves 95 percent of the energy needed to change raw ore into aluminum. Glass makes up 8 percent of all our waste. It can be remelted to make new bottles and jars. Lead batteries can be recycled into new batteries.

Some cities, such as Austin, Texas, make recycling easy. Special containers for glass, plastic, aluminum, and paper are provided to each city customer. Each week trash to be recycled is collected in special trucks, such as the one shown in **Figure 19,** at the same time other waste is collected.

Recycling Resources Waste that can be burned can also be used to generate electricity in factories like the one shown in **Figure 20.** The process of transforming garbage to electricity is called **resource recovery.** The waste collected by all the cities and towns in the United States could produce about the same amount of electricity as 15 large nuclear power plants. Some companies are beginning to do this with their own waste. It saves them money, and it is responsible management.

Recycling is not difficult. Yet in the United States, only about 11 percent of the garbage is recycled. This compares with about 30 percent in Europe and 50 percent in Japan.

Figure 20 A waste-to-energy plant can provide electricity to many homes and businesses.

REVIEW

1. Define and explain *conservation*.
2. Describe the three main ways to conserve natural resources.
3. **Analyzing Relationships** How does conservation of resources also reduce pollution and other damage to the Earth?

Answers to Review

1. Conservation is the wise use and preservation of natural resources. Consuming as few manufactured products as possible and then reusing them in some way is one way to conserve natural resources.
2. The three main ways to conserve natural resources are to reduce, reuse, and recycle.
3. Conservation of resources reduces damage to the Earth by reducing the amount of resources extracted and by reducing the waste and pollution created to alter and package those resources into products people buy.

Maintaining Biodiversity

Imagine a forest with just one kind of tree. If a disease hits that species, the entire forest might be wiped out. Now imagine a forest with 10 different kinds of trees. If a disease hits one kind of tree, nine different species will remain. Look at **Figure 21.** This field is growing a very important crop—cotton. But it is not very diverse. For the crop to thrive, the farmer must carefully manage the crop with weedkillers, pesticides, and fertilizers. Biodiversity helps to keep communities naturally stable.

How much biodiversity is in your part of the world? Investigate by turning to page 758 in your LabBook.

Figure 21 *What could happen if a cotton disease hits this cotton field? Biodiversity is low in fields of crops like this one.*

Species variety is also important because each species makes a unique contribution to an ecosystem. In addition, many species are important to humans. They provide many things, such as foods, medicines, natural pest control, beauty, and companionship, to name just a few.

Species Protection One way to maintain biodiversity is through the protection of individual species. In the United States, the Endangered Species Act is designed to do just that. Endangered organisms are included in a special list. The law forbids activities that would damage a plant or animal on the endangered species list. It also requires the development of programs to help endangered populations recover. Some endangered species are now increasing in number, such as the California condor in **Figure 22.**

Unfortunately, the process of getting a species on the endangered list takes a long time. Many new species need to be added to the list. Many species become extinct even before they are listed!

Figure 22 *The California condor is returning from the verge of extinction thanks to careful captive breeding.*

LabBook PG 758
Biodiversity—What a Disturbing Thought!

Multicultural CONNECTION

Although Costa Rica is a small country (51,000 km^2), an estimated 505,660 species live there, which is about 4 percent of all living species. In 1989, the Costa Rican government set up the National Institute of Biodiversity (Instituto Nacional de Biodiversidad, or INBio) to catalog native species and to educate residents about the importance of preserving biodiversity. Some of the collecting and cataloging is done by local people who have been trained by scientists. Invite interested students to use the Internet to find out how INBio shares information about beneficial and sustainable uses for some of the unique species found in Costa Rica.

MISCONCEPTION ALERT

In the recent past, humans caused extinction primarily by overhunting and overharvesting. Today extinction of whole groups of species is more likely to result from habitat loss and the introduction of foreign species than from hunting. Saving species today requires protecting not just the animals but the ecosystems that support them.

internetconnect
TOPIC: Maintaining Biodiversity
GO TO: www.scilinks.org
sciLINKS NUMBER: HSTL525

IS THAT A FACT!

Just outside Detroit, Michigan, looms a 50 m high former landfill once known as Mount Trashmore. From the 1970s to the mid-1990s, Mount Trashmore was used as a ski slope; it even had ski lifts! In addition, methane gas tapped from the decomposing wastes within the landfill was converted to electricity, which fulfilled the energy needs of some 2,000 households. Today the former landfill, renamed Riverview Highlands, is a recreational area offering ice skating, tubing (using recycled tractor tire tubes), and other sporting activities.

Section 2 • The Good News: Solutions

3) Extend

MEETING INDIVIDUAL NEEDS

Advanced Learners There are numerous volunteer activities that seek to protect and maintain animal and plant habitats. A few activities are as follows: an organized cleanup of a beach or a riverfront; tree planting; or removing alien species from a forest, prairie, or wetland preserve. Have interested students contact local environmental organizations to find out how they can help organize and lead a group of classmates in volunteer field work.
Sheltered English

CROSS-DISCIPLINARY FOCUS

Art and Design As a habitat disappears, many birds have difficulty obtaining food and shelter. Have students or groups of students research, design, and build a simple birdhouse or bird feeder. Birdhouses and bird feeders are also a good way to make use of scrap lumber.
Sheltered English

INDEPENDENT PRACTICE

Concept Mapping Have students make a concept map with the terms *reduce, reuse,* and *recycle* arranged around the phrase *Things I Can Do to Conserve Natural Resources*. Have them include as many ideas as they can on the map.

Deciding About Environmental Issues PG 760

Figure 23 Setting aside public lands for wildlife is one way to protect habitats.

Habitat Protection Waiting until a species is almost extinct to begin protecting it is like waiting until your teeth are rotting to begin brushing them. Scientists want to prevent species from becoming endangered as well as from becoming extinct.

Plants, animals, and microorganisms do not live independently. Each is part of a huge interconnected web of organisms. To protect the entire web and to avoid disrupting the worldwide balance of nature, complete habitats, not just individual species, must be preserved. *All* species, not just those that are endangered, must be protected. All of the species that live in the nature preserve pictured in **Figure 23** are protected because the entire habitat is protected.

Strategies

Laws have been enacted to help conserve the Earth's environment. The purposes of such laws are listed below along with some of the ways citizens can help achieve these goals.

- **Reduce pesticide use.**
  Spray only pesticides that are targeted specifically for harmful insects. Use natural pesticides that interfere with the ways certain insects grow, develop, and live. Develop more biodegradable pesticides that will not injure birds, animals, or plants.

- **Reduce pollution.**
  Regulations prohibit the dumping of toxic substances and solid wastes into rivers, streams, lakes, and oceans and onto farmland and forests.

- **Protect habitats.**
  Conserve wetlands. Reduce deforestation. Practice logging techniques that consider the environment. Use resources at a rate that allows them to be replenished. Protect entire habitats.

- **Enforce the Endangered Species Act.**
  Speed up the process of getting endangered organisms listed.

- **Develop alternative energy sources.**
  Increase the use of solar power, wind power, and other renewable energy sources.

QuickLab

Trash Check

Keep track of all the trash you produce in one day. Classify it into groups. How much is food scraps? What might be considered a hazardous waste? What can be recycled? What can be reused? How can you reduce the amount of trash you produce?

TRY at HOME

Q: What are people who damage the habitat of endangered birds engaging in?

A: fowl play

What *You* Can Do

Reduce, reuse, recycle. Protect the Earth. These are jobs for everyone. Children as well as adults can help to save the Earth. The following list offers some suggestions for how *you* can help. How many of these things do you already do? What can you add to the list?

1. Buy things in packages that can be recycled.
2. Give away your old toys.
3. Use recycled paper.
4. Fill up both sides of a sheet of paper.
5. If you can't use permanent dishes, use paper instead of plastic-foam cups and plates.
6. Recycle glass, plastics, paper, aluminum, and batteries.
7. Don't buy anything made from an endangered animal.
8. Use rechargeable batteries.
9. Turn off lights, CD players, and computers when not in use.
10. Wear hand-me-downs.
11. Share books with friends, or use the library.
12. Walk, ride a bicycle, or use public transportation.
13. Carry a reusable cloth shopping bag to the store.
14. Use a lunch box or reuse your paper lunch bags.
15. Turn off the water while you brush your teeth.
16. Make a compost heap.
17. Buy products made from biodegradable plastic.
18. Use cloth napkins and kitchen towels.
19. Buy products with little or no packaging.
20. Repair leaking faucets.

REVIEW

1. Describe why biodiversity is important.
2. Why is it important to protect entire habitats?
3. **Applying Concepts** In the list above, identify which suggestions involve reducing, reusing, or recycling. Some suggestions will involve more than one of the three Rs.

internet connect

SC_iLINKS NSTA
TOPIC: Recycling, Maintaining Biodiversity
GO TO: www.scilinks.org
*sci*LINKS NUMBER: HSTL520, HSTL525

511

4) Close

Quiz

1. Give one example each of how you could reduce and reuse natural resources, and one example of how you could recycle a natural resource. (Reduce: Ride a bike to a friend's house instead of getting a ride. Reuse: Buy refillable water jugs, and refill them rather than discarding them when empty. Recycle: Recycle aluminum cans.)

2. How does the Endangered Species Act protect endangered organisms? (The law forbids activities that would damage any organism that is listed. It also requires the development of programs that help the endangered species recover.)

ALTERNATIVE ASSESSMENT

Writing Organize students into small groups, and have them create a "Test Your Environmental IQ" quiz. Have them use the information they learned in this section to write 10 multiple-choice questions. Have them also devise a scoring system. If possible, have students post their quizzes on a school Web site.

Reinforcement Worksheet 21
"It's 'R' Planet!"

Critical Thinking Worksheet 21
"Bud Kindfellow Has a Plan"

Interactive Explorations CD-ROM "Moose Malady"

▼ Answers to Review

1. Biodiversity helps to keep biological communities naturally stable.
2. Entire habitats must be preserved and protected in order to preserve biodiversity because each organism is connected to all others in a huge web. The entire web must be protected to avoid disrupting the worldwide balance of nature.
3. 1—reduce, recycle; 2—reduce, reuse; 3—reduce, recycle; 4—reduce; 5—reduce; 6—reduce; 7—reduce; 8—reduce, reuse; 9—reduce; 10—reduce, reuse; 11—reduce, reuse; 12—reduce, reuse; 13—reduce, reuse; 14—reduce, reuse; 15—recycle; 16—recycle; 17—reduce; 18—reduce; 19—reduce; 20—reduce

Chapter Highlights

Vocabulary Definitions

SECTION 1

pollution the presence of harmful substances in the environment

renewable resource a natural resource that can be used and replaced over a relatively short time

nonrenewable resource a natural resource that cannot be replaced or that can be replaced only over thousands or millions of years

overpopulation a condition that occurs when the number of individuals becomes so large that there are not enough resources for all individuals

biodiversity the number and variety of living things

biodegradable capable of being broken down by the environment

Chapter Highlights

SECTION 1

Vocabulary
pollution (p. 498)
renewable resource (p. 501)
nonrenewable resource (p. 501)
overpopulation (p. 502)
biodiversity (p. 503)
biodegradable (p. 504)

Section Notes
- The Earth is being polluted by solid wastes, hazardous chemicals, radioactive materials, noise, and heat.
- Some of the Earth's resources renew themselves, and others do not. Some of the nonrenewable resources are being used up.
- Alien species often invade foreign lands, where they may thrive, become pests, and threaten native species.
- The human population is in danger of reaching numbers that the Earth cannot support.
- The Earth's habitats are being destroyed in a variety of ways, including deforestation, the filling of wetlands, and pollution.
- Deforestation may cause the extinction of species and often leaves the soil infertile.
- Air, water, and soil pollution can damage or kill animals, plants, and microorganisms.
- Humans depend on many different kinds of organisms. Pollution, global warming, habitat destruction—anything that affects other organisms will eventually affect humans too.

✓ Skills Check

Math Concepts

NET WATER LOSS Suppose that water seeps into an underground water supply at the rate of 10 cm/year. The underground water supply is 100 m deep, but it is being pumped out at about 2 m/year. How long will the water last?

First convert all measurements to centimeters.

(100 m = 10,000 cm; 2 m = 200 cm)

Then find the net loss of water per year.

200 cm − 10 cm = 190 cm (net loss per year)

Now divide the depth of the underground water supply by the net loss per year to find out how many years this water supply will last.

10,000 cm ÷ 190 cm = 52.6 years

Visual Understanding

THINGS YOU CAN DO Obviously, the strategies listed on page 510 to help preserve the Earth's habitats are strategies that scientists and other professionals are developing. To help you understand some of the things that you can do now, review the list on page 511.

Lab and Activity Highlights

Biodiversity—What a Disturbing Thought! PG 758

Deciding About Environmental Issues PG 760

 Datasheets for LabBook (blackline masters for these labs)

SECTION 2

Vocabulary
conservation (p. 505)
recycling (p. 507)
resource recovery (p. 508)

Section Notes
- Conservation is the wise use of and preservation of the Earth's natural resources. By practicing conservation, people can reduce pollution and ensure that resources will be available to people in the future.
- Conservation involves the three Rs: Reduce, Reuse, and Recycle. Reducing means using fewer resources to begin with. Reusing means using materials and products over and over. Recycling involves breaking down used products and making them into new ones.
- Biodiversity is the variety of life on Earth. It is vital for maintaining stable, healthy, and functioning ecosystems.
- Habitats can be protected by using fewer pesticides, reducing pollution, avoiding habitat destruction, protecting species, and using alternative renewable sources of energy.
- Everyone can help to save the Earth by practicing the three Rs in their daily life.

Labs
Biodiversity—What a Disturbing Thought! (p. 758)
Deciding About Environmental Issues (p. 760)

VOCABULARY DEFINITIONS, continued

SECTION 2
conservation the wise use of and preservation of natural resources
recycling the process of making new products from reprocessed used products
resource recovery the process of transforming into useable products things normally thrown away

 Vocabulary Review Worksheet 21

 Blackline masters of these Chapter Highlights can be found in the **Study Guide.**

---

internet connect

 GO TO: go.hrw.com

Visit the **HRW** Web site for a variety of learning tools related to this chapter. Just type in the keyword:

KEYWORD: HSTENV

 GO TO: www.scilinks.org

Visit the **National Science Teachers Association** on-line Web site for Internet resources related to this chapter. Just type in the sciLINKS number for more information about the topic:

TOPIC: Air Pollution **sciLINKS NUMBER:** HSTL505
TOPIC: Resource Depletion **sciLINKS NUMBER:** HSTL510
TOPIC: Population Growth **sciLINKS NUMBER:** HSTL515
TOPIC: Recycling **sciLINKS NUMBER:** HSTL520
TOPIC: Maintaining Biodiversity **sciLINKS NUMBER:** HSTL525

Lab and Activity Highlights

LabBank

 EcoLabs & Field Activities, A Filter with Culture, EcoLab 8

Long-Term Projects & Research Ideas, Let's Talk Trash, Project 21

Interactive Explorations CD-ROM

 CD 2, Exploration 3, "Moose Malady"

Chapter Review Answers

USING VOCABULARY

1. Pollution
2. Radioactive waste
3. nonrenewable
4. Biodiversity
5. Recycling

UNDERSTANDING CONCEPTS

Multiple Choice

6. d
7. b
8. c
9. b
10. c
11. b

Short Answer

12. ride a bicycle, recycle cans and bottles, wear secondhand clothing, use rechargeable batteries, and others
13. Alien species thrive without their native predators and often crowd out native organisms. Sometimes the habitat of a rare species is taken over by an alien species, causing the native species to become endangered.

Concept Mapping Transparency 21

Blackline masters of this Chapter Review can be found in the **Study Guide**.

Chapter Review

USING VOCABULARY

To complete the following sentences, choose the correct term from each pair of terms listed below:

1. ___?___ is the presence of harmful substances in the environment. *(Pollution* or *Biodiversity)*

2. ___?___ is a type of pollution produced by nuclear power plants. *(CFC* or *Radioactive waste)*

3. A ___?___ resource can be used only once. *(nuclear* or *nonrenewable)*

4. ___?___ is the variety of forms among living things. *(Biodegradable* or *Biodiversity)*

5. ___?___ is the breaking down of trash and using it to make a new product. *(Recycling* or *Reuse)*

UNDERSTANDING CONCEPTS

Multiple Choice

6. Habitat protection is important because
   a. organisms do not live independently.
   b. protecting habitats is a way to protect species.
   c. without it the balance of nature could be disrupted.
   d. All of the above

7. The Earth's resources can be conserved
   a. only by the actions of industry.
   b. by reducing the use of nonrenewable resources.
   c. if people do whatever they want to do.
   d. by throwing away all our trash.

8. Endangered species
   a. are those that are extinct.
   b. are found only in tropical rain forests.
   c. can sometimes be brought back from near extinction.
   d. are all protected by the Endangered Species Act.

9. Global warming is a danger
   a. only to people living in warm climates.
   b. to organisms all over the planet.
   c. only to life at the poles.
   d. to the amount of carbon dioxide in the air.

10. Overpopulation
    a. does not occur among human beings.
    b. helps keep pollution levels down.
    c. occurs when a species cannot get all the food, water, and other resources it needs.
    d. occurs only in large cities.

11. Biodiversity
    a. is of no concern to scientists.
    b. helps to keep ecosystems stable.
    c. causes diseases to destroy populations.
    d. is found only in temperate forests.

Short Answer

12. Describe how you can help to conserve resources. Include strategies from all of the three Rs.

13. Describe the connection between alien species and endangered species.

Concept Mapping

14. Use the following terms to create a concept map: pollution, pollutants, CFCs, cancer, PCBs, toxic, radioactive wastes, global warming.

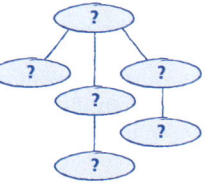

CRITICAL THINKING AND PROBLEM SOLVING

Write one or two sentences to answer the following question:

15. Suppose that the supply of fossil fuels were going to run out in 10 years. What would happen if we ran out without being prepared? What could be done to prepare for such an event?

MATH IN SCIENCE

16. If each person in a city of 150,000 throws away 12 kg of trash every week, how many metric tons of trash does the city produce per year? (There are 52 weeks in a year and 1,000 kg in a metric ton.)

INTERPRETING GRAPHICS

The illustration above shows how people in one home use natural resources.

17. Identify ways in which the people in this picture are wasting natural resources. Describe at least three examples, and tell what could be done to conserve resources.

18. Identify which resources in this picture are renewable.

19. Identify any sources of hazardous waste in this picture.

20. Explain how the girl wearing headphones is reducing pollution in the air. How could such a choice cause her harm?

Reading Check-up

Take a minute to review your answers to the Pre-Reading Questions found at the bottom of page 496. Have your answers changed? If necessary, revise your answers based on what you have learned since you began this chapter.

Concept Mapping

14. An answer to this exercise can be found at the end of this book.

CRITICAL THINKING AND PROBLEM SOLVING

15. We would have severe transportation problems, and most people would not be able to get to work or school. Some places would not have electricity or gas for heating, cooling, or refrigeration. Our survival might even be threatened if needed supplies, such as food and medicine, could not be transported and delivered. We could prepare for such an event by developing alternative sources of fuel, such as solar energy.

MATH IN SCIENCE

16. 93,600 metric tons per year

INTERPRETING GRAPHICS

17. The water is running while the boy is brushing his teeth. He should turn off the water while he brushes. The water sprinklers are running while it is raining. The sprinklers should be turned off; the rain will water the lawn. A boy is throwing away a plastic container that can be recycled.

18. The water is a renewable resource as long as it is replenished faster than it is used.

19. If the girl is not using rechargeable batteries in the radio, the batteries are a source of hazardous waste. The father is pouring oil from the car into the gutter, where it will be a hazardous pollutant.

20. Headphones help reduce noise pollution. If she has the volume too high, it could damage her hearing.

CAREERS
Biologist— Dagmar Werner

Background
The green iguana (*Iguana iguana*) is native to Central America, where it was used by native people as a food source. Iguana meat is tasty, is high in protein, and has a relatively low fat content.

The green iguana population in Costa Rica has declined because people have hunted iguana eggs and adults and because so much of the iguana's habitat has been destroyed. Iguanas are tree-dwelling lizards, so they require a forest habitat to survive.

Teaching Strategy
Ask students why iguana farming might provide Central Americans with environmental benefits. Lead them to conclude that since iguanas are adapted to the forest that is already there, farming them requires preserving areas of forest. Preserving forest and reforesting cleared areas in turn helps preserve fragile tropical forest soils and helps preserve the variety of other creatures that make their home in the forest.

CAREERS

BIOLOGIST

Dagmar Werner works at the Carara Biological Preserve, in Costa Rica, protecting green iguanas. Suffering from the effects of hunting, pollution, and habitat destruction, the iguana was nearly extinct. Since the 1980s, Werner has improved the iguanas' chances of survival by breeding them and releasing thousands of young iguanas into the wild. She also trains other people to do the same.

At Werner's "iguana ranch" preserve, female iguanas lay their eggs in artificial nests. After they hatch, the young lizards are placed in a temperature- and humidity-controlled incubator and given a special diet. As a result, the iguanas grow faster and stronger and are better protected from predators than their wild counterparts. Ordinarily, less than 2 percent of all iguanas survive to adulthood, but Werner's iguanas have an 80 percent survival rate. Once the iguanas are released into the wild, Werner tracks and monitors them to determine whether they have successfully adapted to their less-controlled environment.

Chicken of the Trees
Because she knew the iguana was close to extinction, Werner took an immediate and drastic approach to saving the lizards. She combined her captive-breeding program at the preserve with an education program that shows farmers a new way to make money from the rain forest. Instead of cutting down rain forest to raise cattle, Werner encourages farmers to raise iguanas. The iguanas can be released into the wild or sold for food. Known as "chicken of the trees," this lizard has been a favored source of meat among rain-forest inhabitants for thousands of years.

With Werner's methods, farmers can protect iguanas and still earn a living. But convincing farmers hasn't been easy. According to Werner, "Many locals have never thought of wild animals as creatures that must be protected in order to survive." To help, Werner has established the Fundación Pro Iguana Verde (the Green Iguana Foundation), which sponsors festivals and education seminars. These activities promote the traditional appeal of the iguana, increase pride in the animal, and heighten awareness about the iguana's economic importance.

Find Other Solutions
▶ The green iguana is just one animal that is nearing extinction in the rain forest. Research another endangered species and find out what scientists and local communities are doing to protect the species. Does it seem to be working?

▶ *A green Iguana at Carara Biological Preserve, in Costa Rica*

Answer to Find Other Solutions
Students' answers will vary.

SCIENTIFIC DEBATE

Where Should the Wolves Roam?

The U.S. Fish and Wildlife Service has listed the gray wolf as an endangered species throughout most of the United States and has devised a plan to reintroduce the wolf to Yellowstone National Park, central Idaho, and northwestern Montana. The goal is to establish a population of at least 100 wolves at each location. If the project continues as planned, wolves may be removed from the endangered species list by 2002. But some ranchers and hunters are uneasy about the plan, and some environmentalists and wolf enthusiasts think that the plan doesn't go far enough to protect wolves.

Does the Plan Risk Livestock?

Ranchers are concerned that the wolves will kill livestock. These losses could result in a tremendous financial burden to ranchers. There is a compensation program currently established that will pay ranchers if wolves kill their livestock. But this program will end if the wolf is removed from the endangered species list. Ranchers point out that the threat to their livestock will not end when the wolf is removed from the list. In fact, the threat will increase, but ranchers will no longer receive any compensation.

On the other hand, some biologists offer evidence that wolves living near areas with adequate populations of deer, elk, moose, and other prey do not attack livestock. In fact, fewer than five wolf attacks on livestock were reported between 1995 and 1997.

Are Wolves a Threat to Wildlife?

Many scientists believe that the reintroduction plan would bring these regions into ecological balance for the first time in 60 years. They believe that the wolves will eliminate old and weak elk, moose, and deer and help keep these populations from growing too large.

Hunters fear that the wolves will kill many of the game animals in these areas. They cite studies that say large game animal populations cannot survive hunting by both humans and wolves. Hunting plays a significant role in the economy of the western states.

Are the People Safe?

Some people fear that wolves will attack people. However, there has never been a documented attack on humans by healthy wolves in North America. Supporters say that wolves are shy animals that prefer to keep their distance from people.

Most wolf enthusiasts admit that there are places where wolves belong and places where wolves do not belong. They believe that these reintroduction zones offer places for wolves to thrive without creating problems.

What Do You Think?

▶ Some people argue that stories about "the big, bad wolf" give the wolf its ferocious reputation. Do you think people's fears are based on myth, or do you think that the wolf is a danger to people and livestock living in the reintroduction zones? Do some research and provide examples to support your opinion.

◀ A Gray Wolf in Montana

SCIENTIFIC DEBATE

Where Should the Wolves Roam?

Background

In the 1920s, the gray wolf was exterminated from much of the northwestern United States. Ranchers and federal agents killed wolves to protect livestock. Those in favor of wolf reintroduction cite biologists' claims that wolf attacks on livestock are neither as widespread nor as serious as is generally believed. Some opponents of the reintroduction plan argue that wolves should not be classified as endangered at all. According to data from biologists, there are 1,500 to 2,000 wolves in Minnesota, 6,000 to 10,000 in Alaska, and 40,000 to 50,000 in Canada. With such numbers, many people feel that the animal should not receive the special treatment given to endangered species.

Activity

Research Have interested students research the latest news on the wolf reintroduction issue and present a report to the class.

Answer to What Do You Think?
Students' answers might vary, but most of the fears associated with wolves are based on myths.

UNIT 7

TIMELINE
Human Body Systems

Your body is made up of many systems that all work together like a finely tuned machine. Your lungs take in oxygen. Your heart pumps blood that delivers the oxygen to your tissues. Your brain reacts to things you see, hear, and smell, and sends signals through your nervous system that cause you to react to those things. Your digestive system converts the food you eat into energy that the cells of your body can use. And those are just a few things that your body can do!

In this unit, you will study the systems of your body. You'll discover how the parts of your body work together so that you can complete all your daily activities.

3000 B.C.
Ancient Egyptian doctors are the first to study the human body scientifically.

1824
Prevost and Dumas prove that sperm is essential for fertilization.

1893
Daniel Hale Williams, an African American surgeon, becomes the first to repair a tear in the pericardium, the sac around the heart.

1922
Insulin is discovered.

1930
Karl Landsteiner receives a Nobel Prize for his discovery of the four human blood types.

500 B.C.
Indian surgeon Susrata performs operations to remove cataracts.

1492
Christopher Columbus lands in the West Indies.

1543
Andreas Versalius publishes the first complete description of the structure of the human body.

1766
Albrecht von Haller determines that nerves control muscle movement and that all nerves are connected to the spinal cord or to the brain.

1619
William Harvey discovers that blood circulates and that the heart acts as a pump.

1941
During World War II in Italy, Rita Levi-Montalcini is forced to leave her work at a medical school laboratory because she is Jewish. She sets up a laboratory in her bedroom and studies the development of the nervous system.

1982
Dr. Robert Jarvik implants an artificial heart in Barney Clark.

1998
The first hand transplant is performed in France.

Human Body Systems

Chapter Organizer

CHAPTER ORGANIZATION	TIME MINUTES	OBJECTIVES	LABS, INVESTIGATIONS, AND DEMONSTRATIONS
Chapter Opener pp. 520–521	45	National Standards: UCP 3, SAI 2, LS 3a	**Start-Up Activity** Too Cold for Comfort, p. 521
Section 1 Body Organization	90	▶ Identify the major tissues found in the body. ▶ Compare an organ with an organ system. ▶ Describe a major function of each organ system. UCP 1, 3, LS 1a, 1d, 1e, 3a	
Section 2 The Skeletal System	90	▶ Identify the major organs of the skeletal system. ▶ Describe the functions of bones. ▶ Illustrate the internal structure of bones. ▶ Compare three types of joints. ▶ Discuss how bones function as levers. UCP 2–5, SAI 1, SPSP 1, 4, LS 1a, 1d, 1e	**QuickLab,** Pickled Bones, p. 527 GENERAL **Demonstration,** Bone Dissection, p. 527 in ATE GENERAL
Section 3 The Muscular System	90	▶ List the major parts of the muscular system. ▶ Describe the different types of muscle. ▶ Describe how skeletal muscles move bones. ▶ Compare aerobic exercise with resistance exercise. ▶ Give an example of a muscle injury. UCP 1, 4, SPSP 1, LS 1d, 1e; LabBook UCP 2, 3, SAI 1, 2	**QuickLab,** Power in Pairs, p. 531 GENERAL **Design Your Own,** Muscles at Work, p. 762 GENERAL **Datasheets for LabBook,** Muscles at Work, Datasheet 47 GENERAL **Inquiry Labs,** On a Wing and a Layer, Lab 6 GENERAL
Section 4 The Integumentary System	90	▶ Describe the major functions of the integumentary system. ▶ List the major parts of the skin, and discuss their functions. ▶ Describe the structure and function of hair and nails. ▶ Describe some common types of damage that can affect skin. UCP 5, SPSP 1, LS 1c–1f, 3a, 3b; LabBook UCP 3, SAI 2	**Skill Builder,** Seeing Is Believing, p. 763 BASIC **Datasheets for LabBook,** Seeing Is Believing, Datasheet 48 BASIC **Long-Term Projects & Research Ideas,** Project 22 ADVANCED

See page T20 for a complete correlation of this book with the **NATIONAL SCIENCE EDUCATION STANDARDS.**

TECHNOLOGY RESOURCES

 Guided Reading Audio CD English or Spanish, Chapter 22

 One-Stop Planner CD-ROM with Test Generator

 Scientists in Action, Segments 8 and 27
 Science, Technology & Society, Manufactured Body Parts, Segment 27
 Multicultural Connections, African-American Burial Ground, Segment 5

Chapter 22 • Body Organization and Structure

Chapter 22 • Body Organization and Structure

CLASSROOM WORKSHEETS, TRANSPARENCIES, AND RESOURCES	SCIENCE INTEGRATION AND CONNECTIONS	REVIEW AND ASSESSMENT
Directed Reading Worksheet 22 BASIC **Science Puzzlers, Twisters & Teasers,** Worksheet 22 ADVANCED		
Directed Reading Worksheet 22, Section 1 BASIC **Transparency 78,** Organ Systems	**Cross-Disciplinary Focus,** p. 523 in ATE	**Review,** p. 525 GENERAL **Quiz,** p. 525 in ATE GENERAL **Alternative Assessment,** p. 525 in ATE GENERAL
Directed Reading Worksheet 22, Section 2 BASIC **Transparency 79,** What's in a Bone? **Transparency 231,** Machines Change the Size or Direction (or Both) of a Force **Math Skills for Science Worksheet 53,** Mechanical Advantage GENERAL **Reinforcement Worksheet 22,** The Hipbone's Connected to the… GENERAL **Critical Thinking Worksheet 22,** The Tissue Engineering Debate ADVANCED	**Multicultural Connection,** p. 527 in ATE **Connect to Physical Science,** p. 528 in ATE BASIC	**Review,** p. 529 GENERAL **Quiz,** p. 529 in ATE GENERAL **Alternative Assessment,** p. 529 in ATE GENERAL
Teaching Transparency 80, Types of Muscle **Directed Reading Worksheet 22,** Section 3 BASIC **Math Skills for Science Worksheet 31,** The Unit Factor and Dimensional Analysis GENERAL **Reinforcement Worksheet 22,** Muscle Map GENERAL	**Chemistry Connection,** p. 532 **Math and More,** p. 532 in ATE GENERAL **MathBreak,** Runner's Time, p. 533 GENERAL	**Self-Check,** p. 532 **Homework,** p. 532 in ATE ADVANCED **Review,** p. 533 GENERAL **Quiz,** p. 533 in ATE GENERAL **Alternative Assessment,** p. 533 in ATE GENERAL
Teaching Transparency 81, The Skin **Directed Reading Worksheet 22,** Section 4 BASIC	**Real-World Connection,** p. 536 in ATE **Science, Technology, and Society:** Engineered Skin, p. 542 GENERAL **Eureka!** Hairy Oil Spills, p. 543 GENERAL	**Self-Check,** p. 535 **Review,** p. 537 GENERAL **Quiz,** p. 537 in ATE GENERAL **Alternative Assessment,** p. 537 in ATE BASIC

END-OF-CHAPTER REVIEW AND ASSESSMENT

Chapter Review in Study Guide
Vocabulary and Notes in Study Guide
Chapter Tests with Performance-Based Assessment, Chapter 22 Test
Chapter Tests with Performance-Based Assessment, Performance-Based Assessment 22
Concept Mapping Transparency 22

internetconnect

Holt, Rinehart and Winston On-line Resources
go.hrw.com
For worksheets and other teaching aids related to this chapter, visit the HRW Web site and type in the keyword: **HSTBD1**

National Science Teachers Association
www.scilinks.org
Encourage students to use the sciLINKS numbers listed in the internet connect boxes to access information and resources on the **NSTA** Web site.

Chapter Resources & Worksheets

Visual Resources

TEACHING TRANSPARENCIES

TEACHING TRANSPARENCIES

CONCEPT MAPPING TRANSPARENCY

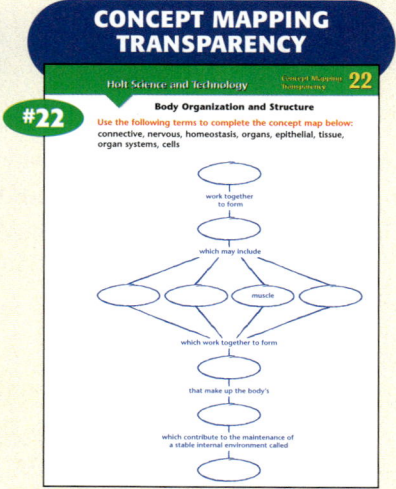

Meeting Individual Needs

DIRECTED READING

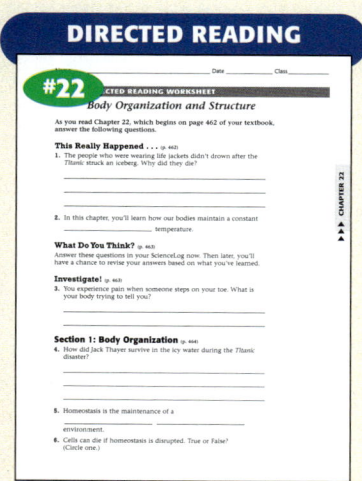

REINFORCEMENT & VOCABULARY REVIEW

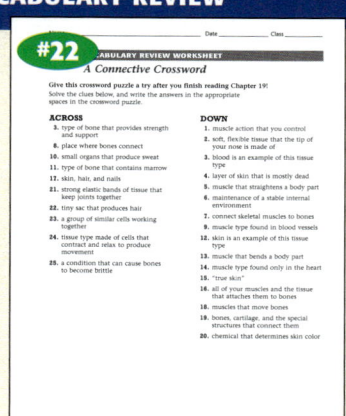

SCIENCE PUZZLERS, TWISTERS & TEASERS

Chapter 22 • Body Organization and Structure

Chapter 22 • Body Organization and Structure

Review & Assessment

STUDY GUIDE
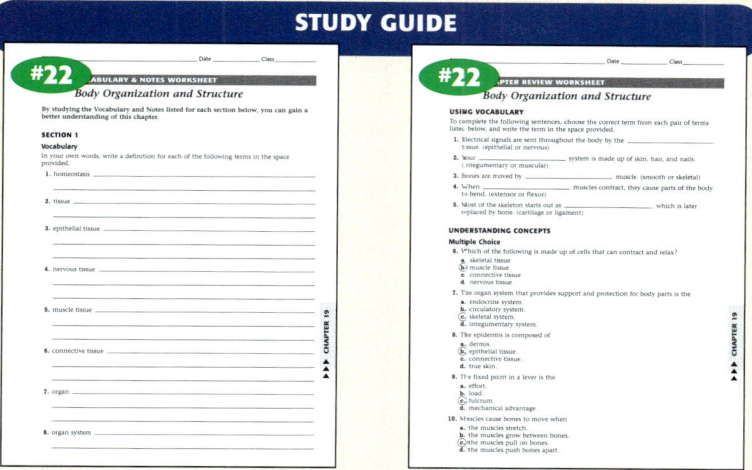

CHAPTER TESTS WITH PERFORMANCE-BASED ASSESSMENT
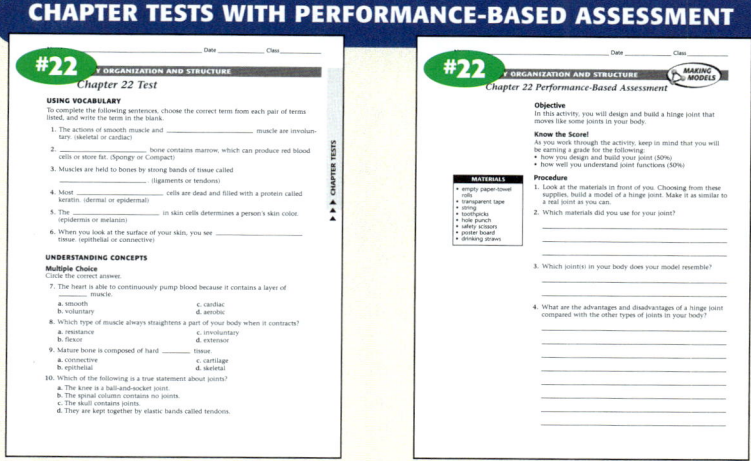

Lab Worksheets

INQUIRY LABS

LONG-TERM PROJECTS & RESEARCH IDEAS

DATASHEETS FOR LABBOOK
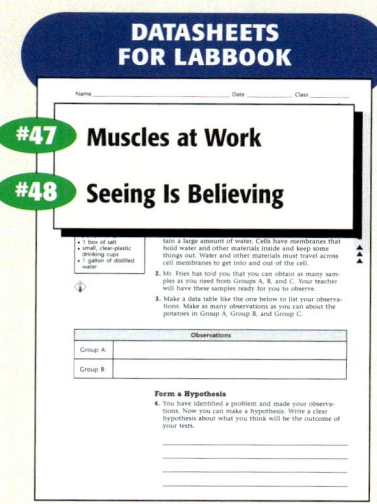

Applications & Extensions

CRITICAL THINKING & PROBLEM SOLVING

MULTICULTURAL CONNECTIONS

SCIENCE TECHNOLOGY

SCIENTISTS IN ACTION
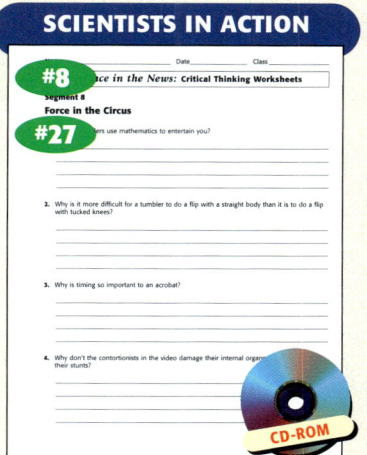

Chapter 22 • Chapter Resources & Worksheets

Chapter Background

SECTION 1

Body Organization

▶ **Tissues**

Tissues differ from each other in a number of ways: shape and size of cells, amount and kind of material between the cells, and the special functions they perform to maintain proper functioning of the body.

- The cells that make up epithelial tissue have little space between them; most are welded to adjacent cells, creating a barrier to movement of materials between them; they form continuous sheets of tissue.

- Connective tissue is the most abundant tissue in the body, and it displays the most variety in form and type. All connective tissue, however, can be classified into one of four types: dense connective tissue—cartilage and bone; loose connective tissue—beneath the skin and around nerves, blood vessels, and body organs; liquid connective tissue—blood and lymph; and fat (adipose) tissue, where the body stores energy as droplets of fat.

- Although bone is considerably harder than other body tissues, it accounts for only about 14 percent of a person's total body weight.

SECTION 2

The Skeletal System

▶ **The Human Skeleton**

The skeleton provides more than just support for soft tissue. It is key to the regulation of body minerals. It also produces both red and white blood cells. There are officially 206 bones in the adult human, but extra bones, particularly those in the hands and feet, increase that number. The number of bones in children varies with age. This is because the skeleton forms from over 800 centers of ossification. All of the bony elements are generally not completely united to form an adult skeleton until a person reaches his or her mid-20s. The clavicles are usually the last bones to complete fusion.

- The skeletons of male and female humans are slightly different. The most pronounced differences are in the pelvis. That is because a female's pelvis is adapted for childbearing and thus has a larger pelvic inlet. Women who are malnourished during their childhood typically do not develop the wider pelvis. This can make childbirth dangerous or even fatal for them.

- It is possible to determine an individual's age by looking at the skeleton alone. A younger individual's dentition and bone fusion patterns are indicative of his or her age. In adults, age determination is much more difficult because one must rely solely on signs of skeletal deterioration.

▶ **Bones**

Each bone is surrounded by a strong fibrous covering called a periosteum. Articular surfaces are also covered in cartilage.

- Bones are made of three types of cells: osteoblasts, osteocytes, and osteoclasts. Osteoblasts are bone-producing cells. Osteocytes are bone-maintaining cells. Osteoclasts are bone-destroying cells.

- For its weight, bone is five times stronger than steel.

▶ **Joints**

Doctors typically classify joints by structure rather than movement. The three types of joint structures are called fibrous, cartilaginous, and synovial. Fibrous joints are immovable joints (such as those in the skull) in which a fibrous tissue or a hyaline cartilage connects the bones. Cartilaginous joints are slightly moveable joints (such as those in the rib cage) in which cartilage connects the

Chapter 22 • Body Organization and Structure

Chapter 22 • Body Organization and Structure

bones. Synovial joints are freely moving joints (such as the knee) in which slick synovial membranes cover the cartilage and ligaments connecting the bone.

SECTION 3
The Muscular System

▶ **The Muscular System**
There are more than 600 skeletal muscles in the human body. To simplify the study of these muscles, they are organized into the following groups: muscles of the head and the neck, muscles of the trunk, muscles of the upper limbs (arms and hands), and muscles of the lower limbs (legs and feet).

▶ **Types of Muscle Cells**
When observed through a microscope, the three types of muscles are clearly identifiable. Cells of smooth muscles have a long tapered shape, no clearly defined striations, and a large central nucleus. Skeletal muscle cells are characterized by distinct light- and dark-colored bands across the long tapered cell; each cell has multiple nuclei because several cells merge and the cell membranes become indistinct. The cells of cardiac muscle have one or more nuclei and have an irregular, branched shape.

SECTION 4
The Integumentary System

▶ **The Skin**
One square inch of the skin can hold as many as 650 sweat glands, 20 blood vessels, and more than 1,000 nerve endings.

- Each person has a unique series of ridges and indentations on the tips of his or her fingers called fingerprints. No two people have the same fingerprints. Fingerprints help the fingers to grip slippery surfaces. Toes also have a unique pattern on their tips, so along with fingerprints, we all have toe prints as well.

IS THAT A FACT!
▰ More than three-quarters of the dust in some homes is made up of dead skin cells!

▶ **Hair and Nails**
Only mammals have true hair; all mammals have hair somewhere on their bodies.

- The body's most visible signs of aging occur in the integumentary system. Skin becomes thin, dry, wrinkled, and less supple. Dark-colored age spots may develop. Hair turns gray or white and may begin to fall out; hair follicles decrease in number. Sweat glands become less active, causing older people to be less tolerant and adaptable to extremely hot weather.

- Hair that is kept short grows an average of 2 cm per month. Growth slows to about 1 cm per month when the hair reaches about 30 cm long. Fingernails grow about 2 cm each year. The fastest-growing nail is on the middle finger. Toenails grow three to four times more slowly than fingernails.

For background information about teaching strategies and issues, refer to the *Professional Reference for Teachers.*

CHAPTER 22

Body Organization and Structure

Pre-Reading Questions

Students may not know the answers to these questions before reading the chapter, so accept any reasonable response.

Suggested Answers

1. Organs are made of tissues, and tissues are made of cells.
2. Skin provides protection from the elements; muscles provide movement; and bones provide structure and protection.

Directed Reading Worksheet 22

Science Puzzlers, Twisters & Teasers Worksheet 22

Guided Reading Audio CD
English or Spanish, Chapter 22

CHAPTER 22

Body Organization and Structure

Sections

1. **Body Organization** 522
   Internet Connect 525
2. **The Skeletal System** ... 526
   QuickLab 527
3. **The Muscular System** ... 530
   QuickLab 531
   Chemistry
     Connection 532
   MathBreak 533
   Internet Connect 533
4. **The Integumentary
   System** 534
   Internet Connect 537

Chapter Review 540
Feature Articles 542, 543
LabBook 762–765

Pre-Reading Questions

1. What is the relationship between cells, tissues, and organs?
2. How do your skin, muscles, and bones help to keep you well?

A Winning Effort

For several consecutive years, Lance Armstrong won the Tour de France. These victories were amazing because a few years earlier, Lance was diagnosed with cancer, which had weakened him. But with medicine and hard work, Lance's body grew strong again—strong enough for him to win one of the toughest races in all of sports. In this chapter, you will learn more about how each of the organ systems of the human body works to keep you healthy.

---

internet connect

HRW On-line Resources

go.hrw.com

For worksheets and other teaching aids, visit the HRW Web site and type in the keyword: **HSTBD1**

SCILINKS. NSTA

www.scilinks.com

Use the *sci*LINKS numbers at the end of each chapter for additional resources on the **NSTA** Web site.

CNNfyi.com

www.cnnfyi.com

Visit the CNN Web site for current events coverage and classroom resources.

START-UP Activity

TOO COLD FOR COMFORT

Did you know that your nervous system sends you messages about your body's cells? For example, the pain you feel when someone steps on your toe is a message that you should move your toe to safety. Try this exercise to watch your nervous system in action.

Procedure

1. Hold a **few pieces of ice** in one hand. Allow the melting water to drip into a **dish.** Hold the ice until the cold is uncomfortable. Then release the ice into the dish. What message did you receive from your nervous system?

2. Look at the hand that held the ice, and then look at your other hand. What changes in your skin do you see? How quickly does the cold hand return to normal?

Analysis

3. What organ systems do you think were involved in restoring your hand to normal?

4. Think of a time when your nervous system sent you a message, such as an uncomfortable feeling of heat, cold, or pain. How did your body react? Which organ systems do you think were involved in the reaction?

START-UP Activity

TOO COLD FOR COMFORT

MATERIALS
For Each Group: • ice • waterproof dish

Safety Caution

Students should clean up the water that results from the melting ice.

Answers to START-UP Activity

1. Answers will vary, but students should feel some discomfort intense enough to make them want to drop the ice.

2. Students might notice redness when their hand becomes very cold. Individuals will experience warming at different rates.

3. Answers will vary, but students might suggest the cardiovascular system. Point out to students that the redness is an increased blood supply to the cold area. The blood brings warmth to the hand, helping to restore it to normal.

4. Answers will vary, but students may know that the nervous system detected the discomfort and sent signals to other body systems to respond.

SECTION 1

Focus

Body Organization

This section introduces the basic organization of the human body. Students identify the four major tissues of the body and describe how the body's tissues are organized into organs. Students also learn that the body's organs are arranged by function into 11 organ systems. Students will be able to describe the major functions of each body system.

Bellringer

Write the names of the body systems below and their functions on the board or an overhead projector. Scramble the columns so that systems and functions do not match. Ask students to copy both columns in their ScienceLog and draw a line between the body system and its correct function.

- Respiratory system—absorbs oxygen
- Muscular system—moves bones
- Digestive system—breaks down food
- Circulatory system—pumps blood
- Endocrine system—regulates body functions

Directed Reading Worksheet 22 Section 1

TOPIC: Tissues and Organs
GO TO: www.scilinks.org
sciLINKS NUMBER: HSTL530

Section 1

Terms to Learn

homeostasis
tissue
epithelial tissue
nervous tissue
muscle tissue
connective tissue
organ

What You'll Do

- Identify the major tissues found in the body.
- Compare an organ with an organ system.
- Describe a major function of each organ system.

Figure 1 *Your body has four types of tissue, and each type has a special function in your body.*

Body Organization

Your body has an amazing ability to survive, even in the face of harsh conditions. How did Jack Thayer stay alive even though the environment around him was so cold? A short answer is that his body did not allow its internal conditions to change enough to stop his cells from working properly. The maintenance of a stable internal environment is called **homeostasis** (HOH mee OH STAY sis). If homeostasis is disrupted, cells suffer and sometimes die.

Four Types of Tissue

Making sure your internal environment remains stable enough to support healthy cells is not an easy task. Many different "jobs" must be done to maintain homeostasis. Fortunately, not every cell has to do all those jobs because the cells are organized into different teams. Just as each member of a soccer team has a special role in the game, each cell in your body has a specific job in maintaining homeostasis. A group of similar cells working together forms a **tissue.** Your body contains four main types of tissue—epithelial tissue, connective tissue, muscle tissue, and nervous tissue, as shown in **Figure 1.**

Epithelial tissue covers and protects underlying tissue. When you look at the surface of your skin, you see epithelial tissue. The cells stick tightly and form a continuous sheet.

Nervous tissue sends electrical signals through the body. It is found in the brain, nerves, and sense organs.

IS THAT A FACT!

The Pompeii worm, *Alvinella pompejana*, can survive a temperature difference of 60°C between its head and its tail! Scientists theorize that a coating of furry bacteria living on the worm's back allow the worm to endure such extreme temperature differences.

522 Chapter 22 • Body Organization and Structure

Tissues Form Organs

Two or more tissues working together form an **organ.** One type of tissue alone cannot do all the things that several types working together can do. Your stomach, as shown in **Figure 2,** uses several different types of tissue to carry out digestion.

Organs Form Systems

Your stomach does much to help you digest your food, but it doesn't do it all. It works together with other organs, such as the small intestine and large intestine, to digest your food. Organs working together make up an *organ system.* The failure of any part can affect the entire system. Your body has 11 major organ systems, which are illustrated on the next two pages. Are there any that you have not heard of before?

The Stomach Is an Organ

- **Nervous tissue** in the stomach partly controls the production of acids that aid in the digestion of food. Nervous tissue signals when the stomach is full.
- **Epithelial tissue** lines the stomach.
- Layers of **muscle tissue** break up stomach contents.
- Blood and a **connective tissue** called collagen are found in the wall of the stomach.

Figure 2 The four types of tissue work together so that the stomach can carry out digestion.

Muscle tissue is made of cells that can contract and relax to produce movement.

Connective tissue joins, supports, protects, insulates, nourishes, and cushions organs. It also keeps organs from falling apart.

---

1) Motivate

DISCUSSION

Homeostasis Before students read this section, ask them to think about what they've already learned about endotherms and ectotherms and how each adjusts to outside temperatures. How does the idea of homeostasis fit into what they already know?

2) Teach

READING STRATEGY

Prediction Guide Before students read the pages that describe the body's tissues and organs, ask whether the following statements are true or false. Students will discover the answers as they read Section 1.

- Homeostasis is the body's ability to maintain a stable internal environment. (true)
- The human body has four main types of tissues. (true)
- An organ is a group of tissues that work together. (true)

USING THE FIGURE

Refer to **Figure 2** as you review with students the four types of body tissue. Encourage students to consider what role each tissue might play in other organs, such as the heart. Sheltered English

---

CROSS-DISCIPLINARY FOCUS

History The first transplant of a human heart was performed in Cape Town, South Africa, on December 3, 1967, by Dr. Christiaan Barnard and a team of 30 physicians. In an operation that lasted 5 hours, Barnard removed a heart from the body of a 25-year-old woman and transplanted it into a 55-year-old man named Louis Washkansky. Washkansky lived for 18 days following the transplant before he died of pneumonia. Have interested students conduct research to find out when other organs such as kidneys and livers were first transplanted.

2) Teach, continued

DEBATE

Transplant Ethics There are more than 53,000 people in the United States waiting for organ transplants. There are approximately 20,000 organ transplants performed every year in the United States. The average cost of an organ transplant is $120,000 for an American citizen. Encourage students to research the topic, and have them debate the ethical issues surrounding transplants. Some suggested topics:

- Should transplants happen at all?
- Who should get a transplant?
- Should a child receive a transplant before an older person?

MEETING INDIVIDUAL NEEDS

Learners Having Difficulty To help students understand and identify the 11 major organ systems of the body, have them make a table with the following headings: Name of organ system, Function(s), and Main organs. Have students use the table to organize the information presented on these pages. Encourage students to continue to fill in their tables as they read the remainder of this book.

Sheltered English

Teaching Transparency 78 "Organ Systems"

TOPIC: Body Systems
GO TO: www.scilinks.org
sciLINKS NUMBER: HSTL535

Organ Systems

Integumentary system
Your skin, hair, and nails protect underlying tissue.

Muscular system
Your skeletal muscles move your bones.

Skeletal system
Your bones provide a frame to support and protect body parts.

Cardiovascular system
Your heart pumps blood through all your blood vessels.

Respiratory system
Your lungs absorb oxygen and release carbon dioxide.

Urinary system
Your urinary system removes wastes from the blood and regulates the body's fluids.

Reproductive system (male)
The male reproductive system produces and delivers sperm.

Reproductive system (female)
The female reproductive system produces eggs and nourishes and shelters the unborn baby.

IS THAT A FACT!

Can you learn about the human body by cutting open animals instead of human bodies? In ancient Rome, physician Galen (129–199) did just that! He wrote more than 500 treatises on the human body and, because of the Roman belief that it was wrong to cut open a human corpse, Galen studied animals and the wounds of fallen gladiators. He never saw inside the human body!

Organg Systems

Nervous system
It is the role of the nervous system to receive and send electrical messages throughout the body.

Lymphatic system
Your lymphatic system returns leaked fluids to blood vessels. It also helps you get rid of germs that can harm you.

Digestive system
Your digestive system breaks down the food you eat into nutrients that can be absorbed into your body.

Endocrine system
Glands regulate body functions by sending out chemical messengers. The ovaries, in females, and testes, in males, are part of this system.

REVIEW

1. Explain the relationship between cells, tissues, organs, and organ systems.
2. Compare the four kinds of tissue found in the human body.
3. **Using Graphics** Make a chart that lists the major organ systems and their functions.
4. **Relating Concepts** Describe a time when homeostasis was disrupted in your body. Which body systems do you think were affected?

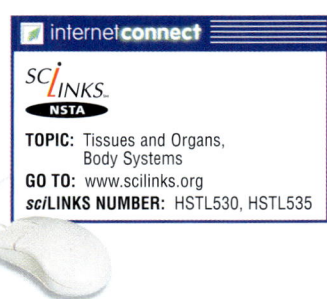

internetconnect

SCILINKS NSTA

TOPIC: Tissues and Organs, Body Systems
GO TO: www.scilinks.org
sciLINKS NUMBER: HSTL530, HSTL535

---

3) Extend

GROUP ACTIVITY
Divide the class into 11 equal groups. Assign each group one of the body's organ systems. Have students use library references or the Internet to prepare an oral report for the class that identifies the main organs of each system and their functions. Encourage students to include a labeled diagram with their reports. In each group, assign two students as researchers and one or two students as poster artists and report writers.

4) Close

Quiz
Ask students whether these statements are true or false. Have them correct the false statements to make them true.

1. Homeostasis is the maintenance of a stable internal environment. (true)
2. Epithelial tissue sends electrical signals throughout the body. (False; this is the function of nervous tissue.)
3. Blood is a type of connective tissue. (true)
4. The lymphatic system returns leaked fluids to blood vessels. (true)

ALTERNATIVE ASSESSMENT

Writing In their ScienceLog, have students describe in as much detail as possible three of the organ systems covered in this chapter. Have them describe the functions and primary organs of each system and include drawings of each system.

▼ Answers to Review

1. The body is organized into cells, tissues, organs, and organ systems. Cells that have similar functions make up tissue; two or more types of tissue work together to form an organ; organs work together to form a system.
2. Nervous tissue sends electrical signals or messages; epithelial tissue covers and protects underlying tissue; muscle tissue is made of cells that can contract and relax to produce movement; connective tissue joins, supports, protects, insulates, nourishes, cushions, and keeps organs from falling apart.
3. The chart should reflect the material found on the last two pages of this section.
4. Answers will vary.

Section 1 • Body Organization

SECTION 2

Focus

The Skeletal System

This section introduces the major organs of the skeletal system and describes the function of bones. The section also illustrates the major internal structure of bones and compares the three major types of joints. The section concludes with a discussion of how bones and joints form levers.

Have students write in their ScienceLog five problems they would have if they lacked bones. (They would have no defined structure, mineral storage, protection, red blood cells, or mobility.)

1) Motivate

ACTIVITY

Locating Bones Review with students that the skeletal system supports the body and protects delicate body parts. Ask students to name the main organ of the skeletal system. (bones)

Encourage students to press the skin in various parts of their body, to feel their bones. Ask students to describe any parts of their body where they cannot feel their bones. (Answers will vary but should include the abdomen.)

As you point to various parts of the body, ask students what organ the bones protect. The skull, for example, protects the brain, and the ribs protect the heart and lungs.
Sheltered English

Section 2

Terms to Learn
skeletal system
compact bone
spongy bone
cartilage
joint
ligament

What You'll Do
- Identify the major organs of the skeletal system.
- Describe the functions of bones.
- Illustrate the internal structure of bones.
- Compare three types of joints.
- Discuss how bones function as levers.

Protection Your heart and lungs are shielded by your ribs, your spinal cord is protected by your vertebrae, and your brain is protected by your skull.

Storage Bones store minerals that help the nerves and muscles function properly. Your arm and leg bones also store fat that can be used for energy.

Movement Skeletal muscles pull on the bones to produce movement. Without bones, you would not be able to sit, stand, walk, or run.

Blood Cell Formation Some of your bones are filled with a special material that makes blood cells.

The Skeletal System

When you hear the word *skeleton,* you may think of the remains of something that has died. But your skeleton is not dead; it is very much alive. Your bones are not dry and brittle. They are just as alive and active as the muscles that are attached to them. Bones, cartilage, and the special structures that connect them make up your **skeletal system.**

The Burden of Being a Bone

Bones do a lot more than just hold you up. Your bones perform several important functions inside your body. The names of some of your bones are identified in **Figure 3.**

Figure 3 The adult human skeleton has approximately 206 bones. Several major bones are identified in this skeleton.

 Directed Reading Worksheet 22 Section 2

Q: Why didn't the skeleton cross the road?

A: It didn't have the guts.

526 Chapter 22 • Body Organization and Structure

What's in a Bone?

A bone may seem lifeless, but it is a living organ made of several different tissues. Bone is composed of connective tissue and minerals that are deposited by living cells called *osteoblasts*.

If you look inside a bone, you will notice there are two different kinds of bone tissue. If the tissue does not have any visible open spaces, it is called **compact bone.** Bone tissue that has many open spaces is called **spongy bone.** Spongy bone provides most of the strength and support for a bone. It acts like the trusses of a bridge.

Down to the Marrow Bones contain a soft tissue called *marrow*. Red marrow, sometimes found in spongy bone, produces red blood cells. Yellow marrow, found in the central cavity of long bones, stores fat. Tiny canals within the compact bone contain small blood vessels. **Figure 4** shows a cross section of a femur.

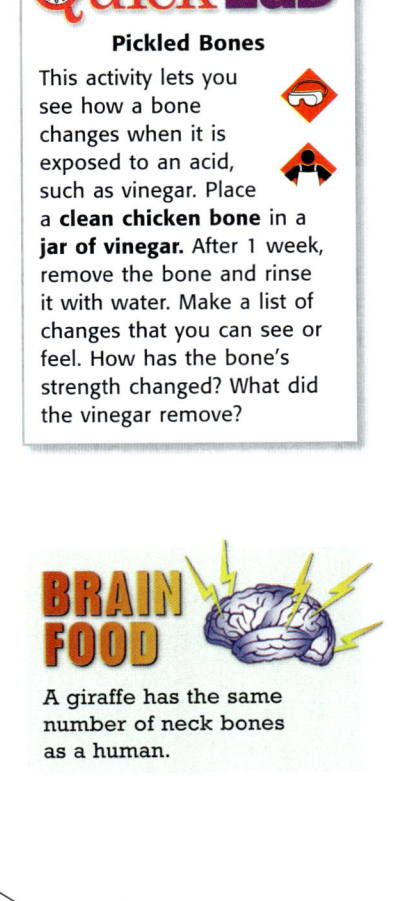

QuickLab

Pickled Bones

This activity lets you see how a bone changes when it is exposed to an acid, such as vinegar. Place a **clean chicken bone** in a **jar of vinegar.** After 1 week, remove the bone and rinse it with water. Make a list of changes that you can see or feel. How has the bone's strength changed? What did the vinegar remove?

BRAIN FOOD

A giraffe has the same number of neck bones as a human.

Figure 4 In children, red marrow fills the center of long bones. It is replaced with yellow marrow by adulthood.

On November 2 each year, people across Mexico celebrate *El Día de los Muertos* (the Day of the Dead). They take food and gifts to the graves of their loved ones and set up elaborate shrines and altars in their homes. These shrines are often decorated with figures of skeletons depicting the person's job when he or she was alive, such as that of a doctor or a teacher. Foods eaten during this holiday are *pan del muerto* (bread of the dead) and candies shaped like skulls. Have interested students write a research paper on this holiday to share with the class.

2) Teach, continued

DISCUSSION

Joint Review After students read about the different kinds of joints, ask them the following questions. You may want to have students move their own bodies before they answer each question.

- What kind of joint do you use when you bend your elbow? (hinge joint) your knee? (hinge joint)
- What kind of joint moves when you swing your arm back and forth? (ball-and-socket joint) Name another location in your body where this type of joint is located. (the hips) **Sheltered English**

CONNECT TO PHYSICAL SCIENCE

Students may be surprised to learn that their arms and legs are "machines." Our limbs are levers, and levers are the simplest kind of machine. They allow us to apply, increase, and change the direction of force. Have students think of other levers they may use or know about. (Examples include a seesaw, the claw end of a hammer, a crowbar, and a garlic press.)

Use Teaching Transparency 231 to help students understand how levers make work easier.

Teaching Transparency 231
"Machines Change the Size or Direction (or Both) of a Force"
LINK TO PHYSICAL SCIENCE

Growing Bones

Did you know that most of your skeleton used to be soft and rubbery? Most bones start out as a soft, flexible tissue called **cartilage**. When you were born, you had little true bone. But as you grew, the cartilage was replaced by bone. During childhood, growth plates of cartilage remain in most bones, providing a place for those bones to continue to grow.

Feel the end of your nose, or bend the top of your ear. As shown in **Figure 5**, some areas, like these, never become bone. The flexible material beneath your skin in these areas is cartilage.

Figure 5 *The skull and neck bones in this computer-colored X ray are shown mostly in blue.*

What's the Point of a Joint?

The place where two or more bones connect is called a **joint**. Your joints have special designs that allow your body to move when your muscles contract. Some joints allow a lot of movement, while other joints are fixed, which means they allow little or no movement. For example, the joints in the skull are fixed. Joints that have a wide range of movement tend to be more susceptible to injury than those that are less flexible. Some examples of movable joints are shown in **Figure 6**.

Figure 6 *Joints are shaped according to their function in the body.*

Sliding joint

Sliding joints allow bones in the hand to glide over one another, giving some flexibility to the area.

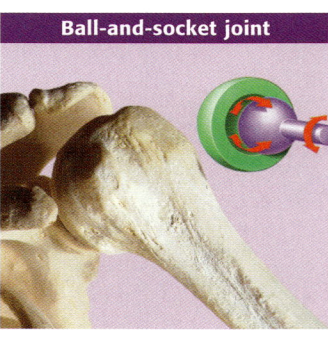

Ball-and-socket joint

Like a joystick on a computer game, the shoulder enables your arm to move freely in all directions.

Hinge joint

Like a hinge on a door, the knee enables you to flex and extend your lower leg.

Math Skills Worksheet 53 "Mechanical Advantage"

IS THAT A FACT!

The only bone in the human body that is not connected to another bone is the hyoid bone. The hyoid bone is found in the throat above the larynx. This bone is easily broken when a person is strangled, and it is often an important piece of evidence in suspected strangulation deaths.

Bone to Bone Joints are kept together with strong elastic bands of connective tissue called **ligaments.** If a ligament is stretched too far, it becomes strained. A strained ligament will usually heal with time, but a torn ligament will not. A torn ligament must be repaired surgically. Cartilage helps cushion the area where two bones meet. If cartilage wears away, the joint becomes arthritic.

Can Levers Lessen Your Load?

You may not think of your limbs as being machines, but they are. The action of a muscle pulling on a bone often works like a type of simple machine called a *lever*. A lever is a rigid bar that moves on a fixed point known as a *fulcrum*. Any force applied to the lever is called the *effort*. A force that resists the motion of the lever, such as the downward force exerted by a weight on the bar, is called the *load* or the *resistance*. **Figure 7** shows how three types of levers are used in the human body.

Figure 7 *There are three classes of levers, based on the location of the fulcrum, the load, and the effort.*

First-class lever
The fulcrum lies between the load and the effort.

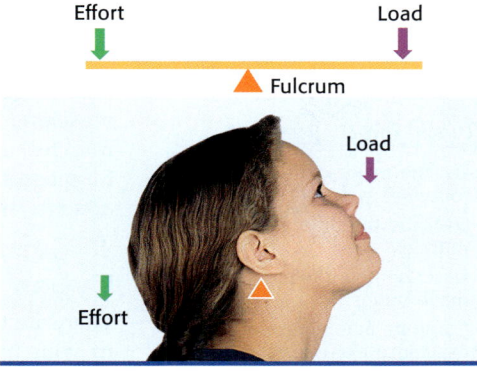

Second-class lever
The load lies between the fulcrum and the effort.

Third-class lever
The effort lies between the fulcrum and the load.

REVIEW

1. Describe four important functions of bones.
2. Draw a bone, and label the inside and outside structures. Use colored pencils to color and label spongy bone, blood vessels, marrow cavity, compact bone, and cartilage.
3. List three hinge joints in your body.
4. **Interpreting Models** Study the models of levers pictured in Figure 7. Use a small box (load), a ruler (bar), and a pencil (fulcrum) to create models of each type of lever.

3) Extend

RESEARCH

Have students work in pairs or groups of three to do library research on the different kinds of bone fractures. Encourage students to make posters or models showing each type of fracture, including a caption or label on how each type of fracture is treated.

4) Close

Quiz

1. What is the difference between compact bone and spongy bone? (Compact bone has no visible, open spaces. Spongy bone has many visible spaces and contains a tissue called marrow.)
2. Where in the body are ball-and-socket joints found? (hip and shoulder) hinge joints? (knee and elbow) fixed joints? (skull)

ALTERNATIVE ASSESSMENT

Writing Have students write an essay about bones. Essays should address what bones do, how they are specialized, and how they are joined.

Reinforcement Worksheet 22
"The Hipbone's Connected to the . . ."

Critical Thinking Worksheet 22
"The Tissue Engineering Debate"

Answers to Review

1. Bones support your body, store and release minerals, and enable your muscles to move the body; some bones make blood cells.
2. Illustrations will vary but should reflect the structures shown in **Figure 4**.
3. examples include: knee, knuckles, toes, elbow, jaw
4. Models will vary but should reflect the information on levers described in **Figure 7**.

SECTION 3

Focus

The Muscular System

This section introduces students to the major parts of the muscular system and describes the different types of muscle. This section also describes how skeletal muscles move bones. Students compare aerobic exercise to resistance exercise. The section concludes with a discussion of typical muscle injuries and how to prevent them.

Bellringer

On the board or an overhead projector, write the following:

In your ScienceLog, list at least five parts of your body that you use to drink a glass of water. (Sample answer: fingers, hands, arm, lips, tongue)

When the students are done, remind them that all the parts needed, including the eyes they used to see the glass, are controlled by muscles.

1) Motivate

Activity

Poster Project Have students draw an outline of a human body. Have them add smooth muscles, skeletal muscles, and cardiac muscles to their drawings. Point out that certain kinds of muscles are located in certain parts of the body. Ask students to identify the function of each type of muscle. Make sure that students understand that all tissue movement in the body is caused by muscle movement. Sheltered English

---

Section 3

Terms to Learn

muscular system   skeletal muscle
smooth muscle   tendon
cardiac muscle

What You'll Do

- List the major parts of the muscular system.
- Describe the different types of muscle.
- Describe how skeletal muscles move bones.
- Compare aerobic exercise with resistance exercise.
- Give an example of a muscle injury.

The Muscular System

Have you ever tried to be perfectly still for just 1 minute? Try as you might, you just can't do it. Somewhere in your body, certain muscles are always working. For example, muscles continuously push blood through your blood vessels. A muscle makes you breathe. And muscles hold you upright. If all your muscles rested at the same time, you would collapse. Your muscles are made of muscle tissue and connective tissue. Muscles that attach to bones and the connective tissue that attaches them make up the **muscular system.**

Types of Muscle

There are three types of muscle tissue that make up the muscles in your body. **Smooth muscle** is found in the digestive tract and the blood vessels. **Cardiac muscle** is a special type of muscle found only in your heart. **Skeletal muscles** are attached to your bones for movement, and they help protect your inner organs. The three types of muscles are shown in **Figure 8.**

Muscle action can be voluntary or involuntary. Muscle action that is under your control is *voluntary*. Muscle action that is not under your control is *involuntary*. The actions of smooth muscle and cardiac muscle are involuntary. The actions of skeletal muscles can be both voluntary and involuntary. For example, you can blink your eyes any time you want to, but your eyes will also blink automatically if you do not think about it.

Figure 8 Your body has smooth muscle, cardiac muscle, and skeletal muscle.

Skeletal muscle enables bones to move.

Smooth muscle moves food through the digestive system.

Cardiac muscle causes the heart to beat.

Teaching Transparency 80
"Types of Muscle"

IS THAT A FACT!

Horses can sleep standing up. Their legs can support their weight on their bones and tendons without the use of any muscles at all. When they fall asleep and their muscles relax, their leg bones lock in place underneath them, holding them upright for the duration of their nap.

530 Chapter 22 • Body Organization and Structure

Making Your Move

Skeletal muscles produce hundreds of different voluntary movements. This is demonstrated by a ballet dancer, a swimmer, or even someone making a funny face, as shown in **Figure 9.** When you want to make a movement, you cause electrical signals to travel from the brain to the skeletal muscle cells. The muscle cells respond to these signals by contracting or getting shorter.

Muscles to Bones Strands of tough connective tissue called **tendons** connect your skeletal muscles to your bones. When a muscle gets shorter, a pulling action occurs, bringing the bones closer to each other. For example, the biceps muscle, shown in **Figure 10,** is attached by tendons to a bone in your shoulder and to another bone in your forearm. When the biceps contracts, your arm bends.

Working in Pairs Your skeletal muscles work in pairs to cause smooth, controlled movements. Many basic movements are the result of muscle pairs that cause bending and straightening. If a muscle bends part of your body, then that muscle is called a *flexor*. If the muscle straightens part of your body, then it is called an *extensor*. The flexor muscle of the arm is the biceps. The extensor muscle of the arm is the triceps. Discover some of your own flexor and extensor muscles by doing the QuickLab at right.

Figure 9 *It takes an average of 13 muscles to smile and an average of 43 muscles to frown.*

 QuickLab

Power in Pairs

1. While sitting in a chair, place one of your hands palm up under the edge of a **table.** Apply gentle upward pressure.
2. With your free hand, feel the front and back of your upper arm.
3. Next place your hand palm down on top of the table. Apply pressure downward.
4. Again with your free hand, feel the front and back of your upper arm.
5. What did you notice when you were pressing up? when you were pressing down?

Figure 10 *Skeletal muscles, such as the biceps and triceps muscles, work in pairs. When the biceps muscle contracts, the elbow bends. When the triceps muscle contracts, the elbow straightens.*

SCIENTISTS AT ODDS

In the early part of this century, tens of thousands of people, mostly children, were stricken with polio, a viral disease that paralyzes muscles. Often, polio would leave its victims unable to walk or move. One Australian nurse, Sister Elizabeth Kenny, treated patients using flexible hot wraps and exercise instead of hard, immobilizing casts. Using her treatments, patients avoided paralysis. Largely because Kenny was self-taught and had no formal medical education, the doctors and hospital administrators of the time fought against her practices. Eventually, she and her successes became well known, and her contributions became the beginning of the field of physical therapy. Have students research and report to the class Sister Kenny's story and the opposition she faced in Australia and the United States.

3) Extend

MATH and MORE

Explain to students that a regular program of aerobic exercise enables the heart to work more efficiently, pumping the same volume of blood in fewer beats. Ask students to imagine that their heart normally beats 75 times per minute. After a 3-month program of aerobic exercise, their heart now beats 65 times per minute. What is the difference in heart rate per minute?
(75 beats − 65 beats = 10 beats)

How many fewer times will the heart beat in 1 hour?
(10 beats/minute × 60 minutes/hour = 600 beats/hour)

How many fewer times will the heart beat in 1 day?
(600 beats/hour × 24 hours/day = 14,400 beats/day)

 Math Skills Worksheet 31 "The Unit Factor and Dimensional Analysis"

GOING FURTHER

Concept Mapping Divide the class into cooperative groups of three or four students. Have each group create a concept map for the ideas in this lesson. They should connect at least 10 terms and link them with apt phrases. Have students record their finished concept maps in their ScienceLog. **Sheltered English**

Answers to Self-Check
Curl-ups use flexor muscles; push-ups use extensor muscles.

Chemistry CONNECTION

Body chemistry is very important for healthy muscle functioning. If there is a chemical imbalance in a muscle due to excessive sweating, poor diet, tension, or illness, spasms or cramping may occur. Sodium, calcium, and potassium—three chemicals called *electrolytes*—must be in proper balance to avoid cramps and spasms. Relaxation and massage usually help the muscle restore its chemical balance.

Figure 12 Aerobic exercise is a great way to have fun while strengthening your heart.

Use It or Lose It

When someone breaks an arm and has to wear a cast, the muscles surrounding the injured bone change. That's because these muscles are not exercised, and they become smaller and weaker. On the other hand, exercised muscles are stronger and larger. Certain exercises can give muscles more endurance. This means they're able to work longer without getting tired. Strong muscles benefit other systems in your body too. When a muscle contracts, blood vessels in that muscle get squeezed. This helps push blood along, increasing blood flow without demanding more work from the heart.

Resistance Exercises To develop the size and strength of your skeletal muscles, resistance exercises are the most effective form of exercise. Resistance exercises require muscles to overcome the resistance (weight) of another object. Some resistance exercises, like the bent knee curl-up shown in **Figure 11,** require you to overcome your own weight.

Figure 11 Resistance exercises are tough, but they can really help you build strong muscles.

Aerobic Exercise Steady, moderate-intensity activity, such as jogging, cycling, skating, swimming laps, or walking, is called aerobic exercise. Aerobic exercise increases the size and strength of your skeletal muscles somewhat, but mostly it strengthens the heart while increasing the endurance of your skeletal muscles. Many people, like the girl in **Figure 12,** enjoy doing aerobic exercise.

✓ Self-Check
Which kind of skeletal muscle do you use to perform a curl-up? Which kind do you use to do a push-up? *(See page 782 to check your answers.)*

Homework

Researching Injuries For one month, have students read the sports section in the local newspaper or look for articles in sports magazines about injuries to the muscular and skeletal systems sustained by athletes. Have them research and write about these injuries in their ScienceLog. Ask students to identify and count the types of injuries—such as sprained ankles, torn or pulled muscles, bruised ribs, and torn or damaged ligaments. Have students compile their information on bar graphs in which they record the kinds of injuries on the *x*-axis and the number and frequency of injuries on the *y*-axis.

Chapter 22 • Body Organization and Structure

Muscle Injury

Any exercise program should be started gradually so that the muscles gain strength and endurance without injury. Muscles should also be warmed up gradually to reduce the risk of injury. However, as shown in **Figure 13,** the muscular system can experience damage. A muscle strain, commonly called a pulled muscle, is the overstretching or even tearing of a muscle. Muscle strain often occurs because the muscle has not been properly conditioned for the work it is doing.

Tendons, as well as muscles, can get injured from overuse. A damaged tendon can become hot or inflamed as your body tries to repair it. This painful condition is called tendinitis, and an extended period of rest is often required for the tendon to heal.

Figure 13 A pulled hamstring is a tear or strain of one of the muscles or tendons on the back of the thigh.

The Dangers of Anabolic Steroids Some people try to make their muscles larger and stronger by taking hormones called *anabolic steroids*. Anabolic steroids are powerful chemicals that resemble testosterone, a male sex hormone. Using anabolic steroids not only gives athletes an unfair advantage in competition but also puts the user at risk for serious long-term health problems. The use of anabolic steroids threatens the heart, liver, and kidneys, and it can cause high blood pressure. If taken before the skeleton is mature, anabolic steroids can cause the bones to stop growing.

MATH BREAK

Runner's Time

Jan, who has been a runner for several years, has decided to enter a race. She now runs 5 km in 30 minutes. She would like to decrease her time by 15 percent before the race. What will her time be when she meets her goal?

REVIEW

1. List three types of muscle tissue, and describe their functions in the body.
2. Compare aerobic exercise with resistance exercise, and give two examples of each.
3. **Applying Concepts** Describe the muscle action required to pick up a book. Make a sketch that illustrates the muscle action.

internetconnect

SCILINKS NSTA

TOPIC: The Muscular System
GO TO: www.scilinks.org
sciLINKS NUMBER: HSTL540

SECTION 4

Focus

The Integumentary System

This section introduces students to the major functions of the integumentary system; it also describes the major parts of the skin and discusses their functions. Students learn about the structure and functions of hair and nails and about common injuries to the skin.

🔔 Bellringer

Write the following questions on the board or an overhead projector, and ask students to write their answer in their ScienceLog:

When do you see dogs panting? Why do you think they pant? (Dogs cannot sweat, and panting cools them down on hot days or after strenuous activity. A dog pants in order to regulate its body temperature.)

1) Motivate

DISCUSSION

Homeostasis Relay the following story to students:

Dr. Charles Blagden was secretary of the Royal Society of London more than 200 years ago. He wanted to test how mammals regulate their body temperature. He spent 45 minutes in a room with a few friends, a dog, and a steak. The temperature in the room measured 126°C (260°F). Ask students what they think happened to the man, the dog, and the steak after the 45 minutes were up. (Everyone and the dog emerged from the room unharmed, but the steak was cooking! Mammals can regulate their temperature.)

Section 4

Terms to Learn

integumentary system
sweat glands
melanin
epidermis
dermis
hair follicle

What You'll Do

- Describe the major functions of the integumentary system.
- List the major parts of the skin, and discuss their functions.
- Describe the structure and function of hair and nails.
- Describe some common types of damage that can affect skin.

The Integumentary System

Here's a quiz for you. What part of your body has to be partly dead to keep you alive? Here are some clues: it comes in a variety of colors, it is the largest organ in the body, and it protects you from the outside world. Oh, and guess what—it is showing right now. Did you guess your skin? If you did, you guessed correctly.

Your skin, hair, and nails make up your **integumentary** (in TEG yoo MEN tuhr ee) **system.** (*Integument* means "covering.") Like all organ systems, the integumentary system helps your body maintain a healthy internal environment.

The Skin: More than Just a "Coat"

Why do you need skin? Here are four good reasons:

■ Skin protects you by keeping moisture in your body and foreign particles out of your body.

■ Skin keeps you "in touch" with the outside world. The nerve endings in your skin allow you to feel what's around you.

■ Skin helps regulate your body's temperature. For example, small organs in the skin called **sweat glands** produce sweat, a salty liquid that flows to the surface of the skin. As sweat evaporates, the skin cools.

■ Skin helps get rid of wastes. Several types of waste chemicals can leave the bloodstream and be removed in sweat.

What Determines Skin Color? A darkening chemical in skin called **melanin** determines skin color, as shown in **Figure 14.** If a lot of melanin is present, the skin is very dark. If only a little melanin is produced, the skin is very light. Melanin in the upper layer of the skin absorbs much of the harmful radiation from the sun, reducing DNA damage that can lead to cancer. However, *all* skin is vulnerable to cancer and therefore should be protected from sun exposure whenever possible.

Figure 14 *Variety in skin color is caused by the pigment melanin. The amount of melanin varies from person to person.*

IS THAT A FACT!

In an average adult, the skin has a surface area of about 2 m^2 and weighs about 4 kg. The skin on the human body varies in thickness from about 5 mm on the soles of the feet to about 0.5 mm on the eyelids.

A Tale of Two Layers

As you already know, the skin is the largest organ of your body. In fact, the skin of an adult covers an area of about 2 m²! However, there's a lot more to skin than meets the eye. The skin has two main layers: the dermis and the epidermis. The **epidermis** is the thinner layer of the two. It's what you see when you look at your skin. (*Epi* means "on top of.") The deeper, thicker layer is known as the **dermis**.

Epidermis The epidermis is composed of a type of epithelial tissue. Even though the epidermis has many layers of cells, it is only as thick as two sheets of notebook paper over most of the body. It is thicker in the palms of your hands and the soles of your feet. Most epidermal cells are dead and are filled with a protein called keratin, which helps make the skin tough.

Dermis The dermis lies underneath the epidermis. It is mostly connective tissue, and it contains many fibers made of a protein called collagen. The fibers provide strength and allow skin to bend without tearing. The dermis also contains a variety of small structures, as shown in **Figure 15**.

Self-Check

To what system do the skin's blood vessels belong? *(See page 782 to check your answer.)*

Your epidermis is showing!

Figure 15 Beneath the surface, your skin is a complex organ made of blood vessels, nerves, glands, and muscles.

Blood vessels transport substances and help regulate body temperature.

Nerves carry messages to and from the brain.

Muscle fibers attached to a hair follicle can contract, causing the hair to stand up.

Hair follicles in the dermis produce hair.

Oil glands release oil that keeps hair flexible and helps waterproof the epidermis.

Sweat glands release sweat. As sweat evaporates, the body is cooled. Sweat also contains waste materials taken out of the body.

A hippo's sweat is a natural sunscreen. Hippopotamuses secrete a pink fluid onto the surface of their skin that helps protect them from the sun's harmful rays.

② Teach, continued

Seeing Is Believing PG 763

READING 📖 STRATEGY

Prediction Guide Before students read this page, ask them if they agree or disagree with the following statements. Students will discover the answers as they explore Section 4.

- Dark hair gets its color from melanin. (true)
- Hair is made up of both living and dead cells. (true)
- Nails grow longer as new cells form at the nail roots. (true)

REAL-WORLD CONNECTION

Protection from the Sun Skin cancer is the most common kind of cancer. More than 800,000 new cases of skin cancer are reported each year. You can take several preventive measures to reduce your risk of skin cancer. Avoid being in the sun from 10:00 A.M. to 3:00 P.M., when the sun's rays are most direct. Wear sunglasses, a wide-brimmed hat, and a long-sleeved shirt and long pants. Wear plenty of sunscreen with an SPF (sun protection factor) of 15 or higher.

TOPIC: Integumentary System
GO TO: www.scilinks.org
sciLINKS NUMBER: HSTL545

How fast do your fingernails grow? Find out on page 763.

Hair and Nails

A hair, shown in **Figure 16,** is formed at the bottom of a tiny sac called a **hair follicle**. The hair grows as new cells are added at the hair follicle and older cells get pushed upward. The only living cells in a hair are in the hair follicle, where the hair is produced.

Letting Your Hair Down Hairs protect skin from ultraviolet light and can help keep particles, such as dust and insects, out of your eyes and nose. Like skin, hair gets its color from the pigment melanin. Dark hair contains more melanin than blond hair. In most mammals, hair also helps regulate body temperature. A contraction of a tiny muscle attached to the hair follicle causes the follicle to bend. In humans, the bending follicle pushes up the epidermis to make a goose bump. If the follicle contains a hair, the hair "stands up." The lifted hairs function like a sweater to trap warm air around the body.

A Nail Tale Nails protect the tips of your fingers and toes so that they can remain soft and sensitive. This allows you to have a keen sense of touch. Nails form from *nail roots* under the skin at the base and sides of nails. As new cells form, the nail grows longer. The parts of a nail are shown in **Figure 17.**

Figure 16 A hair is actually layers of dead, tightly packed, keratin-filled cells.

Figure 17 In nails, new cells are produced in the nail root, just beneath the lunula. The new cells push older cells toward the outer edge of the nail.

IS THAT A FACT!

Chemicals in human skin use the energy in ultraviolet light to make vitamin D.

Q: Where do sheep get their hair cut?

A: at the baa-baa shop

536 Chapter 22 • Body Organization and Structure

Living in Harm's Way

Skin is often damaged. The damage may be minor—a blister, an insect bite, or a small cut. Fortunately, your skin has an amazing ability to repair itself, as shown in **Figure 18**.

Figure 18 How Skin Heals

1. When you get a cut, a blood clot forms to prevent bacteria from entering the wound. Bacteria-fighting cells then come to the area to kill bacteria.

2. Damaged cells are replaced through cell division. Eventually, all that is left on the surface is a scar.

Other damage to the skin is very serious. Damage to the genetic material in skin cells can result in uncontrolled cell division, producing a mass of skin cells called a tumor. The term *cancer* is used to describe a tumor that invades other tissue. Darkened areas on the skin, such as moles, should be watched carefully for signs of cancer. **Figure 19** shows an example of a mole that has possibly become cancerous.

Your skin may also be affected by hormones that cause the oil glands in your skin to produce excess oil. This oil combines with dead skin cells and bacteria to clog hair follicles and cause infections. Proper cleansing and daily skin care can be helpful in decreasing the amount of infections.

Figure 19 This mole has two halves that do not match, a characteristic that might indicate skin cancer.

REVIEW

1. Why does skin color vary from person to person?
2. List six structures found in the dermis and the function of each one.
3. **Making Inferences** Why do you feel pain when you pull on your hair or nails but not when you cut them?

TOPIC: Integumentary System
GO TO: www.scilinks.org
***sci*LINKS NUMBER:** HSTL545

Answers to Review

1. The amount of melanin in the skin determines skin color.
2. nerves, sense; blood vessels, transport; muscle, motion; oil glands, waterproofing; sweat glands, heat regulation; fat cells, insulation
3. The hair and nails don't contain nerves, but the hair follicle and nail root do.

3) Extend

DEBATE

Sun Safety Is sun tanning beneficial or dangerous? Lead students in a debate about the benefits of sunlight and the potential dangers and safety issues associated with getting a suntan.

4) Close

Quiz

1. What are five functions of the skin? (keeps moisture in and foreign particles out; provides information about the outside world; helps to regulate body temperature; and removes some wastes)
2. Describe the two layers of the skin. (The epidermis is the thinner outer layer of the skin and contains epithelial tissue and mostly dead cells. The dermis, the deeper, thicker layer of skin, is made up mostly of connective tissue.)
3. How are pimples formed? (Oil glands in the skin produce excess oil that combines with dead skin cells and bacteria to clog hair follicles and cause an infection. The result is a pimple.)

ALTERNATIVE ASSESSMENT

Have students make a colorful drawing in their ScienceLog of a cross section of skin. Have students make their drawings from memory and label the parts and describe the function of each: dermis, epidermis, fat cells, blood vessels, nerves, muscle, hair follicle, oil gland, sweat gland.
Sheltered English

Section 4 • The Integumentary System

Chapter Highlights

VOCABULARY DEFINITIONS

SECTION 1

homeostasis the maintenance of a stable internal environment

tissue a group of similar cells that work together to perform a specific job in the body

epithelial tissue one of the four main types of tissue in the body; the tissue that covers and protects underlying tissue

nervous tissue one of the four main types of tissue in the body; the tissue that sends electrical signals through the body

muscle tissue one of the four main types of tissue in the body; contains cells that contract and relax to produce movement

connective tissue one of the four main types of tissue in the body; functions include support, protection, insulation, and nourishment

organ a combination of two or more tissues that work together to perform a specific function in the body

SECTION 2

skeletal system a collection of organs whose primary function is to support and protect the body; the organs in this system include bones, cartilage, ligaments, and tendons

compact bone the type of bone tissue that does not have open spaces; the tissue that gives a bone its strength

spongy bone the type of bone tissue that has many open spaces and contains marrow

cartilage a flexible, white tissue that gives support and protection but is not rigid like bone

joint the place where two or more bones connect

ligament a strong band of tissue that connects bones to bones

Chapter Highlights

SECTION 1

Vocabulary
homeostasis (p. 522)
tissue (p. 522)
epithelial tissue (p. 522)
nervous tissue (p. 522)
muscle tissue (p. 523)
connective tissue (p. 523)
organ (p. 523)

Section Notes

- Your body maintains a stable internal environment called homeostasis.
- Four types of tissues work to maintain homeostasis. Each tissue has a special job to do.
- Tissues work together to form organs.
- A group of organs working together for a common purpose is called an organ system.
- There are 11 major organ systems in the human body.

SECTION 2

Vocabulary
skeletal system (p. 526)
compact bone (p. 527)
spongy bone (p. 527)
cartilage (p. 528)
joint (p. 528)
ligament (p. 529)

Section Notes

- The skeletal system includes bones, cartilage, and ligaments.
- Bones support and protect the body, store minerals and fat, and produce blood cells.
- A typical bone contains marrow, spongy bone, compact bone, blood vessels, and cartilage.

✓ Skills Check

Math Concepts

CALCULATING A PERCENTAGE In the MathBreak on page 533 you were asked to calculate a percentage of a number. To do this, first express the percentage as a decimal or a fraction. Then multiply it by the number. For example, 25 percent can be written as 0.25 or $25 \div 100$. To find 25 percent of 48, multiply by either 0.25 or $25 \div 100$.

$$0.25 \times 48 = 12$$
or
$$(25 \div 100) \times 48 = 12$$

Visual Understanding

MOVING WITH JOINTS Take another look at the three kinds of joints on page 528. Consider how your joints work when you throw a ball or walk up stairs. The hinge joint in your knee can move freely in only two directions. The ball-and-socket joint in your shoulder can move in many directions. The sliding joints in your hand allow bones to glide over one another.

Lab and Activity Highlights

Muscles at Work PG 762

Seeing Is Believing PG 763

 Datasheets for LabBook (blackline masters for these labs)

SECTION 2

- A joint is where two bones meet. Some joints allow a lot of movement, and some allow little or no movement.
- Bones are attached to bones by connective tissue called ligaments.
- The action of muscle on bone and joints often works like a simple machine called a lever.

SECTION 3

Vocabulary
muscular system (p. 530)
smooth muscle (p. 530)
cardiac muscle (p. 530)
skeletal muscle (p. 530)
tendon (p. 531)

Section Notes
- Skeletal muscles and tendons make up the muscular system.
- You have three types of muscle: smooth, cardiac, and skeletal.
- Muscles are attached to bones by tendons.
- Exercise helps keep your muscular system healthy.

Labs
Muscles at Work (p. 762)

SECTION 4

Vocabulary
integumentary system (p. 534)
sweat glands (p. 534)
melanin (p. 534)
epidermis (p. 535)
dermis (p. 535)
hair follicle (p. 536)

Section Notes
- Your skin, hair, and nails make up your integumentary system.
- Your skin has two layers that contain a variety of small organs.
- Your hair and nails help protect your body.
- Skin can be damaged, but it has an amazing ability to repair itself.

Labs
Seeing Is Believing (p. 763)

---

internetconnect

GO TO: go.hrw.com

Visit the **HRW** Web site for a variety of learning tools related to this chapter. Just type in the keyword:

KEYWORD: HSTBD1

GO TO: www.scilinks.org

Visit the **National Science Teachers Association** on-line Web site for Internet resources related to this chapter. Just type in the *sci*LINKS number for more information about the topic:

TOPIC: Tissues and Organs	*sci*LINKS NUMBER: HSTL530
TOPIC: Body Systems	*sci*LINKS NUMBER: HSTL535
TOPIC: Skeletal System	*sci*LINKS NUMBER: HSTL537
TOPIC: The Muscular System	*sci*LINKS NUMBER: HSTL540
TOPIC: Integumentary System	*sci*LINKS NUMBER: HSTL545

VOCABULARY DEFINITIONS, continued

SECTION 3

muscular system a collection of organs whose primary function is movement; organs in this system include the muscles and the connective tissue that attaches them to bones

smooth muscle the type of muscle found in the blood vessels and the digestive tract

cardiac muscle the type of muscle found in the heart

skeletal muscle the type of muscle that moves the bones and helps protect the inner organs

tendon a tough connective tissue that connects skeletal muscles to bones

SECTION 4

integumentary system a collection of organs whose primary function is to help the body maintain a stable and healthy internal environment; the organs in this system include skin, hair, and nails

sweat glands small organs in the dermis layer of the skin that release sweat

melanin a darkening chemical in the skin that determines skin color

epidermis the outermost layer of the skin; also the outermost layer of cells covering roots, stems, leaves, and flower parts

dermis the layer of skin below the epidermis

hair follicle a small organ in the dermis layer of the skin that produces hair

---

Lab and Activity Highlights

LabBank

Inquiry Labs, On a Wing and a Layer, Lab 6

Long-Term Projects & Research Ideas, Mapping the Human Body, Project 22

Vocabulary Review Worksheet 22

Blackline masters of these Chapter Highlights can be found in the **Study Guide.**

Chapter Review Answers

USING VOCABULARY

1. nervous
2. integumentary
3. skeletal
4. flexor
5. cartilage

UNDERSTANDING CONCEPTS

Multiple Choice
6. b
7. c
8. b
9. c
10. c
11. b

Short Answer
12. Epithelial tissue—covers and protects; muscle tissue—produces movement; nervous tissue—communicates by transfer of electrical signals or messages throughout the body; connective tissue—joins, supports, and transports other tissues. (Illustrations will vary but should be similar to those in **Figure 1**.)
13. Skin protects underlying tissue from dehydration, germs, and harmful radiation from the sun.
14. Muscle attached to the hair follicle contracts, pushing up the epidermis as it pulls on the hair follicle.
15. a. Skeletal muscle is attached to bone by tendons and causes bones to move; cardiac muscle does not attach to bone.
    b. Skeletal muscle can be voluntary or involuntary, but cardiac muscle is involuntary.
16. Bones in your skeleton depend on muscles to move them. Bones give muscles a frame on which to move, and bones supply muscles with calcium. Bones protect muscles that carry out vital functions. The ribs protect the heart and lungs, which in turn supply the bones with oxygenated blood.

Chapter Review

USING VOCABULARY

To complete the following sentences, choose the correct term from each pair of terms listed below:

1. Electrical signals are sent throughout the body by the __?__ tissue. (*epithelial* or *nervous*)
2. Your __?__ system is made up of skin, hair, and nails. (*integumentary* or *muscular*)
3. Bones are moved by __?__ muscle. (*smooth* or *skeletal*)
4. When __?__ muscles contract, they cause parts of the body to bend. (*extensor* or *flexor*)
5. Most of the skeleton starts out as __?__, which is later replaced by bone. (*cartilage* or *ligaments*)

UNDERSTANDING CONCEPTS

Multiple Choice

6. Which of the following is made up of cells that can contract and relax?
   a. skeletal tissue
   b. muscle tissue
   c. connective tissue
   d. nervous tissue

7. The organ system that provides support and protection for body parts is the
   a. endocrine system.
   b. circulatory system.
   c. skeletal system.
   d. respiratory system.

8. The epidermis is composed of
   a. dermis.
   b. epithelial tissue.
   c. connective tissue.
   d. true skin.

9. The fixed point in a lever is the
   a. effort.
   b. load.
   c. fulcrum.
   d. mechanical advantage.

10. Muscles cause bones to move when
    a. the muscles stretch.
    b. the muscles grow between bones.
    c. the muscles pull on bones.
    d. the muscles push bones apart.

11. Ligaments are the connective tissue that attaches
    a. bones to muscles.
    b. bones to other bones.
    c. muscles to other muscles.
    d. muscles to dermis.

Short Answer

12. Summarize the functions of the four types of tissues, and draw a sketch of each type.
13. How does the skin help protect the body?
14. What is a goose bump?
15. What are two ways skeletal muscle differs from cardiac muscle?
16. How do the functions of the skeletal system relate to the functions of the muscular system?

Concept Mapping

17. An answer to this exercise can be found at the end of this book.

Concept Mapping Transparency 22

Concept Mapping

17. Use the following terms to create a concept map: bones, marrow, skeletal system, spongy bone, compact bone, cartilage.

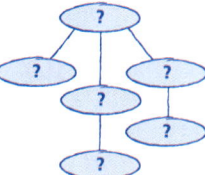

CRITICAL THINKING AND PROBLEM SOLVING

Write one or two sentences to answer the following questions:

18. Why do some muscles not work when a bone is broken?

19. Unlike human bones, some bird bones have air-filled cavities. What advantage does this give birds?

20. Compare the shapes of the bones of the human skull with the shapes of the bones of the human leg. Why is their shape important?

21. Compare the texture and sensitivity of the skin on your elbows with those of the skin on your fingertips. How can you explain the differences?

MATH IN SCIENCE

22. Your muscles make up about 40 percent of your overall mass. What is the muscle mass of a person whose total body mass is 60 kg?

23. The average person blinks 700 times an hour. How many times would the average person blink in a week if he or she were awake for 16 hours each day?

INTERPRETING GRAPHICS

Look at the picture below, and answer the questions that follow.

24. What is *D* called? What type of tissue is most abundant in this layer?

25. What is the name and function of *A*?

26. What is the name and function of *B*?

27. What part of the skin is made up of epithelial tissue that contains dead cells?

28. How does skin help regulate body temperature?

 Take a minute to review your answers to the Pre-Reading Questions found at the bottom of page 520. Have your answers changed? If necessary, revise your answers based on what you have learned since you began this chapter.

CRITICAL THINKING AND PROBLEM SOLVING

18. A muscle needs a bone for leverage. If that bone is broken in two, the muscle can only move part of the bone, or none of it depending on where the break is in relation to where the muscle's tendon attaches to the bone.

19. Hollow bones are lighter, which makes flight possible.

20. The bones in the skull are shaped to form a strong helmet-like protection around the brain. The leg bone has a design that makes standing upright and moving around possible.

21. Students should notice that the skin on their elbows is hard and rough compared with the delicate, sensitive skin on their fingertips. The skin on an elbow has to be tough and insensitive because we rest our upper body on it.

MATH IN SCIENCE

22. Forty percent of 60 kg is 24 kg.

23. $700 \frac{\text{blinks}}{\text{hours}} \times 16 \frac{\text{hours}}{\text{day}} \times 7 \frac{\text{days}}{\text{week}} = 78,400 \frac{\text{blinks}}{\text{week}}$

INTERPRETING GRAPHICS

24. the dermis, connective tissue

25. Sweat glands produce sweat that helps regulate body temperature.

26. Oil glands produce oil, which waterproofs the skin.

27. C. Epidermis

28. Sample answer: Sweat glands produce sweat, which helps cool the body.

 Blackline masters of this Chapter Review can be found in the **Study Guide**.

Chapter 22 • Chapter Review

SCIENCE, TECHNOLOGY, AND SOCIETY
Engineered Skin

Background

The engineered skin is far better than the scar tissue that would form without it. Scar tissue is weaker and more brittle than the skin it replaces. It does not stretch and grow, making a particularly difficult problem for children suffering from burns. Engineered skin also helps reduce the disfigurement associated with scarring.

One significant limitation of the engineered skin is that when it is new, it lacks sweat glands. Because patients cannot perspire in the areas that have skin grafts, patients with large grafts need to be cautious about overexercising and exposure to the sun.

Science, Technology, and Society

Engineered Skin

Your skin is more than just a well-fitting suit—it's your first line of defense against the outside world. Your skin keeps you safe from dehydration and infection, and the oil glands in your skin keep you waterproof. But what happens when a significant portion of skin is damaged?

More Skin Is the Answer

Sometimes doctors perform a skin graft, transferring some of a person's healthy skin to a damaged area of skin. This is because skin is really the best "bandage" for a wound. It protects the wound but still allows it to breathe. And unlike manufactured cloth or plastic bandages, skin can regenerate itself as it covers a wound. Sometimes, though, a person's skin is so severely damaged (as often occurs in burn victims) that the person doesn't have enough skin to spare.

Tissue Engineering

In the past few years, scientists have been studying tissue engineering to learn more about how the human body heals itself naturally. Using a small piece of young, healthy human skin and some collagen from cows, scientists can now engineer human skin. During the engineering process, cells form the dermal and epidermal layers of skin just as they would if they were still on the body. The living human skin that results can even heal itself if it is cut before it is used for a skin graft. Because it is living, the skin must be kept on a medium that provides it with nutrients until it is placed on a wound. Over time, the color of the grafted skin changes to match the color of the skin that surrounds it.

A Woven Dermis

Tissue engineers have also created another kind of skin, except this one has an unusual dermal

▲ *This is a piece of engineered skin used for grafting.*

and epidermal layer. In this skin, the dermis is made of woven collagen fibers. The wounded area digests these fibers and uses them as a guide to create a new dermis. The epidermal layer is a temporary layer of silicone. It shields the body from infection and protects against dehydration while new skin is being made.

After a new dermal layer forms under the protective silicone epidermis, the body is in better condition to accept a skin graft. Doctors can also graft a thinner portion of skin. A thinner graft is better for the body in the long run because it is easier to take from another part of the body. The new dermal layer also gives the body more time to strengthen on its own before the trauma of transplanting healthy skin to other areas.

On Your Own

▶ In the past, doctors have harvested skin from the bodies of people who, before they died, chose to be organ donors. What kinds of problems could arise if this harvested skin were used on burn victims?

Answer to On Your Own

Skin harvested from cadavers can be rejected, and it can also introduce viruses and disease. The bits of skin used to create engineered skin are from the foreskins of babies, and there seems to be a readily available supply. Additionally, youthful skin grows very quickly.

Eureka!
Hairy Oil Spills

Oil and water don't mix, right? Oil floats on the surface of water and is clearly visible to the naked eye. Proving this in your kitchen isn't difficult, nor is it dangerous. But what happens when the water is the ocean and the oil is crude oil? You have an environmental disaster that costs millions of dollars to clean up. The worst example in American waters was in 1989 when the *Exxon Valdez* oil tanker spilled nearly 42 million liters of crude oil into the waters of Prince William Sound on the Alaskan coast.

▲ *Phil McCrory among bags of discarded human hair.*

▲ *This otter was drenched with oil spilled from the* Exxon Valdez.

Backyard Testing

A Huntsville, Alabama, hairdresser asked a brilliant question when he saw an otter whose fur was drenched with oil from the *Valdez* spill. If the otter's fur soaked up all the oil, why wouldn't human hair do the same? The hairdresser, Phil McCrory, gathered hair from the floor of his salon and took it home to perform his own experiments. He stuffed 2.2 kg of hair into a pair of his wife's pantyhose and tied the ankles together to form a bagel-shaped bundle. After filling his son's wading pool with water, McCrory floated the bundle in the pool. Next, McCrory poured used motor oil into the center of the ring. When he pulled the ring closed, not a drop of oil remained in the water!

How Does Hair Do This?

What McCrory discovered was that hair *ad*sorbs oil instead of *ab*sorbing it. To adsorb means to collect a liquid or gas in layers on a surface. Because tiny cuticles cover every hair shaft like fish scales, the oil can bind to the surface of hair. Compare this process with the way a sponge works. A sponge completely absorbs a liquid. This means it is wet throughout, not just on the surface.

McCrory approached the National Aeronautics and Space Administration (NASA) with his discovery. In controlled tests performed by NASA, hair proved to be the fastest adsorber around. A little more than 1 kg of hair can adsorb over 3.5 L of oil in just 2 minutes!

It is estimated that within a week, 64 million kilograms of hair in reusable mesh pillows could have soaked up *all* of the oil spilled by the *Valdez.* Unfortunately, the $2 billion spent on the cleanup removed only about 12 percent of the spill. Did you ever think that the hair from your head could have a purpose beyond keeping your head warm?

Compare the Facts
▶ Research how McCrory's discovery compares with the methods currently used to clean up oil spills. Share your findings with the class.

Eureka!
Hairy Oil Spills

Background

Bioremediation is the use of biological processes and products to eliminate organic contaminants from soils. Hair is a biological waste product that doesn't degrade well in landfills. Using hair for the bioremediation of oil spills would reduce the amount of waste in landfills. Also, since the hair adsorbs the oil, wringing the hair out means the oil can be recovered and the hair can be used again. As a last resort, the oil-saturated mesh pillows can be burned as fuel in order to recover the value of the oil they contain.

Activity

Have a few students work in a group, and ask them to research the current state of Prince William Sound. Has the ecosystem fully recovered? Are there still problems? Ask these students to report their findings to the class.

Answer to Compare the Facts

Current methods of cleanup include skimmers, booms, and dispersing agents. Skimmers recover oil from the water's surface. There are three types of skimmers—weir, oleophilic, and suction. Dispersing agents contain surfactants, which break liquids such as oil into small drops. Booms are used for containment so that other areas are not contaminated. Booms also concentrate the oil into thicker layers on the water's surface, which facilitates recovery. One type of boom has natural oil-eating microbes within it. These microbes biodegrade the contaminants and then the boom biodegrades itself.

McCrory's method has the potential to save millions of dollars. Current remediation procedures cost about $10 per 3.8 L of oil, while his method may cost as little as $2.

Chapter Organizer

CHAPTER ORGANIZATION	TIME MINUTES	OBJECTIVES	LABS, INVESTIGATIONS, AND DEMONSTRATIONS
Chapter Opener pp. 544–545	45	National Standards: UCP 2, SAI 1, ST 2, SPSP 5, LS 1e, 3b	**Start-Up Activity** Exercise and Your Heart, p. 545
Section 1 The Cardiovascular System	90	▶ Describe the functions of the cardiovascular system. ▶ Compare and contrast the three types of blood vessels. ▶ Describe the path that blood travels as it circulates through the body. ▶ Distinguish between blood types. UCP 1–3, 5, ST 2, SPSP 1, 4, 5, LS 1a, 1c–1f, 3b	**Whiz-Bang Demonstrations,** Get the Beat! Demo 12 BASIC
Section 2 The Lymphatic System	90	▶ Discuss the functions of the lymphatic system. ▶ Identify the relationship between lymph and blood. ▶ Describe the organs of the lymphatic system. UCP 1, 5, LS 1a, 1c–1f	
Section 3 The Respiratory System	90	▶ Describe the flow of air through the respiratory system. ▶ Discuss the relationship between the respiratory system and the cardiovascular system. ▶ Identify respiratory disorders. UCP 1, 2, 4, 5, SPSP 1, 4, LS 1a, 1c–1f; LabBook UCP 2, 5, SAI 1, 2, LS 1a	**QuickLab,** Why Do People Snore? p. 559 GENERAL **Making Models,** Build a Lung, p. 766 GENERAL **Datasheets for LabBook,** Build a Lung, Datasheet 49 GENERAL **Skill Builder,** Carbon Dioxide Breath, p. 767 GENERAL **Datasheets for LabBook,** Carbon Dioxide Breath, Datasheet 50 GENERAL **EcoLabs & Field Activities,** There's Something in the Air, Field Activity 9 GENERAL **Whiz-Bang Demonstrations,** Take a Deep Breath, Demo 13 GENERAL **Long-Term Projects & Research Ideas,** Project 23 ADVANCED

*See page **T20** for a complete correlation of this book with the*

NATIONAL SCIENCE EDUCATION STANDARDS.

TECHNOLOGY RESOURCES

 Guided Reading Audio CD English or Spanish, Chapter 23

 One-Stop Planner CD-ROM with Test Generator

 CNN. Science, Technology & Society, Breakthrough Bandage, Segment 30 Modern Acupuncture, Segment 31

Chapter 23 • Circulation and Respiration

CLASSROOM WORKSHEETS, TRANSPARENCIES, AND RESOURCES	SCIENCE INTEGRATION AND CONNECTIONS	REVIEW AND ASSESSMENT
Directed Reading Worksheet 23 BASIC **Science Puzzlers, Twisters & Teasers,** Worksheet 23 ADVANCED		
Directed Reading Worksheet 23, Section 1 BASIC **Math Skills for Science Worksheet 31,** The Unit Factor and Dimensional Analysis GENERAL **Transparency 82,** The Flow of Blood Through the Heart **Transparency 83,** The Flow of Blood Through the Body **Reinforcement Worksheet 23,** Matchmaker, Matchmaker GENERAL **Reinforcement Worksheet 23,** Colors of the Heart BASIC **Critical Thinking Worksheet 23,** Doctor for a Day ADVANCED	**Math and More,** p. 548 in ATE GENERAL **Apply,** p. 552 GENERAL **MathBreak,** The Beat Goes On, p. 553 GENERAL **Health Watch:** Goats to the Rescue, p. 565 GENERAL	**Homework,** pp. 548, 549 in ATE GENERAL **Self-Check,** p. 550 **Review,** p. 551 GENERAL **Review,** p. 553 GENERAL **Quiz,** p. 553 in ATE GENERAL **Alternative Assessment,** p. 553 in ATE GENERAL
Directed Reading Worksheet 23, Section 2 BASIC		**Self-Check,** p. 554 **Review,** p. 555 GENERAL **Quiz,** p. 555 in ATE GENERAL **Alternative Assessment,** p. 555 in ATE ADVANCED
Transparency 84, The Respiratory System **Directed Reading Worksheet 23,** Section 3 BASIC **Transparency 225,** Air Pressure and Breathing	**Chemistry Connection,** p. 557 **Multicultural Connection,** p. 557 in ATE **Connect to Physical Science,** p. 558 in ATE **Weird Science,** Catching a Light Sneeze, p. 564 GENERAL	**Review,** p. 559 GENERAL **Quiz,** p. 559 in ATE GENERAL **Alternative Assessment,** p. 559 in ATE ADVANCED

END-OF-CHAPTER REVIEW AND ASSESSMENT

Chapter Review in Study Guide
Vocabulary and Notes in Study Guide
Chapter Tests with Performance-Based Assessment, Chapter 23 Test
Chapter Tests with Performance-Based Assessment, Performance-Based Assessment 23
Concept Mapping Transparency 23

 Holt, Rinehart and Winston On-line Resources
go.hrw.com
For worksheets and other teaching aids related to this chapter, visit the HRW Web site and type in the keyword: **HSTBD2**

 National Science Teachers Association
www.scilinks.org
Encourage students to use the *sci*LINKS numbers listed in the internet connect boxes to access information and resources on the **NSTA** Web site.

Chapter Resources & Worksheets

Visual Resources

TEACHING TRANSPARENCIES

TEACHING TRANSPARENCIES

CONCEPT MAPPING TRANSPARENCY

Meeting Individual Needs

DIRECTED READING

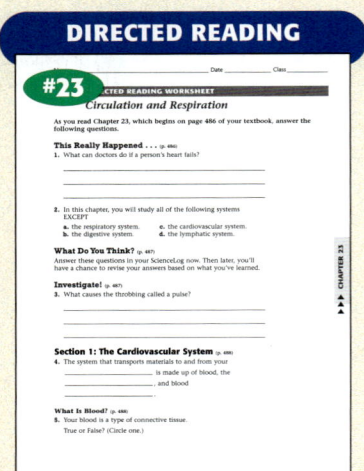

REINFORCEMENT & VOCABULARY REVIEW

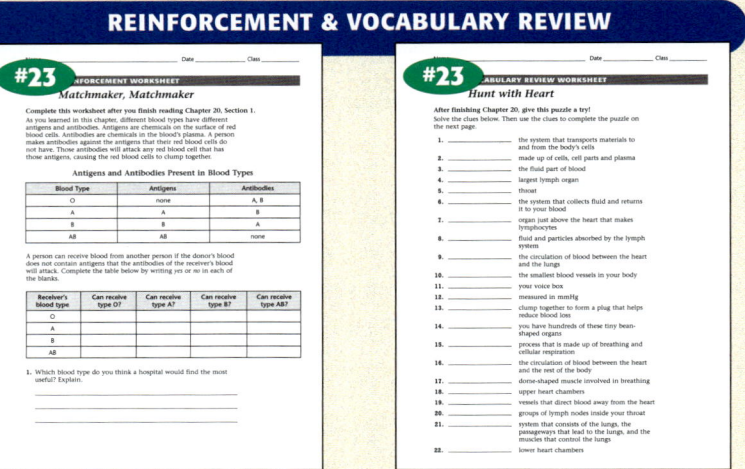

SCIENCE PUZZLERS, TWISTERS & TEASERS

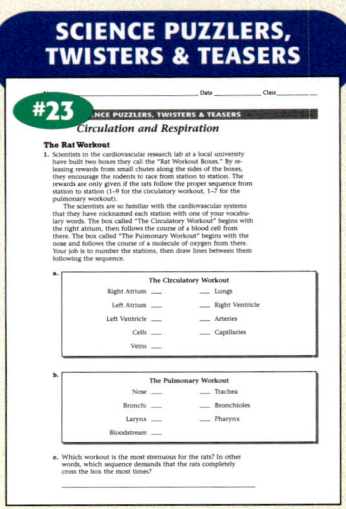

Chapter 23 • Circulation and Respiration

Chapter 23 • Circulation and Respiration

Review & Assessment

STUDY GUIDE

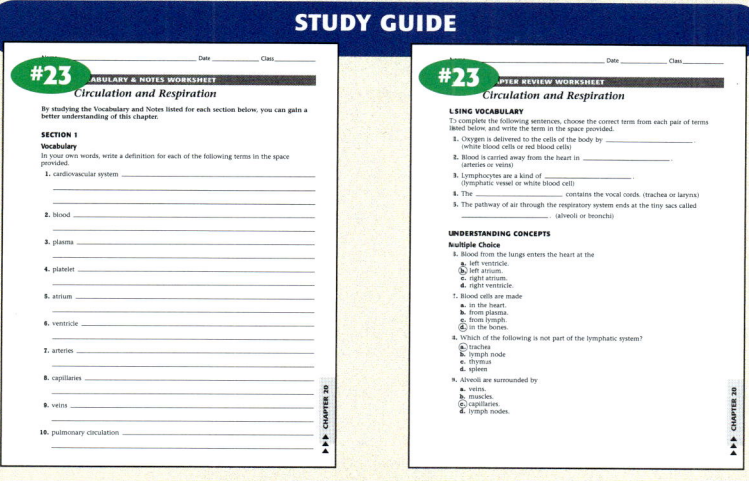

CHAPTER TESTS WITH PERFORMANCE-BASED ASSESSMENT

Lab Worksheets

ECOLABS & FIELD ACTIVITIES

WHIZ-BANG DEMONSTRATIONS

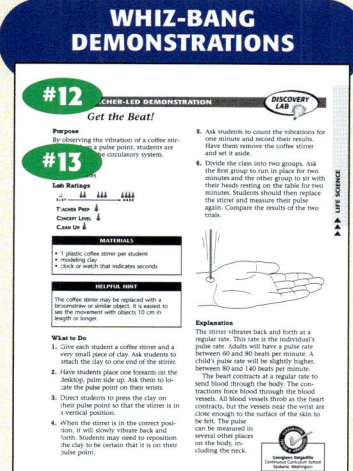

LONG-TERM PROJECTS & RESEARCH IDEAS

DATASHEETS FOR LABBOOK

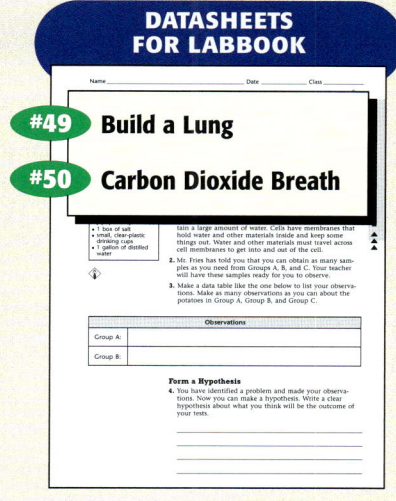

Applications & Extensions

CRITICAL THINKING & PROBLEM SOLVING

SCIENCE TECHNOLOGY

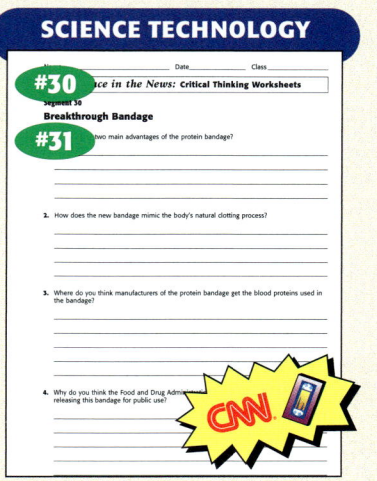

Chapter 23 • Chapter Resources & Worksheets   543D

Chapter Background

SECTION 1

The Cardiovascular System

▶ **The Flow of Blood**
William Harvey (1578–1657) is credited with being the first European to discover the circulation of the blood through the body.

- Based on his dissections of animals, Harvey rightly concluded that the heart was a muscle that served to pump blood through the body. In contrast to conventional wisdom and theories of the famous physician Galen (A.D. 129–c. 201), Harvey also correctly maintained that arteries carry blood away from the heart and veins carry blood toward the heart. Harvey was ridiculed for his views by many other physicians.

▶ **Atherosclerosis**
Atherosclerosis is a disease of the arteries in which the inside layer of the arterial walls thickens with plaque. The plaque forms in areas of turbulent blood flow. As the walls of an artery thicken, the diameter of the vessel narrows, impeding blood flow.

- Cigarette smoking, high blood pressure, obesity, inactivity, high cholesterol level, and a family history of heart disease are all risk factors for atherosclerosis.

▶ **Hypertension**
Like atherosclerosis, people afflicted with hypertension may not exhibit symptoms of the disease for years. In fact, hypertension is often called "the silent killer." Although blood pressure varies within a wide range across the population, a person whose resting blood pressure is consistently at the high end of that range is said to have hypertension.

- Smoking, obesity, stress, excessive consumption of alcohol, and diabetes mellitus all exacerbate high blood pressure.

▶ **Stroke**
A stroke occurs when the brain is damaged due to an interruption in the blood flow or leaking of blood from the blood vessels. Atherosclerosis and hypertension are some of the causes of strokes.

▶ **Heart Attack**
A heart attack occurs when part of the heart muscle dies due to blood and oxygen deprivation. About 1 million people in the United States suffer a heart attack each year.

▶ **Blood**
If red blood cells (RBCs) have an Rh antigen (a particular kind of protein on the surface of the cell), the blood is positive (+). If an Rh antigen is not present, the blood is negative (−). People have one of the following blood types: A+, A−, B+, B−, AB+, AB−, O+, or O−.

- People make antibodies against the antigens that they do not have on their own RBCs. However, people who have Rh− blood do not always have antibodies against the Rh antigen. These antibodies are made only after the Rh− person has been exposed to blood that is Rh+. For example, type B− people make A antibodies that attack any blood cell with an A antigen on it. They may also make Rh antibodies that will attack any blood cell with an Rh antigen on it. This means that people with type B− blood can't be given A+, A−, B+, AB+, or AB− blood. Type O− blood can be given to anyone because its RBCs have no antigens on their surface that a patient's antibodies could attack. Because of this, a type O− person is said to be a *universal donor*. Type AB+ people are *universal recipients;* they can be given any type of blood because they do not make any antibodies against A, B, or Rh antigens.

Chapter 23 • Circulation and Respiration

SECTION 2

The Lymphatic System

▶ **Lymphocytes**
Lymphocytes are white blood cells that specialize in fighting pathogens. The two main kinds of lymphocytes are B cells and T cells.

- About 10 percent of lymphocytes are B cells. When confronted with foreign antigens, B cells produce antibodies that destroy the antigens. This process is called humoral immunity.

- About 90 percent of lymphocytes are T cells, which are formed in the bones and mature in the thymus. Killer T cells locate and attack cells that have foreign antigens on their surface. This type of immunity is called cell-mediated immunity.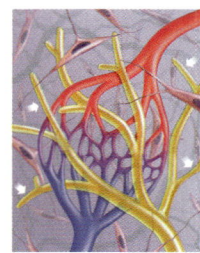

- HIV infects and destroys lymphocytes called helper T cells. When a person's helper T cell count falls below 200 cells per cubic millimeter of blood, the person is diagnosed with AIDS.

IS THAT A FACT!

- The tonsils reach their largest size when a person is about seven years old. Then the tonsils begin to shrink.

SECTION 3

The Respiratory System

▶ **Control of Breathing**
Unless a person consciously holds his or her breath or changes the rate of his or her breathing, breathing is controlled automatically by breathing control centers in the base of the brain (in the medulla oblongata and in the pons).

- Hiccups are caused by a sudden jerky contraction of the diaphragm. When a person eats too much food, the full stomach may irritate the diaphragm muscle, causing it to contract jerkily. Generally, though, the cause of hiccups is unknown.

- Yawning is caused by a buildup of carbon dioxide in the lungs. The brain controls breathing by monitoring carbon dioxide, rather than oxygen, levels in the body. Thus, shallow breathing may result in the accumulation of carbon dioxide in the lungs, resulting in a signal from the brain to take a deep breath and exhale the extra carbon dioxide.

▶ **Smoking**
Tobacco smoking has been implicated in more than 90 percent of lung cancers among men. Among people who do not smoke, 3,000 cases of lung cancer are linked to secondhand cigarette smoke each year.

IS THAT A FACT!

- More than 3,000 adolescents in the United States start to smoke each day. The habit will eventually kill one-third of these children.

- Each year, parents who smoke at least 10 cigarettes a day cause 8,000 to 26,000 new cases of asthma in children. Moreover, each year between 200,000 and 1 million children who already have asthma have their condition worsened by parental secondhand smoke.

For background information about teaching strategies and issues, refer to the *Professional Reference for Teachers*.

CHAPTER 23

Circulation and Respiration

 Pre-Reading Questions

Students may not know the answers to these questions before reading the chapter, so accept any reasonable response.

Suggested Answers

1. Blood is a type of connective tissue made of cell parts, plasma, and two types of cells. Blood carries nutrients and oxygen to all the cells of the body and carries carbon dioxide and wastes away. White blood cells fight infection, and platelets aid in clotting.

2. Inhaling brings oxygen into the lungs, where it is transferred to the blood and transported throughout the body. Exhaling allows carbon dioxide in the lungs to leave the body.

 Directed Reading Worksheet 23

 Science Puzzlers, Twisters & Teasers Worksheet 23

 Guided Reading Audio CD English or Spanish, Chapter 23

CHAPTER 23

Circulation and Respiration

Sections

1. **The Cardiovascular System** 546
   - Apply 552
   - MathBreak 553
   - Internet Connect 553
2. **The Lymphatic System** 554
   - Internet Connect 555
3. **The Respiratory System** 556
   - Chemistry Connection 557
   - QuickLab 559
   - Internet Connect 559

Chapter Review 562
Feature Articles 564, 565
LabBook 766–767

 **Pre-Reading Questions**

1. What is blood, and what is its function in your body?
2. Why do you need to breathe?

SMALL BUT MIGHTY!

These donut-shaped objects are red blood cells like those that can be found throughout your body. Red blood cells are smaller than most other body cells. In fact, millions of them can be found in a single drop of blood. These cells may be small, but they perform a very important function. They are so important that your body makes about 200 billion new red blood cells every day. Why does your body need so many red blood cells? In this chapter, you will learn how these tiny cells enable all your body cells to carry out cellular respiration.

---

internet connect

 HRW On-line Resources
go.hrw.com
For worksheets and other teaching aids, visit the HRW Web site and type in the keyword: **HSTBD2**

 SCILINKS NSTA
www.scilinks.com
Use the *sci*LINKS numbers at the end of each chapter for additional resources on the **NSTA** Web site.

 CNNfyi.com
www.cnnfyi.com
Visit the CNN Web site for current events coverage and classroom resources.

START-UP Activity

EXERCISE AND YOUR HEART

Your heart pumps blood throughout your body. How does your heart respond to exercise? You can determine this reaction by measuring your pulse. You can take your pulse by placing your fingers on the inside of your wrist just below your thumb.

Procedure

1. Take your pulse while remaining still. Using a **watch with a second hand,** count the number of beats in 15 seconds. Then multiply this number by 4 to calculate the number of beats in 1 minute

2. Do jumping jacks or jog in place for 30 seconds. Then stop and calculate your heart rate again.

   Caution: Do not perform this exercise if you have difficulty breathing, have high blood pressure, or easily get dizzy.

3. Rest for 5 minutes, and then take your pulse again.

Analysis

4. How did exercise affect your heart rate? Why do you think this happened?

5. How does your heart rate affect the rate at which red blood cells travel throughout your body?

6. Why did your heart rate return to normal after you rested?

START-UP Activity

EXERCISE AND YOUR HEART

MATERIALS

FOR EACH GROUP:
- watch with a second hand

Safety Caution

Have students bring in a signed permission slip for this activity. Any students who have a health problem that is worsened by exercise should be excused from the exercise portion of this activity. Instruct students who feel pain or become dizzy or tired to stop exercising immediately. Some students may feel embarrassed to exercise in front of their peers. You may want to invite a few volunteers to perform this part of the activity instead of having all students exercise.

Answers to START-UP Activity

4–5. Students should notice that their heart rate goes up when they are exercising. Explanations will vary. Students might suggest that while exercising, more blood is needed to deliver energy and oxygen to the muscles.

6. Once exercise is complete, less blood is needed, so the heart can slow down.

Chapter 23 • Circulation and Respiration   **545**

SECTION 1

Focus

The Cardiovascular System

This section introduces the structures and functions of the cardiovascular system. Students compare and contrast three different types of blood vessels and trace the path of blood through these vessels in the body. Students also learn to distinguish between the different blood types.

Ask students to list in their ScienceLog as many song titles, phrases, and slogans that contain the word *heart* as they can in 2–3 minutes. Ask for examples, and list them on the board. Ask for reasons why the word *heart* is the focus of so many songs and slogans.

1) Motivate

DISCUSSION

Invite students to describe a time when their skin was cut. Encourage students to describe not only what happened but also what their blood looked like. Make a list of the words students use to describe their blood. Based on students' experiences with blood and bleeding, lead a discussion about the structure and functions of blood. Then have students read these pages and compare their descriptions of blood with the one in the textbook. Ask:

Can you see individual blood cells when you bleed? Why or why not? How are red blood cells different from other cells in the body? **(They lack a nucleus, organelles, and DNA, and they carry oxygen to other cells in the body.)**

546 Chapter 23 • Circulation and Respiration

Section 1

Terms to Learn

cardiovascular system
blood
arteries
capillaries
veins
pulmonary circulation
systemic circulation
blood pressure

What You'll Do

◆ Describe the functions of the cardiovascular system.
◆ Compare and contrast the three types of blood vessels.
◆ Describe the path that blood travels as it circulates through the body.
◆ Distinguish between blood types.

The Cardiovascular System

When you hear the word *heart*, what do you think of first? Many people think of romance. But the heart is much more than a symbol of love. It's the pump that drives your cardiovascular system. The **cardiovascular system** transports materials to and from your cells. The word *cardio* means "heart," and the word *vascular* means "vessel." The cardiovascular system, which is shown in **Figure 1**, is made up of three parts: blood, the heart, and blood vessels.

Figure 1
The Cardiovascular System

What Is Blood?

The human body contains about 5 L of blood. **Blood** is a connective tissue made up of two types of cells, cell parts, and plasma. *Plasma* is the fluid part of blood. It is a mixture of water, minerals, nutrients, sugars, proteins, and other substances. Red blood cells, white blood cells, and platelets float in the plasma.

Figure 2 Red blood cells deliver oxygen.

Red Blood Cells Red blood cells, or RBCs, are the most abundant cells in blood. RBCs, shown in **Figure 2**, supply your cells with oxygen. As you have learned, cells need oxygen to carry out cellular respiration. Each RBC contains a protein called *hemoglobin* (HEE moh GLOH bin). Hemoglobin, which gives RBCs their red color, clings to the oxygen you inhale. This allows RBCs to transport oxygen throughout the body. The shape of RBCs gives them a large amount of surface area for absorbing and releasing oxygen.

RBCs are made in the bone marrow. Before RBCs enter the bloodstream, they lose their nucleus and other organelles. Without a nucleus, which contains DNA, the RBCs cannot replace worn-out proteins. RBCs therefore can live only about 4 months.

546

internet connect

SC/**LINKS**
NSTA

TOPIC: The Cardiovascular System
GO TO: www.scilinks.org
***sci*LINKS NUMBER:** HSTL555

IS THAT A FACT!

About half of the volume of blood is cells. The other half is plasma. Plasma consists of 95 percent water.

White Blood Cells Sometimes *pathogens*—bacteria, viruses, and other microscopic particles that can make you sick—are able to enter your body. When they do, they often encounter your white blood cells, or WBCs. WBCs, shown in **Figure 3,** help you stay healthy by destroying pathogens and helping to clean wounds.

WBCs fight pathogens in several ways. Some squeeze out of vessels and move around in tissues, searching for pathogens. When they find a pathogen, they engulf it. Other WBCs release chemicals called *antibodies,* which help destroy pathogens. WBCs also keep you healthy by engulfing body cells that have died or been damaged. WBCs are made in bone marrow. Some of them mature in lymphatic organs, which will be discussed later.

Platelets Drifting among the blood cells are tiny particles called platelets. *Platelets* are pieces of larger cells found in bone marrow. These larger cells remain in the bone marrow, but they pinch off fragments of themselves, which enter the blood. Although platelets last for only 5 to 10 days, they are an important part of blood. When you cut or scrape your skin, you bleed because blood vessels have been opened. As soon as bleeding occurs, platelets begin to clump together in the damaged area and form a plug that helps reduce blood loss, as shown in **Figure 4.** Platelets also release a variety of chemicals that react with proteins in the plasma and cause tiny fibers to form. The fibers create a blood clot.

Figure 3 *White blood cells defend the body against pathogens. These white blood cells have been colored yellow to make their shape easier to see.*

Figure 4 *Platelets release chemicals in damaged vessels and cause fibers to form. The fibers make a "net" that traps blood cells and stops bleeding.*

MISCONCEPTION ALERT

Students may think that deoxygenated blood is blue because it is often depicted that way in illustrations and because blood appears blue in vessels through the skin. The color of blood does change depending on the amount of oxygen it contains; however, human blood is not blue. It varies in color from scarlet to deep red.

Directed Reading Worksheet 23 Section 1

② Teach

READING STRATEGY

Activity Before students read the text on this page, have them read the headings aloud. Then ask students to formulate one question that they expect the text under each heading to answer. Have students write the questions in their ScienceLog.

USING THE FIGURE

Have students compare **Figure 2,** which shows red blood cells, with **Figure 3,** which shows white blood cells. Ask students to relate any differences in shape or size to the different functions of these two types of blood cells. Help students understand that the flat shape and small size of red blood cells enable them to carry oxygen through tiny capillaries to cells throughout the body. Help students link the larger size and sticky-looking surface of white bloods cells to their ability to fight pathogens. **Sheltered English**

MEETING INDIVIDUAL NEEDS

Learners Having Difficulty
To help students visualize the components of blood, have them make a model of blood. Provide students with a variety of materials, such as a resealable plastic sandwich bag, thick corn syrup, plastic-foam balls, and other craft materials. Then have students use the materials to make a model of the parts of blood. Encourage students to be creative in their representations of the parts of blood. **Sheltered English**

Section 1 • The Cardiovascular System **547**

2) Teach, continued

MATH and MORE

Your heart beats about 100,800 times per day. With every beat, about 70 mL of blood is pumped out of your heart. In 1 hour, how much blood does your heart pump out? **(294 L)**

About how much blood does your heart pump out in a day? **(7,056 L)**

Help students visualize this amount by showing them a liter of water.

Math Skills Worksheet 31
"The Unit Factor and Dimensional Analysis"

Homework

Making Models Have students make a model of the human heart to show the path of blood through it. Models can be drawings or three-dimensional constructions. Have students present their completed model to the class. Provide yarn or a pen light so that students can demonstrate to the class the flow of blood through their model heart.
Sheltered English

Teaching Transparency 82
"The Flow of Blood Through the Heart"

Have a Heart

Your heart is a muscular organ about the size of your fist. It is found in the center of your chest cavity. The heart pumps oxygen-poor blood to the lungs and oxygen-rich blood to the body. Like the hearts of all mammals, your heart has a left side and a right side that are separated by a thick wall. As you can see in **Figure 5,** each side has an upper chamber and a lower chamber. Each upper chamber is called an *atrium* (plural, *atria*). Each lower chamber is called a *ventricle*.

Flaplike structures called *valves* are located between the atria and ventricles and also where large arteries are attached to the heart. As blood moves through the heart, the valves close and prevent blood from going backward. The lub-dub, lub-dub sound that a beating heart makes is caused by the closing of the valves. The flow of blood through the heart is shown in the diagram below.

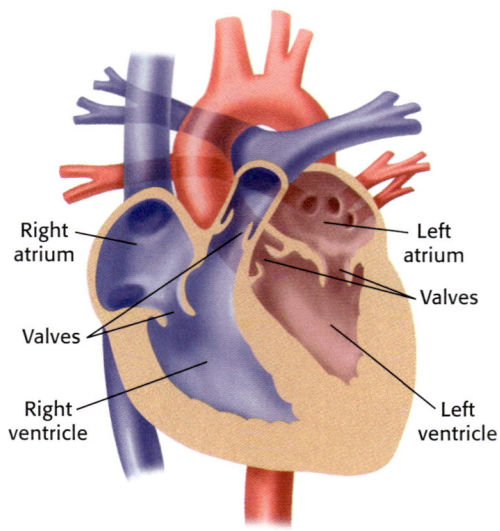

Figure 5 The heart is a four-chambered organ that pumps blood through cardiovascular vessels. The vessels carrying oxygen-rich blood are shown in red. The vessels carrying oxygen-poor blood are shown in blue.

The Flow of Blood Through the Heart

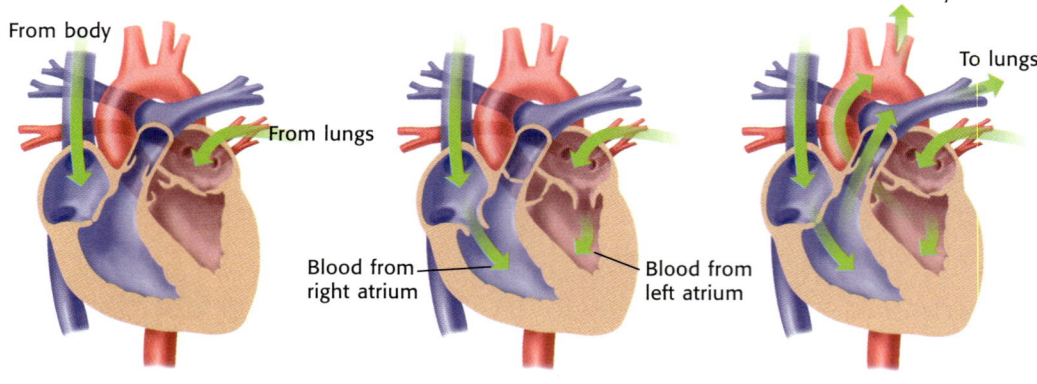

❶ Blood enters the atria first. The left atrium receives oxygen-rich blood from the lungs. The right atrium receives oxygen-poor blood from the body.

❷ When the atria contract, blood is squeezed into the ventricles.

❸ While the atria relax, the ventricles contract and push blood out of the heart. Blood from the right ventricle goes to the lungs. Blood from the left ventricle goes to the rest of the body.

MISCONCEPTION ALERT

The words *left* and *right* as used to diagram the anatomy of the heart might confuse students. When students are looking at a picture of the heart, the left atrium appears on their right, and the right atrium appears on their left. Help students understand anatomical left and right by facing them and asking them to identify your left and right hands in relation to their own.

Blood Vessels

Blood travels throughout your body in blood vessels. A blood vessel is a hollow tube that transports blood. There are three types of blood vessels—arteries, capillaries, and veins. Their structures and their relationship to each other are shown in **Figure 6.**

Figure 6 *Large arteries branch into smaller arteries, which branch into capillaries. Capillaries join small veins, which join to form large veins.*

Arteries Arteries are blood vessels that direct blood away from the heart. Arteries have thick elastic walls that contain a layer of smooth muscle. Each time the heart beats, blood is pumped out of the heart at high pressure. The thick walls of arteries have the strength to withstand this pressure. The rhythmic change in blood pressure is called a *pulse*.

Capillaries A strand of hair is about 10 times wider than a capillary. **Capillaries** are the smallest blood vessels in your body. Capillary walls are only one cell thick. As shown in **Figure 7,** capillaries are so narrow that blood cells must pass through them in single file. The simple structure of a capillary allows nutrients, oxygen, and many other kinds of substances to diffuse easily through capillary walls. No cell in the body is more than three or four cells away from a capillary.

Veins After leaving capillaries, the blood enters veins. **Veins** are blood vessels that direct the blood back to the heart. As blood travels through veins, valves keep the blood from flowing backward. When skeletal muscles contract, they squeeze nearby veins and help push blood toward the heart.

Figure 7 *These red blood cells are traveling through a capillary.*

BRAIN FOOD

If all the blood vessels in your body were strung together, the total length would be more than twice the circumference of the Earth.

READING STRATEGY

Mnemonics Help students use a mnemonic device to remember that arteries carry blood away from the heart and veins carry blood to the heart. Point out that both terms *artery* and *away* begin with the letter *a.* Then challenge students to think of other mnemonic devices to help them recall the flow of blood through the body.

GUIDED PRACTICE

Have students rank the types of blood vessels discussed on this page in order of the thickness of their walls. Have students begin with the vessel that has the thickest walls. (arteries, veins, capillaries) **Sheltered English**

ACTIVITY

Viewing Blood Vessels Set up microscope stations with prepared slides of an artery and a vein. Have students take turns viewing the slides and comparing the images with the descriptions of arteries and veins in the textbook. Then have students draw a sketch of what they saw under the microscope and write descriptive words beside each sketch. **Sheltered English**

Homework

Poster Project Have students draw a diagram of the heart. Have them label each chamber and use arrows to indicate the flow of blood.

WEIRD SCIENCE

Babies born with certain congenital heart defects are blue at birth. The condition, called cyanosis, can be caused by low levels of oxygen in the blood. The low levels of oxygen can be a result of defects in the anatomy of the heart. Deoxygenated blood is pumped to the body before it is pumped to the lungs. This defect can be repaired surgically.

Section 1 • The Cardiovascular System   **549**

2) Teach, continued

GROUP ACTIVITY
Circulation Relay

MATERIALS

FOR EACH CLASS:
- 5 inflated red balloons (or paper disks)
- 5 inflated blue balloons (or paper disks)
- diagram of The Flow of Blood Through the Body
- 8 stations (cardboard boxes, flags, and so on)

Divide the class into five teams for a relay race.

1. Students begin in the left ventricle carrying a red balloon, which represents an oxygenated blood cell.
2. They travel through the aorta.
3. After passing through the aorta, students carry oxygenated blood to the muscles and exchange the red balloon for a blue one.
4. From the muscles, students carry blood loaded with CO_2 to the right atrium.
5. From the right atrium, students travel into the right ventricle.
6. Students travel through the pulmonary artery.
7. From the pulmonary artery, students travel into the lungs, where they exchange their CO_2 for oxygen (exchange blue balloons for red ones).
8. Carrying oxygenated blood (red balloons), students enter the left atrium and are ready to begin again or hand off their balloons.

Walk one student at a time through the pathway; then have the teams send students through in a relay race.

Self-Check

How are the structures of arteries and veins related to their functions? *(See page 782 to check your answer.)*

Going with the Flow

As you read earlier, one important function of your blood is to supply the cells of your body with oxygen. Where does blood get this oxygen? It gets it from your lungs during pulmonary circulation. **Pulmonary circulation** is the circulation of blood between your heart and lungs.

When oxygen-rich blood returns to the heart from the lungs, it must be pumped to the rest of the body. The circulation of blood between the heart and the rest of the body is called **systemic circulation**. Both types of circulation are diagrammed below.

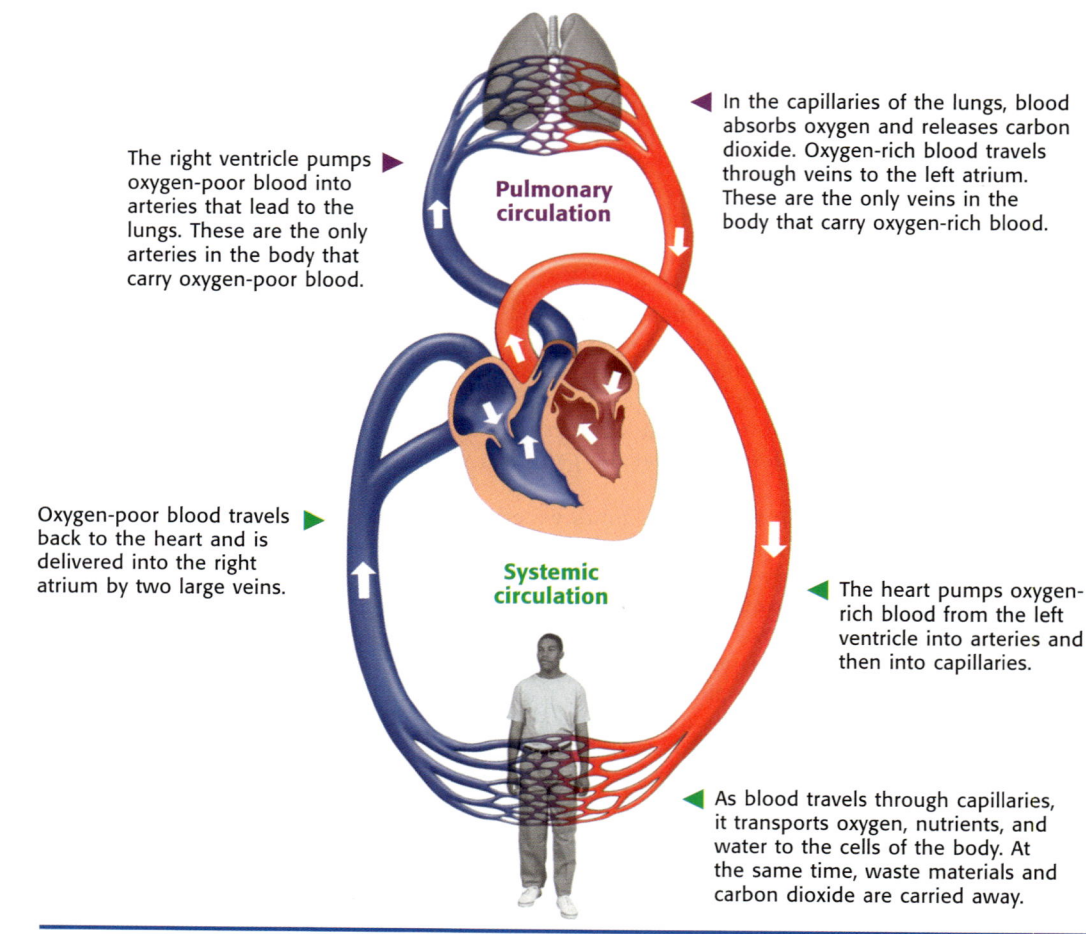

The Flow of Blood Through the Body

◀ In the capillaries of the lungs, blood absorbs oxygen and releases carbon dioxide. Oxygen-rich blood travels through veins to the left atrium. These are the only veins in the body that carry oxygen-rich blood.

The right ventricle pumps oxygen-poor blood into arteries that lead to the lungs. These are the only arteries in the body that carry oxygen-poor blood. ▶

Pulmonary circulation

Oxygen-poor blood travels back to the heart and is delivered into the right atrium by two large veins. ▶

Systemic circulation

◀ The heart pumps oxygen-rich blood from the left ventricle into arteries and then into capillaries.

◀ As blood travels through capillaries, it transports oxygen, nutrients, and water to the cells of the body. At the same time, waste materials and carbon dioxide are carried away.

Answers to Self-Check

The hollow tube shape of arteries and veins allows blood to reach all parts of the body. Valves in the veins prevent blood from flowing backward.

MISCONCEPTION ALERT

Students may think that blood from the heart enters one lung and leaves from the other. Actually, each lung is serviced by vessels carrying blood to and from the heart.

550 Chapter 23 • Circulation and Respiration

Blood Flows Under Pressure

When you run water through a hose, you can feel the hose stiffen as the water pushes against the inside of the hose. Blood has the same effect on your blood vessels. The force exerted by blood on the inside walls of a blood vessel is called **blood pressure.**

Like the man shown in **Figure 8,** many people get their blood pressure checked on a regular basis. Blood pressure is reported in millimeters (mm) of mercury, Hg. A blood pressure of 120 mm Hg means the pressure on the vessel walls is great enough to push a narrow column of mercury 120 mm high.

A normal blood pressure is about 120/80. The first number is called the systolic pressure. *Systolic pressure* is the pressure inside large arteries when the ventricles contract. As you read earlier, the surge of blood causes the arteries to bulge and produce a pulse. The second number is called the diastolic pressure. *Diastolic pressure* is the pressure in the arteries when the ventricles relax.

Figure 8 *This nurse is measuring a patient's blood pressure. Consistently high or low blood pressure may suggest a problem with the cardiovascular system.*

Exercise and Blood Flow

When you exercise, your muscles require much more oxygen and nutrients. To solve this problem, the heart beats faster. Physical activity causes as much as 10 times more blood to be sent to the muscles than when your body is at rest.

During exercise, some organs do not need as much blood as the skeletal muscles do. Less blood is sent to the kidneys and the digestive system so that more blood can go to the skeletal muscles, brain, heart, and lungs. This is like turning off certain water faucets in a house to allow more water to flow through other faucets.

Activity

Imagine that you are a scientist that has been chosen to explore the cardiovascular system. After being shrunk down to the size of a red blood cell, you board a miniature submarine and begin your travels. Describe where you go and what you see.

TRY at HOME

REVIEW

1. What is the function of the cardiovascular system?
2. What are the three kinds of blood vessels? Compare their functions.
3. **Identifying Relationships** How is the structure of capillaries related to their function?

3) Extend

GOING FURTHER

Nobel Prize–winning scientist Karl Landsteiner (1868–1943) discovered that some mixtures of blood are compatible and others are not. He found that he could divide the population into different groups based on how their blood reacted with blood from other people. Encourage interested students to research how Landsteiner's experiments led to the discovery of the ABO and Rh blood groups.

USING THE TABLE

Review the material in the table to reinforce the material presented in the text. Help students compare the shapes of the antigens on each red blood cell with the shapes of the antibodies that bind to the antigens. Then ask the following questions:

- Which antibodies will a person with type AB blood produce? (none)

- Can a person with type O blood receive blood from a person with blood type AB? Why or why not? (No; the type O blood will have antibodies that attack the A and B antigens in the AB blood.)

- Can a person with type O blood donate blood to someone with type A blood? Why or why not? (Yes; the type O red blood cells lack antigens.)

Answer to APPLY
You could bring back type A, B, or O.

Figure 9 *This table shows which antigens and antibodies may be present in each blood type.*

What's Your Blood Type?

When a person loses a lot of blood, the person is given blood that has been donated from someone else. The person receiving the blood cannot be given blood from just anyone because people have different blood types. It's safe to mix some blood types, but mixing others causes a person's RBCs to clump together. The clumped cells may form blood clots, which block blood vessels, causing death.

Every person has one of the following blood types: A, B, AB, or O. Your blood type refers to the type of chemicals you have on the surface of your RBCs. These chemicals are called *antigens*. Type A blood has A antigens; type B has B antigens; and type AB has both A and B antigens. Type O blood has neither the A nor B antigen.

To Mix or Not to Mix Different blood types not only have different chemicals on their RBC surfaces but also may have different chemicals in their plasma, the liquid part of blood. These chemicals are *antibodies*. When antibodies bind to RBCs, they cause the RBCs to clump together.

As shown in **Figure 9**, the body makes antibodies against the antigens that are not on its own RBCs. For example, people with type B blood make A antibodies, which attack any blood cell with an A antigen on it. Therefore, people with type B blood can't be given type A or AB blood. Type O blood can be given to anyone because its RBCs don't have any A or B antigens on their surface. A person with type O blood is therefore said to be a *universal donor*. People with type AB blood are *universal recipients*, meaning they can receive any type of blood because they do not make any antibodies against A or B antigens.

Blood Delivery

A young woman is brought into the emergency room and needs a blood transfusion. Her blood type is AB. You call the blood bank to order AB blood, but you are told the bank is out of that type. What other type or types could the blood bank deliver for her transfusion?

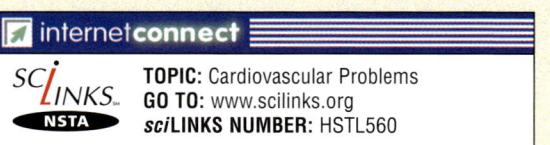

TOPIC: Cardiovascular Problems
GO TO: www.scilinks.org
*sci*LINKS NUMBER: HSTL560

IS THAT A FACT!

The first heartbeat occurs in the human embryo at four weeks of age. Although the heart looks like a simple tube at this stage, it begins to beat. This starts blood circulation through the first blood vessels, which eventually grow and develop into the entire circulatory system.

Cardiovascular Problems

When something is wrong with a person's cardiovascular system, the person's health will be affected. Some cardiovascular problems involve the heart and the blood vessels, while other problems affect the blood. Cardiovascular problems can be caused by smoking, high levels of cholesterol in blood, stress, heredity, and other factors.

Atherosclerosis The leading cause of death in the United States is a cardiovascular disease called *atherosclerosis* (ATH uhr OH skluh ROH sis). Atherosclerosis occurs when fatty materials, such as cholesterol, build up on the inside of blood vessels. The fatty buildup causes the blood vessels to become narrower and less elastic. **Figure 10** shows how the pathway through a blood vessel can become clogged. When a major artery that supplies blood to the heart becomes blocked, a person has a heart attack, and part of the heart can die.

Figure 10 Atherosclerosis is a common cardiovascular problem. Fatty deposits build up on the inside of blood vessels and block blood flow.

A Point About Pressure Atherosclerosis also promotes *hypertension*, which is abnormally high blood pressure. Hypertension is dangerous because it overworks the heart and can weaken vessels and make them rupture. If a blood vessel in the brain becomes clogged or ruptures, certain parts of the brain will not receive oxygen and nutrients and may die. This is called a *stroke*.

The Beat Goes On
Your heart beats about 100,800 times per day. How many times does it beat per year?

REVIEW

1. Where does blood travel to and from during pulmonary circulation? during systemic circulation?
2. What happens to the oxygen level in blood as it moves through the lungs?
3. **Applying Concepts** Billy has type A blood.
   a. What kind of antigens does he have on his RBCs?
   b. What blood-type antibodies can Billy make?
   c. Which blood types could be given to Billy if he needed a transfusion?

internetconnect

sciLINKS
NSTA

TOPIC: The Cardiovascular System, Cardiovascular Problems
GO TO: www.scilinks.org
sciLINKS NUMBER: HSTL555, HSTL560

Section 2

Focus

The Lymphatic System
This section introduces the lymphatic system. Students will also learn about the relationship between blood and lymph.

Draw the following shapes on the board or on an overhead projector:

a circle, a triangle, a straight line, and a cluster of several dots

Ask students to choose the shape(s) that best represents a circulatory system and to explain in their ScienceLog. (The circle and the triangle best represent a circulatory system because they both form a continuous loop.)

Answers to Self-Check
Like blood vessels, lymph capillaries receive fluid from the spaces surrounding cells. The fluid absorbed by lymph capillaries flows into lymph vessels. These vessels drain into large neck veins instead of into an organ, such as the heart. Lymph does not deliver oxygen and nutrients.

1) Motivate

DISCUSSION
Ask students if a doctor has ever felt around their neck when they were sick. Encourage students who have had this experience to share it with the class. Then invite students to explore the purpose of this type of examination. **Sheltered English**

Section 2

The Lymphatic System

Terms to Learn
lymphatic system
lymph
lymph nodes
thymus
spleen
tonsils

What You'll Do
- Discuss the functions of the lymphatic system.
- Identify the relationship between lymph and blood.
- Describe the organs of the lymphatic system.

Your cardiovascular system is not the only circulatory system in your body. As blood flows through your cardiovascular system, fluid leaks out of the capillaries and mixes with the fluid that bathes your cells. Most of the fluid is reabsorbed by the capillaries, but some is not. To deal with this, your body's **lymphatic system** collects the excess fluid and returns it to your blood.

In addition to collecting the excess fluid surrounding your cells and returning it to your blood, your lymphatic system helps your body fight pathogens. Pathogens are microorganisms and viruses that make you sick.

Vessels of the Lymphatic System

The fluid collected by the lymphatic system is transported through vessels. The smallest vessels of the lymphatic system are *lymph capillaries*. From the spaces between cells, lymph capillaries absorb fluid and any particles too large to enter the blood capillaries. Some of these particles are dead cells or cells that are foreign to the body. The fluid and particles absorbed into lymph capillaries are called **lymph**.

As shown in **Figure 11**, lymph capillaries carry lymph into *lymphatic vessels*, which are larger vessels that have valves. Lymph is not pushed by a pump. Instead, the squeezing of skeletal muscles provides the force to move lymph through vessels, and valves help prevent backflow. Lymph travels through your lymphatic system and then drains into large neck veins of the cardiovascular system.

Self-Check
How are the lymphatic system and the cardiovascular system similar? How are they different? *(See page 782 to check your answer.)*

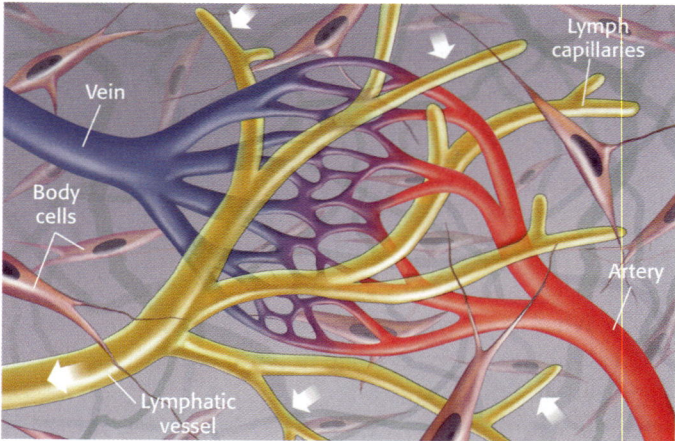

Figure 11 The white arrows show the movement of lymph into lymph capillaries and through lymphatic vessels.

SCIENTISTS AT ODDS

The Danish physician Thomas Bartholin (1616–1680), known as the Elder, is credited with being the first person to describe the lymphatic system. His Swedish contemporary Olof Rudbeck (1630–1702) also studied the lymphatic system.

Rudbeck was furious when French anatomist Jean Pecquet and Thomas Bartholin published their findings before he did. Rudbeck spent the rest of his life studying botany.

Lymphatic Organs

In addition to vessels and capillaries, a variety of other organs are part of the lymphatic system, as shown in **Figure 12.**

Lymph Nodes As lymph travels through lymphatic vessels, it passes through lymph nodes. **Lymph nodes** are small bean-shaped organs where particles, such as pathogens or dead cells, are removed from the lymph.

Lymph nodes contain many white blood cells. Some of these cells engulf pathogens. Other WBCs produce chemicals that become attached to pathogens and mark them for destruction. When the body becomes infected with bacteria or viruses, the WBCs multiply and the nodes sometimes become swollen and painful.

Thymus Your **thymus,** which is located just above your heart, releases WBCs. The WBCs travel to other areas of the lymphatic system.

Spleen The largest lymph organ is your spleen, which is located in the upper left side of your abdomen. The **spleen** filters blood and, like the thymus, releases WBCs. When red blood cells are squeezed through the spleen's capillaries, the older and more fragile cells rupture. The RBCs are broken down, and some of their parts are reused. For this reason, the spleen can be thought of as the red-blood-cell recycling center.

Tonsils **Tonsils** are made up of groups of lymphatic tissue located at the back of your nasal cavity, on the inside of your throat, and at the back of your tongue. WBCs in the tonsils defend the body against infection. Tonsils sometimes become badly infected and must be removed.

Figure 12 The Lymphatic System

REVIEW

1. What are the main functions of the lymphatic system?
2. Where does lymph go when it leaves the lymphatic system?
3. **Identifying Relationships** How are lymph nodes similar to the spleen?

TOPIC: The Lymphatic System
GO TO: www.scilinks.org
sciLINKS NUMBER: HSTL565

2) Teach

RESEARCH

Writing Have students use library and on-line resources to find out about the role of the lymphatic system in protecting the body against disease. Have them write and present reports to the class based on their findings.

3) Close

Quiz

1. What is one function of the tonsils? (The tonsils contain white blood cells, which help fight pathogens.)
2. How is the lymphatic system a circulatory system? (The lymphatic system collects fluid that is not reabsorbed by the capillaries and returns it to the bloodstream.)

ALTERNATIVE ASSESSMENT

Have students make a life-size model of the lymphatic system. Provide students with butcher paper, dried beans, glue, and markers. Then have students use their model to demonstrate the interaction of the lymphatic system with the cardiovascular system. **Sheltered English**

Directed Reading Worksheet 23 Section 2

TOPIC: The Lymphatic System
GO TO: www.scilinks.org
sciLINKS NUMBER: HSTL565

Answers to Review

1. The lymphatic system collects excess fluid surrounding cells and returns it to the bloodstream. It also helps the body fight pathogens.
2. Lymph drains into large veins in the neck.
3. The spleen and lymph nodes are lymph organs involved in the production of white blood cells.

Section 3

Focus

The Respiratory System

This section introduces the structures and functions of the respiratory system. Students will learn to trace the flow of air through the respiratory system and to recognize problems in respiratory function. Students will also find out how the respiratory system and the circulatory system are related.

🔔 Bellringer

Write the following on the board or overhead projector:

In your ScienceLog, explain whether the following statements are true or false:

- Breathing and respiration are the same thing. (False; breathing is only one part of respiration.)
- The nose is the primary doorway into and out of the respiratory system. (true)
- The vocal cords are located in the trachea. (False; they are located in the larynx.)

1) Motivate

ACTIVITY

Have students place their hands on either side of their rib cage and breathe deeply several times. Then ask students to describe what they felt while they breathed in and out. (Students should feel their rib cage moving up and expanding during inhalation and moving down and returning to its initial size during exhalation.)

Explain to students that this section focuses on what happens inside the body during breathing.

Sheltered English

556   Chapter 23 • Circulation and Respiration

Section 3

Terms to Learn

respiration
respiratory system
pharynx
larynx
trachea
bronchi
alveoli

What You'll Do

- Describe the flow of air through the respiratory system.
- Discuss the relationship between the respiratory system and the cardiovascular system.
- Identify respiratory disorders.

The Respiratory System

Breathing. You do it all the time. You're doing it right now. You hardly ever think about it, though, unless your ability to breathe is suddenly taken away. Then it becomes all too obvious that you must breathe in order to survive. Why is breathing important?

Out with the Bad Air; In with the Good

Your body needs a continuous supply of oxygen in order to obtain energy from the foods you eat. That's where breathing comes in handy. The air you breathe is a mixture of several gases. One of these gases is oxygen. When you breathe, your body takes in air and absorbs the oxygen. Then carbon dioxide from your body is added to the air, and the stale air is exhaled.

The words *breathing* and *respiration* are often thought to mean the same thing. However, breathing is only one part of respiration. **Respiration** is the entire process by which a body obtains and uses oxygen and gets rid of carbon dioxide and water. Respiration is divided into two parts: breathing, which involves inhaling and exhaling, and cellular respiration, which involves the chemical reactions that release energy from food.

Figure 13 Air moves into and out of the body through the respiratory system.

Breathing: Brought to You by Your Respiratory System

Breathing is made possible by the respiratory system. The **respiratory system** consists of the lungs, throat, and passageways that lead to the lungs. **Figure 13** shows the parts of the respiratory system.

Nose Your nose is the primary passageway into and out of the respiratory system. Air is inhaled through the nose, where it comes into contact with warm, moist surfaces. Air can also enter and leave through the mouth.

TOPIC: The Respiratory System
GO TO: www.scilinks.org
sciLINKS NUMBER: HSTL570

IS THAT A FACT!

You sneeze when your breathing muscles respond to mucus or dirt that irritates the lining of your nasal cavity. A sneeze consists of a deep breath followed by a 160 km/h surge of air out of the nose!

Pharynx From the nose, air flows into the **pharynx** (FER ingks), or throat. You can use a mirror to see the walls of your pharynx behind your tongue. In addition to air, food and drink also travel through the pharynx on the way to the stomach. The pharynx branches into two tubes. One leads to the stomach and is called the esophagus. The other leads to the lungs and is called the larynx.

Larynx Tilt your head up slightly, and rub a finger up and down the front of your throat. The ridges you feel are the outside of the larynx (LER ingks). The **larynx,** or voice box, contains the vocal cords. The vocal cords are a pair of elastic bands that are stretched across the opening of the larynx. Muscles attached to the larynx control how much the vocal cords are stretched. When air flows between the vocal cords, they vibrate and make sound.

Trachea The larynx guards the entrance to a large tube called the **trachea** (TRAY kee uh), or windpipe. The trachea is the passageway for air traveling from the larynx to the lungs.

Bronchi The trachea splits into two tubes called **bronchi** (BRAHNG kie) (singular, *bronchus*). One bronchus goes to each lung and branches into thousands of tiny tubes called *bronchioles*.

Lungs Your body has two large spongelike lungs. In the lungs, each bronchiole branches to form thousands of tiny sacs called **alveoli** (singular, *alveolus*). Capillaries surround each alveolus. **Figure 14** shows the arrangement of the tubes in the respiratory system.

Chemistry CONNECTION

When people who live at low elevations travel to the mountains, they usually find that they have difficulty exerting themselves. This is because the concentration of oxygen in the air at high elevations is lower than that at low elevations. Until they become used to the change, people have to take more breaths to supply their bodies with the oxygen they need.

Figure 14 *Inside your lungs, the bronchi branch into bronchioles. The bronchioles lead to tiny sacs called alveoli.*

Multicultural CONNECTION

Suppose a newcomer to a Peruvian village in the Andes Mountains gets headaches, feels nauseated, and is very short of breath. What is going on? The newcomer is suffering from a lack of oxygen. The villagers don't have these problems; they are extremely well adapted to this high elevation. Because there is very little oxygen in the air, these people have developed lungs and chests that are much larger than those of the newcomer. They also carry more blood in their bloodstream.

2) Teach

ACTIVITY

Investigating Speech Ask students to place their hands lightly on their neck near the larynx and to say, "ah." Have students keep their hands in place and alternate between blowing as they would blow out candles on a birthday cake and saying, "ah." Then ask:

- What happened when you said, "ah"? (The neck vibrated.)
- What happened when you blew without saying anything? (The neck stopped vibrating, but air still rushed out of the mouth.)
- What caused the sound and the vibrations when you said "ah"? (Air rushing past the vocal cord muscles in the larynx caused the muscles to vibrate. This caused the sound.)

Point out that speech is made up of sounds produced both ways, with voicing and without voicing. If students are unconvinced, have them say *sssssss* (the snake sound) while touching their neck near the larynx. Then have them say *zzzzz* (buzz like a bee) while touching their neck. Students should find that their neck vibrates when they pronounce *z*, which is voiced, but does not vibrate when they pronounce *s*, which is not voiced.

==Sheltered English==

Teaching Transparency 84 "The Respiratory System"

Directed Reading Worksheet 23 Section 3

3) Extend

ACTIVITY

Concept Mapping Have students create a concept map using the following terms:

respiration, respiratory system, pharynx, larynx, cellular respiration, trachea, bronchi, alveoli, diaphragm

Build a Lung

RESEARCH

Writing Ask students if they have ever seen a professional football player inhale oxygen using an oxygen mask. Encourage students to find out why football players do this and to write the results of their research in a short report. As a class, discuss whether the practice is useful. (Although panting from physical exertion is a sign of an oxygen deficit, the additional oxygen does not alleviate the problem because the oxygen deficit occurs in the muscles, not in the lungs. In other words, the oxygen deficit is not a result of inadequate respiratory function but of the muscles' inability to take in more oxygen.)

CONNECT TO PHYSICAL SCIENCE

Lead a discussion of how the body creates changes in air pressure to make breathing possible. The following Teaching Transparency, "Air Pressure and Breathing," is a helpful illustration.

Teaching Transparency 225
"Air Pressure and Breathing"
LINK TO PHYSICAL SCIENCE

How Do You Breathe?

When you breathe, air is sucked in or forced out of your lungs. However, your lungs do not contain muscles that force air in and out. Instead, breathing is done by rib muscles and the *diaphragm*, a dome-shaped muscle underneath the lungs. When the diaphragm contracts and moves down, it increases the chest cavity's volume. At the same time, some of your rib muscles contract and lift your rib cage, causing it to expand. Air is sucked in.

What Happens to the Oxygen? When oxygen has been absorbed by red blood cells, it is transported through the body by the cardiovascular system. Oxygen diffuses inside cells, where it is used in an important chemical reaction known as cellular respiration. During *cellular respiration*, oxygen is used to release energy stored in molecules of carbohydrates, fats, and proteins. When the molecules are broken apart during the reaction, energy is released along with carbon dioxide and water. The carbon dioxide and water leave the cell and return to the bloodstream. The carbon dioxide is carried to the lungs and exhaled. **Figure 15** shows how breathing and blood circulation are related.

Would you like to linger longer on lungs? Then look at page 766.

Figure 15 Blood has an important role in respiration.

- CO_2 enters the air in the alveolus.
- O_2 is picked up by blood.
- Tissues and cells pick up O_2 from the blood.
- CO_2 enters the blood.

TOPIC: Respiratory Disorders
GO TO: www.scilinks.org
***sci*LINKS NUMBER:** HSTL575

IS THAT A FACT!

The lungs contain about 300 million alveoli. The alveoli provide a tremendous surface area for gas exchange. In fact, a person can breathe easily with only one lung.

Respiratory Disorders

Millions of people suffer from respiratory disorders. There are many types of respiratory disorders, including asthma, bronchitis, pneumonia, and emphysema.

In *asthma*, irritants cause tissue around the bronchioles to constrict and secrete large amounts of mucus. As the bronchiole tubes get narrower, the person has difficulty breathing. *Bronchitis* can develop when something irritates the lining of the bronchioles. *Pneumonia* is caused by bacteria or viruses that grow inside the bronchioles and alveoli and cause them to become inflamed and filled with fluid. If the alveoli are filled with too much fluid, the person may suffocate.

The Hazards of Smoking

You probably already know that smoking cigarettes is bad for your health. In fact, smoking is the leading cause of cardiovascular diseases and lung diseases, such as *emphysema* and *lung cancer*. People with emphysema have trouble getting the oxygen they need because their lung tissue erodes away, as shown in **Figure 16**.

QuickLab

Why Do People Snore?

Get a **15 cm² sheet of wax paper.** Hum your favorite song. Then take the wax paper, press it against your lips, and hum the song again. Now answer the following questions:

1. How was your humming different when wax paper was pressed to your mouth?
2. Use your observations to guess what might cause snoring.

Figure 16 The photo on the left shows healthy lungs. The photo on the right shows the lungs of a person who had emphysema.

REVIEW

1. Describe the path that air travels as it moves through the respiratory system.
2. What is the difference between respiration and cellular respiration?
3. **Identifying Relationships** How is the function of the respiratory system related to that of the cardiovascular system?

internet connect

TOPIC: The Respiratory System, Respiratory Disorders
GO TO: www.scilinks.org
sciLINKS NUMBER: HSTL570, HSTL575

Chapter Highlights

VOCABULARY DEFINITIONS

SECTION 1

cardiovascular system a collection of organs whose primary function is to transport blood to and from your body's cells; the organs in this system include the heart, the arteries, and the veins

blood a connective tissue made up of platelets, white blood cells, red blood cells, and plasma

arteries blood vessels that carry blood away from the heart

capillaries the smallest blood vessels in the body

veins blood vessels that direct blood to the heart

pulmonary circulation the circulation of blood between the heart and lungs

systemic circulation the circulation of blood between the heart and the body (excluding the lungs)

blood pressure the amount of force exerted by blood on the inside walls of a blood vessel

SECTION 2

lymphatic system a collection of organs whose primary function is to collect extracellular fluid and return it to the blood; the organs in this system include the lymph nodes and the lymphatic vessels

lymph fluid and particles absorbed into lymph capillaries

lymph nodes small, bean-shaped organs that contain small fibers that work like nets to remove particles from the lymph

thymus a lymph organ that produces lymphocytes

spleen an organ that filters blood and produces lymphocytes

tonsils small masses of soft tissue located at the back of the nasal cavity, on the inside of the throat and at the back of the tongue

Chapter Highlights

SECTION 1

Vocabulary
cardiovascular system (p. 546)
blood (p. 546)
arteries (p. 549)
capillaries (p. 549)
veins (p. 549)
pulmonary circulation (p. 550)
systemic circulation (p. 550)
blood pressure (p. 551)

Section Notes

- The cardiovascular system delivers oxygen and nutrients to the body's cells, takes away the cells' waste products, and helps the body stay healthy. The cardiovascular system is made up of blood, the heart, and blood vessels.

- Blood is a connective tissue made of plasma, red blood cells, white blood cells, and platelets. The heart is a muscular organ that pumps blood through blood vessels.

- Blood moves away from the heart through arteries and then enters capillaries. After leaving capillaries, blood is carried back to the heart through veins.

- In pulmonary circulation, blood vessels carry blood from the heart to the lungs and back to the heart. In systemic circulation, blood flows from the heart to the rest of the body and then back to the heart.

- People have different blood types. Blood type is determined by the presence of certain chemicals on red blood cells.

SECTION 2

Vocabulary
lymphatic system (p. 554)
lymph (p. 554)
lymph nodes (p. 555)
thymus (p. 555)
spleen (p. 555)
tonsils (p. 555)

Section Notes

- The lymphatic system returns excess fluid to the cardiovascular system and helps the body fight infections.

- The lymphatic system includes lymph, lymph capillaries, lymphatic vessels, lymph nodes, the spleen, tonsils, and the thymus.

✓ Skills Check

Math Concepts

A CONTINUOUS BEAT Your heart beats about 100,800 times per day. That means that your heart beats about 4,200 times every hour.

100,800 beats ÷ 24 hours = 4,200 beats

That also means that your heart beats about 70 times every minute.

4,200 beats ÷ 60 minutes = 70 beats

Visual Understanding

AIR PASSAGEWAYS Take another look at Figure 13 on page 556. With your finger, trace the path air takes to reach the lungs. As you do this, reconsider what roles the nose, pharynx, trachea, bronchi, lungs, and diaphragm play in respiration.

Lab and Activity Highlights

Build a Lung PG 766

Carbon Dioxide Breath PG 767

 Datasheets for LabBook (blackline masters for these labs)

SECTION 3

Vocabulary

respiration *(p. 556)*
respiratory system *(p. 556)*
pharynx *(p. 557)*
larynx *(p. 557)*
trachea *(p. 557)*
bronchi *(p. 557)*
alveoli *(p. 557)*

Section Notes

- The respiratory system moves air into and out of the body. The respiratory system includes the nose, the mouth, the pharynx, the larynx, the trachea, and the lungs.
- Air enters the lungs through bronchi and travels to the alveoli, which are gas-filled sacs surrounded by capillaries of the cardiovascular system.
- The blood in the capillaries of the lungs absorbs oxygen and releases carbon dioxide. The carbon dioxide is exhaled. The oxygen is carried by the blood to the heart and then on to the cells of the body.
- The body's cells must have oxygen to carry out cellular respiration. Cellular respiration is a chemical process that releases the energy in carbohydrates, fats, and proteins and makes the energy available to the cells.
- Inhaling and exhaling are caused by the contraction and relaxation of the diaphragm and the muscles of the rib cage.

Labs

Build a Lung *(p. 766)*
Carbon Dioxide Breath *(p. 767)*

VOCABULARY DEFINITIONS, continued

SECTION 3

respiration the exchange of gases between living cells and their environment; includes breathing and cellular respiration

respiratory system a collection of organs whose primary function is to take in oxygen and expel carbon dioxide; the organs of this system include the lungs, the throat, and the passageways that lead to the lungs

pharynx the upper portion of the throat

larynx the area of the throat that contains the vocal cords

trachea the air passageway from the larynx to the lungs

bronchi the two tubes that connect the lungs with the trachea

alveoli tiny sacs that form the bronchiole branches of the lungs

Vocabulary Review Worksheet 23

Blackline masters of these Chapter Highlights can be found in the **Study Guide**.

---

internet connect

 GO TO: go.hrw.com

Visit the **HRW** Web site for a variety of learning tools related to this chapter. Just type in the keyword:

KEYWORD: HSTBD2

 GO TO: www.scilinks.org

Visit the **National Science Teachers Association** on-line Web site for Internet resources related to this chapter. Just type in the sciLINKS number for more information about the topic:

TOPIC	sciLINKS NUMBER
TOPIC: The Cardiovascular System	sciLINKS NUMBER: HSTL555
TOPIC: Cardiovascular Problems	sciLINKS NUMBER: HSTL560
TOPIC: The Lymphatic System	sciLINKS NUMBER: HSTL565
TOPIC: The Respiratory System	sciLINKS NUMBER: HSTL570
TOPIC: Respiratory Disorders	sciLINKS NUMBER: HSTL575

Lab and Activity Highlights

LabBank

Whiz-Bang Demonstrations
- Get the Beat! Demo 12
- Take a Deep Breath, Demo 13

Long-Term Projects & Research Ideas, Getting to the Heart, Project 23

EcoLabs & Field Activities, There's Something in the Air, Field Activity 9

Chapter Review Answers

USING VOCABULARY

1. red blood cells
2. arteries
3. Blood
4. larynx
5. alveoli

UNDERSTANDING CONCEPTS

Multiple Choice

6. b
7. d
8. a
9. c
10. b
11. a

Short Answer

12. Pulmonary circulation carries blood through the lungs and back to the heart. Systemic circulation carries blood from the heart to the rest of the body.
13. The first number is the systolic pressure, or the pressure inside the artery when the ventricles contract. The second number, the diastolic pressure, is the pressure in the arteries when the ventricles relax.
14. Carbon dioxide is a product of cellular respiration which occurs in the body's cells.

Chapter Review

USING VOCABULARY

To complete the following sentences, choose the correct term from each pair of terms listed below:

1. Oxygen is delivered to the cells of the body by __?__. (*white blood cells* or *red blood cells*)
2. Blood is carried away from the heart in __?__. (*arteries* or *veins*)
3. __?__ carries nutrients to the body's cells. (*Lymph* or *Blood*)
4. The __?__ contains the vocal cords. (*trachea* or *larynx*)
5. The pathway of air through the respiratory system ends at the tiny sacs called __?__. (*alveoli* or *bronchi*)

UNDERSTANDING CONCEPTS

Multiple Choice

6. Blood from the lungs enters the heart at the
   a. left ventricle.
   b. left atrium.
   c. right atrium.
   d. right ventricle.

7. Blood cells are made
   a. in the heart.
   b. from plasma.
   c. from lymph.
   d. in the bones.

8. Which of the following is not part of the lymphatic system?
   a. trachea
   b. lymph node
   c. thymus
   d. spleen

9. Alveoli are surrounded by
   a. veins.
   b. muscles.
   c. capillaries.
   d. lymph nodes.

10. What prevents blood from flowing backward in veins?
    a. platelets
    b. valves
    c. muscles
    d. cartilage

11. Air moves into the lungs when the diaphragm muscle
    a. contracts and moves down.
    b. contracts and moves up.
    c. relaxes and moves down.
    d. relaxes and moves up.

Short Answer

12. What is the difference between pulmonary circulation and systemic circulation in the cardiovascular system?
13. Walton has a blood pressure of 110/65. What do the two numbers mean?
14. What body process produces the carbon dioxide you exhale?

Concept Map

15. Use the following terms to create a concept map: blood, oxygen, alveoli, capillaries, carbon dioxide.

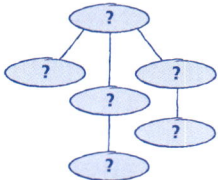

CRITICAL THINKING AND PROBLEM SOLVING

Write one or two sentences to answer the following questions:

16. Why do you think there are hairs in your nose?

17. When a person is not feeling well, sometimes a doctor will examine samples of the person's blood to see how many white blood cells are present. Why would this information be useful?

18. How is the function of the lymphatic system related to the function of the cardiovascular system?

MATH IN SCIENCE

19. After a person donates blood, the blood is stored in one-pint bags until it is needed for a transfusion. A healthy person normally has 5 million RBCs in each cubic millimeter (1 mm^3) of blood.
    a. How many RBCs are there in 1 mL of blood? One milliliter is equal to 1 cm^3 and to 1,000 mm^3.
    b. How many RBCs are there in 1 pt? One pint is equal to 473 mL.

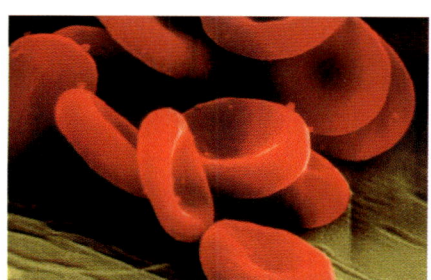

INTERPRETING GRAPHICS

The diagram below shows how the human heart would look in cross section. Examine the diagram, and then answer the questions that follow:

20. Which letter identifies the chamber that receives blood from systemic circulation? What is this chamber's name?

21. Which letter identifies the chamber that receives blood from the lungs? What is this chamber's name?

22. Which letter identifies the chamber that pumps blood to the lungs? What is this chamber's name?

 Take a minute to review your answers to the Pre-Reading Questions found at the bottom of page 544. Have your answers changed? If necessary, revise your answers based on what you have learned since you began this chapter.

Concept Mapping

15. An answer to this exercise can be found at the end of this book.

CRITICAL THINKING AND PROBLEM SOLVING

16. The hairs catch dust and other foreign particles. This helps keep your lungs as clean as possible.
17. Doctors will need to know if the immune system is producing large numbers of white blood cells; this would indicate an infection.
18. The lymphatic system returns leaked fluids back to your blood.

MATH IN SCIENCE

19. a. 5 billion (5,000,000,000) cells
    b. 2.365 trillion (2,365,000,000,000) cells

INTERPRETING GRAPHICS

20. *a*, the right atrium
21. *b*, the left atrium
22. *c*, the right ventricle

 Concept Mapping Transparency 23

 Blackline masters of this Chapter Review can be found in the **Study Guide.**

WEIRD SCIENCE
Catching a Light Sneeze

Activity
Divide the class into pairs. Have students use a flashlight to make their partner's pupils contract. (Be careful not to let them look directly into a bright light for too long.) They should conduct their test for the photic sneeze reflex as a scientific experiment. Have them write a hypothesis, test the hypothesis, and report their results.

CATCHING A LIGHT SNEEZE

Do you sneeze when you come out of a dark movie theater into bright sunlight? If not, look around you next time. Chances are several people will sneeze.

Reflex Gone Wrong
For some reason, about one in five people sneeze when they step from a dimly lit area into a brightly lit area. In fact, some may sneeze a dozen times or more! Fortunately, the sneezing usually stops after a few times. This reaction is called a *photic sneeze reflex*. No one knows for certain why it happens.

Normal sneezing is a reflex, which means you do it without thinking about it. Most people sneeze when something tickles the inside of their nose. They sneeze, and moving air pushes the tickling intruder out. For instance, if you get dust in your nose, sneezing pushes the dust out. In the case of people with the photic sneeze, it's a reflex gone wrong.

ACHOO!
A few years ago, some geneticists studied the photic sneeze reflex. They named it the Autosomal Dominant Compelling Helio-ophthalmic Outburst syndrome, or the ACHOO syndrome. Scientists know that the ACHOO syndrome runs in families. So the photic sneeze can be passed from parent to child. Sometimes even the number of times in a row that each person sneezes is the same throughout a family.

Possible Answers
Some scientists have offered a possible explanation for the ACHOO syndrome. First, everyone's pupils contract when they

▲ *Do you sneeze when you see bright light after exiting a dark room?*

encounter bright light. And the nerves from the eyes are right next to the nerves from the nose. Thus, people with the ACHOO syndrome may have their wires slightly crossed: bright light triggers the pupil reflex, and it also triggers the sneeze reflex!

Sneeze Fest
Sunlight is not the only strange trigger for sudden sneezes. Some people sneeze when they rub the inner corner of their eye. Others sneeze when tweezing their eyebrows or brushing their hair. In rare individuals, even eating too much has been known to cause sneezing fits!

Research the Facts
▶ Yawning is also a reflex. Do some research to find out why we yawn.

Answer to Research the Facts
Sample answer: Yawning is a response to a buildup of carbon dioxide or the sight of another person yawning.

Health Watch

Goats to the Rescue

They're called transgenic (tranz JEHN ik) goats because their cells contain a human gene. They look just like any other goats, but because of their human gene they produce a chemical that can save lives.

Lifesaving Genes

Heart attacks are the number one cause of death in the United States. Many heart attacks are triggered when large blood clots interfere with the flow of blood to the heart. Human blood cells produce a chemical called *tissue plasminogen activator* (TPA) that dissolves small blood clots. If TPA is given to a person having a heart attack, it can often dissolve the blood clot, stop the attack, and save the person's life. But TPA is difficult to produce in large quantities in the laboratory. This is where the goats come in. Researchers at Tufts University, in Grafton, Massachusetts, have genetically engineered goats to produce this lifesaving drug.

Hybrid Goats

Producing transgenic goats is a complicated process. First, fertilized eggs are surgically removed from normal female goats. The eggs are then injected with hybrid genes that consist of human TPA genes "spliced" into genes from the mammary glands of a goat. Finally, the altered eggs are surgically implanted into female goats, where they develop into young goats, or kids. Some of the kids actually carry the hybrid gene. When the hybrid kids mature, the females' milk contains TPA. Technicians then separate the TPA from the goats' milk for use in heart-attack victims.

The Research Continues

Transgenic research in farm animals such as goats, sheep, cows, and pigs may someday produce drugs faster, cheaper, and in greater quantities than are possible using current methods. The way we view the barnyard may never be the same.

Find Out for Yourself

▶ Using chemicals produced by transgenic animals is just one of many gene therapies. Do some research to find out more about gene therapy, how it is used, and how it may be used in the future.

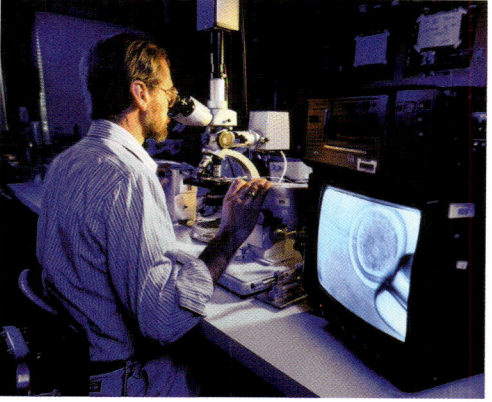

▲ *A scientist at Tufts University injects human TPA genes into fertilized goat eggs.*

HEALTH WATCH
Goats to the Rescue

Background

Many proteins that are produced naturally by the human body could be produced by other animals through genetic engineering. This raises the possibility of turning animals into "drug factories." Genetically altered pigs have been used to produce blood and to grow organs that can be used for human transfusions and transplants. Cows have been altered to produce milk that is more like human milk. A dozen different human proteins have been produced in the milk of various transgenic animals.

However, there are serious safety issues concerning these new animal products. Host animals may carry pathogens that are dangerous to humans. For example, some sheep and goats carry a brain disease known as scrapie. Research companies that offer transgenic drugs must be sure that pathogens are not present in their products. They must ensure that any animal proteins that might trigger allergic reactions or other side effects are removed during the purification process. In addition, these companies must be able to prove that their products will function in the same way as their natural counterparts.

Answer to Find Out for Yourself

Another form of gene therapy is to obtain healthy genes and insert them into the cells of a person with a genetic disorder. Such methods are still highly experimental.

Chapter Organizer

CHAPTER ORGANIZATION	TIME MINUTES	OBJECTIVES	LABS, INVESTIGATIONS, AND DEMONSTRATIONS
Chapter Opener pp. 566–567	45	National Standards: UCP 2, SAI 1, SPSP 5, HNS 2, 3, LS 1e	**Start-Up Activity** Changing Foods, p. 567
Section 1 The Digestive System	90	▶ Describe the parts and functions of the digestive system. ▶ Compare mechanical digestion with chemical digestion. ▶ Describe some disorders of the digestive system. UCP 1, 2, 5, SAI 1, SPSP 1, 5, HNS 1, 3, LS 1a, 1d–1f, 3b; LabBook UCP 2, 5, SAI 1, LS 1a	**Demonstration,** Measuring Saliva, p. 568 in ATE GENERAL **QuickLab,** Break It Up! p. 569 GENERAL **Demonstration,** Peristalsis, p. 571 in ATE GENERAL **Skill Builder,** As the Stomach Churns, p. 768 GENERAL **Datasheets for LabBook,** As the Stomach Churns, Datasheet 51 GENERAL **Discovery Lab,** Enzymes in Action, p. 770 GENERAL **Datasheets for LabBook,** Enzymes in Action, Datasheet 52 GENERAL **Whiz-Bang Demonstrations,** Liver Let Live, Demo 14 GENERAL
Section 2 The Urinary System	90	▶ Describe the parts and functions of the urinary system. ▶ Explain how the kidneys filter blood. ▶ Describe some disorders of the urinary system. UCP 1–5, SAI 1, HNS 1, LS 1a, 1c–1f, 3a, 3b	**Demonstration,** Kidney Structure, p. 577 in ATE GENERAL **Long-Term Projects & Research Ideas,** Project 24 ADVANCED

*See page **T20** for a complete correlation of this book with the*

NATIONAL SCIENCE EDUCATION STANDARDS.

TECHNOLOGY RESOURCES

 Guided Reading Audio CD English or Spanish, Chapter 24

 One-Stop Planner CD-ROM with Test Generator

 CNN. Science, Technology, & Society, Animal Organ Transplants, Segment 32

Chapter 24 • The Digestive and Urinary Systems

Chapter 24 • The Digestive and Urinary Systems

CLASSROOM WORKSHEETS, TRANSPARENCIES, AND RESOURCES	SCIENCE INTEGRATION AND CONNECTIONS	REVIEW AND ASSESSMENT
Directed Reading Worksheet 24 BASIC **Science Puzzlers, Twisters & Teasers,** Worksheet 24 ADVANCED		
Directed Reading Worksheet 24, Section 1 BASIC **Transparency 86,** Enzymes Break Down Proteins **Transparency 108,** Mohs' Hardness Scale **Transparency 87,** The Stomach **Transparency 87,** The Small Intestine **Critical Thinking Worksheet 24,** Frankenstein's Food ADVANCED	**Multicultural Connection,** p. 568 in ATE **Connect to Earth Science,** p. 570 in ATE **Multicultural Connection,** p. 571 in ATE **Connect to Chemistry,** p. 572 in ATE GENERAL **Math and More,** p. 573 in ATE BASIC **Environment Connection,** p. 574 **Health Watch:** A Voiceless Companion, p. 585 GENERAL	**Homework,** p. 567 in ATE ADVANCED **Homework,** p. 569 in ATE GENERAL **Review,** p. 571 GENERAL **Self-Check,** p. 573 **Homework,** p. 574 in ATE GENERAL **Review,** p. 575 GENERAL **Quiz,** p. 575 in ATE GENERAL **Alternative Assessment,** p. 575 in ATE GENERAL
Directed Reading Worksheet 24, Section 2 BASIC **Transparency 88,** How the Kidneys Filter the Blood **Reinforcement Worksheet 24,** Annie Apple's Amazing Adventure BASIC	**MathBreak,** How Much Water? p. 578 GENERAL **Apply,** p. 578 GENERAL **Across the Sciences:** Quench Your Thirst! p. 584 ADVANCED	**Homework,** p. 578 in ATE GENERAL **Review,** p. 579 GENERAL **Quiz,** p. 579 in ATE GENERAL **Alternative Assessment,** p. 579 in ATE GENERAL

 Holt, Rinehart and Winston On-line Resources
go.hrw.com

For worksheets and other teaching aids related to this chapter, visit the HRW Web site and type in the keyword: **HSTBD3**

 National Science Teachers Association
www.scilinks.org

Encourage students to use the *sci*LINKS numbers listed in the internet connect boxes to access information and resources on the **NSTA** Web site.

END-OF-CHAPTER REVIEW AND ASSESSMENT

Chapter Review in Study Guide
Vocabulary and Notes in Study Guide
Chapter Tests with Performance-Based Assessment, Chapter 24 Test
Chapter Tests with Performance-Based Assessment, Performance-Based Assessment 24
Concept Mapping Transparency 24

Chapter 24 • Chapter Organizer   **565B**

Chapter Resources & Worksheets

Visual Resources

TEACHING TRANSPARENCIES

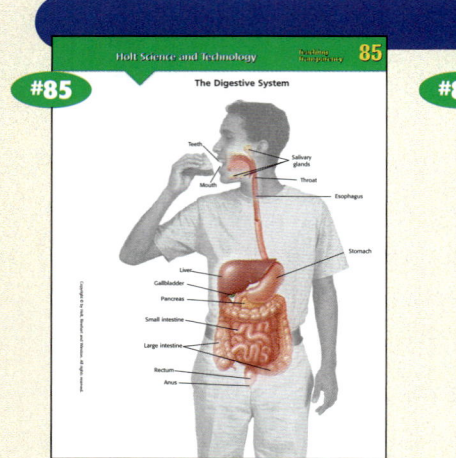
#85 — The Digestive System

#86 — Enzymes Break Down Proteins

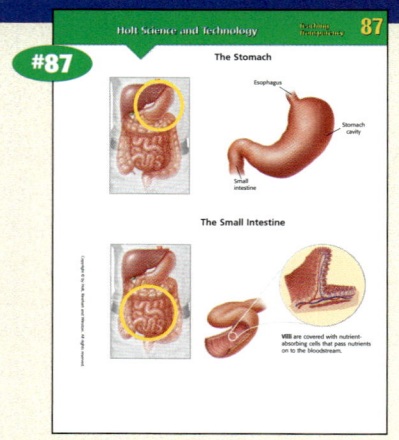
#87 — The Stomach / The Small Intestine

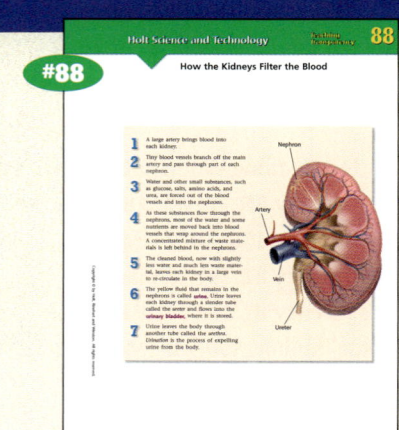
#88 — How the Kidneys Filter the Blood

TEACHING TRANSPARENCIES

#108 — LINK TO EARTH SCIENCE

CONCEPT MAPPING TRANSPARENCY

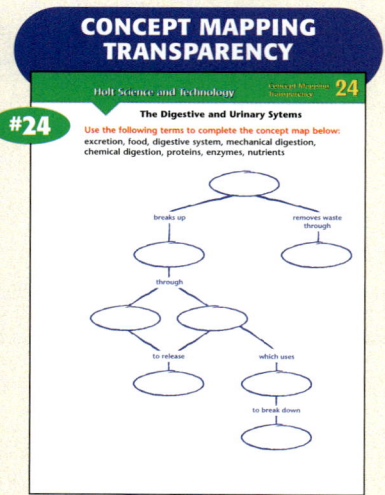
#24 — The Digestive and Urinary Systems

Meeting Individual Needs

DIRECTED READING

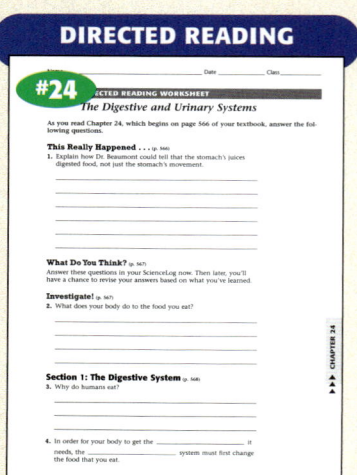
#24 — The Digestive and Urinary Systems

REINFORCEMENT & VOCABULARY REVIEW

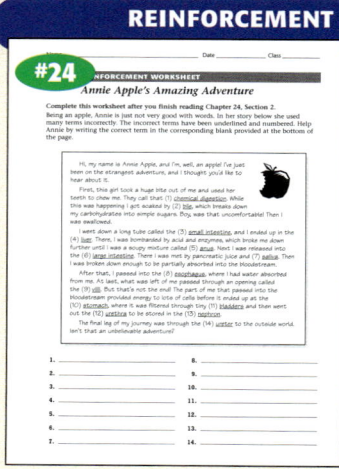
#24 — Annie Apple's Amazing Adventure

#24 — Alien Anagrams

SCIENCE PUZZLERS, TWISTERS & TEASERS

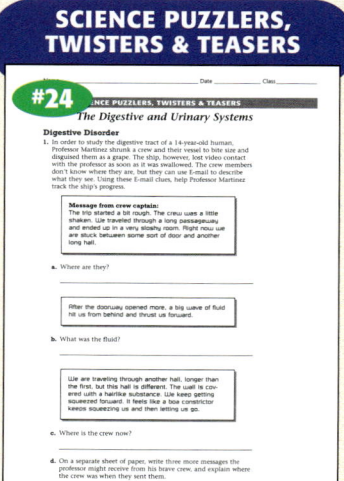
#24 — The Digestive and Urinary Systems

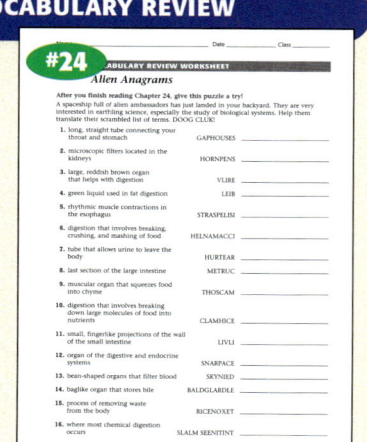

565C Chapter 24 • The Digestive and Urinary Systems

Chapter 24 • The Digestive and Urinary Systems

Review & Assessment

STUDY GUIDE

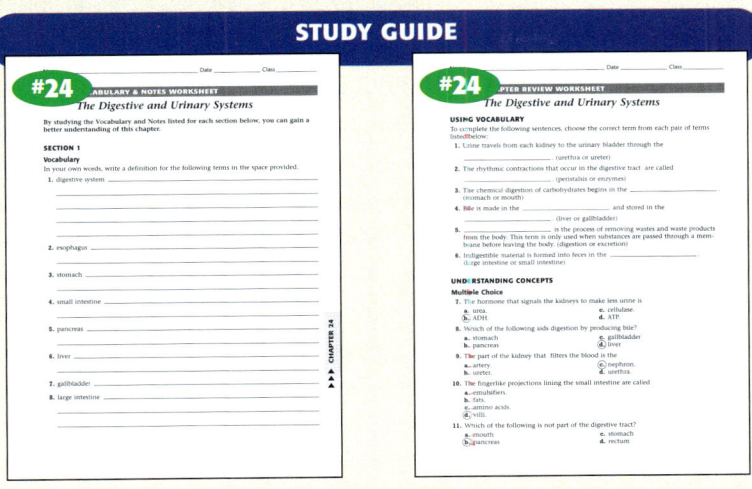

CHAPTER TESTS WITH PERFORMANCE-BASED ASSESSMENT

Lab Worksheets

LONG-TERM PROJECTS & RESEARCH IDEAS

WHIZ-BANG DEMONSTRATIONS

DATASHEETS FOR LABBOOK

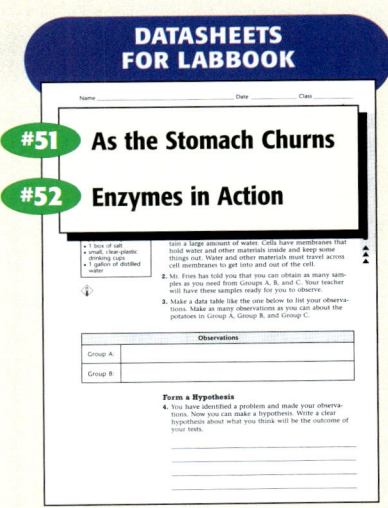

Applications & Extensions

CRITICAL THINKING & PROBLEM SOLVING

SCIENCE TECHNOLOGY

Chapter 24 • Chapter Resources & Worksheets

Chapter Background

SECTION 1

▶ The Digestive System
The digestive system is composed of two sets of organs: those that make up the digestive tract and those that are called accessory organs. The digestive tract is a continuous tube consisting of the mouth, including the teeth and the tongue, the pharynx, the esophagus, the stomach, the small intestine, and the large intestine.

- The accessory digestive organs include the salivary glands, the gallbladder, the liver, and the pancreas.

IS THAT A FACT!
▬ The digestive tract in a cadaver is about 9 m long. However, because of muscle tone, the digestive tract of a living person is considerably shorter.

▶ The Stomach
In short people, the stomach is found high on the abdomen and runs horizontally. In tall people, the stomach tends to run vertically, forming a J shape.

IS THAT A FACT!
▬ It takes about 4–8 seconds for food to pass from the top of the throat to the stomach.

▬ It takes less than 2 seconds for liquids to pass from the top of the throat to the stomach.

▶ The Intestines
The small intestine is the longest portion of the digestive tract. It is about 6 m long and 2.5 cm in diameter.

- Unlike the small intestine, the large intestine does not have villi, nor does it secrete digestive enzymes.

▶ The Appendix
The appendix is a 9 cm long offshoot of the large intestine. Like the tonsils, the appendix contains a large amount of lymphoid tissue.

- Doctors have begun an appendectomy on patients thought to have appendicitis. Instead of appendicitis, however, the patients had holes in the lining of their intestines made by parasitic worms. The incidence of intestinal parasitic worms is increasing as eating raw fish, such as sushi and sashimi, becomes more popular.

▶ Food Poisoning
Food poisoning is characterized by nausea, vomiting, abdominal cramps, and diarrhea. The two most common culprits are the bacteria *Salmonella* and *Shigella*.

- *Shigella* is commonly found among people who have visited developing countries. It is spread via food, feces, fingers, flies, and contaminated public bodies of water, such as swimming pools.

- *Salmonella* is typically spread by contaminated eggs and feces-contaminated hands. *Salmonella* infects the microvilli in the intestinal lining, causing blisters. If *Salmonella* poisoning is not treated promptly, the bacteria may spread throughout the body.

▶ Eating Disorders
Anorexia nervosa and bulimia are two common eating disorders that are characterized by an obsessive fear of becoming too fat. There are often underlying psychological factors that initiate these disorders.

- Anorexia nervosa is an eating disorder characterized by self-induced starvation. People with this condition refuse to eat and often exercise obsessively. Although the disorder can affect anyone, adolescent girls and young women are commonly afflicted. Boys, especially those involved in weight-conscious sports such as wrestling, can also become anorexic.

Chapter 24 • The Digestive and Urinary Systems

- Bulimia nervosa is a binge-purge syndrome in which those afflicted binge on enormous amounts of food and then regurgitate it or use laxatives to eliminate it. The binge-purge cycle may be repeated several times per day.

- Although bulimics are generally at or slightly above a normal body weight and appear to be healthy, they are not healthy. Bulimics tend to have swollen salivary glands, pancreatitis, and liver and kidney problems. In addition, they are at risk of heart failure due to electrolyte imbalance and stomach rupture, both of which can result in death. Excessive vomiting damages the esophagus and the stomach and wears away tooth enamel.

- Treatment for these eating disorders includes control of diet, often by means of hospitalization, behavior modification, nutrition education, and use of anti-depressants.

IS THAT A FACT!

- The volume of liquid that passes through the kidneys in a single day is equivalent to 60 times the body's entire volume of plasma.

- The kidneys require up to one-fourth of the body's oxygen supply to carry out their functions.

- The kidneys filter about 180 L of fluid from the blood each day. About 99 percent of this fluid is returned to the bloodstream. The other 1 percent leaves the body in the form of urine.

- A person who donates a kidney can maintain normal kidney functions. The remaining kidney enlarges and carries out the functions previously performed by two kidneys.

SECTION 2

▶ The Urinary System
The urinary system functions primarily to remove metabolic, nitrogen-containing wastes, such as urea, from the body in the form of urine and to maintain the correct balance of salts and water.

- The digestive system, the circulatory system, and the respiratory system also excrete wastes. The digestive system excretes undigested food in the form of feces. The circulatory and respiratory systems work together to rid the body of carbon dioxide.

- The yellow color of urine comes from the yellow pigment urochrome.

▶ The Kidney
The kidneys are surrounded and kept in their proper place in the body by fat. People who become too thin risk damage to the kidneys and related urinary problems. As much as 1,200 mL of blood passes through the nephrons each minute.

▶ The Urinary Bladder
Like the stomach, the size of the bladder varies with the amount of its contents. The bladder can hold 300 mL of urine without increasing its internal pressure significantly. At 500 mL of urine, the bladder is fairly full and may be 12.5 cm in length.

IS THAT A FACT!

- Urinary bladders of average size can contain as much as 1 L of urine!

For background information about teaching strategies and issues, refer to the Professional Reference for Teachers.

CHAPTER 24

The Digestive and Urinary Systems

Pre-Reading Questions

Students may not know the answers to these questions before reading the chapter, so accept any reasonable response.

Suggested Answers

1. The stomach squeezes the food to break it down mechanically. Acids and enzymes digest the food chemically.
2. Both your urinary system and your skin excrete wastes.

Teaching Transparency 85
"The Digestive System"

Directed Reading Worksheet 24

Science Puzzlers, Twisters & Teasers Worksheet 24

Guided Reading Audio CD
English or Spanish, Chapter 24

CHAPTER 24

The Digestive and Urinary Systems

Sections

1. The Digestive System .. 568
   - QuickLab 569
   - Internet Connect 571
   - Environment Connection 574
   - Internet Connect 575
2. The Urinary System ... 576
   - MathBreak 578
   - Apply 578
   - Internet Connect 579

Chapter Review 582
Feature Articles 584, 585
LabBook 768–771

Pre-Reading Questions

1. What happens to food when it reaches your stomach?
2. What does your urinary system have in common with your skin?

---

internet connect

HRW On-line Resources
go.hrw.com
For worksheets and other teaching aids, visit the HRW Web site and type in the keyword: **HSTBD3**

sciLINKS NSTA
www.scilinks.com
Use the *sci*LINKS numbers at the end of each chapter for additional resources on the **NSTA** Web site.

CNNfyi.com
www.cnnfyi.com
Visit the CNN Web site for current events coverage and classroom resources.

566 Chapter 24 • The Digestive and Urinary Systems

AHHH!!!

You can easily see the stream of water going into this girl's mouth. What you cannot see is where that refreshing gulp of water goes after she swallows it. How do water and food travel through the body and get absorbed for use by the cells? What are the body systems for getting rid of excess water or wastes? In this chapter, you will learn about the organs of the digestive and urinary systems and what happens inside your body to the food and liquids you eat and drink.

START-UP Activity

CHANGING FOODS

During digestion, the stomach squeezes and relaxes as food passes through it. You can see the role this squeezing motion plays in the digestion of food by using a plastic bag to model your stomach.

Procedure

1. Add **200 mL of flour** and **100 mL of water** to a **resealable plastic bag.** Mix **100 mL of vegetable oil** with the flour and water.
2. Seal the plastic bag, and shake it until the flour, water, and oil are well mixed.
3. Remove as much air from the bag as possible, and reseal the bag carefully.
4. Squeeze the bag with your hands for 5 minutes. Record your observations in your ScienceLog. Be careful to keep the bag sealed.

Analysis

5. Describe the mixture before and after you kneaded the bag.
6. How might the changes you saw in the mixture relate to what happens to food you eat?
7. Do you think this is a good model of how your stomach works? Why or why not?

START-UP Activity

CHANGING FOODS

MATERIALS
FOR EACH STUDENT: • 200 mL flour • 100 mL water • clear resealable plastic bag • 100 mL vegetable oil

Safety Caution

Tell students not to ingest any of the materials used in this investigation. Strong or double bags work best. Have paper towels on hand, and clean up any spills immediately. Spilled liquids are a slipping hazard.

Answers to START-UP Activity

4. Students should observe that the oil separates from the flour mixture. Tell students that in this exercise, the oil represents fats consumed in a meal. In the human body, these fats separate from the food mixture, and bile breaks them down into smaller particles.
5. Before the students squeezed the bag, the contents were well dispersed. Once the students began squeezing the bag, the oil separated from the flour mixture.
6. The stomach is a muscular, baglike organ that is involved in the physical and chemical digestion of a meal. By squeezing the bag, the students are modeling the muscular contractions of the stomach. Note: This activity does not model the chemical digestion that occurs in the stomach.
7. Answers will vary.

Chapter 24 • The Digestive and Urinary Systems

SECTION 1

Focus

The Digestive System

This section introduces the structures and functions of the digestive system. Students will compare mechanical digestion with chemical digestion and will learn to trace the path of food through the digestive system. Students will also learn about some ailments of the digestive system and their causes.

🔔 Bellringer

Ask students to answer the following questions in their ScienceLog:

How does your circulatory system obtain the nutrients that it brings to your cells? (from the digestive system)

Describe as best you can the process that turns food into nutrients that cells can use. (Accept all reasonable responses.)

1 Motivate

DEMONSTRATION

Measuring Saliva Show students a 2 L beaker or other transparent container. Pour 1.2 L (2.6 pt) of water into the container, and explain that this amount of water represents the amount of saliva an average person produces in 1 day. Then ask students to discuss what roles saliva might play in the body, specifically in the process of digestion. (Answers might include lubrication of the mouth and related organs, moistening food, and breaking down molecules into nutrients that cells can use.)

Section 1

Terms to Learn

digestive system   pancreas
esophagus   liver
stomach   gallbladder
small intestine   large intestine

What You'll Do

◆ Describe the parts and functions of the digestive system.
◆ Compare mechanical digestion with chemical digestion.
◆ Describe some disorders of the digestive system.

The Digestive System

It's your last class before lunch, and you're starving! You are so hungry you can hardly concentrate. Finally the bell rings and you get to eat your peanut butter and jelly sandwich. Yum!

You feel hungry because your brain receives signals that your cells need energy, but eating is only the beginning of the story. Your body must change a meal into substances it can use. Your **digestive system** is a group of organs that work together to digest food so that it can be used by the body.

Digestive System at a Glance

The most obvious part of your digestive system is the *digestive tract*, a series of tubelike organs that are joined end to end. The digestive tract includes your mouth, throat, esophagus, stomach, small intestine, large intestine, rectum, and anus. The human digestive tract may be more than 9 m long! The food you eat is digested as it passes through these organs. The liver, gallbladder, pancreas, and salivary glands are also part of the digestive system because they secrete substances that are used in digestion. The digestive system is shown in **Figure 1**.

Figure 1 The digestive tract is basically a long tube with an opening at each end.

🌐 Multicultural CONNECTION

Encourage students to research the diets of people in countries such as Japan, India, Israel, Egypt, Mexico, and Russia. Encourage students to discover strategies that people in these countries use to obtain a nutritious diet, and have them compare the diets of people in each country with the diets of people in the United States. You may also want to have students compare the diets based on fat or cholesterol intake.

568 Chapter 24 • The Digestive and Urinary Systems

The Journey of a Sandwich

Digestion is the process of breaking down food, such as a peanut butter and jelly sandwich, into a form that can pass from the digestive tract into the bloodstream. There are two types of digestion—mechanical and chemical. The breaking, crushing, and mashing of food is called *mechanical digestion*. In *chemical digestion,* large molecules are broken down into nutrients. Nutrients are substances in food that the body needs for normal growth, maintenance, and repair.

Three major types of nutrients—carbohydrates, proteins, and fats—make up most of what you eat. In fact, a peanut butter and jelly sandwich contains all three of these nutrients. Special substances called *enzymes* break some nutrients into smaller particles that the body can use. For example, proteins are chains of smaller molecules called amino acids. Proteins are too large to be absorbed into the bloodstream, but enzymes chop up the chain into amino acids. These amino acids are small enough to pass into the bloodstream. This process is illustrated in **Figure 2.**

Break It Up!

1. Drop **one piece of hard candy** into a **clear plastic cup of water.**
2. Wrap an **identical candy** in a **towel,** and crush it with a **hammer.** Drop the crushed candy into a **second clear cup of water.**
3. The next day, examine both cups. What is different about the two candies?
4. What part of digestion is represented by breaking the hard candy?
5. How does chewing your food help the process of digestion?

Figure 2 *Enzymes in the stomach and small intestine break down proteins.*

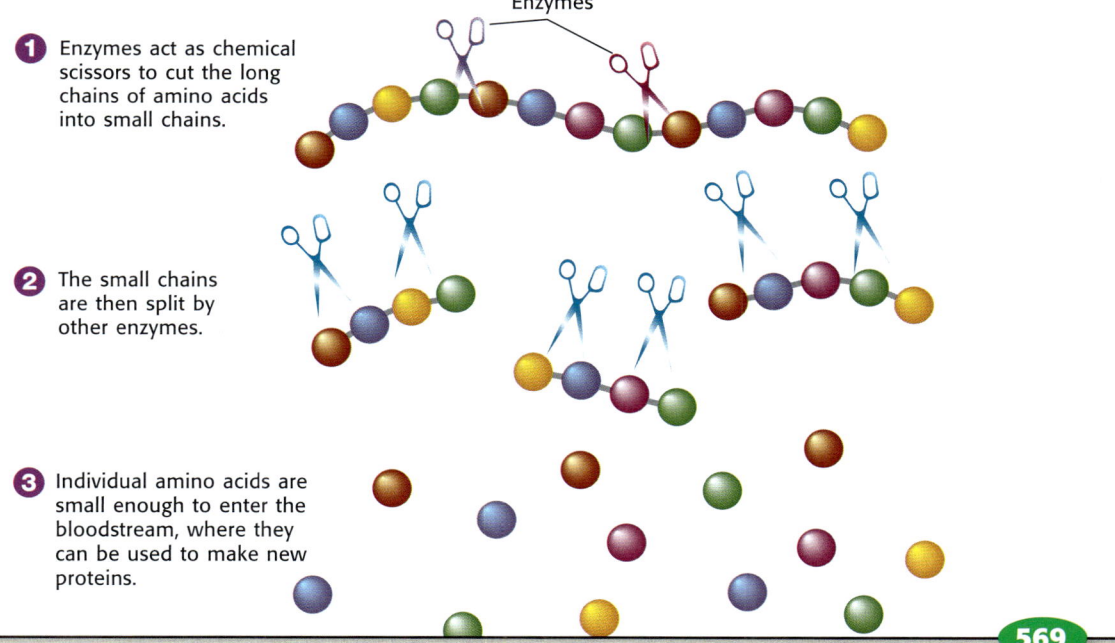

1. Enzymes act as chemical scissors to cut the long chains of amino acids into small chains.
2. The small chains are then split by other enzymes.
3. Individual amino acids are small enough to enter the bloodstream, where they can be used to make new proteins.

2) Teach

QuickLab

MATERIALS

FOR EACH STUDENT:
- safety goggles
- 2 identical pieces of hard candy
- 2 identical clear plastic cups of water
- towel
- hammer

Safety Caution: Tell students not to ingest or taste any of the materials, including the candy, in this QuickLab. Students should wear safety goggles while crushing the candy. Students should strike hammers away from their face and hands. Instruct students to be sure their hands and their classmates' hands are out of the way before pounding the candy with the hammer.

Answers to QuickLab

3. The crushed candy dissolved in the water. The whole candy did not dissolve as much.
4. Breaking the candy represents chewing, one form of physical digestion.
5. Chewing breaks the large chunks of food into smaller pieces. Greater surface area is then available for enzymes to digest the food.

 Teaching Transparency 86 "Enzymes Break Down Proteins"

 Directed Reading Worksheet 24 Section 1

Homework

Provide students with the following list of activities of the digestive system:

The teeth cut and grind food, the stomach churns food, enzymes in saliva break down carbohydrates in food, and enzymes break down proteins in food.

Ask students to indicate which activities represent mechanical digestion and which represent chemical digestion. (mechanical—the teeth cutting and grinding food, the stomach churning food; chemical—enzymes in saliva breaking down carbohydrates in food, enzymes breaking down proteins in food)

Section 1 • The Digestive System

2) Teach, continued

READING STRATEGY

Writing Activity Before students read the text on this page, have them read aloud the headings. Then ask students to formulate one question that they expect the text under each heading to answer. Have students write the questions in their ScienceLog. Possible questions include the following:

- "What happens in the mouth?"
- "Why is chewing important?"
- "What makes the stomach's environment harsh?"

CONNECT TO EARTH SCIENCE

Tooth enamel is an extremely hard material made primarily of carbonated calcium hydroxyapatite. Cavities (also called dental caries) form when acids produced by the bacteria on teeth demineralize the enamel, weakening it. Fluoride compounds, taken internally while the teeth are growing, strengthen the enamel by forming the enamel out of fluoroapatite, an apatite material more acid resistant than natural enamel. Applying fluoride to the outside of teeth after the teeth have formed can also help strengthen the enamel by changing the natural hydroxyapatite in the tooth to fluoroapatite. Use the following Teaching Transparency to illustrate that in geology, apatite is in the middle of the hardness scale for minerals.

Teaching Transparency 108 "Mohs' Hardness Scale" — LINK TO EARTH SCIENCE

Digestion Begins in the Mouth

Why is chewing so important? There are two reasons. First, chewing creates small, slippery pieces of food that are easier to swallow than big, dry pieces. Second, small pieces of food are easier to digest.

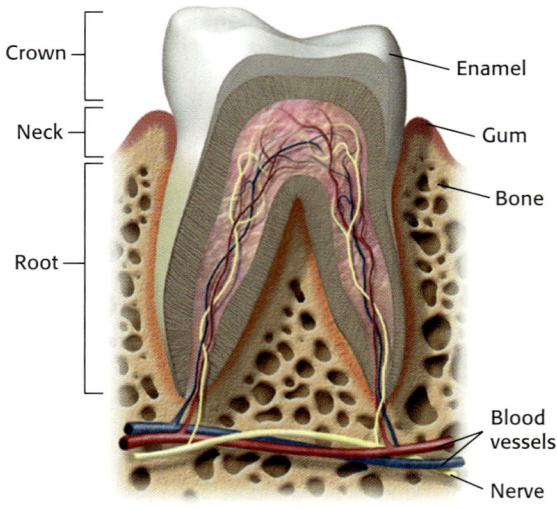

Figure 3 The crown of a tooth, such as this molar, is visible above the gum line. The root is below the gum line.

Through the Teeth Teeth are very important organs for mechanical digestion. With the help of strong muscles and your jaw bones, teeth are able to break and grind food. The outermost layer of a tooth, the *enamel*, is the hardest material in the body. Enamel protects nerves and softer material inside the tooth. **Figure 3** shows the major parts of the tooth.

Have you ever noticed that your teeth have different shapes? Look at **Figure 4** to locate the different kinds of teeth. The *molars* in the back are well suited for grinding food. The *premolars* are perfect for mashing food. The sharp teeth at the front of your mouth, the *incisors* and *canines*, are for shredding food.

And Over the Gums As you chew, the food gets mixed with a liquid called *saliva*. Saliva is made in salivary glands located in and around the mouth. Saliva contains an enzyme that begins the chemical digestion of carbohydrates. Saliva turns complex carbohydrates into simple sugars.

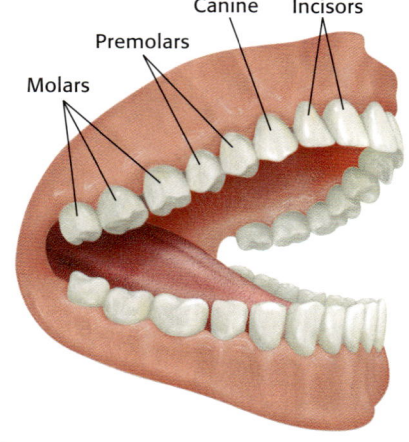

Look Out Stomach, Here It Comes! Once the food has been reduced to a soft mush, the tongue pushes it into the throat, which leads to a long, straight tube called the **esophagus** (i SAWF uh guhs). The esophagus squeezes the mass of food with rhythmic muscle contractions called *peristalsis* (PER uh STAHL sis). Peristalsis forces the food into the stomach.

Figure 4 Most adults have 32 permanent teeth. Each type of permanent tooth has a different function in breaking up food before it is swallowed.

MISCONCEPTION ALERT

Students may mistakenly assume that teeth are made of bone. Point out that although enamel and dentin are similar to bone in appearance and calcium content, they are not bone. Bone contains blood vessels, but enamel and dentin do not.

IS THAT A FACT!

The average human eats about 455 kg (1,000 lb) of food every year.

Chapter 24 • The Digestive and Urinary Systems

The Stomach's Harsh Environment

The **stomach** is a muscular, baglike organ attached to the lower end of the esophagus. It is pictured in **Figure 5**. The stomach continues the physical digestion of your meal by squeezing its contents with muscular contractions. While all this squeezing is going on, tiny glands in the stomach produce enzymes and acid. These work together to break food into nutrients. Stomach acid also kills most bacteria that you might swallow with your food. After a few hours of combined physical and chemical action, your peanut butter and jelly sandwich has been reduced to a soupy mixture called *chyme* (kiem).

A thick substance called mucus covers the stomach's lining and offers some protection from its harsh environment. However, the acids still damage the lining, and the entire lining must be replaced every few days.

Figure 5 *The stomach grinds and mixes food for hours before it releases the mixture into the small intestine.*

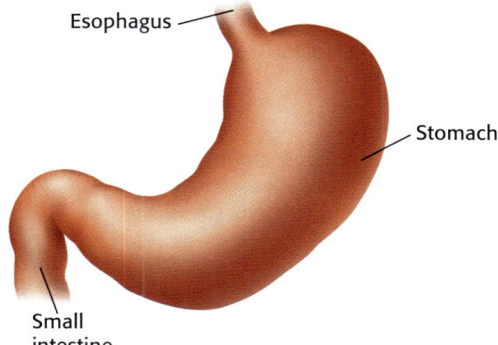

Doorway to the Small Intestine The chyme is slowly released into the small intestine through a small ring of muscle that works like a valve. This valve keeps food in the stomach until it has been thoroughly mixed with digestive fluids. Then the valve opens and closes, letting a small amount of chyme squirt into the small intestine each time. Releasing chyme slowly from the stomach gives the intestine more time to mix the chyme with fluids from the liver and pancreas.

REVIEW

1. What is the difference between mechanical digestion and chemical digestion?
2. **Inferring Conclusions** Give two reasons why the following statement is true: Digestion begins in the mouth.

2) Teach, continued

LabBook — PG 768
As the Stomach Churns

CONNECT TO CHEMISTRY

As food is digested, it undergoes both physical and chemical changes. Ask students to categorize the following activities as either physical changes or chemical changes:

- chewing food (physical change)
- enzymes in saliva breaking down carbohydrates (chemical change)
- squeezing and churning food in the stomach (physical change)
- breaking down food with pancreatic juice (chemical change)

MEETING INDIVIDUAL NEEDS

Advanced Learners Provide students with a compound light microscope and prepared slides of several different digestive organs. You might want to include cross sections of tissue from the stomach, the small intestine, the liver, and the pancreas. Review the proper use of microscopes before allowing students to operate them, and make sure that students do not work with broken or cracked slides. Have students observe the specimens, compare the different cross sections, and make sketches in their ScienceLog. Encourage students to link the structures they observe with the functions of each organ. For example, students may relate the structure of villi to the function of nutrient absorption of the small intestine.

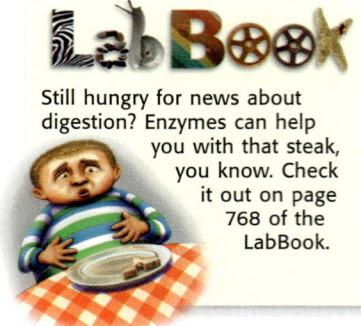

Still hungry for news about digestion? Enzymes can help you with that steak, you know. Check it out on page 768 of the LabBook.

The Gigantic Small Intestine?

The **small intestine** is a muscular tube that is about 2.5 cm in diameter. Other than its diameter, it's really not that small at all. In fact, if you stretched it out, it would be longer than you are tall—about 6 m!

Villi If you flattened out the surface of the small intestine, it would be larger than a tennis court! How is this possible? The inside wall of the small intestine is covered with fingerlike projections called *villi*, shown in **Figure 6.** The villi are covered with tiny nutrient-absorbing cells. Because the villi extend into the chyme, these cells have greater exposure to nutrients. Once absorbed, the nutrients enter the bloodstream.

Most chemical digestion takes place in the small intestine. Chyme from the stomach moves very slowly through the small intestine by peristalsis. Proteins, carbohydrates, and fats in the chyme are digested with the help of enzymes produced in the small intestine and the pancreas.

Figure 6 The highly folded lining of the small intestine has many fingerlike extensions called villi.

Villi are covered with nutrient-absorbing cells that pass nutrients on to the bloodstream.

The Pancreas

The **pancreas** is a fish-shaped organ located between the stomach and small intestine. It makes pancreatic juice that flows into the small intestine. This juice contains digestive enzymes and bicarbonate that neutralizes the acid in chyme. Without bicarbonate, acids would damage the lining of the intestine and prevent enzymes from doing their work. The pancreas also functions as a part of the endocrine system, making hormones that regulate blood sugar. The pancreas is shown in **Figure 7** on the next page.

SCIENCE HUMOR

A man walks into a doctor's office with a stalk of celery in one ear and a carrot in the other. The man says, "Doc, I'm just not feeling well these days." The doctor replies, "I think that's because you haven't been eating right."

The Liver and Gallbladder

The **liver** is a large reddish brown organ that helps with digestion. A human liver can be as large as a football. Your liver is located toward your right side, slightly higher than your stomach, as shown in **Figure 7**. Here are a few of the liver's important jobs:

- Your liver makes a green liquid called *bile* that is used in fat digestion
- Your liver stores nutrients
- Your liver breaks down toxic substances in the blood
- Your liver makes cholesterol for cell membranes

Bile Breaks Up Fat Although bile is made by the liver, it is temporarily stored in a small baglike organ called the **gallbladder,** shown in Figure 7. Bile is squeezed from the gallbladder into the small intestine, where it breaks up large fat droplets into very small droplets. This physical process allows more fat molecules to be exposed to digestive enzymes.

Storing Nutrients and Protecting the Body After nutrients are broken down, they are absorbed into the bloodstream and carried through the body. Nutrients that are not needed right away are stored in the liver. The liver then releases the stored nutrients into the bloodstream as needed. The liver also captures and detoxifies many substances in the body. For instance, it produces enzymes that break down alcohol and many other drugs.

If three-fourths of the liver were removed, the rest would go on working and would eventually grow to replace the part that was removed.

Self-Check

Is bile used for chemical or mechanical digestion? Explain. *(See page 782 to check your answer.)*

Figure 7 *The liver, gallbladder, and pancreas are linked to the small intestine, but food does not move through them.*

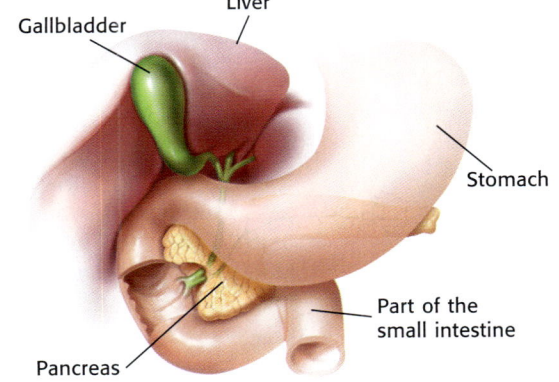

IS THAT A FACT!

Weighing as much as 1.5 kg, the liver is the most massive internal organ in the human body.

3 Extend

RESEARCH

Writing Have students research and report on the effects of one of the following eating disorders on the digestive system:

bulimia, anorexia nervosa, obesity, overeating

COOPERATIVE LEARNING

Activity Have students work in groups of three to five to make a life-size model of the digestive system. First have students in each group trace the outline of one of their classmates on a piece of butcher paper. Then provide each group with an assortment of craft materials—including plastic foam, modeling clay, construction paper, and fabric—with which to make models of the digestive organs. Encourage students to make digestive organs that fit together on their body silhouette. You may want to have students practice naming the digestive organs while tracing the path of food through their model of the digestive system. Sheltered English

Homework

Creating Graphs Provide students with the following average lengths of the digestive organs:

esophagus—25 cm, stomach—25 cm, small intestine—6 m, large intestine—1.5 m.

Then have students prepare a bar graph or another graphic to compare the average lengths of each digestive organ listed. You might also want to have students measure and label the lengths using adding-machine tape or a skein of yarn and compare them to the illustration of the digestive system in this chapter.

Figure 8 The large intestine is the final organ of digestion.

Feces and other human wastes contain microorganisms and other substances that can contaminate drinking water. Every time you flush a toilet, the water and wastes go through the sewer to a sewage treatment plant. Here the disease-causing microorganisms are removed, and the clean water is released back to rivers, lakes, and streams.

The End of the Line

Whatever can't be absorbed into the blood gets pushed into the large intestine. The **large intestine** is the organ of the digestive system that stores, compacts, and then eliminates indigestible material from the body. The large intestine, shown in **Figure 8,** is called "large" because it has a larger diameter than the small intestine. It is about 1.5 m long, and its diameter is about 7.5 cm.

In the Large Intestine Undigested material enters the large intestine as a soupy mixture. The large intestine reabsorbs most of the water in the mixture, changing the liquid into a solid mass called *feces* or *stool*.

Whole grains, fruits, and vegetables contain a carbohydrate, called cellulose, that humans cannot digest. We commonly refer to this material as fiber. Fiber keeps the stool soft and keeps things moving through the large intestine.

A Way Out The *rectum* is the last section of the large intestine. It stores feces until they can be expelled. Feces pass to the outside through an opening called the *anus*. It has taken your sandwich about 24 hours to make this journey.

Problems in the Digestive System

Disorders of the digestive system are frequently related to eating behaviors. However, digestive problems can also be caused by diseases. Some common digestive disorders are described below.

Heartburn The stomach is blocked off at either end by bands of muscle called *sphincters* (SFINGK tuhrz). Occasionally, backflow of chyme from the stomach to the esophagus causes a burning pain in the chest called heartburn. Eating too much, eating right before going to bed, and eating very acidic foods sometimes cause heartburn.

IS THAT A FACT!

In the past, medical professionals have attributed peptic ulcers to stress and heredity. However, in 1982, Australian scientists Robin Warren and Barry Marshall discovered a species of bacteria that was common to many ulcer patients. Dr. Marshall finally proved his hypothesis that the species of bacteria was responsible for ulcers by infecting himself with it, succumbing to peptic ulcers, and then curing himself with antibiotics.

Constipation and Diarrhea When the body does not get enough fiber, water, or exercise, the contents of the large intestine can become dry. Bowel movements become difficult and less frequent. This condition is called *constipation*. When bowel movements are frequent and watery, the condition is called *diarrhea*. Diarrhea occurs when too little water is removed from digested food in the large intestine. Diarrhea may cause dehydration and is especially dangerous for infants and small children, such as the girl in **Figure 9**.

Figure 9 *This child is being given fluids to replace those lost to diarrhea.*

Colon Cancer *Colon cancer* is a serious disease of the digestive tract that can lead to death. The colon is the long tubular portion of the large intestine. When certain colon cells divide uncontrollably, a tumor forms. Tumors interfere with the normal functioning of organs. Cells from a tumor can also break away and start tumors in other areas in the body. Colon cancer can often be treated and cured if detected early.

Gastric Ulcer An open sore in the stomach lining is called a *gastric ulcer*. **Figure 10** shows stomach tissue from a gastric ulcer. Gastric ulcers are often caused by bacteria and can be treated successfully with antibiotics. A high-fat diet, smoking, caffeine, and alcohol may make this condition worse.

Figure 10 *This stomach lining has openings, seen in red, that indicate a gastric ulcer.*

REVIEW

1. What happens to the food that you eat when it gets to the stomach?
2. Describe the roles of the liver, the gallbladder, and the pancreas in digestion.
3. **Analyzing Relationships** How would the inability to make saliva affect digestion?

TOPIC: Problems in the Digestive System
GO TO: www.scilinks.org
*sci*LINKS NUMBER: HSTL585

Section 2

Focus

The Urinary System

This section introduces the structures and the functions of the urinary system. Students will learn how the kidneys filter blood. Students will also learn about some major problems of the urinary system and their causes.

Bellringer

Tell students that the blood must be cleaned regularly. Then ask students to speculate, without looking in the textbook, how the body cleans blood. Once students have written a description of the cleaning process, allow them to check their answers against their textbook.

1) Motivate

DISCUSSION

Mongolian gerbils Tell students that Mongolian gerbils are desert animals that never drink. Ask students how they think Mongolian gerbils obtain water. (They get water from the foods they eat.)

Ask students: How have the gerbils adapted to their habitat? (These animals have adapted to use water very efficiently, losing little or none from their lungs, skin, and urine.)

Directed Reading Worksheet 24 Section 2

internetconnect
SC_INKS **TOPIC:** The Urinary System
GO TO: www.scilinks.org
NSTA **sciLINKS NUMBER:** HSTL590

Section 2

Terms to Learn

urinary system urine
kidney urinary bladder
nephron

What You'll Do

◆ Describe the parts and functions of the urinary system.
◆ Explain how the kidneys filter blood.
◆ Describe some disorders of the urinary system.

The Urinary System

As your body performs the chemical activities that keep you alive, waste products such as carbon dioxide and nitrogen are produced. Your body has to get rid of these waste products in order to stay healthy. *Excretion* is the process of removing wastes and excess products from the body. Three of your body systems are involved in excretion: your skin releases waste products and water when you sweat, your lungs expel carbon dioxide and water when you exhale, and the **urinary system** removes waste products from your blood. Notice that the digestive system is not involved in excretion. The term *excretion* is used only when substances must pass through a membrane in order to leave the body.

Cleaning the Blood

As blood travels through the tissues, it collects all of the waste products produced by the body's cells. Your blood is like a supply train that comes into a town to drop off supplies and take away garbage. The train has to find a way to get rid of the garbage before it can load up with more supplies. If the garbage is not removed, the townspeople will be in a very unhealthy environment. If the cells in your body cannot get rid of their waste products, they can actually be poisoned! On the next few pages, you will see how the urinary system removes waste materials from your blood so that the blood can transport nutrients again. The urinary system is shown in **Figure 11**.

Figure 11 *The urinary system removes many of the waste products produced by the body.*

Q: What does the kidney say when it plays baseball with the other urinary organs?

A: Bladder up!

576 Chapter 24 • The Digestive and Urinary Systems

Flow-Through Filters

The **kidneys** are a pair of bean-shaped organs that constantly clean the blood. Your kidneys filter about 2,000 L of blood each day. Your body only holds 5.6 L of blood, so your blood cycles through the kidneys about 350 times a day!

Inside each kidney are more than 1 million microscopic filters called **nephrons,** shown below. Nephrons remove a variety of harmful substances from the body. Among the most important of these substances is urea, which contains nitrogen and is formed when cells use protein for energy.

Science CONNECTION

Why does your mouth get so dry when the rest of you is so hot and sweaty? Turn to page 584 to find out.

How the Kidneys Filter Blood

1. A large artery brings blood into each kidney.
2. Tiny blood vessels branch off the main artery and pass through part of each nephron.
3. Water and other small substances, such as glucose, salts, amino acids, and urea, are forced out of the blood vessels and into the nephrons.
4. As these substances flow through the nephrons, most of the water and some nutrients are moved back into blood vessels that wrap around the nephrons. A concentrated mixture of waste materials is left behind in the nephrons.
5. The cleaned blood, now with slightly less water and much less waste material, leaves each kidney in a large vein to recirculate in the body.
6. The yellow fluid that remains in the nephrons is called **urine.** Urine leaves each kidney through a slender tube called the *ureter* and flows into the **urinary bladder,** where it is stored.
7. Urine leaves the body through another tube called the *urethra. Urination* is the process of expelling urine from the body.

IS THAT A FACT!

In a lifetime, a person's kidneys clean more than 1 million gallons (4 million liters) of liquid. That's enough to fill a small lake.

Teaching Transparency 88
"How the Kidneys Filter the Blood"

2 Teach

MEETING INDIVIDUAL NEEDS

Learners Having Difficulty Help students with limited English proficiency with the terms on this page. Write the terms *urine* and *urinary* on the chalkboard or on a transparency. As a class, define these terms and write working definitions of the terms beside each word. You may want to allow students to use their textbook for this exercise. Then point out that the term *urine* is a noun and that the term *urinary* is an adjective. **Sheltered English**

USING THE FIGURE

Have students trace the path of blood into, through, and out of the kidney illustrated in the figure. **Sheltered English**

DEMONSTRATION

Kidney Structure Obtain a beef or sheep kidney from your local supermarket or butcher. Cut the kidney into two symmetrical halves. Allow students to observe and sketch the internal and external structures of the kidney and to compare the kidney with the kidney illustration on this page. Have students wear goggles, disposable gloves, and aprons during their examination of the kidney. Students should keep their hands away from their face and eyes during examination and should wash their hands after examining the kidney. Dispose of the kidney as you would any other biohazard. Following the examination of the kidney, ask students why this kidney is so similar to a human kidney. **(Both are mammalian.)** **Sheltered English**

Section 2 • The Urinary System

2) Teach, continued

Answer to MATHBREAK

You need to drink 10.6 8-oz glasses of water per day.

2500 mL ÷ 29.6 mL/oz = 84.5 oz
84.5 oz ÷ 8 oz/glass = 10.6 glasses

READING STRATEGY

Prediction Guide Before students read this page, ask them whether the following statements are true or false. Students will discover the answers as they read this page.

1. When you sweat a lot, you produce less saliva. (true)
2. When you are thirsty, your tissues need more water. (true)
3. When you are thirsty, your kidneys return more water to the blood. (true)

MISCONCEPTION ALERT

Students may think that taking large doses of vitamin C can prevent or cure a cold. In fact, vitamin C has not been shown to prevent or cure colds. However, continued doses of vitamin C of 1 g or more may eventually cause kidney stones, diarrhea, and other conditions.

Answer to APPLY

Answers will vary. Caffeine is a diuretic, a substance that causes the kidneys to make more urine, thereby decreasing the amount of water in the blood. Water is needed to produce energy for the body, so not having enough water might decrease the energy level of an athlete.

Reinforcement Worksheet 24
"Annie Apple's Amazing Adventure"

MATH BREAK

How Much Water?
Most adults need to consume about 2,500 mL of water per day. How many 8 oz glasses of drinking water would you need to get enough water?
Hint: 1 oz = 29.6 mL

Fortunately, your kidneys are very efficient. In fact, if you lost one to disease, you could still survive.

APPLY

Beverage Ban
During football season, a football coach insists that all members of the team avoid caffeinated beverages. Many of the players are upset by the news. Pretend that you are the coach. Write a letter to the team explaining why it is better for them to drink water than drinks containing caffeine.

Water In, Water Out

Our bodies take in water every day. If we did not excrete an equal amount of water, our bodies would swell up with all the excess. Losing water through sweat and urine is necessary to stay healthy. So how does the body keep the water levels in the proper balance? The balance of fluids is controlled by chemical messengers in the body called *hormones*.

Sweat and Thirst When you get hot, you lose more water in the form of sweat. The evaporation of water from your skin cools you down. As the water content of the blood drops, the salivary glands produce less saliva. This is one of the reasons you feel thirsty.

Antidiuretic Hormone When you get thirsty, other parts of your body react to the water shortage, too. A hormone called *antidiuretic* (AN tie DIE yoo RET ik) *hormone*, or *ADH*, is released. ADH signals the kidneys to take back water from the nephrons and return it to the bloodstream, thereby making less urine. When your blood is too watery, smaller amounts of ADH are released. The kidneys react by allowing more water to stay in the nephron and leave the body as urine.

Diuretics When you are thirsty, your tissues are asking for more water. Some beverages contain caffeine, which is a *diuretic* (DIE yoo RET ik). Diuretics cause the kidneys to make more urine, which decreases the amount of water in the blood. So instead of giving your body more water, caffeinated beverages cause additional water to be lost in urine.

Homework

Poster Project Have students make a poster following the path of blood through the kidney. Have them create their own diagram with a labeled pathway using the steps and the figure on this page as a starting point.

WEIRD SCIENCE

Although urea can be toxic to the body and must be eliminated, it also has a number of medical uses. It is used in some creams to treat dry-skin ailments, such as psoriasis. Urea is also used as a diuretic to reduce pressure caused by glaucoma or edema in the brain.

Urinary System Ailments

Since the urinary system regulates body fluids and removes wastes from the blood, any malfunction can become life-threatening. Some common urinary system disorders are described below.

Bacterial Infections Bacteria can get into the bladder and ureters through the urethra and cause painful infections. It is important to treat such an infection early because it could spread to the kidneys and lead to permanent damage to the nephrons.

Figure 12 *This kidney stone had to be removed from a patient's urinary system.*

Kidney Stones Sometimes salts and wastes collect inside the kidneys and form kidney stones, like the one in **Figure 12.** Kidney stones interfere with urine flow and cause pain. Most kidney stones pass naturally from the body, but sometimes a medical procedure is necessary. For example, shockwaves can be used to break the stones into pieces small enough to pass through the urethra.

Kidney Disease Damage to nephrons can prevent normal kidney functioning, leading to kidney disease. If the kidneys do not function properly, a kidney machine can be used to filter waste from the blood. As shown in **Figure 13,** blood is pumped from an artery in the forearm or wrist to a kidney machine, where it is filtered. The cleaned blood is then pumped back into a vein in the arm.

Figure 13 *The kidney machine will filter this man's blood before returning it to his body.*

REVIEW

1. Put the following statements about the urinary system in their proper order:
   a. Water is absorbed back into blood vessels.
   b. Urine leaves the kidney through the ureter.
   c. A large artery brings blood into the kidney.
   d. Water and other small substances, including glucose and urea, leave the blood vessels and enter the nephron.
2. What is the main function of the urinary system?
3. **Applying Concepts** Which contains more water, the blood going into the kidney or the blood leaving the kidney? Explain.

internetconnect

SC_**LINKS**_ NSTA

TOPIC: The Urinary System, Urinary System Ailments
GO TO: www.scilinks.org
sciLINKS NUMBER: HSTL590, HSTL595

Section 2 • The Urinary System   **579**

Chapter Highlights

VOCABULARY DEFINITIONS

SECTION 1

digestive system a collection of organs that break down food so that it can be used by the body; the organs in this system include the stomach, the pancreas, the liver, the gallbladder, the small intestine, and the large intestine

esophagus a long, straight tube that connects the mouth and throat to the stomach

stomach a muscular, baglike organ of the digestive tract; attached to the lower end of the esophagus

small intestine a muscular tube about 6 m long; the site of most chemical digestion

pancreas an organ between the stomach and small intestine that produces enzymes for chemical digestion

liver a large, reddish organ that produces bile and stores nutrients

gallbladder a small, baglike organ that stores bile

large intestine a large organ that reabsorbs water from the digestive tract and stores, compacts, and eliminates indigestible material from the body

Chapter Highlights

SECTION 1

Vocabulary
- digestive system (p. 568)
- esophagus (p. 570)
- stomach (p. 571)
- small intestine (p. 572)
- pancreas (p. 572)
- liver (p. 573)
- gallbladder (p. 573)
- large intestine (p. 574)

Section Notes
- Your digestive system is a group of organs that work together to digest food so that it can be used by the body.
- The breaking, crushing, and mashing of food is called mechanical digestion. Chemical digestion is the process in which large molecules are broken down to simpler molecules.
- Chewed food is pushed through the digestive tract by rhythmic contractions called peristalsis.
- The stomach mixes the food with enzymes and acid to break down nutrients. The mixture is called chyme.
- In the small intestine, pancreatic juice and bile are mixed with chyme.
- From the small intestine, nutrients enter the bloodstream and are circulated to the body's cells.
- The large intestine receives undigested material from the small intestine. As water is absorbed back into the body, this material becomes a solid mass called feces.

- Digestive system disorders include heartburn, constipation, diarrhea, colon cancer, and gastric ulcers.

Labs
As the Stomach Churns (p. 768)
Enzymes in Action (p. 770)

✓ Skills Check

Math Concepts
DRINK UP In the MathBreak on page 578, you determined how many glasses of water you need in order to drink 2,500 mL each day. First you must determine how many ounces are in 2,500 mL:

$$\frac{2{,}500 \text{ mL}}{1 \text{ day}} \times \frac{1 \text{ oz}}{29.6 \text{ mL}} = 84.5 \text{ oz of water}$$

You need to drink 84.5 oz of water each day.

Each glass contains 8 oz, so:

$$\frac{84.5 \text{ oz}}{1 \text{ day}} \times \frac{1 \text{ glass}}{8 \text{ oz}} = 10.6 \text{ glasses}$$

You need to drink 10.6 8-oz glasses of water each day.

Visual Understanding
KIDNEY FUNCTION Look at the illustration on page 577 to review how the kidneys filter the blood.

Lab and Activity Highlights

Enzymes in Action   PG 770

As the Stomach Churns   PG 768

Datasheets for LabBook
(blackline masters for these labs)

SECTION 2

Vocabulary
- **urinary system** (p. 576)
- **kidney** (p. 577)
- **nephron** (p. 577)
- **urine** (p. 577)
- **urinary bladder** (p. 577)

Section Notes
- Your skin, lungs, and urinary system are all involved in excretion.
- The urinary system cleans the blood and removes liquid waste as urine. The filtering structures in the kidneys are called nephrons.
- Most of the water and some nutrients that enter nephrons are moved back into the blood vessels.
- When urine leaves the kidneys, it passes into the urinary bladder through a tube called the ureter. The urinary bladder stores the urine until it can be eliminated.
- Urine travels from the urinary bladder to the outside through a tube called the urethra.
- Some disorders of the urinary system include bacterial infections, kidney stones, and kidney disease.

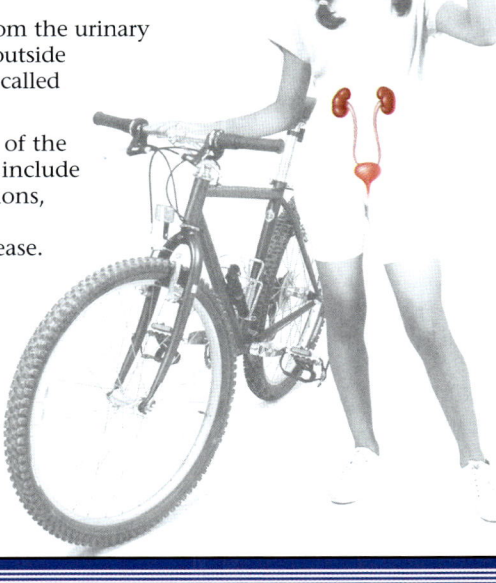

VOCABULARY DEFINITIONS, continued

SECTION 2

urinary system a collection of organs that remove waste from the blood; the organs in this system include the kidneys, ureters, urethra, and urinary bladder

kidney a bean-shaped organ that removes many harmful substances from the blood

nephron a microscopic filter in the kidney that removes a variety of harmful substances from the blood

urine a concentrated mixture of waste materials that forms in the nephrons of the kidney

urinary bladder a baglike organ that stores urine until it can be eliminated through the urethra

 Vocabulary Review Worksheet 24

 Blackline masters of these Chapter Highlights can be found in the **Study Guide.**

---

internet connect

 GO TO: go.hrw.com

Visit the **HRW** Web site for a variety of learning tools related to this chapter. Just type in the keyword:

KEYWORD: HSTBD3

 GO TO: www.scilinks.org

Visit the **National Science Teachers Association** on-line Web site for Internet resources related to this chapter. Just type in the *sci*LINKS number for more information about the topic:

TOPIC: The Digestive System — *sci*LINKS NUMBER: HSTL580
TOPIC: Problems in the Digestive System — *sci*LINKS NUMBER: HSTL585
TOPIC: The Urinary System — *sci*LINKS NUMBER: HSTL590
TOPIC: Urinary System Ailments — *sci*LINKS NUMBER: HSTL595
TOPIC: Tapeworms — *sci*LINKS NUMBER: HSTL600

Lab and Activity Highlights

LabBank

 Whiz-Bang Demonstrations, Liver Let Live, Demo 14

Long-Term Projects & Research Ideas, Copying the Kidney, Project 24

Chapter Review Answers

USING VOCABULARY

1. ureters
2. peristalsis
3. mouth
4. liver, gallbladder
5. Excretion
6. large intestine

UNDERSTANDING CONCEPTS

Multiple Choice

7. b
8. d
9. c
10. d
11. b
12. a

Short Answer

13. Bicarbonate neutralizes the acidic chyme coming in from the stomach. This allows pancreatic enzymes and enzymes made in the intestine to work. By neutralizing the acid, the bicarbonate also protects the lining of the intestine.
14. The long length, folds, and villi increase the surface area that comes into contact with the food that is being digested in the small intestine.
15. A diuretic is a substance that causes the kidneys to produce more urine.

Chapter Review

USING VOCABULARY

To complete the following sentences, choose the correct term from each pair of terms listed below:

1. Urine travels from each kidney to the urinary bladder through the __?__. (*urethra* or *ureter*)
2. The rhythmic contractions that occur in the digestive tract are called __?__. (*peristalsis* or *enzymes*)
3. The chemical digestion of carbohydrates begins in the __?__. (*stomach* or *mouth*)
4. Bile is made in the __?__ and stored in the __?__. (*liver* or *gallbladder*)
5. __?__ is the process of removing wastes and waste products from the body. This term is only used when substances are passed through a membrane before leaving the body. (*Digestion* or *Excretion*)
6. Indigestible material is formed into feces in the __?__. (*large intestine* or *small intestine*)

UNDERSTANDING CONCEPTS

Multiple Choice

7. The hormone that signals the kidneys to make less urine is
   a. urea.
   b. ADH.
   c. cellulase.
   d. ATP.

8. Which of the following aids digestion by producing bile?
   a. stomach
   b. pancreas
   c. gallbladder
   d. liver

9. The part of the kidney that filters the blood is the
   a. artery.
   b. ureter.
   c. nephron.
   d. urethra.

10. The fingerlike projections lining the small intestine are called
    a. emulsifiers.
    b. fats.
    c. amino acids.
    d. villi.

11. Which of the following is not part of the digestive tract?
    a. mouth
    b. pancreas
    c. stomach
    d. rectum

12. The soupy mixture of food, enzymes, and acids in the stomach is called
    a. chyme.
    b. villi.
    c. urea.
    d. vitamins.

Short Answer

13. Give two reasons why it is important that the pancreas releases bicarbonate into the small intestine.
14. How does the structure of the small intestine improve its nutrient absorption?
15. What is a diuretic?

582 Chapter 24 • The Digestive and Urinary Systems

Concept Mapping

16. Use the following terms to create a concept map: teeth, stomach, digestion, bile, saliva, mechanical digestion, gallbladder, chemical digestion.

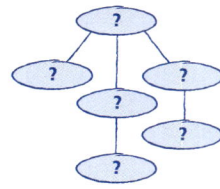

CRITICAL THINKING AND PROBLEM SOLVING

Write one or two sentences to answer the following questions:

17. How would digestion be affected if the liver were damaged?

18. Think about what happens when you put a piece of carbohydrate-dense food, such as bread, potato, or a cracker, in your mouth. If you let a small piece sit near the tip of your tongue, it might begin to taste sweet. What digestive process would explain this change?

MATH IN SCIENCE

19. Mr. Jones has lost all of his molars and two of his premolars. How many teeth does Mr. Jones have?

20. During a one-day water-balance study, a woman drank 1,500 mL of water. The food that she ate contained 750 mL of water, and 250 mL of water was produced internally during normal body processes. She lost 900 mL of water by sweating, 1,500 mL in urine, and 100 mL in feces. Overall, how much water did she gain or lose during the day?

INTERPRETING GRAPHICS

The bar graph below shows how long the average meal spends in each portion of your digestive tract. Use this graph to answer the questions below.

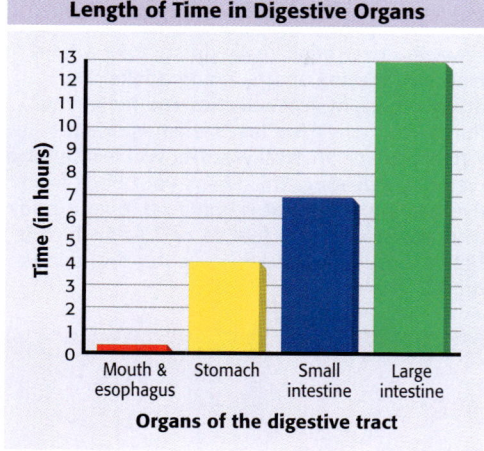

21. Where does the food spend the longest amount of time?

22. On average, how much longer does food stay in the small intestine than in the stomach?

23. Which organ mixes food with special substances to make chyme? Approximately how long does food remain in this organ?

24. Bile breaks up large fat droplets into very small droplets. How long is the food in your body before it comes into contact with bile?

 Take a minute to review your answers to the Pre-Reading Questions found at the bottom of page 566. Have your answers changed? If necessary, revise your answers based on what you have learned since you began this chapter.

Concept Mapping

16. An answer to this exercise can be found at the end of this book.

CRITICAL THINKING AND PROBLEM SOLVING

17. Sample answer: Digestion would be poor because the liver makes bile, which aids in the digestion of fats.

18. Sample answer: Saliva causes chemical digestion of the carbohydrate-dense food, breaking it down to become simple sugars, which taste sweet.

MATH IN SCIENCE

19. 18 remaining teeth
20. 0 gain, 0 loss

INTERPRETING GRAPHICS

21. in the large intestine
22. 3 hours
23. The stomach mixes food with enzymes and acid to make a soupy mixture called chyme. Food stays in the stomach for approximately 4 hours.
24. just over 4 hours

 Concept Mapping Transparency 24

 Blackline masters of this Chapter Review can be found in the **Study Guide**.

Chapter 24 • Chapter Review

ACROSS THE SCIENCES
Chemistry
Quench Your Thirst!

Background
A portion of the brain called the hypothalamus contains nerve cells that monitor the concentration of sodium in the blood. When the concentration of sodium is high, these cells perform two important functions. First, they send messages to the pituitary gland, which releases antidiuretic hormone (ADH). This hormone signals the kidneys to return water to the bloodstream. Aside from signaling the pituitary gland, these nerve cells also signal the salivary glands to produce less saliva. With less saliva, the mouth becomes dry. This creates a sensation of thirst and signals the person to get a drink.

As body heat rises, the body begins to lose potassium. This is due mainly to the fact that a hormone is released that increases the amount of potassium in urine. This hormone, called aldosterone, signals the kidneys to force potassium out of the blood vessels and into the nephron tubes. The potassium is then eliminated from the body in the urine. Sports drinks help replace this essential ion in the blood. But water is the most important component of these drinks, and plain water is often just as helpful as a sports drink to a person exercising.

LIFE SCIENCE • CHEMISTRY

Quench Your Thirst!

Have you ever been really thirsty after a hard workout? Playing sports, riding a bike, and doing other physical activities can make you thirsty—but why? The first reason is sweat. When you are physically active, you lose a lot of water by sweating. This keeps your body from overheating. But what is going on in your body to make your mouth feel so dry? And which is better to quench your thirst, water or a sports drink?

▲ *Activities that make you hot and sweaty make you want to take a drink, but why?*

Thirsty Chemistry
When you lose water, your blood becomes more concentrated. Think about how you make a powdered drink, such as lemonade. If you use the same amount of powder in 1 L of water as you do in 2 L, the drinks will taste different. The lemonade made with 1 L of water will be stronger because it is more concentrated.

Losing water to sweat increases the concentration of sodium and potassium in your blood. The kidneys force the extra potassium out of the blood vessels and into nephrons. From the nephrons, the potassium is eliminated from the body in urine. Nerve cells in your brain react to the high concentration of sodium by sending out two important messages. One message tells the pituitary gland to release antidiuretic hormone. This hormone signals the kidneys to return water to the bloodstream. The second message signals the salivary glands to produce less saliva. With less saliva, your mouth becomes dry, and then you know it's time to get that drink!

With Flavor or Without?
But which is better to drink—water or a sports drink? If you have been exercising, you might think a sports drink is probably better. But studies by Kathy Grunewald, a professor at Kansas State University, indicate that sports drinks may not be necessary unless you have exercised very hard or for more than an hour and a half.

When you drink fluids, you lower the concentration of all the minerals in your blood by adding more water. This is like adding water to the 1 L of strong lemonade. The body also needs to replace the potassium that was lost from the blood. A sports drink can help replace this potassium. But if you drink water, the kidneys will eventually return the potassium concentration to normal. The most important reason for drinking fluids after physical exercise is to get water to your tissues. So whatever physical activity you choose, drink up!

Going Further
▶ If you want to investigate how much you need to drink, weigh yourself before and after your next strenuous activity. Every kilogram that you lose represents about 1 L of water. You should make sure that you drink at least as much water as you lose.

Answer to Going Further
Make sure students know that dehydration is very dangerous. Remind them to drink plenty of fluids during and after strenuous activity.

Health Watch

A Voiceless Companion

If you decided to eat the last piece of pizza in the refrigerator, someone just might ask you for a bite, right? But what if you found out that you had a constant mealtime companion who didn't want just a bite but wanted it all? And what if that companion never asked for your permission?

How to Be a Host

This constant mealtime companion might be a tapeworm. Tapeworms are invertebrate flatworms. These flatworms are parasites. A parasite is an organism that obtains its food by living in or on another living organism. The organism in which a parasite makes its home is called a host. People, cows, pigs, fish, cats, dogs, and many insects are the perfect hosts for tapeworms. Without a host, tapeworms can't survive.

Food broken down in the stomach continues to be broken down in the small intestine. Since a tapeworm doesn't have a digestive tract of its own, it borrows its host's. By attaching itself to the inside of its host's small intestine with clamps and suckers, a tapeworm can eat as much as it likes.

Although tapeworms aren't much thicker than a ribbon, they can grow to more than 6 m in length! They do this by adding one postage-stamp-sized segment at a time. Each segment has both male and female reproductive organs and can be filled with thousands of eggs.

Saying "Goodbye" and Avoiding "Hello"

When an egg-filled segment breaks off, it passes through the rest of the host's digestive tract and ends up in the feces. If another animal eats or drinks something contaminated with these feces, the eggs grow into worms in that animal's intestines. The eggs can then spread to muscle tissues (called meat in animals used for food). If humans eat this meat but don't cook it thoroughly enough to kill tapeworm larvae, the cycle begins all over again.

Getting rid of a tapeworm requires removing the head, or scolex. If the scolex is left behind, it simply produces new segments, and the tapeworm regrows itself. Sometimes humans don't realize they have a tapeworm, even though they suffer from symptoms such as weight loss and nausea. And occasionally there are no symptoms at all.

The best way to avoid these parasites is to avoid eating undercooked beef, pork, and fish. If you do this, you won't have any uninvited guests at your next meal!

▲ *What is 10 m long, looks like it's made of postage stamps, and eats your dinner after you do?*

Think About It

▶ Doctors prescribe certain medications to get rid of tapeworms. Research the different ways people got rid of tapeworms before modern medicines were available.

Chapter Organizer

CHAPTER ORGANIZATION	TIME MINUTES	OBJECTIVES	LABS, INVESTIGATIONS, AND DEMONSTRATIONS
Chapter Opener pp. 586–587	45	National Standards: SAI 1, HNS 3, LS 1e	**Start-Up Activity** Act Fast! p. 587
Section 1 The Nervous System	90	▶ Explain how neurons in the nervous system work together. ▶ Compare the central nervous system with the peripheral nervous system. ▶ Describe the major functions of the brain and the spinal cord. UCP 1, 2, 4, 5, SAI 1, 2, SPSP 1, 5, LS 1a, 1d–1f, 3a–3c	**Demonstration,** Simulating Neuronal Impulses, p. 590 in ATE GENERAL **QuickLab,** Knee Jerks, p. 594 GENERAL
Section 2 Responding to the Environment	90	▶ List four sensations that are detected by receptors in the skin. ▶ Describe how light relates to vision. ▶ Explain the functions of photoreceptors, taste buds, and olfactory cells. UCP 2, 4, 5, SPSP 1, 5, LS 1a, 1d 1e, 3a; LabBook UCP 2, SAI 1, LS 3a	**Quick Lab,** Where's the Dot? p. 597 GENERAL **Skill Builder,** You've Gotta Lotta Nerve, p. 772 BASIC **Datasheets for LabBook,** You've Gotta Lotta Nerve, Worksheet 53 BASIC **Whiz-Bang Demonstrations,** Now You See It, Now You Don't, Demo 15 GENERAL **Labs You Can Eat,** A Salty Sweet Experiment, Lab 9 GENERAL
Section 3 The Endocrine System	90	▶ Explain the function of the endocrine system. ▶ List the glands of the endocrine system and describe some of their functions. ▶ Describe how feedback controls stop and start hormone release. UCP 1, 3, 4, SPSP 5, LS 1e, 1f, 3a–3c	**Long-Term Projects & Research Ideas,** Project 25 ADVANCED

See page **T20** for a complete correlation of this book with the

NATIONAL SCIENCE EDUCATION STANDARDS.

TECHNOLOGY RESOURCES

 Guided Reading Audio CD English or Spanish, Chapter 25

 One-Stop Planner CD-ROM with Test Generator

 CNN Science, Technology & Society, Correcting Colorblindness, Segment 2
Brain Cell Visuals, Segment 23
Learning from Frog Ears, Segment 26
Easy Touch Toys, Segment 33

Chapter 25 • Communication and Control

CLASSROOM WORKSHEETS, TRANSPARENCIES, AND RESOURCES	SCIENCE INTEGRATION AND CONNECTIONS	REVIEW AND ASSESSMENT
Directed Reading Worksheet 25 BASIC **Science Puzzlers, Twisters & Teasers,** Worksheet 25 ADVANCED		
Transparency 89, The Neuron **Directed Reading Worksheet 25,** Section 1 BASIC **Transparency 90,** What's in a Nerve? **Reinforcement Worksheet 25,** This System Is Just "Two" Nervous! BASIC **Transparency 91,** Regions of the Brain **Transparency 92,** The Spinal Cord	**Math Break,** Time to Travel, p. 589 GENERAL **Real-World Connection,** p. 591 in ATE **Cross-Disciplinary Focus,** p. 593 in ATE GENERAL **Eureka!** Pathway to a Cure, p. 609 GENERAL	**Homework,** p. 592 in ATE ADVANCED **Self-Check,** p. 593 **Review,** p. 594 GENERAL **Quiz,** p. 594 in ATE GENERAL **Alternative Assessment,** p. 594 in ATE GENERAL
Directed Reading Worksheet 25, Section 2 BASIC **Transparency 281,** Wavelength **Reinforcement Worksheet 25,** The Eyes Have It GENERAL **Critical Thinking Worksheet 25,** There's a Microchip in My Eye! ADVANCED	**Real-World Connection,** p. 596 in ATE **Connect to Physical Science,** p. 596 in ATE **Math and More,** p. 598 in ATE GENERAL **Physics Connection,** p. 598 **Science, Technology, and Society:** Light on Lenses, p. 608 ADVANCED	**Review,** p. 599 GENERAL **Quiz,** p. 599 in ATE GENERAL **Alternative Assessment,** p. 599 in ATE GENERAL
Directed Reading Worksheet 25, Section 3 BASIC **Reinforcement Worksheet 25,** Every Gland Lends a Hand BASIC	**Apply,** p. 601 GENERAL **Math and More,** p. 602 in ATE ADVANCED	**Homework,** p. 602 in ATE ADVANCED **Review,** p. 603 GENERAL **Quiz,** p. 603 in ATE GENERAL **Alternative Assessment,** p. 603 in ATE GENERAL

internet connect

Holt, Rinehart and Winston On-line Resources
go.hrw.com

For worksheets and other teaching aids related to this chapter, visit the HRW Web site and type in the keyword: **HSTBD4**

National Science Teachers Association
www.scilinks.org

Encourage students to use the *sci*LINKS numbers listed in the internet connect boxes to access information and resources on the **NSTA** Web site.

END-OF-CHAPTER REVIEW AND ASSESSMENT

Chapter Review in Study Guide
Vocabulary and Notes in Study Guide
Chapter Tests with Performance-Based Assessment, Chapter 25 Test
Chapter Tests with Performance-Based Assessment, Performance-Based Assessment 25
Concept Mapping Transparency 25

Chapter Resources & Worksheets

Visual Resources

TEACHING TRANSPARENCIES

TEACHING TRANSPARENCIES

CONCEPT MAPPING TRANSPARENCY

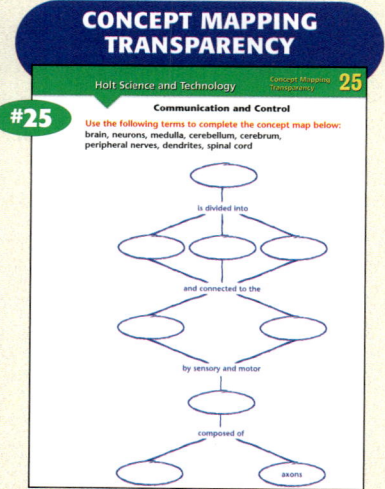

Meeting Individual Needs

DIRECTED READING

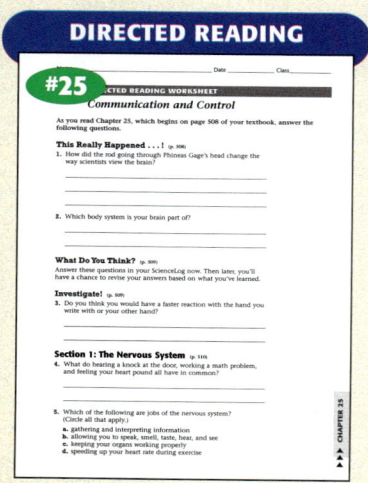

REINFORCEMENT & VOCABULARY REVIEW

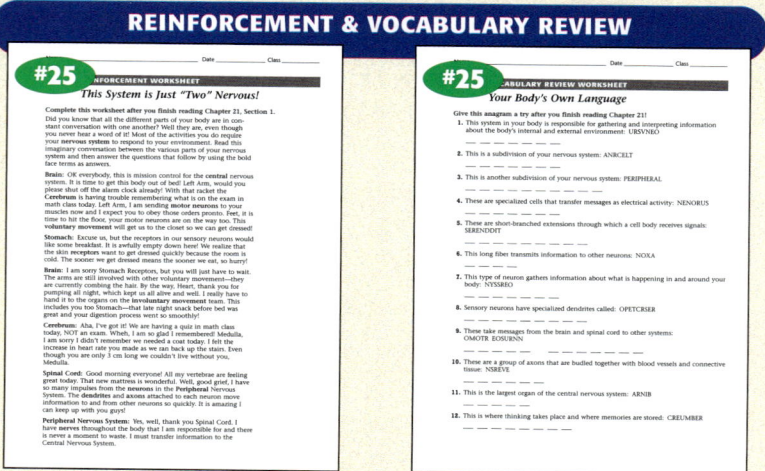

SCIENCE PUZZLERS, TWISTERS & TEASERS

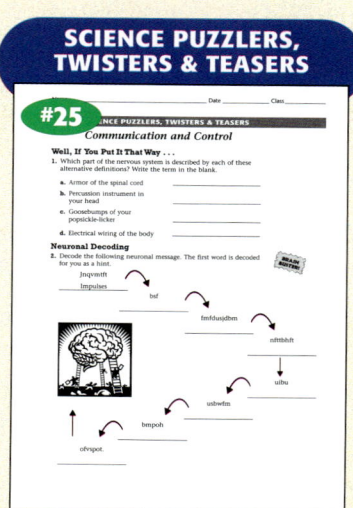

585C Chapter 25 • Communication and Control

Chapter 25 • Communication and Control

Review & Assessment

STUDY GUIDE

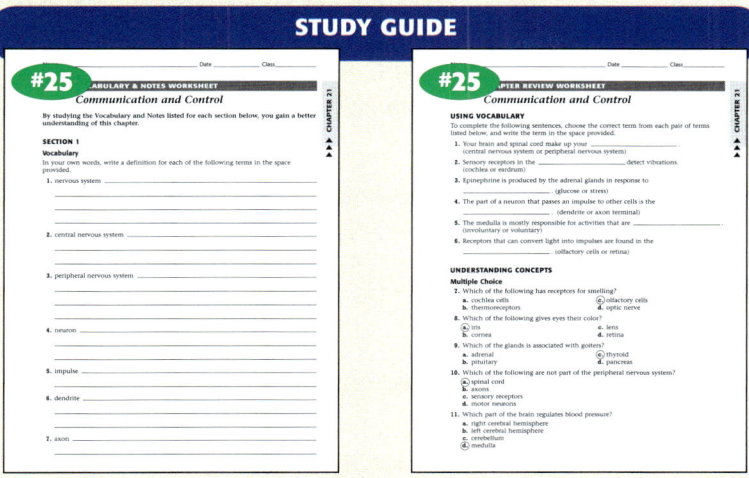

CHAPTER TESTS WITH PERFORMANCE-BASED ASSESSMENT

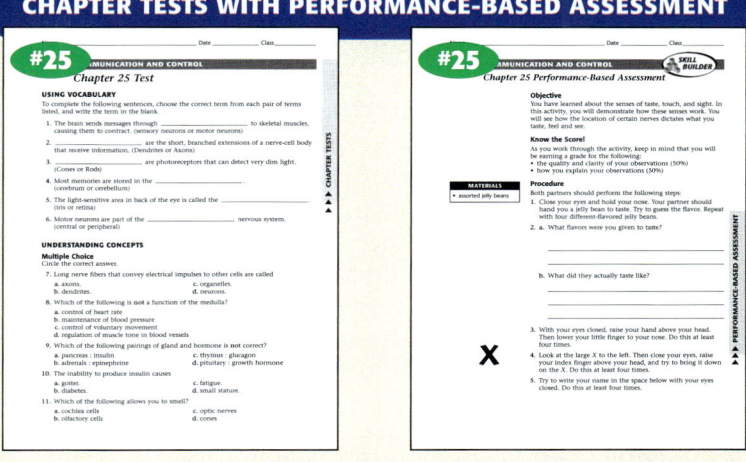

Lab Worksheets

WHIZ-BANG DEMONSTRATIONS

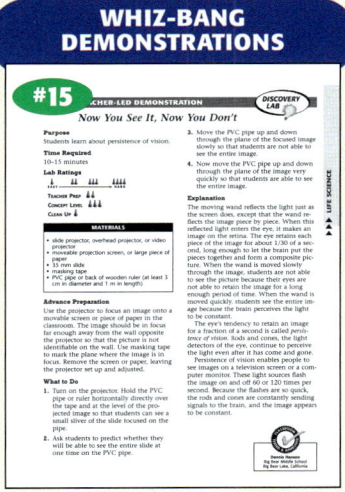

LABS YOU CAN EAT

LONG-TERM PROJECTS & RESEARCH IDEAS

DATASHEETS FOR LABBOOK

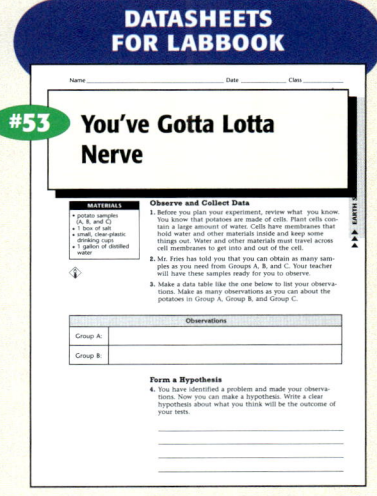

Applications & Extensions

CRITICAL THINKING & PROBLEM SOLVING

SCIENCE TECHNOLOGY

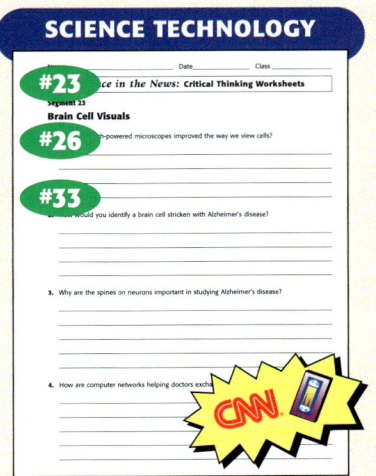

Chapter 25 • Chapter Resources & Worksheets   585D

Chapter Background

SECTION 1

The Nervous System

▶ **The Brain**
The cerebrum's surface area is a more significant indicator of an organism's ability to think and perform than is the brain's volume or weight. The surface area of a porpoise's cerebrum relative to its body size is second to that of the human cerebrum.

- Computerized scanning techniques allow physicians to take pictures of the brain to detect abnormalities. Scanning techniques include CT scanning, MRI scanning, radionucleotide scanning, ultrasound scanning, and PET scanning.

IS THAT A FACT!

◆ The cerebral cortex makes up more than 80 percent of the total human brain mass.

▶ **The Spinal Cord**
Like the brain, the spinal cord contains both gray matter and white matter. The center of the spinal cord is made up of neuron cell bodies and is called gray matter. The outer layer of the spinal cord is made up of axons that traverse the spinal cord. This part of the spinal cord is called white matter.

- The spinal cord is protected by 25 bones, the vertebrae and the sacrum. These bones are connected by joints and separated by cartilaginous disks.

SECTION 2

Responding to the Environment

▶ **Hearing Loss**
There are two principal kinds of deafness: conductive deafness and sensorineural deafness. Conductive deafness results when transmission of sound from the outer ear to the inner ear fails. It may occur as a result of earwax buildup or damage to the middle ear.

- Sensorineural deafness results when sounds reach the inner ear but are not transmitted to the brain due to either damaged inner ear structures or damaged nerves that carry information from the ear to the brain.

IS THAT A FACT!

◆ Sensorineural deafness occurs in 1 out of every 1,000 babies.

▶ **The Eye Doctor**
Ophthalmologists are physicians who specialize in the eyes. An ophthalmologist can examine eyes, prescribe corrective lenses, treat eye disorders, and perform eye surgery.

- An optician may only fit and adjust glasses and contact lenses.

- An optometrist can examine and test eyes and prescribe corrective lenses in the form of glasses or contact lenses.

IS THAT A FACT!

◆ The idea of using contact lenses to correct poor vision was first recorded by Leonardo da Vinci (1452–1519) in 1508.

◆ The first contact lens was made of glass. It covered the entire frontal surface of the eyeball. This first lens was made by Adolf Fick in 1887.

▶ **The Sense of Taste**
Saliva dissolves chemicals in the food and drink we consume. After passing through pores in the taste buds, these chemicals stimulate small nerve endings, which send messages to the brain. These messages form our sense of taste.

Chapter 25 • Communication and Control

- People often lose their sense of taste when they lose their sense of smell. This occurs when olfactory bulbs are damaged or when the person has a stuffy nose. It is rare for a person to maintain the sense of smell and to lose the sense of taste.

Section 3

The Endocrine System

▶ **Endocrine Glands**

There are two main types of glands in the body: exocrine glands and endocrine glands. Exocrine glands, such as sweat glands and salivary glands, secrete substances through ducts to a local area. Unlike exocrine glands, endocrine glands secrete substances directly into the bloodstream (no ducts are involved). The substances secreted by endocrine glands are carried, often to distant parts of the body, by the bloodstream and have effects throughout the body.

▶ **The Pituitary Gland**

The pituitary gland is often called the master gland because its secretions regulate several other endocrine glands.

- About 10 percent of brain tumors affect the pituitary gland. Although usually benign, these tumors can have a great effect on the body because they can affect the production of the pituitary hormones.

- Because of the pituitary gland's location in the brain, enlargement of the gland can cause vision disorders by creating pressure on the nearby optic nerve.

▶ **Diabetes**

The term *diabetes* refers to more than one disorder. There is diabetes insipidus (a rare condition) and diabetes mellitus, of which there are two types. Type I requires regular injections of insulin. Type II can often be controlled by changes in diet and exercise, although insulin injections might also be necessary.

IS THAT A FACT!

- As many as 200 of every 100,000 people in the United States suffer from Type I diabetes.

- About 2,000 of every 100,000 people in the United States have Type II diabetes.

For background information about teaching strategies and issues, refer to the *Professional Reference for Teachers*.

Chapter 25 • Chapter Background

Chapter 25

Communication and Control

Pre-Reading Questions

Students may not know the answers to these questions before reading the chapter, so accept any reasonable response.

Suggested Answers

1. Answers will vary, but some students may suggest that the senses provide the brain with information that can help the individual respond appropriately to environmental changes.

2. Answers will vary, but some students may suggest that during a fight-or-flight response, your body needs extra blood supply to either run or fight for survival.

3. Lenses help bring images into focus. A concave lens corrects nearsightedness, and a convex lens corrects farsightedness.

Directed Reading Worksheet 25

Science Puzzlers, Twisters & Teasers Worksheet 25

Guided Reading Audio CD
English or Spanish, Chapter 25

Chapter 25

Communication and Control

Sections

1. **The Nervous System** .. 588
   - MathBreak 589
   - QuickLab 594

2. **Responding to the Environment** 595
   - QuickLab 597
   - Physics Connection .. 598
   - Internet Connect 599

3. **The Endocrine System** 600
   - Apply 601
   - Internet Connect 603

Chapter Review 606
Feature Articles 608, 609
LabBook 772–773

1. What are your senses? How do senses help us survive?
2. Why does your heart beat faster when something frightens you?
3. How do eyeglasses and contact lenses help some people see better?

586

Outta Sight!

This may look like a flower garden or an oceanic reef. But it's really something much closer to home. It's the human tongue (magnified thousands of times, of course). You know these round bumps as *taste buds*. You use taste and other senses to gather information about your surroundings. This information helps your body respond to its environment. In this chapter, you will find out how the human body senses the world and controls its own functions.

---

 internet connect

HRW On-line Resources
go.hrw.com
For worksheets and other teaching aids, visit the HRW Web site and type in the keyword: **HSTBD4**

www.scilinks.com
Use the *sci*LINKS numbers at the end of each chapter for additional resources on the **NSTA** Web site.

www.cnnfyi.com
Visit the CNN Web site for current events coverage and classroom resources.

586 Chapter 25 • Communication and Control

START-UP Activity

ACT FAST!

If you want to catch an object, your brain sends a message to your arm's muscles. In this exercise, you will see how long that takes.

Procedure

1. Sit in a **chair** with one arm in a "handshake" position. Your partner should stand facing you, holding a **meterstick** vertically. The stick should be positioned to fall between your thumb and fingers.

2. Tell your partner to let go of the meterstick without warning. Catch the stick between your thumb and fingers. Your partner should catch the meterstick if it tips over.

3. Record the number of centimeters the stick dropped before you caught it. That distance represents your reaction time.

4. Repeat steps 1–3 three times. Calculate the average distance.

5. Repeat steps 1–4 with your other hand.

6. Trade places with your partner, and repeat steps 1–5.

Analysis

7. Compare the reaction times of your own hands. Why might one hand react faster?

8. Compare your results with your partner's. Why might one person react faster than another?

START-UP Activity

ACT FAST!

MATERIALS

FOR EACH GROUP:
- meterstick

Safety Caution

Remind students to handle the meterstick carefully and to keep it away from their face and far away from the faces and eyes of their classmates. Allow students to have a practice trial. Instruct students to look only at the ruler and not at their partner.

Teacher's Notes

Point out to students that looking at their partner could distort the results of the investigation because the partner might give a clue about when he or she will drop the meterstick. Remind students to use the correct units of measurement when calculating average distances.

Answers to START-UP Activity

7. Answers will vary, but some students might notice a difference between the reaction time of the left hand and that of the right hand. We use each hand differently, so each has different abilities.

8. Student answers will vary, but possible inferences include how rested an individual feels or if distractions occur in the room.

Chapter 25 • Communication and Control

SECTION 1

Focus

The Nervous System

This section introduces the structures and functions of the nervous system. Students will learn the differences between the central nervous system, which includes the brain and spinal cord, and the peripheral nervous system, which consists of nerves that connect every area of the body to the central nervous system.

Ask students to list as many different functions of the brain as they can in their ScienceLog. After students complete their list, you may want to make a master list on the board or on a transparency. Explain that in this chapter, students will learn how the brain coordinates these many different activities.

1) Motivate

DISCUSSION

Reacting to Stimuli Invite students to describe a time when they reacted quickly. Encourage students to describe not only what happened but also how quickly they were able to react and what they were thinking about as they reacted. Sample experiences include jerking a hand away from a hot object, quickly catching a falling object, and extending one's hand out to brace for a fall. Based on students' experiences, lead a discussion about how quickly the nervous system is able to respond to a stimulus.
Sheltered English

Section 1

Terms to Learn

central nervous system
peripheral nervous system
neuron
impulse
receptor
nerve
brain
reflex

What You'll Do

- Explain how neurons in the nervous system work together.
- Compare the central nervous system with the peripheral nervous system.
- Describe the major functions of the brain and the spinal cord.

The Nervous System

What do the following events have in common? You hear a knock at the door, you write a book report, you feel your heart pounding after a run, you work a math problem, you are startled by a loud noise, and you enjoy eating a sweet mango. These events are all activities of your nervous system. The nervous system gathers and interprets information about the body's internal and external environments and responds to that information. The nervous system keeps your organs working properly and allows you to speak, smell, taste, hear, see, move, think, and experience emotions.

Two Systems Within a System

Your nervous system controls and coordinates many things that happen in your body. It acts as a central command post, collecting and processing information and making sure appropriate information gets sent to all parts of the body. These tasks are accomplished by two subdivisions of the nervous system, the *central nervous system* and the *peripheral nervous system*. The **central nervous system** (CNS) includes your brain and spinal cord. It processes all incoming and outgoing messages. The **peripheral nervous system** (PNS) consists of communication pathways, or *nerves*, that connect all areas of your body to your CNS. **Figure 1** shows the major divisions of the nervous system.

Figure 1 *The CNS (in orange) acts as the control center for your body. The PNS (in purple) carries information to and from the CNS.*

WEIRD SCIENCE

Human skulls from 20,000 years ago provide evidence that ancient humans cut and drilled holes into each other's heads. This ancient practice is called trephining, and it may have been intended to release evil spirits believed to cause mental problems or illnesses such as migraines or epilepsy. Evidence of this surgery has been found in skulls from Europe, North Africa, parts of Asia, New Zealand, some Pacific Islands, and South America.

The Peripheral Nervous System

How long does it take for a light to come on when you flip a light switch? The light seems to come on immediately. In a similar way, specialized cells called **neurons** transfer messages throughout your body in the form of fast-moving electrical energy. A typical neuron is shown in **Figure 2**. The electrical messages that pass along the neurons are called **impulses**. Impulses may travel as fast as 150 m/s or as slow as 0.2 m/s.

Neuron Structure A neuron consists of a cell body, dendrites, and axons. The enlarged region called the cell body contains a nucleus and cell organelles. Look again at Figure 2. The neuron generally receives information from other cells through short, branched extensions called *dendrites*. A neuron may have many dendrites, allowing it to receive impulses from thousands of other cells.

From the cell body, information is transmitted to other cells by a fiber called an *axon*. Axons can be very short or quite long. You have some really long axons that extend almost 1 m from your lower back to your toes. The end of an axon often has branches that allow information to pass to yet more cells. The tip of each branch is called an *axon terminal*.

MATH BREAK

Time to Travel
To calculate how long it takes for an impulse to travel a certain distance, you can use the following equation:

$$\text{Time} = \frac{\text{distance}}{\text{speed}}$$

If an impulse travels 100 m/s, about how long would it take for an impulse to travel 10 m?

Figure 2 Neurons are special cells that transfer electrical messages throughout the body.

IS THAT A FACT!

Unlike humans, canaries replace old brain cells with new neurons each year. Male canaries even sing a new song every spring. Their brain-cell clusters associated with vocalization grow larger during the spring, when males compose their new melodies and females learn to recognize them. In the fall, the brain clusters shrink, neurons die, and the males forget what they sang. Scientists theorize that this happens so that these birds can acquire new information without having to carry around a large and heavy brain.

② Teach, continued

MEETING INDIVIDUAL NEEDS

Learners Having Difficulty
To help students visualize the central and peripheral nervous systems, have them work in pairs to trace the outline of one student's body on butcher paper. Next have each pair fill in the outline, using different colors for each of the nervous systems. Models should include the brain and the spinal cord (the central nervous system), and sensory and motor neurons throughout the body (the peripheral nervous system). **Sheltered English**

DEMONSTRATION

Simulating Neuronal Impulses
Ask students to form a circle and hold hands. Explain that each person in the circle represents a neuron. Every left hand represents a dendrite, every body represents a cell body, and every right hand represents an axon. Join the circle, and initiate a nerve impulse by gently squeezing the hand of the student to your right. Instruct students to pass the nerve impulse to the person to their right by gently squeezing his or her hand. Once students understand the mechanics of the activity, have them call out *dendrite, cell body,* and *axon* as the impulse is passed along the circle. **Sheltered English**

Teaching Transparency 90
"What's in a Nerve?"

Reinforcement Worksheet 25
"This System Is Just 'Two' Nervous!"

BRAIN FOOD
The number of neurons in your brain is about 100 billion, which is about the same as the number of stars in the Milky Way galaxy!

Information Collection Special neurons called *sensory neurons* gather information about what is happening in and around your body and send this information on to the central nervous system for processing. Sensory neurons have specialized dendrites called **receptors** that detect changes inside and outside the body. For example, receptors in your eyes detect the light around you. Receptors in your stomach let your brain know when your stomach is full or empty.

Delivering Orders Neurons that send impulses from the brain and spinal cord to other systems are called *motor neurons*. Motor means "to move"; when muscles get impulses from motor neurons, they respond by contracting. For example, motor neurons cause the muscles around your eyes to move when the sensory neurons in your eyes detect bright light. This movement makes you squint, which reduces the amount of light entering the eye. Motor neurons also send messages to your glands, such as sweat glands. These messages tell the sweat glands to release sweat.

Just a Bundle of Axons

The central nervous system is connected to the rest of your body by nerves. **Nerves** are axons bundled together with blood vessels and connective tissue. Nerves extend throughout your body. Most nerves contain the axons of both sensory and motor neurons. **Figure 3** shows the structure of a nerve. The axon in this nerve transmits information from the spinal cord to muscle fibers.

Spinal cord
Nerve

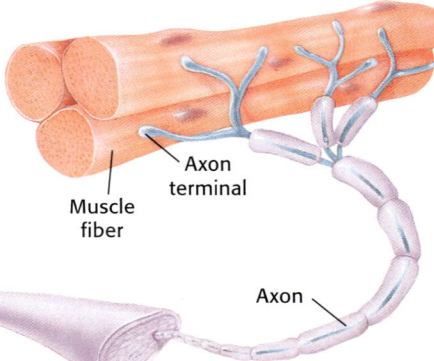
Axon terminal
Muscle fiber
Axon

Figure 3 *In order for a muscle to contract, a message must travel from the spinal cord to the muscle. The message travels along the axon of a motor neuron inside the nerve.*

TOPIC: The Nervous System
GO TO: www.scilinks.org
*sci*LINKS NUMBER: HSTL605

SCIENCE HUMOR
Q: How do nerves shop?
A: They buy only on impulse.

590   Chapter 25 • Communication and Control

The Central Nervous System

The central nervous system works closely with the peripheral nervous system. It receives information from the sensory neurons and responds by sending messages to various parts of the body via motor neurons.

Mission Control The **brain,** part of your central nervous system, is the nervous system's largest organ. It has hundreds of different jobs. Many of the processes that the brain controls happen automatically and are referred to as *involuntary*. For example, you couldn't stop digesting the food you have eaten even if you tried. Other activities controlled by your brain are *voluntary*. When you want to move your arm, your brain sends signals along motor neurons to muscles in your arm. This causes the muscles to contract and your arm to move. The brain has three connected parts—the cerebrum, the cerebellum, and the medulla. Each part has its own functions.

The organism with the largest brain is the sperm whale. Its brain is six times the size of a human brain!

Your Thinking Cap The largest part of your brain is called the *cerebrum*. Its shape resembles a mushroom cap over a stalk. This dome-shaped area is where you think and where most memories are stored. It controls voluntary movements and allows you to detect touch, light, sound, odors, taste, pain, heat, and cold.

The cerebrum has two halves called *hemispheres*. The left hemisphere directs the right side of the body, and the right hemisphere directs the left side of the body. This is because axons cross over to the opposite side of the body in the spinal cord. **Figure 4** gives a general model of the activities that each hemisphere controls. However, most brain activity involves both hemispheres.

Figure 4
The Cerebral Hemispheres

▼ The **right hemisphere** primarily controls activities that involve imagination, appreciation, and creativity.

The **left hemisphere** ▶ primarily controls activities such as speaking, reading, writing, and solving problems.

READING STRATEGY

Prediction Guide Before students read this section, ask them whether the following statements are true or false.

1. The brain is the body's largest organ. (false)
2. The largest part of the brain is the cerebrum. (true)
3. The medulla is responsible for speech and balance. (false)
4. The spinal cord is about as big around as your thumb. (true)

Have students evaluate their answers after they have read these pages.

REAL-WORLD CONNECTION

Students have probably watched people faint in movies or television shows. Point out that fainting and other forms of unconsciousness, except sleeping, are usually the result of some problem in the brain. Fainting is often caused by suddenly low blood pressure and insufficient blood flow to the cerebrum.

IS THAT A FACT!

What is most amazing about the human brain is not its size—a sperm whale's brain is about six times larger. It is the high proportion of brain size to body size as well as the huge surface area. The cerebral hemispheres are folded and wrinkled; but laid out flat, the brain would cover the surface of an office desk. This large surface provides room for highly complex and sophisticated connections.

2) Teach, continued

RETEACHING

If students have difficulty distinguishing the structures of the brain, make a life-size model of the brain as a class. Invite two volunteers to make a silhouette of the head; one student should be the model; the other, the tracer. Then draw in a brain. Have students take turns drawing and labeling the parts of the brain on the silhouette. Include the cerebrum, cerebellum, medulla, and the top of the spinal cord. Also have students label the hemisphere that is shown in the diagram. When the life-size model is complete, post it so students can refer to it as they review this section.
Sheltered English

Early anatomists Herophilus (C.335–C.280 B.C.) and Eristratus (C.276–c.194 B.C.) were experts at dissection, and they produced extensive work on human anatomy and physiology that is now on display at the Museum at Alexandria, in Egypt. Their dissections were discontinued, however, because of the Egyptian belief that the body must be kept intact for the afterlife. Another 15 centuries passed before dissection again was used to study human anatomy. You may want to have students compare the Egyptian views about dissection with modern-day views about organ donation.

Teaching Transparency 91
"Regions of the Brain"

Figure 5 Your cerebellum causes skeletal muscles to make adjustments in order to keep you upright.

The Balancing Act The second largest part of your brain is the *cerebellum* (SER uh BEL uhm). It lies underneath the back of your cerebrum and receives sensory impulses from skeletal muscles and joints. This allows the brain to keep track of your body's position. For example, if you begin to lose your balance, like the girl in **Figure 5,** the cerebellum sends impulses to different skeletal muscles to make them contract, keeping you upright.

The Mighty Medulla The part of your brain that connects to your spinal cord is called the *medulla* (mi DOOL uh). The medulla is only about 3 cm long, but you couldn't live without it. The medulla controls your blood pressure, heart rate, involuntary breathing, and some other involuntary activities.

Your medulla constantly receives sensory impulses from receptors in your blood vessels. It uses this information to regulate your blood pressure. If your blood pressure gets too low, the medulla sends out impulses that tell blood vessels to tighten up to increase the blood pressure. The medulla also sends impulses to the heart to make it beat faster or slower as necessary. **Figure 6** shows the location of each part of the brain and some of the functions associated with each part.

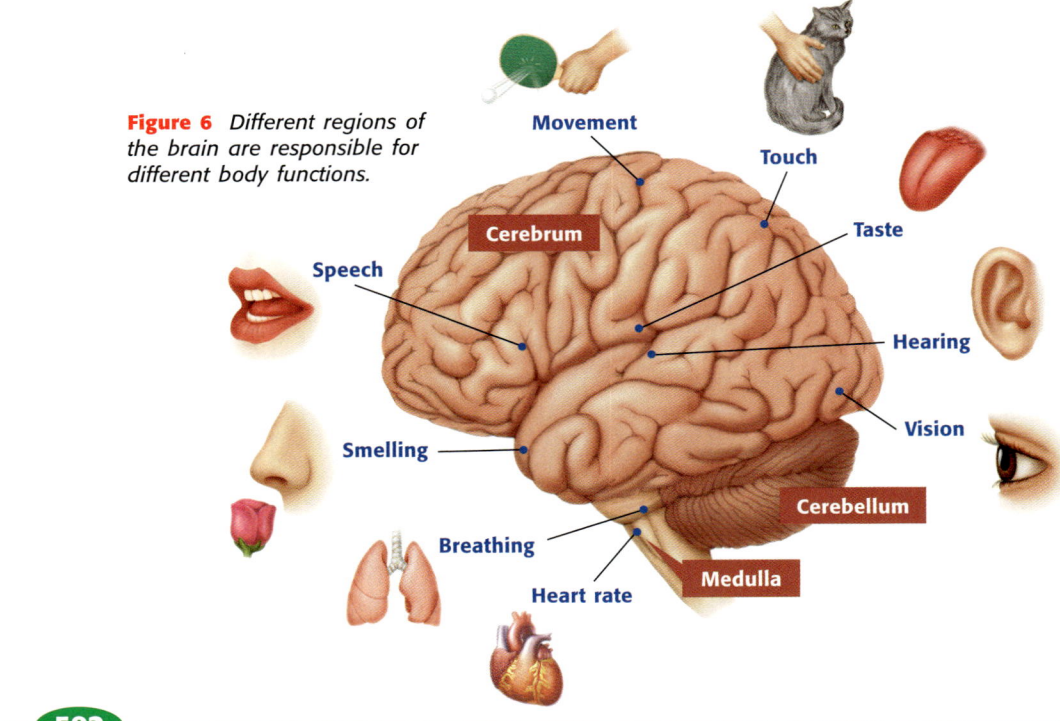

Figure 6 Different regions of the brain are responsible for different body functions.

Homework

Dream Research Dreaming, sleepwalking, and daydreaming are all phenomena of the brain. Have students research one of these topics and give group presentations before the class. They may use posters, signs, songs, skits, oral reports, and other techniques for their presentations.

IS THAT A FACT!

Synapses form in a human baby's brain at the rate of 3 billion a second. At 8 months, a baby's brain has about 1,000 trillion connections. After that, the number begins to decline. Half the connections die off by the time the child reaches age 10, leaving about 500 trillion.

The Spinal Cord

Your spinal cord, part of the central nervous system, is about as big around as your thumb. It contains neurons and bundles of axons that pass impulses to and from the brain. As shown in **Figure 7**, the spinal cord is surrounded by protective bones called *vertebrae* (VUHR tuh BRAY).

The nerve fibers in your spinal cord enable your brain to communicate with your peripheral nervous system. Sensory neurons in your skin and muscles send impulses along their axons to your spinal cord. The spinal cord then conducts impulses to your brain, where they can be interpreted as pain, heat, cold, or other sensations. Impulses moving from the brain down the cord are relayed to motor neurons, which carry the impulses along their axons to muscles and glands all over your body.

Spinal Cord Injury If the spinal cord is injured, any sensory information coming into it below where the damage occurred may be unable to travel to the brain. Likewise, any motor commands the brain sends to an area below the injury may not get through to the peripheral nerves. Thousands of people each year are paralyzed by spinal cord injuries. Many of these injuries occur in automobile accidents. Among young people, spinal cord injuries are often sports related.

Figure 7 The spinal cord carries information to and from the brain. It is protected by vertebrae.

Self-Check

1. What part of the brain do you use to do your math homework?
2. What part of the brain helps a gymnast maintain balance on the balance beam?
3. What is the function of the vertebrae?

(See page 782 to check your answers.)

IS THAT A FACT!

Sometimes it is not possible to inject anesthetic into a part of the body that needs to be anesthetized. In these cases, a *nerve block* is performed. In this procedure, anesthetic is injected into or around a nerve that feeds into the part of the body that needs to be anesthetized. Nerve blocks are often performed on nerves that carry messages away from the spine. This blocks the pain impulses before they reach the brain.

---

3) Extend

GUIDED PRACTICE

Concept Mapping List the following terms on the board:

brain, hemispheres, cerebrum, cerebellum, medulla, spinal cord, central nervous system, peripheral nervous system, sensory neurons, motor neurons

Have students construct a concept map that uses these terms.

CROSS-DISCIPLINARY FOCUS

Language Arts Long-term memory enables us to recall events that happened to us long ago. These memories can be triggered by a chance stimulus or can be deliberately recalled. Recalling memories helps us to refresh them and makes them last a lifetime. Ask students to write down their earliest memory, their happiest recollection, or their most embarrassing moment in their ScienceLog.

Answer to Self-Check

1. cerebrum
2. cerebellum
3. to protect the spinal cord

Teaching Transparency 92 "The Spinal Cord"

Section 1 • The Nervous System

4 Close

Quiz

Ask students whether these statements are true or false.

1. Typically, a dendrite will transmit an electrical impulse to a neighboring axon. (false)
2. Most neurons are made up of either axons or dendrites; few neurons have both. (false)
3. The central nervous system is made up of the brain and the spinal cord. (true)

ALTERNATIVE ASSESSMENT

Writing Have students develop an owner's guide for their central nervous system. The guide should include information about the various components of the central nervous system and a diagram showing their location in the body. Encourage students to share their guide with the class in the form of a presentation or a poster.

QuickLab

Safety Caution: Students should tap their partner's knee gently. There is no pain involved in a true reflex. Instruct students to tap while standing to the side of their partner to avoid being accidentally kicked.

Answers to QuickLab

2. Students should observe movement in the lower leg; no, an individual has no control over a reflex.
3. Students should indicate that the impulse traveled from the knee to the spinal cord and back to the thigh muscle that moves the lower leg.

Ouch! That Hurt!

Have you ever stepped on something sharp? You probably pulled your foot up without thinking. This quick, involuntary action is called a **reflex**. Reflexes help protect your body from damage.

When you step on a sharp object, the message "pain" travels to your spinal cord, and a message to move your foot travels back to the muscles in your leg. The muscles in your leg respond before the information ever reaches the brain. By the time your brain finds out what happened, your foot has already moved. If you had to wait for your brain to get the message, your foot might be seriously injured! The man in **Figure 8** lifted his foot before he realized he had stepped on a toy.

Figure 8 When pain impulses from your foot reach your spine, a message is sent immediately to your leg muscles to lift your foot.

QuickLab

Knee Jerks

1. Sit on the edge of a desk or table so your feet don't touch the floor.
2. While your leg is completely relaxed, have a classmate *gently* tap on your knee slightly below the kneecap with the edge of his or her hand. How did your leg respond? Did you have any control over what happened? Explain.
3. Describe the pathway taken by the impulse that started with the tap on the knee.

REVIEW

1. Make a labeled diagram that shows the path of an electrical message from one neuron to another neuron.
2. Explain how the peripheral nervous system connects with the central nervous system.
3. If a spider is crawling up your left arm, which cerebral hemisphere controls the movement that you will use to knock it off?
4. List the three major parts of the brain, and describe their functions.
5. **Applying Concepts** Describe a time when you experienced a reflex.

Answers to Review

1. Diagrams will vary but should show the following path: dendrite, cell body, axon, axon terminal, dendrite.
2. The peripheral nervous system consists of communication pathways, or nerves, that connect all areas of your body to your central nervous system.
3. You would use the left hemisphere, since you would have to use your right hand to knock it off.
4. The three major parts of the brain are the cerebrum, cerebellum, and medulla. Functions are described on pages 191 and 192.
5. Answers will vary but should demonstrate an understanding that reflexes involve involuntary muscle actions.

Section 2

Responding to the Environment

Terms to Learn

retina   iris
rods   lens
cones   cochlea

What You'll Do

- List four sensations that are detected by receptors in the skin.
- Describe how light relates to vision.
- Explain the functions of photoreceptors, taste buds, and olfactory cells.

How do you know when someone taps you on the shoulder or calls your name? How do you feel the touch or hear the sound? Impulses from sensory receptors in your shoulder and in your ears travel to your brain, sending information about your external environment. Your brain depends on this information to make decisions that affect your survival.

Come to Your Senses

Information about your surroundings and the conditions in your body is detected by sensory receptors. This information is converted to electrical signals and sent to your brain for interpretation. Once the signals reach your brain, you become aware of them. This awareness is called a *sensation*. It is in your brain that you have thoughts, feelings, and memories about sensations.

There are many different kinds of sensory receptors in your body. For example, receptors in your eyes detect light. Receptors in your ears detect vibrations called sound waves. The taste buds on your tongue have receptors that detect chemicals in the foods you eat. You have special receptors in your nose that detect tiny particles in the air. Your skin has a variety of receptors as well. Look at **Figure 9** to see some of the different kinds of receptors in the skin.

I've got to hand it to you—you've gotta lotta nerve. See for yourself on page 772 of your LabBook.

Figure 9 This diagram shows some of the receptors in your skin and what they detect.

Labels: Pressure and heat; Pressure; Light touch and pressure; Light touch; Deep pressure

WEIRD SCIENCE

One out of every 25,000 people has *synesthesia*. These people experience a blend of senses. They can hear colors, taste shapes, or other combinations of senses. When one of their senses is stimulated, another sense is also stimulated.

internet connect

TOPIC: The Senses
GO TO: www.scilinks.org
*sci*LINKS NUMBER: HSTL610

2) Teach

REAL-WORLD CONNECTION

Vision is commonly tested by using a Snellen's chart. This familiar chart consists of rows of letters set in decreasing size. A person who can correctly read a line of letters near the bottom of the chart from a distance of 6 m (20 ft) is said to have normal, or 20/20, vision. **Sheltered English**

MISCONCEPTION ALERT

Students may think that people who are colorblind see in black and white. People who are colorblind can usually perceive colors, but certain colors may appear very similar to one another. This is caused by a lack of at least one of the three cones in the eye. Many people do not know that they are colorblind because they have learned to distinguish other differences in their perception of colors.

CONNECT TO PHYSICAL SCIENCE

In the retina there are three types of cones that only respond to red, blue, or green light. When red cones and green cones are stimulated at the same time, the color yellow is perceived. White is perceived when all three kinds of cones are equally stimulated. Different colors of visible light have different wavelengths. Red has the longest wavelength, and violet has the shortest. Use the Teaching Transparency below to illustrate how wavelengths are measured.

Teaching Transparency 281 "Wavelength" *LINK TO PHYSICAL SCIENCE*

BRAIN FOOD

Carrots and other foods rich in vitamin A can improve your night vision. Vitamin A is important in maintaining proper functioning of the rods in your retina.

Something in My Eye

As you read this sentence, you are using one of your most important senses—*vision*. Vision is your awareness of light energy. Your eyes have special receptors that detect visible light, a portion of the sun's energy that reaches the Earth.

An Eyeful The eye is a complex sensory organ. Examine the eye in **Figure 10.** The outer surface of the eye is covered by the cornea, a transparent membrane that protects the eye but allows light to enter. Visible light that is reflected by objects around you enters through an opening at the front of your eye called the *pupil*. Light is detected by cells at the back of your eye in a light-sensitive layer called the **retina.**

The retina is packed with special neurons called *photoreceptor* (*photo* means "light") *cells* that respond to light. There are two types of photoreceptors in the retina—rods and cones. **Rods** can detect very dim light. They are important for night vision. Impulses from rods are perceived in tones of gray. In bright light, the **cones** give you a very colorful view of the world.

Light energy produces changes in photoreceptors that trigger nerve impulses. These impulses travel along axons, leaving the back of each eye through an *optic nerve*.

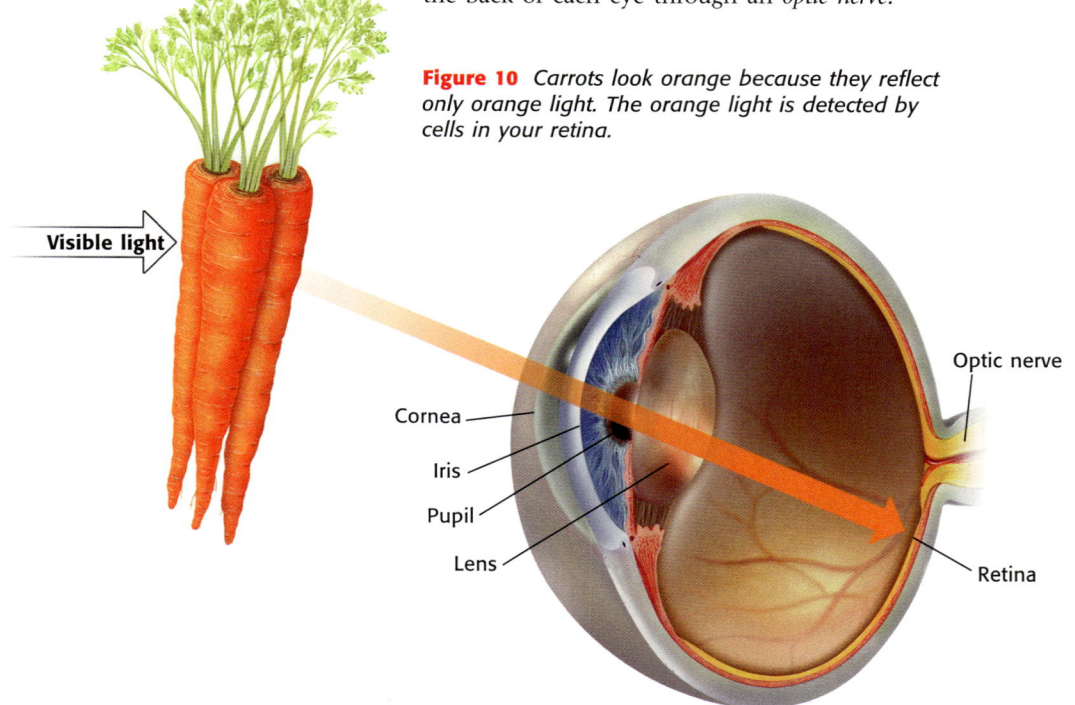

Figure 10 Carrots look orange because they reflect only orange light. The orange light is detected by cells in your retina.

WEIRD SCIENCE

Have students research and report on the tuatara, a reptile that has three eyes.

Seeing the Light Light rays enter the eye through the *pupil*. Your pupil looks like a black dot in the center of your eye, but it is actually an opening. It is surrounded by the **iris**, the part of the eye that gives the eye color. A ring of muscle fibers causes the iris to open and close, making the pupil change size. This regulates the amount of light that passes to the retina. In bright light, your pupil is small, and in dim light, your pupil is large.

Hocus Focus Light travels in straight lines until it passes through the cornea and the *lens*. A **lens** is a piece of curved material behind the pupil that allows light to pass through but changes its direction. The lens focuses the light entering the eye on the retina. The lens of an eye changes shape to adjust focus. When you look at objects close to the eye, the lens becomes more curved. When you look at objects far away, the lens gets flatter.

In some eyes, the lens focuses the light just in front of the retina (resulting in nearsightedness) or just behind the retina (resulting in farsightedness). Glasses or contact lenses can usually correct these vision problems. Focus on **Figure 11** to see how corrective lenses work.

What are some other uses of lenses? Turn to Light on Lenses on page 608 to find out.

Figure 11 *A concave lens bends light rays outward to correct nearsightedness. A convex lens bends light rays inward to correct farsightedness.*

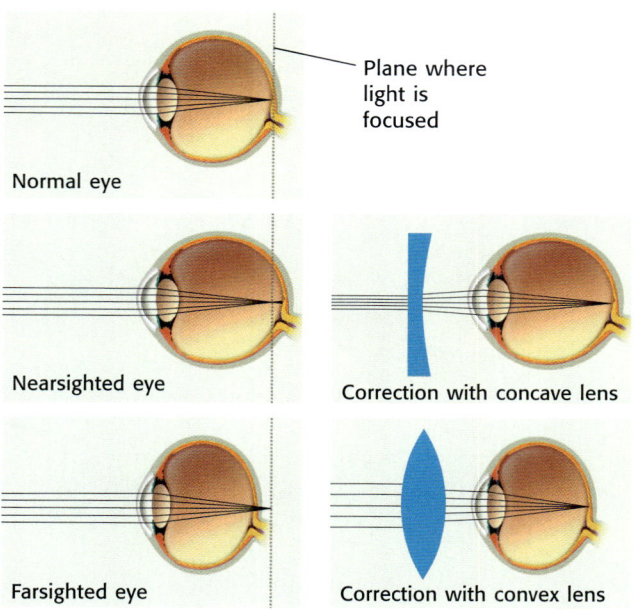

QuickLab

Where's the Dot?

1. Hold this book at arm's length, and close your right eye. Focus your left eye on the solid dot below.

2. Slowly move the book toward your face. Stay focused on the solid dot.
3. What happens to the white dot?
4. Do some research on the optic nerve to find out why this happens.

TRY at HOME

IS THAT A FACT!

Students may have noticed that young people are likely to hold a book very close to their face when reading, while adults tend to hold a book farther away from their face. Explain that the closest point on which a person can focus, called the near point of vision, changes with age. A typical child can focus on an object about 10 cm from his or her eyes (objects closer than the near point of vision can be seen but appear fuzzy). The change in the near point of vision is caused by the lens's decreasing elasticity over time.

Activity

Writing **Pupil Action** Ask students to write a paragraph that explains what happens to their eyes and vision when they first leave a dark movie theater on a sunny day. Students should discuss the change from dim to bright light and its effects on the pupils as well as on their ability to see.

Discussion

Eye Strain For us to see objects within a distance of 6 m, the muscles in the eye must work constantly to focus. Long periods of focusing on very near objects, such as a book, can tire the eye muscles and cause eyestrain. Ask students to suggest ways to avoid straining the eye muscles during these activities. (Answers may include taking breaks from the activity once an hour and looking up and allowing the eyes to relax occasionally.)

Answers to QuickLab

3. Students should observe that the white dot "disappears" when the image is held about 10 cm from their face. The exact point where this happens will vary from person to person. Encourage the students to try this several times until they get this result.
4. Students should discover that the area where the optic nerve leaves the back of the eyeball does not contain any photoreceptors and is called the blind spot. So when the white dot was focused on the eye's blind spot, it disappeared.

3) Extend

RESEARCH

Writing Prolonged exposure to loud sounds can result in a partial or complete loss of hearing. Have students research at what threshold noises are detrimental to hearing. Encourage students to arrange the information they gather into a report or a visual aid. **(Students should find that sounds greater than 90 dB can cause hearing loss over long periods of time.)**

MATH and MORE

Tell students that taste buds are shed approximately every 10 days. Ask students how many times a single taste bud is replaced in a year.

(365 $\frac{days}{year}$ ÷ 10 $\frac{days}{cycle}$ = 36.5 replacements in 1 year)

BRAIN FOOD

Owls have great hearing. In fact, some owls actually hunt by listening for mice tunneling under the snow. They have many adaptations that help them to hear so well. Feathers on the side of an owl's head are arranged to direct sound waves to very large ear openings. Furthermore, the feathers on an owl's face are rigid, and tightly packed into two parabolic formations which also direct sound waves toward the ears. This system works so well that owls can find mice in complete darkness and, according to experiments, are great hunters even when blindfolded.

Physics CONNECTION

Sound is produced by vibrating objects. Objects that vibrate more than 20,000 times a second produce sounds too high for humans to hear. Dolphins can detect sounds from objects that vibrate up to 150,000 times per second.

Did You "Ear" That?

When a guitar string is plucked, what enables you to hear the sound? A sound begins when an object, such as the guitar string, begins to vibrate. The vibrations push on surrounding air particles. These air particles push on other air particles, transferring energy in waves away from the source. Hearing is the sensation experienced in response to these sound waves.

Journey of a Sound Wave

Your ears are organs specialized for hearing. Each ear has an outer, middle, and inner part. The parts of the ear are shown in **Figure 12**. When sound waves reach the outer ear, they are funneled into the middle ear, where they cause the eardrum to vibrate. The vibrating eardrum makes tiny ear bones vibrate. One of the tiny bones vibrates against the **cochlea** (KAHK lee uh), a tiny snail-shaped organ of the inner ear. Inside the cochlea, the vibrations create waves that are similar to the waves you can make by tapping on a glass of water. Neurons in the cochlea convert these waves to electrical impulses and send them to the area of the brain that interprets sound.

Figure 12 A sound wave travels into the outer ear. It is converted to bone vibrations in the middle ear, then to liquid vibrations in the inner ear, and finally to nerve impulses.

IS THAT A FACT!

Although many people think that the perception of taste occurs primarily in the mouth, 80 percent of the perception of taste is actually the sense of smell.

SCIENCE

Some spicy foods, such as chile peppers, actually stimulate pain receptors in the mouth. This is why spicy foods feel like they are "burning" your mouth.

Does This Suit Your Taste?

When you put food in your mouth, your sense of what the food tastes like comes mostly from your tongue. Taste is the sensation you feel when the brain is made aware of certain dissolved chemicals in your mouth. The receptors for taste are clustered in the *taste buds*. The tongue is covered with tiny bumps called *papillae* (puh PIL ee). The taste buds are embedded in these bumps, as shown in **Figure 13.** Taste buds respond to the four basic tastes: sweet, sour, salty, and bitter.

Your Nose Knows

Have you ever noticed that when you have a congested nose you can't taste food very well? Try eating a piece of peppermint while holding your nose. The mint taste is not very intense until you inhale through your nose. That's because smell and taste are closely related. The brain combines information from your taste buds and nose to give you a sense of flavor. The receptors for smell are located on *olfactory cells* in the upper part of your nasal cavity. They react to chemicals that are inhaled and dissolved in the moist lining of the nasal cavity. The woman in **Figure 14** is using her sense of smell to test the effectiveness of underarm deodorants.

Figure 13 *Taste buds are located in tiny bumps on your tongue called papillae.*

Figure 14 *This woman's nose is detecting chemicals in the sweat and in the deodorants used by this man. Her brain will generate opinions about the smells that she will then record in her report.*

REVIEW

1. List three sensations that receptors in the skin can detect.
2. Explain why you would have trouble seeing bright colors at a candlelit dinner.
3. How is your sense of taste similar to your sense of smell?
4. **Applying Concepts** If you can focus on objects close to you but things become blurry when they are far away, would a concave or convex lens correct your vision?

internet connect

SC**INKS**
NSTA

TOPIC: The Senses, The Eye
GO TO: www.scilinks.org
sciLINKS NUMBER: HSTL610, HSTL615

SECTION 3

Focus

The Endocrine System

This section introduces students to the endocrine system. Students will learn how endocrine glands control the body's slower, long-term processes via hormones. They will also learn the location and function of specific endocrine glands. Hormonal imbalances that cause diabetes and goiter are also discussed.

Bellringer

Write the following on the board or overhead projector:

Unscramble the following words, and write them in your ScienceLog:

nalgd	(gland)
meornoh	(hormone)
noclotr	(control)

1) Motivate

DISCUSSION

Endocrine System Ask students how their pulse and breathing rate differed before and after being scared. (Both should be elevated.)

Tell students that the endocrine system is responsible for the changes that occurred in their pulse and breathing rate. Ask the students in each pair to tell their partner about a time when they were frightened and to describe the physical responses they had. Make a list on the board of the types of physical responses named. Return to this list when students read about the adrenal glands and the fight-or-flight response in this section.

Section 3

Terms to Learn

endocrine system
gland
hormone
feedback control

What You'll Do

- Explain the function of the endocrine system.
- List the glands of the endocrine system and describe some of their functions.
- Describe how feedback controls stop and start hormone release.

The Endocrine System

You already know that the job of the nervous system is to communicate with all the other body systems. Its main role is to respond to stimuli. But it is not the only system that has this role. Your **endocrine system** is involved with the control of slower, long-term processes, such as fluid balance, growth, and sexual development. Instead of electrical messages, the endocrine system sends messages via chemicals.

Chemical Messengers

The endocrine system controls body functions with the use of chemicals that are released from endocrine glands. A **gland** is a group of cells that makes special chemicals for your body. Chemicals that are produced by the endocrine glands are called **hormones.** The chemicals made by endocrine glands are released into the bloodstream and carried to other places in the body. Because hormones act as chemical messengers, an endocrine gland near your brain can control the actions of an organ located somewhere else in your body.

Glands at Work Endocrine glands often affect many organs at one time. For example, your adrenal glands prepare your organs to deal with stress. They make the hormone *epinephrine* (ep ih NEF rihn), also known as *adrenalin*. Epinephrine speeds up your heartbeat and breathing rate to prepare your body either to run from danger or to fight for survival. This hormone effect is often referred to as the fight-or-flight response. You may have noticed these effects when you were frightened or angry.

Figure 15 *When you have to move quickly to avoid danger, your adrenal glands help by making more blood glucose available for energy.*

IS THAT A FACT!

Epinephrine occurs naturally in the human body, but it is also administered as a drug by doctors. It can be injected into the heart to help revive a person who has suffered a heart attack. It also dilates the bronchioles of people with asthma.

Fight or Flight?

Maria was working late at the library. She was worried about walking home alone. As she started home, she noticed a shadowy figure walking quickly behind her. The figure was gaining on her! She could feel her heart pounding in her chest. She began to run, and then a familiar voice called out her name. It was her father. He had walked to the library to check on her. What a relief!

Maria had a fight-or-flight response. Write a paragraph describing a time when you had a fight-or-flight experience. Include in your story the following terms: *hormones*, *fight-or-flight*, and *epinephrine*.

Your body has several other endocrine glands, some with many different functions. For example, your pituitary gland stimulates skeletal growth, helps the thyroid function properly, regulates the amount of water in the blood, and stimulates the birth process in pregnant women. The names and some of the functions of this and other endocrine glands are summarized in **Figure 16**.

Figure 16 Your endocrine glands produce chemicals called hormones that control many of your body functions.

The **pituitary gland** secretes hormones that affect other glands and organs.

Your **thyroid gland** increases the rate at which you use energy.

The **parathyroid glands** (behind the thyroid) regulate calcium levels in the blood.

The **adrenal glands** help the body respond to stress and danger.

The **thymus gland** regulates the immune system, which helps your body fight disease.

The **pancreas** regulates blood sugar levels.

The **ovaries** produce hormones involved in reproduction.

The **testes**, in males, produce hormones involved in reproduction.

IS THAT A FACT!

Since the mid 1980s research at Rutgers University shows that some potent hormones in the last third of pregnancy prepare and motivate mothers to care for their young. The most important of these hormones is oxytocin. It is thought to reach the brain at the same time the mother meets her newborn, helping them to bond.

2) Teach

Answer to APPLY

Paragraphs will vary. Students should write about a time when they experienced a fight-or-flight response to stress and include the terms *hormone*, *fight-or-flight*, and *epinephrine*.

USING THE FIGURE

Write the following terms on a board or a transparency:

endocrine, pituitary, thyroid, parathyroid, thymus, adrenals, pancreas, ovaries, testes

As a class, pronounce each term. Then locate each gland shown in **Figure 16**.

BRAIN FOOD

Some cells found in tumors secrete hormones that are identical to those secreted by endocrine glands. Typically, the tumor cells secrete too much of the hormone and do not respond to feedback control. Ask students to speculate on the effects on the body of these tumor cells and the hormones they produce. (Students should recognize that when hormones are produced in improper amounts or in an uncontrolled way, the body's homeostasis will be disrupted. The specific effects will depend on the body's internal environment and on which hormones the tumor cells secrete.)

Directed Reading Worksheet 25 Section 3

3) Extend

USING THE FIGURE

Have students relate the events in **Figure 17** to the events that affect a thermostat. Ask: What happens when the temperature becomes too warm? (The air conditioner turns on and cools the room.)

What happens if the temperature becomes too cool? (The air conditioner turns off, and the room warms up.)

What is the overall effect of feedback control? (The level of the variable remains within a narrow range. It never becomes extremely high or extremely low and thus maintains homeostasis.)

MATH and MORE

After students have analyzed **Figure 17,** ask them to draw a graph that shows the changing levels of glucose in the blood over the course of the figure. (Graphs should approximate a sine curve.)

Have students label their graph "Negative feedback." Then draw a graph that shows a line at a nearly 45° angle on the board or a transparency, and label it "Positive feedback." Ask students to compare the graph with the "Negative feedback" curve they drew. Point out that the "Negative feedback" curve shows that the glucose level stays within a narrow range. The "Positive feedback" line shows a variable that constantly increases.

Controlling the Controls

How do endocrine glands know when to start and stop hormone release? They know because your body has special systems called **feedback controls** that turn endocrine glands on and off. Feedback controls work something like a thermostat on an air conditioner. Once a room reaches the required temperature, the thermostat sends a message to the air conditioner to stop sending in cold air. Much in the same way, a feedback control sends a message to an endocrine gland to stop sending in a particular hormone. **Figure 17** traces the steps of a feedback control that regulates blood sugar.

Figure 17 In this feedback-control system, the pancreas produces hormones that help your body maintain the correct blood sugar level.

Glucose Feedback Control

1. After you eat a meal, glucose is absorbed into the bloodstream from the small intestine.
2. When the glucose level in the blood is high, the pancreas releases the hormone insulin into the blood.
3. Insulin signals the liver to take in glucose from the body, convert it to glycogen, and store it for future energy needs.
4. When the blood sugar level returns to normal, the pancreas stops releasing insulin.
5. To keep your blood sugar level from falling below normal, you must eat again.

Homework

Researching Steroids Tell students that hormones are used as medicines to treat endocrine disorders. However, other hormones, such as anabolic steroids, are abused to increase athletic prowess. Have students research the effects and dangers of abusing anabolic steroids. Have them write a brief report or prepare an oral presentation to share their findings.

Hormone Imbalances

Insulin is a hormone made by the pancreas. When the blood sugar level rises after a person has eaten something, insulin triggers the cells to take in glucose and sends a message to the liver to store glucose. A person whose pancreas cannot make enough insulin has a condition called *diabetes mellitus*. A person with diabetes mellitus may need daily injections of insulin to keep his or her blood glucose levels within safe limits. Some patients, like the woman in **Figure 18**, receive their insulin automatically from a small machine they wear next to their body.

Growth Hormone Sometimes a child may have a pituitary gland that doesn't make enough growth hormone. This causes the child's growth to be stunted. Fortunately, if this problem is detected soon enough, a doctor can prescribe hormone replacement medication and monitor the child's growth. If the pituitary makes too much growth hormone at an early age, the person becomes much taller than expected.

Figure 18 This young woman has diabetes and must have daily injections of the hormone insulin.

Thyroxine When a person doesn't get enough iodine in the diet, the thyroid gland cannot make enough of the hormone *thyroxine*. This causes the thyroid to swell up and form a mass called a *goiter*. Because thyroxine increases metabolism, this person's cells are less active than normal, causing fatigue, weight gain, and other problems.

REVIEW

1. What is the function of the endocrine system?
2. Why are feedback controls important?
3. Name four endocrine glands, and tell what each one does in the body.
4. **Applying Concepts** Epinephrine, the fight-or-flight hormone, increases the level of glucose in the blood. Why would this be important in times of stress?
5. **Illustrating Concepts** Look around your house for an example of a feedback control. Draw a diagram explaining how this feedback control works to start and stop an action.

internetconnect

TOPIC: Hormones
GO TO: www.scilinks.org
*sci*LINKS NUMBER: HSTL620

Section 3 • The Endocrine System   **603**

Chapter Highlights

Vocabulary Definitions

Section 1

central nervous system a collection of organs whose primary function is to process all incoming and outgoing messages from the nerves; includes the brain and the spinal cord

peripheral nervous system the nerves whose primary function is to exchange information from all areas of the body and the outside environment to the central nervous system and from the central nervous system to the rest of the body

neuron a specialized cell that transfers messages throughout the body in the form of fast-moving electrical signals

impulse an electrical message that passes along a neuron

receptor a specialized dendrite that detects changes inside or outside the body

nerve an axon bundled together with blood vessels and connective tissue

brain mass of nerve tissue that is the main organ of the nervous system

reflex a quick, involuntary response to a stimulus

Chapter Highlights

SECTION 1

Vocabulary
central nervous system (p. 588)
peripheral nervous system (p. 588)
neuron (p. 589)
impulse (p. 589)
receptor (p. 590)
nerve (p. 590)
brain (p. 591)
reflex (p. 594)

Section Notes

- The central nervous system includes the brain and spinal cord. The peripheral nervous system includes nerves and sensory receptors.

- A neuron receives information at branched endings called dendrites and passes information to other cells along a fiber called an axon.

- Sensory neurons detect information about the body and its environment. Motor neurons carry messages from the brain and spinal cord to other parts of the body.

- The cerebrum is the largest part of the brain and is involved with thinking, sensations, and voluntary muscle control.

- The cerebellum is the second largest part of the brain. It keeps track of the body's position and helps maintain balance.

- The medulla controls involuntary activities such as heart rate, blood pressure, and breathing.

- Pain signals can trigger a quick, involuntary action, called a reflex, in which a motor neuron sends a message to a muscle without first receiving a signal from the brain.

✓ Skills Check

Math Concepts

THE SPEED OF AN IMPULSE An impulse travels very fast. As shown in the MathBreak on page 589, to calculate the amount of time that it takes for an impulse to travel a certain distance, you must first know the speed it is traveling. Then you can divide the distance by the speed to get the time. For example, if an impulse travels 150 m/s, it would take it 0.02 seconds to travel 3 m.

$$\text{time} = \frac{3 \text{ m (distance)}}{150 \text{ m/s (speed)}} = 0.02 \text{ s}$$

Visual Understanding

PATH OF LIGHT Look back at Figure 10 on page 596 to review the path of light entering the eye. The light first passes through the transparent cornea, then through the opening called the pupil, and then through the lens. At the back of the eye, the light is detected by receptors in the retina.

Lab and Activity Highlights

You've Gotta Lotta Nerve

 Datasheets for LabBook
(blackline masters for this lab)

VOCABULARY DEFINITIONS, continued

SECTION 2

retina layer of light-sensitive cells in the back of the eye

rods photoreceptors that can detect very dim light

cones photoreceptors that can detect bright light and that help you see colors

iris the colored part of the eye

lens a curved, transparent object that forms an image by refracting light

cochlea an ear organ that converts sound waves into electrical impulses

SECTION 3

endocrine system a collection of organs, called glands, whose primary function is to control body fluid balance, growth, and sexual development

gland a group of cells that make special chemicals for the body

hormone a chemical messenger that carries information from one part of an organism to the other; made by the endocrine glands

feedback control the system that turns endocrine glands on or off

SECTION 2

Vocabulary
retina (p. 596)
rods (p. 596)
cones (p. 596)
iris (p. 597)
lens (p. 597)
cochlea (p. 598)

Section Notes
- Different kinds of receptors in the skin are responsible for detecting touch, pressure, temperature, and pain.
- The retina of the eye contains photoreceptors that react to light and cause impulses to be sent to the brain.
- The lens of the eye can change shape to adjust the point of focus so that the image is focused on the retina. Improper focus can usually be corrected with glasses or contact lenses.
- Special receptors inside the cochlea of the ear react to sound waves and send impulses to the brain.
- Receptors for taste are located in taste buds on the bumps of the tongue.
- Receptors for smell are on olfactory cells located in the upper part of the nasal cavity.

Labs
You've Gotta Lotta Nerve (p. 772)

SECTION 3

Vocabulary
endocrine system (p. 600)
gland (p. 600)
hormone (p. 600)
feedback control (p. 602)

Section Notes
- The endocrine system communicates with other systems using chemicals called hormones.
- Hormones are made in endocrine glands.
- The adrenal glands secrete hormones that help the body cope with stress. Epinephrine is the hormone most associated with fight-or-flight situations.
- Feedback control is the body's way of turning glands on and off so that they release hormones only when necessary.

---

internet connect

GO TO: go.hrw.com

Visit the **HRW** Web site for a variety of learning tools related to this chapter. Just type in the keyword:

KEYWORD: HSTBD4

GO TO: www.scilinks.org

Visit the **National Science Teachers Association** on-line Web site for Internet resources related to this chapter. Just type in the *sci*LINKS number for more information about the topic:

TOPIC:	*sci*LINKS NUMBER:
The Nervous System	HSTL605
The Senses	HSTL610
The Eye	HSTL615
Hormones	HSTL620

Vocabulary Review Worksheet 25

Blackline masters of these Chapter Highlights can be found in the **Study Guide.**

Lab and Activity Highlights

LabBank

Whiz-Bang Demonstrations, Now You See It, Now You Don't, Demo 15

Labs You Can Eat, A Salty Sweet Experiment, Lab 9

Long-Term Projects & Research Ideas, Man Versus Machine, Project 25

Chapter Review Answers

USING VOCABULARY

1. central nervous system
2. cochlea
3. stress
4. axon terminal
5. involuntary
6. retina

UNDERSTANDING CONCEPTS

Multiple Choice

7. c
8. a
9. c
10. a
11. d
12. c

Short Answer

13. Answers will vary but should describe dangerous or stressful situations that the student has encountered.
14. Light stimulates a ring of muscle fibers, which enable the iris to open and close.
15. A reflex is a quick, involuntary action. Because the impulse does not need to travel to the brain before a muscle can respond, this reaction can be very quick.
16. The vibrations of the eardrum make the ear bones vibrate, one of which vibrates against the cochlea, creating waves that are detected by neurons.

Concept Mapping Transparency 25

Chapter Review

USING VOCABULARY

To complete the following sentences, choose the correct term from each pair of terms listed below:

1. Your brain and spinal cord make up your __?__. (*central nervous system* or *peripheral nervous system*)

2. Sensory receptors in the __?__ detect vibrations. (*cochlea* or *eardrum*)

3. Epinephrine is produced by the adrenal glands in response to __?__. (*glucose* or *stress*)

4. The part of a neuron that passes an impulse to other cells is the __?__. (*dendrite* or *axon terminal*)

5. The medulla is mostly responsible for activities that are __?__. (*involuntary* or *voluntary*)

6. Receptors that can convert light into impulses are found in the __?__. (*olfactory cells* or *retina*)

UNDERSTANDING CONCEPTS

Multiple Choice

7. Which of the following has receptors for smelling?
   a. cochlea cells
   b. thermoreceptors
   c. olfactory cells
   d. optic nerve

8. Which of the following gives eyes their color?
   a. iris
   b. cornea
   c. lens
   d. retina

9. Which of the glands is associated with goiters?
   a. adrenal
   b. pituitary
   c. thyroid
   d. pancreas

10. Which of the following is not part of the peripheral nervous system?
    a. spinal cord
    b. axons
    c. sensory receptors
    d. motor neurons

11. Which part of the brain regulates blood pressure?
    a. right cerebral hemisphere
    b. left cerebral hemisphere
    c. cerebellum
    d. medulla

12. Which of the following is associated with the endocrine system?
    a. reflex
    b. salivary gland
    c. fight-or-flight response
    d. voluntary response

Short Answer

13. Describe several situations in which your adrenal glands might release epinephrine, causing you to have a fight-or-flight reaction.

14. What causes the size of your pupils to change?

15. What is a reflex? How does a reflex enable you to act quickly?

16. What is the function of the middle-ear bones?

17. Using the terms you learned in this chapter, write down a step-by-step sequence for the path taken by an impulse, beginning at a pain receptor in your left big toe. Be sure to mention each kind of neuron and its parts as well as specific organs in the nervous system.

Concept Map

18. Use the following terms to create a concept map: the nervous system, spinal cord, medulla, peripheral nervous system, brain, cerebrum, central nervous system, cerebellum.

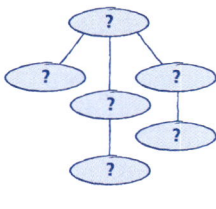

CRITICAL THINKING AND PROBLEM SOLVING

Write one or two sentences to answer the following questions:

19. Why is it important to have a lens that can change shape inside the eye?

20. Why can the nervous system have a faster effect on the body than the endocrine system?

21. Why is it important that reflexes occur without thought?

MATH IN SCIENCE

22. Sound travels about 335 m/s (1 km is equal to 1,000 m). How many kilometers would a sound travel in 1 minute?

23. Some axons can send one impulse every 0.4 milliseconds. One second is equal to 1,000 milliseconds. How many impulses could one of these axons send every second?

INTERPRETING GRAPHICS

Look at the drawing below, and answer the following questions:

24. Which letter identifies the gland that regulates blood sugar?

25. Which letter identifies the gland that releases a hormone that stimulates the birth process in pregnant women?

26. Which letter identifies the gland that helps the body fight disease?

 Take a minute to review your answers to the Pre-Reading Questions found at the bottom of page 586. Have your answers changed? If necessary, revise your answers based on what you have learned since you began this chapter.

---

17. The impulse travels from sensory receptors in the toe along axons leading to the spinal cord. Motor neurons carry a new message to the muscles in the leg telling them to move the foot. The pain message continues along the spinal cord to the cerebrum.

Concept Mapping

18. An answer to this exercise can be found at the end of this book.

CRITICAL THINKING AND PROBLEM SOLVING

19. The lens must change shape to focus objects that are varying distances from the eye.
20. Electrical messages travel along nerves faster than chemicals can travel in the bloodstream.
21. The speed of a reflex might prevent serious harm to the body.

MATH IN SCIENCE

22. 20.1 km/min
23. 2,500 impulses/second

INTERPRETING GRAPHICS

24. *e* (pancreas)
25. *d* (pituitary)
26. *c* (thymus)

 Blackline masters of this Chapter Review can be found in the **Study Guide**.

Science, Technology, and Society

Light on Lenses

Background
Many students may be familiar with lenses because they wear eyeglasses. Lenses mounted in frames and used to improve vision were first developed in both Europe and China, probably during the thirteenth century.

Benjamin Franklin invented bifocals in 1784. These were a new type of eyeglasses in which each lens was divided in half. One lens corrected for nearsightedness and the other for farsightedness. Today, single lenses can be ground to include both features. In Franklin's version, each bifocal lens was made of two separate pieces of glass held together by the frame.

Science, Technology, and Society

Light on Lenses

Can you see in pitch darkness? No, of course not! You need light to see. But there is something else you need in order to see. You need a lens. A **lens** is a curved transparent object that *refracts*, or bends, light.

Lenses are necessary to focus light in all kinds of applications, including in telescopes, microscopes, binoculars, cameras, contact lenses, eyeglasses, and magnifying lenses.

Light Bounces
To learn how lenses work, you must first know something about how light travels. A ray of light travels in a straight path from its source until it strikes an object. When light strikes an object, much of the light bounces off, or is reflected. The light reflects from the object at the same angle that it struck the object in the first place.

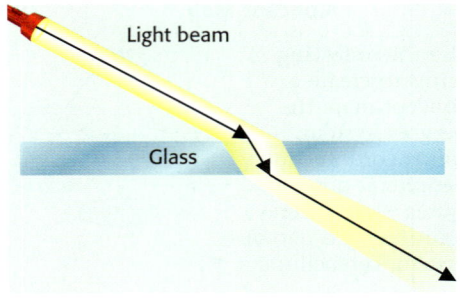

▲ *Light changes speed and direction when it passes from one material into another.*

▲ *The angle formed by the incoming light (angle of incidence) always equals the angle of the reflected light (angle of reflection).*

Lenses Bend Light
A lens allows light to travel through it. However, as the light passes through the lens, it is refracted. **Refraction** is the bending of a light ray as it passes from one transparent material into another, such as when light traveling through air passes through a glass lens.

The type of lens determines how much and in which direction the light is bent. A lens that is thicker in the middle than at its edges is called a **convex lens.** This type of lens bends light toward its center. Convex lenses are used in magnifying glasses, microscopes, and telescopes. The lenses in your eyes are convex lenses.

A lens that is thinner in the middle than at its edges is called a **concave lens.** This type of lens bends light away from its center. Both convex lenses and concave lenses are often used to help correct vision. Convex lenses are also used in combination with concave lenses in cameras to focus light on the film.

Light Your Way
▶ Do some additional research to find out what a photorefractive keratectomy (PRK) is and how it works to correct a person's vision.

Answer to Light Your Way
PRK modifies the cornea to correct a person's myopic vision. A surgeon uses an excimer laser to remove a 5–9 mm diameter portion of the cornea. For mild or moderate cases of myopia, the surgeon removes about 5–10 percent of the cornea's thickness, while for extreme cases, up to 30 percent is removed. This procedure has an advantage over RK (radial keratotomy) in that the integrity of the cornea's dome is not compromised, as it is when cuts are made in the cornea during an RK procedure. In the RK procedure, deep incisions are made in a spokelike pattern. The drawbacks of this method are that it is viable only in mild cases of myopia and is ineffective at correcting hyperopia (farsightedness). The incisions in the cornea flatten it, and over time, it continues to flatten, which increases the person's farsightedness.

Eureka!
Pathway to a Cure

Do you know what would happen if your brain sent out too many impulses to the muscles in your body? First the overload would increase the number of contractions in your muscles, and it would be difficult to carry out simple movements, like scratching your arm or picking up a glass. Even when you wanted to rest, your muscles would continue to tremble. This is what happens to people with Parkinson's disease, and unfortunately, there is still no cure.

The Disease
Parkinson's disease affects the cells in the brain that regulate muscles. These cells require the chemical dopamine, which slows down the activity of nerves so they can function properly. But if the cells that supply the muscle-regulating cells with dopamine are damaged, the brain will send continuous impulses to the muscles. This results in Parkinson's disease.

Parkinson's disease is often diagnosed only after a person has already lost about 80 percent of his or her dopamine-supplying cells. Although there is no known cure for Parkinson's disease, some patients can be treated with chemicals that act like dopamine. Unfortunately, these substitutes are not as good as the real thing. Dopamine itself cannot be given because it cannot pass from the blood into the brain tissue.

Breakthrough
Dr. Bertha Madras studies the effects of drug addiction on the brain. While studying the effects of cocaine addiction, she discovered that a chemical called tropane attaches itself to the same nerves that release dopamine in the brain. This discovery may be used to detect and diagnose Parkinson's disease earlier and at a lower cost to the patient.

A Glow in the Darkness
Madras and her colleagues thought they could use tropane to study the cells that release dopamine. They added a radioactive component to the tropane to make a chemical called altropane. Altropane also attaches to the dopamine-releasing cells. But unlike tropane, altropane glows, so it shows up in a brain scan. Healthy people have large areas where the altropane attaches. Among patients with Parkinson's disease, because of the nerve loss, the altropane attaches to fewer nerves. Therefore, brain scans from these patients do not have as many glowing collections of altropane.

Using this new procedure to diagnose Parkinson's disease could allow doctors to find the disease in people before the neurons are severely damaged or completely lost.

Healthy subject   Parkinson's subject

▲ *Brain scans, such as the ones above, can be used to diagnose Parkinson's disease.*

Activity
▶ Find out what a Single Photon Emission Computed Tomography (SPECT) image is and how it is used to study Parkinson's disease.

Eureka!
Pathway to a Cure

Background
Parkinson's disease was first described by James Parkinson more than 180 years ago. No one knows the cause of Parkinson's disease, although it does tend to run in families. Most people with Parkinson's disease are elderly, but young people can also have the disease. Major signs of Parkinson's disease include stiffness, trembling, and difficulty moving muscles. Dr. Madras was working on the effects of cocaine use on the brain when she discovered tropane. Tropane has the same chemical backbone as cocaine, and it binds specifically to the neurons that transmit dopamine in the brain. By radioactively labeling the tropane molecule and turning it into altropane, scientists could use the tracer molecule to visualize the status of dopamine-producing neurons in the brain.

Several techniques have been used to visualize nerve damage in the brain due to Parkinson's disease. Many of these techniques are very costly, and none of them are as good as the altropane method. The other procedures use chemicals that bind to other neurons besides the ones that produce dopamine. Altropane is very specific to the neurons that transport dopamine.

Answer to Activity
The type of brain scan done with altropane is called single photon emission computed tomography (SPECT) imaging. The other imaging method used to diagnose Parkinson's is positron emission tomography (PET). Only seven locations in the United States use the PET method, and it is a complicated procedure. A PET imaging can cost $2,500. SPECT imaging is cheaper than PET, costing about $1,000, and is more widely available at hospitals. SPECT imaging relies on the use of radioactively labeled molecules to create an image.

Chapter Organizer

CHAPTER ORGANIZATION	TIME MINUTES	OBJECTIVES	LABS, INVESTIGATIONS, AND DEMONSTRATIONS
Chapter Opener pp. 610–611	45	National Standards: UCP 3, SAI 1, LS 2a, 3a	**Start-Up Activity** How Grows It? p. 611
Section 1 Animal Reproduction	90	▶ Distinguish between asexual and sexual reproduction. ▶ Explain the difference between external and internal fertilization. ▶ Describe the three different types of mammalian development. UCP 5, SAI 1, LS 2a, 2b, 2d	**Demonstration,** Eggs, p. 614 in ATE BASIC
Section 2 Human Reproduction	90	▶ Describe the functions of the male and female reproductive systems. ▶ Discuss disorders and diseases that are associated with human reproduction. UCP 1, 5, SAI 1, SPSP 1, 4, LS 1a, 1d–1f, 2b	**Demonstration,** Multiple Births, p. 617 in ATE GENERAL
Section 3 Growth and Development	90	▶ Summarize the processes of fertilization and implantation. ▶ Describe the course of human development. UCP 2, 3, 5, SAI 1, ST 2, SPSP 1, 5, LS 1a, 1b, 1d, 2b; LabBook UCP 2, 3, SAI 1, ST 1	**QuickLab,** Life Grows On, p. 625 GENERAL **Skill Builder,** It's a Comfy, Safe World! p. 774 GENERAL **Datasheets for LabBook,** It's a Comfy, Safe World! Datasheet 54 GENERAL **Skill Builder,** My, How You've Grown! p. 775 BASIC **Datasheets for LabBook,** My, How You've Grown! Datasheet 55 BASIC **Long-Term Projects & Research Ideas,** Project 26 ADVANCED

*See page **T20** for a complete correlation of this book with the*

NATIONAL SCIENCE EDUCATION STANDARDS.

TECHNOLOGY RESOURCES

 Guided Reading Audio CD English or Spanish, Chapter 26

 CNN Eye on the Environment, Eagles and DDT, Segment 5

One-Stop Planner CD-ROM with Test Generator

Chapter 26 • Reproduction and Development

CLASSROOM WORKSHEETS, TRANSPARENCIES, AND RESOURCES	SCIENCE INTEGRATION AND CONNECTIONS	REVIEW AND ASSESSMENT
Directed Reading Worksheet 26 BASIC **Science Puzzlers, Twisters & Teasers,** Worksheet 26 ADVANCED		
Directed Reading Worksheet 26, Section 1 BASIC **Reinforcement Worksheet 26,** Reproduction Review GENERAL	**MathBreak,** Chromo-Combos, p. 613 GENERAL	**Homework,** p. 612 in ATE GENERAL **Homework,** p. 615 in ATE ADVANCED **Self-Check,** p. 613 **Review,** p. 615 GENERAL **Quiz,** p. 615 in ATE GENERAL **Alternative Assessment,** p. 615 in ATE GENERAL
Transparency 93, The Male Reproductive System **Directed Reading Worksheet 26,** Section 2 BASIC **Transparency 94,** The Female Reproductive System **Math Skills for Science Worksheet 3,** Multiplying Whole Numbers GENERAL **Math Skills for Science Worksheet 5,** Dividing Whole Numbers with Long Division GENERAL	**MathBreak,** Counting Eggs, p. 617 GENERAL **Cross-Disciplinary Focus,** p. 617 in ATE **Apply,** p. 618 GENERAL **Math and More,** p. 618 in ATE GENERAL **Chemistry Connection,** p. 619	**Review,** p. 619 GENERAL **Quiz,** p. 619 in ATE GENERAL **Alternative Assessment,** p. 619 in ATE GENERAL
Directed Reading Worksheet 26, Section 3 BASIC **Transparency 154,** How Sonar Works **Transparency 95,** Growth Chart **Reinforcement Worksheet 26,** The Beginning of a Life GENERAL **Critical Thinking Worksheet 26,** One to Grow On! ADVANCED	**Math and More,** p. 622 in ATE ADVANCED **Connect to Earth Science,** p. 623 in ATE **Cross-Disciplinary Focus,** p. 623 in ATE **Across the Sciences:** Acne, p. 630 ADVANCED **Science, Technology, and Society:** Technology in Its Infant Stages, p. 631 GENERAL	**Self-Check,** p. 621 **Review,** p. 625 GENERAL **Quiz,** p. 625 in ATE GENERAL **Alternative Assessment,** p. 625 in ATE GENERAL

END-OF-CHAPTER REVIEW AND ASSESSMENT

Chapter Review in Study Guide
Vocabulary and Notes in Study Guide
Chapter Tests with Performance-Based Assessment, Chapter 26 Test
Chapter Tests with Performance-Based Assessment, Performance-Based Assessment 26
Concept Mapping Transparency 26

 Holt, Rinehart and Winston On-line Resources
go.hrw.com
For worksheets and other teaching aids related to this chapter, visit the HRW Web site and type in the keyword: **HSTBD5**

 National Science Teachers Association
www.scilinks.org
Encourage students to use the sciLINKS numbers listed in the internet connect boxes to access information and resources on the **NSTA** Web site.

Chapter 26 • Chapter Organizer 609B

Chapter Resources & Worksheets

Visual Resources

Meeting Individual Needs

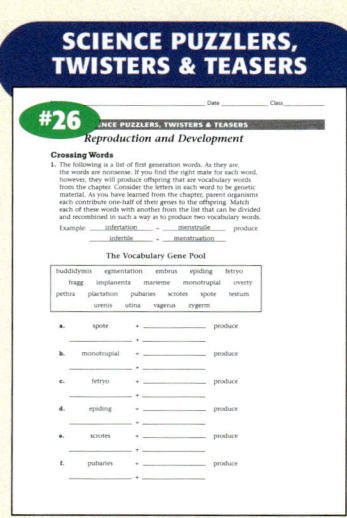

Chapter 26 • Reproduction and Development

Review & Assessment

STUDY GUIDE

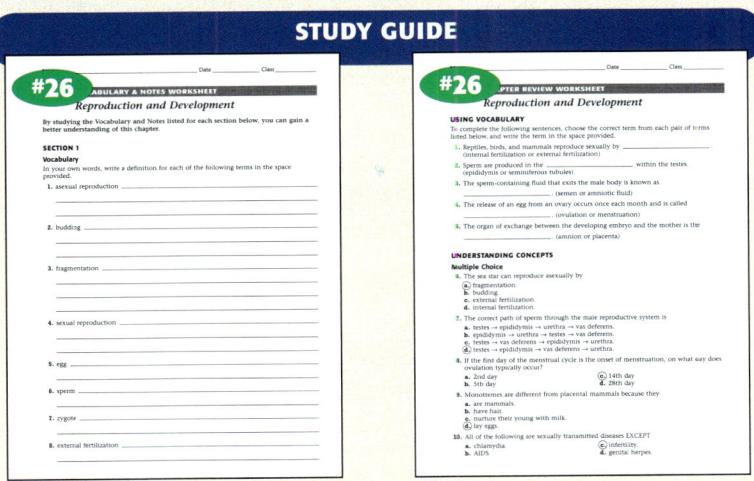

CHAPTER TESTS WITH PERFORMANCE-BASED ASSESSMENT

Lab Worksheets

LONG-TERM PROJECTS & RESEARCH IDEAS

DATASHEETS FOR LABBOOK

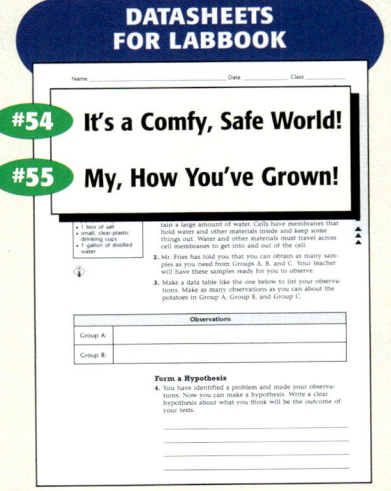

Applications & Extensions

CRITICAL THINKING & PROBLEM SOLVING

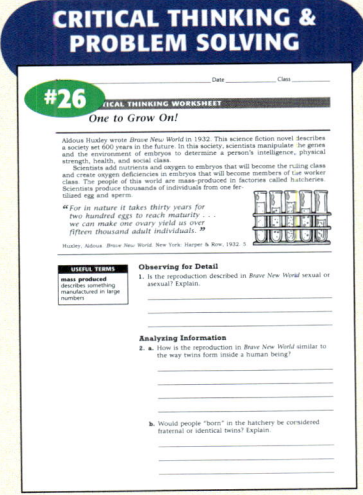

EYE ON THE ENVIRONMENT

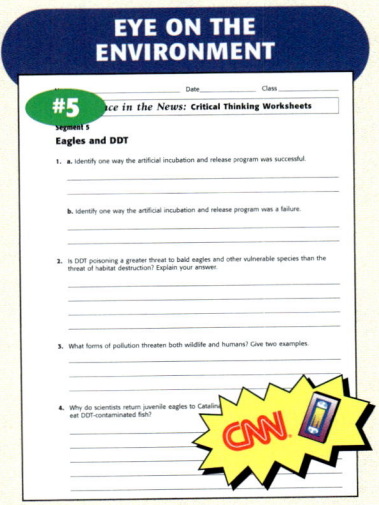

Chapter 26 • Chapter Resources & Worksheets   609D

Chapter Background

SECTION 1

Animal Reproduction

▶ **Asexual Reproduction**
The most widespread forms of asexual reproduction are binary fission, budding, and fragmentation. Binary fission is used mainly by bacteria.

- A major advantage of asexual reproduction is that it does not require a mate. Asexual reproduction also allows animals to produce many offspring in a short period of time. Many animals that do not move around, like sea sponges, reproduce asexually.

▶ **Sexual Reproduction**
Because sexual reproduction brings together genetic material from two parents, there is greater variation among animals that reproduce sexually versus those that reproduce asexually.

▶ **Fertilization**
In external fertilization, eggs can be fertilized without physical contact between the parents. Instead, chemical signals coordinate the fertilization process, ensuring that the parents release their sex cells at the appropriate time.

- Internal fertilization requires a more sophisticated reproductive system, including organs for delivering and storing sperm. Fertilized eggs can develop externally, as with birds, or internally, as with placental mammals. Internally protected embryos are more likely to survive, but placental females do not usually produce as many offspring as do egg-laying females.

IS THAT A FACT!

▰ Some animal species that reproduce sexually don't have separate sexes. Instead, every individual contains male and female sexual characteristics. This situation is known as *hermaphrodism*.

▰ Hermaphrodites can exchange sex cells with one another and some can reproduce by themselves as well.

SECTION 2

Human Reproduction

▶ **The Male Reproductive System**
Male reproductive functions mainly concern sperm production. The head of a sperm contains DNA, and the tail region contains mitochondria. The mitochondria are "engines" for the sperm, providing the sperm's tail with the energy to whip back and forth.

- The process of maturation of sperm from germ cells to spermatozoa takes about 74 days. Even then, they cannot yet penetrate an ovum. First they must "ripen" in the epididymis, a process that takes about 10 days. Though the maturation process is lengthy, once sperm are fully mature, they can remain viable for about 6 weeks.

IS THAT A FACT!

▰ If the seminiferous tubules—the bundle of tubes that makes up each testicle—were joined together and extended, they would be more than 200 m long!

▶ **The Female Reproductive System**
The ovaries are the primary female reproductive organs. About the size of large almonds, the ovaries are located on either side of the uterus, each anchored by an ovarian ligament. These tiny organs secrete the hormones largely responsible for development during puberty. They are also responsible for releasing eggs.

Chapter 26 • Reproduction and Development

- Every menstrual cycle, several ova begin to ripen. In most cases, however, only one egg reaches maturity at a time. This mature, ripened ovum, encased in a Graafian follicle, travels to the surface of the ovary, where it remains until midcycle, when ovulation occurs. Then the Graafian follicle, distended with fluid, ruptures, sending the egg into the abdominal cavity. The fallopian tube then captures the ovum, and it begins the descent to the uterus.

▶ Sexually Transmitted Diseases

Chlamydia is the most prevalent sexually transmitted disease (STD) in North America. Caused by an organism called *Chlamydia trachomatis,* its symptoms include a frequent desire to urinate, pain with urination, and penile or vaginal discharge.

In women, there are often few symptoms in the early stages. Troublesome as the symptoms are, the consequences are worse: chlamydia is a major cause of infertility. If left untreated, it can cause pelvic inflammatory disease and, in women, the subsequent inability to conceive. In men, infection that reaches the testes results in infertility.

- Also known as salpingitis, pelvic inflammatory disease (PID) is an infection of the fallopian tubes, uterus, and cervix. While a number of bacteria can cause PID, the usual culprits are chlamydia and gonorrhea. Though these infections can be completely cured with antibiotics, PID often leaves the fallopian tubes—the conduits between the ovaries and the uterus—scarred, making conception difficult or impossible. Other potential consequences of PID include ectopic pregnancy, peritonitis, and death.

Section 3

Growth and Development

▶ Sex Determination

One pair of human chromosomes determines the sex of a baby. There are two types of these sex chromosomes: X and Y. Because the egg contains only the X chromosome, the gender of the baby is determined by the father's sperm, which may contain either an X or a Y chromosome. If a sperm containing an X chromosome joins with an egg, the baby will be a girl. If a sperm containing a Y chromosome fertilizes the egg, the baby will be a boy.

▶ Fetal Development

The development of a baby from a single cell progresses at an astounding rate. Early in development, the embryo resembles a tiny tadpole, with a rounded body and tail. By about 7.5 weeks of gestation, however, limb buds—with knee and elbow joints evident—form, and facial features are recognizable. By the ninth week, nerves and muscles have developed enough that the fetus can move independently. By 12 weeks, the fetus is about 7.6 cm long and has a mass of about 28 g.

For background information about teaching strategies and issues, refer to the *Professional Reference for Teachers.*

CHAPTER 26

Reproduction and Development

Pre-Reading Questions

Students may not know the answers to these questions before reading the chapter, so accept any reasonable response.

Suggested Answers

1. No; animals that can reproduce asexually—such as sea stars—can have only one parent.
2. Adults are larger and more sexually developed than children.
3. You inherit an equal number of chromosomes from both your parents.

 Directed Reading Worksheet 26

 Science Puzzlers, Twisters & Teasers Worksheet 26

 Guided Reading Audio CD English or Spanish, Chapter 26

CHAPTER 26

Reproduction and Development

Sections

1. **Animal Reproduction** . . 612
   - MathBreak 613
   - Internet Connect 615
2. **Human Reproduction** . . 616
   - MathBreak 617
   - Apply 618
   - Chemistry Connection 619
   - Internet Connect 619
3. **Growth and Development** 620
   - QuickLab 625
   - Internet Connect 625

Chapter Review 628
Feature Articles 630, 631
LabBook 774–775

Pre-Reading Questions

1. Do all animals have two parents?
2. What makes you physically different from an adult?
3. What percentage of genes do you inherit from your mother? your father?

610

Sneak Preview

If someone had taken your picture when your mother was about seven months pregnant with you, it would have looked very much like this photograph. By the eighth month, your eyes opened and you could see light. Can you believe how much you changed in such a short time? In this chapter, you will learn about how a single cell grows and develops into a complete person. You will also learn how you continue to change from infancy through adulthood.

---

internet connect

 HRW On-line Resources
go.hrw.com
For worksheets and other teaching aids, visit the HRW Web site and type in the keyword: **HSTBD5**

www.scilinks.com
Use the *sci*LINKS numbers at the end of each chapter for additional resources on the **NSTA** Web site.

www.cnnfyi.com
Visit the CNN Web site for current events coverage and classroom resources.

610 Chapter 26 • Reproduction and Development

START-UP Activity

HOW GROWS IT?

As you read this, you are aging. Your body is growing into the body of an adult. But does your body have the same proportions that an adult's body has? Do this exercise to find out.

Procedure

1. Have a classmate help you measure your total height, head height, and leg length with a **tape measure** and **meterstick.** Your teacher will tell you how to take these measurements.

2. Calculate your head-to-body proportion and leg-to-body proportion. Use the following equations:

$$\text{head proportion} = \left(\frac{\text{head height}}{\text{body height}}\right) \times 100$$

$$\text{leg proportion} = \left(\frac{\text{leg length}}{\text{body height}}\right) \times 100$$

3. Your teacher will give you the head, body, and leg measurements of three adults. Calculate their proportions. Record all the measurements and calculations.

Analysis

4. Using the direct evidence you collected, evaluate how your proportions compare with the proportions of adults.

START-UP Activity

HOW GROWS IT?

MATERIALS

FOR EACH PAIR:
- tape measure
- meterstick

Teacher's Notes

The head height can be measured by having the student stand next to a sheet of paper with one ear against it. The top of the head and bottom of the chin can be marked with a pencil. That length can then be measured. Total body height can be measured in a similar way. Length should be measured from where the leg bends when the student sits down. The student can hold a meterstick perpendicular to the floor at that level and can mark that height on paper taped to the wall or drop a tape measure down to the floor from the tip of the meterstick. Demonstrate measuring techniques for your students.

Before students come to class, write the measurements of at least three adults on the board. The measurements can be of you and two other teachers.

Answer to START-UP Activity

4. The student's head height should take up a greater proportion of his or her overall height than the adults' head height. The student's leg length should be about 50 percent of his or her overall height. This should match the leg-length proportion of the adults.

Chapter 26 • Reproduction and Development

SECTION 1

Focus

Animal Reproduction

In this section, students learn about two types of asexual reproduction. Students will review meiosis and learn that sexual reproduction unites an egg and sperm using an internal or external fertilization process. The final section focuses on differences in mammalian reproduction.

🔔 Bellringer

Write the following list on the blackboard or on a transparency:

a. bird   c. ants
b. human   d. sea stars

Ask students to write a paragraph explaining how they think reproduction differs among these four animals.

1) Motivate

DISCUSSION

Reproduction Lead a discussion based on students' answers to the Bellringer. Ask students to think about the similarities and differences among the ways animals reproduce. Birds and ants lay eggs, but humans and sea stars don't. Females and males mate to reproduce in humans and birds, but not in sea stars. Help them understand that the end result of reproduction is the same for all animal species, but the means differ widely.

Section 1

Terms to Learn

asexual reproduction
sexual reproduction
egg
sperm
zygote
external fertilization
internal fertilization

What You'll Do

◆ Distinguish between asexual and sexual reproduction.
◆ Explain the difference between external and internal fertilization.
◆ Describe the three different types of mammalian development.

Animal Reproduction

The life span of some living things is very short compared with ours. For instance, a fruit fly lives only about 80 days. Other organisms live for a long time. A bristlecone pine can live for 2,000 to 6,000 years. But all living things eventually die. If a species is to survive, its members must reproduce.

A Chip off the Old Block

Some animals, particularly simpler ones, reproduce asexually. In **asexual reproduction,** a single parent has offspring that are genetically identical to itself.

One kind of asexual reproduction is called *budding*. This occurs when a small part of the parent's body develops into an independent organism. The hydra shown in **Figure 1** is reproducing asexually by budding. The young hydra is genetically identical to its parent.

Fragmentation is another type of asexual reproduction. In fragmentation, an organism breaks into two or more parts, each of which may grow into a separate individual. Sea stars can reproduce by fragmentation. Because sea stars eat oysters, people used to try to kill sea stars by chopping them into pieces and throwing the pieces back into the water. They didn't know that each arm of a sea star can grow into an entire organism! This can be seen in **Figure 2.**

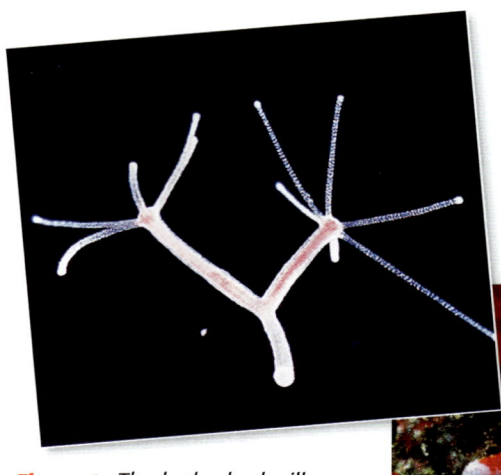

Figure 1 *The hydra bud will separate from its parent. Buds from other organisms, such as coral, remain attached to the parent.*

Figure 2 *The largest arm on this sea star was a fragment, from which the rest of the sea star has grown. In time, all of the sea star's arms will grow to the same size.*

612

Homework

Making Tables Ask students to make a table in their ScienceLog. In one column they will list 10 mammals. In the next column they will indicate how each mammal produces young. From the information in this section, students should be able to indicate whether the animal is a monotreme, a marsupial, or a placental. Students should fill in the table to the best of their knowledge, research the correct answers, and put them in an additional column.

612 Chapter 26 • Reproduction and Development

It Takes Two

Sexual Reproduction produces offspring by combining the genetic material of more than one parent. Most animals, including humans, reproduce sexually. Sexual reproduction most commonly involves two parents, a male and a female. The female parent produces sex cells called **eggs**. The male parent produces sex cells called **sperm**. When an egg's nucleus joins with a sperm's nucleus, a new kind of cell, called a **zygote**, is created. This joining of an egg and sperm is known as *fertilization*.

Review of Meiosis Genes are located in *chromosomes*. All human cells except egg and sperm cells contain 46 chromosomes. Eggs and sperm each contain only 23 chromosomes. Eggs and sperm are formed by a process known as *meiosis*.

In humans, meiosis involves the division of one cell with 46 chromosomes into four sex cells with 23 chromosomes each. When an egg and sperm join to form a zygote, the original number of 46 chromosomes is restored. This combination of genes from the father and mother results in a zygote that will grow into a unique individual. **Figure 3** shows how genes are intermixed through three generations.

MATH BREAK

Chromo-Combos

A cell undergoes meiosis. This cell has 6 chromosomes in 3 pairs. How many chromosomal combinations are possible in the formed sex cells? To find out, use the following formula:

2^x = possible variations where x = the number of pairs.

2^3 (or $2 \times 2 \times 2$) = 8

Therefore, 8 variations are possible.

A typical human cell has 46 chromosomes in 23 pairs. If the cell undergoes meiosis, how many chromosomal combinations are possible in the resulting sex cells?

Figure 3 *Eggs and sperm contain genes. You inherit genes from both of your parents. Your parents each inherited genes from both of their parents.*

Self-Check

What is the difference between sexual and asexual reproduction? *(See page 782 to check your answer.)*

MISCONCEPTION ALERT

In certain species, a single animal can sexually reproduce alone. For example, in some species of nematodes, sperm are produced and then stored until eggs are produced. This is followed by self-fertilization.

3) Extend

GOING FURTHER

 Encourage interested students to investigate the role that the endocrine system plays in reproduction. Have them draw diagrams illustrating the interactions among the hypothalamus, pituitary, and ovaries (in females) or testes (in males). Allow time for students to present their findings to the class.

DEMONSTRATION

Eggs Bird eggs are fertilized internally, but they develop externally. This requires good packaging. The shell of the egg provides the developing embryo with a stable, safe environment. Show students an ordinary chicken egg. Demonstrate for them that the shape of the egg keeps it from rolling away from the mother. Next, wrap your hand around the egg and demonstrate that the shape of the egg is quite protective against squeezing pressure from the outside. Tell students that the egg is shaped to withstand the pressure of the passage through the chicken and the pressure of incubation. It is also designed to be easy to break from within so that even a weak young chick can peck its way out.

Internal and External Fertilization

Depending on the animal, fertilization may occur either outside or inside the female's body. Some fishes and amphibians reproduce by **external fertilization,** in which the sperm fertilize the eggs outside the female's body. External fertilization must take place in a moist environment so the delicate zygotes won't dry out.

Many frogs, such as those pictured in **Figure 4,** mate every spring. The female frog releases her eggs first. The male frog then releases sperm over the eggs to fertilize them. The frogs leave the fertilized eggs to develop on their own. In about two weeks, the eggs hatch into tadpoles.

Figure 4 Frogs fertilize their eggs externally. Some species can produce more than 300 offspring in one season.

The Inside Story With **internal fertilization,** eggs and sperm join inside the female's body. Reptiles, birds, mammals, and some fishes reproduce by internal fertilization. Many animals that use internal fertilization lay fertilized eggs. The female penguin in **Figure 5,** for example, usually lays one or two eggs after internal fertilization has occurred.

In most mammals, internal fertilization is followed by the development of a fertilized egg inside the mother's body. Many mammals give birth to young that are well developed. Young zebras, like the one in **Figure 6,** can stand up and nurse almost immediately after birth.

Figure 5 Instead of leaving the eggs to develop on their own, penguin parents take turns crouching over them to keep them warm.

Figure 6 This zebra has just been born, but he is already able to stand. Within an hour, he will be able to run.

 Reinforcement Worksheet 26 "Reproduction Review"

IS THAT A FACT!

There are only 2 or 3 days each month when fertilization can occur in a human female.

614 Chapter 26 • Reproduction and Development

Making Mammals

All mammals reproduce sexually and nurture their young with milk. There are some differences in how mammals produce offspring, but every mammal follows one of three types of development.

Monotremes Mammals that lay eggs are *monotremes*. Two families of monotremes live today—the echidna and the platypus. After these animals lay their eggs, there is an incubation period that lasts up to 2 weeks. When the eggs hatch, the babies are very undeveloped. They crawl into a fold of their mother's skin and are nourished by the milk that oozes from her pores.

Marsupials Mammals that give birth to live young that are only partially developed are *marsupials*. There are about 260 species of marsupials. Most of them have pouches where their young develop, but some South American species do not have this feature. Marsupials with pouches have extra bones to help support the weight of their young, as can be seen in **Figure 7**. When a baby marsupial attaches itself to its mother's nipple, the nipple expands in the baby's mouth to prevent the baby from separating from its mother.

Placental Mammals There are almost 4,000 different species of placental mammals. These include whales, elephants, armadillos, bats, horses, and humans. *Placental mammals* nourish their young internally before birth. Newborn placental mammals are highly developed compared with newborn marsupials or monotremes.

Figure 7 The skeleton of this opposum has two extra bones extending forward from its pelvis to help support the weight of its young.

REVIEW

1. How many parents are needed to reproduce asexually?
2. What is the difference between monotremes and marsupials?
3. How is a zygote formed?
4. **Applying Concepts** Birds lay eggs, but they are not considered monotremes. Explain why.

TOPIC: Reproduction
GO TO: www.scilinks.org
*sci*LINKS NUMBER: HSTL630

---

4) Close

Quiz

1. How do the offspring created by asexual reproduction differ from those created by sexual reproduction? (Offspring from asexual reproduction are genetically identical to the parent, while offspring from sexual reproduction have genetic material from two parents.)
2. How do internal and external fertilization differ? How are they alike? (Internal fertilization occurs inside the female's body, while external fertilization occurs outside the female's body. Both result in the creation of single cells with combined genetic information from the parents.)

ALTERNATIVE ASSESSMENT

Concept Mapping Have students create a concept map using the new terms in this section and the section title.

Homework

 Encourage students to research an egg-laying mammal. Then have them write a short story about how the egg develops into a new individual.

▼ Answers to Review

1. one
2. Monotremes lay eggs and marsupials give birth to live young.
3. A zygote is formed when a sperm enters an egg and the nuclei of the egg and sperm join.
4. Birds are not mammals. They do not nurture their young with milk, and they are not covered with hair.

SECTION 2

Focus

Human Reproduction
In this section, students are introduced to the male and female reproductive systems. Students then learn about some of the irregularities and problems that affect the human reproductive system, including multiple births, ectopic births, and sexually transmitted diseases.

Bellringer

Ask students if they think that cloning human beings could be considered reproduction. Why or why not? What kind of reproduction is it? Have students write answers to these questions in their ScienceLog.

1 Motivate

DISCUSSION
Ask students to compare reproduction in birds with reproduction in humans. (Both birds and humans fertilize their eggs internally. Birds lay eggs and must protect and keep the eggs warm while obtaining food for themselves. Human mothers carry their baby inside their body, so the baby is always protected.)

 Teaching Transparency 93 "The Male Reproductive System"

 Directed Reading Worksheet 26 Section 2

Section 2

Terms to Learn
testes   ovaries
puberty   fallopian tube
vas deferens   uterus
semen   vagina
penis   infertile

What You'll Do
- Describe the functions of the male and female reproductive systems.
- Discuss disorders and diseases that are associated with human reproduction.

Human Reproduction
When a human sperm and egg combine, a new human begins to grow. About 9 months later, a mother gives birth to her baby. But what happens before that? Where do eggs and sperm come from?

The Male Reproductive System
The male reproductive system, shown in **Figure 8,** produces sperm and delivers it to the female reproductive system. The **testes** (singular, *testis*) make sperm and testosterone. Testosterone is the principal male sex hormone. It regulates the production of sex cells and the development of male characteristics.

Sperm Production The human body is usually around 37°C, but sperm cannot develop properly at such high temperatures. That is why the two testes rest in the *scrotum,* a skin-covered sac that hangs from the body. The scrotum is about 2 degrees cooler than the body. Inside each testis are masses of tightly coiled tubes called *seminiferous* (SEM uh NIF uhr uhs) *tubules* (TOO BYOOLZ), where sperm are produced. A healthy adult male produces several hundred million sperm each day! This massive, continuous sperm production begins at puberty. **Puberty** is the time of life when the sex organs of both males and females become mature.

Before sperm leave a testis, they are stored in a tube called an *epididymis* (EP uh DID i mis). Another tube called a **vas deferens** (vas DEF uh RENZ) passes from each epididymis into the body. As sperm swim through the vas deferens, they mix with fluids from several glands. The mixture of sperm and fluids is called **semen.**

To leave the body, semen passes through the vas deferens into the *urethra,* the tube that runs through the penis. The **penis** transfers semen into the female's body during sexual intercourse.

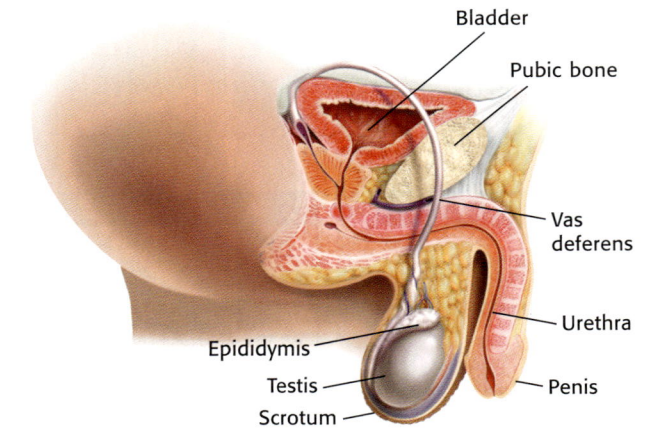

Figure 8 The Male Reproductive System
(Bladder, Pubic bone, Vas deferens, Urethra, Penis, Testis, Scrotum, Epididymis)

IS THAT A FACT!
Mumps, a common childhood disease, poses a risk to males who contract it during puberty or adulthood. When mumps occurs after childhood, it can cause inflammation of the testes, known as acute orchitis, which in rare cases can result in sterility.

The Female Reproductive System

The female reproductive system, shown in **Figure 9**, produces eggs, nurtures fertilized eggs, and gives birth. The **ovaries** produce the eggs. The two ovaries also produce sex hormones, such as estrogen and progesterone, that regulate the release of eggs and direct the development of female characteristics.

The Egg's Journey An ovary contains eggs in various stages of development. As an egg matures, it becomes a huge cell, growing to almost 200,000 times the size of a sperm. During *ovulation,* an egg is ejected through the ovary wall. Then the egg passes into a fallopian (fuh LOH pee uhn) tube. A **fallopian tube** leads from each ovary to the uterus. The **uterus** is the organ where a baby grows and develops.

Every month starting at puberty, the lining of the uterus thickens in preparation for pregnancy. If fertilization occurs, the zygote moves down a fallopian tube and embeds in the lining of the uterus. When a baby is born, it passes from the uterus through the vagina. The **vagina** is the same passageway that received the sperm during sexual intercourse.

Menstrual Cycle To prepare for pregnancy, a female's reproductive system goes through several changes. These changes, called the menstrual cycle, usually occur every 28 days. The first day of the cycle is the beginning of *menstruation,* the monthly discharge of blood and tissue from the uterus. Menstruation lasts about 5 days. As soon as menstruation is over, the uterus's lining begins to build up again in preparation for ovulation. Ovulation typically occurs around the 14th day of the cycle. If the egg isn't fertilized by the time it reaches the uterus, it will deteriorate. Menstruation will flush the egg away, starting the cycle over again. A female's menstrual cycle begins at puberty and continues until late middle age.

Figure 9 The Female Reproductive System

MATH BREAK

Counting Eggs

1. The average human female ovulates every month from about age 12 to about age 50. How many mature eggs can she produce during that time period?

2. A female's ovaries typically house 2 million immature egg cells. If she ovulates regularly from age 12 to age 50, what percentage of her eggs will mature?

CROSS-DISCIPLINARY FOCUS

Language Arts The words *male* and *female* actually originate from two unrelated Latin words. *Female* comes from *femella,* meaning "girl," while *male* comes from *masculus,* meaning "male."

---

2) Teach

READING STRATEGY

Activity Draw students' attention to **Figures 8** and **9**. Have them write the new terms in their ScienceLog, leaving a few lines between each term. As students read the section, they should fill in definitions that explain the new terms in their own words.

DEMONSTRATION

Multiple Births A Russian woman in the eighteenth century gave birth to 69 children, with 67 living to reach adulthood. Ask students: If she began ovulation at age 12 and stopped at age 50, and pregnancy lasts nine months, how could she have had so many children?

Write the following answer on the board to demonstrate how it is possible that she had 69 children: She had 27 pregnancies, all of them producing two or more children. She had 16 pairs of twins, 7 sets of triplets, and 4 sets of quadruplets.

$(16 \times 2) + (7 \times 3) + (4 \times 4) = 69$

Answers to MATHBREAK

1. 50 y − 12 y = 38 y
   38 y × 12 eggs/year = 456 eggs. She can produce about 456 mature eggs.

2. $\frac{456 \text{ eggs}}{2,000,000} \times 100 = 0.0228$ percent of her eggs will probably mature.

Teaching Transparency 94 "The Female Reproductive System"

Math Skills Worksheet 3 "Multiplying Whole Numbers"

Section 2 • Human Reproduction

2) Teach, continued

MATH and MORE

Ask students: If one set of identical twins is born for every 250 births, and one set of quadruplets is born for every 705,000 births, how many sets of identical twins are born for every quadruplet birth? ($\frac{705,000}{250} = 2,820$)

 Math Skills Worksheet 5 "Dividing Whole Numbers with Long Division"

MEETING INDIVIDUAL NEEDS

Advanced Learners Encourage interested students to research how fertility drugs cause multiple births. (They will find that fertility drugs stimulate egg ripening and ovulation, which often results in the release of more than one egg at a time.)

Ask them to prepare a brief report and to share their findings with the class.

ACTIVITY

Puzzle Making Divide the class into small groups, challenging each to create a crossword puzzle using section vocabulary and concepts. Have students write clues and construct puzzles and then trade with another group. Allow time for students to solve the puzzles.

Irregularities and Disorders

In most cases, the human reproductive system completes its functions flawlessly. However, as with any body system, there can sometimes be irregularities or disorders.

Multiple Births Have you ever seen a pair of identical twins? Sometimes they are so similar that even their parents can't tell them apart. About one pair of identical twins is born for every 250 births. Another type of twins, called fraternal twins, is also born frequently. Fraternal twins can look very different from each other.

Twins, such as those shown in **Figure 10,** are the most common type of multiple births, but humans can also have triplets (3 babies), quadruplets (4 babies), quintuplets (5 babies), and so on. These types of multiple births are extremely rare. For instance, quadruplets occur only about once in every 705,000 births. Do you know what circumstances result in a multiple birth? To find out, do the Apply exercise at the bottom of this page.

Figure 10 Identical twins have the exact same genes. Many identical twins who are reared apart have similar personalities and interests.

Ectopic Pregnancy In a normal pregnancy, the fertilized egg travels to the uterus and attaches itself to the uterus's wall. In an *ectopic* (ek TAHP ik) *pregnancy,* the fertilized egg attaches itself to a fallopian tube or another area of the reproductive system. Because the zygote cannot develop correctly outside of the uterus, an ectopic pregnancy can be very dangerous for both the mother and child.

Two Types of Twins

Zach and Drew are fraternal twins. They don't look much alike. Emily and Carol are identical twins. They are hard to tell apart. Why are some twins identical and others fraternal? Consider the two possibilities illustrated at right: In *A,* the mass of cells from a single fertilized egg separates into two halves early in development, and in *B* two eggs are released by an ovary and fertilized by two different sperm cells. Record the answers to the following questions in your ScienceLog:

1. Which instance, *A* or *B*, would produce identical twins? Explain your answer.
2. Could fraternal twins be (a) both boys, (b) both girls, (c) one girl and one boy, or (d) all of the above?

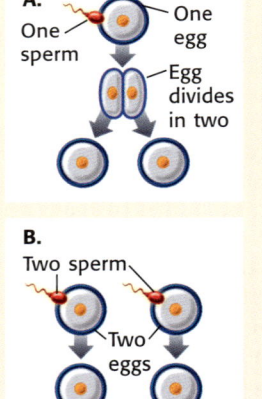

Answers to APPLY

1. *A* would produce identical twins because the two halves of the split egg have identical genetic material.
2. d

 TOPIC: Reproductive System Irregularities or Disorders
GO TO: www.scilinks.org
*sci*LINKS NUMBER: HSTL640

618 Chapter 26 • Reproduction and Development

Infertility In the United States, about 15 percent of married couples have difficulty producing offspring. Many of these couples are **infertile,** which means they are unable to have children. Men may be infertile because they cannot produce enough healthy sperm. This is called a low sperm count. Women may be infertile because they do not ovulate normally. Sexually transmitted diseases can also cause infertility.

STDs *Sexually transmitted diseases* (STDs) are diseases that can pass from an infected person to an uninfected person during sexual contact. An STD you may have heard about is the acquired immune deficiency syndrome (AIDS). Other common STDs are shown in the table below.

One in four American youths catches an STD before age 21.

The Spread of STDs in the U.S.	
STD	Approximate new cases each year
Chlamydia	3–10 million
Genital herpes	1 million
Genital warts	1 million
Gonorrhea	650,000
Syphilis	70,000
AIDS	40,000–50,000

Many chemicals in pollutants are similar to female hormones. Studies are beginning to link these chemicals with early menstruation and low sperm counts.

Cancer Cancer, the uncontrolled division of cells, sometimes occurs in the reproductive organs. The testes and the prostate gland, a gland that produces the fluid in semen, are common sites of cancer in men over age 50. In women, the ovaries and breasts are common sites of cancer.

REVIEW

1. What is the difference between sperm and semen?
2. Can a woman become pregnant at any time of the month? Explain.
3. Define *sexually transmitted diseases,* and give three examples.
4. **Applying Concepts** How are the ovaries similar to the testes? How are they different?

TOPIC: Reproductive System Irregularities or Disorders
GO TO: www.scilinks.org
*sci*LINKS NUMBER: HSTL640

619

Section 2 • Human Reproduction **619**

SECTION 3

Focus

Growth and Development

In this section, students learn about egg fertilization and implantation. Students are also introduced to the different stages of growth of a baby *in utero*, culminating in its birth. Finally, they learn about the stages of human development, from birth through adulthood.

Write this statement on the board or an overhead projector: Name the stages of physical development you have passed through thus far in your life.

Have students list the stages in their ScienceLog. Remind students that their growth and development began while they were still in the uterus. (Students will likely respond with the following: crawling, walking, talking, growing taller, perhaps developing lower voices for some of the boys.)

1 Motivate

DISCUSSION

Life Stages Ask students to list as many characteristics of each of the following as they can:

infancy, childhood, adolescence, adulthood

Tell students that while there are individual differences, all people go through these stages.

Section 3

Terms to Learn

embryo
implantation
placenta
umbilical cord
fetus

What You'll Do

◆ Summarize the processes of fertilization and implantation.
◆ Describe the course of human development.

Growth and Development

Every one of us starts out as a single cell that will become a complete person. We are made of millions of cells, each with its own job to do. You, of course, are no exception. You have become a very complex individual, capable of thousands of different thoughts and actions. It is hard to believe that a person as remarkable as you began your life as a single cell, but that is just what happened.

A New Life

The natural process of creating a human baby starts when a man deposits millions of sperm into a woman's vagina during sexual intercourse. Most of the sperm will die because of the vagina's acidic environment, but a few hundred are able to make it through the uterus and into the fallopian tube, as can be seen in **Figure 11.** The surviving sperm cover the egg, releasing enzymes that help dissolve the egg's outer covering. As soon as one sperm gets through, a membrane closes around the fertilized egg. This membrane keeps other sperm cells from entering.

Implantation The fertilized egg travels down the woman's fallopian tube toward her uterus. The journey takes about 5 days. The zygote undergoes cell division many times during the trip. By the time it reaches the uterus, it is a tiny ball of cells called an **embryo.** During the next few days, the embryo must embed itself in the thick, nutrient-rich lining of its mother's uterus. This process is called **implantation,** and only about 30 percent of all embryos successfully do it. **Figure 12** shows an implanted embryo.

Figure 11 Fertilization and Implantation

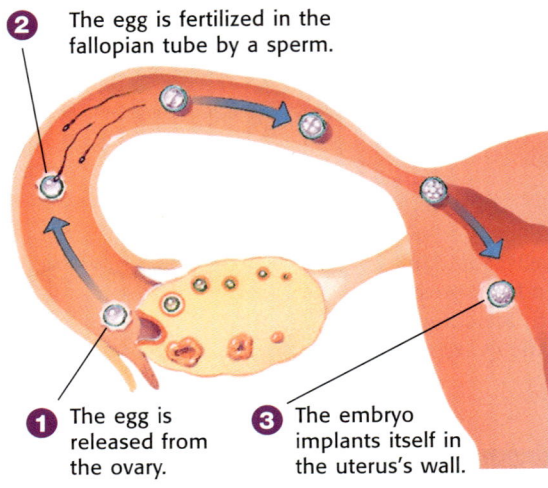

① The egg is released from the ovary.

② The egg is fertilized in the fallopian tube by a sperm.

③ The embryo implants itself in the uterus's wall.

The embryo's actual size is slightly smaller than the period at the end of this sentence.

Figure 12 This embryo has implanted in the wall of its mother's uterus.

Embryo

 Directed Reading Worksheet 26 Section 3

IS THAT A FACT!

The longest gestation period, 22 months, belongs to the Indian elephant. The shortest, 12 days, belongs to the Virginia opossum.

620 Chapter 26 • Reproduction and Development

Before Birth

When the embryo implants itself in a woman's uterus, the woman is officially pregnant. For the embryo to survive, a special two-way exchange organ called a **placenta** begins to grow. The placenta contains a network of blood vessels that provide the embryo with oxygen and nutrients from the mother's blood. Wastes that the embryo produces are removed by the placenta and transported to the mother's blood for her to excrete. Although the embryo's blood and the mother's blood flow very near each other inside the placenta, they never actually mix.

Self-Check

Why is it important that the embryo be implanted in the uterus and not elsewhere? *(See page 782 to check your answer.)*

First Month About 1 week after implantation, the embryo's blood cells and a heart tube form. Then the heart tube begins to twitch, starting the rhythmic beating that will continue for the individual's entire life. By the fourth week, the embryo is almost 2 mm long. Surrounding the embryo is a thin, fluid-filled membrane called the *amnion*, which is formed to protect the growing embryo from shocks. The **umbilical cord** is another new development. It connects the embryo to the placenta. The umbilical cord, amnion, and placenta can be seen in **Figure 13**.

Second Month By the time the embryo is 4 weeks old, it has the beginnings of a brain and spinal cord. It also has tiny limb buds that will eventually develop into arms and legs. Its nostrils, eyelids, hands, and feet then begin to form. Its muscles begin to develop, and for the first time in its life, its brain begins to send signals to other parts of its body. Despite all these transformations, the embryo is still only about the size of a peanut. **Figure 14** shows a 5-week-old embryo.

Figure 13 *The placenta, amnion, and umbilical cord are the life support system for the fetus.*

Figure 14 A 5-Week-Old Embryo

Actual size

2 Teach

Answer to Self-Check

The uterus provides the nutrients and protection that the embryo needs to continue growing. The uterus is also the only place the placenta will form.

READING STRATEGY

Activity Ask students to write down the following question and fill in the correct answers as they read the section. At what stage of development does each of the following events take place? The fetus is felt kicking (3–6 months); the brain and spinal cord begin to form (1–2 months); the fetus practices breathing by moving its lungs up and down (7–9 months).

TOPIC: Growth and Development
GO TO: www.scilinks.org
sciLINKS NUMBER: HSTL645

IS THAT A FACT!

The European badger and the American marten each have a 250-day gestation period. Due to delayed implantation, the embryo grows during only 50 of those days. The fertilized egg develops for a few days immediately after conception in July or August, remains dormant in the uterus until January, and then completes its growth between January and March, at which time the baby is born.

Section 3 • Growth and Development **621**

2 Teach, continued

RESEARCH

Writing Tell students that the first few months of pregnancy are crucial for the healthy mental and physical development of the fetus. Drinking alcohol during this period can lead to birth defects and miscarriages. Have students research the causes and consequences of fetal alcohol syndrome (FAS) and present their findings in a short report.

USING THE FIGURE

Ask students to identify in **Figure 16** the trimester during which the major organs and body structures form. **(the first trimester)**

Ask them to describe the events that occur during the remainder of the pregnancy. **(The structures formed earlier in pregnancy grow and mature during the second and third trimesters.)**

MATH and MORE

Have students calculate the factor of increase in a fetus's body length from the eighth week, when it is about 2.5 cm long, to the fifth month, when it is about 25 cm, to birth, when it is about 50 cm long. **(2.5 cm to 25 cm is an increase by a factor of 10; 25 cm to 50 cm is an increase by a factor of 2; 2.5 cm to 50 cm is an increase by a factor of 20)**

My, How You've Grown! PG 775

Figure 15 A 12-Week-Old Fetus

Actual size

Third Month The next stage comes as tiny movements begin to flutter through the embryo's body. The embryo stretches its legs and twitches its arms. It is now 8 weeks old and is developed enough to be called a **fetus.** Three more weeks pass, and it continues to grow at a fast rate, doubling and then tripling its size within a month. The fetus's hands are now the size of teardrops, and its body weighs as much as two pieces of paper. A 12-week-old fetus can be seen in **Figure 15.**

Fourth to Sixth Month The fetus's 13th week of life passes, and suddenly new movement! It can blink its eyes for the first time, swallow, hiccup, make a fist, and curl its toes that now have tiny nails. By the fourth month, the fetus starts to make even bigger movements. The mother now knows when her baby kicks its legs or stretches its arms.

During the fifth month, the fetus is about 20 cm long. Taste buds form on its tongue, and eyebrows form on its face. The fetus begins to hear sounds through the wall of its mother's uterus. Look at the timeline in **Figure 16** to review the changes that take place in the fetus.

Figure 16 Pregnancy Timeline

Weeks of the First Three Months	
1 and 2	The egg is fertilized by a sperm. The fertilized egg makes its way to the uterus, where it burrows into the lining. The fertilized egg is now called an embryo.
3 and 4	Most major organ systems have started to form. The heart starts to beat around day 22. The placenta is completely formed by the fourth week.
5 and 6	Facial features begin to take shape. The skeleton begins to form.
7 and 8	Muscle movement begins. The embryo is now called a fetus.
9 and 10	Arms, legs, hands, and feet have formed.
11 and 12	The internal organs have formed.

Weeks of the Second Three Months	
13 and 14	The circulatory system is working.
15 and 16	The mother may start to feel the fetus move.
17 and 18	The fetus responds to sound.
19 and 20	The fetus is now about 20 cm long.
21 and 22	
23 and 24	Eyelashes and eyebrows appear.

Weeks of the Third Three Months	
25 and 26	The eyes open.
27 and 28	The fetus can "practice breathe."
29 and 30	Layers of fat form beneath skin.
31 and 32	
33 and 34	Organs are fully functional.
35 and 36	The fetus responds to light.
Birth	The baby is born.

internet connect

SCiLINKS NSTA
TOPIC: Before Birth
GO TO: www.scilinks.org
sciLINKS NUMBER: HSTL635

IS THAT A FACT!

Between conception and birth, the developing fetus increases in size from a single cell to 6 trillion cells!

Seventh to Ninth Month The seventh month is when the fetus's memories begin to form. During this time, its lungs start to "practice breathe," moving up and down continuously as if breathing real air. If the fetus's mother smokes one cigarette during this stage, the fetus's lung movement will stop for up to an hour. The fetus in **Figure 17** is starting its first lung movement.

By the eighth month, the fetus's open eyes can perceive light through its mother's abdominal wall, and its sleeping pattern starts to be influenced by sunlight. When the fetus is asleep, it dreams. Can you imagine what its dreams might be about?

Figure 17 A 21-Week-Old Fetus

Actual size of hand

Birth

After about 9 months, the fetus is ready to live outside of its mother. The mother goes through a series of muscular contractions called *labor*. During labor, the fetus is usually squeezed headfirst through the vagina. There is little room to spare, and the fetus's head is temporarily squashed out of shape as the fetus passes through its mother's pelvis. Suddenly bright lights and cold air surround the newborn baby. It gasps, fills its lungs with air for the first time, and cries.

The baby in **Figure 18** is still connected to the placenta by its umbilical cord. The doctor or midwife assisting the mother ties and cuts the umbilical cord. The baby's navel is all that will remain of the point where the umbilical cord was attached. After the mother expels the placenta from her body, labor is complete.

Figure 18 *This newborn baby is still attached to its umbilical cord. The average mass of a newborn baby is 3.3 kg. The average length is 50 cm.*

From Birth to Death

Of all the animals on this planet, humans have one of the longest life spans. Human infancy lasts 2 years—the same time it takes for most rabbits to be born, grow old, and die. Our childhood extends over a full decade, longer than many cats or dogs live. Humans can live for more than 100 years!

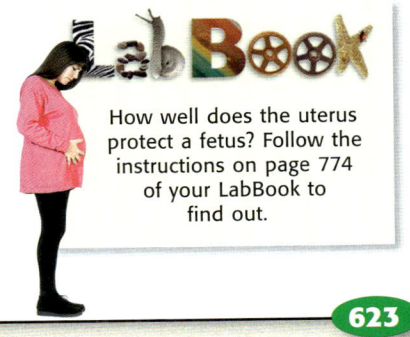

How well does the uterus protect a fetus? Follow the instructions on page 774 of your LabBook to find out.

BRAIN FOOD

Sea horses are one of very few kinds of organisms in which the male carries the fertilized eggs. After courtship, the female deposits eggs into the pouch of her male mate. The male then fertilizes the eggs and carries them until they develop. After a gestation period of between 10 and 60 days, depending on the species, tiny, fully formed sea horses emerge from an opening in the pouch.

CONNECT TO EARTH SCIENCE

It is possible to create pictures using sound waves. Sonograms are pictures obtained by bouncing high-frequency sound waves off of an object. Doctors can use sonograms to "see" a human fetus while it is still in the womb. Sonar, which uses the same principle, is used for navigating and determining an object's position.

Use the following Teaching Transparency to illustrate how sonar works.

Teaching Transparency 154 "How Sonar Works"

PG 774

It's a Comfy, Safe World!

CROSS-DISCIPLINARY FOCUS

Language Arts After the umbilical cord is cut and falls off, all that remains is the navel. The word *navel* comes from the Anglo-Saxon word *nafu*, which means "the hub of the wheel." Early Anglo-Saxons believed the navel was the center of the body.

3) Extend

RETEACHING

Divide the class into small groups, and challenge each group to create a board game. Provide each group with a piece of poster board, plain index cards, and markers. Direct them to create a game board that leads players through prenatal development. The first player who is "born" wins the game. Have them use the index cards to write clues that direct players' movements through "gestation." For example, they might write, "Advance to 4 months if you can describe my abilities at 13 weeks." (At 13 weeks, the fetus can blink its eyes, swallow, hiccup, make a fist, and curl its toes.)

Have students create written rules. Then have them exchange games and play. Sheltered English

Teaching Transparency 95 "Growth Chart"

Reinforcement Worksheet 26 "The Beginning of a Life"

Critical Thinking Worksheet 26 "One to Grow On!"

Figure 19 Five different stages of development are shown the same size so you can see how body proportions change as a person develops.

Activity

Create a poster or timeline illustrating the different stages of human growth. TRY at HOME

Infancy What life stages have you gone through since you were born? You have probably gone through most of the stages shown in **Figure 19.** You were an infant from birth to 2 years of age. During this time, you grew rapidly. Your teeth began to appear. You also became more coordinated as your nervous system developed. This enabled you to begin to walk.

Childhood Your childhood extends from 2 years to puberty. This is also a period of rapid growth. Your first set of teeth were slowly shed and replaced by permanent teeth. Your muscles became more coordinated, allowing you to do activities such as riding a bicycle and jumping rope. Your intellectual abilities also developed during this time.

Adolescence You are considered an adolescent from puberty to adulthood. During puberty, the reproductive systems of young males and females become mature. Puberty occurs in most boys sometime between the ages of 11 and 16. The young male body becomes more muscular, the voice becomes deeper, and body and facial hair appear. In most girls, puberty occurs between the ages of 9 and 14. During puberty in females, the amount of fat in the hips and thighs increases, the breasts enlarge, and body hair appears in areas such as the armpits. At this time, the young female also begins to menstruate.

IS THAT A FACT!

Girls attain three-quarters of their adult height by the age of $7^{1}/_{2}$. Boys attain three-quarters of their adult height by the age of 9.

Adulthood From about age 20 to age 40, you will be considered a young adult. You will be at the peak of your physical development. Beginning around age 30, certain changes associated with aging begin. The changes will be gradual and slightly different for everyone. Some of the early signs of aging include decreasing muscle flexibility, deteriorating eyesight, increasing body fat, and increasing hair loss.

The aging process will continue in a middle-aged adult (someone between 40 and 65). During this period, hair may become gray, athletic abilities will decline, and skin will wrinkle. Any person over 65 years old is considered an older adult. Although aging persists during this period of an individual's life, older adults can still lead active lives. Some of this country's most productive citizens are older adults, as can be seen in **Figure 20**.

Figure 20 John Glenn, the first American to orbit Earth, returned to space at the age of 77.

Life Grows On

Use Figure 19 on the previous page to complete this activity.

1. Use a **ruler** to measure the infant's head height. Then measure the infant's entire body height, including the head.
2. Calculate the percentage of the infant's head height to the infant's total height.
3. Repeat these measurements and calculations for the other stages shown in the figure.

Answer the following question in your ScienceLog:

As a baby grows into an adult, does the head grow faster or slower than the rest of the body? Why do you think this is so?

TRY at HOME

REVIEW

1. What is the difference between an embryo and a fetus?
2. Why does a membrane enclose an egg once a sperm has entered?
3. What developmental changes take place from birth to puberty?
4. **Applying Concepts** When astronauts work in space, they are sometimes attached to the spacecraft by a line called an umbilical. Why do you think the line has been given this name?

TOPIC: Before Birth, Growth and Development
GO TO: www.scilinks.org
sciLINKS NUMBER: HSTL635, HSTL645

Chapter Highlights

Vocabulary Definitions

Section 1

asexual reproduction reproduction in which a single parent produces offspring that are identical to the parent

sexual reproduction reproduction in which two sex cells join to form a unique individual

egg sex cell produced by a female

sperm sex cell produced by a male

zygote a fertilized egg

external fertilization fertilization of an egg by sperm that occurs outside the body of the female

internal fertilization fertilization of an egg by sperm that occurs inside the body of the female

Section 2

testes organs in the male reproductive system that make sperm and testosterone

puberty the time of life when the sex organs become mature

vas deferens the tube in males where sperm is mixed with fluids to make semen

semen a mixture of sperm and fluids

penis the male reproductive organ that transfers semen into the female's body during sexual intercourse

Chapter Highlights

SECTION 1

Vocabulary
- asexual reproduction (p. 612)
- sexual reproduction (p. 613)
- egg (p. 613)
- sperm (p. 613)
- zygote (p. 613)
- external fertilization (p. 614)
- internal fertilization (p. 614)

Section Notes
- During asexual reproduction, a single parent produces offspring that are genetically identical to the parent. Budding and fragmentation are examples of asexual reproduction.
- During sexual reproduction, there is a union of an egg and a sperm.
- Each egg and sperm is the product of meiosis and contains half the usual number of chromosomes. The usual number of chromosomes is restored in the zygote.
- Sperm fertilize eggs outside the female's body in external fertilization. Sperm fertilize eggs inside the female's body in internal fertilization.
- Monotremes are egg-laying mammals. Marsupials are mammals that give birth to partially developed young. Placentals are mammals that give birth to well-developed young.

SECTION 2

Vocabulary
- testes (p. 616)
- puberty (p. 616)
- vas deferens (p. 616)
- semen (p. 616)
- penis (p. 616)
- ovaries (p. 617)
- fallopian tube (p. 617)
- uterus (p. 617)
- vagina (p. 617)
- infertile (p. 619)

☑ Skills Check

Math Concepts

EGGS IN EXILE A woman does not ovulate while she is pregnant. Therefore, if a woman has three children, she will release at least 27 fewer eggs from her ovaries than she would if she never became pregnant.

3 children × 9 months of pregnancy = 27 eggs

Visual Concepts

MALE AND FEMALE REPRODUCTIVE SYSTEMS The diagrams on pp. 616 and 617 show the male and female reproductive systems. Take another look at them, and make sure you recognize all the structures. Also note the similarities between the two systems. For instance, the ovaries have a similar function to the testes, and the fallopian tubes have a similar function to the vas deferens.

Lab and Activity Highlights

My, How You've Grown!   **PG 775**

It's a Comfy, Safe World!   **PG 774**

Datasheets for LabBook
(blackline masters for these labs)

SECTION 2

Section Notes

- The male reproductive system produces sperm and delivers it to the female reproductive system. Sperm are produced in the seminiferous tubules and stored in the epididymis. Sperm leave the body through the urethra.

- The female reproductive system produces eggs, nourishes the developing embryo, and gives birth. An egg leaves one of two ovaries each month and travels to the uterus. If the egg is not fertilized, it disintegrates and menstruation occurs.

- Reproductive system disorders include infertility, cancer, and sexually transmitted diseases.

SECTION 3

Vocabulary
embryo (p. 620)
implantation (p. 620)
placenta (p. 621)
umbilical cord (p. 621)
fetus (p. 622)

Section Notes

- Fertilization occurs in a fallopian tube. From there, the zygote travels to the uterus and implants itself in the uterus's wall.

- After implantation, the placenta develops. The umbilical cord connects the embryo to the placenta. The amnion surrounds and protects the embryo.

- The embryo grows, developing limbs, nostrils, eyelids, and other features. By the eighth week, the embryo is developed enough to be called a fetus.

- Human life stages are infant (birth to 2 years), child (2 years to puberty), adolescent (puberty to 20 years), young adult (20 to 40 years), middle-aged adult (40 to 65 years), and older adult (older than 65 years).

Labs
It's a Comfy, Safe World! (p. 774)
My, How You've Grown! (p. 775)

VOCABULARY DEFINITIONS, continued

ovaries in animals, organs in the female reproductive system that produce eggs

fallopian tube the tube that leads from an ovary to the uterus

uterus an organ in the female reproductive system where a zygote grows and develops

vagina the passageway in the female reproductive system that receives sperm during sexual intercourse

infertile the state of being unable to have children

SECTION 3

embryo an organism in the earliest stage of development

implantation the process in which an embryo embeds itself in the lining of the uterus

placenta an organ that provides a developing fetus with nutrients and oxygen from the mother

umbilical cord a cord that connects the embryo to the placenta

fetus an embryo during the later stages of development within the uterus

---

internetconnect

GO TO: go.hrw.com

Visit the **HRW** Web site for a variety of learning tools related to this chapter. Just type in the keyword:

KEYWORD: HSTBD5

GO TO: www.scilinks.org

Visit the **National Science Teachers Association** on-line Web site for Internet resources related to this chapter. Just type in the sciLINKS number for more information about the topic:

TOPIC: Reproduction — sciLINKS NUMBER: HSTL630
TOPIC: Before Birth — sciLINKS NUMBER: HSTL635
TOPIC: Reproductive System Irregularities or Disorders — sciLINKS NUMBER: HSTL640
TOPIC: Growth and Development — sciLINKS NUMBER: HSTL645

Vocabulary Review Worksheet 26

Blackline masters of these Chapter Highlights can be found in the **Study Guide.**

Lab and Activity Highlights

LabBank

Long-Term Projects & Research Ideas,
Get a Whiff of This! Project 26

Chapter Review Answers

USING VOCABULARY

1. internal fertilization
2. seminiferous tubules
3. semen
4. ovulation
5. placenta

UNDERSTANDING CONCEPTS

Multiple Choice

6. a
7. d
8. c
9. d
10. c
11. d

Short Answer

12. The testes produce sperm, and the ovaries produce eggs.
13. the placenta
14. (must list 4) infancy, childhood, adolescence, young adulthood, middle-aged adulthood, older adulthood
15. an egg and a sperm
16. Budding is a type of asexual reproduction in which a young organism develops off a small part of the parent. Fragmentation is a type of asexual reproduction in which an organism develops from a separated piece of the parent.

Chapter Review

USING VOCABULARY

To complete the following sentences, choose the correct term from each pair of terms listed below:

1. Reptiles, birds, and mammals reproduce sexually by __?__. (*internal fertilization* or *external fertilization*)
2. Sperm are produced in the __?__ within the testes. (*epididymis* or *seminiferous tubules*)
3. The sperm-containing fluid that exits the male body is known as __?__. (*semen* or *amniotic fluid*)
4. The release of an egg from the ovary occurs once each month and is called __?__. (*ovulation* or *menstruation*)
5. The organ of exchange between the developing embryo and the mother is the __?__. (*amnion* or *placenta*)

UNDERSTANDING CONCEPTS

Multiple Choice

6. The sea star can reproduce asexually by
   a. fragmentation.
   b. budding.
   c. external fertilization.
   d. internal fertilization.

7. The correct path of sperm through the male reproductive system is
   a. testes → epididymis → urethra → vas deferens.
   b. epididymis → urethra → testes → vas deferens.
   c. testes → vas deferens → epididymis → urethra.
   d. testes → epididymis → vas deferens → urethra.

8. If the first day of the menstrual cycle is the onset of menstruation, on what day does ovulation typically occur?
   a. 2nd day
   b. 5th day
   c. 14th day
   d. 28th day

9. Monotremes are different from placental mammals because they
   a. are mammals.
   b. have hair.
   c. nurture their young with milk.
   d. lay eggs.

10. All of the following are sexually transmitted diseases *except*
    a. chlamydia.
    b. AIDS.
    c. infertility.
    d. genital herpes.

11. Fertilization occurs in the __?__, and implantation occurs in the __?__.
    a. uterus, fallopian tube
    b. fallopian tube, vagina
    c. uterus, vagina
    d. fallopian tube, uterus

Short Answer

12. What human reproductive organs produce sperm? egg cells?
13. Through what structure does oxygen from the mother pass into the fetus's body?
14. What are four stages of human life following birth?
15. What two cells combine to make a zygote?
16. What is the difference between budding and fragmentation?

628 Chapter 26 • Reproduction and Development

Concept Mapping

17. Use the following terms to create a concept map: asexual reproduction, budding, external fertilization, fragmentation, reproduction, internal fertilization, sexual reproduction.

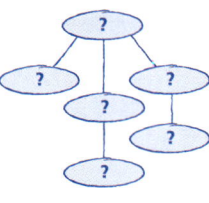

CRITICAL THINKING AND PROBLEM SOLVING

Write one or two sentences to answer the following questions:

18. Explain why the testes are found in the scrotum instead of inside the male body.

19. What is the function of the uterus? How is its function related to the menstrual cycle?

20. How is meiosis important to human reproduction?

MATH IN SCIENCE

21. Hardy Junior High School has 2,750 students. If 1 pair of identical twins is born for every 250 births, about how many pairs of identical twins will be attending the school?

22. Mrs. Schmidt had a baby April 30th. Her baby developed inside her uterus for 9 months. What month was her egg fertilized?

23. In the United States, seven infants die before their first birthday for every 1,000 births. Convert this figure to a percentage. Is your answer greater than or less than 1 percent?

24. In Haiti, a small country in the Caribbean, 74 infants die before their first birthday for every 1,000 births. Convert this figure to a percentage. Is your answer greater or less than 1 percent? Why do you think there is such a difference between the United States and Haiti?

INTERPRETING GRAPHICS

The following graph illustrates the cycles of the male hormone, testosterone, and the female hormone, estrogen. The blue line shows the estrogen level in a female over a period of 28 days. The red line shows the testosterone level in a male over a period of 28 days.

25. What is the major difference between the two hormone levels over the 28-day period?

26. What cycle do you think estrogen affects?

27. Why might the level of testosterone stay the same?

Take a minute to review your answers to the Pre-Reading Questions found at the bottom of page 610. Have your answers changed? If necessary, revise your answers based on what you have learned since you began this chapter.

629

Concept Mapping

17. An answer to this exercise can be found at the end of this book.

CRITICAL THINKING AND PROBLEM SOLVING

18. Sperm develop best at a temperature three degrees lower than normal body temperature. Therefore, the testes are suspended away from the body to keep them cooler.

19. The uterus is the organ in the female reproductive system in which an embryo can develop into a fetus. Every month it builds up tissue that can help nourish a developing embryo. If no embryo is present, the tissue will discharge and cause menstruation.

20. Meiosis ensures that the characteristic human chromosome number remains the same. Since two cells must combine to form a zygote, each sex cell needs only half the 46 chromosomes that all other human body cells have.

MATH IN SCIENCE

21. 11
22. August
23. Approximately 0.7 percent of American infants die before their first birthday. This is less than 1 percent.
24. Approximately 7.4 percent of Haitian infants die before their first birthday. This is more than 1 percent. This is higher than the American percentage because Americans generally have access to better health care than Haitians.

INTERPRETING GRAPHICS

25. Estrogen levels fluctuate, but testosterone stays at the same level throughout the month.
26. Estrogen affects the menstrual cycle.
27. Testosterone levels stay the same because men continually produce sperm.

Chapter 26 • Chapter Review   629

Concept Mapping Transparency 26

Blackline masters of this Chapter Review can be found in the **Study Guide.**

ACROSS THE SCIENCES
Acne

Background
This feature will provide students with a look at some of the changes affecting their body. Puberty is a dynamic time because hormone levels fluctuate from day to day. During puberty, acne will be more severe at times. Students should realize that the physical changes that cause acne are a necessary part of maturation and that acne is not necessarily caused by poor hygiene. Students may be reassured to learn that acne generally clears up after puberty, when hormone levels fluctuate less.

Most importantly, students should know that acne is a treatable condition and should understand how common treatments, such as over-the-counter topical creams and antibiotics, work.

Students may be interested to find out that the male sex hormones, called *androgens*, cause acne in both men and women. Indeed, men and women share the same hormones, only in different quantities and levels of activity.

LIFE SCIENCE • CHEMISTRY

Acne

If you are a teenager, you probably have some firsthand experience with acne. If you don't, you probably will. And contrary to what you may have heard, acne is not caused by greasy foods and candy, though these foods can aggravate the problem. The hormonal fluctuations that occur as young people mature into adults often cause acne.

What Are Pimples?
Skin contains thousands of tiny pores. Each pore contains sebaceous (suh BAY shuhs) glands that produce sebum, the oil you may have noticed on the surface of your skin. This oil is necessary to maintain healthy skin. The production and release of sebum is stimulated by androgens, the male sex hormones, which become active in both girls and boys during puberty.

Sebum usually escapes from the pores without a problem. But sometimes skin cells do not shed properly, and they clog the pores. The sebum that collects in the pores causes lesions, commonly called pimples.

▲ *Acne is caused by the buildup of sebum and dead cells in the pores of the skin.*

Learn Your Lesions
There are two kinds of lesions—noninflamed lesions and inflamed lesions. Noninflamed lesions include blackheads and whiteheads. Some people think blackheads are pores filled with dirt. The dark color of these lesions is actually the result of dark skin pigments or oil trapped in the pores. Whiteheads are white because their contents are hidden under the skin's surface. Inflamed lesions are caused by bacteria and are often red and swollen. Bacteria live in healthy pores, and when pores become clogged, the bacteria are trapped and can cause irritation and infection.

Heredity
Family history appears to be a factor in the development of acne. Unfortunately, if your parents or brothers and sisters had acne, you are likely to have acne too. The causes of hereditary acne remain unclear. Your skin may be genetically programmed to produce more sebum than is produced in other teenagers.

Is There Hope?
Certain over-the-counter products can clean the dead skin cells and sebum out of the pores. Many medications inhibit the production of sebum or encourage the shedding of skin cells. Sometimes doctors prescribe antibiotics, such as tetracycline or erythromycin, to treat severe cases of acne. Most acne clears up as people become adults.

On Your Own
▶ Find out what the active ingredient is in an over-the-counter acne medication. Do some research on this ingredient to find out how it works. Report your findings to the class.

Answer to On Your Own
The primary ingredient in over-the-counter acne medications is benzoyl peroxide, a strong oxidizing agent that kills bacteria. Once absorbed into the skin, benzoyl peroxide is metabolized into benzoic acid, which then exits the body as benzoate through the urine. Some of the side effects of using medications with this ingredient can include different types of skin irritations, such as burning, blistering, crusting, itching, or severe redness.

Science, Technology, and Society

Technology in Its Infant Stages

Every year thousands of babies are born with life-threatening diseases or severe birth defects. What if medical treatments were available to these babies before they were born? Doctors at San Francisco, Harvard, and Vanderbilt Universities are performing experimental fetal surgery with encouraging results.

When Is Fetal Surgery an Option?

To date, approximately 100 fetal operations have been performed across the country. Corrective treatments can take place between the 18th and 30th weeks of pregnancy. Many factors determine whether fetal surgery is appropriate. Surgery is considered to be an option only if the condition is life threatening. However, fetuses with several defects or chromosomal abnormalities are not eligible for surgery.

Successful surgeries have been performed on fetal patients with spina bifida, diaphragmatic hernias, malformations of the lungs, and urinary tract obstructions. Spina bifida is a defect that leaves the spine exposed. A diaphragmatic hernia is a hole in the diaphragm. This condition causes severe breathing difficulties.

Surgery on a Small Scale

Fetal surgery can fall into one of three categories. The least traumatic type of treatment uses a laser scalpel or an endoscope. The scalpel is used to remove chest tumors. An *endoscope* is a video-guided tool that combines a camera lens and scissors that are less than 0.2 cm wide. The doctor guides the scissors through a tiny cut in the abdominal and uterine walls. The doctor is unable to see the fetus directly during this surgery because the cut is so small. Therefore, he or she must watch the video images provided by the endoscope during the operation.

A more traumatic option is open fetal surgery. In this treatment, the mother's abdomen and uterus are opened, and the fetus is partially exposed.

The third, and relatively new, option is called fetal stem cell transplant. This treatment is essentially a bone marrow transplant for the fetus. It is used to treat genetic diseases and diseases of the immune system.

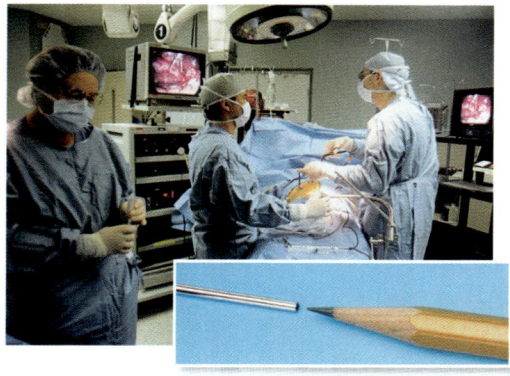

▲ *The endoscope shown here is used to perform fetal surgery.*

What the Future Holds

Each fetal surgery results in the improvement of techniques and treatments, as well as in the expansion of the types of defects and diseases that can be treated. As the number of fetal surgeries increases, fetal surgery will become much more routine.

Going Further

▶ The endoscopes used in fetal surgery use a technology called fiber optics. Research what items around your home also use fiber optics.

UNIT 8

TIMELINE
Human Health

In many ways, living in the twenty-first century is good for your health. Many deadly diseases that plagued our ancestors now have cures. Some diseases, like smallpox, have been wiped out entirely. And others can be prevented by vaccines and other methods. Many researchers, including the people on this timeline, have worked to understand diseases and to find cures.

But people still get sick, and many diseases have no cure. In this unit you will learn how your body protects itself and fights illness. You will also learn about ways to keep yourself healthy so that your body can operate in top form.

1403
The first quarantine is imposed in Venice, Italy, to stop the spread of the plague, or Black Death.

1717
Lady Mary Wortley Montague introduces a smallpox vaccine in England.

1900
Walter Reed discovers that yellow fever is carried by mosquitoes.

1906
Upton Sinclair writes *The Jungle,* which describes unsanitary conditions in the Chicago stockyards and leads to the creation of the Pure Food and Drug Act.

1921
A tuberculosis vaccine is produced.

1816
R. T. Laennec invents the stethoscope.

1853
Charles Gerhardt synthesizes aspirin for the first time.

1895
X rays are discovered by Wilhelm Roentgen.

1855
Nurse Florence Nightingale introduces hygienic standards to military hospitals during the Crimean War.

1977
Smallpox is eradicated.

1953
Cigarette smoking is linked to lung cancer.

1997
Researchers discover that high doses of alcohol in early pregnancy switch off a gene that controls brain, heart, limb, and skull development.

Human Health

Chapter Organizer

CHAPTER ORGANIZATION	TIME MINUTES	OBJECTIVES	LABS, INVESTIGATIONS, AND DEMONSTRATIONS
Chapter Opener pp. 634–635	45	National Standards: UCP 2, SAI 1, 2, HNS 3	**Start-Up Activity** Invisible Invaders, p. 635
Section 1 Disease	90	▶ Explain the difference between infectious diseases and noninfectious diseases. ▶ Identify five ways that you might come into contact with a pathogen. ▶ Discuss four methods that have helped reduce the spread of disease. SAI 1, 2, ST 2, SPSP 1, 5, HNS 1, 3, LS 1f; LabBook UCP 2, SAI 1	**Discovery Lab,** Passing the Cold, p. 778 **GENERAL** **Datasheets for LabBook,** Passing the Cold, Datasheet 57 **GENERAL**
Section 2 Your Body's Defenses	90	▶ Describe how your body keeps out pathogens. ▶ Explain how the immune system works. ▶ Discuss the purpose of a fever. UCP 1–5, SAI 1, HNS 3, LS 1b, 1d–1f, LS 3a, 3b; LabBook UCP 2, SAI 1	**QuickLab,** It's Only Skin Deep, p. 641 **GENERAL** **Making Models,** Antibodies to the Rescue, p. 776 **GENERAL** **Datasheets for LabBook,** Antibodies to the Rescue, Datasheet 56 **GENERAL**
Section 3 Challenges to the Immune System	90	▶ Explain the difference between allergies and autoimmune diseases. ▶ Discuss what cancer is. ▶ Describe how HIV affects the immune system. UCP 3, 4, LS 1d–1f, 3b	**Long-Term Projects & Research Ideas,** Project 27 **ADVANCED**

*See page **T20** for a complete correlation of this book with the*

NATIONAL SCIENCE EDUCATION STANDARDS.

TECHNOLOGY RESOURCES

 Guided Reading Audio CD English or Spanish, Chapter 27

 One-Stop Planner CD-ROM with Test Generator

 Scientists in Action, In Search of Nature's Cures, Segment 29

Science, Technology, & Society, Computer Healing, Segment 34

633A Chapter 27 • Body Defenses and Disease

Chapter 27 • Body Defenses and Disease

CLASSROOM WORKSHEETS, TRANSPARENCIES, AND RESOURCES	SCIENCE INTEGRATION AND CONNECTIONS	REVIEW AND ASSESSMENT
Directed Reading Worksheet 27 BASIC **Science Puzzlers, Twisters & Teasers,** Worksheet 27 ADVANCED		
Directed Reading Worksheet 27, Section 1 BASIC **Critical Thinking Worksheet 27,** Vaccine for Super Bug Found! ADVANCED **Transparency 233,** Thermal Energy	**Physics Connection,** p. 638 **Connect to Physical Science,** p. 638 in ATE **Apply,** p. 639 GENERAL **MathBreak,** p. 639 GENERAL **Careers:** Naturopathic Physician, p. 652 GENERAL	**Self-Check,** p. 637 **Review,** p. 639 GENERAL **Quiz,** p. 639 in ATE GENERAL **Alternative Assessment,** p. 639 in ATE GENERAL
Directed Reading Worksheet 27, Section 2 BASIC **Transparency 96,** An Antibody's Shape Matches a Pathogen **Transparency 97,** The Eight Steps of the Immune System: A **Transparency 98,** The Eight Steps of the Immune System: B **Reinforcement Worksheet 27,** Immunity Teamwork GENERAL	**Multicultural Connection,** p. 641 in ATE **Scientific Debate:** Frogs in the Medicine Cabinet?, p. 653 GENERAL	**Review,** p. 644 GENERAL **Quiz,** p. 644 in ATE GENERAL **Alternative Assessment,** p. 644 in ATE GENERAL
Directed Reading Worksheet 27, Section 3 BASIC	**Real-World Connection,** p. 646 in ATE	**Homework,** p. 646 in ATE ADVANCED **Review,** p. 647 GENERAL **Quiz,** p. 647 in ATE GENERAL **Alternative Assessment,** p. 647 in ATE GENERAL

internetconnect

Holt, Rinehart and Winston On-line Resources
go.hrw.com

For worksheets and other teaching aids related to this chapter, visit the HRW Web site and type in the keyword: **HSTBD6**

National Science Teachers Association
www.scilinks.org

Encourage students to use the *sci*LINKS numbers listed in the internet connect boxes to access information and resources on the **NSTA** Web site.

END-OF-CHAPTER REVIEW AND ASSESSMENT

Chapter Review in Study Guide
Vocabulary and Notes in Study Guide
Chapter Tests with Performance-Based Assessment, Chapter 27 Test
Chapter Tests with Performance-Based Assessment, Performance-Based Assessment 27
Concept Mapping Transparency 27

Chapter Resources & Worksheets

Visual Resources

Meeting Individual Needs

Chapter 27 • Body Defenses and Disease

Chapter 27 • Body Defenses and Disease

Review & Assessment

STUDY GUIDE

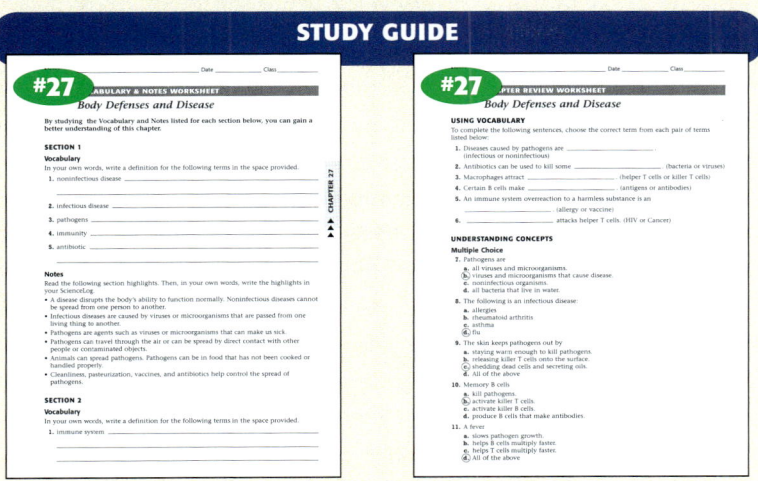

CHAPTER TESTS WITH PERFORMANCE-BASED ASSESSMENT

Lab Worksheets

LONG-TERM PROJECTS & RESEARCH IDEAS

DATASHEETS FOR LABBOOK

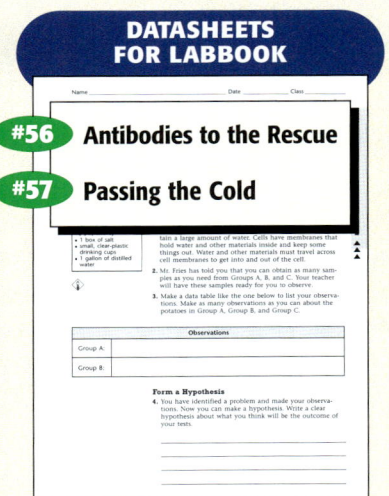

Applications & Extensions

CRITICAL THINKING & PROBLEM SOLVING

SCIENCE TECHNOLOGY

SCIENTISTS IN ACTION

Chapter 27 • Chapter Resources & Worksheets

Chapter Background

SECTION 1

Disease

▶ **Pathogens and the Diseases They Cause**
Pathogens are agents that cause disease. Pathogens can be living or nonliving. Living pathogens include bacteria, protists, fungi, worms, and insects. Nonliving pathogens include viruses, viroids, and prions.

- Bacterial diseases include bubonic plague, cholera, dental caries, lyme disease, pneumonia, and typhoid fever.

- Viral diseases include colds, influenza, chickenpox, measles, rubella, mumps, smallpox, infectious hepatitis, polio, and AIDS.

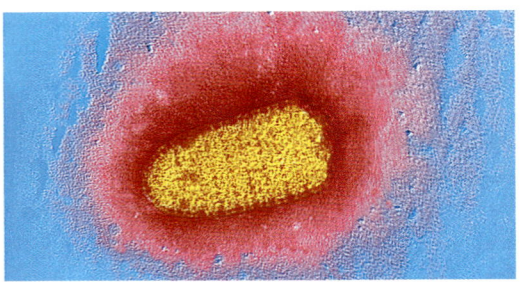

- Protists cause malaria, Chagas' disease, toxoplasmosis, and giardiasis. Common fungal diseases include ringworm, athlete's foot, vaginal yeast infections, jock itch, and histoplasmosis.

IS THAT A FACT!

- Bacteria were the first organisms to inhabit Earth. They are thought to have been the only organisms on Earth for about 1 billion years.

- All other life-forms are thought to have evolved from ancestral forms of bacteria.

- Some species of bacteria can reproduce every 20 minutes. Given unlimited resources, one bacterium could produce 1 million kilograms of bacteria in a day!

▶ **Emerging Viruses**
The news is full of instances in which new viruses have suddenly begun to infect people. Examples include HIV, which became common in the 1980s, hantavirus, which caused an outbreak in 1993, and new strains of Ebola, which were announced in the 1990s. Such viruses are called emerging viruses.

- Emerging viruses can evolve or mutate from an existing virus that was not infectious. They can also spread from one species to another. Another way that a virus can suddenly emerge is through globalization. When people build roads through a previously isolated area or travel to new places, viruses can spread.

▶ **Types of Vaccines**
Vaccines are harmless forms of a pathogen that are introduced into the body, helping the immune system develop antibodies against the pathogen should the disease-causing form enter the body in the future.

- There are several ways that vaccines are prepared today. One way to make a vaccine is to inactivate the viruses or to kill the bacteria that cause the disease. Another way is to use a similar strain of pathogen or an attenuated or weakened version of the pathogen. The latter kind of vaccine is sometimes called a live attenuated vaccine.

IS THAT A FACT!

- Not all vaccines are injections. One form of the polio vaccine is given orally, in a sugar cube.

- Researchers at the Boyce Thompson Institute for Plant Research at Cornell University are working to make a vaccine that subjects receive by eating a genetically engineered banana.

SECTION 2

Your Body's Defenses

▶ **The Body's Defenses Against Pathogens**
The body has two main kinds of defenses against disease—specific and nonspecific defenses.

- The body's so-called first and second lines of defense are its nonspecific defense mechanisms. The first line

Chapter 27 • Body Defenses and Disease

of defense is the skin, the mucous membranes, and the secretions of the mucous membranes. Oil, sweat, tears, mucus, and saliva wash pathogens away and contain proteins that digest the cell walls of microbes.

- The body's second line of defense includes white blood cells that ingest or destroy foreign agents that they detect in the body. The second line of defense also includes proteins that help cells avoid infection by foreign agents. Antimicrobial proteins include complement proteins and interferons. Also part of the body's second line of defense is its inflammatory response, which occurs in response to cuts or other incisions through the skin.

▶ Fever
A fever occurs when the body's temperature rises above 98.6°F (37°C) when measured orally.

- Fevers, which commonly accompany infectious diseases, help the body thwart invading pathogens. However, fevers may also accompany noninfectious conditions, such as dehydration and heart attack.

IS THAT A FACT!
- A very high fever can cause a coma, seizures, or brain damage.

SECTION 3
Challenges to the Immune System

▶ AIDS
AIDS is the final stage in an HIV infection. Upon infection, the viruses first multiply quickly and are also quickly fought off by immune system cells. Some viruses remain in the body and replicate slowly over time. Immune system cells continue the fight, sometimes for many years. HIV attacks T4 helper cells, and when the number of helper T cells falls below a certain level, a person is said to have AIDS.

- HIV is spread through the exchange of blood and other body fluids. It is not spread through casual contact, however.

- There is no cure for AIDS at this time. There are only drug regimens that may prolong the life of some patients.

- The best way to avoid contracting AIDS is to avoid the behaviors known to put one at risk for acquiring HIV. These behaviors include sharing needles and engaging in unprotected sexual contact.

▶ Allergic Reactions
The first time a person is exposed to an allergen, such as pollen, he or she usually shows no allergic response. As when a vaccine is administered, the body produces antibodies against the allergen. Thus prepared, the body develops the allergic response upon subsequent exposures to the allergen.

IS THAT A FACT!
- Allergic responses may be a defense mechanism left over from the body's defenses against parasitic worms. This hypothesis comes from the observation that the body's method of combating parasitic worms is very similar to the allergic response seen in hay fever and asthma.

- Large, colorful flowers are not usually the culprits for pollen allergies. Pollen allergies are typically the result of small, plain flowers whose pollen is dispersed via wind.

For background information about teaching strategies and issues, refer to the *Professional Reference for Teachers*.

CHAPTER 27

Body Defenses and Disease

Pre-Reading Questions

Students may not know the answers to these questions before reading the chapter, so accept any reasonable response.

Suggested Answers

1. A pathogen, more specifically a virus, infects your body.
2. A fever helps cells in your immune system reproduce faster and also inhibits the growth of many pathogens.

Directed Reading Worksheet 27

Science Puzzlers, Twisters & Teasers Worksheet 27

Guided Reading Audio CD
English or Spanish, Chapter 27

CHAPTER 27

Body Defenses and Disease

Sections

1. Disease 636
   Physics Connection .. 638
   MathBreak 639
   Apply 639
   Internet Connect 639
2. Your Body's Defenses .. 640
   QuickLab 641
   Internet Connect 644
3. Challenges to the
   Immune System 645
   Internet Connect 647
   Chapter Review 650
   Feature Articles 652, 653
   LabBook 776–779

Pre-Reading Questions

1. When you "catch a cold," what is it that infects your body?
2. How does a fever help you get well?

Alien Invaders

No, this photo is not from a sci-fi movie. It is not an alien insect soldier. This is, in fact, a greatly enlarged image of a house dust mite that is tinier than the dot of an *i*. Huge numbers of these creatures live in carpets, beds, and sofas in every home. Dust mites often cause problems for people who have asthma or allergies. In this chapter, you will learn how the body's immune system fights diseases and alien factors, such as dust mites, that cause allergies. You will also get some tips on controlling the spread of disease.

---

internet connect

HRW On-line Resources
go.hrw.com
For worksheets and other teaching aids, visit the HRW Web site and type in the keyword: **HSTBD6**

www.scilinks.com
Use the sciLINKS numbers at the end of each chapter for additional resources on the **NSTA** Web site.

www.cnnfyi.com
Visit the CNN Web site for current events coverage and classroom resources.

INVISIBLE INVADERS

In this activity, you will use a technique that makes "invisible" life-forms become visible.

Procedure

1. Obtain two **Petri dishes containing nutrient agar.** Label them "Washed" and "Unwashed."
2. Rub two **marbles** between the palms of your hands. Observe the appearance of the marbles.
3. Roll one marble in the Petri dish labeled "Unwashed."
4. Put on a pair of **disposable gloves.** Wash the other marble with **soap** and **warm water** for 4 minutes. Does the appearance of the marble change after it is washed?
5. Roll the washed marble in the Petri dish labeled "Washed."
6. Secure the lids of the Petri dishes with **transparent tape.** Place the dishes in a warm, dark place. **Caution:** Do not open the Petri dishes after they are sealed.
7. Observe the Petri dishes each day for a week. Record your observations in your ScienceLog.

Analysis

8. How did the washed and unwashed marbles compare? How did the Petri dishes differ after several days?
9. Why is it important to wash your hands before eating?

START-UP Activity

INVISIBLE INVADERS

MATERIALS

For Each Group:
- 2 Petri dishes
- nutrient agar
- 2 marbles
- sterile disposable gloves
- soap
- warm water
- transparent tape

Safety Caution

Remind students to review all safety cautions and icons before beginning this lab activity. Tell students not to open the Petri dishes once they are sealed. Treat all growth in the Petri dishes as pathogenic, and dispose of the dishes as you would any other biohazard.

Teacher's Notes

Keep the lids on the Petri dishes except when rolling the marble on the agar. This helps keep outside contamination to a minimum. In step 6, it might be helpful to use an incubator set at 37°C.

Answers to START-UP Activity

8. Descriptions can vary. The Petri dish labeled "Unwashed" should have the most bacterial growth.
9. It is important to wash to help decrease the number of microorganisms you put in your mouth.

Chapter 27 • Body Defenses and Disease

SECTION 1

Disease

You've probably heard it before: "Cover your mouth when you sneeze!" "Wash your hands!" "Don't put that in your mouth!" What is all the fuss about? When people say these things to you, they are concerned about the spread of disease.

What Causes Disease?

When you have a *disease,* your normal body functions are disrupted. Some diseases, such as most cancers and heart disease, are not spread from one person to another. They are called **noninfectious diseases.**

Noninfectious diseases can be caused by a variety of factors. For example, a genetic disorder causes the disease hemophilia, in which a person's blood does not clot properly. The disease scurvy is caused by a lack of vitamin C in the diet. Smoking, lack of physical activity, and a high-fat diet can greatly increase a person's chances of getting certain noninfectious diseases. Avoiding harmful habits may help you avoid noninfectious diseases.

A disease that can be passed from one living thing to another is an **infectious disease.** Infectious diseases are caused by agents called **pathogens.** Viruses and some bacteria, fungi, protists, and worms may all cause diseases. **Figure 1** shows some common pathogens.

Terms to Learn

noninfectious disease
infectious disease
pathogen
immunity

What You'll Do

◆ Explain the difference between infectious diseases and noninfectious diseases.
◆ Identify five ways that you might come into contact with a pathogen.
◆ Discuss four methods that have helped reduce the spread of disease.

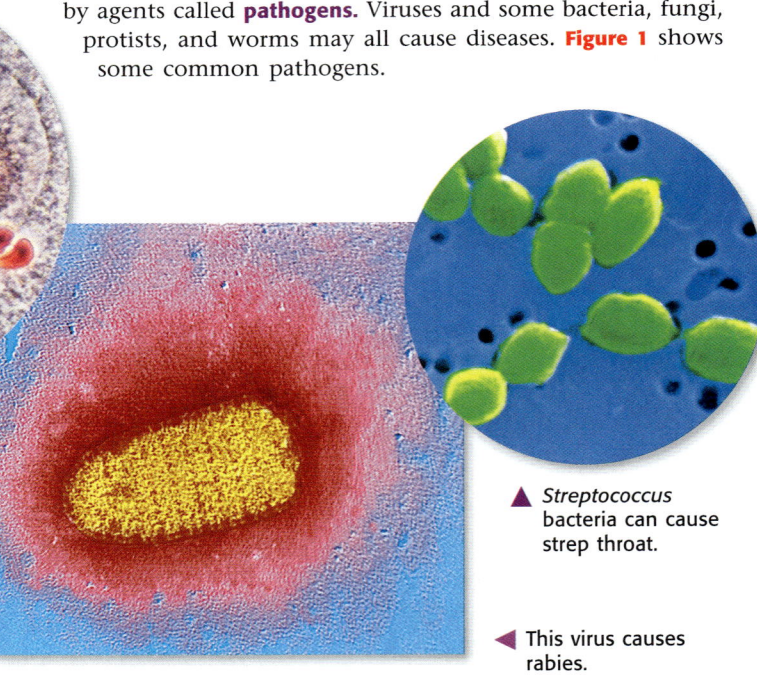

Figure 1 Pathogens, such as these, are often referred to as germs.

▲ This protist, *Entamoeba,* can infect the intestines of humans, causing a disease called dysentery.

▲ *Streptococcus* bacteria can cause strep throat.

◀ This virus causes rabies.

636

Pathways to Pathogens

There are many ways pathogens can be passed from one person to another. Being aware of them can help you stay healthy.

Through the Air Some pathogens travel through the air. For example, a single sneeze, like the one shown in **Figure 2,** releases thousands of tiny droplets of moisture that can carry pathogens.

Contaminated Objects A person who is sick may leave bacteria or viruses on objects such as doorknobs, keyboards, drinking glasses, towels, or combs. If you drink from a glass that an infected person has just used, you could become infected with a pathogen.

Person to Person Some pathogens are spread by direct person-to-person contact. You can become infected with some illnesses by kissing, shaking hands, or touching the sores of an infected person.

Animals Some pathogens are carried by animals. For example, humans can get a fungus called ringworm from handling an infected dog or cat. Also, ticks may carry bacteria that cause Lyme disease or Rocky Mountain spotted fever.

Food and Water Drinking water in the United States is generally safe, but water lines can break, or treatment plants can become flooded, allowing microorganisms to enter the public water supply. Bacteria growing in foods and beverages can cause illness too. Refrigerating foods can slow the growth of many of these pathogens, but meat, fish, and eggs that are not cooked enough can still contain dangerous bacteria or parasites. Leaving food out at room temperature can give bacteria such as *Salmonella* time to grow and produce toxins in the food. For these reasons, it is important to wash all used cooking tools.

Figure 2 A sneeze can force thousands of pathogen-carrying droplets out of your body at up to 160 km per hour.

In developing countries, 80 percent of diseases are related to contaminated drinking water.

Self-Check

Jackie cut up raw meat on her kitchen counter. If her brother makes a sandwich on the same counter later, how could he come in contact with a pathogen? *(See page 782 to check your answer.)*

1) Motivate

DISCUSSION

Diseases Invite students to describe a time when they were sick. Encourage students to describe how they felt, how they may have caught the disease, and how they were treated or cured. Based on students' experiences, lead a discussion about how diseases are caused and treated.

Was the disease you described infectious or noninfectious? (Answers will depend on the disease the students describe.)

What kind of pathogen caused the disease? (Answers will depend on the disease the students describe. Allow students to research the cause of the disease if time permits. Most high school and college biology textbooks have a chart of common diseases and their pathogenic causes.)

2) Teach

MEETING INDIVIDUAL NEEDS

Advanced Learners Provide students with a compound light microscope and prepared slides of different kinds of bacteria, including rod-shaped bacteria. Have them observe the specimens, compare the different kinds of bacteria, and make sketches in their ScienceLog.
<mark>Sheltered English</mark>

Answer to Self-Check

If Jackie did not wash the counter after cutting up the meat, bacteria could grow on the counter where the meat was. This bacteria could contaminate her brother's sandwich.

Passing the Cold

3) Extend

GOING FURTHER

Writing Certain strains of bacteria that were first noticed in the 1950s have genes that make them resistant to antibiotics. Because bacteria can share genes with one another and reproduce rapidly, the number of bacteria that are resistant to antibiotics is increasing. The misuse of antibiotics, such as taking antibiotics for viral infections, can cause the number of antibiotic-resistant bacteria to increase. Have students research and report on the health hazards of these resistant bacteria.

CONNECT TO PHYSICAL SCIENCE

Pasteurization is the process of killing harmful bacteria using thermal energy. Milk is pasteurized one of two ways: by heating it to 66°C for 30 minutes or by heating it to 75°C for 16 seconds. The organisms that can survive pasteurization will eventually spoil the milk, but they are not generally harmful to people. Boiling the milk would kill even more of the bacteria in it—not just the harmful ones—but it would also change the milk. Use Teaching Transparency 233 to illustrate how increasing the temperature of a substance increases its thermal energy.

Teaching Transparency 233
"Thermal Energy"
LINK TO PHYSICAL SCIENCE

Critical Thinking Worksheet 27
"Vaccine for Super Bug Found"

Physics CONNECTION

Hospitals use a machine called an autoclave to kill bacteria on surgical instruments. An autoclave works by increasing the pressure of steam as its temperature increases. The combined effect of pressure and temperature kills bacteria at a lower temperature than would normally be needed.

Putting Pathogens in Their Place

Until the twentieth century, surgery patients often died of bacterial infections. But as doctors learned more about disease, it became clear that simple cleanliness could help prevent the spread of some diseases. Today, hospitals and clinics use a variety of technologies to prevent the spread of pathogens. For example, ultraviolet radiation, boiling water, and chemicals are used in health facilities to kill pathogens.

Pasteurization During the mid-1800s, Louis Pasteur, a French scientist, discovered that microorganisms caused wine to spoil. The uninvited microorganisms were bacteria. Pasteur devised a method of using heat to kill most of the bacteria in the wine. This method is called *pasteurization* (PAS tuhr i ZAY shuhn), and it is still used today. The milk that the girl in **Figure 3** is drinking has been pasteurized.

Vaccines and Immunity In the late 1700s, no one knew what a pathogen was. It was during this time that Edward Jenner, the physician discussed on page 634, studied a disease called smallpox. He observed that people who had been infected with cowpox seemed to have protection against smallpox. This protection, or resistance to a disease, is called **immunity**. Jenner's work led to the first modern *vaccine*. A vaccine is a substance that helps your body develop immunity to a disease.

Today vaccines are used all over the world to prevent many serious diseases. Modern vaccines contain pathogens that are killed or specially treated so that they can't make you very sick. The vaccine is enough like the pathogen to allow your body to develop a defense against the disease.

Figure 3 Today pasteurization is used to kill pathogens in many different types of food, including dairy products, eggs, meats, and juices.

WEIRD SCIENCE

During the Civil War some surgeons began to find links between unclean conditions and certain infections, such as gangrene and blood poisoning. By 1867, a British surgeon named Joseph Lister insisted on cleanliness during surgery. So it came as a shock in 1872 when an American surgeon, Addinell Hewson, claimed that the best way to treat ulcers, burns, and gunshot wounds was with dirt. Although Hewson was much criticized at the time, 93 of his severely wounded patients recovered. It appears he may have stumbled onto natural antibiotics found in the soil, more than 50 years before penicillin was discovered.

Antibiotics Bacterial infections can be a serious threat to your health. Fortunately, doctors can usually treat these kinds of infections with antibiotics. An *antibiotic* is a substance that can kill bacteria or slow the growth of bacteria. Antibiotics may also be used to treat infections caused by other microorganisms, like fungi. If you take an antibiotic when you are sick, it is important that you take it according to your doctor's instructions to ensure that all the pathogens are killed.

Viruses, such as those that cause colds, are not affected by antibiotics. The only way to destroy viruses in your body is to locate and kill the cells they have invaded. In the next section, you'll see how a healthy immune system does just that.

MATH BREAK

Epidemic!
You catch a cold and return to your school while sick. Your friends don't have immunity to your cold. On the first day, you expose five friends to your cold. The next day, each of those friends passes the virus to five more people. If this pattern continues for 5 more days, how many people will be exposed to the virus?

Cold Calamity

Frank caught a bad cold just before the opening night of his school play. He visited his doctor and asked her to prescribe antibiotics for his cold. The doctor politely refused and suggested that Frank stay home and get plenty of rest. Why do you think the doctor refused to give Frank antibiotics? Explain your answer.

REVIEW

1. How is an infectious disease different from a noninfectious disease?
2. List five ways that you might come into contact with a pathogen.
3. How does a vaccine work?
4. **Inferring Relationships** Why might the risk of infectious disease be high in a community that has no water-treatment facility?

internet connect

SCILINKS NSTA

TOPIC: What Causes Diseases?, Pathogens
GO TO: www.scilinks.org
*sci*LINKS NUMBER: HSTL655, HSTL660

Answers to Review

1. An infectious disease can be transmitted to other organisms. A noninfectious disease cannot be transmitted to another organism.
2. Answers can vary, but may include being sneezed upon by an infected person, touching an infected person, having sexual contact with an infected person, eating infected food, or breathing in the pathogen.
3. A vaccine is enough like a pathogen to help a body develop a defense against that pathogen.
4. Without water treatment, a community's water supply can become easily infected with pathogens. These pathogens can be ingested or can contaminate objects washed in the water.

SECTION 2

Focus

Your Body's Defenses

This section introduces the means by which the body protects itself from pathogens. Students will learn how the skin keeps pathogens out of the body and how the immune system works. Students will also learn the purpose of a fever.

Bellringer

Have students make a list in their ScienceLog of the ways that pathogens might enter the body. (*Examples include through the mouth, ears, nose, and cuts in the skin. Pathogens can travel in the water, air, and food.*)

1) Motivate

ACTIVITY

Reactions to Illness Ask students to think of a time when they were ill. Have students make a list of the ways their body reacted to the illness. (*Answers might include having fever, chills, sweating, running nose, sore throat, a rash, and throbbing pain.*)

Encourage students to share their lists with a partner. Then have students skim this lesson and try to link their body's reactions with the reactions of the immune system to pathogenic invasions.

Directed Reading Worksheet 27 Section 2

Section 2

Terms to Learn
immune system   B cell
macrophage   antibody
T cell   memory B cell

What You'll Do
- Describe how your body keeps out pathogens.
- Explain how the immune system works.
- Discuss the purpose of a fever.

Your Body's Defenses

Although you probably don't realize it, your body must constantly protect itself against pathogens that are trying to invade it. But how does your body do that? Luckily, your body has its own built-in defense system.

Your Suit of Armor

For a pathogen to harm you, it must attack a part of your body. Usually, though, only a small percentage of the pathogens around you ever make it past your first lines of defense.

Eyes, Nose, and Mouth Many organisms that try to enter your eyes or mouth are destroyed by special enzymes. Pathogens that enter your nose are washed down the back of your throat by mucus. The mucus carries the pathogens to your stomach, where most are quickly digested.

Skin Your skin is made of many layers of flat cells. The outermost layers are dead. As a result, any pathogen that lands on your skin cannot find a live cell to infect. As **Figure 4** shows, the dead skin cells are constantly dropping off of your body as new skin cells grow from beneath. As the dead skin cells flake off, they carry away viruses, bacteria, and other microorganisms. In addition, glands secrete oil onto your skin's surface. The oil contains chemicals that kill many pathogens.

Figure 4 *Your body loses and replaces approximately 1 million skin cells every 40 minutes. In the process, countless pathogens are sloughed off.*

Earwax is one of your body's defenses against foreign invaders. Wax collects dirt, bacteria, fungi, and other foreign matter that could cause an ear infection.

---

640 Chapter 27 • Body Defenses and Disease

A Forced Entry

Sometimes skin is burned, cut, or punctured. When this happens, pathogens can enter the body. The body acts quickly to keep out as many pathogens as possible. Blood flow to the injured area increases. Cell parts in the blood called *platelets* help seal the open wound so that no more pathogens can enter.

The increased blood flow also brings cells that belong to the **immune system**, the body system that fights pathogens. The immune system is not localized in any one place in your body, nor is it controlled by any one organ, such as the brain. Instead, it is an army of individual cells, tissues, and organs that work together to combat invading pathogens.

Soldiers of the Immune System

The immune system consists mainly of three kinds of cells. One kind is the **macrophage** (MAK roh FAYJ). Macrophages engulf, or eat, any microorganisms or viruses floating around. If only a few microorganisms and viruses have entered the wound, the macrophages can easily stop them.

The other two main types of immune-system cells are **T cells** and **B cells.** T cells play an important role in coordinating the immune system. Many B cells make **antibodies,** which are proteins that attach to specific pathogens. Your body is capable of making billions of different antibodies, but each antibody usually attaches to only one type of pathogen, as illustrated in **Figure 5.**

QuickLab
It's Only Skin Deep

Cut an **apple** in half. Place **plastic wrap** over both halves. The plastic wrap will act as skin. Use **scissors** to cut the plastic wrap on one of the apple halves, then use an **eyedropper** to drip **food coloring** on each apple half. The food coloring represents pathogens coming into contact with your body. Now, answer the following questions:

1. What happened to each apple half?
2. How is the plastic wrap similar to skin?
3. How is the plastic wrap different from skin?

Figure 5 *An antibody's shape is very specialized. It matches a pathogen like a key fits a lock.*

What are antibodies tailored to fit? Find out on page 776 of your LabBook.

Multicultural CONNECTION

In the sixteenth century, Hernando Cortes and the Spanish conquistadors overwhelmed and conquered the flourishing cultures of what is now Mexico. One reason the Europeans were able to overtake the Native Americans so quickly is that the Europeans incidentally brought with them diseases such as smallpox. These diseases were new to the populations in the Americas, and they devastated entire nations. In the span of just two generations, an estimated 12,000,000 to 25,000,000 Native Americans died as a result of European diseases.

2) Teach, continued

MEETING INDIVIDUAL NEEDS

Learners Having Difficulty
Have students trace the proper sequence of the pictures across these two pages. Point out that each picture has its own caption that begins with a bold heading. Then have students outline the information on these two pages by listing the bold headings in order on a sheet of paper. Have pairs of students compare their outlines. Sheltered English

USING THE FIGURE

As students look at the pictures on these pages, point out that the pictures are numbered. After students have studied the sequence of events portrayed in the pictures, have them point to each kind of white blood cell shown in the pictures on these two pages as you call out their names: helper T cell, killer T cell, B cell, macrophage. Then ask students to describe the role of each kind of white blood cell. Sheltered English

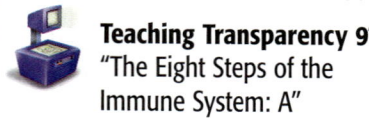

Teaching Transparency 97
"The Eight Steps of the Immune System: A"

TOPIC: Body Defenses
GO TO: www.scilinks.org
sciLINKS NUMBER: HSTL665

1 Enemy Invasion! A macrophage displays the pieces of bacteria it has engulfed for other cells to notice. The pieces of bacteria are called *antigens*.

A War Within

Macrophages can take care of a small invasion of pathogens, but what would happen if millions of pathogens invaded your body? Imagine that bacteria have just moved into your throat. A macrophage discovers a bacterium and engulfs it. But the macrophage does not digest the whole pathogen. Instead, the macrophage saves little pieces of the bacterium and sticks them to its surface. This starts the immune system response . . .

2 The Troops Are Called In The antigens on the outside of the macrophages activate special T cells called **helper T cells.**

3 More Commandos The helper T cells begin dividing as fast as they can to make more helper T cells.

4 Assassins The helper T cells send word to another kind of T cell called a **killer T cell.** Killer T cells kill any cell infected with pathogens. They recognize an infected cell because the cell places antigens on its surface.

5 Foot Soldiers The helper T cells also activate **B cells.** The B cells then make millions of antibodies.

IS THAT A FACT!

In 1918, a strain of flu viruses called the Spanish flu killed at least 20 million people. That's more people than were killed in combat in World War I. Other flu pandemics include the Asian flu, which broke out in 1957, and the Hong Kong flu, which occurred in 1968. All three of these serious flu outbreaks were caused by the A form of the influenza virus. Type A influenza viruses are unstable and can mutate into different, infectious forms fairly quickly. Thus, new vaccines are developed before each flu season.

6 The Battle Intensifies The **antibodies** cling to many of the bacteria. The antibodies also act as markers. Once a bacterium has an antibody attached to it, all kinds of immune cells and proteins swarm to attack the bacterium.

7 Take No Prisoners Special proteins attach themselves to the antibodies stuck on pathogens. They then punch holes in the sides of the pathogens, destroying them.

8 Cleanup Crew Macrophages engulf pathogens tagged with antibodies.

3 Extend

RESEARCH

Writing Have students research the immune problems of "bubble" children, such as David Vetter (the "Bubble Boy"). These children suffer from severe combined immune deficiency (SCID). **(Students should find that children afflicted with this disease lack T cells and B cells and have a very weak immune system. Childhood illnesses that most children can shrug off can kill a child with SCID. People with SCID must live in a germ-free environment, such as in a sterile plastic bubble or cubicle in which the air is cleaned.)**

ACTIVITY

Immunity Skit Have students perform a skit that demonstrates the immune system's response to an invasion of bacteria. Assign a role to each student, and have students study the text to learn about their role. Allow students time to prepare their skit and any props they feel are necessary. For example, the students playing B cells may wish to make antibodies, and the students playing bacteria may wish to construct simple body cells to infect.

Teaching Transparency 98
"The Eight Steps of the Immune System: B"

WEIRD SCIENCE

In some cases, a pregnant woman may form antibodies against the blood of the baby she is carrying. The situation is likely to occur when the mother's blood is Rh-negative, meaning it lacks the Rh antigen, and the baby's blood is Rh-positive, meaning it carries the Rh antigen. The mother's immune system recognizes the Rh antigen as foreign and begins to attack the baby's blood cells.

Section 2 • Your Body's Defenses

4) Close

Quiz

Ask students whether these statements are true or false.

1. As dead skin cells drop off your body, some pathogens may enter your skin. (false)
2. Oil secreted by oil glands in your skin have chemicals that kill pathogens. (true)
3. Antibodies are specific to certain pathogens. (true)
4. Fevers are dangerous because they can increase the growth of pathogens in your body and make you sicker. (false)

ALTERNATIVE ASSESSMENT

Making Models Provide students with an assortment of craft materials, including colored modeling clay, construction paper, pipe cleaners, plastic foam, and other materials. Have students use the materials to construct a "battlefield" that shows the fight among immune system cells and invading pathogens. Allow students to work with a partner to portray the battle. Students should identify the pathogens, the disease they cause, and the following aspects of the immune system: B cells, helper T cells, killer T cells, macrophages, and antibodies. Sheltered English

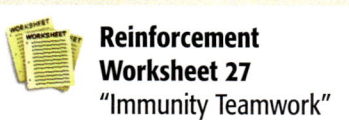

Reinforcement Worksheet 27 "Immunity Teamwork"

Figure 6 A fever can help you feel better faster. However, a high fever can cause tissue damage and blood vessels to burst.

- 41°C Dangerously high temperature
- 39°C Best temperature for B cells and T cells to reproduce
- 37°C Normal body temperature

Heating Things Up

When macrophages activate the helper T cells, they also send a chemical signal that tells your brain to turn up the thermostat. In a few minutes, your body's temperature can rise several degrees. A moderate fever of one or two degrees actually helps you get well faster because it slows the growth of some pathogens. As is shown in **Figure 6,** a fever also helps B cells and T cells multiply faster than usual.

Haven't We Met Somewhere Before?

The immune system responds very quickly if your B cells recognize the invading pathogen and can produce antibodies for it. However, B cells must have had previous contact with a pathogen before they can make the correct antibodies. During the first encounter with a new pathogen, specialized B cells make antibodies that are effective against that particular invader. This process takes about 2 weeks, which is far too long to prevent an infection. Therefore, the first time you are infected, you usually get sick.

A few of the B cells become **memory B cells** that "remember" how to make an antibody for a particular pathogen. If the pathogen shows up again, the memory B cells produce B cells that make enough antibodies to protect you in just 3 or 4 days.

internet connect
SCILINKS NSTA
TOPIC: Body Defenses
GO TO: www.scilinks.org
sciLINKS NUMBER: HSTL665

REVIEW

1. List three ways your body defends itself against pathogens.
2. Name three different cells in the immune system, and describe how they respond to pathogens.
3. Can you make antibodies for diseases you have never come in contact with? Why or why not?
4. **Applying Concepts** If you had chickenpox at age 7, what would be your chances of getting chickenpox again if your memory B cells lived only 2 months?

▼ **Answers to Review**

1. Sample answer: Skin keeps most pathogens out. Chemical defenses are in your eyes, stomach, and mouth. If you have a cut in your skin, blood platelets help to close the wound so more microorganisms cannot enter. Any microorganisms that do enter encounter immune system cells.
2. Sample answer: **macrophages**—they engulf pathogens and stick antigens on their outer membranes; **helper T cells**—they activate killer T cells and B cells; **killer T cells**—they kill any body cell infected with pathogens
3. No; B cells can't make antibodies for a disease until they have encountered that disease at least once before.
4. You could get chickenpox every other month, because there would be no memory B cells to "remember" the pathogen.

644 Chapter 27 • Body Defenses and Disease

Section 3

Terms to Learn
allergy
autoimmune disease
cancer

What You'll Do
- Explain the difference between allergies and autoimmune diseases.
- Discuss what cancer is.
- Describe how HIV affects the immune system.

Challenges to the Immune System

The immune system is a very effective body-defense system, but it is not invincible. There are some diseases that the immune system is unable to deal with. There are also conditions in which the immune system does not work properly.

Ragweed pollen

A-a-achoo!

Sometimes the immune system overreacts to antigens that are not dangerous to the body. This inappropriate reaction is called an **allergy**. Allergies may be caused by many things, including certain foods and medicines. Some of the culprits behind allergic reactions are shown in **Figure 7**. Symptoms can range from a runny nose and itchy eyes to more serious conditions, such as asthma.

Doctors are not sure why the immune system overreacts in some people. Scientists think allergies might be useful because the mucus draining from your nose carries away pollen, dust, and microorganisms.

Figure 7 Things That Cause Allergies

Pollen

Dust mite

Animal hair and dander (skin flakes)

Cigarette smoke

IS THAT A FACT!
Peanuts are dangerous, even potentially deadly, to people who are allergic to them. A person nearly died from eating a tuna sandwich because the knife used to cut the sandwich had just been used to make a peanut butter sandwich.

internetconnect

TOPIC: Allergies
GO TO: www.scilinks.org
sciLINKS NUMBER: HSTL670

SECTION 3

Focus
Challenges to the Immune System

This section introduces several different challenges to the human immune system. Students will learn to recognize the differences between allergies and autoimmune diseases. Students will also learn how a tumor forms and how HIV affects the immune system.

Bellringer

Writing Students will have heard of HIV or AIDS. Have students take a few minutes to write a paragraph describing what AIDS is and how it is related to HIV. Emphasize that students are to write what they already know, that they will not be graded on the accuracy of their answers, and that they will learn about this topic further in Section 3.

1 Motivate

DISCUSSION

Allergies Ask students to tell you about any allergies they have, and about how their bodies react when exposed to the particular allergens. Write their responses on the board or overhead, and use this list, especially the body responses, as a way of introducing how the immune system can make our lives miserable—or at least uncomfortable—when it does not function properly.

Directed Reading Worksheet 27 Section 3

Section 3 • Challenges to the Immune System **645**

2) Teach

REAL-WORLD CONNECTION
Allergies are usually treated two ways once the allergen is identified. An allergist may try to desensitize a patient to the allergen with small, periodic doses of the allergen. In addition, an allergist may prescribe drugs to minimize the body's reactions to allergens.

Homework

Writing Ask students to research and report on the topic anaphylactic shock. *(Students should find that anaphylactic shock is a serious allergic reaction that can result in death. A small amount of an allergen can produce anaphylactic shock. People who are prone to such an allergic reaction may carry with them a syringe containing the hormone epinephrine to combat the onset of anaphylactic shock.)*

3) Extend

GOING FURTHER

Writing Have students find an article or news report about one of the immune disorders discussed in this lesson. Have students work in small groups to summarize their article and link it to the concepts presented in this chapter, either in writing or orally.

internetconnect
SCLINKS **TOPIC:** Cancer and HIV
NSTA **GO TO:** www.scilinks.org
sciLINKS NUMBER: HSTL675

Figure 8 In rheumatoid arthritis, immune-system cells cause joint-tissue swelling, which can lead to joint deformities.

Autoimmune Diseases

An **autoimmune disease** is a disease in which the immune system attacks the body's own cells. This happens when immune-system cells are not able to tell the difference between pathogens and particular body cells. One autoimmune disease is rheumatoid arthritis, in which the immune system attacks the joints. The most common location for rheumatoid arthritis is the joints of the hands, as shown in **Figure 8.** Other autoimmune diseases include type 1 diabetes, Graves' disease, multiple sclerosis, and lupus.

Cancer

Healthy cells divide at a carefully regulated rate. Occasionally, though, a cell doesn't respond to the body's regulation and begins dividing at an uncontrolled rate. As can be seen in **Figure 9,** killer T cells destroy this type of cell. But sometimes division of these cells gets out of the control of the immune system. This causes a condition known as **cancer.**

Many cancers will invade nearby tissues. They can also enter the cardiovascular system or lymphatic system. This way, cancers can be transported to other places in the body. Cancers disrupt the normal activities of organs they have invaded, often leading to death. Today, though, there are many treatments for cancer. Radiation and certain drugs can be used to kill cancer cells or slow their division.

Figure 9 The Destruction of an Unregulated Cell

❶ A killer T cell attacks an unregulated cell.

❷ The cell's membrane ruptures as the cell dies.

WEIRD SCIENCE

There is much evidence to suggest that emotional stress affects a person's immune system. Nearly 2,000 years ago, the Greek physician Galen (A.D. 129–c. 199) observed that people who were mentally depressed tended to be more susceptible to certain diseases than those who were mentally healthy. Today, it is known that hormones secreted in response to stressful situations can affect the number of white blood cells in the blood and can weaken the immune system.

AIDS

The human immunodeficiency virus (HIV) causes the acquired immune deficiency syndrome (AIDS). Most viruses infect cells in the nose, mouth, lungs, or intestines, but HIV is different. As you can see in **Figure 10,** HIV infects the immune system itself, using helper T cells as factories to produce more viruses. The helper T cells are destroyed in the process. Remember that the helper T cells put the B cells and killer T cells to work.

People with AIDS have very few helper T cells, so nothing activates the B cells and killer T cells. Therefore, the immune system cannot attack HIV or any other pathogen. People with AIDS don't usually die of AIDS itself. They die of other diseases that they are unable to fight off.

Figure 10 The blue particles on this helper T cell are human immunodeficiency viruses. They were made inside the cell and can now go and infect other cells.

REVIEW

1. What is the difference between allergies and autoimmune diseases?
2. Why is it important for immune-system cells to be able to recognize all of the body's own cells?
3. What characterizes a cancerous cell?
4. **Interpreting Graphs** Over time, people with AIDS become very sick and are unable to fight off infection. Use the information in the graph below to explain why this occurs.

T Cell Count of a Person with AIDS

internet**connect**

SC*i*LINKS
NSTA

TOPIC: Allergies, Cancer and HIV
GO TO: www.scilinks.org
*sci*LINKS NUMBER: HSTL670, HSTL675

4) Close

Quiz

Ask students whether these statements are true or false.

1. An allergy is caused by the immune system attacking its own body's cells. (false)
2. Killer T cells are useful at killing cancer cells. (true)
3. *HIV* and *AIDS* are two terms for the same disease. (false)
4. The AIDS virus causes HIV. (false)
5. People with AIDS have too many killer T cells. These cells begin to attack the body's cells, and this results in AIDS. (false)

ALTERNATIVE ASSESSMENT

Writing Have students choose one of the disorders discussed in Section 3 and prepare a report or a presentation about it. Projects may take the form of a poster, a pamphlet, a composition, or an oral presentation. Students should research the disorder and provide information on the role of the immune system in the disorder. Encourage students to discuss the immune response and the cells of the immune system.

ACTIVITY

Writing **Concept Mapping** Have students define the new terms presented in this chapter and then use the terms in a concept map. Have students use the chapter title as the first concept in their map.

▼ Answers to Review

1. In allergies, the immune system attacks harmless antigens. In autoimmune diseases, the immune system attacks healthy body cells.
2. Immune system cells must be able to recognize the body's own cells so they can determine when the body has been invaded.
3. A cell becomes cancerous when it starts dividing at an uncontrolled rate.
4. People with AIDS become less able to fight infections because their helper T cell count decreases over time.

Section 3 • Challenges to the Immune System

Chapter Highlights

VOCABULARY DEFINITIONS

SECTION 1

noninfectious disease a disease that cannot spread from one person to another

infectious disease a disease caused by a pathogen

pathogen an agent that causes disease

pasteurization a method of heating food and beverages to kill bacteria

immunity resistance to a disease

SECTION 2

immune system a collection of cells that fight pathogens; these cells include macrophages, B cells, memory B cells, helper T cells, and killer T cells

macrophage an immune-system cell that engulfs pathogens

T cell an immune-system cell that matures in the thymus

B cell an immune-system cell that matures in bones and makes antibodies

antibody a special protein that can recognize specific pathogens

memory B cell an immune-system cell that "remembers" how to make a specialized antibody for a particular pathogen

Chapter Highlights

SECTION 1

Vocabulary
noninfectious disease *(p. 636)*
infectious disease *(p. 636)*
pathogen *(p. 636)*
immunity *(p. 638)*

Section Notes
- A disease disrupts the body's ability to function normally.
- Noninfectious diseases cannot be spread from one person to another.
- Infectious diseases are caused by pathogens that are passed from one living thing to another.
- Pathogens are agents such as viruses or microorganisms that can make us sick.
- Pathogens can travel through the air or can be spread by contact with other people, contaminated objects, animals, or food.
- Cleanliness, pasteurization, vaccines, and antibiotics help control the spread of pathogens.

Labs
Passing the Cold *(p. 778)*

SECTION 2

Vocabulary
immune system *(p. 641)*
macrophage *(p. 641)*
T cell *(p. 641)*
B cell *(p. 641)*
antibody *(p. 641)*
memory B cell *(p. 644)*

Section Notes
- Enzymes in your eyes, nose, and mouth kill most pathogens that try to enter. Other pathogens are washed down the throat and destroyed in the stomach.
- Dead skin cells and oil help to keep germs out of the body.

✓ Skills Check

Math Concepts
SPREAD OF DISEASES It is easy to infect a large group of people with a disease. For instance, suppose a man with the flu gets onto an empty train. The train stops at 10 different towns. If five people get off and five people get on at every stop, how many people could the man expose to his illness?

10 stops × 5 people = 50 people exposed

Visual Understanding
IMMUNE RESPONSE Look at the immune response illustration on pp. 642–643. Review each step to make sure you understand how your immune system works. Think about how many different cells the immune system uses to destroy pathogens. Also, notice that each cell has a special job.

Lab and Activity Highlights

Antibodies to the Rescue PG 776

Passing the Cold PG 778

 Datasheets for LabBook (blackline masters for these labs)

648 Chapter 27 • Body Defenses and Disease

SECTION 2

- When pathogens get into your blood or tissues, the immune system reacts.
- Macrophages engulf pathogens. Macrophages then display parts of the pathogens, called antigens, on their surface.
- Macrophages activate helper T cells. The helper T cells put the killer T cells and B cells to work.
- Killer T cells kill infected cells. B cells make antibodies.
- Antibodies cling to antigens and attract macrophages and other cells. Special proteins kill pathogens with antibodies stuck to them.
- Macrophages cause fever, which speeds the division of T cells and B cells.
- Memory B cells stand ready to produce more B cells that make antibodies if the pathogen appears again.

Labs
Antibodies to the Rescue (p. 776)

SECTION 3

Vocabulary
allergy (p. 645)
autoimmune disease (p. 646)
cancer (p. 646)

Section Notes
- The immune system can overreact to a harmless antigen. This reaction is called an allergy.
- Autoimmune diseases are diseases in which the immune system attacks the body's healthy tissue.
- Cancer cells can enter the body's circulatory systems and infect other areas of the body.
- HIV attacks helper T cells, preventing the immune system from functioning properly.

VOCABULARY DEFINITIONS, continued

SECTION 3

allergy an inappropriate immune-system reaction to a harmless antigen

autoimmune disease a disease in which the immune system attacks the cells of the body it is meant to protect

cancer a condition in which certain body cells begin dividing at an uncontrolled rate

 Vocabulary Review Worksheet 27

 Blackline masters of these Chapter Highlights can be found in the **Study Guide**.

internet connect

GO TO: go.hrw.com

Visit the **HRW** Web site for a variety of learning tools related to this chapter. Just type in the keyword:

KEYWORD: HSTBD6

GO TO: www.scilinks.org

Visit the **National Science Teachers Association** on-line Web site for Internet resources related to this chapter. Just type in the *sci*LINKS number for more information about the topic:

TOPIC: What Causes Diseases?	*sci*LINKS NUMBER: HSTL655
TOPIC: Pathogens	*sci*LINKS NUMBER: HSTL660
TOPIC: Body Defenses	*sci*LINKS NUMBER: HSTL665
TOPIC: Allergies	*sci*LINKS NUMBER: HSTL670
TOPIC: Cancer and HIV	*sci*LINKS NUMBER: HSTL675

649

Lab and Activity Highlights

LabBank

 Long-Term Projects & Research Ideas,
A Chuckle a Day Keeps the Doctor Away, Project 27

Chapter 27 • Chapter Highlights **649**

Chapter Review Answers

USING VOCABULARY

1. infectious
2. bacteria
3. helper T cells
4. antibodies
5. allergy
6. HIV

UNDERSTANDING CONCEPTS

Multiple Choice

7. b
8. d
9. c
10. d
11. d
12. d

Short Answer

13. When a macrophage engulfs a pathogen, it places pieces of the pathogen called antigens on its outer membrane. The antigens attract helper T cells.
14. Helper T cells activate B cells and killer T cells.

Concept Mapping Transparency 27

Blackline masters of these Chapter Highlights can be found in the **Study Guide**.

Chapter Review

USING VOCABULARY

To complete the following sentences, choose the correct term from each pair of terms listed below:

1. Diseases caused by pathogens are __?__. (*infectious* or *noninfectious*)

2. Antibiotics can be used to kill some __?__. (*bacteria* or *viruses*)

3. Macrophages attract __?__. (*helper T cells* or *killer T cells*)

4. Certain B cells make __?__. (*antigens* or *antibodies*)

5. An immune system overreaction to a harmless substance is a(n) __?__. (*allergy* or *vaccine*)

6. __?__ attacks helper T cells. (*HIV* or *Cancer*)

UNDERSTANDING CONCEPTS

Multiple Choice

7. Pathogens are
   a. all viruses and microorganisms.
   b. viruses and microorganisms that cause disease.
   c. noninfectious organisms.
   d. all bacteria that live in water.

8. The following is an infectious disease:
   a. allergies
   b. rheumatoid arthritis
   c. asthma
   d. common cold

9. The skin keeps pathogens out by
   a. staying warm enough to kill pathogens.
   b. releasing killer T cells onto the surface.
   c. shedding dead cells and secreting oils.
   d. All of the above

10. Memory B cells
    a. kill pathogens.
    b. activate killer T cells.
    c. activate killer B cells.
    d. produce B cells that make antibodies.

11. A fever
    a. slows pathogen growth.
    b. helps B cells multiply faster.
    c. helps T cells multiply faster.
    d. All of the above

12. Macrophages
    a. make antibodies.
    b. release helper T cells.
    c. live in the gut.
    d. engulf pathogens.

Short Answer

13. Explain how macrophages start an immune response.

14. Describe the role of helper T cells in responding to an infection.

Concept Mapping

15. Use the following terms to create a concept map: macrophages, helper T cells, B cells, antibodies, antigens, killer T cells, memory B cells.

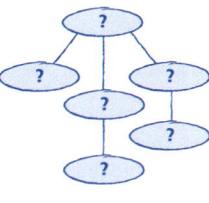

CRITICAL THINKING AND PROBLEM SOLVING

Write one or two sentences to answer the following questions:

16. Why does the disappearance of helper T cells in AIDS patients damage the immune system?

17. Many people take fever-reducing drugs as soon as their temperature exceeds 37°C. Why might it not be a good idea to immediately reduce a fever with drugs? What are the benefits of taking fever-reducing drugs?

18. The risk of dying from a whooping cough vaccine is about one in 1 million. In contrast, the risk of dying from whooping cough itself is about one in 500. Discuss the pros and cons of this vaccination.

MATH IN SCIENCE

19. Suppose you have 50,000 flu viruses on your fingers and you rub your eyes. Only 20,000 viruses make it into your eyes, 10,000 dissolve in chemicals, and 10,000 are washed down into your nose. Of those, you sneeze out 2,000. How many viruses are left to wash down the back of your throat and start an infection?

INTERPRETING GRAPHICS

The graph above compares the concentration of antibodies in the blood the first time you are exposed to a pathogen with the concentration of antibodies the next time you are exposed to the pathogen.

20. Are there more antibodies present during the first week of the first exposure or the first week of the second exposure? Why do you think this is so?

21. What is the difference in recovery time between the first exposure and second exposure? Why?

 Take a minute to review your answers to the Pre-Reading Questions found at the bottom of page 634. Have your answers changed? If necessary, revise your answers based on what you have learned since you began this chapter.

Concept Mapping

15. An answer to this exercise can be found at the end of this book.

CRITICAL THINKING AND PROBLEM SOLVING

16. Helper T cells are needed to activate B cells and killer T cells. Without B cells, the immune system cannot produce antibodies. Without killer T cells, the immune system cannot destroy infected cells.

17. Fevers can help T cells and B cells multiply faster. Fevers can also slow the growth of some pathogens. High fevers can be dangerous, though. If a fever exceeds 40.6°C, fever-reducing drugs can help bring the body's temperature down to a safer temperature.

18. The vaccine gives you an immunity to whooping cough, which is a dangerous disease. However, you may never come into contact with whooping cough and, therefore, may not need the vaccine. If you receive the vaccine anyway, you will have a small risk of dying from the vaccine. If no one is vaccinated, however, the risk of contracting the disease rises.

MATH IN SCIENCE

19. 8,000 viruses

INTERPRETING GRAPHICS

20. There are more antibodies present in the second exposure because memory B cells recognize the pathogen and immediately start the production of antibody-producing B cells.

21. Recovery time is much shorter for the second exposure because your body can produce more antibodies in less time than during the first exposure.

CAREERS
Naturopathic Physician— Stacey Kargman

Background

One kind of sensitivity involves what are called the IgE antibodies. These antibodies engender an immediate reaction. For example, when a person who is allergic to strawberries eats a strawberry, and a few minutes later that person breaks into hives or notices that he or she has a swollen, irritated tongue, that is an IgE response.

To help establish which foods are problematic for someone, naturopaths such as Kargman rely on specialized blood tests. After taking blood, the naturopath will send it to a lab, where it is exposed to different substances and tested for reactions. Once a sensitivity has been discovered, a patient can avoid the foods that have a negative impact on his or her immune system.

CAREERS

NATUROPATHIC PHYSICIAN

Dr. Stacey Kargman of Tucson, Arizona, is a doctor of naturopathic medicine (NMD), commonly referred to as a naturopath. An NMD has similar training to an MD but is less likely than a traditionally trained doctor to use prescription drugs or surgery to treat a patient's symptoms. Naturopaths tend to look for a natural way to treat a patient, using drugs or surgery as a last resort. Dr. Kargman tries to strengthen her patients' immune systems by focusing on things like nutrition.

Dr. Kargman attended the Southwest College of Naturopathic Medicine, where she studied all the sciences a medical doctor would study—like biochemistry, anatomy, pharmacology, and physiology. Beyond the standard medical school sciences, naturopaths spend an additional four years studying subjects like botanical medicines, homeopathy, acupuncture, counseling, and nutrition. "Naturopathy is a way of looking at the person as a whole," says Kargman.

The Keystone to Good Health

Many naturopaths believe that nutrition is the keystone to good health. "Most MDs don't talk to their patients about their diets," Kargman explains. "I'm in a position to talk to them about what they eat and how it may be affecting their health. Food allergies can cause an immune reaction in the body—anything from depression to skin problems to migraine headaches. Even though I can prescribe prescription medications, I usually defer to MDs when it comes to prescription medications."

Dr. Kargman treats many HIV and AIDS patients. She encourages these patients and others who need prescription medications to work with their medical doctor and their naturopath at the same time. That way, patients get the best care.

A Fulfilling Career

Dr. Kargman says the best part of her work is making people feel better. "Someone might come to me and say they have terrible migraines that they can no longer live with and that they've seen every doctor. After examining them, I might be able to tell them something as simple as, 'Stop eating wheat.' The simplest thing can change someone's life . . . It's not like putting a bandage on it. It's fixing the cause of the problem."

▲ *Stacey Kargman, NMD, tries to treat the patient as a whole.*

On Your Own

▶ Do some research about naturopaths. Find out how an NMD's training and practice differ from the training and practice of an MD.

Answer to On Your Own
Answers will vary. Students might contact the American Naturopathic Medical Association to learn more about how naturopaths are trained and how they practice.

Frogs in the Medicine Cabinet?

Frog skin, mouse intestines, cow lungs, and shark stomachs—sounds like the ingredients for a witch's brew, doesn't it? Actually, these animal parts are being tested in an effort to create more effective medicines to combat harmful bacteria.

Leapin' Lily Pads—It's Infection Protection

In 1896, a biologist named Michael Zasloff was studying African clawed frogs. He noticed that cuts in the frogs' skin healed quickly and never became infected. Zasloff decided to investigate further. He found that when a frog was cut, its skin released a liquid antibiotic that killed invading bacteria.

Scientists have found other animals whose bodies contain similar infection fighters. For example, the stomach and tissues of sand sharks (also called dogfish) contain chemicals that kill bacteria and other microorganisms. These useful antibiotics are also in moths, pigs, mice, cows, and even the small intestines of humans!

What's in Dog Spit?

A healthy dog licks cuts, scrapes, and minor wounds to clean them. A mother cat licks her kittens clean. Have you ever wondered why animals do that? Well, dogs, cats, humans, and some other animals have an antibacterial enzyme in their saliva. When animals lick a wound, the enzymes kill the bacteria and help the wound heal.

▲ *African clawed frogs produce a natural antibiotic.*

POW! Punching Holes in Bacteria

Bacteria are becoming resistant to many man-made antibiotics, which means that the drugs no longer affect the bacteria. Scientists now face the challenge of developing new antibiotics that can overcome the resistant strains of bacteria.

Antibiotics from animals pack a different punch than some man-made antibiotics. These substances bore holes through the membranes that surround bacterial cells, causing the cells to disintegrate and die. Bacterial membranes don't mutate often, so they are less likely to become resistant to the animal antibiotics.

Getting Well

▶ When your doctor prescribes antibiotics, you are usually reminded to finish the entire bottle even if you start to feel better. Call or visit a local pharmacy to investigate why this is so important when you are taking antibiotics.

SCIENTIFIC DEBATE

Frogs in the Medicine Cabinet

Background

Antibiotics are drugs used to treat diseases caused by microorganisms. Antibiotics interfere with the disease-causing (pathogenic) bacteria by either damaging the cell membrane or disrupting chemical processes in the cell.

Antibiotics must be used properly to be effective. Some possible side effects from antibiotics include allergic reactions, damage to organs and tissues, and destruction of helpful microorganisms.

Modern scientific study of antibiotics began in the 1800s. Louis Pasteur discovered that bacteria spread infectious diseases, and Robert Koch developed methods for isolating and growing different kinds of bacteria. A breakthrough in treating bacterial diseases came in the early 1900s when Alexander Fleming discovered penicillin, an antibiotic formed from mold. Streptomycin, a fungal antibiotic, was discovered by Selman A. Waksman in 1943. Doctors now use antibiotics to treat diseases such as strep throat, bacterial meningitis, and tuberculosis.

Answer to Getting Well

Not finishing the bottle might enable the remaining bacteria to begin another infection.

Chapter Organizer

CHAPTER ORGANIZATION	TIME MINUTES	OBJECTIVES	LABS, INVESTIGATIONS, AND DEMONSTRATIONS
Chapter Opener pp. 654–655	45	National Standards: SAI 1	**Start-Up Activity** Conduct a Survey, p. 655
Section 1 What We Put into Our Bodies	90	▶ Identify the six groups of nutrients and explain their importance to good health. ▶ Use dietary guidelines and the food pyramid to plan a healthy diet. ▶ Understand nutrition information labels. ▶ Explain the dangers of various nutritional disorders. UCP 1, 4, SAI 1, SPSP 1, 4; LabBook SPSP 1	**QuickLab**, A Healthy Diet, p. 662 GENERAL **Discovery Lab**, To Diet or Not to Diet, p. 780 GENERAL **Datasheets for LabBook**, To Diet or Not to Diet, Datasheet 58 GENERAL **Labs You Can Eat**, Snack Attack, Lab 10 GENERAL
Section 2 Risks of Alcohol and Other Drugs	90	▶ Distinguish between the positive and negative uses of drugs. ▶ Explain the hazards of tobacco, alcohol, and illegal drugs. SAI 1, SPSP 1, 4, 5	**Demonstration**, The Cost of Smoking, p. 665 in ATE GENERAL
Section 3 Healthy Habits	90	▶ Describe four important aspects of good hygiene. ▶ Explain why exercise and sleep are important to good health. ▶ Describe methods of handling stress. ▶ List ways to stay safe at home, on the road, and outdoors. SPSP 1, 3–5; LabBook UCP 2, SAI 1, SPSP 1	**Discovery Lab**, Keep it Clean, p. 781 GENERAL **Datasheets for LabBook**, Keep It Clean, Datasheet 59 GENERAL **Inquiry Lab**, Consumer Challenge, Lab 8 BASIC **Long-Term Projects and Research Ideas**, Project 28 ADVANCED

See page T20 for a complete correlation of this book with the

NATIONAL SCIENCE EDUCATION STANDARDS.

TECHNOLOGY RESOURCES

 Guided Reading Audio CD English or Spanish, Chapter 28

 One-Stop Planner CD-ROM with Test Generator

 CNN **Multicultural Connections**, Muslims and Medicine, Segment 13
 A Healthy Mexican Tradition, Segment 14

Chapter 28 • Staying Healthy

CLASSROOM WORKSHEETS, TRANSPARENCIES, AND RESOURCES	SCIENCE INTEGRATION AND CONNECTIONS	REVIEW AND ASSESSMENT
Directed Reading Worksheet 28 BASIC **Science Puzzlers, Twisters & Teasers,** Worksheet 28 ADVANCED		
Directed Reading Worksheet 28, Section 1 BASIC **Transparency 253,** Covalent Bonds in a Water Molecule **Transparency 99,** The Food Pyramid **Transparency 100,** How to Read a Food Label **Critical Thinking Worksheet 28,** A Daily Routine ADVANCED **Reinforcement Worksheet 28,** To Eat, or Not to Eat . . . BASIC	**Oceanography Connection,** p. 658 **Connect to Physical Science,** p. 658 in ATE **Multicultural Connection,** p. 659 in ATE **Connect to Chemistry,** p. 659 in ATE **Math and More,** p. 660 in ATE GENERAL **MathBreak,** What Percentage? p. 661 GENERAL **Math and More,** p. 661 in ATE GENERAL **Multicultural Connection,** p. 661 in ATE **Health Watch:** Meatless Munching, p. 679 GENERAL	**Homework,** pp. 657, 658 in ATE GENERAL **Review,** p. 659 GENERAL **Self-Check,** p. 661 **Review,** p. 662 GENERAL **Quiz,** p. 662 in ATE GENERAL **Alternative Assessment,** p. 662 in ATE GENERAL
Directed Reading Worksheet 28, Section 2 BASIC	**Multicultural Connection,** p. 664 in ATE **MathBreak,** Deadly Averages, p. 666 GENERAL **Real-World Connection,** p. 666 in ATE **Cross-Disciplinary Focus,** p. 667 in ATE GENERAL	**Self-Check,** p. 664 **Homework,** pp. 664, 667 in ATE **Self-Check,** p. 667 **Review,** p. 668 GENERAL **Quiz,** p. 668 in ATE GENERAL **Alternative Assessment,** p. 668 in ATE GENERAL
Directed Reading Worksheet 28, Section 3 BASIC	**Connect to Earth Science,** p. 669 in ATE **Cross-Disciplinary Focus,** p. 670 in ATE GENERAL **Apply,** p. 671 GENERAL **Real-World Connection,** p. 671 **Science, Technology, and Society:** Bacteria at Your Service, p. 678 GENERAL	**Homework,** p. 670 in ATE BASIC **Homework,** p. 671 in ATE GENERAL **Homework,** p. 672 in ATE ADVANCED **Review,** p. 673 GENERAL **Quiz,** p. 673 in ATE GENERAL **Alternative Assessment,** p. 673 in ATE ADVANCED

internet connect

 Holt, Rinehart and Winston On-line Resources
go.hrw.com
For worksheets and other teaching aids related to this chapter, visit the HRW Web site and type in the keyword: **HSTBD7**

 National Science Teachers Association
www.scilinks.org
Encourage students to use the *sci*LINKS numbers listed in the internet connect boxes to access information and resources on the **NSTA** Web site.

END-OF-CHAPTER REVIEW AND ASSESSMENT

Chapter Review in Study Guide
Vocabulary and Notes in Study Guide
Chapter Tests with Performance-Based Assessment, Chapter 28 Test
Chapter Tests with Performance-Based Assessment, Performance-Based Assessment 28
Concept Mapping Transparency 28

Chapter Resources & Worksheets

Visual Resources

TEACHING TRANSPARENCIES

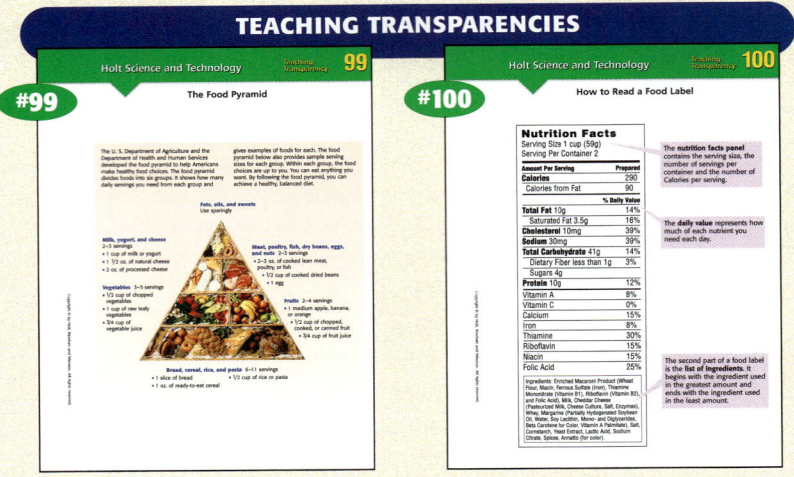

TEACHING TRANSPARENCIES   **CONCEPT MAPPING TRANSPARENCY**

 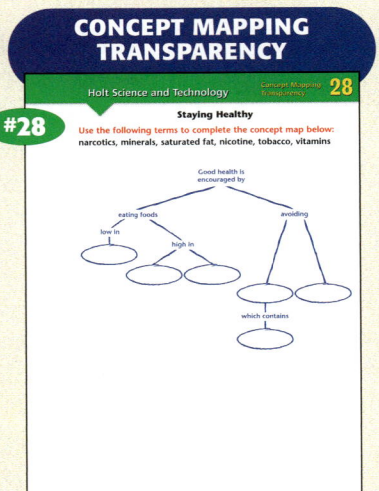

Meeting Individual Needs

DIRECTED READING   **REINFORCEMENT & VOCABULARY REVIEW**   **SCIENCE PUZZLERS, TWISTERS & TEASERS**

653C   Chapter 28 • Staying Healthy

Chapter 28 • Staying Healthy

Review & Assessment

STUDY GUIDE
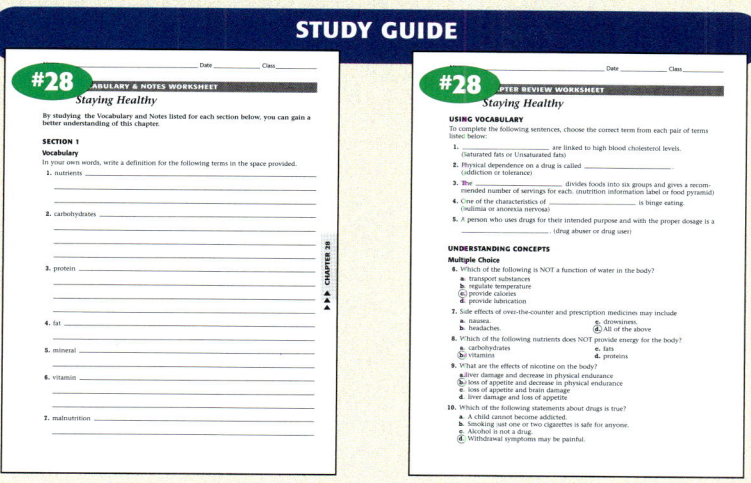

CHAPTER TESTS WITH PERFORMANCE-BASED ASSESSMENT
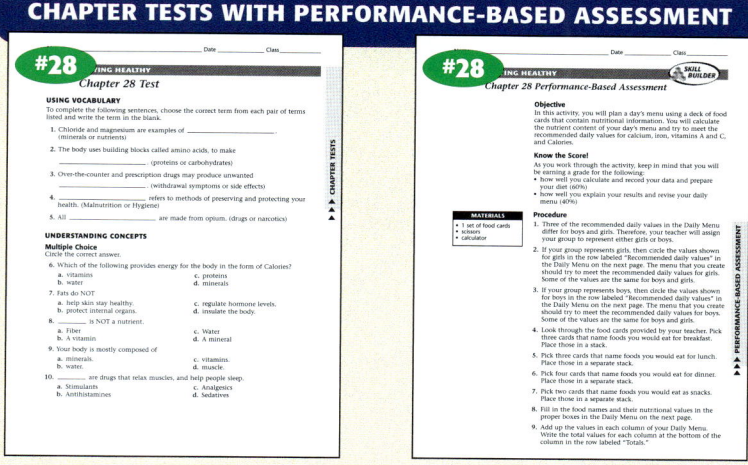

Lab Worksheets

INQUIRY LABS
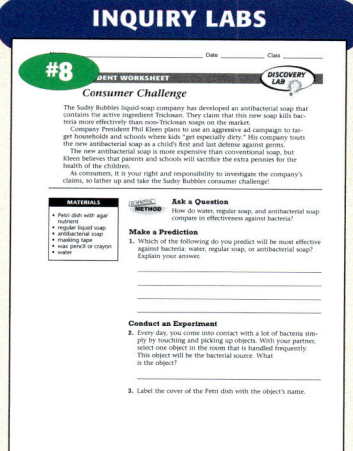

LABS YOU CAN EAT
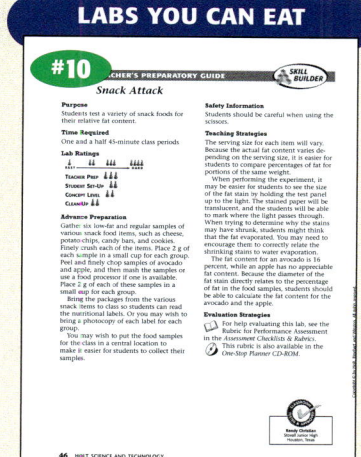

LONG-TERM PROJECTS & RESEARCH IDEAS

DATASHEETS FOR LABBOOK
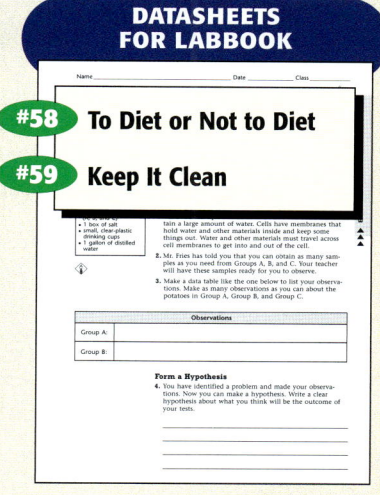

Applications & Extensions

CRITICAL THINKING & PROBLEM SOLVING

MULTICULTURAL CONNECTIONS
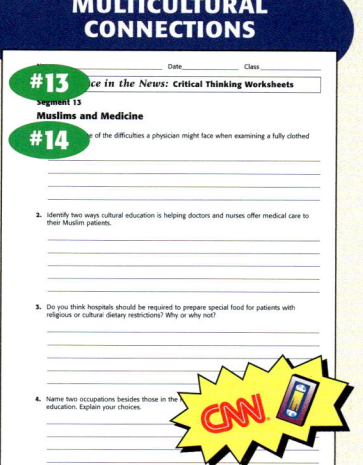

Chapter 28 • Chapter Resources & Worksheets   653D

Chapter Background

SECTION 1

What We Put into Our Bodies

▶ Nutrient Needs in Adolescence

Puberty is a period of rapid growth, and its changes affect every organ of the body. Adolescents need extra nutrients to meet their needs during the growth spurt that accompanies puberty.

- The onset of menstruation in girls and the increase in lean body mass in boys increases the body's need for iron. The Recommended Daily Allowance (RDA) for iron in adolescence is 12–15 mg.

- The increase in skeletal mass that occurs during adolescence boosts the body's calcium needs. Seventy-five to 80 percent of the skeleton is built during this period, increasing the RDA for calcium to 1,200 mg.

- The increased growth rate of adolescents increases the body's caloric needs. Energy needs vary depending on growth rate, body composition, and activity level. In general, boys have a larger proportion of lean body mass to fat and require more calories than girls do.

▶ Fiber

Although fiber contains no vitamins or minerals, it is essential to good health. Insoluble fiber (obtainable from whole-grain foods), along with fluids, helps the colon move waste (fecal matter) out of the bowels. A lack of insoluble fiber can increase a person's risk for constipation, colon and bowel cancer, and diverticulosis.

- Soluble fiber—obtainable from fruit, beans, peas, and other legumes—can reduce the risk of heart disease by lowering cholesterol. Legume-based fiber also aids in the regulation of blood glucose levels.

▶ The Biopsychosocial Nature of Nutrition in Youth

The physical, emotional, and social changes of adolescence have a great impact on teen nutrition. Adolescence is typically a period of increased autonomy. With increased independence comes increased opportunity to make food choices. But rather than making food choices based on long-term health, teens tend to be influenced by social pressures to reach cultural ideals of thinness, gain the acceptance of peers, and assert their independence from their parents.

- The characteristic adolescent preoccupation with body image extends to nutrition. If sound nutritional principles are taught and reinforced during adolescence, long-term health can benefit.

IS THAT A FACT!

- Just before astronauts Neil Armstrong (1930–) and Edwin Aldrin Jr. (1930–1999) embarked on the first moonwalk on July 20, 1969, each astronaut ate four bacon squares, three sugar cookies, and peaches and drank pineapple-grapefruit juice and coffee.

SECTION 2

Risks of Alcohol and Other Drugs

▶ Inhalant Abuse

One of the most disturbing trends in substance abuse today is the increase in inhalant abuse. According to national surveys, one in five eighth graders has used inhalants for the purpose of getting high. Nevertheless, most parents are unaware of the popularity and hazards of inhalant use.

Chapter 28 • Staying Healthy

- More than 1,000 common products are used as inhalants. These seemingly benign, everyday substances can prove deadly when inhaled. Initially, the user may feel slightly stimulated or less inhibited, but nearly all inhalants produce effects similar to anesthesia. The body functions slow down, and loss of consciousness may result.

- A frightening risk associated with inhalant use is the threat of sudden sniffing death syndrome, which may occur any time a person uses an inhalant. Other physical consequences of inhalant use are damage to the brain, heart, liver, lung, and bone marrow.

▶ **Preventing Accidental Drug Poisonings**
Beginning in 1973, the federal government required that all drugs and medications be packaged in child-proof containers. Between 1973 and 1976, there was a 50 percent decrease in childhood poisoning deaths. The development of single-dose packets, product alterations to reduce toxicity, and the creation of poison control centers have also contributed to this decline.

▶ **Smokeless Tobacco**
In recent years, the use of smokeless tobacco among adolescents has increased. Many teens believe that smokeless tobacco is safer than cigarettes are. Unfortunately, ignorance has a high cost: Smokeless tobacco use is linked with many health problems, including mouth ulcers and oral cancer. Furthermore, teens who use smokeless tobacco are more likely to begin to smoke.

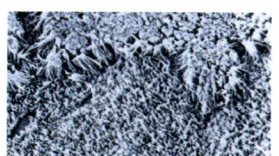

IS THAT A FACT!

▪ In the 1800s, scientists learned how to isolate drug compounds from their natural state in plants. Morphine, cocaine, and heroin became readily available and were welcomed as safe, powerful pain relievers because, at first, no one knew of their addictive properties. By the early 1900s, there was an epidemic of drug abuse in the United States.

SECTION 3
Healthy Habits

▶ **Safety Notes**
In the United States, injuries are the leading cause of death for children and adolescents; in fact, they surpass all major diseases as the cause of death in children between the ages of 1 and 19. Adolescents are particularly prone to accidents, injuries, and death because of their risk-taking behavior, desire to exert autonomy, and sense of invincibility.

- In 1994, motor-vehicle accidents claimed the lives of 5,768 Americans between the ages of 13 and 19. Tragically, almost half of these deaths were easily preventable. Research has shown that the use of seat belts reduces the risk of fatal injury by 45 percent and the risk of critical injury by 50 percent.

▶ **Excuse Me?**
Preventable hearing loss among adolescents is increasing at an alarming rate. Results of hearing tests in a 1995 report showed that 11 percent of ninth graders and 10.6 percent of twelfth graders could not hear high-frequency sounds. Experts attribute this trend to increased exposure to damaging levels of noise, including loud music.

- When sounds enter the ear, they cause the eardrum to vibrate. Tiny hair cells in the inner ear respond to these vibrations by sending nerve impulses to the brain. Ordinarily, these hair cells slowly die as a person ages. When exposed to loud noises, however, more hair cells die than usual. Fewer impulses are sent to the brain. Once damage occurs, it is irreversible. Fortunately, prevention is as simple as inserting a pair of earplugs or turning down the volume.

> For background information about teaching strategies and issues, refer to the ***Professional Reference for Teachers.***

CHAPTER 28

Staying Healthy

Pre-Reading Questions

Students may not know the answers to these questions before reading the chapter, so accept any reasonable response.

Suggested Answers

1. You need to eat foods that will provide all the necessary nutrients. These foods are shown on the food pyramid. Limit your intake of sweets and fats.
2. Drugs are helpful when they are used to cure symptoms or illness. They are harmful when they lead to addiction and health problems.
3. Everyday habits that help keep you healthy include exercise, getting plenty of rest, eating a balanced diet, washing your hands, and taking care of your skin and teeth.

Directed Reading Worksheet 28

Science Puzzlers, Twisters & Teasers Worksheet 28

Guided Reading Audio CD
English or Spanish, Chapter 28

CHAPTER 28

Staying Healthy

Sections

1. **What We Put into Our Bodies** 656
   - Oceanography Connection 658
   - Internet Connect 659
   - MathBreak 661
   - QuickLab 662
   - Internet Connect 662

2. **Risks of Alcohol and Other Drugs** 663
   - MathBreak 666
   - Internet Connect 668

3. **Healthy Habits** 669
   - Apply 671

Chapter Review 676
Feature Articles 678, 679
LabBook 780–781

Pre-Reading Questions

1. What types of foods should you eat daily to have a healthy diet? What foods should you avoid?
2. How are drugs helpful? harmful?
3. What everyday habits can help to keep you healthy?

The Glow of Health

What do you notice most about this photo? Sure, you can see five boys and girls facing the camera. Besides that, though, what else does the picture tell you? The bright eyes, happy smiles, shiny hair, and a certain glow from the faces give off a feeling of radiant health. Having a clear mind, high energy, and a long, active life all depend on having a healthy body. In this chapter, you will learn some basic steps for maintaining the body—your personal "tool kit" for thriving in the world.

---

internet connect

HRW On-line Resources
go.hrw.com
For worksheets and other teaching aids, visit the HRW Web site and type in the keyword: **HSTBD7**

www.scilinks.com
Use the *sci*LINKS numbers at the end of each chapter for additional resources on the **NSTA** Web site.

www.cnnfyi.com
Visit the CNN Web site for current events coverage and classroom resources.

START-UP Activity

CONDUCT A SURVEY

How healthy is your class? Collect data and see for yourself.

Procedure

1. Copy the questionnaire below.
2. Circle *yes* or *no* to answer the questions. Do not put your name on the survey.

Analysis

3. Record the data from your survey and the surveys of your classmates in a chart. Count the number of students who answered *yes* to each question. For each question, calculate the percentage of your class that answered *yes*.
4. What things does your class do well? What health habits can be improved?

---

1. Do you exercise at least three times a week?   Yes   No
2. Do you wear a seat belt every time you ride in a car?   Yes   No
3. Do you eat five or more servings of fruits and vegetables every day?   Yes   No
4. Do you use sunscreen to protect your skin when you are outdoors?   Yes   No
5. Do you eat a lot of high-fat foods?   Yes   No

START-UP Activity

CONDUCT A SURVEY

MATERIALS

FOR EACH GROUP:
- questionnaire
- paper
- pen or pencil

Teacher's Notes

Tell students to use this formula to find the percentages in step 3:

$$\frac{\text{\# of yes answers}}{\text{total \# of students}} \times 100$$

Answers to START-UP Activity

3–4. Answers will vary.

Chapter 28 • Staying Healthy

SECTION 1

Focus

What We Put into Our Bodies

In this section, students learn what the six essential nutrients are and why they are important for good health. Dietary guidelines and the food pyramid are used to illustrate the principles of sound nutrition, and students learn how to use these tools to create a healthy diet. Finally, students learn about the dangers of nutritional disorders.

Bellringer

Post the following on the board or an overhead projector in two columns:

Terms	Descriptions
1. nutrients	a. energy in nutrients
2. calories	b. fats found in meats
3. carbohydrates	c. overweight
4. proteins	d. essential substances
5. saturated fats	e. inorganic elements
6. minerals	f. tissue builders
7. obese	g. main source of energy

Challenge students to recall information from previous chapters and match the terms in column A with the descriptions in column B. **(1. d; 2. a; 3. g; 4. f; 5. b; 6. e; 7. c)**

Section 1

Terms to Learn

nutrient   mineral
carbohydrate   vitamin
protein   malnutrition
fat

What You'll Do

- Identify the six groups of nutrients, and explain their importance to good health.
- Use dietary guidelines and the food pyramid to plan a healthy diet.
- Understand nutrition information labels.
- Explain the dangers of various nutritional disorders.

What We Put into Our Bodies

"You are what you eat." Does this familiar saying mean that you are pizza or candy? Of course not! But, the substances in the pizza and candy enter your body. The protein in the cheese may become part of your hair; the carbohydrates in the crust can give you energy to run your next race. The sugar in the candy can give you a quick energy boost but make you tired later when your blood sugar level drops.

Nutrition

Are you more likely to have potato chips or broccoli for a snack? a candy bar or a banana? If you lean toward foods that are high in sugar and fat, such as potato chips and candy, your food choices probably are not as healthy as they could be. Does that mean you have to cut out all of your favorite foods to eat healthy? No! Broccoli *is* a healthier food than potato chips. But eating only broccoli every day, like the person in **Figure 1**, is not much better than eating only potato chips! Either way, you do not get a balanced diet.

Balancing Act In order to stay healthy, you need to take in more than 40 different substances every day. These substances, or **nutrients**, nourish your body and are essential to life. To get them all, you must eat a wide variety of foods. Nutrients are grouped into six categories: *carbohydrates, proteins, fats, vitamins, minerals,* and *water.* Three of these—carbohydrates, proteins, and fats—provide energy for the body. The energy in these nutrients is measured in units called Calories. The other three nutrients—vitamins, minerals, and water—do not provide energy in Calories but help the body use all of the nutrients properly.

Figure 1 *Eating only one food, even a healthy food, will not give you all the substances your body needs.*

 Directed Reading Worksheet 28 Section 1

IS THAT A FACT!

Frozen vegetables are often just as nutritious as fresh vegetables.

TOPIC: Nutrition
GO TO: www.scilinks.org
***sci*LINKS NUMBER:** HSTL680

656 Chapter 28 • Staying Healthy

Body Fuel A **carbohydrate** is a chemical composed of one or more simple sugars. Carbohydrates are your body's main source of energy. They help digest fats, lubricate joints, and keep skin, bones, and nails healthy. Plant foods are the major source of carbohydrates.

There are two basic types of carbohydrates: simple and complex. *Simple carbohydrates* are sugars. They are easily digested and give your body quick energy. *Complex carbohydrates* are made of many sugar molecules linked together. They are digested more slowly than simple carbohydrates and give your body long-lasting energy.

Body Builders Protein is found in body fluids, muscle, bone, skin, and all other tissues. **Proteins** are nutrients used to build and repair body parts. Your body makes the proteins it needs, but it must have the necessary building blocks, called *amino acids,* to make them. Your digestive system breaks down the protein in food into individual amino acids that are then used to make new proteins. If your body does not get enough carbohydrates, it can also use proteins for energy.

Some foods, such as poultry, fish, milk, and eggs provide all of the essential amino acids. These food sources are called complete proteins. Incomplete proteins contain only some of the essential amino acids. Most plants are incomplete sources of protein, but eating a variety of plant foods each day will provide all of the amino acids your body needs.

Energy Storage **Fats** are energy-storage nutrients that help the body store some vitamins. Too much fat in the diet has been linked to weight gain, heart disease, and some kinds of cancer. But fats are essential to a balanced diet. They are needed to transport vitamins, produce hormones, keep skin healthy, protect vital organs, and provide insulation. Fats provide more than twice as much energy as proteins and carbohydrates per unit mass.

Simple carbohydrates

Complex carbohydrates

Proteins

Fats

Figure 2 **Energy-Producing Nutrients**

2) Teach, continued

BRAIN FOOD

Point out to students that many vitamin manufacturers promote their products by proudly proclaiming that their vitamins are "natural" or "organic," rather than synthetic (manufactured). Vitamins touted as "natural" are almost always more expensive than their synthetic counterparts. Point out that most experts agree that organic vitamins and synthetic vitamins are identical in both structure and function.

Homework

Writing Have students research and write a report about the physical effects of vitamin deficiencies for at least three of the essential vitamins.

CONNECT TO PHYSICAL SCIENCE

Water is a very simple molecule made up of one oxygen atom and two hydrogen atoms. Water is vital to all living organisms. Remind students that water makes up nearly 70 percent of the human body. Illustrate the water molecule using the following Teaching Transparency.

Teaching Transparency 253 "Covalent Bonds in a Water Molecule" LINK TO PHYSICAL SCIENCE

Oceanography CONNECTION

Kelp, a type of brown seaweed, is a nutritious food that is grown on special farms in oceans off the coasts of China and Japan.

Figure 3 *You need to drink about eight glasses of water a day. When you exercise, you need even more.*

There are two types of fats, saturated and unsaturated. *Saturated fats* are found in meats, dairy products, coconut oil, and palm oil. Saturated fats are known to raise blood cholesterol levels. *Cholesterol* is a fatlike substance found naturally in the body. Although cholesterol is important to the body, high levels in the blood increase the risk of heart disease. *Unsaturated fats* may help reduce blood cholesterol levels. Your body can make its own saturated fats, but it cannot make certain unsaturated fats. You must get these from your diet. Vegetable oils and fish contain unsaturated fats.

Flushing the System A human cannot survive for more than a few days without water. Your body is about 70 percent water. Water is in every cell and every kind of tissue. Water's three main functions are to transport substances, regulate temperature, and provide lubrication. You should drink 8 to 10 glasses of water daily, as shown in **Figure 3.** You also get water from the other liquids you drink and the foods you eat. Fresh fruits and vegetables, juices, soups, and milk contain large amounts of water.

Small Necessities **Minerals** are elements that are essential for good health. Six minerals are needed in large amounts: calcium, chloride, magnesium, phosphorus, potassium, and sodium. There are at least 12 minerals that are required in very small amounts. These include fluorine, iodine, iron, and zinc. If you eat a balanced diet, you should get all of the minerals you need. Calcium and magnesium are necessary for strong bones and teeth. Magnesium and sodium help the body use proteins. Potassium is needed to regulate your heartbeat and produce muscle movement, and iron is necessary for red blood cell production.

WEIRD SCIENCE

You are what you eat, as the saying goes, and in some cases, you can even begin to look like it. For example, consuming a lot of carrots or carrot juice can give the skin a yellowish color, a harmless condition that results from consuming the beta carotene found in some vegetables. In 1960, a doctor was puzzled by a patient whose skin looked orange. It turned out that the patient not only was eating large quantities of carrots but also was eating a lot of tomatoes, which can give the skin a reddish color. The two colors mixed, and *voilà,* he had orange skin!

Body Controllers **Vitamins** are organic compounds that control many body functions. Most vitamins cannot be made by the body, so you have to get them from food. The following table provides information about the 13 essential vitamins.

The Essential Vitamins

Vitamin	What it does	Where you get it
A	keeps skin and eyes healthy; builds strong bones and teeth	yellow and orange fruits and vegetables; dark, leafy greens; meat; and milk
B_1 (thiamine)	helps body use carbohydrates; helps nerves and heart function	meats, whole grains, beans, peas, nuts, and seafood
B_2 (riboflavin)	helps cells use carbohydrates and oxygen; keeps skin and eyes healthy	dairy products, fruits, whole grains, eggs, leafy vegetables, and poultry
B_3 (niacin)	helps body use carbohydrates; helps cells use oxygen; helps digestion	meats, peanuts, whole grains, peas, and beans
B_6	helps body use proteins, carbohydrates, and fats	poultry, fish, meat, eggs, potatoes, avocados, and bananas
B_{12}	keeps blood and nerves healthy	meats, poultry, eggs, fish, and milk
Folic acid (a B vitamin)	helps red blood cell formation	leafy greens, peas, beans, nuts, whole grains, liver, and oranges
Pantothenic acid (a B vitamin)	helps body use protein, carbohydrates, and fat; keeps body tissues healthy	meats, fish, whole grains, beans, peas, eggs, and corn
Biotin (a B vitamin)	helps body use protein, carbohydrates, some B vitamins, and fat	eggs, milk, meats, nuts, peas, beans, and whole grains
C	strengthens blood vessels and connective tissue; helps the body absorb iron; helps the body fight disease	citrus fruits; dark, leafy greens; broccoli; peppers; cabbage; tomatoes; potatoes; and strawberries
D	builds strong bones and teeth; helps the body use calcium and phosphorus	sunlight, enriched milk, eggs, and fish
E	protects red blood cells from destruction; needed for some enzymes to work	oils, fats, eggs, whole grains, wheat germ, liver, and leafy greens
K	assists with blood clotting	leafy greens, tomatoes, and potatoes

REVIEW

1. Name the six groups of nutrients, and explain why each is important to the body.
2. If vitamins and minerals do not supply energy, why are they important to a healthy diet?
3. **Applying Concepts** Name some of the nutrients that can be found in a glass of milk.

TOPIC: Nutrition, Vitamins
GO TO: www.scilinks.org
*sci*LINKS NUMBER: HSTL680, HSTL685

CONNECT TO CHEMISTRY

Vitamins are important because they enable enzymes to function. Enzymes perform their functions by fitting together with other body chemicals, and either combining them or breaking the chemicals down. In order for this to happen, vitamins bind to these enzyme proteins, activating them by changing the proteins' shape so that they fit properly with the chemicals they act upon. Without vitamins, many enzymes cannot do their jobs.

Multicultural CONNECTION

In many parts of the world, especially the tropics, insects are part of people's diet. Besides being plentiful and high in protein, insects can be quite tasty. Termites taste like pineapple, and baked bees have a nutty taste, similar to breakfast cereal.

MEETING INDIVIDUAL NEEDS

Writing **Advanced Learners**
Encourage students to use library or Internet resources to learn about vitamin D. (Vitamin D is produced by the body when the skin is exposed to sunlight.)

Have students share their findings with the class.

TOPIC: Vitamins
GO TO: www.scilinks.org
*sci*LINKS NUMBER: HSTL685

Answers to Review

1. Sample answer: Carbohydrates provide energy to the body. Proteins provide amino acids so the body can make other proteins. Fats are an energy source, and they provide insulation to the body. Vitamins and minerals control many body functions. Water transports substances, regulates body temperature, and provides lubrication.
2. Vitamins and minerals help the body use other nutrients properly, and they control many body functions.
3. Milk contains carbohydrates; protein; saturated fat; vitamins A, B_2 (riboflavin), B_{12}, and D; biotin; calcium; magnesium; potassium; and water.

② Teach, continued

MATH and MORE

Have students keep track of all the food they eat in a day. Have them determine how many servings from each of the food groups they consume. Then have them determine the percentage of recommended servings these numbers represent. For example, two glasses of milk and a grilled cheese sandwich represents 100 percent of the recommended dairy servings. One apple is 25–50 percent of the recommended fruit servings. Encourage students to identify how they could change their diet to make it more healthful.

PG 780

To Diet or Not to Diet

Reinforcement Worksheet 28
"To Eat, or Not to Eat . . ."

Critical Thinking Worksheet 28
"A Daily Routine"

Teaching Transparency 99
"The Food Pyramid"

TOPIC: Food Pyramids
GO TO: www.scilinks.org
sciLINKS NUMBER: HSTL690

Eating for Good Health

Now you know what nutrients you need for good health. But how can you be sure to get them all in the right amounts? To begin, keep in mind that most teenage girls need about 2,200 Calories a day and most boys need 2,800 Calories. Since different foods contain different nutrients, *where* you get your Calories is as important as *how many* you get. The food pyramid below can help you make good food choices.

The Food Pyramid

The U.S. Department of Agriculture and the Department of Health and Human Services developed the food pyramid to help Americans make healthy food choices. The food pyramid divides foods into six groups. It shows how many daily servings you need from each group and gives examples of foods for each. This food pyramid also provides sample serving sizes for each group. Within each group, the food choices are up to you. You can eat anything you want. By following the food pyramid, you can achieve a healthy, balanced diet.

Fats, oils, and sweets Use sparingly.

Milk, yogurt, and cheese 2–3 servings
- 1 cup of milk or yogurt
- 1 1/2 oz of natural cheese
- 2 oz of processed cheese

Vegetables 3–5 servings
- 1/2 cup of chopped vegetables
- 1 cup of raw, leafy vegetables
- 3/4 cup of vegetable juice

Meat, poultry, fish, dry beans, eggs, and nuts 2–3 servings
- 2–3 oz of cooked poultry, fish, or lean meat
- 1/2 cup of cooked dried beans
- 1 egg

Fruits 2–4 servings
- 1 medium apple, banana, or orange
- 1/2 cup of chopped, cooked, or canned fruit
- 3/4 cup of fruit juice

Bread, cereal, rice, and pasta 6–11 servings
- 1 slice of bread
- 1 oz of ready-to-eat cereal
- 1/2 cup of rice or pasta
- 1/2 cup of cooked cereal

MISCONCEPTION ALERT

Snacking is a well-established eating pattern among teenagers, and popular wisdom has long held that it should be discouraged. This is not necessarily true, however. Snacks, when balanced with healthy food choices for the rest of the day, can be an important source of nutrients and calories.

IS THAT A FACT!

It's not a lack of food, per se, that makes us hungry. Lack of nutrients in the bloodstream to keep our vital organs functioning causes a message to be sent to the brain, which then stimulates the stomach and the intestines—also known as "stomach growling"!

Chapter 28 • Staying Healthy

How to Read a Food Label

Packaged foods are required by law to have nutrition information labels. The illustration below shows a nutrition information label for a box of macaroni and cheese. Reading labels will help you make healthy eating choices.

Some of the nutrients found in each serving are listed on the label. The daily values shown are based on a 2,000-Calorie-per-day diet. You will need to calculate your own daily values based on your personal Calorie needs.

▶ The **nutrition facts panel** contains the serving size, the number of servings per container, and the number of Calories per serving.

▶ The **daily value** represents how much of each nutrient you need each day.

▶ The second part of a food label is the **list of ingredients**. It begins with the ingredient used in the greatest amount and ends with the ingredient used in the least amount.

Nutrition Facts
Serving Size 1 cup (59g)
Serving Per Container 2

Amount Per Serving	Prepared
Calories	290
Calories from Fat	90
	% Daily Value
Total Fat 10g	14%
Saturated Fat 3.5g	16%
Cholesterol 10mg	39%
Sodium 30mg	39%
Total Carbohydrate 41g	14%
Dietary Fiber less than 1g	3%
Sugars 4g	
Protein 10g	12%
Vitamin A	8%
Vitamin C	0%
Calcium	15%
Iron	8%
Thiamine	30%
Riboflavin	15%
Niacin	15%
Folic Acid	25%

Ingredients: Enriched Macaroni Product (Wheat Flour, Niacin, Ferrous Sulfate (Iron), Thiamine Mononitrate (Vitamin B1), Riboflavin (Vitamin B2), and Folic Acid), Milk, Cheddar Cheese (Pasteurized Milk, Cheese Culture, Salt, Enzymes), Whey, Margarine (Partially Hydogenated Soybean Oil, Water, Soy Lecithin, Mono- and Diglycerides, Beta Carotene for Color, Vitamin A Palmitate), Salt, Cornstarch, Yeast Extract, Lactic Acid, Sodium Citrate, Spices, Annatto (for color).

MATH BREAK

What Percentage?

Use the nutrition information label on this page to answer the following questions for yourself, based on the Calorie needs of teenagers described on the previous page.

1. What percentage of your daily Calorie needs does one serving of macaroni and cheese provide?
2. The recommended daily value of fat is 72 g for teenage girls and 90 g for teenage boys. What percentage of the daily recommended fat value is provided by one serving of packaged macaroni and cheese?

Self-Check

For breakfast, you eat 1 cup of hot cereal with a banana and 1 cup of milk. What servings from the food pyramid have you eaten? *(See page 782 to check your answer.)*

Multicultural CONNECTION

In Japan, the incidence of breast cancer is very low. After moving to United States, however, Japanese women develop the disease nearly as often as American women do. Scientists attribute this to cultural dietary differences. They believe that the high-fat diet of many Americans plays a pivotal role in the development of breast cancer.

Section 1 • What We Put into Our Bodies

3) Extend

Answers to MATHBREAK

1. One serving will give girls 13 percent of their daily Calories and will give boys 10 percent.
2. One serving provides 14 percent for girls and 11 percent for boys.

GOING FURTHER

Have students check out a popular diet book from the library. Have them evaluate the diet in terms of its ability to meet the nutrient and energy needs of the body, and encourage them to identify any necessary changes, if any, to make the diet healthful. Have them prepare brief reports, and allow them to share their findings with the class.

MATH and MORE

If there are 3,312 Cal in a pound of butter, and a single serving of butter is 14.2 g (1tbsp), how many Calories are in a single serving of butter?

$$\frac{3{,}312\text{ Cal}}{1\text{ lb}} = \frac{x\text{ Cal}}{2.2\text{ lbs/kg}} = 7{,}286\text{ Cal/kg}$$

$$\frac{7{,}286\text{ Cal}}{1{,}000\text{ g}} = \frac{x\text{ Cal}}{14.2\text{ g}} = 103\text{ Cal in 14.2g}$$

Answer to Self-Check

You have eaten two servings from the bread, cereal, rice, and pasta group; one serving from the fruit group; and one serving from the milk, yogurt, and cheese group.

Teaching Transparency 100
"How to Read a Food Label"

4 Close

QuickLab

MATERIALS

FOR EACH STUDENT:
- food pyramid
- daily-servings table
- paper
- pen or pencil

Answers to QuickLab

3. Answers will vary. Girls should base their menu on a 2,200 Cal diet, and boys should base their menu on a 2,800 Cal diet. Answers will vary as the students compare this diet with their normal diet.

Quiz

1. What needs must a healthy diet meet? (It must provide enough essential nutrients and meet the body's energy needs.)

2. Why should people strive to limit the fat in their diet? How might a very low-fat diet affect the body? (Too much fat in the diet has been linked to weight gain, heart disease, and some kinds of cancer. Too little fat, however, might result in hormone imbalances, dry skin, and vitamin deficiencies.)

ALTERNATIVE ASSESSMENT

Concept Mapping Have students create a concept map using the new terms of the section and any additional words that are necessary. Have them begin their map with the concept, "What we put into our bodies."

TOPIC: Nutritional Disorders
GO TO: www.scilinks.org
sciLINKS NUMBER: HSTL695

QuickLab

A Healthy Diet

1. Use the recommended daily Calories for teenagers and the **table** below to estimate how many servings from each group in the food pyramid you should eat daily.

2. Create a menu for 2 days that includes the correct number of servings from each group in the food pyramid.

3. Compare this diet with your normal diet. How different are they? What can you do to improve your diet?

Daily Number of Servings

Food group	2,200 Calories	2,800 Calories
Bread	9	11
Fruit	3	4
Vegetable	4	5
Dairy	3	3
Meats	6 oz	7 oz

TRY at HOME

TOPIC: Food Pyramids, Nutritional Disorders
GO TO: www.scilinks.org
sciLINKS NUMBER: HSTL690, HSTL695

Nutritional Disorders

Unhealthy eating habits can cause nutritional disorders. For example, malnutrition can result from consuming too few Calories or too few of the right nutrients. Eating too many Calories or too many of the wrong nutrients can also cause malnutrition. **Malnutrition** occurs when you do not consume the right combination of nutrients.

Anorexia Nervosa and Bulimia Anorexia nervosa and bulimia can lead to malnutrition. Many of the people who suffer from anorexia nervosa and bulimia are teenage girls. *Anorexia nervosa* is an eating disorder characterized by self-starvation and an intense fear of gaining weight. This can cause weak bones, low blood pressure, and heart problems. *Bulimia* is a disorder characterized by binge eating followed by induced vomiting. Sometimes people suffering from bulimia also use laxatives and diuretics to rid the body of food and water. Bulimia can damage the teeth and digestive system and can also lead to kidney or heart failure. These disorders can both be fatal, but they can be cured with medical help.

Obesity *Obesity* is a condition characterized by an extremely high percentage of body fat. Eating too many foods from the top of the food pyramid and having an inactive lifestyle that involves little exercise can contribute to obesity. Obesity increases the risk of high blood pressure, heart disease, and diabetes.

REVIEW

1. What information is found on a nutrition information label?

2. How do anorexia nervosa and bulimia differ?

3. **Applying Concepts** How can someone who is obese suffer from malnutrition?

Answers to Review

1. The nutrition facts panel includes the serving size, the number of servings per container, the number of Calories per serving, and the percent daily value of each type of nutrient per serving.

2. Anorexia nervosa involves self-starvation. Bulimia involves binge eating followed by induced vomiting or the use of laxatives.

3. An overweight person can suffer from malnutrition by eating too many of the wrong nutrients and too few of the right nutrients.

Section 2

Risks of Alcohol and Other Drugs

Terms to Learn

drug
addiction
nicotine
alcoholism
narcotics

What You'll Do

- Distinguish between the positive and negative uses of drugs.
- Explain the hazards of tobacco, alcohol, and illegal drugs.

You see them in movies and on television. You read about them in magazines. You hear about them in music and in your school. You are exposed to information, and misinformation, about tobacco, alcohol, and other drugs almost every day.

What Is a Drug?

A **drug** is any chemical substance that causes a physical or emotional change in a person. Drugs come in many forms, as shown in **Figure 4.** They can be pills, powders, fumes, liquids, or creams. Some drugs enter the body through the skin, and others are swallowed, inhaled, or injected.

When used safely and correctly, legal drugs can help your body heal a variety of ailments from athlete's foot to pneumonia. They can also provide relief from pain, congestion, and other symptoms. When used illegally or improperly, however, drugs can become killers.

What Effects Do Drugs Have?

Different drugs have different effects. One way to classify drugs is by function. *Analgesics,* like aspirin, are pain-relieving drugs. Drugs that relax muscles and help people sleep are *sedatives.* *Antibiotics* fight bacterial infections, and *antihistamines* help control symptoms of allergies, asthma, and colds.

Another way to classify drugs is by their effect on the central nervous system. *Stimulants* speed up the action of the central nervous system and may cause a person to feel more alert. *Depressants* have the opposite effect. They slow down body functions and may reduce a person's alertness.

Figure 4 All of these products contain drugs.

WEIRD SCIENCE

Humans may not be the only organisms that use drugs. Chimpanzees have been observed swallowing entire leaves of a plant that is known to be effective against infections and parasites. In Ethiopia, baboons actively seek out a fruit that fights parasites. It seems that muriqui monkeys of Brazil are able to control their fertility with a plant eaten only certain times of the year, and howler monkeys may even select the sex of their offspring by eating different plants.

2) Teach

Answer to Self-Check
Regular use of some drugs may cause tolerance or addiction. Withdrawal symptoms occur when the body does not receive a drug that it is addicted to.

USING THE FIGURE
Refer students to **Figure 5.** Encourage them to compare the label of a prescription drug with that of the over-the-counter equivalent. Have them identify the information that both labels contain. (Both OTC and prescription labels list the name of the drug, the means of administration, the dosage, and the frequency with which the drug should be taken. In addition, both labels list possible side effects of the drug.)

Why is it important to read the label before taking an over-the-counter or prescription drug? (to make sure that you take the correct amount in the correct way and so that you are aware of possible side effects)

Homework
Encourage students to visit a pharmacy to make a list of 25 drugs that are available without a prescription. Challenge them to include drugs that have different modes of administration. Have them prepare a table that categorizes the drugs by their active ingredients and by their uses.

✓ Self-Check
How are tolerance, addiction, and withdrawal symptoms related? *(See page 782 to check your answer.)*

Dependence and Addiction Regular use of some drugs can cause the body to develop *tolerance*. This means larger and larger doses of the drug are needed to get the same effect. **Addiction** is physical dependence on a drug. When a person is addicted to a drug, the body has a chemical need for the drug. If the body doesn't receive the drug, withdrawal symptoms may occur. These include nausea, vomiting, pain, and other physical symptoms. Once addicted, it is very difficult to stop taking a drug.

Sometimes dependence on a drug is not due to a physical need. Some people form *psychological dependence* on a drug and feel powerful cravings for it.

Types of Drugs
There are many kinds of drugs and many ways to use them. Some drugs are obtained from plants, and some are made synthetically. You can buy some drugs off the shelf, while others must be taken under the supervision of a doctor. Some drugs are illegal to buy, sell, or even possess.

Over-the-Counter and Prescription Drugs An over-the-counter drug can be purchased legally without a doctor's prescription. A prescription is a note written by a doctor to allow a patient to buy a medicine. It specifies the drug, directions for use, and the amount of the drug to be used.

Many over-the-counter and prescription drugs are powerful healing agents. However, some of these drugs also produce unwanted side effects. Side effects are uncomfortable symptoms such as nausea, headaches, drowsiness, or more serious problems caused by a drug.

Whether purchased with or without a prescription, all drugs must be used with care. Each year about 75,000 people in the United States become ill or die from the misuse of drugs. Information on proper use can be found on the label. **Figure 5** shows an example of a prescription drug label. The table below gives some drug safety tips.

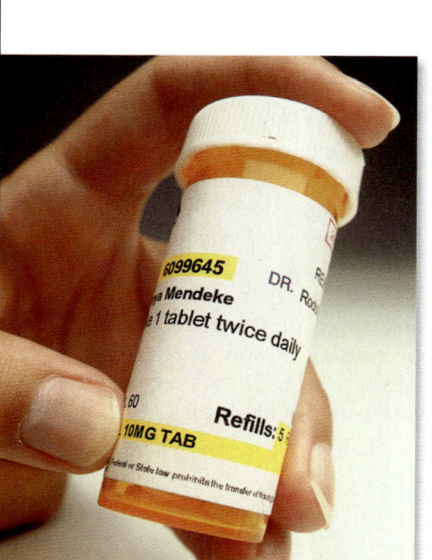

Figure 5 *Prescription drug labels provide instructions for use and list possible side effects.*

Drug Safety Tips
- Never take another person's prescription medicine.
- Read the label before each use. Always follow the instructions on the label and those provided by your doctor or pharmacist.
- Do not take more or less medication than prescribed.
- Consult a doctor if you have any side effects.
- Throw away leftover and out-of-date medicines.

Multicultural CONNECTION
The Chickasaw Indians relieved pain and fever by chewing on the bark of the willow tree. Today many people relieve their minor ills with a chemically related substance—aspirin. Derived from willow, aspirin is the most widely used drug in the world. We have the Chickasaw to thank for the "wonder drug" that relieves pain and fever and prevents blood clotting.

Herbal Medicines Information about medicinal herbs has been handed down by word-of-mouth for centuries. Some plants contain chemicals with important healing properties. However, these herbs are drugs and should be used carefully. **Figure 6** shows some medicinal herbs.

Tobacco About 50 million people in the United States—one-third of all adults—smoke. Smoking has serious health risks, and the nicotine in cigarettes is addictive. **Nicotine** is a chemical stimulant in tobacco that increases heart rate and blood pressure. Many smokers also experience a loss of appetite and a decrease in physical endurance. Smoking increases the chances of lung cancer by 10 times, and it has also been linked to other cancers, emphysema, chronic bronchitis, and heart disease. About 400,000 people die from smoking-related illnesses each year. **Figure 7** shows one of the effects of smoking.

Smokeless tobacco is also a health hazard. Nicotine is absorbed through the lining of the mouth, and the amount of nicotine that reaches the blood can be the same as for a smoker. Smokeless tobacco increases the risk of several types of cancer, including mouth and throat cancer. It also causes gum disease and discoloration of the teeth.

Figure 6 Some herbs can be purchased in health food stores. Medicinal herbs should always be used with care.

Figure 7 Cilia in your airways cleanse debris from the air you breathe and prevent debris from entering your lungs. Compare the cilia from the lungs of a nonsmoker, on the left, with those of a smoker, on the right.

IS THAT A FACT!

The likelihood that a first-time cigarette smoker will become addicted is 90 percent. Fewer than half are able to quit, which puts their health at great risk. About 90 percent of people who get lung cancer are smokers or former smokers. Cigarette smokers are also at greater risk of getting cancers of the larynx, lip, esophagus, bladder, pancreas, and kidneys.

2) Teach, continued

DISCUSSION

The Advertising Age Tell students that beer, liquor, and wine companies in the United States spend more than $2 billion annually on advertising and promotion. The result of this advertising is increased alcohol consumption. Display for students a selection of advertisements for beer, liquor, or wine taken from magazines. Encourage students to identify advertising tactics that seem to target youth. (Students might note that the ads often show groups of young, beautiful, active people in outdoor settings. These ads imply that people cannot have fun without alcohol.)

REAL-WORLD CONNECTION

Current studies suggest that young people are making their first choices about alcohol between the ages of 12 and 14, while only a generation ago those choices were made between the ages of 16 and 18. By ninth grade, 56 percent of students have tried alcohol. By high school, the effects of alcohol abuse have already taken a toll. Furthermore, a recent poll indicated that 66 percent of teenagers believed that drugs and alcohol were the biggest problems facing them. And alcohol-related deaths are the primary killer of Americans between the ages of 15 and 24.

Answers to MATHBREAK

About six people between the ages of 16 and 20 die every day in alcohol-related car crashes. This means that these crashes kill one person every 4 hours.

Figure 8 On average, there is one alcohol-related fatality every 31 minutes.

Deadly Averages

Approximately 2,200 people between the ages of 16 and 20 die in alcohol-related crashes each year. On average, how many die every day?

Alcohol Alcohol depresses the central nervous system and causes relaxation and memory loss. Excessive use of alcohol can damage the liver, pancreas, brain, nerves, and cardiovascular system. In very large quantities, alcohol can cause respiratory failure and even death. In addition, alcohol is a factor in more than half of all accidental deaths, suicides, and murders. **Figure 8** shows one example of an alcohol-related accident. It is illegal in the United States for people under the age of 21 to use alcohol.

About 10 million alcohol users are alcoholics. They suffer from **alcoholism,** which means that they are physically and psychologically dependent on alcohol. Alcoholism is considered a disease, and genetic factors are thought to influence a person's tendency to become an alcoholic.

Marijuana Marijuana is an illegal drug made from the Indian hemp plant. Marijuana produces a mind-altering effect that varies from user to user. It may cause a relaxed feeling or may increase anxiety. Marijuana slows reaction time, impairs thinking, and causes a loss of coordination.

Cocaine Cocaine and its more purified form, crack, are stimulants made from the South American coca plant. Both drugs are illegal and highly addictive, and users can become dependent on them in a very short time. Cocaine and crack produce feelings of intense excitement followed by anxiety and depression. Both drugs increase heart rate and blood pressure and can cause heart attacks even among first-time users.

Hallucinogens Hallucinogens (huh LOO si nuh juhnz) distort the senses and cause changes in mood and thought processes. Users have hallucinations (huh LOO si NAY shuhnz), which means they see and hear things that are not real. Some hallucinations are extremely frightening and can cause people to respond violently. LSD and PCP, or "angel dust," are two powerful and illegal hallucinogens. Sniffing some glues and solvents also causes hallucinations and can cause serious brain damage.

MISCONCEPTION ALERT

One of the most common alcohol-related myths is that beer is not as "strong" as liquor. "It's just beer" is a common refrain heard from teenagers and adults alike. In fact, beer has the same effects as wine or liquor. Alcohol from any source is addictive. It can cause liver damage, memory loss, heart damage, stomach problems, and sexual impotence. It impairs judgment, contributes to traffic deaths, and plays a role in many suicides and homicides.

Narcotics Narcotics are drugs made from opium. Some narcotics are used to treat severe pain and are legal when prescribed by a doctor. But many narcotics are illegal.

One illegal narcotic is heroin. Heroin is one of the most addictive drugs known, and large doses can lead to death. Because it is so strongly addictive, users must continue taking the drug in order to prevent painful withdrawal symptoms. Heroin is usually injected, and users often share needles that are contaminated. Therefore, heroin users have a high risk of infecting themselves with diseases like hepatitis and AIDS.

Designer Drugs There are many other illegal drugs. Examples include inhalants, barbiturates (downers), amphetamines (uppers), and "designer" drugs, which are produced by making small changes to existing drugs. Some inhalants, barbiturates, and amphetamines are legal if prescribed by a doctor.

Drug Use and Drug Abuse

A drug user takes a drug to prevent or improve some medical condition. The drug user obtains the drug legally and uses the drug properly. A drug abuser does *not* take a drug to relieve a medical condition. The drug abuser may take drugs for the temporary good feelings they produce, to escape from problems, or to belong to a group. The drug is often obtained illegally, and it is often taken without knowledge of the strength or purity of the drug.

Drug Abuse: How Does It Start? Nicotine, alcohol, and marijuana are called *gateway drugs* because they are usually the first drugs a person tries. The abuse of other more dangerous drugs may follow the abuse of gateway drugs, as illustrated in **Figure 9.** Most teenagers who start smoking cigarettes, drinking alcohol, or using marijuana do not realize that these drugs are addictive or that they can seriously harm their health.

Peer pressure is the reason most young people begin to use drugs. Teenagers may feel the need to drink, smoke, or try marijuana in order to make friends or to avoid being ridiculed or threatened. Many young people feel that "everyone" is using drugs. Because drug abusers often stand out, the fact that many teenagers do not abuse drugs is sometimes hard to see.

Self-Check

1. What is a hallucination?
2. List three dangers of heroin use.

(See page 782 to check your answers.)

Figure 9 Nicotine, alcohol, and marijuana are called gateway drugs.

4) Close

Quiz

1. What can be done to prevent drug abuse? (Answers will vary but should mention that information about the risks associated with drug use is an effective weapon. Being well informed is the first step toward making informed choices.)

2. How are nicotine and alcohol alike? How do they differ? (Answers will vary but should reflect the understanding that both drugs are legal for adults and that both are addictive. The use of both nicotine and alcohol has been associated with heart disease. The primary physical consequences of smoking are respiratory and cardiac problems; alcohol mostly affects the central nervous system, the liver, and the digestive system. Of the two, only alcohol dangerously impairs judgment.)

ALTERNATIVE ASSESSMENT

Have students prepare tables comparing alcohol, tobacco, marijuana, cocaine, LSD, and heroin. Have them define each and describe their effects on the body. In addition, have them indicate whether the drug is legal or illegal, and whether or not it is addictive.

Answer to Activity

Answers will vary.

TOPIC: Drug and Alcohol Abuse
GO TO: www.scilinks.org
sciLINKS NUMBER: HSTL700

Many people who start using drugs do not recognize the dangers. Misinformation about drugs is everywhere. Several common drug myths are discussed below.

Drug Myths

Myth	Reality
"It's only alcohol, not drugs."	Alcohol is a mood-altering and mind-altering drug. It affects the central nervous system and is addictive.
"I won't get hooked on one or two cigarettes a day."	Addiction is not related to the amount of a drug used. Some people become addicted after using a drug once or twice.
"I can quit any time I want."	Addicts may quit and return to drug usage many times. Their inability to stay drug free shows how powerful the addiction is.

Activity

Write yourself a letter. Tell yourself why you should stay drug free. You may wish to refer to people, goals, activities, or values that are important to you. Put your letter in an envelope, and keep it in a safe place. If you ever find yourself thinking about using drugs, take out your letter and read it.

TRY at HOME

Signs of Use People who begin using drugs generally undergo emotional, physical, and behavioral changes. Teenagers may have problems with school or family. Changes in personality or physical appearance may occur. However, remember that many young people do not take drugs. These changes could be signs of other problems or normal age-related changes.

Getting Off Drugs The first step to quitting drugs is to admit to being a drug abuser and to decide to stop. When quitting drugs, it is important for the addicted person to get proper medical and psychological treatment. Getting off drugs can be extremely difficult. Withdrawal symptoms may be painful, and even after the symptoms are gone, powerful cravings for a drug continue. This is even true of smoking.

REVIEW

1. What is the difference between a prescription drug and an over-the-counter drug?
2. How does addiction occur?
3. **Analyzing Relationships** How are nicotine, alcohol, and cocaine similar? How are they different?

internet connect

TOPIC: Drug and Alcohol Abuse
GO TO: www.scilinks.org
sciLINKS NUMBER: HSTL700

Answers to Review

1. A prescription drug can only be purchased after your doctor writes a prescription telling the pharmacist what drug and what dosage to give you. An over-the-counter drug can be purchased by anyone without a prescription.

2. Addiction occurs when a person takes an addictive drug over a period of time and becomes physically dependent on the drug.

3. Nicotine, alcohol, and cocaine are all addictive drugs. Nicotine and alcohol are legal for use by adults. Cocaine is illegal. Cocaine and nicotine are stimulants. Alcohol is a sedative.

Section 3

Healthy Habits

Terms to Learn
hygiene stress
aerobic exercise

What You'll Do
- Describe four important aspects of good hygiene.
- Explain why exercise and sleep are important to good health.
- Describe methods of handling stress.
- List ways to stay safe at home, on the road, and outdoors.

Do you like playing sports? acting in plays? going to the movies? swimming in the ocean? No matter what you enjoy, the better your health, the easier it will be to take part in the things you like to do. Keeping yourself healthy is a daily task. If you have healthy habits, you are likely to stay healthy for a long time.

Hygiene and Posture

Hygiene refers to methods of preserving and protecting your health. It sounds simple, but washing your hands is the best way to prevent the spread of disease and infection. You should always wash your hands after using the bathroom and before and after eating or preparing food.

Taking care of your skin, hair, and teeth are other important aspects of good hygiene. Using sunscreens can help prevent sunburn, wrinkles, and skin cancer. Shampoo your hair regularly. To prevent cavities and keep your teeth and gums healthy, eat a healthy diet, brush at least twice a day, and floss at least once daily. Get regular dental exams, and replace your toothbrush about every 3 months.

Posture Posture is also important to health. Good posture helps you look and feel good. Bad posture strains your muscles and ligaments and makes breathing difficult. To have good posture when you stand, imagine a vertical line passing through your ear, shoulder, hip, knee, and ankle, as shown in **Figure 10.** When working at a desk, pull your chair forward and plant your feet firmly on the floor.

Figure 10 A slumped posture strains your lower back.

Section 3

Focus
Healthy Habits
In this section, students will learn how hygiene, exercise, rest, and play can enhance their well-being. Students learn how stress affects the body and how it can be reduced. Finally, students learn how injuries can be prevented.

Bellringer
Write this statement and question on the board or on an overhead projector:

> In the 1800s and earlier, people who sustained simple cuts on their skin often ended up with serious infections. That rarely happens now. Why? (We now understand the importance of washing wounds with soap to keep them clean. We also have antiseptics today.)

1) Motivate

ACTIVITY

Don't Kick These Habits! Ask students to list all of their daily hygienic habits. (Answers may vary but will probably include washing their hands, bathing, brushing their teeth, using skin lotions, washing dishes, and using clean utensils to eat.)

CONNECT TO EARTH SCIENCE

Tell students that they may use fossils as part of their daily hygiene. Many toothpastes contain diatomaceous earth, which consists of fossilized diatoms—algae with silica shells. The silica in diatomaceous earth effectively polishes the surface of teeth.

Directed Reading Worksheet 28 Section 3

Keep It Clean

Section 3 • Healthy Habits   **669**

2 Teach

READING STRATEGY

Prediction Guide Before students read this page, have them answer the following question:

Which pair of exercises is aerobic?
a. walking and running
b. swimming and stretching
c. biking and yoga
d. running and weight lifting

(a)

CROSS-DISCIPLINARY FOCUS

Language Arts *Writing* Recite for students the adage, "An apple a day keeps the doctor away." Tell students to write slogans that encourage washing hands, brushing teeth, and good posture.

MEETING INDIVIDUAL NEEDS

Advanced Learners *Writing* Encourage students to use library or Internet resources to investigate how weight-bearing exercise affects bone density. Have them prepare brief reports, and allow them to share their findings with the class.

Figure 11 *To stay with aerobic exercise, it is important to choose an activity you enjoy.*

Only half of a dolphin's brain sleeps at a time. A full, deep sleep would be a problem because dolphins must come to the surface for air every 20–30 seconds.

Exercise and Rest

Imagine that school starts at 7:30 A.M. You drag yourself out of bed at 6:00 every morning. You are tired, but somehow you make it through the school day. In the afternoon, you attend play rehearsal. When you get home, you take a break, eat dinner, and start your homework at 8:00 P.M. When you finish, you do not feel ready to sleep, so you watch TV, then read in bed, and finally, at 10:30, you drift off to sleep.

Keeping your body healthy requires giving it plenty of exercise and plenty of rest. If you have a schedule like the one above, you do not get enough of either.

Exercise Regular aerobic exercise at least three times a week is critical to good health. **Aerobic exercise** is vigorous, sustained exercise of the whole body for 20 minutes or more. Walking, running, swimming, and biking are all examples of aerobic exercise. For another example, see **Figure 11**.

Aerobic exercise increases the heart rate. As a result, more oxygen is taken in and distributed throughout the body. Over time, aerobic exercise strengthens the heart, lungs, and bones. It burns Calories, helps your body conserve nutrients, and aids digestion. It also gives you more energy and stamina. In other words, aerobic exercise protects your physical and mental health, and it's free! What a deal!

Sleep Believe it or not, teenagers actually need more sleep than younger children. Do you ever fall asleep in class, like the girl in **Figure 12**, or feel tired in the middle of the afternoon? If so, you may not be getting enough sleep. Scientists say that teenagers need about 9.5 hours of sleep each night.

At night, the body goes through several cycles of progressively deeper sleep, with periods of lighter sleep in between. If you do not sleep long enough, you will not enter the deepest, most restful period of sleep.

Figure 12 *If you fall asleep easily during the day, you are probably not getting enough sleep.*

Homework

Writing Have students list four benefits of aerobic exercise. (Answers could include the following: improves oxygen distribution; strengthens heart, lungs, and bones; burns calories; aids digestion; conserves proteins and minerals; improves energy and stamina; and reduces stress.)

WEIRD SCIENCE

Regular, intense exercise decreases body fat and therefore, in extreme cases can restrict the release of estrogen in female athletes. When this occurs in prepubescent athletes, it delays the onset of puberty. Menstruation is delayed, and the period of bone growth is extended.

Coping with Stress

You have a big soccer game tomorrow. Are you excited and ready for action? You got a low grade on your math test. Are you upset or angry? The game and the test are causing you stress. **Stress** is the physical and mental response to pressure.

Some stress is a normal part of life, as shown in **Figure 13.** Stress stimulates your body to prepare for difficult or dangerous situations. However, sometimes you may have no outlet for the stress, and it builds up. Excess stress is harmful to your health and can decrease your ability to carry out your daily activities.

You may not even realize you are stressed until your body reacts. Perhaps you get a headache, have an upset stomach, or lie awake at night. You might feel tired all the time or begin an old nervous habit, such as nail-biting. You may become irritable or resentful. All of these things can be signs of too much stress.

Figure 13 *Working under stress can increase an athlete's ability to perform well.*

What to Do Different people are stressed by different things. Once you identify the source of the stress, you can find ways to deal with it. Here are some ideas for handling stress.

- Make a list of all the things you would like to get done, and rank them in order of importance. Do the most important things first.
- Exercise regularly, and get enough sleep.
- Pet a friendly animal.
- If you cannot remove a stressor, spend some quiet time alone or practice deep breathing or other relaxation techniques.
- Share your problems. Talk things over with someone you trust.

APPLY

Stress SOS
Your mother is out of town helping your grandfather move into a nursing home. Your little brother has been snooping in your room. You have a history project due in two days, an oral report due in English, and quizzes in both math and science! You are ready to scream! What are some healthy ways to handle all the stress you are feeling?

Homework

Stress Management Have students think about their life, their activities, and the people around them. Ask them the following question: What are the three things in your life that cause you the most stress? Have students list the sources of stress in their life and come up with three different ways of eliminating, reducing, or coping with stress.

DISCUSSION

Don't Worry, Be Happy Point out to students that although it is commonly believed that the term *stress* refers only to the emotional and physical response that occurs in response to negative events, many *positive* situations also cause stress. Encourage students to identify "happy" events that create stress. (Answers might include starting a new job, the addition of a sibling, and moving to a new house.)

Point out that stress, whatever its source, produces a physiological reaction that is designed to prepare the body for difficult situations.

REAL-WORLD CONNECTION

Sleep Disorders Scientists who study people's sleep patterns have learned that 33 percent of the general population suffers from a sleep disorder. People with insomnia have difficulty falling asleep or staying asleep. Sometimes they simply wake up much too early. Sleep apnea is characterized by brief periods (10–60 seconds) while sleeping during which breathing stops. This may occur because of a narrowing of the upper throat (from health problems, obesity, or alcohol consumption). Sleep apnea can also occur if the brain signal to take a breath is delayed. A person with sleep apnea may wake up hundreds of times during the night to breathe but have no memory of these incidents.

Answer to APPLY
Answers will vary but may include solutions listed on this page.

3) Extend

DISCUSSION

Injuries Tell students that injuries cause more deaths among children ages 1–19 than any of the major diseases. Remind them that many accidents can be prevented. Point out that bicycle injuries alone cause the death of more than 500 children and teens in the United States each year. Most of these deaths involve head trauma. Experts estimate that the simple act of wearing a bicycle helmet can reduce the risk of head injury by 85 percent; yet many children don't wear them. Ask students why they think people don't wear helmets. (Likely responses include: perhaps some people cannot afford helmets; the perception that helmets are "funny-looking" or "uncool.")

Point out that experts believe that one death per day and one head injury every 4 minutes would be prevented if every bike rider wore a helmet.

GROUP ACTIVITY

Poster Project Divide the class into small groups, and provide each group with poster board and markers. Have them create posters designed to educate the public and motivate them to wear bicycle helmets. After students present their posters to the class, display them in the classroom.

672 Chapter 28 • Staying Healthy

Injury Prevention

Have you ever fallen off your bike or sprained your ankle? Maybe you avoided injury, or maybe you ended up in the emergency room. Accidents happen, and they can cause injury and even death. It is impossible to prevent all accidents, but you can decrease your risk by using your common sense and following basic safety rules.

Safety at Home Many accidents can be avoided. **Figure 14** below shows tips for safety around the house.

Figure 14 Home Safety Tips

Bathroom
- Never touch electrical switches or appliances while touching water.
- Use nonslip mats in the shower and tub.
- Use a night light.

Kitchen
- Clean up spills quickly.
- Do not allow pothandles to extend over the edge of the stove.
- Use a stool to reach high shelves.
- Keep grease and drippings away from open flames.

- Have your parents install smoke detectors on every floor.

Living room
- Keep electrical cords out of walkways.
- Do not plug too many electrical devices into one outlet.

Entrance and stairs
- Use a railing.
- Never leave objects on stairs.

Safety Outdoors Always dress appropriately for the weather and the activity. Never hike or camp alone. Tell someone where you are going and when you expect to return. If you do not bring water from home, be sure to purify any water you drink in the wilderness.

Learn how to swim. It could save your life! Never swim alone, and do not dive into shallow water or water of unknown depth. When in a boat, wear a life jacket. If a storm threatens, get out of the water and seek shelter.

Safety on the Road In the car, always wear a seat belt, even if you are traveling only a short distance. Most car accidents happen close to home, and seat belts save lives. When riding a bicycle, always wear a helmet. Ride with traffic, and obey all traffic rules. Be sure to signal when stopping or turning.

Homework

Writing Have students research and write a report about the physical symptoms and emergency treatments for hypothermia and heatstroke.

When Accidents Happen

No matter how well we practice safety measures, accidents can still happen. What should you do if a friend chokes on food and cannot breathe? What if he is stung by a bee and has a violent allergic reaction?

Call for Help Once you've checked for other dangers, call for medical help immediately, like the person in **Figure 15.** In most communities you can dial 911. Speak slowly and clearly. Give the complete address and a description of the location. Describe the accident, the number of people injured, and the types of injuries. Ask what to do and listen carefully to the instructions. Let the other person hang up first to be sure they have no more questions or instructions.

Figure 15 *When calling 911, stay calm and listen carefully to what the dispatcher tells you.*

Learn First Aid You may want to learn more about what to do in an emergency by taking a first-aid course or a CPR course, as shown in **Figure 16.** *CPR* is a lifesaving procedure designed to revive a person who is not breathing and has no heartbeat. If you are over 12 years old, you can become certified in both CPR and first aid. Some babysitting courses also provide basics in first aid and are a good idea for anyone who cares for young children. The American Red Cross, community organizations, and local hospitals offer these classes. You should not attempt any lifesaving procedure unless you have been trained.

Figure 16 *These teenagers are taking a CPR course to prepare themselves for emergency situations.*

REVIEW

1. What is aerobic exercise? Give three examples.
2. What should you do when calling for help in a medical emergency?
3. What is hygiene, and how does it help you stay healthy?
4. **Applying Concepts** What situations are causing excess stress in your life right now? What can you do to help relieve the stress you are feeling?

---

4) Close

Quiz

1. How are healthy habits related to stress? (Practicing healthy habits, such as exercising regularly and getting adequate rest, helps us cope with stress in a positive way.)
2. What do bicycle helmets and seat belts have in common? (They both decrease the risk of injury from accidents.)
3. When you call for emergency help, what should you tell the person who answers the phone? (Tell the person the location of the emergency, the nature of the emergency, the number of people injured, and the type of injuries involved. Always hang up last.)

ALTERNATIVE ASSESSMENT

 Writing Have students write an analysis of their hygienic habits, exercise regimes, sleep patterns, and injury risks or safety measures during play and athletic activities. Tell them to explain whether their activities and habits are encouraging good health and safety or whether they need to make changes to their routines.

▼ Answers to Review

1. Aerobic exercise is vigorous, sustained exercise of the whole body for 20 minutes or more. Some examples of aerobic exercise include biking, in-line skating, jumping rope, and swimming.
2. Dial 911, speak slowly and clearly, and describe where you are, why you called, how many people were injured, and what types of injuries were sustained. Listen carefully to the instructions, and let the other person hang up first.
3. Hygiene includes methods of preserving and protecting your health. It keeps you healthy by keeping your body in top condition.
4. Answers will vary.

Chapter Highlights

VOCABULARY DEFINITIONS

SECTION 1

nutrient a substance that must be consumed or taken in by an organism to promote normal growth, maintenance, and repair

carbohydrate a biochemical composed of one or more simple sugars bonded together; used to provide and store energy

protein a biochemical composed of amino acids; its functions include regulating chemical reactions, transporting and storing materials, and providing support

fat an energy-storage nutrient that helps the body store some vitamins

mineral an element that is essential for good health

vitamin an organic compound that controls many body functions, including cell growth and hormone production

malnutrition a disorder resulting from consuming too few calories or too few nutrients

SECTION 2

drug any chemical substance that causes a physical or emotional change in a person

addiction a physical dependence on a drug

Chapter Highlights

SECTION 1

Vocabulary
- nutrient (p. 656)
- carbohydrate (p. 657)
- protein (p. 657)
- fat (p. 657)
- mineral (p. 658)
- vitamin (p. 659)
- malnutrition (p. 662)

Section Notes
- Carbohydrates, proteins, fats, vitamins, minerals, and water are the six types of nutrients that are essential to life.
- Teenage girls need about 2,200 Calories a day. Boys need about 2,800. It is important to obtain Calories from a variety of foods.
- The food pyramid gives information for eating a balanced diet.
- A nutrition information label on a packaged food lists serving size, Calorie and nutrient content, and the ingredients.
- Anorexia nervosa, bulimia, and obesity can lead to malnutrition.

Labs
To Diet or Not to Diet (p. 780)

SECTION 2

Vocabulary
- drug (p. 663)
- addiction (p. 664)
- nicotine (p. 665)
- alcoholism (p. 666)
- narcotics (p. 667)

Section Notes
- A drug is any chemical substance that causes a physical or emotional change in a person.
- Some drugs can cause addiction or psychological dependence.
- Over-the-counter and prescription drugs are legal drugs, many of which are powerful healing agents. Some also have side effects.
- Alcohol and nicotine are legal drugs for adults. Both are addictive and hazardous to your health.

☑ Skills Check

Math Concepts
PERCENTAGE If your recommended daily value of fat is 72 g and you eat a candy bar that has 12 g of fat, what percentage of your daily value of fat have you eaten? To find the percentage, divide the grams of fat in the candy bar by the daily value. Then multiply by 100.

$$12 \text{ g} \div 72 \text{ g} = 0.17 \times 100\% = 17\%$$

The fat in the candy bar is 17 percent of your total daily value.

Visual Understanding
NUTRITION INFORMATION LABELS All packaged foods in the United States are required to have a nutrition label like the one on page 661. On this label you can see that the serving size is 1 cup and that there are two servings in the container. The number of Calories in a serving and the number of Calories from fat are listed. You will also see the percent daily value for a number of nutrients that can be found in one serving. These percentages are based on 2,000 Calories a day.

Lab and Activity Highlights

To Diet or Not to Diet PG 780

Keep It Clean PG 781

Datasheets for LabBook
(blackline masters for these labs)

SECTION 2

- A drug abuser takes a drug, often illegally, for non-medical reasons.
- Drug abuse oftens begins with the use of tobacco, alcohol, or marijuana—the gateway drugs.
- Getting off drugs requires admitting addiction, deciding to stop, going through withdrawal symptoms, and experiencing cravings for the drug.

SECTION 3

Vocabulary
hygiene (p. 669)
aerobic exercise (p. 670)
stress (p. 671)

Section Notes
- Good hygiene is essential to good health.
- Having a healthy body requires getting regular aerobic exercise and getting enough sleep. Posture is also important to good health.
- Some stress is a normal and necessary part of life. Too much stress can result in poor health.
- It is possible to prevent some accidents by using common sense and following basic rules of safety.
- In an emergency, call for help as soon as possible. Do not attempt any lifesaving procedure for which you are not trained.

Labs
Keep It Clean (p. 781)

VOCABULARY DEFINITIONS, continued

nicotine a chemical stimulant that increases heart rate and blood pressure

alcoholism a disorder in which a person is physically and psychologically dependent on alcohol

narcotics drugs made from opium

SECTION 3

hygiene methods of preserving and protecting your health

aerobic exercise vigorous, sustained exercise of the whole body for 20 minutes or more

stress the physical and mental response to situations that create pressure

 Blackline masters of these Chapter Highlights can be found in the **Study Guide**.

---

internet connect

 GO TO: go.hrw.com

Visit the **HRW** Web site for a variety of learning tools related to this chapter. Just type in the keyword:

KEYWORD: HSTBD7

 GO TO: www.scilinks.org

Visit the **National Science Teachers Association** on-line Web site for Internet resources related to this chapter. Just type in the sciLINKS number for more information about the topic:

TOPIC:		sciLINKS NUMBER:
Nutrition		HSTL680
Vitamins		HSTL685
Food Pyramids		HSTL690
Nutritional Disorders		HSTL695
Drug and Alcohol Abuse		HSTL700

675

Lab and Activity Highlights

LabBank

 Labs You Can Eat, Snack Attack, Lab 10

Inquiry Lab, Consumer Challenge, Lab 8

 Long-Term Projects & Research Ideas, Breakfast, Lunch, and Dinner of Champions, Project 28

Chapter Review Answers

USING VOCABULARY

1. Saturated fats
2. addiction
3. food pyramid
4. bulimia
5. drug user

UNDERSTANDING CONCEPTS

Multiple Choice

6. c
7. d
8. b
9. b
10. d
11. d
12. c

Short Answer

13. Not all narcotics are illegal. Some narcotics are prescription drugs used to treat severe pain.
14. The three nutrients that provide energy in Calories are carbohydrates, proteins, and fats. Three nutrients that do not provide energy are water, vitamins, and minerals.
15. Beer contains alcohol, which depresses the central nervous system. Alcohol is a drug. Therefore, if you drink beer, you are taking a drug.

Concept Mapping

16. An answer to this exercise can be found at the end of this book.

Chapter Review

USING VOCABULARY

To complete the following sentences, choose the correct term from each pair of terms listed below:

1. __?__ are linked to high blood cholesterol levels. *(Saturated fats* or *Unsaturated fats)*
2. Physical dependence on a drug is called __?__. *(addiction* or *tolerance)*
3. The __?__ divides foods into six groups and gives a recommended number of servings for each. *(nutrition information label* or *food pyramid)*
4. One of the characteristics of __?__ is binge eating. *(bulimia* or *anorexia nervosa)*
5. A person who uses drugs for their intended purpose and with the proper dosage is a __?__. *(drug abuser* or *drug user)*

UNDERSTANDING CONCEPTS

Multiple Choice

6. Which of the following is *not* a function of water in the body?
   a. transport substances
   b. regulate temperature
   c. provide Calories
   d. provide lubrication

7. Side effects of over-the-counter and prescription medicines may include
   a. nausea.   c. drowsiness.
   b. headaches.   d. All of the above

8. Which of the following nutrients does *not* provide energy for the body?
   a. carbohydrates   c. fats
   b. vitamins   d. proteins

9. What are the effects of nicotine on the body?
   a. liver damage and decrease in physical endurance
   b. loss of appetite and decrease in physical endurance
   c. loss of appetite and brain damage
   d. liver damage and loss of appetite

10. Which of the following statements about drugs is true?
    a. All drugs are illegal.
    b. Smoking just one or two cigarettes is safe for anyone.
    c. Alcohol is not a drug.
    d. Withdrawal symptoms may be painful.

11. Aerobic exercise does *not*
    a. burn calories.
    b. increase the heart rate.
    c. strengthen the heart, lungs, and bones.
    d. make you weak.

12. When talking to a 911 operator, you should *not*
    a. describe the accident.
    b. ask what to do.
    c. hang up before the dispatcher hangs up.
    d. speak slowly and clearly.

676 Chapter 28 • Staying Healthy

Short Answer

Answer each of the following questions with a few sentences:

13. Are all narcotics illegal? Explain.

14. What are the three types of nutrients that provide energy in Calories? Which three nutrients do not provide energy?

15. If you drink a beer, are you taking a drug? Explain your answer.

Concept Mapping

16. Use the following terms to create a concept map: unsaturated fats, carbohydrates, water, proteins, nutrients, simple sugars, starch, fats, vitamins, minerals, saturated fats.

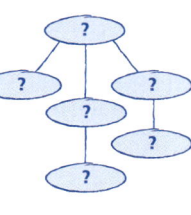

CRITICAL THINKING AND PROBLEM SOLVING

Write one or two sentences to answer the following questions:

17. Many people eat little or no meat. Meat is often the major source of protein in American diets. What other sources of protein can vegetarians choose?

18. You are at a party and a friend offers you a cigarette. He says that one cigarette won't hurt you. Using what you know about tobacco and addiction, explain why his reasoning is false.

MATH IN SCIENCE

19. Assume your diet is 20 percent fat, 30 percent protein, and 50 percent carbohydrates. In order to get 2,000 Calories a day, how many Calories of each nutrient should you be getting?

INTERPRETING GRAPHICS

List the unsafe habits in the following illustrations. For each unsafe habit, tell what the person should be doing instead.

What's wrong here?

20.

21.

 Reading Check-up Take a minute to review your answers to the Pre-Reading Questions found at the bottom of page 654. Have your answers changed? If necessary, revise your answers based on what you have learned since you began this chapter.

CRITICAL THINKING AND PROBLEM SOLVING

17. Sample answer: Other foods that contain protein include eggs, dairy products, and fish.

18. Sample answer: The nicotine in cigarettes is highly addictive. One cigarette could easily lead to many more.

MATH IN SCIENCE

19. 600 Cal from protein, 400 Cal from fat, and 1,000 Cal from carbohydrates

INTERPRETING GRAPHICS

20. The girl in this picture is riding without her seat belt. She needs to wear her seat belt.

21. In this picture, a pot handle is hanging over the edge of the stove. The woman should use a pot holder to turn the handle of the pot so that it is not hanging over the edge of the stove.

Concept Mapping Transparency 28

Blackline masters of this Chapter Review can be found in the **Study Guide.**

Chapter 28 • Chapter Review

SCIENCE, TECHNOLOGY, AND SOCIETY

Bacteria at Your Service

Background

Bacteria have many uses. For instance, some bacteria are currently being used to help break down toxic substances, such as cyanide.

Certain bacteria store energy in the form of a biodegradable plastic called PHB. Originally, researchers found that the plastic was stiff and brittle. It also had a high melting point, which made it difficult to work with. However, scientists found that by feeding the bacteria a mixture of glucose and organic acids, the bacteria could produce a stronger, more flexible plastic with a lower melting point.

Genetically engineered bacteria have been developed to create more-successful fruit and vegetable crops. This technology could provide fresher and more nutritious food for consumption around the world.

Science, Technology, and Society

Bacteria at Your Service

Wanted: Hard worker to clean up trash. You must have experience curing diseases. The ability to make plastics is a plus. Only microorganisms need apply for this position.

What could possibly be flexible enough to perform so many different activities? Would you believe it's bacteria?

Cleaning Up Our Act

Without bacteria, Earth would be littered with the remains of plants and animals. That's because many bacteria decompose once-living matter. Some bacteria also break down other substances. In fact, they offer solutions to some of our toughest pollution problems.

When an oil spill occurs, it often severely damages the environment. However, scientists have engineered bacteria that actually feed on oil! As the bacteria eat the oil, they break it down into harmless substances. Scientists hope to use the bacteria to clean up large oil spills, but they must first be certain that introducing a large number of these bacteria into the ocean will not harm the environment.

Producing Plastics and Pills

Did you know that some bacteria act like factories? For example, one kind of bacteria makes biodegradable plastic! These amazing bacteria store energy as plastic granules, just as animals store energy as fat and plants store energy as starch. Originally, researchers found that the plastic was stiff and brittle. However, scientists found that when certain substances are added to the bacteria's diet, the plastic they produce is flexible enough to be made into consumer products.

Other bacteria can produce important drugs used to fight disease. In fact, some bacteria even produce antibiotics that can fight infections caused by other bacteria!

Helping Plants Grow

Genetic engineers have designed bacteria that can help make plants pest resistant and cold resistant. Some bacteria even keep foods fresh longer on the grocery store shelves. From the garbage dump to the grocery store to the medicine cabinet, bacteria are at our service!

What Do You Think?

▶ Many scientists are concerned about the potential side effects of genetic engineering. What could be some consequences of altering the genetic makeup of crops? Do some research to find out for yourself. Write a report or organize a debate with your classmates.

▲ *These bacteria are used to clean up oil spills.*

Answer to What Do You Think?
Answers will vary.

Health Watch

Meatless Munching

What'll it be today, the hamburger special, chicken surprise, or veggie platter? More and more people are opting for the veggie platter. In fact, research indicates that more than 12 million Americans are now vegetarians, and this number appears to be growing.

It's Not Just Salads
When you think of a vegetarian diet, you might think only of vegetables. Of course, vegetables are important to a vegetarian diet, but not all vegetarian diets are alike. Some vegetarian diets are based solely on plant products, while semivegetarian diets may also include dairy products, eggs, fish, and poultry.

Why the Trend?
There are many different reasons for choosing a vegetarian lifestyle. Some people believe that a vegetarian diet is healthy because a decreased consumption of animal products can lower their intake of saturated fat and cholesterol. Other people have ecological reasons for eating a vegetarian diet. For example, producing a serving of meat requires more land, water, and chemicals than producing a serving of grain. Finally, many vegetarians believe that it is unethical to kill animals for meat when plants are available.

Benefits and Risks
Recent statistics suggest that a vegetarian diet may reduce the risk of heart disease, adult-onset diabetes, and some forms of cancer. However, this type of diet takes careful thought. It is not simply a matter of eliminating meat. People may replace the meat with too many dairy products and eggs, which are higher in fat than most meats. Others may substitute high carbohydrate foods (such as pasta) and junk food (such as french fries) for their meat choices instead of increasing their fruit and vegetable intake. This could lead to nutritional deficiencies. The key to consuming the recommended amount of calories and nutrients for a healthy diet is to eat a wide variety of nutritious, low-fat foods. This is a good idea whether you want to decrease your meat intake or not.

▲ *All of the foods shown here are plant products and are commonly used in vegetarian diets.*

Prepare a Healthy Menu
▶ Choose one of the nutrients that meats provide, and do some research to find a vegetarian substitute. What difficulties did you encounter in your search? Would you eat the substitute you found?

HEALTH WATCH
Meatless Munching

Background
To be nutritionally complete, our bodies need 20 different amino acids, 10 of which we manufacture ourselves. The other 10 are called essential amino acids. By eating a variety of foods, a vegetarian can be assured of getting all the protein he or she needs. Indeed, many experts consider dietary variety to be the primary factor in achieving a nutritionally complete diet and maintaining good health, for both meat eaters and vegetarians.

Teaching Strategy
Explain to the class that a protein consists of a long chain of amino acids. Proteins are used in the body to regulate hormones, to repair damaged tissue, and to help fight infections. Assign each student one of the 20 common amino acids to investigate. Tell students to find out what foods the amino acid can be found in and what function it serves in the body. Then have students write the information in outline form on a small index card, along with illustrations of the foods the amino acid is found in. Use the index cards to make a large poster for the class.

Answers to Prepare a Healthy Menu
Some nutrients found in meats include vitamin B_{12}, iron, zinc, calcium, and protein. Vitamin B_{12} is not found in plants in appreciable amounts, so many vegetarians must eat foods fortified with B_{12} or take supplements.

LabBook

Contents

Safety First! **682**

Chapter 1   The World of Life Science
Does It All Add Up? 686
Graphing Data 688
A Window to a Hidden World 689

Chapter 2   It's Alive!! Or, Is It?
Roly–Poly Races 690
The Best-Bread Bakery Dilemma 692

Chapter 3   Cells: The Basic Units of Life
Elephant-Sized Amoebas? 694
Cells Alive! 696
Name That Part! 697

Chapter 4   The Cell in Action
The Perfect Taters Mystery 698
Stayin' Alive! 700

Chapter 5   Heredity
Bug Builders, Inc. 702
Tracing Traits 704

Chapter 6   Genes and Gene Technology
Base-Pair Basics 706

Chapter 7
The Evolution of Living Things
Mystery Footprints 708
Out-of-Sight Marshmallows 710
Survival of the Chocolates 711

Chapter 8   The History of Life on Earth
Dating the Fossil Record 712
The Half-life of Pennies 715

Chapter 9   Classification
Shape Island 716
Voyage of the USS *Adventure* 718

Chapter 10   Bacteria and Viruses
Aunt Flossie and the Intruder 720
Viral Decorations 721

Chapter 11   Protists and Fungi
Making a Protist Mobile 722
There's a Fungus Among Us! 723

Chapter 12   Introduction to Plants
Leaf Me Alone! 724
Travelin' Seeds 726
Build a Flower 727

Chapter 13   Plant Processes
Food Factory Waste 728
Weepy Weeds 730

Chapter 14   Animals and Behavior
Wet, Wiggly Worms! 732
Aunt Flossie and the Bumblebee 734

Chapter 15   Invertebrates
Porifera's Porosity 736
The Cricket Caper 737

Chapter 16
Fishes, Amphibians, and Reptiles
Floating a Pipe Fish 740
A Prince of a Frog 742

Chapter 17   Birds and Mammals
What? No Dentist Bills? 744
Wanted: Mammals on Mars 745

Chapter 18
Interactions of Living Things
Adaptation: It's a Way of Life 746
Capturing the Wild Bean 748

Chapter 19   Cycles in Nature
Nitrogen Needs 750
A Passel o' Pioneers 752

Chapter 20   The Earth's Ecosystems
Life in the Desert 754
Discovering Mini-Ecosystems 755
Too Much of a Good Thing? 756

Chapter 21   Environmental Problems and Solutions
Biodiversity—What a Disturbing
   Thought! 758
Deciding About Environmental Issues . . 760

Chapter 22
Body Organization and Structure
Muscles at Work 762
Seeing Is Believing 763

Chapter 23   Circulation and Respiration
Build a Lung 766
Carbon Dioxide Breath 767

Chapter 24
The Digestive and Urinary Systems
As the Stomach Churns 768
Enzymes in Action 770

Chapter 25   Communication and Control
You've Gotta Lotta Nerve 772

Chapter 26
Reproduction and Development
It's a Comfy, Safe World! 774
My, How You've Grown! 775

Chapter 27   Body Defenses and Disease
Antibodies to the Rescue 776
Passing the Cold 778

Chapter 28   Staying Healthy
To Diet or Not to Diet 780
Keep It Clean 781

Exploring, inventing, and investigating are essential to the study of science. However, these activities can also be dangerous. To make sure that your experiments and explorations are safe, you must be aware of a variety of safety guidelines.

You have probably heard of the saying, "It is better to be safe than sorry." This is particularly true in a science classroom where experiments and explorations are being performed. Being uninformed and careless can result in serious injuries. Don't take chances with your own safety or with anyone else's.

Following are important guidelines for staying safe in the science classroom. Your teacher may also have safety guidelines and tips that are specific to your classroom and laboratory. Take the time to be safe.

Safety Rules!

Start Out Right

Always get your teacher's permission before attempting any laboratory exploration. Read the procedures carefully, and pay particular attention to safety information and caution statements. If you are unsure about what a safety symbol means, look it up or ask your teacher. You cannot be too careful when it comes to safety. If an accident does occur, inform your teacher immediately, regardless of how minor you think the accident is.

Safety Symbols

All of the experiments and investigations in this book and their related worksheets include important safety symbols to alert you to particular safety concerns. Become familiar with these symbols so that when you see them, you will know what they mean and what to do. It is important that you read this entire safety section to learn about specific dangers in the laboratory.

If you are instructed to note the odor of a substance, wave the fumes toward your nose with your hand. Never put your nose close to the source.

Eye protection • Clothing protection • Hand safety

Heating safety • Electric safety • Chemical safety

Animal safety • Sharp object • Plant safety

Eye Safety

Wear safety goggles when working around chemicals, acids, bases, or any type of flame or heating device. Wear safety goggles any time there is even the slightest chance that harm could come to your eyes. If any substance gets into your eyes, notify your teacher immediately, and flush your eyes with running water for at least 15 minutes. Treat any unknown chemical as if it were a dangerous chemical. Never look directly into the sun. Doing so could cause permanent blindness.

Avoid wearing contact lenses in a laboratory situation. Even if you are wearing safety goggles, chemicals can get between the contact lenses and your eyes. If your doctor requires that you wear contact lenses instead of glasses, wear eye-cup safety goggles in the lab.

Safety Equipment

Know the locations of the nearest fire alarms and any other safety equipment, such as fire blankets and eyewash fountains, as identified by your teacher, and know the procedures for using them.

Be extra careful when using any glassware. When adding a heavy object to a graduated cylinder, tilt the cylinder so the object slides slowly to the bottom.

Neatness

Keep your work area free of all unnecessary books and papers. Tie back long hair, and secure loose sleeves or other loose articles of clothing, such as ties and bows. Remove dangling jewelry. Don't wear open-toed shoes or sandals in the laboratory. Never eat, drink, or apply cosmetics in a laboratory setting. Food, drink, and cosmetics can easily become contaminated with dangerous materials.

Certain hair products (such as aerosol hair spray) are flammable and should not be worn while working near an open flame. Avoid wearing hair spray or hair gel on lab days.

Sharp/Pointed Objects

Use knives and other sharp instruments with extreme care. Never cut objects while holding them in your hands. Place objects on a suitable work surface for cutting.

Safety First! LabBook **683**

Heat

Wear safety goggles when using a heating device or a flame. Whenever possible, use an electric hot plate as a heat source instead of an open flame. When heating materials in a test tube, always angle the test tube away from yourself and others. In order to avoid burns, wear heat-resistant gloves whenever instructed to do so.

Electricity

Be careful with electrical cords. When using a microscope with a lamp, do not place the cord where it could trip someone. Do not let cords hang over a table edge in a way that could cause equipment to fall if the cord is accidentally pulled. Do not use equipment with damaged cords. Be sure your hands are dry and that the electrical equipment is in the "off" position before plugging it in. Turn off and unplug electrical equipment when you are finished.

Chemicals

Wear safety goggles when handling any potentially dangerous chemicals, acids, or bases. If a chemical is unknown, handle it as you would a dangerous chemical. Wear an apron and safety gloves when working with acids or bases or whenever you are told to do so. If a spill gets on your skin or clothing, rinse it off immediately with water for at least 5 minutes while calling to your teacher.

Never mix chemicals unless your teacher tells you to do so. Never taste, touch, or smell chemicals unless you are specifically directed to do so. Before working with a flammable liquid or gas, check for the presence of any source of flame, spark, or heat.

684   LabBook

Animal Safety

Always obtain your teacher's permission before bringing any animal into the school building. Handle animals only as your teacher directs. Always treat animals carefully and with respect. Wash your hands thoroughly after handling any animal.

Plant Safety

Do not eat any part of a plant or plant seed used in the laboratory. Wash hands thoroughly after handling any part of a plant. When in nature, do not pick any wild plants unless your teacher instructs you to do so.

Glassware

Examine all glassware before use. Be sure that glassware is clean and free of chips and cracks. Report damaged glassware to your teacher. Glass containers used for heating should be made of heat-resistant glass.

Safety First! LabBook

Does It All Add Up?
Teacher's Notes

Time Required
One 45-minute class period

Lab Ratings

TEACHER PREP 🧪🧪
STUDENT SET-UP 🧪
CONCEPT LEVEL 🧪🧪
CLEAN UP 🧪

MATERIALS

The materials listed on the student page are enough for 1 student or 1 group of students. Liquid A is plain water. Liquid B is either isopropyl alcohol or denatured ethyl alcohol. Safety thermometers are recommended for this lab.

Safety Caution

Remind students to review all safety cautions and icons before beginning this lab activity.

Caution students to handle mercury thermometers with care. Alcohol is flammable and poisonous. Students should wear goggles and aprons at all times during this lab. A fire extinguisher and fire blanket should be nearby. Know how to use them. The room should be well-ventilated, and students should be familiar with evacuation procedures.

Using Scientific Methods

Does It All Add Up?

Your math teacher won't tell you this, but did you know that sometimes 2 + 2 does not equal 4?! (Well, it really does, but sometimes it doesn't *appear* to equal 4.) In this experiment, you will use the scientific method to predict, measure, and observe the mixing of two unknown liquids. You will learn that a scientist does not set out to prove a hypothesis, but rather to test it, and sometimes the results just don't seem to add up!

Make Observations

1. Examine the two mystery liquids in the graduated cylinders given to you by your teacher.
   Caution: Do not taste, touch, or smell the liquids.

2. In your ScienceLog, write down as many observations as you can about each liquid. Are the liquids bubbly? What color are they? What is the exact volume of each liquid? Touch the graduated cylinders. Are they hot or cold?

3. Pour exactly 25 mL of liquid A into each of two graduated cylinders. Combine these samples in one of the graduated cylinders, and record the final volume in your ScienceLog. Repeat this step for liquid B.

Form a Hypothesis

4. Based on your observations and on prior experience, what do you expect the volume to be when you pour these two liquids together?

Materials

- 75 mL of liquid A
- 75 mL of liquid B
- 100 mL graduated cylinders (7)
- glass-labeling marker
- Celsius thermometer
- protective gloves

Make a Prediction

5. Make a prediction based on your hypothesis using an "if-then" format. Explain why you have made your prediction.

Kevin McCurdy
Elmwood Junior High School
Rogers, Arkansas

686 Chapter 1 • LabBook

Test the Hypothesis

6. In your ScienceLog, make a data table similar to the one below to record your predictions and observations.

	Contents of cylinder A	Contents of cylinder B	Mixing results: predictions	Mixing results: observations
Volume				
Appearance				
Temperature				

DO NOT WRITE IN BOOK

7. Carefully pour exactly 25 mL of Liquid A into a 50 mL graduated cylinder. Mark this cylinder "A." Record its volume, appearance, and temperature in the data table.

8. Carefully pour exactly 25 mL of Liquid B into another 50 mL graduated cylinder. Mark this cylinder "B." Record its volume, appearance, and temperature in the data table.

9. Mark the empty third cylinder "A + B."

10. In the "Mixing results: predictions" column in your table, record the prediction you made earlier. Each classmate may have made a different prediction.

11. Carefully pour the contents of both cylinders into the third graduated cylinder.

12. Observe and record the total volume, appearance, and temperature in the "Mixing results: observations" column of the table.

Analyze the Results

13. Discuss your predictions as a class. How many different predictions were there? Which predictions were supported by testing? Did any of your measurements surprise you?

Draw Conclusions

14. Was your hypothesis supported? Explain why this may have happened.

15. Explain the value of incorrect predictions.

Lab Notes

This lab will be of interest because 25 mL of liquid A + 25 mL of liquid B do not make 50 mL of the mixture! Spaces between molecules of alcohol become filled with water molecules, resulting in less volume. An analogy would be mixing 25 mL of marbles with 10 mL of BBs. The BBs will settle between the marbles, and the result will be less volume. The alcohol-and-water mixture will be cloudy and bubbly for a brief time due to the sudden decrease of volume, leaving tiny bubbles.

 Datasheets for LabBook
Datasheet 1

 Science Skills Worksheet 12
"Working with Hypotheses"

 Science Skills Worksheet 15
"Measuring"

Answers

All answers in this lab are based on student observations and will vary. Students may make some unusual predictions. You may want to lead them into questions about volume. Encourage them to think of as many ways to observe and characterize the two liquids as possible.

15. Incorrect predictions can lead to a new understanding of the way things work.

Graphing Data
Teacher's Notes

Time Required
One 45-minute class period

Lab Ratings

TEACHER PREP 🧪🧪
STUDENT SET-UP 🧪
CONCEPT LEVEL 🧪🧪
CLEAN UP 🧪

Safety Caution

Remind students to review all safety cautions and icons before beginning this lab activity.

Caution students to exercise proper care when handling the beaker of hot water. Also, caution students to be careful when they are moving around an electrical cord. A clip that will hold the thermometer to the side of the beaker and off the bottom of the beaker while it is heating or cooling is safer and more accurate than a thermometer simply propped up inside the beaker. This is also good scientific practice to model.

 Datasheets for LabBook
Datasheet 2

Edith C. McAlanis
Socorro Middle School
El Paso, Texas

Graphing Data

When performing an experiment it is usually necessary to collect data. To understand the data, it is often good to organize them into a graph. Graphs can show trends and patterns that you might not notice in a table or list. In this exercise, you will practice collecting data and organizing the data into a graph.

Procedure

1. Pour 200 mL of water into a 400 mL beaker. Add ice to the beaker until the water line is at the 400 mL mark.

2. Place a Celsius thermometer into the beaker. Use a thermometer clip to prevent the thermometer from touching the bottom of the beaker. Record the temperature of the ice water in your ScienceLog.

3. Place the beaker and thermometer on a hot plate. Turn the hot plate on medium heat and record the temperature every minute until the water temperature reaches 100°C.

4. Using heat-resistant gloves, remove the beaker from the hot plate. Continue to record the temperature of the water each minute for 10 more minutes.
   Caution: Don't forget to turn off the hot plate.

5. On a piece of graph paper, create a graph similar to the one below. Label the horizontal axis (the *x*-axis) "Time (min)," and mark the axis in increments of 1 minute as shown. Label the vertical axis (the *y*-axis) "Temperature (°C)," and mark the axis in increments of ten degrees as shown.

6. Find the 1-minute mark on the *x*-axis, and move up the graph to the temperature you recorded at 1 minute. Place a dot on the graph at that point. Plot each temperature in the same way. When you have plotted all of your data, connect the dots with a smooth line.

Analysis

7. Examine your graph. Do you think the water heated faster than it cooled? Explain.

8. Estimate what the temperature of the water was 2.5 minutes after you placed the beaker on the hot plate. Explain how you can make a good estimate of temperature between those you recorded.

9. Explain how a graph may give more information than the same data in a chart.

Materials

- 200 mL of water
- 400 mL beaker
- ice
- Celsius thermometer with a clip
- hot plate
- clock or watch with a second hand
- graph paper
- heat-resistant gloves

Answers

7. Answers will vary according to several factors, including altitude. Students should notice whether there is a gentle slope of the line (indicating gradual heating or cooling) or a steep slope (indicating rapid heating or cooling).

8. Answers will vary.

9. A list or a chart is organized information, and sometimes it is necessary to put collected data into one of these forms before graphing. Because a graph is like a picture, it can often help scientists to see what is happening when numbers alone would be confusing. A graph can show a trend or a pattern that may not be readily discernible in a list or chart.

A Window to a Hidden World

MAKING MODELS

Have you ever noticed that objects underwater appear closer than they really are? That's because light waves change speed when they travel from air into water. Anton van Leeuwenhoek, a pioneer of microscopy in the late seventeenth century, used a drop of water to magnify objects. That drop of water brought a hidden world closer into view. How did Leeuwenhoek's microscope work? In this investigation, you will build a model of it to find out.

Procedure

1. Punch a hole in the center of the poster board with a hole punch, as shown in (a) at right.

2. Tape a small piece of clear plastic wrap over the hole, as shown in (b) at right. Be sure the plastic wrap is large enough so that the tape you use to secure it does not cover the hole.

3. Use an eyedropper to put one drop of water over the hole. Check to be sure your drop of water is dome-shaped (convex), as shown in (c) at right.

4. Hold the microscope close to your eye and look through the drop. Be careful not to disturb the water drop.

5. Hold the microscope over a piece of newspaper and observe the image.

Analysis

6. Describe and draw the image you see. Is the image larger or the same size as it was without the microscope? Is the image clear or blurred? Is the shape of the image distorted?

7. How do you think your model could be improved?

Going Further
Robert Hooke and Zacharias Janssen contributed much to the field of microscopy. Find out who they were, when they lived, and what they did.

Materials

- hole punch
- 3 × 10 cm piece of poster board
- clear plastic wrap
- transparent tape
- eyedropper
- water
- newspaper

(a)

(b)

(c)

A Window to a Hidden World
Teacher's Notes

Time Required
One 45-minute class period

Lab Ratings

EASY — HARD

- **TEACHER PREP** 🧪🧪
- **STUDENT SET-UP** 🧪🧪
- **CONCEPT LEVEL** 🧪
- **CLEAN UP** 🧪

MATERIALS
The materials listed on the student page are enough for a group of 4–5 students. A 3 × 5 in. index card cut in half lengthwise can substitute for a stiff piece of poster board. It can be difficult to eliminate wrinkles in the plastic over the hole. Some students may need assistance.

Datasheets for LabBook
Datasheet 3

Science Skills Worksheet 24
"Using Models to Communicate"

Answers

6. Answers will vary. Students should see a slightly larger image. It will be blurred, especially around the edges. The image may be distorted.

7. Most students will think their model could be improved by eliminating the wrinkles over the hole.

Going Further
Robert Hooke (1635–1703), one of the world's great inventors, is famous for his discovery of "cells" in cork tissue as seen through his improved microscope. Hooke was also a keen observer with an interest in fossils and geology. Zacharias Janssen, a Dutch lens grinder, mounted two lenses in a tube to produce the first compound microscope in 1590.

Georgiann Delgadillo
East Valley School District
Continuous Curriculum School
Spokane, Washington

Roly-Poly Races
Teacher's Notes

Time Required
One or two 45-minute class periods

Lab Ratings

TEACHER PREP 🧪🧪
STUDENT SET-UP 🧪🧪
CONCEPT LEVEL 🧪
CLEAN UP 🧪

MATERIALS

The materials listed on the student page are enough for 1–2 students. Remind students that they are handling living things that deserve to be treated with respect. The soil used in this lab should be sterilized potting soil to avoid causing allergic reactions among the students.

Safety Caution

Remind students to review all safety cautions and icons before beginning this lab activity.

 Datasheets for LabBook Datasheet 4

 Science Skills Worksheet 10 "Doing a Lab Write-up"

Roly-Poly Races

Have you ever watched a bug run? Did you wonder why it was running? The bug you saw running was probably reacting to a stimulus. In other words, something happened that made it run! One characteristic of living things is that they respond to stimuli. In this activity, you will study the movement of roly-polies. Roly-polies are also called pill bugs. They are not really bugs at all; they are land-dwelling crustaceans called isopods. Isopods live in dark, moist areas under rocks or wood. You will provide stimuli to determine how fast your isopod can move and what affects its speed and direction. Remember that isopods are living things and must be treated gently and with respect.

Materials

- small plastic container with lid
- 1 or 2 cm of soil for the container
- metric ruler
- small slice of raw potato
- piece of chalk
- 4 isopods
- watch or clock with a second hand
- protective gloves

Procedure

1. Choose a partner and decide together how you will run your roly-poly race. Discuss some gentle ways you might be able to stimulate your isopods to move. Choose five or six things that might cause movement, such as a gentle nudge or a change in temperature, sound, or light. Check your choices with your teacher.

2. Make a data table similar to the one below. Label your columns with the stimuli you've chosen. Label the rows "Isopod 1," "Isopod 2," "Isopod 3," and "Isopod 4."

Isopod Responses			
	Stimulus 1: ?	Stimulus 2: ?	Stimulus 3: ?
Isopod 1			
Isopod 2			
Isopod 3			
Isopod 4			

Preparation Notes

Isopods were selected for this lab because they are very common in most areas and can be collected and released. If you choose to use other animals, such as mealworms, that you can obtain at a pet store, be sure to have a plan for appropriate disposal after the lab.

Gladys Cherniak
St. Paul's Episcopal School
Mobile, Alabama

3. Place 1 or 2 cm of soil in a small plastic container. Add a small slice of potato and a piece of chalk. Your isopods will eat these things.

4. Place four isopods in your container. Observe them for a minute or two before you perform your tests. Record your observations in your ScienceLog.

5. Decide which stimulus you want to test first. Carefully arrange the isopods at the "starting line." The starting line can be an imaginary line at one end of the container.

6. Gently stimulate each isopod at the same time and in the same way. In your data table, record the isopods' responses to the stimulus. Be sure to record the distance each isopod traveled. Don't forget to time the race.

7. Repeat steps 5–6 for each stimulus. Be sure to wait at least two minutes between trials.

Analysis

8. Describe the way isopods move. Do their legs move together?

9. Did your isopods move before or between the trials? Did the movement seem to have a purpose, or were the isopods responding to a stimulus? Explain.

10. Did any of the stimuli you chose make the isopods move faster or go farther? Explain.

Going Further

Isopods may not run for the joy of running like humans do. But humans, like all living things, do react to stimuli. Describe three stimuli that might cause humans to run.

Disposal Information

When you are done with the lab, the isopods can be disposed of according to your policy or released into a natural area.

Answers

8. Isopods move their legs in sequence.
9. Answers will be based on students' observations and will vary.
10. Answers will vary.

Going Further

Answers will vary but might include the stimuli of fear, being late, joy, and a need for exercise.

The Best-Bread Bakery Dilemma
Teacher's Notes

Time Required
Two 45-minute class periods

Lab Ratings

TEACHER PREP 🧪🧪
STUDENT SET-UP 🧪
CONCEPT LEVEL 🧪
CLEAN UP 🧪

MATERIALS

The materials listed on the student page are enough for a group of 3–4 students. Yeast is easily obtained from the local grocery store. The school cafeteria may be willing to donate the amount you need.

You may wish to add other materials in anticipation of students' experimental design. For example, some students may recognize that they could collect CO_2 in a balloon attached to the top of a test tube containing live yeast.

Safety Caution

Remind students to review all safety cautions and icons before beginning this lab activity.

Caution students to be careful of the hot plate and the cord. You should demonstrate the proper laboratory technique for determining the presence of an odor. Hold the container away from your face about 25 cm and just below your nose. Use the other hand to "waft" the odor toward your face. Caution students NEVER to put their noses directly in a container and inhale.

The Best-Bread Bakery Dilemma

The chief baker at the Best-Bread Bakery thinks that the yeast the bakery received may be dead. Yeast is a central ingredient in bread. Yeast is a living organism, a member of the kingdom Fungi, and it undergoes the same life processes as other living organisms. When yeast grows in the presence of oxygen and other nutrients, it produces carbon dioxide. The gas forms bubbles that cause the dough to rise. Thousands of dollars may be lost if the yeast is dead.

The Best-Bread Bakery has requested that you test the yeast. The bakery has furnished samples of live yeast and some samples of the yeast in question.

Materials

- yeast samples (live, A, and B)
- magnifying lens
- test tubes or clear plastic cups
- test-tube rack
- 250 mL beaker
- 125 mL of water
- hot plate
- Celsius thermometer with clip
- scoopula or small spoon
- sugar
- graduated cylinder
- 3 wooden stirring sticks
- flour
- heat-resistant gloves

Procedure

1. Make a data table similar to the one below. Leave plenty of room to write your observations.

2. Examine each yeast sample with a magnifying lens. You may want to sniff the samples to determine the presence of an odor. (Your teacher will demonstrate the appropriate way to detect odors in the laboratory.) Record your observations in the data table.

3. Label three test tubes or plastic cups "Live Yeast," "Sample A Yeast," and "Sample B Yeast."

4. Fill a beaker with 125 mL of water, and place the beaker on a hot plate. Use a thermometer to be sure the water does not get warmer than 32°C. Attach the thermometer to the side of the beaker with a clip so the thermometer doesn't touch the bottom of the beaker. Turn off the hot plate when the temperature reaches 32°C.

	Observations	0 min	5 min	10 min	15 min	20 min	25 min	Dead or alive?
Live yeast								
Sample A yeast								
Sample B yeast								

DO NOT WRITE IN BOOK

 Datasheets for LabBook
Datasheet 5

 Science Skills Worksheet 22
"Science Writing"

Susan Gorman
North Ridge Middle School
North Richland Hills, Texas

5. Add a small scoop (about 1/2 tsp) of each yeast sample to the correctly labeled container. Add a small scoop of sugar to each container.

6. Add 10 mL of the warm water to each container, and stir.

7. Add a small scoop of flour to each container, and stir again. The flour will help make the process more visible but is not necessary as food for the yeast.

8. Observe the samples carefully. Look for bubbles. Make observations at 5-minute intervals. Write your observations in the data table.

9. In the last column of the data table, write "alive" or "dead" based on your observations during the experiment.

Analysis

10. Describe any differences in the yeast samples before the experiment.

11. Describe the appearance of the yeast samples at the conclusion of the experiment.

12. Why was a sample of live yeast included in the experiment?

13. Why was sugar added to the samples?

14. Based on your observations, is either sample alive?

15. Write a letter to the Best-Bread Bakery stating your recommendation to use or not use the yeast samples. Give reasons for your recommendation.

Going Further
Based on your observations of the nutrient requirements of yeast, design an experiment to determine the ideal combination of nutrients. Vary the amount of nutrients or examine different energy sources.

Preparation Notes
At least one of the suspect samples should be killed yeast. To do this, place the yeast in an oven at 400°F for 10 minutes or in a microwave oven for a few minutes on high. Do not allow yeast to become moist before use. Toothpicks, coffee stirrers, etc., may be used for stirring. The amounts of each ingredient used are not definite, and you may wish to vary amounts, depending on the results desired.

Lab Notes
To help students prepare for this activity, you may wish to review cellular respiration and fermentation. The equation for respiration is:

$C_6H_{12}O_6 + 6O_2 \rightarrow 6CO_2 + 6H_2O + energy$

Answers

10. Answers are based on students' observations and will vary.

11. Answers will vary.

12. Live yeast is included so students can observe bubble formation from the respiration of living organisms.

13. Sugar is added as a nutrient for the living yeast.

14. Answers will vary according to students' experimental protocol.

15. Student letters will vary, but should recommend the optimal samples they determined in their experiment.

Elephant-Sized Amoebas?
Teacher's Notes

Time Required
Two 45-minute class periods

Lab Ratings

TEACHER PREP
STUDENT SET-UP
CONCEPT LEVEL
CLEAN UP

Safety Caution
Remind students to review all safety cautions and icons before beginning this lab activity.

Preparation Notes
Some students may find it difficult to work with a nonspecific unit of measurement. If so, the cube models easily convert to centimeters. You may want to add some small items, such as peas, beans, popcorn, or peppercorns, to the sand to represent organelles floating in the cytoplasm. Some students may need to review what a ratio is and how ratios are used.

Terry Rakes
Elmwood Junior High School
Rogers, Arkansas

694   Chapter 3 • LabBook

Elephant-Sized Amoebas?

MAKING MODELS

Why can't amoebas grow to be as large as elephants? An amoeba is a single-celled organism. Amoebas, like most cells, are microscopic. If an amoeba could grow to the size of a quarter, it would starve to death. To understand how this can be true, build a model of a cell and see for yourself.

Materials
- cubic cell patterns
- pieces of heavy paper or poster board
- scissors
- transparent tape
- scale or balance
- fine sand

Procedure

1. Use heavy paper to make four cube-shaped cell models from the patterns supplied by your teacher. Cut out each cell model, fold the sides to make a cube, and tape the tabs on the sides. The smallest cell model has sides that are one unit long. The next larger cell has sides of two units. The next cell has sides of three units, and the largest cell has sides of four units. These paper models represent the cell membrane, the part of a cell's exterior through which food and waste pass.

Two-unit cell model

2. In your ScienceLog, copy the data table at right. Use each formula to calculate the data about your cell models. A key to the formula symbols can be found on the next page. Record your calculations in the table. Calculations for the smallest cell have been done for you.

Data Table for Measurements

Length of side	Area of one side $(A = S \times S)$	Total surface area of cube cell $(TA = S \times S \times 6)$	Volume of cube cell $(V = S \times S \times S)$	Mass of cube cell
1	1 unit^2	6 unit^2	1 unit^3	
2				
3				
4				

Data Table for Measurements

Length of side S	Area of one side (square unit)	Total surface area of cube cell (square units)	Volume of cube cell (cubic units)	Mass of cube cell (approximate, in grams)
1	1	6	1	4.5
2	4	24	8	30
3	9	54	27	105
4	16	96	64	230

3. Carefully fill each model with fine sand until the sand is level with the top edge. Find the mass of the filled models using a scale or a balance. What does the sand in your model represent?

4. Record the mass of each cell model in the table. (Always remember to use the appropriate mass unit.)

5. In your ScienceLog, make a data table like the one below.

Data Table for Ratios

Length of side	Ratio of total surface area to volume	Ratio of total surface area to mass
1		
2		
3		
4		

DO NOT WRITE IN BOOK

6. Use the data from your Data Table for Measurements to find the ratios for each of your cell models. Fill in the Data Table for Ratios for each of the cell models.

Analysis

7. As a cell grows larger, does the ratio of total surface area to volume increase, decrease, or stay the same?

8. Which is better able to supply food to all the cytoplasm of the cell—the cell membrane of a small cell or that of a large cell? Explain your answer.

9. As a cell grows larger, does the total surface area to mass ratio increase, decrease, or stay the same?

10. Is the cell membrane of a cell with high mass or the cell membrane of a cell with low mass better able to feed all the cytoplasm of the cell? You may explain your answer in a verbal presentation to the class or you may choose to write a report and illustrate it with drawings of your models.

Key to Formula Symbols
S = the length of one side
A = area
V = volume
TA = total area

Cell Model Template

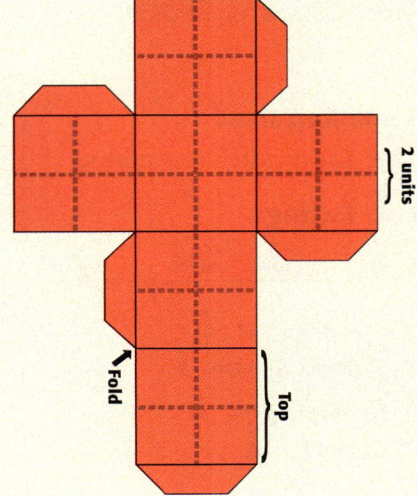

Using the template above, prepare four patterns for students to use to make their cubes. Make one cube 1 unit wide, one cube 2 units wide, one cube 3 units wide, and one cube 4 units wide. The unit can be the size of your choosing.

Answers

3. The sand represents cytoplasm.
4. Masses will vary.
6. See the tables below.
7. decrease
8. A small cell has a higher surface-area-to-volume ratio than a large cell has, allowing more nutrients per cubic unit of volume to enter.
9. decrease
10. low mass

 Datasheets for LabBook
Datasheet 6

Data Table for Ratios

Length of side S	Total surface area/volume ratio	Total surface area/mass ratio
1	$\frac{6}{1} = 6$	$\frac{6}{4.5} = 1.33$
2	$\frac{24}{8} = 3$	$\frac{24}{30} = 0.80$
3	$\frac{54}{27} = 2$	$\frac{54}{105} = 0.51$
4	$\frac{96}{64} = 1.5$	$\frac{96}{230} = 0.42$

Cells Alive!
Teacher's Notes

Time Required
One 45-minute class period

Lab Ratings

- TEACHER PREP
- STUDENT SET-UP
- CONCEPT LEVEL
- CLEAN UP

MATERIALS

The materials listed on the student page are enough for a group of 3–4 students. You may wish to collect the algae ahead of time so they are available for students when they begin the lab. Be sure to keep the algae in a warm, damp place out of direct sunlight; a closed plastic bag with water sprayed into it is ideal.

Safety Caution

Remind students to review all safety cautions and icons before beginning this lab activity.

 Datasheets for LabBook
Datasheet 7

Terry Rakes
Elmwood Junior High School
Rogers, Arkansas

Cells Alive!

You have probably used a microscope to look at single-celled organisms such as those shown below. They can be found in pond water. In the following exercise, you will look at *Protococcus*—algae that form a greenish stain on tree trunks, wooden fences, flowerpots, and buildings.

Euglena *Amoeba* *Paramecium*

DISCOVERY LAB

Materials
- *Protococcus* (or other algae)
- microscope
- eyedropper
- water
- microscope slide and coverslip

Procedure

1. Locate some *Protococcus*. Scrape a small sample into a container. Bring the sample to the classroom, and make a wet mount of it as directed by your teacher. If you can't find *Protococcus* outdoors, look for algae on the glass in an aquarium. Such algae may not be *Protococcus*, but it will be a very good substitute.

2. Set the microscope on low power to examine the algae. In your ScienceLog, draw the cells that you see.

3. Switch to high power to examine a single cell. In your ScienceLog, draw the cell.

4. You will probably notice that each cell contains several chloroplasts. Label a chloroplast on your drawing. What is the function of the chloroplast?

5. Another structure that should be clearly visible in all the algae cells is the nucleus. Find the nucleus in one of your cells, and label it on your drawing. What is the function of the nucleus?

6. What does the cytoplasm look like? Describe any movement you see inside the cells.

Analysis

7. Are *Protococcus* single-celled organisms or multicellular organisms?

8. How are *Protococcus* different from amoebas?

Protococcus

Answers

4. Chloroplasts are the parts of the cell that are responsible for photosynthesis.

5. The nucleus of a cell controls most of the activities that take place in that cell and contains the hereditary information.

6. The cytoplasm is a clear gel-like substance that fills the cell and surrounds the organelles.

7. *Protococcus* is a genus composed of single-celled algae.

8. Many answers are possible, but the following are most likely: *Protococcus* cannot move about like amoebas can; unlike amoebas, they are green and photosynthesize.

Name That Part!

Plant cells and animal cells have many organelles and other parts in common. For example, both plant and animal cells contain a nucleus and mitochondria. But plant cells and animal cells differ in several ways as well. In this exercise, you will investigate the similarities and differences between animal cells and plant cells.

Materials

- colored pencils or markers
- white, unlined paper

Procedure

1. Using colored pencils or markers and white, unlined paper, trace or draw the plant cell and animal cell shown below. Draw each cell on a separate piece of paper. You may color each organelle a different color.
2. Label the parts of each cell.
3. Below each drawing, list all the parts that you labeled and describe their function.

Plant cell

Animal cell

Analysis

4. List at least four structures that plant cells and animal cells have in common.
5. List three structures that plant cells have that animal cells do not have.

Martha Kisiah
Fairview Middle School
Tallahassee, Florida

Datasheets for LabBook
Datasheet 8

Name That Part!
Teacher's Notes

Time Required
One 40-minute class period

Lab Ratings

TEACHER PREP 🧪
STUDENT SET-UP 🧪
CONCEPT LEVEL 🧪
CLEAN UP 🧪

Answers

2. Have students label the following parts: Golgi complex, cytoplasm, nucleus, nucleolus, nuclear membrane, cell membrane, mitochondria, endoplasmic reticulum, vacuole, cell wall, chloroplast, lysosome.

3. **Golgi complex**—area that stores and packages chemicals
cytoplasm—materials between nucleus and cell membrane
nucleus—control center containing genetic information
nucleolus—spherical body in the nucleus
nuclear membrane—membrane surrounding the nucleus
cell membrane—membrane surrounding the cytoplasm and the organelles
mitochondria—releases energy from nutrients
endoplasmic reticulum—location of ribosomal attachment and part of the cell's internal transport system
vacuole—bubblelike storage structure
cell wall—stiff outer covering of a plant cell
chloroplast—plastid that stores chlorophyll used in photosynthesis
lysosome—digests large particles

4. Any four structures are correct except the following: centriole, vacuole, cell wall, chloroplast.

5. vacuole, cell wall, chloroplast

The Perfect Taters Mystery
Teacher's Notes

Time Required
Two 45-minute class periods

Lab Ratings

TEACHER PREP 🧪🧪
STUDENT SET-UP 🧪🧪
CONCEPT LEVEL 🧪🧪🧪
CLEAN UP 🧪

MATERIALS

The materials listed on the student page are enough for 1 class of students. You will need 1 or 2 small potatoes per class. Do not allow students to cut or peel potatoes. You will need to do this ahead of time. Allow students to choose the number of containers they will need for the experiment. They may wish to test several salt concentrations.

Safety Caution

Remind students to review all safety cautions and icons before beginning this lab activity.

Avoid including green or discolored parts of the potato in the pieces students work with. These could cause illness.

Susan Gorman
North Ridge Middle School
North Richland Hills, Texas

698 Chapter 4 • LabBook

Using Scientific Methods

DESIGN YOUR OWN

The Perfect Taters Mystery

You are the chief food detective at Perfect Taters Food Company. The boss, Mr. Fries, wants you to find a way to keep his potatoes fresh and crisp while they are waiting to be cooked. His workers have tried several methods already, but nothing has worked. Workers in Group A put the potatoes in very salty water, and the potatoes did something unexpected. Workers in Group B put the potatoes in water with no salt, and the potatoes did something else! Workers in Group C didn't put the potatoes in any water, and that didn't work either. Now you must design an experiment to find out what can be done to make the potatoes come out crisp and fresh.

Materials
- potato samples (A, B, and C)
- freshly cut potato pieces
- salt
- 6 small, clear plastic drinking cups
- 4 L of distilled water

1. Before you plan your experiment, review what you know. You know that potatoes are made of cells. Plant cells contain a large amount of water. Cells have membranes that hold water and other materials inside and keep some things out. Water and other materials must travel across cell membranes to get into and out of the cell.

2. Mr. Fries has told you that you can obtain as many samples as you need from the workers in Groups A, B, and C. Your teacher will have these samples ready for you to observe.

3. Make a data table like the one below in your ScienceLog to list your observations. Make as many observations as you can about the potatoes tested by workers in Group A, Group B, and Group C.

Observations	
Group A:	
Group B:	
Group C:	

DO NOT WRITE IN BOOK

Ask a Question

4. Now that you have made your observations, state Mr. Fries's problem in the form of a question that can be answered by your experiment.

Lab Notes

Osmosis is often a confusing and misunderstood concept in life science. Quite often, students can repeat the definition of the process but are unable to apply the concept to explain the movement of water in different osmotic environments. In this lab, students will have an opportunity to observe osmosis in a model and obtain measurable results. This lab can be done as a class demonstration if materials and space are limited. The purpose of this lab is to reinforce comprehension of osmosis and to practice the scientific method.

Form a Hypothesis

5. Form a hypothesis based on your observations and your questions. The hypothesis should be a statement about what causes the potatoes to shrivel or swell. Based on your hypothesis, make a prediction about the outcome of your experiments. State your prediction in an "if-then" format.

Test the Hypothesis

6. Once you have made a prediction, design your investigation. Check your experimental design with your teacher before you begin. Mr. Fries will give you potato pieces, water, salt, and no more than six containers.

7. Keep very accurate records. Write out your plan and procedure. Make data tables. To be sure of your data, measure all materials carefully and make drawings of the potato pieces before and after the experiment.

Draw Conclusions

8. Explain what happened to the potato cells in Groups A, B, and C in your experiment. Include a discussion of the cell membrane and the process of osmosis.

Communicate Results

9. Write a letter to Mr. Fries that explains your experimental method, your results, and your conclusion. Then make a recommendation about how he should handle the potatoes so they will stay fresh and crisp.

Datasheets for LabBook
Datasheet 9

Science Skills Worksheet 13
"Designing an Experiment"

Answers

8. The potato cells in group A were placed in very salty water. The potatoes shriveled up because water moved out of the cell and into the salty water (from an area of high concentration of water to an area of low concentration of water). This may be confusing to some students, who may think that because the concentration of salt is high outside the potato, the salt should move to the area of lower concentration. Explain that although water can move through a cell membrane by osmosis, salt must be moved across a cell membrane by a process that requires energy.

   The potato cells in group B were placed in water with no salt. The potatoes swelled because the concentration of water was lower inside the cell. (The concentration of salt and other molecules was higher inside the potato cell.)

   The potato cells in group C turned brown and dried up because the water concentration outside the cell was low. In fact, there wasn't any water at all. The water evaporated as soon as it left the cell membrane. The potato cells turned brown because of chemical reactions with the air.

9. Letters to Mr. Fries will vary according to each student's results. However, all students should explain that through trial and error they found one salt concentration that was closest to the concentration of salt and other molecules inside the potato. This is the concentration that should be used to maintain an osmotic balance in the potato. Furthermore, some students will realize that the potatoes must be kept in water to prevent them from turning brown.

Chapter 4 • LabBook **699**

Stayin' Alive!
Teacher's Notes

Time Required
One 45-minute class period

Lab Ratings

TEACHER PREP 🧪
STUDENT SET-UP 🧪
CONCEPT LEVEL 🧪
CLEAN UP 🧪

MATERIALS

The materials listed on the student page are enough for one group of 5–6 students. You may wish to have your students use a calculator to complete this activity.

Preparation Notes

Some students may consider their height and weight to be personal and won't want to weigh and measure themselves with the others in the class. Give these students the option of using the data of a fictional person, such as one of the following:

Jenny	80 lb	4 ft	age 11
Ben	65 lb	3 ft	age 12
Carlos	110 lb	5 ft 2 in.	age 11
Alexa	120 lb	4 ft 6 in.	age 12
Tasheika	90 lb	4 ft 6 in.	age 13

Stayin' Alive!

Every second of your life, your body's trillions of cells take in, use, and store energy. They repair themselves, reproduce, and get rid of waste. Together, these processes are called *metabolism*. Your cells use the food that you eat to provide the energy you need to stay alive.

Your Basal Metabolic Rate (BMR) is a measurement of the energy that your body needs to carry out all the basic life processes while you are at rest. These processes include breathing, keeping your heart beating, and keeping your body's temperature stable. Your BMR is influenced by your gender, your age, and many other things. Your BMR may be different from everyone else's, but it is normal for you. In this activity, you will find the amount of energy, measured in Calories, you need every day in order to stay alive.

Procedure

1. Find your weight on a bathroom scale. If the scale measures in pounds, you must convert your weight in pounds to your mass in kilograms. To convert your weight in pounds (lb) to mass in kilograms (kg), multiply the number of pounds by 0.454.

| **Example:** If Carlos weighs 125 lb, his mass in kilograms is: | 125 lb
× 0.454
56.75 kg |

2. Use a tape measure to find your height. If the tape measures in inches, convert your height in inches to height in centimeters. To convert your height in inches (in.) to your height in centimeters (cm), multiply the number of inches by 2.54.

| If Carlos is 62 in. tall, his height in centimeters is: | 62 in.
× 2.54
157.48 cm |

Materials
- bathroom scale
- tape measure

Datasheets for LabBook
Datasheet 10

Kathy LaRoe
East Valley Middle School
East Helena, Montana

3. Now that you know your height and mass, use the appropriate formula below to get a close estimate of your BMR. Your answer will give you an estimate of the number of Calories your body needs each day just to stay alive.

Calculating Your BMR

Females

65 + (10 × your mass in kilograms)

+ (1.8 × your height in centimeters)

− (4.7 × your age in years)

Males

66 + (13.5 × your mass in kilograms)

+ (5 × your height in centimeters)

− (6.8 × your age in years)

4. Your metabolism is also influenced by how active you are. Talking, walking, and playing games all take more energy than being at rest. To get an idea of how many Calories your body needs each day to stay healthy, select the lifestyle that best describes yours from the table at right. Then multiply your BMR by the activity factor.

Activity Factors

Activity lifestyle	Activity factor
Moderately inactive (normal, everyday activities)	1.3
Moderately active (exercise 3 to 4 times a week)	1.4
Very active (exercise 4 to 6 times a week)	1.6
Extremely active (exercise 6 to 7 times a week)	1.8

Analysis

5. In what way could you compare your whole body to a single cell? Explain.

6. Does an increase in activity increase your BMR? Does an increase in activity increase your need for Calories? Explain your answers.

7. If you are moderately inactive, how many more Calories would you need if you began to exercise every day?

Going Further

The best energy sources are those that supply the correct amount of Calories for your lifestyle and also provide the nutrients you need. Research in the library or on the Internet to find out which kinds of foods are the best energy sources for you. How does your list of best energy sources compare with your diet?

List everything you eat and drink in 1 day. Find out how many Calories are in each item, and find the total number of Calories you have consumed. How does this number of Calories compare with the number of Calories you need each day for all your activities?

Lab Notes

Some students will think their basal metabolic rate, or BMR, is impossibly low. Emphasize that the BMR is the number of Calories a body needs just to keep the heart beating, the lungs breathing, and the cells respiring. It is not the number of Calories a person needs for an active lifestyle. Of course, a person can consume fewer than that number of Calories for a day, or even for a few days, without dying. Explain that the Calories required to live during starvation conditions are obtained from stored fat. When there is no more fat, then the energy comes from muscle tissue. Under extreme conditions of starvation, the body even begins to shut down some organ functions that use energy but that are not required for survival, such as the uterine cycle in women. Some students may ask why the BMR numbers are so much higher in males than in females. Explain that before puberty, the numbers are much closer together. But as boys approach puberty, they generally develop a higher muscle-to-fat ratio than girls do. Cellular respiration for muscle tissue requires more energy than for fat tissue.

Answers

5. Just as each cell needs energy on a small scale, your body requires energy on a much larger scale.

6. Technically, the BMR does not change with activity. It is the minimum amount of energy a person needs to stay alive. Activity requires that more energy be added to the BMR, thereby increasing the need for Calories.

7. Students should multiply their own BMR by 1.3, then multiply their BMR by 1.8. Students should subtract the smaller number from the larger number. This represents the additional Calories per day a person would expend shifting from a moderately inactive state to an extremely active one.

Bug Builders, Inc.
Teacher's Notes

Time Required
Two 45-minute class periods

Lab Ratings

TEACHER PREP 🧪🧪🧪
STUDENT SET-UP 🧪🧪🧪
CONCEPT LEVEL 🧪🧪🧪
CLEAN UP 🧪

MATERIALS

You will need 14 small brown-paper bags—two sacks for each characteristic listed on this page. Each bag will contain either the mother's alleles or the father's alleles. Cut 1 in. squares of paper to represent alleles. Use a different color paper for each trait (seven colors).

Safety Caution

Remind students to review all safety cautions and icons before beginning this lab activity.

 Datasheets for LabBook
Datasheet 11

Kathy LaRoe
East Valley Middle School
East Helena, Montana

Using Scientific Methods

MAKING MODELS

Bug Builders, Inc.

Imagine that you are a designer for a toy company that makes toy alien bugs. The president of Bug Builders, Inc., wants new versions of the wildly popular Space Bugs, but he wants to use the bug parts that are already in the warehouse. It's your job to come up with a new bug design. You have studied how traits are passed from one generation to another. You will use this knowledge to come up with new combinations of traits and assemble the bug parts in new ways. Model A and Model B, shown below, will act as the "parent" bugs.

Materials

- 14 allele sacks (supplied by your teacher)
- large marshmallows (head and body segments)
- red and green toothpicks (antennae)
- green and blue pushpins (noses)
- pipe cleaners (tails)
- green and black gumdrops (feet)
- map pins (eyes)
- scissors

Model A ("Mom")
- red antennae
- 3 body segments
- curly tail
- 2 pairs of legs
- green nose
- black feet
- 3 eyes

Model B ("Dad")
- green antennae
- 2 body segments
- straight tail
- 3 pairs of legs
- blue nose
- green feet
- 2 eyes

Make a Prediction

1. If there are two forms of each of the seven characteristics, then there are ___?___ possible combinations.

Collect Data

2. Your teacher will display 14 sacks—2 for each characteristic. The sacks will contain slips of paper with capital or lowercase letters printed on them. Take one piece of paper from each sack. (Remember: Capital letters represent dominant alleles, and lowercase letters represent recessive alleles.) For each characteristic, one allele sack carries the alleles from "Mom" and one allele sack carries the alleles from "Dad." After you have recorded the alleles you have drawn, place the slips of paper back into the sacks.

3. In your ScienceLog, create a table like the one below. Fill in the first two columns with the alleles that you selected from the sacks. Next fill in the third column with the genotype of the new model ("Baby").

Bug Family Traits				
Trait	Model A "Mom" allele	Model B "Dad" allele	New model "Baby" genotype	New model "Baby" phenotype
Antennae color				
Number of body segments				
Tail shape				
Number of leg pairs				
Nose color				
Foot color				
Number of eyes				

4. Use the information at right to fill in the last column of the table.

5. Now that you have your table filled out, you are ready to pick the parts you need to assemble your bug. (Toothpicks can be used to hold the head and body segments together and as legs to attach the feet to the body.)

Genotypes and Phenotypes

RR or Rr = red antennae	rr = green antennae
SS or Ss = 3 body segments	ss = 2 body segments
CC or Cc = curly tail	cc = straight tail
LL or Ll = 3 pairs of legs	ll = 2 pairs of legs
BB or Bb = blue nose	bb = green nose
GG or Gg = green feet	gg = black feet
EE or Ee = 2 eyes	ee = 3 eyes

Analyze the Results

6. Take a class poll of the traits of the offspring. What are the ratios for each trait?

Draw Conclusions

7. Do any of the new models look exactly like the parents? Explain your findings.

8. What are the possible genotypes of the parents?

9. How many different genotypes are possible in the offspring?

Going Further

Find a mate for your "baby" bug. What are the possible genotypes and phenotypes of the offspring from this match?

LabBook

Preparation Notes

This lab will take some time to prepare for, but it is well worth the effort for a genetics-reinforcement lesson.

1. Cut enough squares so that each student will have two alleles for each characteristic. You must have an equal number of both dominant and recessive alleles.

2. Half the squares for each characteristic should be marked with capital letters to indicate dominant alleles. The other half should be marked with lowercase letters to indicate recessive alleles.

3. Label each paper bag with one of the seven characteristics. Place both dominant and recessive alleles in their corresponding paper bag.

4. Have students draw one allele from each sack. Tell students that one allele is from "mom" and that the second allele is from "dad."

Going Further

Answers will vary. Have students use Punnett squares to explore possible genotypes.

Answers

1. 128

   two forms of each of seven characteristics so $2 \times 2 \times 2 \times 2 \times 2 \times 2 \times 2$ (or 2^7) = 128

6. Student ratios should be similar to the ratios determined when the alleles where selected by the teacher.

7. If any students have offspring bugs that look like one of the parents, have them compare the genotype of the offspring with the genotype of the parents. They may look alike but still have different genotypes for some traits.

8. Item 6 will lead students to this answer. Answers will vary.

9. Have students construct Punnett squares using the parental traits. Except for the results obtained by parental genotypes that are all homozygous recessive, the student will see other possibilities for genotypes and phenotypes from the same parents.

Chapter 5 • LabBook

Tracing Traits
Teacher's Notes

Time Required
Two 45-minute class periods, separated by several days so students have time to complete their surveys

Lab Ratings

- TEACHER PREP
- STUDENT SET-UP
- CONCEPT LEVEL
- CLEAN UP

Lab Notes
Family histories will vary. Encourage students to include at least three generations in their histories.

Survey results will vary. Make sure that students actually surveyed each family member who was available. Responses will vary. You may check family members with shaded symbols against the survey results for accuracy.

Percentages will vary. A family member may receive a recessive allele from the father and a recessive allele from the mother. In such a case, this family member will exhibit the recessive form of the trait rather than the dominant form.

Because so many children are adopted or live in foster homes or group homes, please emphasize to your students that they may choose any family to study.

Tracing Traits

DESIGN YOUR OWN

Have you ever wondered about the traits you inherited from your parents? Do you have a trait that neither of your parents has? In this project, you will develop a family tree, or pedigree, similar to the one shown in the diagram below. You will trace an inherited trait through a family to determine how it has passed from generation to generation.

Procedure TRY at HOME

1. The diagram at right shows a family history. On a separate piece of paper, draw a similar diagram of the family you have chosen. Include as many family members as possible, such as grandparents, parents, children, and grandchildren. Use circles to represent females and squares to represent males. You may include other information, such as the family member's name, birthdate, or picture.

2. Draw a chart similar to the one on the next page. Survey each of the family members shown in your family tree. Ask them if they have hair on the middle segment of their fingers. Write each person's name in the appropriate square. Explain to each person that it is normal to have either trait. The presence of hair on the middle segment is the dominant form of this trait.

Kerry Johnson
Isbell Middle School
Santa Paula, California

Dominant trait	Recessive trait	Family members with the dominant trait	Family members with the recessive trait
Hair present on the middle segment of fingers (H)	Hair absent on the middle segment of fingers (h)	DO NOT WRITE IN BOOK	

3. Trace this trait throughout the family tree you diagrammed in step 1. Shade or color the symbols of the family members who demonstrate the dominant form of this trait.

Analysis

4. What percentage of the family members demonstrate the dominant form of the trait? Calculate this by counting the number of people who have the dominant trait and dividing this number by the total number of people you surveyed. Multiply your answer by 100. An example has been done at right.

5. What percentage of the family members demonstrates the recessive form of the trait? Why doesn't every family member have the dominant form of the trait?

6. Choose one of the family members who demonstrates the recessive form of the chosen trait. What is this person's genotype? What are the possible genotypes for the parents of this individual? Does this person have any brothers or sisters? Do they show the dominant or recessive trait?

7. Draw a Punnett square like the one at right. Use this to determine the genotypes of the parents of the person you chose in step 7. Write this person's genotype in the bottom right-hand corner of your Punnett square. **Hint:** There may be more than one possible genotype for the parents. Don't forget to consider the genotypes of the person's brothers and sisters.

Example: Calculating percentage

$$\frac{10 \text{ people with trait}}{20 \text{ people surveyed}} = \frac{1}{2}$$

$$\frac{1}{2} = 0.50 \times 100 = 50\%$$

Father / Mother Punnett square with ? in three cells.

Answers

4. Answers will vary.
5. Answers will vary.
6. The genotype of the recessive form of the characteristic must be *hh* (homozygous recessive). Each allele came from one of the individual's parents. Possible genotypes for the parents of the individual expressing the recessive form are *Hh* and *hh*. Does the student know whether either of the parents expresses the recessive form of the trait? Does the student know if the individual chosen has brothers or sisters? Are their genotypes known? If so, have the student decide if each of them has a dominant or recessive genotype. If a dominant genotype is found among the siblings and one of the parents is known to have the recessive form, ask the student what the genotype of the other parent must be *(Hh)*.
7. The Punnett square should show *hh* in the bottom right-hand corner. One of the parents must have the genotype *hh*. The other parent must have either *hh* or *Hh*. If any sibling has the dominant trait, the genotype of the other parent must be *Hh*.

Datasheets for LabBook
Datasheet 12

Base-Pair Basics
Teacher's Notes

Time Required
One 45-minute class period

Lab Ratings

TEACHER PREP 🧪
STUDENT SET-UP 🧪
CONCEPT LEVEL 🧪
CLEAN UP 🧪

MATERIALS
You may want to provide additional materials for the Going Further section.

Safety Caution
Remind students to review all safety cautions and icons before beginning this lab activity.

Students should always exercise care when using scissors.

Lab Notes
You may wish to enlarge the template for your students so the base pairs will be easier to cut out.

Explain to students that the white pieces and the colored pieces indicate an old side and a new side after replication.

Base-Pair Basics

MAKING MODELS

You have learned that DNA is shaped something like a twisted ladder. The side rails of the ladder are made of sugar molecules and phosphate molecules. The sides are held together by nucleotide bases. These bases join in pairs to form the rungs of the ladder. Each nucleotide base can pair with only one other nucleotide base. Each of these pairs is called a base pair. When DNA replicates, enzymes separate the base pairs. Then each half of the DNA ladder can be used as a template to complete a new half. In this activity, you will make and replicate a model of DNA.

Materials
- white paper or poster board
- colored paper or poster board
- scissors
- large paper bag

Procedure

1. Trace the bases below onto white paper or poster board. Label the pieces A (for adenine), T (for thymine), C (for cytosine), and G (for guanine). Draw the pieces again on colored paper or poster board. Use a different color for each base. Draw the pieces as large as you want, and draw as many of the white pieces and as many of the colored pieces as time will allow.

2. Carefully cut out all of the pieces.

3. Gather all of the colored pieces in the classroom into a large paper bag. Spread all of the white pieces in the classroom onto a large table.

4. Withdraw nine pieces from the bag. Arrange the colored pieces in any order in a straight column so the letters A, T, C, and G are right side up. Be sure to match the sugar and phosphate tabs and notches. Draw this arrangement in your ScienceLog.

Sugar notch
Phosphate tab

Debra Sampson
Booker T. Washington
Middle School
Elgin, Texas

706 Chapter 6 • LabBook

5. Find the matching white nucleotide bases for the nine colored bases. Remember the base-pairing rules you have studied, and matching should be easy!

6. Fit the pieces together, matching all tabs and notches. You now have one piece of DNA containing nine base pairs. Draw your results in your ScienceLog.

7. Now separate the base pairs, keeping the sugar and phosphate notches and tabs together. Draw this arrangement in your ScienceLog.

8. Look at each string of bases you drew in step 7. Along each one, write the letters of the bases that should join the string to complete the base pairs.

9. Find all the bases you need to complete your replication. Find white pieces to match the bases on the left, and find colored pieces to match the bases on the right.

Be sure all the tabs and notches fit and the sides are straight. You have now replicated DNA. Are the two models identical? Draw your results in your ScienceLog.

Analysis

10. Name the correct base-pairing rules.

11. What happens when you attempt to pair thymine with guanine? Do they fit together? Are the sides straight? Do all of the tabs and notches fit? Explain.

Going Further

Construct a 3-D model of the DNA molecule, showing its twisted-ladder structure. Use your imagination and creativity to select your materials. You may want to use licorice, gum balls, and toothpicks, or pipe cleaners and paper clips! Display your model in your classroom.

Answers

10. G pairs with C, and A pairs with T.

11. The joining areas of guanine and thymine don't match up. They don't fit together.

Datasheets for LabBook
Datasheet 13

Mystery Footprints
Teacher's Notes

Time Required
Two 45-minute class periods

Lab Ratings

- TEACHER PREP 🧪🧪🧪
- STUDENT SET-UP 🧪🧪
- CONCEPT LEVEL 🧪🧪
- CLEAN UP 🧪

Preparation Notes

To set up this lab, you will need to either construct a long, shallow sandbox out of wood or cardboard for use indoors or find (or build) a sandy area outside. Ask a boy and a girl (preferably students who are not in your science class) or two adults, one male and one female, to walk through the sand with their bare feet. The sand should be about 16 cm deep, and the area they walk through should be long enough that three or four footprints can be seen in the sand. Of course, you may want to make the footprints more permanent by using plaster-of-Paris. If you do not have access to sand, soil that will hold a footprint will substitute for sand nicely.

Maurine Marchani
Raymond Park Middle School
Indianapolis, Indiana

Using Scientific Methods

Mystery Footprints

Sometimes scientists find clues preserved in rocks that are evidence of the activities of organisms that lived thousands of years ago. Evidence such as preserved footprints can provide important information about an organism. Imagine that your class has been asked by a group of paleontologists to help analyze some human footprints. These footprints were found embedded in rocks in an area just outside of town.

DESIGN YOUR OWN

Materials
- large box of slightly damp sand, at least 1 m² (large enough to contain 3 or 4 footprints)
- metric ruler

Form a Hypothesis

1. Your teacher will provide you with some mystery footprints in sand. Examine the mystery footprints, and brainstorm about the information you might learn about the people who walked on this patch of sand. As a class, make as many hypotheses as possible about the people who left the footprints.

2. Form groups of three people, and choose one hypothesis for your group to investigate.

Test the Hypothesis

3. In your ScienceLog, design a table for recording your data. For example, if your hypothesis is that the footprints were made by two adult males who were walking in a hurry, your table would look similar to the one below.

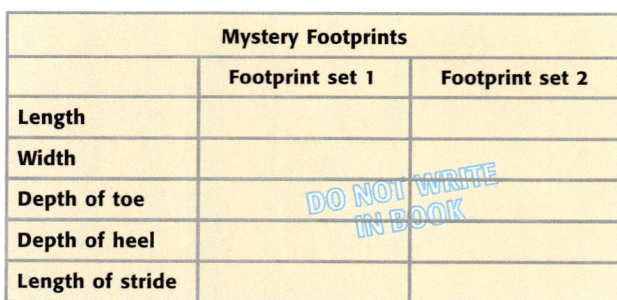

Mystery Footprints		
	Footprint set 1	Footprint set 2
Length		
Width		
Depth of toe		
Depth of heel		
Length of stride		

DO NOT WRITE IN BOOK

4. With the help of your group, you may first want to analyze your own footprints to help you draw conclusions about the mystery footprints. For example, how long is your stride when you are running? How long is it when you are walking? Does your weight affect the depth of the footprint? What part of your foot touches the ground first when you are running? What part touches the ground first when you are walking? When you are running, which part of your footprint is deeper? Make a list of the kind of footprint each different activity produces. For example, you might write, "A deep impression in the toe area and a long stride are produced by running."

Analyze the Results

5. Compare the data of your footprints with that of the mystery footprints. What similarities are there? What differences are there?

6. Were the mystery footprints made by one person or more than one person? Explain your reasoning.

7. Is there enough evidence to tell if the mystery footprints were made by men, women, children, or a combination? Explain.

8. Based on your observations of your own footprints, were the people who made the mystery footprints standing still, walking, or running?

Draw Conclusions

9. Does your data support your hypothesis? Explain.

10. How could you improve your experiment?

Communicate Results

11. Outline your group's conclusions in a document addressed to the scientists who asked for your help. Begin by stating your hypothesis. Then outline your method of gathering information from the study of your own footprints. Include the comparisons you made between your footprints and the mystery footprints. Before stating your conclusions, offer some suggestions about how you could improve your method of investigation.

12. Create a poster or chart, or use a computer if one is available, to prepare a presentation of your findings for the class.

Lab Notes

Tell the students to imagine that a scientist wishes to analyze footprints found in the rocks near fossilized remains, and he has contacted the class, seeking help in the investigation. The scientist wants to know how the students intend to gather information to make inferences about the humans who left the prints. Explain that a scientist should be able to make the same type of inferences about an organism from fresh tracks as from preserved tracks. Use the mystery footprints in the sand to help students design investigations for gathering data. From that data, students can learn to draw inferences.

Much research in evolution is dependent on scientific inferences. To conclude the laboratory experience, lead the students in a discussion of the importance of large sets of data in helping scientists make inferences.

Datasheets for LabBook
Datasheet 14

Answers

The answers for this activity will depend on the footprints your students observe. They should be able to compare their own activities with variations in the footprints they leave. Then they should be able to apply what they've learned to the mystery footprints.

Out-of-Sight Marshmallows
Teacher's Notes

Time Required
One 45-minute class period

Lab Ratings

- TEACHER PREP 🧪🧪
- STUDENT SET-UP 🧪🧪
- CONCEPT LEVEL 🧪
- CLEAN UP 🧪

Safety Cautions
Tell students not to eat the marshmallows after the lab. The marshmallows will have been handled thoroughly.

Preparation Notes
Choose several colors of mini-marshmallows and a piece of cloth or a napkin that will make the marshmallows hard to see at first glance.

 Datasheets for LabBook Datasheet 15

Georgiann Delgadillo
East Valley School District
Continuous Curriculum School
Spokane, Washington

Using Scientific Methods

Out-of-Sight Marshmallows

DISCOVERY LAB

An adaptation is a trait that helps an organism survive in its environment. In nature, camouflage is a form of coloration that enables an organism to blend into its immediate surroundings.

Hypothesis
Organisms that are camouflaged have a better chance of escaping from predators and therefore a better chance of survival.

Test the Hypothesis

1. Working in pairs, count out 50 white marshmallows and 50 colored marshmallows. Your marshmallows will represent the prey (food) in this experiment.
2. Place the white and colored marshmallows randomly on the piece of colored cloth.
3. One student per pair should be the hungry hunter (predator). The other student should record the results of each trial. The predator should look at the food for a few seconds, pick up the first marshmallow he or she sees, and then look away.
4. Continue this process without stopping for 2 minutes or until your teacher signals to stop.

Analyze the Results

5. How many white marshmallows did the hungry hunter choose?
6. How many colored marshmallows did the hungry hunter choose?

Draw Conclusions

7. What did the cloth represent in your investigation?
8. Did the color of the cloth affect the color of marshmallows chosen? Explain your answer.
9. Which marshmallow color represented camouflage?
10. Describe an organism that has a camouflage adaptation.

Materials
- 50 white mini-marshmallows
- 50 colored mini-marshmallows (all one color is preferable)
- 50 cm^2 of colored cloth, matching one of the marshmallow colors
- watch or clock with a second hand

Answers

5. Answers will vary according to the students' experiments.
6. Answers will vary, but the marshmallow that most closely resembles the background cloth is expected to be chosen less often.
7. The cloth represents the organism's background, environment, or surroundings.
8. The marshmallow with the color that does not blend in with the color of the cloth will probably be chosen most often because it is easier to see. So the color of the cloth is important to the "organism's" protection.
9. Answers will vary according to the colors used in the lab.
10. Answers will vary, but students should describe an organism that is difficult to see in its natural surroundings.

Using Scientific Methods

Survival of the Chocolates

Imagine a world populated with candy, and hold that delicious thought for just a moment. Try to apply the idea of natural selection to a population of candy-coated chocolates. According to the theory of natural selection, individuals who have favorable adaptations are more likely to survive. In the "species" of candy you will study in this experiment, shell strength is an adaptive advantage. Plan an experiment to find out which candy characteristics correspond to shell (candy coating) strength.

Materials

- small candy-coated chocolates in a variety of colors
- other materials as needed, according to the design of your experiment

Form a Hypothesis

1. Form a hypothesis and make a prediction. For example, if you chose to study candy color, your prediction might look like this: If the _____?_____ colored shell is the strongest, then fewer of the candies with this color of shell will _____?_____ when _____?_____.

Test Your Hypothesis

2. Design a procedure to determine which candy is best suited to survive by not "cracking under pressure." In your plan, be sure to include materials and tools you may need to complete this procedure. Check your experimental design with your teacher before you begin. Your teacher will supply the candy and assist you in gathering materials and tools.

3. Record your results in a data table you have designed in your ScienceLog. Be sure to organize your data in a clear and understandable way.

Analyze the Results

4. Write a report that describes your experiment. Explain how your data either support or do not support your hypothesis. Include possible errors and ways to improve your procedure.

Going Further

Can you think of another characteristic of these candies that can be tested to determine which candy is best adapted to survive? Explain your choice.

Karma Houston-Hughes
Kyrene Middle School
Tempe, Arizona

Datasheets for LabBook
Datasheet 16

Survival of the Chocolates
Teacher's Notes

Time Required
One or two 45-minute class periods

Lab Ratings

TEACHER PREP 🧪
STUDENT SET-UP 🧪🧪
CONCEPT LEVEL 🧪🧪
CLEAN UP 🧪

Safety Caution
Safety concerns will vary with each design.

Preparation Notes
You will need to be prepared for different experimental designs. Some students may wish to find out if the different colored candy shells differ in hardness by testing which one will crack easiest under physical stress. Others may want to test the colors to see which one will dissolve more readily in water (cold or warm). Encourage different ways of testing. Part of the purpose of this lab is to help students learn how to design an experiment.

Answers

1. The statement made for the student here is for example only. Students may not wish to test for hardness or cracking. Help them make a prediction about their own experiment.

2. Again, students should conduct their own experiment.

Dating the Fossil Record
Teacher's Notes

Time Required

One 45-minute class period

Lab Ratings

EASY ———————→ HARD

- TEACHER PREP 🧪🧪
- STUDENT SET-UP 🧪🧪
- CONCEPT LEVEL 🧪🧪
- CLEAN UP 🧪🧪

Preparation Notes

Think of this lab as a puzzle. Students are told that Sample 2 is the oldest. They must keep in mind that the fossil will not reappear in any sample after it has gone extinct. This should be a challenge, but a fun one. In Part 2 of the procedure, you may want to put the dates given by the geology lab on the board for quick reference. Tell students that *mya* means "million years ago."

James Chin
Frank A. Day Middle School
Newtonville, Massachusetts

712   Chapter 8 • LabBook

Dating the Fossil Record

You have received nine rock samples from a paleontologist in California. Your job is to arrange the samples in order from oldest to youngest according to their fossil content and to determine their relative ages using the process of relative dating. Results from absolute dating methods will not be available from a laboratory for several weeks, and the paleontologist needs the information immediately. You know from previous work that the rocks of Sample 2 are the oldest.

SKILL BUILDER

Materials

- set of nine cards representing rock samples
- pencil and paper
- colored markers
- poster board (61 cm²)

Procedure: Part 1

1. Arrange the fossil cards from oldest to youngest. Begin with Sample 2 because you know this sample is the oldest. You may need to try several different arrangements to get the cards in order. **Hint:** After an organism becomes extinct, it does not reappear in younger rocks.

Fossil Key

 Globus slimius   Bogus biggus

 Circus bozoensis   Microbius hairiensis

 Fungus amongius   Bananabana bobana

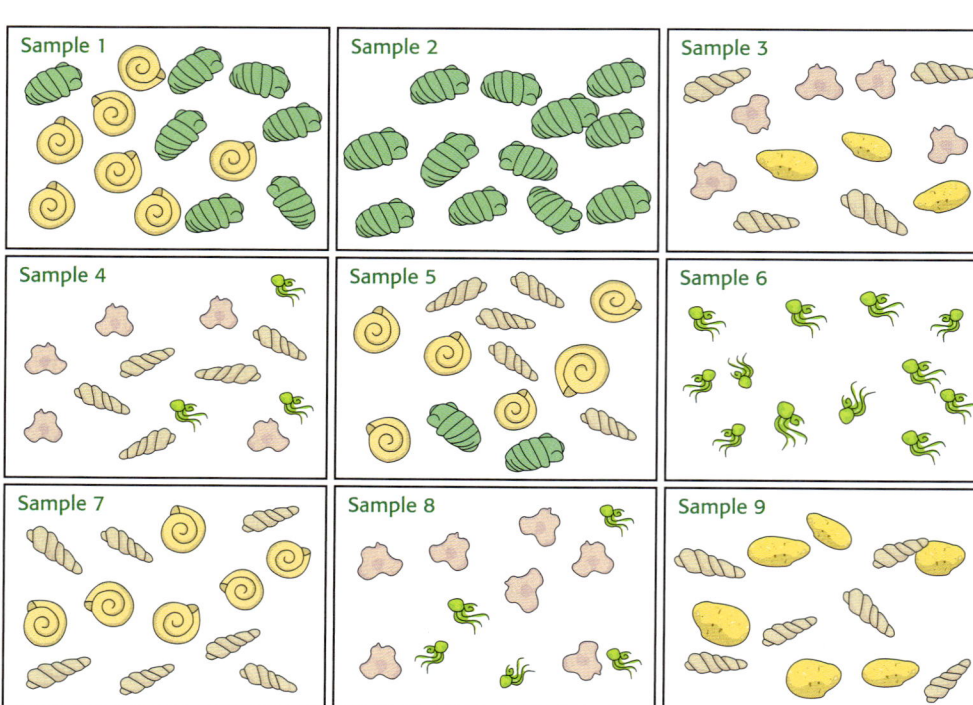

712

2. Prepare a table similar to the one below. Record the samples in order from bottom to top (oldest to youngest) in the first column. Sample 2 has been done for you.

Order of samples	Name of Fossil Organism					
	Globus slimius					
Sample 2	X					

3. Identify the fossils with the fossil key, and write their names in order by age from left to right in the top row of the table. **Hint:** Examine your fossil cards carefully to determine where each fossil appears in the rock record. Write an X in the appropriate column to indicate which fossil or fossils are present in each sample.

Analysis: Part 1

4. Do the Xs make a pattern across the table? What would you conclude if there were an X outside the pattern?

5. Based on the information in your table, which fossil is the youngest?

6. From the information you have, are you able to tell exactly how old a certain fossil is? Why or why not?

7. What information does relative dating provide to paleontologists?

Answers, Part 1

4. The letters do make a pattern. They make a line sloping upward, from left to right. An x outside the pattern might mean that the stray sample is incorrectly placed.

5. Bananabana bobana

6. No; we can determine only an estimate of the relative age of the fossils.

7. Relative dating provides information about which fossils are younger or older than other fossils.

Part 2

Answers are in chart form at the bottom of pages 713–714.

Datasheets for LabBook
Datasheet 17

Name of Fossil Organism

Order of samples	Globus slimius	Microbius hairiensis	Fungus amongius	Circus bozoensis	Bogus biggus	Bananabana bobana
Sample 6						X
Sample 8					X	X
Sample 4			X		X	X
Sample 3			X	X	X	
Sample 9			X	X		
Sample 7		X	X			
Sample 5	X	X	X			
Sample 1	X	X				
Sample 2	X					

Chapter 8 • LabBook   713

Procedure: Part 2

8. You are planning to prepare a timeline for the paleontologist in California. But when the results, shown at right, come in from the geology lab, you discover that the dates have become separated from the appropriate rock samples. Absolute dating is very expensive, and you can't have it done again. But wait! You have already determined the relative ages of the samples. All you have to do is arrange the dates from oldest to youngest and label your table from bottom to top. Add these dates to your data table.

9. Your table now contains all of the information you need to make a timeline for the paleontologist in California. Use colored markers and poster board to make your timeline. You may want to draw a rock wall showing several layers. To do this, label each layer with a date and the names of the fossils found there. Or you may want to draw a line with the dates labeled on the line and the fossils sketched above the appropriate date. Be creative!

Fossil Ages

The dates provided by the geology lab are as follows: 28.5 mya, 30.2 mya, 18.3 mya, 17.6 mya, 26.3 mya, 14.2 mya, 23.1 mya, 15.5 mya, and 19.5 mya.

Analysis: Part 2

10. Based on absolute dating, which fossil organism lived for the longest period of time? Which fossil organism lived for the shortest period of time? Explain your answers.

11. Based on the information in your timeline, what age range would you assign to the fossil of *Circus bozoensis*? **Hint:** Measure from the year that the fossil first appeared in the rock record to the first year it was absent from the rock record.

12. Determine the age ranges of all of your fossil species.

Going Further

Using the library or the Internet, investigate whether the absolute dating of rock surrounding fossils is the most reliable method of dating. Find out what circumstances prevent absolute dating.

Age of sample (in millions of years)	Contents of sample
28.5	Sample 1: *Globus slimius, Microbius hairiensis*
30.2	Sample 2: *Globus slimius*
18.3	Sample 3: *Fungus amongius, Bogus biggus, Circus bozoensis*
17.6	Sample 4: *Fungus amongius, Bogus biggus, Bananabana bobana*
26.3	Sample 5: *Globus slimius, Microbius hairiensis, Fungus amongius*
14.2	Sample 6: *Bananabana bobana*
23.1	Sample 7: *Fungus amongius, Microbius hairiensis*
15.5	Sample 8: *Bogus biggus, Bananabana bobana*
19.5	Sample 9: *Fungus amongius, Circus bozoensis*

The Half-life of Pennies

Carbon-14 is a special unstable element used in the absolute dating of material that was once alive, such as fossil bones. Every 5,730 years, half of the carbon-14 in a fossil specimen decays or breaks down into a more stable element. In the following experiment you will see how pennies can show the same kind of "decay."

SKILL BUILDER

Materials

- 100 pennies
- large container with a cover

TRY at HOME

Procedure

1. Place 100 pennies in a large, covered container. Shake the container several times, and remove the cover. Carefully empty the container on a flat surface making sure the pennies don't roll away.

2. Remove all the coins that have the "head" side of the coin turned upward. Record the number of pennies removed and the number of pennies remaining in a data table similar to the one at right.

3. Repeat the process until no pennies are left in the container. Remember to remove only the coins showing "heads."

4. In your ScienceLog, draw a graph similar to the one at right. Label the *x*-axis "Number of shakes," and label the *y*-axis "Pennies remaining." Using data from your data table, plot the number of coins remaining at each shake on your graph.

Analysis

5. Examine the Half-life of Carbon-14 graph at right. Compare the graph you have made for pennies with the one for carbon-14. Explain any similarities that you see.

6. Recall that the probability of landing "heads" in a coin toss is $\frac{1}{2}$. Use this information to explain why the remaining number of pennies is reduced by about half each time they are shaken and tossed.

Shake number	Number of coins remaining	Number of coins removed
1		
2	*DO NOT WRITE IN BOOK*	
3		

Half-life of Pennies

Half-life of Carbon-14

The Half-life of Pennies
Teacher's Notes

Time Required
One 45-minute class period

Lab Rating

EASY → HARD

- **TEACHER PREP** 🧪
- **STUDENT SET-UP** 🧪
- **CONCEPT LEVEL** 🧪🧪
- **CLEAN UP** 🧪

Lab Notes

It is useful to use coin tosses to explain half-life because approximately half the coins will land heads and half will land tails. Therefore, about half the entire quantity of coins tossed will be eliminated with each successive toss.

Datasheets for LabBook
Datasheet 18

715

Answers

5. The graphs should be very similar in shape. With each half-life and each shake, the number remaining will be reduced by half.

6. The remaining number of pennies is reduced by about half each time the pennies are shaken and tossed because there are only two faces on each coin. The rules of probability suggest that half will land heads and half will land tails, and therefore the amount will be reduced by about half with each shake.

Karma Houston-Hughes
Kyrene Middle School
Tempe, Arizona

Shape Island
Teacher's Notes

Time Required
One 45-minute class period

Lab Rating

TEACHER PREP 🧪
STUDENT SET-UP 🧪
CONCEPT LEVEL 🧪🧪
CLEAN UP 🧪

Lab Notes

This lab will help students demonstrate an understanding of binomial nomenclature by using a key to assign scientific names to fictional organisms. After completing the lab, students should be able to explain the function of the scientific name system.

In the chapter on classification, the vocabulary "two-part scientific name" has been used instead of "binomial nomenclature." You may wish to introduce the latter here.

This activity may be more successful if you review prefixes, suffixes, and root words briefly before beginning. Tell students that the genus name is capitalized but the species name is not and that both words are underlined or italicized.

Shape Island

SKILL BUILDER

You are a biologist exploring uncharted parts of the world looking for new animal species. You sailed for days across the ocean and finally found Shape Island, hundreds of miles south of Hawaii. This island has some very unusual organisms. Each of them has some variation of a geometric shape. You have spent more than a year collecting specimens and classifying them according to Linnaeus's system. You have been able to assign a two-part scientific name to most species you have collected. You must assign all the names to the final 12 specimens before you begin your journey home.

Procedure TRY at HOME

1. In your ScienceLog, draw each of the organisms pictured on this page. Beside each organism, draw a line for its name, as shown on the following page. The first one has been named for you, but you have 12 more to name. Use the glossary of Greek and Latin prefixes, suffixes, and root words below to help you name the organisms.

1

2

3

4

Greek and Latin roots, prefixes, and suffixes	Meaning
ankylos	angle
antennae	external sense organs
tri-	three
bi-	two
cyclo-	circle
macro-	large
micro-	small
mono-	one
peri-	all around
-plast	body
-pod	foot
quad-	four
stoma	mouth
uro-	tail

5   6

7   8

9

10

11

12   13

 Datasheets for LabBook
Datasheet 19

Maurine Marchani
Raymond Park Middle School
Indianapolis, Indiana

1. _Cycloplast quadantennae_
   (cyclo + plast quad + antennae)

2. _____ DO NOT WRITE IN BOOK

3. _____

2. One more organism exists on Shape Island, but you have not been able to capture it. However, your supplies are running out, and you must start sailing for home. You have had a good look at the unusual animal and can draw it in detail. In your ScienceLog, draw an animal that is different from all the others, and give it a two-part scientific name.

Analysis

3. If you gave species 1 a common name, such as round-face-no-nose, would any other scientist know which of the newly discovered organisms you were referring to? Explain. How many others have a round face and no nose?

4. Describe two characteristics shared by all your newly discovered specimens.

Going Further

Look up the scientific names listed below. You can use the library, the Internet, a taxonomy index, or field guides.
- *Mertensia virginica*
- *Porcellio scaber*

For each organism answer the following questions: Is the organism a plant or an animal? How many common names does it have? How many scientific names does it have?

Think of the name of your favorite fruit or vegetable. Find out if it has other common names, and find out its two-part scientific name.

Answers

1. Below are sample answers. Student answers may vary, but they should demonstrate an understanding of the key provided. Each name should consist of two words: the first describes the organism generally, and the second describes it more specifically.

   1. *Cycloplast quadantennae*
   2. *Cycloplast biantennae*
   3. *Quadankylosplast monoantennae*
   4. *Quadankylosplast bipod*
   5. *Triankylosplast triantennae*
   6. *Cycloplast stoma*
   7. *Triankylosplast stoma*
   8. *Quadankylosplast periantennae*
   9. *Cycloplast monopod*
   10. *Triankylosplast uromonopod*
   11. *Triankylos macroplast*
   12. *Quadankylos microplast*
   13. *Cycloplast uro*

2. Answers will vary according to student drawings.

3. No. There are five species that have round faces and lack noses.

4. Answers will vary but should indicate that they all have geometric shapes and two eyes. They are all the same color, all animals, and all living.

Going Further

Mertensia virginica, Virginia bluebells, are common wildflowers found in April and May in shady areas, mostly in moist spots near streams. This plant is quite plentiful in some places. Flower buds are pink, turning blue when the flower is fully opened. This wild flower is very common in western Kentucky.

Porcellio scaber is a species of wood louse. Wood lice are crustaceans, related to shrimps, crabs, and lobsters, and they belong to a class of arthropods called Isopoda. They are the only crustaceans that have been able to invade land without the needing to return to water, although they tend to be restricted to fairly damp places.

Voyage of the USS *Adventure*
Teacher's Notes

Time Required

One 45-minute class period

Lab Ratings

TEACHER PREP 🧪
STUDENT SET-UP 🧪
CONCEPT LEVEL 🧪🧪
CLEAN UP 🧪

Preparation Notes

Some students will find it easier to make the charts on graph paper, so you may wish to add graph paper to the list of materials needed.

Lab Notes

Students should know that we are not yet able to travel outside our solar system. This activity should help students categorize organisms or objects by noticing subtle differences. It is a good activity to begin a study of classification of animals, rocks, or plants. This lab may be useful before introducing dichotomous keys, for example.

Voyage of the USS *Adventure*

DISCOVERY LAB

You are a crew member on the USS *Adventure*. The *Adventure* has been on a 5-year mission to collect life-forms from outside the solar system. On the voyage back to Earth, your ship went through a meteor shower, which ruined several of the compartments containing the extraterrestrial life-forms. Now it is necessary to put more than one life-form in the same compartment.

You have only three undamaged compartments in your starship. You and your crewmates must stay in one compartment, and that compartment should be used for extraterrestrial life-forms only if absolutely necessary. You and your crewmates must decide which of the life-forms could be placed together. It is thought that similar life-forms will have similar needs. You can use only observable characteristics to group the life-forms.

Life-form 1

Life-form 2

Life-form 3

Procedure

Life-form 4

1. Make a data table similar to the one below. Label each column with as many characteristics of the various life-forms as possible. Leave enough space in each square to write your observations. The life-forms are pictured on this page.

Life-form Characteristics				
	Color	Shape	Legs	Eyes
Life-form 1				
Life-form 2				
Life-form 3				
Life-form 4				

DO NOT WRITE IN BOOK

Life-form 5

2. Describe each characteristic as completely as you can. Based on your observations, determine which of the life-forms are most alike.

Life-form 7

Life-form 6

 Datasheets for LabBook
Datasheet 20

Georgiann Delgadillo
East Valley School District
Continuous Curriculum School
Spokane, Washington

3. Make a data table like the one below. Fill in the table according to the decisions you made in step 2. State your reasons for the way you have grouped your life-forms.

Life-form Room Assignments		
Compartment	Life-forms	Reasons
1		
2		
3		

DO NOT WRITE IN BOOK

4. The USS *Adventure* has to make one more stop before returning home. On planet X437 you discover the most interesting life-form ever found outside of Earth—the CC9, shown at right. Make a decision, based on your previous grouping of life-forms, about whether you can safely include CC9 in one of the compartments for the trip to Earth.

Analysis

5. Describe the life-forms in compartment 1. How are they similar? How are they different?

6. Describe the life-forms in compartment 2. How are they similar? How do they differ from the life-forms in compartment 1?

7. Are there any life-forms in compartment 3? If so, describe their similarities. In which compartment will you and your crewmates remain for the journey home?

8. Are you able to safely transport life-form CC9 back to Earth? Why or why not? If you are able to include CC9, in which compartment will it be placed? How did you decide?

CC9

Going Further

In 1831, Charles Darwin sailed from England on a ship called the HMS *Beagle*. You have studied the finches that Darwin observed on the Galápagos Islands. What were some of the other unusual organisms he found there? For example, find out about the Galápagos tortoise.

Answers

There are no right or wrong answers in this activity. The objective is to allow students an opportunity to recognize subtle differences and to recognize that organisms may be more alike than they are different. However, you should make sure the students provide good reasons why they grouped certain life-forms together. There are several ways these seven organisms are similar. For example, four of them are segmented and have no legs. Three of them are geometrically shaped, and three others have mouths. Have students examine them for less observable characteristics, such as what kind of body plan or symmetry they have, how they might obtain food, or whether they might be land dwelling or aquatic.

Going Further

The Galápagos tortoise can have a shell length of 1.3 m, a mass of 180 kg, and live to be 150 years old.

Aunt Flossie and the Intruder
Teacher's Notes

Time Required
Three 20-minute brainstorming and design sessions and five 5-minute observation periods on successive days

Lab Ratings

- TEACHER PREP 🧪🧪
- STUDENT SET-UP 🧪🧪🧪
- CONCEPT LEVEL 🧪🧪🧪🧪
- CLEAN UP 🧪🧪

MATERIALS
Students will need to submit a list of supplies and equipment they will need for their experiment to you for approval.

Safety Caution
Be sure students address any safety concerns in the design of their experiments.

 Datasheets for LabBook
Datasheet 21

Elizabeth Rustad
Crane Junior High School
Yuma, Arizona

Aunt Flossie and the Intruder

DESIGN YOUR OWN

Aunt Flossie is a *really* bad housekeeper! She *never* cleans the refrigerator, and things get really gross in there. Last week she pulled out a plastic resealable bag that looked like it was going to explode! The bag was full of gas that she did not put there! Aunt Flossie remembered from her school days that gases are released from living things as waste products. Something had to be alive in the bag! Aunt Flossie became very upset that there was an intruder in her refrigerator. She said she would not bake another cookie until you determine the nature of the intruder.

Procedure

1. Design an investigation to determine how gas got into Aunt Flossie's bag. In your ScienceLog, make a list of the materials you will need, and prepare all the data tables you will need for recording your observations.

2. As you design your investigation, be sure to include each of the steps listed at right.

3. Get your teacher's approval of your experimental design and your list of materials before you begin.

4. Dispose of your materials according to your teacher's instructions at the end of your experiment.
   Caution: Do not open any bags of spoiled food or allow any of the contents to escape.

Analysis

5. Write a letter to Aunt Flossie describing your experiment. Explain what produced the gas in the bag and your recommendations for preventing these intruders in her refrigerator in the future. Invite her to bake cookies for your class!

Going Further
Research in the library or on the Internet to find out how people kept food fresh before refrigeration. Find out what advances have been made in food preservation as a result of the space program.

Materials
- items to be determined by the students and approved by teacher as needed for each experiment such as resealable plastic bags, food samples, a scale, or a thermometer.
- protective gloves

- Ask a question
- Form a hypothesis
- Test the hypothesis
- Analyze the data
- Draw conclusions
- Communicate your results

Answers
5. Students should explain (in a letter to Aunt Flossie) that it was mold or bacteria in the baggie that produced the gas. The gas was a product of the respiration of the mold or bacteria on the food. Preventing future intruders could be as simple as lowering the temperature of the refrigerator or freezing food.

Going Further
Students should learn that people have developed many ways of preserving food. Salt and sugar have been used as "curing" agents for meat, and home canning of foods has been around for generations. The space program has given us many new technologies of food preservation, particularly freeze-drying.

Viral Decorations

Although viruses are made of only protein and nucleic acids, their structures have many different shapes that help them attach to and invade living cells. One viral shape can be constructed from the template provided by your teacher. In this activity you will construct and modify a model of a virus.

Procedure

1. Obtain a virus model template from your teacher. Carefully copy the template on a piece of construction paper. You may make the virus model as large as your teacher allows.

2. Plan how you will modify your virus. For example, you might want to add the tail and tail fibers of a bacteriophage or wrap the model in plastic to represent the envelope that surrounds the protein coat in HIV.

3. Color your virus model, and cut it out by cutting on the solid black lines. Then fold the virus model along the dotted lines.

4. Glue or tape each lettered tab under the corresponding lettered triangle. For example, glue or tape the large Z tab under the Z-shaded triangle. When you are finished, you should have a closed box with 20 sides.

5. Apply the modifications that you planned. Give your virus a name, and write it on the model. Decorate your classroom with your virus and those of your classmates.

Analysis

6. Describe the modifications you made to your virus model, and explain how the virus might use them.

7. If your virus causes disease, explain what disease it causes, how it reproduces, and how the virus is spread.

Going Further

Research in the library or on the Internet an unusual virus that causes an illness, such as the influenza virus, HIV, or Ebola virus. Explain what is unusual about the virus, what illness it causes, and how it might be avoided.

Materials

- virus model template
- construction paper
- colored markers
- scissors
- glue or tape
- pipe cleaners, twist-ties, buttons, string, plastic wrap, and other scrap materials for making variations of the virus

Viral Decorations
Teacher's Notes

Time Required
One 45-minute class period

Lab Ratings

TEACHER PREP 🧪🧪
STUDENT SET-UP 🧪🧪🧪
CONCEPT LEVEL 🧪🧪🧪🧪
CLEAN UP 🧪🧪

MATERIALS
Enlarge the template below to provide students with patterns.

Safety Caution
Remind students to review all safety cautions and icons before beginning this lab activity.

Answers
6. Answers will vary.
7. Answers will vary.

Going Further
Influenza virus, of course, causes the flu. HIV is the virus that causes AIDS, and Ebola-Zaire is a rare filovirus that causes a deadly hemorrhagic fever.

Datasheets for LabBook
Datasheet 22

Gladys Cherniak
St. Paul's Episcopal School
Mobile, Alabama

Chapter 10 • LabBook   **721**

Making a Protist Mobile
Teacher's Notes

Time Required
One 45-minute class period

Lab Ratings

EASY — HARD
- TEACHER PREP
- STUDENT SET-UP
- CONCEPT LEVEL
- CLEAN UP

MATERIALS
Have students bring materials from home, such as buttons, fringe, pipe cleaners, cotton balls, or anything else that can be used to make a model of a protist.

Safety Caution
Remind students to review all safety cautions and icons before beginning this lab activity.

Answers
6. The kingdom Protista has the greatest diversity of all the eukaryotes with over 65,000 known species. They can live in many different environments. They can drift in the ocean, creep across vegetation in freshwater rivers and ponds, flourish in deep soil, and even reproduce in the bodies of other organisms.

Going Further
Students may choose from any number of disease-causing protists, from amoeba (amoebic dysentery) to *Plasmodium* (malaria). Students' reports should include some of the symptoms of the disease, how prevalent it is, and how or if it is controlled.

722 Chapter 11 • LabBook

Making a Protist Mobile

MAKING MODELS

You have studied many of the diverse species of organisms within the kingdom Protista. This may be the first time you have ever seen many of these single-celled eukaryotes. In this activity you will have an opportunity to express a bit of creativity using what you have learned about these interesting organisms.

Procedure
1. Research the different kinds of protists you have studied. You may cut out pictures of them from magazines, or you may find examples of protists on the Internet. You may want to investigate *Plasmodium*, *Euglena*, amoebas, slime molds, *Radiolaria*, *Paramecium*, *Foraminifera*, various other protozoans, or even algae.

2. Using the paper and recycled materials, make a model of each protist you want to include on your mobile. Be sure to include the special features of each protist, such as vacuoles, pseudopods, shells, cilia, or flagella.

3. Use tape or glue to attach special features to give your protists a three-dimensional look.

4. Provide labels for your protist models. For each protist, provide its name, classification, method of movement (if any), method for obtaining food, and any other interesting facts you have learned about it.

5. Attach your protist models to the wire hanger with wire or string. Use tape or glue to attach your labels to each model.

Analysis
6. Explain what you have learned about the diversity of protists. Include at least three habitats where protists may be found.

Going Further
Choose a disease-causing protist. Write a report describing the disease, its effect on people or the environment, and the efforts being made to control it.

Materials
- heavyweight paper (construction paper or poster board)
- recycled material of your choice
- scissors
- transparent tape or glue
- colored markers
- string, yarn, lightweight wire, or fishing line
- wire coat hanger

722

Datasheets for LabBook
Datasheet 23

CLASSROOM TESTED & APPROVED

Elizabeth Rustad
Crane Junior High School
Yuma, Arizona

There's a Fungus Among Us!

Fungi share many characteristics with plants. For example, most fungi live on land. But fungi have several unique features that suggest that they are not closely related to any other kingdom of organisms. In this activity you will observe some of the unique structures of a mushroom, a member of the kingdom Fungi.

Materials

- mushroom
- tweezers
- 2 sheets of white paper
- masking tape
- fruit-juice agar plate
- incubator
- microscope or magnifying lens
- transparent tape

Procedure

1. Obtain a mushroom from your teacher. Carefully pull the cap of the mushroom from the stem. Place the stem to the side for later use. Using tweezers, remove one of the gills from the underside of the cap. Place the gill on a sheet of white paper.

2. Place the mushroom cap gill-side down on the other sheet of paper and tape it in place with masking tape. Label this sheet of paper with your name, and place the paper aside for at least 24 hours.

3. Use tweezers to take several 1 cm pieces from the stem and place them in your agar plate. Record the appearance of the plate in your ScienceLog. Cover the agar plate, and label it with your name. Incubate your agar plate overnight.

4. Use tweezers to gently pull the remaining mushroom stem apart lengthwise. The individual fibers or strings you see are the hyphae that form the structure of the fungus. Place a thin strand on the same piece of paper with the gill you removed from the cap.

5. Observe the gill and the stem hyphae with a magnifying lens or microscope. Record your observations in your ScienceLog. **Caution:** Never direct sunlight through your magnifying lens or microscope.

6. After at least 24 hours, record any changes that occurred on the agar plate in your ScienceLog. Carefully remove the mushroom cap from the paper. Place a piece of transparent tape over the print left behind on the paper. Record your observations in your ScienceLog.

Analysis

7. Describe the structures you saw on the gill and hyphae.

8. What is the print on the white paper?

9. Describe the structure at the bottom edge of the mushroom gill. Explain how this structure is connected to the print.

10. Explain how the changes that occurred in your agar plate are related to methods of fungal reproduction.

 Datasheets for LabBook
Datasheet 24

There's a Fungus Among Us!
Teacher's Notes

Time Required
Two 45-minute class periods

Lab Ratings

TEACHER PREP 🧪🧪
STUDENT SET-UP 🧪🧪🧪🧪
CONCEPT LEVEL 🧪🧪
CLEAN UP 🧪🧪

Safety Caution
Before beginning this lab, check for any mushroom allergies among students. Caution students not to eat any of the mushrooms.

Preparation Notes
Do not use mushrooms gathered from the wild. Suitable mushrooms can be found in the produce section of a grocery store. Have protective gloves available for students who wish to wear them. This lab works well with groups of 2 to 4 students per mushroom. If you do not have an incubator, place the Petri dishes in a warm place, out of drafts and direct sunlight.

Answers

7. Possible answer: Gills look like ridges and slits. Hyphae are stringlike.

8. The print on the white paper is a spore print produced by basidiospores being released from the gills.

9. The structures at the bottom edge of the mushroom gill are basidia, which contain the nuclei that will develop into the basidiospores.

10. After 24 hours, students may see mycelia growth on the agar plate. (It may take a little longer.) The mycelia constitute the main body of the mushroom and develop from the germinating basidiospores.

Jason Marsh
Montevideo High and Country School
Montevideo, Minnesota

Leaf Me Alone!
Teacher's Notes

Time Required

One 45-minute class period

Lab Ratings

TEACHER PREP 🧪🧪
STUDENT SET-UP 🧪🧪
CONCEPT LEVEL 🧪🧪
CLEAN UP 🧪

MATERIALS

The materials on the student page are enough for a group of 4–5 students. Collect plant specimens ahead of time or have students bring in five specimens that they have collected. Students will need to see the leaves as they appear on the stems, so include as much of the plant as possible.

Safety Caution

Remind students to review all safety cautions and icons before beginning this lab activity.

Lab Note

This exchange activity can be an effective assessment tool for this lab. Students will enjoy challenging their classmates and this is a good way for students to learn from each other.

Leaf Me Alone!

Imagine you are a naturalist all alone on an expedition in a rain forest. You have found several plants that you think have never been seen before. You must contact a botanist, a scientist who studies plants, to confirm your suspicion. Because there is no mail service in the rain forest, you must describe these species completely and accurately by radio. The botanist must be able to draw the leaves of the plants from your description.

In this activity, you will carefully describe five plant specimens using the examples and vocabulary lists in this lab.

Procedure

1. Examine the leaf characteristics illustrated in this lab. These examples can be found on the following page. You will notice that more than one term is needed to completely describe a leaf. The leaf shown at right has been labeled for you using the examples and vocabulary lists found in this lab.

2. In your ScienceLog, draw a diagram of a leaf from each plant specimen.

3. Next to each drawing, carefully describe the leaf. Include general characteristics, such as relative size and color. For each plant, identify the following: leaf shape, stem type, leaf arrangement, leaf edge, vein arrangement, and leaf-base shape. Use the terms and vocabulary lists provided to describe each leaf as accurately as possible and to label your drawings.

Analysis

4. What is the difference between a simple leaf and a compound leaf?

5. Describe two different vein arrangements in leaves.

6. Based on what you know about adaptation, explain why there are so many different leaf variations.

SKILL BUILDER

Materials

- 5 different leaf specimens
- plant guidebook (optional)
- protective gloves

Compound Leaf

- V-shaped leaf base
- Pinnate veins
- Saw-toothed edge
- Opposite leaf arrangement
- Leaflet
- Petiole

Going Further

Choose a partner. Using the keys and vocabulary in this lab, describe a leaf, and see if your partner can draw the leaf from your description. Switch roles, and see if you can draw a leaf from your partner's description.

 Science Skills Worksheet 2 "Using Your Senses"

Jane Lemons
Western Rockingham Middle School
Madison, North Carolina

Leaf Shapes Vocabulary List

cordate—heart shaped
lanceolate—sword shaped
lobate—lobed
oblong—leaves rounded at the tip
orbicular—disk shaped
ovate—oval shaped, widest at base of leaf
peltate—shield shaped
reniform—kidney shaped
sagittate—arrow shaped

Stems Vocabulary List

woody—bark or barklike covering on stem
herbaceous—green, nonwoody stems

Leaf Arrangements Vocabulary List

alternate—alternating leaves or leaflets along stem or petiole
compound—leaf divided into segments or several leaflets on a petiole
opposite—compound leaf with several leaflets arranged oppositely along a petiole
palmate—single leaf with veins arranged around a center point
palmate compound—several leaflets arranged around a center point
petiole—leaf stalk
pinnate—single leaf with veins arranged along a center vein
pinnate compound—several leaflets on either side of a petiole
simple—single leaf attached to stem by a petiole

Datasheets for LabBook
Datasheet 25

Lab Notes

This activity is designed to help students recognize that leaves have many forms and that the variations of leaf shapes are adaptations for a particular function. This exercise also acquaints students with the identification process used in some field or classification guides. Encourage students to recognize the difference between a stem and a petiole and the difference between a leaf and a leaflet.

Answers

4. A simple leaf is a single leaf at the end of a single petiole. A compound leaf has several leaflets on the end of a petiole in various arrangements.

5. Veins can be arranged in three ways—parallel, extending straight up and down the leaf (which is usually elongated); pinnate, which on a single leaf is a network of veins extending out from a central vein; and palmate, which is an arrangement of veins originating from a single point on a leaf that has several lobes.

6. Answers will vary but should include adaptations for water conservation, light reception, and insect resistance, among others. Leaves vary because they serve many functions. Explain that leaf shape is only one of the adaptations leaves can have and that the thickness of the leaf and the waxy coating of the leaf are also adaptations. Have them compare an oak leaf with a conifer leaf.

Chapter 12 • LabBook   **725**

Travelin' Seeds
Teacher's Notes

Time Required
One 45-minute class period

Lab Ratings

EASY ──────► HARD

TEACHER PREP 🧪🧪
STUDENT SET-UP 🧪
CONCEPT LEVEL 🧪🧪
CLEAN UP 🧪

Preparation Notes

Challenge Cards Make up seed-dispersal challenge cards ahead of time. Five basic challenges are listed below. Copy each as needed so that there is one card per student or group.

1. Modify your seed so that it will be carried on an animal's fur as the animal passes by the plant. The seed must travel for at least 1 m. The animal must not be aware that the seed has been attached.

2. Modify your seed so that it will be flung 1 m away from the parent plant (you/group). Be careful that your tests do not fly at others in the class.

3. Modify your seed so that it will glide or float in the air when it falls off the parent plant. The seed must be dropped, not pushed or thrown, and must travel at least 1 m.

4. Modify your seed so that animals will find it desirable to eat and digest.

5. Modify your seed so that it will float on water for at least 1 minute.

Travelin' Seeds

You have learned from your study of plants that there are some very interesting and unusual plant adaptations. Some of the most interesting adaptations are modifications that allow plant seeds and fruits to be dispersed, or scattered, away from the parent plant. This dispersal enables the young seedlings to obtain the space, sun, and other resources they need without directly competing with the parent plant.

In this activity, you will use your own creativity to disperse a seed.

Materials

- bean seed
- seed-dispersal challenge card
- various household or recycled materials (examples: glue, tape, paper, paper clips, rubber bands, cloth, paper cups and plates, paper towels, cardboard)

Procedure

1. Obtain a seed and a dispersal challenge card from your teacher. In your ScienceLog, record the type of challenge card you have been given.

2. Create a plan for using the available materials to disperse your seed as described on the challenge card. Record your plan in your ScienceLog. Get your teacher's approval before proceeding.

3. With your teacher's permission, test your seed-dispersal method. Perform several trials. Make a data table in your ScienceLog, and record the results of your trials.

Analysis

4. Were you able to successfully complete the seed-dispersal challenge? Explain.

5. Are there any modifications you could make to your method to improve the dispersal of your seed?

6. Describe some plants that disperse their seeds in a way similar to your seed-dispersal method.

◄ Mangrove seed

◄ Cottonwood

Wild berry ►

Grass bur ►

Answers
4.–6. Answers will vary.

Datasheets for LabBook
Datasheet 26

Jane Lemons
Western Rockingham
Middle School
Madison, North Carolina

Build a Flower

Scientists often make models in the laboratory to help them understand processes or structures. In this activity, you will use your creativity and your understanding of the structure of a flower to make a model from recycled materials and art supplies.

Procedure

1. In your ScienceLog, draw a flower similar to the one shown below. Label each of the structures on your drawing. The flower shown has both male and female parts. Not all flowers have this arrangement.

2. Examine the available materials. Decide which materials are appropriate for each flower part, and build a three-dimensional model of a flower. The flower you create should contain each of the parts listed below.

Parts of a Flower
- Petals
- Sepals
- Stem
- Pistil (stigma, style, ovary)
- Stamen (anther, filament)

3. Draw a key for your flower model on an index card. Label each of the structures represented on your flower.

Analysis

4. List the structures of a flower, and explain the function of each part.
5. Explain how your model flower might attract pollinators. What modifications could you make to increase the number of pollinators?
6. Describe how self-pollination could take place in your model flower.

Materials

- recycled items (examples: paper plates and cups, yogurt containers, wire, string, beads, buttons, cardboard, bottles)
- art materials (examples: glue, tape, scissors, colored paper, pipe cleaners, yarn)
- index card

Jane Lemons
Western Rockingham Middle School
Madison, North Carolina

5. Answers will vary but should include bright flowers, honey guides on the petals, strong scent, and the position and number of pistils and stamens.

6. Answers should explain how the model flower moves pollen from the anther to the stamen.

Build a Flower
Teacher's Notes

Time Required
One 45-minute class period

Lab Ratings

TEACHER PREP 🧪
STUDENT SET-UP 🧪🧪
CONCEPT LEVEL 🧪🧪
CLEAN UP 🧪

Answers

4. **petal:** the often colorful crown of a flowering plant that attracts pollinators

   sepal: the leaves that form the base of the flower and that enclose and protect the bud before the flower opens

   stem: the main stalk of the aboveground part of a plant from which leaves, flowers, and fruit develop; water and nutrients move through the stem between the flower and roots.

   pistil: the female reproductive organ of a flower

   stigma: the upper tip of the pistil, which receives pollen

   style: the stalklike part of the pistil between the stigma and ovary that holds the stigma where it can receive pollen

   ovary: the enlarged part of the pistil in which ovules are formed

   stamen: the male reproductive organ in flowers

   anther: the top of the stamen, contains pollen

   filament: the threadlike part of the stamen that holds the anther

 Datasheets for LabBook
Datasheet 27

Food Factory Waste
Teacher's Notes

Time Required
One 45-minute class period and about 15 minutes per day for 5 days

Lab Ratings

TEACHER PREP 🧪🧪
STUDENT SET-UP 🧪🧪
CONCEPT LEVEL 🧪🧪🧪
CLEAN UP 🧪🧪

MATERIALS
The materials listed on the student page are enough for 1 student.
- *Elodea* is a common aquarium plant and can be found at some pet stores and most places that sell aquarium fish.
- A 5 percent solution of baking soda and water can be made by dissolving 5 g of baking soda in 95 mL of water.

Safety Caution
Remind students to review all safety cautions and icons before beginning this lab activity.

David Sparks
Redwater Junior High School
Redwater, Texas

Food Factory Waste

Plants use photosynthesis to produce food. We cannot live without the waste products from this process. In this activity, you will observe the process of photosynthesis and determine the rate of photosynthesis for *Elodea*.

Procedure

1. Add 450 mL of baking-soda-and-water solution to a beaker.

2. Put two or three sprigs of *Elodea* in the beaker. The baking soda will provide the *Elodea* with the carbon dioxide it needs for photosynthesis.

3. Place the wide end of the funnel over the *Elodea*. The end of the funnel with the small opening should be pointing up. The *Elodea* and the funnel should be completely under the solution, as shown at right.

4. Fill a test tube with the remaining baking-soda-and-water solution. Place your thumb over the end of the test tube. Turn the test tube upside down, taking care that no air enters. Hold the opening of the test tube under the solution and place the test tube over the small end of the funnel. Try not to let any solution out of the test tube as you do this.

5. Place the beaker setup in a well-lit area near a lamp or in direct sunlight.

6. In your ScienceLog, prepare a data table similar to the one below.

Amount of Gas Present in the Test Tube		
Days of exposure to light	Total amount of gas present (mm)	Amount of gas produced per day (mm)
0		
1		
2		
3		
4		
5		

 Datasheets for LabBook
Datasheet 28

 Science Skills Worksheet 25
"Introduction to Graphs"

 SKILL BUILDER

Materials
- 500 mL of 5% baking-soda-and-water solution
- 600 mL beaker
- 20 cm long *Elodea* sprigs (2–3)
- glass funnel
- test tube
- metric ruler
- protective gloves

7. Record that there was 0 gas in the test tube on day 0. (If you were unable to place the test tube without getting air in the tube, measure the height of the column of air in the test tube in millimeters. Record this value for day 0.) Measure the gas in the test tube from the middle of the curve on the bottom of the upside-down test tube to the level of the solution.

8. For days 1 through 5, measure the amount of gas in the test tube. Record the measurements in your data table under the heading "Total amount of gas present (mm)."

9. Calculate the amount of gas produced each day by subtracting the amount of gas present on the previous day from the amount of gas present today. Record these amounts under the heading "Amount of gas produced per day (mm)."

10. Construct a graph similar to the one at right. Plot the data from your graph.

Amount of Gas Produced by Photosynthesis

Analysis

11. Using information from your graph, describe what happened to the amount of gas in the test tube.

12. How much gas was produced in the test tube after day 5?

13. Write the equation for photosynthesis in your ScienceLog. Explain each part of the equation. For example, what "ingredients" are necessary for photosynthesis to take place? What substances are produced by photosynthesis? What gas is produced that we need in order to live?

14. Write a report describing your experiment, your results, and your conclusions.

Going Further
Hydroponics is the growing of plants in nutrient-rich water, without soil. Research hydroponic techniques, and try to grow a plant without soil.

Lab Notes
You may need to have students practice placing the test tube over the inverted funnel. It may take two or three tries to get the test tube over the funnel stem without letting any air into the tube. First fill the test tube with the solution. Place your thumb over the opening tightly so no air can get in. Submerge your thumb and the top of the test tube underwater. Once the top of the test tube is underwater you can release your thumb to maneuver the test tube over the stem of the funnel. Be sure you have the *Elodea* in place under the funnel before you begin!

You may wish to write the equation for photosynthesis on the board.

Answers

11. Students' graphs should show a gradual increase in the amount of gas in the test tube.

12. Answers will vary according to variables in the classroom, such as the amount of light and temperature.

13. $6CO_2 + 6H_2O + \text{light energy} \rightarrow C_6H_{12}O_6 + 6O_2$
    CO_2 is carbon dioxide and comes from the baking soda solution. H_2O is the water in the solution. Light energy comes from the sun. $C_6H_{12}O_6$ is sugar (glucose), and O_2 is oxygen. Photosynthesis produces sugar and oxygen. Plants produce oxygen as a byproduct of photosynthesis; oxygen is the gas that we breathe and cannot live without.

Weepy Weeds
Teacher's Notes

Time Required
One or two 45-minute class periods

Lab Ratings

- TEACHER PREP 🔺🔺
- STUDENT SET-UP 🔺
- CONCEPT LEVEL 🔺🔺
- CLEAN UP 🔺🔺

MATERIALS
The materials listed on the student page are enough for 1 student. The plant used in this lab can be any leafy plant, such as a bean plant or a coleus. The plant shown is a coleus with all but the top four leaves trimmed away.

Safety Caution
Remind students to review all safety cautions and icons before beginning this lab activity.

Lab Notes
If your lab period is short, you may want to eliminate the measurement of the height of water in the test tube at 40 minutes.

Although it is not essential to the activity, you may want to begin with an exact amount of water in each test tube. Students would then know that the difference can be due only to evaporation and transpiration.

Weepy Weeds

You are trying to find a way to drain an area that is flooded with water polluted with fertilizer. You know that a plant releases water through the stomata in its leaves. As water evaporates from the leaves, more water is pulled up from the roots through the stem and into the leaves. By this process, called transpiration, water and nutrients are pulled into the plant from the soil. About 90 percent of the water a plant takes up through its roots is released into the atmosphere as water vapor through transpiration. Your idea is to add plants to the flooded area that will transpire the water and take up the fertilizer in their roots.

How much water can a plant take up and release in a certain period of time? In this activity, you will observe transpiration and determine one stem's rate of transpiration.

Materials
- 2 test tubes
- test-tube rack
- water
- coleus or other plant stem cutting
- glass-marking pen
- metric ruler
- clock
- graph paper

Procedure

1. In your ScienceLog, make a data table similar to the one below for recording your measurements.

	Height of Water in Test Tubes	
Time	Test tube with plant	Test tube without plant
Initial		
After 10 min		
After 20 min		
After 30 min		
After 40 min		
Overnight		

DO NOT WRITE IN BOOK

2. Fill each test tube approximately three-fourths full of water. Place both test tubes in a test-tube rack.

3. Place the plant stem so that it stands upright in one of the test tubes. Your test tubes should look like the ones in the photograph at right.

4. Use the glass-marking pen to mark the water level in each of the test tubes. Be sure you have the plant stem in place in its test tube before you mark the water level. Why is this necessary?

 Datasheets for LabBook
Datasheet 29

 Science Skills Worksheet 27
"Interpreting Your Data"

David Sparks
Redwater Junior High School
Redwater, Texas

5. Measure the height of the water in each test tube. Be sure to hold the test tube level, and measure from the waterline to the bottom of the curve at the bottom of the test tube. Record these measurements on the row labeled "Initial."

6. Wait 10 minutes, and measure the height of the water in each test tube again. Record these measurements in your data table.

7. Repeat step 6 three more times. Record your measurements each time.

8. Wait 24 hours, and measure the height of the water in each test tube. Record these measurements in your data table.

9. Construct a graph similar to the one below. Plot the data from your data table. Draw a line for each test tube. Use a different color for each line, and make a key below your graph.

10. Calculate the rate of transpiration for your plant by using the following operations:

Rate of Transpiration

red—test tube without plant
blue—test tube with plant

Test tube with plant:
 Initial height
− Overnight height
 Difference in height of water **(A)**

Test tube without plant:
 Initial height
− Overnight height
 Difference in height of water **(B)**

Water height difference due to transpiration:
 Difference **A**
− Difference **B**
 Water lost due to transpiration (in millimeters) in 24 hours

Analysis

11. What was the purpose of the test tube that held only water?

12. What caused the water to go down in the test tube containing the plant stem? Did the same thing happen in the test tube with water only? Explain your answer.

13. What was the calculated rate of transpiration per day?

14. Using your graph, compare the rate of transpiration with the rate of evaporation alone.

15. Prepare a presentation of your experiment for your class. Use your data tables, graphs, and calculations as visual aids.

Going Further

How many leaves did your plant sprigs have? Use this number to estimate what the rate of transpiration might be for a plant with 200 leaves. When you have your answer in millimeters of height in a test tube, pour this amount into a graduated cylinder to measure it in milliliters.

Answers

11. The test tube that holds only water is a control; it will lose water only by evaporation.

12. Water in the test tube containing the plant stem will be lost through evaporation and transpiration. Evaporation is the only means of water loss in the test tube without the plant stem.

13. This answer will vary according to several variables in the classroom, such as the amount of light and the temperature.

14. This answer will vary. Have students compare and contrast the lines on the graph and explain how the graph is easier to interpret than numbers in a data list.

Going Further
Answers will vary.

Wet, Wiggly Worms!
Teacher's Notes

Time Required

One 45-minute class period

Lab Ratings

EASY ———→ HARD

TEACHER PREP △△
STUDENT SET-UP △△
CONCEPT LEVEL △△
CLEAN UP △△

MATERIALS
The materials listed on the student page are enough for a group of 4–5 students.

Safety Caution

Remind students to review all safety cautions and icons before beginning this lab activity. Students may wish to wear protective gloves while handling the worms.

Wet, Wiggly Worms!

DISCOVERY LAB

Earthworms have been digging in the Earth for more than 100 million years! Earthworms fertilize the soil with their waste and loosen the soil when they tunnel through the moist dirt of a garden or lawn. Worms are food for many animals, such as birds, frogs, snakes, rodents, and fish. Some say they are good food for people, too!

In this activity, you will observe the behavior of a live earthworm. Remember that earthworms are living animals that deserve to be handled gently. Be sure to keep your earthworm moist during this activity. The skin of the earthworm must stay moist so that the worm can get oxygen. If the earthworm's skin dries out, the worm will suffocate and die. Use a spray bottle to moisten the earthworm with water.

Materials

- spray bottle
- dissecting pan
- paper towels
- water
- live earthworm
- probe
- celery leaves
- flashlight
- shoe box with lid
- clock
- soil
- metric ruler

Procedure

1. Place a wet paper towel in the bottom of a dissecting pan. Put a live earthworm on the paper towel, and observe how the earthworm moves. Record your observations in your ScienceLog.

2. Use the probe to carefully touch the anterior end (head) of the worm. Gently touch other areas of the worm's body with the probe. Record the kinds of responses you observe.

3. Place celery leaves at one end of the pan. Record how the earthworm responds to the presence of food.

4. Shine a flashlight on the anterior end of the earthworm. Record the earthworm's reaction to the light.

5. Line the bottom of the shoe box with a damp paper towel. Cover half of the shoe box with the box top.

6. Place the worm on the uncovered side of the shoe box in the light. Record your observations of the worm's behavior for 3 minutes.

732

Gladys Cherniak
St. Paul's Episcopal School
Mobile, Alabama

7. Place the worm in the covered side of the box. Record your observations for 3 minutes.

8. Repeat steps 6–7 three times.

9. Spread some loose soil evenly in the bottom of the shoe box so that it is about 4 cm deep. Place the earthworm on top of the soil. Observe and record the earthworm's behavior for 3 minutes.

10. Dampen the soil on one side of the box, and leave the other side dry. Place the earthworm in the center of the box between the wet and dry soil. Cover the box, and wait 3 minutes. Uncover the box, and record your observations. Repeat this procedure 3 times. (You may need to search for the worm!)

Analysis

11. How did the earthworm respond to being touched? Were some areas more sensitive than others?

12. How is the earthworm's behavior influenced by light? Based on your observations, describe how an animal's response to a stimulus might provide protection for the animal.

13. How did the earthworm respond to the presence of food?

14. When the worm was given a choice of wet or dry soil, which did it choose? Explain this result.

Going Further

Based on your observations of an earthworm's behavior, prepare a poster showing where you might expect to find earthworms. Draw a picture with colored markers, or cut out pictures from magazines. Include all the variables that you used in your experiment, such as soil or no soil, wet or dry soil, light or dark, and food. Write a caption at the bottom of your poster describing where earthworms might be found in nature.

Lab Notes

Earthworms are scientifically classified as animals belonging to the order Oligochaeta, class Chaetopoda, and phylum Annelida. There are about 1,800 species of earthworms. Only two of these are grown commercially. Earthworms have setae, or bristles, located on each segment that help them move. Earthworms have both male and female reproductive organs. They usually do not self-fertilize, but they do exchange sperm as they pass in their burrows. Eggs are deposited in the burrow in a cocoon. The cocoon is manufactured by the clitellum that encircles the body of the worm. Different segments of the earthworm perform different functions, just as each of our body parts do. Earthworms have from 95 to 150 segments, depending on the species.

Datasheets for LabBook
Datasheet 30

Answers

11.–14. Students' answers will vary according to their own observations. They will probably observe that the worm squirms when touched and that some areas are more sensitive than others, such as the clitellum. Students will probably observe that earthworms avoid light. Students should describe the worm's behavior as self-protective.

Going Further

Students' posters should describe warm, wet soil, darkness, and partially decayed organic matter for food.

Aunt Flossie and the Bumblebee
Teacher's Notes

Time Required
One to three 45-minute class periods

Lab Ratings

- TEACHER PREP 🧪🧪
- STUDENT SET-UP 🧪🧪🧪
- CONCEPT LEVEL 🧪🧪
- CLEAN UP 🧪🧪

MATERIALS

The materials listed on the student page are enough for a group of 4–5 students. Materials students may need are construction paper in several bright colors, shoe boxes, scents, honey or some other sweet spread, twine, and binoculars or a hand lens. Encourage students to use recycled materials and to bring in their own supplies.

Safety Caution

Remind students to review all safety cautions and icons before beginning this lab activity.

Tell students to avoid wearing bright floral clothing and perfume or cologne while performing this lab.

All students should be cautious when working with wildlife. Students allergic to insect and bee stings should be excused from this exercise.

Using Scientific Methods

DESIGN YOUR OWN

Aunt Flossie and the Bumblebee

Last week Aunt Flossie came to watch the soccer game, and she was chased by a big yellow-and-black bumblebee. Everyone tried not to laugh, but Aunt Flossie did look pretty funny. She was running and screaming, all perfumed and dressed in a bright floral dress, shiny jewelry, and a huge hat with a big purple bow. No one could understand why the bumblebee tormented Aunt Flossie and left everyone else alone. She said that she would not come to another game until you determine why the bee chased her.

Your job is to design an experiment that will determine why the bee was attracted to Aunt Flossie. You may simulate the situation by using objects that contain the same sensory clues that Aunt Flossie wore that day—bright, shiny colors and strong scents.

Materials
- to be determined by each experimental design and approved by the teacher

Ask a Question

1. Use the information in the story above to help you form questions. Make a list of Aunt Flossie's characteristics on the day of the soccer game. What was Aunt Flossie wearing? What do you think she looked like to a bumblebee? What scent was she wearing? Which of those characteristics may have affected the bee's behavior? What was it about Aunt Flossie that affected the bee's behavior?

Form a Hypothesis

2. Write a hypothesis about insect behavior based on your observations of Aunt Flossie and the bumblebee at the soccer game. A possible hypothesis is, "Insects are attracted to strong floral scents." Write your own hypothesis.

 Datasheets for LabBook
Datasheet 31

Barry Bishop
San Rafael Junior High
Ferron, Utah

Test the Hypothesis

3. Outline a procedure for your experiment. Be sure to follow the steps in the scientific method. Design your procedure to answer specific questions. For example, if you want to know if insects are attracted to different colors, you might want to display cutouts of several colors of paper.

4. Make a list of materials for your experiment. You may want to include colored paper, pictures from magazines, or strong perfumes as bait. You may not use living things as bait in your experiment. Your teacher must approve your experimental design before you begin.

5. Determine a place to conduct your experiment. For example, you may want to place your materials in a box on the ground, or you may want to hang items from a tree branch. **Caution:** Be sure to remain at a safe distance from your experimental setup. Do not touch any insects. Have an adult help you release any insects that are trapped or collected.

6. Develop data tables for recording the results of your trials. For example, a data table similar to the one at right may be used to record the results of testing different colors to see which insects are attracted to them. Design your data tables to fit your investigation.

Analyze the Results

7. Describe your experimental procedure. Did your results support your hypothesis? Explain.

8. Compare your results with those of your classmates. Which hypotheses were supported? What conclusions can you draw from the class results?

Communicate Results

9. Write a letter to Aunt Flossie telling her what you have learned. Tell her what caused the bee attack. Invite her to attend another soccer game, and advise her about what she should or should not wear!

Effects of Color

Color	Number of bees	Number of ants	Number of wasps
Red			
Blue			
Yellow			

DO NOT WRITE IN BOOK

Lab Notes

This lab may need to be done during a certain season in your geographical area. Some students may want to extend their data collection period to several days or weeks.

Answers

7. Students should describe their experimental procedure and include as many steps of the scientific method as possible. All answers will depend on student observations.

8. Answers will vary.

9. Letters will vary, but should demonstrate what the students have learned about insect behavior.

Science Skills Worksheet 13 "Designing an Experiment"

Chapter 14 • LabBook

Porifera's Porosity
Teacher's Notes

Time Required
One 45-minute class period

Lab Ratings

EASY → HARD

- TEACHER PREP 🧪🧪
- STUDENT SET-UP 🧪
- CONCEPT LEVEL 🧪
- CLEAN UP 🧪

MATERIALS

Students may choose a very light absorbent material, such as a tissue, for the Going Further. You may need to have access to an electronic scale.

Safety Caution

Remind students to review all safety cautions and icons before beginning this lab activity.

Preparation Notes

Many students have never touched a natural sponge. Allow them a few moments to experience the feel of a natural sponge, and help them identify the structures. Tell them that the sponges are animals even though they don't appear animal-like. Review the life cycle of a sponge, and discuss how sponges obtain food.

Answers

5. Answers will vary.
6. Answers will vary. Students should subtract the mass of the dry sponge from the mass of the wet sponge.
7. Sponges must hold and filter an enormous amount of water to obtain a small amount of food.

Porifora's Porosity

Sponges are aquatic invertebrate animals that make up the phylum Porifera. Sponges pump water through many tiny pores into their interior. Food for the sponge is filtered out of the water, and then the water leaves through an opening at the top of the sponge.

Early biologists thought sponges were plants because they resemble plants in many ways. For example, the adults attach to a surface and do not move. They cannot chase their food. Sponges absorb and filter a lot of water to get food. In this activity, you will determine how much water sponges can absorb.

Procedure

1. Estimate how much water your sponge can hold. Write your predictions in your ScienceLog.
2. Make data tables for recording your observations.
3. Measure the mass of your sponge before you add water. Record the result. Why do you think this is a necessary step?
4. Pour 500 mL of water into the bowl. Soak the sponge in the bowl. If you are unable to completely soak the sponge, add 100 mL of water to the bowl.
5. Measure how much water is left in the bowl when you remove the sponge. How much water did the sponge absorb?

Analysis

6. How many milliliters of water does your sponge hold per gram of sponge tissue? For example, if your sponge has a dry mass of 12 g and it holds 59.1 mL of water, then your sponge holds 4.9 mL of water per gram. (59.1 mL ÷ 12 g)
7. What feeding advantage does a sponge have because of its ability to hold an enormous amount of water?

Going Further

Repeat this experiment using another kind of absorbent material, such as a paper towel or an artificial sponge. How many milliliters of water does it hold per gram? How does it compare with a natural sponge?

SKILL BUILDER

Materials
- natural sponges
- balance
- water
- beaker
- bowl (large enough for sponge and water)
- calculator (optional)

Going Further

Students will probably find that very few other materials hold as much water as a natural sponge. Students may want to measure the absorbency of disposable diapers. In those, liquid is chemically converted to a gel.

 Datasheets for LabBook Datasheet 32

Kathy LaRoe
East Valley Middle School
East Helena, Montana

The Cricket Caper

Insects are a special class of invertebrates with more than 750,000 known species. Insects may be the most successful group of animals on Earth. In this activity you will observe a cricket's structure and the simple adaptive behaviors that help make it so successful. Remember, you will be handling a living animal that deserves to be treated with care.

Procedure

1. Place a cricket in a clean 600 mL beaker, and quickly cover the beaker with plastic wrap. The supply of oxygen in the container is enough for the cricket to breathe while you complete your work.

2. While the cricket is getting used to the container, make a data table in your ScienceLog similar to the one below. Be sure to allow enough space to write your descriptions.

Materials

- 2 crickets
- 600 mL beakers (2)
- plastic wrap
- apple
- hand lens (optional)
- masking tape
- aluminum foil
- lamp
- 2 sealable plastic bags
- crushed ice
- hot tap water

Cricket Body Structures

Number	Description
Body segments	
Antennae	
Eyes	
Wings	

DO NOT WRITE IN BOOK

3. Without making much movement, begin to examine the cricket. Fill in your data table with your observations of the cricket's structure.

4. Place a small piece of apple in the beaker. Set the beaker on a table. Sit quietly for several minutes and observe the cricket. Any movement may cause the cricket to stop what it is doing. Record your observations in your ScienceLog.

5. Remove the plastic wrap from the beaker, remove the apple, and quickly attach a second beaker. Join the two beakers together at the mouths with masking tape. Handle the beakers carefully. Remember, there is a living animal inside.

Alonda Droege
Pioneer Middle School
Steilacom, Washington

Datasheets for LabBook
Datasheet 33

The Cricket Caper
Teacher's Notes

Time Required
One to two 45-minute class periods

Lab Ratings

EASY ——————→ HARD

- **TEACHER PREP** 🧪🧪🧪
- **STUDENT SET-UP** 🧪🧪
- **CONCEPT LEVEL** 🧪🧪
- **CLEAN UP** 🧪🧪

MATERIALS

The materials listed on the student page are enough for a single student or a small group of students. Instead of 600 mL beakers, you may use the bottom halves of 2 clear plastic 2 L bottles. You will need to prepare these ahead of time. The cut on the bottle should be as even as possible to facilitate taping the open ends together in step 5.

Safety Caution
Remind students to review all safety cautions and icons before beginning this lab activity.

Lab Notes
Explain to students that they must move slowly so they won't startle the cricket and alter its behavior. The apple must be removed in step 5 before the containers are taped together. The apple would be an unwanted variable in the tests that follow.

If you decide to extend this activity over two class periods, the cricket will be fine overnight in a covered 500 mL beaker. The cricket will need a slice of potato or apple for food and moisture.

6. Wrap one of the joined beakers with aluminum foil.

7. If the cricket is hiding under the aluminum foil, gently tap the sides of the beaker until the cricket is exposed. Lay the joined beakers on their sides, and shine a lamp on the uncovered side. Record the cricket's location.

8. Record the cricket's location after 5 minutes. Without disturbing the cricket, carefully move the aluminum foil to the other beaker. After 5 minutes, record the cricket's location. Repeat this process one more time to see if you get the same result.

9. Fill a sealable plastic bag halfway with crushed ice. Fill another bag halfway with hot tap water. Seal each bag, and arrange them side by side on the table.

10. Remove the aluminum foil from the beakers. Gently rock the joined beakers from side to side until the cricket is in the center. Place the beakers on the plastic bags, as shown below.

11. Observe the cricket's behavior for 5 minutes. Record your observations in your ScienceLog.

12. Set the beakers on one end for several minutes to allow them to return to room temperature. Repeat steps 10–12 three times. (Why do you think it is necessary to allow the beakers to return to room temperature each time?)

13. Set the beakers on one end. Carefully remove the masking tape, and separate the beakers. Quickly replace the plastic wrap over the beaker containing the cricket. Allow your cricket to rest while you make two data tables in your ScienceLog similar to those at right.

14. Observe the cricket's movement in the beaker every 15 seconds for 3 minutes. Fill in the Cricket (alone) data table using the following codes: 0 = no movement, 1 = slight movement, and 2 = rapid movement.

15. Obtain a second cricket from your teacher, and place this cricket in the container with the first cricket. Every 15 seconds, record the movement of each cricket in the Cricket A and Cricket B data table using the codes given in step 14.

Analysis

16. Describe crickets' feeding behavior. Are they lappers, suckers, or chewers?

17. Do crickets prefer light or darkness? Explain.

18. From your observations, what can you infer about a cricket's temperature preferences?

19. Based on your observations of Cricket A and Cricket B, what general statements can you make about the social behavior of crickets?

Going Further
Make a third data table titled "Cricket and Another Species of Insect." Introduce another insect, such as a grasshopper, into the beaker. Record your observations for 3 minutes. Write a short summary of the cricket's reaction to another species.

Cricket (alone)	
15 s	
30 s	
45 s	
60 s	
75 s	
90 s	
105 s	
120 s	
135 s	
150 s	
165 s	
180 s	

DO NOT WRITE IN BOOK

Cricket A and Cricket B		
	A	B
15 s		
30 s		
45 s		
60 s		
75 s		
90 s		
105 s		
120 s		
135 s		
150 s		
165 s		
180 s		

DO NOT WRITE IN BOOK

Answers
All answers will depend on the students' observations. The following answers are the expected observations.

12. If the beakers are still warm, experimental conditions will not be the same for each trial.
16. Crickets are chewers.
17. Crickets generally prefer darkness.
18. Crickets will prefer the warmer location.
19. If well-fed, crickets generally tolerate each other very well. However, they will fight and even eat each other if they are not fed properly.

Going Further
Explain to students that both threatening actions and submissive responses are agonistic behaviors that often result in producing a "winner." For example, wolves that snarl and bare their teeth at a competitor for a mate are displaying agonistic behavior. Ask students to watch this activity carefully. Ask them to be attentive so that they will observe the first signs of agonistic behavior if any arise. If the animals show signs that they are going to fight, tell students to remove one of them from the container immediately.

Floating a Pipe Fish
Teacher's Notes

Time Required
One 45-minute class period

Lab Ratings

TEACHER PREP 🧪🧪
STUDENT SET-UP 🧪🧪
CONCEPT LEVEL 🧪🧪
CLEAN UP 🧪

MATERIALS
The materials listed on the student page are enough for 1–2 students. PVC pipe ($\frac{3}{4}$ in.) is readily available at a hardware store and is relatively inexpensive. The pieces should be cut in advance. If your school has a shop or Industrial Arts classroom, perhaps you could get the pieces cut there. The hardware store may cut them for you. If not, PVC pipe is not very difficult to cut with a hand saw.

For water containers, students may use anything that is at least 15 cm deep. A bowl, plastic basin, or bucket will do fine.

Safety Caution
Remind students to review all safety cautions and icons before beginning this lab activity.

Christopher Wood
Western Rockingham
Middle School
Madison, North Carolina

Floating a Pipe Fish

 MAKING MODELS

Bony fishes control how deep or shallow they swim with a special structure called a swim bladder. By adding or taking away gases in the swim bladder, they can control how their body rises or sinks in the water. In this activity, you will make a model of a fish with a swim bladder. Your challenge will be to make the fish float halfway between the top of the water and the bottom of the container. It will probably take several tries and a lot of observing and analyzing along the way.

Materials
- water
- container for water at least 15 cm deep
- slender balloon
- small cork
- 12 cm length of PVC pipe, 3/4 in. diameter
- rubber band

Procedure

1. Estimate how much air you will need in the balloon so that your pipe fish will float halfway between the top of the water and the bottom of the container. Will you need to inflate the balloon halfway, just a small amount, or all the way? It will have to fit inside the pipe, but there will need to be enough air to make the pipe float.

2. Inflate your balloon. Hold the neck of the balloon so that no air escapes, and push the cork into the end of the balloon. If the cork is properly placed, no air should leak out when the balloon is held underwater.

Datasheets for LabBook
Datasheet 34

Science Skills Worksheet 1
"Being Flexible"

3. Place your swim bladder inside the pipe, and place a rubber band along the pipe as shown. The rubber band will keep the swim bladder from coming out of either end.

4. Place your pipe fish in the water, and note where the fish floats. Record your observations in your ScienceLog.

5. If the pipe fish does not float where you want, take it out of the water, adjust the amount of air in the balloon, and try again.

6. You can release small amounts of air from the bladder by carefully lifting the neck of the balloon away from the cork. You can add more air by removing the cork and blowing more air into the balloon. Keep adjusting and testing until your fish floats halfway between the bottom of the container and the top of the water.

Analysis

7. Was the estimate you made in step 1 the correct amount of air your balloon needed to float halfway? Explain your answer.

8. In relation to the length and volume of the entire pipe fish, how much air was needed to make the fish float? State your answer in a proportion or percentage.

9. Based on the amount of space the balloon took up inside the pipe in your model, how much space do you estimate is taken up by a swim bladder inside a living fish? Explain.

Going Further
Some fast-swimming fishes, such as sharks, and marine mammals, such as whales and dolphins, do not have a swim bladder. Find out from the library or the Internet how these animals keep from sinking to the bottom of the ocean. Create a poster, and explain your results on index cards. Include drawings of the fish or marine mammals you have researched.

Answers

7. Students may tend to inflate the balloon too much, causing the pipe to float on the surface. They may be surprised to find out how little air is needed in the balloon to make it float in the middle of the water column. Remind students that the cork has some buoyancy of its own. You may want to substitute something less buoyant for the cork.

8. Filling less than 10 percent of the internal volume of the pipe with air will make the pipe float in the middle of the water column.

9. Have students give this answer in a proportion or fraction. Less than one-third of the inside of the pipe is taken by the inflated balloon. Explain that the flesh of a fish is not as dense as PVC pipe and the swim bladder does not need to be very large to adjust the floating depth of the fish.

Going Further
Sharks and marine mammals, such as dolphins and whales, must swim almost constantly to keep from sinking to the bottom. Dolphins and whales must come to the surface to breathe. A shark must constantly move or lie in moving water in order to keep water moving past its gills. Sharks and marine mammals are able to dive to great depths because they don't have a swim bladder that would rupture under pressure.

Chapter 16 • LabBook

A Prince of a Frog
Teacher's Notes

Time Required
One 45-minute class period

Lab Ratings

TEACHER PREP 🧪🧪🧪
STUDENT SET-UP 🧪
CONCEPT LEVEL 🧪🧪
CLEAN UP 🧪

Safety Caution

Remind students to review all safety cautions and icons before beginning this lab activity.

You will need to provide protective gloves for the students. Students' hands may make the frog vulnerable to infection. Also, frogs are known to carry salmonella. Students should wash their hands thoroughly with soap and warm water after handling the frog.

Kerry A. Johnson
Isbell Middle School
Santa Paula, California

A Prince of a Frog

Imagine that you are a scientist interested in amphibians. You have heard in the news about amphibians disappearing all over the world. What a great loss it will be to the environment if all amphibians become extinct! Your job is to learn as much as possible about how frogs normally behave so that you can act as a resource for other scientists who are studying the problem.

In this activity, you will observe a normal frog in a dry container and in water.

Procedure

1. In your ScienceLog, make a table similar to the one below to note all of your observations of the frog in this investigation.

Observations of a Live Frog	
Characteristic	**Observation**
Breathing	
Eyes	
Legs	
Response to food	
Skin texture	
Swimming behavior	
Skin coloration	

DO NOT WRITE IN BOOK

2. Observe a live frog in a dry container. Draw the frog in your ScienceLog. Label the eyes, nostrils, front legs, and hind legs.

3. Watch the frog's movements as it breathes air with its lungs. Write a description of the frog's breathing in your ScienceLog.

4. Look closely at the frog's eyes, and note their location. Examine the upper and lower eyelids as well as the transparent third eyelid. Which of these three eyelids actually moves over the eye?

5. Study the frog's legs. Note in your data table the difference between the front and hind legs.

SKILL BUILDER

Materials

- live frog in a dry container
- live crickets
- 600 mL beaker
- container half-filled with dechlorinated water
- large rock (optional)
- protective gloves

Datasheets for LabBook
Datasheet 35

Science Skills
Worksheet 23
"Science Drawing"

742 Chapter 16 • LabBook

6. Place a live insect, such as a cricket, in the container. Observe and record how the frog reacts.

7. Carefully pick up the frog, and examine its skin. How does it feel?
   Caution: Remember that a frog is a living thing and deserves to be handled gently and with respect.

8. Place a 600 mL beaker in the container. Place the frog in the beaker. Cover the beaker with your hand, and carry it to a container of dechlorinated water. Tilt the beaker and gently submerge it in the water until the frog swims out of the beaker.

9. Watch the frog float and swim in the water. How does the frog use its legs to swim? Notice the position of the frog's head.

10. As the frog swims, bend down and look up into the water so that you can see the underside of the frog. Then look down on the frog from above. Compare the color on the top and the underneath sides of the frog. Record your observations in your data table.

Analysis

11. From the position of the frog's eyes, what can you infer about the frog's field of vision? How might the position of the frog's eyes benefit the frog while it is swimming?

12. How can a frog "breathe" while it is swimming in water?

13. How are the hind legs of a frog adapted for life on land and in water?

14. What differences did you notice in coloration on the frog's top side and its underneath side? What advantage might these color differences provide?

15. How does the frog eat? What senses are involved in helping the frog catch its prey?

Going Further

Observe another type of amphibian, such as a salamander. How do the adaptations of other types of amphibians compare with those of the frog you observed in this investigation?

Answers

11.–15. Have students speculate about the form and function of the frog's structure. Discuss the camouflage coloration of a frog. Ask how the skin of a frog differs from that of a reptile, and how the two different forms have two different functions. Discuss how the frog's skin must stay wet in order for gas exchange to occur. Have students refer to pages 382–386 for more information about frog physiology.

Going Further

Answers will vary, but students should notice several similar adaptations among amphibians.

Preparation Notes

Frogs collected in the wild are best for this activity because they are easily released. Frogs from pet stores must NOT be released into the wild.

If you can divide the class into groups with several observations going on at the same time, you can use a smaller container for each frog. Containers can be a large glass mixing bowl or something similar. Students may bring containers from home as well. Tree frogs are common in pet stores. They are fun to observe, especially if you can find some small crickets to feed them so that students can observe their feeding behavior.

You may substitute another amphibian, such as water doggies, an immature stage of salamanders. Water doggies are especially interesting if they can be kept in the classroom so students can observe their development into salamanders.

Frogs and water doggies may be obtained in pet stores, in the wild, and in bait shops.

Lab Notes

Several years ago, some students who were out collecting frogs for an activity similar to this lab found severe birth defects and mutations among the frogs they found. A good way to introduce this activity may be to find a news clipping from this event or information about frog deformities taken from the Internet. You may also review the material presented in the first chapter of this book.

Chapter 16 • LabBook

What? No Dentist Bills?
Teacher's Notes

Time Required
Two 45-minute class periods

Lab Ratings

TEACHER PREP 🧪🧪
STUDENT SET-UP 🧪🧪
CONCEPT LEVEL 🧪🧪
CLEAN UP 🧪🧪

MATERIALS
Pea gravel is an acceptable substitute for aquarium gravel. It can be obtained from a local hardware store and is much less expensive.

A 4:1 gravel to birdseed ratio works best.

Safety Caution
Remind students to review all safety cautions and icons before beginning this lab activity.

Answers
4. A bird uses a gizzard instead of teeth.
5. Students should be able to demonstrate how their model gizzard grinds birdseed.
6. Gizzard stones are small pebbles that birds sometimes swallow. They settle in the gizzard and aid in digestion.
7. Model gizzards, no more than three-fourths full, will probably be most effective.
8. Answers may include reducing the amount of food, adding gizzard stones, or adding more liquid to the food.

What? No Dentist Bills?

MAKING MODELS

When you and I eat food, we must chew it well. Our teeth are made for chewing because breaking food down into small bits is the first step in the digestive process. But birds don't have teeth. How do birds make big chunks of food small enough to begin digestion? In this activity, you will design and build a model of a bird's digestive system to find an answer to that question.

Procedure
1. Examine the diagram below of a bird's digestive system. Design a model of a bird's digestive system that you can build using the materials provided by your teacher. Include in your model as many of the following parts as possible: esophagus, crop, gizzard, intestine, cloaca.
2. Obtain a plastic bag and the materials you need from your teacher, and build your model.
3. Test your model using the birdseed provided by your teacher.

Analysis
4. How can a bird break down food particles without teeth?
5. Did your bird gizzard grind the food?
6. What are gizzard stones, and what do they do?
7. Does the amount of material added to your model gizzard change its ability to work effectively?
8. Describe how you could improve your model.

Materials
- several sealable plastic bags of various sizes
- birdseed
- aquarium gravel
- water
- string
- drinking straw
- transparent tape
- scissors or other materials as needed

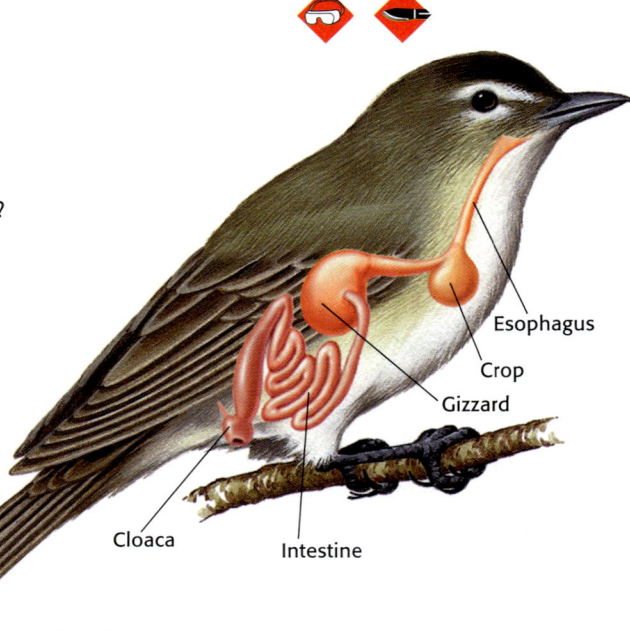

Going Further
Did you know that "gizzard stones" have been found at the sites of fossilized dinosaur skeletons? Look in the library or on the Internet for information about the evolutionary relationship between dinosaurs and birds. List the similarities and differences you find.

Going Further
Scientists have long recognized similarities between birds and some dinosaurs, including an S-shaped neck, a unique ankle joint, and hollow bones.

 Datasheets for LabBook
Datasheet 36

Randy Christian
Stovall Junior High School
Houston, Texas

Wanted: Mammals on Mars

DISCOVERY LAB

The year is 2256. There have been colonies on Mars for almost 50 years. Martian water is scarce but available, and temperatures are still extreme but livable. The Martian planet has slowly developed an atmosphere that humans can breathe due to the efforts of many scientists during the last 200 years. The Interplanetary Commission has decreed that mammals from several different habitats on Earth should be sent to Mars. There they will be housed in a zoo so they can become accustomed to the climate before they are released in the wild.

Your job is to prepare a presentation for the Interplanetary Commission that describes at least three mammals that you think might be able to survive in a zoo on Mars. Select one mammal from a water environment, one mammal from a land environment, and one mammal that lives in the air part of the time.

Materials

- colored markers, crayons, pens, or similar drawing equipment
- poster paper, rolls of newsprint, or other drawing paper
- other materials as needed

TRY at HOME

Procedure

1. Research in the library or on the Internet to obtain information about the Martian environment as it is today. How might an atmosphere change the environment?

2. Research in the library or on the Internet to learn about different species of mammals and their environments on Earth. Use this information to select mammals that you think might be able to live on Mars.

3. Prepare your presentation for the Interplanetary Commission. Your presentation can be a poster, a mural, a diorama, a computer presentation, or any other format that you choose. Make sure your format is approved by your teacher.

Analysis

4. Name and describe the mammals you chose. Explain why you think your choice of mammals would be the right one for a zoo on Mars.

5. Describe what additions or changes should be made at the zoo to accommodate each of your mammals.

Datasheets for LabBook
Datasheet 37

Wanted: Mammals on Mars
Teacher's Notes

Time Required
One or two 45-minute class periods

Lab Ratings

TEACHER PREP 🧪🧪
STUDENT SET-UP 🧪🧪
CONCEPT LEVEL 🧪🧪
CLEAN UP 🧪

Answers

4. Students should remember that this lab is about mammals. Remind them that they should select an aquatic mammal, which would limit their choices to whales, dolphins, sea lions, beavers, and the like. Similarly, the one that lives in the air part of the time might be a bat, a "flying squirrel," or with a little imagination, a mammal that lives high in a tree, such as a sloth. The reasons for choosing a particular animal should have to do with available resources and the habitat the animal requires.

5. Answers will vary according to the animals chosen by the student. All accommodations should have something to do with mammalian characteristics and habitat resources.

Martha Kisiah
Fairview Middle School
Tallahassee, Florida

Adaptation: It's a Way of Life
Teacher's Notes

Time Required
One or two 45-minute class periods

Lab Ratings

TEACHER PREP 🧪🧪
STUDENT SET-UP 🧪🧪
CONCEPT LEVEL 🧪🧪
CLEAN UP 🧪

MATERIALS

The materials listed on the student page are enough for a group of 4–5 students. Materials for this activity can include recycled materials, glue, buttons, pipe cleaners, poster paints and brushes, and any number of other art or craft supplies. Have students bring in as much as they can for their own project and to share.

Lab Notes

This lab provides an opportunity for students to exercise a great deal of creativity and to expand their understanding of adaptations. Most students will probably enjoy choosing the adaptations and inventing a niche where those adaptations are useful. Help them understand that environments and adaptations usually evolve together in the natural world, not one before the other. You may want to make sets of the adaptations and put them in a container for students to draw from. Doing this may lessen duplication in the classroom. Someone might be challenged to design a flying decomposer with armor!

Adaptation: It's a Way of Life

MAKING MODELS

Since the beginning of life on Earth, species have had special characteristics called adaptations that have helped them survive changes in environmental conditions. Changes in a species' environment include climate changes, habitat destruction, or the extinction of prey. These things can cause a species to die out unless the species has a characteristic that helps it survive. For example, a species of bird may have an adaptation for eating sunflower seeds and ants. If the ant population dies out, the bird can still eat seeds and can therefore survive.

In this activity, you will explore several adaptations and design an organism with adaptations you choose. Then you will describe how these adaptations help the organism survive.

Materials
- poster board
- colored markers
- magazines for cutouts
- other arts-and-crafts materials
- scissors

Procedure

1. Study the chart below. Choose one adaptation from each column. For example, an organism might be a scavenger that burrows underground and has spikes on its tail!

Adaptations		
Diet	**Type of transportation**	**Special adaptation**
carnivore	flies	uses sensors to detect heat
herbivore	glides through the air	is active only at night and has excellent night vision
omnivore	burrows underground	changes colors to match its surroundings
scavenger	runs fast	has armor
decomposer	swims	has horns
	hops	can withstand extreme temperature changes
	walks	secretes a terrible and sickening scent
	climbs	has poison glands
	floats	has specialized front teeth
	slithers	has tail spikes
		stores oxygen in its cells so it does not have to breathe continuously
		one of your own invention

 Datasheets for LabBook
Datasheet 38

Alonda Droege
Pioneer Middle School
Steilacom, Washington

2. Design an organism that has the three adaptations you have chosen. Use poster board, colored markers, picture cutouts, or craft materials of your choosing to create your organism.

3. Write a caption on your poster describing your organism. Describe its appearance, its habitat, its niche, and how its adaptations help it survive. Give your animal a two-part "scientific" name based on its characteristics.

4. Display your creation in your classroom. Share with classmates how you chose the adaptations for your organism.

Analysis

5. What does your imaginary organism eat?

6. In what environment or habitat would your organism be most likely to survive—in the desert, tropical rain forest, plains, icecaps, mountains, or ocean? Explain your answer.

7. Is your creature a mammal, a reptile, an amphibian, a bird, or a fish? What modern organism (on Earth today) or ancient organism (extinct) is your imaginary organism most like? Explain the similarities between the two organisms. Do some research outside of the lab, if necessary, to find out about a real organism that your imaginary organism may be similar to.

8. If a sudden climate change occurred, such as daily downpours of rain in a desert, would your imaginary organism survive? What adaptations for surviving such a change does it have?

Going Further

Call or write to an agency such as the U.S. Fish and Wildlife Service to get a list of endangered species in your area. Choose an organism on that list. Describe the organism's niche and any special adaptations it has that help it survive. Find out why it is endangered and what is being done to protect it.

Examine the illustration of the animal at right. Based on its physical characteristics, describe its habitat and niche. Is this a real animal?

Answers

5.–7. All answers will depend on the adaptations that the student chose and the organism the student invented. Students should relate one or more adaptations to the kinds of food the organism eats, where the animal lives, or what kind of animal it is.

8. Several adaptations can be given, but expect a few to say their animals don't survive.

Going Further

This is a good activity to expand your study of the environment. Students can relate problems in the area where they live to adaptations. Often, people wonder why an organism doesn't just "adapt" to changes in its environment. This is a good opportunity to learn firsthand why that can't happen within the span of a single generation and why organisms become endangered.

The animal in the illustration is a duckbilled platypus, an actual mammal. The platypus has webbed feet and a flat tail that help it swim through the water. It also uses claws to dig, and a flat, rubbery bill to search the mud for worms, crayfish, and other food. The duckbilled platypus lives in the rivers and ponds of Australia.

Capturing the Wild Bean
Teacher's Notes

Time Required
One 45-minute class period

Lab Ratings

TEACHER PREP 🧪🧪
STUDENT SET-UP 🧪🧪
CONCEPT LEVEL 🧪🧪
CLEAN UP 🧪

MATERIALS
The materials listed on the student page are enough for a group of 4–5 students. Large, dried beans of any kind will work well in this exercise.

Safety Caution
Remind students to review all safety cautions and icons before beginning this lab activity.

Lab Notes
Explain to students that this is a very common method used in field biology by scientists who need to count a population that is on the move, such as a flock of migratory birds. Explain that scientists always mark their captures in a way that neither harms the organism nor alters its behavior.

Capturing the Wild Bean

When wildlife biologists study a group of organisms in an area, they need to know how many organisms live there. Occasionally, biologists worry that a certain organism is outgrowing the environment's carrying capacity. Other times, scientists need to know if an organism is becoming rare so steps can be taken to protect it. However, animals can be difficult to count because they can move around and hide. Because of this, biologists have developed methods to estimate the number of animals in a specific area. One of these counting methods is called the mark-recapture method.

In this activity, you will enter the territory of the wild pinto bean to get an estimation of the number of beans that live in their paper-bag habitat.

Materials
- small paper lunch bag
- pinto beans
- permanent marker
- calculator (optional)

Procedure

1. Prepare a data table in your ScienceLog like the one below.

Mark-Recapture Data Table				
Number of animals in first capture	Total number of animals in recapture	Number of marked animals in recapture	Calculated estimate of population	Actual total population
		DO NOT WRITE IN BOOK		

2. Your teacher will provide you with a paper bag containing an unknown number of beans. Carefully reach into the bag and remove a handful of beans.

3. Count the number of beans you have "captured," and record this number in your data table under "Number of animals in first capture."

 Datasheets for LabBook
Datasheet 39

 Science Skills Worksheet 30
"Hints for Oral Presentations"

Jason Marsh
Montevideo High and Country School
Montevideo, Minnesota

4. Use the permanent marker to carefully mark each bean that you have just counted. Allow the marks to dry completely. When you are certain that all the marks are dry, place the marked beans back into the bag.

5. Gently mix the beans in the bag so the marks won't rub off. Once again, reach into the bag, "capture," and remove a handful of beans.

6. Count the number of beans in your "recapture." Record this number in your data table under "Total number of animals in recapture."

7. Count the beans in your recapture with marks from the first capture. Record this number in your data table under "Number of marked animals in recapture."

8. Calculate your estimation of the total number of beans in the bag using the following equation:

$$\frac{\text{total number of beans in recapture} \times \text{total number of beans marked}}{\text{number of marked beans in recapture}} = \text{calculated estimate of population}$$

Enter this number in your data table under "Calculated estimate of population."

9. Replace all the beans in the bag. Then empty the bag on your work table. Be careful that no beans escape! Count each bean as you place them one at a time back into the bag. Record the number in your data table under "Actual total population."

Analysis

10. How close was your estimate to the actual number of beans?

11. If your estimate was not close to the actual number of beans, how might you change your mark-recapture procedure? If you did not recapture any marked beans, what might be the cause?

Going Further

How could you use the mark-recapture method to estimate the population of turtles in a small pond? Explain your procedure.

Answers

10. Have students evaluate their estimate. Ask them if they think their estimate was close enough to the actual number of beans in the bag.

11. Samples that are too small can lead to incorrect estimates. If no marked beans were recaptured, then the sample was too small, and increasing the sample size would improve the procedure. A sample should be large enough to allow a scientist to accurately estimate the organisms in the population without having to count every single organism.

Math Skills Worksheet 39 "Random Samples: Estimating Population"

Going Further

Students should state the size of the pond and form a reasonable hypothesis, including how many animals should be in the sample size. Students should describe a way to capture turtles without harming them. They should recommend a marking method that will not harm the turtles or alter the turtles' behavior. The turtles should be returned in their environment immediately and given a day or two to recover from the trauma.

Important: students should recognize the need for the recapture size to be the same size as the original capture size.

Nitrogen Needs
Teacher's Notes

Time Required
One 45-minute class period

Lab Ratings

EASY → HARD

TEACHER PREP 🧪🧪
STUDENT SET-UP 🧪🧪🧪
CONCEPT LEVEL 🧪🧪🧪
CLEAN UP 🧪🧪

MATERIALS
Dead insects may or may not be easy to come by. You may want to go to a pet store and purchase crickets. They are usually small and very inexpensive. If the insects you use are small, you will need more than five of them.

Safety Caution
Remind students to review all safety cautions and icons before beginning this lab activity. Spills should be cleaned up immediately. Hands should be washed thoroughly after all lab activities.

Preparation Notes
Caution students to collect insects carefully, wearing gardening gloves, shoes, and socks.

If you purchase insects, you can humanely kill them by placing them in a jar containing a cotton ball soaked in rubbing alcohol.

Nitrogen Needs

DISCOVERY LAB

The nitrogen cycle is one of several cycles that are vital to living organisms. Without nitrogen, living organisms cannot make amino acids, the building blocks of proteins. Animals obtain nitrogen by eating plants that contain nitrogen and by eating animals that eat those plants. When animals die, decomposers return the nitrogen to the soil in the form of a chemical called ammonia.

In this activity, you will be investigating the nitrogen cycle inside a closed system to discover how decomposers return nitrogen to the soil.

Procedure

1. Fit a piece of filter paper into a funnel. Place the funnel inside a 50 mL beaker, and pour 5 g of soil into the funnel. Add 25 mL of distilled water to the soil.

2. Test the filtered water with pH paper, and record your observations in your ScienceLog.

3. Place some soil in a jar to cover the bottom about 5 cm deep. Add 10 mL of distilled water to the soil.

4. Place the dead insects in the jar, and seal the jar with the lid.

5. Check the jar each day for 5 days for an ammonia odor. (If you do not know what ammonia smells like, ask your teacher.) Record your observations in your ScienceLog.
Caution: Your teacher will demonstrate how to check for a chemical odor by wafting. Do not put your nose in the jar and inhale!

6. On the fifth day, place a second piece of filter paper into the funnel, and place the funnel inside a 50 mL beaker. Remove about 5 g of soil from the jar, and place it in the funnel. Add 25 mL of distilled water to the soil.

7. Once again, test the filtered water with pH paper, and record your observations in your ScienceLog.

Materials
- 2 pieces of filter paper
- funnel
- 50 mL beaker
- balance
- commercially prepared potting soil without fertilizer
- 25 mL graduated cylinder
- 60 mL of distilled water
- pH paper
- 1 pt (or 500 mL) jar with lid
- 5 large, dead insects from home or schoolyard
- protective gloves

Datasheets for LabBook
Datasheet 40

CLASSROOM TESTED & APPROVED

David Sparks
Redwater Junior High School
Redwater, Texas

750 Chapter 19 • LabBook

Analysis

8. What was the pH of the water in the beaker in the first trial? A pH of 7 indicates that the water is neutral. A pH below 7 indicates that the water is acidic, and a pH above 7 indicates that the water is basic.

9. What was the pH of the water in the beaker in the second trial? Explain the difference, if any, between the results of the first trial and the results of the second trial.

10. Based on the results of your pH tests, do you think ammonia is acidic or basic?

11. On which days in your investigation were you able to detect an ammonia odor? Explain what caused the odor.

12. Describe the importance of decomposers in the nitrogen cycle.

Going Further

Test ammonia's importance to plants. Fill two 12 cm flowerpots with commercially prepared potting soil and water. Be sure to use soil that has had no fertilizer added. Plant six radish seeds in each pot. Water your seeds so that the soil is constantly damp but not soaked. Keep your pots in a sunny window. You may plant other seeds of your choice, but do not use legume (bean) seeds. Research to find out why!

Use a plant fertilizer mixed according to the directions on the container to fertilize one of the pots once a week. Water the other pot once a week with tap water.

After the seedlings appear, use a metric ruler to measure the growth of the plants in both pots. Measure the plants once a week, and record your results in your ScienceLog.

Answers

8. The filtered water in the first trial should be slightly acidic; however, this will depend on the type of potting soil you are using. The soil pH may not fall inside the ranges shown in the chart. If not, expand the chart and explain to students that pH is a relative value.

9. If ammonia is present, the filtered water will be more basic than the filtered water in the first trial. Decomposition of the dead insects should be the only difference between the first and second trials.

10. Ammonia is basic.

11. Answers will vary. Students should understand that the odor is from bacterial conversion of nitrogen to ammonia.

12. Decomposers convert nitrogen to a form that plants can use. Nitrogen is essential for plants.

Going Further

The plants grown with ammonia should be bigger and fuller. The plants grown without ammonia may not survive. The only difference between the two pots should be nutrients.

A Passel o' Pioneers
Teacher's Notes

Time Required
One 45-minute class and three 5-minute periodic observation periods

Lab Ratings

TEACHER PREP 🧪🧪
STUDENT SET-UP 🧪🧪
CONCEPT LEVEL 🧪🧪🧪
CLEAN UP 🧪🧪

MATERIALS
The materials suggested for this lab are enough for the entire class. You may want to use a large container, such as a 10 gal aquarium, so each student in the class can contribute a small amount of soil from different areas. Students might be able to bring fishbowls from home. If you have enough fishbowls and sunny windows, students really might enjoy seeing what comes up in their own container. If you do not have a sunny window, the containers can be placed where they will get the most light in the classroom. They need warmth to germinate, and light is necessary after the seedlings emerge from the soil. A local-area field guide might be helpful in identifying plants.

Safety Caution
Remind students to review all safety cautions and icons before beginning this lab activity. Check for any known allergies to molds before having students begin this lab. There may be molds in the soil.

A Passel o' Pioneers

MAKING MODELS

Succession is the natural process of the introduction and development of living things in an area. The area could be one that has never supported life before and has no soil, such as a recently cooled lava flow from a volcano. In an area where there is no soil, the process is called primary succession. In an area where soil already exists, such as an abandoned field or a forest after a fire, the process is called secondary succession.

In this investigation, you will build a model of secondary succession using natural soil.

Procedure

1. Place the natural soil you brought from home or the schoolyard into the fishbowl, and dampen the soil with 250 mL of water. Cover the top of the fishbowl with plastic wrap, and place the fishbowl in a sunny window.
   Caution: Do not touch your face, eyes, or mouth during this activity. Wash your hands thoroughly when you are finished.

2. For 2 weeks, observe the fishbowl for any new growth. Describe and draw any new organisms you observe. Record these and all other observations in your ScienceLog.

3. Identify and record the names of as many of these new organisms as you can.

Materials
- 500 g of soil from home or schoolyard
- balance
- large fishbowl
- 250 mL of water
- 250 mL graduated cylinder
- plastic wrap
- protective gloves

 Datasheets for LabBook
Datasheet 41

Kerry Johnson
Isbell Middle School
Santa Paula, California

Analysis

4. What kinds of plants sprouted in your model of secondary succession? Were they tree seedlings, grasses, or weeds?

5. Were the plants that sprouted in the fishbowl unusual or common for your area?

6. Explain how the plants that grew in your model of secondary succession can be called pioneer species.

Going Further

Examine each of the photographs on this page. Determine whether each area, if abandoned forever, would undergo primary or secondary succession. You may decide that an area will not undergo succession at all. Explain your reasoning.

Bulldozed land

Eutrophic pond

Shipping port parking lot

Mount St. Helens volcano

Going Further

- **Eutrophic pond:** A eutrophic pond will eventually fill with sediment. First aquatic plants will grow. When the pond is completely filled, the area will undergo secondary succession.

- **Bulldozed land:** Left abandoned, this area will undergo secondary succession just as abandoned farmland will.

- **Shipping port parking lot:** If abandoned forever, cracks will appear exposing the soil underneath, and secondary succession will proceed. Some areas of this vast parking lot may even undergo primary succession, where concrete surfaces can be home to lichens.

- **Mount St. Helens volcano:** When Mount St. Helens exploded, it caused an enormous mudslide and released tons of ash. Areas smothered by ash underwent primary succession. The entire region is now in various stages of secondary succession.

Answers

4. Plants that sprout should be plants common to the local area. They can be identified using a local-area field guide as soon as dicot seedlings have developed true leaves. Monocots will probably look like grasses.

5. Answers will vary. Students should recognize common plants.

6. All the plants that come up in students' models of succession are pioneers because they are the first plants to grow in an area. Ask students if a tree can be a pioneer. (Yes; if it is one of the first plants to grow in an area. However, pioneers are usually plants that grow fast and produce many seeds that are dispersed over a large area.)

Life in the Desert
Teacher's Notes

Time Required
One 45-minute class period

Lab Ratings

- TEACHER PREP 🧪
- STUDENT SET-UP 🧪🧪
- CONCEPT LEVEL 🧪🧪
- CLEAN UP 🧪

MATERIALS

The sponges used in this lab can be either natural sponges or the synthetic sponges available in grocery stores. Use 3 × 6 in. sponges, 1 per student, cut in half.

Answers

6. Students should describe the kind of covering or protection they provided for their "adapted" sponge. Effectiveness of the adaptation will be measured by the amount of water lost over 24 hours. Students will want their sponges to dry out as little as possible.

7. The unprotected sponge represents the organism that has no adaptation for conserving water. The unprotected sponge should dry out far more than the protected sponge.

James Chin
Frank A. Day Middle School
Newtonville, Massachusetts

Life in the Desert

Organisms that live in the desert have some very unusual methods for conserving water. Conserving water is an important function for all organisms that live on land, but it is a special challenge for animals that live in the desert. In this activity you will invent an "adaptation" for a desert animal, represented by a piece of sponge, to find out how much water the animal can conserve over a 24-hour period. You will protect your wet desert sponge so it will dry out as little as possible.

Materials

- 2 pieces of dry sponge (8 × 8 × 2 cm)
- water
- balance
- other materials as needed

Procedure

1. Plan a method for keeping your "desert animal" from drying out. Your "animal" must be in the open for at least 4 hours during the 24-hour period. Real desert animals often expose themselves to the dry desert heat in order to search for food. Write your plan in your ScienceLog. Write down your predictions about the outcome of your experiment.

2. Design data tables, if necessary, and draw them in your ScienceLog. Have your teacher approve your plan before you begin.

3. Soak two pieces of sponge in water until they begin to drip. Place each piece on a balance, and record its mass in your ScienceLog.

4. Immediately begin to protect one piece of sponge according to your plan. Place both of the pieces together in an area where they will not be disturbed. You may take your protected "animal" out for feeding as often as you want, for a total of at least 4 hours.

5. At the end of 24 hours, place each piece of sponge on the balance again, and record its mass in your ScienceLog.

Analysis

6. Describe the adaptation you used to help your "animal" survive. Was it effective? Explain.

7. What was the purpose of leaving one of the sponges unprotected? How did the water loss in each of your sponges compare?

Going Further

Conduct a class discussion about other adaptations and results. How can you relate these invented adaptations to adaptations for desert survival among real organisms?

Going Further

Ask students to consider the adaptation they designed for their sponge. Did it compare with a real-life adaptation in a desert organism? In what way? Discuss behavior adaptations for conserving water. Discuss endothermy and ectothermy, and ask students what adaptations conserve water and help regulate body heat.

Datasheets for LabBook
Datasheet 42

Discovering Mini-Ecosystems

In your study of ecosystems you learned that a biome is a very large ecosystem that includes a set of smaller, related ecosystems. For example, a coniferous forest biome may include a river ecosystem, a wetland ecosystem, and a lake ecosystem. Each of those ecosystems may include several other smaller, related ecosystems. Even cities have mini-ecosystems! You may find a mini-ecosystem on a patch of sidewalk, in a puddle of rainwater, under a leaky faucet, in a shady area, or under a rock. In this activity, you will design a method for comparing two different mini-ecosystems found near your school.

Materials

- materials as needed for each investigation

Procedure

1. Examine the grounds around your school, and select two different areas you wish to investigate. Be sure to get your teacher's approval before you begin.

2. Decide what you want to learn about your mini-ecosystems. For example, you may want to know what kind of living things each area contains. You may want to list the abiotic factors of each mini-ecosystem.

3. For each mini-ecosystem, make data tables for recording your observations. You may choose to observe the mini-ecosystems for an hour. You may choose to observe the mini-ecosystems for a short period of time at several different times during the day or at the same time for several days. Get your plan approved by your teacher, and make the appropriate data tables.

Analysis

4. What factors determine the differences between your mini-ecosystems? Identify the factors that set each mini-ecosystem apart from its surrounding area.

5. How do the populations of your mini-ecosystems compare?

6. Identify some of the adaptations that the organisms living in your two mini-ecosystems have. Describe how the adaptations help the organisms survive in their environment.

7. Write a report describing and comparing your mini-ecosystems with those of your classmates.

Discovering Mini-Ecosystems
Teacher's Notes

Time Required
One to two 45-minute class periods

Lab Ratings

EASY ———— HARD

- **TEACHER PREP** 🧪
- **STUDENT SET-UP** 🧪🧪
- **CONCEPT LEVEL** 🧪🧪🧪
- **CLEAN UP** 🧪

MATERIALS
Because this is mainly an observation activity, few materials are needed. If they are available, however, binoculars or magnifying lenses may be helpful.

Lab Notes
Even if your school has no area where there is sand, dirt, grass, or trees, ask students to observe puddles, the underside of eaves, the area under drain spouts, and the ground under rocks. Students should observe the areas they have chosen at least twice a day.

 Datasheets for LabBook
Datasheet 43

Barry Bishop
San Rafael Junior High
Ferron, Utah

Answers

4. Students may have many answers, but they should include answers such as different vegetation, organisms that live there, the soil type, density of vegetation, and amount of water present.

5. Students should recognize that the populations present in each area are adapted for life in that area.

6. Adaptations that students name will probably include camouflage, deep roots, and burrowing behavior.

7. Answers will vary according to student observations.

Chapter 20 • LabBook

Too Much of a Good Thing?
Teacher's Notes

Time Required
One 45-minute class period and one 10-minute observation time every 3 days for 3 weeks

Lab Ratings

- TEACHER PREP 🧪🧪
- STUDENT SET-UP 🧪🧪
- CONCEPT LEVEL 🧪🧪🧪
- CLEAN UP 🧪🧪

MATERIALS
The materials listed on the student page are enough for 1–2 students. This lab is a good opportunity to recycle glass jars or clear plastic 2 L soda bottles. Any container that is transparent and will hold at least 1 L of water will do.

Safety Caution
Remind students to review all safety cautions and icons before beginning this lab activity.

Preparation Notes
A review of the causes of eutrophication might be helpful before beginning this lab.

Jason Marsh
Montevideo High and Country School
Montevideo, Minnesota

Too Much of a Good Thing?

Plants require nutrients, such as phosphates and nitrates. Phosphates are often found in detergents. Nitrates are often found in animal wastes and fertilizers. When large amounts of these nutrients are released into rivers and lakes, algae and plant life grow rapidly and then die off. Microorganisms that decompose the dead matter use up oxygen in the water, causing the death of fish and other animals that depend on oxygen. This process often results in a pond or lake filling unnaturally.

In this activity, you will observe the effect of fertilizers on organisms that live in pond water.

Procedure

1. Use a wax pencil to label one jar "Control," the second jar "Fertilizer," and the third jar "Excess fertilizer."

2. Pour 750 mL of distilled water in each of the jars. Read the label on the fertilizer container to determine the recommended amount of fertilizer. To the "Fertilizer" jar, add the amount of fertilizer recommended for 750 mL of water. To the "Excess fertilizer" jar, add 10 times this amount. Stir the contents of each jar to dissolve the fertilizer.

3. Obtain a sample of pond water. Stir it gently but thoroughly to make sure that the organisms in it are evenly distributed. Pour 100 mL of pond water into each of the three jars.

4. Observe a drop of pond water from each jar under the microscope. Draw at least four of the organisms. Determine whether the organisms you see are algae, which are usually green, or consumers, which are usually able to move. Describe the number and type of organisms in the pond water.

5. Cover each jar loosely with plastic wrap. Place them near a sunny window, but do not place them in direct sunlight.

SKILL BUILDER

Materials
- wax pencil
- 1 qt (or 1 L) jars (3)
- 2.25 L of distilled water
- fertilizer
- graduated cylinder
- stirring rod
- 300 mL of pond water containing living organisms
- eyedropper
- microscope
- microscope slides with coverslips
- plastic wrap
- protective gloves

Common Pond-Water Organisms

Volvox (producer) *Spirogyra* (producer)

Vorticella (consumer) *Daphnia* (consumer)

756 Chapter 20 • LabBook

6. Based on your understanding of how ponds and lakes eventually fill to become dry land, make a prediction about how the pond organisms will grow in each of the three jars.

7. Make three data tables in your ScienceLog. Be sure to allow enough space to record your observations. Title one table "Control," as shown below. Title another table "Fertilizer," and title the third table "Excess fertilizer."

Control			
Date	Color	Odor	Other observations

DO NOT WRITE IN BOOK

8. Observe the jars when you first set them up and at least once every 3 days for the next 3 weeks. Note the color, odor, and any visible presence of organisms. Record your observations.

9. When organisms begin to be visible in the jars, use an eyedropper to remove a sample from each jar, and observe the sample under the microscope. How have the number and type of organisms changed since you first looked at the pond water? Record your observations.

10. At the end of the 3-week period, remove a sample from each jar and observe each sample under the microscope. Draw at least four of the most abundant organisms and describe how the number and type of organisms have changed since your last microscopic observation.

Analysis

11. After 3 weeks, which jar shows the most abundant growth of algae? What may have caused this growth?

12. Did you observe any effects on organisms (other than the algae) in the jar with the most abundant algal growth? Explain.

13. Did your observations match your prediction? Explain.

14. How might the rapid filling of natural ponds and lakes be prevented or slowed?

Answers

11. Answers will vary. Occasionally, the jar with excess fertilizer will grow beyond the carrying capacity of algae or other organisms and will crash.

12. Animal organisms occasionally die from the toxic effects of the fertilizer. When algae growth is overwhelming, the depletion of oxygen in the water will have a detrimental effect on animal organisms.

13. Answers will vary. Students should defend their prediction.

14. Answers will vary, but most students will say that we need to use less fertilizer. Eutrophication is continuously occurring and is a natural process. Fertilizers artificially hasten the process. Have students discuss how the global food supply might be affected if no fertilizers were used to grow crops. Then ask them to brainstorm to come up with some solutions.

Datasheets for LabBook
Datasheet 44

Biodiversity—What a Disturbing Thought!
Teacher's Notes

Time Required
One or two 45-minute class periods

Lab Ratings

- TEACHER PREP 🧪🧪
- STUDENT SET-UP 🧪🧪
- CONCEPT LEVEL 🧪🧪
- CLEAN UP 🧪🧪

MATERIALS
Binoculars may not be available in your classroom. Ask students if they might have some at home they could get permission to bring to class for this activity.

Lab Notes
The lab should be reviewed ahead of time. This lab can be extended to a field trip that can get parents involved. Your school may be in a city where there is no suitable undisturbed area. If you are unable to take students on a field trip, help them understand the difference between severely disturbed (a paved parking lot) and an area that is less disturbed, such as an unimproved lot. Some diversity should exist in every area. You may find this lab interesting to repeat during different seasons.

Using Scientific Methods

Biodiversity—What a Disturbing Thought!

Biodiversity is important for the survival of each organism in a community. Producers, consumers, and decomposers all play a cooperative role in an ecosystem.

In this activity you will investigate areas outside your school to determine which areas contain the greatest biodiversity. You will use the information you gather to determine whether a forest or an area planted with crops is more diverse.

Form a Hypothesis
1. Based on your understanding of biodiversity, do you expect a forest or an area planted with crops to be more diverse?

Make a Prediction
2. Select an area that is highly disturbed (such as a mowed yard) and one that is relatively undisturbed (such as an abandoned flower bed or a vacant lot). Make a prediction about which area contains the greater biodiversity. Get your teacher's approval of your selected locations.

Conduct an Experiment
3. Design a procedure to determine which area contains the greatest biodiversity, and have your plan approved by your teacher before you begin.

4. To discover smaller organisms, measure off a square meter, set stakes at the corners, and mark the area with twine. Use a magnifying lens to observe tiny organisms. Don't worry about the scientific names. When you record your observations, refer to organisms in the following way: Ant A, Ant B, and so on. Observe each area quietly, and make note of any visits by birds or other larger organisms.

DISCOVERY LAB

Materials
- materials and tools necessary to carry out your investigation with your teacher's approval. Possible materials include a meterstick, binoculars, magnifying lens, twine, and forceps.

Terry Rakes
Elmwood Junior High School
Rogers, Arkansas

758 Chapter 21 • LabBook

5. In your ScienceLog, create any data tables that you might need for recording your data. If you observe your areas on more than one occasion, be sure to make data tables for each observation period. Organize your data into categories that are clear and understandable.

Analyze the Results

6. Did your data support your hypothesis? Explain.

7. What factors did you consider before deciding which habitats were disturbed or undisturbed? Explain why those factors were important.

8. What problems did you find in making observations and recording data for each habitat? Describe how you solved them.

9. Describe possible errors in your investigation method. Suggest ways to improve your procedure to eliminate those errors.

Draw Conclusions

10. Do you think the biodiversity outside your school has decreased since the school was built? Why or why not?

11. Both areas shown in the photographs at right are beautiful to observe. One of them, however, is very low in biodiversity. Describe each photograph, and account for the difference in biodiversity.

Going Further

Research rain-forest biodiversity in the library or on the Internet. Find out what factors exist in the rain forest that make that biome so diverse. How might the biodiversity of a rain forest compare with that of a forest community near your school?

Prairie grasses and wildflowers

Wheat field

Datasheets for LabBook
Datasheet 45

Science Skills Worksheet 19
"Researching on the Web"

Answers

6. Students should explain why they predicted one area would be more diverse than the other. If their predictions were confirmed, have them explain if their reasons were also correct.

7. Generally, any area inside a city or even farmland is considered ecologically disturbed. This is the conclusion you want students to come to. Students should consider human impact when deciding if an area is disturbed or undisturbed.

8. Answers will vary.

9. A possible error might be deciding that an area is undisturbed and finding that it is highly disturbed and has little diversity. A bed of petunias is lovely, but it is disturbed and not very diverse, especially if it is well weeded and insect controlled.

10. Answers will vary. Discuss construction and growth in the neighborhood since the school was built.

11. A wheat field is less diverse than a tall-grass prairie. The wheat field grows only one plant and provides little habitat for animal organisms. Some animals may visit and feed there, but their nests or dens would be in danger at harvest time.

Going Further

Have students compare a nearby forest and its diversity with a rain forest and the diversity that is found there.

LabBook

Deciding About Environmental Issues
Teacher's Notes

Time Required
One 45-minute class period

Lab Ratings

EASY → HARD

- **TEACHER PREP** 🧪
- **STUDENT SET-UP** 🧪🧪
- **CONCEPT LEVEL** 🧪🧪🧪
- **CLEAN UP** 🧪

MATERIALS
You may want to have students bring in articles for several days prior to doing this activity. You might also want to limit students' choices to those that are age-appropriate.

Lab Notes
This is a good lab to repeat as environmental issues appear in the news.

You may wish to combine this activity with a video that portrays an international environmental issue. Students can also be encouraged to use the Internet as a source of information.

Debra Sampson
Booker T. Washington Middle School
Elgin, Texas

Deciding About Environmental Issues

You make hundreds of decisions every day. Some of them are complicated, but many of them are very simple, such as what to wear or what to eat for lunch. Deciding what to do about an environmental issue can be very difficult. There are many different factors that must be considered. How will a certain solution affect people's lives? How much will it cost? Is it ethically right?

In this activity you will analyze an issue in four steps to help you make a decision about it. Find out about environmental issues that are being discussed in your area. Examine newspapers, magazines, and other publications to find out what the issues are. Choose one local issue to evaluate. For example, you could evaluate whether the city should spend the money to provide recycling bins and special trucks for picking up recyclable trash.

Procedure

1. In your ScienceLog, write a statement about an environmental issue.

2. **Gather Information** Read about your issue in several publications. Summarize important facts in your ScienceLog.

3. **Consider Values** The values of an issue are the things that you consider important. Examine the diagram below. Several values are given. Which values do you think apply most to the environmental issue you are considering? Are there other values that you believe will help you make a decision about the issue? Consider at least four values in making your decision.

SKILL BUILDER

Materials
- newspapers, magazines, and other publications containing information about environmental issues

A Four-Step Decision-Making Model

- Gather Information
- Consider Values
- Explore Consequences
- Make a Decision

 Datasheets for LabBook
Datasheet 46

4. **Explore Consequences** Consequences are the things that result from a certain course of action. In your ScienceLog, create a table similar to the one below. Use your table to organize your thoughts about consequences related to your environmental issue. List your values at the top. Fill in each space with the consequences for each value.

Consequences Table				
Consequences	**Values**			
Positive short-term consequences				
Negative short-term consequences				
Positive long-term consequences				
Negative long-term consequences				

5. **Make a Decision** Thoroughly consider all of the consequences you have recorded in your table. Evaluate how important each consequence is. Make a decision about what course of action you would choose on the issue.

Analysis

6. In your evaluation, did you consider short-term consequences or long-term consequences to be more important? Why?

7. Which value or values had the greatest influence on your final decision? Explain your reasoning.

Going Further
Compare your table with your classmates' tables. Did you all make the same decision about a similar issue? If not, form teams, and organize a formal classroom debate of a specific environmental issue.

Answers
6. Either short- or long-term consequences can be more relevant, depending on the issue.
7. Answers will vary according to students' perspectives.

Going Further
Encourage students to narrow their topic to a single aspect of an issue, such as the importance of aesthetic value in the preservation of natural areas.

Science Skills Worksheet 3
"Thinking Objectively"

Science Skills Worksheet 12
"Working with Hypotheses"

Chapter 21 • LabBook

Muscles at Work
Teacher's Notes

Time Required

One 45-minute class period

Lab Ratings

TEACHER PREP 🧪
STUDENT SET-UP 🧪
CONCEPT LEVEL 🧪🧪
CLEAN UP 🧪

Safety Caution

Remind students to review all safety cautions before beginning this lab activity.

A digital thermometer that measures temperature from the ear is recommended.

Because of the vigorous nature of the exercise, you may want to ask for volunteers to do the exercising. Also, you should be aware of any health concerns your students have.

 Datasheets for LabBook
Datasheet 47

Kathy LaRoe
East Valley Middle School
East Helena, Montana

Muscles at Work

Have you ever exercised outside on a cold fall day wearing only a thin warm-up suit or shorts? How did you stay warm? The answer is that your muscle cells contracted, and when contraction takes place, some energy is used to do work and the rest is converted to thermal energy. This helps your body maintain a constant temperature in cold conditions. When you exercise strenuously on a hot summer day, your muscles can cause your body to become overheated.

In this activity, it is your job to find out how the release of energy can cause a change in your body temperature.

Materials

- clock or watch with a second hand
- small hand-held thermometer
- other materials as approved by your teacher

Procedure

1. Form a group of four students. In your group, discuss several exercises that can produce a change in body temperature. Form a hypothesis, and write your hypothesis in your ScienceLog.

2. Develop an experimental procedure that includes the steps necessary to test your hypothesis. Be sure to get your teacher's approval before you begin.

3. Assign tasks to individuals in the group, such as note taking, data recording, and timing. What observations and data will you be recording? Design your data tables in your ScienceLog accordingly.

4. Perform your experiment as planned by your group. Be sure to record all observations made during the experiment in your data tables.

Analysis

5. How did you determine if muscle contractions cause the release of thermal energy? Was your hypothesis supported by your data? Explain your results in a written report. Describe how you could improve your experimental method.

Going Further

Why do humans shiver in the cold? Do all animals shiver? Find out why shivering is one of the first signs that your body is becoming too cold.

Answer

5. All answers will depend on the students' observations and their own hypotheses.

Going Further

In a process known as shivering thermogenesis, muscle tone is gradually increased. Shivering increases the workload of the muscles and elevates oxygen and energy consumption. The heat that is produced warms the deep vessels. Shivering can elevate body temperature effectively. It can increase the rate of heat generation by as much as 400 percent. Endothermic animals have the capacity to shiver. Shivering is an automatic response of the body to cold.

Seeing Is Believing

Fingernails are part of your body's integumentary system, which includes the skin that covers your entire body. Nails are a modification of the outer layer of the skin, and they grow continuously throughout your life. In this activity, you will measure the rate at which fingernails grow.

Materials

- permanent marker
- metric ruler
- graph paper (optional)

Procedure

1. Trace around each of your hands. Then fill in some of the details, such as the fingernails, as shown below. Choose one of the fingers you have drawn, and label the parts of the fingernail, as shown at right. Notice that the nail bed is the area where the nail is attached to the finger. The illustration at right shows how far inside your finger your fingernail begins.

Left hand Right hand

Kathy LaRoe
East Valley Middle School
East Helena, Montana

Seeing Is Believing
Teacher's Notes

Time Required
One 45-minute class period, and 5 to 10 minutes every other day for 2 weeks

Lab Ratings

TEACHER PREP
STUDENT SET-UP
CONCEPT LEVEL
CLEAN UP

MATERIALS

The materials listed on the student page are enough for 1–2 students. This lab may be done with several different types of marking methods. The fingernail is very hard and not very porous. Marking the nail permanently is a challenge. A permanent marker, such as a laundry-marking pen, may need to be refreshed only once a day. Fingernail polish may be an acceptable alternative. Acrylic paint may also be used.

Safety Caution
Remind students to review all safety cautions and icons before beginning this lab activity.

Datasheets for LabBook
Datasheet 48

Lab Notes

Few topics are as important to students as acquiring knowledge and understanding of their own body. As they develop, students can't help but observe the ways they are changing physically. One part of the body that grows quickly and requires a great deal of their attention is their fingernails. In this lab, students are able to witness the growth of their own body.

Tell students that the graphed data shown in this lab is only an example and will not be the same as their own data. A female adult index fingernail, for example, may be about 12 mm from the cuticle to the beginning of the free edge.

2. Find the center of the nail bed on your right index finger (the finger next to your thumb). Make a mark with the permanent marker on the center of your nail bed, as shown at right. **Caution:** Do not get the permanent marker ink on your clothing.

3. Measure from the mark to the base of your nail. Record this measurement on your hand drawing. Label this measurement "Day 1."

4. Repeat steps 2–3 for your left index finger. Then switch roles with your lab partner.

5. Let your fingernails grow for 2 days. Normal, daily activity will not wash away the stain completely, but you may need to freshen the mark periodically throughout this lab.

6. Measure the distance from the mark on your nail to the base of your nail. Record this distance on your hand drawing. Label this measurement "Day 3."

7. Continue measuring and recording the growth of your nails every other day for 2 weeks. Refresh the mark as necessary. You may continue to file or trim your nails as usual throughout this lab.

8. After you have completed your measurements and recorded them on your hand drawings, prepare a graph similar to the one below to display your findings.

Analysis

9. Did one hand have a faster-growing nail? Write two possible explanations for why one fingernail might grow faster than another.

10. Who has the fastest-growing nails among your classmates? Who has the slowest-growing nails? What is the difference in the total nail growth between these two students?

11. Among your classmates, is there a difference between nail-growth rates for males and nail-growth rates for females? Is there a relationship between nail growth and other physical characteristics, such as height?

Going Further

Do some research in the library or on the Internet to find answers to the following questions:

- How are nails important to you? What do they help you do? Give at least three examples to support your answers.
- Are your fingernails an indication of your health or state of nutrition?

Answers

All answers to the Analysis questions will depend on student observations and measurements.

Going Further

Nails are extremely versatile. Most of us take for granted the many and unique functions they perform. Fingernails, for example, intensify our tactile sensitivity; they help us when we try to pick up small objects; they protect our fingertips; they serve as tools for scratching; they can be used as weapons. Your students may think of many more ways that toenails and fingernails are important to the body.

Science Skills Worksheet 26 "Grasping Graphing"

Chapter 22 • LabBook **765**

Build a Lung
Teacher's Notes

Time Required
One 45-minute class period

Lab Ratings

TEACHER PREP 🧪🧪
STUDENT SET-UP 🧪🧪
CONCEPT LEVEL 🧪
CLEAN UP 🧪🧪

MATERIALS
You may want to build a model first to use as a reference for students. If so, you may want to substitute a bag smaller than the one that students use to model the diaphragm.

Answers
4. The balloon will inflate when the plastic bag is pulled down.
5. The balloon represents a lung, the plastic wrap represents a diaphragm, and the straw represents a trachea. The bottle represents a body cavity.
6. Air enters the lungs when the diaphragm moves down and creates more space inside the chest cavity. Air is forced out of the lungs when the diaphragm moves up. This should be demonstrated by moving the plastic bag up and down.

Going Further
From the late 1920s to the 1950s, iron lungs were used to treat respiratory paralysis due to poliomyelitis. The patient was encased within an airtight chamber from the neck down. A large set of leather bellows mounted in a separate pumping unit expanded, causing pressure changes inside the chamber. This in turn caused the chest of the patient to expand, drawing fresh air into the lungs through the mouth. Now several models of portable ventilators allow patients much more freedom to move about.

Build a Lung

You have learned that when you breathe, you actually pull air into your lungs because your diaphragm muscle causes your chest to expand. You can see this is true by placing your hands on your ribs and inhaling slowly. Did you feel your chest expand?

In this activity, you will build a model of a lung using some common materials. You will see how the diaphragm muscle works to inflate your lungs. Refer to the diagrams at right as you construct your model.

Materials
- small balloon
- plastic drinking straw
- 2 rubber bands
- golf-ball-sized piece of clay
- metric ruler
- top half of a 2 L bottle
- small plastic trash bag
- transparent tape

Procedure
1. Attach the balloon to the end of the straw with a rubber band. Make a hole through the clay, and insert the other end of the straw through the hole. Be sure at least 8 cm of the straw extends beyond the clay. Squeeze the ball of clay gently to seal the clay around the straw.
2. Insert the balloon end of the straw into the neck of the bottle. Use the ball of clay to seal the straw and balloon into the bottle.
3. Turn the bottle gently on its side. Place the trash bag over the cut end of the bottle. Expand a rubber band around the bottom of the bottle to secure the bag. You may wish to reinforce the seal with tape. Before the plastic is completely sealed, gather the excess material of the bag into your hand, and press toward the inside of the bottle slightly. (You may need to tie a knot about halfway up from the bottom of the bag to take up excess material.) Use tape to finish sealing the bag to the bottle with the bag in this position. This will push the excess air out of the bottle.

Analysis
4. What can you do with your model to make the "lung" inflate?
5. What do the balloon, the plastic wrap, and the straw represent in your model?
6. Using your model, demonstrate to the class how air enters the lung and how air exits the lung.

Going Further
Do some research to find out what an "iron lung" is and why it was used in the past. Find out what is used today to help people who have difficulty breathing.

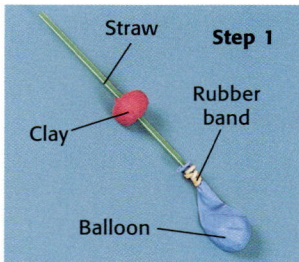
Step 1 — Straw, Clay, Rubber band, Balloon

Step 2 — Bottle neck

Step 3

Datasheets for LabBook
Datasheet 49

Yvonne Brannum
Hine Junior High School
Washington, D.C.

Carbon Dioxide Breath

Plants take in carbon dioxide and give off oxygen as a byproduct of photosynthesis. Animals, including you, use this oxygen and release carbon dioxide as a byproduct of respiration.

In this activity, you will explore your own carbon dioxide exhalation. Phenol red turns yellow in the presence of carbon dioxide. You will use it to detect carbon dioxide in your breath.

Procedure

1. Place 100 mL of water into a 150 mL flask. Using an eyedropper, carefully place four drops of phenol red indicator solution into the water. The water should turn orange.

2. Place a plastic drinking straw into the solution of phenol red and water. Drape a paper towel over the beaker to prevent splashing. Carefully blow through the straw into the solution. **Caution:** Do not inhale through the straw. Do not drink the solution, and do not share a straw with anyone.

3. Have your lab partner time how long it takes for the solution to change color. Begin timing when you start blowing. Record the time in your ScienceLog. What color does the solution become?

Analysis

4. Compare your data with those of your classmates. What was the longest length of time it took to see a color change? the shortest? How do you account for the difference?

5. Is there a relationship between the length of time it takes to change the solution from orange to yellow and the person's physical characteristics, such as gender or whether the tester has an athletic build?

Going Further
Do jumping jacks or sit-ups for 3 minutes, and then repeat the experiment. Did the timing change? Describe and explain any change.

Materials

- 150 mL graduated cylinder
- 100 mL of water
- 150 mL Erlenmeyer flask
- eyedropper
- phenol red indicator solution
- plastic drinking straw
- paper towel
- clock with a second hand or a stopwatch
- protective gloves

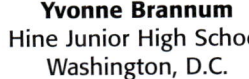
Yvonne Brannum
Hine Junior High School
Washington, D.C.

Answers
4. Answers will depend on student observations. It is typical for the solution to change color faster when the student is breathing fast after exercise.

5. In general, an athlete at rest will take the longest time to generate a color change in the indicator solution. There should be little difference observed between genders. There are exceptions, and all answers will depend on students' observations.

Carbon Dioxide Breath
Teacher's Notes

Time Required
One 45-minute class period

Lab Ratings

TEACHER PREP 🧪🧪
STUDENT SET-UP 🧪🧪
CONCEPT LEVEL 🧪🧪
CLEAN UP 🧪🧪

MATERIALS
You may wish to substitute bromothymol blue indicator solution for the phenol red indicator. The bromothymol blue will turn green in the presence of CO_2. Clear plastic cups (6 oz or 8 oz size) may be used instead of 150 mL flasks if glassware is in short supply or if you have concerns about breakage.

Safety Caution
Remind students to review all safety cautions and icons before beginning this lab activity.

Lab Notes
Tell students that carbon dioxide is in the air of the classroom. They may need to cover their indicator solution to delay the reaction with the air. Tell them not to leave the indicator solution sitting exposed for several minutes before it is used.

 Datasheets for LabBook Datasheet 50

As the Stomach Churns
Teacher's Notes

Time Required
One 45-minute class period and another 15 minutes after 24 hours

Lab Ratings

TEACHER PREP 🧪🧪
STUDENT SET-UP 🧪🧪
CONCEPT LEVEL 🧪🧪
CLEAN UP 🧪🧪

MATERIALS
The materials listed on the student page are enough for 1 student or 1 group of 2 to 4 students. The two tenderizers should be available at the grocery store. You will need to examine the different brands of powdered or liquid tenderizers. You may substitute fresh papaya or pineapple juices if they are available, if both types of tenderizers cannot be found.

Safety Caution
Remind students to review all safety cautions and icons before beginning this lab activity. Caution students that HCl is a chemical they should handle very carefully. You may choose to dispense the HCl yourself. Tell students that if any HCl comes in contact with their skin, they should wash the area with plenty of water immediately and they should notify you as they wash. Tell students not to taste any materials used in this or any lab.

Using Scientific Methods

As the Stomach Churns

The stomach, as you know, performs not only mechanical digestion but also chemical digestion. As the stomach churns, it moves the food particles around while the digestive juices—acid and enzymes—are added to begin protein digestion.

Commercially prepared meat tenderizers contain enzymes from plants that break down, or digest, proteins. Two types of meat tenderizer are commonly available at grocery stores. One type contains an enzyme called papain, from papaya. Another type contains an enzyme called bromelain, from pineapple. In this lab, you will test the effects of these two different types of meat tenderizers on beef stew meat.

Ask a Question
1. Which meat tenderizer will work faster? Which will make the meat more tender? Will there be a color change in the meat or in the water? What might these changes, if any, indicate? Determine what you will look for as you plan your experiment.

Form a Hypothesis
2. Examine the list of ingredients on the labels of each of the meat tenderizers. Form a hypothesis about which tenderizer will make the beef more tender.
   Caution: Do not taste any of the materials in this activity.

Materials
- 4 test tubes
- test-tube rack
- test-tube marker
- masking tape
- 25 mL graduated cylinder
- water
- eyedropper
- 1/4 tsp measuring spoon
- very dilute (0.1 M) hydrochloric acid
- commercially prepared meat tenderizer containing bromelain
- commercially prepared meat tenderizer containing papain
- 1 cm cubes of beef stew meat (3)
- protective gloves

 Datasheets for LabBook
Datasheet 51

Yvonne Brannum
Hine Junior High School
Washington, D.C.

768 Chapter 24 • LabBook

Conduct an Experiment

3. Identify any variables and controls present in your experiment. Make a data table in your ScienceLog to record your observations and results.

4. Label two of the test tubes with the name of the tenderizer being investigated. Label the third test tube "Control." What will be the contents of this tube?

5. Pour 20 mL of water into each test tube.

6. With the eyedropper, add four drops of very dilute hydrochloric acid to each test tube. **Caution:** Hydrochloric acid can burn your skin. If any touches your skin, rinse the area with running water and tell your teacher immediately.

7. Using the measuring spoon, add ¼ tsp of a meat tenderizer to each correspondingly labeled test tube.

8. Add 1 cube of beef to each test tube.

9. Record your observations of each test tube immediately, after 5 minutes, after 15 minutes, after 30 minutes, and again after 24 hours.

Analyze the Results

10. Did you notice any differences in the beef in the three test tubes immediately? At what time interval did you notice a significant difference in the appearance of the beef in the test tubes?

11. Did one meat tenderizer perform better than the other? Explain how you determined which tenderizer was most efficient.

Draw Conclusions

12. Was your hypothesis supported? Explain.

13. Many animals that sting have venom composed of proteins. Explain how applying meat tenderizer to the wound helps relieve the pain of such a sting.

Answers

4. The control tube will contain everything that goes into the other tubes except the meat tenderizer.

10. There should be very little difference in the three test tubes at first. Differences will be mild until after 24 hours, when a significant difference will be noticed between the control tube and the experimental tubes.

11. Both tenderizers should work in a similar way. If one tenderizer is noted to be more efficient, students should be able to describe how they tested the stew meat to demonstrate the difference.

12. Answers will vary, but students should be able to explain how their hypothesis was supported or how their experimental results did not support their hypothesis.

13. Students may conclude that certain digestive enzymes break down proteins. Breaking down the protein in venom often makes the venom less harmful and less painful. Explain to students that using meat tenderizer on an insect bite is first aid only and is not intended to substitute for medical attention. Emphasize that snakebites require immediate medical attention.

Background

Students know that papaya and pineapple fruits are the source of the meat tenderizers they will be using in this lab. They also know about gelatin desserts made with fruit. You might want to show them a dessert made with canned pineapple and one made (or attempted) with fresh pineapple. Tell them that the ingredient that makes the gelatin gel is an animal protein. Ask them to explain why the gelatin with fresh pineapple didn't gel.

Chapter 24 • LabBook

Enzymes in Action
Teacher's Notes

Time Required
One 45-minute class period

Lab Ratings

- TEACHER PREP 🧪🧪
- STUDENT SET-UP 🧪🧪
- CONCEPT LEVEL 🧪🧪🧪
- CLEAN UP 🧪🧪

MATERIALS
The materials listed on the student page are enough for 1 student or 1 group of 2 to 4 students. If you do not have enough mortar and pestles or small plates, you may have students use any small container to mash the liver with a fork. Beef liver is readily obtained at the grocery store.

Safety Caution
Remind students to review all safety cautions and icons before beginning this lab activity. Use a dilute solution of hydrogen peroxide. Hydrogen peroxide can be harmful to skin and clothing. Caution students to be careful not to spill or splatter the solution while pouring. If hydrogen peroxide comes into contact with skin, wash the skin immediately with plenty of running water.

Enzymes in Action

You know how important enzymes are in the process of digestion. This lab will help you see enzymes at work. Hydrogen peroxide is continuously produced by your cells. If it is not quickly broken down, hydrogen peroxide will kill your cells. Luckily, your cells contain an enzyme that converts hydrogen peroxide into two non-poisonous substances. This enzyme is also present in the cells of beef liver. In this lab, you will observe the action of this enzyme on hydrogen peroxide.

Materials
- 1 cm cubes of beef liver (3)
- tweezers
- small plate
- 10 mL graduated cylinder
- water
- 3 test tubes
- test-tube rack
- 4 mL of fresh hydrogen peroxide
- mortar and pestle (or fork and watch glass)
- spatula
- protective gloves

Procedure
1. In your ScienceLog, draw a data table similar to the one below. Be sure to leave enough space to write your observations.

Data Table		
Size and condition of liver	Experimental liquid	Observations
1 cm cube beef liver	2 mL water	DO NOT WRITE IN BOOK
1 cm cube beef liver	2 mL hydrogen peroxide	
1 cm cube beef liver (mashed)	2 mL hydrogen peroxide	

 Datasheets for LabBook
Datasheet 52

James Chin
Frank A. Day Middle School
Newtonville, Massachusetts

2. Get three equal-sized pieces of beef liver from your teacher, and use your forceps to place them on your plate.

3. Pour 2 mL of water into a test tube labeled "Water and liver."

4. Using the tweezers, carefully place one piece of liver in the test tube. Record your observations in your data table.

5. Pour 2 mL of hydrogen peroxide into a second test tube labeled "Liver and hydrogen peroxide."
   Caution: Do not splash hydrogen peroxide on your skin. If you do get hydrogen peroxide on your skin, rinse the affected area with running water immediately, and tell your teacher.

6. Using the tweezers, carefully place one piece of liver in the test tube. Record your observations of the second test tube in your data table.

7. Pour another 2 mL of hydrogen peroxide into a third test tube labeled "Ground liver and hydrogen peroxide."

8. Using a mortar and pestle (or fork and watch glass), carefully grind the third piece of liver.

9. Using the spatula, scrape the ground liver into the third test tube. Record your observations of the third test tube in your data table.

Analysis

10. What was the purpose of putting the first piece of liver in water? Why was this a necessary step?

11. Describe the difference you observed between the liver and the ground liver when each was placed in the hydrogen peroxide. How can you account for this difference?

Going Further

Do plant cells contain enzymes that break down hydrogen peroxide? Try this experiment using potato cubes instead of liver to find out.

Answers

10. The piece of liver in water is the control. It is necessary to have a control so that differences in reactions to other substances can be observed.

11. Students should observe that the cube of liver produced a quick, foaming reaction to the hydrogen peroxide as the solution came into contact with the cells and destroyed them. The mashed liver should also produce a very quick reaction; however, students should observe that the effervescence subsides faster than with the cube. This is because the mashed liver has a greater surface area than the cube, exposing more liver enzymes to the hydrogen peroxide. There should be no reaction in water.

Going Further

Students will discover that plant cells do contain enzymes that will break down hydrogen peroxide. Have them experiment with different types of plants and vegetables so they can observe the different rates of reaction.

You've Gotta Lotta Nerve
Teacher's Notes

Time Required

One 45-minute class period

Lab Ratings

TEACHER PREP 🧪
STUDENT SET-UP 🧪
CONCEPT LEVEL 🧪🧪
CLEAN UP 🧪

MATERIALS

The materials listed on the student page are enough for 1–2 students. Tell students that they will not be testing for pain. The protective cover on the sharp end of the dissecting pin must remain in place at all times.

Safety Caution

Remind students to review all safety cautions and icons before beginning this lab activity.

Remind students to be safe and gentle with each other in this exercise, respecting the sensitivity and comfort of their peers.

Lab Notes

This activity works best if the student whose hand is being tested looks away or is loosely blindfolded while his or her hand is being tested. Often students will say they feel something when they think they should feel something. Students should be given the choice of being blindfolded or looking away.

You've Gotta Lotta Nerve

Your skin has thousands of nerve receptors that detect sensations, such as heat, cold, and pressure. Your brain is designed to filter out or ignore most of the input it receives from these skin receptors. If that were not the case, simply wearing clothes would trigger so many responses that we couldn't function.

Some areas of the skin, such as the back of your hand, are more sensitive than others. In this activity, you will map the receptors for heat, cold, and pressure on the back of your hand.

Procedure

1. Form groups of three. One of you will volunteer the back of your hand to be tested, one will do the testing, and the third will record the results. Check with your teacher to see if you may switch roles so each of you may play each part.

2. Use a fine-point washable marker or pen and a metric ruler to mark off a 3 × 3 cm square on the back of your partner's hand. Draw a grid within the area, spacing the lines approximately 0.5 cm apart. You will have 36 squares in the grid when you are finished. Examine the photograph below to make sure you have drawn the grid correctly.

3. Mark off three 3 × 3 cm areas on the graph paper. Make a grid in each area exactly as you did on the back of your partner's hand. Label one grid "Cold," another grid "Hot," and the third grid "Pressure."

Materials

- fine-point washable pens or markers
- metric ruler
- graph paper
- eyedropper
- very cold water
- hot tap water
- dissecting pin with a small piece of cork or a small rubber stopper stuck on the sharp end

 Datasheets for LabBook
Datasheet 53

 Science Skills Worksheet 11
"Understanding Variables"

Christopher Wood
Western Rockingham
Middle School
Madison, North Carolina

4. Begin locating receptors on your partner's hand. Your partner should not look while his or her hand is being tested! How do you think your partner's looking might influence your results? Use the eyedropper to apply one small droplet of cold water on each square in the grid. On your graph paper, mark an X on the *Cold* grid in the square that corresponds to where the sensation of cold was felt on the hand. You will need to carefully blot the water off your partner's hand after several drops.

5. Repeat the test using hot-water droplets. The water will cool enough as it drops from the eyedropper so that it will not hurt you. Mark an X on the *Hot* grid to indicate where the sensation of heat was felt on the hand.

6. Repeat the test using the head—not the point!—of the pin. Touch the skin to detect pressure receptors. Use a very light touch. Mark an X on the *Pressure* grid to indicate where pressure was felt on the hand.

Analysis

7. Count the number of Xs in each grid. How many heat receptors are there per 3 cm^2? cold receptors? pressure receptors?

8. Do you have areas on the back of your hand where the receptors overlap? Why or why not?

9. How do you think the results of this experiment would be similar or different if you mapped an area of your forearm? the back of your neck? the palm of your hand?

10. Prepare a written report that includes a description of your investigation and a discussion of questions 7–9.

Going Further

In the library or on the Internet research what happens if a receptor is continuously stimulated. Does the kind of receptor make a difference? Does it make a difference how intense the stimulation is? Explain.

Answers

7. Answers will vary. Some students will have more receptors in each category than others.

8. Students may notice that the same square on the grid can feel heat, cold, and pressure. Students may explain this by noting that they have different kinds of receptors in the same spot. Some perceptive students may recognize hot and cold as variations of a single sensation—temperature. They also may perceive that the blunt tip of the dissecting pin might have been cold and that they felt the temperature instead of the pressure.

9. Different areas of the body are more sensitive than others. Results may vary because some areas are not visible to the student, thus the variable of expected sensation is eliminated.

Going Further

Students will find that different responses are made to a constant stimulus according to type and intensity. A person may become insensitive to an odor or even mild pain over time. Intense, sudden, or continued stimuli, such as heat, pain, or noise, may do great damage to a person over time.

It's a Comfy, Safe World!
Teacher's Notes

Time Required
Two 45-minute class periods

Lab Ratings

TEACHER PREP 🔺🔺
STUDENT SET-UP 🔺
CONCEPT LEVEL 🔺
CLEAN UP 🔺🔺🔺

MATERIALS
This lab may require some larger plastic bags, a meterstick, and various other materials, depending on the students' designs. Soft-boiled eggs will simplify the cleanup. Students may wear gloves.

Safety Caution
Remind students to review all safety cautions and icons before beginning this lab activity. Students should wash their hands after handling eggs.

Lab Notes
This lab should be done over a large plastic sheet. You may also want to do this lab outside.

Answers
6. Answers will vary, but an egg inside a viscous liquid in a plastic bag, wrapped in soft cotton and all inside another bag, should not be damaged when dropped from a height of 1 m. An egg protected only by a shell should break.

7. The answers will vary according to students' observations. Most students will observe that the soft wrapping might be thicker to protect the egg better.

774   Chapter 26 • LabBook

It's a Comfy, Safe World!

Before human babies are born, they lead a comfy life. By the seventh month, they just lie around, sucking their thumb, blinking their eyes, and perhaps even dreaming. Baby birds live inside a hard, protective shell until the baby has used up all the food supply. Most mammal babies develop within their mother's uterus, surrounded by fluid and a placenta before they are born. Is the internal environment in a placental mammal safer than a baby bird's environment? In this activity you will create a model of a placental mammal's uterus to see how well it protects a fetus.

Procedure

1. Brainstorm several ideas about how you will construct and test your model. A peeled, soft-boiled egg will represent the fetus in your mammalian model. Build your model.

2. Make a data table in your ScienceLog similar to the First Model Test table at right. Test your model, examine the egg for damage, and record your results.

3. Modify your design as necessary, repeat step 2, and record your results.

4. When you are satisfied with the design of your model, obtain another peeled, soft-boiled egg and an egg in the shell.

5. Make another data table in your ScienceLog similar to the Final Model Test table at right. Repeat step 2 with your new eggs. Record your results in your data table.

Analysis

6. Explain any differences in the test results for the model and the egg in a shell.

7. What modification to your model was the most effective in protecting your fetus?

Going Further
Compare the development of placental mammals with that of marsupial mammals and monotremes.

SKILL BUILDER

Materials
- sealable plastic bags
- water
- mineral oil, cooking oil, syrup, or other thick liquid to represent fluid surrounding the fetus
- cotton, soft fabric, or other soft materials
- 3–5 soft-boiled eggs
- protective gloves

First Model Test	
Original model	Modified model
DO NOT WRITE IN BOOK	DO NOT WRITE IN BOOK

Final Model Test	
	Test Results
Model	DO NOT WRITE IN BOOK
Egg in shell	DO NOT WRITE IN BOOK

Going Further
Students may want to research in the library or on the Internet about marsupials and monotremes.

 Datasheets for LabBook
Datasheet 54

Randy Christian
Stovall Junior High School
Houston, Texas

My, How You've Grown!

In humans, the process of development that takes place between fertilization and birth lasts about 266 days. In 4 weeks, the new individual grows from a single fertilized cell to an embryo whose heart is beating and pumping blood. All of the organ systems and body parts are completely formed by the end of the seventh month. During the last 2 months before birth, the baby grows and its organ systems mature. At birth, the average mass of a baby is about 33,000 times as much as that of an embryo at 2 weeks of development! In this activity you will discover just how fast a fetus grows.

Materials

- graph paper
- colored pencils

Procedure

1. Using graph paper, make two graphs—one titled "Length" and one titled "Mass"—in your ScienceLog. On the length graph, use intervals of 25 mm on the y-axis. Extend the y-axis to 500 mm. On the mass graph, use intervals of 100 g on the y-axis. Extend this y-axis to 3,300 g. Use 2-week intervals for time on the x-axes for both graphs. Both x-axes should extend to 40 weeks.

2. Examine the data table at right. Plot the data in the table on your graphs. Use a colored pencil to draw the curved line that joins the points on each graph.

Increase of Mass and Length of Average Human Fetus

Time (wks)	Mass (g)	Length (mm)
2	0.1	1.5
3	0.3	2.3
4	0.5	5.0
5	0.6	10.0
6	0.8	15.0
8	1.0	30.0
13	15.0	90.0
17	115.0	140.0
21	300.0	250.0
26	950.0	320.0
30	1,500.0	400.0
35	2,300.0	450.0
40	3,300.0	500.0

Analysis

3. Describe the change in mass of a developing fetus. How can you explain this change?

4. Describe the change in length of a developing fetus. How does the change in mass compare to the change in length?

Going Further

Using the information in your graphs, estimate how tall a child would be at age 3 if he or she continued to grow at the same average rate a fetus grows.

My, How You've Grown!
Teacher's Notes

Time Required
One 45-minute class period

Lab Ratings

TEACHER PREP 🧪
STUDENT SET-UP 🧪
CONCEPT LEVEL 🧪🧪
CLEAN UP 🧪

Answers

2. Students' graphs should look like those below.

3. The change in mass of a developing fetus is steadily increasing, approximately tripling each month of the first and second trimesters. This is a period of rapid cell division.

4. The change in length steadily increases, doubling and even tripling each month in the first two trimesters. In the third trimester, the rate of lengthening slows.

Going Further

The child would be 2.45 m (8.04 ft) tall!

Datasheets for LabBook
Datasheet 55

Randy Christian
Stovall Junior High School
Houston, Texas

Chapter 26 • LabBook

Antibodies to the Rescue
Teacher's Notes

Time Required

One 45-minute class period

Lab Ratings

TEACHER PREP 🧪🧪
STUDENT SET-UP 🧪🧪
CONCEPT LEVEL 🧪🧪
CLEAN UP 🧪🧪

MATERIALS

You will be able to expand this activity from very simple to a grand art project! Have students bring craft supplies from home. You may want to include poster paper in the supply list.

Safety Caution

Remind students to review all safety cautions and icons before beginning this lab activity.

Preparation Notes

Encourage students to be imaginative in this exercise. Have them come up with interesting shapes for the viruses and the antibodies that fit them. Remind students that the main lesson of this exercise is that the antibodies can fit only a specific pathogen and in only one specific way, just as a key fits only one lock.

Antibodies to the Rescue

Some cells of the immune system, called B cells, make antibodies that attack and kill invading viruses and microorganisms. These antibodies help make you immune to disease. Have you ever had chickenpox? If you have, your body has built up antibodies that can recognize that particular virus. Antibodies will attach themselves to the virus, tagging it for destruction. If you are exposed to the same disease again, the antibodies remember that virus. They will attack the virus even quicker and in greater number than they did the first time. That is why you will probably never have chickenpox more than once.

In this activity, you will construct simple models of viruses and their antibodies. You will see how antibodies are specific for a particular virus.

Materials

- craft materials, such as buttons, fabric scraps, pipecleaners, and recycled materials
- scissors
- tape or glue
- colored paper

Procedure

1. Draw the virus patterns shown on this page on a separate piece of paper, or design your own virus models from the craft supplies. Remember to design different receptors on each of your virus models.

2. In your ScienceLog, write a few sentences describing how your viruses are different.

3. Cut out the viruses, and attach them to a piece of colored paper with tape or glue.

Viruses

776

 Datasheets for LabBook
Datasheet 56

Martha Kisiah
Fairview Middle School
Tallahassee, Florida

776   Chapter 27 • LabBook

4. Select the antibodies drawn below or design your own antibodies that will exactly fit on the receptors on your virus models. Draw or create each antibody enough times to attach one to each receptor site on the virus.

Antibodies

5. Cut out the antibodies you have drawn. Arrange the antibodies so that they bind to the virus at the appropriate receptor. Attach them to the virus with tape or glue.

Analysis

6. Explain how an antibody "recognizes" a particular virus.
7. After the attachment of antibodies to the receptors, what would be the next step in the immune response?
8. Many vaccines use weakened copies of the virus to protect the body. Use the model of a virus and its specific antibody to explain how vaccines work.
9. Use your model of a virus to demonstrate to the class how a receptor might change or mutate so that a vaccine would no longer be effective.

Going Further

Research in the library or on the Internet to find information about the discovery of the Salk vaccine for polio. Include information on how polio affects people today.

Research in the library or on the Internet to find information about filoviruses. What do they look like? What diseases do they cause? Why are they especially dangerous? Is there an effective vaccine against any filovirus? Explain.

Going Further

Jonas Edward Salk (1914–1995) was born in New York City. His work on an anti-influenza vaccine led him and his colleagues to develop an inactivated vaccine against polio in 1952. After successful wide-scale testing in 1954, the vaccine was distributed nationally, greatly reducing the incidence of the disease. With the Salk vaccine, the cases of polio have drastically gone down year after year—there hasn't been a single case of polio in the Western Hemisphere since 1994, and there were only 4,000 polio cases reported worldwide in 1996. Because we are nearing full eradication of the disease, the World Health Organization plans to end routine polio vaccination sometime around the year 2005.

Filoviruses belong to the family Filoviridae, one of several groups of viruses that can cause hemorrhagic fever, such as Ebola, in animals and humans. When magnified many thousands of times by an electron microscope, filoviruses have the appearance of long filaments or threads. Because filoviruses can be extremely hazardous, laboratory studies of these viruses must be conducted in special maximum-containment facilities. The reservoir and natural history of filoviruses remain unknown. Filoviruses have the highest fatality rates (as high as 90 percent for epidemics of hemorrhagic fever caused by Ebola-Zaire virus). No vaccine exists to protect against filovirus infection, and no specific treatment is available for diseases caused by these viruses.

Answers

6. Sample answer: Antibodies recognize and bind to specific pathogens because they are shaped to match the specific three-dimensional shape of the antigen.
7. Sample answer: Antibodies bind to specific pathogens and either inactivate the pathogen or trigger its destruction by macrophages.
8. Sample answer: Vaccines produce immunity because they contain antigens that stimulate an immune response producing memory cells. Students can use their models to demonstrate or give examples.
9. Sample answer: The antibodies specific for a pathogen are ineffective when the pathogen changes these proteins. Students can show this by slightly changing their model so that the virus and the antibody no longer fit like a lock and key.

Passing the Cold
Teacher's Notes

Time Required

One 45-minute class period

Lab Ratings

TEACHER PREP 🧪🧪
STUDENT SET-UP 🧪🧪
CONCEPT LEVEL 🧪🧪
CLEAN UP 🧪🧪

MATERIALS

Prepare a phenolphthalein indicator solution ahead of time. Dilute the indicator solution in water. Add 10 mL of the indicator to 40 mL of water. This is enough solution for one student. Mix a 1.5 percent NaOH solution. Mix 15 g of NaOH to 1 L of water. All but one student will receive 50 mL of this solution.

Safety Caution

Remind students to review all safety cautions and icons before beginning this lab activity. Also remind students that although they are working with a very low concentration of an alkaline solution, they should work safely with all materials. All spills should be cleaned up immediately. Skin exposed to solutions should be washed immediately with plenty of running water. Remind students that they must never mix unknown solutions without supervision and teacher approval.

778 Chapter 27 • LabBook

Using Scientific Methods

Passing the Cold

DISCOVERY LAB

There are more than 100 viruses that cause the symptoms of the common cold. Any of the viruses can be passed from person to person—through the air or through direct contact. In this activity you will track the progress of an outbreak in your class.

Ask a Question

1. How are cold viruses passed from person to person? How can the progress of an outbreak be modeled?

Conduct an Experiment

2. Obtain an empty cup or beaker, an eyedropper, and 50 mL of one of the solutions from your teacher. Only one of you will have the "cold virus" solution. You will see a change in your solution when you have become infected.

3. Your teacher will divide the class into two equal groups. If there is an extra student, that person will record data on the chalkboard. Otherwise, the teacher will act as the recorder.

4. Each group will form a straight line and face each other.

5. Each time your teacher says "Mix," fill your eyedropper with your solution, and place 10 drops of your solution in the beaker of the person in the line opposite you without touching your eyedropper to the liquid.

6. Gently stir the liquid in your cup with your eyedropper. Do not put your eyedropper in anyone else's solution.

7. If your solution changes color, raise your hand so that the recorder can record the number of students who have been "infected."

8. Your teacher will instruct one line to move one person to the right. The person at the end of the line without a partner should go to the other end of the line.

9. Repeat steps 5–8 nine more times for a total of 10 trials.

Materials

- 200 mL beaker or a cup of similar size
- eyedropper
- 50 mL of an unknown solution
- protective gloves

 Datasheets for LabBook
Datasheet 57

Edith McAlanis
Socorro Middle School
El Paso, Texas

Collect Data

10. Return to your desk, and create a data table in your ScienceLog similar to the one below. The column with the title "Total number of people" will remain the same in every row. Enter the data on the board into your data table.

11. Find the percentage of infected people for the last column by dividing the number of infected people by the total number of people and multiplying by 100 in each line.

Results

Trial	Number of infected people	Total number of people	Percentage of infected people
1			
2			
3			
4			
5			
6			
7			
8			
9			
10			

DO NOT WRITE IN BOOK

Analyze the Results

12. Did you become infected? If so, during which trial did you become infected?

13. Did everyone eventually become infected? If so, how many trials were necessary to infect everyone?

14. Explain at least one reason why this simulation may underestimate the number of people who might have been infected in real life.

15. Use your results to create a line graph showing the change in the infection percentage per trial.

Going Further
Research in the library or on the Internet to find out some of the factors that contribute to the spread of a cold virus. What is the best and easiest way to reduce your chances of catching a cold? Explain your answer.

Preparation Notes

Phenolphthalein is a base indicator and will turn pink in the presence of NaOH. One student (or two, if your class is large) will be given 50 mL of the indicator. This student will represent the original "infected" individual. (It is more fun if no one knows who the original infected student is at first.) All other students will be given the NaOH solution.

Prepare a results chart similar to the student table on the board. You will need to record results while the students are performing the experiment.

When switching the students between trials, the student on the end will need to move to the other end of the line so that all students will have a new partner for each trial. In case of an odd number of students, you will need to participate, or you may use one student volunteer to record results on the board.

Answers

11. The percentage of infected people can be found by dividing column 1 by column 2 and multiplying by 100. For example, if 2 people are infected in trial 1 and there are 16 people in all, then: 2 ÷ 16 × 100 = 11 percent.

12.–13. If there are 10 students (two rows of five facing each other) it will take six trials for everyone to become infected.

14. In real life, colds are spread by more than one means. Coughing, sneezing, touching with unwashed hands are all ways to spread a cold. More than one person in a classroom may have a cold.

Going Further
Colds are usually spread by close contact with a person who is actively infected. Colds may be more prevalent in the winter because we tend to stay indoors where we are in closer contact with each other. The virus is carried on the microdroplets in a cough or sneeze and by unwashed hands. The best and easiest way to reduce your chances of catching a cold is to try to avoid crowded places, wash your hands thoroughly and frequently when people around you have colds, and avoid putting your hands on your face near your eyes. Eat a healthy diet and get plenty of rest and exercise to stay in good general health.

To Diet or Not to Diet
Teacher's Notes

Time Required
Two 45-minute class periods

Lab Ratings

TEACHER PREP 🧪🧪
STUDENT SET-UP 🧪
CONCEPT LEVEL 🧪🧪
CLEAN UP 🧪🧪

MATERIALS
A copy of a chart that fast-food restaurants post in their dining rooms outlining the nutritional information of the food they serve would be very helpful in analyzing a fast-food meal.

Answers
3. Answers will vary. Students may say they might try to eat fewer fatty foods. The nutritional value of foods is a subject that may be new to many students.

 Datasheets for LabBook
Datasheet 58

Ivora Washington
Hyattsville Middle School
Hyattsville, Maryland

To Diet or Not to Diet

There are six main classes of foods that we need in order to keep our bodies functioning properly: water, vitamins, minerals, carbohydrates, fats, and proteins. In this activity you will investigate the importance of a well-balanced diet in maintaining a healthy body. Then you will create a poster or picture that illustrates the importance of one of the three energy-producing nutrients—carbohydrates, fats, and proteins.

Materials
- nutrition reference books
- diet books
- white unlined paper
- crayons or colored markers
- fast-food menus (optional)

Procedure
1. In your ScienceLog, create a table like the one below. Research in the library, on nutrition labels, in nutrition or diet books, or on the Internet to find the information you need to fill out the chart.

Nutrition Data Table			
	Fats	Carbohydrates	Proteins
Found in which foods			
Functions in the body			
Consequences of deficiency			

DO NOT WRITE IN BOOK

2. Choose one of the foods you have learned about in your research, and create a poster or picture that describes its importance in a well-balanced diet.

Analysis
3. Based on what you have learned in this lab, how might you change your eating habits to have a well-balanced diet? Does the nutritional value of foods concern you? Why or why not? Write your answers in your ScienceLog, and explain your reasoning.

Going Further
- Write a paragraph explaining why water is a nutrient.
- Analyze a typical fast-food meal, and determine its overall nutritional value.

Going Further
Sample answer: Without water, most of the reactions that maintain life could not take place. Water carries the other essential nutrients to all parts of the body and is the medium in which waste products are dissolved and carried away from body tissues.

Fast-food restaurants usually post Nutrition Facts in public view. Have students obtain this information and evaluate a fast-food meal based on those Nutrition Facts and daily recommended amounts. Examining the Nutrition Facts on food packaging is helpful before beginning this activity. For example, in a 12 oz can of cola there are 40 g of carbohydrates, which represents 13 percent of the recommended daily amount. 40 g ÷ 0.13 = 308 g. The daily recommended amount of carbohydrates in a 2,000 Calorie diet is 308 g.

Keep It Clean

One of the best ways of preventing the spread of bacterial and viral infections is to wash your hands with soap and water frequently. Many companies advertise that their soap ingredients will destroy bacteria normally found on the body. In this activity you will investigate how effective antibacterial soaps are at killing bacteria.

Materials

- wax pencil
- new scrub brush
- 4 agar plates (Petri dishes filled with sterile nutrient agar)
- liquid antibacterial soap
- incubator
- transparent tape

Procedure

1. Use the wax pencil to label the bottoms of four agar plates with: "control," "unwashed," "no soap," and "soap." Open the control dish for 1 minute. Cover the dish, and leave it closed for the rest of the experiment.

2. Without washing your hands, carefully press different surfaces of your hands on the agar plate marked "unwashed." Replace the cover of the plate immediately.

3. Hold your right hand under running water for two minutes. During this time, ask your partner to scrub all surfaces of your hand with the scrub brush. Be sure to scrub under your fingernails. When you are finished, your partner should turn off the water and open the plate marked "no soap." Without touching anything first, carefully press the same surfaces of your right hand on the plate, as you did in step 2.

4. Repeat step 3 using liquid antibacterial soap on your left hand. Make sure that you do not touch anything before pressing your left hand on the plate marked "soap."

5. Secure the lid of each plate to its bottom half with transparent tape. Place the dishes upside down. Incubate all three plates overnight at 37°C.

6. Remove the plates from the incubator and turn them right side up. Check each plate for the presence of bacterial colonies, and count the number of colonies present on each plate. Record this information in your ScienceLog.
   Caution: Do not remove the lids on any of the plates.

Analysis

7. Compare the bacterial growth on the dishes. Which dish contained the most growth? Which contained the least?

8. Does water alone effectively kill bacteria? Explain.

Going Further

Try this experiment again. This time scrub your hands for 2 minutes with regular liquid soap. Account for any differences you observe.

Keep It Clean
Teacher's Notes

Time Required
Two 45-minute class periods

Lab Ratings

EASY ———————— HARD

- **TEACHER PREP** 🧪🧪
- **STUDENT SET-UP** 🧪
- **CONCEPT LEVEL** 🧪🧪
- **CLEAN UP** 🧪🧪

MATERIALS
You can reduce the number of scrub brushes needed by grouping students and having each group select a volunteer.

Safety Caution
Remind students to review all safety cautions and icons before beginning this lab activity. Check for known allergies to antibacterial or other soaps before beginning. Use plastic Petri dishes if possible.

 Datasheets for LabBook
Datasheet 59

Answers

7. Students should observe that the control dish shows the most bacterial growth. Ideally, the dish inoculated after scrubbing with antibacterial soap should show the least bacterial growth.

8. Water alone kills many bacteria because of the chlorine and other agents used in drinking water. Washing with antibacterial soap for a short time may be only slightly better than washing with water alone.

Going Further

On average, hands must be scrubbed with an antibacterial soap for a minimum total of 4 minutes to see a significant reduction or absence of bacterial growth in nutrient agar. Ask students if they know how long doctors scrub their hands before surgery. (4–5 minutes total)

Elizabeth Rustad
Crane Junior High School
Yuma, Arizona

Self-Check Answers

Chapter 1—The World of Life Science
Page 12: 2. Insecticides caused the frog deformities.
Page 15: Jar C is the control group.

Chapter 2—It's Alive!! Or, Is It?
Page 37: Your alarm clock is a stimulus. It rings, and you respond by shutting it off and getting out of bed.

Chapter 3—Cells: The Basic Units of Life
Page 63: Cells need DNA to control cell processes and to make new cells.
Page 66: 1. The surface-to-volume ratio decreases as the cell size increases. 2. A eukaryotic cell has a nucleus and membrane-covered organelles.
Page 70: Cell walls surround the cell membranes of some cells. All cells have cell membranes, but not all cells have cell walls. Cell walls give structure to some cells.

Chapter 4—The Cell in Action
Page 85: In pure water, the grape would absorb water and swell up. In water mixed with a large amount of sugar, the grape would lose water and shrink.
Page 93: After duplication, there are four chromatids—two from each of the homologous chromosomes.

Chapter 5—Heredity
Page 117: 1. four 2. two 3. They make copies of themselves once. They divide twice. 4. Two, or half the number of chromosomes in the parent, are present at the end of meiosis. After mitosis, there would be four chromosomes, the same number as in the parent cell.

Chapter 6—Genes and Gene Technology
Page 131: TGGATCAAC
Page 137: 1. 1000 amino acids 2. DNA codes for proteins. Your flesh is composed of proteins, and the way those proteins are constructed and combined influences much about the way you look.

Chapter 7—The Evolution of Living Things
Page 165: The population of light-colored moths would increase.

Chapter 8—The History of Life on Earth
Page 179: 5 g, 2.5 g
Page 185: b, c, d, a

Chapter 9—Classification
Page 210: 1. The two kingdoms of bacteria are different from all other kingdoms because bacteria are prokaryotes—single-celled organisms that have no nucleus. 2. The organisms in the kingdom Protista are all eukaryotes.

Chapter 10—Bacteria and Viruses
Page 227: Cyanobacteria were once classified as plants because they use photosynthesis to make food.

Chapter 11—Protists and Fungi
Page 246: No, some funguslike protists are parasites or consumers.
Page 252: 1. Cilia are used to move a ciliate through the water and to sweep food toward the organism. 2. Ciliates are classified as animal-like protists because they are consumers and they move.

Chapter 12—Introduction to Plants
Page 272: Plants need a cuticle to keep the leaves from drying out. Algae grow in a wet environment, so they do not need a cuticle.
Page 288: Stems hold up the leaves so that the leaves can get adequate sunshine for photosynthesis.

Chapter 13—Plant Processes
Page 301: Fruit develops from the ovary, so the flower can have only one fruit. Seeds develop from the ovules, so there should be six seeds.
Page 305: The sun is the source of the energy in sugar.
Page 308: 1. (See concept map below.)
2. During negative phototropism, the plant would grow away from the stimulus (light), so it would be bending to the left.

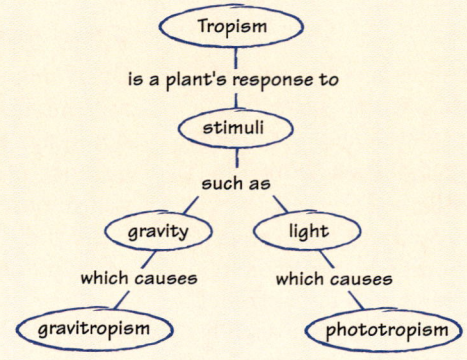

Chapter 14—Animals and Behavior

Page 324: Like other vertebrates, humans have a skull and a backbone.

Chapter 15—Invertebrates

Page 349: Because medusas swim through the water by contracting their bodies, they must have a nervous system that can control these actions. Polyps move very little, so they don't need as complex a nervous system.

Page 359: Segmented worms belong to the phylum Annelida. Centipedes are arthropods. Centipedes have jointed legs, antennae, and mandibles. Segmented worms have none of these characteristics.

Chapter 16—Fishes, Amphibians, and Reptiles

Page 383: Amphibians use their skin to absorb oxygen from the air. Their skin is thin, moist, and full of blood vessels, just like a lung.

Page 389: 1. Thick, dry skin and amniotic eggs help reptiles live on dry land. 2. The hard shell prevents fertilization, so the egg must be fertilized before the shell is added.

Chapter 17—Birds and Mammals

Page 402: 1. Down feathers are not stiff and smooth and could not give structure to the wings. They are adapted to keep the bird warm. 2. Birds need tremendous amounts of food for fuel because it takes a lot of energy to fly.

Page 416: Monotremes are mammals that lay eggs. Marsupials bear live young but carry them in pouches or skin folds before they are able to live independently. Placentals develop inside the mother's body and are nourished through a placenta before birth.

Page 421: 1. Bats bear live young, have fur, and do not have feathers. 2. Rodents and lagomorphs both are small mammals with long sensitive whiskers and gnawing teeth. Unlike rodents, lagomorphs have two sets of incisors and a short tail.

Chapter 18—Interactions of Living Things

Page 439: Humans are omnivores. An omnivore eats both plants and animals. Humans can eat meat and vegetables as well as animal products, such as milk and eggs, and plant products such as grains and fruit.

Page 440: A food chain shows how energy moves in one direction from one organism to the next. A food web shows that there are many energy pathways between organisms.

Page 445: 1. If an area has enough water to support 10 organisms, any additional organisms will cause some to go without water and move away, or die. 2. Weather favorable for growing the food that deer eat will allow the forest to support more deer.

Chapter 19—Cycles in Nature

Page 464: The main difference between primary and secondary succession is that primary succession begins with the formation of soil. Secondary succession begins on preexisting soil, such as when an existing community is disrupted by a natural disaster or by farming. Pioneer species in primary succession are usually lichens, which begin the formation of soil. Pioneer species in secondary succession are usually seed plants, which germinate and take root in the soil.

Chapter 20—The Earth's Ecosystems

Page 479: Deciduous forests tend to exist in mid-latitude or temperate regions, while coniferous forests tend to exist in higher, colder latitudes, closer to the poles.

Page 484: Answers include: the amount of sunlight penetrating the water, its distance from land, the depth of the water, the salinity of the water, and the water's temperature. 2. There are several possible answers. Some organisms are adapted for catching prey at great depths; some feed on dead plankton and larger organisms that filter down from above; and some, such as the bacteria around thermal vents, make food from chemicals in the water.

Chapter 21—Environmental Problems and Solutions

Page 501: 1. We use nonrenewable resources when we burn fossil fuels when driving or riding in a car or burning coal for heat. When we use minerals that are mined, we are using a nonrenewable resource. Pumping ground water is another use of a nonrenewable resource, if the water is used faster than it is replenished. 2. If a nonrenewable resource is used up, we can no longer rely on that resource. Certain oil and coal deposits have been building since life began on the planet. It may take hundreds of years to replace a mature forest that can be cut in a day.

Page 507: 1. Turn off lights, CD players, radios, and computers when leaving a room. Set thermostats a little lower in the winter (wear sweaters). Don't leave the refrigerator door open while deciding what you want. 2. plastic bags, rechargeable batteries, water, clothing, toys; The difference between a reused and a recycled object is that a reused article may be cleaned but is basically unchanged. A recycled article has been broken down and re-formed into another usable product.

Self-Check Answers

Chapter 22—Body Organization and Structure

Page 532: Curl-ups use flexor muscles; push-ups use extensor muscles.

Page 535: Blood vessels belong to the cardiovascular system.

Chapter 23—Circulation and Respiration

Page 550: The hollow tube shape of arteries and veins allows blood to reach all parts of the body. Valves in the veins prevent blood from flowing backward.

Page 554: Like blood vessels, lymph capillaries receive fluid from the spaces surrounding cells. The fluid absorbed by lymph capillaries flows into lymph vessels. These vessels drain into large neck veins instead of into an organ, such as the heart. Lymph does not deliver oxygen and nutrients.

Chapter 24—The Digestive and Urinary Systems

Page 573: Bile is involved in the physical digestion because emulsification does not change the chemical composition of the fat molecules; it only increases the surface area of each fat droplet.

Chapter 25—Communication and Control

Page 593: 1. cerebrum 2. cerebellum 3. to protect the spinal cord

Chapter 26—Reproduction and Development

Page 613: In asexual reproduction, one animal produces offspring that are genetically identical to itself. In sexual reproduction, the genes of two individuals are mixed when sex cells join to form a zygote. This zygote develops into a unique individual.

Page 621: The uterus provides the nutrients and protection that the embryo needs to continue growing. The uterus is also the only place the placenta will form.

Chapter 27—Body Defenses and Disease

Page 637: If Jackie did not wash the counter after cutting up the meat, bacteria could grow on the counter where the meat was. This bacteria could contaminate her brother's sandwich.

Chapter 28—Staying Healthy

Page 661: You have eaten two servings from the bread, cereal, rice, pasta group; one serving from the fruit group, and one from the milk, yogurt and cheese group.

Page 664: Regular use of some drugs may cause tolerance or addiction. Withdrawal symptoms occur when the body does not receive a drug that it is addicted to.

Page 667: 1. A hallucination is a vision or sound that is not real. 2. Heroin is highly addictive and potentially deadly. If shared needles are used to inject it, users risk getting diseases like hepatitis or AIDS.

CONTENTS

Concept Mapping 786
SI Measurement 787
Temperature Scales 788
Measuring Skills 789
Scientific Method 790
Making Charts and Graphs 793
Math Refresher 796
Periodic Table of the Elements 800
Physical Science Refresher 802
The Six Kingdoms 804
Using the Microscope 806

Concept Mapping: A Way to Bring Ideas Together

What Is a Concept Map?

Have you ever tried to tell someone about a book or a chapter you've just read and found that you can remember only a few isolated words and ideas? Or maybe you've memorized facts for a test and then weeks later discovered you're not even sure what topics those facts covered.

In both cases, you may have understood the ideas or concepts by themselves but not in relation to one another. If you could somehow link the ideas together, you would probably understand them better and remember them longer. This is something a concept map can help you do. A concept map is a way to see how ideas or concepts fit together. It can help you see the "big picture."

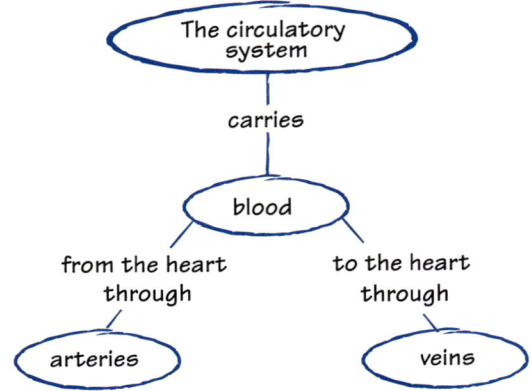

How to Make a Concept Map

1 Make a list of the main ideas or concepts.

It might help to write each concept on its own slip of paper. This will make it easier to rearrange the concepts as many times as necessary to make sense of how the concepts are connected. After you've made a few concept maps this way, you can go directly from writing your list to actually making the map.

2 Arrange the concepts in order from the most general to the most specific.

Put the most general concept at the top and circle it. Ask yourself, "How does this concept relate to the remaining concepts?" As you see the relationships, arrange the concepts in order from general to specific.

3 Connect the related concepts with lines.

4 On each line, write an action word or short phrase that shows how the concepts are related.

Look at the concept maps on this page, and then see if you can make one for the following terms:

plants, water, photosynthesis, carbon dioxide, sun's energy

One possible answer is provided at right, but don't look at it until you try the concept map yourself.

786   Appendix

SI Measurement

The International System of Units, or SI, is the standard system of measurement used by many scientists. Using the same standards of measurement makes it easier for scientists to communicate with one another.

SI works by combining prefixes and base units. Each base unit can be used with different prefixes to define smaller and larger quantities. The table below lists common SI prefixes.

SI Prefixes

Prefix	Abbreviation	Factor	Example
kilo-	k	1,000	kilogram, 1 kg = 1,000 g
hecto-	h	100	hectoliter, 1 hL = 100 L
deka-	da	10	dekameter, 1 dam = 10 m
		1	meter, liter
deci-	d	0.1	decigram, 1 dg = 0.1 g
centi-	c	0.01	centimeter, 1 cm = 0.01 m
milli-	m	0.001	milliliter, 1 mL = 0.001 L
micro-	μ	0.000 001	micrometer, 1 μm = 0.000 001 m

SI Conversion Table

SI units	From SI to English	From English to SI
Length		
kilometer (km) = 1,000 m	1 km = 0.621 mi	1 mi = 1.609 km
meter (m) = 100 cm	1 m = 3.281 ft	1 ft = 0.305 m
centimeter (cm) = 0.01 m	1 cm = 0.394 in.	1 in. = 2.540 cm
millimeter (mm) = 0.001 m	1 mm = 0.039 in.	
micrometer (μm) = 0.000 001 m		
nanometer (nm) = 0.000 000 001 m		
Area		
square kilometer (km^2) = 100 hectares	1 km^2 = 0.386 mi^2	1 mi^2 = 2.590 km^2
hectare (ha) = 10,000 m^2	1 ha = 2.471 acres	1 acre = 0.405 ha
square meter (m^2) = 10,000 cm^2	1 m^2 = 10.765 ft^2	1 ft^2 = 0.093 m^2
square centimeter (cm^2) = 100 mm^2	1 cm^2 = 0.155 $in.^2$	1 $in.^2$ = 6.452 cm^2
Volume		
liter (L) = 1,000 mL = 1 dm^3	1 L = 1.057 fl qt	1 fl qt = 0.946 L
milliliter (mL) = 0.001 L = 1 cm^3	1 mL = 0.034 fl oz	1 fl oz = 29.575 mL
microliter (μL) = 0.000 001 L		
Mass		
kilogram (kg) = 1,000 g	1 kg = 2.205 lb	1 lb = 0.454 kg
gram (g) = 1,000 mg	1 g = 0.035 oz	1 oz = 28.349 g
milligram (mg) = 0.001 g		
microgram (μg) = 0.000 001 g		

Temperature Scales

Temperature can be expressed using three different scales: Fahrenheit, Celsius, and Kelvin. The SI unit for temperature is the kelvin (K). Although 0 K is much colder than 0°C, a change of 1 K is equal to a change of 1°C.

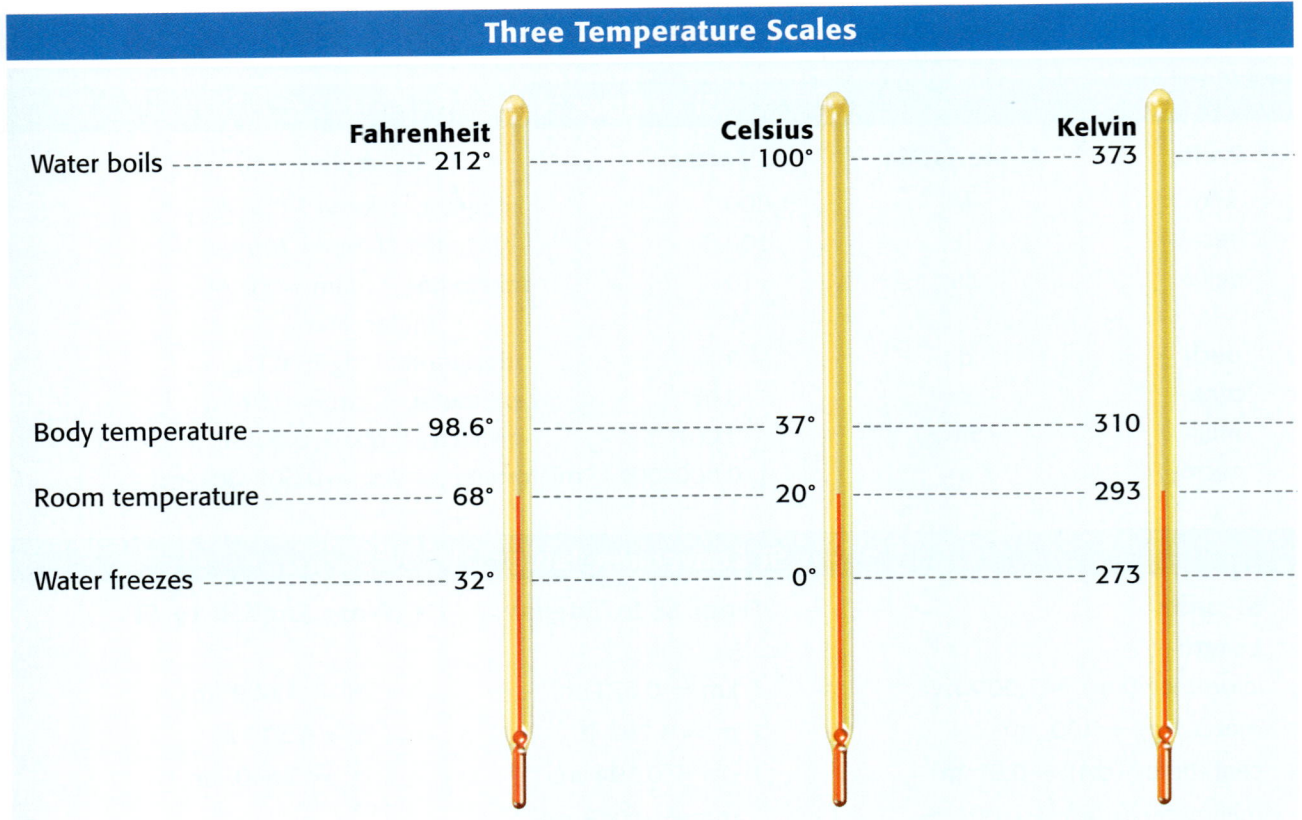

Three Temperature Scales

	Fahrenheit	Celsius	Kelvin
Water boils	212°	100°	373
Body temperature	98.6°	37°	310
Room temperature	68°	20°	293
Water freezes	32°	0°	273

Temperature Conversions Table

To convert	Use this equation:	Example
Celsius to Fahrenheit °C ⟶ °F	°F = $\left(\frac{9}{5} \times °C\right) + 32$	Convert 45°C to °F. °F = $\left(\frac{9}{5} \times 45°C\right) + 32 = 113°F$
Fahrenheit to Celsius °F ⟶ °C	°C = $\frac{5}{9} \times (°F - 32)$	Convert 68°F to °C. °C = $\frac{5}{9} \times (68°F - 32) = 20°C$
Celsius to Kelvin °C ⟶ K	K = °C + 273	Convert 45°C to K. K = 45°C + 273 = 318 K
Kelvin to Celsius K ⟶ °C	°C = K − 273	Convert 32 K to °C. °C = 32 K − 273 = −241°C

Measuring Skills

Using a Graduated Cylinder

When using a graduated cylinder to measure volume, keep the following procedures in mind:

❶ Make sure the cylinder is on a flat, level surface.

❷ Move your head so that your eye is level with the surface of the liquid.

❸ Read the mark closest to the liquid level. On glass graduated cylinders, read the mark closest to the center of the curve in the liquid's surface.

Using a Meterstick or Metric Ruler

When using a meterstick or metric ruler to measure length, keep the following procedures in mind:

❶ Place the ruler firmly against the object you are measuring.

❷ Align one edge of the object exactly with the zero end of the ruler.

❸ Look at the other edge of the object to see which of the marks on the ruler is closest to that edge. **Note:** Each small slash between the centimeters represents a millimeter, which is one-tenth of a centimeter.

Using a Triple-Beam Balance

When using a triple-beam balance to measure mass, keep the following procedures in mind:

❶ Make sure the balance is on a level surface.

❷ Place all of the countermasses at zero. Adjust the balancing knob until the pointer rests at zero.

❸ Place the object you wish to measure on the pan. **Caution:** Do not place hot objects or chemicals directly on the balance pan.

❹ Move the largest countermass along the beam to the right until it is at the last notch that does not tip the balance. Follow the same procedure with the next-largest countermass. Then move the smallest countermass until the pointer rests at zero.

❺ Add the readings from the three beams together to determine the mass of the object.

❻ When determining the mass of crystals or powders, use a piece of filter paper. First find the mass of the paper. Then add the crystals or powder to the paper and re-measure. The actual mass of the crystals or powder is the total mass minus the mass of the paper. When finding the mass of liquids, first find the mass of the empty container. Then find the mass of the liquid and container together. The mass of the liquid is the total mass minus the mass of the container.

Appendix **789**

Scientific Method

The series of steps that scientists use to answer questions and solve problems is often called the **scientific method.** The scientific method is not a rigid procedure. Scientists may use all of the steps or just some of the steps of the scientific method. They may even repeat some of the steps. The goal of the scientific method is to come up with reliable answers and solutions.

Six Steps of the Scientific Method

1 Ask a Question Good questions come from careful **observations.** You make observations by using your senses to gather information. Sometimes you may use instruments, such as microscopes and telescopes, to extend the range of your senses. As you observe the natural world, you will discover that you have many more questions than answers. These questions drive the scientific method.

Questions beginning with *what, why, how,* and *when* are very important in focusing an investigation, and they often lead to a hypothesis. (You will learn what a hypothesis is in the next step.) Here is an example of a question that could lead to further investigation.

Question: How does acid rain affect plant growth?

2 Form a Hypothesis After you come up with a question, you need to turn the question into a **hypothesis.** A hypothesis is a clear statement of what you expect the answer to your question to be. Your hypothesis will represent your best "educated guess" based on your observations and what you already know. A good hypothesis is testable. If observations and information cannot be gathered or if an experiment cannot be designed to test your hypothesis, it is untestable, and the investigation can go no further.

Here is a hypothesis that could be formed from the question, "How does acid rain affect plant growth?"

Hypothesis: Acid rain causes plants to grow more slowly.

Notice that the hypothesis provides some specifics that lead to methods of testing. The hypothesis can also lead to predictions. A **prediction** is what you think will be the outcome of your experiment or data collection. Predictions are usually stated in an "if . . . then" format. For example, **if** meat is kept at room temperature, **then** it will spoil faster than meat kept in the refrigerator. More than one prediction can be made for a single hypothesis. Here is a sample prediction for the hypothesis that acid rain causes plants to grow more slowly.

Prediction: If a plant is watered with only acid rain (which has a pH of 4), then the plant will grow at half its normal rate.

Appendix

3 **Test the Hypothesis** After you have formed a hypothesis and made a prediction, you should test your hypothesis. There are different ways to do this. Perhaps the most familiar way is to conduct a **controlled experiment.** A controlled experiment tests only one factor at a time. A controlled experiment has a **control group** and one or more **experimental groups.** All the factors for the control and experimental groups are the same except for one factor, which is called the **variable.** By changing only one factor, you can see the results of just that one change.

Sometimes, the nature of an investigation makes a controlled experiment impossible. For example, dinosaurs have been extinct for millions of years, and the Earth's core is surrounded by thousands of meters of rock. It would be difficult, if not impossible, to conduct controlled experiments on such things. Under such circumstances, a hypothesis may be tested by making detailed observations. Taking measurements is one way of making observations.

4 **Analyze the Results** After you have completed your experiments, made your observations, and collected your data, you must analyze all the information you have gathered. Tables and graphs are often used in this step to organize the data.

5 **Draw Conclusions** Based on the analysis of your data, you should conclude whether or not your results support your hypothesis. If your hypothesis is supported, you (or others) might want to repeat the observations or experiments to verify your results. If your hypothesis is not supported by the data, you may have to check your procedure for errors. You may even have to reject your hypothesis and make a new one. If you cannot draw a conclusion from your results, you may have to try the investigation again or carry out further observations or experiments.

6 **Communicate Results** After any scientific investigation, you should report your results. By doing a written or oral report, you let others know what you have learned. They may want to repeat your investigation to see if they get the same results. Your report may even lead to another question, which in turn may lead to another investigation.

Appendix

Scientific Method in Action

The scientific method is not a "straight line" of steps. It contains loops in which several steps may be repeated over and over again, while others may not be necessary. For example, sometimes scientists will find that testing one hypothesis raises new questions and new hypotheses to be tested. And sometimes, testing the hypothesis leads directly to a conclusion. Furthermore, the steps in the scientific method are not always used in the same order. Follow the steps in the diagram below, and see how many different directions the scientific method can take you.

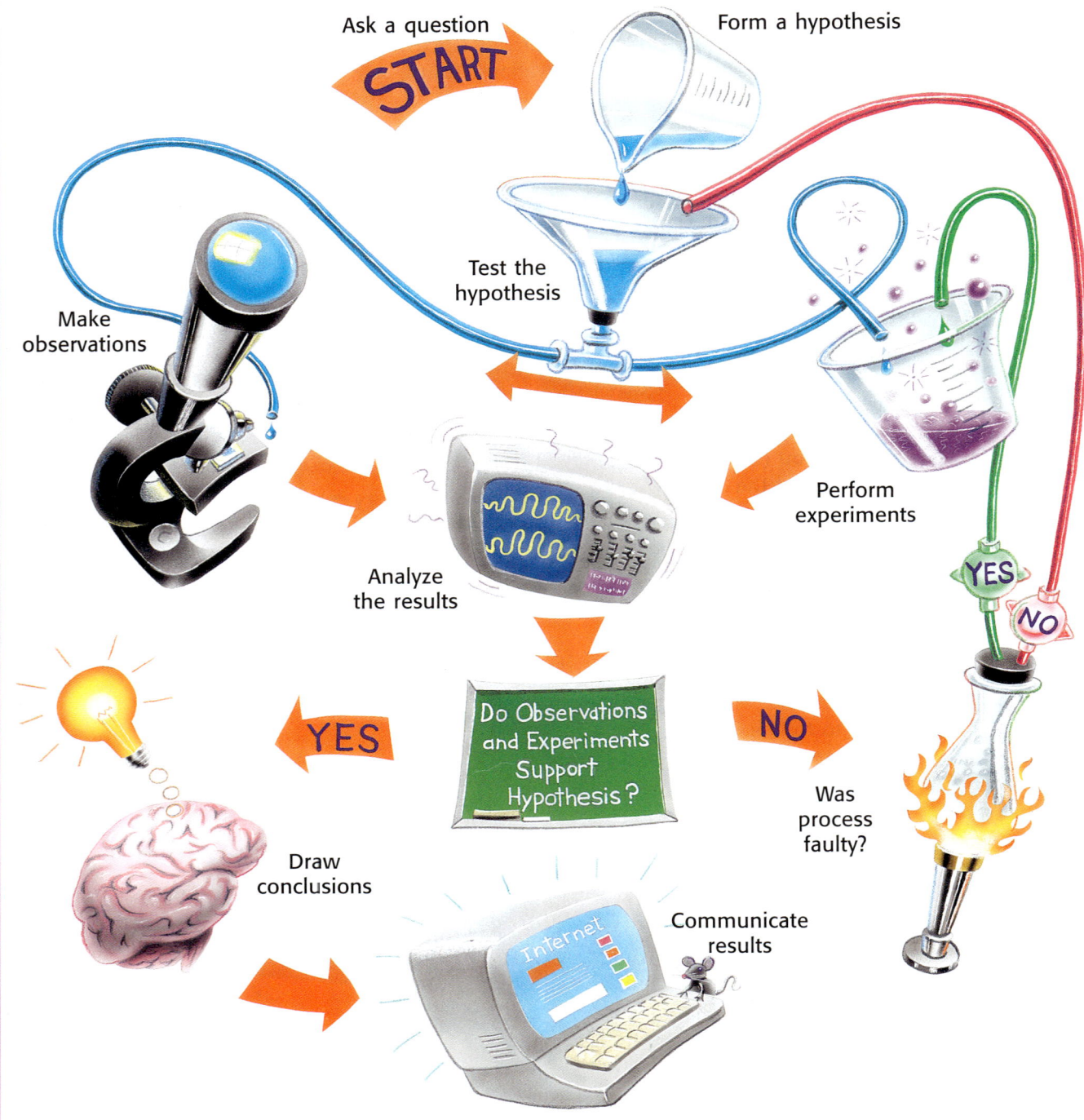

Making Charts and Graphs

Circle Graphs

A circle graph, or pie chart, shows how each group of data relates to all of the data. Each part of the circle represents a category of the data. The entire circle represents all of the data. For example, a biologist studying a hardwood forest in Wisconsin found that there were five different types of trees. The data table at right summarizes the biologist's findings.

Wisconsin Hardwood Trees	
Type of tree	Number found
Oak	600
Maple	750
Beech	300
Birch	1,200
Hickory	150
Total	3,000

How to Make a Circle Graph

1 In order to make a circle graph of this data, first find the percentage of each type of tree. To do this, divide the number of individual trees by the total number of trees and multiply by 100.

$$\frac{600 \text{ oak}}{3,000 \text{ trees}} \times 100 = 20\%$$

$$\frac{750 \text{ maple}}{3,000 \text{ trees}} \times 100 = 25\%$$

$$\frac{300 \text{ beech}}{3,000 \text{ trees}} \times 100 = 10\%$$

$$\frac{1,200 \text{ birch}}{3,000 \text{ trees}} \times 100 = 40\%$$

$$\frac{150 \text{ hickory}}{3,000 \text{ trees}} \times 100 = 5\%$$

2 Now determine the size of the pie shapes that make up the chart. Do this by multiplying each percentage by 360°. Remember that a circle contains 360°.

$20\% \times 360° = 72°$ $25\% \times 360° = 90°$
$10\% \times 360° = 36°$ $40\% \times 360° = 144°$
$5\% \times 360° = 18°$

3 Then check that the sum of the percentages is 100 and the sum of the degrees is 360.

$20\% + 25\% + 10\% + 40\% + 5\% = 100\%$
$72° + 90° + 36° + 144° + 18° = 360°$

4 Use a compass to draw a circle and mark its center.

5 Then use a protractor to draw angles of 72°, 90°, 36°, 144°, and 18° in the circle.

6 Finally, label each part of the graph, and choose an appropriate title.

A Community of Wisconsin Hardwood Trees

Appendix 793

Line Graphs

Line graphs are most often used to demonstrate continuous change. For example, Mr. Smith's science class analyzed the population records for their hometown, Appleton, between 1900 and 2000. Examine the data at left.

Because the year and the population change, they are the *variables*. The population is determined by, or dependent on, the year. Therefore, the population is called the **dependent variable**, and the year is called the **independent variable**. Each set of data is called a **data pair**. To prepare a line graph, data pairs must first be organized in a table like the one at left.

Population of Appleton, 1900–2000

Year	Population
1900	1,800
1920	2,500
1940	3,200
1960	3,900
1980	4,600
2000	5,300

How to Make a Line Graph

1. Place the independent variable along the horizontal (x) axis. Place the dependent variable along the vertical (y) axis.

2. Label the x-axis "Year" and the y-axis "Population." Look at your largest and smallest values for the population. Determine a scale for the y-axis that will provide enough space to show these values. You must use the same scale for the entire length of the axis. Find an appropriate scale for the x-axis too.

3. Choose reasonable starting points for each axis.

4. Plot the data pairs as accurately as possible.

5. Choose a title that accurately represents the data.

How to Determine Slope

Slope is the ratio of the change in the y-axis to the change in the x-axis, or "rise over run."

1. Choose two points on the line graph. For example, the population of Appleton in 2000 was 5,300 people. Therefore, you can define point *a* as (2000, 5,300). In 1900, the population was 1,800 people. Define point *b* as (1900, 1,800).

2. Find the change in the y-axis.
(y at point *a*) − (y at point *b*)
5,300 people − 1,800 people = 3,500 people

3. Find the change in the x-axis.
(x at point *a*) − (x at point *b*)
2000 − 1900 = 100 years

4. Calculate the slope of the graph by dividing the change in y by the change in x.

$$\text{slope} = \frac{\text{change in } y}{\text{change in } x}$$

$$\text{slope} = \frac{3,500 \text{ people}}{100 \text{ years}}$$

slope = 35 people per year

In this example, the population in Appleton increased by a fixed amount each year. The graph of this data is a straight line. Therefore, the relationship is **linear**. When the graph of a set of data is not a straight line, the relationship is **nonlinear**.

794 Appendix

Using Algebra to Determine Slope

The equation in step 4 may also be arranged to be:

$y = kx$

where y represents the change in the y-axis, k represents the slope, and x represents the change in the x-axis.

$$\text{slope} = \frac{\text{change in } y}{\text{change in } x}$$

$$k = \frac{y}{x}$$

$$k \times x = \frac{y \times x}{x}$$

$$kx = y$$

Bar Graphs

Bar graphs are used to demonstrate change that is not continuous. These graphs can be used to indicate trends when the data are taken over a long period of time. A meteorologist gathered the precipitation records at right for Hartford, Connecticut, for April 1–15, 1996, and used a bar graph to represent the data.

Precipitation in Hartford, Connecticut April 1–15, 1996

Date	Precipitation (cm)	Date	Precipitation (cm)
April 1	0.5	April 9	0.25
April 2	1.25	April 10	0.0
April 3	0.0	April 11	1.0
April 4	0.0	April 12	0.0
April 5	0.0	April 13	0.25
April 6	0.0	April 14	0.0
April 7	0.0	April 15	6.50
April 8	1.75		

How to Make a Bar Graph

1. Use an appropriate scale and a reasonable starting point for each axis.
2. Label the axes, and plot the data.
3. Choose a title that accurately represents the data.

Precipitation in Hartford, Connecticut, April 1–15, 1996

Appendix

Math Refresher

Science requires an understanding of many math concepts. The following pages will help you review some important math skills.

Averages

An **average,** or **mean,** simplifies a list of numbers into a single number that *approximates* their value.

Example: Find the average of the following set of numbers: 5, 4, 7, and 8.

Step 1: Find the sum.

$$5 + 4 + 7 + 8 = 24$$

Step 2: Divide the sum by the amount of numbers in your set. Because there are four numbers in this example, divide the sum by 4.

$$\frac{24}{4} = 6$$

The average, or mean, is **6.**

Ratios

A **ratio** is a comparison between numbers, and it is usually written as a fraction.

Example: Find the ratio of thermometers to students if you have 36 thermometers and 48 students in your class.

Step 1: Make the ratio.

$$\frac{36 \text{ thermometers}}{48 \text{ students}}$$

Step 2: Reduce the fraction to its simplest form.

$$\frac{36}{48} = \frac{36 \div 12}{48 \div 12} = \frac{3}{4}$$

The ratio of thermometers to students is **3 to 4,** or $\frac{3}{4}$. The ratio may also be written in the form 3:4.

Proportions

A **proportion** is an equation that states that two ratios are equal.

$$\frac{3}{1} = \frac{12}{4}$$

To solve a proportion, first multiply across the equal sign. This is called cross-multiplication. If you know three of the quantities in a proportion, you can use cross-multiplication to find the fourth.

Example: Imagine that you are making a scale model of the solar system for your science project. The diameter of Jupiter is 11.2 times the diameter of the Earth. If you are using a plastic-foam ball with a diameter of 2 cm to represent the Earth, what diameter does the ball representing Jupiter need to be?

$$\frac{11.2}{1} = \frac{x}{2 \text{ cm}}$$

Step 1: Cross-multiply.

$$\frac{11.2}{1} \diagup\!\!\!\!\diagdown \frac{x}{2}$$

$$11.2 \times 2 = x \times 1$$

Step 2: Multiply.

$$22.4 = x \times 1$$

Step 3: Isolate the variable by dividing both sides by 1.

$$x = \frac{22.4}{1}$$

$$x = 22.4 \text{ cm}$$

You will need to use a ball with a diameter of **22.4 cm** to represent Jupiter.

Percentages

A **percentage** is a ratio of a given number to 100.

Example: What is 85 percent of 40?

Step 1: Rewrite the percentage by moving the decimal point two places to the left.

$$.85$$

Step 2: Multiply the decimal by the number you are calculating the percentage of.

$$0.85 \times 40 = 34$$

85 percent of 40 is **34.**

Decimals

To **add** or **subtract decimals,** line up the digits vertically so that the decimal points line up. Then add or subtract the columns from right to left, carrying or borrowing numbers as necessary.

Example: Add the following numbers: 3.1415 and 2.96.

Step 1: Line up the digits vertically so that the decimal points line up.

$$\begin{array}{r} 3.1415 \\ + 2.96 \\ \hline \end{array}$$

Step 2: Add the columns from right to left, carrying when necessary.

$$\begin{array}{r} {\scriptstyle 1\ 1} \\ 3.1415 \\ + 2.96 \\ \hline 6.1015 \end{array}$$

The sum is **6.1015.**

Fractions

Numbers tell you how many; **fractions** tell you *how much of a whole.*

Example: Your class has 24 plants. Your teacher instructs you to put 5 in a shady spot. What fraction does this represent?

Step 1: Write a fraction with the total number of parts in the whole as the denominator.

$$\frac{?}{24}$$

Step 2: Write the number of parts of the whole being represented as the numerator.

$$\frac{5}{24}$$

$\frac{5}{24}$ of the plants will be in the shade.

Reducing Fractions

It is usually best to express a fraction in simplest form. This is called *reducing* a fraction.

Example: Reduce the fraction $\frac{30}{45}$ to its simplest form.

Step 1: Find the largest whole number that will divide evenly into both the numerator and denominator. This number is called the greatest common factor (GCF).

factors of the numerator 30: 1, 2, 3, 5, 6, 10, **15,** 30

factors of the denominator 45: 1, 3, 5, 9, **15,** 45

Step 2: Divide both the numerator and the denominator by the GCF, which in this case is 15.

$$\frac{30}{45} = \frac{30 \div 15}{45 \div 15} = \frac{2}{3}$$

$\frac{30}{45}$ reduced to its simplest form is $\frac{2}{3}$.

Appendix

Adding and Subtracting Fractions

To **add** or **subtract fractions** that have the **same denominator,** simply add or subtract the numerators.

Examples:
$$\frac{3}{5} + \frac{1}{5} = ? \text{ and } \frac{3}{4} - \frac{1}{4} = ?$$

Step 1: Add or subtract the numerators.
$$\frac{3}{5} + \frac{1}{5} = \frac{4}{} \text{ and } \frac{3}{4} - \frac{1}{4} = \frac{2}{}$$

Step 2: Write the sum or difference over the denominator.
$$\frac{3}{5} + \frac{1}{5} = \frac{4}{5} \text{ and } \frac{3}{4} - \frac{1}{4} = \frac{2}{4}$$

Step 3: If necessary, reduce the fraction to its simplest form.
$$\frac{4}{5} \text{ cannot be reduced, and } \frac{2}{4} = \frac{1}{2}.$$

To **add** or **subtract fractions** that have **different denominators,** first find the least common denominator (LCD).

Examples:
$$\frac{1}{2} + \frac{1}{6} = ? \text{ and } \frac{3}{4} - \frac{2}{3} = ?$$

Step 1: Write the equivalent fractions with a common denominator.
$$\frac{3}{6} + \frac{1}{6} = ? \text{ and } \frac{9}{12} - \frac{8}{12} = ?$$

Step 2: Add or subtract.
$$\frac{3}{6} + \frac{1}{6} = \frac{4}{6} \text{ and } \frac{9}{12} - \frac{8}{12} = \frac{1}{12}$$

Step 3: If necessary, reduce the fraction to its simplest form.
$$\frac{4}{6} = \frac{2}{3}, \text{ and } \frac{1}{12} \text{ cannot be reduced.}$$

Multiplying Fractions

To **multiply fractions,** multiply the numerators and the denominators together, and then reduce the fraction to its simplest form.

Example:
$$\frac{5}{9} \times \frac{7}{10} = ?$$

Step 1: Multiply the numerators and denominators.
$$\frac{5}{9} \times \frac{7}{10} = \frac{5 \times 7}{9 \times 10} = \frac{35}{90}$$

Step 2: Reduce.
$$\frac{35}{90} = \frac{35 \div 5}{90 \div 5} = \frac{7}{18}$$

Dividing Fractions

To **divide fractions,** first rewrite the divisor (the number you divide *by*) upside down. This is called the reciprocal of the divisor. Then you can multiply and reduce if necessary.

Example:
$$\frac{5}{8} \div \frac{3}{2} = ?$$

Step 1: Rewrite the divisor as its reciprocal.
$$\frac{3}{2} \to \frac{2}{3}$$

Step 2: Multiply.
$$\frac{5}{8} \times \frac{2}{3} = \frac{5 \times 2}{8 \times 3} = \frac{10}{24}$$

Step 3: Reduce.
$$\frac{10}{24} = \frac{10 \div 2}{24 \div 2} = \frac{5}{12}$$

Scientific Notation

Scientific notation is a short way of representing very large and very small numbers without writing all of the place-holding zeros.

Example: Write 653,000,000 in scientific notation.

Step 1: Write the number without the place-holding zeros.

$$653$$

Step 2: Place the decimal point after the first digit.

$$6.53$$

Step 3: Find the exponent by counting the number of places that you moved the decimal point.

$$6.53000000$$

The decimal point was moved eight places to the left. Therefore, the exponent of 10 is positive 8. Remember, if the decimal point had moved to the right, the exponent would be negative.

Step 4: Write the number in scientific notation.

$$6.53 \times 10^8$$

Area

Area is the number of square units needed to cover the surface of an object.

Formulas:
Area of a square = side × side
Area of a rectangle = length × width
Area of a triangle = $\frac{1}{2}$ × base × height

Examples: Find the areas.

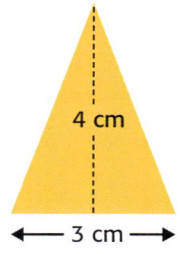

Triangle
Area = $\frac{1}{2}$ × base × height
Area = $\frac{1}{2}$ × 3 cm × 4 cm
Area = **6 cm²**

Rectangle
Area = length × width
Area = 6 cm × 3 cm
Area = **18 cm²**

Square
Area = side × side
Area = 3 cm × 3 cm
Area = **9 cm²**

Volume

Volume is the amount of space something occupies.

Formulas:
Volume of a cube = side × side × side

Volume of a prism = area of base × height

Examples: Find the volume of the solids.

Cube
Volume = side × side × side
Volume = 4 cm × 4 cm × 4 cm
Volume = **64 cm³**

Prism
Volume = area of base × height
Volume = (area of triangle) × height
Volume = $\left(\frac{1}{2} \times 3\text{ cm} \times 4\text{ cm}\right) \times 5\text{ cm}$
Volume = 6 cm² × 5 cm
Volume = **30 cm³**

Periodic Table of the Elements

Each square on the table includes an element's name, chemical symbol, atomic number, and atomic mass.

Atomic number — 6
Chemical symbol — C
Element name — Carbon
Atomic mass — 12.0

The background color indicates the type of element. Carbon is a nonmetal.

The color of the chemical symbol indicates the physical state at room temperature. Carbon is a solid.

Background
- Metals
- Metalloids
- Nonmetals

Chemical symbol
- Solid
- Liquid
- Gas

Period 1
1
H
Hydrogen
1.0

	Group 1	Group 2		Group 3	Group 4	Group 5	Group 6	Group 7	Group 8	Group 9
Period 2	3 Li Lithium 6.9	4 Be Beryllium 9.0								
Period 3	11 Na Sodium 23.0	12 Mg Magnesium 24.3								
Period 4	19 K Potassium 39.1	20 Ca Calcium 40.1		21 Sc Scandium 45.0	22 Ti Titanium 47.9	23 V Vanadium 50.9	24 Cr Chromium 52.0	25 Mn Manganese 54.9	26 Fe Iron 55.8	27 Co Cobalt 58.9
Period 5	37 Rb Rubidium 85.5	38 Sr Strontium 87.6		39 Y Yttrium 88.9	40 Zr Zirconium 91.2	41 Nb Niobium 92.9	42 Mo Molybdenum 95.9	43 Tc Technetium (97.9)	44 Ru Ruthenium 101.1	45 Rh Rhodium 102.9
Period 6	55 Cs Cesium 132.9	56 Ba Barium 137.3		57 La Lanthanum 138.9	72 Hf Hafnium 178.5	73 Ta Tantalum 180.9	74 W Tungsten 183.8	75 Re Rhenium 186.2	76 Os Osmium 190.2	77 Ir Iridium 192.2
Period 7	87 Fr Francium (223.0)	88 Ra Radium (226.0)		89 Ac Actinium (227.0)	104 Rf Rutherfordium (261.1)	105 Db Dubnium (262.1)	106 Sg Seaborgium (263.1)	107 Bh Bohrium (262.1)	108 Hs Hassium (265)	109 Mt Meitnerium (266)

A row of elements is called a period.

A column of elements is called a group or family.

Lanthanides
58	59	60	61	62
Ce Cerium 140.1	Pr Praseodymium 140.9	Nd Neodymium 144.2	Pm Promethium (144.9)	Sm Samarium 150.4

Actinides
90	91	92	93	94
Th Thorium 232.0	Pa Protactinium 231.0	U Uranium 238.0	Np Neptunium (237.0)	Pu Plutonium 244.1

These elements are placed below the table to allow the table to be narrower.

TOPIC: Periodic Table
GO TO: go.hrw.com
KEYWORD: HN0 Periodic

Visit the HRW Web site to see the most recent version of the periodic table.

This zigzag line reminds you where the metals, nonmetals, and metalloids are.

Group 10	Group 11	Group 12	Group 13	Group 14	Group 15	Group 16	Group 17	Group 18
								2 **He** Helium 4.0
			5 **B** Boron 10.8	6 **C** Carbon 12.0	7 **N** Nitrogen 14.0	8 **O** Oxygen 16.0	9 **F** Fluorine 19.0	10 **Ne** Neon 20.2
			13 **Al** Aluminum 27.0	14 **Si** Silicon 28.1	15 **P** Phosphorus 31.0	16 **S** Sulfur 32.1	17 **Cl** Chlorine 35.5	18 **Ar** Argon 39.9
28 **Ni** Nickel 58.7	29 **Cu** Copper 63.5	30 **Zn** Zinc 65.4	31 **Ga** Gallium 69.7	32 **Ge** Germanium 72.6	33 **As** Arsenic 74.9	34 **Se** Selenium 79.0	35 **Br** Bromine 79.9	36 **Kr** Krypton 83.8
46 **Pd** Palladium 106.4	47 **Ag** Silver 107.9	48 **Cd** Cadmium 112.4	49 **In** Indium 114.8	50 **Sn** Tin 118.7	51 **Sb** Antimony 121.8	52 **Te** Tellurium 127.6	53 **I** Iodine 126.9	54 **Xe** Xenon 131.3
78 **Pt** Platinum 195.1	79 **Au** Gold 197.0	80 **Hg** Mercury 200.6	81 **Tl** Thallium 204.4	82 **Pb** Lead 207.2	83 **Bi** Bismuth 209.0	84 **Po** Polonium (209.0)	85 **At** Astatine (210.0)	86 **Rn** Radon (222.0)
110 **Uun** Ununnilium (271)	111 **Uuu** Unununium (272)	112 **Uub** Ununbium (277)						

The names and symbols of elements 110–112 are temporary. They are based on the atomic number of the element. The official name and symbol will be approved by an international committee of scientists.

63 **Eu** Europium 152.0	64 **Gd** Gadolinium 157.3	65 **Tb** Terbium 158.9	66 **Dy** Dysprosium 162.5	67 **Ho** Holmium 164.9	68 **Er** Erbium 167.3	69 **Tm** Thulium 168.9	70 **Yb** Ytterbium 173.0	71 **Lu** Lutetium 175.0
95 **Am** Americium (243.1)	96 **Cm** Curium (247.1)	97 **Bk** Berkelium (247.1)	98 **Cf** Californium (251.1)	99 **Es** Einsteinium (252.1)	100 **Fm** Fermium (257.1)	101 **Md** Mendelevium (258.1)	102 **No** Nobelium (259.1)	103 **Lr** Lawrencium (262.1)

A number in parentheses is the mass number of the most stable isotope of that element.

Appendix

Physical Science Refresher

Atoms and Elements

Every object in the universe is made up of particles of some kind of matter. **Matter** is anything that takes up space and has mass. All matter is made up of elements. An **element** is a substance that cannot be separated into simpler components by ordinary chemical means. This is because each element consists of only one kind of atom. An **atom** is the smallest unit of an element that has all of the properties of that element.

Atomic Structure

Atoms are made up of small particles called subatomic particles. The three major types of subatomic particles are **electrons, protons,** and **neutrons.** Electrons have a negative electric charge, protons have a positive charge, and neutrons have no electric charge. The protons and neutrons are packed close to one another to form the **nucleus.** The protons give the nucleus a positive charge. Electrons are most likely to be found in regions around the nucleus called **electron clouds.** The negatively charged electrons are attracted to the positively charged nucleus. An atom may have several energy levels in which electrons are located.

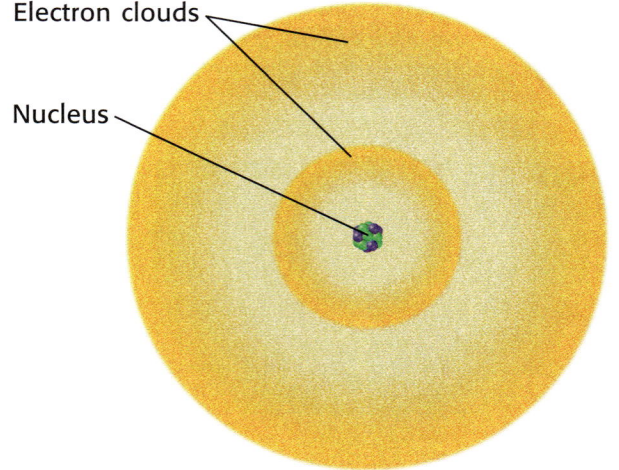

Electron clouds

Nucleus

Atomic Number

To help in the identification of elements, scientists have assigned an **atomic number** to each kind of atom. The atomic number is the number of protons in the atom. Atoms with the same number of protons are all the same kind of element. In an uncharged, or electrically neutral, atom there are an equal number of protons and electrons. Therefore, the atomic number equals the number of electrons in an uncharged atom. The number of neutrons, however, can vary for a given element. Atoms of the same element that have different numbers of neutrons are called **isotopes.**

Periodic Table of the Elements

In the periodic table, the elements are arranged from left to right in order of increasing atomic number. Each element in the table is in a separate box. An atom of each element has one more electron and one more proton than an atom of the element to its left. Each horizontal row of the table is called a **period.** Changes in chemical properties of elements across a period correspond to changes in the electron arrangements of their atoms. Each vertical column of the table, known as a **group,** lists elements with similar properties. The elements in a group have similar chemical properties because their atoms have the same number of electrons in their outer energy level. For example, the elements helium, neon, argon, krypton, xenon, and radon all have similar properties and are known as the noble gases.

Molecules and Compounds

When two or more elements are joined chemically, the resulting substance is called a **compound.** A compound is a new substance with properties different from those of the elements that compose it. For example, water, H_2O, is a compound formed when hydrogen (H) and oxygen (O) combine. The smallest complete unit of a compound that has the properties of that compound is called a **molecule.** A chemical formula indicates the elements in a compound. It also indicates the relative number of atoms of each element present. The chemical formula for water is H_2O, which indicates that each water molecule consists of two atoms of hydrogen and one atom of oxygen. The subscript number is used after the symbol for an element to indicate how many atoms of that element are in a single molecule of the compound.

Acids, Bases, and pH

An ion is an atom or group of atoms that has an electric charge because it has lost or gained one or more electrons. When an acid, such as hydrochloric acid, HCl, is mixed with water, it separates into ions. An **acid** is a compound that produces hydrogen ions, H^+, in water. The hydrogen ions then combine with a water molecule to form a hydronium ion, H_3O^+. A **base,** on the other hand, is a substance that produces hydroxide ions, OH^-, in water.

To determine whether a solution is acidic or basic, scientists use pH. The **pH** is a measure of the hydronium ion concentration in a solution. The pH scale ranges from 0 to 14. The middle point, pH = 7, is neutral, neither acidic nor basic. Acids have a pH less than 7; bases have a pH greater than 7. The lower the number is, the more acidic the solution. The higher the number is, the more basic the solution.

Chemical Equations

A chemical reaction occurs when a chemical change takes place. (In a chemical change, new substances with new properties are formed.) A chemical equation is a useful way of describing a chemical reaction by means of chemical formulas. The equation indicates what substances react and what the products are. For example, when carbon and oxygen combine, they can form carbon dioxide. The equation for the reaction is as follows: $C + O_2 \rightarrow CO_2$.

The Six Kingdoms

Kingdom Archaebacteria
The organisms in this kingdom are single-celled prokaryotes.

	Archaebacteria	
Group	**Examples**	**Characteristics**
Methanogens	*Methanococcus*	found in soil, swamps, the digestive tract of mammals; produce methane gas; can't live in oxygen
Thermophiles	*Sulpholobus*	found in extremely hot environments; require sulphur, can't live in oxygen
Halophiles	*Halococcus*	found in environments with very high salt content, such as the Dead Sea; nearly all can live in oxygen

Kingdom Eubacteria
There are more than 4,000 named species in this kingdom of single-celled prokaryotes.

	Eubacteria	
Group	**Examples**	**Characteristics**
Bacilli	*Escherichia coli*	rod-shaped; free-living, symbiotic, or parasitic; some can fix nitrogen; some cause disease
Cocci	*Streptococcus*	spherical-shaped, disease-causing; can form spores to resist unfavorable environments
Spirilla	*Treponema*	spiral-shaped; responsible for several serious illnesses, such as syphilis and Lyme disease

Kingdom Protista
The organisms in this kingdom are eukaryotes. There are single-celled and multicellular representatives.

	Protists	
Group	**Examples**	**Characteristics**
Sacodines	*Amoeba*	radiolarians; single-celled consumers
Ciliates	*Paramecium*	single-celled consumers
Flagellates	*Trypanosoma*	single-celled parasites
Sporozoans	*Plasmodium*	single-celled parasites
Euglenas	*Euglena*	single-celled; photosynthesize
Diatoms	*Pinnularia*	most are single-celled; photosynthesize
Dinoflagellates	*Gymnodinium*	single-celled; some photosynthesize
Algae	*Volvox*, coral algae	4 phyla; single- or many-celled; photosynthesize
Slime molds	*Physarum*	single- or many-celled; consumers or decomposers
Water molds	powdery mildew	single- or many-celled, parasites or decomposers

Kingdom Fungi

There are single-celled and multicellular eukaryotes in this kingdom. There are four major groups of fungi.

Fungi		
Group	Examples	Characteristics
Threadlike fungi	bread mold	spherical; decomposers
Sac fungi	yeast, morels	saclike; parasites and decomposers
Club fungi	mushrooms, rusts, smuts	club-shaped; parasites and decomposers
Lichens	British soldier	symbiotic with algae

Kingdom Plantae

The organisms in this kingdom are multicellular eukaryotes. They have specialized organ systems for different life processes. They are classified in divisions instead of phyla.

Plants		
Group	Examples	Characteristics
Bryophytes	mosses, liverworts	reproduce by spores
Club mosses	*Lycopodium*, ground pine	reproduce by spores
Horsetails	rushes	reproduce by spores
Ferns	spleenworts, sensitive fern	reproduce by spores
Conifers	pines, spruces, firs	reproduce by seeds; cones
Cycads	*Zamia*	reproduce by seeds
Gnetophytes	*Welwitschia*	reproduce by seeds
Ginkgoes	*Ginkgo*	reproduce by seeds
Angiosperms	all flowering plants	reproduce by seeds; flowers

Kingdom Animalia

This kingdom contains multicellular eukaryotes. They have specialized tissues and complex organ systems.

Animals		
Group	Examples	Characteristics
Sponges	glass sponges	no symmetry or segmentation; aquatic
Cnidarians	jellyfish, coral	radial symmetry; aquatic
Flatworms	planaria, tapeworms, flukes	bilateral symmetry; organ systems
Roundworms	*Trichina*, hookworms	bilateral symmetry; organ systems
Annelids	earthworms, leeches	bilateral symmetry; organ systems
Mollusks	snails, octopuses	bilateral symmetry; organ systems
Echinoderms	sea stars, sand dollars	radial symmetry; organ systems
Arthropods	insects, spiders, lobsters	bilateral symmetry; organ systems
Chordates	fish, amphibians, reptiles, birds, mammals	bilateral symmetry; complex organ systems

Using the Microscope

Parts of the Compound Light Microscope

- The **ocular lens** magnifies the image 10×.
- The **low-power objective** magnifies the image 10×.
- The **high-power objective** magnifies the image either 40× or 43×.
- The **revolving nosepiece** holds the objectives and can be turned to change from one magnification to the other.
- The **body tube** maintains the correct distance between the ocular lens and objectives.
- The **coarse-adjustment knob** moves the body tube up and down to allow focusing of the image.
- The **fine-adjustment knob** moves the body tube slightly to bring the image into sharper focus.
- The **stage** supports a slide.
- **Stage clips** hold the slide in place for viewing.
- The **diaphragm** controls the amount of light coming through the stage.
- The light source provides a **light** for viewing the slide.
- The **arm** supports the body tube.
- The **base** supports the microscope.

Proper Use of the Compound Light Microscope

1. Carry the microscope to your lab table using both hands. Place one hand beneath the base, and use the other hand to hold the arm of the microscope. Hold the microscope close to your body while moving it to your lab table.

2. Place the microscope on the lab table at least 5 cm from the edge of the table.

3. Check to see what type of light source is used by your microscope. If the microscope has a lamp, plug it in, making sure that the cord is out of the way. If the microscope has a mirror, adjust it to reflect light through the hole in the stage.
   Caution: If your microscope has a mirror, do not use direct sunlight as a light source. Direct sunlight can damage your eyes.

4. Always begin work with the low-power objective in line with the body tube. Adjust the revolving nosepiece.

5. Place a prepared slide over the hole in the stage. Secure the slide with the stage clips.

6. Look through the ocular lens. Move the diaphragm to adjust the amount of light coming through the stage.

7. Look at the stage from eye level. Slowly turn the coarse adjustment to lower the objective until it almost touches the slide. Do not allow the objective to touch the slide.

8. Look through the ocular lens. Turn the coarse adjustment to raise the low-power objective until the image is in focus. Always focus by raising the objective away from the slide. *Never focus the objective downward.* Use the fine adjustment to sharpen the focus. Keep both eyes open while viewing a slide.

9. Make sure that the image is exactly in the center of your field of vision. Then switch to the high-power objective. Focus the image, using only the fine adjustment. *Never use the coarse adjustment at high power.*

10. When you are finished using the microscope, remove the slide. Clean the ocular lens and objective lenses with lens paper. Return the microscope to its storage area. Remember, you should use both hands to carry the microscope.

Making a Wet Mount

1. Use lens paper to clean a glass slide and a coverslip.

2. Place the specimen you wish to observe in the center of the slide.

3. Using a medicine dropper, place one drop of water on the specimen.

4. Hold the coverslip at the edge of the water and at a 45° angle to the slide. Make sure that the water runs along the edge of the coverslip.

5. Lower the coverslip slowly to avoid trapping air bubbles.

6. Water might evaporate from the slide as you work. Add more water to keep the specimen fresh. Place the tip of the medicine dropper next to the edge of the coverslip. Add a drop of water. (You can also use this method to add stain or solutions to a wet mount.) Remove excess water from the slide by using the corner of a paper towel as a blotter. Do not lift the coverslip to add or remove water.

Glossary

abdomen the body part of an animal that usually contains the gut and other digestive organs (357)

abiotic describes nonliving factors in the environment (434, 474)

absolute dating determining the age of an object or event in years, usually by measuring the amount of unstable atoms in the sample (177)

active transport the movement of particles through proteins in the cell membrane against the direction of diffusion; requires cells to use energy (86)

adaptation a characteristic that helps an organism survive in its environment (150)

addiction a physical dependence on a drug (664)

adenine (AD uh NEEN) one of the four bases that combine with sugar and phospate to form a nucleotide subunit of DNA; adenine pairs with thymine (128)

aerobic exercise vigorous, sustained exercise of the whole body for 20 minutes or more (670)

alcoholism a disorder in which a person is physically and psychologically dependent on alcohol (666)

algae (AL JEE) protists that convert the sun's energy into food through photosynthesis (246)

alien an organism that makes a home for itself in a new place (502)

alleles different forms of a single gene (111)

allergy an inappropriate immune-system reaction to a harmless antigen (645)

altricial chick (al TRISH uhl) a chick that hatches weak, naked, and helpless (406)

alveoli (al VEE uh LIE) tiny sacs that form the bronchiole branches of the lungs (557)

amnion a thin, fluid-filled membrane surrounding a placental mammal's fetus (621)

amniotic egg (AM nee AH tik) an egg containing amniotic fluid to protect the developing embryo; usually surrounded by a hard shell (400)

amphibian a type of vertebrate ectotherm that usually begins life in the water with gills and later develops lungs (382)

anaerobic describes an organism that does not need oxygen (183)

angiosperm (AN jee oh SPUHRM) a plant that produces seeds in flowers (273)

Animalia the classification kingdom containing complex, multicellular organisms that lack cell walls, are usually able to move around, and possess nervous systems that help them be aware of and react to their surroundings (213)

anorexia nervosa a disorder characterized by self-starvation and an intense fear of gaining weight (662)

antennae feelers on an arthropod's head that respond to touch, taste, or smell (358)

antibiotic a substance used to kill or slow the growth of bacteria or other microorganisms (230, 639)

antibody a special protein that can recognize specific pathogens (641)

antigen pieces of a pathogen that generate an immune response from immune-system cells (642)

anus the opening at the end of the digestive tract through which feces pass to the outside (574)

Archaebacteria (AHR kee bak TIR ee uh) a classification kingdom containing bacteria that thrive in extreme environments (209)

area the measure of how much surface an object has (24)

arteries blood vessels that carry blood away from the heart (549)

asexual reproduction reproduction in which a single parent produces offspring that are genetically identical to the parent (38, 612)

asymmetrical without symmetry (344)

ATP adenosine triphosphate; the molecule that provides energy for a cell's activities (45)

atrium an upper chamber of the heart (548)

australopithecine (ah STRA loh PITH uh seen) an early hominid that evolved more than 3.6 million years ago (190)

autoimmune disease a disease in which the immune system attacks the cells of the body it is meant to protect (646)

axon a long cell fiber in the nervous system that transfers intercellular messages (589)

B

B cell an immune-system cell that matures in bones and makes antibodies (641)

bacteria extremely small, single-celled organisms without a nucleus; prokaryotic cells (66, 209)

bilateral symmetry a body plan in which two halves of an organism's body are mirror images of each other (344)

bile a green liquid made by the liver and stored in the gallbladder; used in fat digestion (573)

binary fission the simple cell division in which one cell splits into two; used by bacteria (92, 225)

biodegradable capable of being broken down by the environment (504)

biodiversity the number and variety of living things (503)

biological clock an internal control of natural cycles (330)

biome a large region characterized by a specific type of climate and certain types of plant and animal communities (474)

bioremediation (BIE oh ri MEE dee AY shun) the use of bacteria and other microorganisms to change pollutants in soil and water into harmless chemicals (230)

biosphere the part of the Earth where life exists (437)

biotic describes living factors in the environment (434)

blood a connective tissue made up of platelets, white blood cells, red blood cells, and plasma (546)

blood pressure the amount of force exerted by blood on the inside walls of a blood vessel (551)

brain the mass of nerve tissue that is the main organ of the nervous system (591)

bronchi (BRAHNG kie) the two tubes that connect the lungs with the trachea (557)

brooding when a bird sits on its eggs until they hatch (405)

budding a type of asexual reproduction in which a small part of the parent's body develops into an independent organism (258, 612)

bulimia a disorder characterized by binge eating followed by induced vomiting to rid the body of food (662)

C

Calorie a unit that expresses the amount of energy found in food (656)

camouflage the coloration and/or texture that enables an animal to blend in with its environment (327)

cancer a condition in which certain body cells begin dividing at an uncontrolled rate (646)

capillaries the smallest blood vessels (549)

carbohydrate a biochemical composed of one or more simple sugars bonded together that is used to provide and store energy (43, 657)

carbon cycle the movement of carbon from the nonliving environment into living things and then back into the nonliving environment (459)

cardiac muscle the type of muscle found in the heart (530)

cardiovascular system a collection of organs that transport blood to and from your body's cells; the organs in this system include the heart, the arteries, and the veins (546)

carnivore a consumer that eats animals (419, 439)

carrying capacity the largest population that a given environment can support over a long period of time (445)

cartilage a flexible tissue that gives support and protection but is not rigid like bone (528)

cell a membrane-covered structure that contains all of the materials necessary for life (36)

cell cycle the life cycle of a cell; in eukaryotes it consists of chromosome duplication, mitosis, and cytokinesis (92)

cell membrane a phospholipid layer that covers a cell's surface and acts as a barrier between the inside of a cell and the cell's environment (44, 63)

cell theory the three-part theory about cells that states: (1) All organisms are composed of one or more cells, (2) the cell is the basic unit of life in all living things, and (3) all cells come from existing cells (62)

cell wall a structure that surrounds the cell membrane of some cells and provides strength and support to the cell membrane (69)

cellular respiration the process of producing ATP in the cell from oxygen and glucose; releases carbon dioxide and water (89, 305, 558)

Cenozoic era the period in the geologic time scale beginning about 65 million years ago and continuing until the present day (187)

central nervous system a collection of organs that processes all incoming and outgoing messages from the nerves; the organs in this system include the brain and the spinal cord (588)

centromere the region that holds chromatids together when a chromosome is duplicated (93)

cephalothorax (SEF uh loh THOR aks) the body part of arachnids that consists of both a head and a thorax and that usually has four pairs of legs attached (359)

cerebellum (SER uh BEL uhm) the part of the brain that keeps track of the body's position (592)

cerebrum the part of the brain that detects touch, sight, sound, odor, taste, pain, heat, and cold and controls all voluntary acts, including thought (591)

chemical digestion the process in which large molecules are broken down into simpler molecules or chemical building blocks (569)

chlorophyll a green pigment in chloroplasts that absorbs light energy for photosynthesis (270, 304)

chloroplast an organelle found in plant and algae cells where photosynthesis occurs (71)

chromatids identical chromosome copies (93)

chromosome a coiled structure of DNA and protein that forms in the cell nucleus during cell division (92)

circadian rhythm a natural, daily cycle (330)

class the level of classification after phylum; the organisms in all phyla are sorted into classes (203)

classification the arrangement of organisms into orderly groups based on their similarities and presumed evolutionary relationships (202)

closed circulatory system a circulatory system in which a heart circulates blood through a network of vessels that forms a closed loop (354)

club fungus a type of fungus characterized by umbrella-shaped mushrooms (259)

cochlea (KAHK lee uh) an ear organ that converts sound waves into electrical impulses (598)

coelom (SEE luhm) a cavity in the body of some animals where the gut and organs are located (345)

coevolution (KOH ev uh LOO shuhn) the long-term changes that take place in two species because of their close interactions with one another (448)

combustion the process of burning; includes the burning of fossil fuels (460)

commensalism (kuh MEN suhl iz uhm) a symbiotic relationship in which one organism benefits and the other is unaffected (447)

communication a transfer of a signal from one animal to another that results in some type of response (332)

community all of the populations of different species that live and interact in an area (60, 436)

compact bone the type of bone tissue that does not have open spaces (527)

competition two or more species or individuals trying to use the same limited resource (445)

compound eye an eye that is made of many identical, light-sensitive cells that work together (358)

compound light microscope a microscope that consists of a tube with lenses, a stage, and a light source (19)

cones photoreceptors that can detect bright light and help you see colors (596)

conifer a tree that produces seeds in cones (476)

connective tissue one of the four main types of tissue in the body; functions include support, protection, insulation, and nourishment (523)

conservation the wise use of and preservation of natural resources (505)

consumer an organism that eats producers or other organisms for energy (40, 227, 325, 439)

contour feather a feather made of a stiff, central shaft with many side branches called barbs (401)

controlled experiment an experiment that tests only one factor at a time (14)

cotyledon (KAHT uh LEED uhn) a seed leaf inside a seed (283)

cuticle a waxy layer that coats the surface of stems, leaves, and other plant parts exposed to air (270)

cytokinesis (SIET oh ki NEE sis) the process in which cytoplasm divides after mitosis (95)

cytoplasm (SIET oh PLAZ uhm) cellular fluid surrounding a cell's organelles (63)

cytosine (SIET oh SEEN) one of the four bases that combine with sugar and phosphate to form a nucleotide subunit of DNA; cytosine pairs with guanine (128)

D

deciduous describes trees with leaves that change color in autumn and fall off in winter (310, 475)

decomposer an organism that gets energy by breaking down the remains of dead organisms or animal wastes and consuming or absorbing the nutrients (40, 439)

decomposition the breakdown of dead materials into carbon dioxide and water (460)

deep-water zone the zone of a lake or pond below the open-water zone where no light reaches (487)

deforestation the clearing of forest lands (503)

dendrite a short, branched extension of a neuron where the neuron receives impulses from other cells (589)

denticles small, sharp, toothlike structures on the skin of cartilaginous fishes (380)

depressant a drug that slows the actions of the central nervous system (663)

dermis the layer of skin below the epidermis (535)

desert a hot, dry biome inhabited by organisms adapted to survive high daytime temperatures and long periods without rain (479)

diaphragm (DIE uh FRAM) the sheet of muscle underneath the lungs of mammals that helps draw air into the lungs (413, 558)

dichotomous key (die KAWT uh muhs) an aid to identifying unknown organisms that consists of several pairs of descriptive statements; of each pair of statements, only one will apply to the unknown organism, and that statement will lead to another set of statements, and so on, until the unknown organism can be identified (206)

diffusion the movement of particles from an area where their concentration is high to an area where their concentration is low (84)

digestive system a collection of organs that break down food so that it can be used by the body; the organs in this system include the stomach, the pancreas, the liver, the gallbladder, the small intestine, and the large intestine (568)

diversity a measure of the number of species an area contains (477)

DNA deoxyribonucleic (dee AHKS ee RIE boh noo KLEE ik) acid; hereditary material that controls all the activities of a cell, contains the information to make new cells, and provides instructions for making proteins (38, 69, 128)

dominant trait the trait observed when at least one dominant allele for a characteristic is inherited (109)

dormant describes an inactive state of a seed (302)

down feather a fluffy, insulating feather that lies next to a bird's body (401)

drug any chemical substance that causes a physical or emotional change in a person (663)

drug abuser a person who takes drugs for a purpose other than to relieve a medical condition (667)

E

ecology the study of the interactions between organisms and their environment (434)

ecosystem a community of organisms and their nonliving environment (60, 436)

ectotherm an animal whose body temperature fluctuates with the environment's temperature (376)

egg a sex cell produced by a female (613)

electron microscope a microscope that uses tiny particles of matter to produce magnified images (20)

embryo an organism in the earliest stage of development (324, 620)

enamel the outermost layer of a tooth; the hardest material in the body (570)

endocrine system a collection of glands that control body-fluid balance, growth, and sexual development (600)

endocytosis (EN doh sie TOH sis) the process in which a cell membrane surrounds a particle and encloses it in a vesicle to bring it into the cell (87)

endoplasmic reticulum (EN doh PLAZ mik ri TIK yuh luhm) a membrane-covered cell organelle that produces lipids, breaks down drugs and other substances, and packages proteins for delivery out of the cell (70)

endoskeleton an internal skeleton (363)

endospore a bacterium surrounded by a thick, protective membrane (225)

endotherm an animal that maintains a constant body temperature despite temperature changes in its environment (376)

energy pyramid a diagram shaped like a triangle that shows the loss of energy at each level of the food chain (441)

enzyme a protein that makes it possible for certain chemical reactions to occur quickly (42, 569)

epidermis the outermost layer of the skin (535); *also* the outermost layer of cells covering roots, stems, leaves, and flower parts (285)

epididymis (EP uh DID i mis) the area of the testes where sperm are stored before they enter the vas deferens (616)

epithelial tissue one of the four main types of tissue in the body; the tissue that covers and protects underlying tissue (522)

esophagus (i SAWF uh guhs) a long, straight tube that connects the throat to the stomach (570)

estivation a period of reduced activity that some animals experience in the summer (329)

estuary an area where fresh water from streams and rivers spills into the ocean (485)

Eubacteria (YOO bak TIR ee uh) a classification kingdom containing mostly free-living bacteria found in many varied environments (209)

eukaryotic cell (eukaryote) (yoo KER ee OHT) a cell that contains a central nucleus and a complicated internal structure (67, 184)

evaporation the change of state from liquid to vapor (458)

evergreen describes trees that keep their leaves year-round (310)

evolution the process by which populations accumulate inherited changes over time (151)

excretion the process of removing wastes from the body; term used only when substances must pass through a membrane in order to leave the body (576)

exocytosis (EK soh sie TOH sis) the process used to remove large particles from a cell; during exocytosis, a vesicle containing the particles fuses with the cell membrane (87)

exoskeleton an external skeleton made of protein and chitin; found on arthropods (358)

extensor a muscle that straightens part of the body (531)

external fertilization the fertilization of eggs by sperm that occurs outside the body of the female (378, 614)

extinct describes a species of organism that has died out completely (179)

F

factor anything in an experiment that can influence the experiment's outcome (14)

fallopian tube the tube that leads from an ovary to the uterus (617)

family the level of classification after order; the organisms in all orders are sorted into families (203)

farsighted describes someone who has better vision for distant objects than for near ones (597)

fat energy-storing nutrients that help the body store some vitamins (657)

feedback controls a system that turns endocrine glands on or off (602)

fermentation the breakdown of sugars to make ATP in the absence of oxygen (89)

fetus an embryo during the later stages of development within the uterus (622)

fibrous root a type of root in which there are several roots of the same size that spread out from the base of the stem (285)

fins fanlike structures that help fish move, turn, stop, and balance (378)

flexor a muscle that bends part of the body (531)

food chain a diagram that represents how the energy in food molecules flows from one organism to the next (440)

food web a complex diagram representing the many energy pathways in a real ecosystem (440)

fossil the solidified remains or imprints of a once-living organism (152, 176)

fossil record a historical sequence of life indicated by fossils found in layers of the Earth's crust (152)

fragmentation a type of reproduction in which an organism breaks into two or more parts, each of which may grow into a separate individual (612)

Fungi a kingdom of complex organisms that obtain food by breaking down other substances in their surroundings and absorbing the nutrients (212)

fungus an organism in the kingdom Fungi (255)

funguslike protist a protist that obtains its food from dead organic matter or from the body of another organism (245)

G

gallbladder a small, baglike organ that stores bile (573)

gametophyte (guh MEET oh FIET) a stage in a plant life cycle during which eggs and sperm are produced (271)

ganglia groups of nerve cells (345)

generation time the period between the birth of one generation and the birth of the next generation (164)

genes segments of DNA that carry hereditary instructions and are passed from parent to offspring; located on chromosomes (111)

genetic engineering the manipulation of genes that allows scientists to put genes from one organism into another organism (141)

genotype the inherited combination of alleles (111)

genus the level of classification after family; the organisms in all families are sorted into genera (203)

geologic time scale the division of Earth's history into distinct intervals of time (178)

gestation period (jeh STAY shuhn) the time during which an embryo develops within the mother (416)

gills organs that remove oxygen from the water and carbon dioxide from the blood (378)

gland a group of cells that make special chemicals for the body (600)

Golgi complex the cell organelle that modifies, packages, and transports materials out of the cell (72)

gravitropism (GRAV i TROH PIZ uhm) a change in the growth of a plant in response to gravity (308)

ground water water stored in underground caverns or porous rock (459)

guanine (GWAH NEEN) one of the four bases that combine with sugar and phosphate to form a nucleotide subunit of DNA; guanine pairs with cytosine (128)

gut the pouch where food is digested in animals (345)

gymnosperm (JIM noh SPUHRM) a plant that produces seeds but not flowers (273)

H

habitat the environment where an organism lives (442)

hair follicle a small organ in the dermis layer of the skin that produces hair (536)

half-life for a particular radioactive sample, the time it takes for one-half of the sample to decay (177)

hallucinogen (huh LOO si nuh juhn) a drug that distorts the senses, causes changes in mood and thought processes, and causes hallucinations (666)

head the body part of animals where the brain is located (357)

helper T cell an immune-system cell that activates killer T cells and B cells (642)

hemoglobin (HEE moh GLOH bin) the protein in red blood cells that attaches to oxygen so that oxygen can be carried through the body (42, 546)

herbivore a consumer that eats plants (439)

heredity the passing of traits from parent to offspring (38, 106)

hibernation a period of inactivity that some animals experience in winter that allows them to survive on stored body fat (329)

homeostasis (HOH mee OH STAY sis) the maintenance of a stable internal environment (37, 522)

hominid the family referring specifically to humans and several extinct, humanlike species, some of which were human ancestors (189)

homologous (hoh MAHL uh guhs) **chromosomes** chromosomes with matching information (93)

812 Glossary

hormone a chemical messenger that carries information from one part of an organism to the other; in mammals, hormones are made by the endocrine glands (600)

host an organism on which a parasite lives (233, 246, 350, 448)

hygiene methods of preserving and protecting your health (669)

hyphae (HIE fee) chains of cells that make up multicellular fungi (256)

hypothesis a possible explanation or answer to a question (12)

I

immune system a collection of cells, tissues, and organs that fight disease-causing agents (641)

immunity resistance to a disease (638)

imperfect fungus a fungus that does not fit into other standard groups of fungi (260)

implantation the process in which an embryo imbeds itself in the lining of the uterus (620)

impulse an electrical message that passes along a neuron (589)

infectious disease a disease caused by a pathogen (636)

infertile the state of being unable to have children (619)

innate behavior a behavior that is influenced by genes and does not depend on learning (328)

integumentary system (in TEG yoo MEN tuhr ee) a collection of organs that helps the body maintain a stable and healthy internal environment; the organs in this system include skin, hair, and nails (534)

internal fertilization the fertilization of an egg by sperm that occurs inside the body of a female (378, 614)

invertebrate an animal without a backbone (323, 344)

iris the colored part of the eye (597)

J

joint the place where two or more bones connect (528)

K

kidney a bean-shaped organ that removes many harmful substances from the blood (577)

killer T cell an immune-system cell that kills body cells infected with pathogens (642)

kingdom the most general of the seven levels of classification (203)

L

lactic-acid bacteria bacteria that digest the milk sugar lactose and convert it into lactic acid (231)

landmark a fixed object used to determine location during navigation (331)

large intestine a large organ that reabsorbs water from the digestive tract and stores, compacts, and eliminates indigestible material from the body (574)

larynx (LER ingks) the area of the throat that contains the vocal cords (557)

lateral line system a row or rows of tiny sense organs along the sides of a fish's body (378)

learned behavior a behavior that has been learned from experience or observation (328)

lens a curved, transparent object that forms an image by refracting light (597)

lichen the combination of a fungus and an alga that grows intertwined and exists in a symbiotic relationship (261)

life science the study of living things (6)

lift an upward force on an object that can be explained by differences in pressure above and below the object; lift opposes the downward pull of gravity (404)

ligament a strong band of tissue that connects bones to bones (529)

limiting factor a needed resource that is in limited supply (444)

lipid a type of biochemical, including fats and oils, that does not dissolve in water; lipids store energy and make up cell membranes (44)

littoral zone the zone of a lake or pond closest to the edge of the land (487)

liver a large, reddish brown organ that produces bile and stores nutrients; the liver has more than 200 functions in the body (573)

lung a saclike organ that takes oxygen from the air and delivers it to the blood (382)

lymph the fluid and particles absorbed into lymph capillaries (554)

lymph nodes small, bean-shaped organs that contain small fibers that work like nets to remove particles from the lymph (555)

lymphatic system a collection of organs that collect extracellular fluid and return it to the blood; the organs in this system include the lymph nodes and the lymphatic vessels (554)

lysosome a special vesicle in a cell that digests food particles, wastes, and foreign invaders (74)

M

macrophage (MAK roh FAYJ) an immune-system cell that engulfs pathogens (641)

malnutrition a disorder resulting from not consuming the right combination of nutrients (662)

mammary glands glands that secrete a nutritious fluid called milk (411)

mandible a jaw found on some arthropods (359)

marine describes an ecosystem based on salty water (481)

marsh a treeless wetland ecosystem where such plants as cattails and rushes grow (488)

marsupial a mammal that gives birth to live, partially developed young that continue to develop inside the mother's pouch or skin fold (415, 615)

mass the amount of matter that something is made of; its value does not change with the object's location (26)

mass extinction a period when a large number of species die out at the same time (179)

matter anything that occupies space and has mass (458)

mechanical digestion the breaking, crushing, and mashing of food (569)

medulla (mi DOOL uh) the part of the brain that connects to the spinal cord and controls many involuntary processes in the body (592)

medusa a body form of some cnidarians; resembles a mushroom with tentacles (348)

meiosis (mie OH sis) cell division that produces sex cells (115, 613)

melanin a darkening chemical in the skin that determines skin color (534)

memory B cell an immune-system cell that "remembers" how to make a specialized antibody for a particular pathogen (644)

menstruation the monthly discharge of blood and tissue from the uterus (617)

Mesozoic era the period in the geologic time scale beginning about 248 million years ago and ending about 65 million years ago (186)

metabolism (muh TAB uh LIZ uhm) the combined chemical processes that occur in a cell or living organism (38)

metamorphosis the process in which an insect or other animal changes form as it develops from an embryo or larva to an adult (361, 384)

meter the basic unit of length in the SI system (23)

migrate to travel from one place to another in response to the seasons or environmental conditions (329)

mineral an element that is essential for good health (658)

mitochondria (MIET oh KAHN dree uh) cell organelles surrounded by two membranes that break down food molecules to make ATP (71)

mitosis nuclear division in eukaryotic cells in which each cell receives a copy of the original chromosomes (93)

mold shapeless, fuzzy fungi (257)

monotreme a mammal that lays eggs (414, 615)

motor neuron a neuron that sends impulses from the brain and spinal cord to other systems (590)

multicellular made of many cells (59, 323)

muscle tissue one of the four main types of tissue in the body; contains cells that contract and relax to produce movement (523)

muscular system a collection of organs whose primary function is movement; organs in this system include the muscles and the connective tissue that attaches them to bones (530)

mutagen anything that can damage or cause changes in DNA (138)

mutation a change in the order of the bases in an organism's DNA; deletion, insertion, or substitution (138, 163)

mutualism (MYOO choo uhl IZ uhm) a symbiotic relationship in which both organisms benefit (447)

mycelium (mie SEE lee uhm) a twisted mass of fungal hyphae that have grown together (256)

N

narcotics drugs made from opium (667)

natural selection the process by which organisms with favorable traits survive and reproduce at a higher rate than organisms without the favorable trait (162)

Neanderthal a species of hominid that lived in Europe and western Asia from 230,000 years ago to about 30,000 years ago (192)

nearsighted describes someone who has better vision for near objects than for distant ones (597)

nephron a microscopic filter in the kidney that removes a variety of harmful substances from the blood (577)

nerve an axon bundled together with blood vessels and connective tissue (590)

nervous system a collection of organs that gather and interpret information about the body's internal and external environment and respond to that information; the organs in this system include the brain, nerves, and spinal cord (588)

nervous tissue one of the four main types of tissue in the body; the tissue that sends electrical signals through the body (522)

neuron a specialized cell that transfers messages throughout the body in the form of fast-moving electrical energy (589)

niche an organism's way of life and its relationships with its abiotic and biotic environments (442)

nicotine a chemical stimulant found in tobacco that increases heart rate and blood pressure (665)

nitrogen cycle the movement of nitrogen from the nonliving environment into living organisms and back again (460)

nitrogen fixation the process of changing nitrogen gas into forms that plants can use (461)

noninfectious disease a disease that cannot spread from one person to another (636)

nonrenewable resource a natural resource that cannot be replaced or that can be replaced only over thousands or millions of years (501)

nonvascular plant a plant that depends on the processes of diffusion and osmosis to move materials from one part of the plant to another (272)

nucleic acid a biochemical that stores information needed to build proteins and other nucleic acids; made up of subunits called nucleotides (45)

nucleotide a subunit of DNA consisting of a sugar, a phosphate, and one of four nitrogenous bases (45, 128)

nucleus the membrane-covered organelle found in eukaryotic cells; contains the cell's DNA and serves as a control center for the cell (66)

nutrient a substance that must be consumed or taken in by an organism to promote normal growth, maintenance, and repair (569, 656)

O

obesity a disorder characterized by an extremely high percentage of body fat (662)

omnivore a consumer that eats a variety of organisms (439)

open circulatory system a circulatory system consisting of a heart that pumps blood through spaces called sinuses (354)

open-water zone the zone of a lake or pond that extends from the littoral zone out across the top of the water and that is only as deep as light can reach through the water (487)

optic nerve a nerve that transfers electrical impulses from the eye to the brain (596)

order the level of classification after class; the organisms in all the classes are sorted into orders (203)

organ a combination of two or more tissues that work together to perform a specific function in the body (57, 324, 523)

organ system a group of organs that works together to perform body functions (58, 523)

organelle (OHR guh NEL) a structure within a cell, sometimes surrounded by a membrane (63)

organism anything that can independently carry out life processes (59)

osmosis the diffusion of water across a cell membrane (85)

ovary in animals, an organ in the female reproductive system producing eggs (617); in flowers, the structure containing ovules that will develop into fruit following fertilization (291)

overpopulation a condition that occurs when the number of individuals within an environment becomes so large that there are not enough resources to support them all (502)

ovulation the process in which an egg is ejected through the ovary wall (617)

ozone a gas molecule that is made up of three oxygen atoms; absorbs ultraviolet radiation from the sun (184)

P

Paleozoic era the period in the geologic time scale beginning about 570 million years ago and ending about 248 million years ago (185)

pancreas a fish-shaped organ between the stomach and small intestine that produces enzymes for chemical digestion (572)

Pangaea the single landmass that contained all the present-day continents 200 million years ago (180)

parasite an organism that feeds on another living creature, usually without killing it (246, 350, 448)

parasitism (PAR uh SIET IZ uhm) a symbiotic association in which one organism benefits while the other is harmed (448)

passive transport the diffusion of particles through proteins in the cell membrane from areas where the concentration of particles is high to areas where the concentration of particles is low (86)

pasteurization (PAS tuhr i ZAY shuhn) a method of heating food and beverages to kill bacteria (638)

pathogen an agent that causes a disease (636)

pathogenic bacteria bacteria that invade a host organism and obtain the nutrients they need from the host's cells (232)

pedigree a diagram of family history used for tracing a trait through several generations (140)

penis the male reproductive organ that transfers semen into the female's body during sexual intercourse (616)

peripheral nervous system the collection of communication pathways, or nerves, whose primary function is to transfer information from all areas of the body and the outside environment to the central nervous system and from the central nervous system to the rest of the body (588)

peristalsis (PER uh STAHL sis) a rhythmic muscle contraction in the digestive tract (570)

permafrost the permanently frozen ground below the soil surface in the arctic tundra (480)

petals the often colorful structures on a flower that are usually involved in attracting pollinators (290)

pharynx (FER ingks) the upper portion of the throat (557)

phenotype an organism's inherited appearance (111)

pheromone (FER uh MON) a chemical produced by animals for communication (333)

phloem (FLOH EM) a specialized plant tissue that transports sugar molecules from one part of the plant to another (284)

phospholipid a type of lipid molecule that forms much of a cell's membrane (44)

photoreceptors specialized neurons in the retina that detect light (596)

photosynthesis (FOHT oh SIN thuh sis) the process by which plants capture light energy from the sun and convert it into sugar (88, 184, 270)

phototropism a change in the growth of a plant in response to light (307)

phylum the level of classification after kingdom; the organisms from all the kingdoms are sorted into several phyla (203)

phytoplankton (FITE oh PLANK tuhn) a microscopic photosynthetic organism that floats near the surface of the ocean (481)

pioneer species the first organisms to grow in an area undergoing ecological succession; usually lichens in primary succession and fast-growing, weedy plants in secondary succession (463)

pistils the female reproductive structures in a flower that consist of a stigma, a style, and an ovary (291)

placenta a special organ of exchange that provides a developing fetus with nutrients and oxygen (416, 621)

placental mammal a mammal that nourishes its unborn offspring with a placenta inside the uterus and gives birth to well-developed young (416, 615)

plankton very small organisms floating at or near the ocean's surface that form the base of the ocean's food web (481)

Plantae the kingdom that contains plants—complex, multicellular organisms that are usually green and use the sun's energy to make sugar by photosynthesis (211)

plasma the fluid part of blood (546)

plate tectonics the study of the forces that drive the movement of pieces of Earth's crust around the surface of the planet (181)

platelet a cell fragment that helps clot blood (547)

pollen the dustlike particles that carry the male gametophyte of seed plants (278)

pollination the transfer of pollen to the female cone in conifers or to the stigma in angiosperms (281)

pollutant a harmful substance in an environment (498)

pollution the presence of harmful substances in an environment (498)

polyp a body form of some cnidarians; resembles a vase (348)

population a group of individuals of the same species that live together in the same area at the same time (59, 436)

Precambrian time the period in the geologic time scale beginning when Earth originated, 4.6 billion years ago, and ending when complex organisms appeared, about 540 million years ago (182)

precipitation water that moves from the atmosphere to the land and ocean, including rain, snow, sleet, and hail (458)

precocial chick (pree KOH shuhl) a chick that leaves the nest immediately after hatching and is fully active (406)

predator an organism that eats other organisms (326, 446)

preening the activity in which a bird uses its beak to spread oil on its feathers (401)

prescription a note written by a doctor to allow a patient to buy a medicine (664)

prey an organism that is eaten by another organism (326, 446)

primate a type of mammal that includes humans, apes, and monkeys; typically distinguished by opposable thumbs and binocular vision (188, 423)

probability the mathematical chance that an event will occur (112)

producer organisms that make their own food, usually by using the energy from sunlight to make sugar (40, 227, 438)

prokaryotic cell (prokaryote) (proh KER ee OHT) a cell that does not have a nucleus or any other membrane-covered organelles; also called a bacterium (66, 183, 224)

prosimian the first primate ancestors; *also* a group of living primates that includes lorises and lemurs (190)

protein a biochemical that is composed of amino acids; its functions include regulating chemical reactions, transporting and storing materials, and providing support (42, 657)

protist an organism that belongs to the kingdom Protista (244)

Protista a kingdom of eukaryotic single-celled or simple, multicellular organisms; kingdom Protista contains all eukaryotes that are not plants, animals, or fungi (210)

protozoa animal-like protists that are single-celled consumers (250)

pseudopodia (soo doh POH dee uh) structures that amoebas use to move around (250)

puberty the time of life when the sex organs become mature (616)

pulmonary circulation the circulation of blood between the heart and lungs (550)

Punnett square a tool used to visualize all the possible combinations of alleles from parents (111)

pupil the opening to the inside of the eye (597)

R

radial symmetry a body plan in which the parts of the body are arranged in a circle around a central point (344)

receptor a specialized cell, sometimes a dendrite, that detects changes inside or outside the body (590)

recessive trait a trait that is apparent only when two recessive alleles for the same characteristic are inherited (109)

rectum the last section of the large intestine; where fecal material is stored until it can be expelled from the body (574)

recycling the process of making new products from reprocessed used products (507)

red blood cell a cell that carries oxygen from the lungs to all cells of the body and carries carbon dioxide back to the lungs to be exhaled (546)

reflex a quick, involuntary response to a stimulus (594)

relative dating determining whether an event or object, such as a fossil, is older or younger than other events or objects (177)

renewable resource a natural resource that can be used and replaced over a relatively short time period (501)

resource recovery the process of transforming into usable products things normally thrown away (508)

respiration the exchange of gases between living cells and their environment; includes breathing and cellular respiration (556); see cellular respiration

respiratory system a collection of organs whose primary function is to take in oxygen and expel carbon dioxide; the organs of this system include the lungs, the throat, and the passageways that lead to the lungs (556)

retina a layer of light-sensitive cells in the back of the eye (596)

rhizoids small, hairlike threads of cells that help hold nonvascular plants in place (274)

rhizome the underground stem of a fern (276)

ribosome a small organelle in cells where proteins are made from amino acids (70, 137)

rods photoreceptors that detect very dim light (596)

S

sac fungus a type of fungus that reproduces using spores, which develop in a sac called an ascus (250)

salivary glands organs located around the mouth that produce a liquid that begins chemical digestion (570)

saturated fat a type of fat found in meats, dairy products, coconut oil, and palm oil; known to raise blood cholesterol levels (658)

savanna a tropical grassland biome with scattered clumps of trees (478)

scales bony structures that cover the skin of bony fishes (380)

scavenger an animal that feeds on the bodies of dead animals (439)

scientific method a series of steps that scientists use to answer questions and solve problems (10)

scrotum a skin-covered sac that hangs from the male body and contains the testes (616)

sediment fine particles of sand, dust, or mud that are deposited over time by wind or water (176)

segment one of many identical or almost identical repeating body parts (355)

selective breeding the breeding of organisms that have a certain desired trait (160)

self-pollinating plant a plant that contains both male and female reproductive structures (107)

semen a mixture of sperm and fluids (616)

seminiferous tubules (SEM uh NIF uhr uhs TOO BYOOLZ) the coiled tubes inside the testes where sperm cells are produced (616)

sensory neuron a special neuron that gathers information about what is happening in and around the body and sends this information on to the central nervous system (590)

sepals the leaflike structures that cover and protect an immature flower (290)

sex cell an egg or sperm; a sex cell carries half the number of chromosomes found in other body cells (114)

sex chromosomes the chromosomes that carry genes that determine the sex of offspring (119)

sexual reproduction reproduction in which two sex cells join to form a zygote; sexual reproduction produces offspring that share characteristics of both parents (38, 613)

sexually transmitted disease a disease that can pass from an infected person to an uninfected person during sexual contact (619)

skeletal muscle the type of muscle that moves bones and helps protect inner organs (530)

skeletal system a collection of organs whose primary function is to support and protect the body; the organs in this system include bones, cartilage, ligaments, and tendons (526)

small intestine a muscular tube about 2.5 cm in diameter and up to 6 m long; the site of most chemical digestion (572)

smooth muscle the type of muscle found in the blood vessels and the digestive tract (530)

social behavior the interaction between animals of the same species (332)

speciation the process by which two populations of the same species become so different that they can no longer interbreed (166)

species the most specific of the seven levels of classification; characterized by a group of organisms that can mate with one another to produce fertile offspring (150, 203)

sperm a sex cell produced by a male (613)

spleen an organ that filters blood and produces lymphocytes (555)

spongy bone a type of bone tissue that has many open spaces and contains marrow (527)

spore a small reproductive cell protected by a thick wall (256)

sporophyte (SPOH roh FIET) a stage in a plant life cycle during which spores are produced (271)

stamen the male reproductive structure in a flower that consists of a filament topped by a pollen-producing anther (291)

stigma the flower part that is located at the tip of the pistil (291)

stimulant a drug that speeds up the action of the central nervous system (663)

stimulus anything that affects the activity of an organism, organ, or tissue (37, 307)

stomach a muscular, baglike organ of the digestive tract that is attached to the lower end of the esophagus (571)

stomata openings in the epidermis and cuticle of a leaf that allow carbon dioxide to enter the leaf (289, 306)

stress a physical and mental response to situations that create pressure (671)

succession the gradual regrowth or development of a community of organisms over time (462)

surface-to-volume ratio the amount of a cell's outer surface in relationship to its volume (64)

swamp a wetland ecosystem in which trees and vines grow (489)

sweat glands small organs in the dermis layer of the skin that release sweat (534)

swim bladder a balloonlike organ that is filled with oxygen and other gases; gives bony fish their buoyancy (380)

symbiosis (SIM bie OH sis) a close, long-term association between two or more species (251, 447)

systemic circulation the circulation of blood between the heart and the body (excluding the lungs) (550)

T

T cell an immune-system cell that matures in the thymus (641)

tadpole the aquatic larvae of an amphibian (384)

taproot a type of root that consists of one main root that grows downward, with many smaller branch roots coming out of it (285)

taxonomy the science of identifying, classifying, and naming living things (204)

technology the application of knowledge, tools, and materials to solve problems and accomplish tasks; technology can also refer to the objects used to accomplish tasks (18)

temperature a measure of how hot or cold something is (26)

tendon a tough connective tissue that connects skeletal muscles to bones (531)

territory an area occupied by one animal or a group of animals from which other members of the species are excluded (332)

testes the organs in the male reproductive system that make sperm and testosterone (616)

theory a unifying explanation for a broad range of hypotheses and observations that have been supported by experimentation (18)

therapsid (thuh RAP sid) a prehistoric reptile ancestor of mammals (387, 410)

thorax the central body part of an arthropod or other animal; where the heart and lungs are located (357)

threadlike fungus a fungus that develops from a spore called a zygospore (257)

thymine one of the four bases that combine with sugar and phosphate to form a nucleotide subunit of DNA; thymine pairs with adenine (128)

thymus a lymph organ that produces lymphocytes (555)

tissue a group of similar cells that work together to perform a specific job in the body (57, 324, 522)

tonsils small masses of soft tissue located at the back of the nasal cavity, on the inside of the throat, and at the back of the tongue (555)

toxic poisonous (499)

trachea (TRAY kee uh) the air passageway from the larynx to the lungs (557)

trait a distinguishing quality that can be passed from one generation to another (160)

transpiration the loss of water from plant leaves through openings called stomata (306)

tributary a small stream or river that flows into a larger one (486)

tropism a change in the growth of a plant in response to a stimulus (307)

true-breeding plant a plant that always produces offspring with the same traits as the parent(s) (108)

tundra a far-northern biome characterized by long, cold winters, permafrost, and few trees (480)

U

umbilical cord the cord that connects an embryo to a placenta (621)

unicellular made of a single cell (59)

unsaturated fat a type of fat that usually comes from plant sources and helps reduce blood cholesterol levels (658)

ureter a slender tube that carries urine from each kidney to the urinary bladder (577)

urethra in males, a slender tube that carries urine and semen through the penis to the outside; in females, a slender tube that carries urine to the outside (577, 616)

urinary bladder a baglike organ that stores urine until it can be eliminated through the urethra (577)

urinary system a collection of organs that remove waste from the blood; this system includes the kidneys, ureters, urethra, and the urinary bladder (576)

urine a concentrated mixture of waste materials that forms in the nephrons of the kidney (577)

uterus the organ in the female reproductive system where a zygote grows and develops (617)

V

vaccine a substance that helps the body develop an immunity to a pathogen (638)

vacuole (VAK yoo OHL) a large membrane-covered structure that serves as a storage container for water and other liquids (73)

vagina the passageway in the female reproductive system that receives sperm during sexual intercourse (617)

variable a factor in a controlled experiment that changes (14)

vas deferens (vas DEF uh RENZ) a tube in males where sperm is mixed with fluids to make semen (616)

vascular plant a plant that has specialized tissues called xylem and phloem, which move materials from one part of the plant to another (273)

veins blood vessels that direct blood to the heart (549)

ventricle a lower chamber of the heart (548)

vertebrae (VUHR tuh BRAY) segments of bone or cartilage that interlock to form a backbone (375)

vertebrate an animal with a skull and a backbone; includes mammals, birds, reptiles, amphibians, and fish (322, 374)

vesicle a membrane-covered compartment in a eukaryotic cell that forms when part of the cell membrane surrounds an object and pinches off (73)

vestigial structure (ves TIJ ee uhl) the remnant of a once-useful anatomical structure (153)

villi fingerlike projections on the inside wall of the small intestine (572)

virus a microscopic particle that invades a cell and often destroys it (233)

vitamin an organic compound that controls many body functions, including cell growth and hormone production (659)

volume the amount of space that something occupies or the amount of space that something contains (24)

W

water cycle the movement of water between the ocean, atmosphere, land, and living things (458)

water vascular system a system of water pumps and canals found in all echinoderms that allows them to move, eat, and breathe (364)

wetland an area of land where the water level is near or above the surface of the ground for most of the year (488)

white blood cell a blood cell that protects the body against pathogens (547)

X

xylem (ZIE luhm) a specialized plant tissue that transports water and minerals from one part of the plant to another (284)

Z

zooplankton (ZOH oh PLANGK tuhn) protozoa that, along with the phytoplankton they consume, form the base of the ocean's food web (481)

zygote a fertilized egg (613)

Spanish Glossary

A

abdomen/abdomen parte del cuerpo de un animal que en general contiene los intestinos y otros órganos del aparato digestivo (357)

abiotic/abiótico describe los factores en el medio ambiente que no están vivos (434, 474)

absolute dating/datación absoluta calcular en años la edad de un objeto o suceso, generalmente midiendo la cantidad de átomos inestables en las rocas que rodean la muestra (177)

active transport/transporte activo el movimiento de partículas a través de las proteínas en la membrana celular contra la dirección de la difusión; requiere que las células usen energía (86)

adaptation/adaptación característica que ayuda a un organismo a sobrevivir en su medio ambiente (150)

addiction/adicción dependencia física de una droga (664)

adenine/adenina una de las cuatro bases que se combinan con azúcar y fosfato para formar una subunidad nucleótida de ADN; la adenina forma un par con la timina (128)

aerobic exercise/ejercicio aeróbico ejercicio vigoroso y sostenido de todo el cuerpo por 20 minutos o más (670)

alcoholism/alcoholismo un problema de salud en el cual una persona depende física y sicológicamente del alcohol (666)

algae/algas protistas que convierten la energía solar en alimento a través de la fotosíntesis (246)

alien/foráneo un organismo que pasa a vivir en un lugar nuevo (502)

alleles/alelos formas alternativas de un gene que regulan las mismas características (111)

allergy/alergia una reacción inadecuada del sistema inmunológico ante un antígeno inofensivo (645)

altricial chick/pollito altricial un pollito que sale del huevo débil, sin plumas, y sin defensas (406)

alveoli/alvéolos pequeños sacos que forman las ramificaciones de los bronquíolos de los pulmones (557)

amnion/amnios una membrana fina, llena de líquido, que rodea al feto en la placenta de un mamífero (621)

amniotic egg/huevo amniótico un huevo que contiene líquido amniótico para proteger el embrión en desarrollo; en general está rodeado de una cáscara dura (400)

amphibian/anfibio tipo de vertebrado ectotérmico que en general comienza su vida en el agua con agallas y más tarde desarrolla pulmones (382)

anaerobic/anaeróbico describe a un organismo que no necesita oxígeno (183)

angiosperm/angiosperma planta que produce las semillas en las flores (273)

Animalia/reino animal la clasificación que contiene organismos complejos, multicelulares, que no tienen paredes celulares, en general se desplazan y tienen sistemas nerviosos que les permiten darse cuenta de lo que pasa a su alrededor y reaccionar (213)

anorexia nervosa/anorexia nerviosa problema caracterizado por dejar de comer por voluntad propia y un miedo intenso de aumentar de peso (662)

antennae/antenas apéndices en la cabeza de un artrópodo que responden al tacto gusto, u olor (358)

antibiotic/antibiótico sustancia que se usa para matar o hacer más lento el crecimiento de bacterias u otros microorganismos (230, 639)

antibody/anticuerpo proteína especial que puede reconocer patógenos específicos (641)

antigen/antígeno partes de un patógeno que generan una respuesta inmunológica de las células del sistema inmunológico (642)

anus/ano la apertura al fin del sistema digestivo a través de la cual las materias fecales pasan al exterior (574)

Archaebacteria/reino arqueobacterial clasificación que contiene las bacterias que prosperan en medios ambientes extremos (209)

area/área la medida de la superficie de un objeto (24)

arteries/arterias vasos sanguíneos que transportan la sangre del corazón (549)

asexual reproduction/reproducción asexual reproducción en la cual un solo progenitor da vida a crías que son genéticamente idénticas a los progenitores (38, 612)

asymmetrical/asimétrico sin simetría (344)

ATP/ATP adenosina trifosfática; la molécula que da energía para las actividades de una célula (45)

atrium/atrio una cavidad superior del corazón (548)

australopithecine/australopitecino un homínido primitivo que evolucionó hace más de 3.6 millones de años (190)

autoimmune disease/enfermedad autoinmune una enfermedad en la que el sistema inmunológico ataca las células del cuerpo que en realidad debe proteger (646)

axon/axón larga fibra celular en el sistema nervioso que transfiere mensajes intercelulares (589)

B

B cell/célula B célula del sistema inmunológico que madura en los huesos y fabrica anticuerpos (641)

bacteria/bacterias organismos muy pequeños, unicelulares y sin núcleo; células procariotas (66, 209)

bilateral symmetry/simetría bilateral plan del cuerpo en el que dos mitades del cuerpo del organismo son imágenes idénticas de la otra (344)

bile/bilis un líquido verdoso hecho por el hígado y almacenado en la vesícula, se usa en la digestión de las grasas (573)

binary fission/fisión binaria la división simple de las células, usada por las bacterias, en la que una célula se divide en dos (92, 225)

biodegradable/biodegradable que se puede desintegrar en el medio ambiente (504)

biodiversity/biodiversidad el número y la variedad de las cosas vivas (503)

biological clock/reloj biológico el control interno de los ciclos naturales (330)

biome/bioma una gran región caracterizada por un tipo de clima específico y ciertos tipos de plantas y de comunidades de animales (474)

bioremediation/bioremediación uso de bacterias y otros microorganismos para cambiar los contaminantes en la tierra y el agua y hacerlos sustancias químicas inofensivas (230)

biosphere/biosfera la parte de la Tierra en que existe la vida (437)

biotic/biótico describe factores vivientes en el medio ambiente (434)

blood/sangre un tejido conjuntivo formado por plateletas, células blancas, células rojas, y plasma (546)

blood pressure/presión sanguínea la cantidad de fuerza que la sangre ejerce sobre las paredes interiores de un vaso sanguíneo (551)

brain/cerebro la masa de tejido nervioso que es el órgano más importante del sistema nervioso (591)

bronchi/bronquios los dos tubos que conectan los pulmones a la tráquea (557)

brooding/camada cuando un pájaro se sienta en el nido sobre sus huevos hasta que nazcan los pichones (405)

budding/gemación tipo de reproducción asexuada en que una pequeña parte del cuerpo del progenitor se desarrolla como un organismo independiente (258, 612)

bulimia/bulimia desorden caracterizado por comer grandes cantidades de comida seguido por purgarse para vomitar y librar al cuerpo de la comida (662)

C

Calorie/caloría unidad que expresa la cantidad de energía que se encuentra en la comida (656)

camouflage/camuflaje la coloración y/o textura que permite que un animal pase inadvertido en su medio ambiente (327)

cancer/cáncer una enfermedad en que ciertas células del cuerpo comienzan a dividirse a una velocidad descontrolada (646)

capillaries/capilares los vasos sanguíneos más pequeños (549)

carbohydrate/hidrato de carbano una sustancia bioquímica formada por dos o más azúcares enlazados que se usa para dar energía y para almacenarla (43, 657)

carbon cycle/ciclo del carbono el movimiento de carbono de un medio ambiente que no está vivo a otro con cosas vivas, y luego de vuelta al medio ambiente no viviente (459)

cardiac muscle/músculo cardíaco tipo de músculo que se encuentra en el corazón (530)

cardiovascular system/sistema cardiovascular colección de órganos que transportan la sangre a y de las células del cuerpo; los órganos en este sistema incluyen el corazón, las arterias, y las venas (546)

carnivore/carnívoro consumidor que come animales (419, 439)

carrying capacity/capacidad de carga la población más grande que un medio ambiente dado puede mantener por un período de tiempo largo (445)

cartilage/cartílago tejido flexible que da apoyo y protección pero que no es rígido como los huesos (528)

cell/célula una estructura cubierta de membrana que contiene todos los materiales necesarios para la vida (36)

cell cycle/ciclo celular el ciclo vital de una célula; en las eucariotas, consiste de duplicación de los cromosomas, mitosis y citokinesis (92)

cell membrane/membrana celular una capa fosfolípida que cubre la superficie de una célula y actúa como barrera entre el interior de una célula y su medio ambiente (44, 63)

cell theory/teoría celular la teoría de tres partes sobre las células que establece: (1) Todos los organismos están compuestos de una o más células, (2) la célula es la unidad básica de la vida en todas las cosas vivas, y (3) todas las células provienen de células ya existentes (62)

cell wall/muro celular estructura que rodea y da resistencia y apoyo a la membrana celular de algunas células (69)

cellular respiration/respiración celular el proceso de producir ATP en la célula de oxígeno y glucosa; libera dióxido de carbono y agua (89, 305, 558)

Cenozoic era/era cenozoica el período en la escala de tiempo geológico que comienza cerca de 65 millones de años atrás y continúa hasta el presente (187)

central nervous system/sistema nervioso central colección de órganos que procesan todos los mensajes que entran y salen de los nervios; los órganos en este sistema incluyen el cerebro y la médula espinal (588)

centromere/centrómero la región que mantiene juntos a los cromátides cuando se duplica un cromosoma (93)

cephalothorax/cefalotórax la parte del cuerpo de los arácnidos que consiste de cabeza y tórax y que en general tiene pegados cuatro pares de patas (359)

cerebellum/cerebelo parte del cerebro que controla la posición del cuerpo (592)

cerebrum/encéfalo parte del cerebro que detecta el tacto, la visión, el sonido, el olor, el gusto, el dolor, el calor, y el frío, y que controla todos los actos voluntarios, incluyendo los pensamientos (591)

chemical digestion/digestión química proceso en el cual las moléculas grandes se dividen en moléculas más simples o bloques químicos de construcción (569)

chlorophyll/clorofila pigmento verde en los cloroplastos que absorbe la energía de la luz para la fotosíntesis (270, 304)

chloroplast/cloroplasto un orgánulo que se encuentra en las células de las plantas y las algas donde tiene lugar la fotosíntesis (71)

chromatids/cromátidos copias idénticas de los cromosomas (93)

chromosome/cromosoma estructura en espiral de ADN y de proteína que se forma en el núcleo de la célula durante la división celular (92)

circadian rhythm/ritmo circadiano el ciclo diario, natural (330)

class/clase el nivel de clasificación luego de phylum; los organismos en todos los phyla están organizados en clases (203)

classification/clasificación la organización de los organismos en grupos ordenados en base a sus similaridades y presuntas relaciones de evolución (202)

closed circulatory system/sistema circulatorio cerrado un sistema circulatorio en que el corazón circula la sangre a través de una red de vasos sanguíneos que forman un lazo cerrado (354)

club fungus/hongo club una clase de hongo caracterizado por su forma de sombrilla (259)

cochlea/cóclea órgano del oído que convierte las ondas sonoras en impulsos eléctricos (598)

coelom/celoma cavidad en el cuerpo de algunos animales en donde están localizados los intestinos y los órganos (345)

coevolution/coevolución los cambios a largo plazo que tienen lugar en dos especies a causa de la intensa interacción de una con otra (448)

combustion/combustión el proceso de quemar; incluye la quema de combustibles fósiles (460)

commensalism/comensalismo una relación simbiótica en la que un organismo se beneficia y el otro no es afectado (447)

communication/comunicación la transferencia de una señal de un animal a otro, que resulta en algún tipo de respuesta (332)

community/comunidad todas las poblaciones de especies diferentes que viven e interactúan en un área (60, 436)

compact bone/hueso denso el tipo de tejido óseo que no tiene espacios vacíos (527)

competition/competición dos o más especies o individuos que tratan de usar los mismos recursos limitados (445)

compound eye/ojo compuesto un ojo formado por muchas células idénticas, fotosensitivas, que trabajan juntas (358)

compound light microscope/microscopio de luz compuesta un miscroscopio que consiste en un tubo con lentes, una plataforma, y una fuente de luz (19)

cones/conos fotoreceptores que pueden detectar luz brillante, y ayudarte a ver los colores (596)

conifer/conífera árbol que produce las semillas en piñas (476)

connective tissue/tejido conectivo uno de los cuatro principales grupos de tejido en el cuerpo; sus funciones incluyen apoyo, protección, aislamiento, y alimentación (523)

conservation/conservación el uso y la preservación inteligentes de los recursos naturales (505)

consumer/consumidor organismo que come a los productores o a otros organismos para tener energía (40, 227, 325, 439)

contour feather/pluma de contorno pluma que está hecha de una varita central dura, con muchas ramas a los costados, llamadas barbas (401)

controlled experiment/experimento controlado experimento que hace pruebas sobre un solo factor por vez (14)

cotyledon/cotiledón hoja de una semilla dentro de una semilla (283)

cuticle/cutícula una capa cerosa que cubre la superficie de los tallos, las hojas, y otras partes de la planta expuestas al aire (270)

cytokinesis/citocinesis el proceso en el que el citoplasma se divide luego de la mitosis (95)

cytoplasm/citoplasma fluido celular que rodea los orgánulos de una célula (63)

cytosine/citosina una de las cuatro bases que se combina con el azúcar y el fosfato para formar una subunidad nucleótida de ADN; la citosina hace par con la guanina (128)

D

deciduous/de hoja caduca describe a los árboles con hojas que cambian de color en otoño y caen en invierno (310, 475)

decomposer/descomponedor organismo que obtiene energía haciendo que se desintegren los restos de organismos muertos o los deshechos de los animales, y consumiendo y absorbiendo los nutrientes (40, 439)

decomposition/descomposición la desintegración de materiales muertos en dióxido de carbono y agua (460)

deep-water zone/zona de aguas profundas área de un lago o laguna bajo la zona de agua superior, adonde no alcanza a llegar la luz (487)

deforestation/deforestación la tala y limpieza de bosques (503)

dendrite/dendrita extensión corta, con ramas, de una neurona, donde la neurona recibe impulsos de otras células (589)

denticles/dientecillos estructuras pequeñas y afiladas, que se parecen a los dientes, en la piel de los peces cartilaginosos (380)

depressant/depresivo droga que hace más lentas las acciones del sistema nervioso central (663)

dermis/dermis la capa de piel bajo la epidermis (535)

desert/desierto un bioma caliente y seco habitado por organismos adaptados a sobrevivir en temperaturas diurnas muy altas y largos períodos sin lluvia (479)

diaphragm/diafragma una capa de músculo bajo los pulmones de los mamíferos, que sirve para traer aire a los pulmones (413, 558)

dichotomous key/clave dicotómica ayuda para identificar los organismos desconocidos, que consiste en un par de oraciones descriptivas; de cada par de oraciones, solamente una se va a aplicar al organismo desconocido, y esta oración va a llevar a otra serie de oraciones, así hasta que se pueda identificar al organismo desconocido (206)

diffusion/difusión movimiento de partículas de un área donde su concentración es alta a otra área donde hay poca concentración (84)

digestive system/sistema digestivo colección de órganos que descompone la comida para que pueda ser usada por el cuerpo; los órganos en este sistema incluyen el estómago, el páncreas, el hígado, la vesícula, y el intestino delgado y el grueso (568)

diversity/diversidad medida del número de especies contenida en un área (477)

DNA/ADN ácido desoxiribonucleico; material hereditario que controla todas las actividades de una célula, contiene la información para hacer nuevas células, y da instrucciones para hacer proteínas (38, 69, 128)

dominant trait/carácter dominante se observa cuando se hereda por lo menos un alelo dominante para una característica (109)

dormant/en reposo describe el estado inactivo de una semilla (302)

down feather/plumas bajas una pluma liviana, aislante, que está junto al cuerpo del pájaro (401)

drug/droga cualquier sustancia química que causa un cambio físico o emocional en una persona (663)

drug abuser/consumidor de droga persona que toma drogas con un propósito que no sea aliviar una enfermedad (667)

E

ecology/ecología el estudio de las interacciones entre los organismos y su medio ambiente (434)

ecosystem/ecosistema comunidad de organismos y su medio ambiente no viviente (60, 436)

ectotherm/ectotérmico animal cuya temperatura corporal varía con la temperatura del medio ambiente (376)

egg/óvulo célula sexual producida por la hembra (613)

electron microscope/microscopio electrónico microscopio que usa pequeñas partículas de materia para producir imágenes aumentadas (20)

embryo/embrión organismo en la primera etapa de desarrollo (324, 620)

enamel/esmalte la capa exterior de un diente; el material más duro en el cuerpo (570)

endocrine system/sistema endócrino colección de glándulas que controlan el equilibrio de los fluidos del cuerpo, el crecimiento, y el desarrollo sexual (600)

endocytosis/endocitosis proceso en el que la membrana celular rodea una partícula y la encierra en una vesícula para traerla al interior de la célula (87)

endoplasmic reticulum/redecilla endoplásmica orgánulo celular cubierto por membranas que produce lípidos, descompone las drogas y otras sustancias, y prepara las proteínas para llevarlas fuera de la célula (70)

endoskeleton/endoesqueleto un esqueleto interno (363)

endospore/endóspora bacteria rodeada por una membrana protectora gruesa (225)

endotherm/endotérmico animal que mantiene una temperatura corporal constante a pesar de los cambios en la temperatura de su medio ambiente (376)

energy pyramid/pirámide de energía un diagrama con forma de triángulo que muestra la pérdida de energía en cada nivel de la cadena alimenticia (441)

enzyme/enzima proteína que permite que ciertas reacciones químicas ocurran rápidamente (42, 569)

epidermis/epidermis la capa exterior de la piel (535); también, la capa exterior de células que cubre las raíces, los tallos, las hojas, y partes de las flores (285)

epididymis/epidídimo área de los testículos en que se almacena el esperma antes de que pase al conducto deferente (616)

epithelial tissue/tejido epitelial uno de los cuatro tipos de tejido en el cuerpo; el tejido que cubre y protege el tejido que está debajo (522)

esophagus/esófago un tubo largo y estrecho que conecta la garganta con el estómago (570)

estivation/estivación período de actividad reducida que algunos animales experimentan en el verano (329)

estuary/estuario área donde el agua dulce de los arroyos y ríos desemboca en el océano (485)

Eubacteria/reino de las eubacterias clasificación que contiene la mayoría de las bacterias de vida independiente que se encuentran en muchos medio ambientes variados (209)

eukaryotic cell (eukaryote)/célula eucariota célula que contiene un núcleo central y una estructura interna complicada (67, 184)

evaporation/evaporación el cambio de estado de líquido a vapor (458)

evergreen/de hoja perenne describe a los árboles que conservan las hojas durante todo el año (310)

evolution/evolución el proceso por el cual las poblaciones acumulan cambios heredados a través del tiempo (151)

excretion/excreción el proceso de quitar los deshechos del cuerpo; el término sólo se usa cuando las sustancias deben pasar a través de una membrana para abandonar el cuerpo (576)

exocytosis/exocitosis el proceso que se usa para extraer partículas grandes de una célula; durante la exocitosis, una vesícula que contiene las partículas se funde con la membrana celular (87)

exoskeleton/exoesqueleto un esqueleto externo hecho de proteína y quitina que se encuentra en los artrópodos (358)

extensor/extensor un músculo que hace que parte del cuerpo se enderece (531)

external fertilization/fertilización externa fertilización de los huevos por el esperma que ocurre fuera del cuerpo de la hembra (378, 614)

extinct/extinto describe una especie de organismo que ha muerto por completo (179)

F

factor/factor cualquier cosa en un experimento que puede influir el resultado (14)

fallopian tube/tuba de Falopio el tubo que va de un ovario al útero (617)

family/familia el nivel de clasificación que viene después de orden; los organismos en todas las órdenes están organizados en familias (203)

farsighted/hipermetropía describe a alguien que puede ver mejor las cosas que están lejos que las que están cerca (597)

fat/grasa nutrientes que almacenan energía y que ayudan al cuerpo a almacenar algunas vitaminas (657)

feedback controls/controles de retroalimentación sistema que hace que las glándulas encócrinas comiencen a funcionar y dejen de hacerlo (602)

fermentation/fermentación la descomposición de los azúcares para hacer ATP en la ausencia de oxígeno (89)

fetus/feto un embrión en las últimas etapas de desarrollo dentro del útero (622)

fibrous root/raíz fibrosa tipo de raíz en la que hay varias raíces del mismo tamaño que se separan de la base del tallo (285)

fins/aletas estructuras con forma de abanico que ayudan a los peces a moverse, a doblar, a detenerse, y a mantener el equilibrio (378)

flexor/flexor músculo que dobla una parte del cuerpo (531)

food chain/cadena alimentaria diagrama que representa cómo la energía en las moléculas de la comida fluye de un organismo al siguiente (440)

food web/ciclo alimentario diagrama complejo que representa las variadas trayectorias de la energía en un ecosistema real (440)

fossil/fósil los restos o impresiones solidificadas de un organismo que vivió en algún momento (152, 176)

fossil record/registro fósil secuencia histórica de la vida indicada por los fósiles encontrados en las capas de la corteza terrestre (152)

fragmentation/fragmentación tipo de reproducción en la que un organismo se divide en dos partes o más, cada una de las cuales puede crecer para ser un individuo separado (612)

Fungi/reino de los hongos reino de organismos complejos que obtienen alimento al desintegrar otras sustancias en sus alrededores y absorber los nutrientes (212)

fungus/hongo organismo en el reino de los Hongos (255)

funguslike protist/semejante de un hongo una protista que obtiene su alimento de materia orgánica muerta o del cuerpo de otro organismo (245)

G

gallbladder/vesícula biliar un órgano pequeño, parecido a una bolsa, que almacena bilis (573)

gametophyte/gametofito período en el ciclo de vida de una planta durante el cual se producen huevos y esperma (271)

ganglia/ganglios grupos de células nerviosas (345)

generation time/período generacional período entre el nacimiento de una generación y el de la siguiente (164)

genes/genes segmentos de ADN que llevan instrucciones hereditarias y se pasan de padres a hijos; están localizados en los cromosomas (111)

genetic engineering/ingeniería genética la manipulación de los genes que permite que los científicos pongan genes de un organismo en otro (141)

genotype/genotipo la combinación de alelos heredada (111)

genus/género el nivel de clasificación que viene después de familia; los organismos en todas las familias están organizados en géneros (203)

geologic time scale/escala de tiempo geológico división de la historia de la Tierra en intervalos de tiempo diferenciados (178)

gestation period/gestación el tiempo durante el cual un embrión se desarrolla dentro de la madre (416)

gills/agallas órganos que extraen el oxígeno del agua y el dióxido de carbono de la sangre (378)

gland/glándula grupo de células que fabrica sustancias químicas especiales para el cuerpo (600)

Golgi complex/complejo Golgi el orgánulo celular que modifica, prepara y transporta materiales fuera de la célula (72)

gravitropism/gravitropismo cambio en el crecimiento de una planta en respuesta a la gravedad (308)

ground water/agua subterránea agua almacenada en cavernas o roca porosa (459)

guanine/guanina una de las cuatro bases que se combina con azúcar y fosfato para formar una subunidad nucleótica de ADN; la guanina forma un par con la citosina (128)

gut/tripa en los animales, la bolsa donde se digiere la comida (345)

gymnosperm/gimnosperma planta que produce semillas, pero que no produce flores (273)

H

hábitat/habitat medio ambiente donde vive un organismo (442)

hair follicle/folículo piloso pequeño órgano en la capa dérmica de la piel que produce pelo (536)

half-life/media vida para una muestra radioactiva en particular, el tiempo que lleva para que se desintegre la mitad de la muestra (177)

hallucinogen/alucinógeno droga que distorsiona los sentidos y causa cambios en el humor y los procesos del pensamiento, y causa alucinaciones (666)

head/cabeza la parte del cuerpo de los animales en donde se encuentra el cerebro (357)

helper T cell/célula T ayudante célula del sistema inmunológico que activa las células T asesinas y las células B (642)

hemoglobin/hemoglobina la proteína en las células sanguíneas rojas que se une al oxígeno para que éste pueda ser transportado por el cuerpo (42, 546)

herbivore/herbívoro consumidor que come plantas (439)

heredity/herencia el pasaje de rasgos de padres a hijos (38, 106)

hibernation/hibernación período de inactividad que experimentan algunos animales en invierno, que les permite sobrevivir consumiendo la grasa acumulada en su cuerpo (329)

homeostasis/homeostasis mantener un medio ambiente interno estable (37, 522)

Spanish Glossary **825**

hominid/homínido la familia que se refiere específicamente a los humanos y a varias especies extintas, similares a los humanos, algunos de los cuales eran antepasados de los humanos (189)

homologous chromosomes/cromosomas homólogos cromosomas con información coincidente (93)

hormone/hormona mensajero químico que lleva la información de una parte a otra de un organismo; en los mamíferos, las hormonas son fabricadas por las glándulas endócrinas (600)

host/huésped organismo en el que vive un parásito (233, 246, 350, 448)

hygiene/higiene métodos para preservar y proteger la salud (669)

hyphae/hifas cadenas de células que forman hongos multicelulares (256)

hypothesis/hipótesis una explicación o respuesta posible a una pregunta (12)

I

immune system/sistema inmunitario colección de células, tejidos, y órganos que luchan contra los agentes que causan enfermedades (641)

immunity/inmunidad resistencia a una enfermedad (638)

imperfect fungus/hongo imperfecto un hongo que no entra en otras categorías estándard de hongos (260)

implantation/implantación proceso en el cual un embrión se fija en el revestimiento del útero (620)

impulse/impulso mensaje eléctrico que pasa por una neurona (589)

infectious disease/enfermedad contagiosa enfermedad causada por un agente patógeno (636)

infertile/infértil la condición de no poder tener hijos (619)

innate behavior/conducta innata un comportamiento influido por los genes que no depende del aprendizaje (328)

integumentary system/sistema tegumentario colección de órganos que ayudan al cuerpo a -mantener un medio ambiente interno estable y sano; los órganos en este sistema incluyen la piel, el pelo, y las uñas (534)

internal fertilization/fertilización interna la fertilización de un huevo por el esperma, que ocurre dentro del cuerpo de una hembra (378, 614)

invertebrate/invertebrado animal sin espina dorsal (323, 344)

iris/iris la parte coloreada del ojo (597)

J

joint/articulación la parte donde se conectan dos o más huesos (528)

K

kidney/riñón órgano con forma de frijol que extrae muchas sustancias dañinas de la sangre (577)

killer T cell/célula T asesina célula del sistema inmunológico que mata las células del cuerpo infectadas con agentes patógenos (642)

kingdom/reino el más general de los siete niveles de clasificación (203)

L

lactic-acid bacteria/bacteria de ácido láctico la bacteria que digiere el azúcar lactosa de la leche y la convierte en ácido láctico (231)

landmark/punto de referencia un objeto fijo que se usa para determinar la posición durante la navegación (331)

large intestine/intestino grueso un órgano grande que reabsorbe el agua del sistema digestivo, y almacena, compacta, y elimina del cuerpo el material que no se puede digerir (574)

larynx/laringe el área de la garganta que contiene las cuerdas vocales (557)

lateral line system/sistema de líneas laterales hilera o hileras de pequeños órganos de los sentidos en los costados del cuerpo de un pez (378)

learned behavior/conducta aprendida un comportamiento que se ha aprendido por experiencia u observación (328)

lens/lente un objeto curvo y transparente que forma una imagen al refractar la luz (597)

lichen/líquen la combinación de un hongo y un alga que crece mezclada, y que existe en una relación simbiótica (261)

life science/ciencias naturales el estudio de las cosas vivas (6)

lift/elevación una fuerza ascendente sobre un objeto causada por las diferencias en la presión arriba y abajo del objeto; la elevación se opone al arrastre hacia abajo de la gravedad (404)

ligament/ligamento una banda fuerte de tejido que conecta a los huesos entre sí (529)

limiting factor/factor limitante un recurso necesario del que hay escasez (444)

lipid/lípido tipo de sustancia bioquímica, que incluye grasas y aceites, que no se disuelve en agua; los lípidos almacenan la energía y forman membranas celulares (44)

littoral zone/zona litoral el área de un lago o laguna que está más cerca de la tierra (487)

liver/hígado un órgano grande, de color rojizo, que produce bilis y que almacena nutrientes; el hígado tiene más de 200 funciones en el cuerpo (573)

lung/pulmón órgano que se parece a una bolsa que toma el oxígeno del aire y lo lleva a la sangre (382)

lymph/linfas el fluido y las partículas absorbidos por los capilares linfáticos (554)

lymph nodes/nódulos linfáticos órganos pequeños, con forma de frijol, que contienen fibras minúsculas que funcionan como redes para quitar partículas de la linfa (555)

lymphatic system/sistema linfático colección de órganos que juntan el fluido extracelular y lo devuelven a la sangre; los órganos en este sistema incluyen los nódulos linfáticos y los vasos linfáticos (554)

lysosome/lisosoma vesícula especial en una célula que digiere las partículas de alimento, los deshechos, y los invasores del exterior (74)

M

macrophage/macrófago una célula del sistema inmunológico que come a los patógenos (641)

malnutrition/malnutrición enfermedad que resulta de no consumir la combinación correcta de nutrientes (662)

mammary glands/glándulas mamarias glándulas que secretan un fluido alimenticio llamado leche (411)

mandible/mandíbula maxilar inferior encontrado en algunos artrópodos (359)

marine/marino describe un ecosistema basado en agua salada (481)

marsh/marisma un ecosistema pantanoso, sin árboles, donde crecen plantas como las aneas y los juncos (488)

marsupial/marsupial mamífero que da a luz a crías vivas, parcialmente desarrolladas, que continúan desarrollándose dentro de la bolsa o pliegue de la piel de la madre (415, 615)

mass/masa la cantidad de materia de que está hecho algo; su valor no cambia con la posición del objeto (26)

mass extinction/extinción masiva período en que un gran número de especies muere al mismo tiempo (179)

matter/materia cualquier cosa que ocupa espacio y tiene masa (458)

mechanical digestion/digestión mecánica despedazar, machacar, y moler la comida (569)

medulla/médula la parte del cerebro que conecta con la médula espinal y controla muchos procesos involuntarios en el cuerpo (592)

medusa/medusa forma del cuerpo de algunos celenterados; se parece a un hongo con tentáculos (348)

meiosis/meiosis división de la célula que produce células sexuales (115, 613)

melanin/melanina una sustancia química que en la piel, que determina su color (534)

memory B cell/célula B de memoria célula del sistema inmunológico que "recuerda" cómo hacer un anticuerpo especializado para un patógeno en particular (644)

menstruation/menstruación la pérdida mensual de sangre y tejidos del útero (617)

Mesozoic era/era mesozoica el período en la escala de tiempo geológico que comienza cerca de 248 millones de años atrás y que dura aproximadamente 183 millones de años (186)

metabolism/metabolismo los procesos químicos combinados que ocurren en una célula o en un organismo vivo (38)

metamorphosis/metamorfosis el proceso en que un insecto u otro animal cambia de forma al desarrollarse de embrión o larva a adulto (361, 384)

meter/metro la unidad básica de longitud en el sistema SI (23)

migrate/migrar viajar de un lugar a otro como respuesta a las estaciones o condiciones ambientales (329)

mineral/mineral elemento que es esencial para la buena salud (657)

mitochondria/mitocondrias orgánulos celulares rodeados por dos membranas que descomponen las moléculas de alimento para hacer ATP (71)

mitosis/mitosis división nuclear en las células eucariotas en la que cada célula recibe una copia de los cromosomas originales (93)

mold/moho hongos sin forma y con pelusa (257)

monotreme/monotrema mamífero que pone huevos (414, 615)

motor neuron/neurona motor neurona que envía impulsos del cerebro y de la médula espinal a otros sistemas (590)

multicelular/multicelular formado por muchas células (59, 323)

muscle tissue/tejido muscular uno de los cuatro tipos principales de tejido en el cuerpo; contiene células que se contraen y se relajan para producir movimiento (523)

muscular system/sistema muscular colección de órganos cuya función primaria es el movimiento; los órganos en este sistema incluyen los músculos y el tejido conjuntivo que los une a los huesos (530)

mutagen/mutágeno cualquier cosa que puede dañar o causar cambios en el ADN (138)

mutation/mutación un cambio en el orden de las bases en el ADN de un organismo; eliminación, inserción, o sustitución (138, 163)

mutualism/mutualismo relación simbiótica en la que se benefician los dos organismos (447)

mycelium/micelio una masa retorcida de hifas que han crecido juntas (256)

N

narcotics/narcóticos drogas hechas del opio (667)

natural selection/selección natural el proceso por el cual los organismos con rasgos favorables sobreviven y se reproducen a más velocidad que los organismos sin el rasgo favorable (162)

Neanderthal/neandertal especie de homínido que vivió en Europa y en el oeste de Asia desde 230,000 años atrás a aproximadamente hace 30,000 años (192)

nearsighted/miope describe a alguien que ve mejor los objetos que están cerca que los que están lejos (597)

nephron/nefrón un filtro microscópico en el riñón que extrae una variedad de sustancias dañinas de la sangre (577)

nerve/nervio un axón; los nervios están agrupados en haces con los vasos sanguíneos y el tejido conjuntivo (590)

nervous system/sistema nervioso colección de órganos que se unen e interpretan información sobre el medio ambiente interno y externo del cuerpo y responden a esa información; los órganos en este sistema incluyen el cerebro, los nervios, y la médula espinal (588)

nervous tissue/tejido nervioso uno de los cuatro tipos principales de tejido en el cuerpo; el tejido que envía las señales eléctricas a través del cuerpo (522)

neuron/neurona una célula especializada que transfiere mensajes a través del cuerpo en la forma de energía eléctrica que se mueve con rapidez (589)

niche/nicho el modo de vida de un organismo y sus relaciones con sus medios ambientes abiótico y biótico (442)

nicotine/nicotina un estimulante químico que se encuentra en el tabaco, que aumenta el ritmo del corazón y la presión arterial (665)

nitrogen cycle/ciclo del nitrógeno el movimiento de nitrógeno del medio ambiente no vivo al interior de los organismos vivos y de vuelta a medio ambiente (460)

nitrogen fixation/fijación de nitrógeno proceso de cambiar el gas nitrógeno a formas que las plantas pueden usar (461)

noninfectious disease/enfermedad no contagiosa una enfermedad que no se contagia de una persona a otra (636)

nonrenewable resource/recurso no renovable un recurso natural que no se puede remplazar o uno que solamente se puede remplazar en miles o millones de años (501)

nonvascular plant/planta no vascular una planta que depende de los procesos de difusión y de osmosis para mover materiales de una parte de la planta a otra (272)

nucleic acid/ácido nucleico una sustancia bioquímica que almacena la información que se necesita para formar proteínas y otros ácidos nucleicos; formada por subunidades llamadas nucleótidos (45)

nucleotide/nucleótido una subunidad de ADN que consiste de un azúcar, un fosfato, y una de cuatro bases nitrógenadas (45, 128)

nucleus/núcleo el orgánulo cubierto por una membrana que se encuentra en las células eucariotas; contiene el ADN de la célula y sirve como centro de control de la célula (66)

nutrient/nutriente sustancia que se debe consumir o tomar por un organismo para promover crecimiento normal, manutención y reparación (569, 656)

O

obesity/obesidad enfermedad caracterizada por un porcentaje extremadamente alto de grasa en el cuerpo (662)

omnivore/omnívoro consumidor que come una variedad de organismos (439)

open circulatory system/sistema circulatorio abierto sistema circulatorio que consiste de un corazón que bombea la sangre a través de espacios conocidos como senos (354)

open-water zone/zona de aguas superiores la zona de un lago o laguna que se extiende desde la zona del litoral por la superficie del agua y que es solamente tan profunda como la luz puede penetrar el agua (487)

optic nerve/nervio óptico nervio que transfiere impulsos eléctricos del ojo al cerebro (596)

order/orden el nivel de clasificación luego de clase; los organismos en todas las clases están organizados en órdenes (203)

organ/órgano combinación de dos o más tejidos que trabajan juntos para llevar a cabo una función específica en el cuerpo (57, 324, 523)

organ system/sistema de órganos grupo de órganos que trabajan juntos para llevar a cabo funciones corporales (58, 523)

organelle/orgánulo estructura dentro de una célula, algunas veces rodeado por una membrana (63)

organism/organismo cualquier cosa que puede realizar independientemente los procesos para la vida (59)

osmosis/osmosis la difusión de agua a través de la membrana celular (85)

ovary/ovario en los animales, un órgano en el sistema reproductor femenino que produce huevos (617); en las flores, la estructura que contiene óvulos y que se va a convertir en fruta después de la fertilización (291)

overpopulation/sobrepoblación condición que ocurre cuando el número de individuos en un medio ambiente se vuelve tan grande que no hay suficientes recursos para que todos se mantengan (502)

ovulation/ovulación proceso por el cual un huevo se expulsa a través de la pared del ovario (617)

ozone/ozono una molécula de gas que está hecha de tres átomos de oxígeno; absorbe radiación ultra-violeta del sol (184)

P

Paleozoic era/era paleozoica el período en la escala de tiempo geológico que comienza aproximadamente 570 millones de años atrás, y que termina hace aproximadamente 248 millones de años (185)

pancreas/páncreas un órgano con forma de pez situado entre el estómago y el intestino delgado que produce enzimas para la digestión química (572)

Pangaea/Pangaea la masa de tierra única que contenía todos los continentes de hoy en día hace 200 millones de años (180)

parasite/parásito organismo que se alimenta de otra criatura viviente, generalmente sin matarla (246, 350, 448)

parasitism/parasitismo una asociación simbiótica en la que un organismo se beneficia y el otro se daña (448)

passive transport/transporte pasivo la difusión de partículas a través de las proteínas en la membrana celular de áreas en que la concetración de partículas es alta a áreas en que la concentración de partículas es baja (86)

pasteurization/pasteurización método de calentar la comida y las bebidas para matar bacterias (638)

pathogen/patógeno un agente que causa una enfermedad (636)

pathogenic bacteria/bacteria patógena bacterias que invaden un organismo huésped y obtienen los nutrientes que necesitan de las células del huésped (232)

pedigree/pedigrí un diagrama de la historia familiar usado para seguir la trayectoria de un rasgo a través de varias generaciones (140)

penis/pene el órgano reproductor masculino que transfiere el semen al cuerpo de la hembra durante las relaciones sexuales (616)

peripheral nervous system/sistema nervioso periférico la colección de trayectorias de comunicación, o nervios, cuya función primaria es transferir información de todas las áreas del cuerpo y el medio ambiente exterior al sistema nervioso central y del sistema nervioso central al resto del cuerpo (588)

peristalsis/peristalsis una contracción muscular rítmica en el sistema digestivo (570)

permafrost/suelo helado el suelo congelado permanentemente bajo la superficie de la tierra en la tundra ártica (480)

petals/pétalos las estructuras con frecuencia coloreadas en una flor que generalmente participan en la atracción de los polinizadores (290)

pharynx/faringe la porción superior de la garganta (557)

phenotype/fenotipo la apariencia heredada del organismo (111)

pheromone/feromona sustancia química producida por los animales para la comunicación (333)

phloem/floema tejido vegetal especializado que transporta moléculas de azúcar de una parte a otra de la planta (284)

phospholipid/fosfolípido tipo de molécula lípida que forma gran parte de la membrana de una célula (44)

photoreceptors/fotoreceptores neuronas especializadas en la retina que detectan la luz (596)

photosynthesis/fotosíntesis el proceso por el cual las plantas capturan la energía de la luz del sol y la convierten en azúcar (88, 184, 270)

phototropism/fototropismo cambio en el crecimiento de una planta en respuesta a la luz (307)

phylum/tipo el nivel de clasificación que viene después de reino; los organismos de todos los reinos están divididos en filas (203)

phytoplankton/fitoplancton organismo microscópico y fotosintético que flota cerca de la superficie del océano (481)

pioneer species/especies pioneras los primeros organismos que crecen en un área que está pasando por sucesión ecológica; generalmente son líquenes, que crecen rápidamente, en sucesión primaria, y plantas herbáceas en sucesión secundaria (463)

pistils/pistilos las estructuras reproductoras femeninas en una flor, que consisten del estigma, un estilo, y un ovario (291)

placenta/placenta órgano especial de intercambio que provee a un feto en desarrollo con nutrientes y oxígeno (416, 621)

placental mammal/mamífero de placenta un mamífero que alimenta a sus crías no nacidas con una placenta dentro del útero, y que da vida a crías bien desarrolladas (416, 615)

plankton/pláncton organismos muy pequeños que flotan en la superficie del océano o cerca de ella, que forman la base de la red alimenticia del océano (481)

Plantae/reino vegetal el reino que contiene las plantas—organismos complejos, multicelulares que en general son verdes y que usan la energía solar para fabricar azúcar por fotosíntesis (211)

plasma/plasma la parte fluida de la sangre (546)

plate tectonics/tectónica de placas el estudio de las fuerzas que llevan al movimiento de los trozos de la corteza terrestre alrededor de la superficie del planeta (181)

platelet/plateletas un fragmento de célula que ayuda a coagular la sangre (547)

pollen/polen las partículas parecidas al polvo que llevan el gametofito masculino de las plantas con semilla (278)

pollination/polinización la transferencia de polen a la piña femenina en las coníferas o al estigma en los angiospermas (281)

pollutant/contaminante una sustancia dañina en el medio ambiente (498)

pollution/contaminación la presencia de sustancias dañinas en un medio ambiente (498)

polyp/pólipo la forma del cuerpo de algunos celenterados; se parece a un florero (348)

population/población grupo de individuos de la misma especie que viven juntos en la misma área, al mismo tiempo (59, 436)

Precambian time/periodo precámbrico el período en la escala de tiempo geológico que comienza con el origen de la Tierra, 4.6 millones de millones de años atrás, y termina con el momento en que aparecieron los organismos complejos, aproximadamente hace 540 millones de años (182)

precipitation/precipitación agua que se mueve de la atmósfera a la tierra y al océano, que incluye la lluvia, la nieve, el aguanieve y el granizo (458)

precocial chick/pollito precocial pollito que sale del nido inmediatamente después de nacer y que está totalmente activo (406)

predator/predador organismo que come otros organismos (326, 446)

preening/limpieza de plumaje la actividad en la que un pájaro usa el pico para esparcir aceite en sus plumas (401)

prescription/prescripción nota escrita por un doctor que permite que un paciente compre una medicina (664)

prey/presa organismo que es comido por otro organismo (326, 446)

primate/primate tipo de mamífero que incluye a los humanos, a los simios, y a los monos, se distigue típicamente por tener pulgares oponibles y visión binocular (188, 423)

probability/probabilidad la chance matemática de que un suceso va a ocurrir (112)

producer/productor organismo que fabrica su propia comida, en general usando la energía solar para hacer azúcar (40, 227, 438)

prokaryotic cell/célula procariota célula que no tiene núcleo o ningún otro orgánulo cubierto por una membrana; también llamada bacteria (66, 183, 224)

prosimian/prosimio los primeros antepasados de los primates; también, un grupo de primates que viven, que incluye las lorias y los lemures (190)

protein/proteína sustancia bioquímica compuesta por aminoácidos; sus funciones incluyen regular las reacciones químicas, transportar y almacenar materiales, y proporcionar apoyo (42, 657)

protist/protisto organismo que pertenece al reino protista (244)

Protista/reino protista reino de organismos eucariotas unicelulares o multicelulares simples; el reino protista contiene a todas las eucariotas que no son plantas, animales, ni hongos (210)

protozoa/protozoarios protistas que se parecen a los animales que son consumidores unicelulares (250)

pseudopodia/seudópodos estructuras que las amibas usan para moverse (250)

puberty/pubertad el momento en la vida cuando maduran los órganos sexuales (616)

pulmonary circulation/circulación pulmonar la circulación de la sangre entre el corazón y los pulmones (550)

Punnett square/cuadrado de Punnett instrumento usado para visualizar todas las posibles combinaciones de alelos de los padres (111)

pupil/pupila la apertura al interior del ojo (597)

R

radial symmetry/simetría radiada un plan del cuerpo en que las partes del cuerpo están organizadas en un círculo alrededor de un punto central (344)

receptor/receptor célula especializada, a veces, una dendrita, que detecta cambios dentro o fuera del cuerpo (590)

recessive trait/carácter recesivo un rasgo que es aparente sólo cuando dos alelos recesivos se heredan para la misma característica (109)

rectum/recto la última sección del intestino grueso; donde se almacenan las materias fecales hasta que se pueden expeler del cuerpo (574)

recycling/reciclaje proceso de hacer productos nuevos con productos usados vueltos a procesar (507)

red blood cell/glóbulo rojo célula que lleva oxígeno de los pulmones a todas las células del cuerpo y que lleva el dióxido de carbono de vuelta a los pulmones para que lo exhalen (546)

reflex/reflejo una respuesta rápida e involuntaria a un estímulo (594)

relative dating/datación relativa determinar si un suceso u objeto, como un fósil, es anterior o posterior a otros sucesos u objetos (177)

renewable resource/recurso renovable recurso natural que se puede usar y remplazar en un período de tiempo relativamente corto (501)

resource recovery/recuperación de recursos proceso de transformar las cosas que normalmente se desechan en productos que se pueden usar (508)

respiration/respiración el intercambio de gases entre las células vivientes y su medio ambiente; incluye la respiración y la respiración celular (556); ver respiración celular

respiratory system/sistema respiratorio colección de órganos cuya función primaria es hacer entrar el oxígeno y expeler el dióxido de carbono; los órganos de este sistema incluyen los pulmones, la garganta, y los pasajes que llevan a los pulmones (556)

retina/retina una capa de células sensibles a la luz en la parte de atrás del ojo (596)

rhizoids/rizoides pequeños hilos de células como pelos que ayudan a mantener a las plantas no vasculares en su lugar (274)

rhizome/rizoma el tallo subterráneo de un helecho (276)

ribosome/ribosoma un pequeño orgánulo en las células en que las proteínas se forman de aminoácidos (70 ,137)

rods/bastones fotorreceptores que detectan luz muy baja (596)

S

sac fungus/hongos saco tipo de hongo que se reproduce usando esporas, que se desarrollan en un saco llamado asca (250)

salivary glands/glándulas salivares órganos situados alrededor de la boca que producen un líquido que comienza la digestión química (570)

saturated fat/grasa saturada tipo de grasa que se encuentra en carnes, productos lácteos, aceite de coco, y aceite de palma; se sabe que aumenta los niveles de colesterol en la sangre (658)

savanna/sabana bioma tropical con pasturas con grupos de árboles esparcidos (478)

scales/escamas estructuras óseas que cubren la piel de los peces (380)

scavenger/carroñero animal que se alimenta de los cuerpos de animales muertos (439)

scientific method/método científico serie de pasos que usan los científicos para responder preguntas y resolver problemas (10)

scrotum/escroto un saco cubierto de piel que cuelga del cuerpo de los especímenes de sexo masculino y que contiene los testículos (616)

sediment/sedimento partículas finas de arena, polvo, o barro que el viento o el agua depositan a través del tiempo (176)

segment/segmento una parte del cuerpo de muchas idénticas o casi idénticas que se repiten (355)

selective breeding/cría selectiva criar organismos que tienen un cierto rasgo deseado (160)

self-pollinating plant/planta autopolinizante planta que contiene las estructuras reproductivas femeninas y masculinas (107)

semen/semen mezcla de esperma y de fluidos (616)

seminiferous tubules/tubos seminíferos los tubos en espiral adentro de los testículos donde se producen los espermatozoides (616)

sensory neuron/neurona sensorial neurona especial que junta información sobre lo que está pasando dentro y alrededor del cuerpo, y envía esta información al sistema nervioso central (590)

sepals/sépalos las estructuras parecidas a las hojas que cubren y protegen una flor que no ha madurado (290)

sex cell/gameto óvulo o espermatozoide; una célula sexual lleva la mitad del número de cromosomas que se encuentra en otras células del cuerpo (114)

sex chromosomes/cromosomas sexuales los cromosomas que llevan los genes que determinan el sexo de las crías (119)

sexual reproduction/reproducción sexual reproducción en la que dos células sexuales se unen para forman un cigoto; la reproducción sexual produce crías que comparten características con ambos padres (38, 613)

sexually transmitted disease/enfermedad de transmisión sexual una enfermedad que se contagia de una persona infectada a otra que no está infectada durante contacto sexual (619)

skeletal muscle/músculo esquelético el tipo de músculo que mueve los huesos y ayuda a proteger los órganos internos (530)

skeletal system/sistema esquelético colección de órganos cuya función primaria es dar apoyo y protección al cuerpo; los órganos en este sistema incluyen los huesos, cartílagos, ligamentos, y tendones (526)

small intestine/intestino delgado tubo muscular de aproximadamente 2.5 cm de diámetro y de hasta 6 m de largo; el lugar de la mayor parte de la digestión química (572)

smooth muscle/músculo liso el tipo de músculo que se encuentra en los vasos sanguíneos y en el sistema digestivo (530)

social behavior/conducta social la interacción entre animales de la misma especie (332)

speciation/especiación el proceso por el que dos poblaciones de la misma especie se vuelven tan diferentes que ya no pueden cruzarse (166)

species/especie el más específico de los siete niveles de clasificación, caracterizado por un grupo de organismos que pueden aparearse uno con otro para producir crías fértiles (150, 203)

sperm/espermatozoide célula sexual producida por el macho (613)

spleen/bazo órgano que filtra la sangre y produce linfocitos (555)

spongy bone/hueso esponjoso un tipo de tejido óseo que tiene muchos espacios libres y que contiene médula (527)

spore/esporo una célula reproductiva pequeña protegida por una pared gruesa (256)

sporophyte/esporofito etapa en el ciclo de vida de una planta durante el cual se producen los esporos (271)

stamen/estambre la estructura reproductiva masculina en una flor, que consiste en un filamento que termina en una antera que produce polen (291)

stigma/estigma la parte de la flor situada en la punta del pistilo (291)

stimulant/estimulante droga que acelera la acción del sistema nervioso central (663)

stimulus/estímulo cualquier cosa que afecte la actividad de un organismo, órgano, o tejido (37, 307)

stomach/estómago un órgano muscular, con forma de bolsa, del sistema digestivo, unido a la parte más baja del esófago (571)

stomata/estomas aperturas en la epidermis y cutícula de una hoja que permiten que el dióxido de carbono entre a la hoja (289, 306)

stress/estrés respuesta física y mental a las situaciones que crean presión (671)

succession/sucesión la gradual vuelta a crecer o desarrollarse de una comunidad de organismos a través del tiempo (462)

surface-to-volume ratio/proporción superficie a volumen la cantidad de superficie exterior de una célula en relación a su volumen (64)

swamp/ciénaga un ecosistema pantanoso en que crecen árboles y plantas trepadoras (489)

sweat glands/glándulas sudoríparas pequeños órganos en la capa de dermis de la piel que liberan el sudor (534)

swim bladder/vejiga natatoria un órgano parecido a un globo lleno de oxígeno y otros gases; les da a los peces óseos la capacidad de flotar (380)

symbiosis/simbiosis una asociación cercana, a largo plazo, entre dos o más especies (251, 447)

systemic circulation/circulación sistémica la circulación de sangre entre el corazón y el cuerpo (excluyendo a los pulmones) (550)

T

T cell/célula T una célula del sistema inmunológico que madura en el timo (641)

tadpole/renacuajo la larva acuática de un anfibio (384)

taproot/raíz fibrosa tipo de raíz que consiste en una raíz principal que crece hacia abajo, con muchas ramificaciones pequeñas que salen de ella (285)

taxonomy/taxonomía la ciencia de identificar, clasificar, y nombrar a las cosas vivientes (204)

technology/tecnología la aplicación del conocimiento, los instrumentos, y los materiales para resolver problemas y realizar tareas; la tecnología también puede referirse a los objetos que se usan para realizar las tareas (18)

temperature/temperatura la medida de cuán caliente o frío es algo (26)

tendon/tendón un tejido conjuntivo fuerte que conecta los músculos esqueléticos a los huesos (531)

territory/territorio área ocupada por un animal o un grupo de animales y de la cual se excluyen otros miembros de la especie (332)

testes/testículos los órganos del sistema reproductor masculino que fabrican esperma y testosterona (616)

theory/teoría explicación unificadora para una gran variedad de hipótesis y observaciones que han sido apoyadas con experimentación (18)

therapsid/teráptido reptil prehistórico, antepasado de los mamíferos (387, 410)

thorax/tórax parte central del cuerpo de un artrópodo o de otro animal; donde están situados el corazón y los pulmones (357)

threadlike fungus/hongo filamentoso un hongo que se desarrolla de un esporo llamado cigosporo (257)

thymine/timina una de las cuatro bases que se combinan con el azúcar y el fosfato para formar una subunidad nucleótida de ADN; la tiamina forma un par con la adenina (128)

thymus/timo órgano linfático que produce linfocitos (555)

tissue/tejido grupo de células similares que trabajan juntas para llevar a cabo una función específica en el cuerpo (57, 324, 522)

tonsils/amígdalas pequeñas masas de tejido blando situadas en la parte de atrás de la cavidad nasal, dentro de la garganta, y detrás de la lengua (555)

toxic/tóxico venenoso (499)

trachea/tráquea el pasaje de aire de la laringe a los pulmones (557)

trait/rasgo una cualidad distintiva que puede pasar de una generación a otra (160)

transpiration/transpiración la pérdida de agua de las hojas de una planta a través de aperturas llamadas estomas (306)

tributary/afluente un arroyo o río pequeño que desemboca en uno más grande (486)

tropism/tropismo un cambio en el crecimiento de una planta en respuesta a un estímulo (307)

true-breeding plant/planta de línea genéticamente pura planta que siempre da crías con los mismos rasgos que los progenitores (108)

tundra/tundra un bioma del extremo norte caracterizado por inviernos largos y fríos, permafrost, y pocos árboles (480)

U

umbilical cord/cordón umbilical el cordón que conecta a un embrión con una placenta (621)

unicellular/unicelular formado por una sola célula (59)

unsaturated fat/grasa no saturada una clase de grasa que en general viene de fuentes vegetales y que ayuda a reducir los niveles de colesterol en la sangre (658)

ureter/uréter un tubo delgado que lleva la orina de cada riñón a la vejiga urinaria (577)

urethra/uretra en los machos, un tubo delgado que lleva la orina y el semen al exterior a través del pene; en las hembras, un tubo delgado que lleva la orina al exterior (577, 616)

urinary bladder/vejiga urinaria órgano con forma de bolsa que almacena la orina hasta que se puede eliminar por la uretra (577)

urinary system/sistema urinario colección de órganos que quita los deshechos de la sangre; este sistema incluye los riñones, los uréteres, la uretra, y la vejiga urinaria (576)

urine/orina mezcla concentrada de materiales de deshecho que se forma en las nefronas del riñón (577)

uterus/útero órgano en el sistema reproductor femenino donde crece y se desarrolla un cigoto (617)

V

vaccine/vacuna sustancia que ayuda al cuerpo a que desarrolle inmunidad contra un patógeno (638)

vacuole/vacuola grandes estructuras cubiertas por membranas que sirven para almacenar agua y otros líquidos (73)

vagina/vagina en el sistema reproductor femenino, el pasaje que recibe el esperma durante las relaciones sexuales (617)

variable/variable un factor que cambia en un experimento controlado (14)

vas deferens/vasos deferentes en el sistema reproductor masculino, el tubo donde el esperma se mezcla con los fluidos para formar semen (616)

vascular plant/planta vascular planta que tiene unos tejidos especializados llamados xilema y floema, que transportan materiales de una parte de la planta a otra (273)

veins/venas vasos sanguíneos que dirigen la sangre al corazón (549)

ventricle/ventrículo la cámara inferior del corazón (548)

vertebrae/vértebras segmentos de hueso o cartílago que se entrelazan para formar una espina dorsal (375)

vertebrate/vertebrado un animal que tiene calavera y espina dorsal; incluyen a los mamíferos, pájaros, reptiles, anfibios, y peces (322, 374)

vesicle/vesícula en una célula eucariota, el compartimiento cubierto por una membrana que se forma cuando parte de la membrana celular rodea un objeto y se separa (73)

vestigial structure/estructura vestigial el resto de una estructura anatómica que en algún momento fue útil (153)

villi/vilis proyecciones que parecen dedos en el interior de la pared del intestino delgado (572)

virus/virus partícula microscópica que invade una célula y con frecuencia la destruye (233)

vitamin/vitamina compuesto orgánico que controla muchas funciones del cuerpo, incluyendo el crecimiento de las células y la producción de hormonas (659)

volume/volumen la cantidad de espacio que algo ocupa, o la cantidad de espacio que algo contiene (24)

W

water cycle/ciclo del agua movimiento del agua entre el océano, la atmósfera, la tierra, y las cosas vivientes (458)

water vascular system/sistema vascular acuífero sistema de bombas de agua y canales que se encuentran en todos los equinodermos que les permite moverse, comer, y respirar (364)

wetland/pantano área de tierra donde el nivel del agua está cerca o por encima del nivel de la tierra la mayor parte del año (488)

white blood cell/leucocito célula de la sangre que protege el cuerpo contra los patógenos (547)

X

xylem/xilema tejido vegetal especializado que transporta el agua y los minerales de una parte de la planta a otras (284)

Z

zooplankton/zooplán cton protozoarios que, junto con el fitoplán cton que consumen, forman la base de la red alimenticia de los océanos (481)

zygote/zigoto un huevo fertilizado (613)

Index

Boldface numbers refer to an illustration on that page.

A

abdomen
  of arachnids, 359, **359**
  of arthropods, 357, **357**, 361, **361**
abiotic factors, 434, 444, 474, 481
ABO blood group, 552, **552**
absolute dating, 177
accidents
  alcohol-related, 666, **666**
  calling for help, 673, **673**
  first aid for victims of, 673, **673**
  prevention of, 672, **672**
active transport, 86, **86**
acupuncture, 652
adaptation, 150
  of predators, 446, **446**
  of prey, 446, **446**
  speciation by, 166, **166**
addiction, 664, 668
adenine, 128–129, **128**
adolescence, 624, **624**
adrenal gland, 600, **601**
adrenaline, 600
adulthood, **624**, 625
aerobic exercise, 670, **670**
Age of Mammals, 187
Age of Reptiles, 178, 186
aging process, 74, 82, 625
AIDS (acquired immune deficiency syndrome), 8, **8**, 233, 619, 647, **647**, 667
air
  composition of, 41
  at high elevation, 557
  pollution, 261, 498, **498**
air sacs, **402**
albumen, **389**
alcohol, 91, **91**
  use of, 654, 666–668, **667**
Aldorasi, Haifa, 496, **496**
algae, 246–249, **246–249**, 272, **272**
  in lichens, 261, **261**
  multicellular, 246, **246**
  mutualism with coral, 447, **447**
  in salt marsh, 436, **436**
  single-celled, **246**, 247
  types of, 247–248
alien species, 455, 502, **502**
alleles, 111
allergy, 645, **645**, 652
alligator, 389–390, **390**, 434, **434**
altricial chick, 406, **406**
alveoli, 557, **557**
amber, 225, **225**
Ambulocetus, 154–155, **154**
amebic dysentery, 250, **636**

amino acids, 42, 70, **70**, 569, **569**
  essential, 657
  making of proteins, 136–137, **136–137**
amnion, 621, **621**
amniotic egg, 388–389, **389**, 400
amoeba, 250–251, **250–251**, 254
amphetamines, 667
amphibians, 382–386
  adaptations to land, 382
  characteristics of, 383–384
  kinds of, 385–386, **385–386**
  metamorphosis in, 384, **384**
  skin of, 383
ampulla, **364**
anabolic steroids, 533
anaerobic, 183
analgesics, 663
angiosperms, 273, **273**, 278, 282–283
  monocots and dicots, 283, **283**
animal breeding, 160, **160**
animal cells, 323
  compared with plant cells, 75, **75**
Animalia (kingdom), **203**, 213, **213**, 322–323, **322–323**, 805
animal-like protists, 250–253, **250–253**
animals, 322–341, **322–341**
  antibiotics from, 653
  appearance on land, 185
  characteristics of, 322–325
  as consumers, 325
  development of, 324, **324**
  evolution of, 185–187
  human pathogens spread by, 637
  movement of, 325, **325**
  multicellular nature of, 323
  navigation by, 330–331, **330**
  pollination by, 282, **282**
  seasonal behavior of, 329, **329**
  sexual reproduction in, 324, **324**
  survival behavior in, 326–327, **326–327**
annelid worms, 355–356, **355–356**
anorexia nervosa, 662
antennae, 358, **359**
anther, 108, **107–108**, **290**, 291
antibiotic-resistant microorganisms, 164, 241, 653
antibiotics, 241, 663
  produced by animals, 653
  produced by bacteria, 230, 678
  produced by fungi, 258, 260, **260**
  treatment of bacterial disease with, 230, 639
antibodies, 547, 552, **552**, 641, **641**, 643–644
antidiuretic hormone, 578, 584
antigens, 552, **552**

antihistamines, 663
ants, **323**, 327, 333, **345**, 362, 416
  coevolution with acacia trees, 448, **448**
anus, 568, **568**, 574, **574**
aquarium, 457
aquatic ecosystem, 60
arachnids, 359–360, **359–360**
archaebacteria, 209, **209**, 224, 228, **228**
Archaeopteryx, 218, **218**, 398, **398–399**
area, 24, **24**, 799, **799**
artery, 549, **549–550**
arthritis, 528
  rheumatoid, 646, **646**
arthropods, **323**, 357–362
  characteristics of, 357–358, **357–358**
  exoskeleton of, 358
  kinds of, 358–360, **358–361**
  nervous system of, 358
  segmentation in, 357
artificial heart, 544
artificial selection, 160, **160**
ascus, 258
asexual reproduction, 38, **38**, 114, 254, **254**, 256, 303, **303**, 324, 612, **612**
aspirin, 663
asthma, 645
asymmetrical, 344
  animals, 344–345, **345**
atherosclerosis, 553, **553**
athlete
  water requirement of, 578, 584, 658, **658**
athlete's foot 255, 260
atmosphere
  carbon dioxide in, 500
  of early Earth, 91, 183, **183**
atomic number, 802
atoms, 42, 177, **177**, 802, **802**
ATP (adenosine triphosphate), 45, **45**, 86, 89
  production of, 71, 89–90, **89–90**
australopithecines, 190–191, 193
autoimmune disease, 646, **646**
averages, 16, 796
Aves (class), 400
axon, 589, **589**

B

bacilli, 226
backbone, 375, **375**
bacteria, 66, **66**, 92, **92**, 209, **209**, 224–228
  antibiotic resistance in, 241, 653
  "bait" of anglerfish, 432

Index 835

classification of, 224, 227–228
decomposers, 439, **439,** 678
in environment, 222–224
in food production, 231, **231**
genetically engineered, 230–231, **230**
in intestine, 447, 454
in nitrogen cycle, 229, **229**
obtaining nutrients, 227, **227**
pathogens, 232, **232,** 241, 579, 636, **636**
products useful to humans, 678
reproduction in, 225, **225**
role in environment, 229–230, **229–230**
shape of, 226
size of, 224, **224**
bacterial infection, 232, **232,** 636, **636**
treatment of, 241, 639
of urinary system, 579
bacteriophage, 241
balanced diet, 656–659, **656**
ball-and-socket joint, **528**
barbiturates, 667
bar graphs, 795, **795**
base pairs in DNA, 130–131, **130–131**
bases, 803
basidia, 259
basket star, 365, **365**
bat, 329, 418, **418,** 449
B cells, 641–642, **641,** 644
bear, **38,** 204, **329,** 413, **413,** 419
Beaumont, Dr. William, 566
bees, 282, **282, 323,** 327, **327,** 334, 362, 499
bumblebee, **360**
honeybee, 335
waggle dance, 334, **334**
beetles, **323,** 362
behavior
innate, 328
learned, 328, **328**
seasonal, 329, **329**
social, 332–335, **332, 334–335**
benthic zone, 483, **483**
Bernoulli effect, 404
bicarbonate, 572
bilateral symmetry, 344–345, **345,** 363, **363**
bile, 573
binary fission, 92, **92,** 225, **225**
binocular vision, 188, **188**
biodegradable, 504, 506, **506,** 678
biodiversity, 477, 503
maintenance of, 509, **509**
biological clock, 330
biome, 474, **474**
bioremediation, 230, **230**
biosphere, 435, **435,** 437, 456
biotic factors, 434, 444
biotin, 659
bipedalism, 189–190, **190**

birds
body temperature of, 401
characteristics of, 400–406
eggs of, 400
evolution of, 218, 398, 400
feeding by, 401
flight of, 402, **402–404,** 404–405
kinds of, 407–409
migration of, 405, **405**
nests of, **255,** 405, **405**
bison, 439
blood, **57, 523,** 546–547, **547**
amount of water in, 578, 584
removal of waste products from, 576, **576**
blood cells, 62
formation of, 526–527, 546–547
blood clotting, 356, 547, **547**
blood flow, 532, 551
through body, 550, **550**
exercise and, 551
through heart, 548, **548**
blood pressure, 551, **551,** 592, 662, **666**
blood-sugar level, 37, **602,** 603
blood type, 552, **552**
blood vessels, 549, **549**
of skin, **535**
body language, 334, **334**
body temperature, 376, 520
of birds, 401
of ectotherms, 376
of endotherms, 376
fever, 644, **644**
of humans, **26**
of mammals, 411–412
regulation of, 37, 534, 536
of reptiles, 388
bone
of birds, **403**
compact, 527, **527**
composition of, 527, **527**
functions of, 526, **526**
growth of, 528
spongy, 527, **527**
bony fishes, 380, **380**
bracket fungi, 260, **260**
brain, 586, 591, **591**
of arthropods, 358
CT scan of, 21, **21**
of fish, 378
of flatworms, 350, **350**
of invertebrates, 345, **345**
of mammals, 413
of mollusks, 354
regions of human, **592**
branching diagrams, 204, **204**
breathing, 89, 413, 556–558, **558**
bristle worms, 355–356, **356**
brittle star, 363, **363,** 365
bronchioles, 557, **557**
bronchitis, 665
bronchus, **556,** 557, **557**
brooding, 405

brown algae, 247, **247**
bubonic plague, 232, **232**
budding, **38,** 324, 612, **612**
in yeast, 258, **258**
bulimia, 662
buoyancy, 380
butterflies, **323,** 325, 329, **329,** 333, **333,** 344, 362
monarch, 329, **329**
queen, 333, **333**

C

cactus, 283, **286,** 289, **479**
caecilians, 385, **385**
caffeine, 578
calcium, 658
California condor, 509, **509**
Calorie, 656
Cambrian period, **178**
camouflage, **150,** 327, **327,** 446, **446,** 484
cancer, 504, 537, 646, **646,** 657, 679
breast, 619
colon, 575
destruction of cancer cell, 646, **646**
lung, 559, 665
mouth and throat, 665
prostate, 619
skin, 138, 184, 500, 534, 537, **537**
canine teeth, 570, **570**
canopy
of rain forest, 477, **477**
capillary, 549, **549–550**
carbohydrates, 43, **43**
complex, 43, **43,** 657
in diet, 656–657, **657**
digestion of, 569, 572
energy in, 45, **45**
simple, 43, **43,** 657
carbon cycle, 459–460, **459**
carbon dioxide
in atmosphere, 459–460, **459,** 500
in carbon cycle, **459**
diffusion into leaf, 306, **306**
photosynthesis and, 41, 88, **88,** 90, **90,** 305, **305**
production in cellular respiration, 89–90, **89,** 558, **558**
production in fermentation, 83, 91, **91**
transport in blood, 550, 558, **558**
Carboniferous period, **178**
cardiovascular system, **524,** 546–553, **546,** 559
careers, 7
biologist, 516
ecologist, 495
ethnobotanist, 297
naturopathic physician, 652

paleobotanist, 199
paleontologist, 176
zoologist, 32
caribou, 480, **480**
Carnivora (order), **203**
carnivore, 419, **419, 438,** 439
carrying capacity, 445
Carson, Rachel, 499, **499**
cartilage, 375, 379, **527–528,** 528
cartilaginous fishes, 379–380, **379**
caterpillar, 325, 327, **327,** 362
cats, 412, 419, **419**
    classification of, 203–204, **203–204**
cell, 36, **36,** 42–45, **44–45,** 56–57, **56–57, 59,** 61–75, **63, 66–75**
    discovery of, 61–62
    eukaryotic, 67, 68–75, **67–75**
    exchange of materials with environment, 84–87
    osmosis, 85, **85**
    prokaryotic, 66, **66**
    similarities among, 63
    size of, 56, 63–65
    specialized, 36, 56, 65
    surface-to-volume ratio of, 64, **64,** 65
cell cycle, 92–95, **94–95**
cell energy, 88–91
cell membrane, 36, 44, **44,** 63, **63,** 66–69, **66, 68–69,** 75, 86, **86,** 87, **87,** 653
cell plate, 95, **95**
cell theory, 62
cellular respiration, 89, **90,** 305, 556, 558
    compared with photosynthesis, 90
cell wall, 66–67, **66,** 69, **69,** 75, 95, 271, **271**
    of archaebacteria, 228
    of fungi, 266
Celsius temperature scale, 26, **26,** 788, **788**
Cenozoic era, 148, **178,** 187, **187**
centipede, 34, 357–358, **358**
central nervous system, 588, **588,** 591–593
centriole, 94, **94**
centromere, 93, **93**
cephalothorax
    of arachnids, 359, **359**
cerebellum, 591–592, **592**
cerebrum, 591, **591–592**
cetaceans, 422, **422**
CFCs (chlorofluorocarbons), 499–500
Chargaff's rules, 129
cheese production, 231, **231,** 260
chelicerae, 359, **359**
chemical digestion, 569–571, **569**
chemical equations, 803
chicken, 56, 406
    embryo of, 157, **157**
childhood, 624, **624**

chimpanzee, 156, 189, 326, **326,** 329
chitin, 358
Chlamydomonas, 246
chloride, 658
chlorophyll, 71, 88, 227, 246–247, 270, **304,** 311, **311**
chloroplast, 71, **71,** 74, **74,** 75, 88, **88, 90, 249,** 270, 304
    ancestors of, 72, **72**
cholesterol, 553, 573, 658, 679
Chordata (phylum), **203,** 374
chordates, 374–375
chromatids, 93, **93,** 115–116
chromosomes, 92–95, **93,** 613
    DNA in, **132–133**
    genes on, 115
    homologous, 93, **93,** 114–117, **114, 116**
    human, 93, **93,** 613
    in mitosis, 94–95, **94–95**
    sex, 119, **119**
chrysanthemum, 309
chyme, 571–572
cigarette smoking, 138, 553, 559, **559,** 623, 636, **645,** 654, 665, **665,** 667–668
cilia, **665**
    of ciliates, 252, **252**
ciliates, 252, **252**
circadian rhythm, 330
circle graph, 793, **793**
circulation
    pulmonary, 550, **550**
    systemic, 550, **550**
circulatory system
    closed, 354–355
    open, 354
citric acid, 260
clams, 325, 344, 352–353, **352–353,** 439, **482,** 485–487
class, 203, **203,** 343
classification, 202–204, 343
    basis for, 204
    defined, 202
    importance of, 202
    levels of, 203, **203**
    six-kingdom, 208–213
climate changes, 179, 186
club fungi, 259–260, **259**
club mosses, 273, **273,** 275, **275,** 277, **277**
Cnidaria (phylum), 348
cnidarians, 348–349, **348**
    feeding in, 349
    kinds of, **348,** 349
    nervous system of, 349
    polyp and medusa of, 348, **348**
    stinging cells of, 349, **349**
cocci, 226
coelacanth, 372, **372,** 381
coelom, 345, **345,** 355
coevolution, 448–449, **448–449**
collagen, **523,** 535
collar cells, 347, **347**

colon cancer, 575
colony
    bacterial, 223
    Volvox, 247, **247**
coloration (warning), 327, **327,** 446
combustion, **459,** 460
commensalism, 447, **447**
common cold, 233, 639
common name, 205–206
communication, 332–334, **332–334**
community, 60, **60,** 435–436, **435**
compact bone, 527
competition, 445, **445**
    between populations, 445, **445**
    within a population, 445
complete protein, 657
complex carbohydrates, 657
compound, 803
compound light microscope, 19, **19,** 806–807, **806**
concave lens, **597**
concept mapping, 786
condensation, **458,** 459
cones (photoreceptors), 596
cones (plant), **280–281,** 281
conifer, 280–281, **280–281,** 476, **476**
conjugation, 254, **254**
connective tissue, 522, **523,** 535
conservation, 505, **505**
    role of individual in, 506, 511
    strategies for, 510
constipation, 575
consumers, 40, **40,** 227, 325, **438,** 439, **440**
    fungi, 255
    gray wolves, 442, **442**
    protists, 244
    slime molds, 245, **245**
contact lenses, 597
continents
    formation of, 180, **180**
contractile vacuole, **249,** 250, **252**
control group, 14, **15,** 791
controlled experiment, 14, **15,** 791
conversion tables
    SI, 787
convex lens, **597**
Cooley, Denton, 544
coral, 349, 482, 484
    mutualism with algae, 447, **447**
coral reef, 349, 484, **484**
cordgrass, 436, **436–437**
cornea, **596**
cotyledon, 283, **283**
courtship display, 332–333, **332**
cowpox, 634, 638
coyote, 419, **419,** 438, **438,** 441, **441**
CPR course, 673, **673**
crab, **343, 357,** 359, 439, 482, 485
crabgrass, 464
cramping, 532
crane, 332, **332,** 408
crayfish, 439
Cretaceous period, **178**

Index   **837**

Crick, Francis, 129, **129**
crocodile, 388–390, **390**
Cro-Magnons, 174, 192–193, **192–193**
crop (bird), 401, **401**
cross-pollination, 108, **108**
crustacean, 359, **359**
crust of the Earth, 152, 181
cuticle (plant), 270, **289**, 306, **306**
cyanobacteria, 184, **184**, 227, **227**
cycles of matter, 458–461
cyclosporin, 266
cystic fibrosis, 8, 140, **140**
cytokinesis, 95, **95**
cytoplasm, 63, **63**, 68, 74
cytosine, 128–129, **128**

D

dart-poison frog, 150, **150**, 327, 383, **383**
Darwin, Charles, 158–163, **158**
   his voyage on HMS *Beagle* and, 159, **159**
   theory of natural selection, 162
Darwin's finches, 159, **159**
data analysis, 16, **16**
data collection, 11, **11**
dating
   absolute, 177
   relative, 177
Dead Sea, **228**
deciduous, 310, **310**, 475, **475**
decomposers, 40, **40**, 439, **439**
   bacteria 227, **227**, 229, 439, **439**, 678
   fungi, 255, 439, **439**
   water molds, 246
decomposition
   in carbon cycle, **459**, 460
   in nitrogen cycle, **460**
deep-water zone, 487, **487**
deforestation, 503, **503**
dehydration, 575
dendrite, 589, **589**
dental cavities, 232
denticles, 380, **380**
depressants, 663
dermis, 535, **535**
desert, 60, 465, **465**, 474, 479, **479**
development, 56, 74, 610
   of amphibians, 383–384, **384**
   of birds, 405–406
   as a characteristic of living things, 39, **39**
   in echinoderms, 363
   of fruit, 301, **301**
   of humans, **56**, 620–625, **620–624**
   of insects, 361–362, **361–362**
   of mammals, 414–416
   of reptiles, 388–389
   of seeds, 301, **301**

Devonian period, **178**
diabetes mellitus, 231, 646, 662, 679
diaphragm, 413, **556**, 558
diarrhea, 575, **575**
diastolic pressure, 551
diatoms, 248, **248**
dichotomous key, 206–207, **207**
dicots, 283, **283**, 285
diet
   balanced, 656–659, **656**
   healthy, 660–661
   of teenagers, 654
   vegetarian, 679
diffusion, 84–86, **84**
digestion, **523**, 568–575
   chemical, 569–571, **569**
   mechanical, 567, 569–571, **571**
digestive enzymes, 569, **569**, 572
digestive system, 58, **58**, **525**, 568, 568–575
   of birds, 401, **401**
   disorders of, 574–575
   Dr. Beaumont's observations of, 566
   of roundworms, 351
digestive tract, 568, **568**
dinoflagellates, 248, **248**
dinosaurs, 178–179, **179**, 186, **186**, 218, 387, 398, 410
disease, 636–639
   autoimmune, 646, **646**
   causes of, 636, **636**
   infectious, 636
   noninfectious, 636
diuretics, 578
diversity
   biological, 477, 503, 509, **509**
DNA (deoxyribonucleic acid), 38, 45, 63, 128
   base pairs in, 130–131, **130–131**
   of birds, 403
   cell cycle and, 92–93
   in chromosomes, 93, **132–133**
   code for making proteins, 136–137, **136–137**
   comparisons among different species, 156
   double helix, 129–130, **130–131**
   of eukaryotic cells, 67, 69, **69**, 93, **93**
   genes and, 132, **132–133**
   as genetic material, 128
   making copies of, 131, **131**
   mutations of, 138–139, **138–139**
   of prokaryotic cells, 66, **66**
   structure of, 128–131, **130**
   subunits of, 128, **128**
dogs, 334, **334**, 412
   breeding, 160, **160**
dolphin, **213**, 333, 422, **422**, 482, 599
dominant allele, 111
dominant trait, 109–110, **110**

drug abuse, 667–668
   getting off drugs, 668
   signs of, 668
drugs, 663
   dependence, addiction, and tolerance, 664
   effects of, 663–664
   from fungi, 266
   gateway, 667, **667**
   myths about, 668
   products containing, **663**
   side effects of, 664
   types of, 664–667
   use of, 667–668
duck, 406, 408, **408**
duckbilled platypus, 204, 414, **414**, 615

E

eagle, **213**, 402, 408
ear, 598, **598**
Earth
   age of, 151, 161
   atmosphere of early, 183
   changes in life on, 151, **151**
   history of, 178
   layers of, 152
earthworm, 344, **345**, **352**, 355, **355**
eating disorder, 662
echidna, 414, **414**, 615
Echinodermata (phylum), 363
echinoderms
   development in, 363
   endoskeleton of, 363
   kinds of, 365, **365**
   nervous system of, 364, **364**
   symmetry in, 363, **363**
   water vascular system of, 364, **364**, 440
echolocation
   in bats, 418
   in cetaceans, 422
ecology, 434
ecosystems, 60, 435–436, **435**
   aquatic, 60
   energy movement through, 440
   freshwater, 486–489, **487**
   land, 60, 474–480
   marine, 481–485
ectotherm, 376, **376**, 397
eel, 381
eggs, 56, **56**, 114–115, 118, **118**, 324, **324**, **373**, 613, **613**, 617
   amniotic, 388–389, **389**
   of amphibians, 383, **388**, 608, **614**
   of birds, **391**, 400, 405, **405**
   of humans, 119, 613, 617–618, **620**
   of insects, 361–362
   of monotremes, 414, **414**, 615, **615**
   of reptiles, 388–389, **388**

egg shell, **373**
   of amniotic egg, 388–389, **389,** 400
electrolytes
   muscle function and, 532
electron, 20, 100, 802
electron cloud, 802, **802**
electron microscope, 20, **20**
element, 42, 802
elephant, **65,** 333, **333,** 412, 421, **421,** 478
elk, 442–443, 445
embryo, 157, **157,** 324, **324,** 620–621, **620–621**
enamel
   tooth, 570, **570**
endangered species, 509, **509,** 516–517, **516–517**
Endangered Species Act, 509–510
endocrine system, **525,** 600–603, **601**
endocytosis, 87, **87**
endoplasmic reticulum, 70, **70,** 72, **74,** 75, 87
endoskeleton
   of echinoderms, 363
endospore, 225, **225**
endotherm, 376, 411
energy
   alternative sources of, 506, **506,** 508, 510
   in ATP, 45, **45,** 71, 89–90, **89**
   cell, 88–91
   from food, 89, **89,** 656, **657**
   from hydrogen sulfide, 34
   movement through ecosystem, 440, **440**
   use by living things, 34, 38, 88–91, 438–443
energy pyramid, 441, **441**
   wolves and, 442, **442**
environment
   abiotic part of, 434, 444
   biotic part of, 434, 444
   human responses to, 595–599
   interactions of living things with, 444–445
   organization in, 435–437, **435–437**
   phenotype and, 135
   plant responses to, 307–311, **307–311**
   protection of, 9, 505–511
environmental problems, 9, 498–504
enzymes, 42, 138
   digestive, 569, **569,** 572
   in small intestine, 572
   in stomach, 571
epidermis
   of leaf, 289, **289**
   of root, 285
   of skin, 535, **535**
epididymis, 616, **616**
epinephrine, 600

epithelial tissue, 522, **522–523,** 535
era, 178
Escherichia coli, 209, **209,** 230–231, 454
esophagus, 557, 568, **568,** 570, **571,** 574
essential amino acids, 657
estivation, 329
estrogen, 617
estuary, 485
eubacteria, 209, **209,** 224, 227, **227**
Euglena, 208, **208,** 210, 254, **254**
euglenoids, 249, **249**
eukaryotes, 184, 210
   evolution of, 184
   protists, 244–254
eukaryotic cells, 66, 67, **67,** 323
   cell cycle in, 93–95, **94–95**
   compared with prokaryotic cells, 67
   DNA of, 93, **93**
   structure of, 68–75, **68–75**
evaporation, **458,** 459
evergreen, 310
evolution, 149, 151, **151**
   of amphibians, 382
   of animals, 185–187
   of birds, 218, 400
   coevolution, 448–449, **448–449**
   of eukaryotes, 184
   fossil evidence of, 152–153, **153**
   of humans, 188–193, **188–192**
   of mammals, 410
   mutation and, 163
   by natural selection, 162–163
   organisms and evidence of, 156–157, **156–157**
   of photosynthesis, 184
   of plants, 185–186, 227, 272, **272**
   of prokaryotes, 183
   of reptiles, 387, **387**
   taxonomy and, 204
   of whales, 153–155, **153–155**
excretion, 576
exercise, 654, 670–671
   aerobic, 532, **532,** 670, **670**
   blood flow and, 551
   effect on muscular system, 532
   heart and, 551
   lack of, 636
   replacing water lost in, 578, 584, 658, **658**
   resistance, 532, **532**
exocytosis, 87, **87**
exoskeleton, 358
experiment
   analyzing results of, 16, 791
   communicating results of, 17, **17,** 791
   controlled, 14–15, **15,** 791
experimental group, 14, **15,** 791
extinct, 152, 179
extinction, 9, 185, 179, 186, 504, 509

eyes
   of arachnids, 359, **359**
   of birds, **402**
   color of, 135, **135,** 597, **597**
   compound, 358–359, **358**
   defenses against pathogens, 640
   of fish, 378, **378**
   human, **596,** 597
   lens of, **596,** 597
eyespots, **249**
   of flatworms, 350, **350**

F

Fahrenheit temperature scale, 26, **26,** 788, **788**
fairy rings, **259**
fallopian tube, 617, **617**
family (classification), 203, **203**
farsightedness, 597, **597**
fat, 44
   in diet, 636, 654, 656–658, **657**
   digestion of, 569, 572–573
   saturated, 658, 679
   unsaturated, 658
feathers, **42,** 400–401, **400–401**
   contour, **400–401,** 401
   down, **400,** 401
feces, 574, 585
feedback control, 602, **602**
feeding
   in amoebas, 250, **250**
   in birds, 401
   in ciliates, 252, **252**
   in cnidarians, 349
   in mollusks, 353
   in sponges, 347, **347**
female (human)
   chromosomes of, 114, 119, **119**
   reproductive system of, 617, **617**
fermentation, 89, 91, **91**
ferns, 270, **270,** 273, 275–277, **275–276,** 463
   importance of, 277
   life cycle of, 276, **276**
fertilization, 118, **118,** 324, **324,** 613, **613,** 620, **620**
   in amphibians, 383
   in birds, 405
   external, 378, 614, **614**
   in fish, 378
   internal, 378, 614
   in mammals, 363
   in plants, 107, **107,** 271, **271,** 300, **300**
   in reptiles, 389
   twins and, 618, **618–623**
fetal development, 622–623, **622**
fetus, 622, **622–623**
fever, 644, **644**
fiber, 574
fibroblasts, 266
fibrous root, 285, **285**
fight-or-flight response, 600, **600**

filament
    of stamen, 290, 291
fingerprinting
    DNA, 126, 146
fins, 378, **378**
fire ants, 455
first aid, 673, **673**
fir tree, 278, 280
fish, 377–381, **377–381**
    bony, 380–381, **380–381**
    cartilaginous, 379–380, **379**
    characteristics of, 377–378
    eyes of, 378, **378**
    fertilization in, 378
    jawless, 379, **379**
    kinds of, 379–381
fission, 254, **254**
flagella, 208
    of bacteria, 226
    of dinoflagellates, 248
    of euglenoids, 249
    of flagellates, 251, **251**
flagellates, 251, **251**
flatworms, 350–351, **350–351**
    kinds of, 350–351
    nervous system of, 350, **350**
Fleming, Alexander, 230, 241
flight
    of birds, 402–403, **402–404**, 404–405
    mechanics of, 404, **428**
    muscles, **403**
flower, 107, **107**, 282–283, **283**, 290–291, **290–291**, 309, **309**
    coevolution with pollinators, 449, **449**
flower color
    in garden peas, 108, **108**, 110–112, **110–112**
    in snapdragons, 134, **134**
flowering plants. *See* angiosperms
flu, 233
flukes, 350–351, **350**
fluorine, 658
fly, 361–362
folic acid, 659
follicle mite, 454
food
    bacteria in production of 231, **231**
    contaminated with pathogens, 637
    energy from, 89, **89**
    methods to find or catch, 326, **326**
    as a necessity of life, 40
food allergy, 652
food chain, 440–441
food crops, 283
food label, 661
food poisoning, 232
food pyramid, 660, 662
food reserves
    seeds, 279, **279**
food safety, 637
food vacuole, 250, **252**

food web, 440, **440**, 443
foraminiferans, 251
forest, 60, **60**, 440, **440**
    coniferous, **474**, 476, **476**
    destruction of, 9, 501, 503, **503**
    regrowth after fire, 462, **462**
    temperate deciduous, **474–475**, 475
    tropical rain, **474**, 477, **477**, 501
forest fire, 462, **462**, 470
fossil fuel, 277, **459**, 460–461, 501
fossil record, 152–153, **153**
fossils, 148, 151–152, **152**, 158, 176, **176**, 182, **182**, 375
    age of, 177, **177**
    Archaeopteryx, 218, **218**, 398, **398–399**
    of the Cenozoic era, 187, **187**
    footprints, 190, **190**
    formation of, 149, 152–153, 176, **176**
    of the Paleozoic era, 185
    of the Precambrian era, 182, **182**
    of whale ancestors, 154–155, **154**
fox, 440, **440**
fractions
    adding, 798
    defined, 797
    dividing, 798
    multiplying, 798
    reducing, 797
    subtracting, 798
fragmentation, 612, **612**
Franklin, Rosalind, 129, **129**
freshwater ecosystems, 486–489
frogs, **382–384**, 386, **386**, 444, 487–488, 614, **614**
    deformed, 4, **4**, 9–17
    different species of, 150–151, **150**
    metamorphosis of, **384**
frond, 276, **276**
fruit, 278, 282, 291
    development of, 301, **301**
    dispersal of, 282, **282**
fulcrum, 529, **529**
Fungi (kingdom), 212, **212**
fungus, 255–265
    bandages from, 266
    cell walls of, 69, 266
    characteristics of, 255–256
    decomposers, 439, **439**
    food for, 255
    hyphae and mycelium of 256, **256**
    kinds of, 257–261, **257–261**
    in lichens, 261, **261**
    pathogenic, 636, **636**
    reproduction in, 256
funguslike protists, 245–246, **245–246**
fur, 412, **412**
    color in tigers, 134

G

Gage, Phineas, 586
Galápagos Islands, 159, **159**
    finches, 159, **159**, 167, **167**
gallbladder, 568, **568**, 573, **573**
gametophyte, 271, **271**, 278
ganglia, 345, **345**, 350, 354–355
gar, 434, **434**
garbage, 498–499, **498**
garden pea
    flower color in, 108, **108**, 110–112, **110–112**
    Mendel's experiment with, 109–112
    seed characteristics of, 108–110, **108–110**, 118, **118**
    self-pollination in, 107, **107**
    true-breeding plants, 108, **108**, 111, **111**
gas exchange
    in plants, 306, **306**
gastric ulcer, 575, **575**
gastropods, 352, **352**
gateway drugs, 667, **667**
genes, 111
    changes in, 138–139, **138–139**
    on chromosomes, 115
    DNA and, 132, **132–133**
    functions of genetic material, 128
    many influencing a single trait, 135, **135**
    one influencing several traits, 134, **134**
    proteins and, 136, **136**
genetic counseling, 140
genetic engineering, 141, **141**
    of bacteria, 230–231, **230**
genetic variation, 162, **162**
genome, 8
genotype, 111–112, 118, **118**
genotype probability, 113
genus, 203, **203**, 205
geologic time scale, 175, 178, **178**
    eras of, 182–187
germination
    of seeds, 279, 302, **302**
gestation period, 416
Giardia lamblia, 251, **251**
gills
    of amphibians, 384, 385
    of crustaceans, 359, **359**
    of fish, 378, **378**, 380
    of mushrooms, 259
giraffe, 420, **420**, 478
gizzard, 401, **401**
gland, 600
glasses, 597, **597**
global warming, 459, 500
glucose
    blood, **600, 602**, 603
    photosynthesis and, 88, **88, 90**, 305, **305**

use in cellular respiration, 89, **89, 90**
gnetophytes, 280
Golgi complex, 72, **72, 74,** 75, 87
Gondwanaland, 180
gorilla, 156, **189,** 412
graduated beaker, 24
graduated cylinder, 24, 789, **789**
grass, 282–283, 441, 463, 478, **478**
grasshopper, 344, **357,** 361, **361,** 439
grassland, 438, 478, **478**
    temperate, **474,** 478, **478**
gravitropism, 308, **308**
gray wolf, 442–443, **442–443,** 517, **517**
green algae, 247, **247,** 272, **272**
ground water, **458,** 459
group living, 335, **335**
growth
    as a characteristic of living things, 39, **39**
    of humans, 611, 620–625, **624**
    of plants, 299
growth hormone, 603
guanine, 128–129, **128**
guard cells, 289, **289,** 306, **306**
gums (mouth), 570, **570,** 665
gut, 345, **345**
gymnosperms, 273, **273,** 278, 280–281, **280–281**

H

habitat, 442
    destruction, 9, 501, 503–504
    protection, 510, **510**
hair, **42,** 135, 412, **535,** 536
    color of, 536
    functions of, 536
    structure of, 536, **536**
hair follicle, 454, **535,** 536
half-life, 177, **177**
hallucinogens, 666
handwashing, 669
hardwood forest, 464–465
hawk, **438**
hay infusion, 243
hazardous waste, 498–499
head
    of arthropods, 357–358, **357**
    of earthworms, **355**
    of flatworms, 350
    of insects, 361, **361**
head capsule, 358
healthy habits, 669–673
    diet, 660–661
    survey of, 654–655
hearing, 413, 598, **598**
    loss of, 500, **500**
heart
    artificial, 544
    atrium, 548, **548, 550**
    of birds, **402**
    blood flow through, 548, **548**
    exercise and, 545
    failure of, 544, 553
    of humans, 544, 548, **548,** 550
    of mollusks, 354
    valves, 548, **548**
    ventricle, 548, **548, 550**
heart disease, 657–658, 662, 665, 679
heat-loving bacteria, 228
helper T cells, 642, 644, **646–647,** 647
hemispheres
    cerebral, 591, **591**
hemoglobin, 42, 546
hemophilia, 636
herbaceous stem, 287, **287**
herbal medicines, 665, **665**
herbivores, **438,** 439
    coevolution with plants, 448, **448**
hereditary disease, 8, 139–140, **139–140**
hereditary material, 63, 128
heredity, 38, **38,** 106
    exceptions to Mendel's principles, 134–135, **134–135**
hermit crab, **436**
heroin, 667
hibernation, 329–330, **329**
high-fat diet, 636, 654
hinge joint, **528**
HIV, 233–234, 647, **647**
hollow nerve cord, 374, **374**
homeopathy, 652
homeostasis, 37, 522
hominids, 189
    evolution of, 190–193, **190–193**
homologous chromosomes, 93, **93,** 114–117, **114, 116**
hoofed mammals, 420
Hooke, Robert, 61
hormones, 537, 600–603, **601–603**
    control of fluid balance by, 578
horse, 411, 420
horsetails, 273, **273,** 275, **275,** 277, **277**
horseweed, 464
host, 233, 246, 350, 448, **448,** 585
human population
    growth of, 435, 502, **502**
    size of, 161, **161**
humans
    body defenses against pathogens, 640–644
    chromosomes of, 613
    classification of, 188
    digestive system of, 568–575
    diseases of, 636–639
    effects of pollution on, 504
    embryo of, 157, **157**
    evolution of, 188–193, **188–193**
    growth and development of, 611, 620–625, **620–625**
    reproduction in, 616–619
    responses to environment, 595–599, **595–599**
    urinary system of, **576,** 576–579
hummingbird, 449, **449**
humpback whale, 333, **481**
hydra, **38, 348,** 349, 612, **612**
hydrogen, 42
hydrogen sulfide, 34
hyena, 335, 419
hygiene, 669
hypertension, 553
hyphae, 256, **256**
hypothesis, 12–15, **12–13, 15, 17,** 18, 790–792

I

immune system, 641–644
    cells of, 641, **641**
    challenges to, 645–647
    response to pathogens, 642–643
immunity, 638
imperfect fungi, 260, **260**
impulse, 589, **589**
incineration of waste, 499
incisors, 570, **570**
incomplete dominance, 134–135, **134–135**
incomplete protein, 657
infancy, 623–624, **624**
infectious disease, 636
infertile, 619
influenza virus, 234
injury prevention, 672, **672**
innate behavior, 328
insecticide, 164, **164**
insectivores, 417, **417**
insects, **323,** 360–362, **360**
    body of, 361, **361**
    development of, 361–362, **361–362**
    pollination by, 282, **282,** 361
insulin, 231, **602,** 603, **603**
integumentary system, **524,** 534–537, **534–537**
intertidal area, 482, **482,** 485, **485**
invertebrates, 323, **323,** 342–365
    body plan of, 344–345, **344–345**
    gut of, 345, **345**
    types of, 346–365
involuntary muscle, 530
involuntary process, 591
iodine, 658
ions, 803
iris (eye), 597
Irish potato famine, 242, 246
iron, 658

J

jawless fishes, 379
jellyfish, **323**, 326, 344, 348–349, **348**, **436**
Jenner, Edward, 634, 638
joint, 528–529, **528**
jointed limbs, 357
Jurassic period, **178**

K

kangaroo, 415, **415**, 610
kangaroo rat, 40, **479**
Kelvin scale, 26, 788
kidney, **576**, 577, **577**
   diseases of, 579, **579**
   filtration of blood, 577, **577**
kidney machine, 579, **579**
kidney stones, 579, **579**
killer T cells, 642, 646, **646**
kilogram, 22, 26, 787
kingdom, 203, **203**, 208–213, 804–805
   Animalia, **203**, 213, **213**, 322–323, **322–323**, 805
   Archaebacteria, 209, **209**, 804
   Eubacteria, 209, **209**, 804
   Fungi, 212, **212**, 805
   Plantae, 211, **211**, 805
   Protista, 210, **210**, 804
knee-jerk reflex, 594
koala, 326, 415, **415**

L

labor (childbirth), 623
lactic acid, 66, 91
lactic acid bacteria, 231
lagomorphs, 418, **418**
lake, 486–487, **486–487**
   conversion to forest, 489, **489**
Laminaria, 247
lamprey, 379, **379**
land ecosystems, 60, 474–480
landfill, 499
landmarks, 331
language, 328, 332
large intestine, 568, **568**, 574, **574**
larvae, 361–362, **361–362**
larynx, **556**, 557
lateral line system, 378, **378**
Latimer, Marjorie Courtney, 372, **372**
Laurasia, **180**
leaf, 57, 288–289, **288–289**
   adaptations of, 289, **289**
   fossil, **152**
   functions of, 288
   seasonal changes in, 310–311, **310–311**
   structure of, 289, **289**

learned behavior, 328, **328**
leech, 342, **342**, 345, **345**, 355–356, **356**
   medical uses of, 356, **356**
legs
   bones of front limbs, 156, **156**
   evolution of whales and, 154–155
length, 22–23, **23**
   SI units, 22, 787
lens, 19, **19**
   concave, **597**
   convex, **597**
   of eye, **596–597**, 597
   magnifying, 20
   of microscope, 19, **19**, 806
lever, 529, **529**
   first class, 529, **529**
   second class, 529, **529**
   third class, 529, **529**
lichen, 261, **261**, 325, 463, 480
life science, 6–9
   tools of, 19–27
lift, 404, **404**
ligament, 529
light
   in photosynthesis, 88, **88**, 90, 304–305, **305**
   response of eyes to, 35, 596–597, **596**
limiting factors, 444
line graphs, 794, **794**
Linneaus, Carolus, 204–205, **204**
lion, 204, 325, 335, **335**, 419
lipids, 44, **44**
   energy in, **45**
liquids
   volume of, 24
liter, 22, 24
littoral zone, 487, **487**
liver, 568, **568**, 573, **573**
liverworts, 272, 274–275, **272–273**, **275**, 277
living things, 36–39
   cells of, 36, **36**, 62
   chemistry of, 42–45
   energy needs of, 438–443
   interactions of, 432–449
   necessities of, 40–41, **40–41**
   origin of, 183, **183**
   use of energy, 34, 38
   water requirement of, 459
lizards, 376, **376**, 387–389, **387**, 391, **391**
load, 529, **529**
lobe-finned fish, 381
long-day plants, 309
Lucy (fossil), 191
lung cancer, 665
lungfish, 381
lungs, **524**, 556–559, **556–559**
   of amphibians, 382, 383
   pulmonary circulation, 550, **550**
lupus, 646
Lyme disease, 232, 637

lymphatic system, **525**, 554–555, **554–555**
lysogenic cycle, 235, **235**
lysosomes, 74, **74**, 75
lytic cycle, 235, **235**

M

macronucleus, 252, **252**
macrophages, 641–644
magnesium, 658
magnification, 19, **19**
malaria, 253, **253**
male (human)
   chromosomes of, 114, 119, **119**
   reproductive system of, 616, **616**
malnutrition, 662
Mammalia (class), **203**, 204, **204**
mammals, **323**, 410–423, **410–423**
   body temperature of, 411–412
   brain of, 413
   breathing in, 413
   characteristics of, 411–413
   evolution of, 410
   kinds of, 414–423, **414–423**
   parental care in, 413, **413**
   reproduction in, 413, 615, **615**
   teeth of, 412, **412**
mammary glands, 411, 414–415
mandibles
   of centipedes and millipedes, 358
   of crustaceans, 359, **359**
   of insects, 361
mantis, 446, **446**
mantle
   of mollusks, **353**
maple tree, 282, 310, **310**
Margulis, Lynn, 54
marijuana, 666–667, **667**
marine, 481
   ecosystems, 481–485
   destruction of habitat, 503–504, **503**
marrow, 527, 546–547
marsh, 488, **488**
   conversion to forest, 489
marsh crab, **436**
marsupials, 415, **415**
   reproduction in, 610, 614–615, **615**
mass, 22, 26, **26**
   SI units, 22, 787
mass extinction, 179, **179**, 185–186
matter, 802
measurement
   systems of, 22–26
   units, 787
mechanical digestion, 567, 569–571, **571**
medulla, 591–592, **592**
medusa, 348–349, **348**
meiosis, 114–119, **114–119**, 613
   steps in, 116–117, **116–117**

melanin, 534, **534,** 536
memory B cells, 644
Mendel, Gregor, 106–113, **106,** 118
menstruation, 617, 624
Mesozoic era, 178, **178,** 186, **186**
metabolism, 38
   dependence on water, 40
metamorphosis
   in amphibians, 384, **384**
   complete, 361–362, **362**
   incomplete, 361, **361**
   in insects, 361–362, **361–362**
meteorite
   collision with Earth's surface, 179, **179,** 183, 186
meter, 22–23, **23**
meterstick, 789, **789**
methane-making bacteria, 228
metric ton, 26
mice, 417, 478
   embryo of, **324**
micronucleus, 252, **252**
microscope, **11,** 19, **19**
   compound light, 19, **19,** 806–807, **806**
   electron, 20, **20**
   Hooke's, 61, **61**
   parts of, **19,** 806, **806**
   preparing a wet mount, 807
   scanning electron, 20, **20**
   transmission electron, 20, **20**
   use of, 807
middle ear, 598, **598**
migration, 329–330, **329**
   of birds, 405, **405**
milk, 411, **411,** 414–415
   pasteurized, 638
millipede, 34, 358, **358**
minerals, 656, 658
mites
   follicle, 454
mitochondria, **70,** 71, **71, 74,** 89, **89, 90**
   ancestors of, 72, **72**
mitosis, 93–95, **94–95,** 114–115, **115**
molars, 570, **570**
mold (fungi), 257
mole (skin), 537, **537**
molecule, 42, 803
Mollusca (phylum), 352
mollusks, **323,** 352–354, **352–354**
   bivalves, 352, **352**
   body parts in, 353, **353**
   cephalopods, 352, **352**
   feeding in, 353
   gastropods, 352, **352**
   heart of, 354
   nervous system of, 354
monkey, 36, **36,** 188, 328, **328,** 411, 423
monocots, 283, **283,** 285
monotremes, 414, **414,** 615
morels, 258
mosquito, 325, **357,** 361
   carrier of malaria, 253, **253**

mosses, 272, 274–275, **272–274,** 463, 480
   importance of, 275
   life cycle of, 274, **274**
motor neuron, 590, **590,** 593
motor vehicle accident, **666,** 672
mouth, 568, **568,** 570
   cancer, 665
   defenses against pathogens, 640
   dry, 577, 584
movement
   of animals, 325, **325**
   bones and, 526
   muscular system and, 531, **531**
MRI (magnetic resonance imaging), 21, **21**
mud flat, 485
multicellular organism, 36, **36, 56,** 59, **59,** 65, 323
muscle
   fermentation in, 91
   injury to, 533, **533**
   involuntary, 530
   neural control of, 590, **590**
   of skin, **535,** 536
   spasm, 532
   strain, 533, **533**
   types of, 530, **530**
   voluntary, 530
muscle cells, 36
muscle tissue, **57,** 522, **523**
muscular system, **524,** 530–533
mushroom, 259–260, **259**
   poisonous, **212,** 259, **259**
musk ox, 335, 480
mutagens, 138
mutations, 138–139, **138–139**
   deletion, 138, **138**
   evolution and, 163
   insertion, 138, **138**
   substitution, 138–139, **138–139**
mutualism, 447, **447**
mycelium, 256, **256**

N

nails, 536, **536**
narcotics, 667
natural selection, 162–163, **162**
   adaptation to pollution, 165, **165**
   for insecticide resistance, 164, **164**
   reasoning behind theory of, 160–161
   speciation and, 166, **166**
navigation, 330–331, **330**
Neanderthals, 18, **18,** 192, **192**
nearsightedness, 140, 597, **597**
nectar, 325, 326, 334, 449, **449**
needles
   conifer, 476, **476**
needle sharing, 667
nematocyst, 349, **349**
nematodes, 351

nephron, 577, **577**
neritic zone, 482, **482**
nerve, 345, 588, 590, **590**
   auditory, **598**
   optic, 596, **596**
nerve cells, 36
   of invertebrates, 345
   of leeches, 342
nerve cord, 345, **345, 350,** 355
   hollow, 374
nerve endings
   in skin, 534, **535**
nerve net, 349
nerve ring, 349, 364, **364**
nervous system, 58, **525,** 588–594, **588**
   of annelids, 355
   of cnidarians, 349
   of echinoderms, 364, **364**
   of flatworms, 350, **350**
   of humans, 588–594
   of invertebrates, 345, **345**
   of mollusks, 354
   of roundworms, 351
nervous tissue, 522, **522–523**
nest, 405, **405**
neuron, 589
   motor, 590, **590,** 593
   sensory, 590, 593
   structure of, 589, **589**
neutrons, 802
niche, 442
   of gray wolf, 442–443, **442–443**
nicotine, 665, 667, **667**
nitrogen, 42
   in atmosphere, 229, **229,** 460, 461
   levels in Gulf of Mexico, 471
   nitrogen cycle, 229, **229,** 460–461, **460**
   nitrogen fixation, 229, **229,** 460, 461
noise pollution, 500, **500**
noninfectious disease, 636
nonrenewable resource, 501, 506
nonvascular plants, 272, **272,** 273
nose, 556, **556,** 599, **599,** 640
notochord, 374, **375**
nuclear membrane, 69, **69,** 94–95, 115–117
nucleic acids, 45
nucleolus, 69, **69**
nucleotides, 45, 128, **128**
nucleus, 66, 67, **67,** 69, **69, 74,** 75, 802, **802**
nutrients, 656
   absorption from small intestine, 572
   storage in liver, 573
nutrition, 656–659
   healthy eating habits, 660–661
   naturopathic medicine and, 652
nutritional disorders, 662
nutrition facts label, 661

Index

O

oak tree, **39**, 278, 489
obesity, 662
observations, 11, 792
oceanic zone, 483, **482–483**
octopus, 327, 352–354, **354**
oil glands, **535**, 537
oils, 44, 658
oil spill, 230, 503, **503**, 678
olfactory cells, 599
omnivores, 439
onion, 283, **285**
open-water zone, 487, **487**
opossum, 415, **415**, **615**
opposable thumb, **188**, 423
orchid, 283, **290**
order, 203, **203**
Ordovician period, **178**
organ, 57, **57**, 59, 324, **324**, 523, **523**
   transplant, 58
organelles, 63, **63**, 67, **67**, 74
organic farming, 506
organisms, 59, **59**, 435, **435**
   interactions among, 445–449
   multicellular, 59, **59**, 65
   unicellular, 59, **59**
organ system, 58, **58–59**, 523, **524–525**
origin of life, 183, **183**
ornithologist, 320
osculum, 347, **347**
osmosis, 85, **85**
osprey, 408, **408**
ostrich, 407, **407**
outdoor safety, 672
ovary
   of human, **601**, 617, **617**
   of flower, **290–291**, 291, 300–302, **300–302**
overpopulation, 502
over-the-counter drugs, 664
ovulation, 617
ovule, **290–291**, 291, 300–302, **300–302**
owl, 326, 408, **408**, 440, **440**
oxygen, 42
   in air at high elevation, 557
   in atmosphere, 184
   cellular respiration and, 89, **90**, 558, **558**
   levels in the Gulf of Mexico, 471
   photosynthesis and, 88, **90**, 184, **184**, 305, **305**
   release from leaves, 306, **306**
   transport in blood, 546, **546**, **550**, 558, **558**
oyster, **436–437**
ozone, 184, **184**
ozone layer, 138, 184, **184**, **500**
   destruction of, 184, 499–500

P

paleontologist, 176, **176**
Paleozoic era, **178**, 185, **185**
palisade layer, 289, **289**
palm oil, 658
pancreas, 568, **568**, 572, **573**, **601–602**, 603
pancreatic juice, 572
Pangaea, 180, **180**
pantothenic acid, 659
papermaking, 496
Paramecium, **19–20**, 210, **210**, 244, 252, **252**
   conjugation in, 254, **254**
parasite, 350–351, 448, **448**
   amoebas, 250
   bacteria, 227
   flagellates, 251
   follicle mites, 454
   tapeworms, 585
   water molds, 246, **246**
parathyroid gland, **601**
parental care
   among birds, 405–406
   among gray wolves, 443, **443**
   among mammals, 413, **413**
parrots, 409, **409**
passive transport, 86, **86**
Pasteur, Louis, 638
pasteurization, 638, **638**
pathogens, 547, 635–636, **636**
   bacteria, 232, **232**
   body defenses against, 640–644
   preventing spread of, 638
   spread of, 637, **637**
   viruses, 233
PCP, 666
pedigree, 140, **140**
peer pressure, 667
pelvis, **189**, 526
penguins, 407, **407**, 614, **614**
penicillin, **212**, 241, 260
Penicillium, 260, **260**
penis, 616, **616**
peppered moth, 165, **165**
percentages, 273, 661, 797
periodic table, **800–801**
peripheral nervous system, 588–590, **588**
peristalsis, 570
periwinkle snail, **437**
permafrost, 480
Permian period, **178**
pesticide, 499, 510
petal, 290, **290**, **300**
pH, 803, **803**
pharyngeal pouch, 374, **375**
pharynx, **556**, 557
phenotype, 111–112, 134, **134**
   environment and, 135, **135**
pheromones, 333, **333**
phloem, 284, **285**, 286, **287**

phospholipids, 44, **44**
   in cell membranes, 44, **44**, 68, 86
phosphorus, 658
photoreceptors, 596, **596**
photosynthesis, 41, 71, 88, **88**, **90**, 211, 270, 286, 288–289, 304–305, **304–305**, 438, **438**
   in algae, 246
   in bacteria, 227
   capture of light energy, 304, **304**
   in carbon cycle, **459**, 460
   compared with cellular respiration, **90**
   evolution and, 184
   in protists, 244
   sugar production in, 305, **305**
phototropism, 307, **307**
phylum, 203, **203**, 322, 343
phytoplankton, 247–248, 481–482, **481–482**, 487
pika, 418, **418**
pillbug, 34, 359
pine tree, 278, 280–281, **280–281**, 464, 476
pinnipeds, 419
pioneer species, 463
pistil, **290**, 291
pitohui bird, 327, **327**
pituitary gland, **601**, 603
placenta, 416, 621, **621**, 623
placental mammals, 416
   kinds of, 416–423, **416–423**
   reproduction in, 615
plains, 478
planarian, 350, **350**
plant
   asexual reproduction in, 303, **303**
   breeding, 160
   characteristics of, 270–271
   classification of, 211, 272–273, **273**
   evolution of, 185–186, 227, 272, **272**
   fertilization in, 300, **300**
   food from, 269
   gas exchange in, 306, **306**
   genetic engineering of, **141**, 240
   growth of, 299
   life cycle of, 271, **271**
   nonvascular, 272, **272**, 273
   organ systems of, 58, 284–287
   organs of, 57
   reproduction in, 271, **271**, 300–303, **300–303**
   responses to environment, 307–311, **307–311**
   seasonal responses of, 309–311, **309–311**
   seedless, 274–277, **274–277**
   with seeds, 278–291, **278–291**
   vascular, 272–273, **273**
Plantae (kingdom), 211, **211**, 805

plant cells
    cell wall of, 69, **69, 75,** 271, **271**
    chloroplasts in, 71, **71**
    compared with animal cells, 75, **75**
    vacuoles in, 73, **73**
plant disease, 232, **232,** 258, 260
plantlike protists, 246–249, **246–249**
plasma, 546
Plasmodium vivax, 253, **253**
platelets, 546–547, **547,** 641
plate tectonics, 181, **181,** 415
pneumonia, 209, 232, 559
poinsettia, 309, **309**
polar ice, **474,** 485, **485**
pollen, 107, **107–109,** 278, 281, **281, 290,** 300, **300,** 559, 645, **645**
pollen tube, 300, **300**
pollination, 107–108, **107–108,** 281–282, **281,** 300, **300**
    by animals, 282, **282**
    by insects, 282, **282,** 361
    by wind, 282, **282,** 291, **291**
pollutants, 498
    chemical, 499
    similar to female hormones, 619
pollution, 9, 498–500, **498,** 510
    bioremediation, 230, **230**
    effects on humans, 504
pollution cycle, 461
polyp, 348–349, **348**
pond, 487
    conversion to forest, 489, **489**
population, 59, **59,** 435–436, **435**
    human, 435
    interaction between populations, 444, **444**
population growth, 161, **161**
    human, 161, **161,** 502, **502**
    overpopulation, 502
population size, 444–445
pores
    of sponge, 347, **347**
Porifera (phylum), 347
posture, 669, **669**
potassium, 584, 658
potato, 43, **43,** 242, 246, 286, **303**
prairie, 60, 438–439, **438–439,** 478
prairie dog, 438–439, **438,** 441, **441,** 446
Precambrian time, 182–184, **182–184**
precipitation
    in water cycle, 458, **458**
precocial chick, 406, **406**
predator, 326–327, 335, 446, **446**
    adaptations of, 446, **446**
prediction, 13–14, 18
preening, 401
prefixes
    SI, 22–23, 787
pregnancy, 620–623
    ectopic, 618
premolars, 570, **570**

prescription drugs, 664, **664**
prey, 326–327, 446, **446**
    adaptations of, 446, **446**
primary succession, 463
primates, 188–189, **188–189,** 423, **423**
probability, 112, 113
    genotype and, 113
producers, 40, **40,** 227, 244, 438, **438**
prokaryotes, 66, **66,** 92, **92,** 183, **183,** 209, 224
    evolution of, 183, **183**
prokaryotic, 66, **66**
    cells compared with eukaryotic cells, 67
prosimians, 190, **190**
protein, 38, 42, **42,** 70, **70**
    amoebalike, 250–251, **250–251**
    animal-like, 250–253, **250–253**
    characteristics of, 244
    complete, 657
    in diet, 656–657, **657**
    digestion of, 569, **569,** 572
    functions of, 136
    genes and, 136, **136**
    in hay infusion, 243
    in immune response, 643
    incomplete, 657
    making of, 137, **137**
    pathogenic, 636, **636**
    plantlike, 246–249, **246–249**
    protist, 244–254
    reproduction of, 254, **254**
    spore-forming, 253
Protista (kingdom), 208, 210, **210,** 244
protozoa, 210, 250–253, **250–253**
    with shells, 251, **251**
pseudopodia, 250, **250**
puberty, 616, 624
puffball, **256,** 260
pulse, 545, 549
Punnett square, 111–112, **111–112**
pupil (eye), **35,** 596–597, **596**
    response to light, 35
purple loosestrife, 502, **502**

Q

Quaternary period, **178**

R

rabbits, 325, 411, **418,** 440, **440,** 449, **479**
rabies, **636**
raccoon, 419, **419**
radial canals, **364**
radial nerves
    of echinoderms, 364, **364**
radial symmetry, 344–345, **345,** 363, **363**

radioactive waste, 499
radiolarians, 251, **251**
radula, 353, **353**
raffia palm, 288, **288**
ragweed pollen, **645**
rain forest
    canopy of, 477, **477**
    tropical, **474,** 477, **477,** 501
ratios, 110, 796
ray-finned fish, 381, **381**
receptors, 590, 595, **595**
recessive allele, 111
recessive trait, 109–110, **110**
rectum, 568, **568,** 574, **574**
recycling, **439,** 457, 507–508, **507–508**
    of glass, 508
    of newspaper, 508
    of resources, 508, **508**
    of trash, 508, **508**
red algae, 247
red blood cells, 43, **57,** 139, **139,** 526–527, 546, **549**
    blood type and, 552, **552**
    breakdown of, 555
    effects of different concentrations of water on, 85, **85**
    sickled, 139, **139**
red-eyed tree frog, **150**
red fish, **436**
red tide, 248, **248**
reflex, 587, 594, **594**
refrigeration, 637
relative dating, 177
remora, 447, **447**
renewable resource, 501
reproduction
    asexual, 38, **38,** 114, 254, **254,** 256, 612, **612**
    in bacteria, 225, **225**
    as a characteristic of living things, 38, **38**
    in fungi, 256
    in humans, 616–619
    in mammals, 413, 615, **615**
    in marsupials, 610, 614–615, **615**
    in monotremes, 615, **615**
    in placental mammals, 615
    in plants, 271, **271,** 300–303
    in protists, 254, **254**
    sexual, 38, **38,** 114, 254, **254,** 256, 613, **613**
    of viruses, 235, **235**
reproductive success, 162
reproductive system (human)
    diseases of, 619
    female, **524,** 617, **617**
    male, **524,** 616, **616**
reptiles, 387–391
    body temperature of, 388
    characteristics of, 388–389, **388–389**
    eggs of, 388–389, **388–389**
    evolution of, 387, **387**
    skin of, 388, **388**
    types of, 389–391, **389–391**

Index **845**

resource
    depletion, 501, **501**
    nonrenewable, 501, 506
    recovery, 508, **508**
    recycling of, 508, **508**
    renewable, 501
respiration, 556. *See also* cellular respiration
    in carbon cycle, **459,** 460
respiratory system, **524,** 556–559, **556–558**
    air flow through, 556–558, **556, 558**
    cilia in, **665**
    disorders of, 559, **559**
    parts of, 556–557, **556–557**
retina, 596, **596**
rheumatoid arthritis, 646, **646**
rhinoceros, **410,** 420
rhizoids, 274–275
rhizome, 276
rib cage, **526,** 558
ribosomes, 66, **66,** 70, **70, 74,** 75, 137, **137**
ring canal, **364**
ringworm, 637
river, 60, 486, **486**
rodents, 417, **417**
rods (photoreceptors), 596
root cap, 285, **285**
root hair, 285
roots, 284–285, **284–285**
    functions of, 284
    fungi growing on, 255
    gravitropism of, 308, **308**
    structure of, 285, **285**
    types of, 285, **285**
rose, 278, 282–283
roundworms, 351, **351**
runner (plant), **303**
rusts, 260

S

sac fungi, 258, **258**
safety
    drug safety tips, 664
    at home, 672, **672**
    outdoors, 672
    on road, 672
safety rules, 27, 682–685
safety symbols, **27,** 682–685, **682–685**
salamanders, **40,** 382–385, **382–383, 385,** 487
saliva, 570, 578, 584, 653
salivary glands, 568, **568,** 570
Salmonella, 637
salt-loving bacteria, 228, **228**
salt marsh, 436–437, **436–437**
sand dollar, 363, 365, **365**
sandy beach, 482, 485
Sargasso Sea, 484, **484**
Sargassum, 484

saturated fats, 658, 679
savanna, **474,** 478, **478**
scarlet tanager, 409, **409**
scavenger, 439, **439**
Schleiden, Matthias, 62
school (fish), 446
Schwann, Theodor, 62
scientific method, 10–17, **10, 17,** 790–792
    analyzing results of an experiment, 16, **16**
    communicating results of an experiment, 17, **17**
    data collection, 11, **11**
    drawing conclusions, 16
    hypothesis, 12–16, **12**
    observations, 11
    predictions, 13
    testing the hypothesis, 14–15, **15**
scientific name, 205–206
scientific notation, 799
scolex, 585
scrambled egg slime mold, 245
scrotum, 616, **616**
sea anemone, 325, 344, **345, 348,** 349, **482**
sea croaker, **436**
sea cucumber, 363, 365, **365**
seals, 411, 419
seaside sparrow, 436, **437**
seasonal
    behavior of animals, 329, **329**
    responses in plants, 309–311, **309–311**
seasons
    causes of, 309, **309**
sea star, 324, 363–364, **363–364, 482, 484, 485,** 612, **612**
seat belts, 672
sea turtle, 390, **390, 482**
sea urchin, 363, **363,** 365, **483,** 484
seaweed, 246–247, **246, 444**
secondary succession, 464
sedatives, 663
sediment, 176, **176**
seed, 279, **279,** 291
    characteristics in garden pea, 108–110, **108–110,** 118, **118**
    development of, 301, **301**
    dormant, 302
    germination of, 279, 302, **302**
    structure of, 279, **279**
seed coat, 279, **279**
seedless plants, 274–277, **274–277**
seed plants, 278–287, **278–287**
segments
    in annelids, 355, **355**
    in arthropods, 357
selective breeding, 104, 141, 160
self-pollinating plant, 107, **107**
semen, 616, **616**
seminiferous tubules, 616, **616**
semivegetarian diet, 679

senses, 595–599
sensory lobes
    of flatworms, 350, **350**
sensory neuron, 590, 593
sensory receptors, 595, **595**
sepal, 290, **290**
sewage treatment plant, 574
sex cells, 114–115, 271, **271,** 613, **613**
sex chromosomes, 119, **119**
sexually transmitted disease, 619
sexual reproduction, 38, **38,** 114, 254, **254,** 256, 324, **324,** 613, **613**
shark, **324,** 379–380, **379**
    denticles of, 380, **380**
    relationship with remoras, 447, **447**
shell
    of amniotic egg, 373, **373,** 388–389, **389**
    of mollusks, 353
    of protozoa, 251, **251**
    of turtle, 390
shrew, 417, 480
shrimp, **344,** 359, **436**
Siberian tiger, 9, **9,** 419
sickle cell anemia, 139, **139**
sieve plate, **364**
Silurian period, **178**
simple carbohydrates, 657
sinuses, 354
sirenia, 422
SI units, 22, **22,** 787
    conversion chart, 22, 787
    prefixes, 787
skeletal muscle, 526, 530–531, **530–531,** 554
skeletal system, 524, 526–529, **526–529**
    comparing structures from different species, 156, **156**
    differences between hominids and other primates, 189, **190**
    storage function, 526
    support function, 526
skin, 57, **57**
    of amphibians, 383, **383**
    of cartilaginous fishes, 380, **380**
    color of, 534, **534**
    follicle mites on, 454
    functions of, 534
    infections on, 537
    layers of, 535, **535**
    as a protective barrier, 537, 640, **640**
    receptors in, 595, **595**
    of reptiles, 388, **388**
    wound healing, 537, **537**
skin cancer, 138, 184, 500, 534, 537, **537**
skunk, 200, **200,** 206, 327, 329
sleep, 670, **670**
sliding joint, **528**
slime mold, 210, **210, 244–245,** 245

slope, 794–795
slugs, 352–353, **353**
small intestine, 568, **568,** 571–572, **571–572**
    enzymes in, 569, **569**
    tapeworm in, 585
smallpox, 634, 638
smell, 413, 599, **599**
smoky jungle frog, 150, **150**
smooth muscle, 530, **530**
smuts, 260, **260**
snails, 352–353, **352–353,** 439
snakes, 387–389, **388,** 391, **391,** 487
social behavior, 332–335
sodium, 584, 658
soil, 275, 277, 463
solar energy, 506, **506**
sound wave, 598, **598**
speciation
    by adaptation, 166, **166**
    by division of population, 167, **167**
    by separation, 166, **166**
species, 203, **203,** 205
    change over time, 151
    defined, 150
    number of known species, 151, **151**
sperm, 114–115, 118, **118,** 324, **324,** 613, **613,** 616, **618, 620**
sphincter, 574
spicule, 346
spider, **323,** 359–360, **359**
spider web, **42,** 360
spinal cord, **375, 590,** 593, **593**
    injury to, 342, 593
spinal fluid, **375**
spinner dolphin, 422, **422**
spirilla, 226
Spirogyra, 246
spleen, 555, **555**
sponge, 322–324, **322–323,** 345–347, **345–347, 482,** 484
    feeding in, 347, **347**
    kinds of, 346, **346**
    regeneration in, 346
spongin, 346
sporangia, **245,** 257, **257**
spore
    of fungi, 256–259, **256–257**
    plant, 271, **271**
    of *Plasmodium,* 253
    of slime molds, 245, **245**
spore-forming protists, 253
sporophyte, 271, **271,** 278
sporozoan, **253**
spruce tree, 278, **280**
squid, 352–354, **352–353,** 371, **371, 483**
stamen, 290–291, **290**
starch, 43, **43**
    detection with iodine, 43
star-nosed mole, 417, **417**
stem, 286–287, **286**
    bending toward light, 307, **307**
    functions of, 286
    gravitropism, 308, **308**
    structure of, 287, **287**
    underground, 286
steppe, 478
steroids, 533
stigma, **107–108,** 290–291, 291, 300, **300**
stimulants, 663
stimulus, 37, **37**
stinging cells, 348–349, **349**
St. Martin, Alexis, 566
stomach, 523, **523,** 568, **568,** 571, **571**
    enzymes in, 569, **569**
    ulcers of, 575, **575**
stomach acid, **523,** 571
stomata, 289, **289,** 306, **306**
strep throat, 232, **636**
stress, 671, **671**
stroke, 553
succession, 462–465
    primary, 463
    secondary, 464
    stable stage of, 465, **465**
sugar, 43, **43**
sulfur dioxide, 461
surface-to-volume ratio, 64–65, **64,** 67
survival behavior, 326–327, **326–327**
Sutton, Walter, 115
swamp, 489, **489**
sweat, 37, 534, **535,** 578, 584
sweat glands, 534, **535**
swim bladder, 380, **380**
symbiosis, 251, 255, 447–448, **447–448**
symmetry
    bilateral, 344–345, **345,** 363, **363**
    radial, 344–345, **345,** 363, **363**
systolic pressure, 551

T

tadpole, 74, 384, **384**
tail, 374, **375**
    grasping, 423
tapeworms, 350–351, **351,** 448, 585
taproot, 285, **285**
taste, 413, 599, **599**
taste bud, 595, 599, **599**
taxonomy, 204
T cells, 641, 644
    helper, 642, 644, **646–647,** 647
    killer, 642, 646, **646**
technology, 18
tectonic plates, 181, **181,** 415
teeth, **568**
    canine, 412, **412**
    care of, 669
    dental cavities, 232
    incisors, 412, **412**
    of mammals, 412, **412**
    milk, 412
    molars, 412
    tooth structure, 570, **570**
    types of, 570, **570**
temperature, 22, 26, **26**
    conversion table, 788
    scales, 788, **788**
    SI units, 22, 788
tendon, 531, **531**
    injury to, 533
territory, 332, **332**
Tertiary period, **178**
testes, **601,** 616, **616**
testosterone, 533, 616
theory, 18
therapsid, 387, **387,** 410, **410**
thermometer, **11,** 26, **26**
thirst, 578, 584
thorax
    of arthropods, 357, **357**
    of insects, 361, **361**
threadlike fungi, 257
throat, 568, **568,** 665
thumb
    opposable, 188
thymine, 128–129, **128**
thymus gland, 555, **555, 601**
thyroid gland, **601,** 603
tick, 359–360, **360,** 448
tiger, 9, **9,** 335
    fur color in, 134
tissue, 57, **57, 59,** 324, 522
    types of, 522–523, **522–523**
toads, 386, **386**
tobacco, 665, **665**
tobacco mosaic virus, 234
tolerance of drug, 664
tomato, 287, **302**
tomato hornworm, 448, **448**
tongue, 570, 599, **599**
tonsils, 555, **555**
toothless mammals, 416, **416**
tortoise, **213,** 389–390
touch, 413
    for communication, 334, **334**
toxic, 499
trachea, **556,** 557, **557**
traits, 160, 108–113, **108–113**
transfusion, 552
transgenic plants, 240
transpiration, 306, **306, 458,** 459
transport
    active, 86, **86**
    passive, 86, **86**
tree rings, 287
tributary, 486, **486**
trilobite, **152,** 185
tropical rain forest, **474,** 477, **477,** 501
tropism, 307–308, **307–308**
true-breeding plant, 108, **108,** 111, **111**

trunk-nosed mammals, 421, **421**
tube feet, **364,** 365
tuberculosis, 8, 164, 232
tundra, **474,** 480
turkey vulture, 439, **439**
turtles, 388–390, **390,** 487–488, **488**
twins, 618, **618**
typhoid fever, 232
Tyrannosaurus rex, 205, **205**

U

ulcer, 232
    gastric, 575, **575**
ultraviolet light, 183, 500
    absorption by ozone layer, 184, **184,** 500
    DNA damage and, 138
umbilical cord, 621, **621,** 623, **623**
unicellular
    organism, 59, **59**
unsaturated fats, 658
upright posture, **189,** 423
ureter, **576,** 577, **577**
urethra, **576,** 577, 616, **616**
urinary bladder, **576–577,** 577
urinary system, 524, 576–579, **576**
    disorders of, 579, **579**
urination, 577
urine, 577
uterus, 416, 617, **617,** 620, **620**

V

vaccine, 232, 240, 634, 638
vacuoles, 73, **73, 74,** 75
vagina, 617, **617**
valve
    heart, 548, **548**
    venous, 549
van Leuwenhoek, Anton, 62
variable, 14, 791
vascular plants, 272–273, **273**
vas deferens, 616, **616**
vegetarian diet, 697
vein
    circulatory system, 549, **549–550**
    leaf, 289, **289**
Venus' flytrap, **37,** 472, **472**
vertebrae, 375, **375,** 593, **593**
vertebral column, **526**
vertebrate, 322, 374–376
vesicles, 73, 87, **87**
vestigial structures, 153, **153**
villi, 572, **572**
Virchow, Rudolf, 62
viruses, 233–235, **233**
    classification of, 234
    control of Australian rabbit population, 449
    diagnosis of bacterial diseases, 241
    in environment, 222
    living or nonliving things, 233, **233**
    lysogenic cycle of, 235, **235**
    lytic cycle of, 235, **235**
    pathogens, 233
    shape of, 234
    size of, 233
    treatment of viral diseases, 639
vision, 413, 596–597, **596–597**
    binocular, 188, **188**
vitamins, 209, 258, 596, 656, 659
vocal cords, 386, 557
vocal sac, 386, **386**
voice box, 557
volume, 22, 24–25, **25,** 64, **64,** 799, **799**
    calculation of, 799
    SI units, 22, 787
voluntary muscle, 530
Volvox, 247, **247**

W

Wallace, Alfred Russel, 162
walrus, 419, **419**
warbler, 41, **41**
warning coloration, 327, **327,** 446
wasps, 298, **323,** 327, **361,** 362
    parasitic, 448, **448**
waste reduction, 506
water
    balance in human body, 578
    boiling point of, **26**
    contaminated with pathogens, 637
    depletion of, 501
    freezing point of, **26**
    human requirement for, 656, 658, **658**
    loss from leaf, 306, **306**
    as a necessity of life, 40, 459
    osmosis, 85, **85**
    production in cellular respiration, 89
    reabsorption in small intestine, 574
    reuse of, 507, **507**
    underground supply of, 501
    use by persons in the United States, 461
    use in photosynthesis, 88, **90,** 304–305, **305**
water bear, 370, **370**
water cycle, 458–459, **458**
waterlily, 487, 489
water mold, 246, **246**
water pollution, 9, **498**
water vascular system, 364, **364**
Watson, James, 129, **129**
weather
    from fire, 470
web of life, 434–437
Wegener, Alfred, 180
wetlands, 472, 488–489, **488–489**
    destruction of, 503
    reducing pollution in the Gulf of Mexico, 471
whales, 328, 333, 412, 422, **422, 481,** 483
    evolution of, 153–155, **153–155**
white blood cells, 73, **73,** 546–547, **547,** 555
wildebeest, 478, **478**
wildflowers, 463
Wilkins, Maurice, 129
wilting, 73, 85, 306
windpipe. *See* trachea
wings
    of birds, 403–405, **404–405**
    of insects, 361
withdrawal symptoms, 664, 667–668
wolf pack, 443, **443**
wolves, 332, **332,** 412, 419, 480, 517, **517**
wood, 281, 287
woody stem, 287, **287**
worms, 439
wound healing, 537, **537,** 653
    bandages from fungi, 266

X

X chromosome, 119, **119**
X rays, 21, **21**
    DNA damage and, 138
xylem, 284, **285,** 286–287, **287**

Y

Y chromosome, 119, **119**
yeast, 83, 258, **258**
    fermentation by, 91, **91**
Yellowstone National Park
    regrowth after fire, 462, **462**
    restoration of gray wolves to, 442, **442**
yolk, 56, **373,** 389

Z

zebra, 420, 478, **478,** 614, **614**
zebra mussel, 502, **502**
zinc, 658
zooflagellates, **244**
zooplankton, 481
zygote, 613

Credits

Abbreviations used: (t) top, (c) center, (b) bottom, (l) left, (r) right, (bkgd) background

ILLUSTRATIONS

All illustrations, unless otherwise noted below by Holt, Rinehart and Winston.

Table of Contents: Page vii (cr), Morgan-Cain & Associates; viii (bl), Marty Roper/Planet Rep; ix (tl), Frank Ordaz/Dimension; ix (cr), John White/The Neis Group; xi (tl), Will Nelson/Sweet Reps; xi (cr), Morgan-Cain & Associates; xiv (bl), Will Nelson/Sweet Reps; xv (b), Will Nelson/Sweet Reps; xvi (bl), Christy Krames; xvii (tl), Kip Carter; xix, Blake Thornton/Rita Marie.

Unit One: Page 2 (bl), Kip Carter.

Chapter One: Page 12 (c), Michael Morrow Design; 13 (c), Michael Morrow Design; 15 (c), Ralph Garafola/Lorraine Garafola Represents; 16 (c), Ross, Culbert and Lavery; 16 (bl), Morgan-Cain & Associates; 20 (tl), Blake Thornton/Rita Marie; 22 (tl), Blake Thornton/Rita Marie; 22 (bl), Stephen Durke/Washington Artists; 23 (scale), Ross, Culbert and Lavery; 23 (tree), Susan Johnston Carlson/Melissa Turk; 23 (boy), Frank Ordaz/Dimension; 23 (grasshopper), Bob Lange/Dianne Roche Represents; 23 (amoeba), Claire Booth/CBMI; 23 (cell), Network Graphics; 23 (virus), Morgan-Cain & Associates; 23 (helix), Robert Margulies/Margulies Medical Art; 24 (bl), Terry Kovalcik; 26 (bl), Stephen Durke/Washington Artists; 31 (tr), Annie Bissett; 31 (bl), Mark Heine.

Chapter Two: Page 39 (c), Will Nelson/Sweet Reps; 44 (b), Morgan-Cain & Associates; 44 (cl), Blake Thornton/Rita Marie; 45 (tr), David Merrell/Suzanne Craig Represents Inc.; 45 (cr), John White/The Neis Group; 45 (br), Morgan-Cain & Associates; 47 (cr), Blake Thornton/Rita Marie; 48 (tl), Morgan-Cain & Associates.

Chapter Three: Page 58 (br), Christy Krames; 58 (c), Michael Woods/Morgan-Cain & Associates; 59 (b), Morgan-Cain & Associates; 59 (c), Morgan-Cain & Associates; 59 (cr), Christy Krames; 60 (br), Yuan Lee; 62 (bl), David Merrell/Suzanne Craig Represents Inc.; 64 (c), Morgan-Cain & Associates; 64 (tl), Terry Kovalcik; 65 (bc), Terry Kovalcik; 65 (cr), Morgan-Cain & Associates; 66 (b), Morgan-Cain & Associates; 67 (tr), Morgan-Cain & Associates; 68, Morgan-Cain & Associates; 69, Morgan-Cain & Associates; 70, Morgan-Cain & Associates; 71, Morgan-Cain & Associates; 72, Morgan-Cain & Associates; 73, Morgan-Cain & Associates; 74, Morgan-Cain & Associates; 75, Morgan-Cain & Associates; 79, Morgan-Cain & Associates.

Chapter Four: Page 83 (cr), Mark Heine; 85 (tr), Stephen Durke/Washington Artists; 86 (bl,br), Morgan-Cain & Associates; 86 (tl), Terry Kovalcik; 87 (c), Morgan-Cain & Associates; 88 (bl), Morgan-Cain & Associates; 89 (bl), Morgan-Cain & Associates; 90 (tl), Robin Carter; 90 (cl), Morgan-Cain & Associates; 90 (bl), Morgan-Cain & Associates; 90 (c), Morgan-Cain & Associates; 90 (br), Morgan-Cain & Associates; 94 (l), Alexander & Turner; 99 (cr), Morgan-Cain & Associates.

Unit Three: Page 103 (tr), John White/The Neis Group; 103 (tl), John White/The Neis Group.

Chapter Five: Page 107 (b), Mike Wepplo/Das Group; 108, John White/The Neis Group; 109, John White/The Neis Group; 110, John White/The Neis Group; 111, John White/The Neis Group; 115 (r), Alexander & Turner; 116 (l), Alexander & Turner; 117 (r) Alexander & Turner; 118, Alexander & Turner; 119 (bc), Alexander & Turner; 119 (br), Rob Schuster/Hankins and Tegenborg; 119 (cr), Blake Thornton/Rita Marie; 121 (cr), Blake Thornton/Rita Marie; 122, John White/The Neis Group; 123 (bl) John White/The Neis Group.

Chapter Six: Page 126, Stephen Durke/Washington Artists; 128, Rob Schuster/Hankins and Tegenborg; 130 (c), Alexander & Turner; 130 (tl), Marty Roper/Planet Rep; 131 (cl), Alexander & Turner; 132, Morgan-Cain & Associates; 133 (r), Grey Geisler; 134 (bl), John White/The Neis Group; 136–137, Rob Schuster/Hankins and Tegenborg; 138 (tl), Rob Schuster/Hankins and Tegenborg; 139 (b) Rob Schuster/Hankins and Tegenborg; 142 (cr), Marty Roper/Planet Rep.

Chapter Seven: Page 148 (l), Will Nelson/Sweet Reps; 148 (tl), Michael Morrow Design; 148 (br), Will Nelson/Sweet Reps; 151, Steve Roberts; 153 (tr), Ross, Culbert and Lavery; 153 (b), Rob Wood/Wood, Ronsaville, Harlin; 154–155, Rob Wood/Wood, Ronsaville, Harlin; 156, Christy Krames; 157 (c), Sarah Woods; 157 (tr), David Beck; 157 (cr), Frank Ordaz/Dimension; 159 (tr), Tony Morse/Ivy Glick; 159 (b), John White/The Neis Group; 161, Ross, Culbert and Lavery; 162 (r), Will Nelson/Sweet Reps; 164 (c), Carlyn Iverson; 164 (bl), Frank Ordaz/Dimension; 166 (c), Mike Wepplo/Das Group; 166 (bl), Will Nelson/Sweet Reps; 167 (c), Carlyn Iverson; 168 (tc), Rob Wood/Wood, Ronsaville, Harlin; 168 (br), Christy Krames; 169, Carlyn Iverson; 171 (tr), Ross, Culbert and Lavery; 172 (tl), Carlyn Iverson.

Chapter Eight: Page 175 (cr), Michael Morrow Design; 176 (b), Mike Wepplo/Das Group; 177 (cr), Mike Wepplo/Das Group; 177 (b), Rob Schuster/Hankins and Tegenborg; 178, Barbara Hoopes-Ambler; 179, John White/The Neis Group; 180, MapQuest.com; 181 (tr), MapQuest.com; 181 (br), Walter Stuart; 183, John White/The Neis Group; 184, Craig Attebery/Jeff Lavaty Artist Agent; 185, Barbara Hoopes-Ambler; 186, Barbara Hoopes-Ambler; 187 (tr), John White/The Neis Group; 188 (bl), Todd Buck; 188 (br), Will Nelson/Sweet Reps; 189, Christy Krames; 194, Barbara Hoopes-Ambler; 197 (tr), John White/The Neis Group; 197 (tr), John White/The Neis Group; 197 (tr), John White/The Neis Group; 197 (tr), John White/The Neis Group; 197 (tr), John White/The Neis Group; 198 (tr), Greg Harris.

Chapter Nine: Page 201 (bl), Terry Kovalcik; 203 (bear, blue jay, earthworm), Michael Woods/Morgan-Cain & Associates; 203 (boy), Frank Ordaz/Dimension; 203 (whale), Graham Allen; 203 (lynx), David Ashby; 203 (cat, lion), Will Nelson/Sweet Reps; 204 (tl), Will Nelson/Sweet Reps; 204 (bear, platypus), Michael Woods/Morgan-Cain & Associates; 204 (cat, lion), Will Nelson/Sweet Reps; 205 (b), John White/The Neis Group; 205 (b), Blake Thornton/Rita Marie; 206 (c), Marty Roper/Planet Rep; 206 (bl), Will Nelson/Sweet Reps; 207 (br), Cy Baker/WAA; 207 (tl), John White/The Neis Group; 207 (tr), John White/The Neis Group; 214, John White/The Neis Group; 216 (cr), Marty Roper/Planet Rep; 217, (lemur), Will Nelson/Sweet Reps; 217 (baboon), Graham Allen; 217 (chimpanzee), Michael Woods/Morgan-Cain & Associates; 217 (human), Frank Ordaz; 218 (tr), John White/The Neis Group; 218 (tr), Barbara Hoopes-Ambler.

Chapter Ten: Page 222 (t), Blake Thornton/Rita Marie; 225 (cl), Art and Science, Inc.; 226, Kip Carter; 229 (bl), Carlyn Iverson; 234 (cl), Morgan-Cain & Associates; 234 (c), Art and Science, Inc.; 234 (bl), Morgan-Cain & Associates; 234 (bc), Morgan-Cain & Associates; 239 (tr), Art and Science, Inc.

Chapter Eleven: Page 249 (c), Scott Thorn Barrows/The Neis Group; 250 (c), Scott Thorn Barrows/The Neis Group; 252, Morgan-Cain & Associates; 253, Art and Science, Inc.; 256, Will Nelson/Sweet Reps.

Chapter Twelve: Page 268 (t), Marty Roper/Planet Rep; 271 (tr), Morgan-Cain & Associates; 271 (bl), Sidney Jablonski; 273 (c), John White/The Neis Group; 274 (art), Ponde & Giles; 274 (arrows), Sidney Jablonski; 276 (art), Ponde & Giles; 276 (arrows), Sidney Jablonski; 279 (cr), Keith Locke; 279 (cl), Sarah Woods; 279 (br), James Gritz/Photonicia; 281 (art), Will Nelson/Sweet Reps; 281 (arrows), Sidney Jablonski; 283 (art), John White/The Neis Group; 283 (arrows), Sidney Jablonski; 284 (bl), Will Nelson/Sweet Reps; 285 (tr), John White/The Neis Group; 287 (r), Will Nelson/Sweet Reps; 289–290 (tr), Will Nelson/Sweet Reps; 292 (br), Sarah Woods; 295, Will Nelson/Sweet Reps.

Chapter Thirteen: Page 298 (l), Dan McGeehan/Koralick Associates; 300 (b), Will Nelson/Sweet Reps; 301 (c), Will Nelson/Sweet Reps; 302 (b), Will Nelson/Sweet Reps; 304 (c), Stephen Durke/Washington Artists; 305 (cl), Ponde & Giles; 306 (c), Morgan-Cain & Associates; 307 (bl), Carlyn Iverson; 309 (tr), Stephen Durke/Washington Artists; 309 (bl), Rob Schuster/Hankins and Tegenborg; 311 (c), Rob Schuster/Hankins and Tegenborg; 314 (cr), Will Nelson/Sweet Reps; 315 (cr), Carlyn Iverson.

Chapter Fourteen: Page 320 (tr), Tony Morse/Ivy Glick; 323 (chart), Sidney Jablonski; 323 (ant, beetle, bug, fish, mollusk, sponge, starfish, worm), Barbara Hoopes-Ambler; 323 (jellyfish), Sarah Woodward/Morgan-Cain & Associates; 323 (spider, fly), Steve Roberts; 323 (butterfly), Bridgette James; 323 (elephant), Michael Woods/Morgan-Cain & Associates; 324 (bl), Kip Carter; 328 (cl), Keith Locke/Suzanne Craig Represents Inc.; 330 (tr), Gary Locke/Suzanne Craig Represents Inc.; 330 (bl), Tony Morse/Ivy Glick; 334 (b), John White/The Neis Group; 336 (br), John White/The Neis Group; 339 (bl), Sidney Jablonski.

Chapter Fifteen: Page 345 (tl), Barbara Hoopes-Ambler; 345 (tc), Sarah Woodward/Morgan-Cain & Associates; 345 (tr), Alexander & Turner; 345 (cr,br), Alexander & Turner; 347, Alexander & Turner; 348, John White/The Neis Group; 349, Morgan-Cain & Associates; 350, Alexander & Turner; 353 (tr), Alexander & Turner; 357, Felipe Passalacqua; 359 (c), John White/The Neis Group; 359 (cr), Will Nelson/Sweet Reps; 361, Steve Roberts; 362, Bridgette James; 364 (tl), Alexander & Turner; 364 (b), Alexander & Turner; 369 (cr), Barbara Hoopes-Ambler.

Chapter Sixteen: Page 373 (br), Kip Carter; 375 (t), Alexander & Turner; 378 (cl), Will Nelson/Sweet Reps; 380 (br), Kip Carter; 380 (b), Barbara Hoopes-Ambler; 382 (br), Peg Gerrity; 384 (c), Will Nelson/Sweet Reps; 387 (c), Barbara Hoopes-Ambler; 389 (c), Kip Carter; 394 (bl), Will Nelson/Sweet Reps; 395 (bl), Marty Roper/Planet Rep; 395 (tr), Rob Schuster/Hankins and Tegenborg; 396 (bc), Ron Kimball; 397 (bc), Ka Botz.

Chapter Seventeen: Page 399 (tr), John White/The Neis Group; 401 (feather), Will Nelson/Sweet Reps; 401 (bird), Will Nelson/Sweet Reps; 401 (closeup), Kip Carter; 401 (digestive system), Kip Carter; 402 (c), Will Nelson/Sweet Reps; 403, Will Nelson/Sweet Reps; 404 (c), Will Nelson/Sweet Reps; 409 (cr), Kip Carter; 410 (bl), Howard Freidman; 425 (c), Yuan Lee; 427 (tr), Sidney Jablonski.

Chapter Eighteen: Page 433 (br), David Beck; 434 (b), Will Nelson/Sweet Reps; 435 (l), Will Nelson/Sweet Reps; 436–437 (b) John White/The Neis Group; 438–439 (b) Will Nelson/Sweet Reps; 440 (b), John White/The Neis Group; 441 (b), Will Nelson/Sweet Reps; 443 (br), Will Nelson/Sweet Reps; 444 (bl), Blake Thornton/Rita Marie; 449 (cr), Mike Wepplo/Das Group; 450 (cl), Will Nelson/Sweet Reps; 453 (cr), Jared Schneidman Design.

Chapter Nineteen: Page 458 (tr), Robert Hynes/Mendola Artists; 459 (b), Robert Hynes/Mendola Artists; 460 (b), Robert Hynes/Mendola Artists; 463, Robert Hynes/Mendola Artists; 464, Robert Hynes/Mendola Artists; 466 (r), Robert Hynes/Mendola Artists; 468 (br), Robert Hynes/Mendola Artists; 471 (c), MapQuest.com.

Chapter Twenty: Page 474 (b), MapQuest.com; 475 (b), Will Nelson/Sweet Reps; 476 (b), Will Nelson/Sweet Reps; 477 (b), Will Nelson/Sweet Reps; 479 (b), Will Nelson/Sweet Reps; 482–483, Yuan Lee; 486 (bl), Will Nelson/Sweet Reps; 487 (br), Mark Heine; 491 (cr), Mark Heine; 492 (bl), Will Nelson/Sweet Reps; 493 (tr,cr), Rob Schuster/Hankins and Tegenborg.

Chapter Twenty One: Page 515 (t), John White/The Neis Group.

Chapter Twenty Two: Page 522 (c,cl), Morgan-Cain & Associates; 523 (cl), Morgan-Cain & Associates; 523 (c), Morgan-Cain & Associates; 523 (tr), Morgan-Cain & Associates; 524, Christy Krames; 525, Christy Krames; 527, Keith Kasnot; 528, John Huxtable/Black Creative; 529, John Huxtable/Black Creative; 531 (br), Christy Krames; 535 (br), Morgan-Cain & Associates; 535 (cr), Marty Roper/Planet Rep; 537 (t), Morgan-Cain & Associates; 538 (br), John Huxtable/Black Creative; 540 (br), Christy Krames; 541 (tr), Morgan-Cain & Associates.

Chapter Twenty Three: Page 546 (tr), Christy Krames; 547 (b), Keith Kasnot; 548, Kip Carter; 549 (c), Kip Carter; 550 (b), Kip Carter; 552 (tl), Jared Schneidman Design; 552 (br), Marty Roper/Planet Rep; 554 (br), Kip Carter; 555 (tr), Christy Krames; 556 (bl), Christy Krames; 557 (b), Christy Krames; 558 (br), Christy Krames; 558 (bc,bl), Kip Carter; 560 (br), Christy Krames; 562 (tr), Kip Carter; 563 (tr), Kip Carter.

Chapter Twenty Four: Page 568 (bc), Christy Krames; 569 (b), Brian Evans; 570 (tl,bl), Keith Kasnot; 571 (cl), Christy Krames; 571 (cr), Brian Evans; 572 (tl), Marty Roper/Planet Rep; 572 (cl), Christy Krames; 572 (c), Brian Evans; 573, Christy Krames; 574 (tl), Christy Krames; 576 (cl), Christy Krames; 577 (cr), Keith Kasnot; 580 (cr), Brian Evans; 580 (tr), Keith Kasnot; 581 (tr), Christy Krames; 582 (br), Keith Kasnot; 582 (tr), Brian Evans.

Chapter Twenty Five: Page 588 (bl), Christy Krames; 589 (b), Scott Thorn Barrows/The Neis Group; 590 (b), Scott Thorn Barrows/The Neis Group; 591 (bc), Brian Evans; 592 (b), Brian Evans; 593 (tr), Christy Krames; 595 (b), Morgan-Cain & Associates; 596 (bc), Keith Kasnot; 596 (br), Carlyn Iverson; 597 (bl), Keith Kasnot; 598 (b), Christy Krames; 599 (tr), Keith Kasnot; 600 (b), Dan McGeehan/Koralick Associates; 601 (b), Christy Krames; 602, Christy Krames; 604 (br), Keith Kasnot; 605 (cl), Dan McGeehan/Koralick Associates; 606 (tr), Christy Krames; 607 (tr), Christy Krames.

Chapter Twenty Six: Page 613 (bl), Rob Schuster/Hankins and Tegenborg; 616 (bl), Keith Kasnot; 617 (tr), Keith Kasnot; 618 (br), Rob Schuster/Hankins and Tegenborg; 620 (cl), David Fischer; 621 (cr), Christy Krames; 629 (cr), Sidney Jablonski; 630 (bl), Morgan-Cain & Associates.

Chapter Twenty Seven: Page 640 (br), Scott Thorn Barrows/The Neis Group; 641 (bl), Scott Thorn Barrows/The Neis Group; 642–643, Blake Thornton/Rita Marie; 644 (l), Stephen Durke/Washington Artists; 648 (tl), Blake Thornton/Rita Marie; 650 (bc), Scott Thorn Barrows/The Neis Group; 651 (tr), Sidney Jablonski.

Chapter Twenty Eight: Page 667 (br), Marty Roper/Planet Rep; 672 (c), Uhl Studios, Inc.; 675 (tl), Marty Roper/Planet Rep.

LabBook: Page 691 (cr), Keith Locke; 693 (br), Blake Thornton/Rita Marie; 694 (tl), David Merrell/Suzanne Craig Represents Inc.; 694 (cr), Rob Schuster/Hankins and Tegenborg; 697 (c), Morgan-Cain & Associates; 704 (br), Kip Carter; 706 (b), Rob Schuster/Hankins and Tegenborg; 708 (r), Frank Ordaz/Dimension; 709 (tr,br), John White/The Neis Group; 710 (br), Keith Locke; 711 (cr), Keith Locke; 715 (br,cr), Rob Schuster/Hankins and Tegenborg; 716 (b,r), Rob Schuster/Hankins and Tegenborg; 717 (r), Keith Locke; 718, Rob Schuster/Hankins and Tegenborg; 719 (r), Rob Schuster/Hankins and Tegenborg; 720 (br), Keith Locke; 723 (cr), Will Nelson/Sweet Reps;

724 (cr), Will Nelson/Sweet Reps; 725 (tr), Cori Zeller; 725 (br), Will Nelson/Sweet Reps; 727 (cr), Sarah Woodward/Morgan-Cain & Associates; 729 (br), John White/The Neis Group; 733 (br), Carlyn Iverson; 734 (tr), Keith Locke/Suzanne Craig Represents Inc.; 735 (tr), John White/The Neis Group; 737 (br), Marty Roper/Planet Rep; 739 (bc), Keith Locke; 741 (br), David Merrell/Suzanne Craig Represents Inc.; 741 (tr), John Huxtable/Black Creative; 744 (cr), Will Nelson/Sweet Reps; 745 (b), Blake Thornton/Rita Marie; 747 (tr), Blake Thornton/Rita Marie; 747 (br) Lori Anzalone/Jeff Lavaty Artist Agent; 754 (cr), John White/The Neis Group; 756 (br), Carlyn Iverson; 763 (cr), Morgan-Cain & Associates; 763 (b), Annie Bissett; 764 (tr), Kip Carter; 765 (tr), Rob Schuster/Hankins and Tegenborg; 776 (b, c), Rob Schuster/Hankins and Tegenborg; 777 (tc), Rob Schuster/Hankins and Tegenborg; 781, Dan McGeehan/Koralick Associates.

Appendix: Page 785 (cl), Blake Thornton/Rita Marie; 788 (t), Terry Guyer; 792 (b), Mark Mille/Sharon Langley; 800–801, Kristy Sprott; 802 (bl), Stephen Durke/Washington Artists; 803 (tl,c) Stephen Durke/Washington Artists; 803 (b), Bruce Burdick; 803 (cl), Stephen Durke/Washington Artists.

PHOTOGRAPHY

Cover: (tl, spine, back cover), Kim Taylor/Bruce Coleman, Inc.; (cl), Frans Lanting/Minden Pictures; (c), Peter Peterson/Tony Stone Images; (cr), Chris Jaffe; (bl), Carr Clifton; (br), ©Gerry Ellis/GerryEllis.com

Title Page: (cr), Frans Lanting/Minden Pictures; (tc), Kim Taylor/Bruce Coleman, Inc.

Feature Borders: Unless otherwise noted below, all images copyright ©2001 PhotoDisc/HRW. *Across the Sciences:* all images by HRW; *Careers:* (sand bkgd and Saturn), Corbis Images; (DNA), Morgan Cain & Associates; (scuba gear), ©1997 Radlund & Associates for Artville; *Eureka:* copyright ©2001 PhotoDisc/HRW; *Eye on the Environment:* (clouds and sea in bkgd), HRW; (bkgd grass, red eyed frog), Corbis Images; (hawks, pelican), Animals Animals/Earth Scenes; (rat), Visuals Unlimited/John Grelach; (endangered flower), Dan Suzio/Photo Researchers, Inc.; *Health Watch:* (dumbbell), Sam Dudgeon/HRW Photo; (aloe vera, EKG), Victoria Smith/HRW Photo; (basketball), ©1997 Radlund & Associates for Artville; (shoes, bubbles), Greg Geisler; *Scientific Debate:* Sam Dudgeon/HRW Photo; *Science Fiction:* (saucers), Ian Christopher/Greg Geisler; (book), HRW; (bkgd telescope), Dave Cutler Studio, Inc./SIS Illustration Source; *Science Technology and Society:* (robot), Greg Geisler; *Weird Science:* (mite), David Burder/Tony Stone Images; (atom balls), J/B Woolsey Associates; (walking stick, turtle), EclectiCollection.

Table of Contents: v(br), Uniphoto; vi(tl), Leonard Lessin/Photo Researchers, Inc.; vii(bl), Visuals Unlimited/R. Calentine; vii(tr), Robert Brons/BPS/Tony Stone Images; viii(tr), Frans Lanting/Minden Pictures; viii(br), Biophoto Associates/Photo Researchers, Inc.; ix Centre National de Prehistoire, Perigueux, France; x(tl), G. Randall/FPG; x(bl), Fran Heyl Associates; xi(bl), SuperStock; xi(br), Phil Degginger; xii(bl), Richard R. Hansen/Photo Researchers, Inc.; xiii(tl), Daniel Schaefe/HRW Photo; xiii(br), Visuals Unlimited/James Beverigde; xiii(bl), Brian Parker/Tom Stack; xiii(tr), Carl Roessler/FPG; xiv(cr), Edwin & Peggy Bauer/Bruce Coleman; xiv(tl), Tui De Roy/Minden Pictures; xv(tl), Stuart Westmorland/Tony Stone Images; xvii(tc), Dr. Dennis Kunkel/Phototake, Inc.; xvii(br), Image Bank; xviii(bl), Lennart Nilsson/Albert Bonniers Forlag AB, A CHILD IS BORN

Unit One: 2(t), O.S.F./Animals Animals; 2(cr), University of Pennsylvania/Hulton Getty; 3(cl), Hulton Getty; 3(bl), Peter Veit/DRK Photo; 3(c), National Portrait Gallery, Smithsonian Institution/Art Resource; 3(br), O. Louis Mazzatenta/National Geographic Society Image Collection; **Chapter One:** 4(c), Minnesota Pollution Control Agency; 7(tl), NASA; 7(tc), Gerry Gropp; 7(tr), Chip Simmons/Discover Channel; 7(cr), Charles C. Place/Image Bank; 8(tl), Hank Morgan/Photo Researchers, Inc.; 8(bl), Mark Lennihan/AP/Wide World Photos; 9(b), George Holton/Fhoto Researchers, Inc.; 9(cr), Dale Miquelle/National Geographic Image Collection; 12(tl), Fernando Bueno/Image Bank; 13 Mark E. Gibson; 14(tl, bc), John Mitchell/Photo Researchers, Inc.; 18(tl), John Reader/Science Photo Library/Photo Researchers, Inc.; 18(cr), Greg Greico/PENN State; 19(bl), CENCO; 19(bc), Robert Brons/Tony Stone Images; 20(cl), Sinclair Stammers/Science Photo Library/Photo Researchers, Inc.; 20(cr), RJ Lee Instruments Limited; 20(bl), Microworks/Phototake; 20(br), Visuals Unlimited/Karl Aufderheide; 21(tr), Scott Camazine/Photo Researchers, Inc.; 21(cr), Alfred Pasieka/Photo Researchers, Inc.; 21(b), Howard Sochurek/The Stock Market; 23(tr), David Austen/Publishers Network, Inc.; 25(tr), Science Kit & Boreal Laboratories; 27 Dr. Jeremy Burgess/Science Photo Library/Photo Researchers, Inc.; 29(cr), CENCO; 30 Charles C. Place/Image Bank; 32(tl), Eric Pianka/University of Texas; 32(br), Charles C. Place/Image Bank

Chapter Two: 34(tr), Patrick Landmann/Gamma-Liaison; 34(cl, br), Chris Landmann/Gamma-Liaison; 35(bl), Steve Dunwell/Image Bank; 36(tr), Visuals Unlimited/Cabisco; 36(bl), Visuals Unlimited/Science Visuals Unlimited; 36(br), Wolfgang Kaehler/Liaison International; 37(cl, cr), David M. Dennis/Tom Stack and Associates; 37(br), Visuals Unlimited/Fred Rohde; 38(tl), Visuals Unlimited/Stanley Flegler; 38(c), James M. McCann/Photo Researchers, Inc.; 38(bl), Lawrence Migdale/Photo Researchers, Inc.; 40 Robert Dunne/Photo Researchers, Inc.; 41(tr), Wolfgang Bayer; 41(cr), Visuals Unlimited/Rob Simpson; 42(bl), Photo Researchers, Inc.; 42(bc), Hans Reinhard/Bruce Coleman, Inc.; 46 Visuals Unlimited/Stanley Flegler; 47 Wolfgang Bayer; 49(bl), Dede Gilman/Unicorn Stock Photos; 50(tc, c), NASA

Unit Two: 52(tr), Visuals Unlimited/Kevin Collins; 52(c), Ed Reschke/Peter Arnold, Inc.; 52(br), Cold Spring Harbor Laboratory; 52(cl), Glen Allison/Tony Stone Images; 53(tc), Ed Reschke/Peter Arnold; 53(cr), Keith Porter/Photo Researchers, Inc.; 53(br), Dr. Ian Wilmut/Liaison; 53(cl), The National Archives/Corbis; 53(bc), Dan McCoy/Rainbow; **Chapter Three:** 54 Biology Media/Photo Researchers, Inc.; 56(cl), Image Copyright ©2001 Photodisc, Inc.; 56(bl, bcl, bcr), Dr. Yorgos Nikas/Science Photo Library/Photo Researchers, Inc.; 56(br), Lennart Nilsson; 57(tc), Visuals Unlimited/Fred Hossler; 57(tl), National Cancer Institute/Science Photo Library/Photo Researchers, Inc.; 57(tr), GW Willis/BPS/Tony Stone Images; 57(cl), Visuals Unlimited/G. Shih and R. Kessel; 59(tl), Visuals Unlimited/Michael Abbey; 59(tr), Robert Brons/BPS/Tony Stone Images; 59(cl), David M. Phillips/Photo Researchers, Inc.; 59(b), E. S. Ross; 60(tr), Joe McDonald/DRK Photo; 61(cl, c), C. C. Lockwood/DRK Photo; 61(b), Visuals Unlimited/Kevin Collins; 61(br), Leonard Lessin/Peter Arnold; 62(tl), Visuals Unlimited/Doug Sokell; 62(tr), Visuals Unlimited/K. G. Murti; 62(cl), Visuals Unlimited/D. M. Phillips; 63(br), Biophoto Associates/Science Source/Photo Researchers, Inc.; 63(tr), Dr. Petit/Rapho/Liaison International; 65 AP/Wide World Photos; 73(tr), Biology Media/Photo Researchers, Inc.; 76(tr), Robert Brons/BPS/Tony Stone Images; 76(c), Joe McDonald/DRK Photo; 78 Biophoto Associates/Science Source/Photo Researchers, Inc.; 80(l), Hans Reinhard/Bruce Coleman; 80(tr), Andrew Syred/Tony Stone Images; 81 Dr. Smith/University of Akron

Chapter Four: 85(cr), Visuals Unlimited/Stanley Flegler; 85(br), Visuals Unlimited/David M. Philips; 87(tr), Photo Researchers, Inc.; 87(cr), Birgit H. Satir; 88 Runk/Schoenberger/Grant Heilman; 92 CNRI/Science Photo Library/Photo Researchers, Inc.; 93(tr), L. Willatt, East Anglian Regional Genetics Service/Science Photo Library/Photo Researchers, Inc.; 93(br), Biophoto Associates/Photo Researchers, Inc.; 94(all), Ed Reschke/Peter Arnold; 95(tr), Visuals Unlimited/R. Calentine; 95(tr, cr), Biology Media/Photo Researchers, Inc.; 96(tc), Visuals Unlimited/Stanley Flegler; 97 Ed Reschke/Peter Arnold; 98 CNRI/Science Photo Library/Photo Researchers, Inc.; 99(cl, c), Biophoto Associates/Science Source/Photo Researchers, Inc.; 100 Lee D. Simons/Science Source/Photo Researchers, Inc.

Unit Three: 102(t), Library of Congress/Corbis; 102(bl), John Reader/Science Photo Library/Photo Researchers, Inc.; 102(br), NASA; 102(c), Kenneth Eward/Science Source/Photo Researchers, Inc.; 103(bc), Biophoto Associates/Science Source/Photo Researchers, Inc.; 103(c), Marine Biological Laboratory Archives; 103(cl), John Reader/Science Photo Library/Photo Researchers, Inc.; 103(cr), Ted Thai/Time Magazine; **Chapter Five:** 104(tr), Dr. Paul A. Zahl/Photo Researchers, Inc.; 104(tl), Gerard Lacz/Peter Arnold; 104(cl), Runk/Schoenberger/Grant Heilman; 104(br), SuperStock; 106(c), Frans Lanting/Minden Pictures; 106(br), Corbis; 107 Runk/Schoenberger/Grant Heilman Photography; 113(br), Image Copyright ©2001 Photodisc, Inc.; 113(tr), Gerard Lacz/Animals Animals; 114(cl), Phototake/CNRI/Phototake NYC; 114(bc), Biophoto Associates/Photo Researchers, Inc.; 119 Phototake/CNRI/Phototake NYC; 120 Frans Lanting/Minden Pictures; 124 Hank Morgan/Rainbow; 125(t, c), Dr. F. R. Turner, Biology Dept., Indiana University

Chapter Six: 127(cr, whorl), Leonard Lessin/Peter Arnold; 127(cr, arch), Federal Bureau of Investigation; 127(br), Archive Photos; 129(tr), Science Photo Library/Photo Researchers, Inc.; 129(br), Archive Photos; 131 Dr. Gopal Murti/Science Photo Library/Photo Researchers, Inc.; 132(cl), Phil Jude/Science Photo Library/Photo Researcher, Inc.; 133(cl), Biophoto Associates/Photo Researchers, Inc.; 133(bl), J. R. Paulson & U. K. Laemmli/University of Geneva; 133(bl), Dan McCoy/Rainbow; 134(br), Lawrence Migdale/Photo Researchers, Inc.; 139(br, cr), Jackie Lewin/Royal Free Hospital/Science Photo Library/Photo Researchers, Inc.; 141(cl), Remi Benali and Stephen Ferry/Gamma-Liaison; 141(tr), Visuals Unlimited/Science Visuals Unlimited/Keith Wood; 144 Kenneth Eward/Science Source/Photo Researchers, Inc.; 145 Remi Benali and Stephen Ferry/Gamma-Liaison; 146 Volker Steger/Peter Arnold

Chapter Seven: 150(tr), Visuals Unlimited/James Beveridge; 150(cr), Gail Shumway/FPG International; 150(cl), Doug Wechsler/Animals Animals; 152(cl), Ken Lucas; 152(cr), John Cancalosi/ Tom Stack & Associates; 157(cr), Visuals Unlimited/H. W. Robison; 158(b), Christopher Ralling; 158(bl) William E. Ferguson; 160(tr), Jeanne White/Photo Researchers, Inc.; 160(tl), Baines Photo; 160(br), Robert Pearcy/Animals Animals; 160(cl), John Daniels/DANI2/Bruce Coleman, Inc.; 160(bc), Dennis and Catherine Quinn; 160(bl), Yann Arthus-Bertrand/Corbis; 160(cr), Fritz Prenzel/Animals Animals; 161(tl), Library of Congress/Corbis; 163(tr), Image Copyright ©2001 Photodisc, Inc.; 165(l, r), M. W. Tweedie/Photo Researchers, Inc.; 170 Ken Lucas; 171(bl), Breck P. Kent/Animals Animals; 171(bc), Pat & Tom Leeson/Photo Researchers, Inc.; 172(tr), Doug Wilson/Westlight

Chapter Eight: 174(br), Jerome Chatin/Gamma-Liaison; 174(t), Centre National de Prehistoire, Perigueux, France; 176 Louie Psihoyos/Matrix; 182 SuperStock; 183 Visuals Unlimited/NMSM; 184 M. Abbey/Photo Researchers, Inc.; 188(cr), Daniel J. Cox/Tony Stone Images; 188(c), Art Wolfe/Tony Stone Images; 190(bl), John Reader/Science Photo Library/Photo Researchers, Inc.; 190(tl), Daniel J. Cox/Gamma-Liaison; 191(tr), David Brill; 191(br), John Gurche; 192(bl), John Reader/Science Photo Library/Photo Researchers, Inc.; 192(bl), E. R. Degginger/Bruce Coleman; 192(tl, br), Neanderthal Museum; 193 David Brill/National Geographic Society Image Collection; 195 Renee Lynn/Photo Researchers, Inc.; 196 John Reader/Science Photo Library/Photo Researchers, Inc.; 198(c), Thomas W. Martin, APSA/Photo Researchers, Inc.; 199(tl, b), Bonnie Jacobs/Southern Methodist University

Chapter Nine: 200 Jeff Lepore/Photo Researchers, Inc.; 202 Ethnobotany of the Chacabo Indians, Beni, Bolivia, Advances in Economic Botany/The New York Botanical Gardens; 204(tl), Library of Congress/Corbis; 208 Biophoto Associates/Photo Researchers, Inc.; 209(tr), Sherrie Jones/Photo Researchers, Inc.; 209(bl, bc), Dr. Tony Brian & David Parker/Science Photo Library/ Photo Researchers, Inc.; 210(tl), Visuals Unlimited/M. Abbey; 210(cl), Visuals Unlimited/Stanley Flegler; 210(br), Chuck Davis/Tony Stone Images; 211(c), Corbis Images; 211(bl), Art Wolfe/Tony Stone Images; 212(tl), Robert Maier; 212(c), Visuals Unlimited/Sherman Thomson; 212(br), Visuals Unlimited/Richard Thom; 213(cr), Telegraph Colour Library 1997/FPG; 213(tr), SuperStock; 213(cl), G. Randall/FPG; 213(c), SuperStock; 215 Robert Maier; 219 Peter Funch

Unit Four: 220(cl), David L. Brown/Tom Stack; 220(cr), Oliver Meches/MPI-Tubingen/Photo Researchers, Inc.; 221(tl), Dr. Tony Brian & David Parker/Science Photo Library/Photo Researchers, Inc.; 221(tr), Larry Ulrich/DRK Photo; 221(c), Frederick Warne & Co./Courtesy of the National Trust; 221(br), Gelderblom/Photo Researchers, Inc.; 221(bl), Charles O'Rear/Westlight; **Chapter Ten:** 224(cr), Robert Yin/Corbis; 224(cr), Dr. Norman R. Pace and Dr. Esther R. Angert; 225(cr), Institut Pasteur/CNRI/Phototake; 225(br), Heather Angel; 226(bl), Visuals Unlimited/David M. Phillips; 226(cl), Fran Heyl Associates; 226(br), CNRI/Science Photo Library/Photo Researchers, Inc.; 227(tr), SuperStock; 227(b), Larry Ulrich/DRK Photo; 228 Richard T. Nowitz/Corbis; 230(cr), Bio-Logic Remediation LTD; 230(cl), Sergio Purtell/FOCA; 232(tl), R. Sheridan/Ancient Art & Architecture Collection; 232(bl), Visuals Unlimited/Sherman Thomson; 233(b), E.O.S./Gelderblom/Photo Researchers, Inc.; 234(cl), Visuals Unlimited/Hans Gelderblom; 234(cr), Visuals Unlimited/K. G. Murti; 234(bl), Dr. O. Bradfute/Peter Arnold; 234(br), Oliver Meckes/MPI-Tubingen/Photo Researchers, Inc.; 236(b), Institut Pasteur/CNRI/Phototake; 236(c), Robert Yin/Corbis; 236(cr), Dr. Norman R. Pace and Dr. Esther R. Angert; 238 Fran Heyl Associates; 240 HRW Photo composite; 241 Oliver Meckes/MPI-Tubingen/Photo Researchers, Inc.

Chapter Eleven: 242(t), Art Resource; 242(br), Astrid & Hanns-Frieder Michler/Science Photo Library/Photo Researchers, Inc.; 243(c), Spike Walker/Tony Stone Images; 244(tr), Visuals Unlimited/David Phillips; 244(bl), Matt Meadows/Peter Arnold; 244(bc), Breck Kent; 244(c), Michael Abbey/Photo Researchers, Inc.; 245(cr), David M. Dennis/Tom Stack; 245(b), Matt Meadows/Peter Arnold; 246(tl), Dr. Bruce Kendrick; 246(bl, br), Dr. E. R. Degginger; 247(cr), Kenneth W. Fink/Photo Researchers, Inc.; 247(br), Manfred Kage/Peter Arnold; 248(tl), Robert Brons/BPS/Tony Stone Images; 248(b), Kevin Schafer/Peter Arnold; 250 P. Parks/OSF/Animals Animals; 251(bl), Manfred Kage/Peter Arnold; 251(bc), George H. Harrison/Grant Heilman; 251(bc), Dr. Hossler/Custom Medical Stock Photo; 254(cl), Dr. Hilda Canter-Lund; 254(c), Eric Grave/Science Source/Photo Researchers, Inc.; 255(cr), Runk/Schoenberger/Grant Heilman; 255(cl), Visuals Unlimited/Stan Flegler; 255(bl), David M. Dennis/Tom Stack; 255(c), R. Carr/Bruce Coleman; 256 A. Davies/Bruce Coleman; 257(tr), Ralph Eague/Photo Researchers, Inc.; 257(b), Andrew Syred/Science Photo Library/Photo Researchers, Inc.; 258(tl), Gamma-Liaison; 258(c), J. Forsdyke/Gene Cox/Science Photo Library/Photo Researchers, Inc.; 258(b), Laurie Campbell/NHPA; 259(tr), Visuals Unlimited/Wally Eberhart; 259(c, cl), Dr. E. R. Degginger; 260(tr), Michael Fogden/DRK; 260(c), Visuals Unlimited/Inga Spence; 260(b), Walter H. Hodge/Peter Arnold; 261(c), John Gerlach/DRK Photo; 261(tr), Visuals Unlimited/Walt Anderson; 261(cr), Visuals Unlimited/Gerald & Buff Corsi; 262 Visuals Unlimited/David Phillips; 263 David M. Dennis/Tom Stack; 264 David M. Dennis/Tom Stack; 265(all), Omikron/Photo Researchers, Inc.; 266(all), Paul F. Hamlyn, BTTG; 267 Dr. James A. Pisarowicz/Wind Cave National Park

Chapter Twelve: 270(cl), Robert Shafer/Tony Stone Images; 270(bl, tr), SuperStock; 272(tc), Runk/Schoenberger/Grant Heilman; 272(bl), John Gerlach/Earth Scenes; 272(tl), Bruce Coleman, Inc.; 275(tr), Runk/Schoenberger/Grant Heilman; 275(br), John Weinstein/The Field Museum, Chicago, IL; 276(tl), Larry Ulrich/DRK Photo; 276(c), SuperStock; 277(tr), Ed Reschke/Peter Arnold; 277(cr), Runk/Schoenberger/Grant

Heilman; 278(tr), Robert Barclay/Grant Heilman; 278(cl), Heather Angel; 278(br), Phil Degginger; 280(tl), Tom Bean; 280(tc), Jim Strawser/Grant Heilman; 280(br), Visuals Unlimited/John D. Cunningham; 280(bl), Walter H. Hodge/Peter Arnold; 281 Patti Murray/Earth Scenes; 282(tl), William E. Ferguson; 282(bl), Werner H. Muller/Peter Arnold; 282(bc), Grant Heilman; 282(br), SuperStock; 285(bc), Runk/Schoenberger/Grant Heilman; 285(br), Nigel Cattlin/Holt Studios International/Photo Researchers, Inc.; 285(bl), Dwight R. Kuhn; 285(tr), Ed Reschke/Peter Arnold, Inc.; 285(tc), Runk/Rannels/Grant Heilman Photography; 286(tc), Harry Smith Collection; 286(cl), Larry Ulrich/DRK Photo; 286(bc), Albert Visage/Peter Arnold; 286(br), Dale F. Boyer/Photo Researchers, Inc.; 287(bl), Stephen J. Krasemann/Photo Researchers, Inc.; 287(tr), Tom Bean; 287(tl), Index Stock Photography; 288(tl, bc), Dr. E. R. Degginger; 288(tr), Gary B. Braasch; 289 Ken W. Davis/Tom Stack; 290(tl), SuperStock; 290(bl), Kevin Adams/Liaison International; 291(tr), George Bernard/Science Photo Library/Photo Researchers, Inc.; 291(c), Patrick Jones/Corbis; 292 The Field Museum, Chicago, IL; 293 SuperStock; 294 Kevin Adams/Liaison International; 296 Carl Redmond/University of Kentucky; 297(tl), Mark Philbrick/Brigham Young University; 297(br), Phillip-Lorca DiCorcia

Chapter Thirteen: 302(tl), Visuals Unlimited/W. Ormerod; 302(tc), George Bernard/Earth Scenes; 302(tr), Image Copyright ©2001 Photodisc, Inc.; 303(tr), Paul Hein/Unicorn; 303(cr), Jerome Wexler/Photo Researchers, Inc.; 303(cl), George Bernard/Earth Scenes; 304(br), Gregg Hadel/Tony Stone Images; 306(tl), Dr. Jeremy Burgess/Science Photo Library/Photo Researchers, Inc.; 307(br), Cathlyn Melloan/Tony Stone Images; 308(cl, cr), R. F. Evert; 309(c), Dick Keen/Unicorn; 309(b), Visuals Unlimited/E. Webber; 310(tr), W. Cody/WestLight; 310(bl, bc, br), Rich Iwasaki/Tony Stone Images; 311(tl), Visuals Unlimited/Bill Beatty; 311(cl), Visuals Unlimited/Bill Beatty; 313 R. F. Evert; 315(bl), W. Cody/Westlight; 316(cl), Discover Syndication/Walt Disney Publications; 316(bc), David Littschwager & Susan Middleton / Discover Magazine; 316(br), Discover Syndication/Walt Disney Publications; 317(cr), Cary S. Wolinsky

Unit Five: 318(t), Runk/Schoenberger/Grant Heilman; 318(bl), Grant Heilman; 318(br), M. Gunther/Peter Arnold; 319(tl), Johnny Johnson/DRK Photo; 319(tr), Gail Shumway/FPG; 319(c), John James Audobon/Collection of the New York Historical Society; 319(cl), M. Corsetti/FPG; 319(bl), Art Wolfe/Tony Stone Images; 319(br), Susan Erstgaard; **Chapter Fourteen:** 320(b), Doug Wechsler/VIREO; 320(bc), G. Bilyk/Academy of Natural Sciences/VIREO; 321(t), James L. Amos/Peter Arnold; 322(t), David B. Fleetham/FPG International; 324(tl), David M. Phillips/Photo Researchers, Inc.; 324(c), Visuals Unlimited/Fred Hossler; 325(tl), Gerard Lacz/Peter Arnold; 325(cr), Manoj Shah/Tony Stone Images; 325(tr), Stephen Dalton/Photo Researchers, Inc.; 325(bc), Stephen Dalton/Photo Researchers, Inc.; 326 Tim Davis/Tony Stone Images; 327(t), J. H. Robinson/Photo Researchers, Inc.; 327(bl), W. Peckover/Academy of Natural Sciences Philadelphia/VIREO; 327(br), Visuals Unlimited/Leroy Simon; 328(tl), Visuals Unlimited/A. J. Copley; 329(tr), George D. Lepp/Tony Stone Images; 329(bl), Michio Hoshino/Minden Pictures; 331(t), FPG International; 332(cl), Fernandez & Peck/Adventure Photo & Film; 332(bl), Peter Weimann/Animals Animals; 333(tr), Lee F. Snyder/Photo Researchers, Inc.; 333(br), Johnny Johnson/Animals Animals; 334(tl), Ron Kimball; 335(tl), Planet Earth Pictures; 335(cr), Richard R. Hansen/Photo Researchers, Inc.; 336(c), Keren Su/Tony Stone Images; 336(tr), Stephen Dalton/Photo Researchers, Inc.; 337 Lee F. Snyder/Photo Researchers, Inc.; 338 Visuals Unlimited/Leroy Simon; 340 John Elk/Tony Stone Images; 341 Wayne Lawler/AUSCAPE

Chapter Fifteen: 342 Tim Branning; 343(tc), Norbert Wu/Peter Arnold, Inc.; 343(cr), Larry West/FPG; 343(cl), Tom Corner/Unicorn Stock Photos; 343(bl), James H. Carmichael Jr./Image Bank; 343(bc), Dr. E. R. Degginger, FPSA; 343(tr), Larry West/FPG; 343(b), G. K. & Vikki Hart/Image Bank; 343(tl), Visuals Unlimited/Barbara Gerlach; 344(tr), SuperStock; 344(cl), Carl Roessler/FPG; 344(c), J Carmichael/Image Bank; 344(bl), David B. Fleetham/Tom Stack; 346(tl), Jeffrey L. Rotman/Peter Arnold, Inc.; 346(br), Dr. E. R. Degginger; 346(bl), Keith Philpott/Image Bank; 347(br), Nigel Cattlin/Holt Studios International/Photo Researchers, Inc.; 348(bl), Randy Morse/Tom Stack & Associates; 348(cl), Biophoto Associates/Science Source/Photo Researchers, Inc.; 348(tl), Lee Foster/FPG; 350(tl), Visuals Unlimited/T. E. Adams; 350(b), CNRI/Science Photo Library/Photo Researchers, Inc.; 351(tr), Visuals Unlimited/R. Calentine; 351(c), Visuals Unlimited/A. M. Siegelman; 352(cl), SuperStock; 352(cr), Dr. E. R. Degginger, FPSA; 352(c), Stephen Frink/Corbis; 352(tr), Holt Studios Int./Photo Researchers, Inc.; 353 Visuals Unlimited/David M. Phillips; 354 David Fleetham/FPG; 355(br), Daniel Schaefer/HRW Photo; 355(tr), Milton Rand/Tom Stack & Associates; 356(cl), St. Bartholomew's Hospital/Science Photo Library/Photo Researchers, Inc.; 356(tl), Mary Beth Angelo/Photo Researchers, Inc.; 357(tr), SuperStock; 357(cl), Will Crocker/Image Bank; 357(bl), Sergio Purcell/FOCA; 358(tl), CNRI/Science Photo Library/Photo Researchers, Inc.; 358(cl), Visuals Unlimited/A. Kerstitch; 358(bl), Dr. E. R. Degginger, FPSA; 359 David Scharf/Peter Arnold; 360(tl), Visuals Unlimited/R. Calentine; 360(c), SuperStock; 360(bc), Uniphoto; 360(cl), Stephen Dalton/NHPA; 360(br), Gail Shumway/FPG; 361(cr), Joe McDonald; 363(cl), Darryl Torckler/Tony Stone Images; 363(blb), Visuals Unlimited/Cabisco; 363(blt), Paul McCormick/Image Bank; 363(tr), Robert Dunne/Photo Researchers, Inc.; 363(cr), Chesher/Photo Researchers, Inc.; 365(cr), Visuals Unlimited/Marty Snyderman; 365(tr), Andrew J. Martinez/Photo Researchers, Inc.; 365(bl), Visuals Unlimited/Daniel W. Gotshall; 366 Keith Philpott/Image Bank; 367(c), Uniphoto; 367(tc), SuperStock; 368 Ken Philpott/Image Bank; 370(c), Visuals Unlimited/Diane R. Nelson; 371(br), Mark Norman/Archfull

Chapter Sixteen: 372(br, bc), Hans Fricke/National Geographic Society Image Collection; 372(t), Visuals Unlimited; 373 Visuals Unlimited/Dale Jackson; 374(c), Louis Psihoyos/Matrix; 374(bc), Norbert Wu/Peter Arnold; 374(bl), Randy Morse/Tom Stack; 375 Grant Heilman; 376 Uniphoto; 377(bl), Doug Perrine/DRK Photo; 377(br), Brian Parker/Tom Stack; 377(cl), Animals Animals; 377(br), Visuals Unlimited/Ken Lucas; 377(c), Bruce Coleman; 379(tr), Hans Reinhard/Bruce Coleman; 379(c), Index Stock; 379(b), Martin Barraud/Tony Stone Images; 380(tl), Visuals Unlimited/Science Visuals Unlimited; 380(cl), Navaswan/FPG; 381(tr), Bruce Coleman; 381(cl), Steinhart Aquarium/Tom McHugh/Photo Researchers, Inc.; 382(cl), Michael Fogden/DRK Photo; 382(bl), Visuals Unlimited/Nathan W. Cohen; 383(tr), David M. Dennis/Tom Stack & Associates; 383(br), C. K. Lorenz/Photo Researchers, Inc.; 384 Michael and Patricia Fogden; 385(tr), M.P.L. Fogden/Bruce Coleman; 385(bc), Zig Leszczynski/Animals Animals; 385(cr), Stephen Dalotrn/NHPA; 386(tr), Leonard Lee Rue/Photo Researchers, Inc.; 386(tr), Breck P. Kent; 386(cl), Telegraph Color Library/FPG; 387 Visuals Unlimited/Rob & Ann Simpson; 388(tc), Gail Shumway/FPG; 388(tl), Gail Shumway/FPG; 388(bc), Stanley Breeden/DRK Photo; 388(br), Visuals Unlimited/Joe McDonald; 390(tl), Bruce Coleman; 390(c), Mike Severns/Tony Stone Images; 390(bl), Kevin Schafer/Peter Arnold; 390(br), Wayne Lynch/DRK Photo; 391(t), Wolfgang Kaehler; 391(cr), Michael Fogden/DRK Photo; 392 Uniphoto; 393(cl), Michael Fogden/DRK Photos; 393(tr), Brian Parker/Tom Stack & Assoc.; 394 Steven David Miller/Animals Animals Earth Scenes

Chapter Seventeen: 398(bl), James L. Anos/Photo Researchers, Inc.; 398(bc), O. Louis Mazzatenta/National Geographic Society Image Collection; 400(cl), Anthony Mercieca/Photo Researchers, Inc.; 400(tr), Stan Osolinski/FPG; 400(c), Gail Shumway/FPG; 400(b – inset), Runk/Schoenberger/Grant Heilman; 400(bl), Douglas Faulkner/Photo Researchers, Inc.; 404(c), Ben Osborne/Tony Stone Images; 405(b), D. Cavagnaro/DRK Photo; 405(tr), Frans Lanting/Minden Pictures; 405(cr), Joe McDonald/DRK Photo; 406(tr), Thomas McAvoy/Time Life Syndication; 406(br), Hal H. Harrison/Grant Heilman; 407(bc), Gavriel Jecan/Tony Stone Images; 407(cr), APL/J. Carnemolla/Westlight; 407(bl), Kevin Schafer/Tony Stone Images; 408(cl), Tui De Roy/Minden Pictures; 408(cr), Wayne Lankinen/Bruce Coleman; 408(tr), S. Nielsen/DRK Photo; 408(bl), Greg Vaughn/Tony Stone Images; 408(br), Fritz Polking/Bruce Coleman; 409(tl), Stephen J. Krasemann/DRK Photo; 409(cr), Visuals Unlimited/S. Maslowski; 409(tr), Frans Lanting/Minden Pictures; 410(cl), Gerard Lacz/Animals Animals; 410(cr), Tim Davis/Photo Researchers, Inc.; 410(c), Nigel Dennis/Photo Researchers, Inc.; 411(cl), Hans Reinhard/Bruce Coleman; 411(tr), World Perspective/Tony Stone Images; 412(tl), David E. Myers/Tony Stone Images; 412(cl), Tom Tietz/Tony Stone Images; 412(bl), Konrad Wothe/WestLight; 413 Kathy Bushue/Tony Stone Images; 414(cl), Edwin & Peggy Bauer/Bruce Coleman; 414(bl), Dave Watts/Tom Stack; 415(tr), Jean-Paul Ferrero/AUSCAPE; 415(cl), Hans Reinhard/Bruce Coleman; 415(bc), Art Wolfe/Tony Stone Images; 416(bl), Wayne Lynch/DRK Photo; 416(br), Visuals Unlimited/John D. Cunningham; 417(tr), Gail Shumway/FPG; 417(tl), D. R. Kuhn/Bruce Coleman; 417(br), Lynda Richardson/Peter Arnold; 417(bl), Frans Lanting/Minden Pictures; 418(tr), David Cavagnaro/Peter Arnold; 418(tl), John Cancalosi; 418(c), S. C. Bisserot/Bruce Coleman; 418(b), EyeWire, Inc.; 419(cl), Uniphoto; 419(tr), Gail Shumway/FPG; 419(bl), Arthur C. Smith III/Grant Heilman; 419(cl), Joe McDonald/Bruce Coleman; 420(tr), Scott Daniel Peterson/Liaison; 420(cl), Gail Shumway/FPG; 420(b), Roberto Arakaki/International Stock; 421 Art Wolfe/Tony Stone Images; 422(c), Francois Gohier; 422(tr), Flip Nicklin/Minden Pictures; 422(b), Tom & Therisa Stack; 423(l), J. & P. Wegner/Animals Animals; 423(tr), Inga Spence/Tom Stack; 424, Frans Lanting/Minden Pictures; 425 Gerard Lacz/Animals Animals; 426 S. C. Bisserot/Bruce Coleman; 428(b), Will & Deni McIntyre/Tony Stone Images; 428(c), Tom & Pat Leeson/Photo Researchers, Inc.; 429(br), Raymond A. Mendez/Animals Animals

Unit Six: 430(t), Carr Clifton/Minden Pictures; 430(c), SuperStock; 430(b), Tom Brakefield/Corbis; 430(b), SuperStock; 431(tr), Photo Researchers, Inc.; 431(c), FPG; 431(cl), Erich Hartmann/Magnum; 431(bc), David Young Wolff/Tony Stone Images; 431(br), Tom Smart/Gamma-Liaison; **Chapter Eighteen:** 432(t, bc), Norbert Wu; 442(bl), Gamma-Liaison; 442(tl), Laguna Photo/Liaison International; 443(cr), Jeff Lepore/Photo Researchers, Inc.; 444(c), Jeff Foott/AUSCAPE; 445 Ross Hamilton/Tony Stone Images; 446(tl), Visuals Unlimited/Gerald & Buff Corsi; 446(bl), Hans Pfletschinger/Peter Arnold; 447(b), Ed Robinson/Tom Stack & Associates; 447(cr), Telegraph Color Library/FPG; 447(tr), Peter Parks/Animals Animals Earth Scenes; 448(tl), Gay Bumgarner/Tony Stone Images; 448(bl), Carol Hughes/Bruce Coleman; 449(tr), CSIRO Wildlife & Ecology; 451(cr), Gay Bumgarner/Tony Stone Images; 454(tc), Darlyne Murawski/National Geographic Society Image Collection; 455(tr), Sanford D. Porter/U.S. Department of Agriculture

Chapter Nineteen: 456 Michael J. Howell/Index Stock Photography; 457 Ecosphere Associates, Ltd.; 461 Ray Pfortner/Peter Arnold, Inc.; 462(t), Diana L. Stratton/Tom Stack; 462(b), Stan Osolinski/FPG; 465 Kim Heacox/DRK Photo; 466(tl), Ray Pfortner/Peter Arnold, Inc.; 467 Kim Heacox/DRK Photo; 470 Charles O'Rear/Westlight

Chapter Twenty: 472(t), Visuals Unlimited/David Sieren; 472(br), Runk/Schoenberger/Grant Heilman; 472(cl), J. H. Robinson/Photo Researchers, Inc.; 478(c), Grant Heilman; 478(b), Tom Brakefield/Bruce Coleman; 480 Kathy Bushue/Tony Stone Images; 481(bc), Stuart Westmorland/Tony Stone Images; 481(bl), Manfred Kage/Peter Arnold; 484(tl), Jeff Hunter/Image Bank; 484(bl), Zig Leszczynski/Animals Animals; 485 Johnny Johnson/DRK Photo; 485(c), Nancy Sefton/Photo Researchers, Inc.; 488(b), Dwight Kuhn; 488(tr), Unicorn Stock Photos; 489(tr), Don Fawcett/Photo Researchers, Inc.; 489(cr), Don & Pat Valenti/DRK Photo; 489(tr), Hardie Truesdale; 491(tl), Jeff Hunter/Image Bank; 494 Dr. Verena Tunnicliffe; 495(tl, br), Lincoln P. Brower

Chapter Twenty One: 496(b), Richard Aldorasi; 496(bkgd), HRW Photo; 498(c), Grant Heilman; 498(bl), Arthur Tilley/Tony Stone Images; 499(tr), Peter Darro; 499(br), Ken Griffiths/Tony Stone Images; 500(c), Roy Morsch/Stock Market; 500(tl), Owen Garrett/Centre for Atmospheric Science at Cambridge University, UK/NASA; 501 Jacques Jangoux/Tony Stone Images; 502(c), Runk/Schoenberger/Grant Heilman; 502(cl), John Eastcott/VVA Momatiuk/Woodfin Camp; 503(tr), Rex Ziak/Tony Stone Images; 503(br), Martin Rogers/Uniphoto; 504(cl), Fed Bavendam/Peter Arnold; 506(tl), Argonne National Laboratory; 506(bl), Emile Luider/Rapho/Liaison; 507(tr), PhotoEdit; 507(bl), Kay Park-Rec Corp.; 507(bc), J. Contreras Chacel/International Stock; 508(cl), Martin Bond/Science Photo Library/Photo Researchers, Inc.; 509(cl), Uniphoto; 509(bl), K. W. Fink/Bruce Coleman; 509(tr), Toyohiro Yamada/FPG; 10 Stephen J. Krasemann/DRK Photo; 511(tr), Will & Deni McIntyre/Tony Stone Images; 511(cr), Stephen J. Krasemann/DRK Photo; 512(cl), Arthur Tilley/Tony Stone Images; 512(cr), K. W. Fink/Bruce Coleman, Inc.; 514 Runk/Schoenberger/Grant Heilman; 516(b, tr), Karen M. Allen; 517(bc), Art Wolfe

Unit Seven: 518(t), Geoffrey Clifford/Woodfin Camp; 518(c), CNRI/Science Photo Library/Photo Researchers, Inc.; 518(bl), Brown Brothers; 518(br), SuperStock; 519(tl), J & L Weber/Peter Arnold; 519(bl), AP/Wide World Photos; 519(tc), Gamma-Liaison; 519(cr), Enrico Feroreli; **Chapter Twenty Two:** 520(br), C. J. Ashford/Denis Cochrane Collection/E.T. Archive; 520(tr), New York Times/Corbis-Bettmann; 521(tr), Simon Fraser/Science Photo Library/Photo Researchers, Inc.; 522–523(b), David Madison/Tony Stone Images; 528(tl), Peter Dazeley/Tony Stone Images; 528(bc, br, bl), SP/FOCA/HRW Photo; 530(bc), Bob Torrez/Tony Stone Images; 530(bl), Dr. E. R. Degginger; 530(br), Manfred Kage/Peter Arnold, Inc.; 530(cl), G. W. Willis/BPS/Tony Stone Images; 532(bl), Chris Hamilton; 533 Shelby Thorner/David Madison; 536(c), Dr. Robert Becker/Custom Medical Stock Photo; 537(cr), Dr. P. Marazzi/Science Photo Library/Photo Researchers, Inc.; 539 Peter Dazeley/Tony Stone Images; 542(tr), Dan McCoy/Rainbow; 543(cl), Gamma-Liaison; 543(tr), Huntsville Times

Chapter Twenty Three: 544(t), Enrico Feroreli, 546(bl), Dr. Dennis Kunkel/Phototake NYC; 549(cl, tr), O. Meckes/Nicole Ottawa/Photo Researchers, Inc.; 549(cr), David Phillips/Science Source/Photo Researchers, Inc.; 551(tr), Custom Medical Stock Photo; 551(br), James Wilson/Woodfin Camp & Associates; 553(tr), Ken Wagner/Phototake NYC; 559(cl, cr), Matt Meadows/Peter Arnold, Inc.; 560(c), Dr. Dennis Kunket/Phototake, Inc.; 561(br), Don Fawcett/Photo Researchers, Inc.; 563(bl), Dr. Dennis Kunkel/Phototake NYC; 564(tr), Index Stock Photography; 565(tr), Russell Dian/HRW Photo;565(bl), Jim Gripe/Pivot Media

Chapter Twenty Four: 566(t), National Library of Medicine/Visual Image Presentations; 575(br), Prof. P. Motta/Dept. of Anatomy/University "La Sapienza" Rome/Science Photo Library/Photo Researchers, Inc.; 575(tr), The Stock Market; 578(br), Image Bank; 579(tr), Stephen J. Krasemann/DRK Photo; 579(cr), E.K. Martin and Associates; 585 J. H. Robinson/Photo Researchers, Inc.

Chapter Twenty Five: 586(tr), Warren Anatomical Museum/Harvard Medical School; 586(b), Vermont Historical Society; 597 Bruno Joachim/Liaison; 599 Louis Psihoyos/Matrix; 603 Will & Deni McIntyre/Photo Researchers, Inc.; 609 Journal of Nuclear Medicine

Chapter Twenty Six: 610 SuperStock; 612(bl), Visuals Unlimited/Cabisco; 612(br), Innerspace Visions; 614(tl), Michael Fogden/Animals Animals; 614(bl), Photo Researchers, Inc.; 614(br), Guy Mannering/Bruce Coleman; 615 Dr. E. R. Degginger/Bruce Coleman; 618(tl), Chip Henderson/Tony Stone Images; 620(b), Lennart Nilsson; 621 Petit Format/Nestle/Science Source/Photo Researchers, Inc.; 622 Lennart Nilsson; 623(tr), Lennart Nilsson/Albert Bonniers Forlag AB, A CHILD IS BORN; 623(cr), Keith/Custom Medical Stock Photo; 623(br), SP/FOCA/HRW Photo; 625 NASA; 626 Guy Mannering/Bruce Coleman, Inc.; 628 Lennart Nilsson/Albert Bonniers Forlag AB,

BEING BORN; 631(inset), Vince Viverito, Jr./Richard Wolf Medical Instruments Corp., Vernon Hills, IL; 631(cr), Tom McCarthy/Rainbow

Unit Eight: 632(c), LSHTM/Tony Stone Images; 632(b), UPI/Corbis-Bettmann; 632(t), Gervase Spencer/E.T. Archive; 633(tl), Mary Evans Picture Library; 633(tr), Wayne Floyd/Unicorn Stock Photos; 633(cl), Erich Schrempp/Photo Researchers, Inc.; 633(cr), Mary Evans Picture Library; **Chapter Twenty Seven:** 634 Image Copyright ©2001 PhotoDisc, Inc.; 636(br), CNRI/Science Photo Library/Photo Researchers, Inc.; 636(bc), Tektoff-RM/CNRI/Science Photo Library/Photo Researchers, Inc.; 636(bl), Manfred Kage/Peter Arnold; 637 Kent Wood/Photo Researchers, Inc.; 645(tr), Visuals Unlimited/George Musil; 645(bc), Image Copyright ©2001 PhotoDisc, Inc.; 645(cr), K. H. Kjeldsen/Science Photo Library/Photo Researchers, Inc.; 645(cl), SuperStock; 646(tl), Clinical Radiology Dept., Salisbury District Hospital/Science Photo Library/Photo Researchers, Inc.; 646(bl, br), Dr. A. Liepins/Science Photo Library/Photo Researchers, Inc.; 647 Lennart Nilsson; 649 Dr. A. Liepins/Science Photo Library/Photo Researchers, Inc.; 652(all), Chris Mooney/HRW Photo; 653 E. R. Degginger/Bruce Coleman

Chapter Twenty Eight: 660 John Kelly/Tony Stone Images; 665(bl), E. Dirksen/Photo Researchers, Inc.; 665(tr), ©1999 Stephen Foster; 665(br), Dr. Andrew P. Evans/Indiana University; 666 Spencer Grant/Photo Researchers, Inc.; 670 Rob Van Petten/Image Bank; 671 Wally McNamee/Corbis; 678 Manfred Kage/Peter Arnold; 679 SuperStock

LabBook: "LabBook Header": "L", Corbis Images, "a", Letraset-Phototone, "b" and "B" HRW, "o" and "k", Images Copyright ©2001 PhotoDisc, Inc. 680(tc), Scott Van Osdol/HRW Photo; 683(cl), Michelle Bridwell/HRW Photo; 683(br), Image Copyright ©2001 Photodisc, Inc.; 684(bl), Stephanie Morris/HRW Photo; 685(tr), Jana Birchum/HRW Photo; 696(tl, tc), Runk/Schoenberger/Grant Heilman; 696(tr), Michael Abbey/Photo Researchers, Inc.; 696(br), Runk/Schoenberger/Grant Heilman; 726(bc), Breck P. Kent; 726(br), Stephen J. Krasemann/Photo Researchers, Inc.; 726(c), Visuals Unlimited/R. Calentine; 726(t), Runk/Schoenberger/Grant Heilman; 740(t), FPG; 742 Rod Planck/Photo Researchers, Inc.; 753(tr), Kenneth Gabrielsen/Liaison International; 753(cl), Visuals Unlimited/Doug Sokell; 753(br), Larry Nielsen/Peter Arnold; 753(bl), Phil Degginger; 757 David Hoffman/Tony Stone Images; 759(tr), Tom Bean/DRK Photo; 759(br), Darrell Gulin/DRK Photo; 774 Dr. E. R. Degginger, FPSA

Appendix: 806 CENCO

Sam Dudgeon/HRW Photos: all Systems of the Body background photos, vii(cl), xvii(bl), xviii(tl), xx, xxi, xxii(tr, bl), 5(bl), 11(b), 12(bl), 17(tr), 26, 35(tr), 42(br), 43(br), 49(tr, cr, br), 55, 579 (bl), 82, 83, 84, 91 (tr), 110, 126(cl), 127(tr–all), 132(tl), 134(tl), 135(tr–all), 269(tr), 299(bl, tr), 304(bl), 305(tr), 473, 504(tr), 511(br), 524, 526, 531(tr, tc), 532(c), 534, 538(c), 545(all), 568–569(t), 587, 592, 594, 595, 601, 602, 604, 611, 627, 669, 675(cr), 680(l, tr), 680(br), 682, 683(bc), 684(br, tl), 684(tr), 685(tl), 686, 687, 689, 690, 693, 695, 696(cr), 698, 699, 700(br, tr), 701, 702–703(all), 710(cr), 713, 714, 715(all), 722, 728, 730, 733, 736, 738(t, b), 748(bc), 748–749(tr), 749(tr), 750, 751(tr, br), 762, 764, 766(tr, cr, br), 767, 768, 769, 770, 771, 772(br, bl), 773, 778, 785(tr, b), 789(br)

Peter Van Steen/HRW Photos: v(tr), vi(bl), xvi(tl), xix(bl), xxiii, 4(t), 5(br), 6, 11(tr), 25(bl, br), 28, 105, 149, 223(tr, cr, br), 231(tr, b), 239, 243(b), 321(br), 322(cl), 399(all), 490, 497, 505(bl, bc, b), 508(tl), 513, 521(bl), 529(all), 536(l, br), 584(cl), 624(all), 634(b), 635, 638, 640, 645(br), 648, 654(tr, bl), 655(b), 656, 657(tr, cr, br), 658, 661, 663, 664, 665(cr), 670(br), 671(br), 673(all), 674, 676, 677(tr, cr), 685(tr), 721(cr, c, bl), 740(b), 743, 752(b), 755, 758, 761, 780, 789(tr)

Victoria Smith/HRW Photos: 126(c), 175, 269(br), 567(tr, b, tc), 707

John Langford/HRW Photos: xii(tl), xix(cl), 89, 96(cr), 639, 683(tr), 732(cr, br)

ANNOTATED TEACHER'S EDITION CREDITS

Cover: (cl), Frans Lanting/Minden Pictures; (c), Peter Peterson/Tony Stone Images; (cr), Chris Jaffe; (b), Carr Clifton; (c)Gerry Ellis/GerryEllis.com; owl: (cover, spine, back title page), Kim Taylor/Bruce Coleman.

Title Page: (c), Frans Lanting/Minden Pictures.

TE Frontmatter: Unless otherwise noted all images: Image Copyright ©2001 PhotoDisc/HRW; T5(br), Frans Lanting/Minden Pictures; T7(br), Peter Van Steen/HRW Photo; T8(l), Gay Bumgarner/Tony Stone Images; T9(r), Digital Stock Corp.; T11(br), Randy Morse/Tom Stack & Associates; T12(tl), Visuals Unlimited/Dale Jackson; T15(br), Peter Van Steen/HRW Photo; T17(br), Visuals Unlimited/Gerald & Buff Corsi.

Master Materials List: Unless otherwise noted all images: Image Copyright ©2001 PhotoDisc/HRW; Page xxviii (CD), HRW Photo; xxix (marshmallows), Sam Dudgeon/HRW Photo; xxx (graph paper), Sam Dudgeon/HRW Photo; xxx (salt, lima bean seeds), Digital Stock Corp.; xxxi (toothpicks), Sam Dudgeon/HRW Photo; xxxi (sugar), Digital Stock Corp.

Lab Approval Portraits: All photos courtesy of the reviewers.

TE Background Illustrations: Page 33E(bc), Morgan-Cain & Associates; 33F(tr), John White/The Neis Group; 53E(tc), Morgan-Cain & Associates; 53E(cl), Christy Krames; 53F Morgan-Cain & Associates; 81E Morgan-Cain & Associates; 81F(tr), Alexander & Turner; 103E(bl), John White/The Neis Group; 103E(cr), Mike Wepplo/Das Group; 103F(cl), Alexander & Turner; 103F(bc), Blake Thornton/Rita Marie; 125E(cl), Alexander & Turner; 125F(cl), Rob Schuster/Hankins and Tegenborg; 147E(tc), Christy Krames; 147E(bl), Rob Wood/Wood, Ronsaville, Harlin; 147E(br), John White/The Neis Group; 147F(tc), John White/The Neis Group; 147F(cl), Mike Wepplo/Das Group; 147F(br), Tony Morse/Ivy Glick; 173E(tc), Mike Wepplo/Das Group; 173F(tc,tr,br), Barbara Hoopes-Ambler; 173F(tc), Barbara Hoopes-Ambler; 173F(tr), Christy Krames; 199E(tc), Frank Ordaz/Dimension; 199E(cl), Graham Allen; 199E(cr) Cy Baker/WAA; 199E(bl), Will Nelson/Sweet Reps; 199E(br), Barbara Hoopes-Ambler; 267F(cl), Sarah Woods; 297E(br), Ponde & Giles; 319F(tl), Tony Morse/Ivy Glick; 319E(c), Barbara Hoopes-Ambler; 319E(cr), Sarah Woodward; 319E(br), Steve Roberts; 341E(bl), John White/The Neis Group; 471E(tl), MapQuest.com; 519F(cl), Christy Krames; 519F(br), Morgan-Cain & Associates; 519E(cl), Morgan-Cain & Associates; 543F(tr), Christy Krames; 565E(tc), Christy Krames; 565E(bc), Brian Evans; 565F(c), Christy Krames; 585E(tc), Brian Evans; 585F(tl), Keith Kasnot; 585F(c), Christy Krames; 609E(cl), Keith Kasnot; 609E(cr), Keith Kasnot; 633F(tr), Scott Thorn Barrows/The Neis Group.

TE Background Photography: Page 3E(tl), Minnesota Pollution Control Agency; (tr), Chip Simons Photography; (br), Dale Miquelle/National Geographic; 3F(tl), John Mitchell/Photo Researchers, Inc.; (tr), Dr. Jeremy Burgess/Science Photo Library/Photo Researchers, Inc.; (bl), John Reader/Photo Researchers, Inc.; (br), Howard Sochurek/The Stock Market; 33E(tl), Visuals Unlimited/Science VU; (br), Visuals Unlimited/Fred Rohde; 33F(tc), Sam Dudgeon/HRW Photo; (tr), Photo Researchers, Inc.; 53E(tr), Photo Researchers, Inc.; (br), Visuals Unlimited/Kevin Collins; 81E(tl), Michael Abbey/Science Source/Photo Researchers, Inc.; (br), Biophoto Associates/Science Source/Photo Researchers, Inc.; 81F(cl), L. Willatt, East Anglian Regional Genetics Service/Science Photo Library/Photo Researchers, Inc.; (bc), Ed Reschke/Peter Arnold Biology; (br), Media/Photo Researchers, Inc.; 103E(tl), Corbis; 103F(cr), Runk/Schoenberger/Grant Heilman Photography; 125E(cr), Jackie Lewin/Royal Free Hospital/Science Photo Library/Photo Researchers, Inc.; (bl), Sam Dudgeon/HRW Photo; 125F(tr), Remi Benali & Stephen Ferry/Gamma-Liaison; (br), Cellmark Diagnostics; 173E(bl), Louis Psihoyos/Matrix International; 173F(bl), Neanderthal Museum/Mettman, Germany; (br), David L. Brill; 199E(bl), Library of Congress/Corbis; 199F(tr), Dr. Tony Brian & David Parker/Science Photo Library/Photo Researchers, Inc.; (br), Biophoto Associates/Photo Researchers, Inc.; (bl) Sherrie Jones/Photo Researchers, Inc.; 221E(cl), Fran Heyl Associates; (c), Visuals Unlimited/David M. Phillips; (cr), CNRI/Science Photo Library/Photo Researchers, Inc.; 221F(br), Visuals Unlimited/Hans Gelderblom; (tl), Dr. O. Bradfute/Peter Arnold; 241E(tl), Visuals Unlimited/David M. Phillips; (cr), Dr. Bruce Kendrick; (bl), Dr. E. R. Degginger; 241F(tl), David M. Dennis/Tom Stack & Associates; (cr), John Gerlach/DRK Photo; (bl), Gamma-Liaison; 267E(l), John Gerlach/Animals Animals Earth Scenes; (cr), Runk/Schoenberger/Grant Heilman Photography; (br), Larry Ulrich/DRK Photo; 267F(cr); Phil Degginger/Color-Pic; 297E(tl), Paul Hein/Unicorn Stock Photos; (cl), George Bernard/Animals Animals Earth Scenes; 297F(tl), Rich Iwasaki/Tony Stone Images; (bl), Visuals Unlimited/E. Webber; (cr), Cathlyn Melloan/Tony Stone Images; 319E(tl), Manoj Shah/Tony Stone Images; 319F(bl), Gerard Lacz/Peter Arnold; (cr), Peter Weimann/Animals Animals Earth Scenes; 341E(tr), E. R. Degginger/Color-Pic; (cl), Ken Philpott/Image Bank; (br), Milton Rand/Tom Stack & Associates; 341F(cl), SuperStock; (cr), Chesher/Photo Researchers, Inc.; (bl), Sergio Purcell/FOCA/HRW Photo; 371E(tl), Randy Morse/Tom Stack & Associates; (bl), Norbert Wu/Peter Arnold; (cr), Index Stock Photography; 371F(tl), FPG International; (cr), Wayne Lynch/DRK Photo; (bl), Stephen Dalton/NHPA; 397E(tl) Ben Osborne/Tony Stone Images; (cr), Fritz Poling/Bruce Coleman; (bl), Anthony Mercieca Photo/Photo Researchers, Inc.; 397F(tr), D. R. Kuhn/Bruce Coleman; (cl), Lynda Richardson/Peter Arnold; (br), Wayne Lynch/DRK Photo; 431E(cr), Laguna Photo/Liaison International; 431F(cl), Michael Fogden & Patricia Fogden/Corbis; (tr), Gregory G. Dimijian/Photo Researchers, Inc.; (br), Telegraph Color Library/FPG International; 455E(tl), Ecosphere Associates, Ltd.; 455F(t), Stan Osolinski/FPG International; (cr), Diana L. Stratton/Tom Stack & Associates; 471F(tl), Stuart Westmorland/Tony Stone Images; (cr), Don & Pat Valenti/DRK Photo; (bl), Jeff Hunter/Image Bank; 495E(tl), National Wildlife Magazine; (cr), Arthur Tilley/Tony Stone Images; (bl), Grant Heilman/Grant Heilman Photography; 495F(tr), J. Conteras Chacel/International Stock; (cl), K. W. Fink/Bruce Coleman; (br), Peter Van Steen/HRW Photo; 519E(tr), Sam Dudgeon/HRW Photo; (br), Fotomas Index; 519F(cr), Robert Becker/Custom Medical Stock Photo; 543E(cl), Ken Wagner/Phototake; (cr), Dr. Dennis Kunkel/Phototake; 543F(br), Matt Meadows/Peter Arnold; 565E(cr), The Stock Market; 585E(cl, cr), Sam Dudgeon/HRW Photo; 585F(cr), Will & Deni McIntyre/Photo Researchers, Inc.; 609E(tl), Innerspace Visions; (bl), Guy Mannering/Bruce Coleman; 609F(tr), Lennart Nilsson/Albert Bonniers Forlag AB, A CHILD IS BORN; (bl), Chip Henderson/Tony Stone Images; (br), Peter Van Steen/HRW Photo; 633E(cl), Tektoff-RM/CNRI/Science Photo Library/Photo Researchers, Inc.; 633F(tl), Peter Van Steen/HRW Photo; (r), SuperStock; 653E(tl, bl), Peter Van Steen/HRW Photo; (cr), John Kelly/Tony Stone Images; 653F(cl), E. Dirksen/Photo Researchers, Inc.; (c), Dr. Andrew P. Evans/Indiana University; (cr), Spencer Grant/Photo Researchers, Inc.; (bl), LeFever/Grushow/Grant Heilman.

Acknowledgments continued from page iv.

Staff Credits

Editorial

Robert W. Todd, Associate Director, Secondary Science
Debbie Starr, Managing Editor
Laura Zapanta, Editor

ANNOTATED TEACHER'S EDITION
David Westerberg

COPYEDITORS
Dawn Spinozza, Copyediting Manager

EDITORIAL SUPPORT STAFF
Jeanne Graham, Mary Helbling, Kenneth G. Raymond, Tanu'e White

EDITORIAL PERMISSIONS
Cathy Paré, Permissions Manager
Jan Harrington, Permissions Editor

Art, Design, and Photo

BOOK DESIGN
Richard Metzger, Design Director
Marc Cooper, Senior Designer
David Hernandez, Designer
Sonya Mendeke, Designer
Alicia Sullivan, Designer (ATE), Cristina Bowerman, Design Associate (ATE), Holly Whittaker, Traffic Coordinator

IMAGE ACQUISITIONS
Elaine Tate, Art Buyer Supervisor
Julie Kelly, Art Buyer
Tim Taylor, Photo Research Supervisor

PHOTO STUDIO
Sam Dudgeon, Senior Staff Photographer
Victoria Smith, Photo Specialist
Lauren Eischen, Photo Coordinator

Production

Mimi Stockdell, Senior Production Manager
Adriana Bardin Prestwood, Senior Production Coordinator
Beth Sample, Production Coordinator
Suzanne Brooks, Sara Carroll-Downs

Answers to Concept Mapping Questions

The following pages contain sample answers to all of the concept mapping questions that appear in the Chapter Reviews. Because there is more than one way to do a concept map, your students' answers may vary.

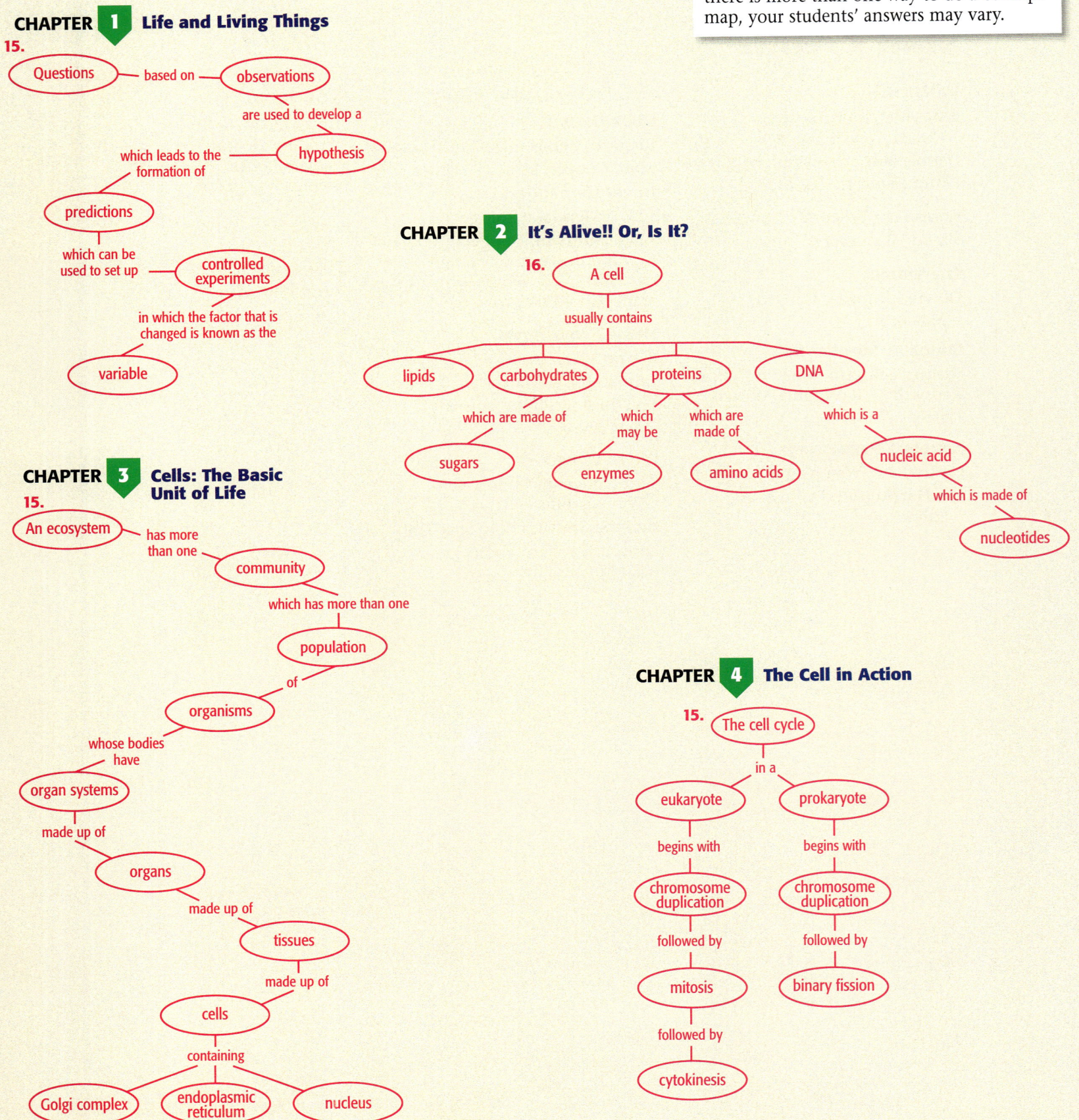

CHAPTER 5 Heredity

16.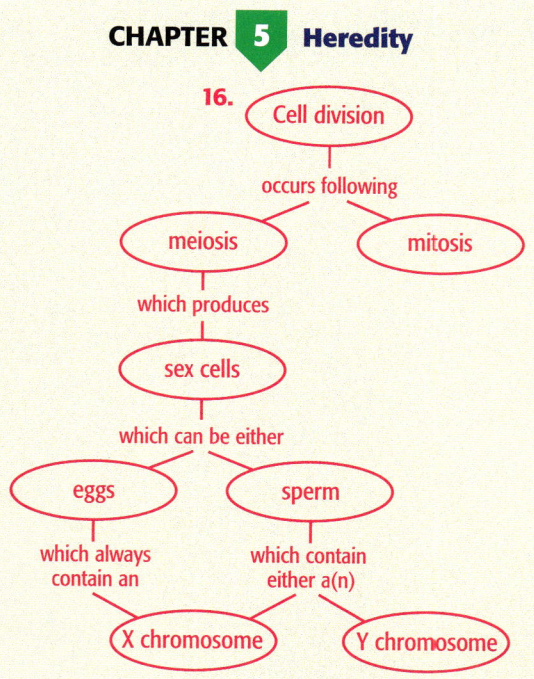

CHAPTER 6 Genes and Gene Technology

14.

CHAPTER 7 The Evolution of Living Things

16.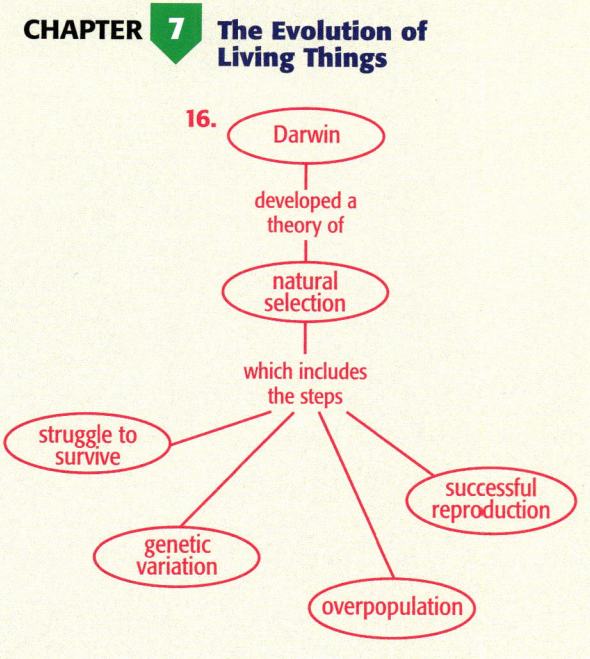

CHAPTER 8 The History of Life on Earth

14.

CHAPTER 9 Classification

15.

CHAPTER 10 Bacteria and Viruses

17.

CHAPTER 11 Protists and Fungi

18.

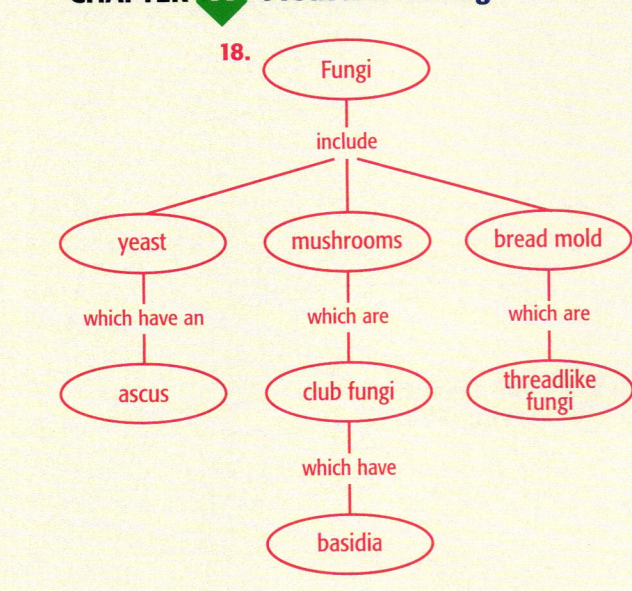

CHAPTER 12 Introduction to Plants

17.

856 Concept Mapping Answers

CHAPTER 13 Plant Processes

15.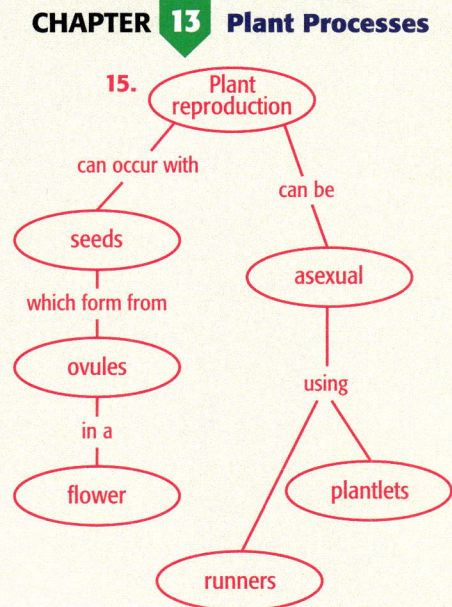

CHAPTER 14 Animals and Behavior

15.

CHAPTER 15 Invertebrates

21.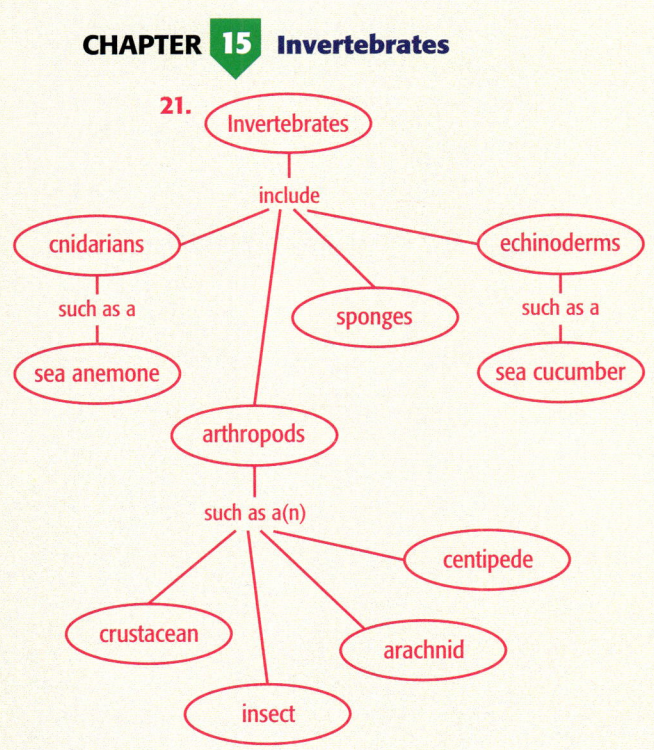

CHAPTER 16 Fishes, Amphibians, and Reptiles

16.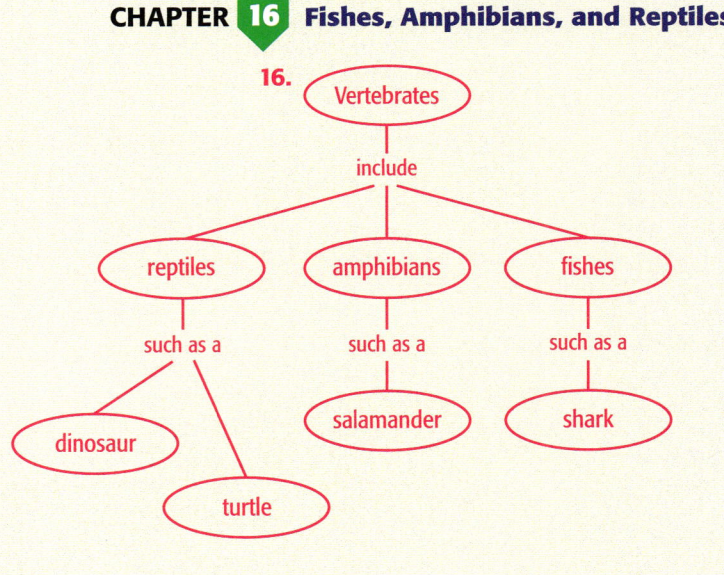

Concept Mapping Answers

CHAPTER 17 Birds and Mammals

CHAPTER 18 Interactions of Living Things

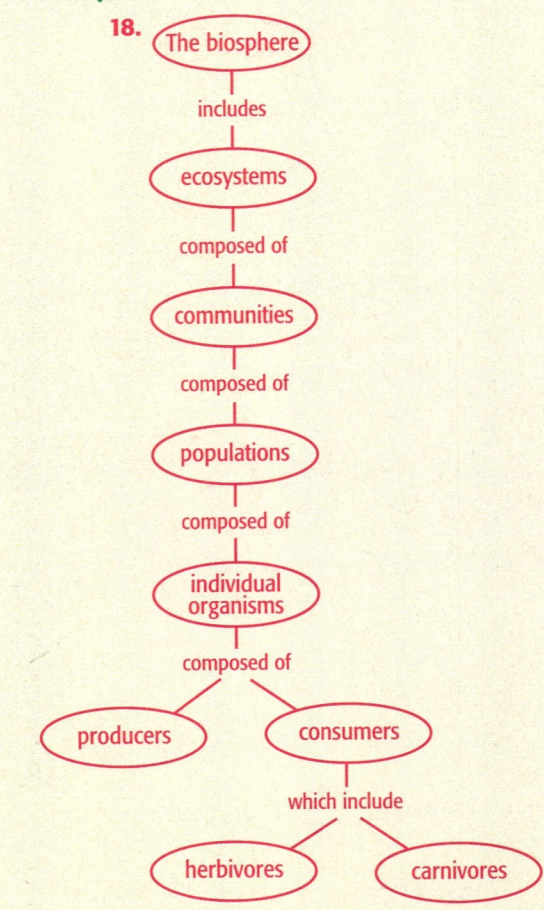

CHAPTER 19 Cycles in Nature

CHAPTER 20 The Earth's Ecosystems

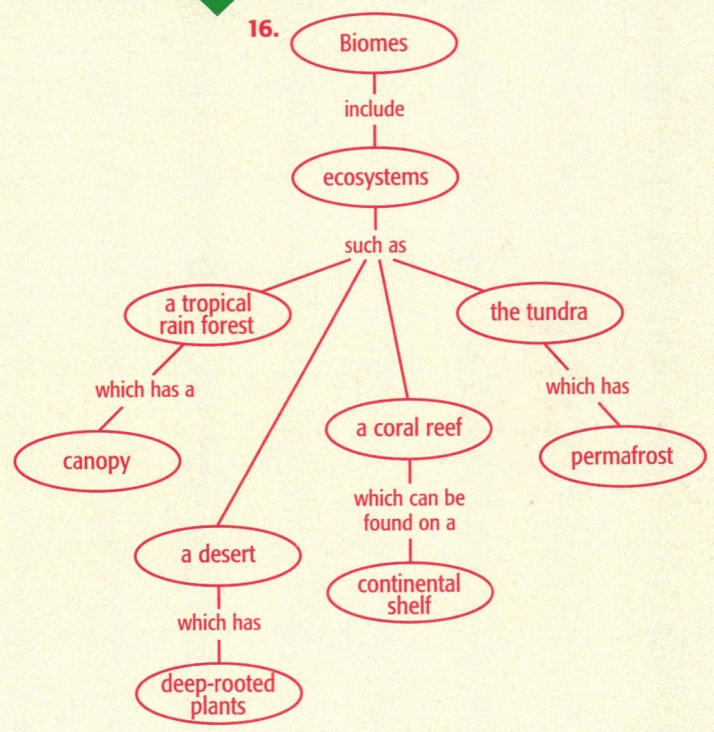

CHAPTER 21 Environmental Problems and Solutions

14.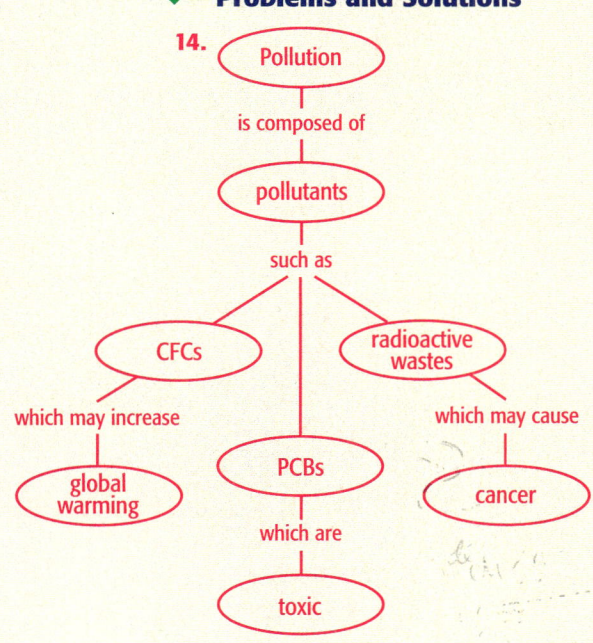

CHAPTER 22 Body Organization and Structure

17.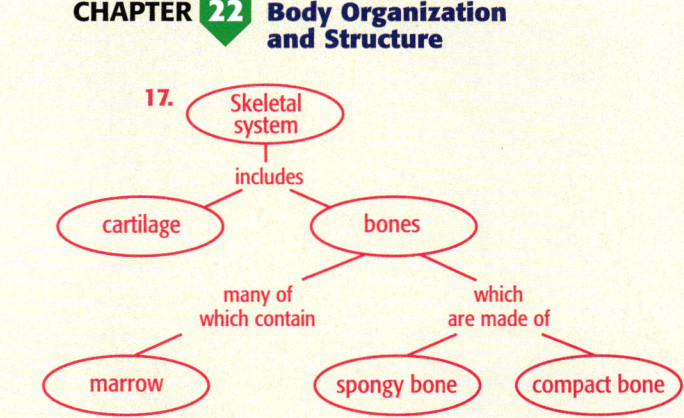

CHAPTER 23 Circulation and Respiration

15.

```
        Blood
          │
     flows through
          │
      capillaries
          │
        of the
          │
        alveoli
         ╱  ╲
where it    where it
releases    picks up
   │            │
carbon       oxygen
dioxide
```

CHAPTER 24 The Digestive and Urinary Systems

16.

Concept Mapping Answers **859**

CHAPTER 25 Communication and Control

18.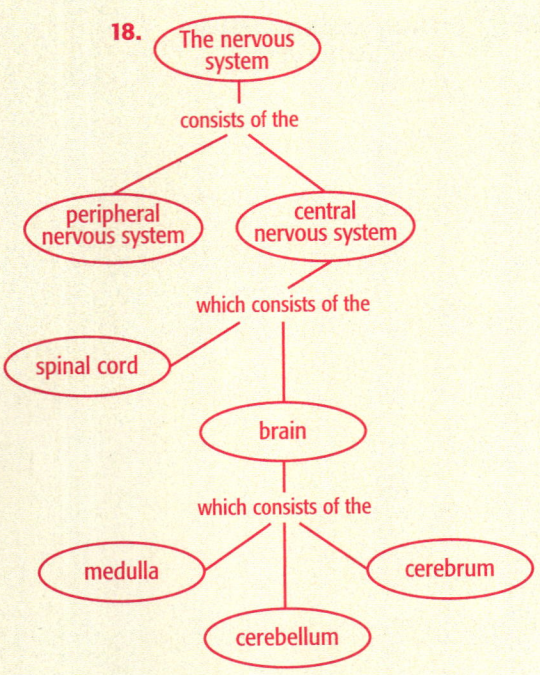

CHAPTER 26 Reproduction and Development

17.

CHAPTER 27 Body Defenses and Disease

15.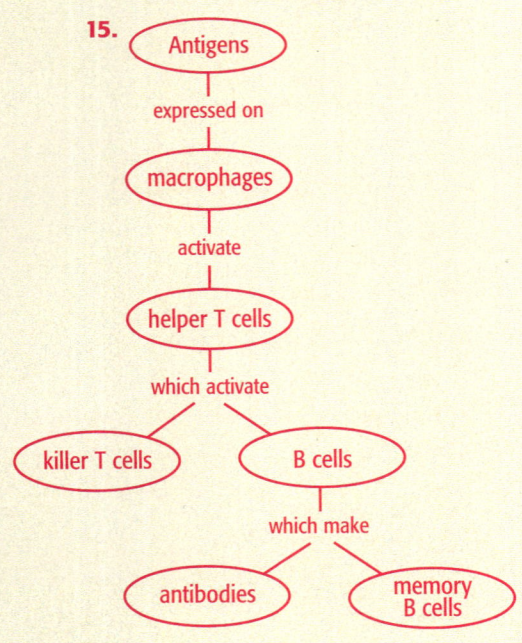

CHAPTER 28 Staying Healthy

16.

860 Concept Mapping Answers